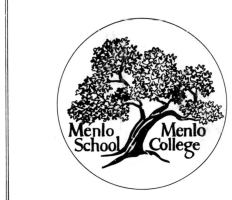

Menlo School   Menlo College

A gift in honor of

Jane Ann Fell

From

Mr. & Mrs. Morris B. Fell

BOWMAN LIBRARY

POST-IMPRESSIONISM
From van Gogh to Gauguin

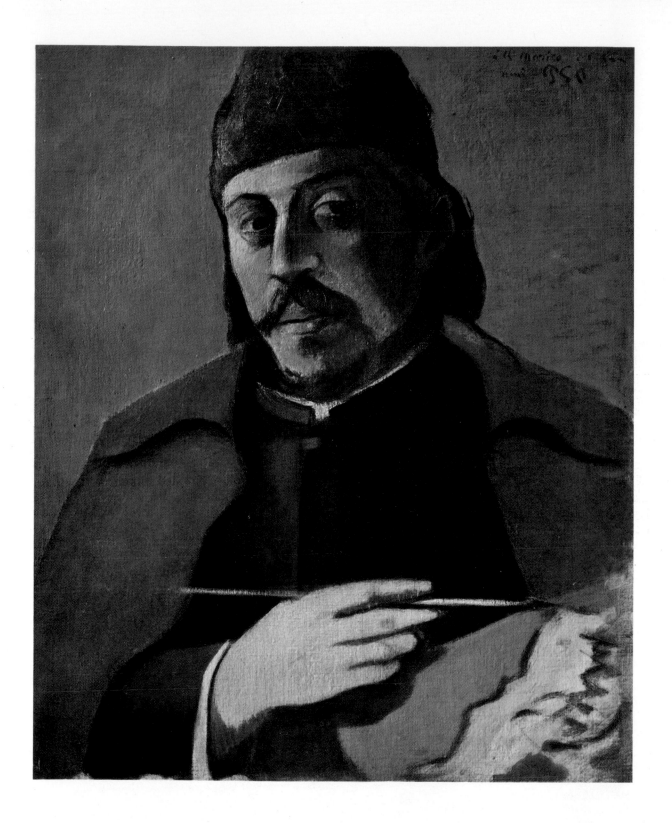

POST-IMPRESSIONISM
From van Gogh to Gauguin

Third Edition, Revised

JOHN REWALD

THE MUSEUM OF MODERN ART, NEW YORK

Distributed by New York Graphic Society, Boston

BOOKS BY JOHN REWALD

GAUGUIN, New York, 1938

MAILLOL, New York, 1939

GEORGES SEURAT, New York, 1943, 1946

THE HISTORY OF IMPRESSIONISM, New York, 1946, 1955, 1961, 1973

PAUL CÉZANNE, New York, 1948

PIERRE BONNARD, New York, 1948

LES FAUVES, New York, 1952

SEURAT—L'ŒUVRE PEINT, BIOGRAPHIE ET CATALOGUE CRITIQUE, *in collaboration with Henri Dorra*, Paris, 1959

CÉZANNE, GEFFROY, GASQUET, Paris, 1959

ODILON REDON—GUSTAVE MOREAU—RODOLPHE BRESDIN, *in collaboration with Dore Ashton and Harold Joachim*, New York, 1961

CAMILLE PISSARRO, New York, 1963

GIACOMO MANZÙ, New York, 1967

EDITED BY THE SAME AUTHOR

PAUL CÉZANNE, LETTERS, London, 1941, New York, 1976

PAUL GAUGUIN, LETTERS TO A. VOLLARD AND A. FONTAINAS, San Francisco, 1943

CAMILLE PISSARRO, LETTERS TO HIS SON LUCIEN, New York, 1943, 1972

THE WOODCUTS OF ARISTIDE MAILLOL (A COMPLETE CATALOGUE), New York, 1943

DEGAS, WORKS IN SCULPTURE (A COMPLETE CATALOGUE), New York, 1944, 1956

RENOIR DRAWINGS, New York, 1946, 1958

PAUL CÉZANNE, CARNETS DE DESSINS, Paris, 1951

GAUGUIN DRAWINGS, New York, 1958

IN PREPARATION

POST-IMPRESSIONISM—FROM GAUGUIN TO MATISSE

CÉZANNE, PAINTINGS (A COMPLETE CATALOGUE)

CÉZANNE, WATERCOLORS (A COMPLETE CATALOGUE), *in collaboration with Adrien Chappuis*

GAUGUIN, LETTERS

Published by The Museum of Modern Art, New York, 1978
All rights reserved
Third edition, revised
Previous editions 1956, 1962
Library of Congress Catalog Card Number 77–77286
ISBN 0–87070–532–6
Printed in Japan by Chanticleer Press, Inc.

The Museum of Modern Art
11 West 53 Street
New York, New York 10019

Frontispiece: GAUGUIN: *Self-Portrait, Dedicated to Charles Morice*, 1891–93. 21½ x 18″. Private collection, Switzerland

CONTENTS

INTRODUCTION

At the height of the short period covered in the present volume the Belgian poet Emile Verhaeren exclaimed: "There is no longer any single school, there are scarcely any groups, and those few are constantly splitting. All these tendencies make me think of moving and kaleidoscopic geometric patterns, which clash at one moment only to unite at another, which now fuse and then separate and fly apart a little later, but which all nevertheless revolve within the same circle, that of the new art."*

It is this "circle of the new art" which is the subject of the present study, but it is indeed an intricate and confusing subject. While in my *History of Impressionism* I endeavored to trace the tribulations of a small group of painters until it disbanded in 1886, the present volume begins with that same year 1886 and tries to tell what happened in the few yet decisive years that followed. But whereas the story of the impressionist movement offered as a central theme the series of group exhibitions which periodically brought together the various painters and maintained a certain link between them, the post-impressionist period presents no such common denominator. The *History of Impressionism* actually called for a "simultaneous" treatment, each fact and document falling almost automatically into its logical place, once the general plan was established. But this does not apply to the succeeding years. The groups which assembled and dispersed with great fluidity were of no particular homogeneity, nor did they follow each other or exist simultaneously in clearly definable form. Even more important is the fact that some of the most remarkable figures of the time did not belong to any of the larger currents but went their way alone.

In these circumstances any strictly chronological presentation of occurrences had to be abandoned. Yet, to study this period with its diversified tendencies as a series of individual portraits would have meant losing track of that intricate interplay of events, that crisscross of ideas, that overlapping of episodes which make those years so fascinating. I have therefore adopted a kind of compromise by singling out some of the leading figures of the period and making all the others revolve around them. This seemed especially indicated, even at the cost of some unavoidable repetition, because there was more than a passing relationship between most of these figures.

It was no small problem to attempt a historical reconstruction which would put every person, every work, every action, and every utterance in its proper place in that big jigsaw puzzle which Verhaeren so aptly likened to a kaleidoscope. To do so required the simplification of many complicated aspects and the unearthing of a mass of little-known or

* E. Verhaeren: Le Salon des Indépendants, *La Nation*; reprinted in *L'Art Moderne*, April 5, 1891.

forgotten evidence to fill in gaps, to establish connections between seemingly unrelated factors, to supply minute details while never losing sight of the whole, in a word to re-create that flowing movement, that incessant forward thrust which alone can convey the vitality of a moment of the past.

I was concerned not so much to tell here what I thought of all the events which took place in the comparatively short period covered by this study, as to relate what I was able to find out about them in years of patient research. However, in presenting this material I have not mechanically registered all the documents and testimonials I have gathered; I have endeavored, on the contrary, to organize this vast material in the way I thought most appropriate to the subject—a way that is true to history. Far from claiming to be right in my picture of those important years, I merely wish to stress the fact that this account comes as close as possible to the truth as I perceive it. To those who disagree, who find that I have unduly underlined one aspect or neglected another, I can reply only that a choice had to be made and that the only liberties I have taken are those of elimination or emphasis in the interest of continuity, clarity, and—let it be said again—truth. If I have succeeded in throwing a more complete light on this short phase of history, if I have managed to show major and minor events in their proper sequence and have established their real significance, my essential aim will have been accomplished.

Nothing is more painful than to have to make choices when at first the eye meets a swarming multitude of facts, anecdotes, documents. In this particular instance this task was made more difficult by the circumstance that many of the important happenings are already very well known while less salient ones have been greatly neglected. Many secondary figures of the time have been disregarded, figures concerning whom I was lucky enough to find much new material. By showing these figures, such as Emile Bernard, Félix Fénéon, Albert Aurier and several others, in their true roles, I have possibly somewhat overweighted my account in their favor, yet to have kept them in the background would have deprived the reader of much lively and captivating information which is not available elsewhere.

While studying the present book, the reader should always bear in mind that to the vast majority of their contemporaries all the painters and their friends treated here in such detail were far from well known. Vincent van Gogh hardly rated obituary notices, and any writer on French art during his lifetime would scarcely have mentioned him, nor would he have done much better by Seurat, Gauguin, or Redon. Their lives and works were of no consequence in their own day and we actually "distort" history by singling them out and remaining silent about many events and figures which their contemporaries considered infinitely more important. But with the distance of a little over half a century that separates us from the period here studied, we are now able to concentrate our attention on the men who did most to shape the art of the following decades. Thus we approach their times with the hindsight of those who, while recording facts, possess the necessary detachment to evaluate them properly.

The place accorded van Gogh in these pages may go somewhat beyond a "reasonable" treatment, but he has not only emerged as the painter of the period who most powerfully captivates today's public, he has also been the subject of much fiction, confusion, and misinterpretation. As the present book afforded an opportunity to set the record straight and as van Gogh was more or less closely connected with everything that happened in the art world between his arrival in Paris and his death four years later, it seemed not inappropriate to dwell at particular length on his life and work.

8

Some of the painters who lived at the same time and even some of those who gained stature during the same years have been mentioned only in passing, so as not to distract from the central theme. These men, above all Toulouse-Lautrec, the *douanier* Rousseau, the Nabis (Bonnard, Vuillard, Sérusier, Denis, Vallotton, etc.), and Cézanne—who only "emerged" in 1895 when Vollard gave him his first one-man show—will be treated in a subsequent volume devoted to the second half of the post-impressionist period.

The term "post-impressionism" is not a very precise one , though it is certainly a very convenient one. In a broad sense it covers the period from about 1886, when the impressionists held their last and incomplete exhibition at which the neo-impressionists appeared for the first time, until some twenty years later, when cubism was born and with it a completely new era which ushered in what we may call contemporary art. The second volume devoted to the post-impressionist period will therefore cover not only those men or movements which, though contemporary with van Gogh and Seurat, were neglected in the present study, but also those who emerged after their death, such as the Fauves and the young Picasso, as well as Gauguin during his second and last trip to Tahiti.

Mark Twain has said somewhere that "in writing, it is usually stronger and more dramatic to have a man speak for himself than to have someone else relate a thing about him." This has been my guiding principle; I have effaced myself wherever possible so as to let the artists and all other available sources speak for themselves. Many of the documents presented here have not been published before; others have been translated into English for the first time; still others have been retranslated when previous versions did not appear satisfactory.

It should be mentioned in passing that since this book may be read separately while at the same time it constitutes a sequel to my *History of Impressionism*, there are some unavoidable repetitions involved in the last two chapters of the earlier and the first chapter of the present volume. It seems equally necessary to inform the reader that in a few instances I have borrowed from my own previous writings, particularly my books on Seurat, Gauguin, and Bonnard, and articles on Fénéon, Gachet, van Gogh, etc., without identifying such minor passages as quotations.

I have received the most generous help from museum officials, art historians, collectors, and art dealers in the United States as well as abroad. To name them all would constitute a duplication of the *Who's Who* of modern art. But in some cases a special expression of gratitude seems called for. I have been fortunate. enough to have known intimately Félix Fénéon and Lucien Pissarro, and somewhat less intimately, among the other protagonists of this book, Paul Signac, Emile Bernard, Henry van de Velde, Maximilien Luce, Maurice Denis, and Comte Antoine de La Rochefoucauld; I have also had an illuminating correspondence with the Danish painter, the late Jens Ferdinand Willumsen. In numerous instances I have consulted the widows or descendants of men discussed here, and was given kind assistance and permitted to copy a multitude of hitherto unknown documents. Among those who were especially helpful were van Gogh's nephew (Theo's son), Ir. Dr. Vincent W. van Gogh of Laren, without whose unselfish coöperation this book could not have been written in its present form; Signac's daughter, Mme Ginette Signac; Théo van Rysselberghe's widow, the late Mme Maria van Rysselberghe (M. Saint-Clair); and Angrand's nephew, M. Pierre Angrand, all of Paris, who helped me in every conceivable way and allowed me to copy innumerable unpublished letters which shed a more complete light on the neo-impressionist movement. Albert Aurier's nephew and niece,

M. Jacques Williame of Châteauroux and Mme Mahé-Williame of Aix-en-Provence, entrusted me with their uncle's invaluable correspondence; Emile Bernard's son and son-in-law, M. Michel-Ange Bernard Fort and M. Clément Altarriba, both of Paris, gave me equally generous assistance through the communication of many revealing manuscripts by Bernard; my friend the late Mrs. Esther L. Pissarro of London bequeathed to me a group of precious documents, letters written to or notes taken by her late husband, Lucien Pissarro; Mme Jeanne Schuffenecker of Paris authorized me to copy important letters among the papers of her father, Emile Schuffenecker; so did my friend the late Ludovic-Rodo Pissarro, who put at my complete disposal the voluminous correspondence of his father, Camille Pissarro. Odilon Redon's son, M. Arï Redon of Paris; Dr. Gachet's son, the late M. Paul Gachet of Auvers-sur-Oise; Hippolyte Petitjean's daughter, Anquetin's niece, the late Mme du Ferron-Anquetin; Sérusier's widow, the late Mme Paul Sérusier and her friend, Mlle H. Boutaric, all of Paris, and Mr. Henri Dorra of Santa Barbara, Calif., were equally helpful with information and documents. For photographic material I have received particularly valuable assistance from the Wildenstein Galleries, Inc., of New York and Paris. Prof. A. M. Hammacher, former Director of the Rijksmuseum Kröller-Müller, Otterlo, and Mr. H. L. C. Jaffé, former Assistant Director of the Stedelijk Museum, Amsterdam, answered numerous queries with unending patience. I am also indebted to Dr. Erwin Ackerknecht, of the University of Zurich, to the late Agnès Huc de Monfreid and to Mme Anne Joly-Segalen of Paris.

I am deeply grateful to my friends Alfred H. Barr, Jr., for reading the manuscript and making many useful suggestions, Monroe Wheeler for his sympathetic encouragement, Frances Pernas for valiantly supervising the production of this book, diligently assisted by John Kirsch, and, last but not least, Gerstle Mack for patiently checking the translations and revising the text.　　　　　　　　　　　　　　　— JOHN REWALD

FOREWORD TO THE THIRD EDITION

While the differences between the first edition of this book in 1956 and its second printing in 1962 were not too great—except for the correction of errors, supplying changes in ownership of works reproduced, and extension of the bibliography—this third edition contains more numerous revisions. The second edition had featured new documents only in chapter V, but in the fifteen intervening years, more data, now duly incorporated into the text, have been brought to light.

I owe a special debt of gratitude to the late Marc E. Tralbaut for his communication of several early Dutch articles on the van Gogh brothers, and to Bengt Danielsson, who most kindly corrected some errors, mainly concerning the topography of Tahiti and the chronology of Gauguin's first sojourn there. Ned Polsky was very helpful in bringing an unexpected number of misprints to my attention, and Mark Roskill made various welcome suggestions. I am deeply indebted to Jane Fluegel for the patience and skill with which she has supervised the preparation of this new edition; to Pauline Di Blasi for her thoughtful attention to detail in adapting the design for this new edition; and to Frances Weitzenhoffer for her devoted help with many aspects of the book.

The bibliography once more has been brought up to date and discusses many of the very important publications that have appeared in recent years.　　— J. R.

I 1886-1888 VAN GOGH IN PARIS

"I shall be in the Louvre from noon on, or earlier, if you wish." With these words, written towards the end of February 1886, Vincent van Gogh informed his brother Theo that he had suddenly left Antwerp for Paris. He added that he would be waiting for him in the famous *Salon carré*. And there, surrounded by the Louvre's proudest possessions, by works of Leonardo, Titian, Raphael and Veronese, of van Eyck, Rubens and Rembrandt, of Holbein, Velásquez and many others, the two brothers met. But it was not precisely to study these masters that Vincent van Gogh had hurried to Paris. He had been there before, in his early twenties, first in 1874 and again for a year from 1875 to 1876, as an employee of the Goupil Galleries in which one of his uncles was a partner. Since then, however, his life had changed completely and after many tribulations he was back now, no longer as an apprentice art dealer rather oblivious to the world around him, but as an art student himself. Matured and hungry for all that life had to offer, he was burning with the desire to perfect his instruction, to establish contact with anything unconventional and promising, to achieve a style of his own in the cosmopolitan maze of the French capital.[1]

Though Paris was then literally bursting with new movements and new ideas, it was by no means the only place in Europe that attracted young painters. In Munich Lenbach taught the wizardry of his brush, and students from all over the globe, including many Americans, flocked to his studio. In Düsseldorf too an international group gathered to imbibe the secrets of anecdotalism and a German version of Pre-Raphaelitism, even more anemic than its British counterpart and less poetic. On the surface Paris offered little more than did Munich or Düsseldorf. Its wide avenues held the same prejudices against all that was new, the same narrow-mindedness, the same provincialism, though more cleverly disguised as worldliness. But in its small side streets one could find a host of young painters, poets, philosophers, scientists, actors, and others, unknown to the crowds yet eager to throw new light on the world and to conquer it. For anyone ready to leave the beaten track Paris presented unforeseen opportunities to study the great currents of new thought at their very source, to plunge into the exciting whirl of revolutionary concepts.

As a matter of fact van Gogh could not have chosen a better place or a better time for his initiation. No less than four important exhibitions, each presenting a different aspect of contemporary tendencies, were held in Paris during that year of 1886. In May the official Salon offered to an appreciative public and complacent critics its annual contingent of academic portraits, pretty nudes, historical scenes, and genre pictures.[2] The works of Puvis de Chavannes, with their simplification of forms and their low-keyed harmonies, large compositions conceived in a semi-classical vein with mystic undertones, shone among these insipidities. Only the preceding year, while in Paris, Strindberg had found that Puvis "stood quite alone, like a contradiction, painting with a believing soul, even while he took passing notice of the taste of his contemporaries for allusion."[3] Yet it was not Puvis de Chavannes who provided the center of attraction at the Salon, but Albert Besnard, former Prix de Rome winner. He showed a portrait which presented a "daring" mixture of the lifeless academic tradition with some features of impressionism, thus achieving a compromise "modernism" that became almost palatable even to die-hard reactionaries.

Concurrently with the Salon the impressionist group opened its eighth exhibition in which, however, few of the original impressionists appeared. Most talked about was a narrow room where Seurat's *Grande Jatte* hung surrounded by canvases signed Signac and Pissarro, done in a similar technique. In a small hallway Odilon Redon presented a series of drawings in black and white, subtle yet full of a mysterious power. Degas exhibited a number of pastels entitled "Series of nudes of women bathing, washing, drying, rubbing down, combing their hair or having it combed." Gauguin, who had just spent the most miserable winter of his life, obliged to post bills in the Gare du Nord to earn a few pennies, was nevertheless able to show nineteen paintings, mostly landscapes, which still clearly demonstrated the influence of his former friend and mentor, Camille Pissarro, though the latter had meanwhile abandoned impressionism and adopted Seurat's theories. In fact Gauguin's paintings, together with those of Guillaumin and Berthe Morisot, as well as some timid works by Schuffenecker, a colleague of Gauguin, constituted the only representation of the impressionist element in the show.[4]

Renoir and Monet, who had not joined their impressionist friends, exhibited in June at the fifth Exposition Internationale in the sumptuous galleries of Georges Petit, where they found themselves in the company of the more fashionable celebrities of the day, among them Boldini, Besnard, Jacques-Emile Blanche and Raffaëlli. Monet was beginning at last to obtain comparatively high prices for his paintings and felt tempted to break with Durand-Ruel, who had been his dealer for fifteen years, in order to work with Petit, Durand-Ruel's most active rival. He believed that it would strengthen the public's confidence in the impressionists if their works were handled by several dealers instead of by Durand-Ruel alone, who had come to be suspected of boosting them solely because he had so many of their paintings. Renoir showed at Petit's several canvases which attested to his effort to break away from impressionism by emphasizing draftsmanship and adopting a much smoother brushwork than in his vibrant and more colorful earlier paintings.

In August the Salon des Indépendants displayed the works of those artists who were treated without mercy by the Salon jury or who did not wish to invite its verdict. There Seurat showed his *Grande Jatte* again, Redon exhibited once more, and the *douanier* Rousseau appeared for the first time before the public eye, stoically defying general hilarity. What most intrigued the visitors was the evidence that Seurat's "divisionism" (as he called it) had acquired more adherents. Seurat now found himself at the head of a small group which comprised not only Camille Pissarro, his eldest son Lucien, and Signac, but also Angrand, Cross, and Dubois-Pillet. Among the new generation the ranks of those whom a friend of Seurat called "dissidents from impressionism" were obviously growing.

Added to these exhibitions which drew large crowds, there were also some one-man and group shows which dealers such as Durand-Ruel, Georges Petit, and Goupil began to organize and which were still quite a novelty at the time. Thus an exhibition of Gustave

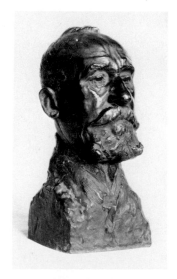

RODIN: *Bust of Puvis de Chavannes,* 1891. Bronze, 16½" high. Philadelphia Museum of Art

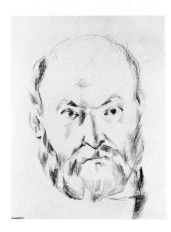

Moreau's illustrations for La Fontaine's *Fables*, held in 1886 at the Goupil Galleries, acquainted van Gogh with yet another aspect of French art: a strange mixture of an unbridled, romantic imagination and linear asceticism, of grandiose visions blurred by a futile application to details, of literary inspiration and a genuine colorist's eye. It was a mixture of the most anachronistic tendencies that seemed to drown the talent of this isolated painter, whom success was just about to consecrate.[5]

During that same year of 1886 Emile Zola, whom van Gogh admired greatly, published his novel *L'Oeuvre*, dealing with the failure of an "impressionist" painter who ultimately loses his mind and commits suicide. Many readers—van Gogh among them—thought they recognized in Zola's hero the author's friend Manet, dead since 1883. Nobody suspected that Zola had actually drawn mostly upon Cézanne for many of the traits of his lamentable artist. Indeed there were very few in Paris who had ever heard of Cézanne, secluded in his native Aix, or of Zola's intimate association with him. Van Gogh, who had already read some installments of the book in Antwerp, found in it much food for meditation and a certain amount of information about the early years of the impressionist movement. But Monet was greatly disturbed by the implications of this novel, and Cézanne himself was so hurt by Zola's lack of understanding that he broke off a friendship which had started on a school-bench in Aix and lasted for thirty years.[6]

In 1886 also, Félix Fénéon, a young critic, wrote a series of articles on *Les Impressionnistes en 1886*, endeavoring to prove that the "naturalistic" impressionism was being superseded by a new "scientific" one, and explaining at length the theories of his friend Seurat. A young scientist, Charles Henry, at the same time concluded a study on *L'Esthétique Scientifique* which appeared, like Fénéon's articles, in the little review *La Vogue*, in which Verlaine published Rimbaud's prose poems, *Illuminations*, while the editor erroneously announced Rimbaud's death in Abyssinia. The *Illuminations* "enraptured several people and frightened some others," according to Fénéon. A little later Verlaine had to be hospitalized for alcoholism. Mallarmé went to see him after his release. It was in 1886 that Mallarmé also first met Monet and Renoir at Berthe Morisot's, wrote his introduction to René Ghil's *Traité du Verbe*, and began to attract a selected group of esthetes, poets and artists to the Tuesday gatherings at his apartment, where Whistler and later Oscar Wilde joined those who silently listened to the master's fascinating monologues. Among the first and most regular attendants were three very young and more or less unknown men: Edouard Dujardin, Teodor de Wyzewa, and Félix Fénéon.

Victor Hugo had died only the preceding year; Zola, Daudet, Maupassant were achieving fame; Flaubert's stature was posthumously increasing, but already the younger generation was beginning to react against naturalism with its "lack of mystery," its careful descriptions rather than suggestions and evocations of moods. Thus in the fall of 1886 Jean Moréas issued a much-discussed *Manifeste du Symbolisme*, announcing the principles of a new literary concept. Moréas was valiantly supported by Gustave Kahn, who had just put the final touches to a volume of poetry written in what he called *vers libre*, a form whose disregard for traditional syntax greatly alarmed Mallarmé. There were also attempts by Antoine to reanimate the theater, and Ibsen was about to be revealed to the Parisian avant-garde. The first French translations of Dostoevsky and Tolstoi were appearing in rapid succession and attracting wide attention; *Crime and Punishment* and *Anna Karenina* were published in 1886 in Paris. A Pole, Teodor de Wyzewa, capably acted as delegate for Slavic letters in France.

The music and philosophy of Richard Wagner, who had died in 1883, continued to pre-occupy French intellectuals because they discovered in his work an echo of medieval mysticism as well as a new musical language related to the recent evolution of French poetry. Fénéon's friend Dujardin, assisted by Wyzewa, had just founded a *Revue Wagnérienne* to which Mallarmé contributed. Yet Paris had listened until then only to concerts of Wagner's music; with the exception of *Tannhäuser*, played as far back as 1861, none of his operas had been presented in France though they were being given all over the globe, including Russia and America. But when the state-subsidized Opéra Comique announced that it would produce *Lohengrin* early in 1886, this project immediately brought vehement protestations from rabble-rousing patriots. A prominent official painter threatened to invade the theater with "two hundred young people from the Ecole des Beaux-Arts, students and models, dressed in togas and provided with whistles."[7] Yielding to pressure, the management declared that the project was abandoned. *Lohengrin* eventually was given in a private theater in 1887, but caused such a turmoil that a second presentation was canceled and tickets were refunded. The Hungarian Franz Liszt, however, shortly before his death in 1886, was officially received by the French president and a banquet was given in his honor.

At least half a dozen little magazines were founded in the course of 1886 to promote new talents in literature, poetry and art, but some of them—and not the most unworthy—did not live until the end of the year. Angry battles raged among the proponents of opposed and even of kindred conceptions; numerous duels took place on the meadows outside Paris. In one of these, Edouard Drumont, a fierce anti-semite, whose book *La France juive* immediately became a "best-seller" in 1886, was slightly wounded; in another a young writer, Robert Caze, a friend of Seurat's, was killed (and a French lady challenged Mrs. Booth, Marshal of the Salvation Army, then visiting Paris, to a fight which never took place).[8] Less sanguinary duels were fought on the terraces of boulevard cafés. There was agitation in the studios and ebullition in editorial offices. In the background sounded the occasional burst of anarchist bombs as the Russian nihilist movement and Kropotkin's writings found a slowly rising following in France. Louise Michel, a famous French revolutionary, and Prince Kropotkin were released from prison in 1886 as a result of a general amnesty. (There was also, on May 1, 1886, a huge strike in Chicago, during which an anarchist bomb exploded among the police force.) The agitation created by anarchists did much to disturb the French middle class which, after a great economic crisis in 1882, was only beginning to catch its breath and now looked with hope to General Boulanger, the power-hungry Minister of War supported by the former socialist Clemenceau. A national loan for five hundred million francs was over-subscribed twenty-one times within a few days, while the young republic solidified its position by banishing from French soil the Bonaparte and Bourbon-d'Orléans pretenders to France's throne and by curbing in 1887 Boulanger's dictatorial ambitions. At the same time an auction sale of the crown jewels was being prepared and a public subscription was voted for the founding of an "Institut Pasteur" after Pasteur had for the first time successfully and dramatically inoculated a man against rabies.

But there was also great noise and fun in Paris. Two dancers, La Goulue and Grille d'Egout, began to attract attention with their lively and somewhat impudent performances and the public flocked to the cabarets generously sprinkled all over Montmartre: the Divan Japonais and the Cabaret des Assassins which later became the Lapin Agile, both of which had just

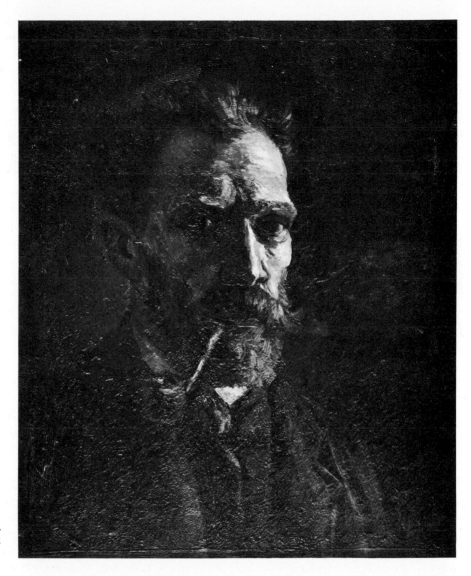

VAN GOGH: *Self-Portrait,* Paris, 1886.
18⅛ x 15". Rijksmuseum Vincent van
Gogh, Amsterdam

opened; the Mirliton, where the picturesque Aristide Bruant entertained his clients by
bullying them unmercifully (Henri de Toulouse-Lautrec, an unknown young painter and
Bruant's friend, exhibited his paintings there); and the Chat Noir, where the customers
were attended by waiters attired in the elaborately embroidered green costumes of the
venerable members of the French Academy. Theo van Gogh was well acquainted with
Henri Rivière, author of Chinese shadow plays given at this cabaret. The Chat Noir was in
the rue Laval, not far from the place Pigalle; in the same street Theo van Gogh had his
small apartment where his brother went to live with him.

Paris presented the sharpest possible contrast to the quietness of van Gogh's parental
home at Nuenen in Brabant or the dusty boredom of the Antwerp Academy, where his
self-consuming ardor had constantly bruised itself against the narrow barriers of prejudice.

He had arrived at the point where new stimuli had become not only an emotional but almost a physical necessity. Paris promised to provide just that. It was up to Theo now to guide his brother's first steps.

Theo van Gogh had lived in Paris for some seven years and was directing for Boussod & Valadon, successors of Goupil, a small gallery on the boulevard Montmartre. This was a minor branch of the main establishment, one of the greatest and most influential galleries in Paris.[9] Whereas on the ground floor of his gallery the customary "merchandise" was on display, Theo van Gogh was permitted, on the second floor, to deal in the works of the impressionists and their immediate predecessors, while his employers looked on skeptically and preferred to handle the more salable masters of the Salon, notably Bouguereau, for whose paintings there was a steady demand in America.[10] Theo's salary was small but was supplemented by his commissions on sales, and since he seems to have lived in modest comfort, this tends to prove that he did not do too badly in his venture. There can be little doubt that in his quest for new talents Theo van Gogh had visited the impressionist group exhibitions, held annually between 1879 and 1882, and that he had thus developed both a taste and a knowledge which he was now ready to pass on to his older brother.

In Theo's gallery Vincent van Gogh could study the works of Corot and Daumier (there were few clients for the latter's paintings), as well as those of Manet and Renoir, Monet and Pissarro, Sisley, Guillaumin and especially Degas. Until then it had been the Barbizon school which in Vincent's mind represented "modern art." He professed a boundless admiration for Corot, Troyon, Daubigny and above all Millet. He not only believed that Millet could never be surpassed, but actually thought that since Millet's death in 1875 there had begun a general artistic decline. He was completely unaware of the fact that the death of Millet had coincided with the rise of the impressionist movement, with its new approach to color and draftsmanship. This could hardly have been otherwise, since the impressionists had by no means achieved an undisputed reputation in France and their work was as yet completely unknown outside their own country. Indeed it was Bastien-Lepage, who had died in 1884 in his middle thirties, whose clever amalgam of Millet's subjects, of Puvis de Chavannes' simplifications, of a somewhat loose and impressionist execution and of attenuated colors dear to the official school had embodied for the world at large the last word in French modernism. Everywhere the younger generation was imitating his work.

Of the impressionists Vincent van Gogh only knew what his brother had told him in his letters, for instance that Monet used bright colors. He had not been particularly impressed by the few paintings by Manet he had seen during his earlier sojourns in Paris, but had since shown interest in such artists as Lhermitte and Raffaëlli, who combined a greatly diluted impressionist palette with conventional draftsmanship and more or less anecdotal subject matter. Actually subject matter had counted for much in van Gogh's appreciation of art; a certain sentimentality, especially in the representation of the humble, had never failed to move him. But he had also paid great attention to execution and had admired many painters, like Meissonier, whose only distinction was skillfulness and complete knowledge of all the tricks of the trade, which he himself lacked.

Although Delacroix's work had interested him profoundly, Vincent van Gogh had been of the opinion that the innovations of Delacroix, his sumptuous colors and nervous line, had left no trace on the evolution of art. The paintings of the impressionists were soon to convince him of his error. At one time, inspired by Delacroix, he had concerned himself with the breaking up of colors, the combination of complementaries and their influence on each other, but he had of course been unable to profit by the experience which the impressionists had gained in this field. Yet at the beginning he was not very much attracted by their works, as he later explained to his sister: "One has heard about the impressionists, one expects much and... when one sees them for the first time, one is very much disappointed and thinks they are ugly, sloppily and badly painted, badly drawn, of a poor color; everything that is miserable. That was my first impression also, when I came to Paris...."[11] But after he had studied them more closely, van Gogh professed great admiration for Monet's landscapes.

Theo van Gogh took his brother to some small dealers: Delarbeyrette, where they marveled at the scintillating impasto of Monticelli (who died in June 1886), and Portier, with whom Theo had already left some of the canvases Vincent had sent him, in the vain hope that he might be able to sell them. Portier did show van Gogh's paintings to his friend Guillaumin. The two brothers also went to see *père* Martin and *père* Thomas who, like Portier, made a modest living by selling at a small profit works by the impressionists and younger painters, though they constantly complained that there was no interest in their art. "Trade is slow here," van Gogh reported to a friend in Antwerp. "The great dealers sell Millet, Delacroix, Corot, Daubigny, Dupré, a few other masters, at exorbitant prices. They do little or nothing for young artists. The second-class dealers sell those, but at very low prices."[12]

The best place to study the impressionists was of course the gallery of Durand-Ruel who,

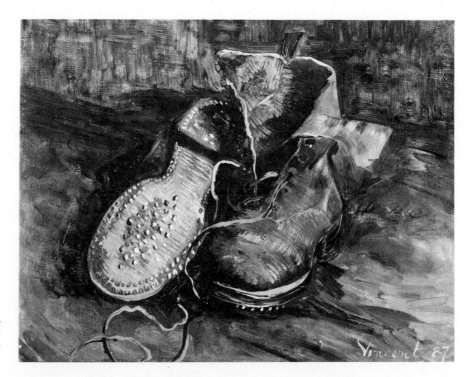

VAN GOGH: *Shoes,* Paris, d. **1887.** 13 x 16⅛". Formerly collection *père* Tanguy. Baltimore Museum of Art (Cone Collection)

since 1871, had accumulated an enormous stock of their paintings and had been reduced almost to bankruptcy by the general apathy towards the painters he represented. Visitors who were genuinely interested were always welcome there, even if they were not buyers; they were allowed to spend hours looking at unsold pictures dragged in by an assistant from the apparently inexhaustible reserves. Indeed it still took great courage to buy impressionist paintings, just as it required daring to praise them in the press or, for that matter, to expose the insipidity of the official masters. Monet's friend, the novelist Mirbeau, was requested by the publisher of a great daily paper *not* to review the Salon, in spite of a previous agreement, because eighty exhibitors at the Salon had been discovered to be subscribers to that newspaper. Bouguereau and Bonnat had even protested in advance against Mirbeau's articles.[13]

Anxious to popularize impressionism abroad, Durand-Ruel had organized in 1885 an exhibition in a Brussels hotel which met with little success, except for leaving a deep impact on a small group of young Belgian artists. In March 1886 Paul Durand-Ruel left for New York with some three hundred paintings, in a desperate effort to win over the new world to an art that could count on so little support at home. He returned to Paris in June, greatly encouraged by his reception in America though by no means at the end of his difficulties.[14] In spite of the fact that some collectors and most of the daily press in New York had manifested a certain sympathy, there had of course been voices which strongly opposed the impressionists. A number of vicious articles had shown that the painters still had to overcome in America enemies as violent as those they had met at their beginnings in France. The impressionists had been called in New York "insolent in the crudity and rudeness of their work,"[15] their show had been branded as "a collection of monstrosities of composition, color and drawing which would not be tolerated in any well regulated barber shop,"[16] and Renoir had been singled out particularly by antagonistic critics who considered that he expressed "his sense of color in a manner which reminds one of a cross between a rainbow and a pinwheel in active operation."[17] As for Degas, whose studies of nudes had enthralled van Gogh, he had been characterized by an American expert as "nothing but a peeping Tom behind the *coulisses* [scenes], and among the dressing-rooms of the ballet dancers, noting only travesties on fallen, debased womanhood, most disgusting and offensive."[15] Indeed, according to some, the worst feature of impressionism was its "low moral standard."

Vincent van Gogh, who had always been sensitive to the ethical values of the works he admired, found in what he saw at Durand-Ruel's none of the qualities that offended some of the American as well as many French critics. It is quite possible, however, that he was not able immediately to grasp the momentum of an art which he had considered a budding experiment but which he now discovered to be an accomplished conquest of a new vision. In any case, he found it easier at first to understand the robust qualities of Guillaumin and the paintings of Pissarro, considered the heir of Millet among the impressionists, than the more delicate art of Renoir.

The overabundance of fresh impressions during his first days or weeks in Paris naturally sharpened van Gogh's desire to set to work himself. Had he not come to Paris just because he wanted to perfect himself, anxious to continue an artistic apprenticeship that had already lasted some six years? In 1880, at the age of twenty-seven, driven by an irresistible urge to express his visual experiences, he had started an uphill fight against his own clumsiness. Though he had been an employee in art galleries, he had not previously shown

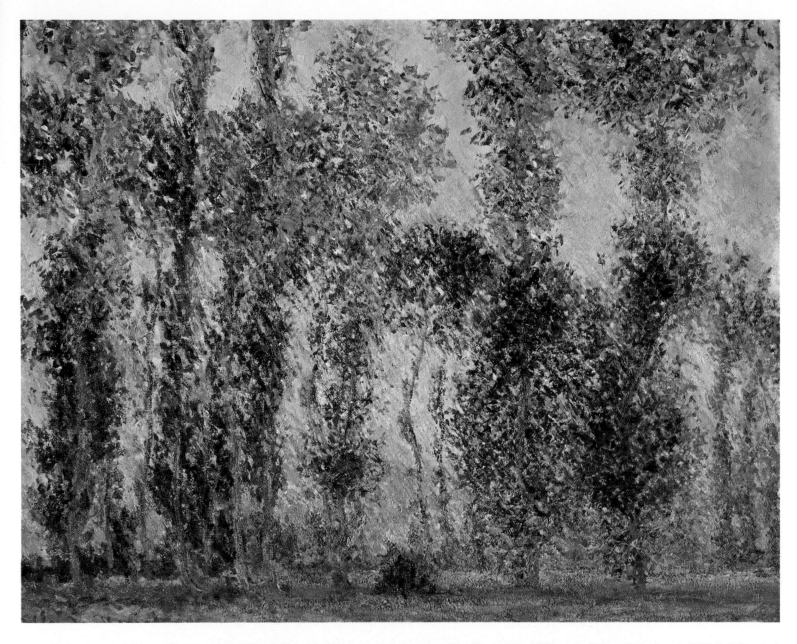

MONET: *Poplars at Giverny, Sunrise*, 1888. 29⅛ x 36½″. The Museum of Modern Art, New York (The William B. Jaffe and Evelyn A. J. Hall Collection)

the slightest inclination towards creativeness, and when the desire to draw had at last taken hold of him, he proved himself in the beginning so touchingly awkward that even the best-intentioned adviser could not have discerned in his first sketches the faintest gleam of promise. But with incredible stubbornness and ardor he had worked in Brussels, in the Hague, in his parents' home in Nuenen, and lastly in Antwerp, until his unskilled hand began to follow more and more closely the dictates of his eye and mind. Thus he had become an artist, not, like most artists, because he had shown precocious gifts or an early interest in matters of art, but rather because he *wanted* to paint and because he knew somehow that through application, patience, and persistence he would find a way to express himself. "That of which my head and heart are full must reappear in drawings or paintings," he had written in the early days of his career as an artist.[18] If there ever was a painter who set out with grim determination and by dint of sheer will power to struggle against the most discouraging odds—an apparently complete absence of talent—it was Vincent van Gogh. What gave him the courage to persevere was precisely the fact that his heart and head were filled with things he had to express. In order to do this with the necessary skill, he had voiced, even before leaving Antwerp, his intention to enter Cormon's studio where he wished to perfect himself in two fields: study from the nude and drawing from plaster casts of the antique. As there was not enough room in Theo's flat for Vincent to paint, he soon presented himself at Cormon's, whose studio was nearby. Since van Gogh was about ten years older than the average art student, of rather blunt manners and with a heavy accent, it is not easy to explain how he gained admission to Cormon's class, which was attended only by some thirty pupils, very few of whom were foreigners. But then Cormon was a rather good-natured man and the Dutchman's humble and ardent desire to work seriously may have decided him in favor of the unusual student.

At the age of forty Fernand Cormon, an academic painter, had already achieved certain fame with enormous and drab compositions of prehistoric scenes. A few years earlier, some pupils of the Ecole des Beaux-Arts, dissatisfied with the teaching of Léon Bonnat, had asked Cormon to take them in hand. Among these was the young Count de Toulouse-Lautrec who later described Cormon as "the ugliest and thinnest man in Paris." Though a very inferior artist, Cormon was not really a bad teacher. Kindness and patience made up to a certain extent for his lack of imagination or talent; and he was not unsympathetic to novelties. According to one of his pupils, however, "the crown of his reputation in the studio was that he kept three mistresses at one time."[19]

In spite of his relative open-mindedness, Cormon did have trouble with some unruly pupils who suffocated in the uninspiring atmosphere of his class. Just before van Gogh entered it, Cormon's studio had been the scene of a minor upheaval, the tale of which apparently spread all over Montmartre, duly exaggerated in the process. One of his favorite students, Emile Bernard, not quite eighteen years old, had been discovered one morning painting the old brown sail that served as a background to the model, in alternate streaks of vermilion and emerald. Outraged, Cormon threw him out, sent for his father and requested the permanent removal of the offender accused of leading a revolt against his master's sacred academic principles.[20]

As a matter of fact, the episode of the old brown sail was merely the culmination of a series of incidents. At Cormon's young Bernard had fallen in with an older student who never did any work but who was well versed in matters of art and regularly visited the galleries in the rue Laffitte, such as Durand-Ruel's. He made Bernard appreciate the

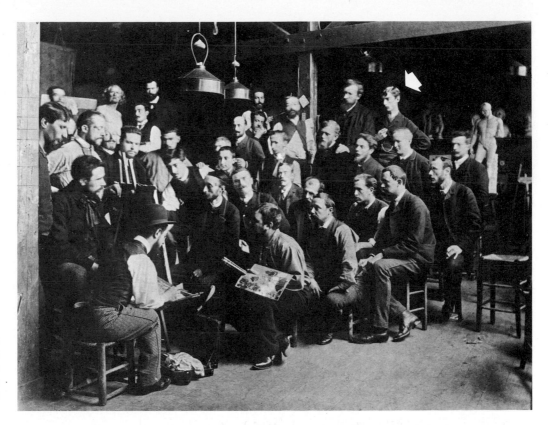

Photograph of Cormon's students in their classroom, c. 1886. In the left foreground, H. de Toulouse-Lautrec, seated; standing in the background, Emile Bernard (see arrow)

paintings of Courbet, Manet, and the impressionists; he also took him to the Louvre to study the works of Velásquez. As a result, as Bernard himself later recalled: "I began to form my own ideas on art and I expressed them at the studio. I said that what we were taught was based on nothing, that the [real] Masters had a much greater knowledge, that the impressionists offered us the theory of colors, that their works were filled with truth, with observation, with feeling, that we should all attempt to achieve a personal style through theories and contact with nature."[21] It is not surprising then that Cormon told Bernard's father: "Your son is very gifted, but he is an independent and I can't keep him." Greatly disappointed, Bernard senior seized the culprit's brushes and paints, threw them in the fire and ordered his son to look for a commercial career. This the young man refused to do.

Young Bernard found an unexpected helper in his predicament in Julien Tanguy, a color grinder and dealer, in whose small shop, not far from the boulevard de Clichy, Cézanne used to leave some of his works. Bernard later told a friend (not without dramatizing the events) what Tanguy had done for him in those days when he was forbidden by his father to paint: "I was without colors, without money, sometimes even without food when I walked [from Asnières] to Paris to see the masterpieces in the Louvre.... Tanguy happened to be on my route, and it is thanks to him that my career opened itself up before me.... I even owe him my initial education. It was he who showed and explained Cézanne's works to me; only through him were the miseries of that life of art revealed to me at the mention of names I admired. Suffering as I was then, and even deprived of what it takes to produce, those paintings fired my enthusiasm. I was happy to have to suffer like the others...."[22] Thus strengthened in his resolve to become an artist, Bernard, a few weeks after the Cormon incident, returned to the studio to bid his former comrades farewell before setting out on foot for Normandy and Brittany. In the dim studio with its low model stand on which a nude held the pose against a dirty drapery that had replaced the one colored by Bernard, he saw for the first time Vincent van Gogh, working arduously on his canvas and substituting for the soiled material of the background a colorful tapestry of his own invention. Thus van Gogh achieved in his sketch what Bernard had attempted to do to the object itself. The others occasionally made fun of van Gogh, but he apparently did not care, nor did Cormon seem to feel as offended by his liberties as he had been by Bernard's. Indeed, when Cormon, on his weekly round, came to correct van Gogh's first oil painting done in vivid colors, he only criticized the drawing and completely avoided comments on the intense blue of the drapery and the golden yellow of the nude which had puzzled the other pupils.

According to François Gauzi, one of Lautrec's best friends, van Gogh was known to Cormon's pupils by his first name only. "He was an excellent comrade but had to be left in peace. A man from the North, he did not appreciate the Parisian 'esprit.' The smart alecs in the studio refrained from teasing him for they were somewhat afraid of him. When the others discussed art, and their opinions, opposed to his own, exasperated him, he was apt to flare up in the most disquieting fashion. Color drove him mad. Delacroix was his god and his lips trembled with emotion when he spoke of him. For a long time van Gogh only made drawings which had nothing excessive about them and did not distinguish themselves by any particular tendency."[23]

Determined as he was to master the rudiments of art and used to being jeered at or misunderstood, van Gogh was no doubt happy to find at Cormon's a model to work from, the technical corrections he needed, and also a few colleagues with whom he could occasionally exchange ideas. Beyond this he did not expect anything and was therefore spared disillusionment. He was completely aware of the fact that technical proficiency was not an end in itself, as it was for most Salon painters. Long before he went to Paris he had explained to a friend: "Do you think that I do not care for technique? Certainly I do, but only in order that I may say what I have to say, and when I cannot yet do that satisfactorily, I try hard to correct myself. But if my language is not to the liking of the speakers, or of the audience, I do not care a rap about it."[24]

So eager was van Gogh to extend his knowledge that in the beginning he also spent his afternoons in the studio, when no other pupils were there. He used to draw then from plaster casts, correcting his lines relentlessly, or untiringly starting all over again, and often erasing with so much passion that he rubbed holes in his paper.[25] "Theo's brother is certainly here for good," Theo's best friend, Andries Bonger, who almost daily dined with the two, reported to his parents in Holland. "In any case, he intends to work for three years in Cormon's studio. I believe I have already told you how strange the life of this brother has been. He knows nothing of a well-regulated existence and cannot get along with anybody. Theo therefore has a good deal of trouble with him."[26]

In June Theo moved to a larger apartment at 54, rue Lepic—farther up the slope of Montmartre and not far from the Moulin de la Galette. Even though Vincent later said that he could never get used to the staircases in Paris—they made him dizzy and filled him with awful nightmares—he was happy at last to get a room where he could work. By then he was no longer thinking of remaining for years at Cormon's but was spending long hours in the Louvre or roaming through the streets of Paris. Their new flat provided the brothers with more space; it also delighted them because of its unique view over all of Paris and even as far as the distant hills of Meudon and Saint-Cloud. This view reminded them of a lyrical description of the Parisian panorama in one of Zola's recent novels and Theo ventured the opinion that it might offer subjects not only for paintings but also for verses. "They have an apartment which is quite large for Paris," Andries Bonger wrote, "and they keep house themselves; they have taken a cook *in optima forma*. Theo continues to look sickly.... The poor fellow has lots of trouble. On top of this his brother makes life almost unbearable for him and continually reproaches him for things over which Theo has no control." [27]

But when Theo himself wrote to their mother, he avoided complaining about Vincent's unruly behavior. "We like the new apartment very much," he said. "You wouldn't recognize Vincent, so much has he changed and it strikes other people even more than it does me.... He makes great progress in his work and has begun to have some success. He is in much better spirits than before and many people here like him.... He has friends who send him every week a bunch of beautiful flowers which he uses for still life. He paints chiefly flowers, especially to make the colors for his future pictures brighter and clearer. If we can continue to live together like this, I think the most difficult period is past and he will find his way." [28]

During the summer of 1886 Theo went to Holland for his vacation and his friend Bonger agreed to live with Vincent so that the painter would not be alone, particularly since he was in poor health. It was then that an odd and somewhat obscure incident occurred: apparently Theo's French mistress, with whom it seems he had just decided to break, unexpectedly moved in with the two men. She must have been rather high-strung, mentally unstable and physically ill; nobody knew quite what to do with her. "These are strange days," Vincent wrote to his brother. "Sometimes we are really frightened by her, but at other times we are terribly gay and turbulent.... You will know only when you see her again without fear of falling once more into her grasp whether everything is really finished between you and her. That you two do not belong together is certain, and that we therefore have to come to a decision is also certain." Vincent was very anxious to see his brother "free again to go his own way" and therefore submitted his own plan: "The solution to the question which you mention in your letter—that is, that either she or I would have to leave the apartment—this solution has to be decisive once and for all, if it can be carried out.... You must be prepared to understand that this can not be settled in the way you imagine, by being abrupt with her; through such conduct you will only obtain from her the opposite of what you want, possibly pushing her to commit suicide or to lose her mind, and that would of course have very sad repercussions on yourself and would break you for the rest of your life.... I have talked with Bonger about this.... You should try to get rid of her by finding somebody else for her, and... a friendly solution, which seems right at hand, would be for you to give her over to me.... Should either you or she insist on this, then I am willing to take her over, though preferably without having to marry her; yet if it looks better to the others, then a marriage of convenience...." [29] To these lines Bonger added a lengthy analysis of his own, concurring with Vincent's description of the girl's condition, but concluding: "It is quite possible to agree upon a plan, yet the one suggested

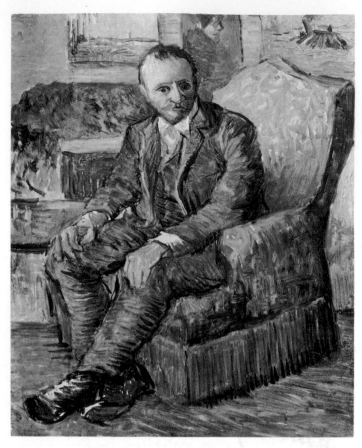

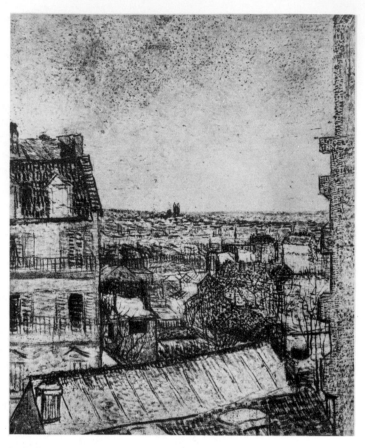

VAN GOGH: *Portrait of Alexander Reid,* Paris, c. 1887. Oil on panel, 16⅛ x 12¾". Collection Mrs. Aaron M. Weitzenhoffer, Oklahoma City

VAN GOGH: *View from van Gogh's Room,* rue Lepic, Paris, Spring 1887. Oil on cardboard, 18⅛ x 15". Formerly collection H. de Toulouse-Lautrec. Private collection, U.S.A.

by Vincent is unworkable." It is not known what happened subsequently. The question does not seem to have been discussed again in any letters of the two brothers; evidently the painter's altruistic offer never received serious consideration.

On another occasion Vincent roomed together at Theo's with the English art dealer Alexander Reid, who for a time worked at Boussod & Valadon's. Reid was then toying with the idea of becoming an artist himself. He shared Vincent's enthusiasm for Monticelli and van Gogh found in him a willing model for portraits. But their friendship did not last long. In his own peculiar English the painter later wrote on the subject of Reid: "I was very much taken in by him during the first six weeks or two months, but after that period he was in pecuniary difficulties and in the same acted in a way that made on me the impression that he had lost his wits, which I still think was the case, and consequently he [is] not responsible even if his doings then were pretty unfair. He is very nervous—as we all are—and can't help being so. He is prompted to act in his crisis of nerves to make money... whilst painters would make pictures...."[30]

Reid's own explanation of their friction was quite different. Being out of favor with his

24

mistress, he one day unburdened himself to Vincent, who was equally depressed because he depended so completely on Theo's financial help. Vincent thereupon "gallantly suggested a suicide pact. This appeared to Reid as altogether too drastic a solution and, as Vincent continued with the gruesome preparations, he decided to make himself scarce."[31]

Theo had gone to Holland in the hope of persuading his uncles to help him set up his own business where he could handle the work of avant-garde artists in whom he believed, a project which Vincent greatly favored. But he failed in his efforts. On the other hand he apparently succeeded in convincing the various members of the van Gogh family of the fact that Vincent was a serious painter whose work held real promise. "I have learned with pleasure," Bonger wrote to Theo, "that Vincent is now being recognized. This must be quite a satisfaction for you who have had such staunch confidence in him." And Bonger went on to report on Vincent's progress: "He has painted a few very beautiful things.... His series of flower still lifes strikes one as gay and colorful on the whole. But some of them I find rather flat, though I can't persuade him that they are. He always replies: 'But it was my intention to bring out this and that in contrasts of colors.' As if I cared what he *intended* to do!"[29] Vincent himself informed his brother that he was working particularly with contrasts of complementaries, painting for instance orange tiger lilies against a blue background, a bunch of purple dahlias against a yellow background, or red gladioli in a blue vase against yellow. A little later he wrote to an English painter whom he had met in

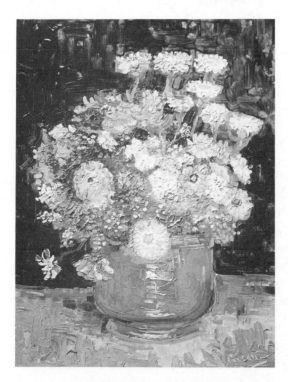

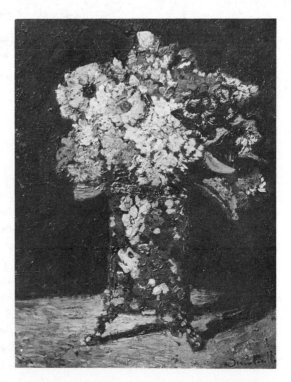

VAN GOGH: *Zinnias,* Paris, c. 1886. 24 x 18″. Present whereabouts unknown.

MONTICELLI: *Vase with Flowers,* 1875–80. 20 x 15⅜″. Formerly collection Theo van Gogh. Rijksmuseum Vincent van Gogh, Amsterdam

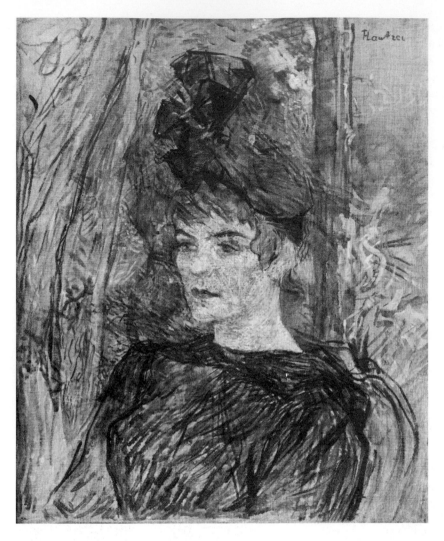

TOULOUSE-LAUTREC: *Portrait of Suzanne Valadon*, 1884. 21⅝ x 17¾". Ny Carlsberg Glyptotek, Copenhagen

Antwerp: "I have lacked money for paying models, else I had entirely given myself to figure painting; but I have made a series of colour studies in painting simply flowers, red poppies, blue cornflowers, and myosotis, white and pink roses, yellow chrysanthemums, seeking oppositions of blue with orange, red, green, yellow, and violet, seeking *les tons rompus et neutres* to harmonise brutal extremes. Trying to render intense *colour*, and not a *grey* harmony. Now after these gymnastics I lately did two heads, which I daresay are better in light and colour than those I did before. So as we said at the time in *colour* seeking *life*—the true drawing is modelling with colour. I did a dozen landscapes—two frankly *green*, frankly *blue*. And so I am struggling for life and progress in art." Van Gogh also told his friend: "There is but one Paris; and however hard living may be here, and if it became worse and harder even, the French air clears up the brain and does one good—a world of good...."[12]

Since he could not afford to hire his own models van Gogh apparently continued for some time to work at Cormon's where he had become acquainted with two fellow students, Anquetin and Toulouse-Lautrec. The latter, as dissatisfied with Cormon's teaching as he had been with Bonnat's, began slowly to drift away from the studio, attending it ever less frequently. He had rented a studio of his own in Montmartre and was interested mostly in doing portraits of the people around him, of studying the physiognomies of relatives or friends, and expressing—with a brush that still showed some indebtedness to the impressionists—his perfect understanding of men and his astonishing psychological insight. According to a friend of his, Lautrec had made at Cormon's "a great effort to copy the model exactly; but in spite of himself he exaggerated certain typical details, sometimes the general character, so that he distorted without trying or even wanting to. I have seen him force himself to 'prettify' his study of a model: in my opinion without success."[32]

In 1884, when not quite twenty, Lautrec had painted a portrait of a young model who in December 1883 had given birth to a child who still bore his mother's name but was eventually to be adopted by a Spaniard named Utrillo. Suzanne Valadon, whose beauty, grace, and youthful charm had made her a favorite model of Puvis de Chavannes and Renoir, appears in Lautrec's likeness sad and unglamorous, as if he had been able to guess how she would look once she had lost the loveliness of her nineteen years. (It is true that Suzanne Valadon, who had begun to draw, was almost as severe when she portrayed herself.) Shortly after doing her portrait Lautrec painted one of Emile Bernard, his ambitious and restless comrade at Cormon's. Bernard sat no fewer than twenty times for this canvas because Lautrec could not manage to harmonize the background satisfactorily with the face. Thus Bernard frequently visited Lautrec's studio in the rue Tourlaque where, according to his recollections, he met the dancer La Goulue, Aristide Bruant, and a good many revelers of whose morals, songs, and jokes he heartily disapproved.[21] In 1887 Lautrec

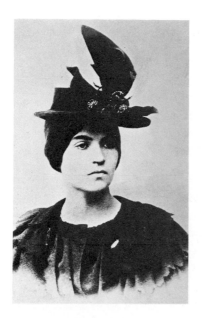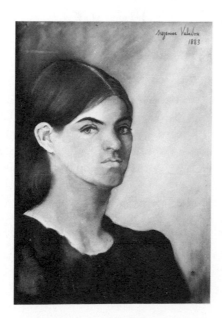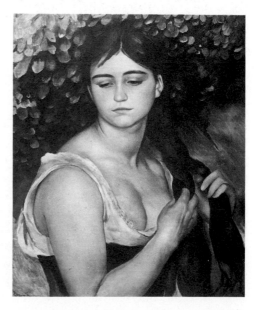

Left: Photograph of Suzanne Valadon, c. 1890. Center: VALADON: *Self-Portrait*, d. 1883. Pastel. Musées Nationaux, Paris. Right: RENOIR: *The Tresses* (Suzanne Valadon), c. 1885, 22 x 18½". Collection Sidney W. Brown, Baden, Switzerland

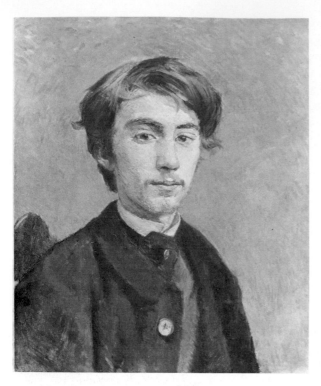

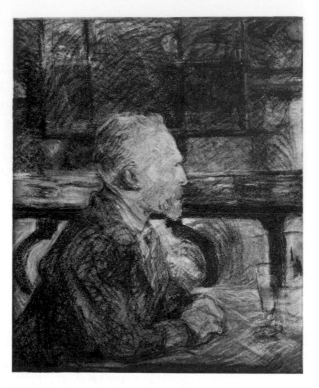

TOULOUSE-LAUTREC: *Portrait of Emile Bernard,* 1885 (?). 21¼ x 17¾″. Tate Gallery, London (Bequest of Arthur Jeffres)

TOULOUSE-LAUTREC: *Portrait of Vincent van Gogh,* Paris, 1887. Pastel, 22½ x 18½″. Rijksmuseum Vincent van Gogh, Amsterdam

also sketched a likeness of van Gogh at a café, showing him in a rather brooding mood and charged with that tension which struck all those who met him in Paris.

While Lautrec was fascinating, sharp-witted, arrogant, tender, loyal, full of incongruous ideas, always casting a curious eye on his surroundings like a hound on the scent of game, his was not a personality which could form an intimate friendship with van Gogh. The Dutchman's idealism and warmth could not easily reconcile themselves with Lautrec's sarcastic spirit and lack of respect for almost everything. Had he not, in 1884, painted a huge parody of Puvis de Chavannes' *Sacred Wood* (for which Suzanne Valadon had posed) in which the paradise of Olympian virgins was invaded by a procession of Lautrec's friends held back by a gendarme? Yet van Gogh and Lautrec must have felt esteem for each other's sincerity. As they apparently did not meet often at Cormon's, it is likely that their acquaintance was maintained through occasional encounters in the studios of friends, such as Anquetin, or in various cafés. Suzanne Valadon, who is believed to have modeled also for van Gogh, later reported that for some time he made regular appearances at Lautrec's studio: "He arrived, carrying a heavy canvas which he stood in a corner where it got a good light and then waited for some attention to be shown. But no one bothered. He sat opposite his picture, scrutinizing the others' glances, taking little part in the conversation, and finally he left wearied, taking his last work with him. But the next week he came back and began the same pantomime all over again."[33] Indignant, Suzanne Valadon thought that painters were very cruel folk, but the truth is that in the carefree atmosphere of Lautrec's studio van Gogh's intensity—even the intensity of his humility—must have made the others feel quite uncomfortable. He simply did not belong there and in the end he probably realized that himself.

Van Gogh got along much better with Lautrec's friend Anquetin. Like Lautrec, Louis Anquetin did not have to worry about supporting himself. His father, though not an aristocrat of glorious ancestry but a butcher, provided for his son's career. He had his own apartment of three small rooms in the avenue de Clichy and a red-haired mistress who not only loved the impressionists but actually owned some paintings by Caillebotte. In contrast to Lautrec's dwarfed body and his fascinatingly ugly features Anquetin was a striking figure, overflowing with health and vigor; he was always active, expending in horseback riding the energy his work could not absorb. His friends, especially Lautrec, admired the ease and forcefulness with which he expressed himself as an artist as well as the passion with which he set out to "invent" painting all over again. Lautrec went so far

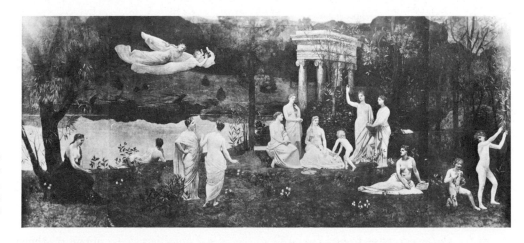

Puvis de Chavannes: *The Sacred Wood Dear to the Arts and the Muses,* 1884. 19′ x 33′4″. Exhibited at the Salon of 1884. Musée des Beaux-Arts, Lyons

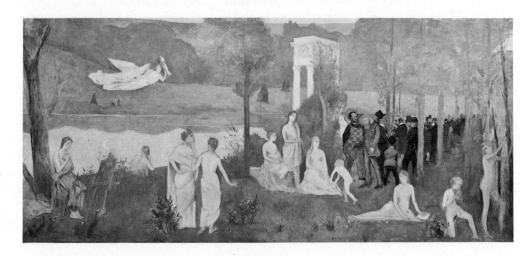

Toulouse-Lautrec: *Parody on "The Sacred Wood" of Puvis de Chavannes,* 1884. 68 x 150″. Henry and Rose Pearlman Foundation, New York

as to say that since Manet no painter had been as richly gifted as Anquetin.[34] But Signac later commented that Anquetin was "too skillful" and subject to too many influences; "the tenth part of that talent in the hands of an original creator would be enough to produce marvels."[35] In the beginning Anquetin's work had shown great indebtedness to Delacroix and Michelangelo (for both of whom Cormon had little taste). He then had manifested the successive influences of Degas, of Japanese prints, and of the impressionists; he even went to work in Vétheuil in order to be near Monet and benefit from his advice.

With many others, Anquetin had believed that the theories of color, dear to Delacroix, had become those of the impressionists, and he expected from Monet an initiation into these theories. But he soon discovered that Monet knew very little about the problems he was so eager to study. As a matter of fact, though working with a palette similar to that of Delacroix, from which black was barred, Monet had never bothered to theorize much; he relied on his instinct more than on any knowledge of the properties of complementary colors, etc. Anquetin returned disappointed from Vétheuil. (Signac had not been more successful when he asked Monet for guidance.)

Whatever Cormon might have thought of Anquetin's evolution, several of his paintings hung in the atelier as works of the most promising student of the class, and it is known that Cormon at one time had hoped to make Anquetin his successor. Vincent van Gogh was enthusiastic about some of Anquetin's canvases which, in spite of all the influences to which he had subjected himself, often showed an undeniable originality. Among the paintings which impressed the Dutchman were *Place Clichy, Evening*, in blue tonalities, and a landscape with a mower, painted in 1887 almost exclusively in various tones of yellow. This canvas with its large flat planes and simplification of design and color appealed so powerfully to van Gogh that it inspired him to paint a similar composition (page 32).

In the summer of 1886, after he had studied Seurat's works at the impressionist show and at the Independents, Anquetin's style underwent another change. Like many other young artists searching for new ways of expression, he was fascinated by Seurat's pointillism and began to try his hand at it (Emile Bernard did likewise). Here he found the firm theoretical basis partly derived from Delacroix which he had sought in vain to acquire from Monet. Thus the issue of Seurat's innovations became the subject of lively debates in Cormon's atelier, debates to which van Gogh could not have listened with indifference.

The Salon des Indépendants was then a very new institution and one that held great hope for all those young artists who felt no inclination to follow the worn and anemic precepts of the perennial Ecole des Beaux-Arts. The Groupe des Artistes Indépendants had been founded in the spring of 1884 by a number of painters whose works had been rejected by the Salon jury. For several decades this jury had systematically endeavored to suppress all efforts which displayed the least disregard for its canons. The impressionists, after their numerous attempts to show at the Salon were thwarted by the jury, finally had resorted to the then novel means of organizing their own exhibitions. But these were restricted to the members of the group and their guests, in order to ensure a semblance of unity. Ten years had passed since the first impressionist show, but the jury—antagonized by these disrespectful occurrences—showed no sign of relenting. To the men rejected in 1884 the problem was therefore not so much one of forming yet another more or less homogeneous group, but rather to establish an organization admitting *all* artists, regardless of their tendencies. In May 1884 they opened their first jury-free exhibition in which four hundred artists participated. Jules Grévy, President of the French Republic, who was expected to

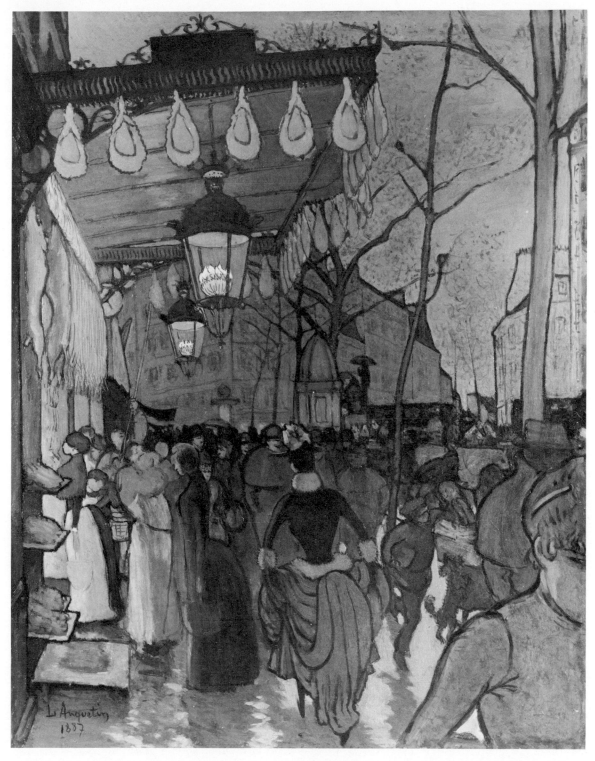

ANQUETIN: *La Place Clichy, Evening,* d. 1887. 27 x 21″. Wadsworth Atheneum, Hartford (Ella Gallup Sumner and Mary Catlin Sumner Collection)

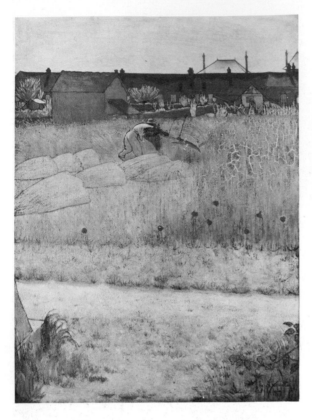

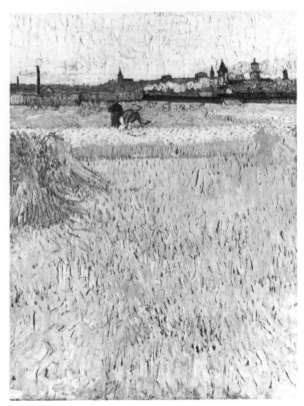

ANQUETIN: *The Mower,* d. 1887. 27½ x 20". Formerly collection Mme C. du Ferron-Anquetin, Paris

VAN GOGH: *The Mower,* Arles, 1888. 28¾ x 21¼". Formerly collections *père* Tanguy and Auguste Rodin. Musée Rodin, Paris

attend the opening, chose not to appear, doubtless because pressure groups had prevailed upon him not to sanction officially such an unorthodox venture.

This exhibition had provided both Seurat and Signac with the first opportunity to show their paintings. Signac, then twenty-one, and Seurat, four years older, had not previously known each other but soon became acquainted at meetings to which they were summoned by Albert Dubois-Pillet. The latter, who made his living as an officer in the Republican Guard, exhibited a canvas representing a dead child, a work which Zola was to describe in *L'Oeuvre* as one of the paintings by the hero.[36] During the run of the show Dubois-Pillet conceived the project of founding a permanent "Société des Artistes Indépendants" for the organization of annual exhibitions without the interference of any jury. In June a general assembly, presided over by Odilon Redon, established the bylaws of this society according to the proposals of Dubois-Pillet. Redon, Seurat, Signac, as well as Angrand and Cross, took an active part in the debates. The first exhibition of the new society was held that same year, in December 1884. Owing to the lateness of the season and unfavorable weather, few people visited the show, in which Seurat exhibited, among other works, a landscape of the island of La Grande Jatte (page 37), a study for the new picture he was then planning. The show, comprising some three hundred works, closed with a deficit of

2,700 francs and the new society was barely kept afloat through special contributions, the organization of an auction sale of donated paintings, etc.[37] No exhibition could be held the following year. Thus the next Salon des Indépendants was opened only in 1886, and this time it registered a profit of 700 francs.

It goes without saying that not all the works shown at the exhibitions of the Independents were of interest. Many lacked only a certain slickness and facility to be acceptable at the official Salon; others were hopeless "duds." Paintings that testified to some talent or promise actually were in the minority. Signac, who in 1886 was a member of the hanging committee, even had some difficulty in securing sufficient space for himself and his friends. But since there was no other place where they could show their work, their few paintings alone justified the new enterprise. Van Gogh must have heartily welcomed this organization free from any yoke of officialdom, as he himself had seen in Paris and heard from his brother (if he hadn't known it already) how hard it was for young painters to win approval unless they were willing to compromise with the Salon jury.

Van Gogh was now extremely eager to put to use all the new things he had learned. Gradually he abandoned the dark and earthy colors he had used in his early work. Already in Antwerp he had begun to brighten his palette under the influence of Rubens' paintings which he had studied there. He now also experimented with wools of different colors, assembling either complementaries or two shades not too distant from each other in small

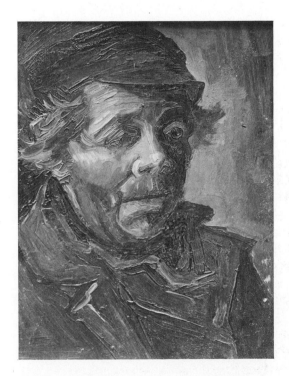

VAN GOGH: *Head of a Peasant, Study for the "Potato Eaters,"* Nuenen, 1885. 15½ x 11¾". Formerly collection G.-A. Aurier. Private collection, Aix-en-Provence

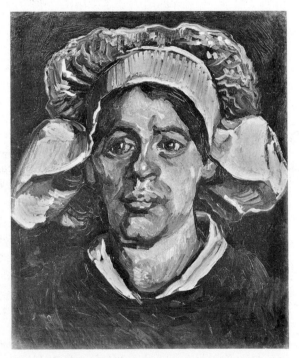

VAN GOGH: *Head of a Peasant Woman, Study for the "Potato Eaters,"* Nuenen, 1885. 17⅜ x 14". Formerly collection G.-A. Aurier. Rijksmuseum Kröller-Müller, Otterlo

33

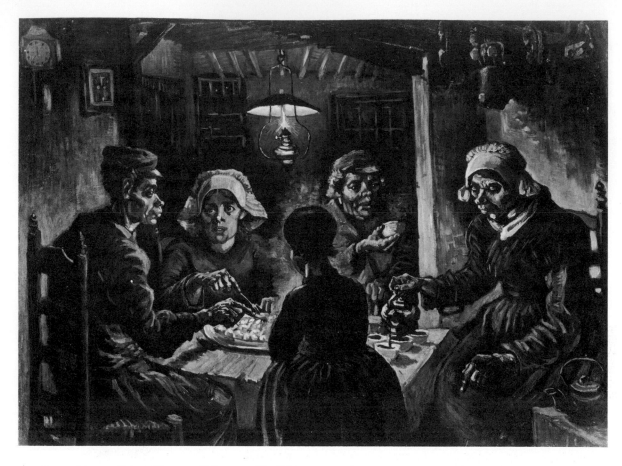

woolly balls.[38] But in Paris his paintings not only became chromatically lighter, their mood also brightened. His favorite subjects, peasants and workers, poor and old people, and humble objects, gave way to others devoid of any social implications: landscapes, still lifes and portraits. They reflect the various influences to which he was subjected in Paris. Especially in his canvases of flowers, often done in heavy impasto, he showed great indebtedness to Monticelli, several of whose still lifes were owned by Theo.

The greatest gain derived by van Gogh from the artists he met personally in Paris was apparently due to the first real impressionist who befriended him there: Camille Pissarro. Theo van Gogh had known Pissarro for some time and had tried to sell his work, particularly his recent pointillist pictures which Durand-Ruel had turned down. He had not been too successful with them, but that had not prevented him from admiring Pissarro's "qualities of a rustic character which show immediately that the man is more at ease in wooden shoes than in patent leather boots."[39] It was precisely this trait which was bound to attract Vincent, together with Pissarro's gentleness and genuine interest in others. Theo van Gogh therefore presented his brother to Pissarro, who was then approaching sixty but, with his long white beard and a crown of white hair surrounding his bald dome, looked even older. Vincent showed him the paintings which he had brought along from Holland, such as his large *Potato Eaters*, and they struck Pissarro by their forcefulness. Pissarro, having previously been the first to recognize the genius of Cézanne and to take an interest in both Guillaumin and Gauguin, generously helping them with advice, did not take long to perceive van Gogh's latent power.[40] He was happy to explain to him the impressionist concepts of light and color as well as Seurat's theories of complementaries, which he himself considered the ultimate achievement of impressionism. In spite of his adherence to these scientific concepts, however, Pissarro stressed his conviction that "originality depends only on the character of the drawing and the vision peculiar to each artist."[41] Pissarro's explanations were clear and persuasive, his own works rendered them even more convincing, and van Gogh was soon able to use brighter colors with a full knowledge of their specific properties. Through Pissarro, van Gogh also met Pissarro's son Lucien, a rather timid young man who worked at his father's side and adopted his views.

It was through the dealer Portier who, like the van Gogh brothers, lived at 54, rue Lepic, that the painter was introduced a little later to Armand Guillaumin. The latter had liked some of Vincent's paintings, and Portier thereupon brought him up to their apartment on the fourth floor. Van Gogh professed a great admiration for Guillaumin and went to see him frequently at the quai d'Anjou where Guillaumin occupied the studio formerly used by Daubigny. Guillaumin was kind and patient but by no means as inclined to theorize as Pissarro, nor did his personality command as much respect, yet van Gogh found him "more sure of his ideas than the others," probably because he was not continually preoccupied with new problems but was satisfied instead to follow quietly his own bent. Guillaumin somewhat dreaded van Gogh's visits as the Dutchman was always so excitable that his conversation could easily degenerate into a violent outburst even when he felt real affection for his opponent. Once, seeing at Guillaumin's a canvas representing men unloading a barge, van Gogh flew into a rage because he thought that the movements of the laborers had not been depicted correctly. With an imaginary spade he started to demonstrate the various attitudes; on other occasions he was likely to strip to the waist for a better display of anatomical details.[42]

At Cormon's van Gogh had also struck up a friendship with an Australian painter, John Russell, who in November introduced him to a young Englishman, Hartrick. The latter had just returned from the Breton village of Pont-Aven where he had met Gauguin. Hartrick now entered Cormon's studio where van Gogh no longer worked, but the Dutchman frequently visited him at his home. Hartrick was impressed less by van Gogh's work than by his unpredictable character: he was often apt to be morose, as if his suspicions were aroused; at other times he would express pleasure or pain loudly and in a childlike manner, but even more commonly he would plunge into heated discussions, pouring out sentences in a wild mixture of Dutch, English, and French, then glance back over his shoulder at his opponent and hiss through his teeth. Hartrick and his comrades thought him "cracked" but harmless, perhaps not interesting enough to bother much about. What most disconcerted them was the direct way in which van Gogh showed his likes and dislikes, though they had to concede that the Dutchman did so without malice or conscious knowledge of giving offense.[43] Van Gogh himself readily admitted his inability to hide his feelings. "I cannot always keep quiet," he once said, "as my convictions are so much part of myself that it is sometimes as if they took me by my throat...."[44] Yet he made a constant effort to approve rather than to criticize, for as he put it: "It always hurts me, it

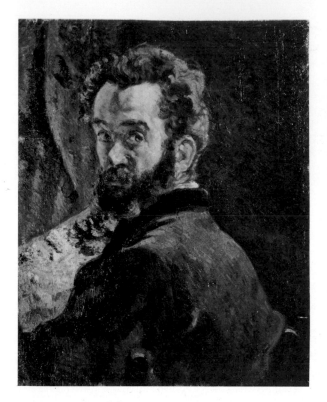

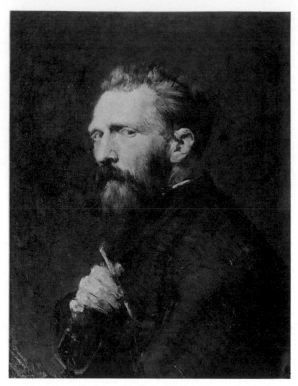

GUILLAUMIN: *Self-Portrait*, 1878. 23½ x 20″. Formerly collection Theo van Gogh. Rijksmuseum Vincent van Gogh, Amsterdam

RUSSELL: *Portrait of Vincent van Gogh*, Paris, c. 1886. 23½ x 18″. Formerly collection Theo van Gogh. Rijksmuseum Vincent van Gogh, Amsterdam

makes me nervous, when I meet somebody about whose principles I have to say: 'But that is neither good nor bad, that really does not look like anything,' and it gives me a sort of choking feeling that stays with me, till some day I find out he has something good in him."[45] In many instances it was thus merely a question of whether he could wait for the revelation of some redeeming quality before a flare of tempers got the better of him. In other cases, where even his good will could detect no reason for leniency, his outbursts were formidable, though he often regretted them afterwards.

It is possible that Hartrick told van Gogh about his acquaintance with Gauguin, whose influence on some of Cormon's pupils drew expressions of amusement and contempt from their master. Emile Bernard too had met Gauguin at Pont-Aven, introduced by Gauguin's friend Schuffenecker. But Gauguin had made it plain that he did not care to be disturbed. Though the Pension Gloanec where he stayed was patronized by many young artists, Gauguin kept to himself. His lofty manners greatly intrigued the others, and so did his paintings, since Mlle Gloanec's boarders were not at all familiar with the outcast art of impressionism. Yet four days after arriving at Pont-Aven Bernard wrote to his parents: "There is also an impressionist here named Gauguin, a rather strong fellow. He is thirty-six years old and draws and paints very well."[46] Indeed Gauguin's work did not fail to strike some of the others, among them several of Cormon's pupils who began to ask his advice.

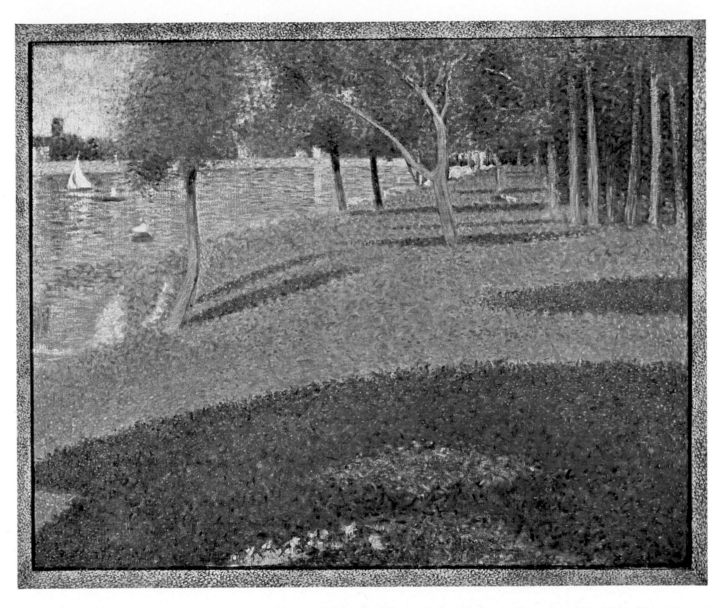

SEURAT: *The Island of La Grande Jatte*, 1884. 25⅝ x 32". Exhibited with the Independents in December 1884. Collection **Mr.** and **Mrs.** John Hay Whitney, New York

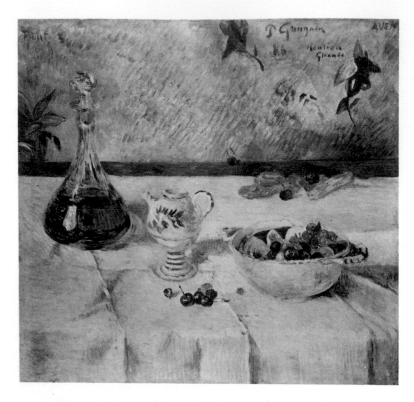

GAUGUIN: *Still Life,* inscribed "Pont-Aven, Pension Gloanec, 1886." Oil on panel, 21¾ x 33". Formerly collection Maurice Denis. Collection the Honorable Michael Astor, London

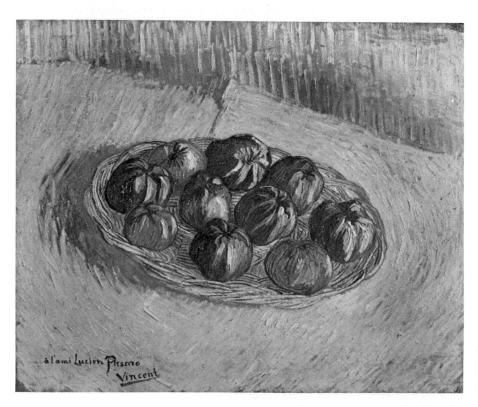

VAN GOGH: *Still Life with Apples,* dedicated to Lucien Pissarro, Paris, 1887. 19¾ x 24". Formerly collection Lucien Pissarro. Rijksmuseum Kröller-Müller, Otterlo

He told them of his admiration for Pissarro and Degas, of whom they knew little, as well as for Cézanne, whose name most of them had never heard. The evenings at the inn were spent in animated debates which seldom ended before midnight, when Marie Gloanec begged everybody to go to bed so that the maids could put up their cots in the dining room.

Though generally self-contained and confident, silent and almost dour, Gauguin could unbend and be quite charming when he wished. He was flattered by the attention of the other boarders, many of whom were foreigners. There were quite a number of Americans who seemed to like his work. "I am respected as the strongest painter in Pont-Aven," Gauguin proudly wrote to his wife.[47] Yet only two painters were actually admitted by him to intimacy: Charles Laval and a wealthy young man who discreetly paid Gauguin's bills.[48] It was mostly through these that the others learned of his ideas, while they could study some of his paintings—which appeared to them extremely crude—in the dining room of the inn for which Gauguin painted some decorations.[49] But these were crude only in comparison with what they themselves had been taught to do, for Gauguin's work still strongly showed the influence of Pissarro and was actually more hesitant and less vigorous than that of his master. Problems of execution were as yet preoccupying him much more than questions of doctrine.

In November 1886, when Gauguin returned to Paris, where he planned to do ceramics with Chaplet, he met van Gogh. A strange friendship soon united the two, in spite of the cold purposefulness of the one and the boiling enthusiasm of the other. All they had in common was the belligerent character of their convictions. Gauguin began to show the certitude of one who has found his way and who has become used to being listened to; van Gogh was animated with the ardor and humility of the devotee who, having witnessed wonders, feels growing in himself the fierce pride of new beliefs. Van Gogh readily recognized the superiority of Gauguin, who was older than himself and who had known the impressionists and participated in their struggles, but he could not possibly always agree with the extreme intolerance of Gauguin's views. Gauguin was very critical of Pissarro's recent work and must have taken pleasure in demolishing van Gogh's respect for Seurat's theories.

Gauguin had had a violent quarrel with Seurat while temporarily using Signac's studio before leaving Paris, when he had been without any abode. Not knowing that Signac had offered him the use of his studio, Seurat apparently had prevented Gauguin from working there. And Gauguin had written bitterly to Signac: "I am a person of no manners or delicacy; you are really a good fellow to accept my bad behavior! That is what Monsieur Seurat has told Pissarro and Guillaumin.... I may be an artist full of hesitancy and with little knowledge, but as a man of the world I *will allow no one* the right to annoy me."[50]

Gauguin now avoided Pissarro and his friends; instead he frequently went to see Degas, though he had once quarreled with him as well. Degas held forth at the Café de la Nouvelle Athènes where earlier the impressionists used to gather around him and Manet. When Pissarro returned there one evening in the company of Seurat, Signac, and Dubois-Pillet, Guillaumin and Gauguin refused to shake hands with Signac, and after some heated explanations, Gauguin left abruptly without saying goodbye to anybody.[51] It seems likely that Gauguin occasionally took van Gogh along to the meetings at the Nouvelle Athènes, especially since Theo was handling Degas' work whenever he could get hold of the few paintings or pastels Degas consented to sell him. At the café and through Gauguin, van Gogh must have learned of the clashes, the gossip, the scarcely hidden enmity which divided the once so united group of impressionists. Saddened by their "disastrous squabbles," van Gogh saw with surprise "each member getting at the other's throat with a passion worthy of a nobler and better aim."[52]

Though Gauguin expressed his opinions rather forcefully, his reasoning was not always too sound. Knowing no pity for others, he claimed to have none for himself, yet he did not succeed at all times in hiding his egotism. But he was constantly ready to explain and excuse his selfishness as the artist's right to do things his own way. There can be little doubt that van Gogh's excitability was greatly increased through his association with Gauguin, the more so since some of Gauguin's characteristics found an easy response in his own personality. And this response could not be a peaceful one, as the traits they had in common were precisely those which invited conflicts.

Van Gogh's restlessness began to cast a shadow even over his relations with his brother. Theo and Vincent had been separated for ten years, during which time, however, a steady flow of letters had kept them in close contact. But each had developed habits adapted to his own way of life, and now they found it increasingly difficult to share an apartment, or rather it was Theo who had great trouble reconciling his love for neatness, order, and calm with Vincent's conduct. The painter was completely oblivious to his surroundings, careless, and too preoccupied with his own thoughts to pay much attention to the comfort of others; he reigned over his brother's household with an unconscious tyranny. Shortly after they had moved to more spacious quarters in the rue Lepic, Theo spoke openly about his worries in a letter to their sister (while trying to conceal his feelings from their mother):

"Can you understand," he wrote, "how hard it is sometimes to have no other conversation than with gentlemen who talk about business, and artists who in most cases have a difficult time themselves...? You have no idea of the loneliness in a big city!" And concerning Vincent he added: "My home life is almost unbearable; no one wants to come to see me any more because it always ends in quarrels; besides he is so untidy that the place looks far from attractive. I wish he would go and live by himself; he sometimes speaks about it, but if I were to tell him to go away, it would be just a reason for him to stay. Since I can do nothing right for him, I only ask him for one thing: that he does not cause me any trouble. But by staying with me he is doing just that, for I can hardly bear it.

"It is as if there were two persons in him—one marvelously gifted, delicate, and tender, the other egotistical and hardhearted! They present themselves in turn, so that one hears him talk first in one way, then in the other, and this always with arguments which are now all for, now all against the same point. It is a pity that he is his own enemy, for he makes life hard not only for others but also for himself."[53]

Their sister advised Theo to abandon Vincent to his own fate, but Theo's faith in his brother's destiny was such that he considered it his duty to stand by him. "If he were someone with another trade," Theo replied, "I am sure I would have done long ago what you advise me to do, for I have often asked myself whether it was not wrong to go on helping him always, and I have often been on the point of letting him fend for himself. After your letter I thought it over again, and I think that in the given circumstances the only thing I can do is to go on. It is quite certain that he is an artist, and while what he is doing now may sometimes not be beautiful, it is sure to be of use to him later on, and then it will perhaps be sublime, and it would be a shame if it were made impossible for him to go on studying. No matter how unpractical he may be, if he only improves himself he is sure to start selling one day. I am firmly determined to go on acting as I have done hitherto."[54] Yet Theo added that he hoped Vincent would eventually find another place to live.

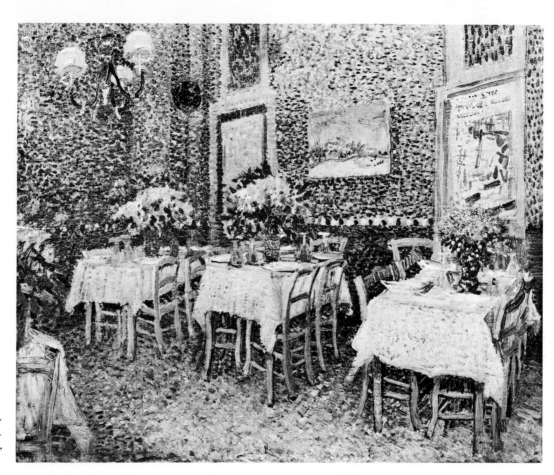

Despite this determination to stand by his brother, and strange as this may seem, Theo in those days was not even fully convinced of Vincent's potentialities. At least that is what his friend Andries Bonger later asserted: "When the two brothers lived together on Montmartre, Theo said one day in summing up his opinion that Vincent had a good average talent as a painter, nothing more."[55]

For several years Theo had been the painter's sole support and he knew that to withdraw his help now that he could see for himself how steadily Vincent was working and progressing would not merely be cruel, it would condemn his brother to despair. Vincent's fate lay in Theo's hands. He had no one else to whom he could turn, no one whom he could trust as he trusted Theo, no one able to summon up enough love to pardon his faults and share his hopes. It was the consciousness of his responsibility that gave Theo the strength to endure and tolerate what he would have accepted from nobody but this brother. Vincent, on the other hand, wrote in those days to their sister Wil: "If I didn't have Theo, it would not be possible for me to attain with my work what I ought to attain, but because I have him as a friend, I believe I shall still make progress and be able to keep on."[56]

But then, as Bonger later remembered: "When at last all had gone well for a week [between the brothers], Vincent again resumed the interminable discussions concerning impressionism, into which he dragged everything else." Indeed, even on the subject of impressionism the two did not always seem to agree, especially in the beginning when Theo came out in support of *plein air* and Vincent retorted that it "would never amount to much." According to Bonger: "Impressionism continually was an apple of discord between them, and sometimes their disputes grew quite serious." At the bottom of all these discussions, as Bonger saw it, lay the fact that "Vincent always tried to dominate his brother, and Theo frequently defended himself vehemently."[55]

Vincent van Gogh knew very well that his character and behavior, his abruptness, his irritability, his frequent changes of mood set him apart from the others. Already in 1880 he had explained to Theo: "I am a passionate man, capable and likely to do more or less foolish things which I sometimes more or less regret. It does happen that I speak or act a little too quickly when it would have been better to wait with more patience.... Since this is so, what should be done ? Should one consider oneself as a dangerous person and one that is incapable of anything ? I don't think so. Rather, one should try by all means to use these very passions to their best advantage.... Thus, instead of abandoning myself to despair, I chose the state of active melancholy, in as much as I had a faculty for activity; in other words, I have preferred the melancholy which hopes and aspires and searches to the melancholy which, dejected and stagnant, is desperate.... Now, someone who is absorbed in all this is sometimes shocking to others and, without wanting to do so, he more or less violates certain forms and usages and social conventions. However, it would be regrettable if this were considered in a bad light. For example, you know well that frequently I have neglected my clothes; this I admit and I admit that it is shocking. Yet straitened circumstances and poverty are to some extent responsible for that, and also a profound discouragement, but beyond that it is sometimes *a very good way to obtain the necessary solitude* so as to be able to delve more or less deeply into this or that problem which preoccupies you."[57]

While the painter occasionally succeeded in isolating himself by being consciously or unconsciously different from the others, at the same time he longed desperately to make friends, was anxious to please and ready to show great self-restraint, on the condition however that his entourage should accept him as he was. Criticism or remonstrances seem in general to have had the effect of stiffening his attitude rather than softening it. Just as he was able to defend opposite viewpoints with equal conviction, so could he justify his own behavior even in cases where it had cost him badly wanted understanding. Sincere as was his humility, it was counterbalanced by a staunch self-righteousness which, at the slightest provocation, was ready to confuse issues and prevent cordial and steady associations. This self-righteousness hung like a menace over all of the painter's friendships; it was the refuge into which he readily withdrew whenever he encountered opposition. Only Theo seems to have completely understood the multiple contradictions of his brother's character, but not even he succeeded in smoothing their sharp angles.

Towards the end of December 1886 Theo fell ill, and Bonger reported to his parents that his friend had suffered "a serious nervous disorder, to the extent that he couldn't move anymore. To my great surprise, I found him yesterday as he had been before [his illness]; he still felt a stiffness as after a fall, but besides that no other aftereffects. Now he will at last take care of his health, which he greatly needs to do." And Bonger added: "He has decided to separate from Vincent; to live together is impossible."[58]

Vincent van Gogh cannot have remained unaware of the tension in his relationship with Theo, though he could not always master himself sufficiently to avoid conflicts. It may have been partly in order to ease this tension that the painter began to spend less time in their home, that he did fewer still lifes, and turned, especially in the spring of 1887, to landscapes instead. After having worked at first mainly in the immediate vicinity of the rue Lepic, painting numerous views of Montmartre with its picturesque windmills dominating the hill (then still strewn with small gardens and vacant lots), van Gogh started to look for motifs in the more distant outskirts of Paris, where his work detained him all day long. This change was possibly also brought about by his acquaintance with Emile Bernard and Paul Signac, both of whom he met early in 1887 in the small shop of the color grinder *père* Tanguy.

It is not known who first took van Gogh to Tanguy's place in the rue Clauzel, half way between their apartment on rue Lepic and Theo's gallery. Many of the artists he had met in Paris, and probably also Theo himself, knew the little old man well and enjoyed visiting his shop. Pissarro had been his customer for years and had persuaded all his friends to buy their colors from him (though these were not always very good) because he liked the humble dealer, a former soldier of the Commune. Pissarro also advised his acquaintances to study Cézanne's works at Tanguy's, for Tanguy dealt not only in paints, brushes, and canvases, but in pictures as well, which he frequently accepted in exchange for his supplies. While this was not a very lucrative arrangement, it permitted *père* Tanguy to handle the works of those painters whom he loved.[59]

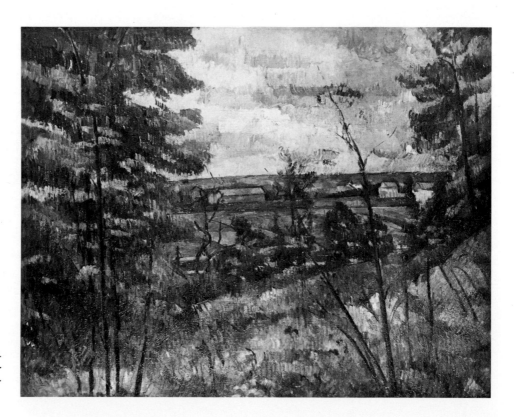

CÉZANNE: *View of the Oise Valley*, c. 1880. 28⅜ x 35¾". Purchased by Signac from *père* Tanguy in 1886. Collection Mme Ginette Signac, Paris

Tanguy was then a man of sixty, short, thickset, with a grizzled beard and large, beaming, profoundly kind, dark blue eyes. He immediately took a fancy to van Gogh in spite of his wife's pronounced aversion for the painter who, in her opinion, used too much canvas and paint for too many unsalable pictures. The painter, in turn, was greatly taken with Tanguy and immediately did a portrait of him which was followed somewhat later by two more ambitious likenesses. In all of them he endeavored to express his new friend's good nature, his deep, almost sacred respect for art, his touching devotion to a cause whose greatness was probably even beyond Tanguy's grasp.

At Tanguy's request van Gogh also painted a portrait of one of his friends, for which he was paid 20 francs (his "regular" price was 50 francs), as well as one of Mme Tanguy, although he reciprocated her hearty dislike for him. This portrait cannot have pleased the sitter very much, for it was sold almost immediately and has since disappeared. Feeling sorry for Tanguy on account of what he had to endure from his wife, van Gogh liked to compare the patient, resigned, yet often cheerful old man to "ancient Christians, martyrs, and slaves."

Whether or not Tanguy was really discerning in art matters is difficult to ascertain, but

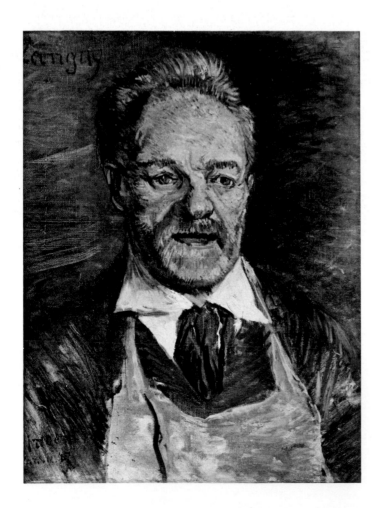

VAN GOGH: *Portrait of Père Tanguy,* Paris, d. 1887. 18½ x 15⅛". Formerly collections *père* Tanguy and Octave Mirbeau. Ny Carlsberg Glyptotek, Copenhagen

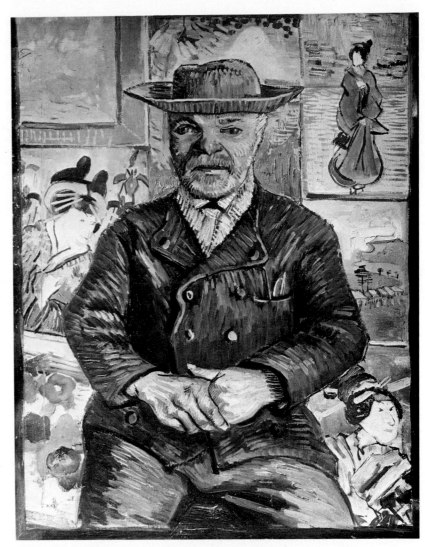

van Gogh: *Portrait of Père Tanguy with Japanese Prints,* Paris, 1887. 25½ x 20″.
Collection Stavros S. Niarchos

one fact cannot be disputed: the painters he patronized and in whom no "respectable" dealer showed any interest were precisely those singled out by fate for great achievements. He may not have fully recognized the extent of their genius, he may have been attracted mostly by their sincerity (though bad painters can be sincere too, and often are), he may have pitied them in their constant struggles more than he understood their aims, but somehow his instinct must have responded to all that was unconventional and daring in art. There was a certain consistency in the choice of artists he favored; whatever the reason, *père* Tanguy did have a "stock" which comprised works by Cézanne and Pissarro, Guillaumin and Gauguin, to which he now added paintings by van Gogh as well as by Seurat, Signac and their friends. A little later works by other and still younger men were to crowd his shelves or to appear in his little show window.

When van Gogh met Tanguy, the latter had been for some ten years practically the sole dealer to handle Cézanne's works (Portier occasionally also had some), and this fact filled him with pride, though there were few people who took any interest in these canvases. Those who did were mostly painters, too poor to buy them even at the low prices Tanguy asked. Cézanne's paintings were then selling for between 80 and 150 francs each, while Monet was already obtaining some 2000 for his. In earlier times, before they had achieved their modest success, Renoir and Monet also had entrusted canvases to Tanguy, but now their works were out of his clients' reach and the little dealer must have been happy that they no longer needed his help. Superbly indifferent to prices and profits, Tanguy lived very simply, insisting that "a man who spends more than 50 centimes a day is a rascal." Many of "his" painters did not have even that much and Tanguy readily shared his frugal meals with them. His best reward was the enthusiasm which his visitors usually expressed for the paintings he showed them, particularly those by Cézanne. Indeed, it was Cézanne's work which brought many of the younger generation to Tanguy's small dark shop. No wonder then that van Gogh liked to linger there and to engage in lengthy conversations about art with whoever happened to come in. According to Emile Bernard, van Gogh once met Cézanne himself at Tanguy's, but Cézanne saw in van Gogh's paintings only the work of a madman.[60]

It was at Tanguy's that van Gogh became acquainted with Charles Angrand, to whom he later proposed an exchange of paintings, because he had seen in the rue Clauzel a canvas which particularly interested him: a farmyard scene of a woman followed by chickens,

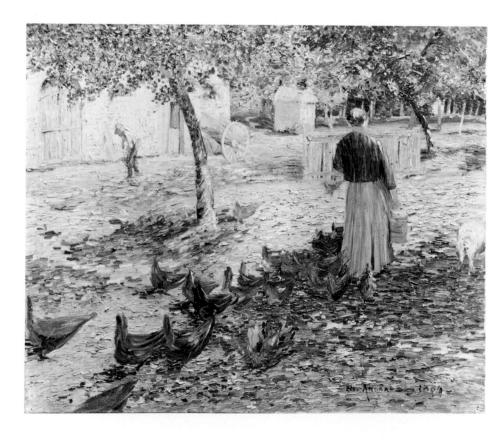

ANGRAND: *Farmyard Scene,* d. 1884. 21⅛" x 25⅝". Ny Carlsberg Glyptotek, Copenhagen

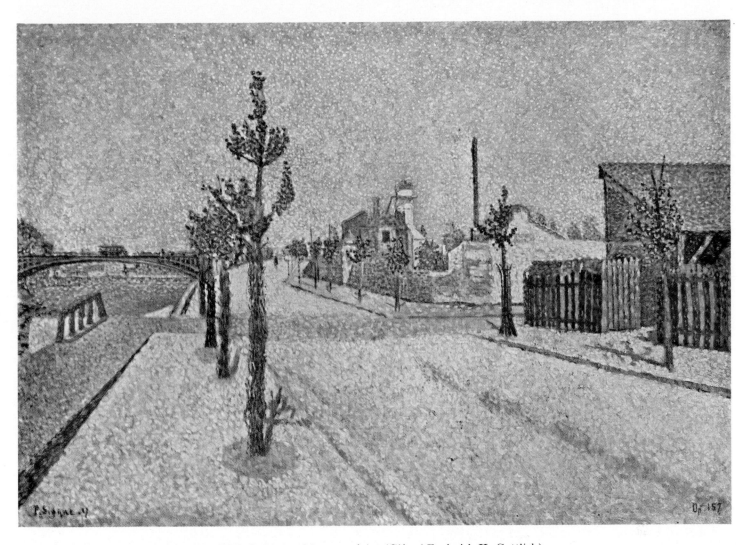

Signac: *Quay at Clichy*, d. 1887. 18¼ x 25¾". Baltimore Museum of Art (Gift of Frederick H. Gottlieb)

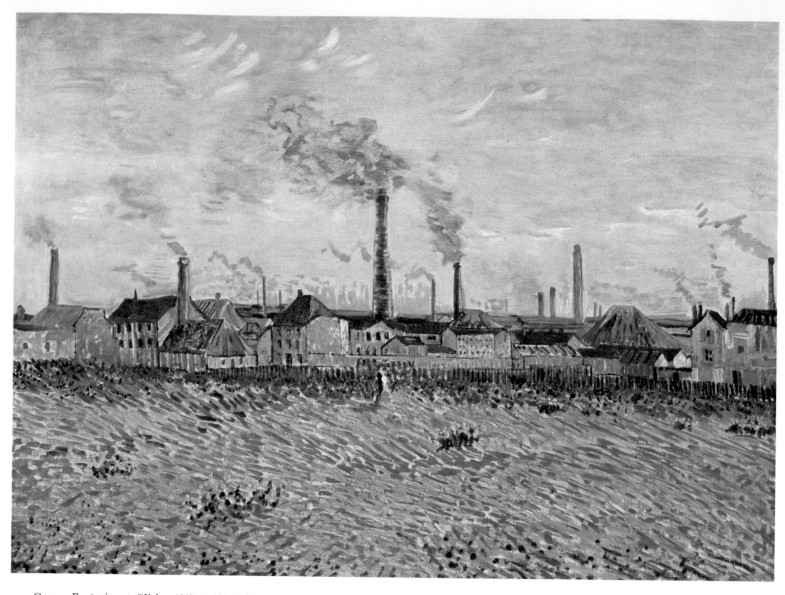

VAN GOGH: *Factories at Clichy*, 1887. 21¼ x 28¾". Formerly collection *père* Tanguy. The St. Louis Art Museum (Gift of Mrs. Mark C. Steinberg)

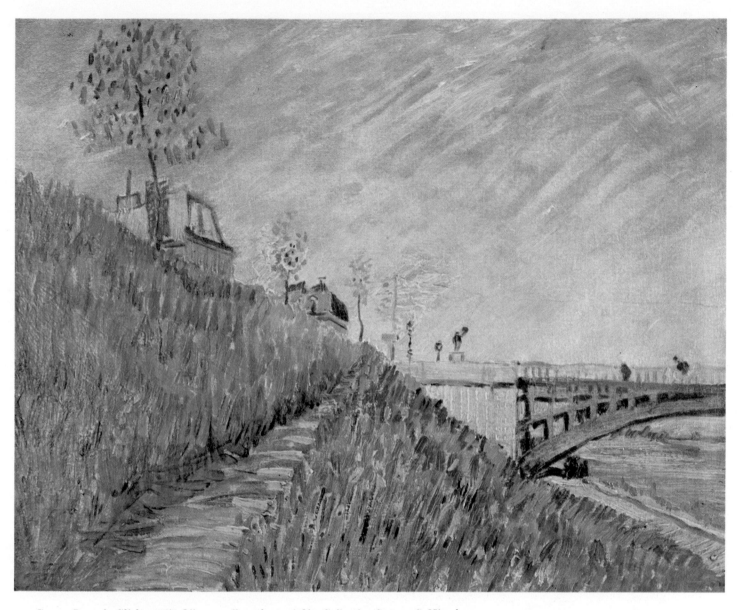

VAN GOGH: *Pont de Clichy,* 1887. Oil on cardboard, 12 x 15⅜". Collection Stavros S. Niarchos

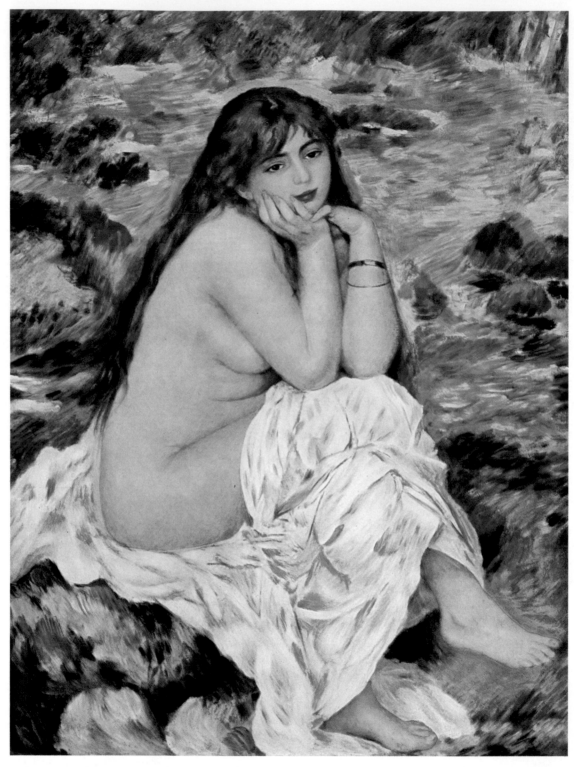

RENOIR: *Seated Bather,* 1885. 47½ x 36″. Fogg Art Museum, Harvard University, Cambridge, Mass. (Maurice Wertheim Collection)

painted in heavy layers of paint, partly in an almost pointillist execution, done in bright colors, with a brilliant pink wall in the background. Van Gogh was then obsessed with the idea of exchanging works with other artists (as the Japanese had done) and actually acquired in this way a group of paintings for himself and Theo—among them a picture by Lautrec—though he did not obtain Angrand's canvas.[61] At Tanguy's also he first saw Signac whom he subsequently met now and then at Asnières or Saint-Ouen, where both of them worked on the banks of the Seine.

Ten years younger than van Gogh, Signac had started to paint very early in life. A passionate sailor, he had inscribed the names of Manet-Zola-Wagner on the stern of his first boat, much to the consternation of his widowed mother. At first Signac had been influenced by Monet, but—unable to meet his chosen master—he had struck up a close friendship with Guillaumin, in whose company he often went to work on the quays in Paris. He had also at times ascended the hill of Montmartre and there painted landscapes with forceful brush strokes and thick layers of pigment, not unlike those which van Gogh did a little later in the same vicinity. Eager to improve further his impressionist technique, Signac had discovered new possibilities in 1884, when he saw Seurat's *Baignade* at the first exhibition of the Independents. Soon, together with Seurat, he had been able to perfect the latter's system. One year later he had met Camille Pissarro through Guillaumin and had succeeded in winning him over to their new concepts and methods. Since then he had never stopped trying to persuade everybody he encountered.

It must have been in 1886 that Signac discovered in a small exhibition in Asnières, organized by some painters of that Parisian suburb, a few pointillist canvases by Emile Bernard, who had just begun experimenting with that technique. According to Bernard's

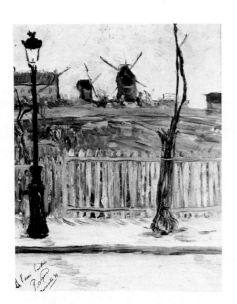
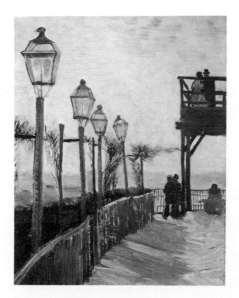
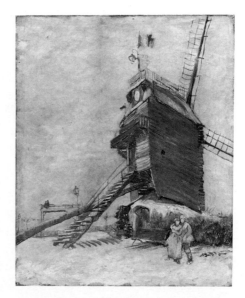

Left: SIGNAC: *View of Montmartre,* d. 1884. 14 x 10″. Musée Carnavalet, Paris (Gift of David-Weill). Center: VAN GOGH: *Montmartre,* Paris, 1886. 17¼ x 13¼″. The Art Institute of Chicago (Helen Birch Bartlett Memorial Collection). Right: VAN GOGH: *The Moulin de la Galette,* Montmartre, 1886–87. 24 x 19¾″. Museo Nacional de Bellas Artes, Buenos Aires

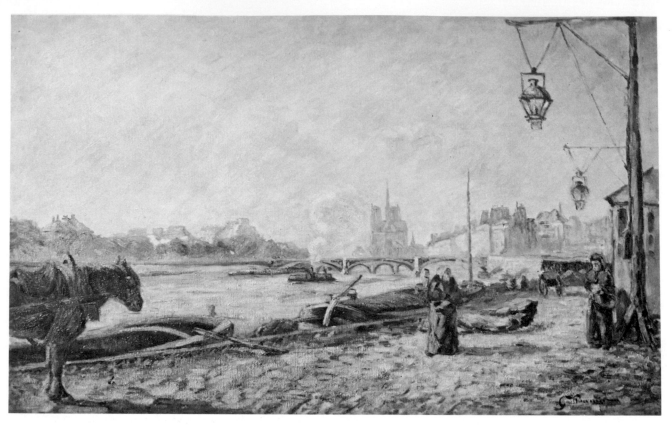

GUILLAUMIN: *Le Quai de la Rapée,* Paris, c. 1884. Formerly collection Paul Signac. Collection Mme Ginette Signac, Paris

somewhat acid recollections, "M. Paul Signac immediately presented himself to my parents, wishing to talk to me. I had no idea what this gentleman wanted from me. He explained to me that he had seen my attempts at 'divisionism' and that he himself was, together with Georges Seurat, the inventor of that method. I thereupon told him that I was happy to know him and he took me to see his paintings. His studio was not far from the place Clichy. I saw there some large landscapes, very luminous, but with little life; some interiors of which all the figures seemed to me quite wooden. I drew the conclusion that while the method was good for the vibrant reproduction of light, it spoiled the color, and instantly I adopted an opposite theory."[21] Bernard subsequently discussed this experience with Anquetin and Lautrec, who also agreed to pursue their researches in a different direction. Whether it was Signac's certainty that had antagonized Bernard or whether it was his stressing of scientific laws, is hard to say, but Signac not only lost a new adherent, he actually made an enemy. Indeed, for reasons that will probably never be known, Bernard thenceforth always expressed himself with a mixture of hatred and contempt on the subject of divisionism. He also seems to have destroyed most of his pointillist studies.

Signac's relations with van Gogh were much more cordial. Signac was a gay and stimulating companion, brimming over with the conviction that he had made great progress in art through the strict application of optical laws. To the sober information that van Gogh had already obtained from Pissarro, Signac must have added ebullient demonstrations of his science. Though Signac was almost as aggressive in his beliefs as was van Gogh himself, his aggressiveness was not caused by exasperation, but rather by an inescapable need to proselytize. Never could he let pass an occasion to prove the infallibility of his theories. Apparently van Gogh did not escape Signac's persuasiveness, for he began to paint, particularly at Asnières, a number of landscapes executed in little dots. He did others from the window of his room in the rue Lepic. Yet, while using the pointillist technique, he let himself be carried away by his enthusiasm instead of accepting the exacting rules of Signac's system. This cannot have failed to bring about animated discussions with his new comrade. As a matter of fact Signac did not show an exaggerated appreciation of van Gogh's work.

Although Signac was as temperamental as van Gogh, he endeavored to control his emotions through the observation of the laws of contrast. He tried not to succumb to the "temptations" of nature and liked to point out that none of the old masters had actually worked direct from nature, that they had thus achieved a greater domination of their subjects. But van Gogh preferred to paint under the pressure of his immediate sensations and to use the execution in little dots merely as an experiment in textures. Still, Signac's theories on complementaries inspired him to the occasional application of "halos," as he

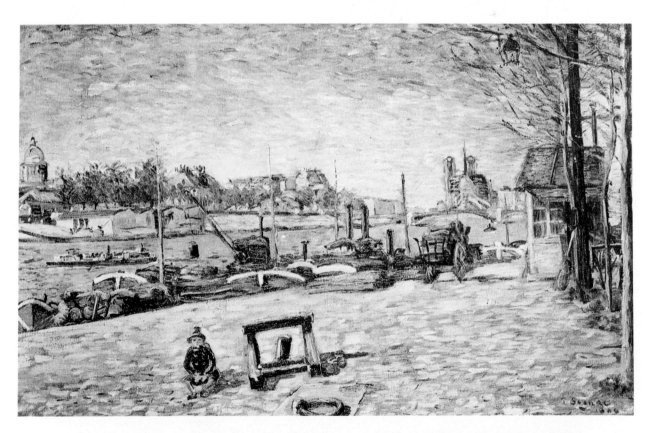

SIGNAC: *Le Quai de la Rapée,* Paris, 1884. 23 x 35½". Formerly coll. F. Fénéon. Collection T. Kakinuma, Tokyo

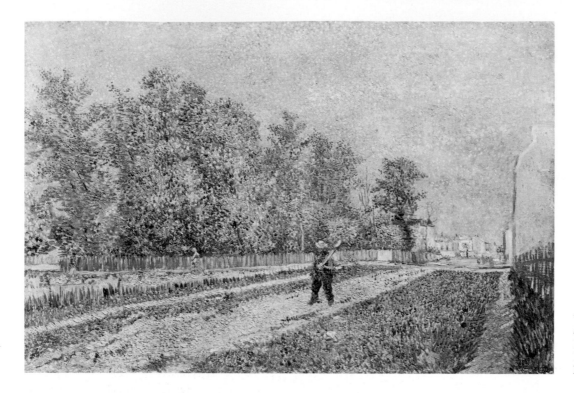

van Gogh: *Road with Peasant Shouldering a Spade,* Paris, 1887. 18⅝" x 28¼". Collection Miss Caren Carter Johnson, Forth Worth, Texas

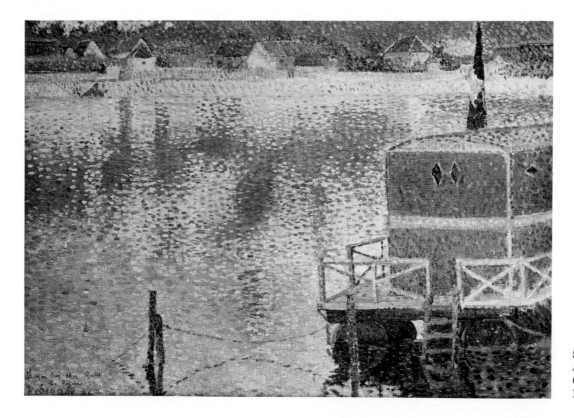

Signac: *Bathhouse on the Seine,* d. 1886. Dedicated to Camille Pissarro. 13 x 18⅛". Private collection, Paris

called them, outlining each object with the complementary color of its background to accentuate it.

Van Gogh's "unorthodoxy" did not prevent his appreciation of the system of Signac and Seurat. "As to pointillist execution and making halos or other things," he explained to his brother, "I think that is a real discovery; yet it is already to be foreseen that this technique will not become a universal dogma any more than any other. This is another reason why Seurat's *Grande Jatte*, the landscapes in large dots by Signac, and Anquetin's *Boat* will become in time still more individual and still more original."[62]

Though van Gogh did not join the small group gathered around Seurat, there can be no doubt that he profited greatly from his contact with Signac. He must have been impressed by Signac's frankness, his great abilities, and the powerful concentration with which he applied himself to his work. When the two met at Asnières, they would, according to Signac's recollections, have lunch together and later walk all the way back to Paris. "Van Gogh, dressed in a blue workman's blouse, had painted little dots of colors on his sleeves. Sticking close to me, he shouted and gesticulated, brandishing his large, freshly covered canvas, and with it he polychromed himself as well as passers-by."[63] Frequently the canvas

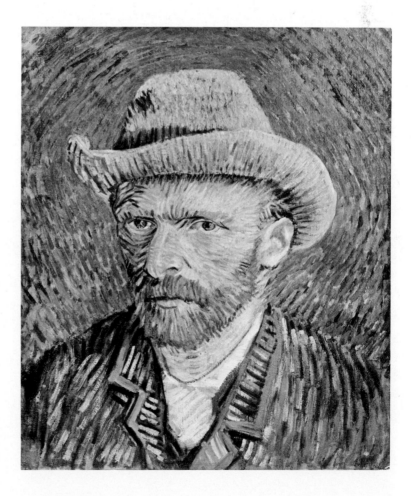

VAN GOGH: *Self-Portrait*, Paris, 1887. 17¼ x 14¾". Rijksmuseum Vincent van Gogh, Amsterdam

van Gogh carried was an unusually big one which he would divide into various rectangles, so as to assemble several studies on it at one sitting. Whenever, on his way home, he met friends for whose judgment he cared, such as Camille Pissarro, he would prop his new work against any wall and invite a verdict, oblivious to the people in the street.[40]

More intimate than van Gogh's relations with Signac were those with the even younger Emile Bernard. They met one day at Tanguy's where Bernard had come for supplies. When they were introduced to each other, the Dutchman immediately complimented Bernard on his work, which he had studied in Tanguy's shop. They left together and van Gogh took his new acquaintance to the rue Lepic where they exchanged paintings in commemoration of their first meeting.[64] They subsequently saw a great deal of each other and even worked together in a little studio which Bernard had constructed in the garden of his parents' house at Asnières, not far from the island of La Grande Jatte. But after a quarrel with Bernard's father, who showed no confidence whatsoever in his son's artistic calling, van Gogh preferred not to return there, though he maintained his close friendship with the young painter. As he had done occasionally with Signac, van Gogh frequently worked side by side with Emile Bernard on the banks of the Seine at Asnières. Bernard was so astounded by his friend's ardor that he later wrote: "I have seen him walk great distances under a blazing sun in order to paint a motif he liked: he never spared himself. Rain, wind snow, he braved them all. He put himself to work no matter what time of day or night, either to paint a starry sky or a noon sun."[65]

Bernard was more inclined to brood than the other artists van Gogh had met in Paris.

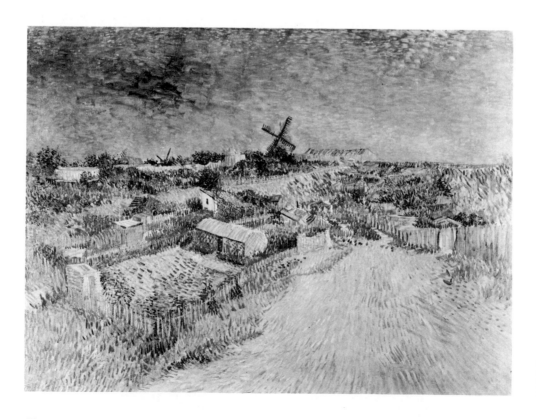

VAN GOGH: *View of Montmartre,* Paris, 1887. 37¾ x 47¼". Stedelijk Museum, Amsterdam

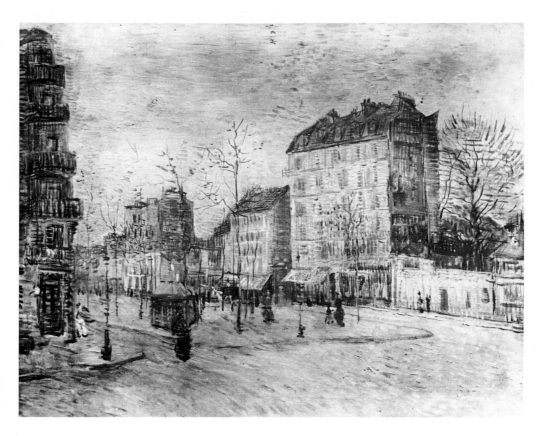

VAN GOGH: *Boulevard de Clichy,* Paris, 1887. 18¼ x 21⅝″. Rijksmuseum Vincent van Gogh, Amsterdam

He was interested in all the new currents, read constantly, kept a diary, wrote poetry, and pondered over philosophical and artistic theories. He presented a strange mixture of sincere self-criticism and of self-righteousness, of a steady search for logic and truth coupled with youthful enthusiasm and even arrogance. He liked to analyze the works of others, past and present, so as to lay bare their components and thus be able to experiment with their various elements: color, line, composition, chiaroscuro, glazes, brushwork. Highly intelligent and constantly driven by a creative urge that drew on many sources yet was strong enough to assimilate them instead of succumbing to them, Bernard must have impressed van Gogh by his knowledge and earnestness, quite uncommon in a youth of nineteen. He in turn attached himself to the Dutchman, who was the first ever to express a favorable opinion of his work and to take him seriously. This, however, did not keep van Gogh from admonishing Bernard on the danger of becoming sectarian and narrow-minded, for he recognized in his young friend's blind absolutism and too quickly pronounced likes or dislikes a lack of experience in life. "I believe," van Gogh told him, "that in time you will come to realize that in the studios one not only does not learn much about painting, but one does not even learn much about a technique of life; so one is obliged to learn how to live, as well as how to paint, without having recourse to the old tricks and optical illusions of the clever ones." He also warned Bernard that "it is better to look at things for a long while and make sure before judging them categorically." [66]

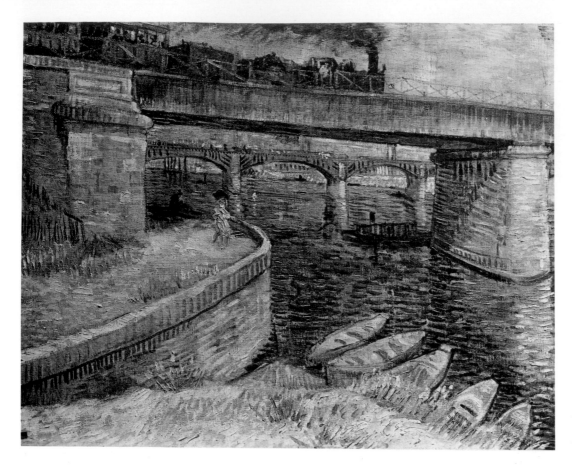

VAN GOGH: *Bridge at Asnières,* Paris, 1887. 20½ x 25½". E. G. Bührle Foundation, Zurich

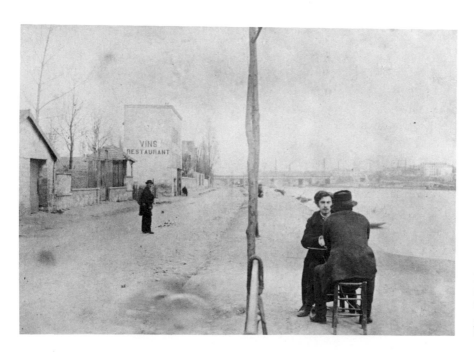

Photograph of Emile Bernard and Vincent van Gogh (seen from the back) taken in 1886 on the Seine quays at Asnières, with the railroad bridge in the background

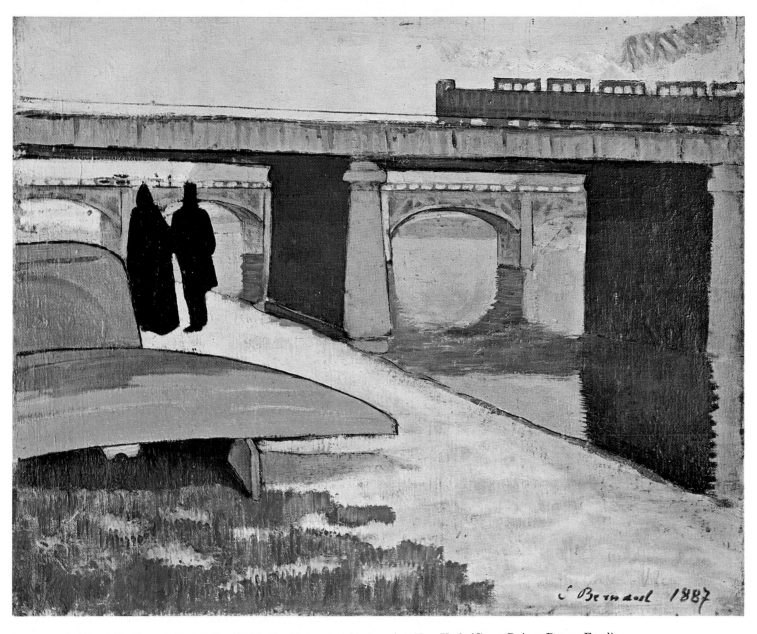

BERNARD: *Bridge at Asnières*, d. 1887. 18⅛ x 21⅜". The Museum of Modern Art, New York (Grace Rainey Rogers Fund)

Van Gogh witnessed with regret the quarrels Bernard was constantly picking with Gauguin (who had shown himself so unfriendly at Pont-Aven) and apologetically explained Bernard's character to Theo: "He is sometimes foolish and crabbed, but I certainly have no right to reproach him with that, because I myself know too well the same disorders of the nerves, and I know that he will not reproach me either...."[67]

Bernard's and van Gogh's discussions on art drew ample material from the exhibitions held in Paris in the spring of 1887. In a new Exposition Internationale at Petit's, Renoir showed a large composition, *Bathers* (opposite), for which Suzanne Valadon had posed. Renoir had labored for several years on this work which signified the farthest reach of his efforts to escape impressionism and re-establish a link with the eighteenth century. His search for a perfect solution of linear harmony, simplification, smooth execution, and cold colors met with great success, though some artists and critics did not hide their disapproval. Van Gogh, however, admired Renoir's "pure, clean line," which represented the painter's conscious break with impressionism. Yet Renoir himself did not for long pursue his efforts in this direction. In the large seated nude (page 50) painted in 1885 he offset the careful modeling of the body and the accurate rendition of the drapery by the spirited execution of the landscape background. A little later, in 1888, Renoir completely abandoned his smooth brushwork reminiscent of Ingres and returned to the vibrant technique of small strokes that he had previously used.

Pissarro was among those who objected to Renoir's composition of bathers because the insistence on draftsmanship resulted, according to him, in a lack of unity which made the figures appear as "separate entities." Pissarro himself was represented at Petit's Exposition Internationale by some of his recent pointillist works, which appeared there for the first time in the company of canvases by his former friends Renoir, Monet, and Sisley. He was happy to conclude from the comparison that the divisionist technique endowed his paintings with greater luminosity than that achieved by the others, whose execution he considered "incoherent." Berthe Morisot, Whistler, Puvis de Chavannes, and Rodin were also among the exhibitors. "Seurat, Signac, Fénéon, all our young friends like only my works, and Mme Morisot's a little," Pissarro wrote to his son Lucien, adding: "Naturally they are motivated by our common struggle. But Seurat, who is colder, more logical, and more moderate, does not hesitate for a moment to declare that we have taken the right position, and that the impressionists are even more retarded than before."[68]

There was also then a great Millet exhibition in Paris which afforded van Gogh an opportunity to study the work of an artist he worshipped. Now that Millet was dead, crowds flocked to his show and people outdid each other in the expression of their deeply moved feelings. The fact that 500,000 francs had recently been refused for the *Angelus* was not altogether irrelevant to this outburst of sentimental admiration.[69] Looking at Millet with new eyes, van Gogh discovered that he was not very colorful, that some of his works were dominated by grays. But his esteem was not much altered by this, since he particularly admired the plasticity of Millet's simple peasant figures and the poetic exactitude with which their characteristic gestures were rendered. He later advised his sister: "I hope you'll go often to the Luxembourg Museum and that you will go and look at the modern paintings in the Louvre, so that you get an understanding of what is a Millet, a Jules Breton, a Daubigny, a Corot. You can have the rest, with the exception of Delacroix. Though now one works in quite a different manner, the work of Delacroix, of Millet, of Corot remains and the changes don't affect it."[70]

More controversial than the Millet retrospective, more important but also less noticed, was the new show of the Independents. Redon exhibited there again, but van Gogh felt unable to share Bernard's enthusiasm for him. For van Gogh and many others, the paintings by Seurat and his friends provided once more the center of attraction among the Independents. His appreciation of these artists led to heated discussions with Bernard, who disdainfully brushed aside their theories and did not care to examine their canvases. Van Gogh was incensed by Bernard's affirmation that he would not exhibit together with Seurat and Signac. This question was not merely of theoretical importance to him, but also had practical implications, since van Gogh was then preoccupied with the idea of assembling the works of some of his friends and of showing them wherever he would have an opportunity to do so.

While, strangely enough, van Gogh did not send anything to the Independents in 1887 (he was to exhibit there for the first time in 1888, *after* he had left Paris), he dreamt of finding a café where he could show his pictures. He eventually succeeded in hanging a number of his paintings, together with works by Anquetin, Bernard, and Lautrec, at Le Tambourin, a cabaret owned by a former artist's model, La Segatori. Le Tambourin, on

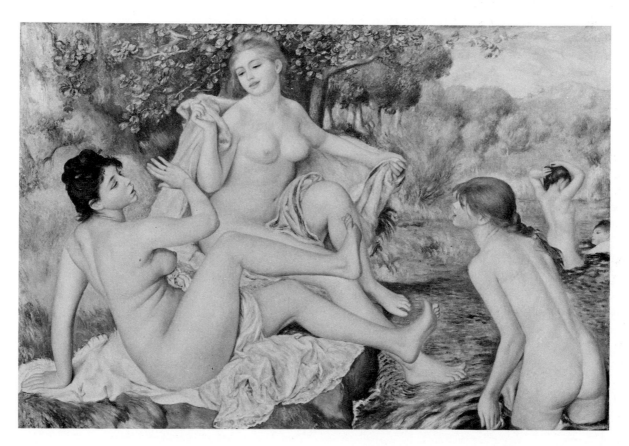

RENOIR: *Bathers,* 1884–87, d. 1887. 45¼ x 67″. Suzanne Valadon posed for this painting. Philadelphia Museum of Art (Mr. and Mrs. Carroll S. Tyson, Jr., Collection)

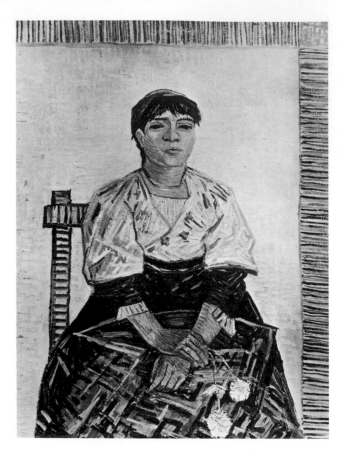

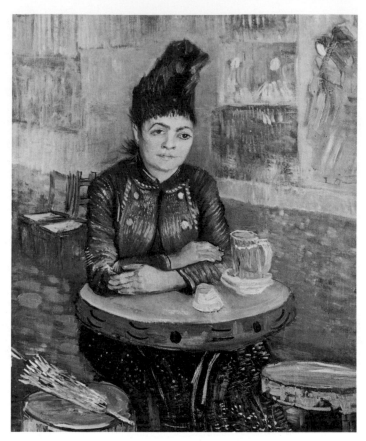

VAN GOGH: *Portrait of an Italian Woman* (La Segatori?), Paris, 1887–88. 31⅞ x 23⅝". Private collection, Paris

VAN GOGH: *Woman at Le Tambourin*, Paris, 1887. 21⅞ x 18¼". Rijksmuseum Vincent van Gogh, Amsterdam

the boulevard de Clichy, was patronized by many writers and painters, as well as by Ernest Hoschedé, a friend of Manet's, Renoir's, and Monet's and an ardent supporter of the Independents, who, between bankruptcies and judiciary sales, used to collect impressionist paintings. Some believed van Gogh to be the lover of La Segatori, a still beautiful Italian woman. All that is known is that after a quarrel with her Vincent told his brother: "I still am attached to her and I hope that she also is to me."[71] He subsequently removed all his canvases from Le Tambourin in a handcart. It was rumored that he had been supplanted in the favors of La Segatori by some regular "du milieu," and Vincent himself took great pains to blame the woman's companions for their misunderstanding, since he considered her "neither free, nor her own mistress."[71]

Van Gogh's ambition was to group as many of his friends as possible in such enterprises as the one which so sadly terminated at Le Tambourin, and if Gauguin did not show there it was because he had left Paris early in April 1887, together with Charles Laval, for Panama and thence for Martinique, where he hoped to satisfy his longing for adventure, new surroundings, tropical colors, and the primitive life of the natives. Nor did Gauguin participate in another exhibition arranged by van Gogh late in 1887 in the huge sky-

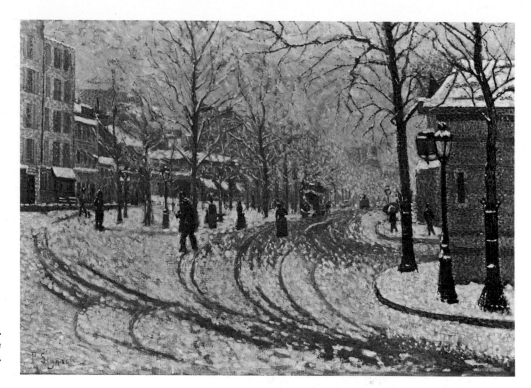

SIGNAC: *Boulevard de Clichy*, 1886. 18 x 25¼″. The Minneapolis Institute of Arts (Bequest of Putnam Dana McMillan)

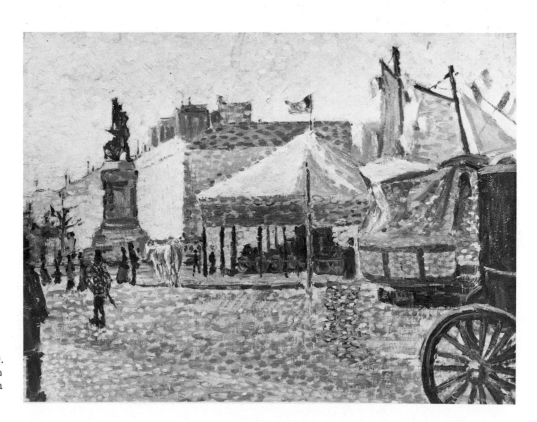

SIGNAC: *Place Clichy* (*La Foire*). 1889. 10¾ x 14″. The Metropolitan Museum of Art, New York (Robert Lehman Collection, 1975)

63

lighted hall of a popular, low-priced restaurant at 43, avenue de Clichy, not far from the junction of the avenues de Clichy and de Saint-Ouen. Emile Bernard later gave this report of the event:

"Vincent van Gogh had undertaken to organize a kind of exhibition of impressionism. The hall was tremendous and provided an area in which over a thousand canvases could be displayed. Vincent therefore asked for help and Louis Anquetin, Koning [a Dutchman who shortly afterwards returned to Holland], as well as Emile Bernard joined him. The regular customers of the place were somewhat horrified by that improvised exhibition (rather out of place there, yet one takes what one can get and wasn't this better than nothing at all?). But unable as they were to appreciate either good or bad, they tolerated the show and continued to take their meals at the restaurant, surrounded by those polychromatic pictures, although they were a little disconcerted by the forbidding aspect of the paintings and the painters. A certain number of artists came there, among them Pissarro, Gauguin [who had returned from Martinique in November 1887], Guillaumin, Seurat, etc., and also several dealers who were well disposed towards the revolutionaries and even made some purchases; among these dealers was M. Georges Thomas...

"There Vincent spread himself out with all the fullness of his vigorous talent. One could already guess the style, the will power, the daring of his later productions, particularly in his *Portrait of Père Tanguy*, of such a delightful joviality, in his *Factories at Clichy* [page 48], which smelled so strongly of coal and gas, and in his sun-drenched landscapes of Asnières. Intensity of life was the most striking feature of these canvases, and even though the feverish activity of his brain was sometimes betrayed by a certain hastiness of execution, one nevertheless felt the powerful traces of logic and of knowledge. As there were about one hundred of his paintings displayed on the walls, the general impression of the hall was dominated by him; it was a joyful, vibrant, harmonious impression."[65]

Van Gogh was very proud when Bernard sold a picture there for the first time, and Anquetin too found a buyer for one of his works. As to van Gogh himself, he exchanged one of his canvases for a painting by Gauguin. Van Gogh would have liked to include some of Signac's pictures in this show, had it not been for the stubborn objections of Bernard. It was at this exhibition in the restaurant that Seurat for the first time spoke to van Gogh.[72] But their contact was not to become a close one.

Together with Seurat and Signac, van Gogh took advantage of an offer by Antoine to hang their paintings and drawings in the lobby of his newly founded Théâtre Libre in the rue Pigalle. Antoine, who dedicated his theater to realistic drama, had informed Zola's friend Paul Alexis: "I have sixty or eighty square meters of wall to decorate in the rehearsal room. I thought of those young people who sometimes paint or sculpture marvelous things and then keep them in their attics... In my theater they can hang the pictures they have ready, and since there will be a coming and going of chic people, this will be a modest but possibly useful exhibition. Remember that I already have some princes and millionaires on my list of subscribers. A bit of canvas has only to strike their fancies to make them buy it. Don't you think the idea is a good one?... No need for frames; I want this foyer of the Théâtre Libre to retain a purely artistic character, and not at all bourgeois."[73] But apparently neither princes nor millionaires were tempted by the works exhibited at the Théâtre Libre.

Vincent van Gogh may also have attended the evening gatherings in this foyer where Antoine assembled his friends among the authors and artists, and where Edmond de Gon-

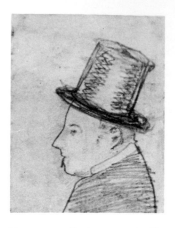

BERNARD: *Caricature of Signac* (detail), c. 1886. Pencil, 4⅛ x 3⅛". Collection Clément Altarriba, Paris

court, whom the painter revered, would occasionally appear. Later van Gogh seems to have participated in an exhibition at offices of the *Revue Indépendante* where Fénéon frequently showed works by Seurat and his associates, as well as by other avant-garde painters. Gauguin rejected an invitation to show there because he did not wish to be taken for a beginner by hanging his canvases where Signac and Dubois-Pillet had previously exhibited. Nor did he approve of Guillaumin's showing there. Van Gogh was greatly disturbed by this lack of generosity he observed around him, the more so as he himself was quite able to admire the works of artists who, he knew, would only despise his own. "Among the artists," he later explained "there is not always a *sufficient* inclination towards friendliness. They either exaggerate people's good qualities or else they neglect them too much. I am inclined to think, however, that justice is more robust than it may appear to be. One should sometimes be able to laugh and to have a little fun, or even quite a lot." [74]

While van Gogh himself complained to his sister that he had lost "the pleasure of laughing" in Paris, he did endeavor not to have his judgment obscured by the rivalries among his friends and to do justice to each according to his artistic merits. Within a year of his arrival in Paris he had met Lautrec and Anquetin, Camille and Lucien Pissarro, Guillaumin and Gauguin, Bernard, Signac, Seurat, Angrand and a host of others, such as Schuffenecker, Vignon, and probably also Degas and Monet. Conversations with these men had helped to clarify his own mind. The study of their works, together with those of Cézanne, Monticelli, Delacroix, and Millet, and of Japanese prints, had also furthered his evolution. These often conflicting influences appear more or less clearly in van Gogh's paintings done in Paris, which show wide divergencies in their execution as well as in their colors: small brush strokes and dots alternate with broad, forceful strokes, thin layers of paint with heavy loads of pigment, emphasis on line and perspective with insistence on large masses, bright colors with pale ones, monochrome compositions with studies in complementaries, impressionistic sketches with robust paintings influenced by Japanese prints, such as a portrait of a woman which supposedly represents La Segatori. But always there is present in his work a vehemence and a tendency towards exaggeration that seems typically his own. It appears as if after every new experience or contemplation of the works of others van Gogh had endeavored to translate into his own language whatever had struck him most. He did so, however, not with the desire to imitate, but rather in order to acquire whatever the others had to offer.

Yet in spite of all the new elements which are apparent in his Paris canvases, van Gogh could write in the fall of 1887 to his sister Wil: "What I think of my own work is that the painting of the *Potato Eaters* [page 34] that I made in Nuenen is after all the best I have done. Only since then I missed the occasion to find models, but I had the occasion to study the question of color, and when I again find models for my figures, then I hope to show that I am looking for something other than little green landscapes or flowers. Last year I scarcely painted anything but flowers, to get used to another color but gray, namely pink, soft or hard green, light blue, purple, yellow, orange, beautiful red. And when I painted landscapes at Asnières this summer, I saw more color therein than formerly. I am now investigating portraiture, and I must say that I am not painting any worse because of that." [75]

Though he did not mention Japanese prints, which he had first discovered in Nuenen and now studied more carefully in Paris, they contributed greatly to van Gogh's new artistic vocabulary. He even organized an exhibition of Japanese prints at Le Tambourin

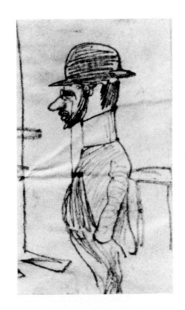

BERNARD: *Caricature of Toulouse-Lautrec*, c. 1886. Pencil, 3½ x 2⅜". Collection Clément Altarriba, Paris

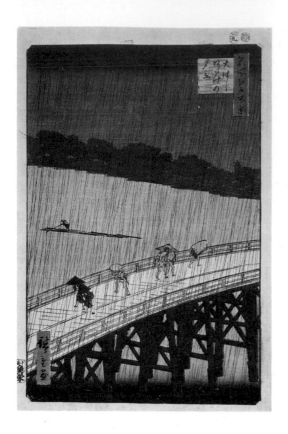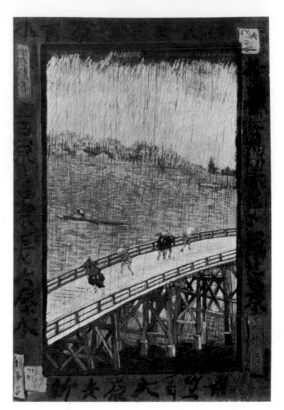

during his ill-fated friendship with La Segatori and spent many hours at the Bing gallery, which specialized in Oriental art, looking at thousands of prints and drawings. He was permitted to roam through Bing's entire building, including cellar and attic, and his enthusiasm knew no limits. He purchased as many prints as he could afford, telling all his acquaintances to do the same. Anquetin and Bernard in particular were deeply impressed by Japanese art; they shared van Gogh's admiration for Hokusai and exchanged prints with him. Gauguin also was greatly attracted by Japanese prints (though his interest in them was probably awakened by Degas and the impressionists even before he met van Gogh). Their preoccupation with these exotic images did not fail to manifest itself in the work of these artists. Van Gogh soon decorated his room with his new acquisitions. He also represented some Japanese prints in the background of two portraits of *père* Tanguy (see page 45), possibly painted in the rue Lepic, as well as in the portrait of a woman at Le Tambourin (page 62). He even copied some of these prints, but in his copies he combined, as always, faithfulness to his model with great freedom of expression and insistence on what seemed essential to him.[76] As to Seurat's friend Fénéon, he was then planning to write a book on Japanese art, a project which he eventually abandoned.

Now that he knew more of the art world in Paris, Vincent's discussions with Theo turned increasingly to the problem of an art dealer's relationship with his painters. Van Gogh later told Gauguin that while he had been absent, "the discussions had taken a wider turn—with Guillaumin, with the two Pissarros, with Seurat.... These discussions often concerned what is so dear to our hearts, my brother's as well as mine: what measures must be taken to safeguard the material existence of artists and their means of production (colors, canvas), and to safeguard for the painters directly their share of the price which their pictures nowadays obtain only long after they have ceased to be the artist's property."[77]

What disturbed van Gogh most was not so much the lack of appreciation for his own work, but to see that men like Pissarro, Guillaumin, and Gauguin had to struggle constantly against difficulties which compromised and even paralyzed their creative efforts. He tried hard to convince his brother that the only solution would be for Theo to leave Boussod & Valadon altogether and establish himself independently. But since the brothers dreamt of providing a number of artists with regular incomes by acquiring all of their works, this was not an easy undertaking and one not exactly encouraged by the difficulties with which Durand-Ruel had to struggle after twelve years of a similar policy. An auction sale which Durand-Ruel had organized in New York in May 1887 had yielded only meager results. According to the *New York Times*, "there were few buyers present, and the bidding was at times rather sluggish. The prices obtained were for the most part rather low." Only Monet's paintings had brought more than $1000 each; Renoir's highest bid was $675, and a Degas pastel, *At the Races*, was sold for $400. None of the works by Sisley and Pissarro reached the $200 mark. Several pictures had to be withdrawn.[78]

In view of the recent depression, of Bismarck's threatening attitude, and above all of his own lack of capital, Theo preferred not to embark on such a venture and to continue instead as an employee of Boussod & Valadon, little though he agreed with their views. While his impetuous brother disliked this compromise, Theo was at least certain in this way to do some good without incurring almost certain bankruptcy. Indeed at Vincent's insistence, Theo was able, during the winter of 1887–88, to buy works by younger artists whom he and Vincent wished to encourage. He was grateful to Vincent for having created for them both a circle of painters and new friends, admitting freely that he would have been unable to do so himself.[79] In addition to the men he had met through his brother —among them apparently Lautrec—Theo was in personal contact with Puvis de Chavannes, Rodin, and Sisley, whom he went to see at Moret. He seems to have been on particularly cordial terms with Degas, and he now also collaborated more closely with Camille Pissarro, whose pointillist paintings Durand-Ruel still declined to handle. Vincent did not conceal his satisfaction when he later wrote to their sister: "Theo is working for all the impressionists; for all of them he has done and sold something, and surely he will go on doing that. But ... that is something quite different from the ordinary dealers who do not care for the painters."[80]

In 1888 Theo van Gogh even managed to sign a contract with Monet who, angered by Durand-Ruel's increasing efforts to open the American market, accused his former dealer of shipping all his works across the Atlantic.[81] Monet had recently painted the tulip fields of Holland, the shores of the Mediterranean, and the rocky coast of Brittany. When he exhibited his paintings from Antibes at Theo's place, Mallarmé complimented him on having outdone himself, while Fénéon accused him of "brilliant vulgarity."

When, in November 1887, Gauguin returned sick and penniless from Martinique, Theo showed interest in his paintings and potteries. After hard times in Panama, during which he had earned his passage to Martinique as a digger on the canal, Gauguin was soon disenchanted with the tropics and their climate. He barely prevented his friend Laval from committing suicide during an attack of illness. Back in Paris, Schuffenecker's limitless

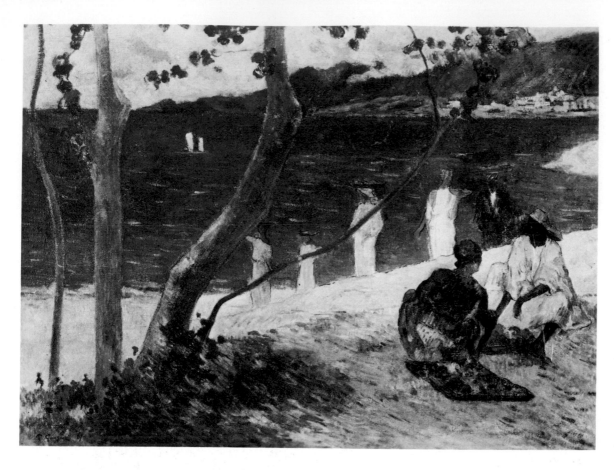

GAUGUIN: *By the Seashore, Martinique,* d. 1887. 18⅛ x 24". Private collection, Paris

hospitality enabled him to get well and meditate on what to do next. "Business in Paris is getting worse and worse," he wrote to his wife in Denmark. "Everybody considers war the only means of getting out of this situation." And he added cynically: "This will have to come one day; on that day there will be many voids and that will make it so much easier for the rest of us." [82]

Gauguin also informed his wife that Boussod & Valadon now had become "the center of the impressionists" and that he had great hopes in their efforts, which were of course those of Theo van Gogh. As a matter of fact, in January 1888 the latter organized a small exhibition of some works by Pissarro, Guillaumin, and Gauguin, in which for the first time one of his landscapes of Martinique appeared. The paintings Gauguin had brought back from there did not differ basically from those he had executed previously in Brittany, except for their richer colors and occasional simplifications of design. His execution and conception were still related to those of the impressionists. But Fénéon reviewed his show benevolently, probably as an encouragement.

Vincent van Gogh seems to have been quite impressed with Gauguin's increasing skill. He himself began to feel somewhat confused by all that he had seen and heard in Paris. He longed for complete solitude in which he might more easily assimilate and put to better use his newly acquired knowledge. Gauguin's plan to return to Brittany and isolation may have contributed to van Gogh's desire to leave Paris. He felt a growing need to come close to nature again, to abandon the city, its excitement and distractions. Paris had finally exhausted his forces; he had started to drink heavily in an effort to gain more stamina, but saw the approach of the moment when his strength would fail him completely. Even though his relationship with Theo had become more harmonious—they went together to several Wagner concerts—he could not overcome a feeling of depression and helplessness. Conditions for working also became increasingly difficult and Theo later remembered that while Vincent had "seen a great many things in Paris which he should have liked to paint, he was always deprived of the possibility of doing so. Models did not want to pose for him, he was forbidden to work in the streets, and in view of his irritability the result was that there were continually scenes which aggravated him to such an extent that it became impossible to get along with him, and Paris itself became highly unbearable to him."[83]

Once more melancholy held the painter in its grip. He desperately needed a new change of environment. Gauguin apparently tried to take him along to Pont-Aven, but van Gogh dreamt of the South and of being alone, at least for a while. In February 1888 Gauguin left for Brittany while van Gogh prepared for his own trip to Provence. "One likes Japanese painting," he explained to his brother, "one has felt its influence—all the impressionists

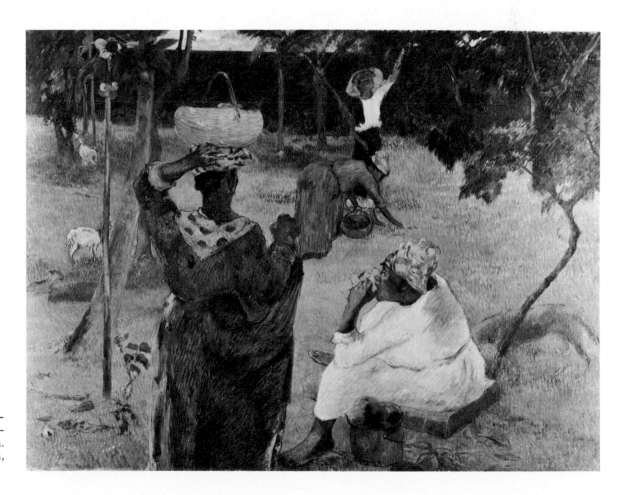

GAUGUIN: *Mango Pickers, Martinique,* 1887. 35¼ x 45¼". Formerly collection Theo van Gogh. Rijksmuseum Vincent van Gogh, Amsterdam

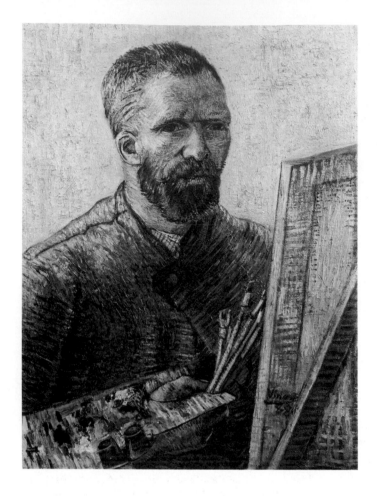

VAN GOGH: *Self-Portrait with Easel*, Paris, d. 1888. 25¾ x 19½". Rijksmuseum Vincent van Gogh, Amsterdam

have that in common—then why not go to Japan, that is to say the equivalent of Japan, the *midi*? Thus I think that after all the future of the new art lies in the South."[84] Van Gogh planned to go first to Arles with the intention of proceeding later to Marseilles, where he would feel himself closer to Monticelli and Cézanne.

Theo in no way opposed Vincent's projects; he actually welcomed them. Indeed, things had become so bad that shortly before the painter's departure, Theo, "unable to take it any longer, had left home, vowing not to return unless Vincent found separate quarters for himself."[55] On the other hand, Theo of course agreed to send his brother a monthly remittance which, though modest, would take care of his needs. The painter considered this a kind of commercial agreement through which his entire output would become Theo's property. He only regretted that Theo could not make similar arrangements with Gauguin and Bernard. Before he left, van Gogh asked Bernard to help him prepare his room in such a way that Theo might believe him still present.[85] He also invited Bernard to join him in the South whenever that would be possible.

A few hours before he took the train, about February 20, 1888, van Gogh, accompanied by his brother, paid his first and last visit to Seurat's studio.

NOTES

1 For a good description of the situation, see R. Welsh-Ovcharov, Vincent van Gogh: His Paris Period, 1886–1888, Utrecht–The Hague, 1976.

2 On the Salons of the period see F. Jourdain: L'Art officiel de Jules Grévy à Albert Lebrun, Le Point, April 1949; also cats. of the exhibitions: "Le Salon entre 1880 et 1900," Galerie Beaux-Arts, Paris, April–May 1934, and "The Two Sides of the Medal," Detroit Institute of Arts, 1954.

3 Strindberg to Gauguin, Paris, Feb. 1, 1895; in J. de Rotonchamp: Paul Gauguin, Paris, 1925, p. 150.

4 On the eighth impressionist exhibition see J. Rewald: The History of Impressionism, New York, 1973, pp. 521–29.

5 On these illustrations see R. von Holten: Gustave Moreau, Illustrateur de la Fontaine, L'Oeil, July–Aug. 1964.

6 On Zola's L'Oeuvre [The Masterpiece] see J. Rewald: Paul Cézanne, New York, 1948, chap. XVIII.

7 See I. de Wyzewa: La Revue Wagnérienne, Paris, 1934, p. 75. (The painter was Boulanger.)

8 On these duels see J. Ajalbert: Mémoires en vrac—Au temps du Symbolisme—1880–1890, Paris, 1938, chaps. VII, XVI; Ferréus: Annuaire du duel, 1880–1889, Paris, 1891.

9 Theo van Gogh's gallery was at 19, boulevard Montmartre; the main establishment was located at 2, place de l'Opéra; while Goupil's publishing firm was at 9, rue Chaptal.

10 According to one of his Dutch acquaintances, Theo, in 1888, was bitter when he managed to sell a Meissonier or a Bouguereau for thousands of francs "but tried in vain to obtain 400 francs for a fine painting by Pissarro." B.v.H. [Boele van Hensbroek]: De Nederlandsche Spectator, Aug. 26, 1893.

11 V. van Gogh to his sister Wil, [Arles, June–July 1888]; Verzamelde Brieven van Vincent van Gogh, Amsterdam, 1952–1954. vol. IV, no. W 4, p. 150. For the various editions and translations of van Gogh's letters, see Bibliography.

12 V. van Gogh to H. M. Levens, [Paris, Aug.–Oct. 1887]; ibid., vol. III, no. 459a, p. 164. Letter written in English.

13 See O. Mirbeau: Lettres à Claude Monet, Cahiers d'Aujourd'hui, 1922, no. 9, p. 162.

14 On Durand-Ruel in America see his Mémoires in L. Venturi: Les Archives de l'Impressionnisme, Paris–New York, 1939, vol. II, pp. 214–17; also H. Huth: Impressionism Comes to America, Gazette des Beaux-Arts, April 1946, and Rewald: History of Impressionism, pp. 518, 523f., 529ff.

15 Unsigned article in The Churchman, June 12, 1886.

16 Unsigned article in the New York Commercial Advertiser, April 10, 1886.

17 Unsigned article in the New York Herald, April 10, 1886.

18 V. van Gogh to his brother, The Hague, [end of Dec. 1881]; Verzamelde Brieven, vol. I, no. 166, p. 295.

19 A. S. Hartrick: A Painter's Pilgrimage through Fifty Years, Cambridge, 1939, p. 48.

20 See ibid., p. 42. Many authors insist that Bernard painted these stripes not on the sail but only on his own canvas. But since Bernard relates that van Gogh painted an imaginary background on his study done at Cormon's without being dismissed, it seems more likely that Hartrick's version of Bernard's defacing the sail itself is accurate.

21 Bernard, unpublished notes, M. M.-A. Bernard, Paris.

22 Bernard to A. Bonger, Port-Said, Feb. 20, 1894; see M. E. Tralbaut: André Bonger, L'Ami des frères van Gogh, Van Goghiana I, Antwerp, Jan. 1963, p. 36.

23 F. Gauzi: Lautrec et son temps, Paris, 1954, pp. 28–31. Bernard later wrote that van Gogh remained at Cormon's for "two months and left behind the reputation of being a diabolical revolutionary. He painted three studies during every sitting, drowning himself in heavy impastos, continually starting all over again on new canvases, painting the model from every possible angle while the miserable pupils who mocked him behind his back spent eight days stupidly copying a single foot." (See note 65.)

24 V. van Gogh to van Rappard, [Nuenen, April 1884]; Verzamelde Brieven, vol. IV, no. R43, pp. 110–12.

25 Bernard: Introduction, Lettres de Vincent van Gogh à Emile Bernard, Paris, 1911, p. 10.

26 A. Bonger to his parents, [Paris, 1886]; Verzamelde Brieven, vol. III, no. 462a, p. 171.

27 A. Bonger to the same, Paris, June 23, 1886; ibid.

28 Theo van Gogh to his mother, [Paris, Summer 1886]; see Introduction, Verzamelde Brieven, vol. I, pp. XXXVII–XXXVIII.

29 V. van Gogh and A. Bonger to Theo van Gogh, Paris, [Aug. to Oct. 1886]; Verzamelde Brieven, vol. III, no. 460a, pp. 165–66.

30 V. van Gogh to John Russell, [Arles, April 1888]; Verzamelde Brieven, vol. III, no. 477a, p. 198. Letter in English.

31 See T. J. Honeyman: Van Gogh, A Link with Glasgow, The Scottish Art Review, vol. II, no. 2, 1948.

32 Gauzi quoted by G. Coquiot: Lautrec, Paris, 1921, p. 23.

33 S. Valadon quoted by F. Fels: Utrillo, Paris, 1930.

34 See J. E. S. Jeanès: D'après nature, Geneva-Besançon, 1946, pp. 18 and 35. On Anquetin see W. Rothenstein: Men and Memories, Recollections, 1872–1900, vol. I, New York, 1931, p. 64; Bernard: Louis Anquetin, La Rénovation Esthétique, Sept. 1905, and Gazette des Beaux-Arts, Feb. 1934; E. Dujardin: Le Cloisonnisme, Revue Indépendante, May 19, 1888; R. H. Sherard: Louis Anquetin, Painter, The Art Journal, 1899, p. 89; also Anquetin: De l'art, Paris, 1970.

35 Signac, diary, May 24, 1897; see Excerpts from the Unpublished Diary of Paul Signac, Gazette des Beaux-Arts, April 1952.

36 This painting is reproduced in S. Lövgren: The Genesis of Modernism, Stockholm, 1959, p. 37. Executed in 1881, it was not painted in the pointillist style.

37 See J. Desclozeaux: Les Artistes Indépendants, La Cravache, June 9, 1888. On the Independents see particularly G. Coquiot: Les Indépendants (1884–1920), Paris, n.d.; Coquiot: Seurat, Paris, 1924, pp. 139–49; and P. Angrand: Naissance des Artistes Indépendants, 1884, Paris, 1965.

38 Information courtesy Ir. V. W. van Gogh, Laren, who long preserved these balls of wool.

39 Theo van Gogh to his brother, Paris, Sept. 5, 1889; Verzamelde Brieven, vol. IV, no. T16, p. 274.

40 Information courtesy the late Lucien Pissarro, London. Pissarro supposedly later said that he had felt very soon that van Gogh "would either go mad or leave all of us far behind. But I didn't know that he would do both." See M. Osborn: Der bunte Spiegel, New York, 1945, p. 37.

41 C. Pissarro to Durand-Ruel, Nov. 6, 1886; see L. Venturi, op. cit., vol. II, p. 24.

42 See Coquiot: Vincent van Gogh, Paris, 1923, pp. 136–37.

43 The preceding passage is quoted almost verbatim from various sections in Hartrick, *op. cit.*, pp. 40, 47, and 45.

44 V. van Gogh to van Rappard, [Sept. 1885]; Verzamelde Brieven, vol. IV, no. R57, p. 135.

45 V. van Gogh to the same, Etten, Nov. 2, 1881; Verzamelde Brieven, vol. IV, no. R3, p. 18.

46 Bernard to his parents, Pont-Aven, Aug. 19, 1886; Lettres de Gauguin à sa femme et à ses amis, Paris, 1946, p. 94, footnote.

47 See Gauguin's letters to his wife, Pont-Aven, end of June and July 1886; *ibid.*, nos. XLI, XLII, pp. 91–94.

48 The Frenchman has been identified only by his initial, P; see Hartrick, *op. cit.*, p. 30.

49 *Ibid.*, pp. 31–33.

50 Gauguin to Signac, [Paris, June–July 1886]; unpublished document, courtesy Mme Ginette Signac, Paris.

51 See Pissarro's letter to his son, Dec. 3, 1886; Camille Pissarro: Letters to his Son Lucien, New York, 1943, p. 82.

52 V. van Gogh to Bernard, [Arles, end of July 1888]; Verzamelde Brieven, vol. IV, no. B11, p. 215.

53 Theo van Gogh to his sister, [Paris, 1886–87]; see Introduction, Verzamelde Brieven, vol. I, p. XXXVIII. On the relationship of the two brothers see: C. Mauron: Vincent et Théo van Gogh, une symbiose, Amsterdam, Instituut voor moderne Kunst, no. 1, 1953.

54 Theo van Gogh to the same; *ibid.*, pp. XXXVIII–XXXIX.

55 Anon. [A. Bonger]: Vincent, *Nieuwe Rotterdamsche Courant*, Sept. 5, 1893; reply to the article quoted in note 10.

56 V. van Gogh to his sister Wil, Paris [summer or autumn 1887]; Verzamelde Brieven, vol. IV, no. W1, p. 144.

57 V. van Gogh to his brother, [Cuesmes], July 1880; Verzamelde Brieven, vol. I, no. 133, p. 195.

58 A. Bonger to his parents, Paris, Dec. 31, 1886; see M. E. Tralbaut, *op. cit.*, p. 6.

59 On Tanguy see C. Waern: Some Notes on French Impressionism, *Atlantic Monthly*, April 1892; O. Mirbeau: Julien Tanguy, *Le Journal*, Feb. 1894, reprinted in Des artistes, Paris, 1922, vol. I, pp. 181–86; E. Bernard: Julien Tanguy, *Mercure de France*, Dec. 16, 1908; G. Lesaulx: Tanguy, *Le Mémorial Artistique*, Feb. 17, 1894; H. Schlittgen: Erinnerungen, Munich, 1926, pp. 250–52; T. Duret: Van Gogh, Paris, 1919, chap. IV; W. Verkade: Le Tourment de Dieu, Paris, 1923, p. 87; M. Dormoy: Tanguy, *Kunst und Künstler*, Aug. 1931; A. de Goaziou: Le "Père Tanguy," Paris, 1951; H. Perruchot: Le Père Tanguy, *L'Oeil*, June 15, 1955; Rewald: History of Impressionism, pp. 301 and 556–58; and Tralbaut, *op. cit.*

60 See Bernard: Julien Tanguy, *op. cit.*

61 On Theo van Gogh's collection see the cat. of the exhibition: "De verzameling van Theo van Gogh," Stedelijk Museum, Amsterdam, 1953 (the collection also contained other works not listed); also V. W. van Gogh: Theo van Gogh without Vincent, *Art News*, Oct. 1953. On the planned exchange with Angrand see Coquiot: Vincent van Gogh, p. 149.

62 V. van Gogh to his brother, [Arles, Aug. 1888]; Verzamelde Brieven, vol. III, no. 528, p. 290. Van Gogh also wrote to his brother, apropos Seurat: "I often think over his method, though I do not follow it at all, but he is an original colorist, and Signac likewise, though to a different degree; the pointillists have found something new, and I like them well, after all." [Arles, Sept. 1888]; *ibid.*, no. 539, p. 312.

63 Signac to Coquiot; see Coquiot: Vincent van Gogh, p. 140.

64 See Bernard: Introduction, Lettres à Bernard, *op. cit.*, p. 16.

65 E. Bernard, excerpt from an unpublished manuscript on Vincent van Gogh [1889], found among the papers of his friend A. Aurier (courtesy M. Jacques Williame, Châteauroux). This text was meant either as a short article or as a source of information for the study on van Gogh which Aurier was preparing in 1889 for the *Mercure de France*; see chapter VII.

66 V. van Gogh to Bernard, [Paris, summer 1887]; Verzamelde Brieven, vol. IV, no. B1, p. 191, also *ibid.*, no. 1, p. 19.

67 V. van Gogh to his brother, [Arles, Sept. 1888]; Verzamelde Brieven, vol. III, no. 539, p. 312.

68 Pissarro to his son Lucien, May 14 and 15, 1887; *op. cit.*, pp. 107–10. See also Fénéon: Quelques Impressionnistes, *La Cravache*, June 2, 1888, reprinted in Fénéon: Oeuvres, Paris, 1948, pp. 137–40.

69 See Pissarro's letter to the same, May 16, 1887; *op. cit.*, p. 110.

70 V. van Gogh to his sister Wil, [Arles, second half of Aug. 1888]; Verzamelde Brieven, vol. IV, no. W6, pp. 157–58.

71 V. van Gogh to his brother, [Paris, summer 1887]; Verzamelde Brieven, vol. III, no. 462, p. 170; also *ibid.*, no. 461, pp. 167–69. On van Gogh and La Segatori see also P. Gauguin: Avant et Après, Paris, 1923, pp. 177–78.

72 See Seurat's letter to Beaubourg, Aug. 28, [1890]; reprod. in R. Rey: La Renaissance du sentiment classique, Paris, 1931, opp. p. 132.

73 Antoine to Alexis, 1887, published by Trublot in *Cri du Peuple*, Sept. 7, 1887; see D. Le Blond-Zola: Paul Alexis, *L'Ordre*, March 2, 1939.

74 V. van Gogh to his sister Wil, [Saint-Rémy, middle of Feb. 1890]; Verzamelde Brieven, vol. IV, no. W20, p. 180.

75 V. van Gogh to the same, [Paris, summer–autumn 1887]; *ibid.*, no. W1, p. 145.

76 On van Gogh and Japanese prints see M. E. Tralbaut: Van Gogh's Japanisme, *Mededelingen* van de Dienst voor Schone Kunsten der gemeente 's-Gravenhage, 1954, no. 1–2. M. de Sablonière: Vincent van Gogh, Amsterdam-Antwerp, n.d., p. 61, has established that van Gogh already knew Japanese prints in Nuenen.

77 V. van Gogh to Gauguin, [Arles, Sept.–Oct. 1888]; Verzamelde Brieven, vol. III, no. 553a, p. 343.

78 See *New York Times*, May 6 and 7, 1887; also cat. of the sale: The Durand-Ruel Collection of French Paintings, Moore's Art Galleries, Sale May 5 and 6, 1887.

79 See Theo van Gogh's letter to his brother, Paris, Oct. 27, 1888; Verzamelde Brieven, vol. IV, no. T3, p. 261.

80 V. van Gogh to his sister Wil, [Arles, June–July 1888]; *ibid.*, no. W4, p. 155.

81 See Monet's letters to Durand-Ruel in Venturi, *op. cit.*, vol. I, pp. 306–15.

82 Gauguin to his wife, Paris, Nov. 24, 1887; *op. cit.*, no. LVIII, p. 118.

83 Theo van Gogh to his fiancée, Johanna Bonger, [April 1889]; see Introduction, Verzamelde Brieven, vol. I, p. XLV.

84 V. van Gogh to his brother, [Arles, June 1888]; Verzamelde Brieven, vol. III, no. 500, p. 237.

85 See Bernard's recollections in: Introduction, Lettres à Bernard, *op. cit.*, p. 12.

II   1886-1890   SEURAT AND HIS FRIENDS

Georges Seurat was a strange man, proud and often almost haughty, whose secretiveness surprised even his closest friends. Yet they all agreed—and Vincent van Gogh with them— that he was the leader among the painters of the new generation. He himself was perfectly aware of being looked to for guidance and simply accepted the place he occupied as a natural consequence of his intellect and efforts. He was always careful that proper acknowledgment should be given him for his discoveries and achievements; indeed nothing hurt him more deeply than not to receive credit when he deserved it. Relentlessly he devoted himself to the pursuit of a goal to which he came closer with each new work. This goal was to reach beyond impressionism and apply to his art the results of scientific research in the field of physics; but it was also, as he admitted unhesitatingly, to find "something new, an art entirely my own."

The early career of Seurat had not been different from that of many young artists of the time. After attending a municipal art school in Paris where he was taught to copy dusty plaster casts, he entered the Ecole des Beaux-Arts in 1878, at the age of eighteen, and for two years attended the classes of Henri Lehmann, a pupil of Ingres. A dutiful and orderly student, but not a particularly brilliant one, he soon began to satisfy his natural curiosity and his taste for the difficult through extensive reading. Thus he was able to resist the deadly grip of academic conceptions which proved fatal to his classmates, among them his friend Aman-Jean.

Seurat cherished a great veneration for the Goncourt brothers and found even more food for thought in the precepts and works of Delacroix, from which he took copious notes, as well as in some of Corot's ideas,[1] in the paintings of Pissarro and Monet, and above all in the writings of Charles Blanc and the scientific treatises of Chevreul, Sutter, Rood, and others. He was fascinated by the idea that color is controlled by fixed laws which "can be taught like music." Among these laws was the one established by Chevreul, according to which "under *simultaneous contrast of colors* are included all the modifications which differently colored objects appear to undergo in their physical composition, and in the height of tone of their respective colors, when seen simultaneously."[2] One of the basic elements of this simultaneous contrast is the fact that two adjacent colors mutually influence each other, each imposing on its neighbor its own complementary (the light one becoming lighter, the dark one darker when they are of unequal value).

During frequent visits to the Louvre Seurat endeavored to find confirmation of these principles in the works of the masters but soon discovered that even those who, like Veronese and Delacroix, had sometimes observed these laws, had done so instinctively rather than with scientific precision. Thus he saw opened before him a field where it would be his task to apply his knowledge methodically and to reconcile the rigid principles of draftsmanship that had been handed down by Ingres with the optical tenets foreseen by the great colorists of the past.

After a year's military service in Brest, on the coast of Brittany, Seurat had returned to Paris late in 1880 to devote two years exclusively to the art of black and white. In his drawings he soon achieved a perfect mastery over the balance of light and dark masses. His preoccupation with gradation and contrast, rather than line, permitted him to study further, with a reduced scale of values, the problems of interpenetration and reflection. Signac was actually to say later that Seurat's drawings, "even simple sketches, are so studied in contrast and gradation that one could paint from them without seeing the model again."[3]

In 1883 one of Seurat's drawings, a large portrait of his friend Aman-Jean, was accepted by the Salon jury while the rest of his entries were refused. During that same year Seurat, then twenty-three years old, worked mostly on his first great composition, *Une Baignade à Asnières*, a painting measuring almost seven by ten feet. Carefully regulating the play of horizontals and verticals, attentively studying the slightest details in a great number of preparatory drawings and small panels, Seurat proceeded with a methodical separation of elements—light, shade, local color, interaction of colors—and their proper balance and proportion.

Une Baignade was one of the numerous paintings rejected by the Salon jury of 1884 to appear subsequently at the exhibition of the Groupe des Artistes Indépendants, in the creation of which Seurat took an active part. It was there that Signac saw the huge paint-

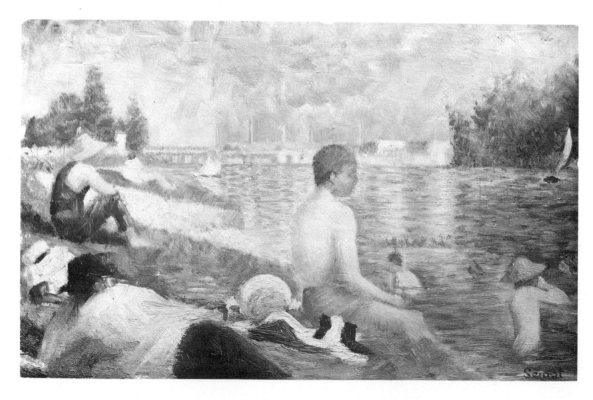

SEURAT: *Study for "Une Baignade,"* 1883. Oil on wood, 6¾ x 9¾". The Art Institute of Chicago

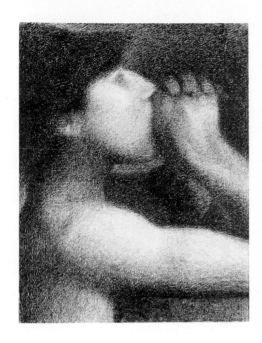 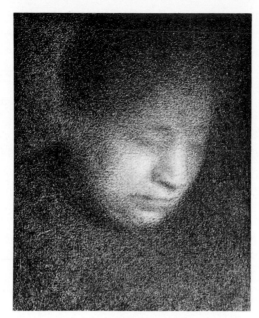 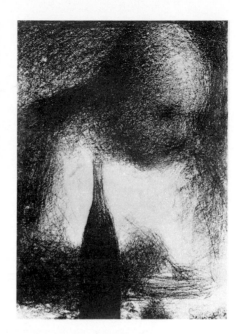

Above, left: SEURAT: *Echo, Study for "Une Baignade,"* 1883–84.
Conté crayon, 12⅛ x 9⅜". Yale University Art Gallery, New
Haven, Conn. (Bequest of Edith Wetmore). Center: SEURAT: *The
Artist's Mother,* c. 1884 Conté crayon, 12 x 9¼". Formerly collec-
tion Lucien Pissarro. Collection Mr. and Mrs. Alex Lewyt, New
York. Right: SEURAT: *The Artist's Father,* c. 1884. Conté crayon,
12½ x 8⅝". Formerly collection Paul Signac. Collection Mme
Ginette Signac, Paris

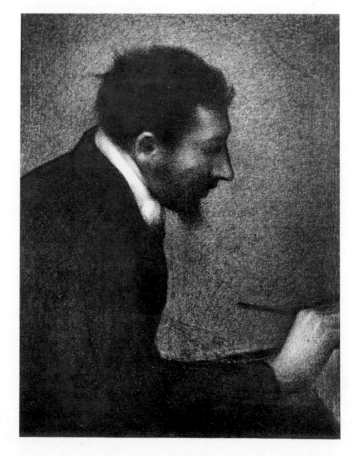

SEURAT: *Portrait of the Painter Aman-Jean,* 1882. Conté crayon,
24¾ x 18¾". The Metropolitan Museum of Art, New York (Bequest of Stephen C. Clark)

ing (it was hung in the canteen) and immediately noticed its qualities. But he was struck by the fact that Seurat had painted it "in great flat strokes, brushed one over the other, fed by a palette composed, like Delacroix's, of pure as well as earth colors. By means of ochres and browns the picture was deadened and appeared less brilliant than those the impressionists painted with a palette limited to prismatic colors."[4]

Signac's own canvases at the Independents, among them a view of a Montmartre street, were executed with small, comma-like strokes and bright colors which he had derived from the greatly admired works of Monet and Guillaumin, neither of whom he knew at that time. When Signac met Seurat at the constituent assemblies of the Independents and began to discuss with him the problems which preoccupied them both, it soon became apparent that each could reap great benefit from the other's experience. Signac was able to replace his intuitive observation of contrasts with Seurat's scientific method, while Seurat, at his friend's insistence, eliminated all earth colors from his palette. He actually even repainted certain parts of *Une Baignade* the following year, adding small dots of bright colors.[5]

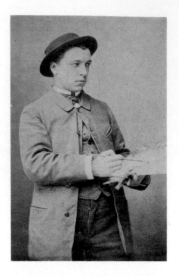

Photograph of Paul Signac, c. 1883

Eager to acquaint himself completely with the theories which formed the basis of Seurat's system, Signac went to call on Chevreul. The scientist, who was then ninety-eight years old, told the young painter that thirty-four years earlier Delacroix had written to him, expressing a desire to discuss the science of color and to question him about certain problems. But a constant sore throat had prevented Delacroix from keeping their appointment.[6] When Signac, accompanied by Angrand, returned somewhat later with the request that Chevreul should arbitrate a discussion about a particularly difficult problem, they discovered sadly that the centenarian was losing his faculties. After asking them to repeat their question several times, Chevreul suddenly seemed to understand and exclaimed: "Ah! Ah! division of light! Oh, yes. I remember, I once wrote a little pamphlet about that. Oh! you are painters. Why don't you see my colleague at the Institut de France, Monsieur Ingres! He will give you all the information."[7] Ingres had been dead for twenty years (moreover he had never been interested in prismatic colors or simultaneous contrast), and Chevreul himself was now unable to be of any assistance. Thenceforth the painters were on their own in their efforts to apply his theories to their art.

In order to study more carefully the interplay of colors and their complementaries, Seurat constructed, according to Chevreul's and Rood's principles, a disc on which he brought together all the hues of the rainbow, joined to one another by a number of intermediate colors: blue, natural ultramarine, artificial ultramarine, violet, purple, purple-red, carmine, red, vermilion, minium, orange, orange-yellow, yellow, greenish yellow, yellow-green, green, emerald green, very greenish blue, greenish cyanic blue, greenish blue, cyanic blue I and cyanic blue II, leading back to blue and thus closing the circle. On his palette Seurat also used white, which he mixed with the primary colors, thereby obtaining a host of *tones* from a color with only a trace of white in it to almost pure white. His disc could thus be completed in such a way that the pure hues would be concentrated around the center from which they would slowly fade toward white, a uniform ring of pure white forming the periphery. With the aid of this disc, Seurat could easily locate the complementary of any color or tone.

Lucien Pissarro later jotted down, for his own use, the various principles which guided Seurat and his friends in the application of Rood's disc to their work. The painters separated the six basic colors into three primary and three composite or binary ones; "the primary colors are red(1), yellow(2) and blue(3); the composite or binary colors are orange (1+2), green(2+3), violet(1+3). United, these colors produce the sensation of white, white

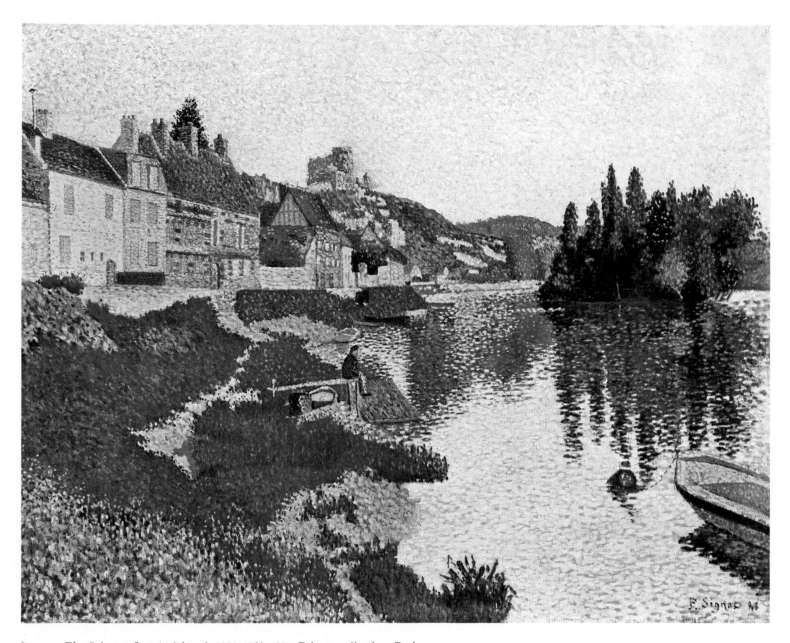

SIGNAC: *The Seine at Les Andelys,* d. 1886. 25½ x 32″. Private collection, Paris

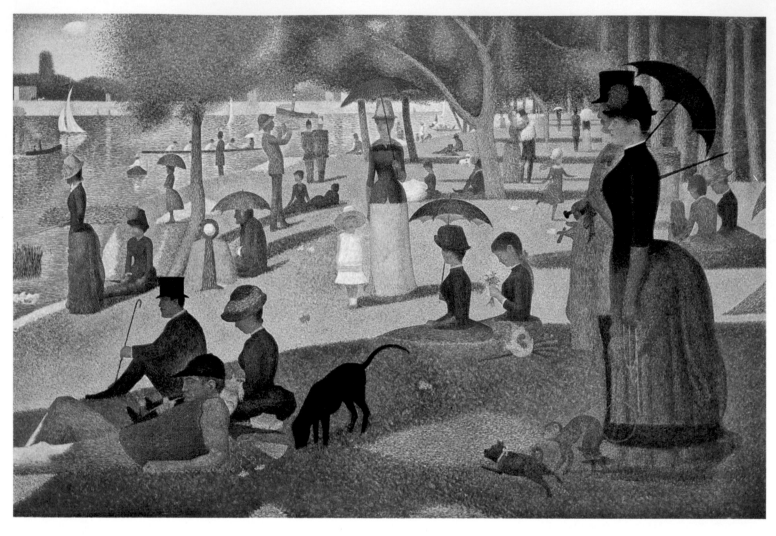

SEURAT: *A Sunday Afternoon on the Island of La Grande Jatte,* 1884–86. 81¼ x 120¼". The Art Institute of Chicago (Helen Birch Bartlett Memorial Collection)

light being the sum of all colors. Each color serves as complementary to two others to form white light. As 1+2+3 are always required to form white light, the

complementary of red (1) = (2+3) = yellow + blue = green
complementary of yellow (2) = (1+3) = red + blue = violet
complementary of blue (3) = (1+2) = red + yellow = orange

and vice versa. According to the law of contrast a color achieves its maximum of intensity when brought close to its complementary. But while two complementaries enhance each other through juxtaposition, they destroy each other when mixed. Complementaries mixed in equal portions produce gray. Two complementaries mixed in unequal portions destroy each other partially and produce a broken color which is a variety of gray, a tertiary color. The law of complementaries permits a color to be toned down or intensified without becoming dirty; while not touching the color itself, one can fortify or neutralize it by changing the adjacent colors. If one juxtaposes in their pure state two equals of different degrees of energy, such as a dark red and a light red, one obtains (a) a contrast through the difference of intensity and (b) a harmony through the similarity of tones. Two colors which do not go well together can be separated by white which serves as an intermediary and unites them."[8]

With such precise concepts and a methodically arranged palette, Seurat endeavored to treat his subjects according to the various optical laws established by Chevreul, Maxwell, Helmholtz, and others, but especially Rood, of which Lucien Pissarro's notes offer only excerpts. He proceeded by first placing on his canvas pigments to represent the local color, that is, the color the chosen object would assume in a completely white light (or if seen from very close by). This color was then "achromatized" by additional strokes corresponding to (a) the portion of colored light which reflected itself, with alteration, on that surface (usually a solar orange); (b) the feeble portion of colored light which penetrated beyond the surface and which was reflected after having been modified by partial absorption; (c) reflections from surrounding objects; and (d) ambient complementary colors.[9]

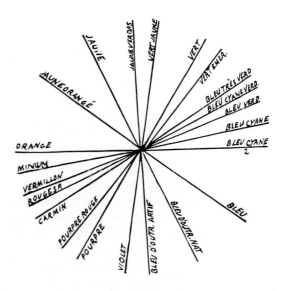

Color wheel drawn by Seurat after O. N. Rood (published in France in 1881). Collection Mme Ginette Signac, Paris

Inseparable from these concepts was Seurat's particular technique of painting. "Achromatization" required the interpenetration of all colors and tones in their pure state. In order to reproduce the exact coloration of a given surface under given light conditions, it was impossible to mix the pigments on the palette. Physical experiments had proved that the mixture of pigments eventually leads to black. The only mixture capable of producing the desired effect was *optical mixture*, which thus became the decisive factor in Seurat's execution. The painter, having assembled separately on his canvas the individual color elements present in nature, assigned to the observer's retina the task of mixing them again. In doing so he based his theory on that of H. W. Dove, among others, according to which the retina, expecting distinct rays of light to act on it, perceives in rapid alternation both the dissociated colored elements and their resultant color.[10]

The principle of optical mixture was in itself not new to art and had been practiced notably by Delacroix and the impressionists. But their execution in hatchings and comma-like strokes, destined to fuse at a certain distance, did not present the mathematical strictness which Seurat needed to apply his system to full advantage. By adopting tiny brush strokes in the form of dots, Seurat managed to accumulate even on small surfaces a great variety of colors and tones, each corresponding to one of the elements which contributed to the appearance of the object. At a given distance—which varied according to the size of the dots chosen for the specific painting—these tiny particles would blend optically. And this optical mixture, according to Seurat and his friends, produced a far greater intensity and luminosity of color than any mixture of pigments.

His system thus perfected in collaboration with Signac, Seurat began the planning of a large composition which would represent his new palette and technique. During the latter part of 1884 he started to make careful studies of the landscape and crowds in the public park on the island of La Grande Jatte, near Asnières, the site of his *Baignade*. For these studies done on the spot, on small wooden panels, Seurat did not use the slow and meticulous execution of little dots, but rather, as in his preparatory studies for *Une Baignade*, vivid brush strokes similar to those of the impressionists. His colors, however, were pure, the elements balanced, and the law of contrasts was observed. These panels, on which Seurat registered the particularities of the site and the incidental figures he saw there, were to provide the necessary "information" for his work, after being subjected to the rigorous requirements of his composition.[11] Whenever he needed further details, he had models pose in his studio for drawings in which he finally determined the attitudes he wanted. Thus his chance observations from nature were eventually integrated on his large canvas, once the spontaneity of his sketches with their record of fugitive effects had furnished the basic elements for a work from which all improvisation was excluded.

Always proceeding with perfect method, Seurat later noted in a letter to a friend: "1884, Ascension Day—*Grande Jatte*, the studies and the painting,"[12] thus specifying that he had begun the preparatory studies on the very same day as the large canvas itself. This appears rather strange, for the small panels and drawings for the *Grande Jatte*, more numerous than those for the *Baignade*, seem to reflect, almost like a diary, the evolution of the composition and the process of elimination or intensification which was to lead to the final version. It is difficult to imagine the artist working simultaneously on the large painting and on the small panels and drawings, since the arrangement of the composition had to be based on the elements provided by the preparatory studies. Yet, in view of Seurat's insistence on this essential point, one has to accept that the artist, from the start, had

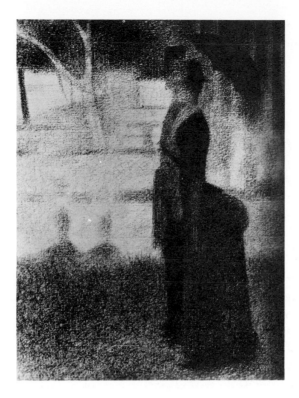

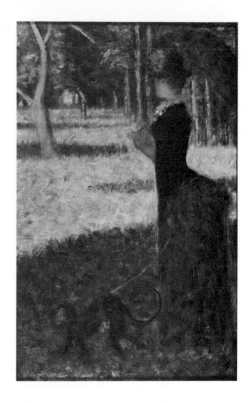

Right: Seurat: *Study for "La Grande Jatte,"* c. 1885. Conté crayon, 12¼ x 9⅜". British Museum, London (Bequest of César M. de Hauke)

Far right: Seurat: *Study for "La Grande Jatte,"* c. 1885. Oil on wood, 9¾ x 6". Smith College Museum of Art, Northampton, Mass.

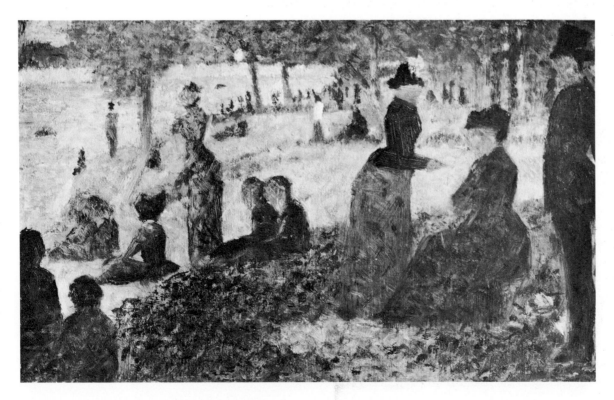

Seurat: *Study for "La Grande Jatte,"* c. 1884. Oil on wood, 6 x 9¾". Formerly collection Maximilien Luce. Collection Mr. and Mrs. Leigh B. Block, Chicago

established the principle of his composition and thereafter advanced systematically in his effort to perpetuate his sensation, to create a synthesis of the landscape, and to avoid, in the figures which animate it, all that is accidental and transitory.[13]

Embarking upon his immense new project, Seurat followed the procedure later outlined by Signac: "It seems that the first consideration of a painter who stands before the white canvas should be to decide what curves and arabesques should cut the surface, what colors and tones should cover it.... Following the precepts of Delacroix he would not begin a composition until he had first determined its organization. Guided by tradition and science, he would adjust the composition to his conception, that is to say he would adapt the lines (directions and angles), the chiaroscuro (tones), the colors, to the features he wished to make dominant."[14]

For several months Seurat went every day to the island of La Grande Jatte. He was so absorbed by his work that he sometimes even refused to lunch with his best friends, fearing to weaken his concentration. Whenever he saw Angrand, who was then also painting on the island, Seurat greeted him without even putting his palette down, scarcely detaching his half-closed eyes from his motif. Working on the island in the morning, Seurat devoted his afternoons to painting on the composition in his studio and hardly paused to eat a roll or a bar of chocolate. Standing on a ladder, he patiently covered his canvas (equal in size to *Une Baignade*) with tiny multi-colored dots, applied over a first layer of pigment which was broadly brushed in. This original layer bound the loosely applied dots together and relieved Seurat from the necessity of always assembling them tightly. At his task, Seurat frequently centered his attention on a single section of the canvas, having previously determined each stroke and color to be applied. Thus he was able to paint steadily without having to step back in order to judge the effect obtained or the result of optical mixture. His great power of concentration also enabled Seurat to keep working late into the night, despite the treacherous character of artificial light. He no more needed to consult Rood's disc than a true poet must count syllables; the law of simultaneous contrast had become the guiding principle of his thinking.

Seurat never considered the various rules which he applied to his art as an encroachment upon his freedom of expression. He found in them a means of controlling his observation, a solemn guide towards truth. They were a challenge to his eye and mind rather than a restriction. And instead of gradually liberating himself from their firm grip, he actually added new rules whenever science offered further data that could be applied to his work.

If Seurat had needed any confirmation for his viewpoint, he had found it in a series of articles on the "Phenomena of Vision," published in 1880 by David Sutter, who had concluded that "one must look at nature with the eyes of the mind and not merely with the eyes of the body, like beings without reason.... There are colorists' eyes as there are tenor voices, but these gifts of nature have to be stimulated by science to develop to the full.... Despite their absolute character, rules do not hamper the spontaneity of invention or execution. Science delivers us from every form of uncertainty and enables us to move freely within a wide circle; it would be an injury both to art and science to believe that one necessarily excludes the other. Since all rules are derived from the laws of nature, nothing is easier to learn or more necessary to know. In art everything should be willed."[15]

Seurat pondered these and similar problems while proceeding with his work on *La Grande Jatte*. He was well enough satisfied with the progress of his new composition to admit friends, notably Dubois-Pillet, Signac and Angrand, to his studio occasionally and show them the huge canvas while he explained his theories.[16] But when some visitors praised his work, he simply remarked to Angrand: "They see poetry in what I have done. No, I apply my method and that is all there is to it."[17]

A Sunday Afternoon on the Island of La Grande Jatte was ready in March 1885, when Seurat left for Grandcamp on the Channel coast, whence he returned with several seascapes. Back in Paris in October, he again went over his large composition. It was while Seurat had been at Grandcamp that Signac, in Paris, had met Camille Pissarro in Guillaumin's studio and had explained to him the principle of Seurat's researches. In October 1885, Guillaumin introduced Seurat to Pissarro at the Durand-Ruel Galleries. Pissarro soon became convinced that the two young painters had indeed discovered a method to assure impressionism of all the benefits of modern science.[18] He had lately been dissatisfied with his own work, especially with a certain roughness in his execution, and was therefore particularly receptive to the constructive elements in Seurat's theories. He immediately started to apply the new method to his own painting.

At the beginning of the following year, the sight of two small divisionist paintings by Pissarro definitely shook Signac and prompted him to execute in Clichy his own first paintings in the divisionist technique and with pure colors. There can be no doubt that Pissarro also had much sound advice to offer, based on his much greater experience; advice, among other things, on the changes many pigments undergo after a certain time, a factor of which Seurat had not been sufficiently aware during his work on *La Grande Jatte*.[19] Pissarro by no means slavishly adopted the theories of his new friends but began to experiment on his own. He was led to the conclusion that a colored surface acts not only through its complementary on neighboring surfaces, but reflects some of its own color onto them, even when it is not brilliant and the eye does not perceive its reflection clearly. Seurat and Signac were less affirmative in this respect, though it is certain that the continual exchange of views among the three painters did much to strengthen their style, increase their sum of observations, and clarify their science.[20]

Pissarro's conversion seemed to assure Seurat and Signac that their theories constituted the logical continuance and perfection of what their forerunners had begun. For Pissarro himself it meant a rather sudden break in his evolution and a completely new start, a step so radical that it must have surpassed the fondest expectations of his new friends who had hardly counted on finding such an ally among the old-guard impressionists. It is therefore understandable that, a little later, Signac wrote enthusiastically to the older painter: "How much misery and trouble your courageous conduct will bring you! For us, the young, it is a great good fortune and a truly great support to be able to battle under your command."[21] But at no time did Pissarro himself consider his role in the new movement to be a leading one; he was always anxious to acknowledge Seurat's initial efforts. He did, however, contribute much towards propagating these efforts, since he was in a better position to reach a wide audience than either Seurat or Signac. At the same time, Pissarro's eldest son, Lucien, who was Signac's age (and four years younger than Seurat), also began to apply the divisionist technique in his work.

Early in December 1885 Pissarro approached Monet concerning the organization of a new exhibition of the impressionist group—there had been none since 1882. At the beginning of 1886 Berthe Morisot and her husband—Manet's brother—took up this suggestion and discussed the project with the various impressionists. Pissarro immediately insisted that his new friends be invited. He met with strong opposition and was only reluctantly sup-

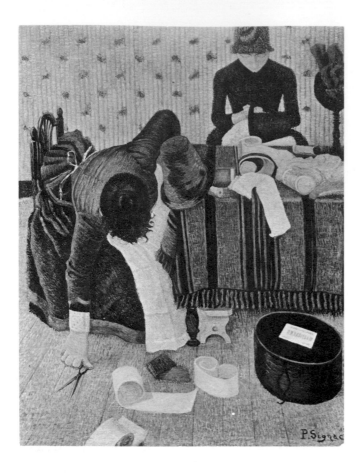

SIGNAC: *Apprêteuse et Garnisseuse (Two Milliners)*, d. 1885. 44 x 35″. Exhibited with the impressionists and at the Independents in 1886. E. G. Bührle Foundation, Zurich

ported by Degas, who had always been defended by Pissarro.[22] In the end he obtained satisfaction, but Monet, Renoir, Sisley, and Caillebotte decided to abstain. Gauguin, who owed his admission to the group to Pissarro's sponsorship since 1879, now managed to have his friend Schuffenecker invited to make up for the defection of the others. At Pissarro's request his own works were shown together with those of Signac, Seurat, and Lucien in a separate room, the last one of the apartment at the Maison Dorée in the rue Laffitte, that the painters had rented for the occasion. Seurat's *Grande Jatte* was the most striking feature of that room, which, however, was not large enough to show it off to full advantage. With the *Grande Jatte* appeared some of Seurat's paintings of Grandcamp as well as three of his drawings and no less than fifteen canvases by Signac, done mostly in the Breton port of Saint-Briac and in various Parisian suburbs, all distinguished by a "frenetic intensity of light."[10] Signac also exhibited a large composition, his most important contribution to the show, *Apprêteuse et Garnisseuse (modes), rue du Caire*, in which he had attempted for the first time to apply the new principle to a view of an interior. The room further contained nine recent paintings by Pissarro, together with some of his gouaches, pastels, and etchings, and a group of paintings, woodcuts, and watercolors by his son.

The show was greeted with considerable curiosity aroused by advance rumors concerning Seurat's large composition, which immediately attracted a laughing crowd.[23] Signac later recalled that on the day of the opening the painter Stevens "continually shuttled back and forth between the Maison Dorée and the neighboring Café Tortoni to recruit those of his cronies who were sipping on the famous terrace, and brought them to look at Seurat's canvas so as to show how his friend Degas had fallen in welcoming such horrors. He threw his money on the turnstile and did not even wait for change, in such a hurry was he to bring in his forces." [24]

What added to the general confusion was the fact that public and critics were unable to distinguish between the works of Seurat, Signac, and the two Pissarros. The novelty of paintings produced by different artists relying on a common method was so striking that it did not allow visitors to note more subtle differences of personal qualities. Even George Moore, a personal friend of Degas and most of the other impressionists, frankly admitted: "Great as was my wonderment, it was tenfold increased on discovering that only six of these pictures were painted by the new man, Seurat, whose name was unknown to me; the other five were painted by my old friend Pissarro. My first thought went for the printer; my second for some *fumisterie* on the part of the hanging committee, the intention of which escaped me. The pictures were hung low, so I went down on my knees and examined the dotting in the pictures signed Seurat, and the dotting in those that were signed Pissarro. After a strict examination I was able to detect some differences, and I began to recognize the well-known touch even through this most wild and most wonderful

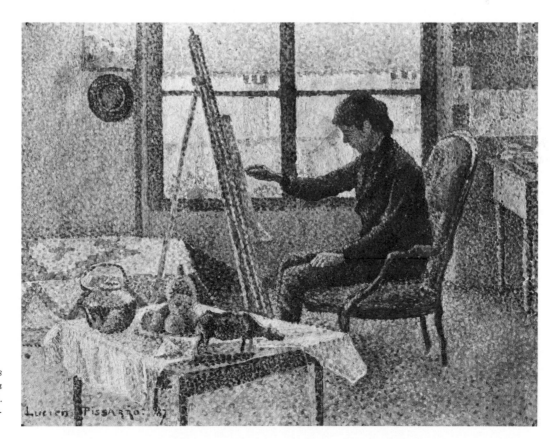

LUCIEN PISSARRO: *Georges [Manzana] Pissarro Painting a Snowscape,* d. 1887. 13 x 16⅛". Collection Mme Paulémile Pissarro, Clécy

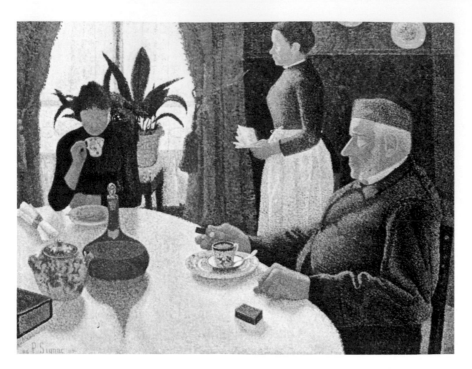

SIGNAC: *The Dining Room (Breakfast)*, d. 1886–87. 35 x 45¼". Exhibited with the Independents in 1887. Rijksmuseum Kröller-Müller, Otterlo

transformation. Yes, owing to a long and intimate acquaintance with Pissarro and his work, I could distinguish between him and Seurat, but to the ordinary visitor their pictures were identical."[25] Thus Seurat's majestic calm and restraint, Signac's more colorful impetuosity, Camille Pissarro's somewhat rigid lyricism, and his son's genuine naiveté were ignored, and the critics claimed that the new technique had completely destroyed the personalities of the painters who used it. Others questioned Seurat's sincerity or spoke openly of a hoax. Since Camille Pissarro was the only known artist and by far the oldest of the small group, many saw him as the inventor of the new style and considered the others to be merely his pupils. Seurat was deeply disturbed by this, although Pissarro took great pains to assert everywhere that it was Seurat who "first conceived the idea and applied the scientific theory after profound study; I have only followed."[18]

Some critics went even further, and one of them declared that Seurat's large painting, besides being influenced by Pissarro, was "an error, a flat imitation of Miss Kate Greenaway."[26] Another claimed that if the logic of Seurat's system were pursued to its conclusion, an effect of sunlight in his work should emit its own rays of light, since a chemist who is given the elements of a body can reconstitute with these the body itself.[27] The opinion was also voiced that these pictures could be seen properly only in the place in which they had been painted, as the different light conditions of the showroom, the colors of its walls, and even the clothes of the visitors were likely to disrupt their carefully calculated harmonies. Even the reproach of a "too hasty execution" was leveled at Seurat and his friends.[28]

With the exception of a few painters who were fascinated by the new concept and who immediately tried their hand at it (such as Anquetin), the artists in general did not show greater comprehension than the critics. When the Belgian poet Emile Verhaeren went to

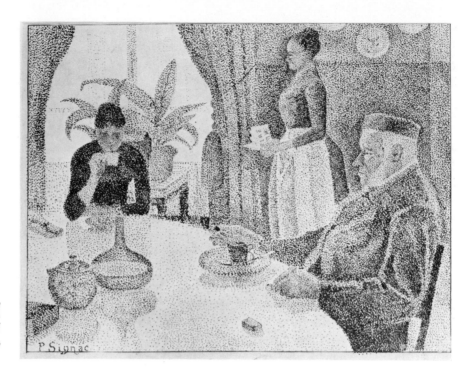

the show accompanied by his friend, the painter Théo van Rysselberghe, the latter was so irritated by *La Grande Jatte* that he broke his cane in front of it.[29] Verhaeren himself, however, was greatly taken by Seurat's canvas but when he told some painters how impressed and intrigued he was with Seurat's work, they answered with laughter and ridicule.[30] Degas' friend Raffaëlli explained that the new technique consisted simply of putting a red next to a blue to obtain a purple, or a yellow next to a blue to obtain a green, without taking the trouble to ascertain that both purple and green existed on Seurat's palette and did not have to be obtained through optical mixture.[31] Renoir seems to have shared Raffaëlli's views. And the American painter Theodore Robinson considered himself authorized by his admiration for Monet to scorn "the men of small talent, with their little invention, who have tacked themselves on to the [impressionist] movement, notably the genius who imagined the fly speck or dot *facture*."[32]

The incredible abuse with which the press and the public greeted Seurat's innovations was equaled only by the reception which the impressionists themselves had experienced when they first exhibited. Yet there was, in 1886, one man who had the courage to proclaim his unqualified admiration for the new art: Félix Fénéon. In 1881, at the age of twenty, he had come to Paris and immediately taken a lively interest in all the unconventional literary and artistic movements. He had been to the museums, to Durand-Ruel's, and to the various exhibitions of the impressionists, when Seurat's art was revealed to him by *Une Baignade* at the Independents in 1884. In that same year Fénéon had participated in the founding of the little *Revue Indépendante*, which was soon to occupy a distinguished place in French literature. But although he became deeply aware of the importance of Seurat's painting, he did not then commit himself in writing. It was only two years later, after he had studied *La Grande Jatte* and met Seurat himself at the impressionist show, that he decided to put his pen at the service of the new movement.[33] His fervor and his serious effort to grasp the full meaning of their art instantly won him the friendship of Seurat, Signac, and Pissarro, who were glad to furnish all the necessary information. Every line Fénéon subsequently wrote was based on meticulous discussions with the painters, if not actually revised by them. Fénéon thus became their spokesman, just as Zola had once been the mouthpiece for Manet and the young impressionists.

It was in the recently founded *Vogue* that Fénéon published a series of articles on current exhibitions, putting particular emphasis on Seurat's innovations. These articles, like all that were to follow, were distinguished by their poetic precision, their cool appraisals —never blurred by Fénéon's own warm enthusiasm—and by their strange style, representative of the quaint syntax and unusual vocabulary in favor with the symbolists. Fénéon explained in detail the particular character of Seurat's conceptions, described his *Grande Jatte* in terms which disclosed the artist's intentions, and analyzed his method in a truly scientific spirit. He stressed above all the effect of the observation of simultaneous contrast on Seurat's execution.

"If you consider," Fénéon told his readers, "a few square inches of uniform tone in Monsieur Seurat's *Grande Jatte*, you will find on each inch of this surface, in a whirling host of tiny spots, all the elements which make up the tone. Take this grass plot in the shadow: most of the strokes render the local value of the grass; others, orange-tinted and thinly scattered, express the scarcely-felt action of the sun; bits of purple introduce the complement to green; a cyanic blue, provoked by the proximity of a plot of grass in the sunlight, accumulates its siftings towards the line of demarcation, and beyond that point progressively rarefies them. Only two elements come together to produce the grass in the sun: green and orange-tinted light, any interaction being impossible under the furious beat of the sun's rays. Black being a non-light, the black dog is colored by the reactions of the grass; its dominant color is therefore deep purple; but it is also attacked by the dark blue arising from neighboring spaces of light... These colors, isolated on the canvas, recombine on the retina: we have, therefore, not a mixture of material colors (pigments), but a mixture of differently colored rays of light. Need we recall that even when the colors are the same, mixed pigments and mixed rays of light do not necessarily produce the same results? It is also generally understood that the luminosity of optical mixture is always superior to that of material mixture, as the many equations worked out by O. N. Rood [a professor at Columbia University] show. For a violet-carmine and a Prussian blue, from which a gray-blue results:

$$\underbrace{50 \text{ carmine} + 50 \text{ blue}}_{\text{mixture of pigments}} = \underbrace{47 \text{ carmine} + 49 \text{ blue} + 4 \text{ black}}_{\text{mixture of rays of light}}$$

for carmine and green:

$$50 \text{ carmine} + 50 \text{ green} = 50 \text{ carmine} + 24 \text{ green} + 26 \text{ black}$$

"We can understand why the impressionists, in striving to express extreme luminosities —as did Delacroix before them—wish to substitute optical mixture for mixing on the palette. Monsieur Seurat is the first to present a complete and systematic paradigm of this new technique. His immense canvas, *La Grande Jatte*, whatever part of it you examine, unrolls, a monotonous and patient tapestry: here in truth the accidents of the brush are

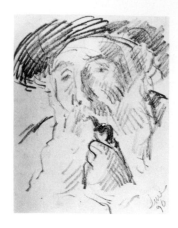

LUCE: *Portrait of Camille Pissarro,* d. 1890. Pencil, 5 x 4″. Private collection, New York

futile, trickery is impossible; there is no place for bravura—let the hand be numb, but let the eye be agile, perspicacious, cunning."[34]

In order to avoid any possible confusion between the "old-time" impressionists on the one hand and Seurat and his associates on the other, Fénéon coined the word "neo-impressionists," although Seurat would have preferred the more precise designation "chromoluminarists." Signac later explained that he and his friends eventually adopted the neo-impressionist label "not in order to curry favor (the impressionists had still not won their own battle), but to pay homage to the efforts of their predecessors and to emphasize that while procedures varied, the ends were still the same: *light and color*. It is in this sense that the term neo-impressionist should be understood, for the technique employed by these painters is utterly unlike that of the impressionists: to the degree that the technique of the latter is instinctive and instantaneous, that of the neo-impressionists is deliberate and constant."[35]

Fénéon further underlined the difference between the two schools by commenting: "The phenomenon of the sky, of water, of shrubbery, varies from second to second, according to the original impressionists. To cast one of these fugitive aspects upon the canvas —that was the goal. Hence the necessity to capture a landscape in one sitting and hence an inclination to make nature grimace in order to prove conclusively that the moment is unique and will never occur again. To synthesize landscapes in a definite aspect which will preserve the sensation implicit in them is the neo-impressionists' endeavor. Moreover, their procedure makes haste impossible and necessitates work in the studio... Objective reality is for them a simple theme for the creation of a higher and sublimated reality into which their personalities are transfused."[36]

Though Fénéon hailed Seurat's system without reservation, there remained one problem for which the painter himself was still seeking a solution. According to one of his friends, Seurat was then asking himself: "If, with the experience of art, I have been able to find scientifically the law of pictorial color, can I not discover an equally logical, scientific, and pictorial system to compose harmoniously the lines of a picture just as I can compose its colors?"[37]

The answer to this question was supplied by the young scientist, Charles Henry, whom the painter met in 1886, doubtless through Fénéon, since Henry was among the contributors to *La Vogue* and an intimate of Fénéon's friends, the poets Gustave Kahn and Jules Laforgue. Henry's extraordinarily brilliant intellect and his universal curiosity, his independent and generous mind had already plunged deeply into problems of poetry, music, literature, philosophy, esthetics, and psychology as well as mathematics, physics, biology, and chemistry. While these last four were then still separate sciences, Charles Henry, according to Paul Valéry, "perceived the only doctrine which could, in those days, allow one to think in terms of physics or biology, music or painting, sensation or action, while applying the same language, by imposing identical conditions on the phenomena and systems considered.... He seems to have conceived already at that early time a kind of program of synthesis tending to establish a unified system of human sensibility and activity. This system appeared to him fertile in applications to all fields of practice; in particular to that of the arts... To the young and adventurous, tired and disappointed by the verbalism of philosophic esthetics, he offered the hope of achieving something *new* based on *truth*; and this *truth*, not the one of the naturalists, which was only a coarse approximation, a truth of common and mediocre observers, was to be a *truth* instituted, if not

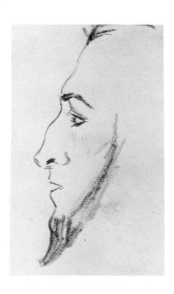

SIGNAC: *Profile of Félix Fénéon,* 1889–90. Pencil, 4 x 3". Study for the painting page 105. Private collection, New York

created, by the effort of criticism, rigor, and coordination which is called Science."[38]

Henry's interests covered an extremely wide field. In addition to scientific research and the study of music, he wrote about the life of the painter Watteau and soon was to publish anonymously an essay entitled "La Vérité sur le Marquis de Sade." Through his friendship with Gustave Kahn and Jules Laforgue he became associated with the symbolist movement in poetry and exerted a certain influence on it. By 1886, when he was twenty-seven years old—he was the same age as Seurat—he had already written or edited nineteen books.

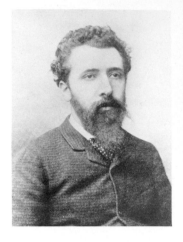

Photograph of Georges Seurat

Occasionally Henry gave popular evening lectures to which he carried two dummies borrowed from a hairdresser, one blonde and one brunette. Draping them with materials of various colors, he demonstrated his theories. The scientist was happy to explain to Seurat and his friends the theory of contrast, rhythm, and measure on which he was then working. "It was with a piece of chalk in his hand that Charles Henry addressed himself to the painters and it was at the blackboard that he discussed art questions with them. I still remember," wrote Pissarro's friend and admirer Georges Lecomte many years later, "an obscure conversation of that kind, at the end of which Charles Henry found himself squatting before a tremendous blackboard which, in the course of this strange, esthetic chat, he had covered with equations and formulas from top to bottom and from left to right. These learned demonstrations of the nature of light—which in fact were none too clear—left Pissarro rather indifferent, as he was a layman, an artist in love with truth and poetry, a sincere interpreter of his own sensations. But the grave and patient Seurat, whose young fervor and enthusiasm had been aroused by these theories to the point where he could listen to them without ever getting tired, clarified them by translating them into the more lucid language of a painter for the benefit of Camille Pissarro, so that he in turn could absorb Henry's discoveries."[39]

Since 1884 Henry had prepared an important treatise on the expression of lines, endeavoring to solve the following problems: (a) given any kind of lines, find the combination able to produce precisely a definite expression; (b) given lines or segments of lines, determine the order or orders of agreeable or disagreeable successions; (c) which are in general the systems of lines which are most agreeable? For solving these problems, the aid of the most delicate theories of modern geometry, of "cinematic" and of solid geometry was indispensable. The new mathematical science created by Charles Henry was not without psychological usefulness; it illuminated vividly the other domains of expression: colors and sounds; and it offered unlimited resources for industrial art.[40]

In 1885 Henry had published *Theory of Directions* as well as the treatise *The Scientific Esthetic*, followed in 1886 by a study of musical esthetics and *Law of the Evolution of Musical Sensations*. He also contemplated an essay on Rameau's theory of music. Seurat, who had been fascinated by the possibility of analogies between musical theories and his own, immediately discovered in Henry's researches a mine of precisely the scientific data he was looking for. While Seurat was studying Henry's findings, Signac began to participate actively in the scientist's work and to draw charts for him.

Since Seurat's method subjected the color harmonies of his paintings to the dictates of physical and optical laws, such elements as structure, composition and line necessarily attained a paramount importance, for here the artist could intervene more freely and impose his creative will upon the "ingredients" of his work. Thenceforth Seurat was to follow Henry's research closely in order to apply the scientist's discoveries to his paintings and to the completion of his own theories.

The showing of *La Grande Jatte* at the eighth—and last—impressionist exhibition thus brought Seurat, besides great abuse, a valiant and capable ally in Félix Fénéon, an acquaintance with Charles Henry which was to prove extremely fruitful, as well as a few more followers among the new generation of painters. It also resulted in his first contact with the avant-garde group the XX (Les Vingt) in Brussels, which was to contribute greatly to his increasing celebrity.

The group of the XX had been established in January 1884, just a few months before the Independents, for the similar purpose of promoting new and unconventional art, but with quite different statutes.[41] Twenty young artists, either Belgian or residing in Belgium, among them James Ensor, Willy Finch, and Théo van Rysselberghe, had founded an association free from any doctrines, whose sole program was to organize yearly exhibitions to which the twenty members would invite an equal number of guests, some from abroad, representatives of new and vital tendencies. This program enabled them to concentrate their efforts on all the significant contributions to modern art (they also arranged concerts and lectures) without the inconvenience of having to admit *everybody*, as the Independents were forced to do. Among the guests for their first show, in 1884, were Rodin, Whistler, Chase, and Sargent. Two years later, after Durand-Ruel had exhibited some impressionist paintings in a hotel in Brussels, not only were Chase and Whistler invited again, but this time also Monet, Renoir, Redon, and Monticelli. It was Redon's work, then still little known even in France, which had been the most discussed, admired, or contested of the show. The secretary of the group (there was no president), the Belgian lawyer Octave Maus, also edited with the collaboration of Verhaeren and Edmond Picart a weekly, *L'Art Moderne*, to assist the association in spreading its views and gaining wider support. Its Paris correspondent naturally wrote at length about the 1886 impressionist show, closing his report with a paragraph on that "odd fellow because of whom, in this exhibition of intransigents, the intransigents themselves battle each other, some praising him beyond measure, others criticizing him pitilessly. This Messiah of a new art, or this cold-blooded mystifier, is Monsieur Georges Seurat. A personality, certainly, but of what kind? Judging him only on the immense canvas which he calls *A Sunday on La Grande Jatte* . . . one might not take him seriously. The figures are wooden . . ., the composition has a geometrical aspect. . . . In Brussels *La Grande Jatte* would cause a scandal. There would be, if it were exhibited, sudden cases of mental disturbance and choking apoplexies. Yet, in this disconcerting canvas, what depth, what exactitude of atmosphere, what radiance of light! A mystification? We do not think so. Several landscapes painted in the same manner reveal an artistic nature singularly able to decompose the phenomena of light, to penetrate the prism, to express, through simple but knowingly employed means, the most complicated and most intense effects. We consider Monsieur Georges Seurat to be a sincere, reflective, observant painter whom the future will appraise."[42]

This was all that was needed to decide the XX to invite Seurat to their show in 1887, together with Camille Pissarro, Berthe Morisot, the Englishman Sickert, and several others. Maus also asked Félix Fénéon to become the Paris correspondent of *L'Art Moderne*, which subsequently published some of his most important articles on the neo-impressionists.[43] Fénéon's first article for *L'Art Moderne* was written on the occasion of the second exhibition of the Independents, held during August and September 1886. There Seurat reigned over the last room, surrounded by Signac, Dubois-Pillet, Angrand, Cross, and Lucien Pissarro. Camille Pissarro decided not to join the Independents since he considered

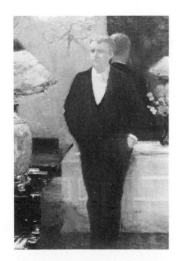

VAN RYSSELBERGHE: *Portrait of Octave Maus* (detail), d. 1885. 38⅝ x 29¾". Musées Royaux des Beaux-Arts, Brussels

it mainly a venture of the young to whom other doors were closed. Similar reasons may have prompted Odilon Redon, though a co-founder of the society, soon to discontinue his participation in these shows, unless it was his distaste for the innumerable dabblers who swamped the jury-free exhibition with their daubs.

At the Independents Seurat again showed his *Grande Jatte*, much better hung there, together with seascapes from Grandcamp and a view of the harbor of Honfleur, painted that same year. Signac, too, exhibited once more his canvas shown with the impressionists, *Apprêteuse et Garnisseuse*, as well as landscapes done during the summer at Le Petit Andely on the Seine, where he had been working with Lucien Pissarro. The latter sent watercolors showing the rural surroundings of his parental home at Eragny. Dubois-Pillet was represented by several views of Paris. Angrand showed various aspects of Parisian suburbs, and Cross showed portraits and some landscapes done in Monaco, where he lived. Although these two men were not yet painting in little dots, their canvases demonstrated the influence of Seurat's concepts, especially in contrast to their previous work.

In his article on the exhibition Fénéon once again stressed the scientific theories of neo-impressionism, discussed some of the paintings, and dwelt on several technical questions such as the chemical composition of certain colors subject to transformation and deterioration. He also touched upon the problem of frames: "With the abandonment of the gold frame, destructive of orange tones, Pissarro, Seurat, Dubois-Pillet, and Signac temporarily

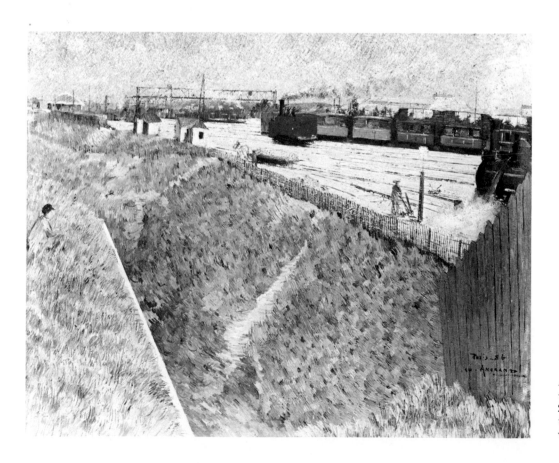

ANGRAND: *Railroad Embankment outside Paris,* d. 1886. 28¼ x 36⅝". Exhibited with the Independents in 1886. Private collection, Paris

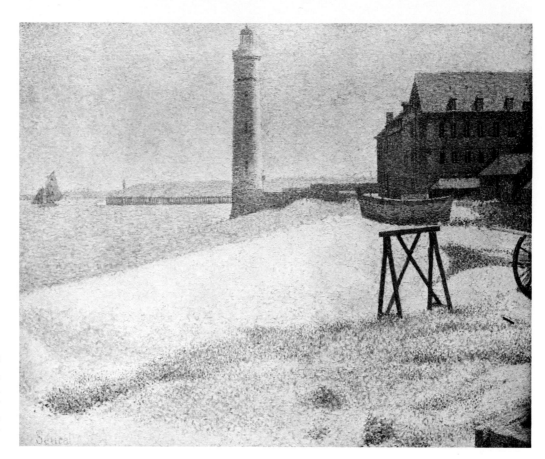

SEURAT: *The Lighthouse of Honfleur*, 1886. 26¼ x 32⅜". Exhibited with the XX in Brussels in 1887; acquired by Verhaeren. Collection Mr. and Mrs. Paul Mellon, Upperville, Va.

adopt the classic frame of the impressionists, the white frame whose neutrality is friendly to everything near it, if it contains, to temper its crudity, clear chrome yellow, vermilion, and lake."[44] Soon Seurat was to begin coloring the frame itself and eventually, in order to soften the contrast between canvas and frame while strengthening the unity of the picture, he was to provide his paintings with a small border applied to the canvas itself, a border which used complementaries to enhance the surfaces it bound.

Since Seurat showed himself increasingly jealous of his theories and was apparently somewhat reluctant to divulge further details of his continued research even to Fénéon, the latter had to rely mostly on information supplied by Pissarro and Signac. In the hope of dispelling Seurat's apprehensions of being too easily imitated, Fénéon insisted that "if Monsieur X spent an eternity studying treatises on optics, he would never paint *La Grande Jatte*.... The truth is that the neo-impressionist method demands an exceptionally delicate eye: its dangerous strictness will frighten off all the clever fellows who mask their visual incapacity beneath digital subtleties. This type of painting is accessible only to *painters*."[44]

Seurat spent the fall of 1886 completing the canvases he had brought back from Honfleur, where he had also done a series of drawings and painted several small panels to guide his work in the studio. His views of Honfleur were ready towards the end of the year when

Seurat prepared to accompany his *Grande Jatte* and six paintings of Grandcamp and Honfleur to Brussels, where they were to be shown at the exhibition of the XX. Though Signac had not been invited to participate in the Belgian show, he went along with Seurat to attend the opening. From Brussels Signac wrote to Camille Pissarro, the other neo-impressionist guest of the XX: "I have just left the exhibition exhausted. An enormous crowd, a terrible throng, very bourgeois and anti-artist. All in all it is a great success for us: Seurat's canvas was practically invisible, it was impossible to get near it, so dense was the crowd. The exhibition room is a magnificent gallery of the museum, very large and with excellent light. It is impossible to find anything better. Your canvases look very well; unfortunately they are somehow too isolated by their small number and their small dimensions. They disappear, lost among the large paintings which surround them. However, the effect produced has been a great one. The pointillist execution intrigues the people and obliges them to think; they realize that there must be something to it." [45]

On his return to Paris, Signac told Pissarro how interested the Belgian artists had been and how they had welcomed a closer contact with the neo-impressionists. As to Seurat's large composition, Signac reported: "In my opinion the *Grande Jatte* loses a little in that big hall. It displays a certain meticulousness which at that distance is unnecessary and disappears. One feels that this large canvas has been painted in a small room without much space for stepping back sufficiently. As a matter of fact this was an observation made by several members of the XX. They told Seurat: 'We like your *Grande Jatte* better at close range than from a certain distance. You probably did not paint it in a large room.' It is evident that this infinitely delicate division, exquisite on smaller canvases, becomes too timid for a canvas of several yards. Obviously, for a ceiling decoration the brush stroke must be larger than for an easel painting." [46]

As was to be expected, the *Grande Jatte* became the center of heated controversies and was greeted with much abuse by the Belgian press. Emile Verhaeren availed himself of the occasion to publish an enthusiastic article on its author. "Monsieur Seurat is described as a savant, an alchemist, who knows what?" he wrote. "However, he uses his scientific experiments only for the purpose of controlling his vision. They give him an extra degree of sureness. Where is the harm? *La Grande Jatte* is painted with a primitive naïveté and honesty.... As the old masters, risking rigidity, arranged their figures in hierarchic order, M. Seurat synthesizes attitudes, postures, gaits. What the masters did to express their time, he attempts for his, and with equal care for exactness, concentration, and sincerity... The gestures of the promenaders, the groups they form, their goings and comings, are *essential*." [47]

Alternately praised and called a *farceur* and ignoramus, Seurat did sell two paintings in Brussels. His *Bec du Hoc, Grandcamp,* found a buyer at 300 francs, and his *Lighthouse of Honfleur* was acquired by Verhaeren. [48] After his return to Paris, Seurat shut himself up in his studio and locked his door for several weeks; even Signac was not admitted. He began to work on a new large composition, *Les Poseuses*, for which he did some preparatory studies, though by no means as many as for his previous big canvases. The painting shows the same nude model in three different poses, represented life size in a corner of Seurat's studio on the wall of which *La Grande Jatte* appears. Since many critics had accused his figures of being lifeless and his technique of being suited only to landscape, Seurat would seem to have intended this new canvas as a reply to such challenges. However, as in *La Grande Jatte,* he chose attitudes showing the model either full face, in profile, or from the back.

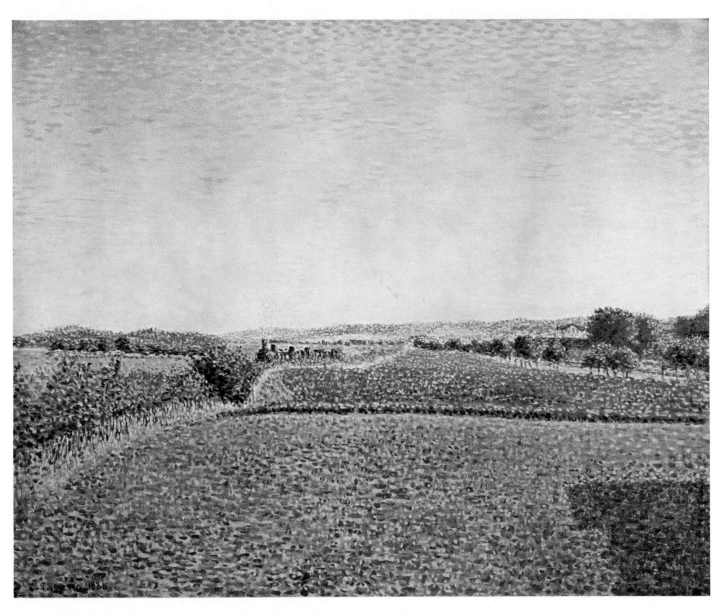

PISSARRO: *The Railroad to Dieppe*, d. 1886. 21¼ x 25¾". Exhibited with the XX in 1887. Philadelphia Museum of Art (Mr. and Mrs. Carroll S. Tyson, Jr., Collection)

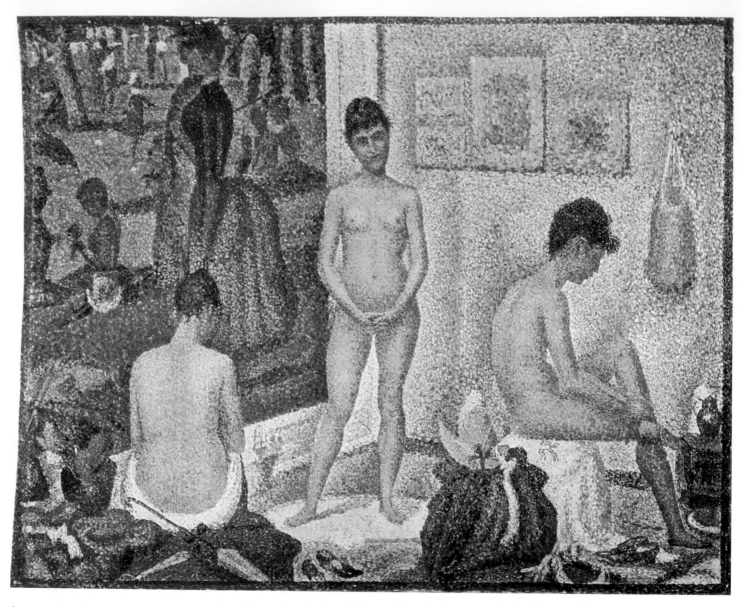

SEURAT: *Les Poseuses* (small version), 1888. 15½ x 19¼". Private collection, Switzerland

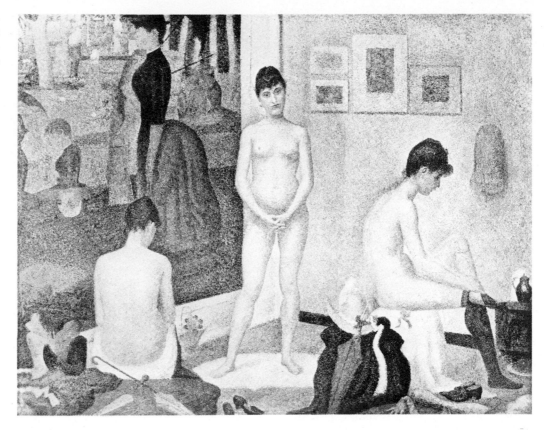

For this composition Seurat apparently experimented with a new ground for his canvas, but was very much dissatisfied with the result. "Gesso-coated canvas deplorable," he wrote to Signac. "Don't understand anything any more. Everything makes a stain—work difficult. I see nobody."[49] Signac, who was then painting at Collioure on the Mediterranean on similarly prepared canvases, also complained in a letter to Lucien Pissarro: "I am deeply unhappy about my gesso-coated canvases—the tones change in two days and become repulsive. Poor Seurat has painted his nude women on a canvas of this kind; in one of his recent letters he too complained of the alteration of his colors."[50] At the same time Seurat also modified his execution, with which he was now particularly concerned, and adopted even smaller dots and a more closely knitted texture, in spite of his friends' criticism.

The technique of small dots which antagonized public and critics while tempting many artists was in no way an intrinsic part of Seurat's system. Actually these dots were merely the most appropriate means of achieving optical mixture, and a by-product rather than an essential feature of his concepts. Besides, Seurat did not exclusively use little dots for his execution, but simply favored very small brush strokes which frequently took the shape of round dots. Nor did he apply these dots mechanically; the dense fabric of small strokes and dots, often applied in two or three superimposed layers, never has the aspect of uniform application. And did he not forego the pointillist execution altogether in most of his small panels, generally painted as preparatory studies for his large compositions? In spite of his

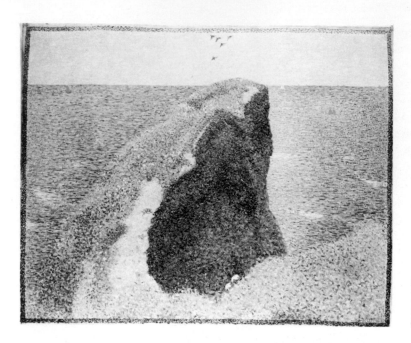

Seurat: *Le Bec du Hoc, Grandcamp,*
1885. 25⅝ x 32″. Exhibited with the XX
in Brussels in 1887 and sold there. Tate
Gallery, London

methodical approach, Seurat felt free to vary his execution not only from canvas to canvas, but also within the same work, and thus saved it from monotony. Indeed, according to Pissarro's explanation: "as far as execution is concerned, we regard it as of little importance; art, as we see it, does not reside in the execution: originality depends only on the character of the drawing and the vision peculiar to each artist."[18]

Seurat and his associates carefully avoided the word "pointillism" in their discussions and always spoke of "divisionism," a term which embraced all their innovations.[51] Some of Seurat's followers and friends, such as Cross and Signac, experimented about 1904 with small square strokes, not unlike mosaic, while a few years later Angrand used still larger squares; they obtained a result similar to that achieved with dots, though the optical blending was not always as smooth. It was compensated for by a greater intensity of color, which had shown a tendency to grow pale when applied in too small particles. (When Signac, at Pissarro's insistence, bought a painting by Cézanne at Tanguy's, he selected a landscape done in heavy layers of small square strokes, but applied with no particular concern for optical mixture—see *View of the Oise Valley*, page 43). Theoretically at least there was no reason why this blending could not be achieved with triangular spots of color.

Because it tended to be too obvious, Seurat's pointillist technique was regarded by several members of his circle as an inconvenience, although an unavoidable one. Signac considered as failures to a certain degree all works in which the execution forced itself upon the onlooker's attention instead of guiding him towards a more complete enjoyment of the work itself. For reasons such as these Signac later noted in his diary apropos of *Les Poseuses*: "Divisionism is carried too far, the dot is too small. This gives that beautiful painting a small and mechanical quality. Parts, such as the background for example, covered with those tiny dots, are disagreeable, and all this work seems unnecessary and harmful, since it gives the whole a gray tonality. Other parts, which are treated more broadly, are of a much more beautiful color."[52] Seurat himself may have realized this, for after the completion of the large canvas he painted a smaller, loosely treated version, which, though much less "readable" at close range, appears more delicate and spontaneous from a short distance.

While the others searched for the most appropriate way to overcome the problems presented by pointillist execution, in the fall of 1886 Signac and Dubois-Pillet conceived the idea of doing pen and ink drawings exclusively in small dots. This tedious work provided a charming texture and rather unusual effects, although the dot obviously here lost most of its meaning, that of binding together tiny particles of different and interacting colors. Their friends were fascinated by the subtleties of the grays thus obtained and Camille Pissarro also did some drawings in this way, distinguished by a general luminosity and more evenly distributed light. Seurat himself made a few such drawings, including one of his standing *Poseuse*. But drawing in dots was apparently only something of a fad that does not seem to have lasted long.

While work on his *Poseuses* progressed, Seurat began to admit friends to his studio to discuss with them the problems which preoccupied him. (It was *Les Poseuses* which van Gogh admired on his visit to Seurat.) "To hear Seurat making his confession before his year's work," Verhaeren later wrote, "was to feel his sincerity and to be conquered by his eloquence. Calmly, with careful gestures, his eye never leaving you, and his slow and unemphatic tones seeking rather didactic formulas, he showed you the results obtained, what was clearly proved, what he called the *basis*. Then he asked your opinion, took you as a witness, awaited the word which would indicate that you had understood. He was very modest, even timid, although you felt all the time his unspoken pride in his accomplishment."[53]

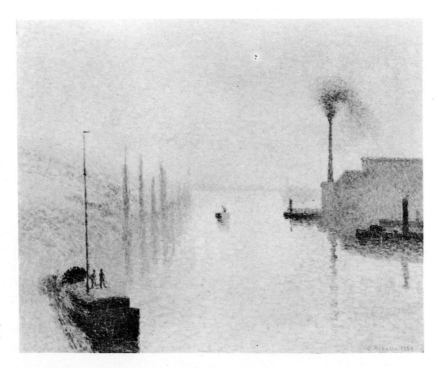

PISSARRO: *River—Early Morning, Rouen,* d. 1888. 17¼ x 21⁵⁄₁₆". Philadelphia Museum of Art (John G. Johnson Collection)

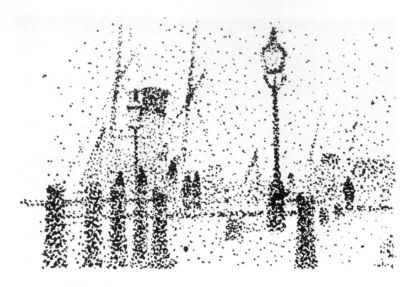

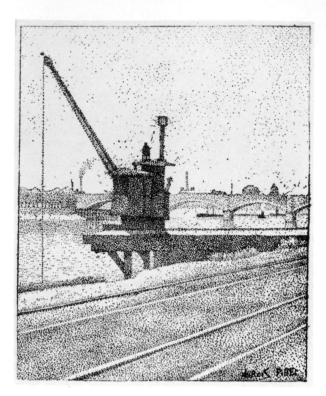

FINCH: *Harbor View,* 1888. Pen and ink. Drawn for the catalogue of the XX. Present whereabouts unknown

Right: DUBOIS-PILLET: *Seine Quay, Paris,* 1888. Pen and ink. Drawn for the catalogue of the XX. Present whereabouts unknown

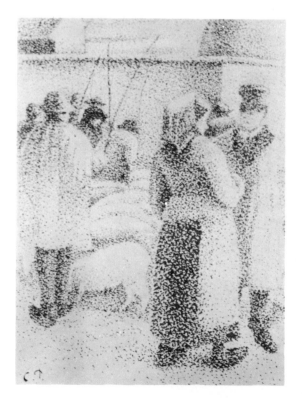

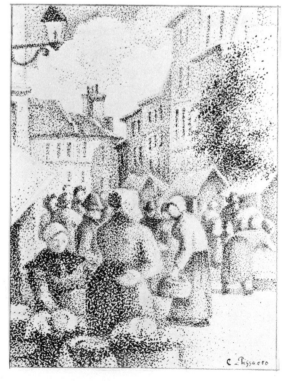

Far left: PISSARRO: *Pig Dealers, Saint-Martin Market,* 1886. Pen and ink, 6⅝ x 5″. Collection Max Kaganovich, Paris

Left: PISSARRO: *Market Scene, Pontoise,* 1886. Pen and ink, 6⅝ x 5″. The Metropolitan Museum of Art, New York (Robert Lehman Collection, 1975)

100

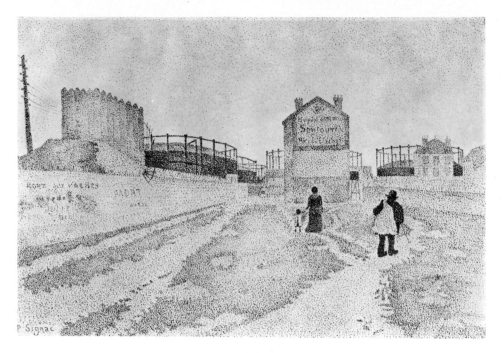

SIGNAC: *Passage du Puits Bertin, Clichy,* 1886. Pen and ink, 9½ x 14⅜". The Metropolitan Museum of Art, New York (Harris Brisbane Dick Fund)

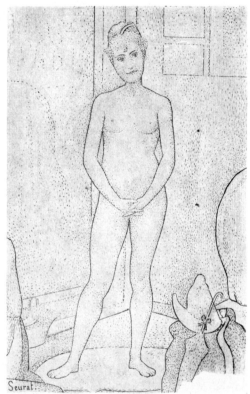

SEURAT: *Model Standing, Study after "Les Poseuses,"* 1888. Pen and ink. Armand Hammer Foundation, Los Angeles

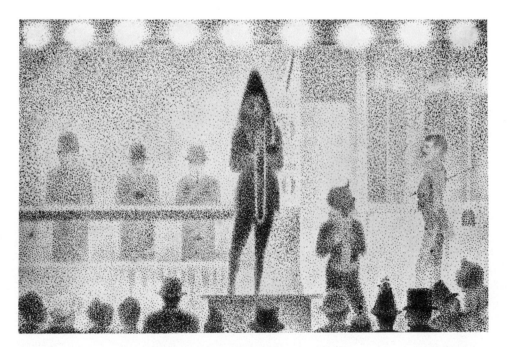

SEURAT: *La Parade,* 1888. Pen and ink, 5 x 7⅜". Estate of Robert von Hirsch, Basel

101

In June 1887 Seurat talked at length with Lucien Pissarro about colored frames, and when Lucien's father came to the studio a little later he noticed that Seurat had begun to color the frame for *Les Poseuses*, gradually, as he proceeded with his work. "His large canvas is progressing," Camille Pissarro reported to Signac. "It is already of a charming harmony. It is evidently going to be a very beautiful thing, but what will be very surprising is the execution of the frame. I have seen a beginning of it. It is obviously unavoidable, my dear Signac. We shall be obliged to do the same. The picture is not at all the same with white or anything else around it. One has positively no idea of the sun or of gray weather except through this indispensable complement. I am going to try it out myself. Of course, I shall exhibit the result only after our friend Seurat has made known the priority of his idea, as is only fair."[54]

In writing these lines, Pissarro was not merely scrupulously honest but also showed the increasing disposition of Seurat's associates to humor their friend's jealous fears. These were indeed anything but subsiding with the steady growth of his following. And grow it did with every exhibition, to the extent that Seurat was tempted to abstain from showing his work anymore, in a futile effort to stem the repercussions of his innovations.

At the Salon des Indépendants of 1887, where Seurat showed only landscapes, drawings and a study for *Les Poseuses*—the large composition itself being not yet ready—Dubois-Pillet and Angrand exhibited paintings now completely executed in little dots. And there was a newcomer, Maximilien Luce, a former pupil of Carolus-Duran at the Ecole des Beaux-Arts. Soon Luce also converted a friend, Léo Gausson, while Lucien Pissarro had already won over a young comrade of his, Louis Hayet, who during his military service in Versailles laboriously prepared chromatic discs of up to 120 colors which he submitted to Camille Pissarro. When Signac, Dubois-Pillet, and Cross were invited to show with the XX in Brussels in 1888, their works helped to convince several Belgian painters whose interest had been aroused by the paintings of Seurat and Pissarro seen there the previous year. Willy Finch was the first to join the neo-impressionists, soon followed by Théo van Rysselberghe, one of the most active members of the group and its Paris talent scout, and by Henry van de Velde and Georges Lemmen, while another member of the XX, Dario de Regoyos, experimented in Spain with "prismatic dots." A little later, in Paris, still another recruit presented himself, Hippolyte Petitjean, and even Gauguin's closest friend, Schuffenecker, temporarily went over to Seurat's camp, where he was not too warmly welcomed and which he soon abandoned. A number of other artists also employed the pointillist technique, as van Gogh had done, but without using Seurat's color scheme or observing the law of contrasts, thus depriving themselves of the sole benefit to be derived from it.

Far from seeing the ever more widespread influence which he exerted as a confirmation of the validity of his theories and their irresistible appeal, Seurat considered these new conversions as something of an attempt to "climb on the bandwagon." Pissarro and Signac naturally could not share his narrow views and the latter exclaimed with undisguised joy: "Our formula is certain, demonstrable, our paintings are logical and no longer done haphazardly, wrong or right, like those of the beginning. We represent an entire movement and no longer just particular and isolated examples as in earlier exhibitions."[55] But at the very same moment Seurat complained to the Parisian art critic Arsène Alexandre that his followers had become too numerous for his taste. His strange attitude was actually to lead to a serious conflict with Signac.

During the summer of 1888, while Seurat was working at Port-en-Bessin, a charming

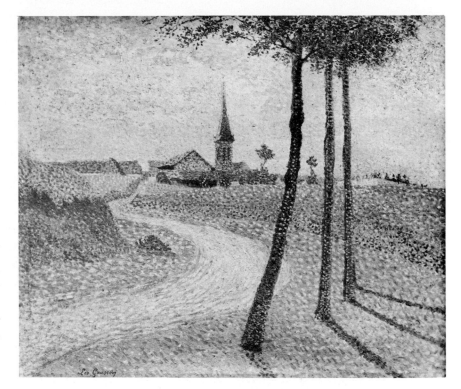

GAUSSON: *The Church of Gouvernes,* 1887–88. 15¾ x 20″. Exhibited with the Independents in 1888. Formerly collection Theo van Gogh. Rijksmuseum Vincent van Gogh, Amsterdam

Below: LUCE: *View of Montmartre,* d. 1887. 18⅛ x 31⅞″. Formerly collection Camille Pissarro. Rijksmuseum Kröller-Müller, Otterlo

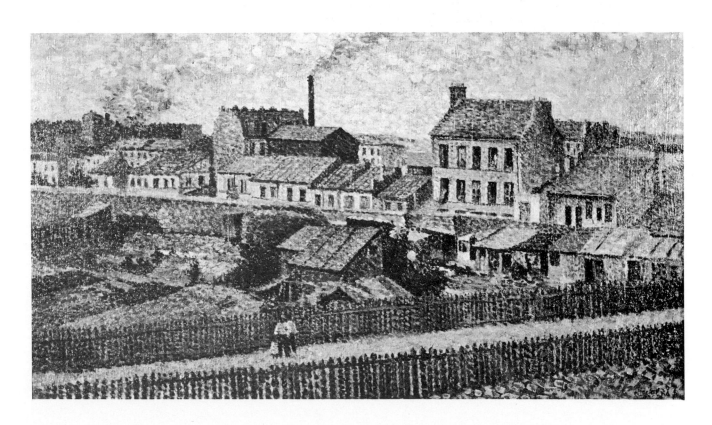

little harbor on the Normandy coast which Signac had "discovered" several years before, Arsène Alexandre in Paris devoted a study to the neo-impressionist movement. His article was by no means friendly, repeating as it did the usual contention that the pointillist technique had "spoiled some notably gifted painters, such as Angrand and Signac," and concluding that "a little bit of science does not do any harm to art; too much science leads away from it." Alexandre did however concede that Seurat was a real painter, speaking of "the true apostle of the lentil, who planted it, who saw it come to life, Seurat, the man of great research and effort who almost sees himself deprived of the paternity of his theory by ill-informed critics or unscrupulous comrades."[56]

Signac was incensed when he read this sentence on the "unscrupulous comrades" which, as he immediately wrote to Pissarro, "questions our honesty and which I cannot let pass. I am writing to Seurat to ask him whether it was he who inspired that phrase.... I am waiting for a *frank* reply. In any case, you will have to admit that if Seurat had not wept like a coward on Alexandre's shoulder, that man would know nothing of our excellent comrade's petty jealousies."[57]

Seurat's reply did not completely dispel Signac's misgivings. "My dear Signac," he wrote, "I know nothing of that article except the phrase quoted in your letter. If M. Alexandre had told me: 'I am going to write this,' I would have replied: 'But you will offend Signac or Pissarro, or Angrand, or Dubois-Pillet.' I do not want to offend anybody. Now, I have never told him anything but what I have always thought: the more numerous we are, the less originality we shall have, and the day when everybody uses this technique, it will no longer have any value and one will look for something else, as has already happened. It is my right to think this and to say so, since I paint in this way only in order to find something new, an art entirely my own." To this letter was attached a little note: "I have never (a) called anyone an "unscrupulous comrade," (b) I still consider Fénéon's pamphlet as the expression of my ideas on painting."[58]

Pissarro tried to calm Signac and told him to judge the incident philosophically: "Really, if Seurat is the instigator of the article you bring to my attention, one might think that he has lost his head.... What, is it not enough to have, from the beginning, taken the greatest precautions, with Fénéon, with Durand-Ruel and with all who were interested in the new art, to leave to Seurat all the glory of having been the first in France to have the idea of demonstrating the application of science to painting? Today he would like to be its sole proprietor!... That's absurd!... But, my dear Signac, one should give Seurat a diploma for having introduced this concept, if that flatters his pride.... After all, all art is not in the scientific theory. If Seurat had only that, I confess he would interest me but moderately.... And you, my dear Signac, do you think that that is the basis of your talent? Fortunately not. Then don't let yourself be influenced by these whines. Be calm, quietly continue your work and let the jealous howl. You have what it takes to make art.... Thus apply the science which belongs to everybody, but keep for yourself the gift you have, to feel as an artist of a free race, and let Seurat solve the problems which of course have their usefulness. That is his task...."[59]

It was indeed Seurat's task to solve new problems. "All his friends," Verhaeren asserted, "the painters and the others, felt that he was the real force in the group.... He was the most persistent seeker, he had the strongest will, and was the one most determined to penetrate the unknown. He had complete concentration, he was an integrator of ideas, a savage synthesizer forcing every chance remark to reveal laws, attentive to the least

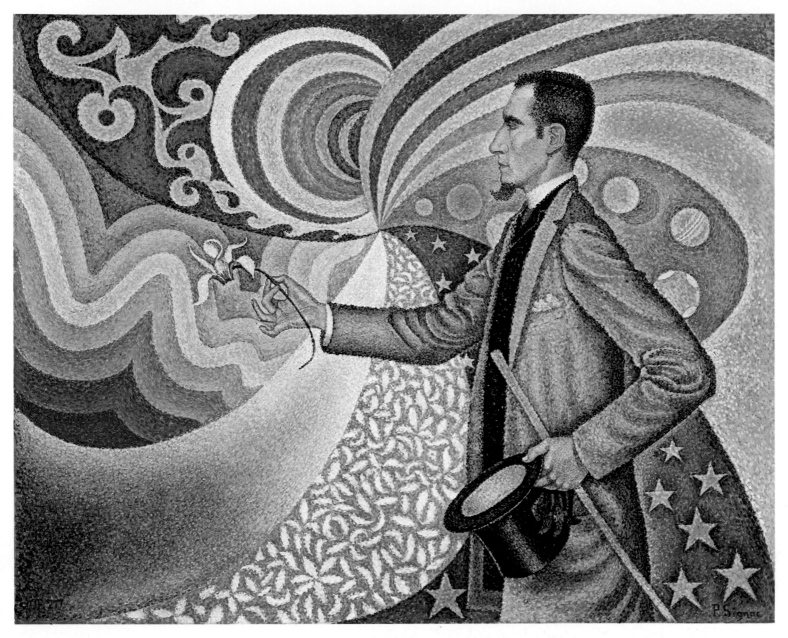

SIGNAC: *Against the Enamel of a Background Rhythmic with Beats and Angles, Tones and Colors, Portrait of M. Félix Fénéon in 1890*, 1890. 29⅛ x 36⅝″. Collection David Rockefeller, New York

105

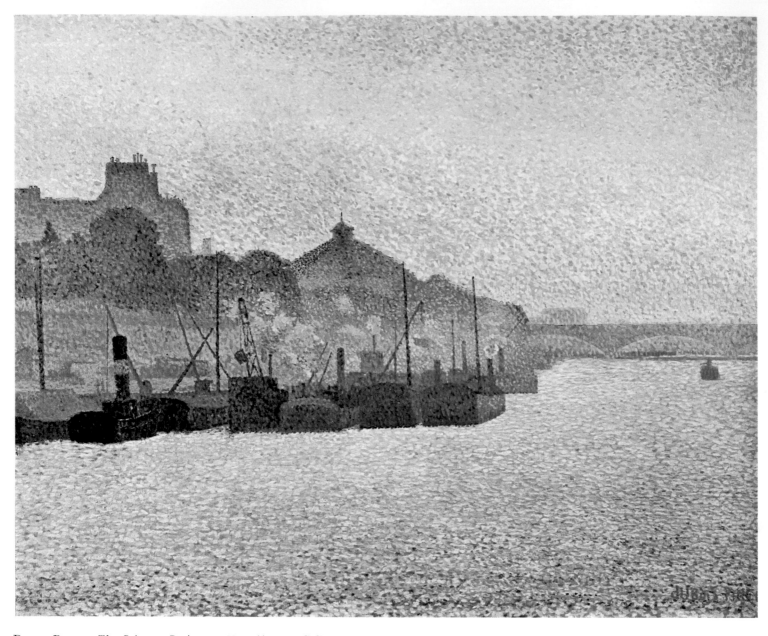

Dubois-Pillet: *The Seine at Paris*, c. 1888. 31½ x 39″. Collection Arthur G. Altschul, New York

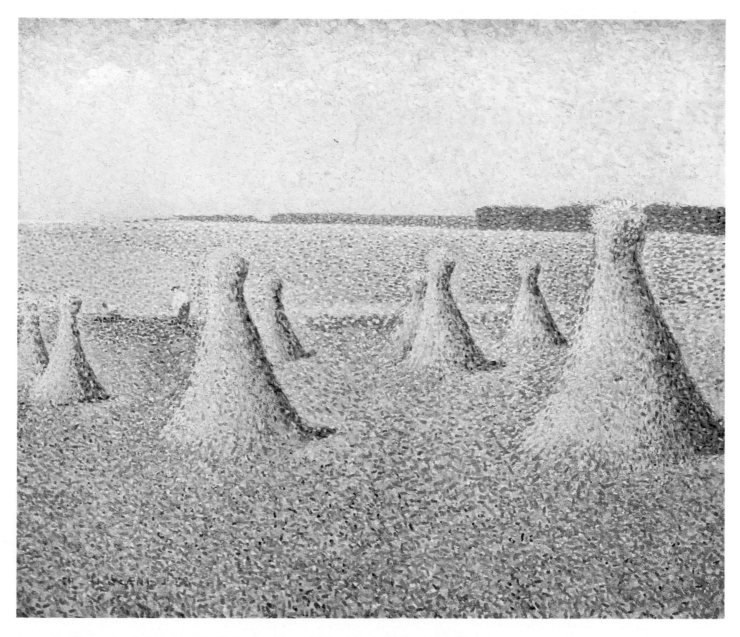

ANGRAND: *Haystacks,* d. 1888. 21 x 25". Collection Mr. and Mrs. Morris Hadley, New York

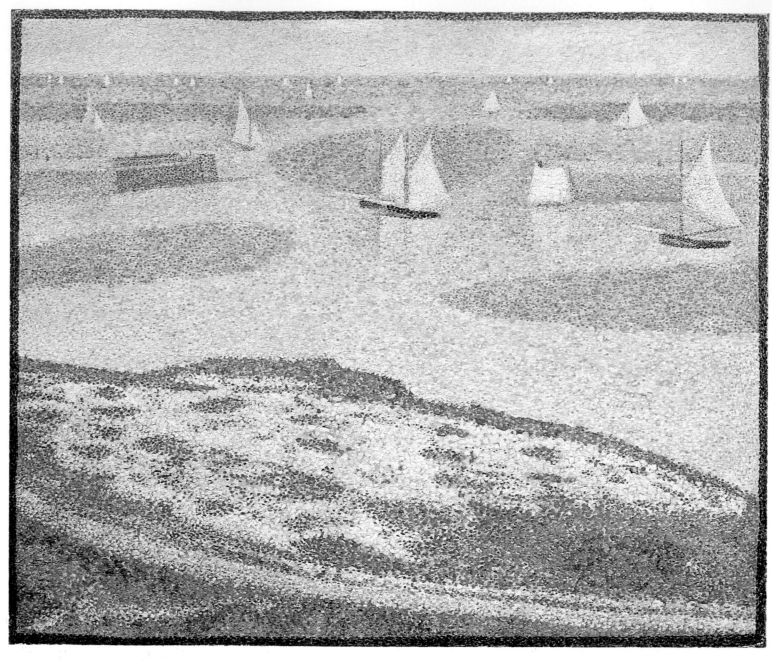

SEURAT: *Port-en-Bessin, Entrance to the Outer Harbor,* 1888. 21⅝ x 25⅝". The Museum of Modern Art, New York (Lillie P. Bliss Collection)

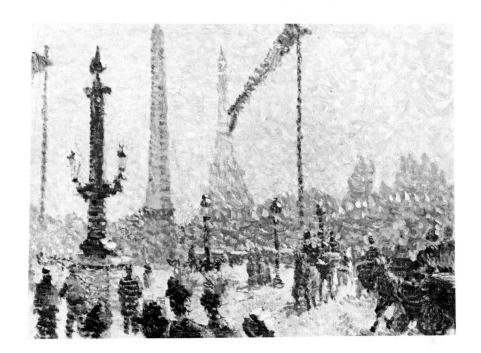

HAYET: *Place de la Concorde, Paris,* 1889.
7¼ x 10⅝". Exhibited with the Independents in 1889. Private collection, New York

detail that might fill out his system. . . . He never regarded his comrades-in-arms as being on the same plane as himself."[60]

While the others readily acknowledged Seurat's leadership, they also suffered from the condescension with which he treated them. This made for hard feelings and disillusionments. It would be unjust, however, to say that Seurat's associates did not sincerely try to make their contributions to the progress of his theories, that they merely copied him. There was a continual exchange of experience and views among the group, each member of which embarked on some specific problem and kept the others apprised of his findings. Every new work was devoted to the exploration of new ideas, and although there were many blind alleys and progress was often slow, Signac later asserted that there were not two years in which the works of any of the painters did not show new elements, fruits of their incessant research.[61]

Dubois-Pillet, who was apparently the first to apply systematic divisionism to portraiture (though Théo van Rysselberghe immediately followed suit), was not satisfied with studying the *Theory of Colors* by the American physicist O. N. Rood. He began experiments with what he called *passages*, based on the findings of Thomas Young. According to a theory formulated by this English scientist in 1807, "each infinitely small element of the retina can receive and transmit three different sensations: one category of nerves is sensitive to the action of long luminous waves (sensation of red), a second category is activated by the waves of medium length (sensation of green), the third is stimulated by short light waves (sensation of violet). Red acts on the first series of nerves, but—always according to Young—it acts also, though less strongly, on the other two series; the same holds for green and violet. Now, if one studies a graph indicating the stimulating energy of the various categories of nerves, one sees, for instance, that if, for the sensation of red, the

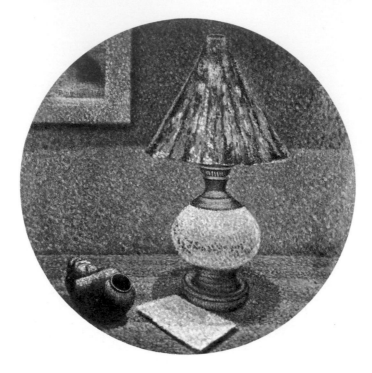

DUBOIS-PILLET: *A Table Lamp,* c. 1888. Diameter, 22¼". Private collection, New York

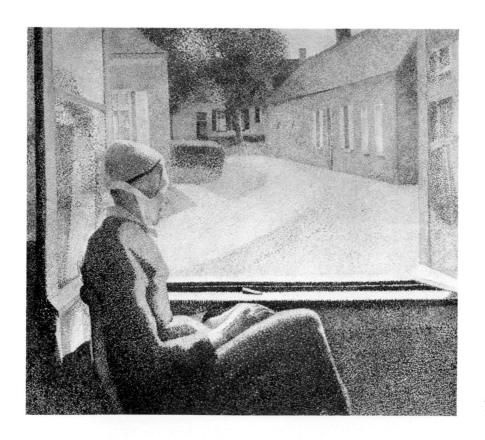

H. VAN DE VELDE: *Woman at a Window,* 1890.
43¾ x 49¼". Exhibited with the XX in
1890. Musée Royal des Beaux-Arts, Antwerp

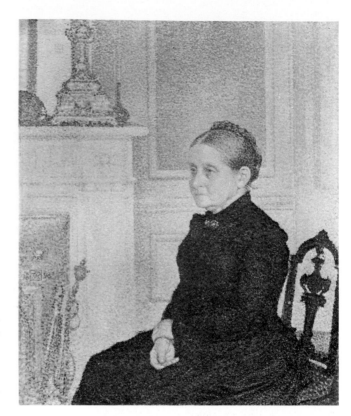

van Rysselberghe: *Portrait of Mme Charles Maus,*
d. 1890. 22 x 18⅛″. Musées Royaux des Beaux-Arts,
Brussels

Below: van Rysselberghe: *La Pointe Perkiridec,*
d. 1889. 27¼ x 41¾″. Rijksmuseum Kröller-Müller,
Otterlo

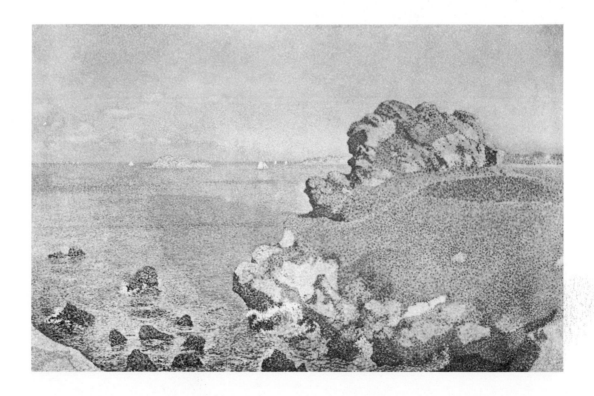

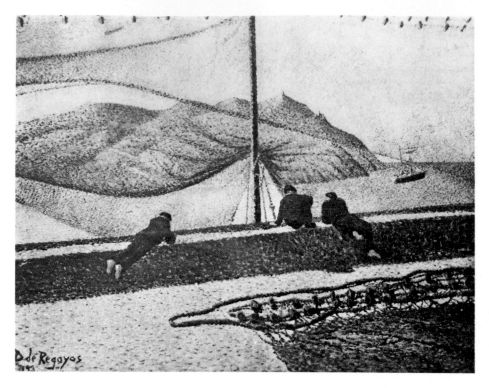

DE REGOYOS: *Fishermen at San Sebastian,* d. 1893. Present whereabouts unknown

Below: LEMMEN: *Thames Scene, The Elevator,* 1892. 24 x 33½". Museum of Art, Rhode Island School of Design, Providence (Anonymous Gift)

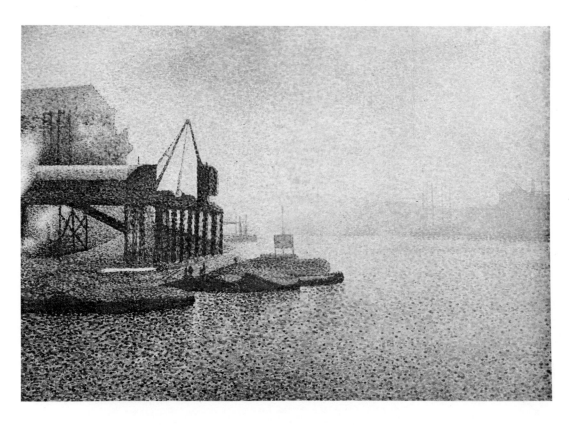

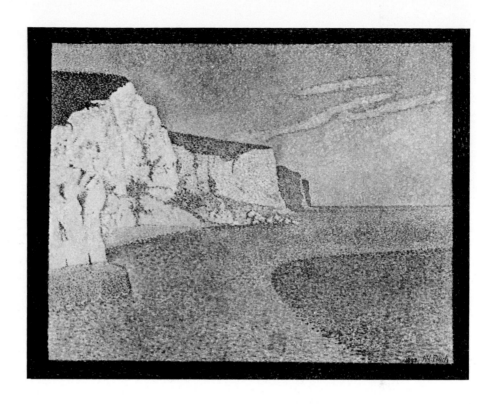

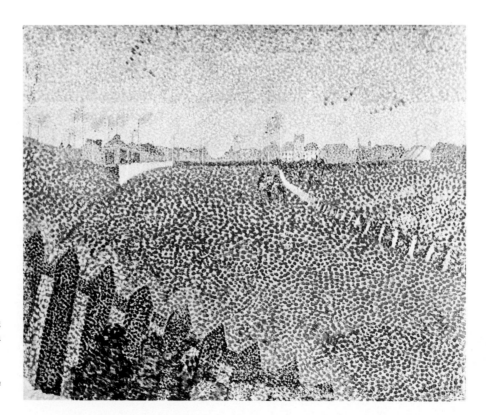

Above: FINCH: *The English Coast at Dover,* d. 1892. 26⅛ x 31⅝″. Ateneumin Taidemuseo, Helsinki

FINCH: *The Horse Race,* 1888. Private collection, Helsinki

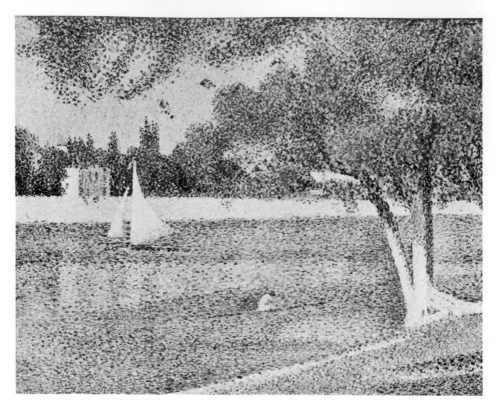

SEURAT: *The Seine at Courbevoie (La Grande Jatte)*, c. 1887. 25⅝ x 32¼". Musées Royaux des Beaux-Arts, Brussels

Below: ANGRAND: *The Seine at Courbevoie (La Grande Jatte)*, 1888. 19½ x 25". Collection H. M. Robinow, London

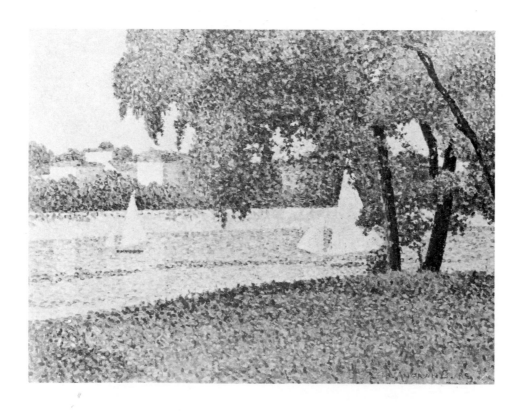

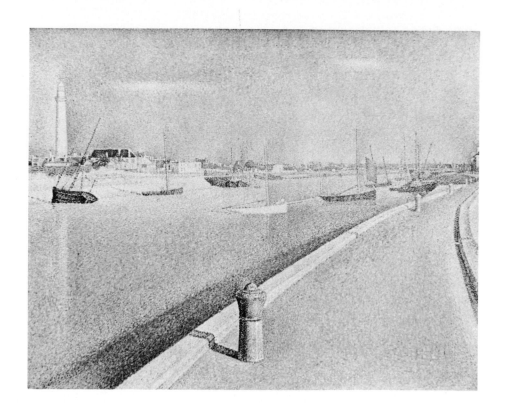

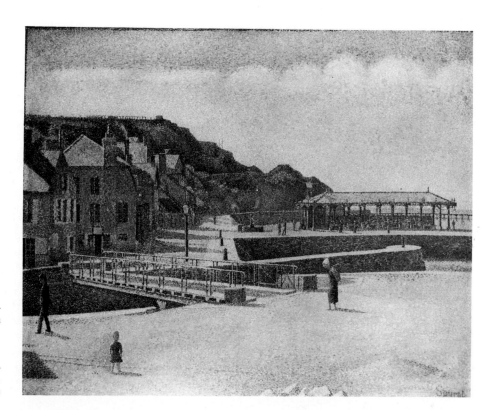

Above: SEURAT: *The Harbor of Gravelines*, 1890. 28¾ x 36¼". Indianapolis Museum of Art

SEURAT: *Port-en-Bessin*, 1888. 25½ x 32". Exhibited with the XX in Brussels in 1889. The Minneapolis Institute of Arts

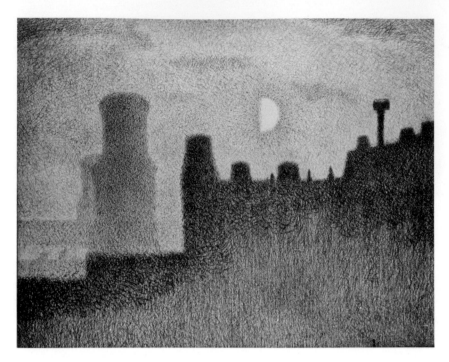

Dubois-Pillet: *Paris Rooftops and Saint-Sulpice by Night,* c. 1888. Charcoal, 18⅞ x 22⅞". Collection Arthur G. Altschul, New York

nerves concerned are strongly acted upon, those for green and violet are also stimulated, although the nerve for green much less and the one for violet very little. Thus one should, in order to express a sensation of red in a painting, take into account these quantities of green and violet; and the same applies to the sensations produced by other colors. If, for a simple sensation of red or green, or violet, etc., one does not take into account the quantities of the other color sensations, the tone of the red will be merely modified; but if this red, green, violet is placed beside other colors, influenced by colored light or reflections, or spotted by shadows, the quantity of the neglected color will be missing and the passage from one color to the other, from light to shadow, etc., will be poor."[62]

Dubois-Pillet's friends were not convinced of the necessity of these complicated calculations. Nor did they choose to follow Léo Gausson, who argued that it was not enough to study the law of complementaries on the basis of binary combinations only.[63] And when Hayet also proclaimed some personal theories on the *passages* and intermediary tones, the others deplored the optical achromatism and the decoloration which they observed in his work.[64] Hayet, on the other hand, explained in a letter to his friend Lucien Pissarro: "The theory should be the same for everybody; each and all should endeavor to complete it while condensing it, but in return they all should apply it differently, otherwise we would be hybrids."[65]

However, the personal research of Seurat's associates did not keep them from imitating him occasionally, either by drawing in large masses as he did, or by using small wooden panels for direct sketches from nature, or simply by giving their work such precise and descriptive titles as the ones he favored, sometimes even by working from motives which he had selected, such as the island of La Grande Jatte. Of course, they also permitted them-

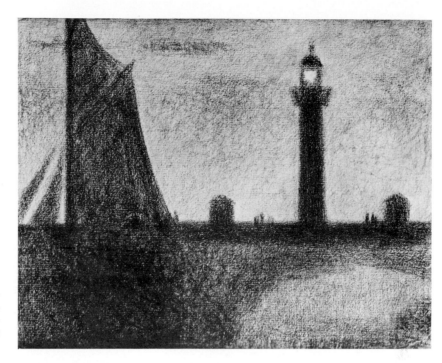

SEURAT: *The Lighthouse of Honfleur,* 1886. Conté crayon with gouache, 9½ x 12⅛″. Formerly collection Félix Fénéon. The Metropolitan Museum of Art, New York (Robert Lehman Collection, 1975)

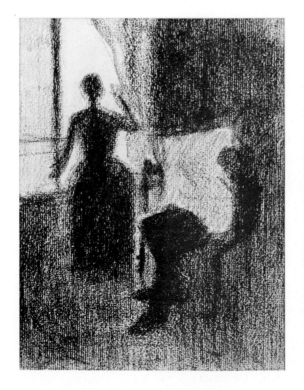

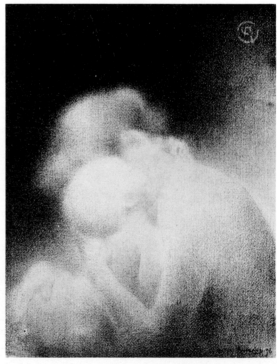

SIGNAC: *Study for "A Sunday,"* 1889. Charcoal, 8¼ x 5¾″. Collection Mme Ginette Signac, Paris

ANGRAND: *Mother and Child,* d. 1896. Charcoal, 23¾ x 17¾″. Private collection, France

selves occasionally to be carried away by his influence, but did they not thus acknowledge his leadership, especially since almost nobody joined the group without the intention of achieving a quite personal expression with the help of the neo-impressionist concepts? They were eager, as Signac put it, to "leave the hard and useful period of analysis, when all our studies resembled one another, to enter into that of personal and varied creation."[66] Those who succumbed to Seurat's influence were weak rather than unscrupulous.

In an era when science seemed to be coming into its own and increasingly impressed wide masses with the unlimited possibilities of its discoveries, exemplified by such men as Darwin, Pasteur and Edison, it must have seemed quite logical to carry scientific concepts into the fields of art and literature. Zola was intensely interested in natural science, Flaubert had foreseen that literature would more and more take on a scientific attitude, and it was a poet, philosopher and scientist, Charles Cros, who died in 1888, whom France credited with the invention of the phonograph and color photography.[67] It is not surprising then that Seurat's theories attracted such wide attention among painters, for here was not only something new but also something perfectly in line with the general trends of the time. Yet those who believed they had found an infallible recipe for art in the concepts of Seurat simply forgot that any technique or theory is never worth more than the one who applies it, and that no method, however subtle, can put a stop to mediocrity. The few opportunists who tried to avail themselves of Seurat's method soon discovered how right Fénéon had been in warning them of its exacting strictness. They either gave up, as Schuffenecker and Anquetin had done, or merely used Seurat's execution for otherwise completely academic works, as did Petitjean, Laurent, Aman-Jean, and later Henri Martin and Le Sidaner.

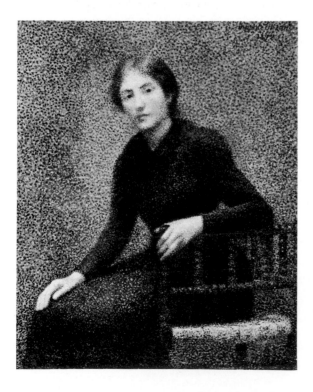

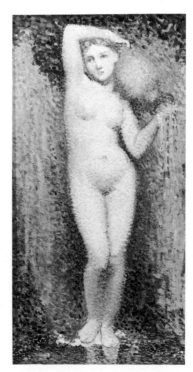

Far left: PETITJEAN: *Portrait of the Artist's Wife,* 1892. 39¾ x 23¾". Musées Nationaux, Paris

Left: PETITJEAN: *"La Source," after Ingres.* 16¾ x 8½". Present whereabouts unknown

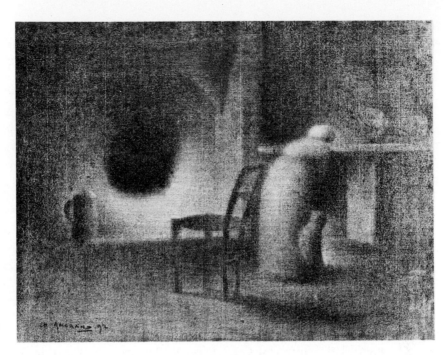

ANGRAND: *The Kitchen,* d. 1892. Charcoal,
18⅛ x 24″. Private collection, Paris

There is even a story that somebody undertook jokingly to copy one of the innumerable and insipid Venuses of Bouguereau in Seurat's technique, only to end up with a painting that was still essentially a Bouguereau.[68] While it is true that those who tried to "cash in" on the researches of Seurat and his group were so weak that they only underlined the strength and originality of the others, it is also true that public success, when it came at last, temporarily went to them, as it always goes to vulgarizers before reaching the initial inventors.

With the exception of Seurat, the members of his group seem to have been little disturbed by such occurrences, especially as they were much too honest and convinced to envy the results of easy virtuosity. They were also too busy perfecting their method. And this they did constantly. Unlike his friends, Théo van Rysselberghe, for instance, tried to combine on a single canvas dots of different sizes, treating backgrounds and other large areas in greater dots than details, such as the features of his sitters, to which he applied tiny dots that allowed for more precise modeling. This procedure did render the small touches individually invisible at a distance at which the larger ones were still quite apparent. Among his Belgian comrades of the XX, the English-born Willy Finch, a highly cultivated and gifted artist, distinguished himself by applying for some time fairly regular, large dots distant enough from each other to show the white ground of the canvas between them (whereas Seurat usually painted on canvases previously covered with large brush strokes on which he could pose his dots more loosely without the interposition of a white ground). As to the third neo-impressionist member of the XX, Georges Lemmen, he showed much less inclination for experiments and seems to have used the method more freely, not unlike Maximilien Luce.

There were also members of the group who did not adhere too strictly to Seurat's principles, such as Luce, who never completely submitted his somewhat romantic temperament to the rigidity of divisionism. He must have complained to Cross about his difficulties in imposing a strict discipline upon his perceptions, for the latter once wrote to him: "In creation there is, together with instinct, a great deal of will power, and will can only derive from a precise basis. This precision preoccupies me. I seek it in the laws of the contrast of colors. I do not permit myself to reason too much, and I think that this is precisely what I lack most. If you are gifted with artistic sensitivity, which the critics call 'poetry'—I speak here only in general—then it is not the fact of searching and perfecting a method which will prevent you from ever abandoning the impressions you have experienced."[69] As to himself, Cross freely admitted: "My sensations as a result of the quality of my artistic temperament, demand grammar, rhetoric and logic." But in the same breath he declared: "I am far from being dogmatic and consider that he is happy who has found adequate means for the expression of his temperament. 'Become what you are' says Nietzsche."[70]

Yet the method not only hampered Luce, it eventually also began to weigh heavily on the spirit of Henry van de Velde, who suffered nervous strain from too great concentration on its requirements. As to Camille Pissarro, he too had difficulties in mastering a "technique which ties me down and prevents me from producing with spontaneity of sensation," as he told Fénéon.[71] He began to look for a substitute for the dot, explaining to his son Lucien: "The actual execution does not seem to me to be rapid enough and does not follow sensation with enough inevitability."[72] But then, Seurat and Signac might have argued that this represented indeed a virtue of their method, since—unlike the impressionists—they were not interested in spontaneous creation and sought to achieve what van de Velde called a "return to style," by letting their sensations be dominated by will power and reflection.

Henri-Edmond Cross, while putting the accent on decorative compositions, at one time tried to simplify his execution by applying the dots in perfectly regular rows and without their touching each other, having previously covered his canvas with a layer of paint. At first Cross devoted himself to rather monochrome compositions which relied on balanced masses and linear arabesques rather than on color accents, but gradually his execution became less restrained and his palette brighter. Signac admired his "progression towards the logic of color, the synthesis of form.... He is both a cold and methodical thinker and a dreamer, strange and troubled."[73]

Explaining his concepts, Cross himself once told his friend Théo van Rysselberghe: "Harmony implies sacrifices. We always proceed from an impression of nature. Well, relative to nature one cannot put everything on a canvas, and it isn't so much that one can't put everything, but that one can put only very little. These few things become every-thing—the work of the man. The sacrifices are of forms, of values, of colors, according to the thought which governs the work to be accomplished."[74]

The great ambition of Cross was to heed the call of his imagination more freely, in con-trast to Seurat, and he later wrote to van Rysselberghe: "Should that be the goal of art, I ask myself, those fragments of nature arranged in a rectangle with more or less perfect taste? And I return to the idea of chromatic harmonies completely invented and established, so to speak, without reference to nature as a point of departure."[75] Signac was similarly obsessed with the desire to liberate himself from the imitation of nature. He once commented to Angrand: "The smallest rhythm, the tiniest measure seem much more important to me than the apparent reality, and I have too often felt the yoke of nature not to dread it. And when nature is not a nuisance, it is often useless. How superior the background of

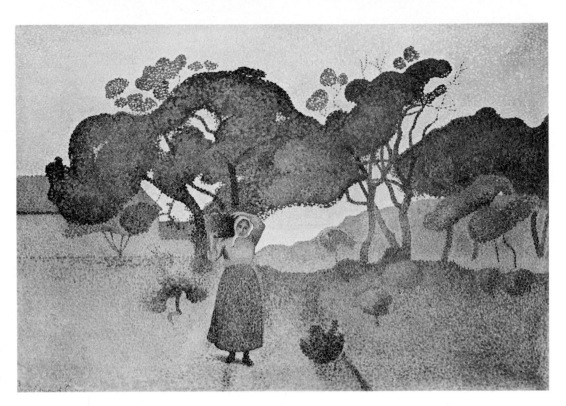

CROSS: *The Farm, Evening; Girl Carrying a Bucket,* d. 1893. 25⅛ x 36½. Private collection, Paris

Paris which I created for my canvas of *Housebreakers* seemed to me—let's get this right: superior for my picture—to the one which I went to sketch on the heights of Montmartre! Yet, what joys that source of all beauty holds for us.—The thing is to choose, to idealize, to simplify—but it is hard, isn't it, this task which may seem so simple ?"[76]

Angrand, who, with Signac, was among Seurat's most intimate friends, and whose drawings particularly were highly appreciated by the others, was preoccupied with the same ideas. "He declares," Signac jotted down one day, "that it is the search for nature which paralyzes us, that we know enough to draw a dog which does not resemble a donkey —and that this is sufficient. For the rest, only the arrangement of lines and colors should preoccupy us." But Signac himself added to this observation: "Unfortunately, it seems to me, if we don't renew our impressions of nature, we shall rapidly fall into monotony."[77]

Signac was without doubt the member of the group who not only worked in closest communion with Seurat (whom he deeply admired in spite of occasional misunderstandings), but who contributed most to its evolution, being both the propagandist and the driving spirit of Seurat's circle. *"All the weight of neo-impressionism rests on your shoulders!"* Pissarro once wrote to him. "Seurat is not attacked because he is always silent; I am looked down upon as being old and senile, but you, well, they are after you because you are belligerent."[78]

Constantly attracted by new ideas, Signac explored them with an enthusiasm that contrasted sharply with Seurat's solemn purposefulness. Always ready to explain the principles of divisionism, whereas Seurat frequently showed great reluctance to do so unless he was

121

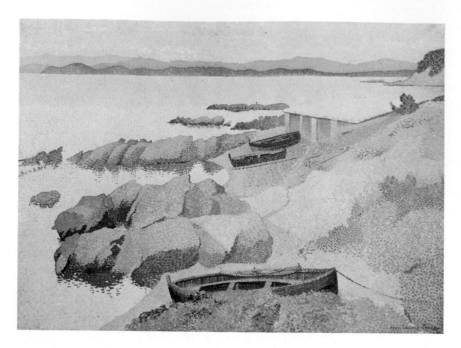

CROSS: *Coast near Antibes*, c. 1892. 25¾" x 36½". Collection Mr. and Mrs. John Hay Whitney, New York

Below: CROSS: *Grape Harvest*, d. 1892. 37½ x 55". Collection Mr. and Mrs. John Hay Whitney, New York

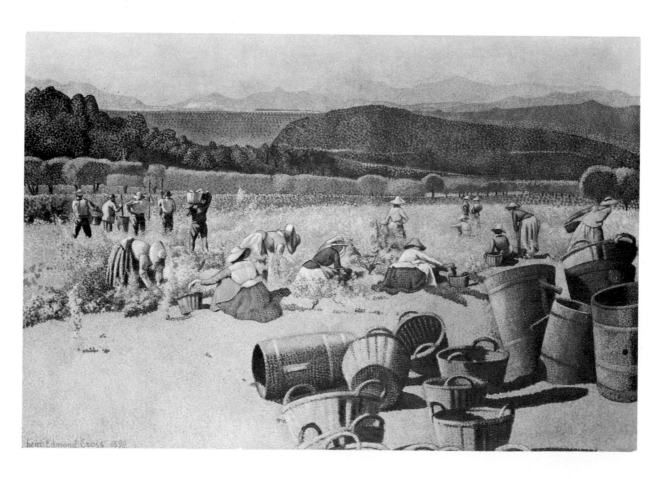

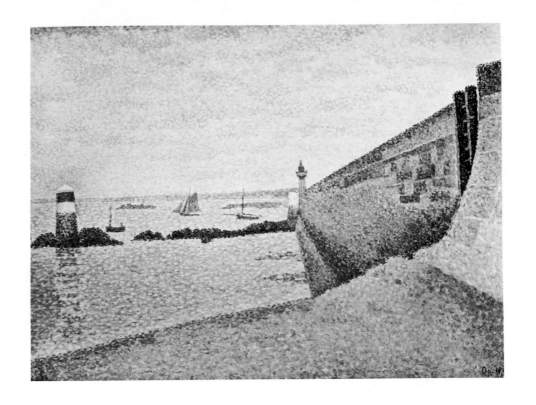

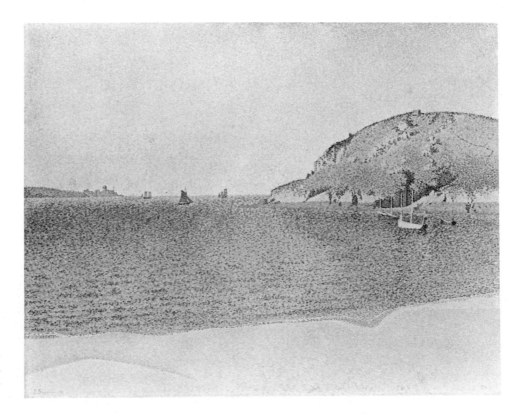

Above: SIGNAC: *Pier at Portrieux*, d. 1888. 19¾ x 25¼″. Rijksmuseum Kröller-Müller, Otterlo

SIGNAC: *The Bay of La Fresnaye*, d. 1890. 25 x 31½″. Collection William Coolidge, Topsfield, Mass.

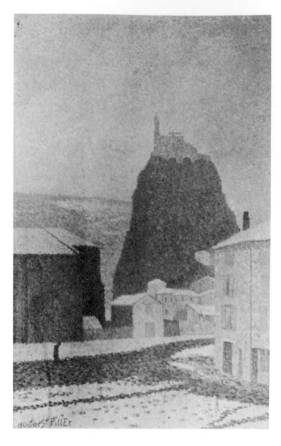

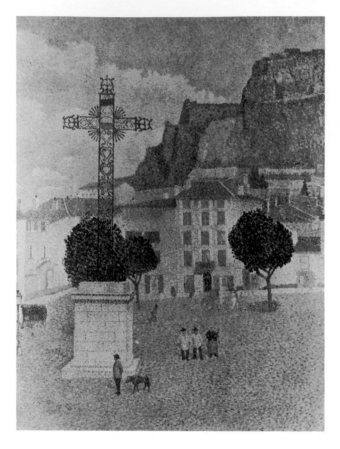

DUBOIS-PILLET: *Saint-Michel d'Aiguilhe in the Snow,* Le Puy, 1889–90. 23⅝ x 14⅜". Musée Crozatier, Le Puy

DUBOIS-PILLET: *Square at Le Puy,* 1889–90. Formerly collection Mme Audiard, Le Puy

certain to find sympathetic understanding, it was indeed Signac who assumed the role of theorist in the group. The others even considered him more precise and scientific than Seurat himself. They also found that his work was apt to be more luminous than that of Seurat.[79] Yet Signac worked hard to overcome a temperamental predisposition towards high color and exclaimed in 1887 in a letter to Pissarro: "Oh, the gray weather! and the local colors which are not pure, in a word the grays! I think it is there that we have to seek now."[80] After a short phase of subdued coloration, however, Signac devoted himself again to the brilliant harmonies which he handled with so much vigor.

Among some of Signac's minor inventions was his idea of numbering his works in the fashion of musical compositions, of giving some of his seascapes such titles as *Adagio, Larghetto, Scherzo,* and of coloring his signatures in accord with the surface to which they were applied. (Fénéon was against signatures altogether, as interfering with the purity of the work of art, and also, probably, on account of his anarchistic convictions.) Fénéon admired in Signac's paintings "exemplary specimens of a highly developed decorative art, which sacrifices the anecdote to the arabesque, nomenclature to synthesis, the fugitive to the permanent, and confers on nature—weary at last of its precarious reality—an authentic reality."[81] Fénéon also remarked that all of Signac's works were subordinated to the character of one dominant direction, the supremacy of which was furthered by the opposition of accessory lines, but he added that Signac proceeded thus more by intuition than by principle.[82]

One of Signac's most significant contributions at this time was probably his close collaboration with Charles Henry on the latter's *Education of the Spirit of Forms* and *Education of the Spirit of Colors*, as well as to some extent on his other works which were completed in 1888. Signac even designed a poster for Henry's publications and illustrated a lithographic announcement which appeared on the reverse of programs for Antoine's Théâtre Libre, while Fénéon endeavored to explain Henry's theories in several articles. Henry's two new publications were: *The Chromatic Circle Giving all the Complementaries and Harmonies of Colors, with an Introduction on the General Theory of Dynamogeny, or of Contrast, Rhythm and Measure,* and the *Esthetic Table with a Notice on Its Application to Industrial Art, to the History of Art, to the Interpretation of the Graphic Method and in General to the Study and Esthetic Rectification of all Forms.*[83] "It is a book on the esthetic of forms," Signac explained to Vincent van Gogh, "with an instrument—the esthetic table by C. Henry— that permits the study of measures and angles. One can thus see whether a form is harmonious or not. This will have a great social importance, especially from the point of view of industrial art. We teach the workers, apprentices, etc., whose esthetic education until now has been based on empirical formulas or dishonest or stupid advice, how to see correctly and well. I shall send you one of these pamphlets as soon as it is printed."[84]

These publications appeared first in the *Revue Indépendante* in 1888 and were followed shortly by yet another study for which Signac drew numerous charts, on the *Application of New Instruments of Precision (Chromatic Circle, Esthetic Table and Esthetic Treble-Decimeter) to Archaeology.*[85] Signac became so preoccupied with problems of linear arrangements that in 1890 he painted a somewhat "symbolical" portrait of Fénéon holding a

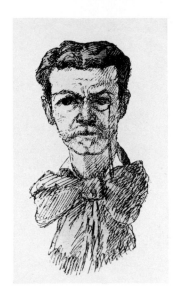

DUBOIS-PILLET: *Self-Portrait,* c. 1890. Pen and ink

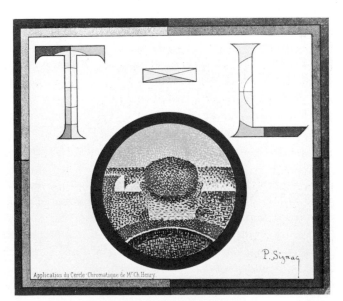

SIGNAC: *Advertisement for Henry's "Cercle Chromatique"* on a program for Antoine's Théâtre Libre, 1888. Color lithograph, 6⅛ × 7". Museum of Fine Arts, Boston

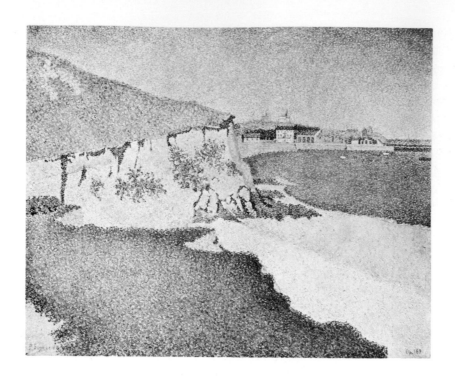

SIGNAC: *The Anchorage of Portrieux*, d. 1888. 9⅞₁₆ x 11⅝″. Private collection

cyclamen "against the enamel of a background rhythmic with beats and angles, tones and colors" as specified in the title (page 105). But Pissarro pointed out that such obvious use of arabesques had no real decorative quality or any value from the point of view of artistic sensation. Signac must have agreed, for he did not persist in this vein of coldly reasoned compositions and endeavored instead to apply his new knowledge of the significance of linear directions to the observation of nature. [86]

The course of his researches had permitted Charles Henry to establish a close relationship between esthetic and physiological problems, after he had set out to discover which spatial *directions* are expressive of pleasure or dynamogeny, and which of pain or inhibition. His findings were that pleasure is associated with an upward direction and with movement from left to right, while the opposite effect is achieved by moving downward or from right to left, intermediary excitations being occasioned by intermediary directions. The scientist also found that certain colors, such as red and yellow (*warm* colors), are more or less agreeable (dynamogenous), whereas others—green, violet, and blue (*cold* colors)—are relatively inhibiting. Henry consequently established a chromatic circle on which agreeable (dynamogenous) colors correspond to agreeable (dynamogenous) directions, and inhibiting colors to inhibiting directions, also taking into consideration the theory of contrast, the wave length of the various colors, etc. Exploring rhythm and measure, Henry arrived at definitions which apply to color as well as to forms. Fénéon hailed his publications as a "flowering mathematical work of art which re-animates all sciences."[87]

Gauguin had already had an inkling of some of the same questions when he wrote in 1885 to Schuffenecker: "...There are noble lines, others which are deceptive, etc.; a straight line creates infinity, a curve limits creation, not to speak of the fatality of numbers. The numbers 3 and 7, how often have they not been discussed! Colors, though less diverse than lines, are nevertheless more explanatory by virtue of their power over the eye. There are noble tonalities and others which are vulgar, calm or consoling harmonies and those which are exciting because of their boldness." [88] But while Gauguin chose to deal empirically with these problems, Seurat preferred the certitude of a scientific approach.

Seurat immediately availed himself of Henry's findings and began to explore the symbolic value of linear directions and of colors in his new compositions. This preoccupation appears clearly in his *Parade* (page 390), on which he started to work in the fall of 1887, with its obvious insistence on verticals and horizontals, enhanced by a bluish-violet coloration, to achieve a certain effect of monotony. Seurat also completely abandoned in his compositions outdoor scenes such as he had portrayed in *Une Baignade* and *La Grande Jatte*, or at least chose, as in his *Parade*, conditions of artificial light. This liberated him from the obligation to study the effects of the sun in nature and enabled him to establish beforehand the general tonalities that were to dominate each work. For, as Signac put it, "it is through the harmonies of lines and colors which he can manipulate in accordance with his needs and will... that the painter should move." [89]

Seurat explained to Gustave Kahn that "Phidias' Panathenaea was a procession. I want to show the moderns moving about on friezes in the same way, stripped to their essentials, to place them in paintings arranged in harmonies of colors—through the direction of hues —in harmonies of lines—through their orientation—line and color fitted for each other." [90]

Yet, in spite of Seurat's increasing insistence on perpendiculars, horizontals, and soon also on diagonals in his compositions, he once told Angrand and Cross "that his vision always made him perceive values before lines, that it would never occur to him to start a canvas with a line. Besides," he added, "colorations do change the design of things." [91]

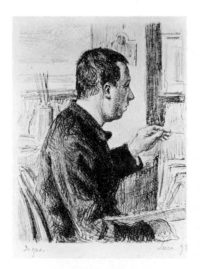 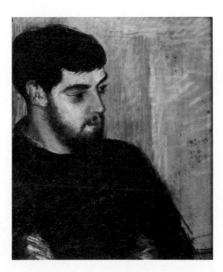 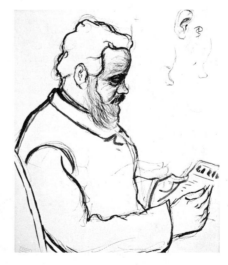

Left: LUCE: *Portrait of Paul Signac,* 1892. Lithograph. Center: PISSARRO: *Portrait of His Son Lucien* (detail), d. 1883. Pastel, 22½ x 14⅝". Ashmolean Museum, Oxford. Right: SIGNAC: *Portrait of Maximilien Luce,* 1890. Pen, brush and ink, 10½ x 8⅝". Marlborough Fine Art, London

This explanation, however, seems to apply less to Seurat's large compositions than to his landscapes, though even there linear directions constantly gained in importance. Each year he undertook in the summer a series of landscapes at the seashore or just outside Paris, "to wash the studio light from his eyes and to transcribe most exactly the vivid outdoor clarity in all its nuances," as he said to Verhaeren, while during the winter he completed a large canvas representing much research and possibly some discoveries. But Seurat disapproved of Verhaeren's suggestion that these winter paintings be called "canvases with a thesis."[92]

It was in his winter work, *La Parade*, followed by *Le Chahut* and *Le Cirque*, that Seurat most clearly endeavored to apply Henry's theories, so as to incorporate into his system all elements that might prove useful to art. At last persuaded that there were no secrets in art, Seurat now felt ready to proclaim his own theory, if only to establish his uncontested priority. He eventually consented to the publication of his esthetic principles which he worded not like a painter but with the precise and factual style of a scientist:[93]

"Esthetic

Art is Harmony. Harmony is the analogy of contrary and of similar elements of *tone*, of *color* and of *line*, considered according to their dominants and under the influence of light, in gay, calm, or sad combinations.

The contraries are:

For *tone*, a more $\left\{ \begin{array}{l} \text{luminous} \\ \text{lighter} \end{array} \right.$ shade against a darker

For *color*, the complementaries, i.e., a certain red opposed to its complementary, etc. (red-green; orange-blue; yellow-violet).

For *line*, those forming a right angle.

Gaiety of *tone* is given by the luminous dominant; of *color*, by the warm dominant; of *line*, by lines above the horizontal.

Calm of *tone* is given by an equivalence of light and dark; of *color*, by an equivalence of warm and cold; and of *line*, by horizontals.

Sadness of *tone* is given by the dominance of dark; of *color*, by the dominance of cold colors, and of *line*, by downward directions.

Technique

Taking for granted the phenomena of the duration of a light-impression on the retina: a synthesis follows as a result. The means of expression is the optical mixture of tones and colors (both of local color and of the illuminating color—sun, oil lamp, gas lamp, etc.) i.e. of the lights and their reactions (shadows) according to the laws of *contrast* and gradation of irradiation.

The frame is in the harmony opposed to that of the tones, colors, and lines of the picture:

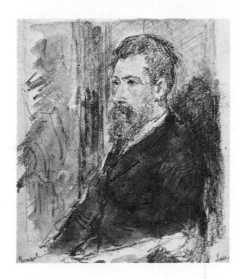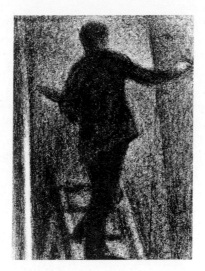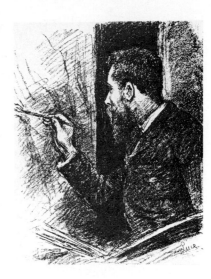

Left: LUCE: *Portrait of Georges Seurat,* 1890. Watercolor, 9¼ x 8″. Private collection, Paris. Center: SEURAT: *The Artist in His Studio,* c. 1884. Conté crayon, 12½ x 9″. Philadelphia Museum of Art (A. E. Gallatin Collection). Right: LUCE: *Portrait of Georges Seurat,* 1890. 7⅝ x 5¾″. Private collection, Paris

Thus, what might have been partly intuition at Seurat's beginnings, strengthened by scientific data, had now crystallized into certitude. If he had ever known any doubts, there is positively no trace of them in his exposé. His friends, who had followed his researches step by step in his work and who had marveled at the "immediate infallibility" with which he attacked each new problem, were now presented with the basic doctrine of his efforts.

It does not seem that the perfection of Seurat's theories aroused any new discussions; they were apparently received with unchallenged respect by his circle, with the same respect with which his associates had always listened to his rare but invariably clear explanations.

Seurat would meet his friends now and then at the Café Marengo where the Independents (whose meetings he attended scrupulously) gathered, at the Nouvelle Athènes, the former rendezvous of the impressionists, who appeared there ever less frequently, at the Taverne Anglaise in the rue d'Amsterdam, where the collaborators of *La Vogue* assembled in 1886 (the little review ceased to appear at the end of that year), at the regular Monday gatherings in Signac's studio, near Seurat's own, in the avenue de Clichy, where Signac welcomed his painter friends and some men of letters such as Henri de Régnier, Paul Adam, and Paul Alexis, or at the Café d'Orient in the rue de Clichy, where Seurat stopped briefly, faultlessly and formally dressed, when he left his studio at dusk to dine at his mother's. He usually listened to the others without saying a word except when directly questioned, but as soon as the conversation turned to problems of art, and especially when *his* method was discussed, he spoke with an extreme lucidity that added weight to his words. He was completely serious and never lapsed into fantasy, remaining a mystery to most of his associates who respected his habits and allowed him to pursue his own ardent and solitary way.

Sometimes Seurat also appeared at the *Revue Indépendante,* whose cofounder and secretary was Fénéon, and where his friends met in the late afternoon. Pissarro, Angrand,

Luce, Charles Henry, Gustave Kahn, the critic Jules Christophe with whom Seurat struck up a close friendship, and many others there exchanged views concerned with politics and literature as much as with art. In the offices of the *Revue Indépendante* small exhibitions were frequently organized, to which the neo-impressionists furnished the dominant element, but to which other painters, like van Gogh, were also invited. On other occasions, Seurat, together with Signac, Dubois-Pillet, and Charles Henry, joined a group of poets and writers at the Brasserie Gambrinus where, from 1884 to 1886, almost every evening were gathered Jean Moréas, Gustave Kahn, Felix Fénéon, Paul Adam, Edouard Dujardin, editor of the *Revue Wagnérienne*, Teodor de Wyzewa, a critic unconvinced by Seurat's theories, Jean Ajalbert, Maurice Barrès, Jules Laforgue, and their friends. At this brasserie the *Revue Indépendante* and the short-lived *Vogue* had been founded, and there according to Jules Christophe, "out of disgust for the coarse, completely external and already old naturalistic formulas, symbolism was born, explorer of souls, of fragile nuances, of sensational commas, of fugitive and—sometimes—quite painful and intense impressions; an esoteric art, necessarily aristocratic, perhaps something of a bluff, if you like, where one finds the semblance of a desire for mystification in revolt against universal foolishness, an art which derives from science and from dreams, evoker... of all forms existing in the intelligence and outside of matter itself, a spiritual and Pyrrhonian art, nihilistic, religious, and atheistic, even Wagnerian."[94]

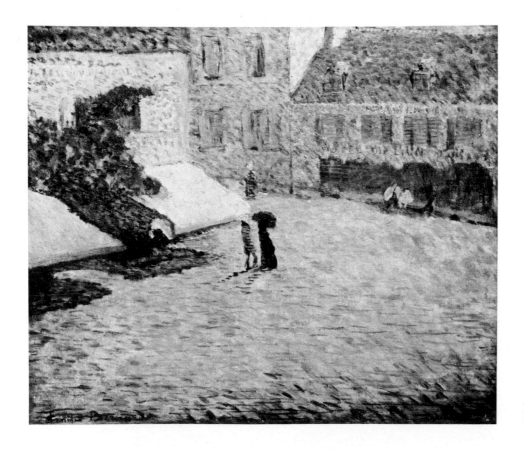

BERNARD: *Place Saint-Briac,* c. 1887. 18⅛″ x 21⅝. Private collection, France

NOTES

1 On Seurat's interest in Corot's theories see: Extraits du journal inédit de Paul Signac, II, *Gazette des Beaux-Arts*, April 1952; diary entry of Nov. 16, 1898.

2 Chevreul: La Loi du contraste simultané des couleurs, Paris, 1839, section II, chap. I, no. 78.

3 Signac diary, Feb. 22, 1895; see Extraits du journal inédit de Paul Signac, I, *Gazette des Beaux-Arts*, July–Sept. 1949.

4 Signac: D'Eugène Delacroix au néo-impressionnisme, Paris, 1899, chap. II.

5 See Signac's diary, Dec. 29, 1894; *op. cit.*, I.

6 Signac: D'Eugène Delacroix au néo-impressionnisme, chap. II.

7 See article on Angrand in *Par chez nous* (Revue normande), Feb.–March 1921.

8 Condensation of unpublished notes by Lucien Pissarro, courtesy the late Mrs. Esther L. Pissarro, London.

9 See Fénéon: Le Néo-impressionnisme, *L'Art Moderne*, May 1, 1887; this important article is not included in Fénéon: Oeuvres, Paris, 1948; see note 43.

10 See Fénéon: Les Impressionnistes en 1886, Paris, 1886; reprinted in his Oeuvres, p. 81. On this subject see also J.C. Webster: The Technique of Impressionism—A Reappraisal, *College Art Journal*, Nov. 1944.

11 See D.C. Rich: Seurat and the Evolution of "La Grande Jatte," Chicago, 1935.

12 See Seurat's letter to Fénéon [June 20, 1890] *in* H. Dorra and J. Rewald: Seurat—L'Oeuvre peint, biographie et catalogue critique, Paris, 1959, p. XXVII, note 34.

13 See Fénéon: Le Néo-impressionnisme, *op. cit.*

14 Signac: D'Eugène Delacroix au néo-impressionisme, chap. III.

15 Sutter: Les Phénomènes de la vision, six articles published in 1880 in *L'Art*; see J. Rewald: Georges Seurat, New York, 1946, pp. 59–60.

16 J. Christophe: Albert Dubois-Pillet, *La Cravache*, Sept. 15, 1892.

17 Angrand to Coquiot, see Coquiot: Seurat, Paris, 1924, p. 41.

18 See Pissarro's letter to P. Durand-Ruel, Nov. 6, 1886; in L. Venturi: Les Archives de l'Impressionnisme, Paris–New York, 1939, vol. II, pp. 24–25.

19 Fénéon in his article: Au Pavillon de la ville de Paris, *Le Chat Noir*, April 2, 1892 (not included in his Oeuvres) stated six years after the completion of *La Grande Jatte* and one year after Seurat's death: "Because of the colors which Seurat used towards the end of 1885 and in 1886, this painting of historical importance has lost its luminous charm: while the reds and blues are preserved, the Veronese greens are now olive-greenish, and the orange tones which represented light now represent nothing but holes."

20 See Fénéon: L'Impressionnisme aux Tuileries, *L'Art Moderne*, Sept. 19, 1886 (not included in his Oeuvres).

21 Signac to Camille Pissarro [May 1887]; unpublished document, courtesy the late Rodo Pissarro, Paris.

22 See Camille Pissarro: Letters to his Son Lucien, New York, 1943, pp. 63–75, and J. Rewald: The History of Impressionism, New York, 1973, pp. 521–23.

23 For criticism of *La Grande Jatte* see Rewald: Seurat, pp. 28–31, and Dorra and Rewald, *op. cit.*, pp. 157–65.

24 Signac: Le Néo-impressionnisme, documents, *Gazette des Beaux-Arts*, 1934.

25 G. Moore: Modern Painting, new edition, London, 1898, p. 89.

26 F. Javel: Les Impressionnistes, *L'Evénement*, May 16, 1886.

27 See J. Antoine: Les Peintres néo-impressionnistes, *Art et Critique*, Aug. 9 and 16, 1890.

28 See L. Pilate de Brinn'Gaubast: L'Exposition des Artistes Indépendants, *Le Décadent*, Sept. 18, 1886.

29 See P. Fierens: Théo van Rysselberghe, Brussels, 1937, p. 16.

30 See Verhaeren: Sensations, Paris, 1927, p. 196.

31 See Signac's diary, Dec. 3, 1894; *op. cit.*, I.

32 T. Robinson: Modern French Masters, New York, 1891, p. 169.

33 See J. Rewald: Félix Fénéon, *Gazette des Beaux-Arts*, July–Aug. 1947 and Feb. 1948.

34 Fénéon: Les Impressionnistes en 1886; Oeuvres, pp. 79–80.

35 Signac: D'Eugène Delacroix au néo-impressionnisme, chap. III.

36 Fénéon: Le Néo-impressionnisme, *op. cit.*

37 See G. Kahn: Seurat, *L'Art Moderne*, April 5, 1891.

38 P. Valéry: Charles Henry, *Cahiers de l'Etoile*, no. 13, Jan.–Feb. 1930; special issue: "Hommage à Charles Henry," with contributions by G. Kahn, P. Signac and many others. On Henry see also Fénéon: Une Esthétique scientifique, *La Cravache*, May 18, 1889 (reprinted in Oeuvres, pp. 167–72); Fénéon: Les Disparus: Charles Henry, *Bulletin de la Vie Artistique*, Nov. 15, 1926; R. Mirabaud: Charles Henry et l'idéalisme scientifique, Paris, 1926; J.-F. Revel: Charles Henry et la science des arts, *L'Oeil*, Nov. 1964; W.I. Homer: Seurat and the Science of Painting, Cambridge, Mass., 1964; and J. Argüelles: Paul Signac's "Against the Enamel of a Background Rhythmic with Beats and Angles, Tones and Colors, Portrait of M. Félix Fénéon in 1890," Opus 217, *Journal of Aesthetics and Art Criticism*, vol. XXVIII, no. 1, Fall 1969.

39 G. Lecomte: Camille Pissarro, Paris, 1922, p. 75.

40 See G.L. in *La Revue Indépendante*, Jan. 1885, p. 268. In 1890 J. Antoine noted in *Art et Critique*, Jan. 4, that one could observe in Jules Chéret's most recent posters the application of the laws of complementaries and contrasts.

41 On "Les Vingt" see M.-O. Maus: Trente années de lutte pour l'art, 1884–1914, Brussels, 1926; also cat. of the exhibition: "Le Groupe des XX et son temps," Musées Royaux des Beaux-Arts de Belgique, Brussels, and Rijksmuseum Kröller-Müller, Otterlo, April–May 1962.

42 Anonymous: Les Vingtistes parisiens, *L'Art Moderne*, June 27, 1886.

43 These articles, like those listed in notes 9, 20, and many others, are not reprinted in Fénéon: Oeuvres, Paris, 1948. They can be found in F. Fénéon: Oeuvres plus que complètes, edited by J.U. Halperin, 2 vols., Geneva–Paris, 1970. Fénéon's writings on Seurat are assembled in Dorra and Rewald, *op. cit.*, pp. XI–XXXI.

44 Fénéon: L'Impressionnisme aux Tuileries, *op. cit.*

45 Signac to Pissarro, [Brussels, Feb. 1887]; unpublished document, courtesy the late Rodo Pissarro, Paris.

46 Signac to Pissarro, [Paris, March–April 1887]; unpublished document, courtesy the late Rodo Pissarro, Paris.

47 E. Verhaeren: Le Salon des Vingt à Bruxelles, *La Vie Moderne*, Feb. 26, 1887.

48 On Seurat and Verhaeren see R.L. Herbert: Seurat and Emile Verhaeren, *Gazette des Beaux-Arts*, Dec. 1959.

49 Seurat to Signac, [Paris, Aug. 1887]; unpublished document, courtesy Mme Ginette Signac, Paris.

50 Signac to Lucien Pissarro, Collioure, Aug. 29, [1887]; unpublished document, courtesy the late Mrs. Esther L. Pissarro, London.

51 Divisionism, according to Signac, means "to assure the benefits of luminosity, color, and harmony: by optical mixture of uniquely pure pigments (all the colors of the prism and all their tones); by the separation of various elements (local color, light, and their interactions); by the balancing of these elements and their proportions (according to the laws of contrast, gradation, and irradiation); by the selection of a brush stroke commensurate with the size of the canvas." D'Eugène Delacroix au néo-impressionnisme, chap. I.

52 Signac diary, Dec. 29, 1897; op. cit., II.

53 Verhaeren: Sensations, op. cit., p. 200.

54 Pissarro to Signac, June 16, 1887; see Rewald: Seurat (French edition), Paris, 1948, p. 113.

55 Signac to Pissarro, [May 1887]; unpublished document, courtesy the late Rodo Pissarro, Paris.

56 Alexandre: Le Mouvement artistique, Paris, Aug. 13, 1888.

57 Signac to Pissarro, Aug. 24, 1888; see Rewald: Seurat (French edition), p. 114.

58 Seurat to Signac, [Port-en-Bessin], Aug. 26, [1888]; ibid., p. 115. The reference to Fénéon's pamphlet alludes to: Les Impressionnistes en 1886, reprinted in Oeuvres, pp. 78–82.

59 Pissarro to Signac, Paris, Aug. 30, 1888; ibid., pp. 115–16.

60 Verhaeren: Sensations, op. cit., p. 201.

61 See Signac diary, March 11, 1898; op. cit., II.

62 J. Christophe: Dubois-Pillet, Les Hommes d'Aujourd'hui, vol. 8, no. 370, 1890.

63 See J. Antoine: Les Peintres néo-impressionnistes, op. cit.

64 See S. P. [Paul Signac]: Catalogue de l'exposition des XX, Art et Critique, Feb. 1, 1890.

65 Hayet to Lucien Pissarro, July 9, 1888; unpublished document, courtesy the late Mrs. Esther L. Pissarro, London.

66 Signac diary, Sept. 1, 1895; op. cit., I.

67 See Fénéon: Feu Cros, La Cravache, Aug. 18, 1888; reprinted in Oeuvres, pp. 246–53.

68 See J. E. Blanche: Les Arts plastiques, Paris, 1931, p. 269. On the other hand, Théo van Rysselberghe, unable in the beginning to completely shed Whistler's influence, did a portrait of a little girl that looks like a Whistler executed in small dots. See Fierens, op. cit., plate 5.

69 Cross to Luce [no date], quoted in L. Cousturier: H.-E. Cross, Paris, 1932, p. 11.

70 Cross to T. van Rysselberghe, March 9 [1907?]; unpublished document, courtesy the late Mme van Rysselberghe, Paris.

71 Pissarro to Fénéon, Feb. 21, 1889; see Pissarro: Letters to his Son Lucien, pp. 134–35, footnote.

72 Pissarro to his son Lucien, Feb. 20, 1889; ibid., p. 135.

73 Signac diary, Dec. 14, 1894; op. cit., I.

74 Cross to T. van Rysselberghe [no date]; unpublished document, courtesy the late Mme van Rysselberghe, Paris.

75 Cross to T. van Rysselberghe [c. 1902]; quoted in M. Saint-Clair: Galerie privée, Paris, 1947, p. 33, footnote.

76 Signac to Angrand, Feb. 1897; unpublished document, courtesy M. Pierre Angrand, Paris.

77 Signac diary, Nov. 27, 1894; op. cit., I.

78 Pissarro to Signac; see G. Cachin-Signac: Autour de la correspondance de Signac, Arts, Sept. 7, 1951.

79 Information courtesy the late Henry van de Velde.

80 Signac to Pissarro, [May 1887]; unpublished document, courtesy the late Rodo Pissarro, Paris.

81 Fénéon: Paul Signac, Les Hommes d'Aujourd'hui, vol. 8, no. 373, 1890. (This text is not in Fénéon's Oeuvres; the study reprinted there as having appeared in Les Hommes d'Aujourd'hui was published in La Plume, Sept. 1, 1891.)

82 See Fénéon: Paul Signac, La Plume, Sept. 1, 1891; reprinted in Oeuvres, p. 69.

83 The original titles are: Education du sens des formes, 1890; Cercle chromatique, présentant tous les compléments et toutes les harmonies de couleurs, avec une introduction sur la théorie générale de la dynamogénie, autrement dit du contraste, du rythme et de la mesure, 1888–89; Rapporteur esthétique avec notice sur ses applications à l'art industriel, à l'histoire de l'art, à l'interprétation de la méthode graphique, en général à l'étude et à la rectification esthétique de toutes formes, 1888–89.

84 Signac to Vincent van Gogh, Cassis, April 1889; see Verzamelde Brieven van Vincent van Gogh, Amsterdam, 1953, vol. III, no. 584a, p. 404.

85 The original title is: Application de nouveaux instruments de précision (cercle chromatique, rapporteur et triple-décimètre esthétique) à l'archéologie, 1890.

86 On this painting see J. Argüelles: op. cit., and F. Cachin: Le Portrait de Fénéon par Signac—Une Source inédite, Revue de l'Art, no. 6, 1969.

87 Fénéon: Une Esthétique scientifique, La Cravache, May 18, 1889; reprinted in Oeuvres, pp. 167–72.

88 Gauguin to Schuffenecker, [Copenhagen], Jan. 14, 1885; Lettres de Gauguin à sa femme et à ses amis, Paris, 1946, no. XI, p. 45.

89 Signac: Le Sujet en peinture, Encyclopédie Française, Paris, 1935, vol. XVI, chap. II.

90 Kahn: Chronique, Revue Indépendante, Jan. 1888. (Seurat is designated merely as "one of the young impressionist innovators.")

91 See: Inédits d'H.-E. Cross, Bulletin de la Vie Artistique, Sept. 15, 1922.

92 See Verhaeren: Sensations, op. cit., p. 199.

93 Seurat to Beaubourg, Aug. 28, [1890]; facsimile first published by R. Rey: La Renaissance du sentiment classique, Paris, 1931, opp. p. 132. See also Rewald: Seurat, op. cit., pp. 61–62.

94 J. Christophe: Symbolisme, La Cravache, June 16, 1888.

III   1886-1890   SYMBOLISTS AND ANARCHISTS FROM MALLARME TO REDON

The year 1886, in which Seurat completed *La Grande Jatte,* the first important painting to embody his new theories, also witnessed the advent of literary symbolism and the impassioned manifesto in which Moréas laid down the principles of that movement. Although this was a coincidence, it was certainly not by chance that both innovators, the poet and the artist, quoted Charles Henry's findings among their justifications and that both hailed Félix Fénéon as the first "scientific" critic of their work. Indeed, there were many affinities between the young poets and painters of the time, though those who took part in the rising symbolist movement were by no means unanimous in their artistic tastes.

Symbolism, which thrust itself quite suddenly and with a definite impact upon an astonished and hostile public, had already been anticipated for several years by a series of almost unnoticed events. The overpowering figure of Victor Hugo, casting a gloomy shadow over the entire poetic life of France, and the robust naturalism of Zola, whose novels met with ever increasing success, had not prevented the younger generation of poets from discovering the works of Verlaine (born in 1844), of Mallarmé (born in 1842) and of Villiers de l'Isle-Adam (born in 1838). This new generation was now ready to overthrow established hierarchies, liquidate the heritage of the immediate past, and proclaim its ideals, confused and unrelated as they might be at first. For it is thus that every new movement attacks the preceding one, the better to assert itself, and erects its own temple on the very ruins to which it has reduced the sanctuary of what has gone before.

Mallarmé was then still in the strange position of being at the same time famous and unknown, venerated and disdained. He was not always understood even by those who admired him; the few who pretended to be able to penetrate his abstruse prose openly boasted about it. Verlaine's erratic life, which took him from prisons to pothouses to brothels to hospitals, had distracted attention from his merits as a poet. The singular personality of Villiers de l'Isle-Adam, who had romantically dissipated a small fortune but in deepest poverty maintained an air of grandeur, was equally appreciated only by a few. Yet the young poets of the new generation, fascinated by the revelation of Wagner's synthetic art, eager to achieve a more intimate fusion of verse and sound, searching for suggestive imagery and a revitalized vocabulary, found in the works of these men examples and inspiration. "Charles Baudelaire should be considered the true precursor of the present movement," proclaimed Moréas. "Stéphane Mallarmé endowed it with a sense of the mysterious and the inexpressible; Paul Verlaine shattered in its honor the cruel chains of verse which the subtle fingers of Théodore de Banville had already made more flexible."[1]

The symbolist poets shared the conviction that only ideas represent that superior

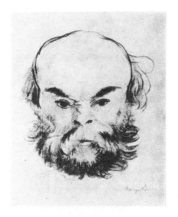

ANQUETIN: *Portrait of Paul Verlaine,* 1896. Pencil, 7½ x 6⅞". Musée Toulouse-Lautrec, Albi

reality which art should elect and retain, quoting Schopenhauer's assertion that there were "as many and probably different worlds as there are thinkers." Their ambition was to transform modern life by introducing into it "phantoms of dreams, of hallucinations, of memories, imaginary creations, because all these are to be found in life and actually compose it."[2] In order to achieve their aim of expressing their individual worlds, it became necessary to resort to new means. Aims and means were explained by Moréas when he wrote in his manifesto:

"Symbolic poetry endeavors to clothe the Idea in a sensitive form which, nevertheless, would not be an end in itself, but would be subordinate to the Idea while serving to express it. The Idea, on the other hand, should not make its appearance deprived of the sumptuous trappings of external analogies,[3] for the essential character of symbolist art consists in never going straight to the conception of the Idea itself.

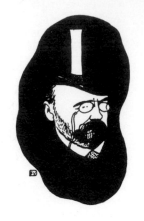

VALLOTTON: *Portrait of Emile Zola.* Pen and ink

"For the exact translation of its synthesis, symbolism requires an archetypal and complex style: unpolluted vocables, a well-composed sentence alternating with a sentence that falters undulatingly, significant pleonasms, mysterious ellipses, suspended anacolutha, every audacious and multiform trope: finally good [French] language." And Moréas concluded by reiterating that "art can derive from objectivity only a simple and extremely succinct point of departure."[1]

This manifesto, published in a widely read newspaper, represented the first attempt to acquaint a literary public with the principles of the new movement. It gave rise to loud protestations, jeers, and a solemn refutation by Anatole France. Fénéon's friend Gustave Kahn—together with Laforgue the first exponent of free verse—immediately set out to emphasize Moréas' statements by explaining in another daily paper that "what unifies this tendency is the negation of the old monochord technique of verse, the desire to divide rhythm, to give in the graphic quality of a stanza the scheme of a sensation. With the evolution of minds, sensations become more complicated, they need more appropriate words that are not worn out by twenty years of hackneyed usage. Moreover there is the normal expansion of a language through inevitable neologisms and through the re-establishment of an ancient vocabulary necessitated by a return of the imagination to the epic and the marvelous.

"The main way in which we distinguish ourselves from all similar endeavors is that we establish the fundamental principle of perpetual inflection of the verse, or better the stanza, which is considered the basic unit. Banal prose is the tool of conversation. We claim for the novel the right to make the sentence rhythmic, to accentuate its oratorical quality; the tendency is towards a poem in prose, very mobile and with a rhythmic pattern that varies according to the turn, the swing, the twisting, and the simplicity of the Idea.

"As to subject matter, we are tired of the quotidian, the near-at-hand, and the compulsorily contemporaneous; we wish to be able to place the development of the symbol in any period whatsoever, and even in outright dreams (*the dream being indistinguishable from life*). We want to substitute the struggle of sensations and ideas for the struggle of individualities, and for the center of action, instead of the well-exploited décor of squares and streets, we want the totality or part of a brain. The essential aim of our art is to objectify the subjective (the externalization of the Idea) instead of subjectifying the objective (nature seen through the eyes of a temperament).

"Analogous reflections have created the multitonal tone of Wagner and the recent technique of the impressionists [meaning neo-impressionism]. This is an adhesion of literature to scientific theories established by induction and controlled by the experimentation of M. Charles Henry, as stated in an introduction to the principles of a mathematical and experimental esthetic. These theories are founded on the purely idealistic philosophical principle which prompts us to spurn all reality of matter and which admits the existence of the world only as representation.

"Thus we carry the analysis of the *Self* to the extreme, we let the multiplicity and intertwining of rhythms harmonize with the measure of the Idea, we create literary enchantment by annulling the pattern of a forced and spiritual modernism, we compose a personal vocabulary based on the entire gamut of our work, and we endeavor to escape the banality of transmitted molds."[4]

These concepts had taken shape gradually in a series of little magazines, sole outlets for an esoteric art which made no claim to win over the masses. In 1882–83 the review *Lutèce*, among the founders of which was Charles Morice, later one of Gauguin's most intimate friends, had been the first to publish, besides Verlaine and Mallarmé, such still unknown and indeed extremely young poets as Moréas, Laforgue, Régnier, and the American Viélé-Griffin.[5] In 1884 the *Revue Indépendante* was founded with Fénéon, then only twenty-three years old, as its chief editor. He recruited contributors from among the "declining naturalists and the rising symbolists," such as Zola, Huysmans, E. de Goncourt, Alexis, and Robert Caze (a friend of Seurat's) on the one hand, Mallarmé, Moréas, and Christophe on the other. The political articles in the *Revue Indépendante* were almost completely anarchistic.

In 1884 Huysmans (born in 1848) suddenly left the entourage of Zola when he published *A Rebours* (*Against the Grain*), in which his decadent hero, des Esseintes, announces that a new poetry is being born but is yet little understood, and proclaims his admiration for Verlaine and Mallarmé. About the latter he wrote: "Perceiving the most remote analogies, he often designates an object or being by a word, giving at the same time, through an effect of similarity, the form, the fragrance, the color, the specific quality, the splendor, whereas it would have been necessary to attach to this object or being numerous and different epithets in order to embrace all its aspects, all its nuances, had it been designated merely by its technical term."[6]

But Huysmans did not speak only of poets; he also expressed his appreciation of such painters as Gustave Moreau and Odilon Redon (who was then practically unknown), while he was less attracted to Puvis de Chavannes. Henri de Régnier later even went so far as to say that it was in part his association with Redon and Moreau that had revived Huysmans' "propensity for the immaculate dream, a tendency towards evasive flights from the present."[7] As Huysmans himself stated: "The important thing is... to be able to detach oneself sufficiently to bring about hallucinations and substitute the dream of reality for reality itself." To Huysmans' hero, des Esseintes, "artificiality appeared to be the distinguishing sign of man's genius. As he used to say, nature has served her purpose; by the disgusting uniformity of her landscapes and her skies she has definitely worn out the attentive patience of the refined.... There can be no doubt, that sempiternal driveler has by now used up the complacent admiration of true artists and the time has come when she should be replaced by artificiality as far as possible."[6]

Huysmans' book was promptly called "decadent" by its enemies, giving the new movement its name. Some of the poets readily accepted this designation, just as the impressionists had decided twenty years earlier to adopt the nickname coined for them by an ironic critic. "Not to admit the state of decadence which we have reached," announced one

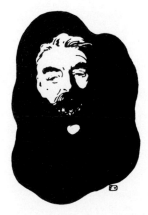

VALLOTTON: *Portrait of Stéphane Mallarmé*. Pen and ink

of the symbolist magazines, "would be the height of nonsense. Religion, morals, justice, everything is in decadence. . . . Refinement of appetites, of sensations, of taste, of luxury, of pleasure; neurosis, hysteria, hypnotism, morphinomania, scientific charlatanism, Schopenhauerism to the utmost, these are the symptoms of social evolution. It is in the language above all that the first signs of it manifest themselves. New ideas, infinitely subtle and varied, correspond to new needs. That explains the necessity of creating un-heard-of words to express this complexity of sentiments and of physiological sensations."[8]

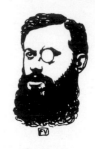

Jean Moréas, however, frowned upon the term "decadent" and saw, on the contrary, characteristics of a renaissance in "the abuse of pomposity, the strangeness of metaphor, a new vocabulary in which harmonies are combined with colors and lines."[1] And Gustave Kahn was soon to state: "Although any label is vain, we feel compelled, for the exact information of those interested, to remind them that *decadent* is pronounced *symbolist*."[4]

These ideas were further explored by a pupil of Théodore de Banville, Maurice Barrès, who at the age of twenty-two published single-handed *Les Taches d'Encre* in 1884–85, writing practically all the articles of this little review himself. In 1885 there also appeared *La Minerve, Le Passant,* and *La Revue Contemporaine,* but the most significant new publi-cation of that year was the *Revue Wagnérienne,* founded by Edouard Dujardin, who had studied at the Paris Conservatory together with Debussy and who now set out to promote Wagner not only as a great musician and poet, but also as a great thinker and, above all, as the creator of a new art form. Edouard Dujardin was assisted chiefly by Teodor de Wyzewa, theorist of the movement, who established the link between Wagner and French literature by pointing out that if an author's aim is to suggest rather than to describe, literature has to become music, since music has supreme suggestive power and can evoke better than words the mystery of life. Thus Villiers de l'Isle-Adam, in Wyzewa's eyes, was a "musician of words" and the perfect transmitter of the new "Wagnerian art."[9] Indeed, Wyzewa related every creative effort to Wagner and even spoke of "Wagnerian painting," into which category he grouped the work of Redon and Puvis de Chavannes as well as that of Degas, Cézanne, and Monet.

Among the contributors to the *Revue Wagnérienne* were Mallarmé and Stuart Merrill, a young American who was soon to publish in the United States a translation of collected poems by the French symbolists. In the fall of 1886 Dujardin, assisted by Fénéon, took over the *Revue Indépendante,* which had been temporarily discontinued but which now quickly achieved a leading role under their guidance. Laforgue, Kahn, Henry, Verhaeren, Wyzewa, George Moore, and a host of others joined the list of authors for the *Revue In-dépendante,* whereas the naturalist writers were dropped from it. The de luxe edition of the magazine contained prints or reproductions of works by Whistler, Redon, Seurat, Signac, Luce, Chéret, Renoir, and others. A little later, at the instigation of Fénéon, the *Revue Indépendante* began to hold small exhibitions in its editorial offices, showing works by Manet, Pissarro, Morisot, Rodin, Raffaëlli, Seurat, Signac, Anquetin (a friend of Dujardin's), and van Gogh. Guillaumin and Luce held their first one-man shows there. Though the *Revue Indépendante* now became the most influential of all the little magazines, it was supported in this task by a host of other more or less ephemeral periodicals, of which the year 1886 saw a truly bewildering number.

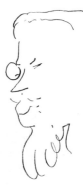

In January 1886 there first appeared in Liège *La Wallonie,* around which gathered all the Belgian symbolists, just as their artistic countrymen were grouped around the still young association of the XX and its official organ, *L'Art Moderne,* which Verhaeren now also steered into symbolist waters. In March *La Pléiade* began publication in Paris, featuring articles by Maeterlinck and René Ghil, who soon after revised his recently published *Traité du Verbe* to include the findings of Helmholtz on vocal tones and harmonies. *La Pléiade* later printed articles by Albert Aurier, the first symbolist critic to appraise the work of Gauguin and van Gogh and to do for them what Fénéon was doing for the neo-impressionists. *La Vogue*, a weekly founded in April 1886 with Gustave Kahn as its driving force, seconded by Fénéon, who there published his defense of Seurat, disappeared in December of that same year, but not without having given space to significant pages by Mallarmé, Rimbaud, Verlaine, Moréas, Adam, Henry, Morice, and many others, as well as to translations of poems by Walt Whitman and Keats. *La Vogue* also reprinted Mallarmé's definition of poetry as "the expression, through human language, reduced to its essential rhythm, of the mysterious meaning of the aspects of life: thus it confers authenticity upon our existence and constitutes the sole spiritual aim."[10] *La Vogue* appeared again in 1889 under Kahn's editorship, with occasional illustrations by Pissarro, Luce, and others.

Le Décadent, founded at the same time as *La Vogue* in April 1886 with a similar roster of contributors, would have preferred a new designation, coined by its editor, "le décadisme," a word in which Verlaine delighted. As it was, *Le Décadent* forced *La Décadence*, which first appeared in October of that same year, to change its title to *Le Scapin*; both reviews were proud to publish Mallarmé's rare articles. *Le Symboliste*, making its appearance in the fall of 1886 with Kahn, Moréas, and Adam as editorial officers, once more listed Henry, Fénéon, Laforgue, Dujardin, Huysmans, Mallarmé, Verlaine, Wyzewa, and several others among its regular contributors, disavowed both *Le Scapin* and *Le Décadent*, and proclaimed *La Vogue* as the only true symbolist periodical. Yet *Le Symboliste* ceased publication after four issues, shortly before *La Vogue* in turn had temporarily exhausted its resources.[11]

During that same year most of the symbolists also contributed to *La Revue Moderne*, and there were more new magazines in 1887, among them the *Revue Exotique*, for which Fénéon wrote, and *Les Ecrits pour l'Art*, which, like the rest, proclaimed Mallarmé its master and included articles by Ghil (who wrote a violent polemic against Wyzewa), Verhaeren, Régnier, and Merrill, as well as Villiers de l'Isle-Adam's reminiscences of Wagner. The year 1887 was marked by the appearance of the first volume of free verse poetry, Kahn's *Palais Nomades*, and by the death at twenty-seven of Laforgue, considered by his friends the most promising protagonist of the new poetry. Laforgue had planned to write a book on art, "a series of studies in which, through the accumulation of well selected words (*meaning* and *sonority*), of facts, of sentiments appropriate to the color scale of a painter, I should *convey the sensation* of the world created by this painter."[12] He was unable to carry out this project. Fénéon, Dujardin, and Wyzewa took it upon themselves to administer his literary estate and edit his unpublished works and letters.

In 1888 the symbolists "seized" the weekly *La Cravache*, entrusting Fénéon's young friend Georges Lecomte with its editorship. For a little over a year most of the symbolists contributed to *La Cravache*, which devoted much space to art criticism. Fénéon wrote about the impressionists and neo-impressionists as well as about Charles Henry's theories, Huysmans spoke of Cézanne, Christophe of Luce and Dubois-Pillet, Octave Maus reported on the Brussels exhibitions of the XX, and so on. Verlaine published there some poems of his forthcoming volume *Parallèlement*. But in the summer of 1889 they all abandoned *La Cravache* and switched back to the re-issued *Vogue* with Gustave Kahn.

In 1891 many of the symbolist writers temporarily converged on *La Vie Moderne*, which

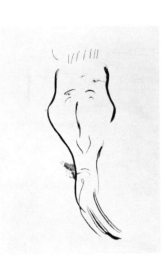

Toulouse-Lautrec: *Caricature of Félix Fénéon*, c. 1896. Pen and ink, 11 x 7¾". Private collection, New York

in 1887–88 had published some of the pointillist and other drawings by Signac, Dubois-Pillet, Seurat, Luce, Hayet, van Rysselberghe, and Lucien Pissarro, together with art criticism by Kahn, Verhaeren, Adam, and others.

All these little reviews had in common a feverish eagerness, a self-righteousness, a lofty intolerance, and an even loftier independence of spirit, together with a great frugality. They practically never paid contributors, and Fénéon, for instance, far from drawing a salary at *La Vogue*, actually sometimes defrayed printer's costs, though he himself was pursued by creditors who tried to confiscate his meager earnings as an employee of the War Ministry. Yet, like fragile plants growing luxuriantly in a hothouse, these poets seemed to thrive in the protected atmosphere of their publications, somewhat oblivious to the climate outside,[13] heroically and almost arrogantly proud of being obscure and eccentric, unintelligible to whoever was not initiated. Their fondness for bizarre and unconventional syntax, spiced with the most precious, archaic, and unusual words (unearthed from the depths of dictionaries and texts of bygone days, if not altogether made up by the various poets) took such proportions that Paul Adam soon felt compelled to issue a "Small Glossary to Serve for the Comprehension of the Decadent and Symbolist Authors."[14] But while these authors consciously cultivated a style which shut them off from the masses, they found in their very inaccessibility a confirmation of their originality, since they apparently shared Wyzewa's belief that "the esthetic value of a work of art is always in inverse relationship to the number of people who can understand it."[15] As Huysmans had already stated: "If the most beautiful tune in the world becomes vulgar and insufferable as soon as the public hums it, as soon as hurdy-gurdies get hold of it, so the work of art which does not leave false artists indifferent, which is not contested by blockheads, which is not satisfied with arousing the enthusiasm of the few, becomes likewise, and on account of this, polluted, banal, almost repulsive for the initiated."[6]

The very few who could understand symbolist poetry did not always present a united front. They were divided by petty jealousies as well as by differences of theory and interpretation. Indeed, the great number of little magazines founded in those years, all of which addressed themselves more or less to the same limited circle of readers, seems to reflect the internal squabbles of the symbolists. Every dissenter appears to have published almost automatically yet another small periodical. There were also frequent and controversial statements as to which were reliable pronouncements on the new movement. Among those quoted were Henry's *Esthétique Scientifique*, Moréas' and Kahn's articles as well as Fénéon's bibliographical notes in the *Revue Indépendante*. As for Mallarmé, he remained aloof from most disputes and apparently endeavored to satisfy the steady demand for contributions to all of these reviews.

The various factions gathered in a number of cafés and editorial offices, such as the Brasserie Gambrinus, the Taverne Anglaise in the rue d'Amsterdam, meeting place of the *Vogue* contributors, and especially the premises of the *Revue Indépendante* where, in the late afternoon, Kahn and Fénéon assembled their associates. Besides Henry, Christophe, Alexis, Verlaine, and occasionally Mallarmé himself, there appeared most of Fénéon's painter friends: Pissarro, Seurat, Signac, Dubois-Pillet, Angrand, Luce, and even Raffaëlli.

The poets and their friends who spent long hours discussing all the topics which preoccupied them formed a strange and widely dissimilar group. Most of them were of approximately the same age, but beyond that they did not always have much in common. Those who were born within the same decade, that is between 1855 and 1865, were Tailhade,

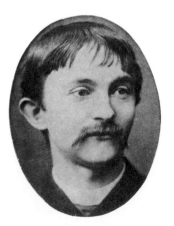

Photograph of Teodor de Wyzewa, 1884

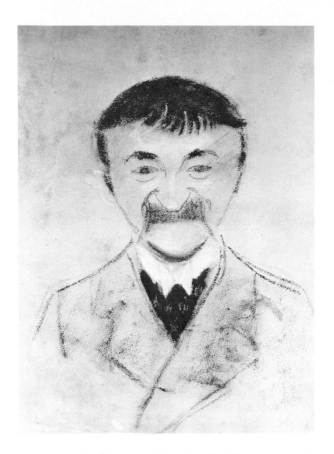

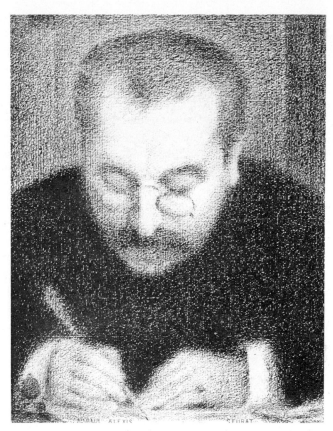

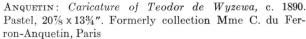

Anquetin: *Caricature of Teodor de Wyzewa,* c. 1890. Pastel, 20⅞ x 13¾″. Formerly collection Mme C. du Ferron-Anquetin, Paris

Seurat: *Portrait of Paul Alexis,* 1888. Conté crayon. Published in 1888 in *La Vie Moderne.* Present whereabouts unknown

Verhaeren (a Belgian), Moréas (a Greek), H.-E. Cross, de Gourmont, Luce, Seurat, Henry, Kahn (an Alsatian), Laforgue, Morice, Dujardin, Anquetin, Ghil, Wyzewa (a Pole educated in France), Maeterlinck (a Belgian), Barrès, Adam, Debussy, Merrill (an American), Signac, Ajalbert, Régnier, Viélé-Griffin (another American), Lautrec, Fontainas (Belgian), Fénéon (born in Italy of French parents), and Aurier. Some of them were aristocrats, others were workmen's sons; some had means which permitted them to live independently, such as Seurat, Signac, Lautrec, and Henry; others, among them Luce, Laforgue, and Wyzewa, were desperately poor. Many had to work for a living at some unrewarding or humiliating job to be able to carry on their creative work. Yet, quite apart from their station in life, many were inclined to some eccentricity; like Baudelaire and Mallarmé, they were by no means opposed to a certain dandyism. They favored eyeglasses and top hats, and showed in their bearing, manners, speech, and dress the same preciosity that distinguished their writings. Moréas, with his well-groomed mustache, was discovered one day wearing a corset, embroidered with his initials surmounted by a nobiliary coronet.[16] Dujardin gave himself the airs of a seducer, a role in which he was portrayed by Lautrec. In the way in which he dressed and even in which he cut his hair, Wyzewa kept an undefinable exotic flavor.[17] Paul

Adam, who bore with modesty the enviable distinction of having been condemned (like Baudelaire and Flaubert) for the alleged immorality of one of his novels, was no less a Beau Brummel than Moréas and in addition was generally accompanied by a "rheumatic greyhound." Fénéon shared their penchant for oddities; when he did not wear his silk top hat (dear also to Seurat, Signac, Henry, and Dujardin), he would sport a greatcoat or full tippet cape, such as the French identified with Anglo-American travelers; his pointed beard contributed to make him look like Uncle Sam. Fénéon's attire was completed by a small black felt hat, dark red gloves, and not exactly appropriate black patent leather shoes.[18] His manners, like those of Wyzewa, were of an exquisite, slightly ironical politeness. These manners notwithstanding, or possibly to heighten a certain effect of absurdity, Fénéon occasionally told stories that would have made young maidens faint. Signac was not only outspoken and loud, he reveled in the use of an extensive but unprintable vocabulary, an exercise in which Lautrec could also hold his own. Alexis, on the other hand, indulged in Parisian slang; in fact he wrote a daily newspaper column in this idiom, a column to which Signac sometimes contributed exhibition reviews that were unblushingly favorable to his own works. But none went as far in eccentricity as the then famous Comte Robert de Montesquiou who attended a concert attired in a pale mauve frock-coat with shirt, collar, and tie to match, explaining that "one should always listen to Weber in mauve."[19] In contrast to the more fanciful habits of many of their friends, Seurat and Henry were always soberly dressed in black or blue, and were equally sober in their deportment.

Though problems of art were, of course, their main interest, these men often discussed political questions. Only Moréas carefully avoided taking sides. But with the notable exception of Barrès who, at the age of twenty-seven, got himself elected in 1889 as a Boulangist deputy and thenceforth remained within the fold of ultra-nationalism, all the others were committed to the extreme left. When, during the electoral campaign of 1889, somebody conceived the hoax of printing a leaflet announcing Boulanger's sudden death, accompanied by his "last will," Signac was on hand to supply a picture of the rabble-rousing general on his fictitious deathbed. Actually, political matters were of grave concern to them, and their convictions were in those years inseparable from their works.

As Marcel Aymé has expressed it so excellently: "... An obscure poem, a violent image, a beautiful verse full of shadows and vagueness, a dim harmony, a rare sound, the mystery of a sumptuous and insignificant word, all produce an effect like alcohol and introduce into the organism itself habits of feeling and of thinking which could not have entered into it through the path of reason. To accept a revolution in the art of poetry and to enjoy its novelty is to familiarize oneself with the idea of revolution *per se* and frequently also with the rudiments of its vocabulary."[20]

The symbolists and most of their friends were anarchists. Was it possible not to be an anarchist when the upper classes showed themselves so resolutely blind to anything new and beautiful? How could they accept without protest a social order in which the artist had no real place, in which he must struggle all his life for recognition, in which the vote of the bourgeois went to reaction in politics and in art as well? Their social ideals seemed to them inseparable from violence. It was not so much that they were in favor of bombs, but rather that dynamite appeared to be a not wholly unjustified means of ending social inequities when other measures had failed or seemed too slow. They were idealists, not agitators. While most of them shunned direct political activities, Fénéon managed to give an anarchistic touch to art criticism by stating dryly in an article on Pissarro: "Everything

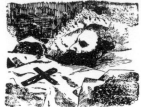

Leaflet announcing General Boulanger's fictitious death, illustrated by Signac, 1889

new, to be accepted, requires that many old fools must die. We are longing for this to happen as soon as possible. This wish is not at all charitable, it is practical."[21]

Time bombs were of course the speediest way to activate this process of elimination. But to these intellectuals, who were anything but blood-thirsty, bombs represented above all the most effective means of attracting attention to their revindications and to those of the underprivileged into whose camp society had relegated them. Whereas the philosophers of anarchism, such as Elysée Reclus, opposed "propaganda by action," Fénéon pointed out that anarchist terrorism did more to spread propaganda than twenty years of pamphlets. Although the movement attracted not only idealists but also adventurers, cynics, desperadoes, and even common criminals,[22] the writers and painters who professed extremist views were anarchists with all the altruism of their hearts, the purity of their souls, and the elegance of their demeanors. In the theories of anarchism they found many elements that corresponded to their own yearnings: an ultra-radical individualism, love of liberty, pity for the disinherited, passionate solidarity, and glorification of humanity. Some, like Pissarro, who had studied Marx as well as Kropotkin, reasoned that "the movement of ideas in present society tends with extraordinary energy towards the elaboration of new philosophical and scientific systems destined to become law in societies of the future."[23] Others explained in more sentimental terms why they were anarchists. Signac, for instance, listed among the reasons for his convictions: "the sufferings of many; logic, kindness, honesty; physiological laws (the rights of the stomach, of the brain, of the eyes, etc.); the need to feel happiness around oneself."[24]

Those who more or less openly manifested their sympathy for the anarchist movement were Pissarro and his sons, Signac, Seurat, and Luce among the painters; Kahn, Tailhade, Régnier, Adam, de Gourmont, Lecomte, Verhaeren, Merrill, Viélé-Griffin, Mauclair, and even Mallarmé among the poets; Fénéon, Mirbeau, Alexandre, and Geffroy among the critics; as well as many of their friends. They admired the logic and particularly the generosity of Kropotkin's writings; they dreamed of a new society which, freed from all bourgeois prejudices, would be a paradise for creative minds. And though they themselves stood high above the masses (and often liked their lofty attitude), they envisioned a society of the future in which the equality of men would assure them the freedom and respect which the present so bitterly denied them. They hoped that one day their tools, their pens and brushes, would be considered equal in importance to the hammer, the sickle, and the plow.

This Utopia became all the more tempting as the weak Third Republic, still in its infancy, entrusted its powers to a group of wealthy reactionaries and corrupt politicians. In 1887 exposés of organized graft on the part of his own son-in-law had forced the French president to resign. No sooner was Boulanger's nationalist movement beaten back than another scandal, that of the Panama Canal, stunned the public by its unprecedented magnitude. And soon France was shaken with bomb detonations. After Ravachol had thrown a number of bombs, Vaillant dropped one in the Chamber of Deputies which proved to be less effective than noisy; after some commotion the session continued. When asked what they thought of such violence, Mallarmé replied that he could "not discuss the acts of those saints," while Tailhade went on record with the proud exclamation: "What does it matter if some vague individualities disappear, as long as the gesture is beautiful?"[25] Ironically, Tailhade himself soon fell victim to a bomb thrown by a fellow anarchist. He had an eye plucked out but felt compelled to state that he didn't mind. Another anarchist was even less fortunate: while trying to destroy the church of La Madeleine, he succeeded

VALLOTTON: *Portrait of Rémy de Gourmont*. Pen and ink

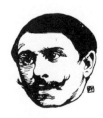

VALLOTTON: *Portrait of Paul Adam*. Pen and ink

only in literally blowing off his own head. But there were colleagues of his who handled detonators more effectively, among them an idealistic youngster, a friend of Fénéon's, with whom the guillotine eventually caught up. When the French president Sadi Carnot succumbed to an anarchist attack, the French lawmakers frantically enacted new legislation to curb these unpleasant activities and began hunting for intellectuals whom they saw as instigators of these crimes. Fénéon and Luce became involved in a famous lawsuit against thirty anarchists.

There can be no doubt that several of the small symbolist periodicals which had set out to shatter some of the traditions of French prose and verse eventually expanded their goals and sought to shatter bourgeois society itself. One of them even published the scientific formula for the composition of dynamite. And many of the new magazines that succeeded the short-lived ones of 1886, among them the *Mercure de France*, which lasted for seventy years, and the *Revue Blanche*, published for some twelve years, made no secret of their sympathy for anarchism. In addition, there were of course a number of specifically anarchist and more or less clandestine periodicals devoted mainly to political questions. To these also, many of the poets, painters, and writers lent their collaboration, though they confined themselves mostly to problems of art and literature rather than to the writing of inflammatory articles.

By joining a movement that claimed to bring about the deliverance of all exploited humanity, it is almost as if the symbolists and their friends atoned for the isolation in which their own works kept them. The step from radicalism in their artistic beliefs to a radicalism that advocated practically raw physical violence seems to have been a logical one to them. Yet they were not merely drawing-room anarchists. They had the courage of their convictions, signed numerous public appeals in favor of the downtrodden, and generously supported their cause, even though this often meant great sacrifices to them. Whenever the proletariat found itself in open conflict with the ruling class, it was certain that these poets, painters, and writers would be on the side of the poor. Their severe and constant criticism of the habits, the blindness, the hypocrisies of the upper class made these intellectuals almost more dangerous than the isolated agitator whose bomb or dagger, more often than not, tended to discredit the movement in the public eye. Eventually, however, the generosity of the initial idea and the abnegation of its supporters were obscured by a flood of petty crimes and senseless attacks which spelled the end of a movement that had offered great hopes to those who believed in the basic goodness of mankind.

While their political convictions and their zeal as reformers united the various factions of symbolism, they were strangely divided in their appreciation of the painters who shared their views, as well as of others who did not. Although there existed bonds of real friendship between many of these poets and painters, there was no artistic movement, as such, that the symbolists recognized as their counterpart in the arts. Indeed, some of the painters they admired had no connection whatsoever either with their own literary tendencies or with their anarchist leanings. As a matter of fact, the symbolists were in open disagreement on questions of art evaluation, and a conflict such as the one that seems to have inflamed Fénéon and Wyzewa may well have had its roots in the former's esteem for Seurat and the latter's avowed hostility to neo-impressionism.

Though the uncontested leader of the poets, Mallarmé made no attempt to impose upon the others his artistic taste which must have appeared to them as definitely on the conservative side. Having been a personal friend of Manet's, Mallarmé felt himself drawn to the impressionists, who belonged to his own generation, rather than to the younger painters.

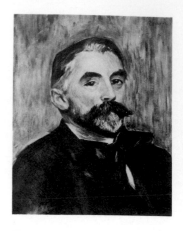

RENOIR: *Portrait of Stéphane Mallarmé,* dedicated to the poet, c. 1890. Musée du Louvre, Paris

He was devoted to Berthe Morisot, Manet's sister-in-law, and in her house enjoyed the company of Renoir (who painted his portrait), of Monet, and of Degas, whom he assisted with advice when the painter took a fancy to write sonnets.[26] He was also on friendly terms with Whistler. Near Fontainebleau, where he spent his summers, Mallarmé was the neighbor of Redon; their cordial relations were based on a profound understanding of each other's work and a common love for the beauties of the mysterious.

Mallarmé's young friend Wyzewa shared his master's predilections: he admired Puvis de Chavannes and Redon for the emotional qualities of their work, but even more Renoir and Berthe Morisot. Renoir eventually admitted Wyzewa to his circle of friends. Jules Laforgue also was very responsive to the art of the impressionists. His early death may have prevented him from following Fénéon in his devotion to neo-impressionism. Fénéon himself adopted a somewhat patronizing attitude towards the impressionists, whose historical role he did not wish to deny, but his loyalty went exclusively to Seurat and his friends. Though he did write a few words of appreciation on Redon and Puvis de Chavannes, it can almost be said that Fénéon was prejudiced against anybody who did not use the divisionist technique.

It was Fénéon's friend Dujardin who, speaking of Anquetin's recent work, formulated some of the guiding principles of symbolist art: "In painting as well as in literature the representation of nature is idle fancy.... On the contrary, the aim of painting, of literature, is to give the sensation of things through means specific to painting and literature; what ought to be expressed is not the image but the character [of the model]. Therefore, why retrace the thousands of insignificant details the eye perceives? One should select the essential trait and reproduce it—or, even better, produce it. An outline is sufficient to represent a face. Scorning photography, the painter will set out to retain, with the smallest possible number of characteristic lines and colors, the intimate reality, the essence of the object he selects. Primitive art and folklore are symbolic in this fashion.... And so is Japanese art.

"What practical lesson can we derive from this? First of all a rigorous differentiation

Right: TOULOUSE-LAUTREC: *Portrait of Jane Avril and Edouard Dujardin* (detail from the poster for the Divan Japonais), 1892. Color lithograph

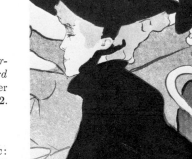

Far right: TOULOUSE-LAUTREC: *Portrait of Félix Fénéon* (detail from the decorations for the booth of La Goulue), 1895. Musée du Louvre, Paris

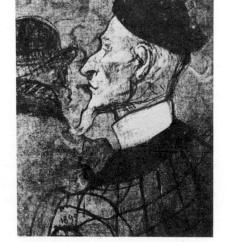

143

between line and coloration. To confuse line and color ... means not to have understood what specific means of expression they are: line expresses what is permanent, color what is momentary. Line, an almost abstract symbol, gives the character of the object; the unity of coloration establishes the general atmosphere, retains the sensation...."[27]

Since impressionism was opposed to these concepts, it was not surprising that the impressionists counted so few friends among the symbolists. Indeed, it was the belief of most of these authors that the impressionist did not think, that his eye took the place of an empty brain. In their opinion, the impressionist followed his sensations almost automatically, observing without seeing, while they themselves expected to find in a work of art some poetic thought sublimated into pictorial language. No wonder then that Huysmans actually contributed greatly to the "discovery" of both Moreau and Redon. Since his approach to art was essentially a literary one, his enthusiasm went to those works which inspired him to verbose and poetical interpretations. Unlike Mallarmé, Huysmans had failed for a long time to grasp the true significance of impressionism, and even though he now professed to like it, his eyes really feasted on paintings that struck his fertile imagination. Fénéon's friend, the poet Francis Poictevin, also was a great admirer of Moreau; so was Gustave Kahn.

There can be no doubt that Moreau's art contained many analogies with symbolist poetry: preciosity, mysticism, complexity, archaism, carefully chiseled details, abundance of unexpected elements, a well disciplined imagination, horror of the vulgar. It could even be said that Moreau's paintings and watercolors reveal the same obsession with jewels as Villiers de l'Isle-Adam's writings. Yet Moreau himself was shocked by the eccentricities of the young symbolists and kept away from them so as to devote himself to the pursuit of a work entirely given over to what he called "imaginative reason."

Born in 1826, son of well-to-do parents, Gustave Moreau had added palatial halls and a tremendous studio to their comfortable house near the Gare Saint-Lazare, where he lived in almost complete seclusion, caring little to exhibit his works and even less to sell them. But in the isolation of his somewhat pompous ivory tower, he followed all the intellectual currents of his time, and Degas aptly characterized Moreau as a "hermit who knows the train schedules." Huysmans was more charitable and less precise when he described the painter as "a mystic shut up in the heart of Paris in a cell which is not reached even by the noise of contemporary life, though it furiously beats against the doors of the cloister. Plunged in ecstasy, he sees the radiance of fairy-like visions, the sanguinary apotheosis of other ages."[28]

Interested in archeology, philosophy, and mythology, Moreau had been in his early years under the influence of Delacroix until he yielded to that of Chassériau, who had replaced Delacroix's romantic passion and spontaneity with elegant and sentimental mannerisms. Eventually spontaneity completely disappeared from Moreau's work, giving way to careful calculation and a strange tendency to surcharge his work with a host of details that threatened to submerge his initial inspiration. He himself said that "my greatest effort, my unique concern, my constant preoccupation, is to direct as best I can that team to proceed with equal pace: my unbridled imagination and my mind which is critical almost to the extent of mania."[29] In this he did succeed, though the flowery unfolding of his fantasy lost all of its sparkle under the domination of cold reason. Nevertheless his bizarre world of beautiful adolescents, of perversely chaste maidens, tame monsters, haunted seas, ethereal architecture, and mysterious landscapes holds an unusual fascination for one who

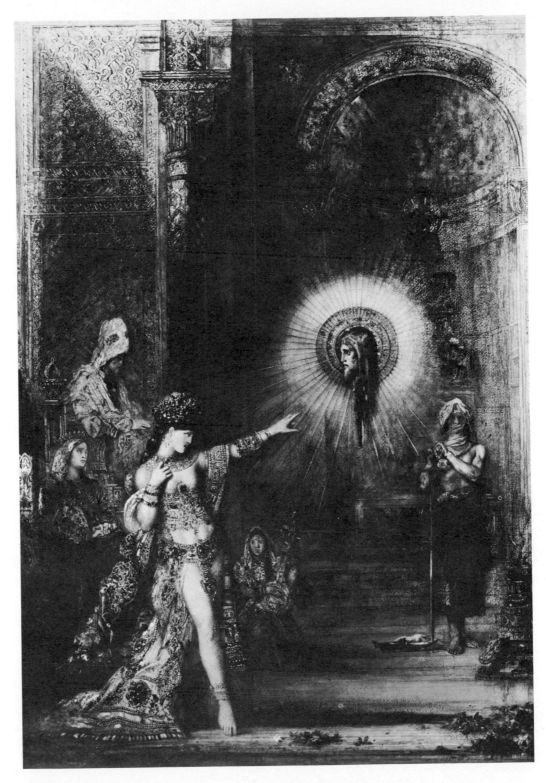

MOREAU: *Salome* (*Apparition*), c. 1875. Watercolor, 41¾ x 28½". Musée du Louvre, Paris

knows how to *read* a work of art (the word *read* was used by Moreau himself). Here are all the "phantoms of dreams, of hallucinations, of memories, imaginary creations," here is the Idea "clothed in a sensitive form," here are the "sumptuous trappings," the "mysterious ellipses," the "unpolluted" elements, and the "ancient vocabulary" which Moréas and his group were so eager to revive in their poems. Huysmans had good reason for des Esseintes' statement that Moreau's paintings "went beyond the limits of painting, borrowing from the art of writing its most subtle evocations." And when Huysmans, in describing Moreau's works, did so in precious and bombastic words, an odd circle was closed. Yet, though his paintings represented an accumulation of literary elements that seemed to defy translation into pictorial language, Moreau managed, through the power of his will, through his patience as well as through his sense of color and composition, to pull together all the ingredients assembled by his restless mind and thus endowed his works with a mystical realism and poetry. Except for small sketches which he kept in his studio and never showed, Moreau's art lacked boldness, and while this could not have displeased those who once called themselves "decadents," there were many among the symbolists who felt drawn rather to neo-impressionism, in which they found more analogies to their own endeavors. Seurat and his friends had a wide following among the symbolists. Next to Fénéon and Verhaeren, who had been the first to recognize Seurat's genius, Kahn, Paul Adam, Henri de Régnier, Jules Christophe, and Ajalbert were fervent admirers. Gustave Kahn later explained what appealed to them in Seurat's austere theories:

"We not only felt that we were leading a struggle for new ideas, we were attracted by something that seemed to parallel our own efforts: the kind of equilibrium, the search for an absolute departure which characterized the art of Seurat. We were sensitive to the mathematical element in his art. Perhaps the fire of youth had stirred up in us a number of half-certitudes which seemed strengthened by the fact that his experiments in line and color were in many respects exactly analogous to our theories of verse and phrase. Painters and poets were mutually captivated by the possibility that this was the case."[30]

However, this connection between neo-impressionism and symbolism was not a very obvious one. When Signac tried to emphasize it in his portrait of Fénéon, by putting a stylized cyclamen into his friend's hand and painting him against what he called "the enamel of a background rhythmic with beats and angles, tones and colors," the result was a strange concoction of disparate elements. It looked like a *tour de force* rather than like a solution of the problem of integrating realism, symbolism, and linear abstractions. In spite of their personal friendship with many of the key figures of literary symbolism, Seurat and his friends were never named among those considered symbolist painters. The praise Seurat received from some poets and critics was counterbalanced by the attacks he suffered from others. George Moore mocked his *Grande Jatte*, refusing to take his efforts seriously; Wyzewa reproached him for lack of sincerity and missed in his works a "complete expression of vivid sensations" such as he found in impressionism. He considered neo-impressionist paintings "interesting only as the exercises of highly mannered virtuosos."[31] As for Huysmans, he violently attacked Seurat's figure compositions (while liking his landscapes) because, as he said, "I very much fear that there have been too many techniques, too many systems; there are not enough sparks of fire, there is not enough life."[32] Huysmans did not bother to explain where he found "sparks of fire" in the greatly admired works of Gustave Moreau.

There are many odd inconsistencies in the preferences of the various symbolists. Each,

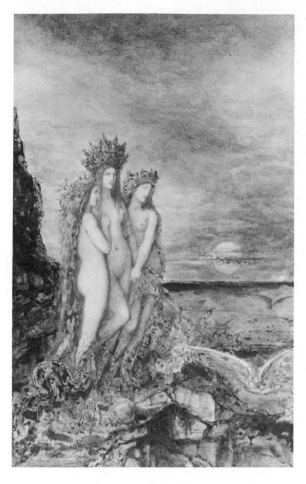 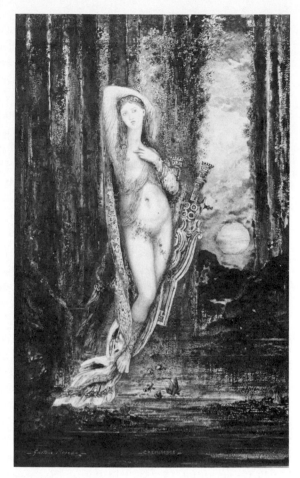

MOREAU: *The Sirens,* c. 1869. Watercolor, 12⅞ x 8⅛″. Fogg Art Museum, Harvard University, Cambridge, Mass. (Grenville L. Winthrop Bequest)

MOREAU: *Twilight.* Watercolor, 14 x 8½″. Private collection, Paris

with the exception of the methodical Fénéon, apparently approached art with the greatest subjectivity, responding only to those qualities in a painting which struck vibrant chords in his own imagination. Where such affinities existed, these men indulged in boundless admiration, but whenever a work of art failed to release the flow of their own dreams, they were highly critical without much regard for consistency. Thus Wyzewa later wrote that in those years, "before I could like a work of art, it had to be really new, that is in keeping with the latest inventions; it had to be a little sickish. I was then in excellent health and nothing is as conducive to a taste for sickly works of art as healthiness."[33] While such a predisposition does explain Wyzewa's liking for Moreau, it is difficult to understand how he could also admire Renoir, who was by no means sickish, or why he disapproved of Seurat, whose work took into account all "the latest inventions." On the whole, however, it was certainly their taste for sickishness which made the "decadents" accept without question the works of Moreau and the anemic grace of Puvis de Chavannes.

147

If there was one painter whose art captivated practically all of the symbolists, it was Puvis de Chavannes. Already in 1885 Strindberg had noticed on a visit to Paris that "in the midst of the last spasms of naturalism, one name was pronounced by all with admiration, that of Puvis de Chavannes."[34] And Gustave Kahn later wrote: "Puvis was the great painter on whose merits we were less divided than on those of any other. Probity, noble ambitions, a new and delicate art of harmonies! He was no longer contested."[35]

Actually, Puvis de Chavannes had hardly been contested during his long career, nor had he been as savagely attacked as the impressionists (he was scarcely older than they). But he came to be fully appreciated only in the 'eighties, after the advent of literary symbolism had created a truly favorable climate for his art.[36] Avoiding the three main currents of his time, academic art, naturalism, and impressionism, Puvis had evolved a style entirely his own, one completely opposite to that of Moreau, with whom the symbolists generally linked him in their admiration. His art tended towards the simplification of ideas, of lines and of color, in a fashion that coincided well with Dujardin's precepts about the roles of color and line. In his works line does express "what is permanent" while "the unity of coloration established the general atmosphere."

"For all clear thoughts," Puvis once explained, "there exists a plastic equivalent. But ideas often come to us entangled and blurred. Thus it is important first to disentangle them, in order to keep them pure before the inner eye. A work of art emanates from a kind of confused emotion in which it is contained as an animal is contained in its egg. I meditate upon the thought buried in this emotion until it appears lucidly and as distinctly as possible before my eyes. Then I search for an image which translates it with exactitude.... This is symbolism, if you like."[37]

Instead of representing what he perceived, Puvis preferred to translate the emotions his perception had released. For these emotions he found equivalents in the tranquil gestures of his figures, in the large rhythms of his compositions, in the use of subdued colors that made for a general feeling of serenity, in simplified drawing that reduced most forms to their essentials, while leaving them naturalistic enough to be immediately understood. He replaced outworn allegories with new ones, and endeavored to convey the symbolic meaning of his works through the general arrangement and color rather than through details. His observations of nature were carefully filtered to produce harmonious shapes and colorations, the poetic content of which he strove to emphasize.

As the creator of numerous murals, indeed as the artist who in France revived the art of mural decoration, Puvis was extremely conscious of the fact that large architectural surfaces demand a treatment different from that of easel paintings. This circumstance permitted him to make further simplifications. He renounced to a certain extent the third dimension, conceiving his murals strictly as embellishments which maintained the walls as what they were: limits of space. Hence his predilection for large flat planes, neutral colorations, and quiet compositions; hence his tendency to express his thoughts not in the overwrought style of Moreau but with an almost naïve limpidity.

Once the symbolists had hailed him for the harmonious ordonnance with which he expressed his emotions, Puvis found himself acclaimed as possibly the greatest master of his time. It is true that Huysmans thought him clumsy, but the others, while they did not deny Puvis' faults, highly valued his *intentions*. Wyzewa clearly stated that to the symbolists Puvis' work meant something that lay beyond its pictorial qualities or defects. "It represents for us," he wrote, "a reaction against opposite excesses of which we have grown

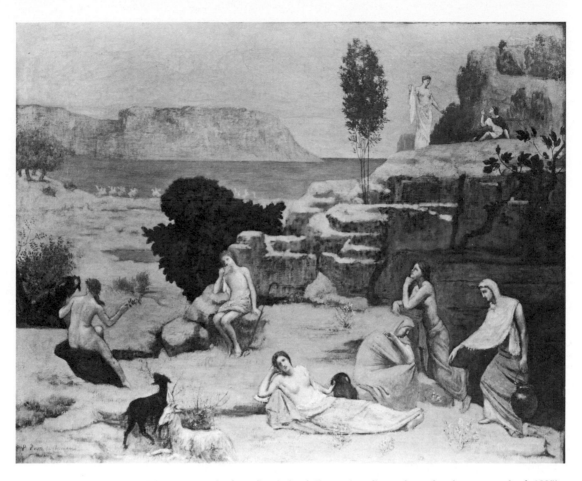

PUVIS DE CHAVANNES: *A Vision of Antiquity—Symbol of Form* (small version of a large mural of 1885). 41½ x 52″. Museum of Art, Carnegie Institute, Pittsburgh

tired. In painting as in literature a moment came... when we had enough and too much of realism, enough and too much of so-called verity, and of that harsh relief (or modeling), and of that blinding color with which some endeavor to overwhelm us. We were struck by a thirst for dreams, for emotions, for poetry. Satiated with light too vivid and too crude, we longed for fog. And it was then that we attached ourselves passionately to the poetic and misty art of Puvis de Chavannes. We liked even its worst mistakes, even its faulty drawing and its lack of color, so weary were we of admiring in other painters what we took naïvely to be drawing and color. Thus the art of Puvis de Chavannes became for us something like a cure; we clung to it as patients cling to a new treatment."[38]

But this statement does not quite do justice to Puvis, for to many symbolists his art meant more than just a lesser evil. The self-imposed restrictions of his means, combined with a strange mixture of naïveté and sophistication, contained indeed many features akin to literary symbolism, although Puvis, like Moreau, disclaimed any link with it. Together with Moreau he had striven, though in an entirely different way, to understand, as Albert

149

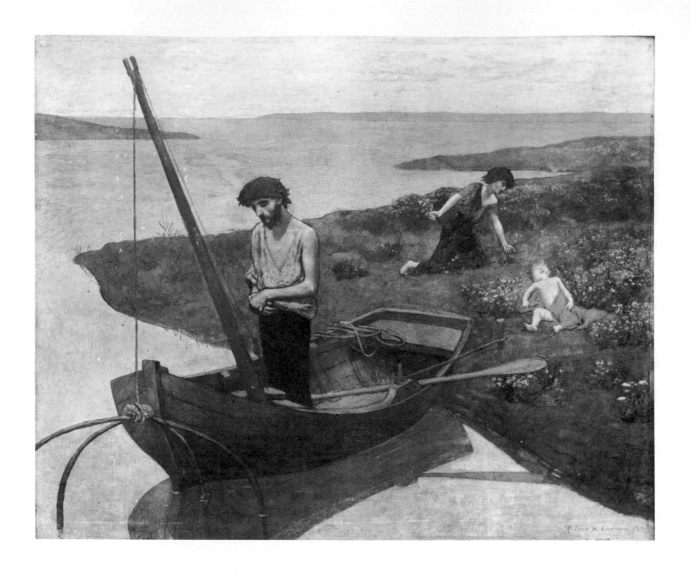

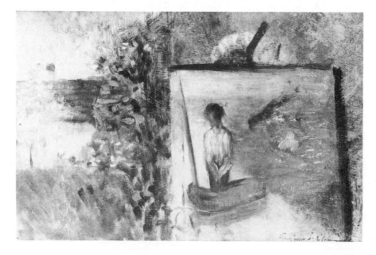

Above: PUVIS DE CHAVANNES: *The Poor Fisher-man,* d. 1881. 59⅞ × 75″. Exhibited at the Salon of 1881. Musée du Louvre, Paris

Left: SEURAT: *Copy after Puvis de Chavannes' "Poor Fisherman,"* c. 1881. Oil on wood, 6¾ × 10½″. Private collection, Paris

Opposite: HODLER: *The Night,* 1890. 41¾ × 118″. Exhibited in Paris in 1891. Kunstmuseum, Bern

Aurier put it, "the mysterious significance of lines, of lights, and of shadows, so as to use these elements, which one might call alphabetical, to write the beautiful poems of their dreams and their ideas."[39]

The efforts of Puvis de Chavannes acted most effectively as a "cure" upon the artists of the younger generation, not excluding Gauguin who, despite strong objections to Puvis' excessively literary allegories, professed real respect for the painter. Vincent van Gogh liked Puvis' works almost as much as he liked those by his idol Delacroix, while Angrand actually preferred Puvis' murals, simple and without oppositions, to those of Delacroix, more tormented and full of contrasts. He explained that the neo-impressionists, considering the simplicity of their colors, likewise needed simple gestures of calmness and nobility.[40] Seurat also admired the arrangement of Puvis' compositions, though he himself went much farther than Puvis in his methodical research into the meaning of lines. In spite of the fact that Lautrec had mocked Puvis' *Sacred Wood*, he too was impressed by the muralist's art. There is no denying that most of his contemporaries found in Puvis' work some means both of overcoming the tradition of academic art and of going beyond the recent achievements of impressionism. To them Puvis was not only a link with the Italian primitives, but also a guide in their endeavor to translate the language of the past into an idiom of their own day. And so Seurat had done a sketch after Puvis, Gauguin was to copy one of his paintings in the background of a still life, and many other young painters tried to acquaint themselves more thoroughly with his style by copying Puvis' works. Among them was a youthful student at the Ecole des Beaux-Arts, Aristide Maillol.

Puvis de Chavannes and Seurat were not the only ones to explore the psychological meaning of linear directions. In Switzerland, Ferdinand Hodler worked during the 'eighties on a theory of parallelism which consisted chiefly of rhythmic repetitions of certain lines and curves throughout his large compositions. Hodler first attracted attention in Paris when he exhibited his *Night* at the Salon of 1891. While his colors were much brighter than those of Puvis, his contours were also much more stylized. Congealed in solemn gestures, his figures seem to reveal their emotions with the studied attitudes of actors. The necessity

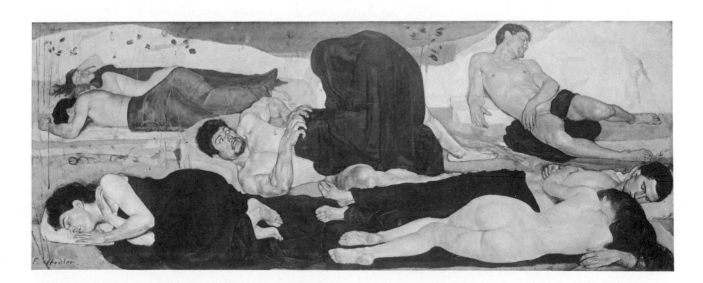

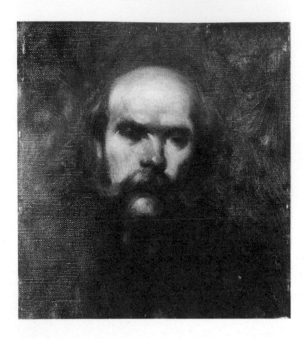

of subordinating these figures to the parallels with which Hodler strove to underline his message, made them appear like prisoners of their roles who were never quite permitted to express their own feelings. Hodler stripped his symbols to their essentials and by the same token always came dangerously near exaggerating sentiment as well as form.

Altogether renouncing line and color as means of expression, Eugène Carrière set out to satisfy the longing for a "misty art" of which Wyzewa had spoken. The colorless vapors out of which he modeled his images offered literary-minded onlookers a welcome occasion to supply in their own imagination all that the artist had left unsaid. Having invented a formula that met with success, Carrière exploited it to the utmost, vulgarizing symbolism without adding anything to it. While poets and critics raved about his work, Fénéon was the only one to point out, and with good reason, that "if a man like Mallarmé sometimes tried to create a sensation of mystery, he always did so with words of great clarity, regulated by an inescapable and unifying syntax."[41] Carrière's mysteries were obtained with obvious devices; his place is not among the truly symbolist painters. But Carrière was a kind and generous man, widely respected in the art world.

Though there was by no means unanimity among the literary symbolists concerning the artistic merits of Odilon Redon, he was the only painter of their day whose concepts and work actually paralleled theirs. Born in 1840, he was somewhat younger than Puvis and Moreau, and belonged in fact to the generation of the impressionists, being of the same age as Monet, Renoir, and Sisley. Although a great admirer of Delacroix and one of the first to recognize Pissarro's talent, Redon had never associated himself with the impressionists, explaining that he considered their art somewhat "low of ceiling." But when Guillaumin, whom he had met at the Independents, invited him in 1886 to show with the impressionist group, Redon accepted, although two years previously he had participated in the creation of the Société des Indépendants and had been for some time its vice-president.

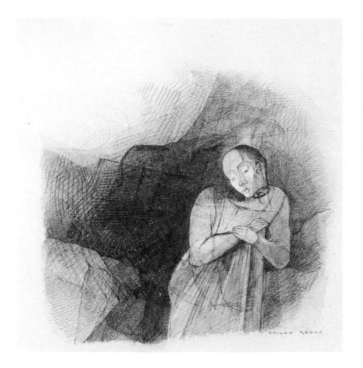

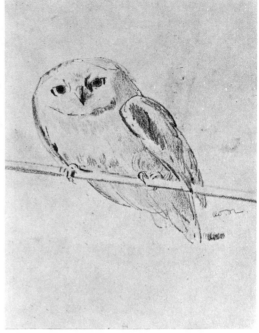

Redon: *Apparition,* c. 1870–75. Pencil, 7¾ x 7½″ (image). Collection Mr. and Mrs. Jack Butler, New York

Redon: *Owl,* c. 1890. Pencil, 10 x 7¼″. Private collection, New York

Redon had always stressed the role of imagination in art. As early as 1868 he had written in a Salon review: "... Some people insist upon the restriction of the painter's work to the reproduction of what he sees. Those who remain within these narrow limits commit themselves to an inferior goal. The old masters have proved that the artist, once he has established his own idiom, once he has taken from nature the necessary means of expression, is free, legitimately free, to borrow his subjects from history, from the poets, from his own imagination...."[42] And he had emphasized: "While I recognize the necessity for a basis of observed reality... true art lies in a reality that is felt."[43]

This continued to be his credo. With great and loving care he scrutinized nature, drew plants and trees with all their details, studied animals, human beings, and landscapes, and from this work there was finally to evolve a language of his own, a language suited to the translation of the strange world of his visions. Soon, observed and felt reality became intimately interlocked in his mind and work. He himself explained their peculiar relationship when he wrote to a friend: "... I have always felt the need to copy nature in small objects, particularly the casual or accidental. It is only after making an effort of will power to represent with minute care a grass blade, a stone, a branch, the face of an old wall, that I am overcome by the irresistible urge to create something imaginary. External nature, thus assimilated and measured, becomes, by transformation, my source, my ferment. To the moments following such exercises I owe my best works."[44]

Redon always insisted that his imagination had its roots in the observation of nature, that his drawings were "true," that the fantastic beings he created, the haunting visions

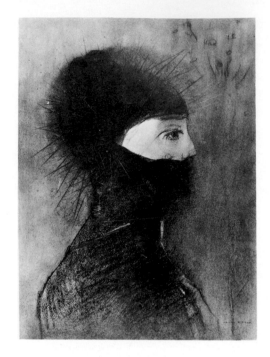

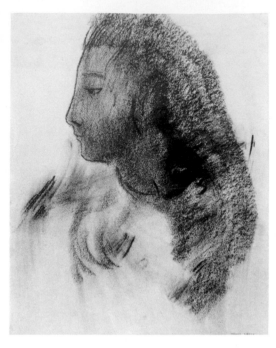

REDON: *Armor,* 1891. Charcoal, 19⅞ x 15″.
The Metropolitan Museum of Art, New York

REDON: *Profile,* c. 1890. Charcoal, 17⅞ x 14½″.
Rijksmusem Kröller-Müller, Otterlo

he translated into black and white, belonged to a world that was never absolutely detached from reality. According to his own words: "My originality consists in bringing to life, in a human way, improbable beings and making them live according to the laws of probability, by putting—as far as possible—the logic of the visible at the service of the invisible."[45] This he could achieve because the objects of his nightmares were not merely elaborate inventions like those of Moreau, nor were they carefully polished images like those of Puvis—they were things he had actually seen with his mind's eye. Thus he was able to record them in a purely pictorial language, attaining mysterious effects through lines, color, and composition without borrowing too many symbols from literature, though he did sequences of lithographs and drawings inspired by Poe and Flaubert. To him poetry was not something achieved with a play of lines only, an assembly of colors; poetry was an inherent part of his imagination, of his vision. He did not have to search for the plastic equivalents of his emotions because his work was not a translation of ideas from one medium into another. Redon lived in a world of beautiful and disquieting dreams that were indistinguishable from reality. Since to him they were real, he hardly bothered to investigate their meaning; all he desired was to express them with the most voluptuous colors, the most powerful or subtle oppositions of black and white.

But it was not easy in a period of naturalism and rationalism to find a public for creations which explored the secrets of a mind that seemed both tormented and serene. As had to be expected, those who witnessed with apprehension the emergence of literary symbolism felt equally uneasy about Redon's art. The still powerful group of literary naturalists,

154

REDON: *Spider,* c. 1881. Charcoal, 19½ × 15⅜″. Musée du Louvre, Paris

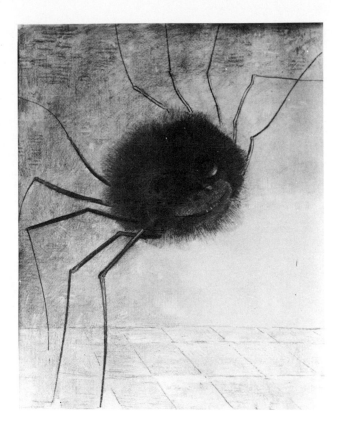

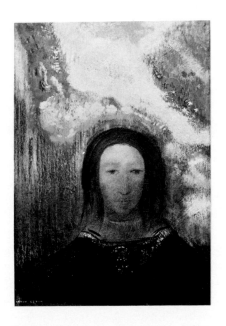

REDON: *Reverie,* c. 1900. Pastel, 21¼ × 14½. Private collection, Japan

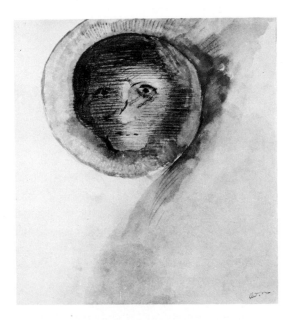

REDON: *Mysterious Head,* c. 1910. Watercolor, 7¼ × 6⅜″. Collection Ian Woodner, New York

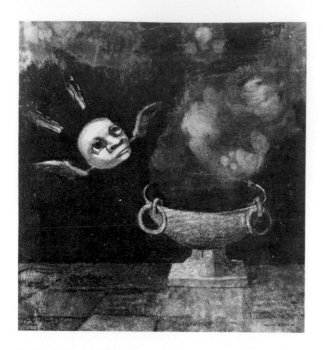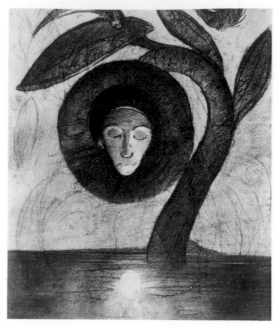

REDON: *Incense Burner,* d. 1880. Charcoal, 13⅜ x 12¼″. Collection R. Dreyfus, Basel

REDON: *Marsh Flower,* 1885. Charcoal, 16¾ x 14″. Private collection, New York

gathered around Emile Zola, was by no means ready to abandon its fight for supremacy, shaken though it was by the defection of Huysmans, who later explained why he had deserted Zola's circle: "There were many things which Zola could not understand; first the need I felt to open the windows [Redon was to use a very similar expression], to flee from a milieu in which I suffocated; then the desire which overtook me to shake prejudices, shatter the limits of the novel, open it to art, science, history, in a word to use it only as a framework into which more serious works could be inserted. That was what struck me most at that time, to suppress the traditional intrigue, even passion, even women, and to concentrate my brush dipped into light on a single figure, to create at any price something new [these are almost Seurat's words]."[46]

For having done something similar, with a brush "dipped into tenebrae," Redon automatically incurred the wrath of the naturalists. One of their most articulate spokesmen, Octave Mirbeau, a long-time companion of Zola and a friend and admirer of the impressionists, in 1886 went over to the attack when he wrote a violent article against Redon (who was then preparing to participate in the last impressionist group show):

"After innumerable battles, all pacific by the way and in which only ink was spattered, everybody agrees that it is necessary for art to approach nature. . . . Among painters there is hardly anybody except M. Odilon Redon who resists the great naturalist current and who opposes the thing dreamed to the thing experienced, the ideal to the truth. Thus M. Odilon Redon draws for you an eye which floats, at the end of a stem, in an amorphous landscape. And the commentators assemble. Some will tell you that this eye exactly represents the eye of Conscience, others the eye of Incertitude; some will explain that this

156

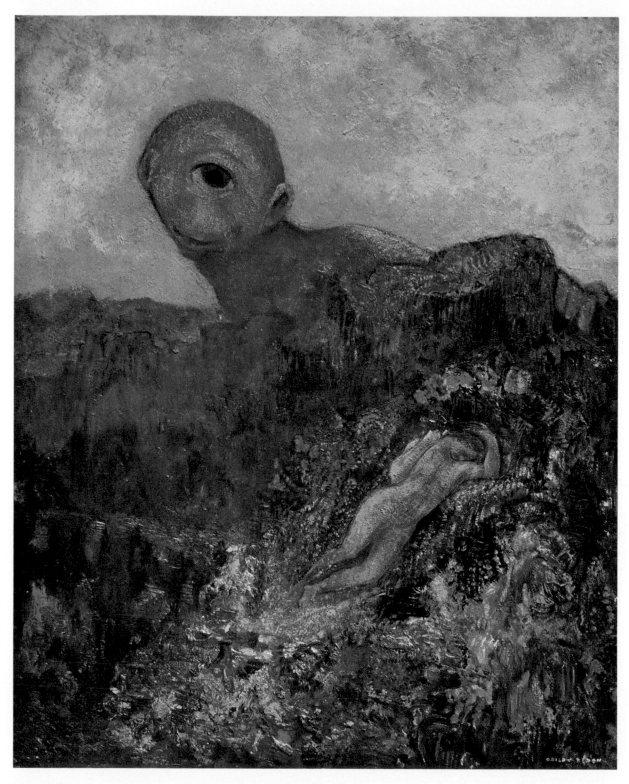

REDON: *Cyclops*, c. 1898. 25¼ x 20". Rijksmuseum Kröller-Müller, Otterlo

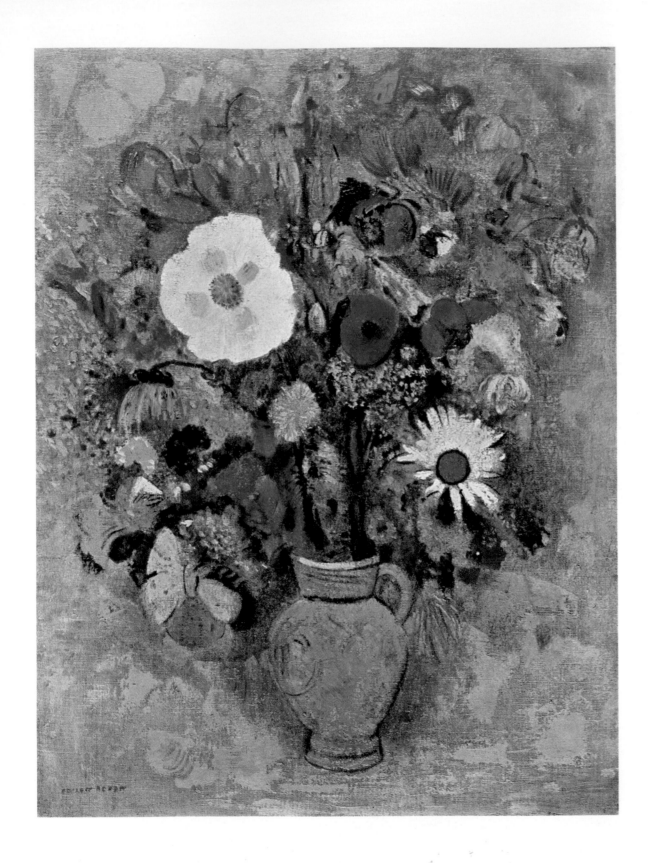

158

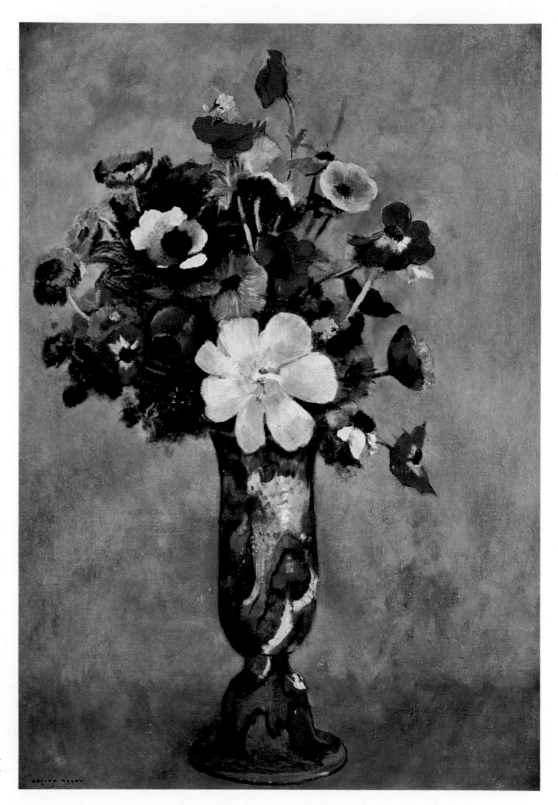

Opposite: REDON: *Flowers in a Vase*. c. 1905. Collection Mrs. Donald S. Stralem, New York

REDON: *Vase with Anemones*, 1912–14. 29 x 20″. Private collection, New York

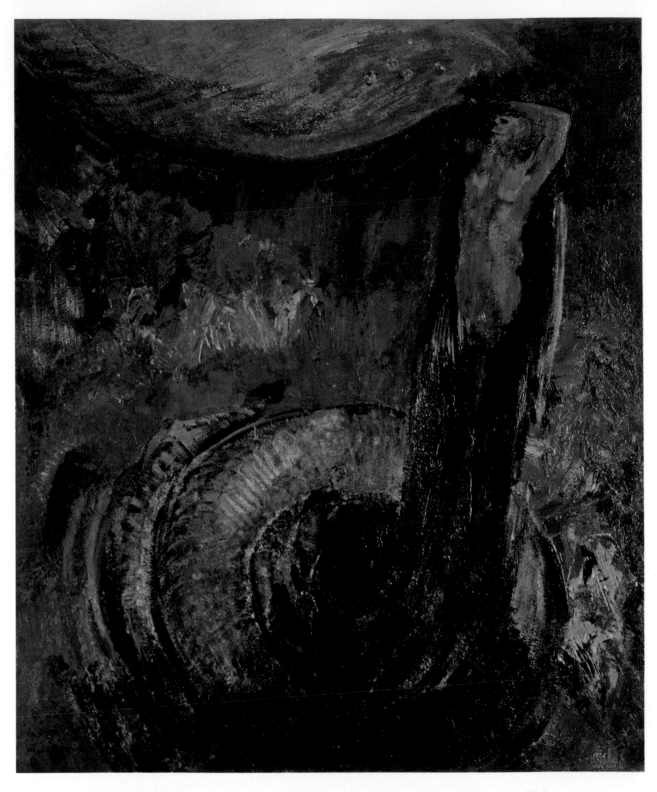

REDON : *Green Death,* after 1905. Oil on cardboard, 22⅜ x 18¾″. Collection Mrs. Bertram Smith, New York

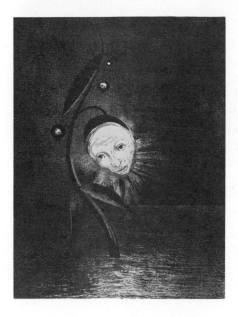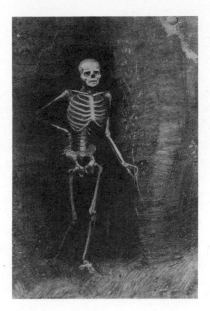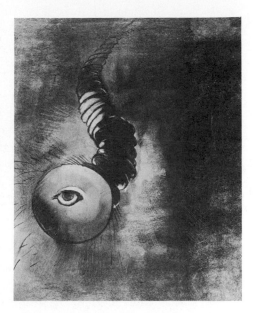

Left: Redon: *Marsh Flower,* 1885. Lithograph, 11 x 8¼". The Art Institute of Chicago (Elizabeth Stickney Collection). Center: Redon: *Skeleton,* c. 1885. Charcoal, 18¾ x 12¼". Collection Mr. and Mrs. James W. Alsdorf, Winnetka, Ill. Right: Redon: *Phantom,* c. 1885. Charcoal, 16 x 13". Collection Mr. and Mrs. Leonard Bernheim, Jr., New York

eye synthesizes a setting sun over hyperborean seas, others that it symbolizes universal sorrow, a bizarre water lily about to blossom on the black waters of invisible Acherons. A supreme exegete arrives and concludes: 'This eye at the end of a stem is simply a necktie pin.' The very essence of the ideal is that it evokes nothing but vague forms which might just as well be magic lakes as sacred elephants, extra-terrestrial flowers as well as necktie pins, unless they are nothing at all. Yet, we demand today that whatever is represented must be precise, we want the figures that emanate from an artist's brain to move and think and live."[47]

Before he thus became a center of controversy, Redon had labored for many years without attracting much attention or without even seeking to make himself known. His first album of lithographs—a medium in which he produced some of his most important works—had appeared in 1879, when he was almost forty. His first modest one-man show took place in 1881 in the offices of the weekly *La Vie Moderne* and was not even advertised in the paper itself. Yet Huysmans took some notice of it. When, the following year, Redon exhibited again, this time in a newspaper office, a young critic, Emile Hennequin, who subsequently became one of Seurat's most outspoken adversaries, was seized with admiration. He interviewed the artist and immediately published a long article on him. "From now on," he wrote, "M. Odilon Redon should be considered as one of our masters and—for those who value above all this touch of strangeness without which, according to Francis Bacon, there is no exquisite beauty—as an outstanding master who, Goya excepted, has no ancestors or emulators. He has succeeded in conquering, somewhere on the border between reality and fantasy, a desolate domain which he peopled with formidable ghosts, monsters, monads, composite beings made of every possible human perversity, bestial baseness, and of all kinds of terrors of inert and noxious things.... As much as Baudelaire, M. Redon deserves the superb praise of having created *'un frisson nouveau.'*"[48]

No wonder then that the symbolist writers, who acknowledged Baudelaire's inspiration, should now discover the originality of Redon, should now acclaim him as one of their own. The rising symbolist movement was creating the necessary climate in which Redon could at last be appreciated. To his work Huysmans devoted long descriptions which, though they reveal more about their author than about Redon, nevertheless contributed greatly to the painter's renown. Wrote Huysmans: "If we except Goya... [and] Gustave Moreau, of whom Redon is, after all, in the healthy parts of his work, a very distant pupil, we shall find his ancestry only among musicians perhaps and certainly among poets."[49] In speaking of the "healthy" part of the artist's work, Huysmans seemed to imply that there was also an unhealthy one: that sickishness to which Wyzewa was so sensitive. As a matter of fact Huysmans had already stated in *A Rebours* that Redon's drawings "were outside of any known category; most of them leap beyond the boundaries of painting, innovating a very special fantasy, a fantasy of sickness and delirium."[6] It may have been partly this that attracted many of the symbolist poets, for indeed Redon now found himself the object of a kind of interested praise that sometimes sprang less from an understanding of his art than from an approval of his tendencies.

Redon felt a little awkward in the midst of his new admirers, unable to satisfy them with the precepts and theories of which the symbolists were so fond. "I am supposed to have much more of an analytical mind than I really have," Redon confided in 1888 to his notebook; "this would at least account for the curiosity that I feel in the young writers who visit me. In contact with me I see them at first somewhat surprised. What did I put into my work to suggest so much subtlety? I placed in it a little door opening on mystery. I made fiction. It is for them to go further."[50]

By opening a door to mystery, Redon did precisely what Mallarmé accused the Parnassian poets of having failed to achieve when he declared: "They lack mystery; they deprive minds of that delicious joy which is to believe that they create."[51] Redon, on the contrary, invited minds to enhance the images he offered them. Whereas Moreau imprisoned the observer's imagination in a profusion of detail, and Puvis guided it towards austere simplifications, Redon knew how to be vague without being vaporous like Carrière; he knew how to suggest moods without being precise, how to indicate things without defining them, always provoking a deep but indescribable impression, like that created by music.

The effect produced by Redon's work was not a result of his creative invention alone, for there were many others who now endeavored to break away from everyday reality. To their ranks had just come James Ensor of the Brussels **XX**, who after a series of sensitive but mildly impressionist works began to give free rein to his fancy. In 1888 he completed his enormous canvas *Christ Entering Brussels* which, if van de Velde's barb were to be given credence, had been inspired by the intention to impress the crowds with a composition even larger than Seurat's *Grande Jatte*. But Ensor's imagination remained pedestrian and never quite spread its wings wide enough to take off from the ground. His subject matter, for all its singularity, always kept close to the anecdotal, and his paintings merely seemed to illustrate incidents cleverly contrived by the artist. The special nature of his inventiveness kept his imagination within the bounds of the grotesque. There was none of the element of the inescapable that seemed always to guide Redon's hand, and that endowed even his naturalistic bouquets of flowers with a mysterious charm. Redon's fertile

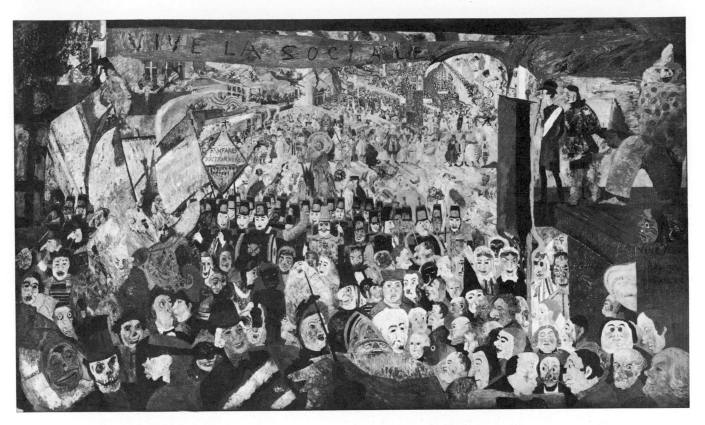

ENSOR: *Christ Entering Brussels in 1889*. 1888. 8'5½" x 14'1½". Casino Communal, Knokke-le-Zoute, Belgium

imagination, and his alone, was able to confer upon the strange, sweet, and haunting unrealities of dreams an authenticity of their own. One of the reasons for this was of course his ability to heed the call of his imagination without breaking its spell. As Redon explained himself: "Nothing is achieved in art by will power alone. Everything is done through docile submission to the 'unconscious.'"[52]

In 1889, when he assembled a series of art studies in his book *Certains*, Huysmans once more praised the works of Redon—particularly his lithographs—as well as those of Moreau, Puvis de Chavannes, Whistler, Degas, Chéret, Raffaëlli, and even Cézanne. (While he wrote of Cézanne with some reservations, Huysmans at least was the first to publicly express admiration for his still lifes and to state that the painter had contributed more than Manet to the evolution of impressionism.)

Though some of the symbolist writers did remain impervious to Redon's art, many of them were attracted by his esotericism, his profound originality, his delicate mysticism, his disquieting imagination. It is a fact that Huysmans, Hennequin, Wyzewa, and others who had remained insensitive to Seurat's innovations, expressed great admiration for Redon. Charles Morice, Paul Adam, Albert Aurier, and Gustave Kahn also praised his work, thus breaking the stubborn silence that had surrounded his efforts for so long. And Mallarmé himself sensed and appreciated the artistic and intellectual qualities that linked

163

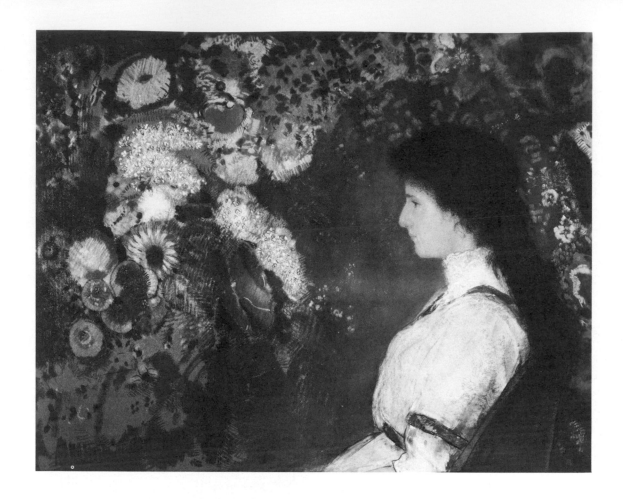

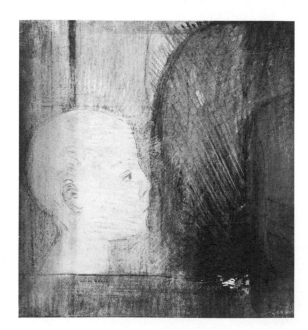

Above: REDON: *Portrait of Mlle Violette H.*, 1910.
Pastel, 28⅜ x 36⅜". The Cleveland Museum of
Art (Hinman B. Hurlbut Collection)

REDON: *Child and Aurora Borealis* (the artist's
son), 1894. Pastel, 11 x 10⅝". Formerly in the collection of Stéphane Mallarmé. Musée des Beaux-
Arts, Dijon (Collection Pierre Granville)

164

Redon to symbolism. A mutual sympathy and admiration soon formed the basis for their friendship. It was apparently Huysmans who introduced Redon to Mallarmé in 1882–83; some five years later Redon began to spend his summers at Samois near Valvins, on the outskirts of the Fontainebleau forest, where Mallarmé had his house and where the two men saw each other almost daily. Mallarmé loved to contemplate Redon's lithographs without ever "exhausting the impression created by each, so far goes the sincerity of your vision, no less than your power to stir it in others!" as he once told the artist.[53] The poet was moved when he discovered in one of Redon's creatures a "delightfully mad hermit, the poor little man that in the depths of my soul I should like to be." At the same time some of the strangeness of Mallarmé's syntax and vocabulary pervaded Redon's own writings; his notes, letters, and diaries are written in a poetic vernacular that can compare favorably with that of many symbolist writers. Mallarmé actually told Redon that he envied the captions with which he accompanied his prints.[54]

While it seemed natural that the symbolists should not escape the appeal of Redon's art, it is a startling fact that no painters of his own generation showed any interest in it or understanding of it. Gustave Moreau announced with condescension: "I see kind and gentle people like M. Redon, who is sincere and certainly shows a development of the intellect that is by no means banal.... But, after all, what sad results!"[55] Even the younger generation of painters was slow to appreciate Redon. The first to become aware of his true importance seems to have been Emile Bernard, who had tried unsuccessfully to rally van Gogh to his views. An admirer of Redon's work for some time, he managed about 1889, when he was barely twenty-one years old, to be introduced to the painter by his friend Schuffenecker. He was well received by Redon who was as yet quite unaccustomed to being treated with "the enthusiastic respect one feels for genius."[56]

Even Mirbeau's hostility was eventually overcome. Ten years after his acid attack he was to write to Redon: "... at first I dismissed you, not for your craftsmanship which I always found to be superb, but for your philosophy. Today there is no artist for whom I feel the impassioned admiration I feel for you, because there is none who has opened to my mind such distant, such luminous, such grievous vistas on the mysterious, that is, on the only real life."[57]

That Redon found a slowly increasing audience in the 'nineties was due as much to Bernard's infectious admiration as to the growing impact of literary symbolism.[58]

NOTES

1 J. Moréas: Le Symbolisme, *Figaro Littéraire*, Sept. 18, 1886.

2 P. Adam: La Presse et le symbolisme, *Le Symboliste*, Oct. 7, 1886.

3 The concept of "analogies" had played a key role in the esthetics and metaphysics of French literary and visual symbolism from the time of Baudelaire. Rimbaud had established analogies between vowels and colors and the symbolist poets emphasized the analogies between words, sounds, and moods. Henry's research into the significance of lines and colors was an extension of their efforts into the visual field, while van Gogh in a similar vein—though empirically—explored the symbolic qualities of colors. A little later, inspired by this same predilection for analogies, Gauguin began to stress the musical side of his art. Poets and painters alike endeavored to convey feelings and ideas through analogies rather than through direct representation.

4 G. Kahn: Réponse des symbolistes, *L'Evénement*, Sept. 28, 1886.

5 See F. Viélé-Griffin: Le Journal Lutèce, *L'Occident*, Feb. 1903.

6 J.-K. Huysmans: A Rebours, Paris, 1884; English translation: Against the Grain.

7 H. de Régnier in *Ecrits pour l'Art*, no. 6, June 7, 1887.

8 Anonymous [A. Baju?]: Aux Lecteurs, *Le Décadent*, no. 1, April 10, 1886.

9 On the *Revue Wagnérienne* see I. de Wyzewa: La Revue Wagnérienne, Paris, 1934. On Wyzewa see: E. Liverman-Duval: Téodor de Wyzewa—Critic without a Country, Paris-Geneva, 1961.

10 Mallarmé in *La Vogue*, no. 2, 1886.

11 On symbolist periodicals see: Le Mouvement symboliste, catalogue of an exhibition at the Bibliothèque Nationale, Paris, 1936, by A. Jaulme and H. Moncel.

12 See M.J. Durry: Jules Laforgue, Paris, 1952, p. 11. (This book contains a complete list of Laforgue's writings as well as an excellent bibliography.)

13 G.Kahn later wrote: "In 1886 and in the following years we paid more attention to our literary development than to the pace of the world." He also stated: "The first criterion, the only one, was to satisfy myself; in so doing, I was certain to please, either immediately or after an unforeseeable time, those of my kind, and that was enough for me." Kahn: Les Origines du symbolisme, 1879–1888, Revue Blanche, Nov. 1, 1901.

14 Jack Plowert [Paul Adam]: Petit Glossaire pour servir à l'intelligence des auteurs décadents et symbolistes, Paris, 1888. Fénéon did not collaborate in the editing of this publication, as it is sometimes stated, though many examples are drawn from his writings, as well as from those of Kahn, Moréas, Laforgue, and Mallarmé.

15 T. de Wyzewa: La Littérature Wagnérienne, Revue Wagnérienne, June 1886.

16 See J.E.S.Jeanès: D'après nature, Geneva-Besançon, 1946, p. 204.

17 See R. Doumic: Téodor de Wyzewa, Revue des Deux Mondes, Sept. 15, 1917.

18 See J. Rewald: Félix Fénéon, Gazette des Beaux-Arts, July–Aug. 1947 and Feb. 1948.

19 W.Rothenstein: Men and Memories, New York, 1931, vol. I. p. 95.

20 M. Aymé: Le Confort intellectuel, Paris, 1949, p. 13.

21 Anonymous [F. Fénéon]: L'Exposition Pissarro, L'Art Moderne, Jan. 20, 1889.

22 On the anarchist movement see A. Zevaès: Histoire de la 3e République, 1870–1925, Paris, 1926; J. Grave: Le Mouvement libertaire sous la 3e République, Paris, 1930; F. Dubois: Le Péril anarchiste, Paris, 1894. Of the unsigned reproductions in this last book, those on pp. 3, 31, 47, 67, 116, 123, 163, 195, 211, 229, 243, and 277 were drawn by Camille Pissarro's sons Lucien, Georges, Félix, and Rodo; those on pp. 13, 17, 37, 85, 87, 161, 175, 187, 197, 205, 217, 237, 271, and 279 are by Luce: the one on p. 93 is by Ibels. Information courtesy the late Rodo Pissarro, Paris.

23 C. Pissarro, undated letter to his nephew; unpublished document, courtesy the late Mrs. Esther L. Pissarro, London. See also E. Nicolson: The Anarchism of Pissarro, The Arts, 1949, vol. II.

24 Signac, excerpts from a reply to a questionnaire, see Dubois, op. cit., pp. 233 and 240.

25 See G.Kahn: Laurent Tailhade, Revue Blanche, Oct. 1, 1901.

26 See D. Rouart: Autour de Berthe Morisot, Paris, 1950.

27 E.Dujardin: Le Cloisonnisme, Revue Indépendante, May 19, 1888. Sections from this article have been mistakenly included in Fénéon: Oeuvres, Paris, 1948, pp. 55–56.

28 J.-K. Huysmans: Salon de 1880, in L'Art moderne, Paris, 1883, p. 152.

29 Moreau quoted by C. Chassé: Le Mouvement symboliste dans l'art du XIXe siècle, Paris, 1947, p. 36.

30 G. Kahn: Les Dessins de Seurat, Paris, 1926, introduction. Mr. Robert Herbert of Yale University has kindly provided me with the following additional information concerning Henry's influence on symbolist poets: "In his theory of poetry (see preface to Premiers Poèmes, 1897) Kahn explains the use of dynamogenic and inhibitory impulses in verse, assonance, continuity, and other elements of rhythm and structure, which leave no doubt that he was influenced by his friend's Cercle Chromatique of 1888. In this book, Henry analyzes language and music much as he did color, his theories of perceptual psychology being at the base of his studies of all three arts: painting, poetry, and music. Kahn relates mood and emotion to sound and rhythm just as does Henry."

31 T. de Wyzewa: L'Art contemporain, Revue Indépendante, Nov.–Dec. 1886.

32 J.-K. Huysmans: Chronique d'art, Revue Indépendante, April 1887.

33 Wyzewa quoted by R. Doumic, op. cit.

34 Strindberg to Gauguin, Paris, Feb. 1, 1895; see J. de Rotonchamp: Paul Gauguin, Paris, 1925, p. 151.

35 G. Kahn: Silhouettes littéraires, Paris, 1925, p. 112.

36 See R. Goldwater: Puvis de Chavannes, Some Reasons for a Reputation, Art Bulletin, March 1946.

37 Puvis de Chavannes quoted by C. Chassé, op. cit., p. 42.

38 Wyzewa: Puvis de Chavannes, 1894, in Peintres de jadis et d'aujourd'hui, Paris, 1903, p. 369.

39 A. Aurier: Les Symbolistes, Revue Encyclopédique, April 1892.

40 See P. Signac, Journal, Nov. 27, 1894, Gazette des Beaux-Arts, July–Sept. 1949.

41 Fénéon: Exposition Carrière, Le Chat Noir, April 25, 1891; reprinted in Oeuvres, p. 185.

42 Redon: Le Salon de 1868, La Gironde, May 19, 1868.

43 Ibid., June 9, 1868.

44 Redon: Confidences d'artiste, L'Art Moderne, August 25, 1894; reprinted in: A soi-même, Paris, 1922, p. 11–30.

45 Redon: A soi-même, p. 29.

46 Huysmans: A Rebours [new edition], Foreword written twenty years after the novel, 1903.

47 O. Mirbeau: L'Art et la nature, Le Gaulois, April 26, 1886.

48 E. Hennequin: Odilon Redon, Revue Littéraire et Artistique, March 4, 1882, quoted by A. Mellerio: Odilon Redon, Paris, 1913. See also J.Rewald: Quelques notes et documents sur Odilon Redon, Gazette des Beaux-Arts, Nov. 1956.

49 Huysmans: L'Art moderne, Paris, 1883, appendix.

50 Redon: A soi-même (note written in 1888), p. 89.

51 Mallarmé to Huret: Enquête sur l'évolution littéraire, 1891, quoted by C. Chassé, op. cit., p. 47.

52 Redon quoted by C. Fegdal: Odilon Redon, Paris, 1929, p. 54.

53 Mallarmé to Redon [spring 1885?], quoted by H. Mondor: Vie de Mallarmé, Paris, 1941, p. 453.

54 See Mallarmé's letter to Redon, Nov. 10, 1891, reproduced in Maandblad voor Beeldende Kunsten, Oct. 1948.

55 Moreau quoted by C. Chassé, op. cit., p. 32.

56 E. Bernard: Odilon Redon, in: Recueil de lettres à Emile Bernard, Tonnerre, 1925–27, p. 103

57 Mirbeau added: "I do believe, and I cannot think of any higher praise, I believe that I have understood and loved you from the day on which I [first] suffered." Mirbeau to Redon [1896]; see Lettres à Odilon Redon, Paris, 1960, p. 249.

58 See Rewald, op. cit., note 48 above.

IV   1888   GAUGUIN
BERNARD
VAN GOGH
BRITTANY AND PROVENCE

When Emile Bernard arrived at Pont-Aven early in August 1888, accompanied by his mother and younger sister, he immediately went to see Gauguin, with whom Vincent van Gogh had advised him to get better acquainted. This time Gauguin gave him a much friendlier reception than two years before. He came to look at Bernard's work, seemed impressed by it, and struck up a firm friendship with the young painter. It is true that Gauguin had also cast an eye upon Madeleine, Bernard's seventeen-year-old sister.

Pont-Aven was a fairly large Breton village with old slate-roofed houses, huddled in the fold of a valley near the Aven river, the rapid waters of which provided motive power for several mills. Craggy hills surrounded the village. Small paths led across them to a fertile upland with farms, chapels, and little woods. From their heights one could see the sand-covered gulf towards which rushed the river. It was not a particularly varied landscape, yet it had a character of peacefulness to which the almost superstitiously devout Catholicism of the peasants in their picturesque Breton costumes added a touch of medieval mysticism.

Pont-Aven had for some years attracted a number of artists: Scandinavians, Americans, Englishmen, and Italians, as well as Frenchmen. Gauguin had gone there first in 1886, partly to get away from Paris and to find a more primitive atmosphere, partly out of "sadness," as he said, and because he longed for quiet and solitude, but also for the very practical reason that life was much cheaper in Brittany than anywhere else. He paid sixty-five francs a month for room and board. Gauguin avoided association with the other painters, most of whom were pupils of such official masters as Cormon, or of the so-called Académie Julian. Yet the others had been intrigued by his unorthodox canvases, and Gauguin had proudly informed his wife: "My work gives rise to many discussions and I must say that it is rather favorably received by the Americans."[1]

Gauguin was then still painting according to the impressionist concepts instilled in him by Pissarro. Though he was at that time primarily interested in purely technical problems, he also seems to have spoken frequently of his desire to achieve a *synthesis*.[2] But nothing in his work showed as yet any radical break with the general principles he had derived from his mentor. However, Gauguin now made experiments in a direction that led away from Pissarro and showed traces of the influence of both Degas and Cézanne, which appears most clearly in a still life with the profile of his young friend Charles Laval. The way in which Laval's head is cut off at the right openly proclaims Gauguin's indebtedness to Degas, while the simplification of the vigorously modeled fruits seems derived from Cézanne. In this still life also figures the somewhat mysterious form of one of the potteries which

Gauguin had begun to make with Chaplet in 1886. Altogether this canvas does indicate a certain departure from impressionism and a preoccupation with more ornamental design. But the vivid texture of small impressionistic brush strokes still prevails.

In Martinique, where Gauguin had gone in 1887 with the painter Laval, whose acquaintance he had made in Brittany, a definite evolution made itself felt in Gauguin's art. His composition began to show a slight Japanese influence and sometimes there appeared in his canvases large and comparatively uniform areas, especially when he included the dark blue ocean in his landscapes. Yet Gustave Kahn later wrote: "What he exhibited [in Theo van Gogh's gallery] upon his return in 1888 disappointed his admirers and the critics. They expected new conquests of color, more radiant and more violent effects of sunlight. In his paintings with their heavy and warm shadows the forms seemed purplish and black. He simplified the colors, contrasting them violently. Pissarro defended him and explained: in those hot countries forms were swallowed up by the light, the nuance did not exist, and therefore one could not think of rendering it but could proceed only through violent oppositions. Just the same, the exhibition had no success; the few collectors of Gauguin's work were disconcerted. This was neither pointillism nor even optical mixture, nor was it exactly an art which broke openly with all the impressionist ideas. People did

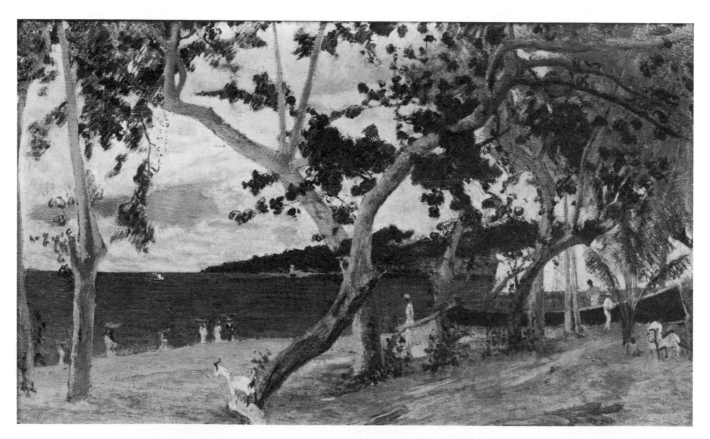

GAUGUIN: *Seashore at Martinique*, 1887. 21¼ x 35⅜". Ny Carlsberg Glyptotek, Copenhagen

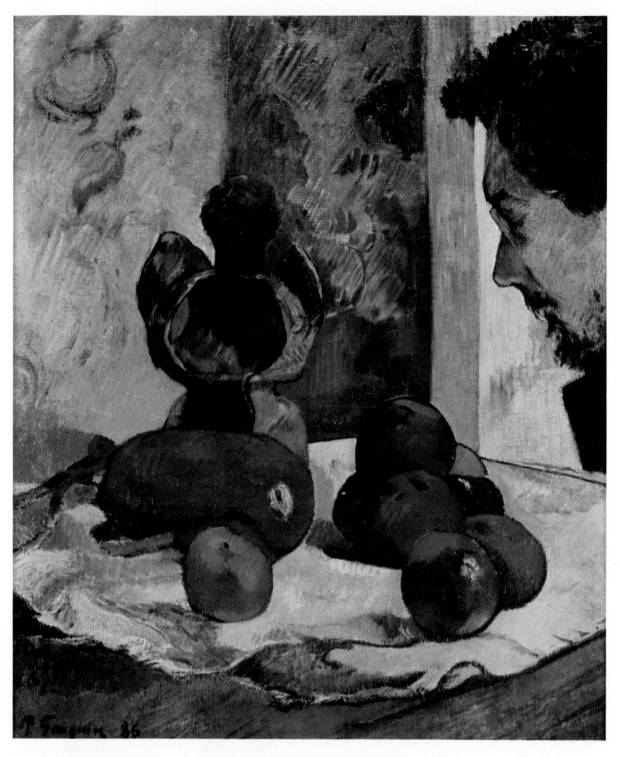

GAUGUIN: *Still Life with Portrait of Charles Laval*, d. 1886. 18⅛ x 15″. Collection Mr. and Mrs. Walter B. Ford II, Grosse Pointe, Mich.

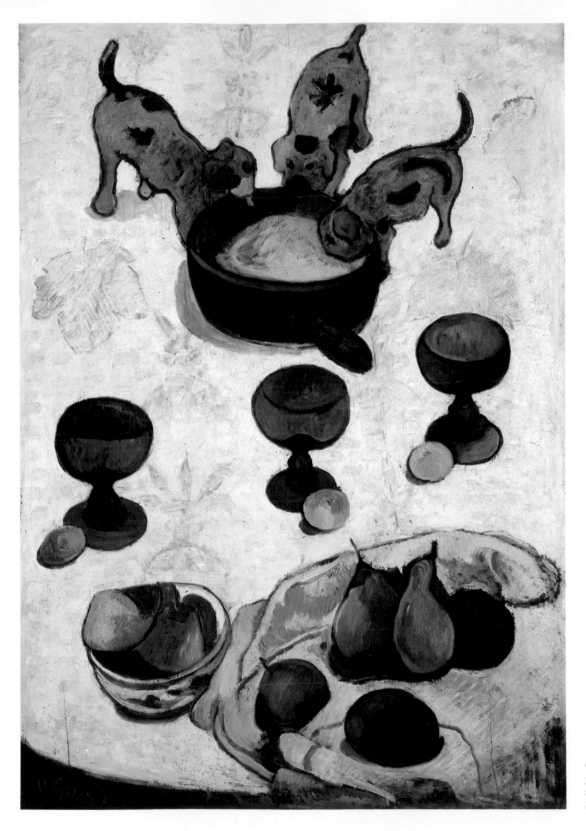

GAUGUIN: *Still Life with Three Puppies*, d. 1888. 36⅛ x 24⅝". The Museum of Modern Art, New York (Mrs. Simon Guggenheim Fund)

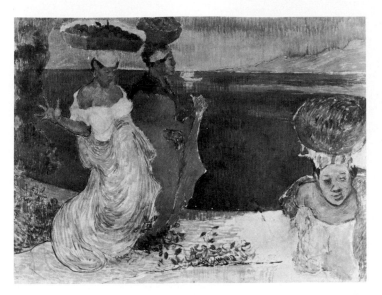

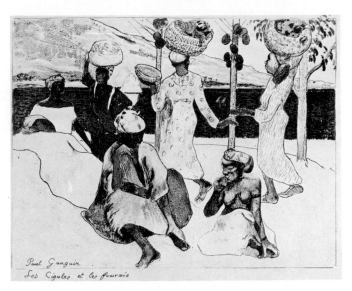

LAVAL: *Martinique, 1887. 25⅝ x 36¼".* Formerly collection Maurice Denis. Private collection, France

GAUGUIN: *The Grasshoppers and the Ants, Souvenir of Martinique,* c. 1889. Lithograph, 8 x 10¼". National Gallery of Art, Washington, D.C. (Lessing Rosenwald Collection)

not understand this foretaste of an evolution which, by the way, did not assert itself with any vigor...." But Kahn added: "Nevertheless this one-year trip had been of great esthetic benefit to Gauguin. He now began to change visibly."[3]

It was in his color schemes, no doubt, that Gauguin's contact with the tropics brought about the greatest change. His palette brightened, contrasts became more accentuated, the pale softness of earlier works slowly disappeared. There were not as yet, however, any very daring combinations of colors, any far-reaching simplifications of outlines.[4] As a matter of fact, what struck van Gogh most in his friend's canvases from Martinique was not so much their novelty as their general mood. "There's great poetry in his pictures of Negresses," van Gogh explained to Bernard. "Everything he does has something gentle, heart-rending, astonishing. People don't understand him yet, and he's very upset he doesn't sell—like other real poets."[5]

When Gauguin went back to Pont-Aven early in 1888—just a short time before van Gogh left Paris for Arles—he felt attracted once more by its simplicity and austere charm. Van Gogh would have liked to persuade Gauguin to accompany him to the South which held so much promise of color and romance, but Gauguin preferred to return to familar surroundings. "I love Brittany," he soon wrote to his friend Schuffenecker. "I find wildness and primitiveness there. When my wooden shoes ring on this granite, I hear the muffled, dull, and powerful tone which I try to achieve in painting."[6] Indeed, Gauguin's first paintings done in Pont-Aven after his return from Martinique appear muffled and dull, though by no means powerful. The subtleties acquired on the tropical island are altogether absent, and their lack cannot be wholly attributed to the difference of subject or the dissimilar aspect of the two places. It seems that at first Gauguin was not quite able to translate his impressions of Brittany in terms of his recent experience. But then it always

171

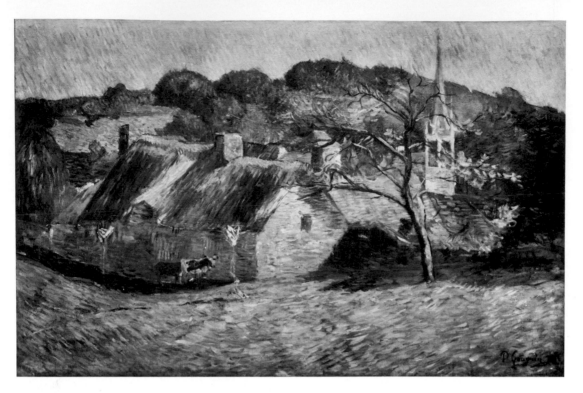

GAUGUIN: *View of Pont-Aven,* d. 1888. 26 x 39⅜″. Barber Institute of Fine Arts, The University of Birmingham, England

took time for him to get accustomed to new surroundings, except that this time they were not really new.

At the Pension Gloanec where he again found board and also practically unlimited credit, Gauguin had been given a studio at the top of the house. He decorated it with reproductions of Manet's *Olympia,* Botticelli's *Triumph of Venus,* Fra Angelico's *Annunciation,* and of works by Puvis de Chavannes; there were also prints by Utamaro. In their company he now brooded over his discouraging past and his uncertain future. Ever since he had lost his lucrative position at a bank, his had been a desperate struggle to keep alive and to work. After separating from his wife and children, he had been forced to accept various menial jobs and to sell some of the impressionist paintings from his collection formed in better days. He had gone through innumerable hardships, but he had never given up hope. Conscious of his inner calling, he had remained convinced that his sacrifices could not be in vain. Though he had still not lost confidence in his own abilities, he did not now see a very clear road before him. Sometimes wild hopes to which he clung all too easily seemed to promise a life of modest successes, even triumphs, but the dreary present never relinquished its bitter grip for long. And he was ill with dysentery contracted in Martinique, worried about his family in Denmark, harassed by debts in spite of occasional remittances from the good Schuffenecker. There were times when he was so poor that he could not even work for lack of canvas and colors. In a letter to his wife written in March 1888, he com-

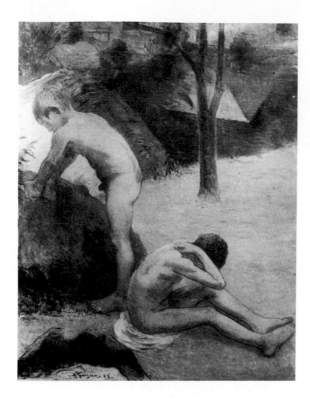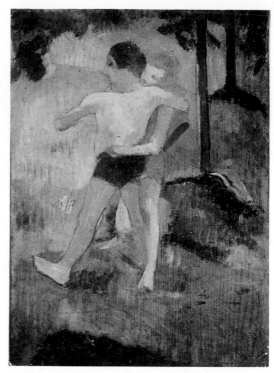

Left: GAUGUIN: *Young Boys Bathing*, Pont-Aven, d. 1888. 36⅛ x 28½". Kunsthalle, Hamburg. Right: GAU-GUIN: *Young Boys Wrestling*, Pont-Aven, 1888. Oil on wood, 13¼ x 9½". Formerly collection Ambroise Vol-lard. Private collection, Switzerland

plained of being "all alone in the room of an inn from morning till night. I have absolute silence, nobody with whom I can exchange ideas."[7]

As summer came, and with it the possibility of working out of doors, the attacks of fever redoubled and confined him to his bed. In June, when he turned forty, Gauguin, in the prime of his manhood, felt weak and old. A little later, being able to work between spells of illness, he painted several pictures of bathers near the river, among them two boys wrestling, executed in what he himself called "an altogether Japanese style... very sketchily done...."[8]

With the good weather the painters flocked once more to Pont-Aven, and Gauguin was no longer quite so isolated, though he still kept away from the others. Charles Laval, who came to join him, was hardly an entertaining companion; in his work he continued to imitate Gauguin timidly.[9] It was then, early in August, that Bernard appeared, perhaps a little too sure of himself and youthfully arrogant, but bursting with ideas, well read, versed in all the theories and achievements of literary symbolism, acquainted with every-thing that was new and startling in Paris. Compared with the mediocre horde of con-formists at the Pension Gloanec, this ardent youngster must have struck Gauguin like a fresh breeze, a welcome relief in the midst of monotony and discouragement.

Before his arrival in Pont-Aven, while he was painting in Saint-Briac (Brittany), Bernard had become friendly with a young symbolist writer, G.-Albert Aurier, only three years

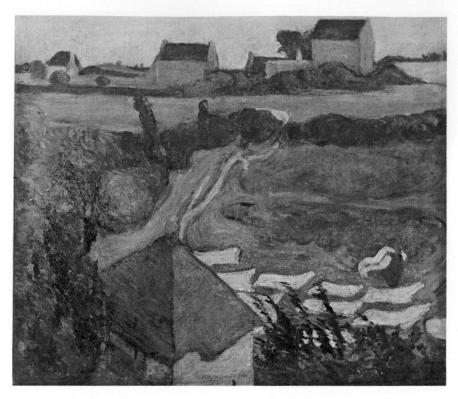

BERNARD: *Landscape of Saint-Briac,* 1888.
19¼ x 22". Private collection, Versailles

older than himself. That very spring of 1888 Aurier, who also painted occasionally, had written a Salon review for *Le Décadent*; in Saint-Briac he sought out Bernard after seeing some of his mural decorations at the local inn. They soon engaged in long discussions and Bernard apparently told him about his own endeavors as well as about Vincent van Gogh's, whose letters and sketches he showed him. Aurier seems to have been greatly impressed with Bernard, who later introduced him to all his painter friends.

Some of the paintings which Aurier had admired earlier in Saint-Briac Bernard now was able to show to Gauguin. These paintings were extremely striking in their radicalism. Gauguin must have easily understood why van Gogh found in his young friend's work "something deliberate, sensible, something solid and self-assured."[10] Bernard had done powerfully modeled still lifes which suggested in certain ways the influence of Cézanne, though more simplified in design. His landscapes showed a tendency to convert his subjects into large, flat patterns, and his portraits, such as the one of his grandmother, were extremely strong in their contrasts of solid planes, in the sharpness of their lines, in the balance of masses. If Gauguin had really been preoccupied with synthesis, here was certainly a far-reaching attempt to achieve it. Three years earlier Gauguin had already confided to Pissarro: "More than ever am I convinced that there is no such thing as *exaggerated art*. I even believe that there is salvation only in the extreme."[11] But his own efforts had nowhere shown a trend towards exaggeration that went as far as Bernard had dared to go.

It is true that Emile Bernard, only twenty years old, had not been alone in the elaboration of this new style, though he claimed a decisive share for himself. While he acknowledged

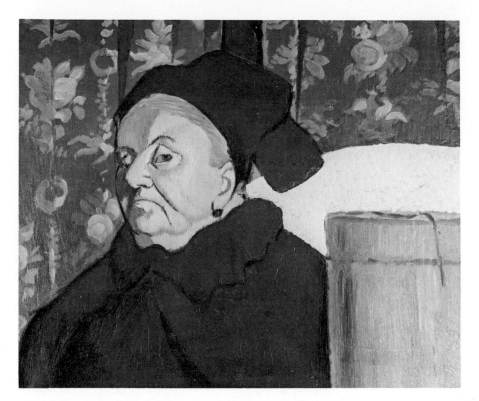

BERNARD: *Portrait of the Artist's Grand-mother*, c. 1887. 20⅞ × 25⅛". Formerly collection van Gogh brothers. Rijksmuseum Vincent van Gogh, Amsterdam

having worked in close communion with his friend Anquetin, the initiative seems to have been Bernard's. When in 1886–87 Anquetin had turned towards neo-impressionism in the hope of finding there a solution for his problems, Bernard, violently opposed to Seurat's innovations, apparently had tried to guide him towards another goal. As Bernard himself related many years later: "I told him of my ideas about art. It seemed to me that one should keep the theory of colors, but move away from the realism of the *trompe l'oeil* either through impression [from memory] or through luminous vibrations. Painting, being decorative, should *above all* please the eye and the mind; and for this there were but two means: color on one hand, invention of the picture on the other. Thus I opposed . . . the *subjective* and the *objective*. Anquetin began to waver. . . ."[12]

There can be little doubt that these concepts were related to those which the literary symbolists expounded at that very same moment. "Anything that overloads a spectacle [of nature]," Bernard contended, as did the symbolists, "covers it with reality and occupies our eyes to the detriment of our minds. We must simplify in order to disclose its meaning . . . I had two ways to achieve this. The first consisted in confronting nature and in simplifying it with utmost rigor . . . in reducing its lines to eloquent contrasts, its shades to the seven fundamental colors of the prism. . . . The second way to obtain this result consisted in relying on conception and memory and in disengaging myself from all direct contact [with nature]. . . . The first possibility meant, so to speak, a simplified handwriting which endeavored to catch the symbolism inherent in nature; the second was an act of my will signifying through analogous means my sensibility, my imagination, and my soul."[13]

175

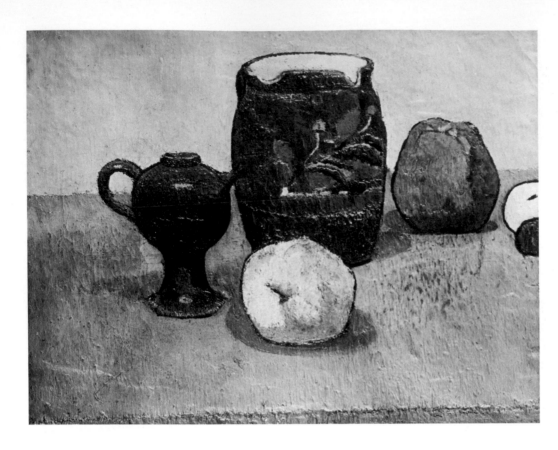

It is hard to say which was Bernard's and which was Anquetin's share in the elaboration of these theories, but the fact is that their paintings of 1887 show a similarity in conception. Anquetin's *Mower* (page 32), which so impressed van Gogh, and Bernard's portrait of his grandmother, which van Gogh obtained through an exchange with his friend, were both executed according to these principles. When Anquetin, though eight years older than Bernard, exhibited his works for the first time early in 1888 with the XX in Brussels and later with the Independents in Paris, his former school friend Edouard Dujardin hailed in the *Revue Indépendante* the advent of a new art form which he called *cloisonnisme*, and for which he gave credit to Anquetin alone. "At first glance," he wrote, "these works give the impression of decorative painting; an outer line, a violent and decisive color inevitably bring to mind folk art and Japanese prints. Then beneath the general hieratic character of drawing and color one perceives a sensational truth which disengages itself from the romanticism of passion; and above all, little by little, it is the intentional, the reasoned, the intellectual and systematic construction that calls for our analysis." And Dujardin explained that according to this new concept "the painter traces his drawing in closed lines between which he puts varied hues, the juxtaposition of which will provide the sensation of the general coloration intended, the drawing emphasizing the color and color emphasizing the design. The work of the painter is something like painting in *compartments*, analogous to the [medieval] *cloisonné*, his technique consisting of a kind of *cloisonnisme*."[14]

Emile Bernard, who was not even mentioned by Dujardin, must have complained about

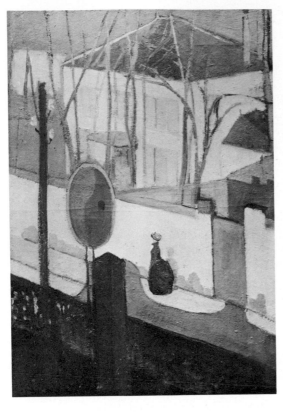

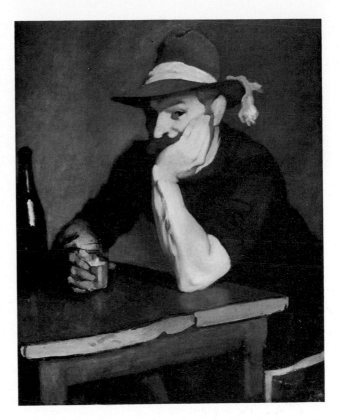

BERNARD: *The House of the Artist's Parents at Asnières*, d. 1887. 21⅝ x 15". Collection Mr. and Mrs. Edgar B. Miller, Chicago

Anquetin: *The Drinker*, d. 1892. 38⅝ x 31½". Formerly collection Mme du Ferron-Anquetin, Paris

this to van Gogh, for Vincent wrote to his brother: "An article has appeared, it seems, in the *Revue Indépendante*, on Anquetin, which calls him the leader of a new tendency, in which Japanese influence is still more apparent, etc. I have not read it, but anyway the leader of the Petit Boulevard [the young, as yet unrecognized painters] is undoubtedly Seurat, and in the Japanese style young Bernard has perhaps gone farther than Anquetin."[15]

Be this as it may, it was Emile Bernard in any event who carried the message of this new tendency to Pont-Aven; it was he who acquainted Gauguin with his own and Anquetin's experiments. And Gauguin discovered in Bernard's works precisely those elements of reason, of intention, of intellectual and systematic construction which Dujardin had hailed. They must have had a particularly strong impact upon Gauguin since, at that very moment, he was going through a phase of doubt and indecision. Just as Camille Pissarro had joined ranks with Seurat and Signac because their theories promised to lead him out of a blind alley, so Gauguin was now tempted to adopt some of Bernard's principles.

While Gauguin was greatly interested in Bernard's work he was apparently no less impressed by the young painter himself. In sharp contrast to Gauguin's somewhat inarticulate mind was Bernard's facility in the formulation of explanations and theories, the ease with which he justified every move by philosophical, historical, esthetic, literary or poetic digressions. Indeed a strange mixture of restlessness and erudition prompted Bernard to accompany each new experiment with soul-searching discussions, to surround it with amazing structures of daring principles or afterthoughts. It was as if each color he used, each line he drew was part of an involved system and became, through clever analysis, an irrefutable argument for whatever point he wished to make. Gauguin, with the fondness of the half-educated for intricate and high-sounding theories, found here numerous appealing terms and concepts which were to enable him to clothe his own endeavors in a seemingly scientific vocabulary. It is possible, of course, that the subjects on which Bernard propounded so elaborately were not entirely new to Gauguin, that similar thoughts had already occurred to him, but if that is the case, he had not been able until then to formulate these ideas or to translate them into his works. It took his meeting with Emile Bernard to put some kind of order, although as yet a rather obscure one, into his mind. His more or less complete assimilation of Bernard's theories and his efforts to harmonize them with his own still vague inclinations are revealed in the artistic tenets which Gauguin himself now began to expound. So great was the younger painter's ascendancy over him that even Bernard's religious fervor was reflected in Gauguin's letters.

Towards the middle of August 1888, less than two weeks after Bernard's arrival in Pont-Aven, Gauguin wrote to their friend Schuffenecker: "Young Bernard is here and has brought from Saint-Briac some interesting things. Here is someone who isn't afraid of anything." And then he went on to say: "One bit of advice, don't copy nature too much. Art is an abstraction; derive this abstraction from nature while dreaming before it, but think more of creating than of the actual result. The only way to rise towards God is by doing as our divine Master does, create.... My latest works are well under way and I believe that you will find in them a special note or rather an affirmation of my previous researches, the *synthesis* of form and color derived from the observation of the dominant element only. Well, be courageous and may God take you in His blessed care by crowning your efforts with success."[16]

How Gauguin himself lived up to these concepts he explained when he wrote a little later: "I have sacrificed everything this year, execution, color, for the benefit of style, forcing upon myself something different from what I know how to do. This is, I believe, a transformation which hasn't yet borne its fruits, but which will bear them."[17] Thus Gauguin did acknowledge having turned over a new leaf at the very moment of his acquaintance with Bernard.

After Bernard had spent less than a month at the inn, agreement between him and Gauguin seems to have been complete. "Gauguin and Bernard talk now of 'painting like children,'" Vincent van Gogh wrote to his brother. "I would rather have that than the painting of the decadents."[18] But their attempt to paint like children was the result of sophistication rather than naïveté. Gauguin and Bernard were far from the true primitiveness that revealed itself so touchingly in the works of the *douanier* Rousseau. Their approach was a highly reasoned one, a conscious attempt to simplify forms and color for the sake of more forceful expression.

As time went by, Gauguin pronounced himself ever more strongly on the transformation his art was undergoing. Discussions and experiments fostered new certitudes in him; they also somewhat obliterated any feeling of indebtedness to Bernard, and Gauguin soon spoke as if the direction taken by his evolution was an inescapable one, the fulfillment of all his earlier efforts. "Of course," he told Schuffenecker, "the road of synthesism is full of perils,

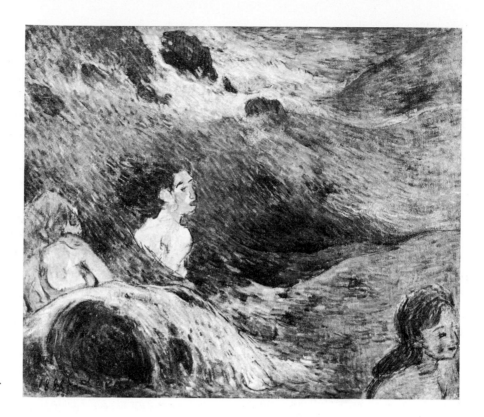

LAVAL: *Bathers,* Brittany, d. 1888.
18⅛ x 21⅝″. Kunsthalle, Bremen

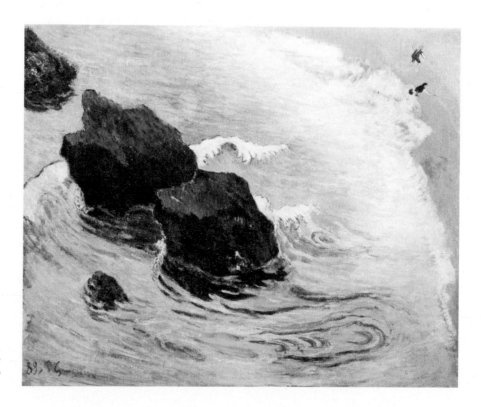

GAUGUIN: *The Wave (Red Beach),* d.
1888. 23¾ x 28⅜″. Private collection,
New York

and I have only just put one foot on it, but it is the road which truly corresponds to my nature and one should always follow one's temperament. I know very well that I shall be *less and less* understood. Yet what does it matter if I move away from the others? For the masses I will be an enigma, for some I will be a poet, and sooner or later that which is good will take its rightful place.... Come what may, I tell you that I shall eventually do *first class things*; I know it and we shall see. You know that in questions of art I am always right in the end."[19]

In his discussions with the others Gauguin adopted an increasingly dogmatic tone. When Bernard and Laval asked him what he thought of the role of shadows, Gauguin replied by referring to Japanese woodcuts, of which Bernard had probably made a more careful study than he had made himself. "You want to know whether I disdain shadows," he said. "In so far as they are an explanation of light, I do. Look at the Japanese who draw so admirably, and you will see there life in the open air and in the sun without shadows. They use color only as a combination of tones, various harmonies, giving the impression of heat, etc.... Moreover, I consider impressionism an altogether new departure which inevitably diverges from anything that is mechanical, such as photography, etc.... Thus I shall get away as much as possible from anything that gives the illusion of an object, and shadows being the *trompe l'oeil* of the sun, I am inclined to eliminate them. But if a shadow enters your composition as a necessary form, that is an altogether different thing.... Therefore, use shadows if you consider them helpful, or don't use them, it amounts to the same thing, as long as you don't consider yourself the slave of shadows. For in a way it is the shadow which is at your service."[20]

Gauguin himself now painted on a large wooden panel a strange still-life composition from which most shadows were absent (page 170). Three pinkish-gray puppies, three deep blue goblets, and some fruit are assembled with an utter disregard for proportion or natural coloration. In all probability it represents one of Gauguin's attempts to paint "like a child." Throughout the summer of 1888 Gauguin seems to have done a number of paintings, often rather small in size, that had an experimental character. Sometimes he relied mostly on an impressionistic execution but used very vivid colors, sometimes he worked with flat planes and accentuated outlines, as Bernard did, and sometimes he combined both techniques. In a small canvas of a goose girl (opposite) he translated his observations of nature into an almost abstract pattern, relieved only by naturalistic elements in the figure of the girl. In a large Breton landscape with a young swineherd (page 277), on the other hand, he abandoned crude simplifications, strong colors, and flat areas for little brush strokes, soft harmonies, and small patches well integrated into the composition. Yet there is an insistence on line and a summarization of forms that show a definite step beyond impressionism, in spite of the execution which, quite unlike the *Still Life with Three Puppies*, features a texture of small strokes.

Bernard, in the meantime, pursued his research in the direction of greater abstraction and more ornamental forms. He painted a group of *Breton Women in the Meadow* without any attempt to model their forms, forcefully setting in opposition the dark masses of their dresses and the peculiar white arabesques of their headgear and collars, whose outlines he set off strongly against the flat background (page 226). Gauguin was quite impressed with this painting and Bernard gladly offered it to him in exchange for one of his. During the weeks that they had spent together, Bernard had increasingly come to respect Gauguin. In a letter to van Gogh he expressed himself with so much fervor that Vincent reported

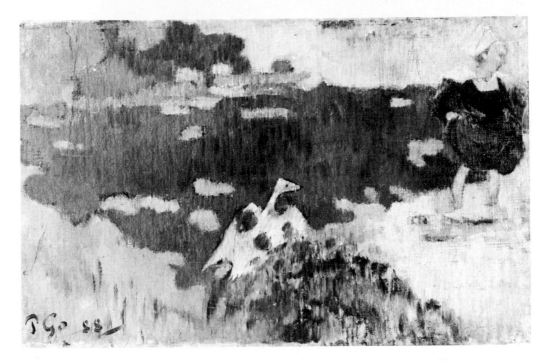

GAUGUIN: *Goose Girl,* Brittany, d. 1888. 9½ x 15″. Estate of Hunt Henderson, New Orleans

to his brother: "Bernard's letter is steeped in admiration for Gauguin's talent. He says that he considers him so great an artist that he is almost afraid of him, and that he finds everything that he himself does poor in comparison."[21]

Bernard's admiration for Gauguin may have been brought about particularly by a canvas which the latter completed early in the fall of 1888. Indeed, after all their philosophizing, there remained for Gauguin the task of embodying his new independence from nature, his freedom in the use of its elements as best suited his purpose, in a painting that would represent strikingly his novel approach. He therefore started in September to work on a large and complex composition, the epitome of his new style. The subject he chose was the struggle of Jacob with the angel, symbolic as well as religious, almost as if he himself meant not to relinquish his grasp on his new ideas until he was blessed (page 189). As a setting for this Biblical episode, he selected a Breton landscape with a group of peasant women in their picturesque bonnets watching the two contestants. These women with their strange and ornamental headdress (which also had attracted Bernard) occupy the entire foreground of the canvas, which is divided diagonally by an apple tree, very much in the fashion of Japanese prints. Jacob and the angel detach themselves in the distance from a bright vermilion ground, while a cow beneath the tree is much too small in proportion to the rest of the figures. As Gauguin explained, the scene witnessed by these women, most of whom kneel down in prayer, represents an apparition that occurs to them after hearing the Sunday sermon in their village church. "I believe," Gauguin reported to van Gogh, "I have attained in these figures a great rustic and *superstitious* simplicity. It is all very severe. . . . To me in this painting the landscape and the struggle exist only in the imagination of these praying people, as a result of the sermon. That is why there is a contrast between these real people and the struggle in this landscape, which is not real and is out of proportion."[22]

Having set out to encompass all forms within their essential outlines, use pure colors, avoid shadows as far as possible, and even renounce modeling to a great extent, Gauguin was well satisfied with the result. He decided to offer this painting to one of the small Breton churches, not out of piety but because he wanted to see the effect his canvas would produce among the crude Romanesque or Gothic forms of the local granite chapels. He selected the old church of Nizon, not far from Pont-Aven, and Laval and Bernard helped him to carry the canvas there. But they failed to convince the *curé*, who apparently feared some artistic hoax; the gift was refused after the priest explained that his parish would not understand the painting. And sadly the three returned with the canvas to Pont-Aven.[23] A little later Gauguin sent it to Paris, requesting Theo van Gogh to ask 600 francs for it.

There can be no doubt that Gauguin's painting greatly impressed his friends, including Schuffenecker, who joined them during the summer months. Together they continued to work and to argue endlessly about the merits of pictorial symbolism. Both Bernard and Gauguin did portraits of Bernard's sister Madeleine but seemed less preoccupied with any literal resemblance than with a stylization derived from Cézanne. (While Gauguin courted the young girl more or less discreetly, Laval, unmarried and much closer to her in age, was more successful and eventually became engaged to her.[24]) Gauguin and Bernard also

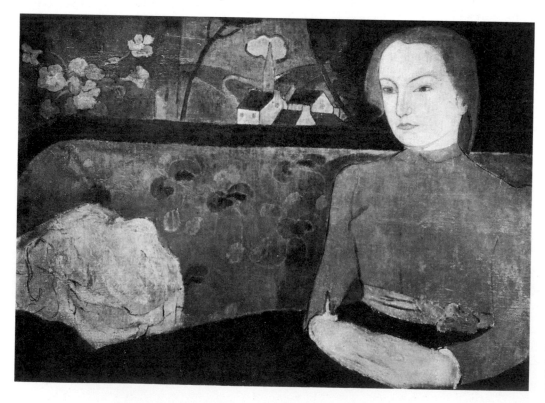

SCHOOL OF PONT-AVEN: *Portrait of Madeleine Bernard.* 28¾ x 38¼". Present whereabouts unknown

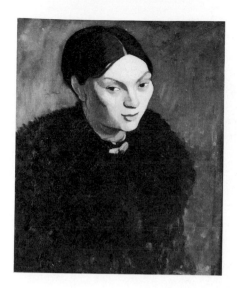

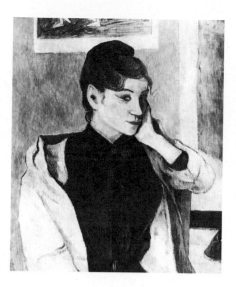

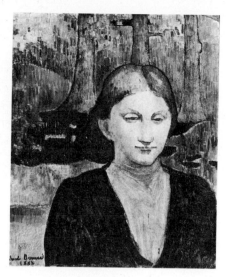

ANQUETIN: *Portrait of Madeleine Bernard* (?), c. 1892. 23¾ x 19½". Collection B. G. Verte, Paris

GAUGUIN: *Portrait of Madeleine Bernard*, Pont-Aven, 1888. 28⅜ x 22¾". Musée des Beaux-Arts, Grenoble

BERNARD: *Portrait of the Artist's Sister*, Pont-Aven, d. 1888. 24 x 19¾". Musée Toulouse-Lautrec, Albi

frequently worked on a hill overlooking Pont-Aven, topped by a little wood poetically called the Bois d'Amour, where Bernard represented his sister on a large canvas, lying among the trees like a contemporary Joan of Arc listening to heavenly voices (page 184). Van Gogh, who knew this painting only from a description by his friends, thought that Bernard had achieved here great "elegance with nothing." The religious fervor of the peasants, their superstitiousness which so struck Gauguin, the crude naïveté of the many granite Calvaries, together with Bernard's own devout Catholicism, seem to have brought about in their works a mixture of pictorial symbolism and religious mysticism.

Though they worked hard the circumstances of their daily life were not pleasant. Bernard even reported to van Gogh that it grieved him "to see how Gauguin is often prevented from doing what he otherwise could, for wholly material reasons, paints, canvas, etc."[25] It may be that Gauguin received some help from a dwarfish Dutchman, Meyer de Haan, son of a wealthy industrialist, whom Pissarro had recommended to Gauguin. Two other young painters, Moret and de Chamaillard, also joined his little group.[26]

At Gloanec's Gauguin and his friends kept to themselves most of the time and occupied in the dining room a small table separated from the large one where the rest of the boarders assembled. But their heated conversations often drew the others into their circle and lively controversies resulted. Gauguin described their life in Pont-Aven to van Gogh, and Vincent thereupon reported to his brother: "They are enjoying themselves very much painting, arguing, and fighting with the worthy Englishmen; Gauguin speaks well of Bernard's work and Bernard speaks well of Gauguin's."[27]

Among the painters from the Académie Julian who spent the summer at Gloanec's was one, Paul Sérusier, who felt greatly attracted to Gauguin and to the small group of his friends, but did not dare to join or even to approach them. Encouraged by Bernard, how-

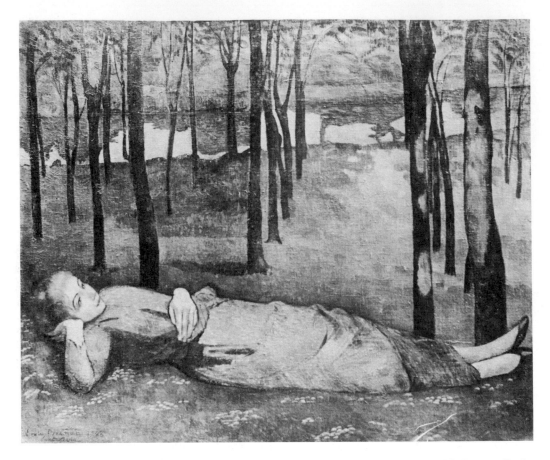

BERNARD: *Madeleine at the Bois d'Amour,* Pont-Aven, 1888. 54⅜ x 64⅛″. Musées Nationaux, Paris. Compare with Sérusier's painting, page 188.

ever, Sérusier decided on the very last day of his stay to talk to Gauguin. He found him in bed—Gauguin was still suffering from dysentery—and showed him one of his own paintings. As there was little time to be lost, Gauguin offered to give him a "lesson" out of doors the next morning. They went to the little Bois d'Amour, and Sérusier painted an autumn landscape on a small panel under Gauguin's guidance (page 188). "How do you see these trees?" Gauguin asked him. "They are yellow. Well then, put down yellow. And that shadow is rather blue. So render it with pure ultramarine. Those red leaves? Use vermilion."[28]

Thus Sérusier was initiated and learned that, according to Gauguin's new principles, "the impression of nature must be wedded to the esthetic sentiment which chooses, arranges, simplifies, and synthesizes. The painter ought not to rest until he has given birth to the child of his imagination... begotten by the union of his mind with reality.... Gauguin insisted on a logical construction of composition, on a harmonious apportionment of light and dark colors, the simplification of forms and proportions, so as to endow the outlines of forms with a powerful and eloquent expression...."[29]

184

Preoccupations with these same problems were also reflected in the letters which Gauguin and Bernard wrote from Pont-Aven to Vincent van Gogh in Arles. Indeed, a steady flow of letters maintained their close contact and kept van Gogh informed of all the experiments, of all the new achievements that grew out of his friends' endeavors. Van Gogh openly envied their community of work and their productive comradeship, in such sharp contrast to his own loneliness in Arles. Every now and then he felt almost tempted to join them in Pont-Aven, but when he once asked Gauguin to give him an idea of material conditions and prices there, Gauguin was in no haste to reply. Could it be that he was not welcome in Brittany? And then there was also the thought that he would have to room at the inn with reactionary Englishmen and with pupils of the Ecole des Beaux-Arts, that he would be dragged into endless discussions every night (and van Gogh knew how these exhausted him). Though life in Pont-Aven was cheaper than in the South, van Gogh preferred his independence in Arles; he believed in "calm, carefully considered actions" rather than in "enormous discussions," as he said. Yet, what was most important to him was the idea of a group of artists working together, an idea he had cherished for a long time. As he once explained to Bernard: "More and more it seems to me that the pictures which must be painted to make present-day painting completely itself and raise it to a height equal to the serene peaks which were attained by the Greek sculptors, the German musicians, and the French novelists, are beyond the power of one isolated individual. They will therefore probably be created by groups of men gathered to execute an idea held in common."[30]

While the old-guard impressionists had to a certain extent formed such a group, it was essential now that the "impressionists of today," as van Gogh and Gauguin considered themselves, should establish a close community of work. There was no doubt in van Gogh's mind that the ground for such a community was being laid in Pont-Aven, but he thought it would prosper much better in the South. He therefore tried to persuade his friends to come to Arles where they could form a more homogeneous group and would not be disturbed. With this in mind he moved in September into a small house which he had previously used only as a studio; there he hoped to establish a "Studio of the South" of which Gauguin would become the head and to which he also invited Bernard and Laval. But Gauguin felt that he could not leave Pont-Aven without paying his many debts, particularly since the owner of the inn had always been very kind to him. These debts meanwhile increased with every day he stayed.

Van Gogh was then especially preoccupied with the suggestive power of color and tried to achieve symbolic meaning or to create specific moods through contrasts, harmonies, or slight variations of tones. When he wrote to Gauguin that he wished to suggest poetic ideas through his coloration, the latter replied that he agreed, though he himself professed to know nothing of *poetic ideas*. "I find *everything* poetic," Gauguin specified, "and it is in the dark corners of my heart, which are sometimes mysterious, that I perceive poetry. Forms and colors, harmoniously established, produce poetry by themselves."[31] Van Gogh was deeply grateful for such pronouncements, vague as they were, having always admired the poetry he discovered in Gauguin's work. Yet he felt that seeing some of his friends' recent paintings would help him to better understand their objectives. And so he suggested that they exchange some canvases. "Japanese artists often used to exchange works among themselves," he explained in a letter to Bernard. ". . . The relationship between them was evidently, and quite naturally, brotherly; they didn't live a life of intrigue. The more we can copy them in this respect the better for us."[32]

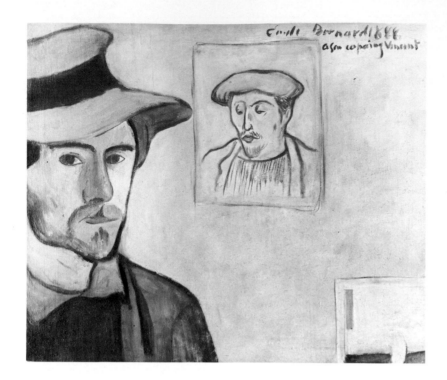

BERNARD: *Self-Portrait,* dedicated to Vincent van Gogh, Pont-Aven, d. 1888. 18⅛ × 21⅝″. Rijksmuseum Vincent van Gogh, Amsterdam

It was planned originally that Gauguin and Bernard should paint each other's portrait for van Gogh. Gauguin did study Bernard for a while but somehow felt that he could not grasp him. "I am observing young Bernard," he wrote to van Gogh in September, "and I do not yet get him. Maybe I shall do him from memory, but in any case it will be an abstraction. Tomorrow possibly, I don't know, it will come to me all of a sudden."[22] Bernard, on the other hand, informed van Gogh that he *dared not* do Gauguin, because he felt himself too timid in front of him.[33] Since Gauguin's inspiration apparently did not materialize and since Bernard so strangely lacked courage, the two friends decided to paint their own portraits instead, but to include in the background a likeness of each other. Thus Bernard painted himself in a bluish-gray harmony, the forms outlined with a blue (*cloisonniste*) contour. His head, partly cropped, appears on the left side of the canvas, while in the background a sketchy portrait of Gauguin, done in *grisaille* and tacked to the wall, occupies almost the center of the painting. His picture, executed in large and sweeping strokes, greatly pleased van Gogh who wrote to his brother that it was "a painter's idea, a few simple colors, a few blackish lines, but done as deftly as a real Manet."[34] Van Gogh actually liked Bernard's self-portrait better than the more elaborate one Gauguin sent him.

Like Bernard, Gauguin represented himself in the left part of his canvas and included a profile of Bernard in the upper right corner. But he used more vivid colors, painting Bernard's likeness in greenish tones, the background chrome yellow with pink flowers, his own face in a purplish red with bluish shadows, set against a blue shirt and a green coat. He too used blue lines to accentuate contours, but his brush strokes were small, even in the large areas of the background; they carefully modeled the artist's features and indicated the texture of his hair, while Bernard had been much more abstract in his painting.

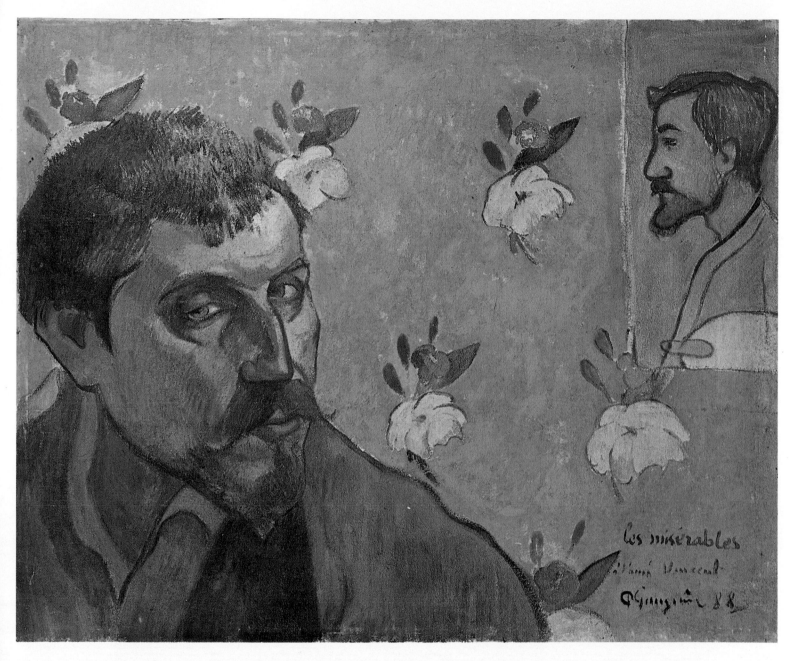

Gauguin: *Self-Portrait, "Les Misérables,"* dedicated to Vincent van Gogh, Pont-Aven, d. 1888. 28⅛ x 35⅝". Rijksmuseum Vincent van Gogh, Amsterdam

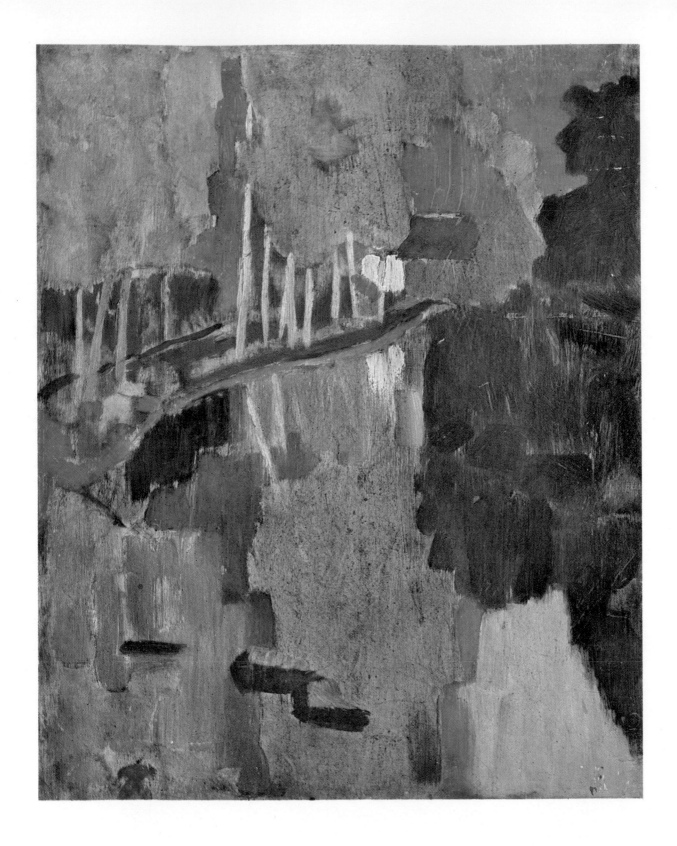

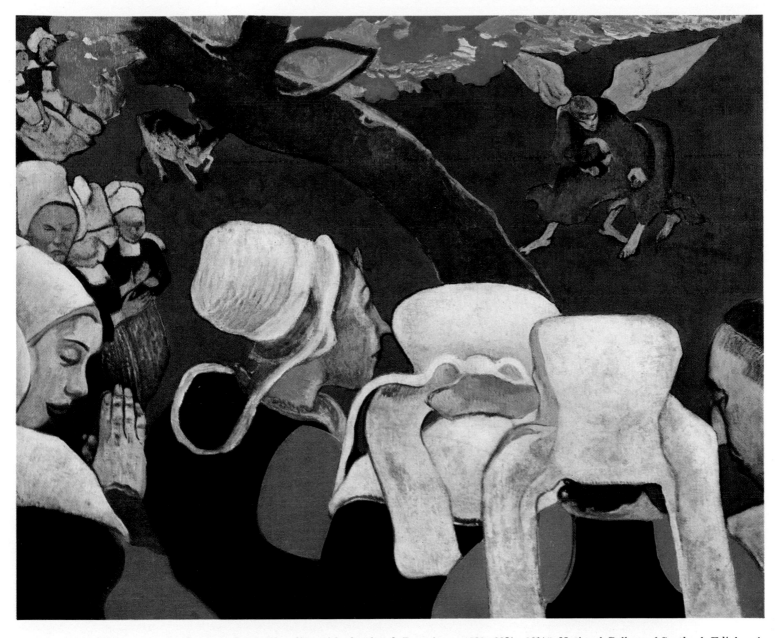

GAUGUIN: *The Vision after the Sermon—Jacob Wrestling with the Angel,* Pont-Aven, 1888. 28¾ x 36¼″. National Gallery of Scotland, Edinburgh

Opposite: SÉRUSIER: *Landscape of the Bois d'Amour at Pont-Aven—The "Talisman,"* 1888. Oil on wood, 10⅝ x 8⅝″. Formerly collection Maurice Denis. Private collection, France

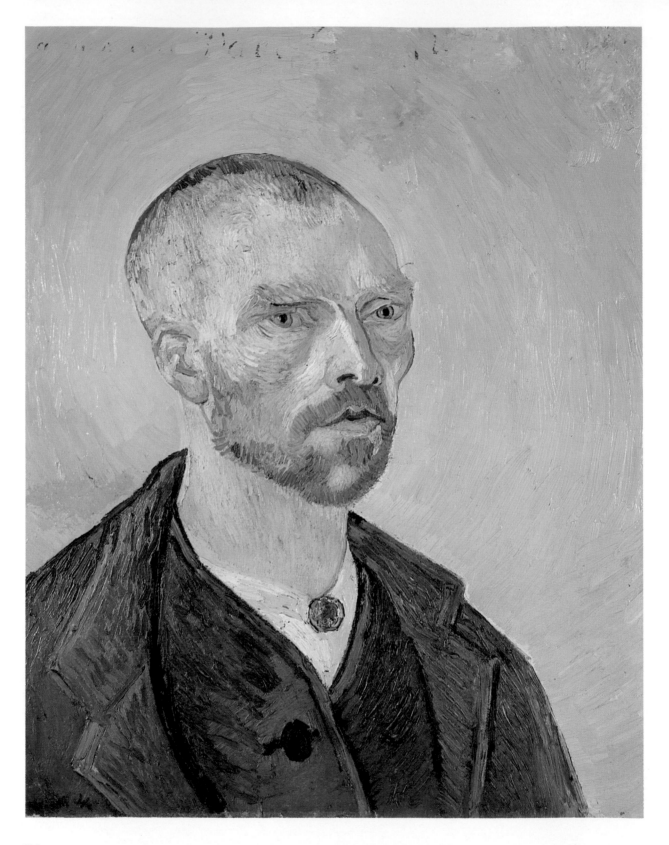

Opposite: VAN GOGH: *Self-Portrait,* dedicated to Paul Gauguin, Arles, Sept. 1888. 24½ x 20½". Fogg Art Museum, Harvard University, Cambridge, Mass. (Maurice Wertheim Collection)

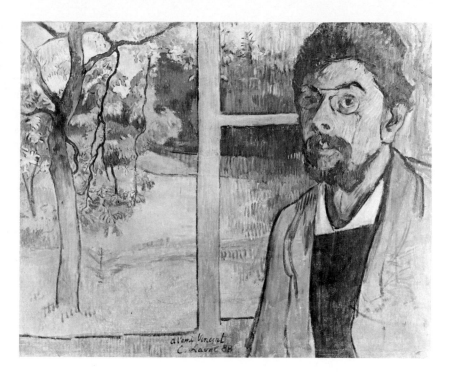

LAVAL: *Self-Portrait,* dedicated to Vincent van Gogh, Pont-Aven, d. 1888. 19¾ x 23⅝". Rijksmuseum Vincent van Gogh, Amsterdam

In a long letter to van Gogh, Gauguin felt compelled to expand in his own peculiar way on the specific meaning of his portrait. This letter, together with the canvas itself, gave van Gogh "above all absolutely the impression of representing a prisoner. Not a shadow of gaiety. Nor is there the least trace of sensuousness. But one can attribute this to his determination to obtain a melancholy effect."[34]

Gauguin began his letter by explaining why he had written *Les Misérables* on his portrait, an allusion to Victor Hugo's novel and its tormented hero Jean Valjean. Gauguin saw in his own head "the mask of a badly dressed and powerful ruffian like Jean Valjean who has a certain nobility and inner kindness. The hot blood pulsates through the face and the tonalities of a glowing forge which surround the eyes indicate the fiery lava that kindles our painter's soul. The design of the eyes and nose, resembling that of flowers in a Persian rug, sums up an abstract and symbolic art. The delicate maidenly background with its childlike flowers is there to signify our artistic virginity. And this Jean Valjean whom society oppresses, an outlaw, with his love, his strength, is he not also the image of an impressionist of today? By painting him in my own likeness, you have an image of myself as well as a portrait of all of us, poor victims of society, who retaliate only by doing good."[35] Gauguin, well content with his portrait, also sent a description of it to Schuffenecker: "It is, I believe, one of my best works, though so abstract that it is absolutely incomprehensible.... The color is rather remote from nature.... The impressionist is an immaculate human being, not yet sullied by the putrid kiss of the Ecole des Beaux-Arts."[17]

Laval, who had never met van Gogh but who had read his letters from Arles and listened to his friends' stories about him, also decided to send him a self-portrait. He painted his face, on the right side of the canvas, in the same reddish tones that Gauguin had used, and his hair and beard in blue; through an open window could be seen a landscape treated impressionistically. Van Gogh later sent him a portrait of himself.[36]

For Gauguin, van Gogh selected a self-portrait (page 190) which he had just completed and which, in his own words, was *"almost colorless, with ashen gray tones against a background of pale Veronese green."*[37] His head detaches itself vigorously from the uniform background, and though in his portrait there is "not a shadow of gaiety" either, there is an almost superhuman intensity and an indescribable glare of will power in the intentionally slanting eyes. "My portrait, which I am sending Gauguin in exchange," van Gogh informed his brother, "holds its own with his, I am sure of that. I have written to Gauguin in reply to his letter that if I too may be allowed to exaggerate my own personality in a portrait, I have done so in trying to convey in my portrait not only myself but an impressionist in general. I have conceived it as that of a Bonze, a simple worshipper of the eternal Buddha. And when I put Gauguin's conception and my own side by side, mine is as grave, but less despairing."[34]

It was only for convenience that van Gogh continued to consider himself an impressionist. "I remain among the impressionists," he explained to his brother, "because it doesn't mean anything and doesn't hold me to anything, and because thus I don't owe any explanations to the others."[38] But van Gogh had come a long way since he had left Paris where he had so eagerly assimilated the discoveries of the old-guard impressionists.

While Gauguin and Bernard in Pont-Aven coldly reasoned every stroke of their brushes, van Gogh in Arles abandoned himself more freely to the excitement of discovering a new world. His dreams of the South had been typical of those of any northerner who aspires to get closer to the sun, its warmth, its greater indolence. "I always remember," van Gogh later wrote to Gauguin, "the emotions which the trip from Paris to Arles evoked. How I kept watching to see if I had already reached Japan! Childish, isn't it?"[39]

Van Gogh's preconception of southern France had combined everything that he cherished in art: the vividness of Moroccan colors which he loved so much in Delacroix's work, the rigid and simple masses he admired in Cézanne's landscapes, the scintillation of Monticelli's palette, vistas with incisive outlines as in Japanese prints, an atmosphere reminiscent of his favorite authors, Zola and Daudet, both southerners, and possibly even some of the tropical luxuriance that Gauguin had found in the West Indies. He was not yet aware that he would not only find all this but would also discover in Arles a serenity not unlike that of Puvis de Chavannes' compositions, peasants who seemed to come straight out of Millet's paintings, townspeople who made him think of Daumier, as well as wide plains which reminded him of the flatness of his native Holland and, except for a more intense coloration, of Ruysdael, Hobbema, Ostade.

Strangely enough, when van Gogh had arrived at Arles in February 1888, the country-side had presented a most unusual aspect: it was covered with snow. But soon the exceptional cold subsided and the flowering almond trees literally drove him into a frenzy of work. Every day he discovered new motifs as well as new reasons to love the ancient city and its beautiful surroundings. At last his wish to use color as in stained glass windows and to achieve a drawing of firm lines seemed to have been granted. The sulphur yellow of the light which made all forms stand out so clearly was for him an unceasing source of wonder. "I am convinced that nature down here is just what one needs to give one color,"[40] he wrote to his brother, also telling him: "Things here have so much style. And I want to manage to get my drawing more deliberate and more exaggerated."[41] He remembered

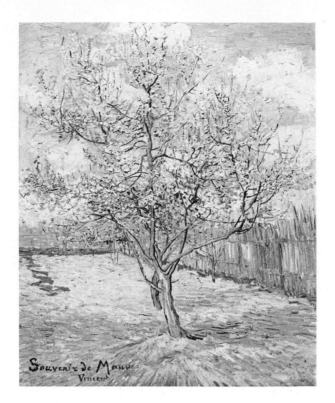

VAN GOGH: *Flowering Tree,* Arles,
April 1888. 28 x 22⅞″. Rijksmuseum
Kröller-Müller, Otterlo

his conversations with Pissarro: "What Pissarro says is true: one should unhesitatingly exaggerate the effects which colors produce by their harmony or by their clashes."[42]

Thus, like his friends in Pont-Aven, van Gogh now strove for simplified lines and more expressive colors; he even painted a landscape closely related to Anquetin's *Mower* (page 32), which he had admired in Paris. Dujardin, in his article on *cloisonnisme* had stated that this particular canvas produced an effect similar to that of a window in a darkened room suddenly opened to reveal a sun-bathed landscape. "All the details of coloration which would emerge after long examination do not at first appear, absorbed as they are by the unity and power of the total impression."[14] This was indeed van Gogh's own experience when he suddenly opened his "window" upon the sun-drenched splendor of southern France.

"I am trying now to exaggerate the essential and, with set purpose, to leave the obvious vague!"[43] van Gogh announced after his first weeks in Arles. Soon he became aware that his vision had changed, that he saw things "with an eye more Japanese," that he felt color differently. "You understand," he explained in a letter to his sister, "that nature in the South can't precisely be painted with the palette... of the North. A palette nowadays is absolutely colorful: sky-blue, pink, orange, vermilion, strong yellow, clear green, pure wine red, purple. But by strengthening *all* colors one again obtains calm and harmony; there happens something similar to Wagner's music which, even though performed by a great orchestra, is none the less intimate."[44] And he also told his sister that studying Japanese prints was certainly the best way for her to understand the direction taken by

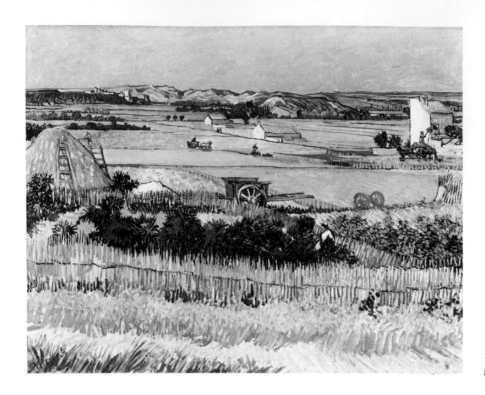

the modern artists who used bright and pure colors. "As for me here," he added, "I have no need for Japanese art, for I always tell myself that here I am *in Japan*, and that consequently I have only to open my eyes and to take in what I have before me."[44]

From his very first contact with it the South stirred van Gogh's deepest feelings and revealed to him the true character of his creative urge. "I am convinced that a long sojourn here is just what I need to enable me to affirm my personality," he wrote to his brother.[15] "Nature here is so *extraordinarily* beautiful!" he exclaimed. "Everywhere and over all the vault of the sky is a marvelous blue, and the sun sheds a radiance of pale sulphur; it is as soft and lovely as the combination of celestial blues and yellows in Vermeer's paintings. I cannot paint it as beautifully as that, but it absorbs me so much that I let myself go without thinking of any rules."[45]

So feverishly was he trying to retain on canvas after canvas the various enticing aspects of the Provençal landscape that he felt obliged to accompany the first batch of paintings he sent to his brother with an explanatory note: "I must warn you that everyone will think that I work too fast. Don't believe a word of it. Is it not emotion, the sincerity of one's feeling for nature, that draws us? And if these emotions are sometimes so strong that one works without knowing one does so, when sometimes the brush strokes come with a sequence and a coherence like words in a speech or in a letter, then one must remember that it has not always been so, and that in time to come there will again be dreary days, devoid of inspiration. So one must strike while the iron is hot...."[46]

When Theo expressed fear that Vincent might get over-excited and try to do too much, the painter replied: "Don't think that I would artificially maintain a feverish state, but do

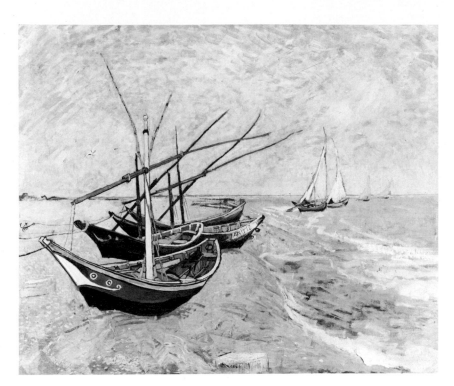

understand that I am in the midst of a complicated calculation, which results in a rapid
succession of canvases quickly executed, but calculated long *beforehand.*"[47]

As far as one can judge from his letters it would seem that van Gogh, despite his exaltation, did not exactly work under the pressure of an overpowering first impression. Long
daily walks took him across the lovely countryside, and whenever he saw a tempting motif
or one that offered elements which challenged his imagination he would decide to return
and work there. Thus each time he set out with a canvas and his box of paints he knew
where he was going and had had at least a few hours to "calculate beforehand" his next
picture. The specific problem of his new motif had thus already found a solution in his
mind, the essential features had already assumed their priority over the obvious ones, the
colors had arranged themselves in such a way as to permit the accentuation of the appropriate mood: gaiety, exuberance, or utter sadness, harmony or violent clash. The minute van
Gogh put up his easel in the field and secured it against the ever-blowing mistral his hand
began to obey two masters: the eye which wandered scrutinizingly over the landscape,
observing each detail, each nuance, and the mind which had already prepared a synthetic
image of the spectacle that nature spread out before him. Even the most banal views were
infused with the dynamism of his urge after he had discovered in them that intangible
quality which released the outpouring of his emotions. His problem then was not so much
to remain photographically faithful to his subject as to find an expression which would
convey his feelings within the framework of accuracy. "When the thing represented," he
asked his brother, "is, in point of character, absolutely in agreement with the manner of
representing it, isn't it just that which gives a work of art its quality?"[48]

195

Toward the middle of June, Vincent met two former students of Cormon's, the Belgian painter Eugène Boch, a member of the XX, and Dodge McKnight, a friend of Anquetin's, who were spending a few weeks near Arles. They had not been acquainted until McKnight "discovered" Vincent, "a completely mad guy but a good fellow." Van Gogh was particularly taken with Boch's tall, lanky, and very northern appearance (though less with his work), which revived his old wish of doing a portrait of an artist, a dreamer. It was to be a mixture of both observation and invention.

"To begin with, I shall paint him as he is, as faithfully as I can," Vincent explained to his brother. "Yet the picture won't be finished that way. In order to finish it, I shall become an arbitrary colorist. By exaggerating the blond of his hair I shall obtain orange tones, chromes, a pale lemon yellow. Behind the head, instead of the banal wall of the shabby apartment, I shall paint infinity by putting there a plain background of the richest and most intense blue I can produce, and through this simple combination of the yellow head, lit up against the rich blue backdrop, I shall obtain an effect as mysterious as a star on deep azure."[49]

But despite these almost literary preoccupations and the symbolic content of the projected work, Vincent's portrait of Boch shows an astonishing degree of resemblance, for he had indeed represented his friend's features most faithfully. On September 3, he was able to report to his brother: "Thanks to him I at last have a first version of that picture which I have dreamed of for so long—the poet. He posed for it. His fine head with that green gaze stands out in my portrait against a starry sky of deep ultramarine; for clothes, a short yellow coat, a collar of unbleached linen, and a striped tie. He gave me two sittings in one day."[50]

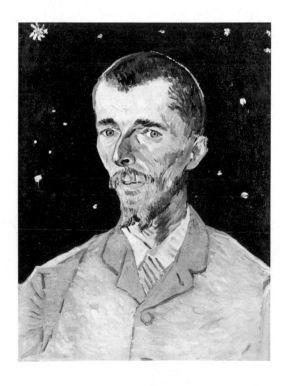

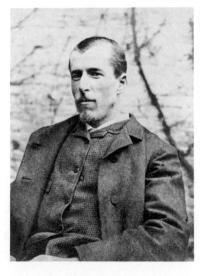

Far left: VAN GOGH: *Portrait of Eugène Boch*, Sept. 1888. 23⅛ x 17¾". Musée du Louvre, Paris

Left: Photograph of Eugène Boch, c. 1888

Right: VAN GOGH: *The Iron Bridge of Trinque-taille,* Arles, Oct. 1888. 28¾ x 36⅛". Collection Mrs. Sonja Binkhorst-Kramarsky, Brooklyn, N.Y.

Below: Photograph of the same bridge, taken before its destruction during World War II. It has since been reconstructed, though not in the same form

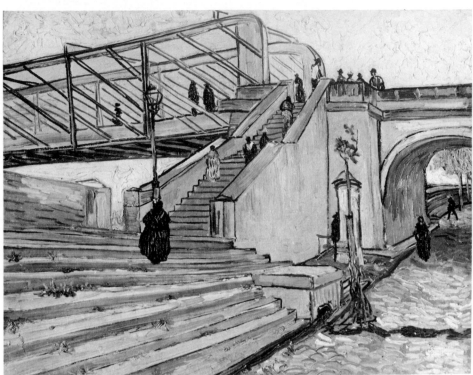

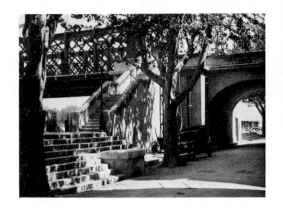

Right: VAN GOGH: *The Railway Viaduct on the Road to Tarascon,* Arles, Oct. 1888. 28¼ x 36¼". Private collection, Switzerland

Below: Photograph of the same subject

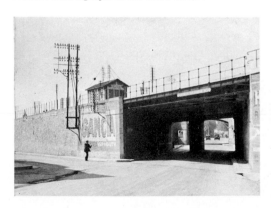

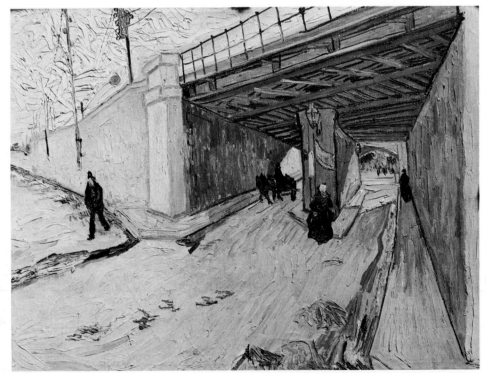

Although van Gogh admired the way in which his friends in Pont-Aven were able to work from memory and even wholly to invent such compositions as *Jacob Wrestling with the Angel*, he insisted that he himself could not yet adopt these methods. In a letter to Emile Bernard he explained: "I can't work without a model. I am not saying I don't disregard nature completely when I am working up a sketch into a picture, arranging the colors, enlarging or simplifying, but as far as the forms are concerned I am terrified of getting away from the possible, of not being accurate. Later perhaps, after another ten years, things may be different; but honestly I am so intrigued by what is possible, by what really exists, that I haven't either enough desire or courage to seek the ideal as it might result from my abstract studies. Others seem to have more feeling for abstract studies than I do, indeed you may be among the number, Gauguin too... myself too perhaps when I am old. Meanwhile I devour nature ceaselessly. I exaggerate, sometimes I make changes in the subject, but still I don't invent the whole picture, on the contrary I find it already there; it's a question of picking out what one wants from nature."[51]

In and about Arles nature offered van Gogh innumerable subjects from which to pick the elements in which he was mainly interested, subjects which helped him to renew constantly the passionate inner struggle for a balance between his vision and his visual experience. Everywhere lovely sites appealed to him: the quays of the broad and lazy Rhone river with its iron bridge, the shady promenade and Roman tombs of the Alyscamps, the romantic ruins of Montmajour to which he returned fifty times, the majestic plain of La Crau, the fields with their canals and willows and even some drawbridges built by Dutchmen, the humble fisherman's cottages in Saintes-Maries with its little fortified church, its lonely beach and picturesque boats. And then there was his yellow house near the station which he

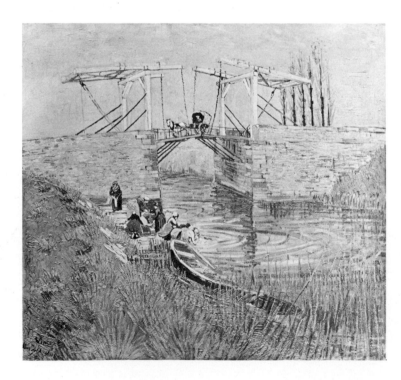

VAN GOGH: *Drawbridge near Arles*, April 1888. 23¼ x 24⅜". Private collection, Paris

furnished when he expected Gauguin's visit, the café where he went frequently, the public park which attracted him particularly and which he liked to call "Garden of a Poet," or the old coaches that went daily to nearby Tarascon, home of Daudet's beloved *Tartarin*. Van Gogh never felt attracted by the famous antique ruins of Arles, the beautiful churches, the sites tourists went to see; he preferred to paint things that were familiar to him or simple subjects, the beauty of which escaped most sightseers but in which he found a hidden poetry and life as well as a challenge to his creative power.

After a first series of canvases which still showed an impressionist approach—among them several of blooming almond trees—van Gogh had slowly tried to heighten his color schemes, to simplify forms. He was of course well aware of this evolution, for though he generally painted under the impact of his emotions, he never failed to analyze his work afterwards. The radical change his art underwent in Arles began with a change in his attitude towards nature, because what he now "wanted from nature" was no longer what he had wanted in Paris where Pissarro and Signac, Guillaumin and Monet had first taught him to see with the eye of an impressionist. But now in Arles, left to his own devices, occasionally strengthened by an exchange of ideas with Pont-Aven, he was able to report to his brother: "I feel that what I learned in Paris is *leaving* me.... And I should not be surprised if the impressionists soon will find fault with my way of painting, which has been fertilized by the ideas of Delacroix rather than by theirs. Because, instead of trying to reproduce exactly what I have before my eyes, I use color more arbitrarily so as to express myself vigorously."[52]

Among the first paintings to show his new approach was a series of views of a drawbridge just outside Arles, which he painted in a fashion suggestive of Japanese prints, with pronounced diagonals, flat planes, sharp outlines and strong contrasts. He returned several times to this motif between March and May; indeed he made it a habit to paint several versions of many of his subjects, since he professed that "in order to grasp the real character of the things here, one must look at them and paint them for a very long time."[53]

Van Gogh's increasing use of flat planes, frequently set off by strong, dark contours, was accompanied by experiments in texture which tended to relieve the monotony of uniform surfaces by the liveliness of clearly apparent brushwork. Painting with brushes practically dripping with color and applying pigments heavily, he would for instance adopt for a background strokes that appear interwoven like lattice work or basket weaves, or he would use a lively stippling for a sky in contrast to the broad strokes in which the landscape underneath is executed. In other cases he would represent each form by undulating lines which peculiarly stress its shape. According to his needs he would thus use all kinds of brush strokes within the same painting, enhancing their contrasts and creating oppositions that add themselves to those produced by colors. Sometimes he not only used hatchings, dots, or forcefully sweeping lines but actually squeezed the pigment directly from the tube onto his canvas. All this contrasted strongly with Gauguin's technique at Pont-Aven, which relied on the effects of flat planes precisely through their smooth and unadulterated flatness.

In many instances van Gogh seems to *draw* with his brushes, applying each stroke in such a way that it forms a line—straight or curved—or a dot and building up the entire painting out of an accumulation of clearly visible strokes. "I have now reached the point," he told his brother in September, "at which I have decided no longer to begin a painting with a [preparatory] charcoal sketch. It leads to nothing; one should attack a drawing directly with color in order to draw well."[54]

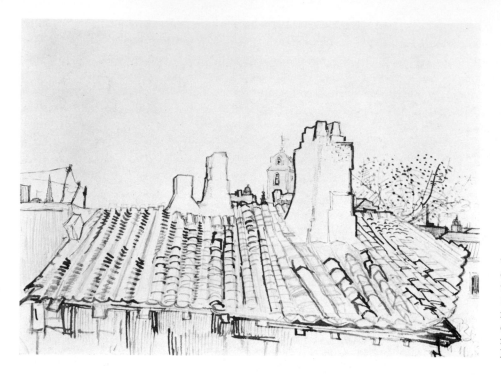

van Gogh: *Arles Roof Tops,* probably drawn from the artist's room above the Restaurant Carrel, March–April 1888. 9¾ x 13¼″. One of van Gogh's first ink drawings executed at Arles, it combines pencil, reed pen, and ordinary pen. Collection Heinz Berggruen, Paris

On the other hand his pen and ink drawings show a use of lines very similar to the application of brush strokes in his canvases, coupled with an analogous insistence on textures. It was apparently at Arles that Vincent employed for the first time oriental reed pens for his ink drawings in an endeavor to come closer to the technique of the Japanese. He sometimes combined their use with that of ordinary pens which trace much thinner lines, and also with pencil, but he generally drew with several reed pens of different widths. With these he obtained an amazing variety of textures and effects, a dazzling accumulation of strokes, commas, dots, hatchings such as no one had ever attempted to achieve. His broad, black lines have an accent of the definitive while they retain at the same time an undefinable vibrancy of spontaneity. Put down rapidly and unhesitatingly, they swarm in various directions, spread out over the large white sheet, densely assembled here and sparsely applied there, imitating undulating blades of grass or stems of wheat, curling and spiraling to represent the verdure of cypresses, extending in waves to depict tiled roofs or the sea, appearing in strong, parallel lines on garments, in thinly spread dots on skies, in tangled masses on bushes or trees, often closely knit and dark next to surfaces left immaculately white. They are like signs of a strange shorthand, swift, powerful, subtle, always unerringly precise and descriptive, always conveying an image of lush vegetation, distant horizons, dynamic forms. And the richness of varying textures, the inventiveness with which these textures are linked or opposed, confer upon his drawings a very special character and attraction which was felt even by those who did not appreciate van Gogh's paintings.

However, in spite of van Gogh's use of Japanese reed pens, his drawings scarcely have an oriental flavor; they are in no way elegant, fluid or deft, nor do they have the decorative qualities found in Japanese brush drawings. They are, instead, statements of tremendous

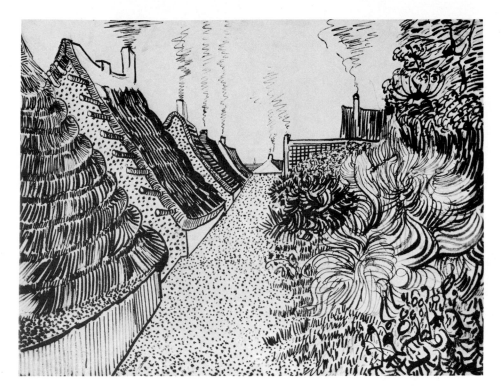

VAN GOGH: *Cottages at Saintes-Maries*, June 1888. Brush, reed pen and ink, traces of pencil, 9⅝ × 12½″. The Museum of Modern Art, New York (Abby Aldrich Rockefeller Bequest)

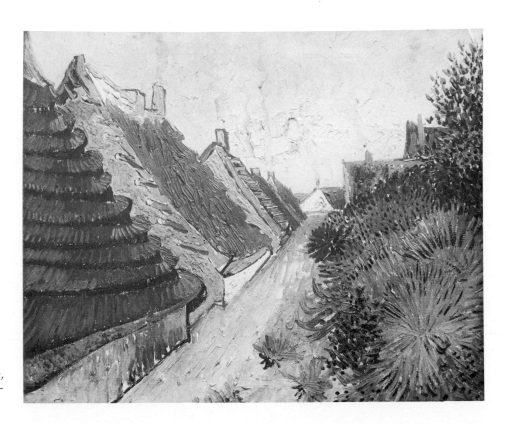

VAN GOGH: *Cottages at Saintes-Maries*, June 1888. 14⅜ × 17⅝″. Present whereabouts unknown

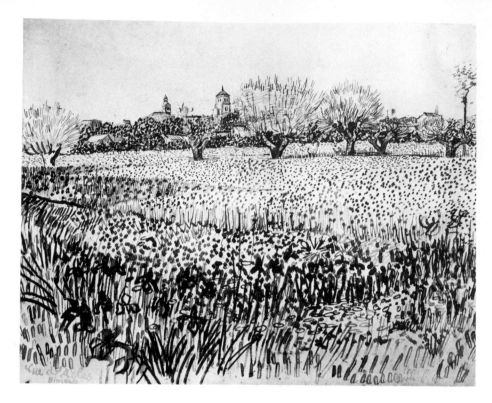

VAN GOGH: *View of Arles,* May 1888. Reed pen and ink, 17 x 21½". Museum of Art, Rhode Island School of Design, Providence

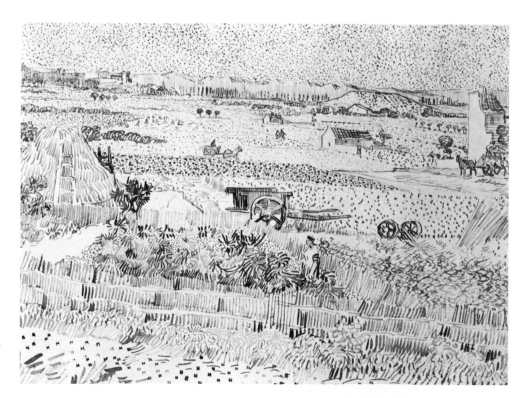

VAN GOGH: *Harvest—The Plain of La Crau,* Arles, June 1888. Reed pen and ink, 9½ x 12¾". Collection Mr. and Mrs. Paul Mellon, Upperville, Va.

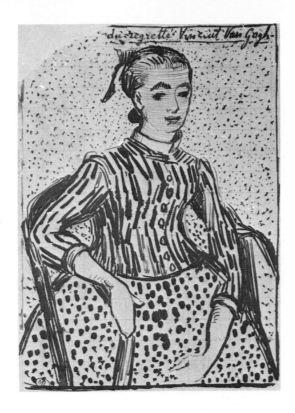

VAN GOGH: *La Mousmé,* Arles, July 1888. Reed pen, pen and ink. Formerly in the collection of Paul Gauguin, who pasted it in his manuscript of "Noa-Noa." Musée du Louvre, Paris

VAN GOGH: *Sailboats at Saintes-Maries,* June 1888. Reed pen and ink with pencil, 9⁹⁄₁₆ x 12⁹⁄₁₆". Justin K. Thannhauser Collection, New York. Courtesy the Thannhauser Foundation and The Solomon R. Guggenheim Museum, New York

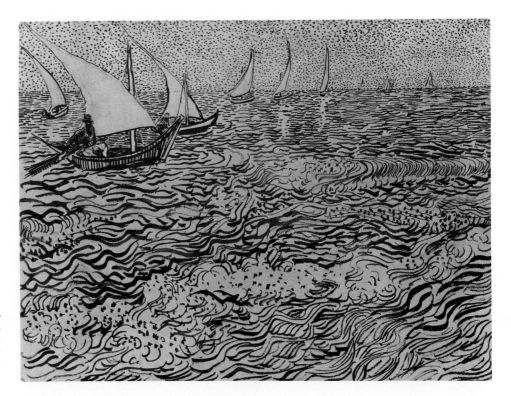

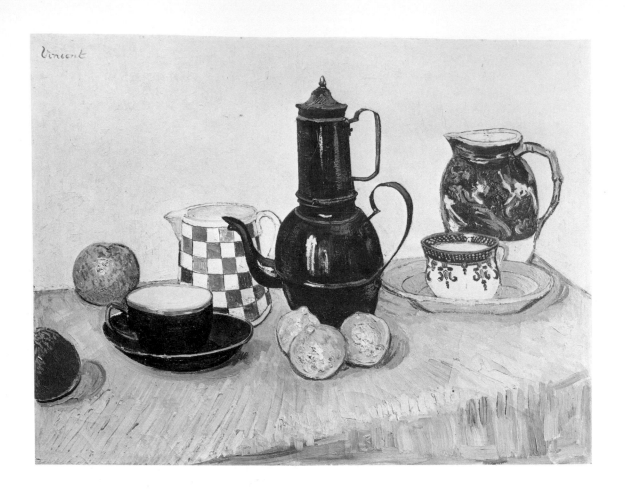

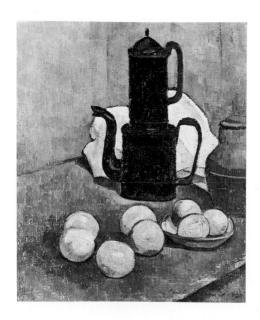

Above: VAN GOGH: *Still Life with Cups and Coffee-pot*, Arles, May 1888. 25⅝ x 31⅞". The Basil P. and Elise Goulandris Collection, Lausanne

Left: BERNARD: *Still Life with Coffeepot*, d. 1888. 21⅝ x 18⅛". Kunsthalle, Bremen

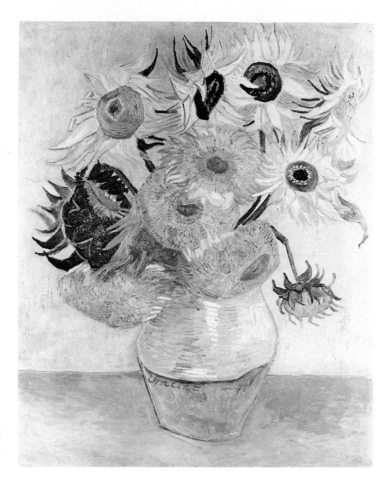

VAN GOGH: *Sunflowers*, Arles, Jan. 1889.
36¼ x 28⅞". Philadelphia Museum of Art
(Mr. and Mrs. Carroll S. Tyson, Jr., Collection)

vitality and force whose character lies not so much in graceful arabesque as in the mastery with which a multitude of pulsating and fluctuating signs is integrated into images of almost brutal simplicity, yet full of poetic evocation.[55]

Stronger than in his drawings, van Gogh's preoccupation with oriental art appears in some of his paintings, such as a still life which he painted in May. It has the same clear-cut outlines as the one with puppies Gauguin did at Pont-Aven, but van Gogh's composition has a unity which Gauguin's lacks, and there is nothing of the whimsical mood that Gauguin expressed. Instead there is a quiet yet vigorous solemnity in his endeavor to build up a powerful harmony based on two colors only. "I have done a still life," the artist wrote to Bernard, "with a blue enameled iron coffeepot, a royal blue cup and saucer, a milk jug checkered pale cobalt and white, a cup with a pattern in blue and orange on a white ground, a blue majolica jug decorated with flowers and foliage in greens, browns, and pinks. All that on a blue tablecloth, against a yellow background; there are also two oranges and three lemons among the crockery. So it's a variety of blues enlivened by a whole range of yellows, running even into orange."[56] Bernard, at about the same time, also painted a still life with an enameled coffeepot.

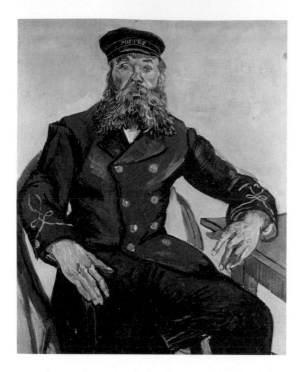

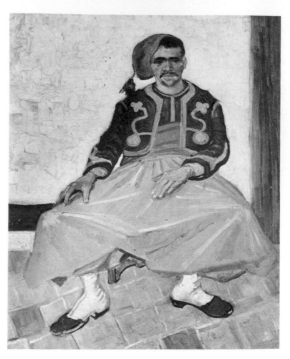

van Gogh: *Portrait of the Postman Roulin*, Arles, Aug. 1888. 31½ x 25″. Museum of Fine Arts, Boston (Robert Treat Paine II Collection)

van Gogh: *Portrait of a Zouave Bugler*, Arles, Aug. 1888. 31 x 25½″. Private collection, South America

Fascinated by the effect he could produce with a reduced scale of colors, the use of large flat planes and strong outlines, van Gogh did a portrait of Roulin,[57] a postman whom he had befriended, in a bright blue uniform against a pale blue background. He also painted a series of pictures all representing sunflowers in a yellow Provençal jug, set on a yellow table against a pale yellow background, composed of a variety of yellows with a few soft green notes. In other paintings he aimed at a forceful opposition of colors. When he painted the *Tarascon Coach* (Daudet had devoted a chapter to such a stagecoach in one of his *Tartarin* novels) with its stark reds, blues, blacks, and greens, he placed it against a background of yellow and a warm white dominated by a blue sky. And when he made a portrait of a Zouave bugler, he reveled in clashes of reds, blues, greens, and white.

Van Gogh doubtless met this bugler through the Zouave Lieutenant Milliet, who, together with Roulin, became one of his closest companions. Milliet was on leave in Arles after having fought in Tonkin, and it is quite likely that the painter sought him out because of his picturesque uniform. Soon Milliet took some drawing lessons from the artist, but he subsequently insisted that under no circumstances would he have allowed van Gogh to teach him how to paint. Indeed, the two friends hardly saw eye to eye when it came to art matters. "He was a strange fellow," Milliet later remembered, "impulsive like someone who has lived a long time in the strong sun of the desert. . . . He drew quite well. A charming companion when he felt like it, which did not happen every day. We would frequently take beautiful walks through the countryside around Arles and out there both of us made a great many

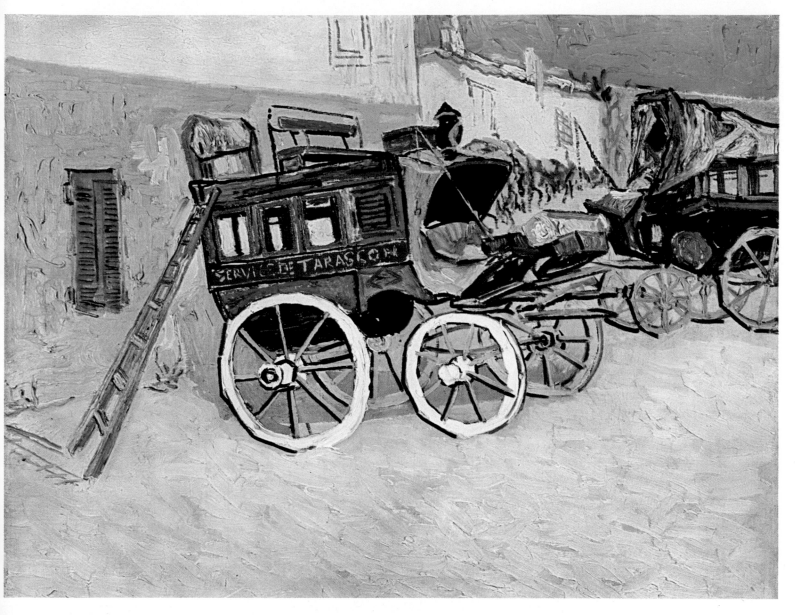

VAN GOGH: *The Tarascon Coach,* Arles, Oct. 1888. 28¼ x 36¼". Henry and Rose Pearlman Foundation, New York

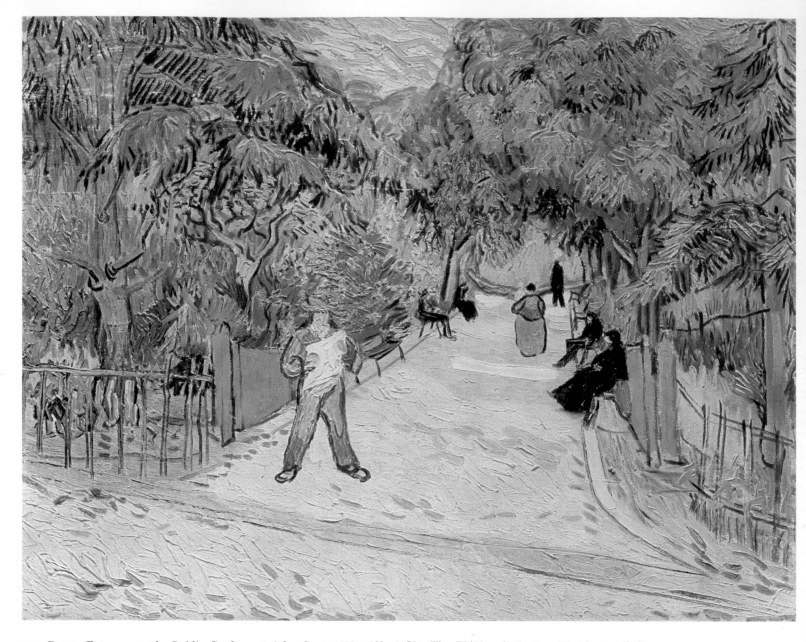

van Gogh: *Entrance to the Public Gardens at Arles,* Sept. 1888. 28½ x 35⅝″. The Phillips Collection, Washington, D.C.

sketches. Sometimes he put his easel up and began to smear away with paints. And that, well, that was no good. This fellow who had a taste and talent for drawing became abnormal as soon as he touched a brush.... Either I walked away, or I refused to voice any opinion, or else we quarreled. He was not easy to get along with and when he was angry, he almost seemed mad. He painted too broadly, paid no attention to details, did not draw first.... He replaced drawing by colors."[58] Milliet obviously did not approve of this and only sat for a portrait in order to be agreeable to his friend. He in no way cared for the likeness van Gogh painted of him (page 214).

Van Gogh was particularly interested in portraits and always regretted not knowing enough people who might be willing to pose for him. "In a picture I want to say something as comforting as music," he informed his brother. "I should like to paint men and women with that certain something of the eternal, which the halo used to symbolize and which we seek to achieve by the actual radiance and vibration of our colorings."[59] But he himself admitted that his portraits appeared to him "hard, and anyhow *ugly* and unsuccessful. All the same, as real difficulties have been tackled, they may open up the path for the future. The figures I do almost always seem to me horrid, not to mention how they seem to others; and yet it is the study of figures which gives the greatest strength."[60]

The word "ugly" was frequently applied by van Gogh to his own work, and he explained that he often could not express himself without an exaggeration that resulted in violence of color. This was the case particularly in his painting representing a café at night, the café where he took his meals. "For three nights running," he wrote to his brother, "I sat up to paint and went to bed during the day. I often think that the night is more alive and more

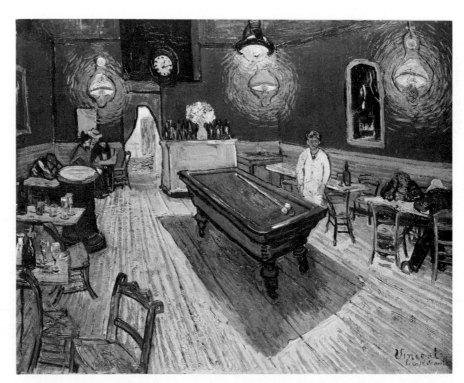

van Gogh: *Night Café,* Arles, Sept. 1888. 28¾ x 36¼". Yale University Art Gallery, New Haven, Conn. (Bequest of Stephen C. Clark)

richly colored than the day.... I have tried to express in this picture the terrible passions of humanity by means of red and green. The room is blood red and dark yellow with a green billiard table in the middle; there are four lemon-yellow lamps with a glow of orange and green. Everywhere there is a clash and contrast of the most alien reds and greens, of violet and blue in the figures of the little sleeping tramps, in the empty dreary room. The blood red and the yellow green of the billiard table for instance contrast with the soft tender Louis XV green of the counter on which there is a pink nosegay. The white coat of the proprietor, on vigil in a corner of this blaze, turns lemon yellow, or pale luminous green.... The color is not locally true from the *trompe-l'oeil* realist point of view; it is a color suggesting some emotions of an ardent temperament."[61] And van Gogh insisted: "In my picture of the *Night Café* I have tried to show that the café is a place where one can ruin one's self, go mad, or commit a crime."[62]

Van Gogh used this same symbolism of colors to express happy moods, as when he painted the yellow house in which he lived against a fresh blue sky. (The Zouave Milliet thought this horrible and professed not to understand how one could choose to paint such dull, stiff houses with no grace whatsoever.) In another painting, that of his own bedroom in the yellow house, van Gogh again selected an "unattractive" subject. "It's just simply my bedroom," he told his brother, "only here color is to do everything and, giving by its simplification a grander style to things, it is here to be suggestive of *rest* or of sleep in general. In a word, to look at the picture ought to rest the brain or rather the imagination.... The broad lines of the furniture also must express undisturbed rest.... The shadows and the shadows thrown are suppressed, the whole is painted in flat and large color areas as in

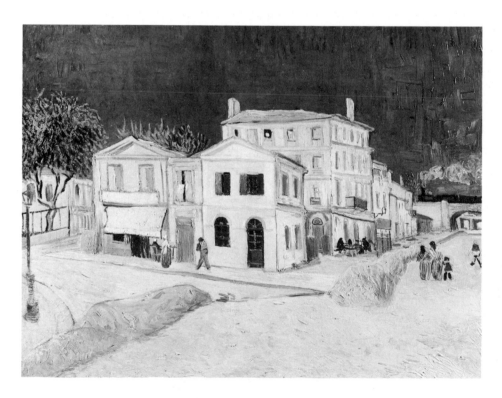

Left: van Gogh: *The Yellow House* (the artist's house at Arles), Sept. 1888. 28½ x 36¼". Rijksmuseum Vincent van Gogh, Amsterdam

Below: Photograph of the same subject taken before its destruction during World War II

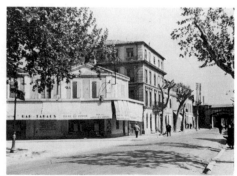

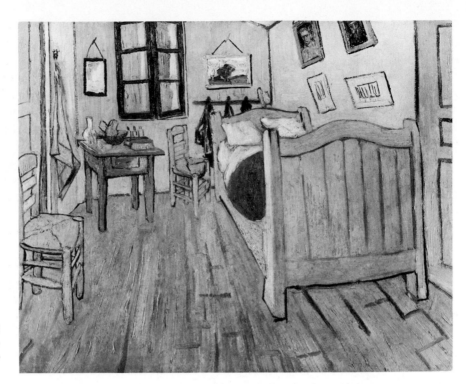

Japanese prints. It is going to be a contrast with, for instance, the *Tarascon Coach* and the *Night Café.*"[63] With real passion van Gogh explored the possibilities of expressing different moods through color combinations. "I am always hoping to make a discovery there," he informed Theo, "to express the love of two lovers by a marriage of two complementaries, their mingling and their opposition, the mysterious vibrations of kindred tones. To express the thought of a brow by the radiance of a light tone against a somber background. To express hope by some star, the eagerness of a soul by a sunset radiance."[59]

It becomes clear from van Gogh's own commentaries that each subject he chose to paint released in him specific emotions or associations of ideas which he sought to express by means of composition, of simplification, and especially of color. Thus every one of his canvases has a spiritual content, crystallizing a genuine feeling. Though his paintings are of course self-sufficient and do not have to be explained, they convey the obscure impression that they say much more, and much graver things, than appear on their surfaces. They are laden with meaningful allusions, reminiscences, meditations, and even forebodings—are pregnant with repressed compassion and tenderness, evangelical fervor or pagan ectasy. Each amplifies its literal, obvious value with a hidden, symbolic one that adds another dimension.[64]

In a certain way, therefore, van Gogh's paintings done in Arles are like a diary, a record of his changing moods and inspirations, of his hopes and desires. In addition to them he kept yet another kind of diary, consisting of his almost daily letters to his brother, in which he discussed his paintings, his life, the books he read, the people he met, and any other topic that presented itself. These letters relieved the isolation in which he lived, for there were days, especially at the beginning, when he hardly spoke to anyone except the waiters from whom he ordered his meals or the shopkeepers from whom he purchased his supplies. Though accustomed to being quite alone, van Gogh always felt an urge to pour himself out, and Theo became again, as he had been before they lived together in Paris, the ideal confidant. In their correspondence now reappeared a certain tenderness, a deep love which their natural shyness had prevented them from expressing while they shared a home. Vincent's letters, written in terse, direct language, though the syntax seems sometimes involved (for he now wrote in French rather than in Dutch) unfold the story of a hard yet poetic life, an odd mixture of sobriety and tenseness, filled with resignation, despair, faith, and consolation. They resemble strangely, even in their style, the pathetic tale of another artist's struggle which Knut Hamsun was putting down at the very same time in his first novel, *Hunger*. But unlike Hamsun who desperately fought off utter poverty and discouragement, Vincent always had his brother to whom he could turn for help. While he sometimes managed his budget rather badly and ordered frames, for instance, when he should have kept his money for food, and while there were occasionally several successive days during which he subsisted on coffee and bread, there was always relief in sight from Paris; there was always a bank note included in Theo's letters to take care of some unforeseen and urgent debts.[65] Though Vincent spoke frequently of financial matters in his letters, he did so with a superb disregard for the practical and the possible, freely putting wishful thinking and pleasant dreams on the credit side of his accounts. It is true that Gauguin, always ready to entertain the most fantastic schemes, was even more expert at mixing facts and fiction. During the summer of 1888 Gauguin, who could not pay his moderate board at Gloanec's, imagined that he might be able to raise no less than 600,000 francs to establish a dealer in impressionist paintings, and that dealer was to be Theo van Gogh.

More level-headed than the painters, as indeed he had to be if he wanted to help them, Theo somehow always managed to support himself and his brother, while also sending occasional remittances to Gauguin. Very seldom does he seem to have reminded Vincent of the limitations of his own means, and not once did he turn a deaf ear when Vincent's demands exceeded his monthly allowance. On the contrary, when Vincent was depressed by the thought of accepting so much money from his brother and expressed the hope that he might be able to repay him with pictures, Theo replied: "I consider the question of money and of selling [your] paintings and all the financial problem non-existent, or rather that it exists merely in the form of an illness.... You speak of the money that you owe me and want to repay. I don't want to hear about this. What I hope is that in time you will never have such preoccupations. I have to work in order to make money. Since neither of us has much, we should not take on more than we can afford, but once we keep this in mind, we can still hold out for some time even without selling anything."[66] And when Vincent lamented that his paintings were unsalable, Theo reassured him: "When we see that the works of Pissarro, Gauguin, Renoir, Guillaumin don't sell, we should be almost happy not to be favored by the public, for those who are in favor now will not always remain so and times may very well change rather soon."[67]

Thus besides his steady financial aid Theo also gave his brother the fullest moral support, manifesting an unflinching confidence in his art. As a matter of fact it seems hardly conceivable that Vincent could have been able to work without the certainty that Theo was always at his side, a safe harbor where he could find protection before, during, or after any storm. The painter realized this, and he often told his brother that he was more than just a dealer, that he had an important share in Vincent's own creative work. "I should like," he

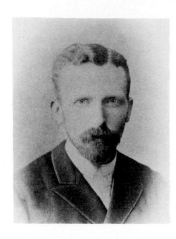

Photograph of Theo van Gogh, c. 1889

once wrote to Theo, "to be able to make you feel the truth of the fact that by giving money to artists you yourself are doing the work of an artist, and that my only desire is to see my canvases become of such a quality that you won't be too dissatisfied with *your* work."[68]

After Vincent left Paris, Theo kept in touch not only with Gauguin and Bernard (whose works Vincent constantly urged him to purchase), but also with Seurat, one of whose drawings he bought, and with Signac, Luce, Lautrec, and many others. Occasionally he would ask Guillaumin and Pissarro to come to see the latest canvases Vincent had sent him, and then would immediately transmit to his brother their encouraging remarks.[69] When Degas showed a liking for Gauguin's pictures from Pont-Aven, Theo also forwarded this good news and succeeded in bolstering the painter's low spirits. But on the commercial side Theo met with little or no success. In the summer of 1888 he took a group of impressionist paintings, among them a canvas by his brother, to Holland, where nobody cared for them. Indeed the head of his firm in Holland commented, on seeing a landscape by Sisley, that he could not help thinking that the artist must have been slightly drunk while painting it. Vincent had to admit that his own picture, in comparison, would have to be considered the result of delirium tremens.

Theo apparently was too shy and self-effacing ever to become a "figure" in the Parisian art world, although the little symbolist reviews frequently carried announcements of the paintings to be seen in his gallery. He went about his task very quietly. While he knew how to express his ardent belief in the future of such artists as Gauguin and his own brother, he preferred to let his customers discover their qualities by themselves and never tried to impose his convictions on others. Occasionally he succeeded in selling some of Gauguin's works, but he apparently felt a certain reluctance in recommending his brother's paintings, possibly because Vincent did not have to depend on his sales for a living.[70]

"Theo van Gogh," Gustave Kahn later wrote, "was pale, blond, and so melancholy that he seemed to hold canvases the way beggars hold their wooden bowls. His profound conviction of the value of the new art was stated without vigor and thus without great success. He did not have a barker's gift. But this salesman was an excellent critic and engaged in discussions with painters and writers as the discriminating art lover he was."[71]

A German painter who in July 1888 had studied Monet's canvases at Theo van Gogh's gallery (Theo had just signed a short-lived contract with Monet) and who returned several times to the exhibition, later reported that "a young and friendly employee with reddish hair, who did not look at all like a Frenchman, soon began to greet us very cordially like old acquaintances. One could see that there was no great interest in the pictures since the gallery was usually empty. We used to look around and admire the paintings while the young man kept to himself, smiled, and seemed pleased. After a few days he spoke to us, saying that he could see that we were interested in modern art and telling us that he had a brother who was a painter and who lived in the country. Could he show us some of his paintings? From another room he brought some unframed pictures of small size. He stood modestly aside, observing the effect these canvases made on us. We were still under the spell of Monet and now were somewhat perplexed. This was something entirely different, nature seen with a powerful will, decorative, the outlines sometimes drawn with blue color, as in old Japanese woodcuts. The gentleman asked for my opinion; I praised the beautiful pure color, though to my taste there was too much stylization. The friendly gentleman thanked as and carried the paintings back. Often when we subsequently passed his place he was looking through the glass of the door on the boulevard and greeted us with a smile. We only learned much later that his name was Theo van Gogh."[72]

It seems obvious that these retiring manners could not lead to many sales. Fortunately, in the late summer of 1888 Theo came into a small inheritance, left him by an uncle in Holland. Since he did not really need the money, he decided to put part of it aside for the support of his brother and to use another part for the realization of Vincent's fondest wish: the signing of a contract with Gauguin through which he guaranteed him 150 francs a month in payment for twelve paintings a year, leaving him free to sell the rest of his production elsewhere. To Gauguin this seemed at long last the solution of all his problems. (Laval had a similar arrangement with an anonymous benefactor and Bernard admittedly envied both of them, for although his parents were not too badly off, they refused to help him as long as he persisted in painting.) While offering to support Gauguin on a regular and permanent basis, Theo van Gogh also suggested that he join Vincent in Arles where the two painters could live more cheaply by sharing expenses.

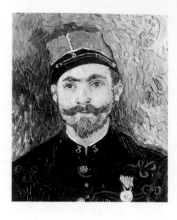

Vincent van Gogh was delighted with his brother's arrangement and hoped that eventually Theo would be able to secure the exclusive rights to Gauguin's work and then be in a position to raise his prices. But Gauguin himself modestly wrote from Pont-Aven to Vincent: "I fear that your brother, who likes my talent, actually overestimates it. I am a man ready for sacrifices and I should like him to understand that I shall always approve of whatever he does."[73] Yet, when he wrote to Schuffenecker at the same time, Gauguin expressed himself quite differently: "You may be assured that, as much as Theo van Gogh likes me, he would not undertake to support me in the South for love of me alone. Like the cold Dutchman he is, he has studied the conditions and intends to push me as much as can be done, and exclusively."[74] Though he knew nothing of Gauguin's suspicion that Theo had acted mainly for the purpose of making money, Vincent appraised his friend perfectly when he told his brother: "I feel by instinct that Gauguin is calculating; seeing himself at the bottom of the social ladder, he wants to regain a position by means which will certainly be honest, but which will be very strategic. Gauguin is unaware that I am able to recognize that."[75] What worried Vincent most was to see another financial burden, another responsibility placed on his brother's shoulders. After having been so anxious to see the deal with Gauguin go through he soon began to dread its consequences.

Now that Gauguin was commercially linked with Theo van Gogh and enjoyed some security, he would at last be able to pay his debts in Pont-Aven, which for so long had been an obstacle to his reunion with Vincent. On the other hand, the two brothers were reluctant to force Gauguin to go south simply because he now depended on them; they wanted him to come to Arles of his own free will. And Gauguin seemed in no particular hurry to do so, although Vincent's letters continuously clamored for his arrival. Gauguin later said that he had a premonition of something abnormal. But when Theo sold over 300 francs' worth of Gauguin's potteries in October and also agreed to pay his fare as well as his room and board in Arles, accepting paintings and drawings in exchange, Gauguin could no longer delay his departure. With Theo's remittances and additional sales he quickly figured that after six months to a year in Arles he might be able to save enough towards another trip to Martinique, for the splendors of the tropics began once more to haunt him, in spite of his unhappy experiences there. Instead of the "studio of the South" of which Vincent dreamt, Gauguin began to think of a "studio of the tropics" which he would establish with some of his companions from Pont-Aven. Yet in order to carry out this project Gauguin seemed to have no choice but to go first to Arles.

1 Gauguin to his wife, [Pont-Aven, end of June 1886]; see *Lettres de Gauguin à sa femme et à ses amis*, Paris, 1946, no. XLI, p. 92. These letters are rather carelessly transcribed and edited. Quotations here are translated directly from the originals, wherever possible, instead of being taken from the American edition of this book. Unless otherwise indicated, source references for Gauguin's letters always refer to the French edition, though its dates for letters are here frequently revised.

2 See C. Chassé: *De quand date le Synthétisme de Gauguin?*, *L'Amour de l'Art*, April 1938.

3 G. Kahn: Paul Gauguin, *L'Art et les Artistes*, Nov. 1925.

4 It is possible that Gauguin later reworked some of his canvases from Martinique to simplify both colors and lines.

5 V. van Gogh to Bernard, [Arles, end of May 1888]; see *Verzamelde Brieven van Vincent van Gogh*, vol. IV, Amsterdam, 1954, no. B5, p. 197.

6 Gauguin to Schuffenecker, [Pont-Aven, Feb. 1888]; see C. Roger-Marx: *Lettres inédites de Vincent van Gogh et de Paul Gauguin*, *L'Europe*, Feb. 15, 1939.

7 Gauguin to his wife, [Pont-Aven, March 1888]; *op. cit.*, no. LXII, p. 127.

8 Gauguin to Schuffenecker, [Pont-Aven, July 8, 1888]; *ibid.*, no. LXVI, p. 133.

9 According to Bernard, Gauguin often begged Laval not to follow him too closely. Indeed Laval's paintings resemble Gauguin's to such an extent that it is probable that many canvases from Martinique and even from Pont-Aven, attributed to Gauguin and now bearing his signature, are actually the work of Laval. Bernard mentions several such instances; the same thing has happened to some of Bernard's work done in Brittany, notably the painting reproduced p. 174 from which Bernard himself subsequently had to remove a forged Gauguin signature.

10 V. van Gogh to Bernard, [Arles, early Aug. 1888]; *Verzamelde Brieven*, vol. IV, no. B14, p. 220.

11 Gauguin to Camille Pissarro, [Copenhagen, March 1885]; unpublished document, courtesy the late Rodo Pissarro, Paris.

12 E. Bernard: Louis Anquetin, *Gazette des Beaux-Arts*, Feb. 1934.

13 Bernard: Mémoire sur l'histoire du symbolisme pictural de 1890, *Maintenant*, April 1946.

14 E. Dujardin: Le Cloisonnisme, *Revue Indépendante*, May 19, 1888.

15 V. van Gogh to his brother, [Arles, June 1888]; see *Verzamelde Brieven van Vincent van Gogh*, vol. III, Amsterdam, 1953, no. 500, p. 238. These letters, written in French, are here translated directly and not quoted from the English edition: *The Complete Letters of Vincent van Gogh*, 3 vols., Greenwich, Conn., 1958.

16 Gauguin to Schuffenecker, [Pont-Aven, Aug. 14, 1888]; *op. cit.*, no. LXVII, pp. 134–35.

17 Gauguin to Schuffenecker, [Pont-Aven, Oct. 8, 1888]; *ibid.*, no. LXXI, p. 140. On the relationship between Gauguin and Bernard see H. Dorra: Emile Bernard and Paul Gauguin, *Gazette des Beaux-Arts*, April 1955 (published Dec. 1955).

18 V. van Gogh to his brother, [Arles, end of Aug. 1888]; *Verzamelde Brieven*, vol. III, no. 527, p. 298.

19 Gauguin to Schuffenecker, [Pont-Aven, Oct. 16, 1888]; *op. cit.*, no. LXXIII, p. 147.

20 Gauguin to Bernard, [Arles, Nov. 1888]; *ibid.*, no. LXXV, p. 150.

21 V. van Gogh to his brother, [Arles, Sept.–Oct. 1888]; *Verzamelde Brieven*, vol. III, no. 539, p. 311.

22 Gauguin to V. van Gogh, [Pont-Aven, Sept. 1888]; unpublished document, courtesy Ir. V. W. van Gogh, Laren.

23 See Bernard: Souvenirs inédits sur l'artiste peintre Paul Gauguin et ses compagnons lors de leur séjour à Pont-Aven et au Pouldu, Lorient, n.d. [1939], pp. 9–10.

24 Laval was to die of tuberculosis in 1894 in Cairo. His fiancée, who had followed him there, apparently contracted his illness; she succumbed a year later, also in Cairo, where her brother then lived.

25 Bernard to V. van Gogh, quoted in van Gogh's letter to his brother, [Arles, Sept.–Oct. 1888]; *Verzamelde Brieven*, vol. III, no. 535, p. 302.

26 See A. Tellegen: Vincent and de Chamaillard, *Museumjournaal*, no. 1–2, 1966, p. 52.

27 V. van Gogh to his brother, [Arles, end of Aug. 1888]; *Verzamelde Brieven*, vol. III, no. 526, p. 288.

28 Gauguin quoted by M. Denis *in* P. Sérusier: ABC de la peinture, suive d'une étude sur la vie et l'œuvre de Paul Sérusier par Maurice Denis, Paris, 1942, p. 42.

29 Dom W. Verkade: Le Tourment de Dieu, Paris, 1923, pp. 75–76. Quotations from this book were translated from the French version, supervised by the author, instead of being taken from the not always adequately translated English edition: Yesterdays of an Artist Monk, London, 1930.

30 V. van Gogh to Bernard, [Arles, second half of June 1888]; *Verzamelde Brieven*, vol. IV, no. B 6, p. 198.

31 Gauguin to V. van Gogh, [Pont-Aven, Sept. 1888]; unpublished document, courtesy Ir. V. W. van Gogh, Laren.

32 V. van Gogh to Bernard, [Arles, end of Sept. 1888]; *Verzamelde Brieven*, vol. IV, no. B 18, p. 228.

33 See V. van Gogh's letter to his brother, [Arles, Sept. 1888]; *Verzamelde Brieven*, vol. III, no. 539, p. 312.

34 V. van Gogh to his brother, [Arles, Sept.–Oct. 1888]; *ibid.*, no. 545, p. 328.

35 Gauguin to V. van Gogh, [Pont-Aven, Sept.–Oct. 1888]; unpublished document, courtesy Ir. V. W. van Gogh, Laren.

36 On the exchange of these portraits see A. Meyerson: Van Gogh and the School of Pont-Aven, *Konsthistorisk Tidskrift*, Dec. 1946.

37 V. van Gogh to his brother, [Arles, Sept. 17, 1888]; *Verzamelde Brieven*, vol. III, no. 537, p. 306.

38 V. van Gogh to his brother, [Arles, Sept. 1888]; *ibid.*, no. 539, p. 312.

39 V. van Gogh to Gauguin, [Arles, Oct. 1888]; *Verzamelde Brieven*, vol. IV, no. B 22, p. 237.

40 V. van Gogh to his brother, [Arles, beginning of May 1888]; *Verzamelde Brieven*, vol. III, no. 480, p. 204.

41 V. van Gogh to his brother, [Arles, beginning of June 1888]; *ibid.*, no. 495, p. 228.

42 V. van Gogh to his brother, [Arles, June 1888]; *ibid.*, no. 500, p. 238. Vincent frequently thought of Camille Pissarro; on March 14, 1888, shortly after his brother had left Paris, Theo wrote to Pissarro at Eragny: "In his last letter my brother asked me to give you his best regards. He works

a great deal and is going to send me some paintings soon. When you come to Paris I hope that you will come to see them and give me your opinion." Unpublished document, courtesy the late Rodo Pissarro, Paris.

43 V. van Gogh to his brother, [Arles, May 1888]; Verzamelde Brieven, vol. III, no. 490, p. 220.

44 V. van Gogh to his sister Wil, [Arles, beginning of April 1888]; Verzamelde Brieven, vol. IV, no. W 3, p. 148.

45 V. van Gogh to his brother, [Arles, Sept. 1888]: Verzamelde Brieven, vol. III, no. 539, p. 310.

46 V. van Gogh to his brother, Arles, [June–July 1888]; *ibid.*, no. 504, pp. 245–46.

47 V. van Gogh to his brother, [Arles, July 1888]; *ibid.*, no. 507, p. 253.

48 V. van Gogh to his brother, [Saint-Rémy, June 9, 1889]; *ibid.*, no. 594, p. 429.

49 V. van Gogh to his brother, [Arles, beginning of Aug. 1888]; *ibid.*, no. 520, p. 276. On V. van Gogh and Boch see the catalogue of the exhibition *Anna und Eugène Boch*, by Th. Faider-Thomas, Saarland-Museum, Saarbrücken, May–June 1971.

50 V. van Gogh to his brother, [Arles, Sept. 3, 1888]; Verzamelde Brieven, *ibid.*, no. 531, p. 293.

51 V. van Gogh to Bernard, [Arles, beginning of Oct. 1888]; Verzamelde Brieven, vol. IV, no. B 19, pp. 229–30.

52 V. van Gogh to his brother, [Arles, first half of Aug. 1888]; Verzamelde Brieven, vol. III, no. 520, p. 276.

53 V. van Gogh to his brother, [Arles, second half of Sept. 1888]; *ibid.*, no. 541, p. 315.

54 V. van Gogh to his brother, [Arles, Sept. 1888]; *ibid.*, no. 539, p. 312.

55 For an excellent study on van Gogh's draftsmanship see F. Novotny: Van Gogh's Teekeningen van het "Straatje te Saintes-Maries," *Maandblad voor Beeldende Kunsten*, Dec. 1936; also F. Novotny: Reflections on a Drawing by van Gogh, *The Art Bulletin*, March 1953; both reprinted in Novotny: Über das "Elementare" in der Kunstgeschichte und andere Aufsätze, Vienna, 1968.

56 V. van Gogh to Bernard, [Arles, end of May 1888]; Verzamelde Brieven, vol. IV, no. B 5, p. 197.

57 Roulin was about six and a half feet tall and lived in the rue de la Cavalerie, where Vincent had also stayed upon his arrival at Arles. Roulin was *not* a letter carrier but was employed at the railroad station—close to the yellow house—to load and unload mail. After he was transferred to Marseilles, he worked on the Lyons-Marseilles trains, sorting mail. See J.-N. Priou: Van Gogh et la famille Roulin, *Revue des PTT de France*, May–June 1955. Van Gogh presented at least five of his paintings to the Roulins, mostly portraits of the members of the family (later sold to Vollard), and Gauguin gave them two canvases, which were subsequently lost or destroyed.

58 Milliet quoted by P. Weiller: Nous avons retrouvé le Zouave de van Gogh, *Lettres Françaises*, no. 561, March 24–31,

1955. Milliet's portrait by van Gogh is de La Faille no. 499 (F. 473). That Vincent's portraits of the bugler represent another Zouave was pointed out by M. Florisoone: Vincent van Gogh, peintre de Zouaves, *Revue Internationale d'Histoire Militaire*, no. 13, 1953.

59 V. van Gogh to his brother, [Arles, beginning of Sept. 1888]; Verzamelde Brieven, vol. III, no. 531, pp. 294–95.

60 V. van Gogh to Bernard, [Arles, end of June 1888]; Verzamelde Brieven, vol. IV, no. B 8, p. 211.

61 V. van Gogh to his brother, [Arles, Sept. 8, 1888]; Verzamelde Brieven, vol. III, no. 533, pp. 297–98.

62 V. van Gogh to his brother, [Arles, first half of Sept. 1888]; *ibid.*, no. 534, p. 300.

63 V. van Gogh to his brother, [Arles, second half of Oct. 1888]; *ibid.*, no. 554, pp. 345–46.

64 The last four sentences are quoted freely from J. Seznec: Literary Inspiration in van Gogh, *Magazine of Art*, Dec. 1950.

65 On the psychological aspects of this financial dependency see G. Kraus: The Relationship between Theo and Vincent van Gogh, Amsterdam, 1954. C. Mauron: Vincent et Théo van Gogh—Une Symbiose, 1955, has stated that the 150 francs a month which the painter received from his brother "would represent at least 30,000 francs today ($86). Before the first World War a schoolmaster was paid 75 francs a month as a starting salary. I am not certain whether Mallarmé, as an English teacher, ever received more than the allowance van Gogh enjoyed."

66 Theo van Gogh to his brother, Paris, Oct. 27, 1888; Verzamelde Brieven, vol. IV, no. T 3, pp. 260–61.

67 Theo van Gogh to his brother, Paris, May 21, 1889; *ibid.*, no. T 9, p. 267.

68 V. van Gogh to his brother, [Arles, Oct. 1888]; Verzamelde Brieven, vol. III, no. 550, p. 335.

69 According to Andries Bonger, though this is not supported by any other evidence, Theo did not really appreciate his brother's work. Bonger subsequently stated: "When the packs of pictures arrived from Arles, it was Vincent's studio pals who were filled with admiration and told Theo of the extraordinary artistic talent that was manifest in them; Theo himself realized this only somewhat later." (Anon. [A. Bonger]: Vincent, *Nieuwe Rotterdamsche Courant*, Sept. 5, 1893.)

70 On Theo as an art dealer, see J. Rewald: Theo van Gogh, Goupil, and the Impressionists, *Gazette des Beaux-Arts*, Jan.–Feb. 1973.

71 G. Kahn: Au temps du pointillisme, *Mercure de France*, May 1924.

72 H. Schlittgen: Erinnerungen, Munich, 1926, pp. 199–200.

73 Gauguin to V. van Gogh, [Pont-Aven, Sept. 1888]; unpublished document, courtesy Ir. V. W. van Gogh, Laren.

74 Gauguin to Schuffenecker, [Quimperlé, Oct. 16, 1888]; *op. cit.*, no. LXXIII, p. 147.

75 V. van Gogh to his brother, [Arles, middle of Sept. 1888]; Verzamelde Brieven, vol. III, no. 538, p. 308.

V   1888   TRAGEDY IN ARLES

As Gauguin's arrival at Arles approached, Vincent van Gogh became increasingly nervous. He admitted to himself that he would not have been able to spend the winter in Arles alone, that he badly needed Gauguin's presence as a relief from his solitude. But he also feared that his friend might be disappointed, that he might regret having left Pont-Aven for the South. Somehow he tried to prepare himself for such a possibility; yet deep inside all his hopes were set on Gauguin's liking Arles, for only then could his own plans for the future succeed. If Gauguin's sojourn at Arles proved to be a success, the road would be open for additional visitors. Already Bernard and Laval had let it be known that they might come south in February 1889, and now Vincent even went so far as to dream of the possibility that Seurat might be persuaded to join them; but of this he hardly dared to speak to Theo and certainly not at all to Gauguin and Bernard.

Meanwhile van Gogh worked more feverishly than ever in order to be ready for Gauguin. "I have carried as far as I can everything I have started," he wrote to his brother, "because of my great desire to show him something new and not to be subjected to his influence (for I certainly hope that he will have some influence on me) before I am able to show him unquestionably my own originality."[1] He stated that "ideas for my work come to me in *throngs* so that, although solitary, I have no time to think or to feel; I go on like a steam engine at painting."[2]

Complete isolation and intensive work, while they elated him, contributed to Vincent's slowly deteriorating health. The irregular meal hours he kept, the cheap and insufficient food he hastily ate—often consisting of bread and coffee or inexpensive wine—and the long, uninterrupted hours of work he crammed into every day soon began to leave their mark. He himself admitted that he was completely exhausted after devoting one long session—lasting an entire day—to a single canvas which he frequently completed between dawn and dusk. During the harvest season he had thus worked day after day, hardly stopping long enough to take a little light nourishment. The result was that he soon felt absolutely numb at the end of his day. "In those moments," he wrote to Theo, "the prospect of not being alone any more is not unpleasant to me. And very often, upon returning from this mental work of harmonizing six essential colors: red—blue—yellow—orange—purple—green, I think of that excellent painter Monticelli, who is said to have been a drinker and demented.... After that, in my case as in many others, the only thing that relieves and distracts one is to forget oneself by drinking heartily and by smoking a good deal, which no doubt is not very virtuous...."[3]

But van Gogh made no complaints about the ardent and consuming life he was leading. There were many things he was willing to give up—comfort, food, peace—as long as he could go on with his work. "Oh, my dear brother," he exclaimed, "sometimes I know so well what I want. In life and in painting too I can easily do without God, but I cannot —I who suffer—go without something that is bigger than I, that is my life: the power to create."[4]

Always attracted by nocturnal scenes, van Gogh painted in September—a few weeks before Gauguin's arrival—a view of the Rhone river at night under a starry sky. So as to be able to work in the dark, he stuck a number of burning candles into his hatband and painted by the light of this strange and flickering crown, a circumstance which prompted the citizens of Arles who watched him to consider Vincent more than a little crazy.[5]

Van Gogh bought some essential furniture for the house, but warned Gauguin not to expect any great luxury, and completed a series of canvases destined for the decoration of their rooms. "I wrote you the other day that my eyes were strangely tired," he told Gauguin in October. "Well, I took a rest for two and a half days and then started to work again, but without yet daring to go out of doors. For my decoration I did a painting about 28 by 36 inches of my bedroom, with the unpainted wood furniture you are familiar with. And it gave me tremendous pleasure to paint this interior without artifice, of a simplicity à la Seurat: flat surfaces, though coarsely brushed with heavy pigment; the walls pale lilac, the floor of a broken and faded red, the chairs and the bed chrome yellow, the pillows and the sheet very pale lemon green, the blanket blood red, the dressing table orange, the washbasin blue, the window green. I should have liked to express absolute peacefulness through all these various colors, you see, where the only white note is given by the small spot of the mirror with its black frame (so as to cram yet the fourth pair of complementaries into the painting). Well, you will see it with the others and we shall talk about it, for I often don't know what I am doing, working almost like a somnambulist.

"It is beginning to be cold, especially on days when the mistral blows. I had gaslight put in the studio so that we shall have good light in the winter. Maybe you will be disappointed in Arles, if you arrive at a time when there is a mistral, but wait.... It is only after some time that the poetry of this place grips one. You will not yet find the house as comfortable as we shall try to make it little by little. There are so many expenses! And this cannot be done all at once. But I think that once you are here you will — like me — be seized by an intense eagerness to paint the effects of autumn during the intervals of the mistral, and that you will understand why I insisted that you come here now when there are some beautiful days."[6]

Yet the excitement of anticipation became almost too much, and in his last letter written to Theo before Gauguin's arrival Vincent confessed: "I am not sick, but I would become so without any doubt if I did not take some strengthening food and did not stop painting for a few days [owing to his working pace he had already had several fainting spells]. Once again I am almost reduced to a state of madness like that of Hugo van der Goes in the painting by Emile Wauters. And if it were not that I have a kind of split personality, being both something of a monk and a painter, I would have been completely reduced to the same condition long ago. But even so I do not believe that my madness would have taken the form of persecution mania since in a state of over-excitement my own feelings lean rather towards preoccupations with eternity and eternal life. But just the same I must beware of my nerves...."[1]

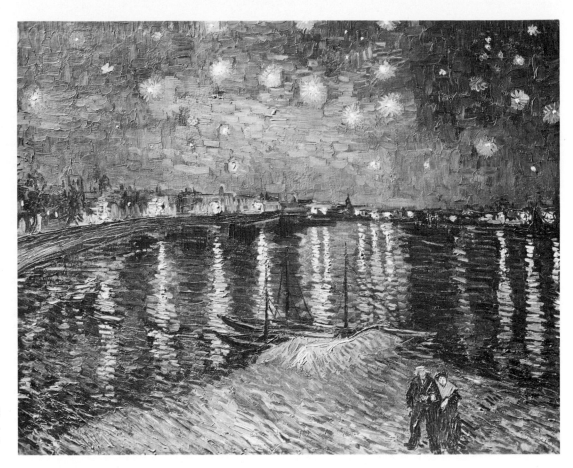

VAN GOGH: *The Rhone River at Night,* Arles, Sept. 1888. 28½ x 36¼". Exhibited with the Independents in 1889. Private collection, Paris

This is the first time van Gogh mentions the word *madness* in his letters from Arles, and he does so in connection with another painter, Hugo van der Goes (Flemish, 1440–82), who at the age of thirty-five had retired to a monastery, taken to drink, and soon shown signs of insanity. In Wauters' canvas, to which van Gogh refers, the artist is seen in a novice's robe, seated, his hands clenched, intently listening to a choir of young boys, while a strange gleam illuminates his eyes.[7] And to this mad painter-monk van Gogh likened himself while waiting for Gauguin.

Gauguin reached Arles some time before dawn on October 23, 1888. Since he did not want to awaken his friend, he went to the "night café," where the proprietor immediately recognized him, for van Gogh had shown him the new arrival's self-portrait. The meeting of the two friends was extremely cordial although Vincent seemed rather agitated, as Gauguin reported to Theo; but Gauguin hoped to be able to calm him soon. Indeed Vincent, who had seriously feared that he might become ill, felt his confidence return now that Gauguin was with him. And Gauguin found himself in excellent spirits when, during his first days in Arles, he received a money order for 500 francs from Theo for a Brittany picture the latter had sold. Gauguin could now pay his last debts in Pont-Aven and even send some money to his wife in Copenhagen.

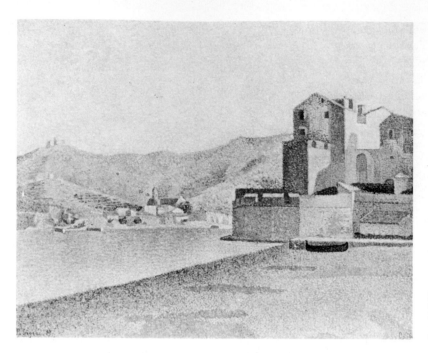

While van Gogh had been overwhelmed by the South and had discovered Japan there, Gauguin was much less struck with Provence, which was unquestionably more colorful and romantic—though less mystic—than Brittany, but which was far from being as luscious and tropical as Martinique. As a matter of fact, the impression the *midi* made on artists was strongly conditioned by what they expected from it as well as by the course their own work was following. Signac, for instance, whose mind was scientifically trained to analyze colors and their interaction, experienced very different sensations from his first contact with the South in 1887. "In this region there is nothing but white," he later wrote in his diary concerning the Mediterranean shore. "The light, reflected everywhere, devours all local colors and makes the shadows appear gray.... Van Gogh's paintings done at Arles are marvelous in their fury and intensity, but they do not at all render the *luminosity* of the South. Just because they are in the *midi* people expect to see reds, blues, greens, yellows.... It is on the contrary the North—Holland for example—that is *colored* (local colors), the South being *luminous*."[8] And to Pissarro he wrote: "Oh, no, I am not at all enthusiastic and I am not sustaining a paradox: the *midi* resembles Asnières; the same dusty roads, the same red roofs, the same slightly gray sky.... This is not subjective, it is entirely objective.... In short, except for certain local colors, the South does not differ too much from our usual landscapes, and those who paint black in the North and blue in the *midi* are charlatans. I see the South quite differently from the way Monet [who had painted on the Côte d'Azur in 1884] sees it. There is much less distance between the tones. The shadow is warmer, one feels the light more—the light in the shade, oh Seurat!"[9] But all this did not prevent Signac from loving the South which he found more harmoniously colored than the North: "Blue sky, blue sea, and all the rest burned, orange;—thus a forced harmony. In that respect the *midi* is splendid."[10]

Whether or not Gauguin shared Signac's views, he was far from smitten with the South. That much is certain: at one time or another Gauguin told van Gogh that he considered Arles "the filthiest place in the *midi*,"[11] though this may not have been his first impression. "When we were together in Arles," he subsequently wrote, "both of us mad, in continuous war for beautiful colors, I adored red—where to find a perfect vermilion? He, with his yellowest brush, wrote on the wall, suddenly purple:

Je suis sain d'esprit
Je suis le Saint-Esprit."[12]

Actually very little is known about the time Gauguin and van Gogh spent together in Arles. When Gauguin, many years later, put down his recollections of that period, he did so with a tendency towards self-justification that heavily weights his report in his own favor. While the facts as he related them were probably exact, there can be no doubt that he left much unsaid. From the beginning van Gogh must have burst forth with all the emotion and enthusiasm pent up for so long; his admiration for Gauguin, his joy at having at last somebody with whom he could discuss those esthetic problems which were so vital to him were expressed with a violent cordiality. Gauguin, on the other hand, tried to remain aloof and to concern himself with his own affairs. During the first days he did not say much about van Gogh's work in general, although the latter eagerly waited for his friend's comments, but he did indicate a real liking for some canvases, such as the *Sunflowers* and Vincent's *Bedroom*. As for himself, Gauguin planned to spend about a month in Arles before doing any serious work, for he needed time to acquaint himself with the new surroundings; in the meantime he intended to paint some studies and to draw. Yet from his very first promenades through Arles with Vincent, who proudly showed him all the beautiful sites he loved so much, Gauguin could not help but feel himself out of place and found it difficult to conceal his disappointment. "I find everything small, paltry, the landscape and the people," he wrote to Bernard.[13] Gauguin's reaction could not escape van Gogh, and while he did not want to hurt Theo by telling him about it, he did write to his brother that Gauguin continually spoke about his nostalgia for the tropics.

In spite of his admiration for Gauguin and the lengthy discussions he had had with him in Paris, van Gogh did not really know his friend intimately. He now observed him intently and soon reported to Bernard: "Gauguin interests me very much as a person, very much indeed. For a long time I have thought that in our damned artist's trade we have the greatest need for people who have hands and stomachs like workers, more natural appetites, temperaments more loving and more charitable than those decadent and rotten Parisian boulevardiers. And here, without the slightest doubt, we find ourselves in the presence of a virginal being with the instincts of a savage. In Gauguin blood and sex dominate ambition. But enough of this. You have seen him at close quarters longer than I have; I just wanted to give you my first impressions in a few words. You won't be very much surprised if I tell you that our discussions have a tendency to touch upon the terrible subject of an association of certain painters. This association might or might not have a commercial character. We haven't reached any conclusions yet... but I certainly believe in the possibility of a tremendous renewal of art; I believe that this new art will have the tropics as its homeland."[14]

To these lines Gauguin added the following comment: "Don't listen to Vincent; as you know, admiration comes easily to him and indulgence ditto. His idea of the future for a new generation in the tropics seems perfectly correct to me as a painter and I continue to have the intention of returning there whenever I find the means. Who knows — maybe with a little bit of good luck?..."[15]

While he pursued his dreams of the tropics, Gauguin went on to show how little he liked Arles. He glorified Pont-Aven to such an extent that Vincent felt impelled to admit that in Brittany everything was better, more beautiful, and of a purer character than in parched Provence.[16] Not content with scuttling his friend's attachment for his beloved South, Gauguin soon made it plain that he did not approve of the way in which Vincent ran their "household." Indeed, there was practically nothing he did like. "To begin with," he later wrote, "I found everywhere a disorder that shocked me. His box of colors was scarcely large enough to contain all the squeezed tubes which were never closed, yet in spite of all this disorder, this mess, there was something brilliant in his canvases; in his words too. His Dutch brain was afire with the Bible. In Arles, the quays, the bridges, and the boats, in fact all of the *midi* became Holland to him. He even forgot how to write Dutch.... From the first month I saw our joint finances take on the same aspects of disorder. What was to be done? The situation was delicate, the cash-box being modestly filled by his brother.... Only with great precaution and much coaxing, little in keeping with my character, did I refer to the matter. I must admit that I succeeded much more easily than I had expected."[17]

There was actually nothing surprising in the fact that van Gogh should have given in so readily. He was determined to make a success of Gauguin's visit and was perfectly willing to arrange their daily life in any fashion that would suit his friend; he was probably prepared to make many more concessions, had that been the price of Gauguin's happiness. Long before he succeeded in persuading Gauguin to come to Arles, van Gogh had already outlined to him some of the aspects of their future life in common when he wrote:

"It seems to me that if I find another painter who would like to exploit the *midi* and like me would be sufficiently absorbed by his work to be willing to live like a monk who goes to the brothel once every two weeks, but otherwise is held by his work and little disposed to waste his time, then it would be an excellent arrangement.... Yet my brother cannot send you money to Brittany and also money to me in Provence. But wouldn't you share things with me here? Then, in combining our expenses, there might be enough for two; I am even certain of this.... Although life here seems to me more expensive [than in Brittany], isn't it also true that there are better chances for doing pictures here? Be this as it may, if my brother sent us 250 francs a month for the two of us, would you care to come? We would share them. But in that case we should have to eat at home as often as possible and hire some cleaning woman for a few hours a day so as to avoid all hotel expenses. And you would give my brother one painting a month whereas you would be free to do with the rest as you please."[18]

As a matter of fact the two friends now agreed to put all their money into two boxes and to divide it into various categories: for rent and food, for nocturnal and "hygienic" promenades, for tobacco, and so on. To cut down on their expenses, Gauguin was to do the cooking himself while van Gogh did the shopping. To Vincent's delight Gauguin turned out to be an excellent cook. But their budget was never well-balanced in spite of their careful bookkeeping. As Vincent later explained to Theo: "What is good is that he [Gauguin] knows marvelously how to arrange expenses on a day-by-day basis. Whereas I am often absent-minded, anxious to arrive at a good *result*, he has much more of a feeling for money

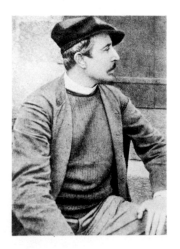

Photograph of Paul Gauguin, 1888

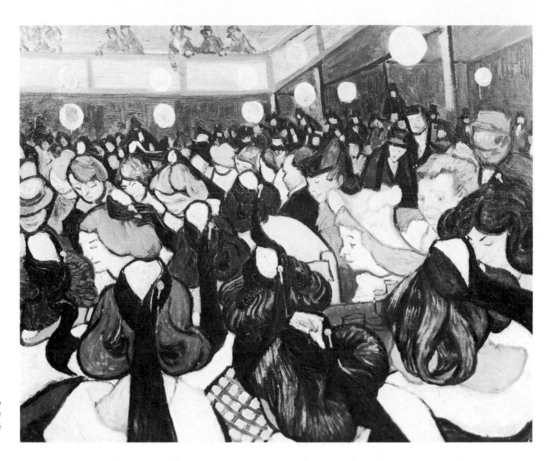

van Gogh: *Dance Hall at Arles,* Nov. 1888. 25⅝ × 31⅞″. Musée du Louvre, Paris (Gift of André Meyer)

and for daily equilibrium than I have. But his weakness is that he ruins all his calculations by going on binges and indulging in sordid escapades."[19]

There remained many subjects of disagreement. In a somewhat cryptic letter to Theo, Vincent later said: "On various occasions I have seen Gauguin do things which you or I would not allow ourselves to do, since our consciences work differently, and I have heard a couple of things said about him of the same kind. However, I who have seen him from very nearby, believe that he is carried away by his imagination, by his pride perhaps, but is not to be held responsible."[19]

On the other hand Gauguin revealed himself a fascinating storyteller who entertained his companion with accounts of his apprenticeship as a seaman. These inspired van Gogh not only with respect but also with complete confidence in his friend and reminded him of Loti's *Pêcheur d'Islande*. After having insisted somewhat cruelly on the advantages of Brittany, Gauguin provided lively descriptions of Martinique which appeared extremely enticing to Vincent.[16] In this fashion Gauguin acquainted his comrade with an enchanting world utterly unknown to him, and this may explain why van Gogh now began to dream of an art to be created in the tropics.

As soon as the newness of their meeting had worn off, the two friends settled down to work, Gauguin doing some sketches whereas van Gogh continued his canvases under his

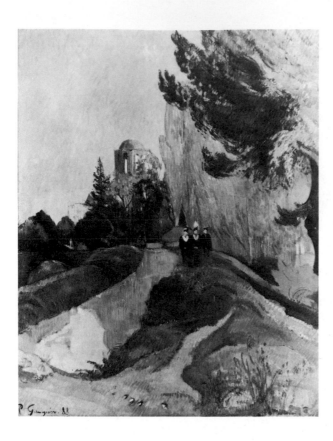

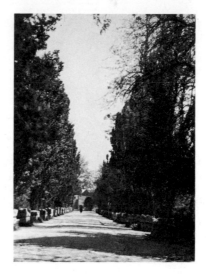

Left: GAUGUIN: *The Alyscamps,* Arles, d. 1888. 36¼ x 28¾″. Included in Gauguin's auction of 1891. Musée du Louvre, Paris

Below: Photograph of the Alyscamps, Arles

companion's watchful eye. They apparently first began to work together at the Alyscamps; yet while they painted there at the same time, they did not choose the same motifs, nor did they set up their easels side by side. Gauguin's painting of the Alyscamps had nothing unusual in design, but he did accentuate the flaming autumn hues. Van Gogh's version was not only more colorful—he used pure colors, a vivid yellow against a pale green, with some red accents—it was also more powerful and brutal, executed in vibrant and sweeping strokes in contrast to Gauguin's more subtle and less temperamental technique.

At the beginning of November, Theo opened in Paris the first one-man show of Gauguin, consisting of canvases from Brittany which the artist had sent him before leaving for Arles. On November 14, Gauguin received a letter from Theo, informing him: "You will probably be pleased to know that your paintings have a great success ... Degas is so enthusiastic about your works that he speaks to many people about them and plans to buy the picture which shows a spring landscape with a meadow in the foreground and two women, one seated, the other standing. Two canvases are definitely sold; one is the vertical landscape with two dogs in a meadow, the other a pond near a path. Since there is a combination of a trade-in, I put the first one at 375 francs *net for you,* the other at 225. I could also sell the *Breton Girls Dancing* [see page 264], but there is a small retouching job to be done.

Opposite: VAN GOGH: *The Alyscamps,* Arles, Oct. 1888. 36½ x 29″. Private collection, Paris

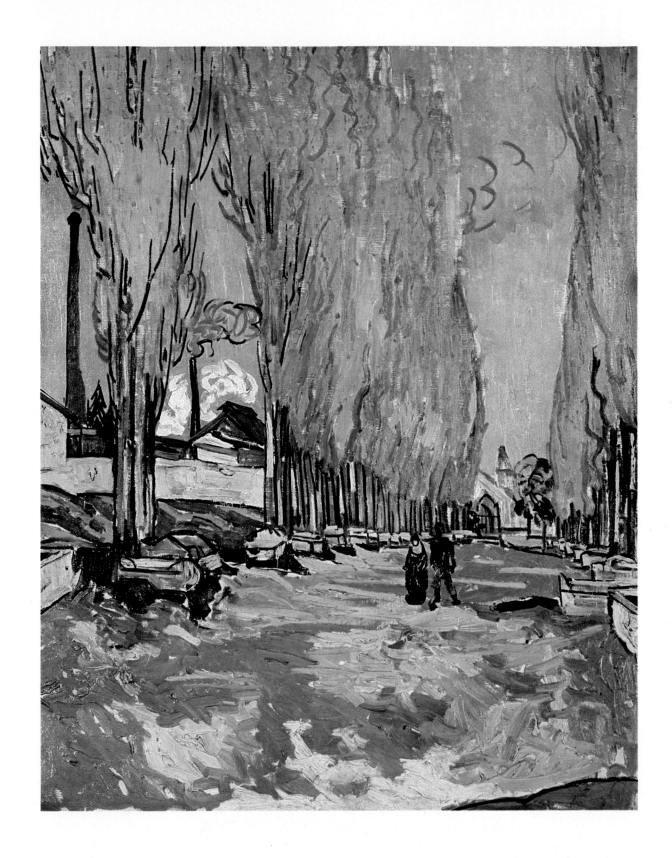

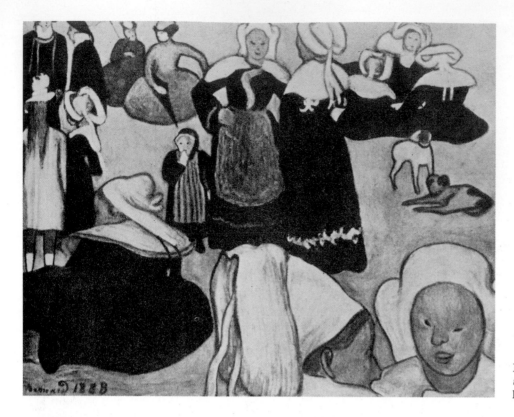

BERNARD: *Market in Brittany—Breton Women in the Meadow,* Pont-Aven, d. 1888. 29⅛ x 36¼″. Collection Dominique Denis, Paris

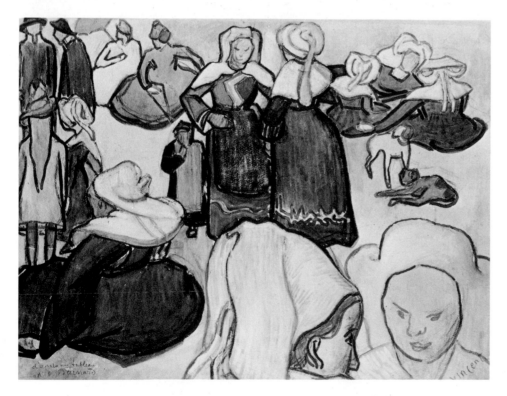

VAN GOGH: *Copy after Bernard's "Breton Women in the Meadow,"* Arles, Oct.–Dec. 1888. Watercolor and gouache, 18¾ x 24⅜″. Galleria d'Arte Moderna, Milan (Collezione Grassi)

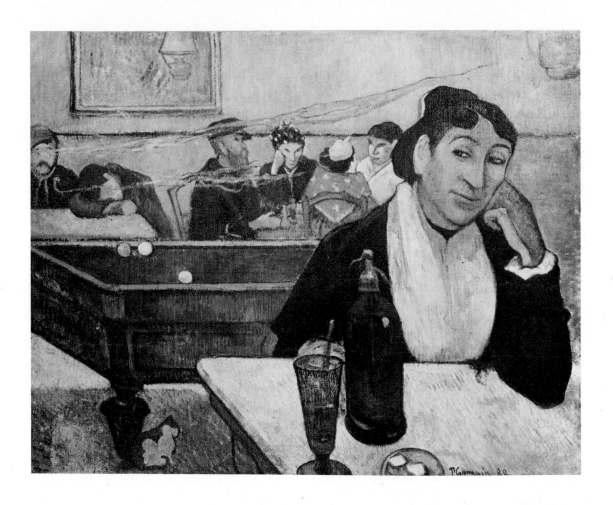

Above: GAUGUIN: *The Night Café,* Arles, Nov. 1888. 28¾ x 36¼". Pushkin State Museum of Fine Arts, Moscow

Right: GAUGUIN: *L'Arlésienne,* Nov. 1888. Charcoal, 22 x 19". The Fine Arts Museums of San Francisco, M. H. de Young Museum (Hanley Collection)

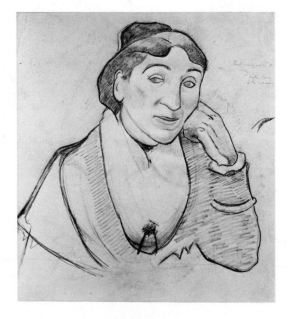

The hand of the young girl close to the edge of the frame takes on an importance which it does not seem to deserve.... My client would like you to alter somewhat the form of this hand without otherwise changing anything in the picture. It seems to me that you won't have any difficulty doing this and I therefore send you the canvas. My client will pay 500 francs for this painting which I provided with a frame that cost almost 100 francs.... For the picture I sold recently, I deducted 15%, which is the minimum commission the gallery requests. Many artists give us 25%. In case we could manage to sell your work more or less regularly, I should engage you to do likewise, if you will be so kind.... Tell me your opinion concerning this matter.

"I was happy to learn that you two are getting along well together and that you were able to set immediately to work. How I should have liked to be with you!"[20]

Gauguin acceded to the collector's desire and modified the painting after it arrived in Arles. But when Vincent compared it with the recent works of his friend, he by far preferred the latter.

Since Gauguin had apparently not brought with him any of his own paintings from Pont-Aven but had taken Bernard's *Breton Women in the Meadow*, it was actually this picture which Vincent studied at first to acquaint himself with his friends' radical synthesism. He even copied it, and also painted a view of a *Dance Hall* (page 223), for which he drew inspiration from Bernard's work. Gauguin himself soon made a broadly conceived drawing of an Arlesian woman which he planned to use, in spite of his dislike for the subject, for an interior of the night café that Vincent had already painted. Van Gogh was pleased with this drawing. "I believe," he soon wrote to Theo, "that we'll wind up spending our evenings making drawings and writing; there is more work to be done than we can accomplish."[21]

"We have made several excursions to the brothels," van Gogh informed Bernard two or three weeks after Gauguin's arrival, "and it is probable that we will go there frequently to work. Gauguin is at this moment working on a canvas of the same night café which I too have painted, but with figures seen in the brothels. It promises to be a beautiful thing. As for me, I have painted two studies of falling leaves in an alley of poplar trees [the Alyscamps], and a third one of the entire alley, completely yellow."[14] Gauguin added in a postscript that these two studies of falling leaves "are in my room; you would like them very much. They are on very heavy but very good burlap [see page 232]."[15]

At the same time van Gogh became enraptured with another subject, a red vineyard turning to yellow in the distance, under a green sky, with violet and yellow earth, wet from the rain, in which the setting sun was reflected. This *Red Vineyard* was to become one of the paintings he valued most. Gauguin, simultaneously, painted some women picking grapes. In a short note to Bernard, Gauguin himself explained his recent work: "Purple vines forming triangles against the upper part which is chrome yellow. On the left a Breton woman of Le Pouldu in black with a gray apron. Two Breton women bending down in light blue-green dresses with black bodices. In the foreground pink earth and a poor woman with orange hair, white blouse, and green skirt mixed with white. All this done with bold outlines enclosing tones which are almost uniform and are laid on very thickly with a palette knife on coarse sackcloth. It is a view of a vineyard which I have seen at Arles. I have put Breton women into it—so much the worse for *exactitude*. It is my best canvas of this year and as soon as it is dry I shall send it to Paris. I have also done [a painting of] a café which Vincent likes a lot and I like less. Actually that's not in my line and those vulgar local colors don't suit me. I like them well enough in the works of others but always

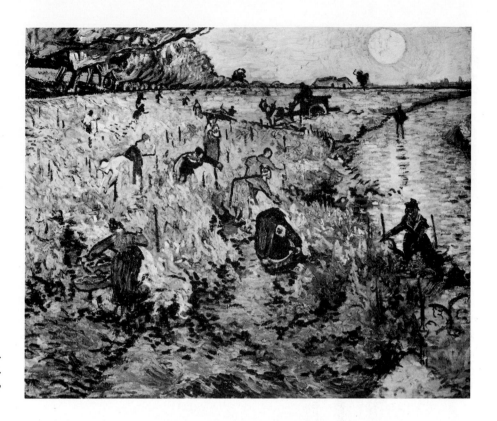

van Gogh: *The Red Vineyard—Mont-majour*, Arles, Nov. 1888. 28¾ x 36¼".
Pushkin State Museum of Fine Arts, Moscow

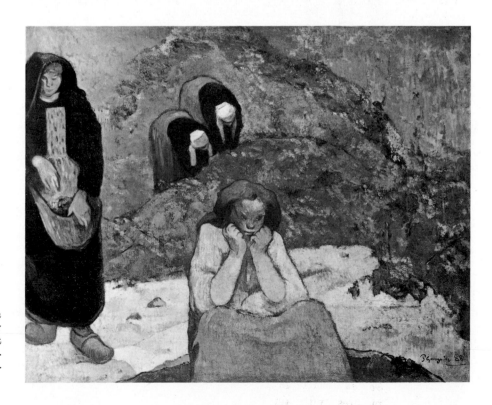

Gauguin: *Vineyard at Arles with Breton Women*, d. 1888. 28¾ x 36⅝". Formerly collection Schuffenecker. Exhibited at Volpini's and the XX as *Misères humaines*. Ordrupgardsamlingen, Copenhagen

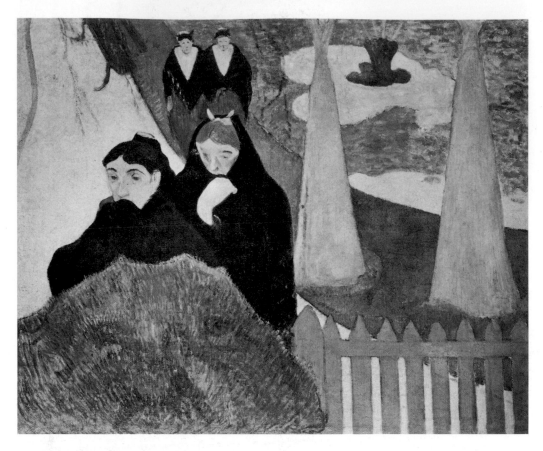

GAUGUIN: *Women in a Garden,* Arles, 1888. 28¾ x 36″. The Art Institute of Chicago (Gift of Annie Swan Coburn to the Lewis Coburn Memorial Collection)

feel apprehensive about them myself. It's a matter of education and one cannot change oneself. In the upper part red wallpaper; three prostitutes: one bristling with curl-papers, the second seen from behind wearing a green shawl, the third in a vermilion shawl; on the left a man asleep. A billiard table—in the foreground a rather carefully executed figure of an Arlésienne with a black shawl and a white front. Marble table. Across the picture runs a streak of *blue smoke*, yet the figure in the foreground is *much too* conventional...."[22]

The women in their picturesque black Provençal costumes were possibly the only things that attracted Gauguin in Arles, though it was not their attire alone that interested him. "It is strange," Gauguin reported to Bernard, "Vincent is inspired here to paint like Daumier, while I on the contrary find here a combination of a colorful Puvis and Japanese art. The women here have elegant headdresses and a Greek beauty. Their shawls fall into folds as in primitive paintings.... Well, it is worth seeing. In any event here is a source of beautiful *modern style.*"[23] Gauguin exploited this source in his painting *Women in a Garden* with large patterned forms, similar to those featured in some of his Brittany pictures, and again Vincent expressed great enthusiasm for this work. "He likes my paintings very much," Gauguin wrote to Bernard, "but when I do them he always finds that

230

I am wrong here and there. He is a romantic and I am rather drawn towards the primitive. In regard to color, he likes the accidental quality of impasto, such as Monticelli uses, and I detest the messiness of execution."[13]

Though van Gogh was much too sincere not to express his views freely, he must have done so only with humility, so awed was he by Gauguin's knowledge. Indeed it is hard to believe that Gauguin was not touched by Vincent's complete and almost naïve confidence in his superiority. For van Gogh certainly repeated now what he had already told Gauguin in a letter: "In comparison with yours I find my own artistic concepts extremely vulgar. I always have the coarse appetites of a beast. I forget everything for the exterior beauty of things *which I do not know how to represent*, because I make it appear ugly and uncouth in my painting whereas nature seems to me so perfect."[24]

Gauguin himself later recorded what influence he exerted on his friend, insisting that van Gogh was then still "trying to find himself, whilst I, much older, was a completed man." (Vincent was then thirty-five and Gauguin forty, which is not so much older.) According to Gauguin: "Vincent, at the time of my arrival at Arles, was up to his ears in the neo-impressionist school, and he was floundering considerably, which made him unhappy. Not that this school, like all schools, was bad, but because it was not in harmony with his

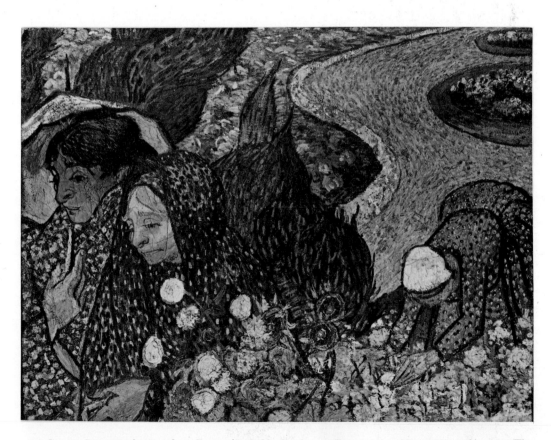

VAN GOGH: *Promenade at Arles—Souvenir of the Garden at Etten,* Arles, Nov. 1888. 28¾ x 36". The Hermitage, Leningrad

impatient and independent nature. With all his yellows and violets, all this work with complementaries—a disorderly work on his part—he only achieved soft, incomplete, and monotonous harmonies; the sound of the bugle was lacking. I undertook the task of explaining things to him, which was easy for me, for I found a rich and fruitful ground. Like all original natures marked with the stamp of personality, Vincent was without distrust or obstinacy. From that day van Gogh made astonishing progress; he seemed to become aware of everything that was in him, and thence came all the series of sunflowers after sunflowers in brilliant sunshine.... Without losing an inch of his originality, van Gogh learned valuable lessons from me. And every day he was grateful to me for them."[17]

While it is certain that van Gogh was grateful to Gauguin for all his stimulating ideas, it is also certain that he had painted most of his still lifes of sunflowers *before* his friend's arrival. Though he listened willingly to Gauguin, Vincent seems to have always been determined to follow him only when his advice coincided with the direction of his own research. He was perfectly prepared to submit to Gauguin's influence and eager to improve his work under Gauguin's guidance, yet he had no desire to give up what he had acquired by himself during the months of his solitude in Arles.

The first advice Gauguin gave van Gogh was to work from memory or, as Vincent put it, to do "abstractions." Van Gogh now painted a composition inspired by Gauguin's *Women*

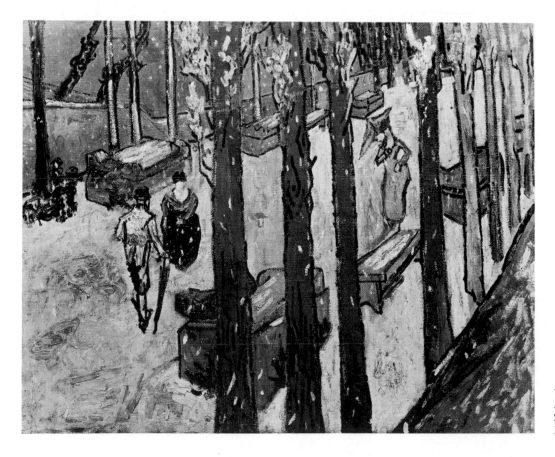

VAN GOGH: *The Alyscamps— Falling Leaves*, Arles, Nov. 1888. 28 x 35¾". Rijksmuseum Kröller-Müller, Otterlo

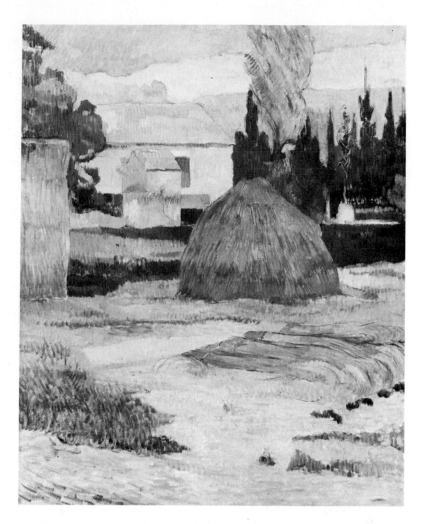

GAUGUIN: *Landscape near Arles*, 1888.
36 x 28½". Indianapolis Museum of Art

in a Garden as well as by his recollections of his family's garden in Holland. He was fascinated by the possibilities which work from the imagination opened up for him, as he would thenceforth have a wider range of subjects during the winter when he could usually do only portraits or still lifes in his studio. Apparently echoing Gauguin's theories, Vincent wrote to his brother: "Paintings done from memory are always less awkward and have a more artistic character than studies done from nature." [25]

But soon van Gogh discovered that he was not very successful when he tried to work from memory without the stimulus provided by the observation of nature. And thus he wrote later to Bernard: "When Gauguin was in Arles, I once or twice allowed myself to turn to abstraction... and at that time abstraction seemed to me to offer a charming path. But it's an enchanted territory, old man, and one quickly finds oneself up against a wall."[26] In this respect, therefore, Gauguin's advice went unheeded.

Though Gauguin may have objected to Vincent's neo-impressionistic use of complementaries — van Gogh admitted having thought of Seurat when he painted his *Bedroom*

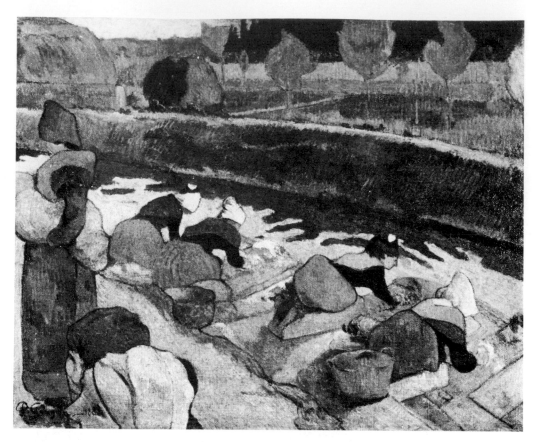

(page 211)—Gauguin could certainly not maintain that his friend employed Seurat's time-consuming technique (and had therefore spoken of a "disorderly work with complementaries"). As a matter of fact van Gogh's *Bedroom* was specifically one of the canvases which Gauguin had liked. It is true that from that time on Vincent changed his palette, yet he did so in order to achieve softer harmonies and thus strove exactly for the opposite of what Gauguin later claimed to have told him to do. Far from aiming for the "sound of the bugle" —and there had been such a sound in the portrait of the Zouave bugler (page 206), for example—van Gogh became more intent on mellower sonorities.

The strangest instance of van Gogh's artistic relationship with Gauguin concerns Vincent's predilection for basing some of his paintings on the variations of a single color, as he had done in his *Sunflowers*, a tendency that Gauguin mocked mercilessly.[17] Yet many years later Gauguin claimed that it was he who had taught van Gogh "the orchestration of a pure tone from all the derivatives of that tone."[27] In any event, when van Gogh himself subsequently analyzed his debt to Gauguin—a debt which he never denied—it was not of color that he spoke: "I assure you," he wrote to a friend, "that I owe much to the things Gauguin told me about draftsmanship, and I value very, very highly his specific love for nature."[28]

It is possible that van Gogh alluded to recommendations by Gauguin, about which the latter was more specific shortly before his death, when he declared that, due to his intervention, in Vincent's landscapes "all the litter of still-life objects, which had once been necessary, had been replaced by tonalities of solid colors in conformity with the total harmony; hence the literary or, if you prefer, explanatory element became of secondary importance. Naturally this procedure made his drawing more flexible. No doubt this is merely a question of craftsmanship, but it is very important just the same. As all this forced him into further experimentation befitting his intelligence and ardent temperament, he thereby developed his originality and personality." And Gauguin asserted: "I have no desire to diminish van Gogh's merit even if I claim credit for a tiny share in it."[27]

When they discussed the works of other painters, van Gogh and Gauguin seem almost always to have been in disagreement. "Generally speaking," Gauguin reported to Bernard, "Vincent and I hardly see eye to eye, especially in regard to painting. He admires Daumier, Daubigny, Ziem, and the great [Théodore] Rousseau, all people whom I cannot tolerate. On the other hand he hates Ingres, Raphael, Degas, all of whom I admire. I keep replying: 'Yes, you are right!' merely to keep peace."[13] But though he tried not to enter into arguments with Vincent, Gauguin was exasperated by his friend's inconsistencies, or at least by what he considered such. As he later wrote in his recollections: "In spite of all my efforts to unravel in his disorderly mind a logical reasoning in his critical opinions, I was

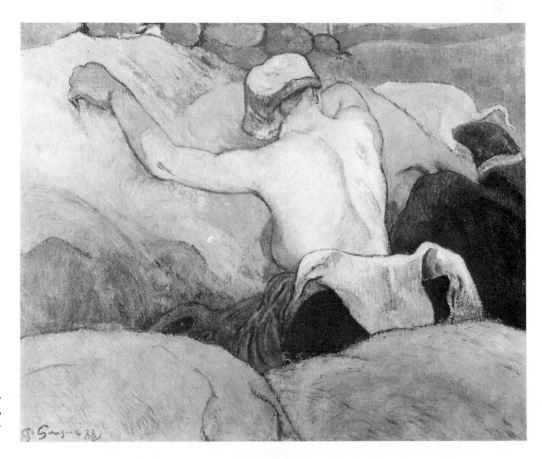

GAUGUIN: *Woman against a Haystack* (*Woman with Pigs*), Arles, d. 1888. 28¾ x 36¼". Collection Stavros S. Niarchos

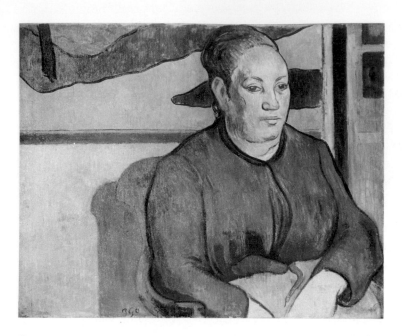

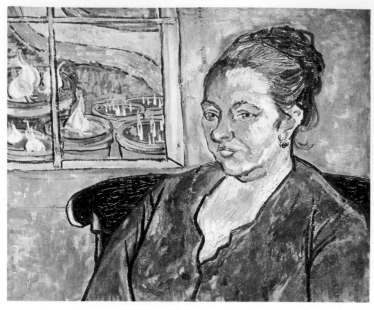

GAUGUIN: *Portrait of Mme Roulin,* Arles, 1888. 19½ x 24½". The St. Louis Art Museum (Gift of Mrs. Mark C. Steinberg)

VAN GOGH: *Portrait of Mme Roulin,* Arles, Nov.–Dec. 1888. 21¼ x 25½". Oskar Reinhart Foundation, Winterthur, Switzerland

not able to explain to myself all the contradictions between his painting and his opinions." Gauguin added that he began very soon to feel that "between two personalities, his and mine, one a volcano, the other boiling also, but within, a struggle was in some way brewing."[17]

If van Gogh had the same premonitions, his letters to his brother revealed nothing about them. He kept on writing to Theo about how well they worked together. He reported regularly on the paintings Gauguin was doing, always saying how much he admired them, and how interesting Gauguin was as a companion. "He is a very great artist and an excellent friend."[29]—"It does me a great deal of good to have such intelligent company as that of Gauguin and to see him work."[30] Indeed, work was the *leitmotif* of all his letters, for it was work that counted, and little did it matter to Vincent if they disagreed or had arguments as long as they made some progress in their paintings. Thus he was not really complaining when he wrote to his brother: "Our days are occupied by work, always work; in the evening we are so exhausted that we go to the café and then early to bed. That's our life."[31]

After having painted several landscapes, Gauguin now seemed to have grasped what he later called the "rough savor" of Arles, though many of his pictures done there could almost have been painted in Brittany.[32] This is true particularly of a *Woman against a Haystack* and of a group of washerwomen whose costumes alone testify to their Provençal origin; but Vincent considered these two canvases superior to those of Pont-Aven. Schuffenecker shared this opinion. When, in December, Gauguin sent his first batch of paintings done in Arles to Theo van Gogh, he received a dithyrambic letter from Schuffenecker:

"I went on Saturday with my wife to Goupil's to see your latest paintings. I am absolutely enthusiastic. This is much more beautiful even than your shipment from Brittany, more abstract and more powerful. And besides, what astounds me is the abundance and fecundity of your production. Poor devil that I am, drudging for several months on one little canvas! Everybody does what he can, it's true, but you, my dear Gauguin, how far will you not go? Our comrades probably rejoice only halfheartedly; but as I am seeing nobody (except Guillaumin), I can't very well find out what they think, if they should show it at all. The more I think and observe, the more I am convinced that you will overwhelm them all, with the exception of Degas. He is a colossus, but you, you are a giant; you know, one of those who stormed the skies. You are piling Ossa on Pelion to reach the sky of painting. You won't reach it because it is the absolute, that is to say God, but you will clasp the hand of those who have come nearest to it. Yes, my dear Gauguin, the fate in art that is awaiting you is not only success, it is fame beside such men as Rembrandt and Delacroix. And you will have suffered as they have. I hope that now at least you will be spared material suffering (money)."[33]

For the time being Gauguin certainly did not suffer. Vincent's reverent approval and Schuffenecker's lyrical admiration can only have incited him to work harder. He finished his *Night Café* as well as a still life and, together with van Gogh, did a portrait of Mme Roulin, the wife of Vincent's friend the postman.[34] Both these likenesses are painted with strong outlines and a minimum of modeling, but Gauguin's appears even flatter than van Gogh's, because the brushwork is much less turbulent; it also features in the background an extremely synthesized landscape that he had executed at Arles.

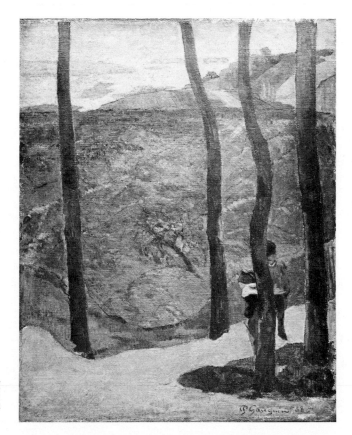

GAUGUIN: *Landscape with Blue Trees,* Arles, d. 1888. 36¼ x 28¾". This landscape appears in the background of Gauguin's portrait of Mme Roulin, opposite. Exhibited with the XX in 1889. Ordrupgardsamlingen, Copenhagen

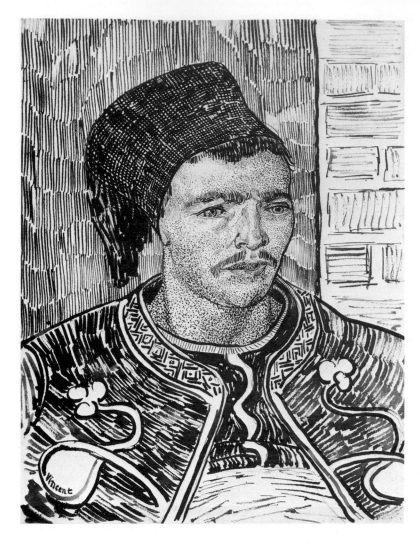

VAN GOGH: *Portrait of a Zouave Bugler*, Arles, June 1888. Reed pen and ink, 12⁹⁄₁₆ × 9⁹⁄₁₆″. Justin K. Thannhauser Collection, New York. Courtesy the Thannhauser Foundation and The Solomon R. Guggenheim Museum, New York

Little by little Gauguin had met all of van Gogh's friends, particularly the Zouave officer Milliet, whose account of Indo-China may actually have inspired him with the idea of focusing his dreams of the tropics upon Tonkin, though at first he had spoken of returning to Martinique. But later Gauguin planned for a while to make Tonkin the destination of his next escape from civilization. Yet Gauguin did not ask Milliet to pose for him as he had done for Vincent, though he was just as interested in portraiture as was van Gogh. Subsequently Vincent was to recall their discussions about portraits: "Gauguin and I talked about this and similar questions in such a way that our nerves became very tense until all vital warmth was extinguished."[35]

Gauguin now decided to do a portrait of van Gogh while the latter was painting yet another bunch of sunflowers (p. 244). Meanwhile Vincent worked on a whole series of portraits; he painted a friendly neighbor, Mme Ginoux, in the costume of an Arlésienne (a purple dress against a yellow background—a juxtaposition of complementaries which Gauguin so

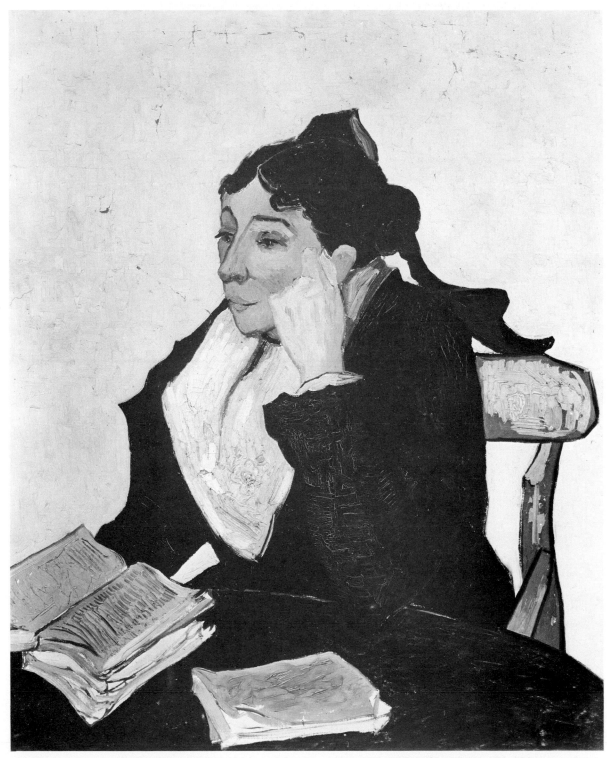

VAN GOGH: *Portrait of Mme Ginoux—L'Arlésienne*, Arles, Nov. 1888. 35⅜ x 28⅜". The Metropolitan Museum of Art, New York (Sam A. Lewisohn Bequest)

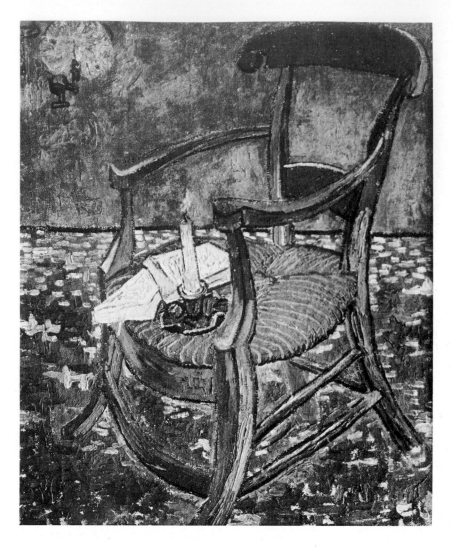

van Gogh: *Gauguin's Chair*, Arles, Dec. 1888. 35⅝ x 28⅜″. Rijksmuseum Vincent van Gogh, Amsterdam

disliked), and also did likenesses of the various other members of Roulin's family. Yet he who had always been so eager to do portraits apparently never attempted to do one of Gauguin. Did Gauguin lack the patience to pose for him or was it that Vincent, like Bernard, felt intimidated and did not "dare" to paint his friend? What van Gogh did paint, strangely enough, was Gauguin's chair, his "empty place" as he later called it.

When Gauguin showed his finished portrait to van Gogh, a portrait which he himself admitted was not a very good likeness but in which he thought he had caught something of his friend's intimate character, Vincent exclaimed: "It is certainly I, but I gone mad."[36] The same evening the two went together to the café, as usual. Van Gogh ordered a weak absinthe; he had begun to drink rather heavily by that time and Gauguin no doubt also indulged freely. According to Gauguin's subsequent testimony (a testimony which cannot be challenged since there were no other witnesses), van Gogh suddenly threw his glass and its contents at the head of Gauguin, who ducked it.

240

Gauguin immediately took his companion by the arm and brought him home where Vincent fell asleep in a few seconds. The next morning van Gogh told Gauguin that he had a vague remembrance of having offended him. "I forgive you willingly and gladly," Gauguin replied, "but yesterday's incident might happen again, and if I were hit I might not remain master of myself, and might strangle you. Allow me therefore to write to your brother to announce my return."[37]

Thus Gauguin informed Theo van Gogh: "Everything considered, I am obliged to return to Paris. Vincent and I simply cannot live together without trouble, due to the incompatibility of our characters, and we both need tranquillity for our work. He is a man of remarkable intelligence whom I esteem very highly and whom I leave with regret, but I must repeat, it is necessary that I leave."[38] At the same time Gauguin also wrote to Schuffenecker to ask whether he might again count on his hospitality in Paris.

The days that followed were harassing. Vincent must have felt everything crumbling around him, his dreams of the "studio of the South" possibly destroyed forever. All his thoughts were now turned towards one goal: to make Gauguin reconsider his departure. At Gauguin's suggestion they decided to make an excursion to nearby Montpellier to visit the museum there with the famous Bruyas collection, especially rich in works by Delacroix and Courbet. Their discussions on art, which had until then been theoretical, became even more heated in front of these paintings. And this time it was Vincent himself who reported to his brother: "Our discussions are excessively electric and we emerge from them sometimes with our heads as tired as a battery after it has been discharged."[39] Yet it was after this trip that Gauguin decided to remain in Arles and begged Theo not to pay any heed to his previous letter; he also offered Theo his portrait of Vincent. Simultaneously Gauguin wrote to Schuffenecker to apprise him of the change in his plans: "Unfortunately I am not coming yet. My situation here is very awkward; I owe a great deal to [Theo] van Gogh and to Vincent and, in spite of some discord, I cannot be angry with an excellent fellow who is sick, who suffers, and who asks for me. Remember the life of Edgar Poe who became an alcoholic as the result of grief and a nervous condition. Some day I shall explain all this to you. In any event I stay here, but my departure will always be a possibility."[40]

Vincent somehow suspected that Gauguin's decision to stay was not a final one. "I believe," he told his brother, "that Gauguin is a bit disappointed in the good town of Arles, in the little yellow house where we are working, and especially in me. Indeed there still remain for him as well as for me great difficulties that have to be overcome here. But these difficulties lie rather in ourselves than anywhere else. As a result I myself believe that he will definitely decide either to go or to stay. But before he acts, I told him to think it over and to weigh his decision. Gauguin is very strong, a great creative mind, but precisely for this reason he needs peace. Will he find it elsewhere if he doesn't find it here? I am waiting for him to make up his mind in absolute serenity."[41]

While Vincent waited for Gauguin to come to a decision in absolute serenity, his own condition was far from serene. Gauguin later told Emile Bernard that "ever since the question arose of my leaving Arles he had been so queer that I hardly breathed any more. He even said to me: "You are going to leave,' and when I said 'Yes,' he tore a sentence from a newspaper and put it into my hand: 'The murderer had fled.'"[42]

It may well be that a factor completely unrelated to Gauguin's presence also contributed to van Gogh's uneasiness. After more than a year's courtship Theo had just become engaged to a young Dutch girl, Johanna Bonger, sister of his friend Andries Bonger. It

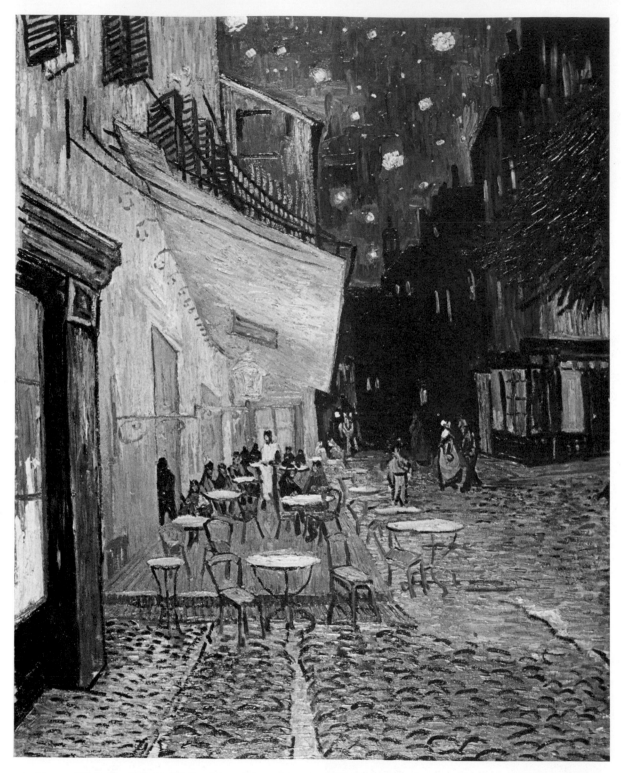

VAN GOGH: *Sidewalk Café at Night,* Arles, Sept. 1888. 31 x 24¾". Formerly in the collection of G.-Albert Aurier. Rijksmuseum Kröller-Müller, Otterlo

242

seems quite possible that Vincent—always extremely possessive in his affections—feared he might thus lose some of his brother's solicitude since Theo would soon have a family of his own.[43]

After the incident at the café Vincent had grown ever more agitated. His moods had changed from excessive brusqueness and boisterousness to complete silence. At night he had sometimes risen and gone over to Gauguin's bed, as if to see whether his friend was still there. At the end the suspense became too much for him. How could he go on living and working without knowing what the next day might bring? And Gauguin, sullen and brooding, did nothing to reassure him. On Sunday, December 23, the very day on which Vincent had written to Theo and analyzed the situation, Gauguin left their home after dinner for a walk by himself. According to Gauguin's recollections (put down in *Avant et Après* in 1903), he had almost crossed the large square in front of their house when he heard behind him familiar little steps, rapid and jerky. He turned around just in time to see Vincent on the point of throwing himself upon him with an open razor in his hand. Gauguin's look must have been overpowering at that moment, for Vincent stopped and, lowering his head, returned to the house. Gauguin later often asked himself whether he should have disarmed his friend and tried to pacify him; yet instead he went to a hotel for the night.[44]

Van Gogh returned to his room and there, assailed by auditory hallucinations, suddenly cut off his left ear.[45] After he succeeded in stopping the abundant flow of blood, he covered his head with a large beret, washed his severed ear, wrapped it up, and rushed to the brothel which the two friends usually patronized. It is not impossible that Vincent went there in the hope of finding Gauguin. But his friend was not there. What happened at the brothel was subsequently reported in an Arles newspaper under the heading: *Local News.* "Last Sunday night at half past eleven, a painter named Vincent van Gogh, a native of Holland, appeared at the *maison de tolérance* No. 1, asked for a girl called Rachel, and handed her his ear with these words: 'Keep this object carefully.' Then he disappeared. The police, informed of these happenings which could be attributed only to an unfortunate maniac, looked the next morning for this individual, whom they found in his bed with barely a sign of life."[46]

The event caused quite a commotion in the rue du Bout d'Arles where the brothels were located.[47] According to the recollections of the policeman Robert, who was that night on duty in the ill-famed sector, "passing before the *maison de tolérance* No. 1, run by a woman named Virginie... the prostitute [Rachel] whose *nom de guerre* was Gaby, in the presence of the owner, handed me a newspaper... saying: 'This is what the painter gave us as a present.' I questioned them a little and opened the package in which I discovered a whole ear. It was my duty to inform my superior... who went with other gendarmes to his home."[48]

When Gauguin, unaware of all this, went to their yellow house early the next morning, he found a police commissioner at the door who asked him why he had assassinated his friend. It took him some minutes to recover from the shock, and then they went upstairs together to Vincent's room. It was not long before Gauguin realized that his companion's body was still warm. Relieved, he told the commissioner to wake Vincent gently and to tell him that his friend had gone to Paris.[49]

Once awake, van Gogh asked for Gauguin, for his pipe and tobacco, and also for the box in which the two friends kept their money; apparently he wanted to ascertain whether Gauguin had actually taken the amount for his fare.[50] While Vincent was transported to

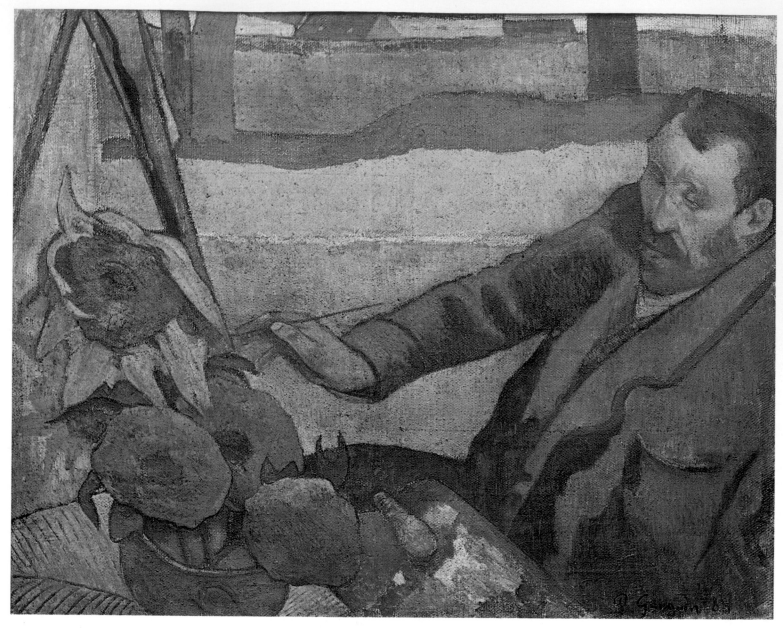

GAUGUIN: *Portrait of Vincent van Gogh*, Arles, d. 1888. 28¾ x 36½". Formerly collection Theo van Gogh. Rijksmuseum Vincent van Gogh, Amsterdam

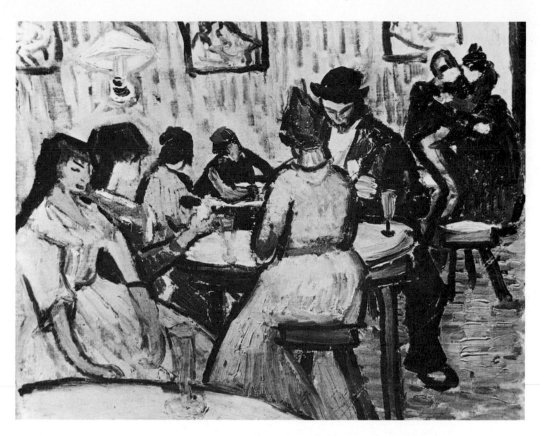

VAN GOGH: *Bordello at Arles*, Oct. 1888. 13 x 16⅛″. The Barnes Foundation, Merion, Pa.

the hospital, Gauguin telegraphed Theo that his presence was urgently needed in Arles, and himself prepared to leave.

Four days after his return to Paris, where he stayed again at Schuffenecker's, Gauguin received a visit from Emile Bernard who had heard of Vincent's hospitalization and was anxious to know all the details. In a long and sad letter to Aurier, Bernard immediately transcribed everything he had just learned from Gauguin:

"I am so sad that I need somebody who will listen to me and who can understand me. My best friend, my dear friend Vincent is mad. Since I have found out, I am almost mad myself.... I rushed to see Gauguin who told me this: 'The day before I left [Arles], Vincent ran after me—it was at night—and I turned around, for Vincent had been behaving strangely for some time and I was on my guard. He then said to me: "You are taciturn, but I shall be likewise." I went to sleep in a hotel and when I returned the entire population of Arles was in front of our house. It was then that the gendarmes arrested me, for the house was full of blood. This is what had happened: Vincent had gone back after I left, had taken a razor and had cut off his ear. He had then covered his head with a large beret and had gone to a brothel to give his ear to one of the inmates, telling her: "Verily I say unto you, you will remember me."'"[51]

There is one remarkable difference between the version of the incident as Gauguin wrote it down some fifteen years later in his recollections, *Avant et Après*, and the version which he told Bernard almost immediately after the event. In Bernard's report there is *no* mention of van Gogh having tried to throw himself upon Gauguin with an open razor in his hand. Indeed Bernard states clearly, repeating of course Gauguin's words, that Vincent had taken the razor *after* returning to the house, in order to mutilate himself. It may well be that Gauguin, writing his memoirs in 1903 (at a time when the strange details of this incident had already been widely reported), chose to emphasize van Gogh's aggressiveness so as to better justify his having abandoned a friend in a moment of crisis.

Bernard also obtained from Gauguin some details about what had happened to van Gogh at the hospital, details which he transmitted to Aurier: "Vincent was taken to the hospital; his condition is worse. He wants to be quartered with the other patients, refuses assistance from the nurse, and washed himself in the coal bin. One might almost think that he pursues Biblical mortifications. They were forced to shut him up in a room by himself." And Bernard exclaimed: "My dear friend is lost and it will probably be only a question of time until his approaching death!"[51]

These apprehensions seemed justified, for at the hospital Vincent's condition had been considered serious; he remained unconscious for three days. The devoted postman Roulin, who visited his friend daily, thought two days after van Gogh's admission that the end had come, but the same day the patient rallied. When Theo arrived, there was little for him to do but comfort his brother. To his fiancée of a few days Theo reported: "He had, while I was with him, moments in which he acted normally, but then after a short while he wandered off into divagations on philosophy and theology. It was deeply saddening to witness all this, for from time to time he became conscious of his illness and in those moments he tried to cry—yet no tears came. Poor fighter, and poor, poor sufferer. For the time being nobody can do anything to alleviate his suffering, though he himself feels it deeply and strongly. If he had been able to find somebody to whom he could have opened his heart, maybe it would never have come to all this."[52]

Vincent was greatly distressed at causing his brother so much anxiety and also bitterly resented the fact that Gauguin had urged Theo to make the trip to Arles, which he considered wholly superfluous. "I am utterly desolate about your trip," he told his brother. "I should have wished that this could have been avoided, for after all nothing serious has happened to me and there was no reason for you to go to this trouble."[53] After a few days Theo left, his brother being greatly improved.

As soon as he was able to write Vincent composed a letter to Gauguin: "My dear friend Gauguin, I take advantage of my first leave from the hospital to write you a few words of very sincere and profound friendship. I have thought of you very often at the hospital, even while I was very feverish and quite weak. Tell me—was my brother Theo's trip really so necessary, my friend? Now at least please reassure him completely and I beg you to have confidence yourself.... What I want most ... is that you should abstain, until we have more thoroughly considered the whole situation, from saying anything uncomplimentary about our poor little yellow house."[54]

And even later, when he had been forced to abandon his yellow house, and to abandon with it all his dreams of a "studio of the South," van Gogh bore no grudge and always insisted that he owed much to Gauguin. Yet his comments on Gauguin were rather unexpected. "In my opinion," Vincent once wrote, "he is worth even more as a man than as an artist."[28]

NOTES

1 V. van Gogh to his brother, [Arles, middle of Oct. 1888]; Verzamelde Brieven van Vincent van Gogh, Amsterdam, vol. III, no. 556, pp. 350–51.

2 V. van Gogh to his brother, [Arles, Sept. 10, 1888]; *ibid.*, no. 535, p. 301.

3 V. van Gogh to his brother, [Arles, July 1888]; *ibid.*, no. 507, p. 253.

4 V. van Gogh to his brother, [Arles, beginning of Sept. 1888]; *ibid.*, no. 531, p. 294.

5 See V. Doiteau and E. Leroy: La Folie de van Gogh, Paris, 1928, p. 41.

6 V. van Gogh to Gauguin, [Arles, Oct. 1888]; see Verzamelde Brieven, vol. IV, no. B 22, pp. 237–38.

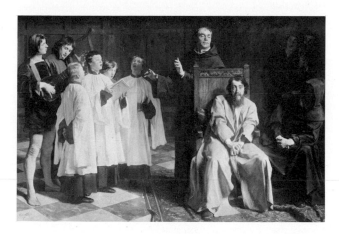

7 WAUTERS: *The Madness of Hugo van der Goes*, 1872. $73^1/_4 \times 108^1/_4''$. Musées Royaux des Beaux-Arts, Brussels.

8 Signac, diary, Saint-Tropez, Sept. 29, 1894; see Extraits du journal inédit de Signac, I, *Gazette des Beaux-Arts*, July–Sept. 1949.

9 Signac to Camille Pissarro, [Collioure, Sept. 1887]; unpublished document, courtesy the late Rodo Pissarro, Paris.

10 Signac to Lucien Pissarro, Collioure, Aug. 29, [1887]; unpublished document, courtesy the late Mrs. Esther L. Pissarro, London.

11 Gauguin quoted by V. van Gogh in a letter to his brother, [Arles, Feb. 3, 1889]; Verzamelde Brieven, vol. III, no. 576, p. 386.

12 Gauguin: Natures mortes, *Essais d'Art Libre*, Jan. 1894. Translation: "I am of a healthy mind — I am the Holy Ghost." (This article was not incorporated into Gauguin's volume of recollections: Avant et Après, Paris, 1923).

13 Gauguin to Bernard, [Arles, Dec. 1888]; see Lettres de Gauguin à sa femme et à ses amis, Paris, 1946, no. LXXVIII, pp. 154–55.

14 V. van Gogh to Bernard, [Arles, Oct.–Nov. 1888]; Verzamelde Brieven, vol. IV, no. B 19a, pp. 230–31. (This letter was given by Bernard to Aurier who used it for his article on van Gogh; see chapter VII, p. 342 and note 74.)

15 Gauguin to Bernard, postscript to the preceding letter; unpublished document, courtesy Ir. V. W. van Gogh, Laren.

16 See V. van Gogh's letter to his brother, [Arles, end of Oct. 1888], not included in Verzamelde Brieven; the Complete Letters of Vincent van Gogh, Greenwich, Conn. n.d. [1958], vol. III, no. 558b, pp. 97–99.

17 Gauguin: Avant et Après, [written in Atuana, Marquesas Island, 1903], Paris, 1923, pp. 15–19.

18 V. van Gogh, draft of a letter to Gauguin, [Arles, beginning of June 1888]; Verzamelde Brieven, vol. III, no. 494a, p. 227.

19 V. van Gogh to his brother, [Arles, Jan. 17, 1889]; *ibid.*, no. 571, p. 373.

20 Theo van Gogh to Gauguin, Paris, Nov. 13, 1888; see M. Bodelsen: An Unpublished Letter by Theo van Gogh, *Burlington Magazine*, June 1957. It would seem that the client refused the picture despite Gauguin's alterations, for it was exhibited the next year, under the title *Ronde dans les foins*, at the Volpini show (see chapter VI, p. 289, note 14), where it was catalogued as no. 36 without any mention of ownership and must therefore still have belonged to the artist. Subsequently Gauguin was to take the painting back to Brittany.

21 V. van Gogh to his brother, [Arles, Nov. 1888]; *ibid.*, no. 560, p. 356.

22 Gauguin to Bernard, [Arles, Nov. 1888]; see Vincent van Gogh: Letters to Emile Bernard, London–New York, 1938, pp. 106, 119–20, plates 31 and 32.

23 Gauguin to Bernard, [Arles, Nov. 1888]; see Lettres de Gauguin, *op. cit.*, no. LXXV, p. 151.

24 V. van Gogh to Gauguin, [Arles, beginning of Oct. 1888]; Verzamelde Brieven, vol. III, no. 553a, p. 344.

25 V. van Gogh to his brother, [Arles, Nov. 1888]; *ibid.*, no. 561, p. 358.

26 V. van Gogh to Bernard, [Saint-Rémy, Nov.–Dec. 1889]; Verzamelde Brieven, vol. IV, no. B 21, p. 234.

27 Gauguin to Fontainas, [Atuana, Sept. 1902]; see Lettres de Gauguin, *op. cit.*, no. CLXXVI, p. 306.

28 V. van Gogh to J. Russell, [Saint-Rémy, end of Jan. 1890]; see H. Thannhauser: Van Gogh and John Russell, Some Unknown Letters and Drawings, *Burlington Magazine*, Sept. 1938, and Verzamelde Brieven, vol. III, no. 623a, p. 494.

29 V. van Gogh to his brother, [Arles, Nov.–Dec. 1888]; *ibid.*, no. 562, p. 359.

30 V. van Gogh to his brother, [Arles, Dec. 1888]; *ibid.*, no. 563, p. 361.

31 V. van Gogh to his brother, [Arles, Nov. 1888]; *ibid.*, no. 560, p. 355.

32 In some cases paintings done by Gauguin in Arles have been attributed to this Brittany period; thus the landscape reproduced in Rewald: Gauguin, New York, 1938, p. 65, as *Brittany Landscape* was doubtlessly painted at Arles. (Here reproduced p. 233.)

33 Schuffenecker to Gauguin, Paris, Dec. 11, 1888; unpublished document, coll. Pola Gauguin, courtesy Henri Dorra, Santa Barbara, Calif.

34 See Ir. V. W. van Gogh: Madame Roulin—La Berceuse—door Vincent van Gogh en Paul Gauguin, *Museumjournaal*, Oct. 1955.

35 V. van Gogh to his brother, [Saint-Rémy, Nov. 1889]: Verzamelde Brieven, vol. III, no. 604, p. 453.

36 In a letter to Theo, Vincent later explained: "It was I, all right, extremely tired and charged with electricity as I then was." [Saint-Rémy, Sept. 10, 1889]; *ibid.*, no. 605, p. 458.

37 Gauguin: Avant et Après, *op. cit.*, p. 20. As related there by Gauguin, fifteen years after the incident, the sequence of events was that he painted van Gogh's portrait and the same evening Vincent threw a glass at him, then apologized the next morning, only to attempt an attack on Gauguin's life the *same* night and subsequently mutilate himself. But according to van Gogh's and Gauguin's own letters, the portrait was painted late in November or early in December 1888, several weeks before the fateful night of December 23. The glass-throwing episode may or may not have followed the completion of the portrait and prompted Gauguin's letter to Theo (see note 38), which is not dated. However, it is certain that after Vincent's apologies the two friends went together to Montpellier, since Gauguin wrote to Theo to discard his intention of going to Paris *after* their return from this trip. While the events are presented here more correctly than in Gauguin's notes, there is no guarantee that the narration given here follows them accurately; it merely tries to establish a likely sequence based on all available documents. A detailed chronology of Gauguin's paintings executed in Arles and a new sequence for van Gogh's letters written during Gauguin's visit, differing from the one adopted in Verzamelde Brieven, have been established by Mark Roskill: Van Gogh, Gauguin and the Impressionist Circle, London–New York, 1970.

38 Gauguin to Theo van Gogh, [Arles, Dec. 1888]; see Introduction to Verzamelde Brieven, vol. I, p. XLII.

39 V. van Gogh to his brother, [Arles, Dec. 1888]; Verzamelde Brieven, vol. III, no. 564, p. 363.

40 Gauguin to Schuffenecker, [Arles, Dec. 1888]; see C. Roger-Marx: Lettres inédites de Vincent van Gogh et de Paul Gauguin, *Europe*, Feb. 15, 1939.

41 V. van Gogh to his brother, [Arles, Dec. 23, 1888]; Verzamelde Brieven, vol. III, no. 565, pp. 363–64.

42 Bernard to Aurier, [Paris, Jan. 1, 1889]; see note 51.

43 On this question see C. Mauron: Notes sur la structure de l'inconscient chez Vincent van Gogh, *Psyché*, nos. 75–78, Jan.–April 1953.

44 See Gauguin: Avant et Après, *op. cit.*, pp. 20–21.

45 The question of whether van Gogh cut off his whole ear or only the lobe has given rise to many discussions. Dr. Rey and the policeman Robert agreed that van Gogh had severed his entire ear (a version supported by Gauguin although he probably did not see Vincent without bandages), but Dr. Gachet and his son, as well as Theo's wife and Signac, maintained that the painter had only cut off the lobe of his ear; see Doiteau and Leroy: Vincent van Gogh et le drame de l'oreille coupée, *Aesculape*, July 1936. According to Dr. Rey (*ibid.*), the severed ear was delivered to the Arles hospital the day after the incident, too late for him to try to put it back into place. Dr. Peyron in his report, Saint-Rémy, May 9, 1889 (quoted p. 305) stated that van Gogh had mutilated himself "by *cutting off* his ear." In Verzamelde Brieven, vol. IV, no. A 13, J. Olivier has likened van Gogh in his self-mutilation to both the vanquished bull and the victorious matador, who, when awarded the bull's ear, presents it to a lady of his choice.

46 *Le Forum républicain*, quoted in H. Perruchot: La Vie de van Gogh, Paris, 1955, p. 284, footnote 2.

47 In her recollections (Introduction to Verzamelde Brieven, vol. I, p. XLII) Theo's widow—who was not in Arles—later reported that, aroused by the clamor, the postman Roulin had rushed to the scene and taken his friend Vincent back to his yellow house. But this seems somewhat doubtful since it appears most unlikely that the devoted Roulin would then have left van Gogh alone without calling a doctor and without attempting to clean up the blood spattered all over the room. Roulin's daughter, whom I interviewed in Arles in 1955, could not remember ever having heard her father say that he took Vincent home during that fateful night.

48 Robert, letter dated Arles, Sept. 11, 1929, quoted in Doiteau and Leroy: *op. cit.*, Aesculape, July 1936.

49 According to an interview with Dr. Rey, it was Gauguin who alerted the physician, telling him merely that a discussion "on matters of art" had caused Vincent's overexcitement. See B. Stokvis: Van Gogh in Arles, *Kunst und Künstler*, Sept. 1929, p. 470.

50 See Gauguin: Avant et Après, *op. cit.*, pp. 20–23.

51 Bernard to Aurier, [Paris, Jan. 1, 1889]. According to a passage in this letter, it was written "four days after Gauguin's precipitate return" from Arles. Unpublished document, courtesy Jacques Williame, Châteauroux.

52 Theo van Gogh to his fiancée, Johanna Bonger, [Arles, end of Dec. 1888]; see Introduction to Verzamelde Brieven, vol. I, p. XLII.

53 V. van Gogh to his brother, [Arles, Jan. 1, 1889]; Verzamelde Brieven, vol. III, no. 566, p. 364.

54 V. van Gogh to Gauguin, [Arles, Jan. 1, 1889]; letter enclosed in the one to his brother of the same date, *ibid.*, pp. 364–65.

THE ACADEMIE JULIAN
THE SYNTHESIST EXHIBITION AT VOLPINI'S
AND THE PONT-AVEN GROUP

After his sudden return from Arles in December 1888 Gauguin remained for about three months in Paris, taking advantage once more of Schuffenecker's hospitality. He pinned great hopes on the exhibition of the XX in Brussels to which he had received an invitation while in Arles and where he expected to "dethrone" the neo-impressionists. Indeed, Gauguin had felt quite bitter to see that Seurat and his friends were regular guests at the Belgian shows while he was ignored. It is not impossible that he actually owed his invitation to a recommendation from Degas which he himself may have solicited. Among those who were invited in addition to Gauguin were Seurat, Camille Pissarro, Cross, and Luce, as well as Monet and Degas; the last-named refused. Gauguin even planned to go to Brussels but was unable to raise the fare. However, the smashing success on which he had counted did not materialize; in fact the only encouraging note came from Octave Maus, who reported on the Brussels show in a Paris weekly: "Of all the exhibitors the one who has the distinction of exciting the utmost hilarity is M. Paul Gauguin . . . . Because one of his landscapes shows blue tree trunks and a yellow sky [p. 237], people conclude that M. Gauguin does not have the most elementary notions of color, and a *Vision after the Sermon*, symbolized by the struggle of Jacob with the angel on a vermilion field [p. 189], makes them believe that the artist intended to pull the visitors' legs in a most presumptuous way. I myself humbly admit my sincere admiration for M. Gauguin, one of the most refined colorists I know and a painter who, more than any other, avoids the customary tricks. I am attracted by the primitive character of his paintings as well as by the charm of his harmonies. There is something of Cézanne in him, and something of Guillaumin, but his most recent canvases show that he is developing and that the artist is already freeing himself from all obsessive influences. . . . None of his paintings have been understood by the public. . . all are praised by Degas, which should amply compensate the artist for all other opinions, the ironic echoes of which must have come to his ears."[1]

His failure to sell anything in Brussels temporarily shattered Gauguin's plan to save money for another voyage to the tropics, and he decided to go once more to Brittany, to live there cheaply with his friend Meyer de Haan. Meanwhile he occupied himself with pottery and some small sculptures.

Before he left, Gauguin also made, together with Emile Bernard, a series of lithographs representing Breton subjects, and painted a large portrait of Schuffenecker, his wife, and his two small daughters, assembled in Schuffenecker's studio. This canvas was much bolder in composition, execution, and color than the likeness of van Gogh that Gauguin had done

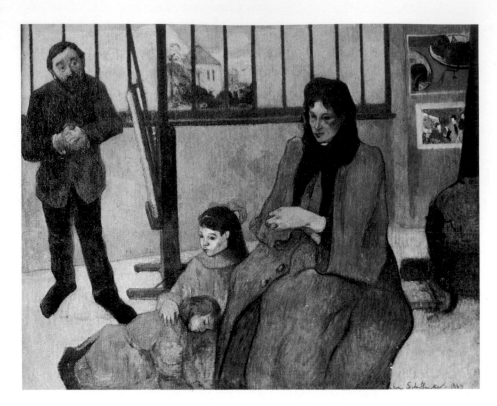

GAUGUIN: *The Schuffenecker Family,* Paris, d. 1889. 28¾ x 36¼″. Musée du Louvre, Paris

in Arles. While in Paris, Gauguin kept in touch with Theo van Gogh and also corresponded with Vincent, yet he does not seem to have seen again his "pupil of a day," Paul Sérusier. But then Gauguin could not know that the little panel Sérusier had painted under his guidance in the Bois d'Amour at Pont-Aven had had a tremendous influence on Sérusier as well as on his friends at the Académie Julian.

Strictly speaking the Académie Julian was not an "academy" at all but merely an art school which furnished models and a not too close supervision of its pupils' work. Theoretically all art education in France was free, as were the public schools, yet the official Ecole des Beaux-Arts was unable to admit all those who applied for its tuition. In order to relieve the French taxpayers from the burden of providing free courses for foreign students without repudiating the generosity of the lawmakers, the Ministry of Fine Arts had hit upon this very clever device: it obliged foreigners to take an extremely difficult, indeed vicious, examination in the French language, with the result that practically all those who had come from abroad with the desire to be taught by France's official masters saw themselves rejected. A similar fate, of course, befell many Frenchmen, though for reasons of insufficient talent. It was this condition which, in 1873, had prompted Rodolphe Julian, a painter of no particular gifts (he looked more like a prizefighter), to open an "academy" of his own, for which he astutely engaged as visiting professors four of the most famous teachers of the Ecole des Beaux-Arts who generally made one weekly appearance to look over the students' work. Julian's enterprise proved so successful that he soon had to open several branches throughout Paris, including a special one for women artists.

Julian's prosperity can be easily explained by the fact that he enabled hundreds, if not thousands, of young artists, especially foreigners, who had been rejected by the Ecole des Beaux-Arts, to study at an "academy" under the direction of some of the Ecole's own masters. Profitable though this venture was for Julian himself, it turned out to be equally advantageous for his pupils and their teachers. Indeed, as members of the Salon jury, the various professors saw to it that works of each other's pupils were admitted, while the pupils in turn re-elected their teachers to the jury by overwhelming majorities every year. The students could thus proudly write home that they were pupils of famous painters, were exhibiting at the Salon, and were well on the way to recognition. The benefits from this smug system seemed well worth the fees charged by Julian.

But among Julian's pupils there were also others, young artists who deliberately forsook the Ecole des Beaux-Arts and its threadbare principles and who attended his classes precisely because they could work there without too much interference from any teacher; there were many older painters who went to Julian's to avail themselves of his life classes. And as the reputation of his establishment grew, those who came from abroad eventually no longer presented themselves at the Ecole des Beaux-Arts at all, but went straight to Julian's; in fact it was the Académie Julian that drew them to Paris. Whatever they learned there they owed less to the pallid personalities of their teachers than to themselves, to their own eagerness and receptiveness. Julian's was a starting point from which many roads led each student to his self-made destiny.

To a certain extent the fame of the Académie Julian was derived from the unruly behavior of its pupils, their legendary coarseness, merciless chaff, the crude practical jokes with which newcomers were greeted, and their wild parades through the streets of Paris. Foreign students, always easy targets for jests, sometimes had a rather rugged life at Julian's, and more than one gave up in despair.

The Académie Julian was a group of studios crowded with pupils, the walls thick with palette scrapings, covered with caricatures, hot, airless, and extremely noisy. Over the entrance were written such words of Ingres as "Drawing is the probity of art," "Look for the character in nature," and "The navel is the eye of the torso." To find a place among the closely packed easels and stools was not easy; wherever one settled one was in somebody's way. Old-timers and those who had already won medals at the Salon had the coveted places near the model stand; newcomers were relegated to the last rows where they could hardly see the models (frequently two posed simultaneously). Among the students all nationalities were represented: Russians, Turks, Egyptians, Serbs, Rumanians, Finns, Swedes, Germans, Englishmen, Scots, and many Americans, besides a great number of Frenchmen, who constituted the leading element as far as general hubbub was concerned. The reserved English were most frequently imitated and mocked; the Germans, victors of the recent war against France, were not too well liked, though they were not treated worse than the others and were always expected to yodel; but the Americans were for the most part let alone because they knew how to use their fists. During intermissions they occasionally staged boxing bouts among themselves and were the only ones permitted to wear their top hats during work, a disregard for "rules" suffered from nobody else. An extremely tall American attracted attention by fastening his brushes to a long stick in order to force himself to paint from a distance and judge his work at the same time. Keeping his palette between his legs while seated on a stool, he covered a canvas in front of the man before him, wielding his extended brush over the head of his unfortunate neighbor. Among the many painters who at one time or another worked at Julian's were the Irishman George Moore, who later turned to writing, the German Lovis Corinth, the Swiss Félix Vallotton, the Spaniard Ignacio Zuloaga, the Englishman William Rothenstein, and later, among the Americans, Alfred Maurer.

In the stifling atmosphere of the studios the noise was often deafening. Sometimes there was silence for a few minutes and then suddenly the students would burst into wild songs. Tunes of all kinds and of all nations were sung. The Frenchmen were extremely quick to catch foreign melodies and the sounds of foreign words. They loved Negro songs and the so-called war cries of American Indians. Besides "singing," the students liked to imitate animal voices, frogs, pigs, tigers, and so on, or to whistle on their door keys. One of their favorite ditties was sung by a leading pupil:

> *La peinture à l'huile*
> *est très difficile*

whereupon the chorus would join in:

> *Mais c'est bien plus beau*
> *que la peinture à l'eau.*[2]

There were no rules and no discipline; even the teachers were not always respected on their infrequent rounds. Some pupils, in open defiance, turned their paintings around when the professor approached. It is true that the advice of the various teachers did not always follow the same lines. Bouguereau, the most famous of them and the least imaginative, rigidly insisted on "correct" drawing, while some of the others were apt to make occasional allowances for color. Lefebvre, a skillful but thoroughly conventional painter of nudes, managed to correct some seventy works in two hours. Straightforward and unaffected, he was chiefly concerned with accurate proportions and always had encouraging words for everybody. His colleague Robert-Fleury, elegant in bearing as well as in speech, would often examine studies without uttering a word, unless he informed their authors that he could not condescend to correct such daubs. His favorite bit of advice was that shadows had no colors but were always neutral. As to Doucet, a suave and polished Parisian, he actually showed some benign sympathy for the experimental eccentricities current in the studios. Indeed, among the pupils there were many who had no desire to adopt the precepts of the Ecole des Beaux-Arts and who preferred to follow their own inclinations. Puvis de Chavannes and Monet were the dominant influences among the more intelligent students.[3]

There was in each studio a *massier*, chosen from among the pupils and elected by them, whose task it was to prevent flagrant disorders, to attend to the stove, hire the models, and take care of other administrative duties. Paul Sérusier was the *massier* of what was called the "little studios" of the Académie Julian in the faubourg Saint-Denis, where Lefebvre and Boulanger taught. Surrounded by more or less vulgar and uncouth students, he was a man of superior culture, a stimulating force, an intellectual and artistic guide. Yet at the same time he was an admirable and gay companion, ready for mischief though defending the weak, proud of his physical strength, his good appearance, his splendid voice. Born in 1863, Sérusier had received an excellent higher education, had been interested in the theater, writing some plays in verse, painting sets, and fashioning marionettes; but he had also read a great deal and had even started to learn Arabic. After some parental opposition

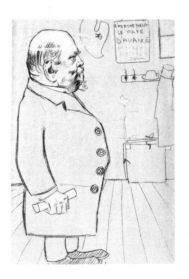

ROTHENSTEIN: *Caricature of M. Julian.* 1889. Pencil

252

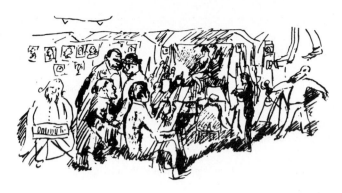

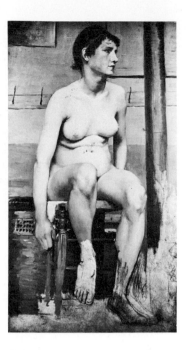

Above: BONNARD: *At the Académie Julian, 1888–1889,* drawn
c. 1910. Pen and ink, c. 3 x 4″. Private collection, France

Right: VALLOTTON: Unfinished study of a nude, Académie
Julian, 1885. 31¾ x 17½″. Private collection, France

to a career in the arts he had been permitted to enter Julian's where he made rapid progress.
A painting of his, done in accordance with all the conventional concepts of his masters, had
even obtained an "honorable mention" at the Salon of 1888. But in that same year his short
acquaintance with Gauguin had suddenly opened new horizons to him.

Returning from Pont-Aven to Paris in October 1888, Sérusier had shown his small panel
to the little group of his intimate friends at Julian's. Rising above the doltish majority,
these friends of his were interested in new ideas, ready to embark upon untraveled roads.
They were all beginners, several years younger than himself: Pierre Bonnard, Edouard
Vuillard, Maurice Denis, Félix Vallotton, and Paul Ranson. Sérusier's panel at first looked
almost formless to them because of the extreme degree to which all elements had been synthesized. With the enthusiasm of the proselyte Sérusier had in fact gone much farther in
abstraction than Gauguin himself. His small painting almost resembled a crazy quilt with
large patches of uniform color and an absolute minimum of naturalistic elements; it was
actually hard to say where its top or bottom was. Pale blue tree trunks were crowned by
flat masses of yellow and green, a blue spot signified a piece of sky appearing among the
leaves, and crude reflections in the water, brushed in with utmost freedom, occupied the
whole lower half of the painting (reproduced page 188). Explaining this work, Sérusier
conveyed to his friends Gauguin's "message" that instead of copying nature as one perceived it, one should *represent* it, transmute it into a play of vivid colors, emphasizing
simple, expressive, original arabesques for the pleasure of the eye.

Sérusier's interpretation of Gauguin's aims was fascinating, but his friends tried not to
be carried away by his enthusiasm. They were suddenly being offered a solution to many
problems which they had hardly had time to approach, some of which they may not yet
have even become aware of. It would have been too simple just to rally around Gauguin

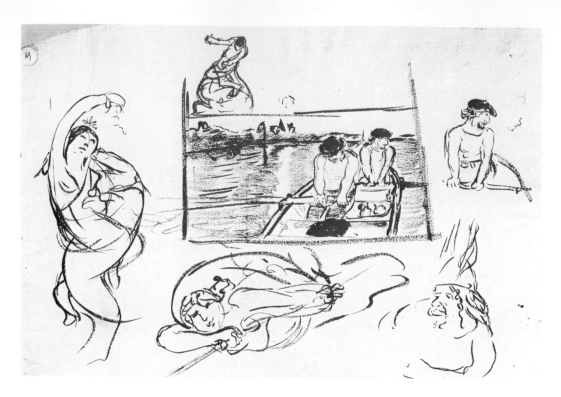

SÉRUSIER: *Gauguin Rowing in Brittany*, 1888–90. Brush and ink drawing, 12¾ x 18¾″. Collection Mlle H. Boutaric, Paris

and accept his theories. Could they renounce their healthy curiosity, the joy of experimenting, the thrill of sudden discoveries, by adopting Sérusier's gospel? Could they exchange their enterprising youthfulness for a mature certitude? There was much, certainly, that could be of help in freeing them from the conventions of naturalism, but there seemed to be also much that presented the danger of too narrow a formula. And above all, there were still many questions to which Sérusier himself did not yet know the answers, his exchange of ideas with Gauguin having been limited to a few hours.

While Gauguin's concepts became almost an obsession with Sérusier, he realized how little he knew as yet about them and was anxious to meet Gauguin once more. During the Easter vacation he went, accompanied by some other pupils of Julian's, to Pont-Aven, whence Gauguin reported to Bernard: "Sérusier has just arrived and speaks of nothing but his evolution. He intends to resist Lefebvre's influence and is carrying along all those around him, he says. I have not yet seen anything of what he [does]. . . ."[4]

Strangely enough, Sérusier at first experienced a great disillusionment at Pont-Aven and wrote to his friend Maurice Denis: "As soon as I arrived I became aware that Gauguin, who is with me, is not the artist I thought he was. I have seen points in his reasoning on which we do not at all agree and I find in his works a lack of delicacy, an illogical and puerile affectation of drawing, a search for originality which borders on deception. I have therefore refrained from showing him what I am doing."[5] But three days later Sérusier concluded this letter on a more cheerful note, written at Le Pouldu, a small seaside resort not far from Pont-Aven: "I arrived yesterday on these beautiful beaches where I shall spend two weeks alone with Gauguin, without distractions, without cares, and without *apéritifs*. I am seized

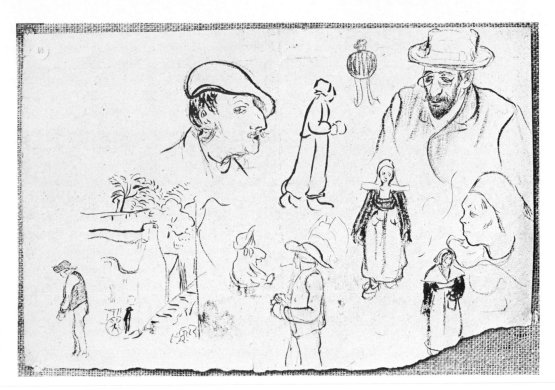

SÉRUSIER: *Sketches of Gauguin and Paul Ranson,* Brittany, 1888–90. Brush and ink drawing, 14¾ x 17⅞". Collection Mlle H. Boutaric, Paris

by a fever to work, all is well.... I believe that I shall at last do something worth while."[6]

In his enthusiasm Sérusier inscribed on the wall of the inn the following *credo* taken from Wagner's writings: "I believe in a Last Judgment at which all those who in this world have dared to traffic with sublime and chaste art, all those who have sullied and degraded it by the baseness of their sentiments, by their vile lust for material enjoyment, will be condemned to terrible punishments. I believe on the other hand that the faithful disciples of great art will be glorified and that—enveloped in a celestial tissue of rays, of perfumes, of melodious sounds—they will return to lose themselves forever in the bosom of the divine source of all Harmony."[7]

Inspired by this mystical devotion to his calling, Sérusier had yet to find a proper expression for his innate gifts. The problem which above all preoccupied him and which he must have discussed at length with Gauguin was set forth by him in these words: "What part should nature play in a work of art? Where should the line be drawn? And from the standpoint of practical procedure, should one work directly from nature or merely study and remember it? Too much freedom frightens me, poor copyist that I am, and yet my head is filled with so many images evoked by what I see around me at all times that nature seems insignificant and banal."[5]

The advice which Gauguin gave Sérusier doubtless followed the same lines as that which he had given van Gogh, but dogmatic though he may have been and eager though Sérusier was to learn, it does not seem that Sérusier returned to Paris wholly convinced that he had discovered the truth.

All Paris meanwhile was active and excited about the forthcoming great World's Fair

255

that was to open in the spring of 1889 under the sign of the newly completed Eiffel Tower, symbol of the novel ways in which iron could be used in architecture. But apparently few artists were tempted by this elegant structure, with the exception of Seurat, who painted a small, luminous sketch of the tower even before its completion. Subsequently the *douanier* Rousseau included it in several of his canvases.

The art section of the 1889 World's Fair was to contain a Centennial Exhibition (opened after some delay) in which the critic Roger Marx had had the courage to include a few works by many still controversial painters such as Manet, Monet, and Pissarro. Renoir, in a moment of doubt and despondency, had informed Roger Marx that he "considered bad all that I have done and that it would be extremely distressing to me to see it exhibited."[8] Degas was even more modest — or proud; he simply refused to avail himself of the special room that had been reserved for his works. As for Cézanne, Roger Marx was able to admit one of his paintings through some subterfuge and the intervention of Victor Chocquet, friend of both Renoir and Cézanne. There was of course the inevitable contingent of official masters but there were no provisions to exhibit younger artists, such as Gauguin, since Roger Marx had already encountered fierce resistance as far as their immediate predecessors were concerned.

The only way for Gauguin to appear at the Fair would have been to follow the example previously set by Courbet and Manet when in 1867 they built their own pavilions on the exposition grounds. But for that he lacked the means. Gauguin had given up any hope of being represented at the Fair when, quite by accident, Schuffenecker discovered a place where he and his friends could show their works. He had noticed the large hall of a café appropriately called "Grand Café des Beaux-Arts" and situated right next to the official art section. When Schuffenecker had spoken to the owner, an Italian by the name of Volpini, he found him quite discouraged because the 250,000 (?) francs worth of mirrors which he had ordered as mural decorations would not be ready in time. It was apparently not difficult for Schuffenecker to convince the proprietor that it would be cheaper to forego the mirrors, cover the walls with pomegranate-red material, and let him and his friends hang their paintings there.[9] Gauguin received the unexpected news at Pont-Aven and immediately replied to Schuffenecker: "Bravo! You have succeeded. Go to see [Theo] van Gogh and arrange everything until the end of my stay here. But do remember that this is not an exhibition for the *others*. Consequently, let's arrange to have a small group of friends, and from that point of view I desire to be *represented* by as many works as possible. Please see to it that everything is done to my best advantage, according to the space available. [Here follows a list of ten paintings from Martinique, Arles, and Brittany that Gauguin wished to show.] Remember that it is we who are inviting the others, therefore...

Schuffenecker	10 paintings	
Guillaumin	10	,,
Gauguin	10	,,
Bernard	10	,,
Roy	2	,,
The man from Nancy	2	,,
Vincent	6	,,

40 paintings

10 paintings

50 paintings

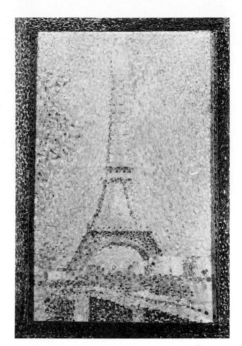

SEURAT: *The Eiffel Tower,* 1888–89. Oil on wood,
9⅝ x 6¼". Collection Mr. and Mrs. Germain Seligman,
New York

That should be sufficient. I refuse to exhibit with the *others*, Pissarro, Seurat, etc. It's our group! I intended to show only a few works, but Laval tells me that this is my turn and that I would be wrong to work for the others."[10]

From the beginning Gauguin took a rather aggressive stand with regard to the artists he did not want to invite, and it seems strange that he should have offered such a large representation to Guillaumin who, after all, belonged to the old-guard impressionists much more than to Gauguin's group. It was true, however, that Guillaumin had no contract with Durand-Ruel and was seldom included among the impressionists. Yet he must have felt antagonized by Gauguin's position towards his impressionist friends, for he refused to participate in the show. Gauguin later explained that if Guillaumin had exhibited with him, he would have invited fewer of the younger and unknown artists. As a matter of fact he considered Guillaumin's refusal as a desertion.

Gauguin forgot to include his friend Laval in his initial list; he was subsequently added to it. As to Roy and the "man from Nancy," the painter Léon Fauché, they were two young artists whom Gauguin had recently met in Brittany and who had asked his advice. Sérusier, on the other hand, was apparently ruled out. A further addition to the list was made when Daniel de Monfreid, a friend of Schuffenecker's whom Gauguin had first known early in 1889, was included. But it seems odd that no place was found for Meyer de Haan.

It appears natural that Schuffenecker, in spite of his mediocrity as a painter, should have been represented by ten canvases, for after all he was not only the originator of the whole project but also Gauguin's most faithful and patient friend. More significant is the fact that Gauguin allotted to young Emile Bernard as much space as to himself (while giving less to Vincent van Gogh). As Gauguin later explained to Theo van Gogh, he regarded himself and Bernard as the pillars of the new movement, whereas he saw the others only as "substitutes."

When, in accordance with Gauguin's instructions, Schuffenecker went to see Theo van Gogh about their show, he unexpectedly found him opposed to the entire enterprise. "I said at first that you would show with them," Theo reported to his brother, "but the thing took on such an air of noisy virulence that it became really bad to be part of it.... It looks somewhat like entering the World's Fair through a back door."[11] Thus, without even consulting his brother, Theo declined Vincent's participation. The painter subsequently ratified this decision, though he by no means condemned the venture itself; indeed, had it not been for his utter confidence in Theo, Vincent might well have disagreed with him. "I think you are right," he wrote to his brother, "not to show any of my pictures at the exhibition of Gauguin and the others, and there is a valid reason for me to abstain without offending them, as long as I myself am not completely cured. For me there is no question that Gauguin and Bernard have real and great merit. For men like them, who are very much alive and young, and who *must* live and try to get ahead, it is impossible to turn all their canvases against the wall until it pleases other people to admit them somewhere, in the official salad. By showing in cafés one does make a noise which, I don't deny it, may be in bad taste, but I myself have this same crime on my conscience twice, having exhibited at the Tambourin and in the avenue de Clichy.... Thus in any event I am worse and more to blame than they, as far as making a noise is concerned, though Heaven knows I did it unintentionally. Young Bernard, in my opinion, has already painted some absolutely astonishing canvases in which there is a gentleness and something essentially French and candid of rare quality. Anyhow, neither he nor Gauguin is an artist who could possibly give the impression of trying to enter the World's Fair through the service entrance. You may be sure of that. It is understandable that they *could not* keep quiet."[12]

In spite of van Gogh's defection Gauguin was determined to go ahead and gather his friends and followers around him in order to prove that it was possible to appear before the public as a more or less homogeneous group. Thus Bernard's comrade Anquetin was added to the list of exhibitors. But there was one painter who let it be known that he would have accepted an invitation had he received one: Toulouse-Lautrec. Yet, having once shown with a group of which Gauguin did not approve, he found himself excluded, despite his friendship with both Bernard and Anquetin.[13] It is true, however, that Lautrec had no stylistic connection with Gauguin's circle.

Gauguin returned to Paris so as to organize the exhibition personally. On a pushcart he helped to transport the canvases, framed in white, to Volpini's, where they were hung by him and his friends on the pomegranate-red walls under the benevolent eye of the proprietor.[9] The hall at Volpini's apparently turned out to be much more spacious than expected. Instead of the fifty paintings Gauguin had counted on assembling, the group was able to hang almost one hundred pictures, drawings, and watercolors. Of these the largest contingent was furnished by Bernard, who showed over twenty works and even listed in the catalogue some *peintures au pétrole* under the name of Ludovic Nemo. Schuffenecker exhibited twenty works and Gauguin only seventeen. Laval, somewhat lazy and always dissatisfied with his works, was represented by ten paintings. Anquetin and Roy each contributed seven, Fauché five, and Daniel de Monfreid three. The printed catalogue was made up handsomely, with reproductions of drawings by Gauguin, Bernard, Schuffenecker, and Roy. Among Gauguin's works were paintings from Martinique, Brittany, and Arles; Laval also sent works from Martinique and Brittany; Breton subjects formed an important part of Bernard's exhibit as well.[14]

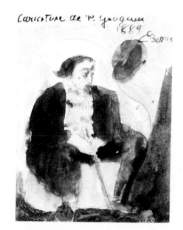

BERNARD: *Caricature of P. Gauguin*, d. 1889. Watercolor

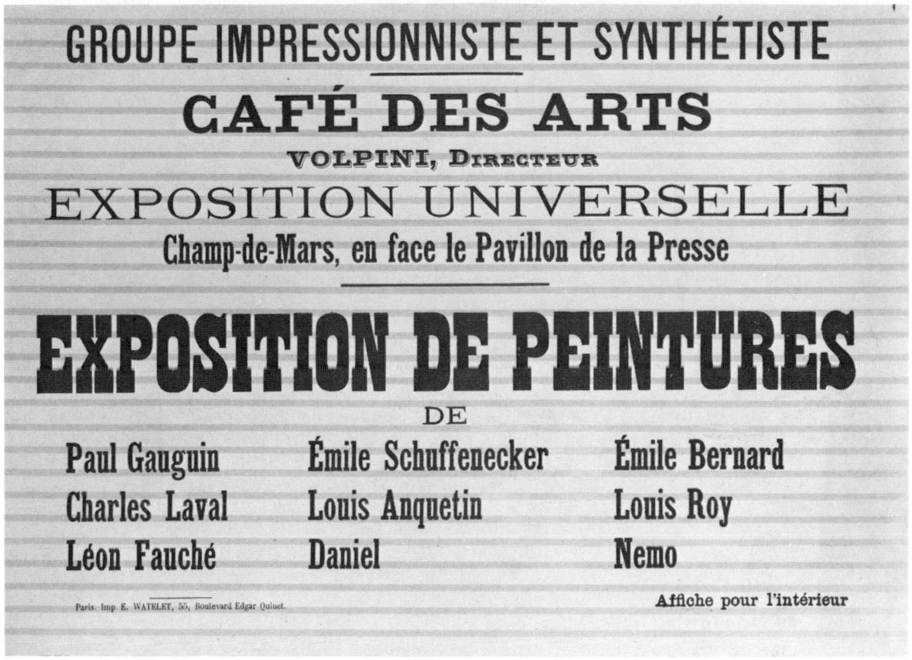

GROUPE IMPRESSIONNISTE ET SYNTHÉTISTE

CAFÉ DES ARTS

VOLPINI, Directeur

EXPOSITION UNIVERSELLE

Champ-de-Mars, en face le Pavillon de la Presse

EXPOSITION DE PEINTURES

DE

Paul Gauguin	Émile Schuffenecker	Émile Bernard
Charles Laval	Louis Anquetin	Louis Roy
Léon Fauché	Daniel	Nemo

Paris. Imp. E. WATELET, 55, Boulevard Edgar Quinet.

Affiche pour l'intérieur

Poster for the Volpini Exhibition, 1889

When it came to announcing the show Gauguin must have felt some uncertainty as to a proper name for it. He and those round him were striving for a synthesis of their sensations and had cut off all links with the impressionists, and yet Gauguin had continued to think of himself—as did van Gogh—as being an impressionist. At Gloanec's he and his friends were always called impressionists. Whereas Seurat and his group had stressed their indebtedness to their forerunners by calling themselves "neo-impressionists," Gauguin might have proclaimed himself a "new" or "modern" impressionist, but this must have appeared too subtle to him. He simplified matters by naming his group "impressionist and synthesist." In this way he probably expected to benefit from the sympathy which the impressionists were slowly acquiring among a small unprejudiced section of the public, and he also had a common denominator for all the paintings by his associates that did not reflect his own new style. According to Bernard this name was actually suggested by his friend Albert Aurier. In any event Gauguin never bothered to explain the choice of these two words though they did lead to numerous misunderstandings.

Posters were now printed which, on a background of horizontal stripes in red and white, announced in bold type the exhibition of paintings by a "Groupe Impressionniste et Synthétiste" in the Café des Arts, and which also listed the names of the participants. So as to assure a wide distribution of these posters, Gauguin, Laval, Schuffenecker, and Bernard went out at night to paste them all over town. They climbed on each other's shoulders to post them where they could not be torn off easily. "Schuffenecker claims that this manifestation will knock out all the other painters," Theo van Gogh reported to his brother, "and if he could have had his way, I believe he would have paraded through the streets of Paris with multicolored banners, so as to show that he is the great victor."[11]

A few days before the opening, Bernard wrote to Aurier, whom he had meanwhile introduced to several of his friends and with whom he had visited a number of exhibitions. (Together with his colleague Julien Leclercq, Aurier had also gone to Tanguy's to admire van Gogh's paintings from the South, an admiration in which they were joined by Octave Mirbeau.) Bernard now asked Aurier for some free publicity in the various symbolist periodicals: "As the result of all kinds of efforts we are entering the Exposition Universelle at last. We have found a place; it is a café, the best place in the world to see paintings which one should examine at leisure and discuss. This café must be made known, people should learn where it is and what it contains. I appeal to your friendship and especially to your ideas on art, so that you may assist us as much as possible, that is to publish in all the periodicals you know... an announcement as follows:

'To be seen at the Café des Arts (Fine Arts Pavilion, opposite the Pavilion of the Press) an exhibition of a new group of impressionists. The hall was made available through the enlightenment of Monsieur Volpini, artistic director of the Grand Café. The exhibitors are Paul Gauguin, Emile Bernard, Emile Schuffenecker, Charles Laval, Louis Anquetin, Vincent [sic] Roy. (We shall publish a detailed review of this exhibition.)'"[15] Bernard added that the available surface was twenty-six yards long and over seven and one-half yards high. He also suggested that the *Moderniste*, of which Aurier was editor-in-chief, publish a catalogue of the show in a special issue to be sold at the exhibition. Aurier did not follow this suggestion, nor did he apparently agree that a café was "the best place in the world" to examine paintings, but he did start his general review of the Exposition Universelle with the following paragraph:

"I am happy to have been informed that individual initiative has just attempted what the forever incurable imbecility of the administration would never have consented to accomplish. A small group of independent artists has managed to break, not into the Palace of Fine Arts, but into the Exposition and to create a minute competition with the official exhibition. Oh! the installation is somewhat primitive, rather strange and—as will no doubt be said—*bohemian!*... But what can you expect? If those poor devils had had a palace at their disposal, they would certainly not have hung their canvases on the walls of a café."[16]

The exhibition seems to have been opened late in May or early in June and must have startled the patrons of the café who went there to see a "Princess Dolgorouka" direct an orchestra of women violonists, supposedly Russians, with the accompaniment of a single male cornet player.[17] Whereas the show did not attract any attention among the reviewers of the daily press, Aurier apparently did what Bernard had expected of him and it received short write-ups in several symbolist periodicals. Gustave Kahn in *La Vogue* (republished after suspension) regretted that Gauguin's paintings were shown under such bad conditions and expressed little liking for the works of the other exhibitors.[18] Félix Fénéon wrote about the show in *La Cravache* with more sympathy for Gauguin and his friends, but ventured the opinion that Anquetin might have influenced Gauguin: "It is likely that the manner of M. Anquetin, impenetrable contours, flat and intense tones, was not without some influence upon M. Paul Gauguin; but this is a purely formal influence, as it does not appear that the slightest feeling circulates in these [Anquetin's] intelligent and decorative works."[19] Gauguin, who did not know Anquetin, never forgave Fénéon for this statement, although the critic, while wrong in fact, was right at least insofar as Anquetin's *cloisonniste* style was perfectly known to Gauguin through Anquetin's co-cloisonnist Bernard.[20]

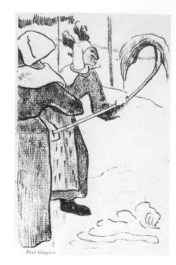

GAUGUIN: *Breton Haymakers,* 1889

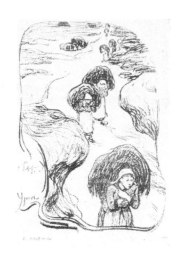

SCHUFFENECKER: *Seaweed Gatherers,* 1889. Illustrations on these two pages are from the catalogue of the Volpini show

260

In his review Fénéon also reported: "It is not easy to approach these canvases on account of the sideboards, beer pumps, tables, the bosom of M. Volpini's cashier, and an orchestra of young Moscovites whose bows unleash in the large room a music that has no relation to these polychromatic works."[19]

The strangest article on the show appeared in *Art et Critique* over the signature of Jules Antoine, who endeavored to divide the exhibitors into impressionists and synthesists. His highest praise went to Schuffenecker. He considered only Anquetin and Bernard as synthesists, while he saw in Gauguin an impressionist. On the other hand he accused Laval as well as Bernard of copying Gauguin.[21] Bernard himself later said that the exhibition had had a rather heterogeneous character and that only he, Gauguin, and Laval had represented synthesism, whereas he classified all the others as impressionists. It became obvious that this division of the exhibitors into two groups only created confusion, especially since nobody seemed to agree about who belonged in which category.

Gauguin was exasperated by the constant speculations as to whether he had influenced Bernard or been influenced by him. "I do not resemble him any more than he resembles me," he explained to Theo van Gogh, "except that both of us make *different* attempts to reach the same goal, a goal about which I have thought for a long time but which I have formulated only recently."[22]

Fénéon, however, was not convinced of this and a couple of years later was to emphasize that Gauguin had met "in Brittany a young painter of an adventurous and well informed mind, M. Emile Bernard, who today is possibly his pupil but who seems to have once been his mentor. For M. Bernard was the first to paint with saturated colors those capsized Breton women with meshed outlines of stained-glass windows, wrapped in a décor devoid of atmosphere and tonal modulations. The characteristics of this work derived partly from the artist's purpose and partly from his clumsiness. M. Gauguin . . . outdid the Breton women of M. Bernard, but being a sophisticated painter, he put some logic into their barbarism, which, behind a savage exterior, is very controlled."[23]

By far the most perceptive notice and actually the first one to appear was written by Albert Aurier, next to Fénéon the only one among the symbolist poets and writers to devote himself seriously to the study of contemporary art (he was even listed in the show's catalogue as owner of one of Bernard's paintings). In his subsequent writings Aurier was to explore at length the relation between impressionism and the synthesism of Pont-Aven. He insisted that the former appellation be reserved exclusively "for those painters to whom art is but a translation of the artist's sensations and impressions," while he saw in Gauguin's paintings a trend which paralleled the symbolist movement in literature and which indeed he preferred to call "symbolism" rather than "synthesism."[24] But he formulated his definitions only later, after he had become more thoroughly acquainted with Gauguin's art. At the time of the Volpini exhibition he merely urged the readers of his newly founded *Moderniste* to visit the café, explaining: "In most of the works shown, and especially in those of Gauguin, Bernard, Anquetin, etc., I seem to have noticed a marked tendency towards a synthesis of drawing, composition, and color, as well as an effort to simplify the means of expression which appears very interesting to me at this particular moment when empty prowess and cheap tricks are the rule."[25]

On the whole Gauguin was deeply disappointed by the reception his show received. Not a single painting was sold at Volpini's. Yet, it may have been of some comfort to him that his canvases aroused tremendous interest among many artists of the new generation.

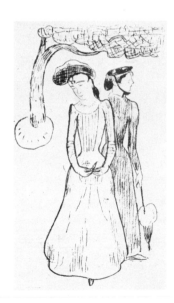

BERNARD: *Two Women Walking*, 1889

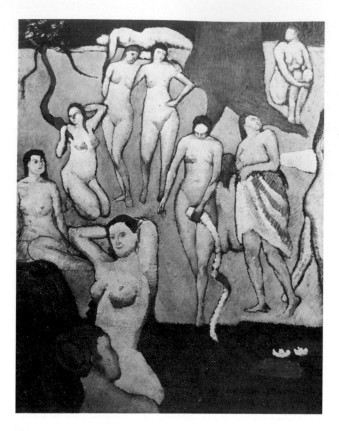 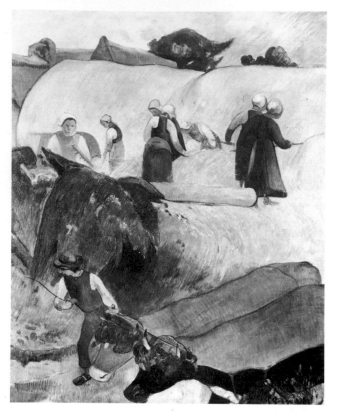

BERNARD: *Bathers,* Pont-Aven, d. 1889. 35 × 27¾″. Present whereabouts unknown

GAUGUIN: *Harvesting,* Pont-Aven, d. 1889. 36¼ × 28¾″. Courtauld Institute Galleries, London

Sérusier and his friends, for instance, were frequent visitors at the café, where they at last became familiar with synthesism as a collective effort. As one of Sérusier's comrades later put it, they felt drawn towards Gauguin by "the presentiment of a higher reality, a predilection for the mysterious and the unusual, a tendency towards reverie, a mental luxury...."[26] Owing to Sérusier's reports, Gauguin's ideas had already germinated in their minds; now they could study for the first time a representative series of his works. In these they discovered remnants of impressionistic execution combined with simplification of forms, a strange mixture of naïveté and sophistication, of brutality and subtlety, of dogmatism and primitiveness. They may even have found some traces of bad taste and grandiose visions. They were startled by these contradictions and stimulated by all that Gauguin had to offer. But only one of them, only Sérusier, was now completely convinced and converted. He told Gauguin: "From now on I am one of yours."[27]

Another profoundly stirred visitor was Aristide Maillol, who had left Cabanel's class at the Ecole des Beaux-Arts to devote himself to designing and executing tapestries strongly influenced by Puvis de Chavannes. Sérusier's friend, Maurice Denis, had already spoken to him about Gauguin. "Gauguin's art was a revelation to me," Maillol later acknowledged. "The Ecole des Beaux-Arts, instead of enlightening me, had obscured my vision. Looking

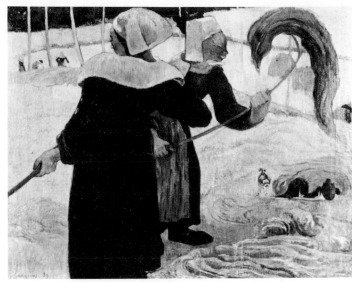

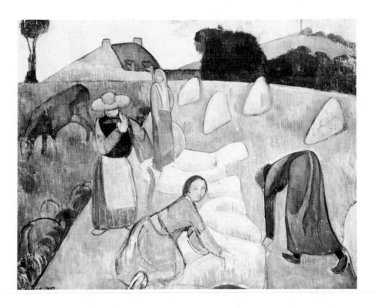

Above: GAUGUIN: *Breton Haymakers*, Pont-Aven, d. 1889. 29⅞ x 37⅜". Collection S. Schwarz-von Spreckelsen, Basel

Left: BERNARD: *Wheat Harvest*, Pont-Aven, d. 1889. 28⅜ x 35¾". Present whereabouts unknown

Left: GAUGUIN: *Seated Breton Girl*, Le Pouldu, d. 1889. 28⅛ x 35⅝". Ny Carlsberg Glyptotek, Copenhagen

Below: GAUGUIN: *Landscape at Le Pouldu,* d. 1889. 23½ x 29". Private collection, New York

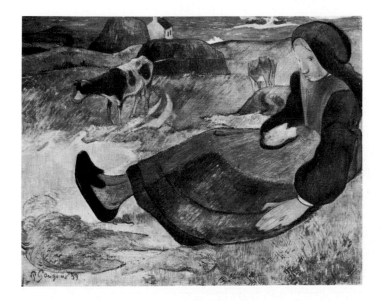

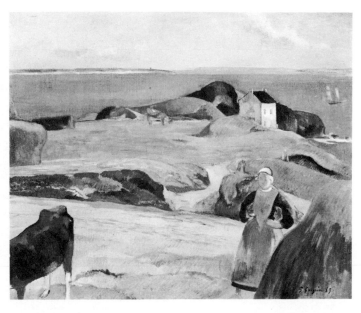

at his paintings of Pont-Aven I felt that I would be able to work in the same vein. I told myself at once that what I was doing would be satisfactory when Gauguin would approve of it."[28] A little later Maillol was to meet his chosen master and submit his work to him.

Unknown to Gauguin, another fledgling artist also derived great benefit from his show. This was Suzanne Valadon, then twenty-three years old. Since the birth of her son in December 1883 she had devoted herself to her child but also continued to draw in her spare time. Though she almost never went to the Louvre or to exhibitions, she must have gone to Volpini's, for she later said, when listing the decisive events of her artistic career, that she had felt "intrigued by the technique of Pont-Aven" which she had decided to apply to more naturalistic subjects, "without any trace of estheticism or artiness."[29]

On the other hand some of the old-guard impressionists seem to have voiced their disapproval of Gauguin's venture. But the painter was unaffected by their criticism and defiantly told Theo van Gogh: "Pissarro and others do not like my exhibition, *therefore* it must be good for me."[22] In spite of the slight recognition he had received, Gauguin was by no means ready to admit that Theo van Gogh's advice against showing at Volpini's might, to some extent at least, have been justified. As a matter of fact this exhibition opened a new

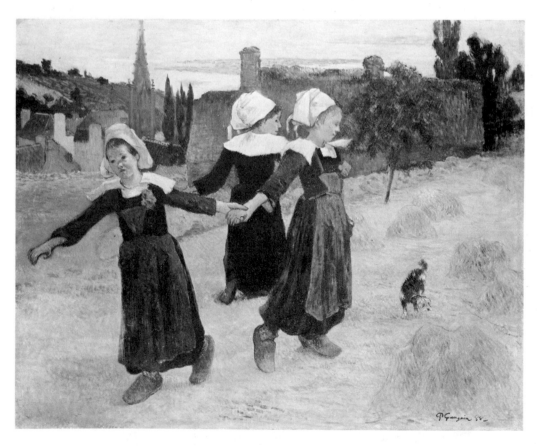

GAUGUIN: *Breton Girls Dancing*, Pont-Aven, d. 1888 (retouched in Arles). 36¼ x 28⅜". Exhibited at the Volpini show. Collection Mr. and Mrs. Paul Mellon, Upperville, Va.

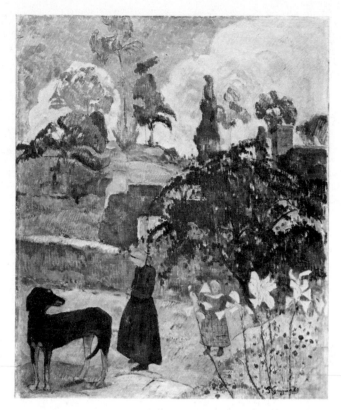

GAUGUIN: *Breton Landscape with Children and Dog,* d. 1889. 36¼ x 28⅜″. Öffentliche Kunstsammlung, Basel (on extended loan from the R. Staechelin Foundation)

chapter in Gauguin's life, for it earned him a few new friends among young authors and painters and greatly contributed to his emergence as the head of a new art movement.

While in Paris during the World's Fair, Gauguin was particularly attracted by a reconstructed village from Java where he went frequently to observe native dances. He was impressed by the close connection of these dances with the art from India and especially with photographs from Cambodia, which he liked to study and which he was to take back with him to Brittany. His longing for the tropics was revitalized by these impressions; Gauguin began to be obsessed with the idea of leaving either for Tonkin or for Madagascar.

During his stay in Paris Gauguin also met Albert Aurier through Bernard; he as well as Bernard wrote several articles for Aurier's *Moderniste.* These articles of Gauguin's are rather clumsy in style, awkward in their reasoning, and primitive in their polemic. He vituperates against official art without the necessary detachment that might have made his conclusions persuasive, and adopts on the whole a rather negative attitude instead of setting forth his own views on the new currents in art.[30]

After his return to Pont-Aven, Gauguin again went to work, though he was greatly depressed by his lack of success at Volpini's. "Guillaumin has written to me that nobody pays any attention to it," he wrote bitterly to Schuffenecker regarding their show.[31] Bernard was even more downcast. He had left Paris after depositing the remaining catalogues with *père* Tanguy and complained to Schuffenecker: "Nothing sold! Nothing either in the daily papers or in the so-called art periodicals. Isn't that fine?"[32] But while Bernard

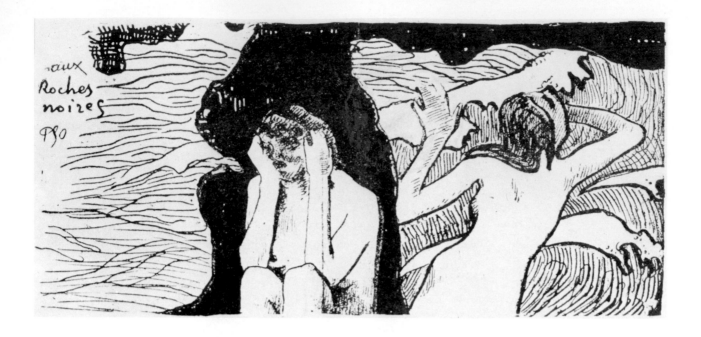

was completely discouraged, Gauguin made a valiant effort not to let this mishap interfere with the progress of his work. "I have been in a horrible state of depression," he wrote to Bernard, but he added immediately: "In works which it takes me a certain length of time to complete I experience the pleasure not so much of going further in what I had prepared previously, but in finding something additional. I feel it but do not quite express it yet. I am certain to find it, though slowly in spite of all my impatience. Under these conditions my groping studies yield only quite awkward and shallow results. However, I hope that this winter I shall be able to show you an almost entirely new Gauguin; I say almost because everything is linked together and I don't claim to have invented something new. What I wish is to explore an as yet unknown part of myself...."[33] And Bernard reported enviously to Schuffenecker: "Gauguin experiments and has few doubts—how lucky he is. Laval doubts and is somnolent."[32]

By now Gauguin had become tired of Pont-Aven, where there were too many artists of the official type and where his canvases, when hung at Gloanec's among theirs, were jeered at by the others. Though he boasted to Schuffenecker: "The battle at Pont-Aven is finished; everybody is checkmated and the Atelier Julian begins to tack about and make fun of the Ecole des Beaux-Arts,"[31] and though he was proud to be looked upon as chief of a new movement, he felt an increasing need for isolation. Pont-Aven no longer offered a propitious atmosphere for his meditations and for an exchange of views with the small group of his faithful friends. When Signac passed through the village a little later, he mockingly reported to his comrade Luce: "Yesterday I was at Pont-Aven. It's ridiculous countryside with little nooks and cascades, as if made for female English watercolorists. What a strange cradle for pictorial Symbolism.... Everywhere painters in velvet garments, drunk and bawdy. The tobacco merchant has a sign in the form of a palette: 'Artist's Material' [in English], the maidservants in the inns wear arty ribbons in their headdresses

266

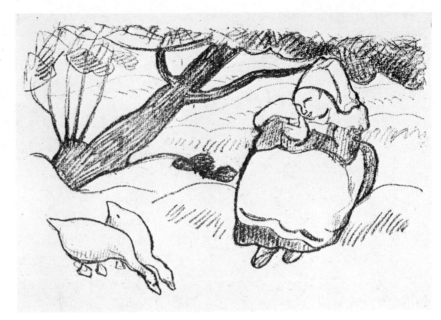

Opposite page: GAUGUIN: *Aux Roches noires*, 1889. Illustration from the catalogue of the Volpini show

Right: BERNARD: *Reverie*, 1889. Illustration from the catalogue of the Volpini show

and probably are syphilitic."[34] And Bernard himself later wrote from Pont-Aven: "This is the country of atrocious dreams, of hideous nightmares, of walls garnished with larvae and sea-eagles, with owls and vampires, fit to die."[35]

No wonder then that Gauguin preferred to return to Le Pouldu, where he had already been with Sérusier and where he was sure to be left alone with the few painters he liked to gather round him. He went there with Meyer de Haan, who continued to provide discreetly for his friend. Bernard would have joined them had it not been for his father's opposition to his going to Le Pouldu; but Bernard did spend some time in Pont-Aven. Instead Sérusier arrived at Le Pouldu in order, as he put it, "to ask the master's forgiveness for not having understood him right away."[36]

At the mouth of the Quimper river, about fifteen miles from Pont-Aven, Le Pouldu was an exciting place because of its dramatic strangeness. It was in a country of gigantic sand dunes, like the waves of a solid sea, between which appeared glimpses of the Bay of Biscay and the Atlantic rollers. According to a painter who had gone there a little while before Gauguin, it was peopled by a savage-looking race of men, who seemed to do nothing but search for driftwood or collect seaweed with curious sledges drawn by shaggy ponies, and by women in black dresses, who wore great black *coiffes* resembling huge sunbonnets.[37] Here Gauguin came as close to a primitive way of life as he could ever expect to come in France. He remained there for the rest of 1889 and, after a short trip to Paris early in 1890, for part of that year as well.

After having stayed at first at the larger of the two inns at Le Pouldu, Gauguin and his friends moved in October 1889 to the smaller one owned by Mlle Marie Henry (also called Marie Poupée), who from the beginning surrounded them with motherly care. There was hardly anybody else at her inn so that the painters had the place practically to themselves. It must have been shortly after their arrival that there came to the inn a young man

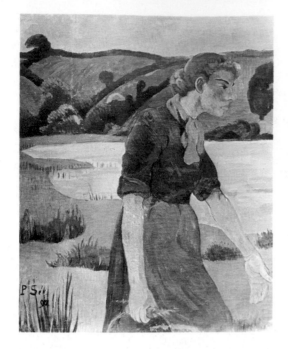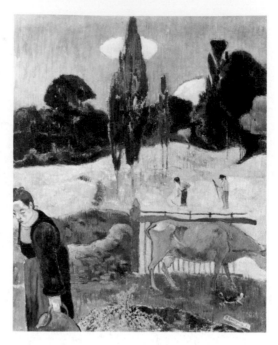

Left: Sérusier: *Peasant Girl Carrying Water*, d. 1892. 29½ x 23¼". Collection Mme Bontemps, Paris
Right: Gauguin: *Brittany Landscape with Mowers*, d. 1889. 36 x 29". Los Angeles County Museum of Art
(Mr. and Mrs. George Gard de Sylva Collection)

who, as Emile Bernard had done before, was exploring Brittany on foot. His name was
André Gide, and he set down, many years later, what he remembered of that day: "As I
was following the seashore.... I arrived one day, towards evening, in a small village: Le
Pouldu.... This village was composed only of four houses, two of which were inns; the
more modest of the two seemed to me the pleasanter, and I entered because I was very
thirsty. A maidservant showed me into a large room with whitewashed walls where she
left me with a glass of cider. The scarcity of furniture and the bareness of the walls made me
particularly aware of a rather large number of canvases piled up on the floor, their faces
against the wall. No sooner was I alone than I ran towards these canvases; one by one
I turned them round and contemplated them with increasing astonishment; I had the impression that these were only childish daubs, but with such vivid colors, so strange, so gay
that I no longer thought of leaving. I wished to meet the artists capable of such amusing
foolishness; I ... took a room for the night and asked when dinner would be served.

"'Would you like to be served separately or will you eat in the same room with those
gentlemen?' the servant asked. 'Those gentlemen' were the creators of these paintings:
they were three who soon arrived with their paint-boxes and easels. Of course I had asked
to be served with them provided that this would not inconvenience them. But they showed
that I did not embarrass them at all, that is to say, they were completely at ease. All
three of them were barefoot, dressed with superb negligence, and spoke with loud voices.
During the entire meal I remained gasping, gobbling up their words, tortured by the
desire to talk to them, to introduce myself, to learn who they were, and to tell the tall one

268

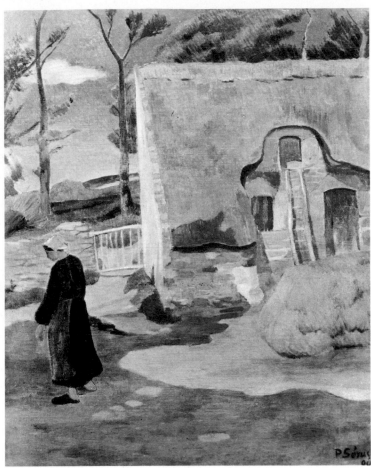

SÉRUSIER: *Farmhouse at Le Pouldu,* d. 1890. 28½ × 23⅝″. Present whereabouts unknown

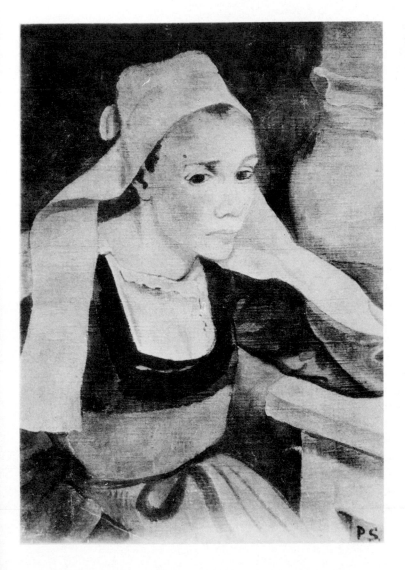

SÉRUSIER: *Portrait of Marie Derrien* (erroneously called "Portrait of Marie Poupée"), d. 1891. 24⅜ × 18½″. Collection Mlle Bernadette Maurice-Denis, Saint-Germain-en-Laye. Compare with Gauguin's portrait, page 287

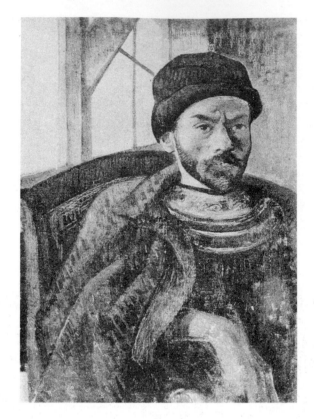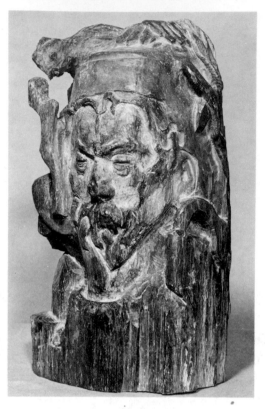

Left: MEYER DE HAAN: *Self-Portrait,* Le Pouldu, 1890. 28⅜ x 21⅝″. Formerly collection Mme Henry Cochennec, Rosporden, France. Right: GAUGUIN: *Bust of Jacob Meyer de Haan,* 1889–90. Polychromed oak, 23 x 11¾″. Formerly collection Marie Henry, Le Pouldu. National Gallery of Canada, Ottawa

with the clear eyes that the aria which he was singing at the top of his voice and which the others repeated in chorus was not by Massenet, as he believed, but by Bizet...."[38] Later Gide was to find out that one of the three was Gauguin, another Sérusier; the third may have been Filiger.

The walls of the dining room at Marie Henry's in Le Pouldu did not remain bare for long. Soon Gauguin and his friends began to decorate them rather lavishly, leaving hardly any space uncovered. They either painted murals directly on the plaster or else hung their pictures, drawings, and lithographs wherever there was room for them. According to Marie Henry's recollections, the center of the wall opposite the entrance was occupied by a large portrait of the innkeeper, painted by Meyer de Haan, for which Gauguin conceived such an admiration that he himself made and painted a frame for it before hanging it in the place of honor. This portrait was flanked by two landscapes from Pont-Aven, a still life, a drawing by Gauguin, etc. The mantelpiece on the wall to the right was dominated by a more than life-size bust of Meyer de Haan which Gauguin had hewn from a massive piece of oak and colored. Above it hung Gauguin's *Breton Girls Dancing* (page 264). On either side of the bust stood earthen pots with humorous decorations; there were also some statuettes. On the upper panel of one door Gauguin painted his own portrait to the right (page 275), while his likeness of de Haan was on the left. On another door was a small version of his *Bonjour Monsieur Gauguin*—inspired by a painting by Courbet which Gauguin had seen with van Gogh in Montpellier—and beneath it *Caribbean Woman with Sunflowers* (page 411), both painted directly on the wood.[39] Over one of the doors Gauguin put a large white goose with the legend: *Maison Marie Henry*. Between the doors was Sérusier's transcription of Wagner's creed. The windows which faced the road leading to the sea were also painted by the friends who covered them simply with oil colors, worrying little about their preservation; they succumbed to the weather after a few years. As to the ceiling, it was richly decorated, the central motive being a travesty of the mythological subject of Leda. It showed a swan which looked more like a goose, its beak caressing the hair of a woman who was none other than Marie Henry. But since Gauguin was then actively and successfully courting the maid of the inn rather than the hostess, he thought it well to adorn this allegory with the inscription: *Homis* [sic] *soit qui mal y pense*. (Actually Marie

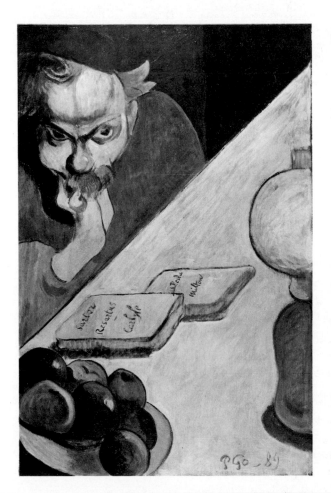 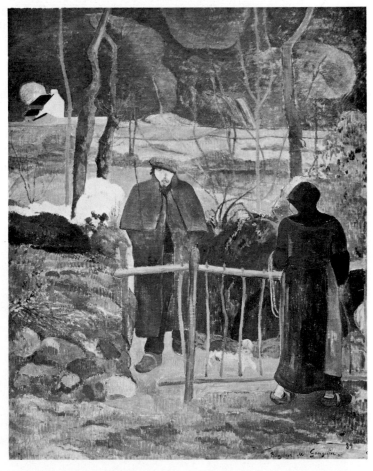

Left: GAUGUIN: *Portrait of Jacob Meyer de Haan,* Le Pouldu, d. 1889. Oil on wood, 31½ x 20½". The Museum of Modern Art, New York (Gift of David Rockefeller, Donor Retaining Life Interest). Right: GAUGUIN: *Bonjour Monsieur Gauguin,* Le Pouldu, d. 1889. 44½ x 36¼". Museum of Modern Art, Prague

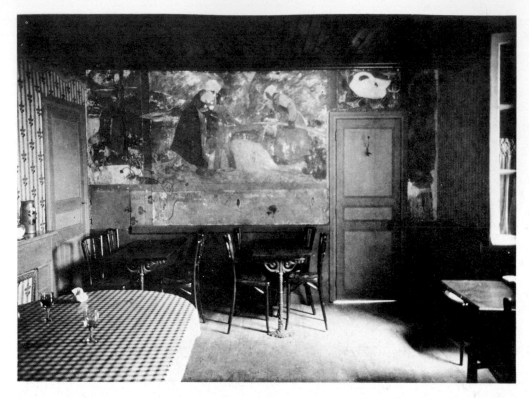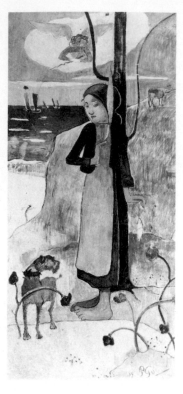

Left: Photograph of the dining room of Marie Henry's Inn at Le Pouldu (courtesy Abraham Rattner, New York). Right: GAUGUIN: *Joan of Arc,* Le Pouldu, d. 1889. Fresco, 52 x 22¾". Collection Mr. and Mrs. Frederick W. Ziv, Cincinnati

Henry was the mistress of Meyer de Haan, to whom she bore a child; Gauguin is said to have been very jealous of his friend.)

Some paintings were also hung in the entrance hall of the inn and behind the bar. Moreover the display in the dining room may have been changed periodically, for there are photographs of it, taken many years later, which show still other paintings, mostly done directly on the wall.[40] Among them is a very stylized decoration, four feet high, of a standing Brittany girl (supposed to be Joan of Arc) by Gauguin, and a mural seven feet wide by Meyer de Haan, showing Breton women stretching hemp. Gauguin liked this mural so much that he sent a sketch and description of it to Vincent van Gogh.

Gauguin and his friends led a strange, quiet, and yet exciting life at Le Pouldu. Besides de Haan and Sérusier there were several painters who at one time or another joined them at Marie Henry's, or who remained at Pont-Aven but with whom Gauguin and his group exchanged periodic visits. Among them were the former lawyer Henri de Chamaillard whose work strongly resembled Gauguin's; the Swiss Filiger, a very retiring man who painted small gouaches with minute care and managed to escape Gauguin's influence, drawing his inspiration from Byzantine sources; Maufra, more truly a follower of Monet; Louis Roy; Moret, a silent soul who liked to listen rather than to talk; somewhat later Laval again, who for six months did not touch his brushes; and several others. There were even a countess and her daughter who both fell under Gauguin's spell, a fact of which he

272

was particularly proud. Those who were unable to join them, such as Schuffenecker and Bernard, maintained a regular correspondence with their friends in Le Pouldu. Occasionally there was also an exchange of letters with Vincent van Gogh.

Among the members of Gauguin's group Sérusier and de Haan seem to have been the most erudite thinkers, the most ardent theorists. Where Bernard had formerly provided Gauguin with the harvest of his diversified reading, Sérusier was now able to supply the others with his extended knowledge of philosophy. As for de Haan, he too was equipped with a mind well trained in religious and metaphysical philosophy. A trace of this can be found in the portrait (page 271) in which Gauguin appears to have overemphasized the weird features of his friend and into which he has introduced two books: Carlyle's *Sartor Resartus* and Milton's *Paradise Lost.*

In long discussions and daily experiments the ideas of these men took shape more and more. "I live between Gauguin and de Haan," Sérusier reported to his friend Maurice Denis, "in a dining room at the inn that we have decorated and embellished. I am working a little and learning a lot; how many things I shall have to tell you when we see each other again. Above all my drawing has changed...."[41]

One of the favorite topics of discussion seems to have been Seurat's pointillism, about which Gauguin was especially sarcastic. The previous year at Pont-Aven he and Bernard

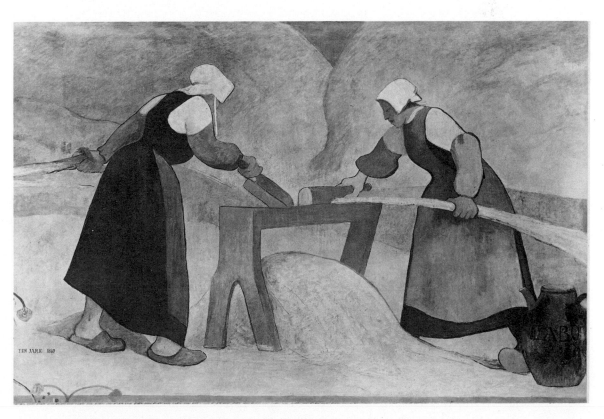

MEYER DE HAAN: *Breton Women Stretching Hemp,* Le Pouldu, d. 1889. Fresco transferred to canvas, 52 x 79″. Present whereabouts unknown

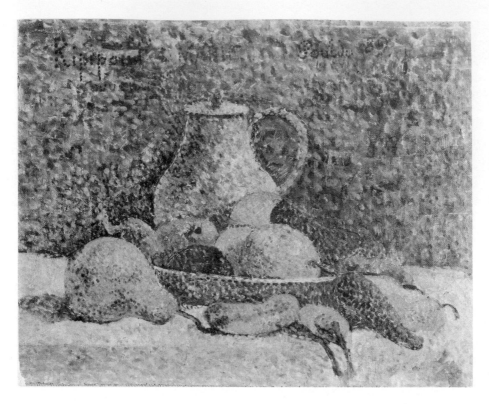

GAUGUIN: *Still Life "Ripipoint à Marie, Souvenir Pouldu 89,"* d. 1889. 12¾ x 15½". Present whereabouts unknown

had amused themselves by inventing a character representing a neo-impressionist, whom they had named *Ripipoint*. Bernard had written a series of ditties which the friends delighted in singing together.[42] Gauguin had brought along and hung in the dining room a pointillist landscape, and now at Le Pouldu he did a small still life, executed in dots, which he actually signed *Ripipoint*. (Laval had listed a Martinique watercolor in the catalogue of the Volpini show as "owned by M. Rippipoint.")

Even the subject of synthesism was by no means always treated in a serious way. On an earthen pot he gave Filiger, Gauguin mockingly wrote: "Vive la sintaize!"[43] and he was often apt to deride all systems in art, including synthesism. Gauguin "always spoke in a jesting manner, which gave rise to many errors and fables about him," a friend later reported.[44] Gauguin also painted an ironical portrait of himself as a synthesist "saint" with a halo, surrounded by ornamental flowers, some apples, and the stylized image of a snake or swan.[45] He even adopted a synthesized signature at that time, signing most of his works merely P. Go.

While they talked incessantly about art and occasionally made music together, the friends—with the possible exception of de Haan and Sérusier—apparently never read anything, neither books nor periodicals nor newspapers; they kept completely aloof from the world outside. Their life was well regulated and exclusively devoted to work. They got up early in the morning and painted out of doors, returning to the inn only for lunch. After the meal they worked again in the open until dusk. They usually went to bed about nine o'clock, having spent the early evening hours debating or making drawings.[46] A

274

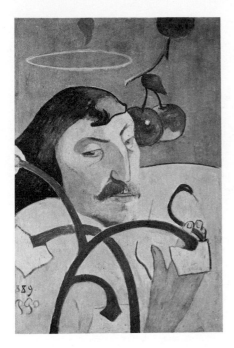 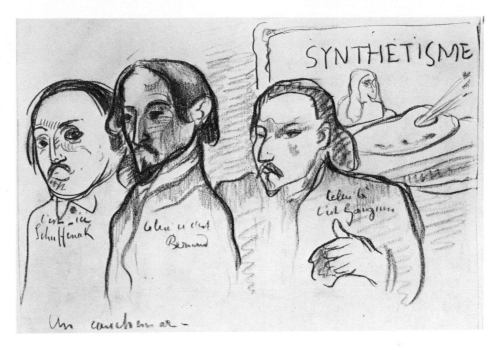

Left: GAUGUIN: *Symbolist Self-Portrait with Halo,* Le Pouldu, d. 1889. Oil on wood, 31¼ x 20¼″. National Gallery of Art, Washington, D.C. (Chester Dale Collection). Right: BERNARD or GAUGUIN: *A Nightmare—Portraits of Schuffenecker, Bernard, and Gauguin,* c. 1888. 7⅛ x 10⅝″. Musée du Louvre, Paris

number of their sketches together with others done in 1888 were later pasted into an album by Schuffenecker. Since many of them are not signed, it is difficult to determine the individual draftsmen. Among these drawings is one, satirically titled *A Nightmare,* which shows Schuffenecker, Bernard, and Gauguin before a composition that bears in large letters the inscription: *Synthétisme.*[47]

For the winter season the friends (or rather de Haan) had rented the attic of a neighboring villa as a studio. This was a tremendous room measuring about 36 by 45 feet, which Gauguin decorated with lithographs by himself and by Bernard, as well as with Japanese prints. But as long as the weather permitted, the painters preferred to work outdoors rather than in this studio, which they used mostly for their sculpture. Indeed, seized by an overpowering urge for creation, Gauguin and his friends were no longer satisfied with painting alone. It may well be that the decoration of the dining room at Marie Henry's had inspired them to branch out into the fields of applied art. Gauguin tried his hand not only at sculpture (which he had already done before) but also at bas-reliefs; he made designs for plates and for fans; he adorned pieces of furniture with carvings and even decorated his wooden shoes. Among his more ambitious efforts was a large polychrome relief with the inspiring advice, addressed to women: *Be in love and you will be happy* (page 410).

Of course Gauguin was the uncontested leader of the little group. In the words of an unidentified admirer: "Gauguin was the chief. He had followers whom he prodded unmercifully, whom he encouraged, and to whom he showed the road to be followed, as a friend. He also demonstrated what work really was and set the example, he who could

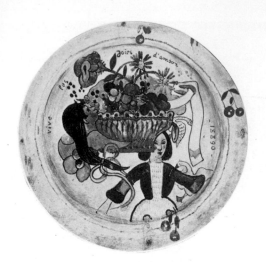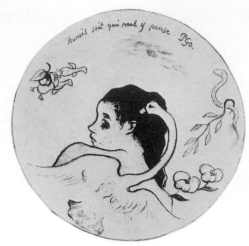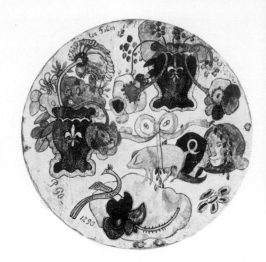

GAUGUIN: Three designs for plates. Left: *"Vive les joies d'amour,"* d. 18890 (sic). Gouache, 10½" in diameter. Formerly collection Justin K. Thannhauser, New York. Center: *"Homis [sic] soit qui mal y pense,"* d. 1889. Lithograph, 8" in diameter. Exhibited at the Volpini show. Right: *"Les folies de l'[amour],"* d. 1290 (sic). Gouache, 10½" in diameter. Present whereabouts unknown

never remain idle for a single moment. . . . He made use of wood, clay, paper, canvas, walls, anything on which to record his ideas and the result of his observations. I still remember a cask on the staves of which he carved a series of fantastic animals that seemed to dance. Some envious people have said that he pontificated, but wouldn't he have had the right to do so, even if this had been the case? Yet he was without pretension when he showed his most recent experiments, though, like every great artist, he was well aware of his own worth. . . . He opened new horizons to those who followed him. Everybody can see the influence he exerted. He brought to light individualities of the most diversified kind; nothing would ever have been produced by those in whom was dormant only a vague spark of art, had it not been for his magic presence. Yet he never had any pupils. . . ."[44]

This testimony notwithstanding, it seems debatable that Gauguin really had no pupils. His was the strongest personality among the painters in Brittany, and even though he owed some of his own ideas to the more pioneering spirit of Bernard, his power was greater, and so were his gifts. The fecundity with which he produced, the ease with which he created, the inventiveness he displayed, the daring with which he explored new avenues placed him head and shoulders above his surroundings. Those who had gathered about him were either too weak to withstand his influence or else had no desire to do so, for they sought his company precisely in order to learn from him. In the continuous give and take that resulted from the close association of a group of men intent upon the same purpose, it may well have been that Gauguin occasionally received some inspiration from his friends or at least that their approval strengthened his own convictions, but on the whole there can be no doubt that it was he who gave rather than received, and even that he gave generously. The fact is that no other important personality was to emerge from the group at Pont-Aven and Le Pouldu and that none of its members has any claim to immortality except as the friends and followers of Gauguin.

It is true however that Gauguin did not *like* to give advice, out of respect for the per-

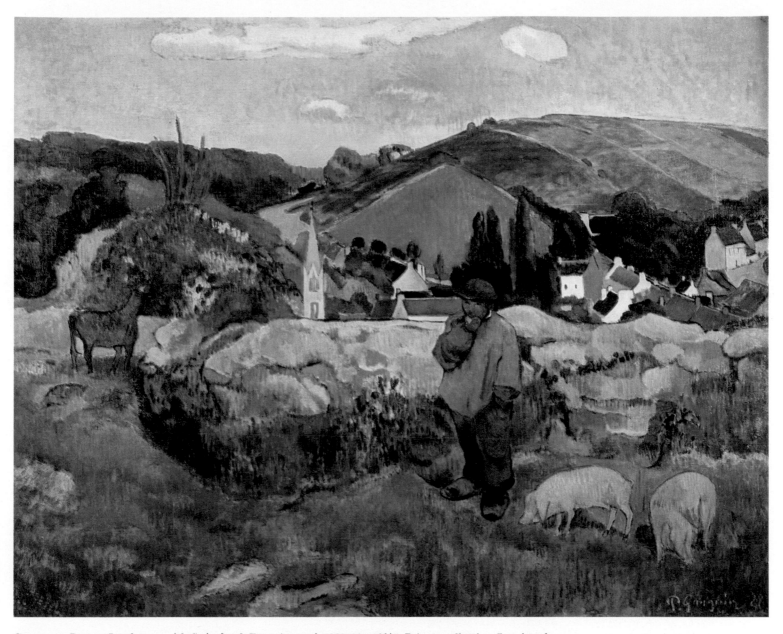

GAUGUIN: *Breton Landscape with Swineherd*, Pont-Aven, d. 1888. 29 x 36½". Private collection, Los Angeles

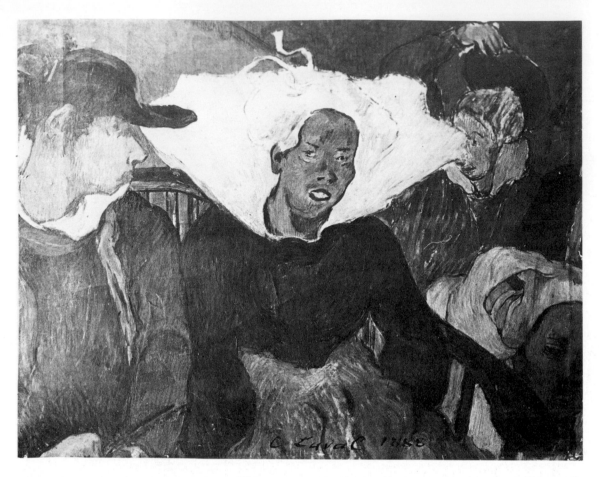

LAVAL: *Breton Peasants*, d. 1888. 14½ x 18¾″. Private collection, Paris

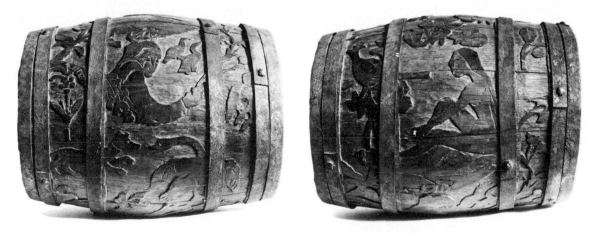

GAUGUIN: Carved cask (two views), c. 1890. Originally polychromed, 14½″ high, 12″ in diameter. Formerly collection Marie Henry, Le Pouldu. Present whereabouts unknown

sonalities of his friends. But while Gauguin himself may not have "pontificated," Sérusier's philosophically inclined intelligence transformed the least of his sayings into scientific doctrines. Sérusier kept regularly in touch with his friends from Julian's in Paris, with Maurice Denis above all, with Bonnard, Vuillard, and the others. To all of them, as Denis later put it, Gauguin was "the undisputed Master, the one whose paradoxical pronouncements were collected and spread, whose talent, eloquence, gestures, physical strength, biting irony, inexhaustible imagination, capacity for alcohol, and romantic bearing were generally admired. The mystery of his ascendance can be explained by the fact that he furnished us with one or two simple and obviously true ideas at a moment when we were completely at a loss for guidance. Thus, without ever having sought for beauty in the classical sense, he almost immediately led us to be preoccupied with it. He wanted above all to catch the character of things, express their 'inner meaning' even in their ugliness.... He was ferociously individualistic, and yet he clung to popular tradition, the most universal and the most anonymous ones. We derived a law, an instruction, a method from these contradictions."[48] During the summer of 1890 Denis formulated in an article the principles of Gauguin's art as they had been transmitted to him by Sérusier.[49]

Gauguin was of course fully aware of his role as leader. "At that time." he later explained to Denis, "I wanted to try everything, to *liberate*, as it were, the younger generation."[50] Gauguin's influence was actually so strong that it made itself felt even in the works of many artists who had never met him or seen his canvases but who lived in Brittany during that period; it seemed almost inescapable. Those who were not directly in touch with him were likely at least to have heard about him through Sérusier or Bernard. Thus "synthesist"

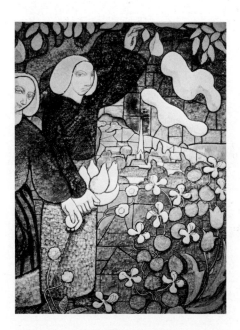

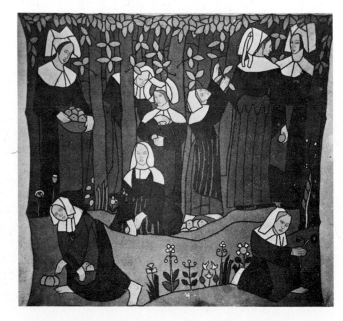

BERNARD: Painted-glass window, Pont-Aven, c. 1890 (?). 42½ x 40⅛″. Musée de Lille, France

BERNARD: *Breton Women Picking Apples,* Pont-Aven, 1892. Wall hanging, 78¾ x 157½″. Made of colored fabrics for Count Antoine de La Rochefoucauld

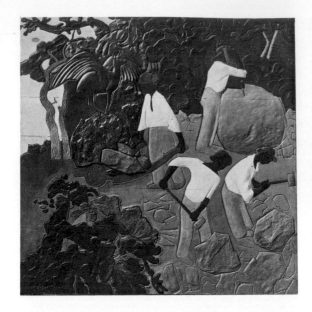

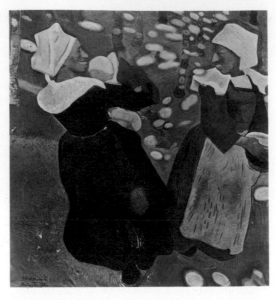

WILLUMSEN: *Men Working in a Quarry,* Paris, 1891. Relief in colored wood and bronze, 39½ x 39½". Statens Museum for Kunst, Copenhagen

WILLUMSEN: *Two Breton Women Parting after a Chat,* d. 1890. 39½ x 37". Collection Generalkonsul H. Duelund, Copenhagen

elements can be detected, for instance, in the paintings of a young Dane, J. F. Willumsen, who came to Pont-Aven during the summer of 1890. It was while Willumsen was working on his canvas of two Breton women that Gauguin, on one of his short visits to Pont-Aven, noticed him and engaged him in conversation. Despite his strong dislike for Danes (his wife being Danish), Gauguin spent two days with Willumsen at Gloanec's and took him to see Maurice Denis, who was then staying in a small house outside the village. Although Denis was not at home, Gauguin was able to show Willumsen some of his works. During the short time they spent together, Gauguin made a great many drawings after dinner on ordinary grocery paper, among them a sketch of Willumsen's painting, as well as a portrait of his young friend. But Willumsen has always claimed that all he owed to Gauguin was some technical information as to how to prepare his canvases, how to mix his colors, etc. Gauguin also taught him how to carve wooden panels and how to decorate them in polychrome.[51]

In spite of the fact that everybody around him listened eagerly to whatever he had to say, Gauguin was profoundly unhappy and bitter. At that time he intensely dreaded isolation and seemed to feel a great need for the company of his young friends, though their admiration for him did not succeed in dispelling his somber moods. All his letters of this period sound downcast and depressed. "As a result of all my efforts this year nothing remains but the howls from Paris which reach me here and discourage me to such an extent that I do not dare to paint any more, and I drag my old body along the shores of Le Pouldu while the north wind blows! Almost mechanically I make some studies (if one can call studies a few brush strokes determined by the eye). But the soul is not there; sadly it observes the gaping hole in front of it."[52]

Gauguin grew suddenly bitter about Degas, who apparently had not found to his liking some of Gauguin's recent works he had seen at Theo van Gogh's. "He doesn't find in my canvases," Gauguin complained, "what he sees himself (the nasty smell of the model). He senses in us a movement that is contrary to his own. Oh! if only I had, like Cézanne, the material means to engage in the struggle, I should certainly do so with pleasure. Degas is growing old and is furious because he hasn't pronounced the last word...."[52]

Those who were with Gauguin at Le Pouldu apparently remained unaware of his depressed moods. What they did notice, however, was the variety of directions which he explored and which reflected his restlessness. "Some thought that he was going to change his style," one of his companions later wrote. "What an error! Yet that was the essence of each day's work, for he was daily... in search of the Unknown, of a new art formula, and this of course without any effort, by merely letting his temperament go where it carried him."[44]

Since he had painted, early in 1889, his boldly conceived portrait of the Schuffenecker family, Gauguin had striven to soften somewhat the definite outlines with which he surrounded all forms, and he had also replaced large flat planes by more subtly modeled areas. But even in canvases where he resorted to an execution of accumulated small brush strokes, densely interwoven, he maintained his favorite device for striking composition, that of placing large and broadly treated figures against a more impressionistically painted background. His colors were bright though he avoided too violent contrasts. Still he continued to show complete freedom from realism and consistently combined simplified forms with exaggerated colorations, so as to sever as far as possible any connection with the "model and that damned nature."[53] But occasionally, as for example in a still life which he presented

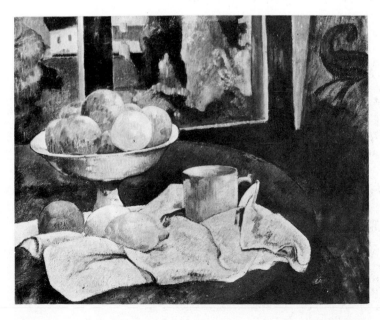

GAUGUIN: *Still Life with Oranges*, Brittany, c. 1890. 19¾ x 23⅝".
Collection Brown-Boveri, Baden, Switzerland

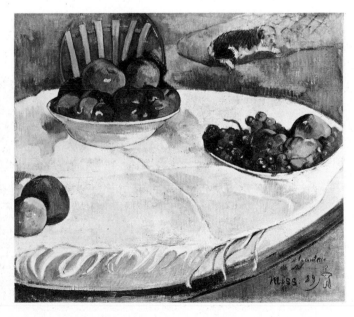

GAUGUIN: *Still Life*, dedicated to the Countess de Nimal, Brittany, d. 1889. Collection Terence Kennedy, London

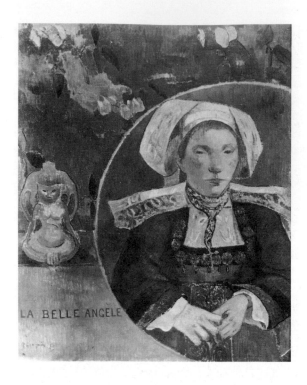

LA BELLE ANGELE

GAUGUIN: *La Belle Angèle* (Mme Angèle Satre), Pont-Aven, d. 1889. 36¼ x 28¾". Purchased by Edgar Degas at Gauguin's auction, 1891. Musée du Louvre, Paris

to his new admirer, Countess de Nimal, he reverted to careful modeling, whereas he adopted the opposite approach, that of a far-reaching abstraction, in such paintings as his portrait of Meyer de Haan (page 271).

"Gauguin has sent me a few new canvases," Theo van Gogh reported to his brother in September 1889. "He wrote that he hesitated to send them, since he had not attained in them what he was searching for. He says that he found it in other canvases which are not yet dry. Be this as it may, his shipment does not seem to me to be as good as the one of last year, but there is *one* painting which is again a really beautiful Gauguin. He calls it *La Belle Angèle* [a likeness of Mme Satre, wife of a builder at Pont-Aven who had refused the painting]. It is a portrait arranged on the canvas like the big heads in Japanese prints; there is the bust-length portrait with its frame, and then the background. It shows a seated Breton woman, her hands joined, black costume, violet apron, and white collar; the frame is gray and the background is of a beautiful lilac-blue with pink and red flowers. The expression of the head and the position [of the model] are very well achieved. The woman somewhat resembles a young cow, but there is something so fresh and also so full of rustic flavor that it is very pleasant to behold."[54] A little later Theo van Gogh again discussed Gauguin's recent work in a letter to his brother, regretting the over-abundance of "reminders of the Japanese, the Egyptians, etc. As far as I am concerned, I prefer to see a Breton woman from Brittany rather than a Breton woman with gestures of a Japanese; but in art there are no limits and one can thus do as one pleases."[55]

Gauguin also relied on local traditions for his work. Inspired by the crude stone crucifixes frequently found by the wayside in Brittany, he produced several compositions in which he endeavored to capture the "great rustic and superstitious simplicity" which so struck

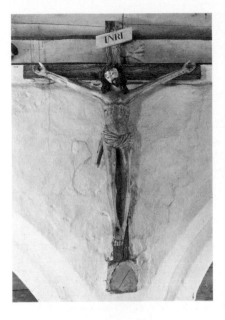

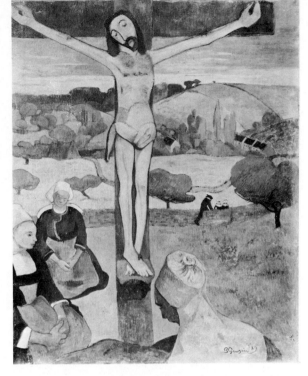

Above: Photograph of yellow Christ, chapel of Trémalo, Pont-Aven

Right: GAUGUIN: *The Yellow Christ,* Pont-Aven–Le Pouldu, d. 1889.
36⅜ x 28¾". Formerly collection Emile Schuffenecker. Albright-Knox
Art Gallery, Buffalo

Right: GAUGUIN: *The Calvary—Green Christ,* Le Pouldu, d. 1889.
36¼ x 29". Musées Royaux des Beaux-Arts, Brussels

Below: Photograph of the moss-covered stone Pietà from the Calvary of Nizon, Brittany

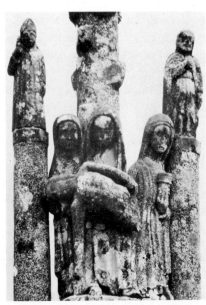

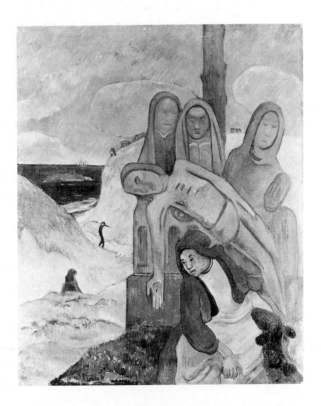

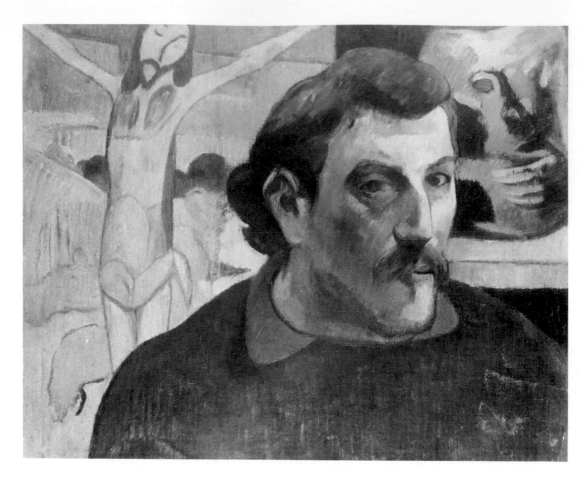

GAUGUIN: *Self-Portrait in Front of the "Yellow Christ,"* c. 1890. 14½ x 17¾". Formerly collection Maurice Denis. Private collection, Paris

him among the peasant folk. One of these paintings, his *Yellow Christ,* is unquestionably based on a wooden, polychromed sculpture of a Christ to be found in the ancient chapel of Trémalo near Pont-Aven, where the primitive, ivory-colored figure detaches itself from a bluish-white wall beneath a blue-painted arch which enhances its own yellow appearance.[56] Gauguin merely accentuated the yellow of the body and used it in an open-air setting. He subsequently painted his own likeness in front of this canvas (which appears in reverse, being seen in a mirror), while to his left he reproduced one of the tobacco pots fashioned by himself. Another painting done in a similar vein shows a Calvary with a green Christ, doubtlessly derived from the moss-covered stone Pietà of Nizon near Pont-Aven.[57] The deep religious feelings released by his surroundings as well as by Bernard's profound belief also expressed themselves in another painting in which Gauguin represented himself in the guise of *Christ in Gethsemane,* a striking symbol of his own loneliness in spite of the "apostles" that had gathered around him; his face betrays the resignation and suffering of which he so often spoke in his letters. Meanwhile Bernard too painted scenes from the life of Christ, and in one of these (reproduced page 337) Gauguin thought he recognized himself in the features of Judas; but he did not object.[53]

Theo van Gogh does not seem to have liked Bernard's recent works any more than those

284

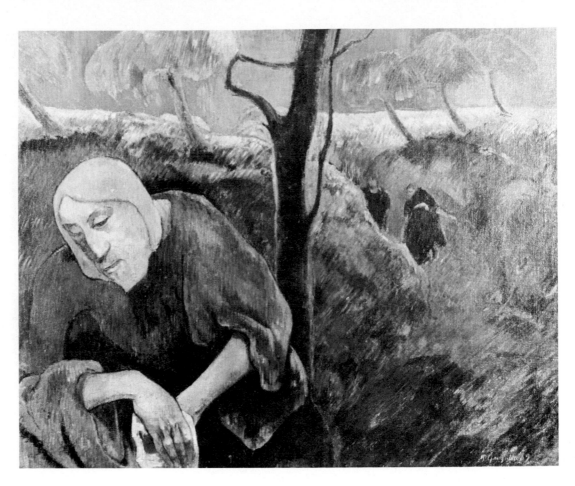

GAUGUIN: *Christ in Gethsemane—Self-Portrait*, d. 1889. 29 x 36". Norton Gallery and School of Art, West Palm Beach, Fla.

of Gauguin. "There is more subtlety in his [Bernard's] brushwork," he wrote to Vincent. "In his paintings there is a more direct influence of the primitives.... He too has painted a *Christ in the Garden of Olives*; a violet Christ with red hair and a yellow angel. It is very difficult to understand; his search for a style often makes his figures appear somewhat ridiculous; but maybe something good will come of this."[58]

When Vincent van Gogh received from Bernard some photographs of the latter's recent canvases he completely agreed with his brother: "They resemble dreams or nightmares," he wrote to Theo. "They are erudite enough—one feels that they are done by somebody who is obsessed by the primitives—but frankly, the English Pre-Raphaelites have done this so much better, and then Puvis de Chavannes and Delacroix, who are much more healthy than the Pre-Raphaelites. It is not that this leaves me cold, but it does give me a painful feeling of degeneration instead of progress."[59]

In a letter he wrote to Bernard himself, Vincent reacted much more violently, almost accusing his friend of attempting a revival of medieval tapestries. "It is undoubtedly wise and just to be moved by the Bible," he wrote, "but the realities of today have so taken hold of us that, even when attempting abstractly to reconstruct ancient times in our thoughts, our meditations are broken into by the minor events of our daily life and we

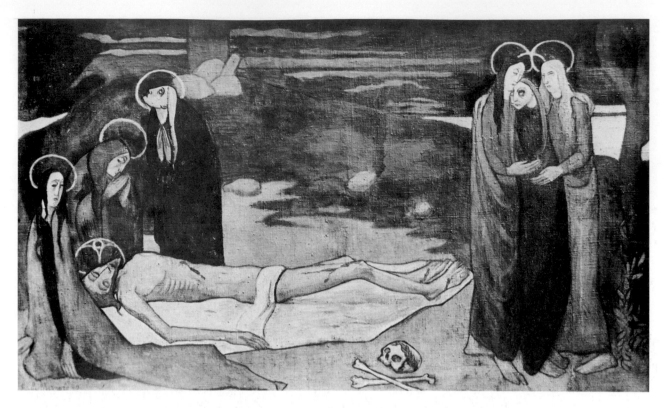

BERNARD: *Christ Taken from the Cross* d. 1890. 59¼ x 35½". Collection Clément Altarriba, Paris

are brought back forcibly by our own experiences into the world of personal sensations —joy, boredom, suffering, anger, and laughter."[60] Unlike Bernard, Gauguin had indeed tried to infuse into his religious paintings the reflections of his own experiences.

This mystical inspiration is only one aspect of Gauguin's work during the years 1889–90. On the whole he seems to have been intent on renouncing the more spectacular devices of synthesism in favor of the "solid" qualities of "pure" painting. If he submitted to the influence of any painter during this crucial period, it was that of Cézanne. He apparently even kept with him at Le Pouldu a still life of Cézanne's, a remnant of his collection with which he refused to part and which he represented in the background of a portrait of a young Breton woman, Marie Lagadu, who used to model for Gauguin and Sérusier.[61] Gauguin always spoke of Cézanne with great reverence. It is even reported that when he started work on a new canvas in Le Pouldu, Gauguin used to say: "Let's make a Cézanne."[62] In various still lifes his indebtedness to the master is quite evident, and the way in which he handled his pigments very often came close to Cézanne's method (the same applies to some of Bernard's works). But whereas Cézanne remained scrupulously faithful to his "motif," never detaching his eyes from it while he worked, Gauguin adopted Cézanne's plastic language, his brush strokes and shifting planes rather than his approach to nature. For Gauguin studied nature around him for elements of form and color which he reconstructed in his paintings not so much in an attempt to reproduce what he had observed,

286

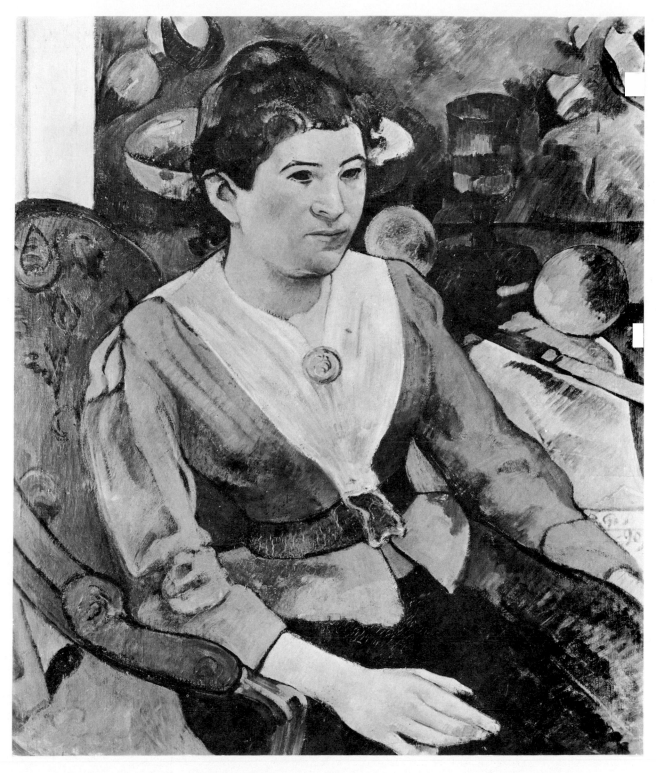

GAUGUIN: *Portrait of Marie Derrien,* nicknamed Marie "Lagadu" (black eyes) (erroneously called "Portrait of Marie Henry"), Le Pouldu, d. 1890. 24¼ x 20¼". The Art Institute of Chicago (Joseph Winterbotham Collection)

but as if preoccupied with capturing the sensations which the sight of his subject had released in him.

In his words as well as in his own canvases Gauguin brought Cézanne's art near to those round him; not, as Denis later stated, "as the work of an independent genius, of an 'irregular' of Manet's school, but as what it really is, the result of a long effort, the necessary outcome of a great crisis."[48]

Whereas the exhibition at Volpini's had promoted the rising reaction against impressionism (even though it had used its name)—a reaction which elsewhere manifested itself less brutally in the work of Seurat and his followers—Gauguin now turned towards Cézanne, the only member of the impressionist group who had set out to bring painting back to a firmer basis. But Cézanne was isolating himself in the south of France, working in silence, out of touch even with his very few friends, while Gauguin, partly through the force of circumstances, partly because of his need for communication and his desire to influence others, drew more and more remote groups into his orbit. Yet at the same time his friend van Gogh was striving towards a similar goal. Gauguin however had no intention of joining forces with him again, though at the exhibition of the Independents in the spring of 1890 he considered van Gogh's works the most noteworthy.

Only very seldom does Gauguin seem to have mentioned Vincent van Gogh to his entourage in Brittany, and then he usually spoke of him as his would-be assassin at Arles. It is true that van Gogh now wrote very infrequently and complained in a letter to Bernard that he felt out of touch with what Gauguin and his friends did in Brittany. But when van Gogh once inquired about the possibility of joining Gauguin and his companions at Le Pouldu, Gauguin burst out: "Never in my life! He is mad! He tried to kill me!"[63]

NOTES

1 O. Maus: Le Salon des XX à Bruxelles, *La Cravache*, March 2, 1889. The catalogue lists Gauguin's entries as follows: Paul Gauguin, 2 place Lamartine, Arles [the painter having accepted the invitation while staying with van Gogh]. 1. *Aux Mangos* (Tropiques) [probably the painting owned by Theo van Gogh, reproduced p. 69]; 2. *Conversation* (Tropiques); 3. *Paysage breton*; 4. *Breton et veau*; 5. *Berger et Bergère*; 6. *Lutteurs en herbe* [probably the painting reproduced p. 173]; 7. *Vision du sermon* [reproduced p. 189]; 8. *En pleine chaleur*; 9. *Misères humaines* [reproduced p. 229]; 10. *Au presbytère*; 11. *Les mas* [painted in Arles]; 12. *"Vous y passerez, la belle!"*

2 Translation: "To paint in oils is very difficult, but it's much more beautiful than to paint with watercolors."

3 On the Académie Julian see W. Rothenstein: Men and Memories, Recollections, 1872–1900, New York, 1931, vol. I, pp. 36–43; H. Schlittgen: Erinnerungen, Munich, 1926, pp. 173–79; L. Hevesi: Altkunst–Neukunst, Wien, 1894–1908, Vienna, 1909, pp. 579–88 (chapter: Beim berühmten Julian); L. Corinth: Legenden aus dem Künstlerleben, Berlin, 1908, pp. 50–68; A. S. Hartrick: A Painter's Pilgrimage through Fifty Years, Cambridge, 1939, pp. 13–27 (chapter: The Atelier Julian).

4 Gauguin to Bernard, [Pont-Aven, March 1889]; see Lettres de Gauguin à sa femme et à ses amis, Paris, 1946, no. CVIII, p. 197.

According to Bernard himself this undated letter—the last part of which is lost—was written in 1890, but since it refers elsewhere to an exhibition which was to open in June 1889 it must date from the spring of that same year.

It is extremely difficult to arrive at an exact chronology of Gauguin's movements throughout 1889, especially concerning his different sojourns in Pont-Aven and Le Pouldu. The various writers on this subject have confused the issue rather than clarified it; none of the documents referring to this period are dated. There is no actual record of Gauguin's stay in Le Pouldu with Sérusier in the spring of 1889 and all the letters relating to their meeting in Le Pouldu are commonly supposed to have been written during the summer of that same year when they did spend some time there together. Yet in this author's mind there is little doubt that the sequence of events as narrated here is more correct, or at least more plausible.

5 Sérusier to Denis, Pont-Aven, [March] 1889; see P. Sérusier: ABC de la peinture, Correspondance, Paris, 1950, pp. 39–40. (This letter is generally supposed to have been written during the summer of 1889. It should be remembered that Sérusier, well read and trained in philosophy, must have

found Gauguin's reasoning frequently rather primitive and uninformed.

6 *Ibid.*, p. 41.

7 *Ibid.*, p. 42.

8 Renoir to Roger Marx, July 10, 1889; see C. Roger-Marx: Renoir, Paris, 1937, p. 68.

9 See E. Bernard: Souvenirs inédits sur l'artiste peintre Paul Gauguin et ses compagnons lors de leur séjour à Pont-Aven et au Pouldu, Lorient, n.d. [1939], pp. 14–15.

10 Gauguin to Schuffenecker, [Pont-Aven, March 1889]; *op. cit.*, no. LXXVII, pp. 152–53 (described erroneously as written in Arles, Dec. 1888).

11 Theo to V. van Gogh, [Paris], June 16, 1889; see Verzamelde Brieven van Vincent van Gogh, vol. IV, no. T 10, p. 268.

12 V. van Gogh to his brother, [Saint-Rémy, June 19, 1889]; Verzamelde Brieven, vol. III, no. 595, pp. 431–32.

13 Emile Bernard, sometimes very unreliable in his recollections, later wrote that Lautrec *had* participated in the show, introduced by himself; see Bernard: L'Aventure de ma vie, in Lettres de Paul Gauguin à Emile Bernard, Geneva, 1954, p. 33. However, neither the poster nor the catalogue of the Volpini exhibition lists Lautrec's name and no reviewer of the show mentioned his works.

14 The catalogue reads as follows: PAUL GAUGUIN, chez M. Schuffenecker, 29, Rue Boulard [Paris]. 31. *Premières fleurs*, Bretagne; 32. *Les Mangos*, Martinique (owned by M. van Gogh) [reproduced p. 69]; 33. *Conversation*, Bretagne; 34. *Hiver*, Bretagne; 35. *Presbytère de Pont-Aven*; 36. *Ronde dans les foins* [reproduced p. 264]; 37. *Paysage d'Arles*; 38. *Les Mas*, Arles; 39. *Pastel décoratif*; 40. *Jeunes Lutteurs*, Bretagne [probably the painting reproduced p. 173]; 41. *Fantaisie décorative*, pastel; 42. *Eve*, aquarelle; 43. *Misères humaines* (owned by M. Paul Schuffenecker) [reproduced p. 229]; 44. *Dans les vagues*; 45. *Le modèle*, Bretagne; 46. *Portrait*, Arles [possibly the painting reproduced p. 236]; 47. *Paysage*, Pont-Aven.

EMILE SCHUFFENECKER, 29, Rue Boulard [Paris]. 55. *Danseuse*, pastel; 56. *Nature Morte*; 57. *Notre-Dame par la neige*; 50. *Paysage de neige*; 59. *Coin de plage à Concarneau* (owned by M. Gautereau); 60. *Coucher de soleil à Concarneau*; 61. *Ramasseuses de varech*, Yport [see the drawing p. 260]; 62. *Pivoines* (owned by M. Choquart); 63. *Falaises*, Yport; 64. *Cirque de Fécamp*; 65. *Rochers*, Yport; 66. *Au parc de Montsouris*; 67. *Paysage parisien*; 68. *Nature morte*, *Oranges*; 69. *Square*; 70. *A Vanves*; 71. *Matinée à Yport*; 72. *Dans la neige*; 73. *Effet de neige*; 83. *Portrait de Monsieur B**** (peinture pétrole).

EMILE BERNARD, 5, Avenue Beaulieu, Asnières. 7. *Chiffonnières*, Clichy; 8. *Fleurs en pots*; 9. *Paysage à Asnières*; 10. *Paysage Pont-Aveniste*; 11. *Paysage Saint-Briacois*; 12. *Portrait de Monsieur Q****; 13. *L'ami Marcel* (owned by M. Hérissé); 14. *Les Bretonnes* (owned by Mme Berthe); 15. *Château de Kerlaouen*; 16. *Floréal*; 17. *Paysage Asniérois*; 18. *Marche au Calvaire*; 19. *Moisson*, Bretagne [probably the painting reproduced p. 263]; 19 bis. *Paysage à Saint-Briac*; 75. *Baigneuses* (owned by M. Albert Aurier) [probably the painting reproduced p. 262]; 76. *Château de Kerlaouen* (owned by Mme La Valle); 77. *Nues* (owned by M. de Laval); 79. *Peupliers*; 80. *Croquis à Pont-Aven*, aquarelle; 81. *idem.*; 82. *idem.*; 86. *Femme et oies* (owned by M. Régis Delbœuf)

[see the drawing reproduced p. 267]; 88. *Caricatures bretonnes* (owned by Mlle Jeanne Simons).

LOUIS ANQUETIN, 86, Avenue de Clichy [Paris], 1. *Bateau*, *Soleil déclinant*; 2. *Effet du soir*; 3. *Eté*; 4. *Etude de cheval*; 5. *Etude de cheval*; 6. *Rosée*; 6 bis. *Eventail*.

LOUIS ROY, Lycée Michelet, Vanves, 49. *Poires*; 50. *A Gif* (owned by M. Filliger); 51. *Paysage à Gif*; 52. *Primevères*; 53. *A Gif*; 54. *Chemin des Glaises*, Vanves; 54 bis. *Crépuscule*.

LÉON FAUCHÉ, 5, Rue Boissonnade [Paris]. 22. *Le Soir*, pastel; 23. *Femme et enfant*; 25. *Paysanne cousant*; 26. *La carriole*; 28. *Cantonnier*.

CHARLES LAVAL, à Pont-Aven (Finistère). 84. *Entrée de bois*, Martinique; 85. *Allant au marché*, Bretagne; 89. *Les Palmes*; 90. *Sous les bananiers*; 91. *Femmes au bord de la mer*, esquisse; 92. *Rêve Martiniquais*; 93. *Le Saule*, Pont-Aven; 94. *Dans la mer* (owned by M. Bernard); 95. *L'Aven*, *Ruisseau* (owned by Mme la Comtesse de Z***); 96. *Course au bord de la mer*, aquarelle Martinique (owned by M. Rippipoint).

GEORGE DANIEL [DE MONFREID], 55, Rue de Château [Paris]. 20. *Fleurs*; 21. *Paysage*; 21 bis. *Portrait du peintre*.

LUDOVIC NÉMO [EMILE BERNARD]. 74. *Portrait d'un jeune ouvrier*, peinture pétrole (1887), (owned by M. Jacques Tasset); 87. *Après-midi à Saint-Briac*, peinture pétrole (1887), (owned by M. Emile Schuffenecker).

Visible sur demande: ALBUM DE LITHOGRAPHIES par Paul Gauguin et Emile Bernard.

15 Bernard to Aurier, [Paris], Monday morning, [May 1889]; unpublished document, courtesy M. Jacques Williame, Châteauroux.

16 Aurier: A propos de l'Exposition Universelle de 1889, May 26, 1889; see Aurier: Oeuvres posthumes, Paris, 1893, pp. 334–35.

17 See A. Retté: Bars et brasseries à l'Exposition, *La Vogue*, no. 2, Aug. 1889.

18 See G. Kahn: L'Art français à l'Exposition, *ibid.* Kahn stated: "M. Gauguin shows in a café, in the worst conditions, his paintings which are interesting although they appear harsh and hammered; around him are hung canvases of no particular interest, with excessive colorations applied in flat surfaces, with modeling that is unnecessary and in no way attractive."

19 F. Fénéon: Autre groupe impressionniste, *La Cravache*, July 6, 1889; reprinted in Fénéon: Oeuvres, Paris, 1948, p. 180.

20 Although he practically never agreed with Fénéon on artistic matters, Teodor de Wyzewa, exactly two years later, expressed the same thought even more bluntly when he wrote: "The style of M. Gauguin derives ... simply from M. Anquetin who practiced it some four or five years ago with a much more original feeling for its strange possibilities." But it is likely that Gauguin never read this statement for it appeared shortly after his departure for Tahiti. See T. de Wyzewa: Le Nouveau Salon du Champ-de-Mars, *L'Art dans les Deux Mondes*, June 13, 1891.

21 See J. Antoine: Impressionnistes et Synthétistes, *Art et Critique*, Nov. 9, 1889.

22 Gauguin to Theo van Gogh, [Le Pouldu, Nov. 1889]: unpublished document, courtesy Ir. V. W. van Gogh, Laren.

23 F. Fénéon: Paul Gauguin, *Le Chat Noir*, May 23, 1891; reprinted in F. Cachin: Fénéon, Paris, 1966, pp. 112–13.

24 See A. Aurier: Le Symbolisme en peinture, Paul Gauguin, *Mercure de France*, March 1891.

25 A. Aurier: Concurrence, *Le Moderniste*, no. 10, June 27, 1889.

26 W. Verkade: Le Tourment de Dieu, Paris, 1926, p. 70.

27 M. Denis: Paul Sérusier, sa vie, son œuvre, in: P. Sérusier: ABC de la peinture, Paris, 1942, p. 46.

28 See J. Rewald: Maillol, New York, 1939, pp. 9–10.

29 See Suzanne Valadon par elle-même, *Prométhée*, March 1939.

30 These articles, all published in *Le Moderniste*, were: Gauguin: Notes sur l'art à l'Exposition Universelle, June 4 and 13, 1889; Bernard: Au Palais des Beaux-Arts, Notes sur la peinture, July 27, 1889; Gauguin: Qui trompe-t-on ici?, Sept. 21, 1889.

31 Gauguin to Schuffenecker, [Le Pouldu], Sept. 1, 1889; *op. cit.*, no. LXXXVI, p. 165.

32 Bernard to Schuffenecker, [Saint-Briac], Aug. 26, 1889; unpublished document, courtesy Mme Jeanne Schuffenecker, Paris.

33 Gauguin to Bernard, [Le Pouldu, Aug. 1889]; *op. cit.*, no. LXXXIV, pp. 162–63.

34 Signac to Luce, [summer 1891]; unpublished document, courtesy Mme Ginette Signac, Paris.

35 Bernard to Schuffenecker, Pont-Aven, [1892]; unpublished document, courtesy Mme Jeanne Schuffenecker, Paris.

36 Sérusier to Denis, Paris, 1889; see ABC de la peinture, Paris, 1950, p. 38.

37 See Hartrick: A Painter's Pilgrimage through Fifty Years, *op. cit.*, p. 30.

38 A. Gide: Si le grain ne meurt, Paris, 1924, vol. II, pp. 195–96. According to Gide this occurrence took place in 1888, but there can be no doubt that the correct date is 1889.

39 See Mothéré (husband of Marie Henry) quoted by C. Chassé: Gauguin et le groupe de Pont-Aven, Paris, 1921, pp. 46–50.

40 These murals were discovered in 1924 by the American painters Abraham Rattner and Isadore Levy (see *Life*, May 1, 1950), who kindly supplied the photograph of the dining room before removal of the paintings.

41 Sérusier to Denis, [Le Pouldu, fall 1889]; see ABC de la peinture, 1942, p. 54.

42 See Bernard: Souvenirs, *La Rénovation Esthétique*, Nov. 1907 and April 1909, the latter reprinted in Rewald: Seurat, Paris, 1948, p. 152 (note 81). In his Souvenirs, *op. cit.*, Bernard later wrote that in those days "we derided everything, and particularly the ridiculous, from the members of the Institut de France to the divisionists and pointillists who were then represented mainly by Messrs. Signac, Seurat, and Pissarro. The last, like every convert, had become the militant and dangerous apostle of that movement. How many painters has not the dignity of his long beard and of his old talent committed to that theory?"

43 See Mothéré, *op. cit.*, p. 38. Spelled this way the word *synthèse* takes on an almost vulgar connotation. There are a number of more or less obvious puns in the titles or dates on Gauguin's works of this period; he also dated designs for plates (ill. p. 276) 18890 and 1290.

44 Anonymous: Gauguin et l'Ecole de Pont-Aven, by "un de ses admirateurs de l'Ecole de Pont-Aven," *Essais d'Art Libre*, Nov. 1893.

45 See K. van Hook: A Self-Portrait by Paul Gauguin, *Gazette des Beaux-Arts*, Dec. 1942.

46 See Mothéré, *op. cit.*, pp. 33–34.

47 See C. Chassé: De quand date le Synthétisme de Gauguin? *L'Amour de l'Art*, April 1938.

48 M. Denis: L'Influence de Paul Gauguin, *L'Occident*, Oct. 1903; reprinted in Denis: Théories, 1890–1910, Paris, 1912, p. 163.

49 See M. Denis: Définition du Néo-Traditionnisme, *Art et Critique*, Aug. 23 and 30, 1890; reprinted *ibid.*, pp. 1–13.

50 Gauguin to Denis, [Tahiti, June 1899]; *op. cit.*, no. CLXXI, pp. 290–91.

51 Information courtesy the late J. F. Willumsen, Cannes, and Sigurd Schultz, Copenhagen. Willumsen had a tendency to belittle his indebtedness to Gauguin. His relationship to the latter has been studied by M. Bodelsen: Willumsen i 90'ernes Paris *in* Festskrift for Professor Ragnar Josephson, Stockholm, 1957.

52 Gauguin to Bernard, [Le Pouldu, Nov. 1889]; *op. cit.*, no. XCII, pp. 173–74.

53 Gauguin to Bernard, [Le Pouldu, end of Nov. 1889]; *ibid.*, no. XCV, p. 178.

54 Theo to V. van Gogh, Paris, Sept. 5, 1889; see Verzamelde Brieven van Vincent van Gogh, vol. IV, no. T 16, p. 274.

55 Theo to V. van Gogh, [Paris], Oct. 22, 1889; *ibid.*, no. T 19, p. 277.

56 See F. Dauchot: Le *Christ Jaune* de Gauguin, *Gazette des Beaux-Arts*, July–Aug. 1954.

57 This connection was discovered by C. Chassé: Gauguin et son temps, Paris, 1955 (plate LX). (It was the *curé* of the Church of Nizon who had refused the gift of Gauguin's *Jacob Wrestling with the Angel*, p. 189).

58 Theo to V. van Gogh, Paris, Nov. 16, 1889; *op. cit.*, no. T 20, p. 278.

59 V. van Gogh to his brother, [Saint-Rémy, Nov. 1889]; Verzamelde Brieven, vol. III, no. 615, p. 478.

60 V. van Gogh to Bernard, [Saint-Rémy, beginning of Dec. 1889]; Verzamelde Brieven, vol. IV, no. B 21, p. 236.

61 Information courtesy Mlle H. Boutaric, Paris, according to whom the late Mme Cochennec of Rosporden (Brittany), supposed to have been the daughter of Marie Henry and Meyer de Haan, always maintained that this portrait does *not* represent her mother although it is generally accepted as being a likeness of Marie Henry. On Gauguin and Cézanne see M. Bodelsen: Gauguin's Cézannes, *Burlington Magazine*, May 1962.

62 See R. Rey: Gauguin, Paris, 1928, p. 25.

63 See Mothéré, *op. cit.*, p. 36.

VII   1889-1890   VAN GOGH IN SAINT-REMY
AURIER'S ARTICLE ON VAN GOGH

Vincent van Gogh had been able to leave the hospital after only two weeks, on January 7, 1889. He was taken to his home by the devoted postman Roulin, who faithfully kept Theo informed about Vincent's progress. At the hospital van Gogh had made friends with the Pastor Salles and the intern Dr. Rey (whose portrait he was to paint), both of whom his brother had met on his hurried visit to Arles; they, too, remained in touch with Theo.

Now that he was back in his yellow house—though he went daily to the hospital to have his wound dressed—Vincent received a letter from Gauguin who explained that he had returned to Paris for fear of disturbing him during his illness. Van Gogh was not quite satisfied with this explanation and wrote to Theo: "How can Gauguin pretend that he feared his presence might have upset me, since he can hardly deny knowing that I continually asked for him; he was told and retold that I insisted on seeing him immediately. It was precisely because I meant to ask him to keep all this to himself and not to disturb you. He didn't want to listen."[1]

Van Gogh grew bitter when he turned over and over again in his mind what had happened, but made an effort not to reveal his feelings. Yet in one of his letters to Theo he said frankly: "In making a bold analysis, nothing prevents us from seeing in him [Gauguin] the little Bonaparte tiger of impressionism, in so far as... I do not quite know how to put it, his eclipse—let's call it that—from Arles may be compared or considered parallel to the return from Egypt of the above-mentioned little corporal who also went to Paris afterwards and who always abandoned his armies in adversity."[1]

Of his own condition van Gogh spoke very calmly. "Although today everybody will be afraid of me," he wrote to Theo, "as time passes this may disappear. We are all mortal and may be afflicted by all possible kinds of illnesses. Is it our fault when these are not precisely of a pleasant kind? The best thing is to try to get well again." And he added: "I feel some remorse when I think of the trouble which, though involuntarily, I have caused Gauguin. But before that, during those last days, I saw only one thing: that he was working with his heart torn between life in Arles and the desire to go to Paris in order to devote himself to his projects."[2]

Vincent even summoned up enough courage to poke fun at himself. Discussing Gauguin's renewed plan to go to the tropics, he told his brother: "With this little country here I don't have to go to the tropics at all. I believe and always shall believe in an art to be created in the tropics, and I think that it will be wonderful, yet personally I am too old and (particularly if I have myself fitted with a papier-mâché ear) made too much of cardboard to go there."[3]

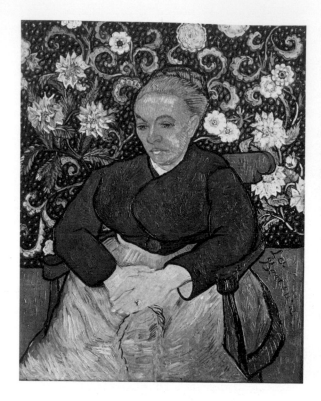

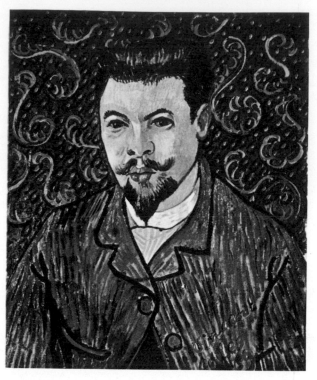

VAN GOGH: *La Berceuse—Mme Roulin,* Arles, Jan. 1889.
35½ x 28". Rijksmuseum Kröller-Müller, Otterlo

VAN GOGH: *Portrait of Dr. Rey,* Arles, Jan. 1889.
25⅛ x 20⅞". Pushkin State Museum of Fine Arts, Moscow

In spite of his unhappy experience van Gogh was perfectly ready to share his house once more with Gauguin, writing to Theo: "The best thing that he [Gauguin] could do, and the one thing he certainly will not do, would be simply to come back here.... I venture to think that after all, as far as our natures are concerned, Gauguin and I like each other sufficiently to be able, if need be, to start again together."[4]

But van Gogh's hope received a cruel blow when, exactly one month after his release and just after he had started painting again, he had to be taken to the hospital. This time his internment came about because he suddenly imagined that somebody tried to poison him. Once admitted to the hospital he refused to utter a single word. After about one week, however, Dr. Rey was able to report to Theo that Vincent was much better and that there was great hope for his recovery. A few days later the painter himself wrote to his brother: "There are so many moments when I feel myself completely normal. It seems to me indeed that if what I have is only an illness indigenous to this region, I must quietly wait here until it is over, even if it should repeat itself (which presumably will not be the case)." Vincent now even resigned himself to giving up his fondest dream when he added: "I no longer dare to urge [other] painters to come here after what has happened to me; they risk losing their minds as I did...."[5]

After he had left the hospital once more, van Gogh was eager to go back to work and painted several canvases which he himself considered perfectly "calm." One of the first

292

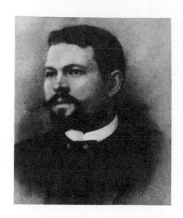

things he did was to continue a likeness of Mme Roulin on which he had worked before his illness. He was particularly anxious to finish this canvas because Roulin was being assigned to a new postal job at Marseilles, whither his family was to follow him, and van Gogh feared that the postman's wife would not care to pose for him any more after her husband had left. (Many years later Mme Roulin confided to her daughter that she had always been somewhat frightened by the artist.) In his new painting, *La Berceuse*, van Gogh represented Mme Roulin rocking an invisible cradle against a background enlivened by imaginary flowers. The canvas had been inspired by Pierre Loti's novel about Icelandic fishermen which he had discussed with Gauguin. Thinking of their monotonous and dangerous life, Vincent wished to paint a picture which, hung in the cabin of their boat, would make the sailors feel the old sense of cradling come over them and remind them of lullabies. His canvas thus became an expression of his preoccupation with "abstractions" and "consoling" art, but it was also, as he explained, "an attempt to get all the *music* of the color." Van Gogh was so fascinated with this theme that he painted altogether five versions of it. One of these—the best according to Vincent—was selected by Mme Roulin; another he later presented to Gauguin, who also expressed the desire to own one of his *Sunflowers*. But van Gogh agreed to this only on condition that Gauguin should give him an equally important work in exchange, remembering that "Gauguin liked the *Sunflowers* only after he had seen them for a long time."[6]

Vincent van Gogh was so composed that he was actually able to paint his own likeness with his still bandaged ear and, a little earlier, had even returned to the brothel where he was told that incidents such as the one he had caused were not considered unusual.[7] (Van Gogh eagerly recorded any information tending to show that what had happened to him was not "unusual," was caused by the climate, etc., in other words could have happened to anybody.) But no sooner had he taken up his work again than he ran into new trouble. What he himself had feared, namely, that as a result of his first attack people might become afraid of him, now found its expression in a petition that some thirty neighbors (not eighty, as Vincent and Pastor Salles later said) addressed to the mayor.

"The undersigned citizens of Arles," they wrote, "residing on place Lamartine, have the honor to inform you that the Dutch subject named Vood (Vincent), landscape painter, residing on place Lamartine, has for some time and on various occasions furnished proof of the fact that he does not dispose of his full mental faculties, that he indulges in excessive drinking after which he finds himself in such a state of excitement that he does not know what he says or what he does, and that his instability inspires public fear for the residents of the sector, especially for the women and children.

"For this reason the undersigned have the honor to request, in the name of public safety, that said Vood (Vincent) be as soon as possible returned to his family or that his family take the necessary steps to have him admitted to a mental institution so as to prevent whatever mishap is bound to happen one of these days if energetic measures are not taken."[8]

Vincent later spoke bitterly of the "cannibals" who had ganged up against him; yet the various people who signed this letter showed a certain restraint by asking first of all that he merely be sent home. All they wanted was to get rid of him. Their undated petition brought forth, on February 27, 1889, an investigation by a police commissioner consisting in the interrogation of five neighbors, each of whom signed his or her deposition; but the similarity of their testimony strongly suggests that they had been asked somewhat leading questions, to which they replied in more or less the same fashion.

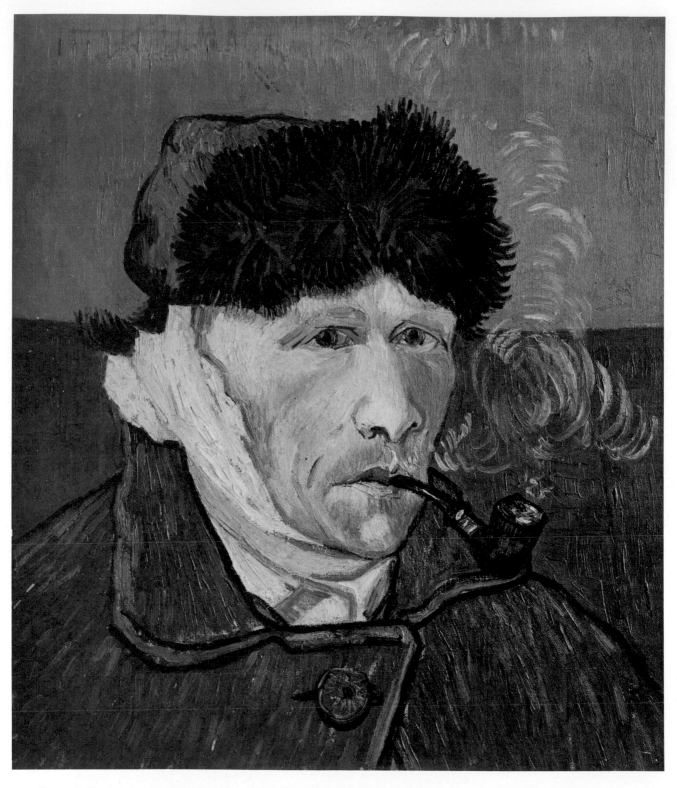

van Gogh: *Self-Portrait with Bandaged Ear*, Arles, Jan. 1889. 20 x 17¾". Collection Stavros S. Niarchos, Athens

A sixty-three-year-old proprietor living on avenue Montmajour declared: "As manager of the building occupied by Vincent van Goghe I have had occasion to talk with him yesterday and to ascertain that he is suffering from mental alienation, for his conversation is incoherent and his reasoning is impaired. On the other hand I have been told that this man indulges in touching women who live in the neighborhood; I have been assured that they are not even safe in their homes, which he enters. Thus it is urgent that this madman be confined in an asylum since the presence of van Goghe in our sector constitutes a public danger."

A thirty-two-year-old woman who had a shop for fruit and produce on place Lamartine told the police commissioner: "I live in the same building as Vincent van Goghe who is truly mad. This individual enters my shop and asserts himself. He insults my clients and indulges in touching women of the neighborhood whom he even pursues into their homes. Everybody in the sector is frightened because of the presence of said van Goghe, who will certainly become a public danger."

A forty-year-old tobacco dealer, residing on place Lamartine, confirmed the declaration of the preceding witness. A forty-two-year-old seamstress, residing at 24, place Lamartine, declared: "The man van Goghe, who lives in the same sector as I do, has, during the last few days, become increasingly mad; consequently everybody in the neighborhood is frightened. The women especially no longer feel secure because he indulges in touching them and also makes obscene remarks in their presence. As a matter of fact, this individual has taken me by the waist in front of the shop of the second witness and has lifted me into the air, on Monday, day before yesterday. This madman is becoming a public danger, and everybody clamors for his internment in a special institution."

Finally, a forty-five-year-old café-keeper, domiciled on place Lamartine, confirmed that the facts related by the preceding witness were true and honest, and declared that he had nothing to add to them.

Having transcribed these statements, the police commissioner summed up his interrogations: "The man Vincent van Goghe is really suffering from mental derangement; however, we were able to observe on various occasions that this madman has moments of lucidity. Van Goghe does not yet constitute a public danger; yet there are fears that he may become one. All his neighbors are alarmed and have good reason to be, since a few weeks ago the madman in question, in a fit of madness, cut one of his ears; such a fit could occur again and be fatal for some person in his vicinity.

"The result of the preceding investigation and of our personal observations is that Vincent van Goghe is mentally deranged and might become a public danger. We feel that this madman should be detained in a special asylum."[8]

It is noteworthy that only the police commissioner alluded to the incident of the ear, although it had been reported in the local press, and that most witnesses as well as he himself insisted that the painter was "not yet" to be considered a public danger though he "might become" one. This could be considered as a further, admittedly indirect, indication that Vincent had *not* attacked Gauguin with an open razor on the place Lamartine, for such an act would certainly have earned him the designation of a "public danger."

As a result of the commissioner's report, a police officer was dispatched on February 28 to close Vincent's house and to take him back to the hospital. Many months later van Gogh regretted having followed the officer obediently and told his brother: "I reproach myself for my cowardice; I should have defended my studio better, even if this had meant an

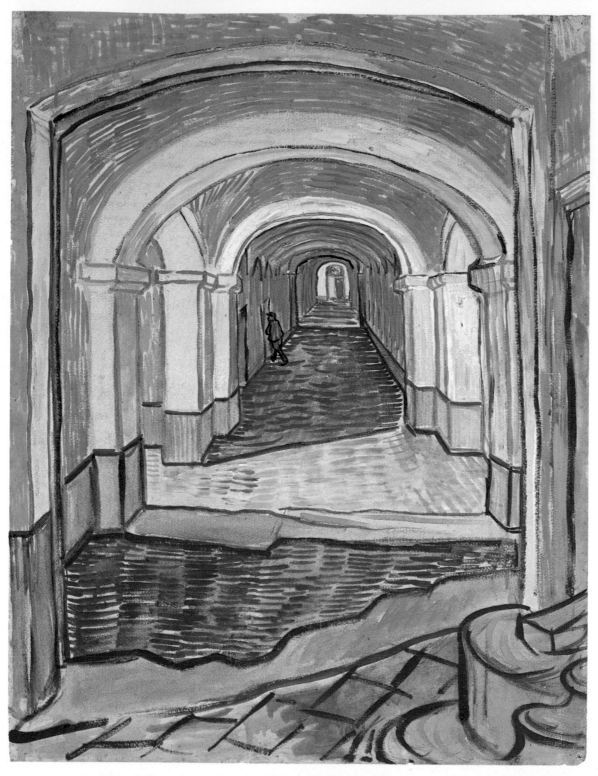

VAN GOGH: *Hospital Corridor at Saint-Rémy* May–June 1889. Gouache and watercolor 24⅛ x 18⅝″. The Museum of Modern Art, New York (Abby Aldrich Rockefeller Bequest)

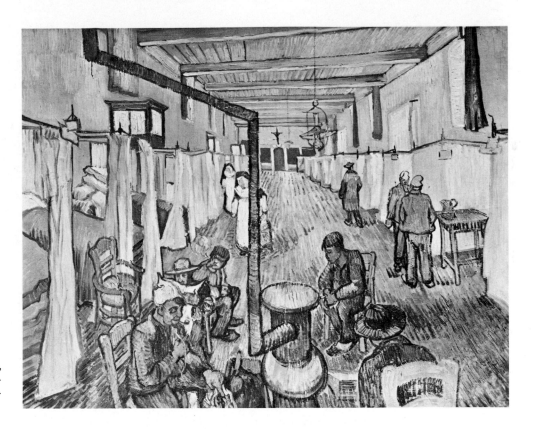

open fight with those gendarmes and neighbors. Others in my place have used a gun, and certainly if—as an artist—I had killed a few blockheads, I would have been acquitted. I would have come off better that way, yet I was a coward and a drunkard."[9]

Fortunately van Gogh did not resort to a gun (no doubt he did not have one) and instead swallowed his pride, making an effort to remain quiet for fear that he might be considered dangerously mad should he emphatically express his indignation. In the agonizing days that followed, and while he was left completely to himself—without books and even his pipe—he had ample time to think about his fate and a future which, indeed, took on ever more gloomy aspects. But the strain was too great and a new attack developed which, however, did not last long. Vincent was so downcast that he did not even care to write to Theo; Pastor Salles took it upon himself to keep the latter informed, reporting after the seizure had passed: "Your brother spoke to me with great calm and perfect lucidity about his situation, and also of the petition signed by his neighbors. This petition distresses him a great deal. 'If the police,' he said to me, 'would protect my liberty by preventing children and even grown-ups from gathering round my home and climbing up the windows, as they have done (as if I were some strange animal), then I would have remained much calmer; in any case I haven't harmed anybody.' In short, I found your brother *transformed* and may God help to maintain this improvement. His condition is somehow indefinable and it is impossible to account for the sudden and complete changes which take place in him."[10]

When Vincent himself wrote again to Theo, after a silence of almost one month, he urged him *not* to interfere with the local authorities as he hoped to regain his freedom by remaining calm and reasonable. He discussed his illness with Dr. Rey, who explained to him that his condition was partly due to the fact that, instead of eating enough and regularly, he had subsisted mostly on coffee and alcohol. His reply was: "I admit all this, but it is none the less true that in order to reach that high note of yellow which I reached last summer, I had to force the pace somewhat. After all, an artist is a man who works, and it isn't right that a few old fools [meaning the signers of the petition] should be allowed to finish him off." And he added sadly: "I am thinking of accepting explicitly my role as a madman, just as Degas has taken on the appearance of a notary. However, I don't think I am quite strong enough to play such a part."[11]

· Theo, on the eve of his marriage, was deeply disturbed by the news. When he heard that Signac was planning to leave for the South, he begged him to pass through Arles. Thus, towards the end of March, Signac called on van Gogh at the hospital. He was permitted to take him for a walk, and they went to Vincent's house, which was still locked by the police. But they got in eventually, and van Gogh was able to show Signac all his paintings accumulated there; he even offered Signac a small still life of two herrings. Signac later said about this visit: "All day long he talked about painting, literature, socialism. In the evening he was a little tired. There was a terrific mistral blowing, which may have unnerved him. He wanted to drink a liter of turpentine directly out of the container, which was on the table in the bedroom. It was time for him to return to the hospital."[12]

Signac came back the next day and then took his leave. Though his visit was a great stimulus to van Gogh, Signac does not seem to have been over-enthusiastic about Vincent's work. At least his report to Theo sounds rather cautious on this subject. "I found your brother in perfect physical and mental condition," Signac wrote. "We went out together yesterday afternoon and again this morning. He took me to see his pictures, several of which are really fine and all of which are very interesting."[13] As to Vincent himself, he delighted in this interruption of his dreary life. "I am writing to you," he informed his brother, "to tell you that I saw Signac whose visit has done me a lot of good. He was very kind and straightforward and simple when the question arose whether or not to force the door locked by the police. . . . I found Signac very calm, though he is said to be so violent; he gave me the impression of somebody who has poise and equilibrium, that's all. Seldom or never have I had with any impressionist a conversation so devoid of disagreements or annoying irritations on either side. . . ."[11]

In the last days of March van Gogh was permitted to take walks by himself again and he was happy to discover that his immediate neighbors had not taken part in the move for his internment. But in agreement with his doctors it was decided that he would still be lodged at the hospital, where he now did a painting of the courtyard and made some drawings.[14] While he was eager to start working again, he had at the same time to give up his yellow house and to store his furniture. Dr. Rey let two small rooms to him; towards the middle of April Vincent was able to inform his brother, still on his honeymoon in Holland, that he was doing six studies simultaneously.

His work helped him to recover although it did not prevent him from meditating about his future. "I read very little so as to be able to think more," he wrote to his sister Wil. "It is most likely that I shall still have to suffer a great deal. To tell you the truth this does not suit me too well, for by no means do I wish for the career of a martyr. I have always been searching for something other than heroism, of which I have none, which I certainly admire

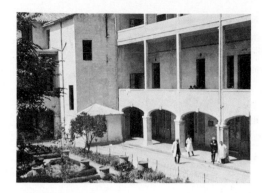

Above: Photograph of the courtyard of the hospital at Arles

Right: VAN GOGH: *The Courtyard of the Hospital at Arles,* April 1889. 28¾ x 36¼″. Oskar Reinhart Foundation, Winterthur, Switzerland

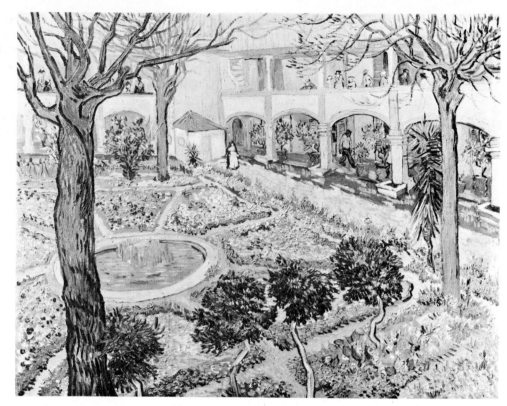

in others but which, I repeat, I *don't* think is my duty or my ideal.... Every day I am taking the remedy that the incomparable Dickens prescribes against suicide. It consists in a glass of wine, a piece of bread, some cheese, and a pipe of tobacco. That does not sound complicated, you may say, and you may not believe that melancholy sometimes drives me near to it; however there are moments, well...."[15]

Van Gogh could not help realizing that he now lacked the courage to live and work altogether by himself. He had a long talk with Pastor Salles who reported to Theo: "Sometimes it would seem that there is no trace left of the illness which affected him so strongly .... He is fully aware of his condition and speaks to me with a touching candor and simplicity about what has happened and what, he fears, may happen again. 'I am unable,' he told me day before yesterday, 'to look after myself and control myself; I feel that I am quite different from what I used to be.'"[16] It was the Pastor who, in agreement with the doctors, suggested that the painter have himself committed to the asylum of nearby Saint-Rémy, and Vincent fully approved. On April 21 he wrote at great length to his brother:

"It will be enough, I hope, if I say that I feel myself definitely incapable of starting once more to take a new studio and to remain there alone, either here in Arles or elsewhere.... I have tried to get accustomed to the idea of beginning all over again, yet for the time being it is not possible. I should fear losing the faculty for work which is coming back now, if I forced myself and if I had besides all the responsibilities of having a studio. And thus I wish to remain interned provisionally for my own tranquillity as well as for that of others.

What consoles me somewhat is that I am beginning to consider madness as an illness like any other, and that I accept it as such, whereas during the seizures it seemed to me that everything that I imagined was real. I really don't want to think or talk about it. Don't press me for explanations, but I ask you, Pastor Salles, and Dr. Rey to arrange things in such a way that by the end of this month or the beginning of May I can go there as an interned boarder. To start the life of a painter again as I led it before, isolated in the studio once more and without any distraction except going to a café or a restaurant under the critical eyes of the neighbors, etc., *that I can't do.* As for living with another person, even another artist, that is difficult, very difficult; one takes too much of a responsibility. I don't even dare to think about it. So let us try for three months, and then we shall see.... I shall do some paintings and drawings, but without all the furor of last year. Don't be too distressed about all this. It was sad these last days, the moving, the transportation of my furniture, the packing of the canvases which I am going to send you; but it seemed sad to me above all because all this had been given to me by you with so much brotherly love, and for so many years it has been you alone who sustained me, and now I have once more to come to you with this sad story; but it is difficult for me to express this the way I feel it. The kindness which you have shown me is not lost since you have had it and it remains yours, even if the actual results are nil....

"You will understand now that if alcohol was certainly one of the main causes of my madness, then it came about very slowly and can only go again slowly, in case it should go at all, of course. Or if it came from smoking, the same thing.... Well, we have to take our share of the illnesses of our time, and it seems after all only right that—having lived for years in relatively good health—we should sooner or later receive our part. As for me, you must know that I shouldn't precisely have chosen madness if there had been any choice, but once such a thing has taken hold of you, you can't very well get out of it. Nevertheless, there may still be the additional consolation that I can continue to do a little painting.... I clasp your hand in my thoughts, but I don't know whether I shall write to you very frequently, since all my days are not sufficiently lucid to permit me to write quite logically."[17]

Theo thought that it might be better if Vincent went to Pont-Aven instead of being committed to Saint-Rémy, but his brother turned this project down. When Theo's young wife suggested that the painter might join them in Paris, her husband tried to explain to her the peculiar character of the brother-in-law she had never met: "One of the greatest difficulties is created by the fact that his life is so ill prepared for any outside influence, regardless of whether he is sick or healthy. If you knew him you would realize more clearly how difficult it is to solve the question of what should be done. As you know, he has long since broken with anything that is called convention. His way of dressing and his manners show immediately that he is a man of a different kind, and for years now those who have seen him have said: 'He is a madman.' I don't mind all that, but at home it wouldn't work. Even in his way of speaking there is something which makes people either think a great deal of him or else unable to bear him. He always finds people who are attracted to him, but he also has very many enemies. It is impossible for him to have indifferent relationships. It is always either one thing or the other. Even for those who are his best friends it is not always easy to get along with him, since he spares nothing and nobody. If I had the time I would go to him and possibly go on an extended excursion with him, as this is now the only thing that I believe might really calm him somewhat. If I could find somebody among the painters who would be willing to undertake such a project with him, then I would send him the fellow. But those with whom he can get along at all are somewhat frightened by him, and Gauguin's sojourn with him has not changed that—quite the contrary. Then there is still something else which explains why I haven't the courage to ask him to come here ...."[18] And Theo went on to say how overexcited Vincent had been in Paris and how unlikely it seemed that another stay in the city would be good for him. Yet he added: "If he himself wants to come here, then I shall not hesitate for a moment.... But I repeat, I believe one cannot do anything more for him than to let him do as he pleases. For him there are no quiet surroundings outside of nature and with such very simple people as the Roulins. Wherever he goes, his presence leaves its mark. It is impossible for him to keep silent when he sees something that is not as it should be, and thus quarrels arise.... It hurts me to be so powerless and not to be able to do something for him, yet with extra-ordinary beings extraordinary measures are necessary and I hope they will be found where ordinary people would not even look for them."[18]

Vincent van Gogh was perfectly willing to resort to an extraordinary measure when he informed his brother that it might be best for him to enlist for five years in the French Foreign Legion, since he felt physically stronger then he had in years, although he admitted being mentally far from stable. Theo of course would not hear of such a solution, suspecting Vincent of wanting to sacrifice himself rather than to create more complications and expenses. Theo could not help thinking that even Vincent's desire to be shut up in an asylum was prompted by his wish to simplify matters; he therefore once more, and against his better judgment, suggested a trip to Brittany or Paris. But the painter declined: "I don't feel able to go to Paris or to Pont-Aven; besides, most of the time I have no strong inclinations, or any strong regrets, for that matter."[19] And to Theo's wife Vincent explained a little later that to himself and to Theo "Paris is certainly already something of a cemetery where quite a number of artists whom we have known directly or indirectly have perished."[20] Theo eventually consented to Vincent's internment, but made it clear: "I do not consider your going to Saint-Rémy as a retreat, as you put it, but merely as a rest for a short time, so that you can come back soon with renewed strength."[21]

On the whole Vincent van Gogh was considerably mellowed by his illness, even to the extent of admitting that his often uncontrolled temper had antagonized those who surrounded him, and of fearing that his judgments had sometimes been too peremptory. Meanwhile Pastor Salles had been to Saint-Rémy and had returned with the sobering news that the monthly rates there were higher than expected and that Vincent would *not* be permitted to work outside of the establishment. While this greatly distressed the painter, Theo was willing to accept the added financial burden. "If I were without your friendship," Vincent wrote to him, "they would have driven me without remorse to suicide, and cowardly as I may be, I might nevertheless have resorted to it."[22] At the very moment when he prepared to go to Saint-Rémy, van Gogh spoke once more and for the last time of his favorite dream: "The idea of an association of painters, of having several of them live together, remains, even though we did not succeed, even though we met with a deplorable and painful failure, but the idea itself, like so many others, is still true and reasonable. Yet not to be started again."[23]

On April 24, 1889, Theo van Gogh wrote from Paris to the director of the Saint-Rémy asylum: "With the consent of the person in question, who is my brother, I request the admission to your institution of Vincent Willem van Gogh, painter, 36 years old, born at

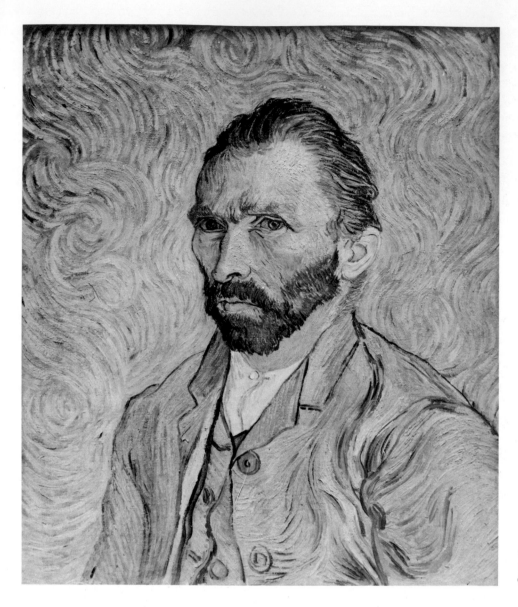

Groot Zundert (Holland), now living in Arles. I ask that he be admitted among your patients of the third class. In view of the fact that his internment is desired mainly to prevent the recurrence of previous attacks and not because his mental condition is unsound, I hope that you will find it possible to permit him to do some painting outside of your establishment, should he so desire. Moreover, without insisting on the care which he will need and which, I suppose, is given with the same solicitude to all your patients, I beg you to be kind enough to allow him at least a half liter of wine with his meals. Sincerely, T. van Gogh."[24]

On May 8, 1889, Vincent van Gogh, accompanied by the faithful Pastor Salles, undertook the short trip of about seventeen miles to Saint-Rémy via Tarascon and was introduced to the asylum's director, Dr. Peyron. The very next day the pastor reported to Theo van Gogh: "Our trip to Saint-Rémy was accomplished under excellent conditions. Mr. Vincent was perfectly calm and explained his case himself to the director, as a man who is fully aware of his situation. He remained with me until my departure, and when I took leave of him he thanked me profusely and seemed somewhat moved at the thought of the completely new life he was going to lead in that establishment."[25] The painter was given a fairly comfortable room and was even promised the greatly desired permission to leave the institution should he wish to work in its peaceful and picturesque surroundings.

The asylum of Saint-Rémy is located in a pleasant but rather lonely spot some two miles from Saint-Rémy itself, a sleepy town of but a few thousand inhabitants, birthplace of Nostradamus. The institution lies in a fertile plain amidst fields of wheat, vineyards, and olive groves, while towards the south it is close to the rugged mountains of the Alpilles, last chain of the distant Alps. Originally an Augustinian monastery, built in the twelfth and thirteenth centuries, of which a small but exquisite cloister and church (see page 339) still exist, the establishment was later augmented by two low and extremely long wings which extend on both sides of the ancient buildings. These housed the male and female patients when the asylum was founded early in the nineteenth century. The whole complex is surrounded by walled-in gardens and fields; a beautiful alley of pine trees and a path

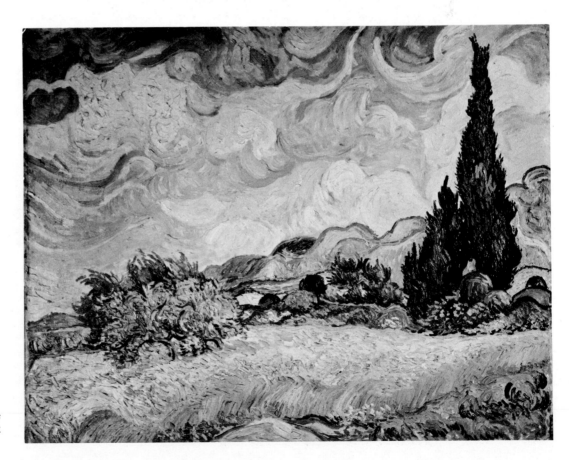

VAN GOGH: *Yellow Corn—Cypresses at Saint-Rémy,* June–July 1889. 28¾ × 36⅝". Private collection, Zurich

profusely bordered by irises and laurels leads to the doctor's residence. On one side the wing for men has a view of tilled acres, while the other side faces a stately though completely desolate park with stone benches, a circular fountain, high and knotty pines twisted by the frequently blowing mistral, and grass and undergrowth in abundance. Whereas the general aspect of the buildings and enclosures is not too unpleasant, in spite of a strong impression of neglect and isolation, the inside of the quarters for men is quite depressing, with long and ill-lighted hallways and monotonous rows of small rooms whose windows are secured by bars. The one occupied by van Gogh looks out on the fields with gentle mountain ranges in the distance. To the left of the hallway is a large room, in which the only furniture consists of wooden benches attached to the walls; its windows face the park but the large trees, many of which have since been felled, must have shut out most of the light. There were only about ten male inmates when van Gogh was admitted to the asylum. They were cared for by several attendants, assisted by some nuns who were in charge of cooking, sewing, etc. On the whole the patients were pretty much left to themselves since Dr. Peyron ran the establishment on an extremely parsimonious budget and seems to have been concerned mainly with keeping his patients alive rather than with treating their afflictions by the best means science could afford in those days.

Dr. Théophile Peyron had first been a physician in the Navy and subsequently established himself as an oculist at Marseilles.[26] Although he was apparently familiar with pathology, it may be doubted whether he should be considered a specialist on mental ills.

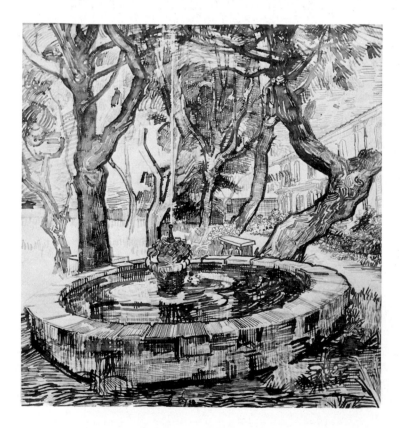

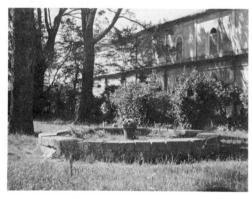

Photograph of the fountain in the garden of the Saint-Rémy asylum

VAN GOGH: *Fountain in the Garden of the Saint-Rémy Asylum,* May–June 1889. Reed pen, pen and ink, 20¼ x 18½″. Rijksmuseum Vincent van Gogh, Amsterdam

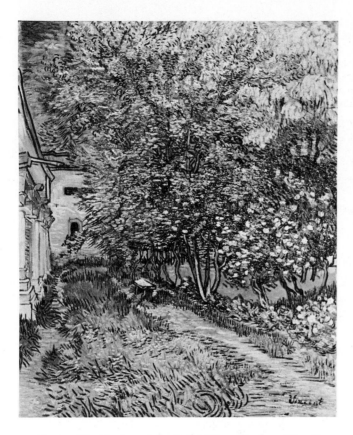

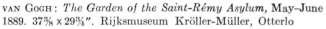

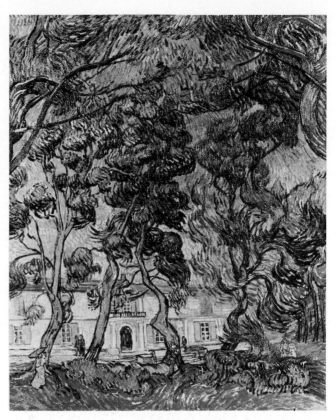

VAN GOGH: *The Garden of the Saint-Rémy Asylum,* May–June 1889. 37⅜ x 29¾″. Rijksmuseum Kröller-Müller, Otterlo

VAN GOGH: *Asylum at Saint-Rémy,* Oct. 1889. 35⅜ x 27⅞″. Collection Armand Hammer, Los Angeles

Twenty-four hours after the painter arrived at the asylum, the doctor entered the following observations in the register of the voluntarily interned: "The undersigned, director of the asylum of Saint-Rémy, certifies that van Gogh (Vincent), age thirty-six, born in Holland and presently domiciled in Arles, having been treated at the hospital in that town, is suffering from acute mania with hallucinations of sight and hearing which have caused him to mutilate himself by cutting off his ear. At present he seems to have recovered his reason, but he does not feel that he possesses the strength and the courage to live independently and has voluntarily asked to be admitted to this institution. As a result of the preceding it is my opinion that M. van Gogh is subject to epileptic fits at very infrequent intervals, and that it is advisable to keep him under prolonged observation in this establishment."[27]

Dr. Peyron's diagnosis was evidently based on reports from the hospital in Arles and on what the painter himself and Pastor Salles had just told him. Since then many doctors have studied van Gogh's case; they have advanced various theories, from schizophrenia to syphilis, either inherited or acquired—though neither can be proven—but most of them agree that he did suffer from an epileptic disorder.[28] Van Gogh told Dr. Peyron that there had been epilepsy in his mother's family. His illness is now generally considered to have been an "epileptoid psychosis (latent mental epilepsy)," the symptoms of which are

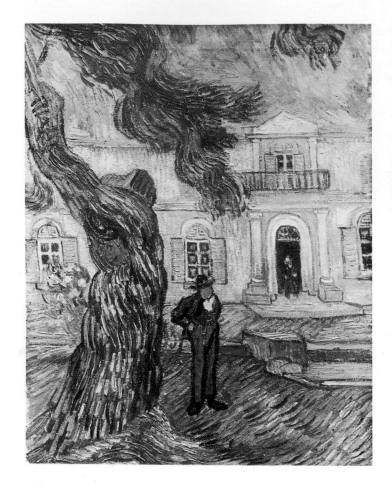

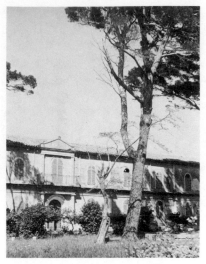

Above: Photograph of the quarter for men of the Saint-Rémy asylum

Left: VAN GOGH: *Dr. Peyron (?) in Front of the Quarter for Men of the Saint-Rémy Asylum*, Oct. 1889. 27⅞ x 17¾". Private collection, Switzerland

that the patient is gloomy, taciturn, defiant, suspicious, always ready to take offense, to injure others, to be carried away by fits of temper, to hit out at people.[29] What characterizes this affliction is the fact that it manifests itself periodically in attacks of indefinite duration, preceded by what is called crepuscular stages and followed by torpor. But in the interval between attacks the patient behaves in a perfectly rational way. In the case of Vincent van Gogh these fits usually lasted from two weeks to a month; they started more or less suddenly and recurred at fairly long intervals. During his seizures he committed various acts of violence, repeatedly tried to swallow his poisonous paints, etc., and suffered from terrifying hallucinations. It goes without saying that all his normal activities, such as painting, drawing, and letter-writing, ceased completely as soon as he was overcome by his illness, which produced a state of profound lassitude whenever he was not agitated. But of all this he retained only a vague recollection, once he had regained his composure. In the intervals between attacks he was in complete possession of his faculties and able to work, write, and reason with undiminished lucidity; this lucidity enabled him to discuss his own affliction with an admirable detachment and with full acceptance of the unavoidable. Occasionally he even tried to describe—as far as his hazy memory would allow—the sensations of terror he experienced during paroxysms. In any event, the letters he wrote at Saint-Rémy and the work he did there are those of a man in control of his emotions. The "blackouts" from which he suffered left no traces on his work since his periods of illness and of artistic activity were always completely separated.

Although Dr. Peyron may have diagnosed van Gogh's illness correctly, he provided little or no proper care for his patient, outside of two long baths a week. (Baths were apparently administered by groups in a small room on the ground floor—with two rows of clumsy and primitive tubs facing each other—the dreariness of which defies description.) It is true that medical science did not then command all the insight and methods it possesses today, but on the other hand the director of the Saint-Rémy asylum was renowned for his stinginess. The other inmates fared no better than the painter; they were all similarly neglected. "The treatment of the patients in this establishment is certainly easy to follow," Vincent reported to his brother, "for absolutely *nothing* is done."[30] Yet, strangely enough, van Gogh was not at first displeased with the institution, possibly because he was left alone and allowed to work. This, after all, was precisely what he had bargained for, although there is no denying that more intensive and individual care could have done much to relieve his mind of the terrific strain caused by the suspicion that his illness was incurable. What he needed most but received in wholly insufficient doses was the assurance that there was still hope and that somehow ways might be found to restore his health. Even pious lies might have accomplished wonders, had he only been led to believe that his attacks might possibly be shortened and eventually be completely eliminated. Like all who are doomed, he would

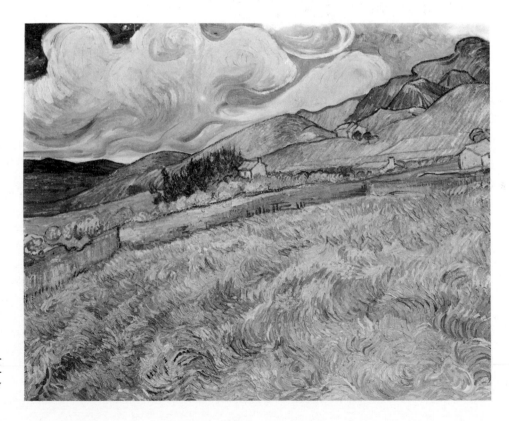

VAN GOGH: *Enclosed Field at Saint-Rémy, Seen from the Artist's Workroom,* June 1889. 27½ x 35⅞". Ny Carlsberg Glyptotek, Copenhagen

doubtless have welcomed the solace of soothing illusions. Indeed, there were moments when he himself clung to this hope with brave self-deceit. Yet his depressing surroundings reminded him only too constantly of his condition, although he professed that the company of the other patients reconciled him somewhat to his own affliction.

On the very day after his admission to the asylum, van Gogh wrote to his brother and sister-in-law: "I think that I did well to come here, mainly because by seeing the *reality* of the life of the various madmen and crazy fellows in the menagerie, I am losing the vague fear, the dread of the thing. And little by little I may succeed in considering madness as an illness like any other.... It may well be that I shall stay here for quite awhile; never have I had such tranquillity as here and in the hospital in Arles so as to be able to paint a little at last."[31] He wrote less often now than he had done before, probably because the monotony of his life failed to stimulate him to make frequent reports, but whenever he did write, his letters were long and descriptive. Some two weeks after his first letter he sent Theo a detailed account of his new life:

"Since I arrived here, the desolate garden ... has been sufficient for my work and I have not yet been outside. Nevertheless the scenery at Saint-Rémy is very beautiful, and sooner or later I shall probably spend some time there.... I have a small room with grayish-green wallpaper and with two curtains, aquamarine with a design of very pale roses enlivened by narrow stripes of blood red. These curtains, probably a legacy from a ruined and defunct rich [patient], are very pretty. From the same source probably comes a very worn-out armchair, covered with a spotted tapestry *à la* Diaz or *à la* Monticelli: brown, red, pink, white, cream, black, forget-me-not blue and bottle green. Beyond the window with its iron bars I can see an enclosed field of wheat ... above which I see the sun rise in the morning in all its glory. Besides, since there are more than thirty empty rooms, I have another room to work in.

"The room where we spend the rainy days is like a third class waiting room in some stagnant village, especially as there are respectable lunatics who always wear a hat, spectacles, a cane, and a traveling outfit, more or less as in a seaside resort—these represent the passengers.

"The food is so-so. It smells of course a little bit musty, as in one of those cockroach-infested Parisian restaurants or in a boarding school. Since these unfortunates do absolutely nothing (not a book, nothing to entertain them but a bowling alley and a game of checkers), they have no other daily diversion than to stuff themselves at regular hours with rationed portions of chick-peas, beans, lentils, and other groceries and colonial produce. As the digestion of these victuals presents certain difficulties, they thus fill their days in a fashion which is as inoffensive as it is cheap. But, without joking, I am losing to a great extent the *fear* of madness when I see from close at hand those who are stricken with it as I myself may easily be some day.... Although there are some who scream and who are usually incoherent, there is also a good deal of real friendship here.... They say: we must bear with the others in order that the others may bear with us.... And among ourselves we understand each other very well.... If someone falls down during a fit, the others look after him and see to it that he doesn't hurt himself. The same goes for those who have the mania of flying into a rage; the old habitués of the menagerie immediately separate the fighters if there is any fight....

"I am also grateful for something else: I notice that the others, too, during their attacks, hear sounds and strange voices, just as I do, and that before their eyes also things seem to

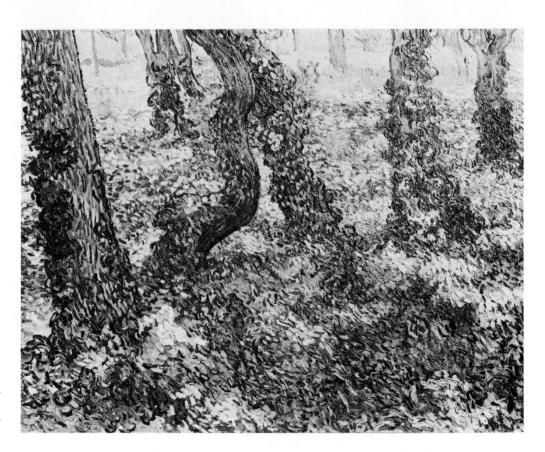

VAN GOGH: *Tree Trunks and Ivy—Garden of the Saint-Rémy Asylum*, July 1889. 29⅛ x 36¼″. Rijksmuseum Vincent van Gogh, Amsterdam

change. And that diminishes the horror which I felt at first at the seizure I had.... Once one knows that this is part of the sickness, one takes it in one's stride like many other things... I believe that once one knows what it is, once one is aware of one's condition and knows that one is subject to attacks, then one can prepare oneself so as not to be inordinately surprised by sensations of anguish or fright.... The shock I received [during the first fit] was so great that I shrank even from making any movement, and nothing would have been more pleasant to me than never to wake up again. At present this *horror of life* is less pronounced and the melancholy is less acute. But I still have no *will power* at all and few or no desires.... That is why I am not ready to leave here soon; I should still be melancholy anywhere. It is only during these last few days that my revulsion against life has been somewhat radically modified....

"My hope is that after one year I shall know better than now what I can do and what I want. Then, little by little, I shall find a way to start all over again. To return to Paris or to go somewhere else does not at all appeal to me at present. This is where I belong. In my opinion those who have been here for years suffer above all from an extreme apathy. Yet to a certain degree my work will preserve me from such a condition." [32]

While this report constitutes a gallant attempt to analyze his situation calmly, Vincent van Gogh also tried hard to spare his brother any anxieties and at the same time to quiet his own apprehensions. Whereas he humorously described the inmates and even insisted on the advantage of being near other madmen, he tried to hide from his brother how utterly depressing it was to live in the company of imbeciles and paranoiacs. Though he made fun of the stale nourishment, he did not tell Theo—as he admitted several months later—that from the very beginning he had refused to eat the asylum food, preferring to subsist only on bread and soup.[33] On the whole it may be true that at first the disadvantages of his new life did not appear too clearly to him, partly because of his reduced will power, partly because the change in itself took his mind off other things, but mostly because he felt the resurgence of his wish to work. More than anything else, he hoped that his work would provide a cure, that it would help him to overcome his depressive moods and give him the courage to face the future.

Within a month after his arrival at Saint-Rémy, van Gogh was permitted to work not only in the garden of the asylum, but also in the environs of the institution, where a guard accompanied him. But while he was satisfied with his work and even felt that his paintings might now become better than before, he was still not ready to face normal surroundings. "I went to the village [of Saint-Rémy] once," he reported in June, "and even though I was accompanied, the sight of people and things was enough to produce a sensation as though I was going to faint, and I felt quite sick. In the presence of nature it is the feeling of work that sustains me."[34] Yet he was careful now not to overwork himself. His regulated and uneventful existence as well as his painting did much to restore his confidence. "With all the precautions I am taking now," he wrote to Theo in June, "I shall not become ill so easily again, and I hope that the attacks will not recur."[35]

Of course van Gogh's life at the asylum was in every respect more bearable than that of the other unfortunate inmates. He could isolate himself and could work, could leave the institution occasionally, and could read a great deal. Through his correspondence with his brother he was kept informed about all the events that interested him, and Theo sent him not only books but also newspapers and periodicals. Thus he learned of the great exhibition of sculpture by Rodin and paintings by Monet held concurrently at Petit's during the World's Fair and also read about Gauguin's show of the "Groupe Impressionniste et Synthétiste" at Volpini's. This title must have puzzled him somewhat, for he commented: "I am led to believe that there has been formed yet another new sect, by no means less infallible than those already in existence. Is that the exhibition about which you wrote me ? What a tempest in a teacup!"[34] But in a letter to his sister Wil, Vincent discussed Gauguin's show with more sympathy: "The friend who was with me in Arles and some others have organized an exhibition in which I would have participated had I been in good health. And what have they been able to achieve? Almost nothing. And yet in their canvases there is something new, something good, something that gives me pleasure and, I assure you, even arouses my enthusiasm."[36]

Although there was hardly any exchange of letters now between van Gogh and Gauguin or Bernard, he continued to think of his two friends and frequently felt close to them while he worked. He particularly remembered how he had discussed with them the need for a "consoling art," and how he had tried to explain to Gauguin that such an art had already been achieved by the painters of the Barbizon school.[37] He seems to have had in mind the observation of humble objects of nature, rendered without too much concern for composition, just as if they had been singled out haphazardly. Indeed, among his first paintings done at Saint-Rémy, obviously in the asylum's garden, are several depicting flowers or plants with butterflies or insects that completely fill the canvas. The most important of

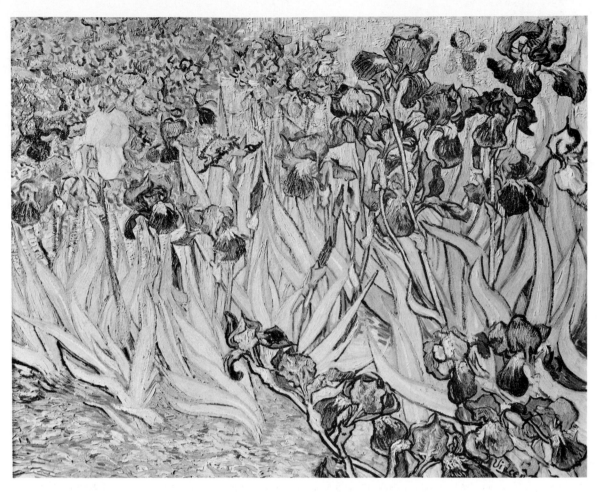

VAN GOGH: *Iris,* Saint-Rémy, May 1889. 29⅛ x 37″. Exhibited with the Independents in 1889. Formerly collection Octave Mirbeau. The Joan Whitney Payson Gallery of Art, Westbrook College, Portland, Me.

these and the largest is a painting of iris, resembling a tapestry of flowers and leaves skillfully interwoven, in which hardly any ground or sky appears; the entire surface is only a single dazzling composition repeating the same shapes of blossoms, the same design of foliage, the same colors, thus conveying a sensation of luxuriant bloom. He also painted aspects of the garden itself: tree trunks covered with ivy (page 309) and a row of trees and flowering bushes along the façade of the men's quarters (page 305). Besides these he did a series of views of the field that stretched out behind his barred window, with its enclosure and the mountains beyond it. Among the few pictures that were apparently painted outside the asylum during May and June 1889 are three of cypresses.

"Cypresses still preoccupy me," Vincent wrote to Theo. "I should like to do something with them like my canvases of sunflowers, because it is surprising to me that they haven't been done yet the way I see them. They are beautiful in line and proportion like an Egyptian obelisk. And the green is of such a distinguished quality. It is the *black* spot in a sunlit

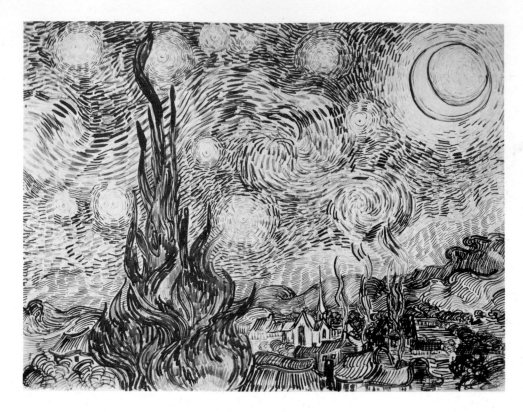

landscape, but it is one of the most interesting black notes, one of the most difficult to hit right that I can imagine."[38] In another letter the painter reported: "I did a landscape with olive trees and also a new study of a starry sky. Although I have not seen the last canvases painted by either Gauguin or Bernard, I am fairly convinced that these two studies which I just mentioned are done in a similar spirit [to theirs]. When you will have had these two studies before your eyes for a certain time, as well as the one of ivy, then I may be able to give you a better idea than through words of the things that Gauguin, Bernard and I have sometimes discussed and that preoccupied us. This is not a return to the romantic or to religious ideas, no. Nevertheless, while deriving from Delacroix more than might appear, in color and through a draftsmanship that is more intentional than the exactness of *trompe-l'oeil,* one can express a rustic nature that is purer than the suburbs, the taverns of Paris. One would also try to paint human beings who would be more serene as well as purer than those Daumier observed, although of course one would follow Daumier's drawing in this... Gauguin, Bernard or I, we may all devote our lives to this and we may not win, but we will not be vanquished either; we may not be destined for one or the other, being here to console or to prepare a more consoling art."[39]

When Vincent sent the first batch of paintings done at Saint-Rémy to Theo in June, these two last paintings, *Landscape with Olive Trees* and *Starry Night,* were not among them, probably because they were not yet dry. Van Gogh only sent them to Paris in October. Meanwhile Theo was delighted with his brother's first shipment, the more so as he viewed with apprehension the increasingly "symbolist-synthesist" art of Gauguin and Bernard.

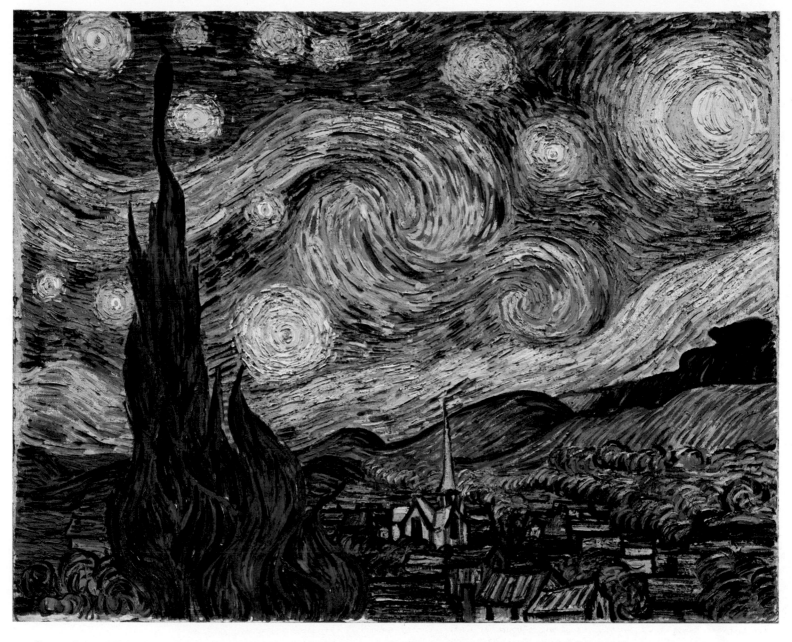

VAN GOGH: *Starry Night,* Saint-Rémy, June 1889. 29 x 36¼". The Museum of Modern Art, New York (Acquired through the Lillie P. Bliss Bequest)

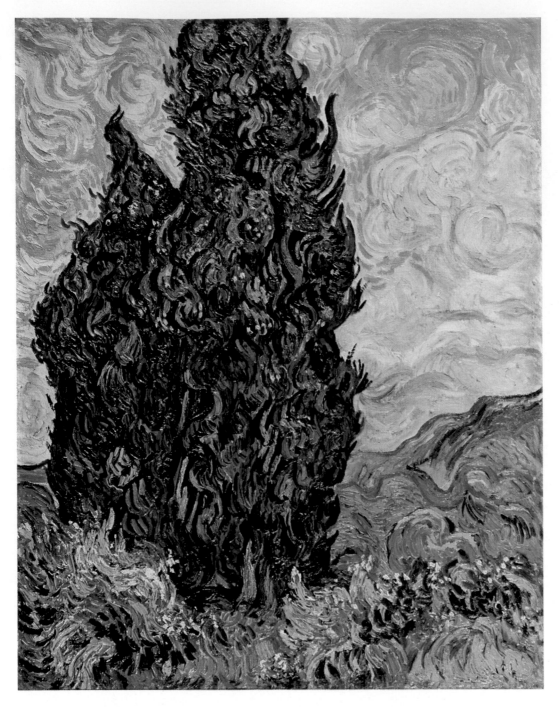

VAN GOGH: *Cypresses,* Saint-Rémy, June 1889. 36¾ x 29⅛″. The Metropolitan Museum of Art, New York (Rogers Fund, 1949)

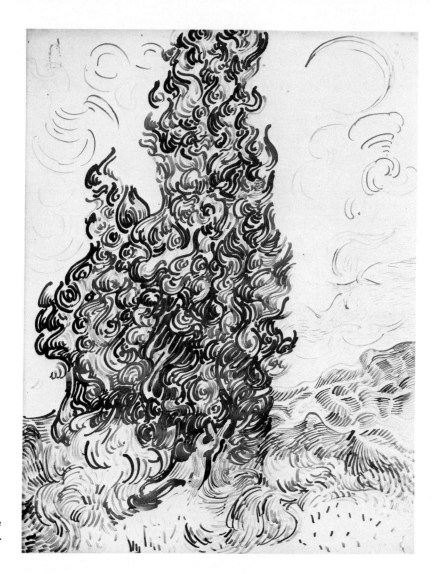

van Gogh: *Cypresses,* Saint-Rémy, June 1889. Reed pen, pen and ink, 24⅝ x 18½″. Brooklyn Museum, New York

He apparently found something too obvious, too contrived, too intellectual in the work now being done at Pont-Aven and Le Pouldu and was pleased to see that Vincent had remained closer to nature and searched less for stylistic singularities. "Your last pictures," he wrote Vincent, "have given me a great deal to think of about your state of mind when you did them. There is in all of them a vigor in the colors that you have never achieved before, which is a rare quality in itself, but you have gone even further: while there are some who are preoccupied with the search for symbols to such an extent that they torture forms, I find these [symbols] in many of your canvases in the expression of the sum total of your thoughts about nature and the living beings which you feel are so strongly attached to it."[40] Theo liked somewhat less his brother's recent drawings because—as he put it—they "seem to have been done in a frenzy and are somehow less close to nature."[41]

Theo was happy to show Vincent's latest works to all their friends. Gauguin, who was then doing mostly sculpture, had just left for Brittany after arranging the show at Volpini's, but Meyer de Haan came to see van Gogh's latest shipment. So did Camille Pissarro and his son, as well as several foreign painters.

Possibly encouraged by the favorable comments he received from Paris, Vincent decided early in July, exactly two months after his arrival at Saint-Rémy, to return for a day to Arles to fetch the last batch of paintings he had left there because they were not dry, and to send them to his brother. In view of the fact that a short while ago even a simple walk to the village of Saint-Rémy had made him feel dizzy, it seems surprising that the painter should have been allowed to undertake this trip, accompanied though he was by one of the surveillants of the asylum. The excursion was probably motivated in part by van Gogh's desire for what he and Gauguin had called "nocturnal hygienic promenades" (Saint-Rémy could not boast of any appropriate institution). Everything went well apparently, although Vincent failed to meet Dr. Rey and Pastor Salles, who were both absent. He returned the same evening and prepared the shipment of his pictures. It was not long afterwards, and very shortly after Theo's wife had written him that she was expecting a baby in February 1890 (she counted on having a boy whose name would be Vincent), that he was seized by a new fit while painting outside the asylum on a windy day. But this fit was not sudden enough to prevent him from finishing his canvas (page 335).

Van Gogh's first attack at Saint-Rémy was as painful as, if not worse than, his seizures at Arles. It was accompanied by suicidal intentions and frightful hallucinations, the intensity of which subsided but slowly;[42] it was followed by a profound depression, since this recurrence made the chronic character of the painter's infirmity only too obvious. Dr. Peyron was honest with him to the extent of telling him that he did not hold too much hope for the immediate future, but he provided at least better food for his patient—meat and wine added to the regular fare—although van Gogh hated to receive special consideration. What contributed to his despondency was the religious atmosphere of the asylum, which now began to suffocate him, the Protestant, in these devoutly Catholic surroundings. And he had also reached the point where he feared the other inmates, avoiding all contact with them. He remained mostly in his bedroom as for some time he was not allowed to work without asking permission, a fact which struck him as humiliating, particularly since he insisted again and again that only work could take his mind off his illness and help him to overcome his dejection. For six weeks he did not go out of the building, not even into the garden—part of that time he had been ill, of course—and when he started at last to paint again, he did so indoors.

"The weather outside is beautiful," he wrote to his sister Wil, "yet for a very long time— I don't know why—I haven't left my room. . . . I need courage which I often lack. It is also because since my sickness a feeling of solitude seizes me in the fields in such a dreadful way that I hesitate to go out. But as time passes this will change again. Only when I am working in front of my easel do I still feel some life. . . . My health is so good that my physical condition will once more gain the upper hand."[43]

Strangely enough, van Gogh's latest and, at least to some extent, unexpected attack stiffened his will power instead of weakening it. "During these fits I feel cowardly towards the anguish and suffering," he explained to his brother, "more cowardly than I should, and maybe it is this very cowardice which now prompts me to eat for two, to work hard, to diminish my contacts with the other patients, for fear of a relapse, whereas previously I had no desire to get better; in a word, I am anxious to recover at present, like someone who,

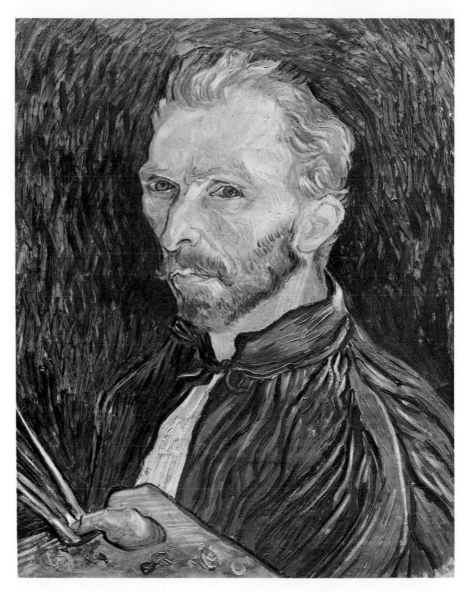

having attempted to kill himself but having found the water too cold, tries to return to the shore."[44]

The first canvas van Gogh painted after he recovered was a portrait of himself, thin and pale, his white face with the yellow hair and reddish beard set against an intensely blue background. He holds a palette in his hand; the piercing glance of his blue eyes indicates determination rather than discouragement; the flame was still far from being extinguished and he now kindled it firmly. He worked slowly but without respite, from morning to night. At the same time he calmly told Theo that he expected a new attack about Christmas. Should it come and so prove that the asylum "treatment" could do nothing for his health, then he would consider going back north, the more so as under the influence of a regulated existence he was reverting to less colorful harmonies. The landscape he had been painting when he was overcome had been, as he wrote Theo, "a more sober essay, dull colors without impasto, broken greens, reds, and ferruginous ochre-yellows, just as I told you that at times I felt the desire to start all over again with a palette like [the one I used] in the North."[45]

In many of his paintings done at Saint-Rémy van Gogh showed a predilection for "muddy" colors: browns, ochres, dull purples. The violence and brilliance of his palette was gradually replaced by muffled tones and more somber harmonies, by the avoidance of clashes or contrast. At times he also favored soft tonalities of pinks and pale greens without the strong accents of his Arles period. There was a subdued quality in many of his canvases that seemed to announce a new departure, although, towards the end of his stay, he once more reverted to more outspoken and vibrant colors, the expression of a vitality regained.

The news from Paris which van Gogh had received shortly before his most recent attack had been good and even exciting, but it was over a month before his mind was clear enough for him to answer. He now replied with words of deep joy and emotion to the notice of Jo's pregnancy. Theo also informed him that they were planning to move and that he had rented a room in the building where Tanguy lived, in order to store Vincent's canvases there and also to enable Tanguy to show as many of them as possible. Tanguy helped with the transfer. "You can imagine," Theo reported, "how enthusiastic he is about such colorful things as the [red] vineyard, the night effect, etc. I wish you could hear him!"[41] But more important was the announcement that a secretary of the association of the XX in Brussels had approached Theo to ask whether Vincent would consider showing with the Belgian group in 1890; Bernard was also to be invited.

Until then van Gogh had exhibited only in various small shows while he was in Paris, shows which had been partly organized by him. Since he had gone south, Theo had sent three paintings and several drawings of his to the Independents in 1888 and again two paintings in September 1889: the *Iris* and *Starry Night over the Rhone,* of which the latter was badly hung. But never before had Vincent been invited to an important and selective exhibition. While Pissarro and Monet, Seurat and Signac, Lautrec and Anquetin, and lastly Gauguin had been guests of the XX between 1887 and 1889, he himself apparently had not expected to follow them so closely. Yet van Gogh showed no excitement over the invitation and actually told Theo that it did not matter to him and that he was not particularly anxious to exhibit, although he did not plan to refuse participation. At about the same time he asked his brother to intercede with the Dutchman Isaäcson, whom Theo had met through Meyer de Haan, in order to prevent him from writing an article on Vincent's work. He felt it would be better to wait until, with improved health, he could assemble a whole group of paintings which he planned to call "Impressions of Provence." It seems evident therefore that at this particular moment van Gogh felt not yet quite ready to confront the public. But when the official invitation from the XX eventually reached him, he accepted it without even knowing who had been invited with him. There was to be, as usual, a contingent of pointillists (this time Signac, Lucien Pissarro, Dubois-Pillet, and Hayet), plus Redon, Renoir, and Toulouse-Lautrec. Whereas most of them had already previously shown with the XX, there were also two newcomers besides van Gogh: one was Sisley, who had declined an invitation in 1888, and the other was Paul Cézanne. As to Emile Bernard, he was either not invited after all, or he refused once again to show with Signac and his friends; in any case his name does not appear among the exhibitors of 1890.

It is to the tremendous credit of Octave Maus and the members of the XX that they unfailingly recognized the great innovators of their time despite the confusing richness of new talents, of conflicting tendencies, of imitators and short-lived reputations. Since 1886, when they had invited Seurat for the first time to their 1887 exhibition, they had continued to send invitations to men of the new generation whose names were not even known in France. Thus, in 1887, their Paris "talent scout," Théo van Rysselberghe, had reported after a visit to Toulouse-Lautrec (who had never before participated in any major exhibition and had not yet shown with the Independents): "The little Bas-du-Cul not bad at all. The fellow has talent! Definitely for the XX! *Has never exhibited.* At present is doing very amusing things, Cirque Fernando, whores, and all that. Is well acquainted with a great many people. He is the right kind, in a word. The idea of being represented at the XX with some ⌊painters⌋ of the rue de Sèze [where the Georges Petit galleries were located] and the rue Laffitte [Durand-Ruel] strikes him as very chic. . . ."[46]

When Cézanne received an invitation to show with the XX in January 1890, he had not exhibited since 1877, in which year he took part for the last time in a group show of his impressionist comrades. However, one of his paintings had just been hung at the Paris World's Fair because his friend Chocquet had interceded on his behalf. Thus, like Gauguin, though in another and much less conspicuous way, he had entered the World's Fair through a back door. Outside of the small group of art lovers and of painters who came to see his work at *père* Tanguy's, nobody knew of Cézanne. But the envoy of the XX apparently went to Tanguy's, where he saw both Cézanne's and van Gogh's paintings. Cézanne must have been just as surprised as was van Gogh to be invited by the XX. Whereas van Gogh was well informed about the Belgian group through Seurat, Signac, Pissarro, and particularly Gauguin, who had received an invitation while he was in Arles, Cézanne may never have heard about the organization. Apparently he declined at first—as did Degas, who consistently refused to show with the XX or anywhere else and who even had his paintings removed from the World's Fair — but when Octave Maus thereupon accused him of disdainfully isolating himself and told him who were the other invited guests, Cézanne relented and replied:

"Having learnt the contents of your flattering letter, I should like to thank you in the first place and to accept with pleasure your kind invitation. May I, however, be permitted to refute the accusation of *disdain* which you attribute to me with reference to my refusal to take part in exhibitions of painting? I must tell you with regard to this matter that the many studies I have made having given only negative results, and fearing criticisms that are only too well justified, I had resolved to work in silence until the day when I should feel myself able to defend in theory the results of my experiments. In view of the pleasure of finding myself in such good company I do not hesitate to modify my resolution. . . ."[47]

Cézanne pledged three paintings; van Gogh planned to send twice as many. "I accept with pleasure your invitation to show with the XX," he wrote to Octave Maus. "This is the list of canvases intended for you: (1) *Sunflowers*; (2) *Sunflowers*; (3) *Ivy*; (4) *Orchard in Bloom* (Arles); (5) *Field of Wheat at Sunrise* (Saint-Rémy); (6) *The Red Vineyard* (Montmajour). All these canvases are of the size 30 [c. $36 \times 29''$]. I am perhaps exceeding the space of about thirteen feet [accorded to each guest], but believing that the six together, thus selected, will present a somewhat varied color effect, maybe you will find a way to place them."[48]

In the meantime van Gogh was preoccupied with but one thing: work. He felt that a more

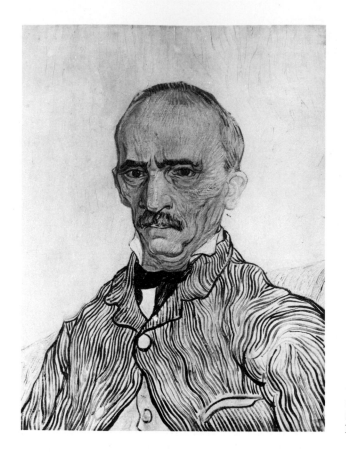

violent attack might destroy forever his capacity to paint and he was determined to take fullest advantage of whatever time he had left. He also became increasingly convinced that less morbid surroundings would enhance his resistance and his productivity. Moreover he experienced a strong desire to communicate again with friends, to discuss art with fellow painters, to escape the complete and oppressive isolation in which he had now lived in Saint-Rémy for almost six months. Besides Dr. Peyron, with whom he never established as friendly a relationship as he had had with the intern Rey, and whom he did not see very frequently, there was actually nobody with any education whom he could engage in conversation. The nuns had, as was to be expected, a low opinion of his art, and he does not seem to have talked much with any of them.[49] He saw more of the guards, especially the two who ordinarily accompanied him by turn when he worked outside of the asylum, but he did not become very loquacious with them, although he occasionally questioned one of them about the field work and the peasants. This guard later reported that he had never seen the painter laugh, or even smile.[50] Van Gogh was better acquainted with the head guard and painted a portrait of him as well as of his wife. But the lack of stimulating company, added to all the other inconveniences, prompted him in the fall of 1889 to think more and more about returning to the North. It was in this state of mind that he recapitulated in a letter to his brother both his reasons for going to the South and for wanting to leave it:

"You know that there were thousands of reasons why I went south and threw myself into my work there. I wanted to see a different light; I thought that to observe nature under a clearer sky would give me a better idea of the way in which the Japanese feel and draw. I also wanted to see this stronger sun because I felt that without knowing it I could not understand paintings by Delacroix from the standpoint of execution and technique, and because I felt that the colors of the prism were blurred by mist in the North. All this remains somewhat true. To this should be added a heartfelt longing for the South that Daudet described in *Tartarin*, and the fact that here and there I also have found friends and things that I love. Can you understand then that while I consider my affliction horrible, I nevertheless feel that here I have created for myself attachments which are a little bit too strong—attachments which later may again bring about the desire to take up my work here once more—yet just the same I might return to the North in the not too distant future. Yes, for though I won't deny that I eat heartily at present, I also feel a terrific desire to see my friends again and to see once more the countryside of the North."[44]

Van Gogh did not as yet have any clear idea of how he would live in the North. He was somewhat apprehensive of joining Gauguin at Pont-Aven, where there were too many people for his taste, and thought it might be better to board with one of the painters living in the country round Paris. He considered staying with Vignon or, preferably, Camille Pissarro, of whom Theo often spoke in his letters. The two brothers had the highest esteem for Pissarro; it seemed quite evident that his even temper and benevolent character could not but exert a favorable influence on Vincent. Pissarro apparently was not opposed to the project, though only the previous year he had had to decline a similar proposition from Meyer de Haan, mainly for lack of space. He promised to consider the question, but Theo did not feel too hopeful. "I don't think that he has a great deal to say at home where his wife wears the pants," he wrote to Vincent. Indeed, Mme Pissarro was afraid of the effect an unbalanced man might have on her children, the last two of whom were not yet ten years old. Pissarro thereupon looked elsewhere and came up with the suggestion of Dr. Gachet at Auvers, who presented the triple advantage of being a doctor, of being interested in modern art, a friend of Cézanne, Guillaumin, and Pissarro himself among others, and even of being something of an artist since he did etchings as a hobby.[51]

While Pissarro and Theo explored the possibility of sending Vincent in the coming spring to Auvers-sur-Oise, not far from Paris, where Gachet could discreetly watch over him, van Gogh continued to work incessantly. Although he felt at present little desire to be near Gauguin and Bernard, he was still thinking of them frequently when he painted. He seems to have been particularly conscious of his connection with the Pont-Aven group when he had painted in June a strange and haunting view of a starry night over a village that looks like a cross between Saint-Rémy and reminiscences of the North. This canvas is one of the few where he departed from the direct observation of nature and let his imagination invent forms and colors to create a specific mood. His *Starry Night* (page 313), with its sleeping houses, its fiery cypresses surging into a deep blue sky animated by whirlpools of yellow stars and the radiations of an orange moon, is a deliberate attempt to represent a vision of incredible urgency, to liberate himself from overpowering emotions rather than to study lovingly the peaceful aspects of nature round him. The same tendency and the same use of heavy outlines appear in several other paintings done at that time, particularly a landscape with silver-green olive trees in a rolling field with a range of undulating blue mountains in the background, over which hovers a solid white cloud. In a letter to

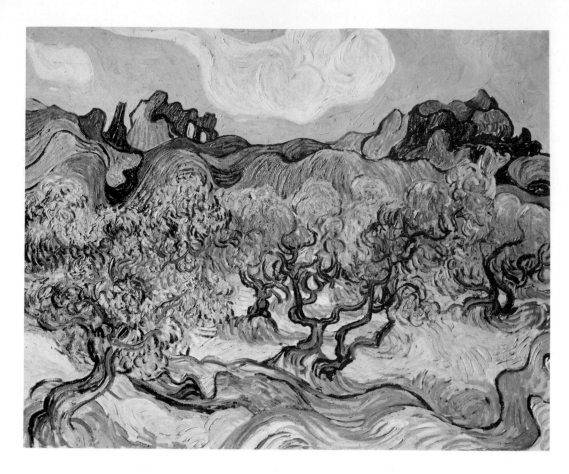

his brother van Gogh tried to explain what he had wanted to achieve: "The olive trees with the white cloud and the mountains behind, as well as the rise of the moon and the night effect, are exaggerations from the point of view of the general arrangement; the outlines are accentuated as in some of the old woodcuts." And he went on to say: "Where these lines are tight and purposeful, there begins the picture, even if it is exaggerated. This is a little bit what Bernard and Gauguin feel. They do not care at all about the exact form of a tree, but they do insist that one should be able to say whether its form is round or square—and, by God, they are right, exasperated as they are by the photographic and silly perfection of some painters. They won't ask for the exact color of mountains, but they will say: 'Damn it, those mountains, were they blue? Well then, make them blue and don't tell me that it was a blue a little bit like this or a little bit like that. They were blue, weren't they? Good—make them blue and that's all!'"[52] (This was precisely the advice Gauguin had given young Sérusier.)

Theo did not fail to notice the similarity of his brother's new tendencies to those of Gauguin. When he received in October a group of Vincent's recent canvases as well as some of Gauguin's from Brittany, he wrote to Saint-Rémy: "In the last shipment from Gauguin there are the same preoccupations as in your work. . . ." But he also made it clear that he did not like this new approach in his brother's paintings any better than he

322

did in Gauguin's. Speaking of the *Iris*, which had just been returned from the Independents, he explained: "I think that you are strongest when you do true things like that, or like the *Tarascon Coach* . . . or the *Underbrush with Ivy* . . . . The form is so well defined and the whole so full of colors. I do understand what interests you in the new paintings, such as the village in the moonlight [*Starry Night*] or in the mountains, but I find that the search for style takes away from the real feeling for things."[53]

"In spite of what you say," Vincent replied, "that the search for style frequently does harm to other qualities, the fact remains that I feel strongly driven to search for style, if you want to call it that, but I mean by that a more masculine and firm drawing. If this should make me resemble more closely Bernard or Gauguin, I can't help it. But I am inclined to believe that as time passes you will get used to it." And as an afterthought the painter specified: "I know well that the studies drawn with large and knotty lines in my last shipment were not yet what these endeavors ought to be, yet I beg you to believe that in landscape painting one will continue to attempt to mass things by means of drawing which tries to express the entanglement of masses. . . . Bernard has really found perfect things in this direction. So do not too hastily adopt a prejudice against it."[54]

But while van Gogh thus maintained a spiritual link with Gauguin and Bernard, whose recent paintings he had not seen and to whom he scarcely wrote because of the pressures of his own work, he actually spent the fall of 1889 under the spell of artists quite different from those at Pont-Aven. From lithographs, reproductions, and woodcuts he copied the works of other masters. He was attracted by Delacroix, Rembrandt, and even by such sentimental products as a painting by Virginie Demont-Breton; but above all he copied works of Millet. Early in 1890 he also painted after Daumier. Theo sent him a series of

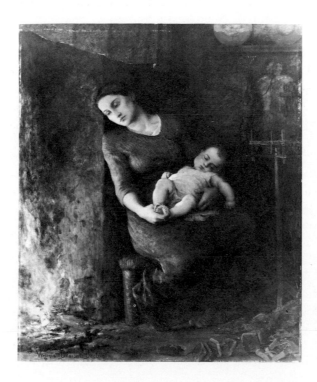
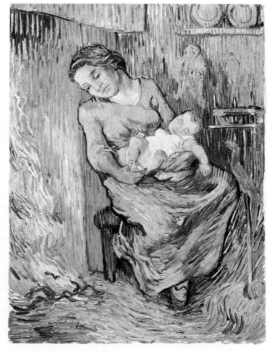

Right: DEMONT-BRETON: *Husband at Sea,* exhibited at the Salon of 1889 and reproduced in a periodical. Walker Art Center, Minneapolis

Far right: VAN GOGH: *Husband at Sea,* after Demont-Breton, Saint-Rémy, Oct. 1889. 26 x 20⅛". Formerly collection Dr. Gachet. Private collection, Philadelphia

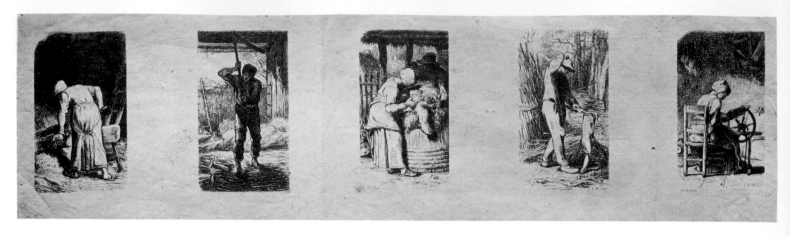

Series of wood engravings by Lavieille after Millet, sent by Theo van Gogh to his brother and copied by the latter at Saint-Rémy. Rijksmuseum Vincent van Gogh, Amsterdam

woodcuts by Lavieille after Millet, as well as reproductions of drawings by Millet. Ever since he had started to draw the peasants of his native Brabant, Vincent had been impressed by the monumental simplicity of Millet's figures, by the acute observation of their typical poses and gestures. He may have remembered that Pissarro used to consider Millet's drawings "a hundred times better than his paintings," although he found his work "infected with sentimentality."[55] But in the woodcuts and drawings which he now studied, this sentimentality was much less apparent, the use of lights and shadows more accentuated than in the paintings, and the figures themselves much more powerfully detached. In making copies from these models or from the more romantic, nervous, and inspired works by Delacroix, van Gogh could do once again what he had wanted to do in the South: use colors more arbitrarily. "It seems to me," he wrote to his brother, "that to make paintings after these drawings by Millet means to *translate them into another language* rather than to copy them."[54]

Indeed, working from black-and-white reproductions, van Gogh not only invented the color schemes but also emphasized forms, striving for those "large and knotty lines" which he also sought in his work from nature. Between the fall of 1889 and the spring of 1890 he did no fewer than twenty-three paintings — mostly small — after Millet, and it was doubtless the forcefulness and plasticity with which Millet usually set out single figures of peasants in typical attitudes against a landscape background that inspired van Gogh.

"I can assure you," Vincent informed Theo, "that I am enormously interested in making copies, and since I have no models for the time being, through these copies I shall not neglect figure studies. I use the black-and-whites by Delacroix or Millet (or after them) as I would a real life subject. And then I improvise colors, though of course I do this not as if I were quite myself, but rather trying to remember *their* paintings. Yet this recollection, the vague harmony of their colors which, though not exact, are in the feeling, that is an interpretation all my own."[56]

It seems as if towards the close of that fateful year of 1889 van Gogh's inspiration had somewhat slackened. He would have liked to paint sunsets but was not permitted to work

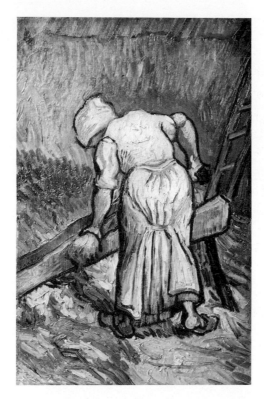

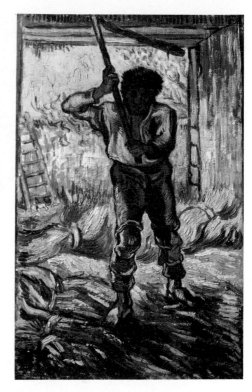

Right: VAN GOGH: *Woman Cutting Straw,* after Millet, Saint-Rémy, Sept. 1889. 16 x 10⅜″. Rijksmuseum Vincent van Gogh, Amsterdam

Far right: VAN GOGH: *Thresher,* after Millet, Saint-Rémy, Sept. 1889. 17⅜ x 10⅝″. Rijksmuseum Vincent van Gogh, Amsterdam

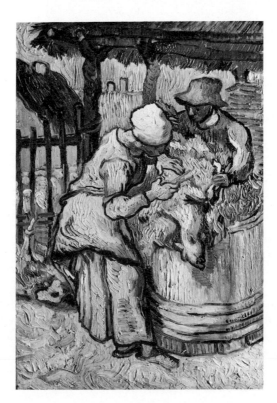

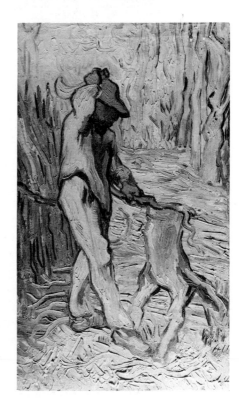

Right: VAN GOGH: *Peasants Shearing Sheep,* after Millet, Saint-Rémy, Sept. 1889. 17 x 11½″. Rijksmuseum Vincent van Gogh, Amsterdam

Far right: VAN GOGH: *Woodcutter,* after Millet, Saint-Rémy, Feb. 1890. 17⅛ x 9⅞″. Rijksmuseum Vincent van Gogh Amsterdam

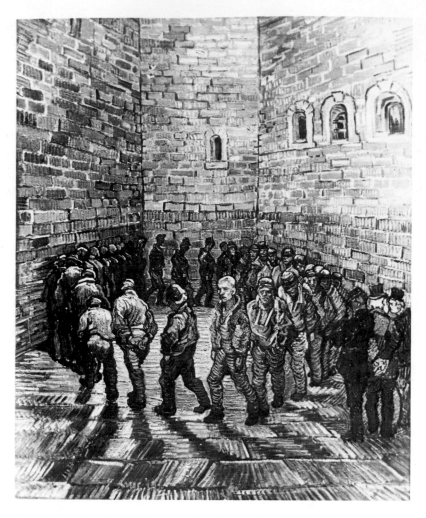

VAN GOGH: *Round of Prisoners,* after Gustave Doré, Saint-Rémy, Feb. 1890.
31½ x 25⅛". Pushkin State Museum of Fine Arts, Moscow

outdoors late in the day. He was extremely bored during the evening hours in the asylum, although he read a great deal, particularly Shakespeare's historical dramas. When he could not paint in the open, he no longer turned to still lifes as he had so often done in Paris and in Arles. Instead, whenever he was not engaged in copying, he now painted replicas of his own pictures—some of them meant for his mother or his sister—such as of his *Bedroom in Arles,* which Theo shipped from Paris to Saint-Rémy for that purpose. He even planned to paint second versions of his *Tarascon Coach* and the *Red Vineyard.* In other instances he executed on the spot replicas of paintings done at Saint-Rémy. He also finished a view of the ward for the mentally ill in the hospital at Arles (page 297), which he had begun there.[57] Eventually he was to ask his brother as well as his mother to send him some of his early drawings and small sketches of peasants so as to work anew from them. In this way he used a drawing (or lithograph) he had made in the Hague

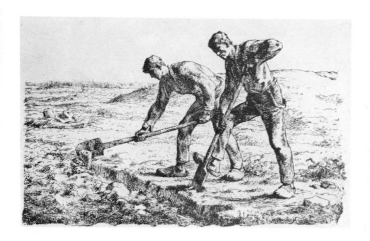

After MILLET: *Men Digging*. Wood engraving, 9¼ x 13¼"

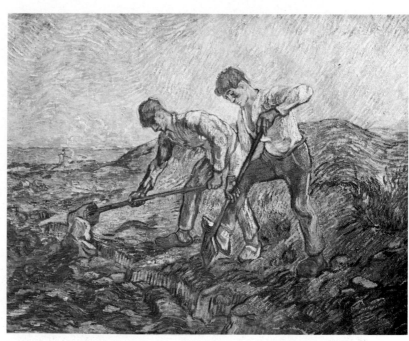

VAN GOGH: *Men Digging*, after Millet, Saint-Rémy, Oct.–Nov. 1889. 28⅜ x 36¼". Rijksmuseum Vincent van Gogh, Amsterdam

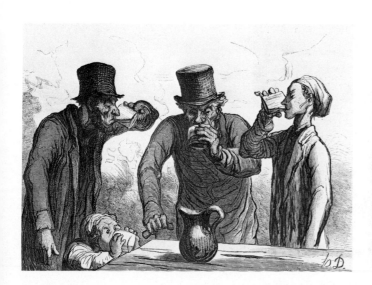

After a drawing by DAUMIER: *Men Drinking—The Four Ages of Drinkers*. Wood engraving

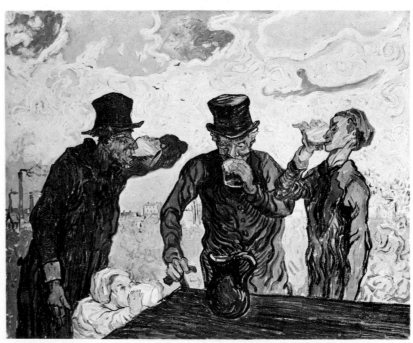

VAN GOGH: *Men Drinking*, after Daumier, Saint-Rémy, Jan.–Feb. 1890. The Art Institute of Chicago (Joseph Winterbotham Collection)

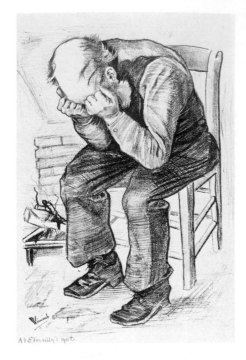
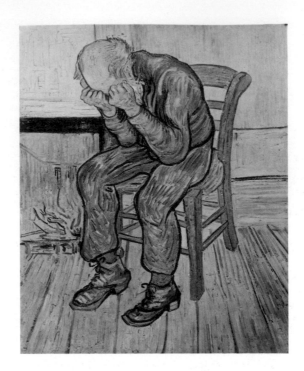

Left: VAN GOGH: *At Eternity's Gate*, 1882–85. Lithograph, 19¾ x 13¾". Private collection, New York. Right: VAN GOGH: *At Eternity's Gate,* after the artist's own lithograph, Saint-Rémy, May 1890. 31½ x 25¼". Rijksmuseum Kröller-Müller, Otterlo

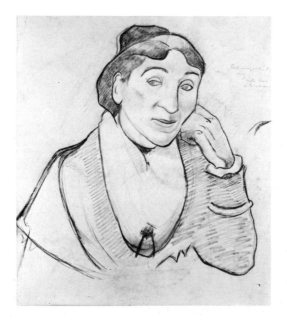
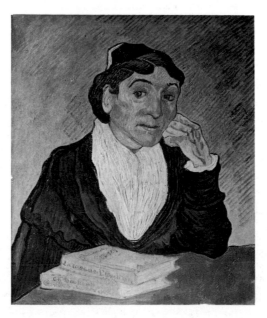

Left: GAUGUIN: *L'Arlésienne,* Arles, Nov. 1888. Charcoal, 22 x 19". The Fine Arts Museums of San Francisco, M. H. de Young Museum (Hanley Collection). Right: VAN GOGH: *L'Arlésienne,* after Gauguin's drawing, Saint-Rémy, Jan.–Feb. 1890. 23⅝ x 19¾". Galleria Nazionale d'Arte Moderna, Rome

between 1882 and 1885 for a painting of an old man mourning, *At Eternity's Gate*. He even derived inspiration from the drawing of an *Arlésienne* which Gauguin had done for his own version of the *Night Café*.[58]

"I have endeavored to respect your drawing faithfully," Vincent later explained to his friend, "and yet have taken the liberty of interpreting it by means of a coloration in harmony with the sober character and the style of the original drawing. One might call it a synthesis of an Arlésienne; as syntheses of Arlésiennes are scarce, consider this one as a work by you and me, as the summing up of our months of working together."[59] Van Gogh actually painted several oils of this subject. It may have been that Gauguin's study helped him to do portraits, since Vincent always regretted his inability to find models for portraiture at Saint-Rémy. In any event, with the coming winter season the number of his landscapes diminished — though he painted a view from his window of the enclosed field he had done so often, this time under a heavy rain — while the work done indoors is almost exclusively based on "sources" found in the works of other artists or in his own.

But making copies and duplicates did not keep van Gogh from painting in the open, sometimes in spite of the cold weather. While he did so less frequently than before, he undertook many walks through the countryside which subsequently enabled him to paint a few landscapes from memory. At the same time he was on the lookout for new subjects and told his brother: "I have the pictures already ripe in my head; I know in advance the places which I still want to paint these coming months."[60] On some occasions, when such subjects could not "wait" for him, he tackled them immediately, as he did for instance when he observed in Saint-Rémy a group of men repairing the pavement of a large boulevard among the gigantic trunks of gnarled plane trees whose leaves were turning yellow (page 333). Within a few days he painted a second version of this canvas.

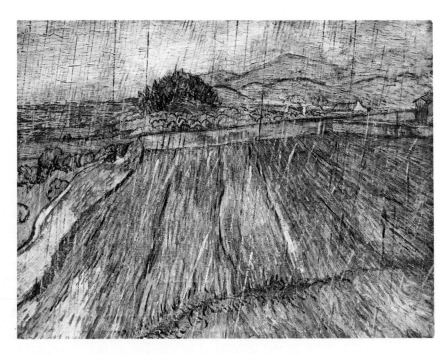

van Gogh: *The Enclosed Field under Rain,*
Saint-Rémy, Oct. 1889. 28⅞ x 36⅜". Collection
Henry P. McIlhenny, Philadelphia

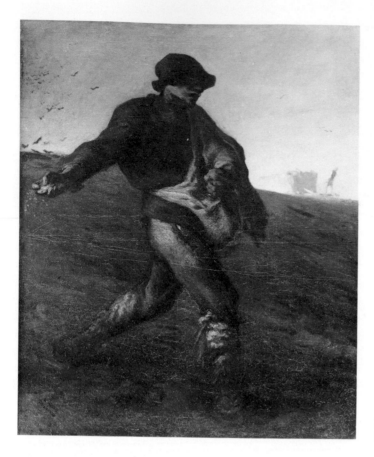

MILLET: *The Sower.* 39¾ x 32½".
Museum of Fine Arts, Boston

The question of the "newness" of a subject occurred often in Vincent's thoughts and letters; he always seemed concerned about whether particular motifs had already been painted by other artists. He felt that Provence offered many subjects which had not been sufficiently explored, such as vineyards, cypresses, and olive trees; to these he devoted special attention since he did not want to leave the South without taking back a group of canvases that would be "new." Thus the subjects which attracted him most during the last months of 1889 were the rugged mountains near the asylum (the Alpine foothills), the elegant dark cypresses whose tapering forms seemed so fraught with mystery, and above all the tender, silver-green olive trees, which he had not painted before. He was preoccupied with a whole series of pictures showing olive-pickers, although he felt that Puvis de Chavannes would probably have known better than he did how to "explain" these picturesque trees. But he also remembered Gauguin and Bernard, telling Theo: "I have worked this month in the olive groves, for they made me mad with their 'Christs in the Garden' where nothing is observed. Of course, with me there is no question of doing anything from the Bible and I have written to Bernard as well as to Gauguin that I believed that our duty lay in thoughts and not in dreams, and that I was therefore surprised to see that in their work they let themselves go in that direction...."[61]

It had been exactly a year since van Gogh had last written to Bernard, but now, in the

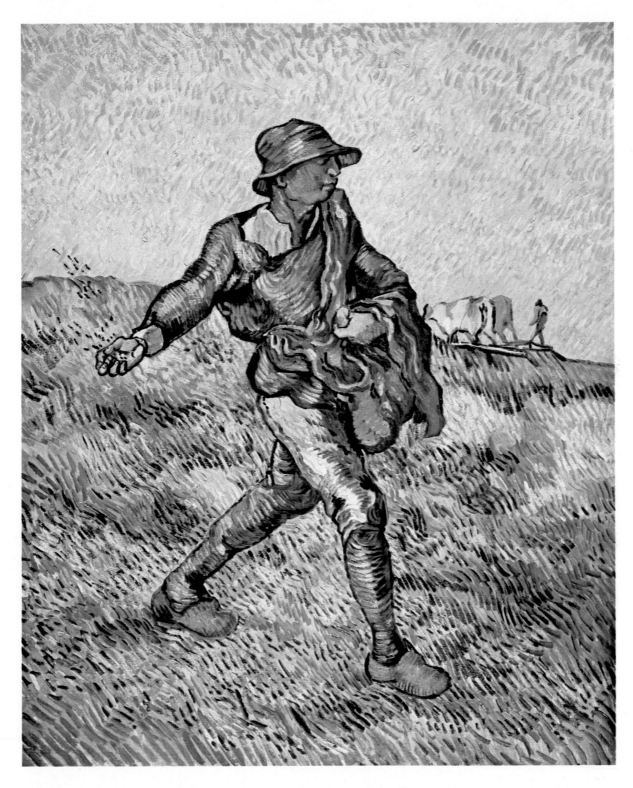

VAN GOGH: *The Sower,* after Millet, Saint-Rémy, Jan. 1890. 31⅞ x 25½". Collection Stavros S. Niarchos, Athens

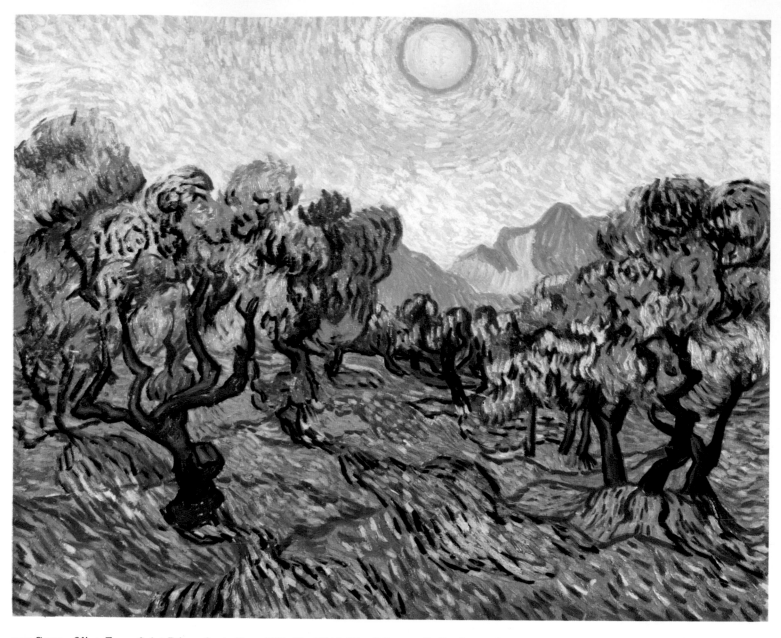

van Gogh: *Olive Trees*, Saint-Rémy, Sept.–Nov. 1889. 29 x 36½". The Minneapolis Institute of Arts

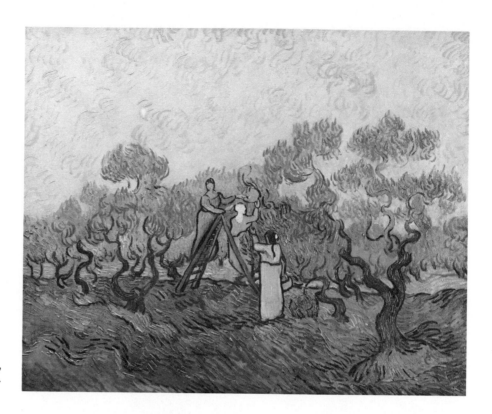

VAN GOGH: *Olive Pickers*, Saint-Rémy,
Nov. 1889. 28¾ × 35½″. Collection Mrs.
Enid A. Haupt, New York

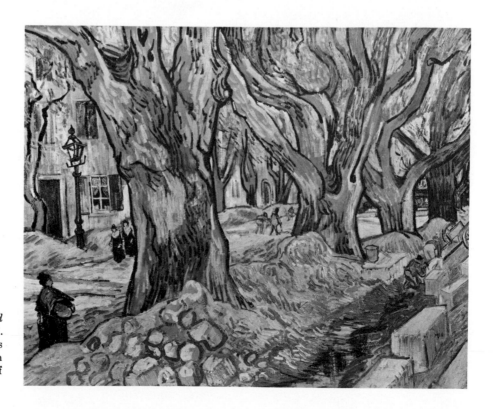

VAN GOGH: *Road Menders—Boulevard
at Saint-Rémy*, Dec. 1889. 29 × 36¼″.
One of two versions, of which one was
exhibited with the Independents in
1890. Cleveland Museum of Art (Gift of
Hanna Fund)

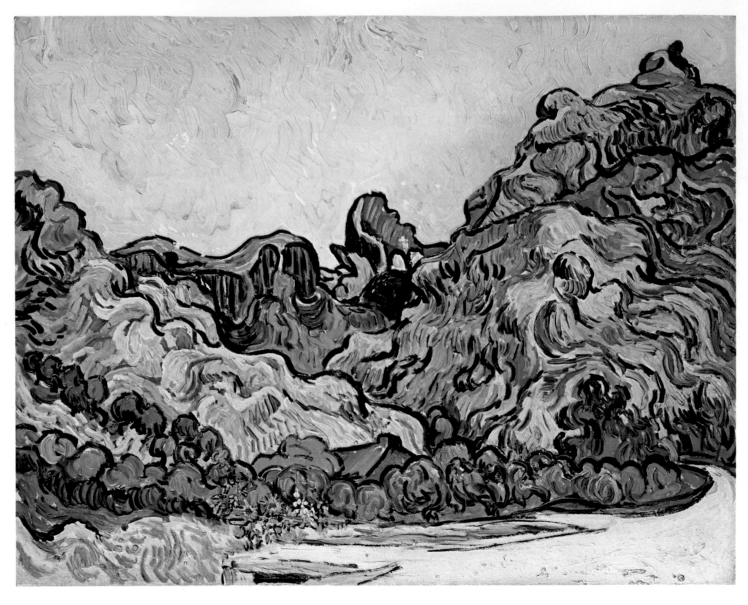

VAN GOGH: *Mountains at Saint-Rémy*, July 1889. 28¼ x 35¾". Justin K. Thannhauser Collection, New York. Courtesy the Thannhauser Foundation and The Solomon R. Guggenheim Museum, New York

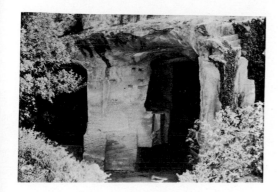

Above: Photograph of quarry near Saint-Rémy

Right: VAN GOGH: *Entrance to a Quarry near the Asylum of Saint-Rémy,* July 1889. 20½ x 25¼″. This is the painting on which the artist was working when he was overcome by his first seizure at Saint-Rémy. Collection Mrs. Morton M. Palmer, Jr., and Mr. George A. Forman, New York

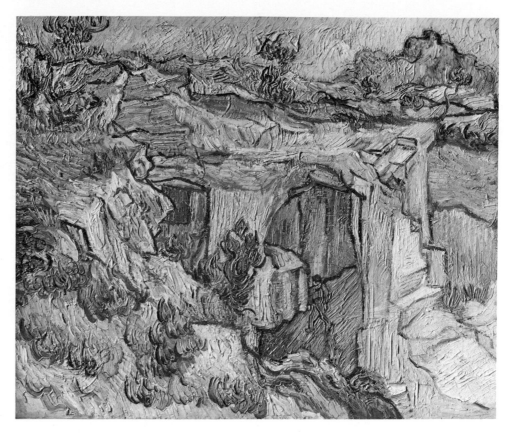

fall of 1889, he was eager to resume their correspondence. "My brother wrote me that you were coming to see my pictures," he said. "Thus I know that you are back [in Paris] and I am very pleased that you should have thought of going to see what I have done. On my side I am very anxious to know what you have brought back from Pont-Aven. I haven't really got much of a head for correspondence, but I feel quite lost when I am no longer in touch with everything that Gauguin, you, and the others are doing.... I have another dozen studies here which will probably be more to your taste than those of this summer which my brother will have shown you. Among these studies is an *Entrance to a Quarry*: pale lilac rocks against a reddish soil, as in certain Japanese drawings. In design and in the use of large planes of color it has quite a lot in common with what you are doing at Pont-Aven. I have been more master of myself in these last studies, because my condition has greatly improved.... That will prove to you, I hope, that I'm not yet washed up. My God, it's a mighty tricky bit of country this, everything is difficult to do if one wants to get at its inner character so that it is not merely something vaguely experienced, but the true soil of Provence. And to manage that one has to work very hard, whereupon the results become naturally a bit abstract; for it's a question of giving the sun and the sky their full force and brilliance, of retaining the fine aroma of wild thyme which pervades the baked and melancholy earth. It's the olive trees here, old man, which would be your cup of tea. I haven't had much luck with them myself this year, but I'll come back to

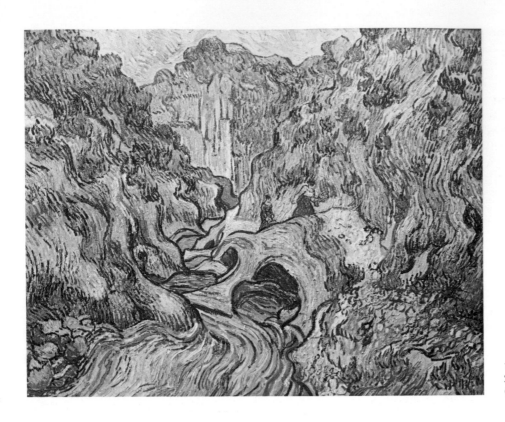

them, at least I intend to. They are like silver in an orange or purplish landscape under a large white sun.... So you see there's still plenty for me to get my teeth into here.... I am working on a big canvas of a *Ravine,* a subject very much like that study of yours with a yellow tree which I still have; two masses of extremely solid rock between which flows a thin stream of water, and at the end of the ravine a third mountain, which blocks it. Such subjects have a fine melancholy, and moreover it's fun working in very wild places where one has to wedge the easel in between the stones to prevent everything from being blown over by the wind."[62]

Having thus re-established contact with Bernard by telling him what he himself was doing, Vincent, a few weeks later, was ready to lash out against the new tendency of religious mysticism which his brother had noticed in the recent works of Gauguin and Bernard, a tendency of which Theo did not approve any more than did his brother. It is strange to think that Vincent van Gogh, the former lay preacher and religious fanatic, should have so violently opposed any revival of Biblical subjects, but his contacts in Paris with such atheists and anarchists as Pissarro, Signac, Seurat, and *père* Tanguy, the books he read (Voltaire, Renan, Flaubert, Zola, Daudet, Turgenev, Maupassant, Huysmans, Goncourt, most of whom were freethinkers, to say the least), and his own visual experiences as a painter had shaken his faith. While he still believed in a God, as an artist he was passionately attached to the world of reality. And he now tried to explain his viewpoint in a long letter to Bernard, discussing his friend's religious paintings, of which Bernard had sent him photographs. After a few complimentary words he wrote bluntly that he did not consider Bernard's approach healthy. He analyzed an *Adoration of the Magi* by Bernard, stating that he thought it was "going too far beyond the bounds of possibility to imagine a delivery in the middle of a road" and comparing this birth of Christ to the birth of a calf as painted by Millet. "Personally I love things that are real. that are possible," he wrote. "If I am at all capable of a spiritual thrill, then I bow before that study by Millet which is powerful enough to make one tremble: peasants carrying back to the farm a calf just born in the fields. That, my friend, all people have felt from France to America. Are you now going to follow this up with a revival of medieval tapestries? Is it really a sincere conviction? Surely not! You can do better than that, and you know that what you must strive for is the possible, the logical, the real, even if you have to forget the Baudelairean aspects of Paris. How I prefer Daumier to that fellow!

"... But it's enough if you understand that I am longing to hear that you are doing things like the picture of yours which Gauguin has, the *Breton Women in the Meadow* [reproduced page 226], so beautifully ordered and so naïvely distinguished in its color. And now you exchange that for what is—must I say the word—artificial and affected! ... But when I compare such things with that nightmare, *Christ in the Garden of Olives*, I am sad indeed; so in this letter I urge you once more, reviling you with all the force of my lungs, to become your own self again. The *Christ Carrying the Cross* is atrocious. Are they

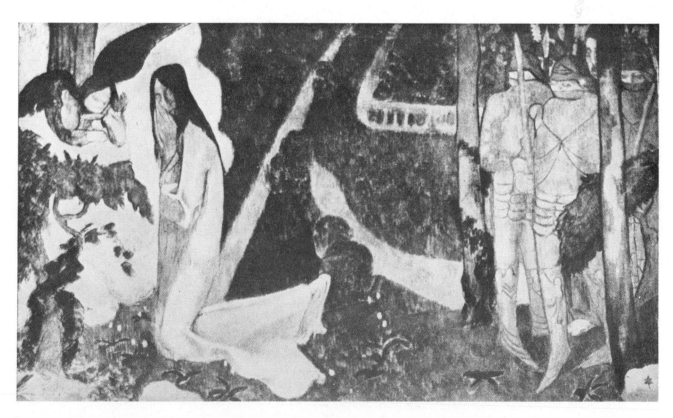

BERNARD: *Christ in the Garden of Olives,* 1889. Formerly collection A. Vollard, Paris. Gauguin thought he recognized himself in the figure partly hidden by the tree at the right

337

harmonious, those patches of color in it? I won't forgive you for the banality — indeed *banality* — of the composition. When Gauguin was in Arles, as you know, I once or twice allowed myself to turn to abstraction.... I don't say that after a manly lifetime of research, of hand to hand battles with nature, one might not risk it; but for my part I don't want to bother my head with such things. All year I have pottered about with nature, hardly giving a thought either to impressionism or anything else. However, once again I let myself go and reached for stars that were too big; once more a failure, and now I have had enough. So at the moment I am doing olive trees, seeking after different effects with a gray sky against yellow soil, and a green-black note in the foliage.... These interest me far more than all the abstractions mentioned above.

"... If I haven't written for a long while it is because, what with having to wrestle with my illness and to calm my mind, I had but little desire for discussion, I found danger in these abstractions. If one goes on working quietly, the fine subjects will come along of their own accord; above all it is really a question of plunging oneself anew in reality with no preconceived plan and none of the Parisian prejudices.... I have absorbed as well as I could the atmosphere of the little mountains and the olive groves; after that we'll see. I don't want anything more than a few sods of earth, some sprouting wheat, an olive grove, a cypress — the latter not easy to do by any means...."[63] Van Gogh went on to describe several of his own landscapes, saying that in some he had endeavored to produce a sensation of anguish through certain combinations of colors and through heavy black outlines, while in other paintings he had striven to express calm and peacefulness. He summed this up by declaring that "there are other means of attempting to convey an impression of anguish without making straight for the historic Garden of Gethsemane; to create something gentle and consoling it is not necessary to portray the figures of the Sermon on the Mount."[63]

In a letter to Theo, written at the same time, Vincent compared his own recent works to those of Gauguin and Bernard: "What I have done is somewhat hard and of a coarse realism compared with their abstractions, however it will strike a rustic note and will smell of the earth."[61] In spite of his "coarse realism" van Gogh felt that the period of calm he was enjoying reflected itself even in his colors and his execution. He seemed to forgo the clashes of complementaries which had so often sounded dramatic notes in his paintings, explaining to his mother: "All the colors are much softer than usual."[64] And to Theo he wrote: "I think it is likely that I shall no longer do anything with heavy impasto; this is a result of the quiet secluded life I am leading, which makes me feel better. After all, I am not as violent as all that, I feel more *myself* in calmness."[65] His frenzied efforts to catch up with all the onrushing impressions, to paint as fast as he saw, were likewise gone. "I try to live from one day to the next," he told his mother, "to finish one thing before beginning another."[64]

Van Gogh seemed to have so well established the routine of his work that in November he could spend two days in Arles—during which he visited Pastor Salles—without any noticeable ill effects. He was amazed to find that this venture did not provoke any new attack. An attack did come about, however, around Christmas, just as he had foreseen, yet this time it lasted but one week, a circumstance from which he derived a certain comfort. A few weeks later, during the last days of January 1890, he had a second seizure after another day in Arles, but this one again was very short and does not appear to have upset him too much. Although he had declared earlier that he would definitely leave the asylum should there be any more attacks, his resolve was evidently modified by the mildness of his last two

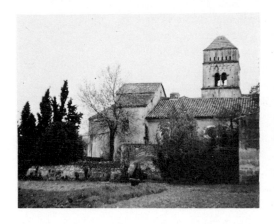

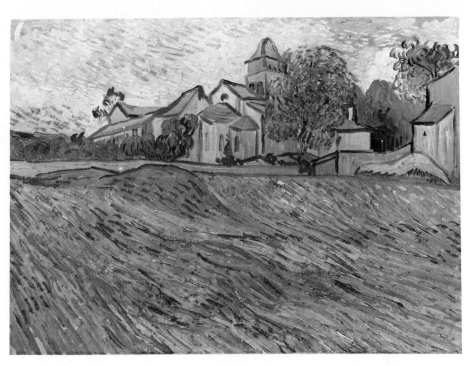

Above: Photograph of the Church of Saint-Paul at the Saint-Rémy asylum, as seen from the surrounding fields

Right: VAN GOGH: *The Church of Saint-Paul at the Saint-Rémy Asylum,* 1889. Private collection

fits. But in spite of his willingness to stay on a little longer at Saint-Rémy, where he planned to do yet another series of paintings, Vincent was slowly beginning to prepare for his eventual departure. After the first of his two slight attacks he had informed Theo: "I shall write a short note to Gauguin and de Haan to find out whether they intend to stay in Brittany, whether they would like me to send my furniture [from Arles] there, and also whether they would like me to come too. I shall not make any pledges; all I shall say is that in all probability I shall not remain here."[66]

Van Gogh's note reached Gauguin at a time when the latter was greatly depressed. "There are moments," Gauguin wrote in January 1890 to his friend Schuffenecker, "when I ask myself whether I should not do better to give up; you'll have to admit that there is plenty of reason for dropping everything. I have never been as discouraged as I am right now, and as a result I do very little work, asking myself: 'What is the good of it and to what end?' ...[Meyer de Haan] has begged me to leave Pont-Aven for Le Pouldu in order to instruct him in impressionism; as I do not have the credit he enjoys, he pays for my bed and board as a loan while I wait for Goupil [Theo van Gogh] to sell something. I have given up smoking, which is a painful sacrifice for me; I secretly do some of my own laundry; in fact, except for ordinary food I am deprived of everything. What is to be done? Nothing, except to wait like a rat on a barrel surrounded by water...."[67]

When Gauguin received van Gogh's letter, sounding him out about the possibility of his coming to Brittany, he was not exactly in a state of mind for further complications. His reply was therefore extremely guarded. "Thanks for your letter and for what you say about your *projects*," he wrote. "I have thought about them a great deal and I must admit that I believe it would be possible, very possible, for us to live together, but only with a great many precautions. Your ailing condition which is not yet completely cured calls for calm and a lot of forethought. You yourself say that when you go to Arles you are agitated by memories. Don't you fear that I too may be a similar reminder? In any event it does not seem wise to me to settle in a town where you would find yourself isolated and consequently would lack immediate care in case of a recurrence. Therefore I have been looking for an appropriate place. Meyer de Haan (who is a very sensible fellow) and I have discussed this and I think that *Antwerp* would be just the right spot, because life is just as cheap there as in some little hole in the provinces, because there are museums, which are not to be despised by painters, and finally because one can work there *in order to sell*. Why shouldn't we establish a studio [there] in my name? With some connections, with our names somewhat known [in Belgium] through the group of the XX, the thing should be possible. And however little one gains, one always takes a profitable step. In my opinion impressionism will not really become firmly established in France until it returns there from abroad. For it is outside of France that it finds the best reception, that it is debated; thus it is there that one should work...."[68]

For a short time Vincent seems to have toyed with this idea, yet he did not consider the project a very practical one and soon gave it up. In any event he did not discuss it with Theo.

It was possibly because Theo did not want to excite his brother unduly that he in turn does not seem to have mentioned in any of his letters the fact that Bernard had brought a young art critic to his apartment who had greatly admired Vincent's works. Indeed, prompted by Bernard, Aurier had decided to write an article on Vincent van Gogh and it appears unlikely that Theo knew nothing about this. But since Vincent had already asked their countryman, the painter Isaäcson, *not* to speak of his paintings in a series on the impressionists which Isaäcson had been doing for a Dutch paper (and in which he did mention van Gogh in a footnote), it may well have been that Theo preferred not to inform his brother of Aurier's project. Little as Theo himself liked the whole symbolist movement, of which Aurier, then twenty-five, was a promising member, Theo must have realized how important it would be to have his brother's work discussed in print at last, and he probably felt that it might be better if such an undertaking were not thwarted once more by Vincent's objections.

Ever since Albert Aurier had met Bernard at Saint-Briac early in the summer of 1888, he had kept in touch with him. When Bernard returned from Pont-Aven in the fall of that same year, Aurier reported from Paris to his mother: "I have seen Emile Bernard again, the impressionist painter from Saint-Briac. He made me visit a series of exhibitions and introduced me to Guillaumin...."[69] Of course Bernard acquainted his new friend with all the recent trends in art — Aurier soon shared Bernard's aversion for Seurat's pointillism — spoke at length about his own and Gauguin's endeavors and also gave him a detailed account of van Gogh's life and work, showing him the sketches and letters he had received from Arles. Aurier was fascinated by them and accompanied Bernard to *père* Tanguy's shop as well as to Theo's apartment, to see Vincent's paintings. When, in January 1889, Bernard learned from Gauguin about the tragic event in Arles, Aurier was the first to whom he unburdened his grief.[70] During the summer of 1889 Aurier obliged Bernard with some free publicity in symbolist periodicals for the Volpini exhibition and also published in *Le Moderniste*, of which he was editor-in-chief, some articles on the World's Fair written by Bernard and Gauguin. It was during the run of the Volpini show that Aurier met Gauguin

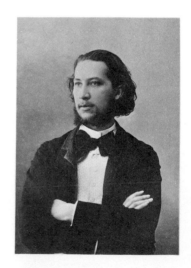

Photograph of G.-A. Aurier, c. 1890

for the first time. But though he was by then thoroughly conversant with their impression-ist-symbolist-synthesist art, Aurier had not yet written anything of consequence on this movement, in spite of its obvious link with symbolist literature. Bernard must have felt that the time had come to use Aurier's talent and renown to boost the efforts of his friends.

During the second part of the year 1889, Bernard sent Aurier some notes on Vincent van Gogh with the following letter: "Enclosed is a short article on my friend Vincent. Should you consider it worth publishing in *Le Moderniste*, please do so. As far as possible I am anxious that something should be said about my good friend, since he is truly an artist and some mention should be made of him in our time; not that his work is something absolutely complete, but on account of the surprising perceptions which he sometimes has. It seems to me that it would be well — if you share this opinion — to do this in such a way that you would complete this article yourself with a critical appraisal of his canvases which are at Tanguy's, expressing the hope that his brother will not hesitate some day to show his paintings either by organizing an exhibition, which should be easy, or by showing them at Goupil's. . . . I do not know whether you will agree with me on this. In any event, do as you like, but it might be interesting to review in this manner a certain number of young and old impressionists in a series of articles written by them about one another."[71]

The idea seems to have interested Aurier, though he decided that he himself would write a series on "isolated" artists. There is no question that the prospect of studying the work of Vincent van Gogh must have appealed to any symbolist author: to reveal to the public the art of a man utterly unknown who had attempted, with colors and forms, something akin to what the symbolists tried to do with word images and sound: to express moods (just as Seurat endeavored to convey these through the direction of lines). Had not Teodor de Wyzewa stated that before he "could like a work of art, it had to be really new, that is in keeping with the latest inventions; it had to be a little sickish"?[72] Here was a work that was altogether new by a man who was sick, passionate, inspired, who worked in an insane asylum, wrote soul-searching letters in a strange, awkward, and yet eloquent style, a man whose life and behavior had always been outside the ordinary, not because he wanted to be different, like so many of Aurier's symbolist friends, but because he really *was* different. Aurier no doubt remembered what Bernard had told him about van Gogh's early years:

"Moved by the most profound mysticism, reading the Bible and delivering sermons in all kinds of bawdy places to the most contemptible people, my dear friend had come to believe himself a Christ, a God. His life of suffering and of martyrdom seems to me such as to make of this astonishing intellect a being of the *beyond*. And this has indeed happened. A preacher at the age of twenty-five, he saw the need to reform protestant concepts . . . . Thwarted, rejected by the world, he began to live like a saint. Somewhat later he went into the mining district and, at la Sorcière, cared for a workman half burned by firedamp who showed on his forehead *traces of a crown of thorns*. Then his long walks through the Dutch fields and his heart-rending paintings of peasants. These are some of the aspects of his existence before his stay in Paris. And in Paris his extreme humanity for prostitutes, for I myself have been a witness to sublime scenes of devotion on his part. Finally his departure for Arles, Gauguin's precipitate return from there. . . and the news of Vincent being at the hospital. . . ."[73]

Yet Aurier chose not to insist on these biographical details and instead presented van Gogh as a symbolist painter. Indeed, his article, the first of the series he planned and the first ever to appear on the painter, was to be published in January 1890 in the first issue of the *Mercure de France*, a symbolist bimonthly, in the founding of which Aurier had taken an active part; it succeeded several short-lived periodicals, such as Aurier's own *Le Moderniste*, as well as *La Pléiade*. Aurier's article was entitled "Les Isolés, Vincent van Gogh." In it he described van Gogh's canvases in the precious, obscure, and verbose language affected by all the members of the symbolist movement. But besides its redundance of literary appreciations and poetic interpretations, Aurier's article also contained passages of penetrating evaluation.

"In the case of Vincent van Gogh," Aurier wrote, "despite the sometimes disconcerting strangeness of his work, it is difficult . . . to contest the naïve truthfulness of his art, the ingenuity of his concepts. Indeed, independently of that undefinable aroma of good faith and of things really seen which all his pictures exhale, his choice of subjects, the constant harmony of the most excessive colors, the honesty in the study of characters, the continuous search for the essential meaning of each object, a thousand significant details unquestionably proclaim his profound and almost childlike sincerity, his great love of nature and of truth — of his own truth. . . . What particularizes his entire work is the excess, excess in strength, excess in nervousness, in violence of expression. In his categorical affirmation of the character of things, in his frequently headstrong simplification of forms, in his insolence in depicting the sun face to face, in the vehement ardor of his drawing and of his color, and even in the slightest particularities of his technique, he reveals a powerful being, a male, a bold man, often brutal and sometimes ingenuously delicate. This can be seen in the almost orgiastic excesses of everything that he has painted; he is a fanatic, an enemy of bourgeois sobriety and of trifling details, a kind of drunken giant, better able to move mountains than to handle bibelots, an ebullient brain which irresistibly pours its lava into all the ravines of art, a terrible and highstrung genius, often sublime, sometimes grotesque, almost always on the edge of the pathological. Lastly and above all, he is a hyperesthete with obvious symptoms who perceives with abnormal and possibly even painful intensity the imperceptible and secret character of lines and forms, and even more of colors, of light, of the magic iridescence of shadows, of nuances which are invisible to healthy eyes. And that is why the realism of this neurotic, why his sincerity and his truth are so different. . . . He is no doubt very conscious of pigment, of its importance and beauty, but also, and most frequently, he considers this enchanting pigment only as a kind of marvelous language destined to express the Idea. Almost always he is a symbolist . . . feeling the constant urge to clothe his ideas in precise, ponderable, tangible forms, in intensely corporeal and material envelopes. Beneath this physical envelope, beneath this very carnal flesh, beneath this very material matter, there lies in practically all his canvases, for those who know how to find it, a thought, an Idea, and this Idea, the essential substratum of the work, is also at the same time its efficient and final cause. . . . Indeed, Vincent van Gogh is not only a great painter, enraptured with his art, with his palette and with nature, he is also a dreamer, a fanatical believer, a devourer of beautiful Utopias, who lives on ideas and illusions. For a long time he has taken delight in imagining a renovation of art made possible through a displacement of civilization: an art of tropical regions. . . . [74]

"As a consequence of his conviction that there was a need to start everything all over in art, he had and for a long time cherished the idea of inventing an art of painting that was very simple, popular, almost childlike, capable of touching the humble people who do not care for subtlety, and of being understood even by the most naïve among the feeble-minded.... Are all these theories, are all these hopes of Vincent van Gogh really practical? Are they not merely vain and beautiful chimeras? Who knows?..."

Aurier then proceeded to study van Gogh's technique: "The external and material side of his painting is absolutely in correlation with his artistic temperament. In all his works the execution is vigorous, exalted, brutal, intense. His nervous, powerful, often awkward and somewhat heavy draftsmanship exaggerates the character, simplifies, and like a master and conqueror, it ignores details, achieves a bold synthesis and sometimes, but not always, a great style. His color... is unbelievably dazzling. He is, as far as I know, the only painter who perceives the coloration of things with such intensity, with such a metallic, gem-like quality....

"This robust and true artist, with the brutal hands of a giant, with the nerves of a hysterical woman, with the soul of a mystic, so original and so alone in the midst of the pitiful art of our time, will he experience some day — anything is possible — the joy of rehabilitation, the repentant cajoleries of fashion? Possibly. But whatever happens, and even if it should become fashionable, as is very unlikely, to pay for his canvases the prices commanded by the dwarfish infamies of M. Meissonier, I do not think that much real sincerity will ever enter into the belated admiration of the public at large. Vincent van Gogh is both too simple and too subtle for the contemporary *esprit bourgeois*. He will never be fully understood except by his brothers, the true artists, and the happy ones among the little people, the very little people...."[75]

Vincent van Gogh received this article late in January 1890, together with the good news that Theo had become the father of a boy who was to be named Vincent, after his uncle. The painter read Aurier's words with mixed feelings. "I was very much surprised," he wrote to his mother, "by the article that has been written about me. Isaäcson once wanted to write one about me, but I asked him not to. I was saddened when I read this article because it is so exaggerated; the truth is quite different. What encourages me in my work is precisely the feeling that there are others who are doing exactly what I do. Then why an article about me and not about those six or seven others? Yet I must admit that once my surprise had calmed down I began to feel quite elated by this publication."[76] In a letter to his sister Wil he expressed the same feeling: "When I read the article, it made me almost sad just to think: this is how I should be and I feel myself to be so inferior. Pride can make you tipsy like drink. When one is praised or when one drinks, one becomes sad; well, I don't know how to express this, but I feel it and it seems to me that the best work would be that which would be done together in a group, without applause."[77] And to Theo he repeated that he felt Aurier's article had shown how he *should* paint. Eventually he sat down to write a long reply to Aurier himself, whom he had never met:

"Dear Monsieur Aurier: Many thanks for your article in the *Mercure de France*, which surprised me greatly. I like it very much as a work of art in itself; it seems to me that you create colors with your words. I rediscover my canvases in your article, but much better than they really are, much richer and more significant. However, I feel ill at ease when I think that what you say applies to others much more than to myself. For example mainly to Monticelli. You write: 'He is, as far as I know, the only painter who perceives the coloration of things with such intensity, with such a metallic, gem-like quality.' If it would please you to go and see at my brother's one of Monticelli's bouquets of flowers, a bouquet in white, forget-me-not blue, and orange, then you would feel what I mean.... I do not know of any colorist who derives so straightforwardly and directly from Delacroix.... This is only to say that you have credited me with things that it would have been better for you to say about Monticelli, to whom I owe a great deal. I also owe a great deal to Paul Gauguin, with whom I worked for several months at Arles and whom, besides, I already knew in Paris. Gauguin, this strange artist, this alien whose bearing and gaze remind one vaguely of the *Portrait of a Man* by Rembrandt in the Lacaze Collection [in the Louvre], this friend who likes to make you feel that a good picture should be the equivalent of a good deed, not that he says this, yet it is difficult to associate with him without perceiving a certain moral responsibility. A few days before we separated, when illness forced me to enter a hospital, I tried to paint his 'empty place.' It is a study of his armchair in dark, brown-red wood, the seat of greenish straw and, at the place of the absent [Gauguin], a lighted candle and some modern novels [reproduced page 240]. I beg you, if the occasion presents itself, to look a little at this study again, which is completely done in broken tones of green and red. You may possibly realize then that your article would have been more correct and consequently, it seems to me, more powerful if, in treating the question of the future of 'art in the tropics' as well as the question of color, you had, before speaking of me, done justice to Gauguin and to Monticelli. *For the share that is mine or that will be mine, will always, I assure you, remain a very secondary one.*

"And then I should also like to ask you something else. Let us say that the two canvases of *sunflowers* which are presently exhibited with the XX have certain qualities of color, and also that they express an idea symbolizing 'gratitude.' Is that so different from all the other paintings of flowers [by other artists], painted with greater skill and which are not yet sufficiently appreciated... ? You see, it seems to me so difficult to make a distinction between impressionism and other things; I do not see the necessity for so much sectarian spirit as we have seen in these last years; *in fact I fear its absurdity.* And, in closing, I must declare that I do not understand how *you* can speak of Meissonier's 'infamies.' ...I have inherited a boundless admiration for Meissonier....

"In the next shipment that I shall send to my brother, I shall include a study of cypresses for you, if you will give me the pleasure of accepting it as a souvenir of your article. I am still working on it at this moment, wanting to put a figure into it. The cypress is characteristic of the Provençal landscape, and you sensed that when you said: 'even the black color.' Until now I have not been able to paint it as I feel it; the emotions which seize me when I am confronted with nature sometimes produce fainting spells, and then the result is a fortnight during which I am incapable of working. Nevertheless, before leaving here, I count on going back again to this subject and challenging the cypresses.... In the meantime I beg you to accept the expression of my gratitude for your article. If I go to Paris in the spring, I shall certainly not fail to come and thank you in person."[78]

Vincent sent a copy of this reply to Gauguin. In a letter to his brother, written at the same time, he considered Aurier's article more from a practical side. After having stated that "a painter should work really just as a cobbler," he conceded that Aurier's publication "renders us indeed a great service for the day when we shall be obliged, like everybody else, to try to recover what the pictures cost. Beyond that it leaves me fairly cold, but in order to continue painting it is essential that the cost of producing pictures shall be repaid."[79] Apparently the painter was reluctant to discuss at greater length Aurier's endeavors to make him appear as a symbolist, endeavors of which he had tactfully disposed in his reply to Aurier by taking a stand against any sectarianism. Undoubtedly most of the subtleties and refinements of the literary symbolists were lost on him; their squabbles and their

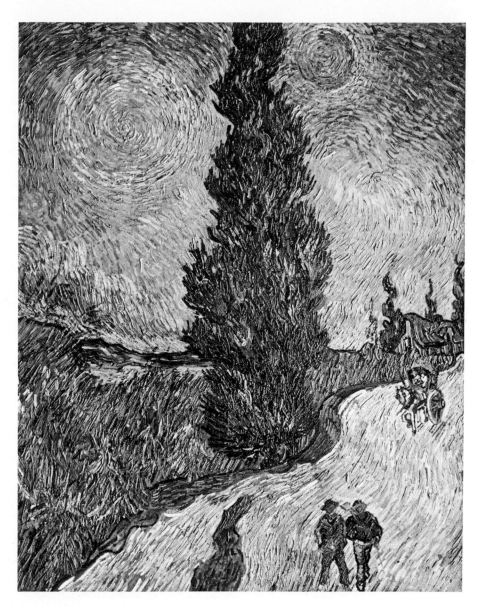

van Gogh: *Road with Cypresses,* Saint-Rémy, Feb. 1890. 36¾ x 29". Presented by the artist to Aurier. Exhibited in March 1890 with the Independents, where Gauguin commented very favorably on it. Rijksmuseum Kröller-Müller, Otterlo

efforts to obtain attention actually seemed ridiculous to van Gogh. Without wasting any more words on this subject, Vincent simply confided to Theo: "Aurier's article might have encouraged me, if I dared to let myself go, to venture farther away from reality and to make with colors something like a music of tones, such as are some of Monticelli's canvases. But truth is so dear to me, and the *search for being truthful* too. Well, I think I still prefer being a cobbler to being a musician who works with colors."[79]

Vincent van Gogh's mild objections and his sincere humility notwithstanding, Aurier's article created quite a stir (excerpts from it were published in the January 19, 1890, issue of *L'Art Moderne,* Belgian organ of the XX group), and that in spite of the fact that very few of his readers could have been familiar with the painter's works. He had not even indicated where they might be seen. Yet Aurier's friend Rémy de Gourmont stated a short while later that this first study of a series on living artists "met with an unexpected success. It was excellent, by the way, said the truth without regard for [generally accepted] opinions and praised the painter of the sun and of sunflowers without those puerile flatteries which are the vice of enthusiasm.... Aurier's art criticisms were greatly appreciated; one felt the strength of his originality. They had real authority in the circle in which impressionist-symbolist painting is known and admired, a new and small yet strong circle...."[80] Aurier was soon invited, as a result of his article on van Gogh, to write art reviews for the *Revue Indépendante*, then still much more influential than the newly founded *Mercure de France*.[81]

Aurier's article was but one of the elements which made the weeks of January and February 1890 exciting ones for Vincent van Gogh. There was also the opening of the exhibition of the XX, the birth of his nephew and namesake, the forthcoming new show of the Independents, scheduled for March, in which he planned to participate, and finally the news that for the first time one of his canvases, the *Red Vineyard*, had been sold in Brussels. On February 15 he informed his mother: "Theo wrote me yesterday that one of my paintings had been sold for 400 francs in Brussels. This is little in comparison with the prices of other pictures and with what is now being paid in Holland, but I am trying to be productive enough to be able to continue working at reasonable prices."[76]

The purchaser of van Gogh's painting was a painter, Anna Boch, for Aurier had been right: for the time being only artists seem to have appreciated his work. In a review which appeared in *La Wallonie*, the Belgian mouthpiece of the symbolist movement, a critic actually wrote: "We do not share the enthusiasm which the art of M. Vincent van Gogh evokes in some profound and sincere artists. His *Sunflowers*, which are very strong in color and beautiful in design, are above all decorative and pleasant to behold; in his *Red Vineyard* the use of vivid, specially arranged colors produces certain metallic effects, a very curious light, which are interesting. The virtues of his other canvases escape us completely."[82] Signac, in an article published anonymously (which allowed him to speak at some length of his own works), discussed the paintings by Cézanne and Redon, spoke of his friends Dubois-Pillet and Hayet, but found very little to say about Lautrec and even less about van Gogh, to whose canvases he devoted one short and cryptic sentence: "The tomb of yellow, of chrome and of Veronese green: *Sunflowers, Ivy, Red Vineyard*."[83]

It is not certain whether Vincent ever read these lines, since Theo may have preferred not to mail them to him. In one of his letters Theo merely told him that he had gathered from a newspaper that the works which most struck the Belgian visitors to the exhibition were the outdoor studies by Cézanne, the landscapes by Sisley, the color symphonies by van Gogh, and the paintings by Renoir.[84] On the other hand Vincent probably received no echo of the disturbances which his shipment had unleashed among the members of the XX. On January 16, two days before the opening, Henry de Groux, a realist-religious painter whom van Gogh had once greatly admired, declared that he was withdrawing his own works since he did not want them to be shown in the same room with the "abominable *Pot of Sunflowers* by Monsieur Vincent or any other *agent provocateur*."[85] Two days later, however, de Groux participated in the banquet which officially celebrated the opening of the show. Among the guests were Toulouse-Lautrec and Signac, who had come from Paris especially for the occasion. During this dinner de Groux once more loudly railed against van Gogh and, according to Octave Maus' recollections, called him "an ignoramus and a

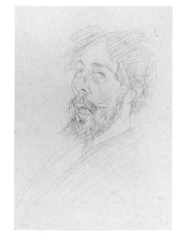

ENSOR: *Self-Portrait,* d. 1887. Pencil, 8½ x 6⅛". Collection Sam Salz, New York

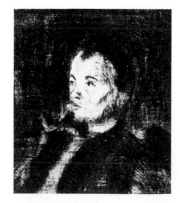

C. PISSARRO: *Portrait of Paul Signac* (detail), c. 1890. Etching, 9 x 8¼"

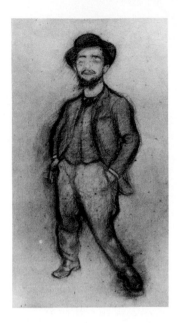

charlatan. At the other end of the table Lautrec suddenly bounced up, with his arms in the air, and shouted that it was an outrage to criticize so great an artist. De Groux retorted. Tumult. Seconds were appointed. Signac announced coldly that if Lautrec were killed he would assume the quarrel himself."[86]

This incident was not without its comical side since de Groux, sickly, with a complexion like clay, was no taller than Lautrec, dwarfed by his short legs. The other members of the XX immediately expelled de Groux from their association, and the next day Maus obtained, not without trouble, an apology from de Groux, through which the duel was averted; at the same time de Groux was permitted to resign from the group. Two new members were subsequently elected by the XX. One of them was Signac.

After the close of the show Octave Maus wrote to Theo: "When the occasion presents itself, please tell your brother that I was very happy about his participation in the exhibition of the XX, where strong artistic sympathy for him was manifested in the heat of animated discussions."[87] But this comforting news reached the painter only after considerable delay.

The events of the last weeks had been too much, after all. As van Gogh later explained to his mother: "When I learned that my work was being recognized in an article, I immediately feared that this might completely unnerve me. It is almost always like that in an artist's life that success is one of the worst things."[88] On February 24, Dr. Peyron informed Theo that Vincent had had another attack after spending two days in Arles, where he apparently had been permitted to go unaccompanied. He had been brought back to Saint-Rémy in a carriage and it was not known where he had spent the night. A painting of the *Arlésienne*, which he had taken along with him—probably as a gift to the model, Mme Ginoux—had disappeared. A few days later the doctor wrote again, saying that the attack was lasting longer this time and that it definitely proved that these trips to Arles were bad for the painter.

Those were dark days again of complete blackout, anguish, and terror, of hallucinations and fear, of torpor or agitation, of silence or rage. And the endless nights were worse. Nothing but delirium, despair, resignation, suffering. This time the crisis lasted longer than ever before. At his wits' end, Dr. Peyron apparently decided to let the patient have it his own way and even allowed him to paint. "Just when I felt worst," Vincent later remembered, "I did do some paintings, among them a souvenir of Brabant, cottages with moss covered roofs and beech hedges on a stormy autumn evening with a red sun setting in a pink sky. Also a field of beets with women picking the green sprouts in the snow [page 348]."[88]

It seems that van Gogh tried to swallow some of his poisonous paints during his work, whether in a conscious attempt at suicide or merely as an irrational act it is hard to say; but it is likely that this was merely an uncontrolled urge, like his attempt to drink turpentine when Signac visited him at Arles. After that his colors had to be taken away and he was again left in demoralizing seclusion and idleness. Towards the end he felt no pain, but his head was completely numb and he was absolutely exhausted. It took almost two months before he was able to write again to his brother. He did so without trying to analyze the reasons for his latest fit, without connecting it with his trip to Arles (about which he remained silent),[89] without even insisting on how depressed he was by the severity of his new seizure which shattered all the hopes created by the shortness of his previous attacks. All he would say was: "And now I almost give up hope altogether. Maybe, maybe I shall indeed be cured if I live in the country [in the North] for a while."[90]

This time the chips were down. Dr. Peyron's usual and vague consolations: "Let's hope

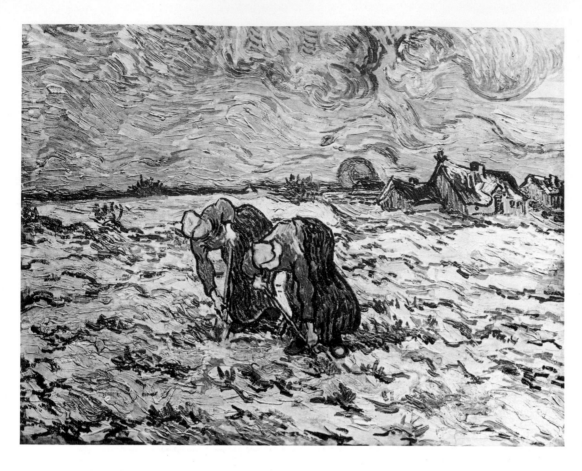

van Gogh: *Women Picking Green Sprouts in the Snow*, Saint-Rémy, March–April 1890. 19¾ x 25⅛″. Present whereabouts unknown

that this will not occur again" and similar ready-made phrases were powerless before Vincent's determination to leave the asylum. He even had a violent argument with the doctor, but they made up somewhat later.

After his recovery, towards the middle of April, Dr. Peyron handed van Gogh a batch of letters that had arrived during his illness, letters from his mother, his sister, from Gauguin, Aurier, Russell, probably also from Pissarro, and of course from Theo. But at first he was too downcast and weak even to read his mail. As soon as he felt well enough, he wrote to his brother: "Please ask M. Aurier not to write any more articles about my paintings; do insist on the fact that, above all, he is mistaken on my account and that I am really much too shaken by mortification to be able to face any publicity. To paint pictures cheers me up, but if I hear talk about them, it hurts me more than he can possibly know."[91]

On the whole the news he received from Paris was excellent and encouraging. Theo's baby was doing well, and so was the child's mother, in spite of complications that had been expected. Theo reported at length on the new exhibition of the Independents, which opened on March 19 on the Champs-Elysées and where Vincent was represented by ten paintings done in Arles and Saint-Rémy, among them: *Cypresses* (the picture promised to Aurier), *Boulevard at Saint-Rémy, Alpine Foothills, Sunflowers,* and *Olive Grove.* Those whose interest had been aroused by Aurier's article could now see at last a representative display of van

348

Gogh's work. After attending the opening accompanied by his wife, Theo wrote that the President of the Republic had been present (by now the Independents had become "respectable") and added: "Your pictures are very well hung and make a good effect. Many people have come to ask me to convey their compliments to you. Gauguin said that your paintings are the high point of the show.... Seurat is exhibiting a really curious picture [*Le Chahut*] in which he endeavors to express things through the direction of lines. He certainly does express movement, but his canvas has a rather strange aspect and does not seem to reflect a very generous idea. Guillaumin shows several things among which are some good ones; by Lautrec there is an excellent *Portrait of a Woman at the Piano* [page 375]

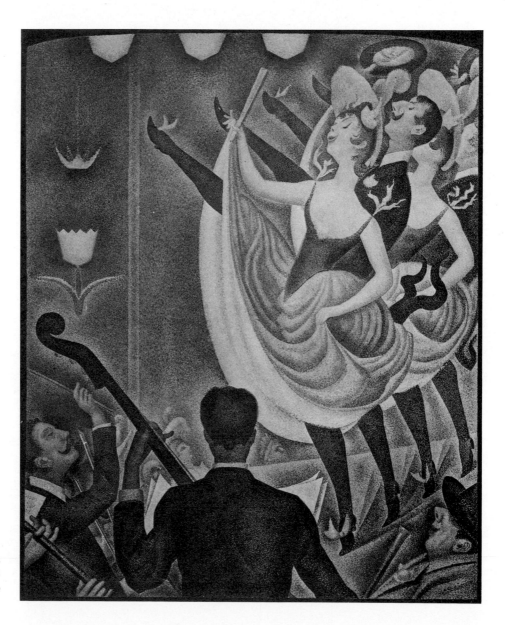

SEURAT: *Le Chahut,* 1889–90. 67 × 55½".
Exhibited with the Independents in 1890. Rijksmuseum Kröller-Müller, Otterlo

and a large painting [a Moulin-Rouge scene] which holds up very well. Despite its unsavory subject it has real distinction. In general it is to be noticed that the public shows an ever increasing interest in the young impressionists; there are at least a certain number of collectors who begin to buy them. Pissarro's exhibition [at Goupil's] is closed. A great many people came to see it and five paintings were sold. For the moment that was all we counted on. Next Sunday Bernard and Aurier are coming to see your latest pictures."[92] Theo also wrote that Aurier intended to study the paintings by Gauguin on whom he expected to write an article. In subsequent letters Theo continued his reports on the exhibition: "I have not yet been back to the Independents, but Pissarro who goes there every day tells me that you have a real success among the artists. There are also some collectors who spoke to me about you even before I could draw their attention to your canvases there. The newspapers which publish reviews of the exhibition are silent on the subject of the room with the impressionists. That is the best thing they could do, for you know well what most of those write-ups are worth."[93]

Vincent van Gogh was not the only one to have ten paintings at the Independents; Seurat, Signac, Luce, and Guillaumin had the same number; the *douanier* Rousseau had nine works, Dubois-Pillet eight, Théo van Rysselberghe seven. Anquetin, Cross, Lucien Pissarro, van de Velde, and Lautrec were represented by fewer works. But even Monet agreed that van Gogh's contribution was the best in the show.[94] Gauguin expressed his opinion in a particularly friendly letter to Vincent. He had come to Paris in February when de Haan was no longer able to provide for him and had been looking for a job, but without success, while Theo did his best so sell some of his canvases, sculptures, and ceramics. He now planned to go back to Brittany for another two months with de Haan at Le Pouldu.

"I have studied with great attention the work you have done since we parted," Gauguin wrote, "first at your brother's and then at the show of the Independents.—It is particularly at this last place that one can well judge what you are doing, partly because your pictures are hung together, partly because they are surrounded by other things. I want to pay you my sincere compliments. To many artists you are the most remarkable one in the whole exhibition. Among those who work from nature, you are the *only one who thinks*. I have talked about it with your brother and there is one canvas that I should like to *exchange with you for anything of mine you choose*. The one I mean is a mountainous landscape; two very small travelers seem to be climbing in search of the unknown. There is in it an emotion like in Delacroix, with very suggestive colors. Here and there some red notes, like lights, and the whole in a violet harmony. It's beautiful and impressive. I've talked at length about it with Aurier, Bernard, and many others. All congratulate you. Only Guillaumin shrugs his shoulders when he hears it mentioned. I do understand him, by the way, since all he sees is pigment with an eye devoid of thought. Towards my own canvases of these last years he reacts the same way; he understands nothing.

"I have hesitated a good deal to write to you, knowing that you have just had a rather lengthy attack. Therefore I am asking you not to reply until you feel completely fit again. Let's hope that with the warm weather which will soon be back you will at last be cured; winter has always been dangerous for you."[95]

Winter may indeed have been a bad season for van Gogh, but spring was a time when he always felt stimulated. It had been almost spring when he had joined Theo in Paris and had

Opposite: VAN GOGH: *White Roses,* Saint-Rémy, May 1890. 36⅝ x 28¾". Formerly collection Mrs. Albert D. Lasker, New York

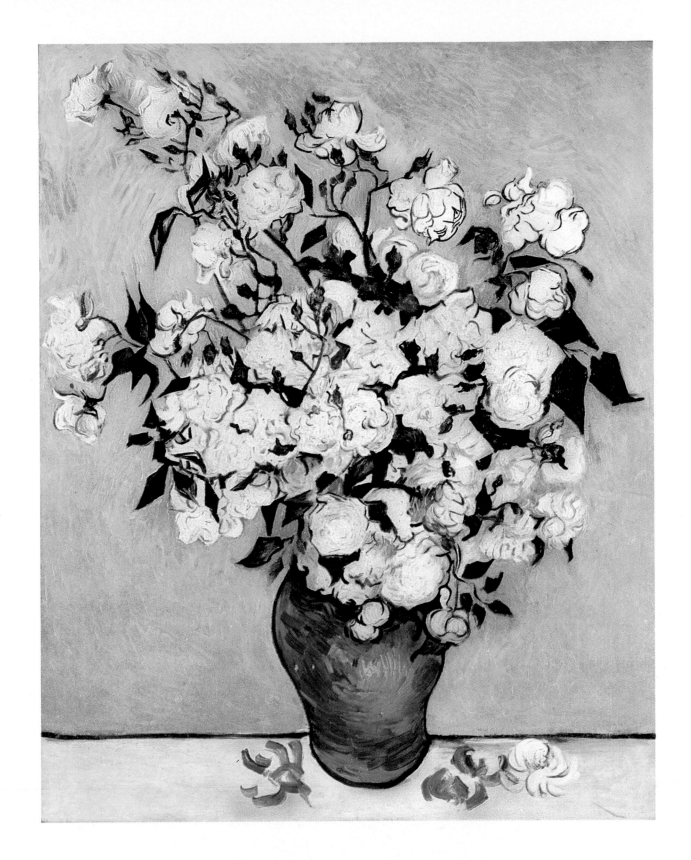

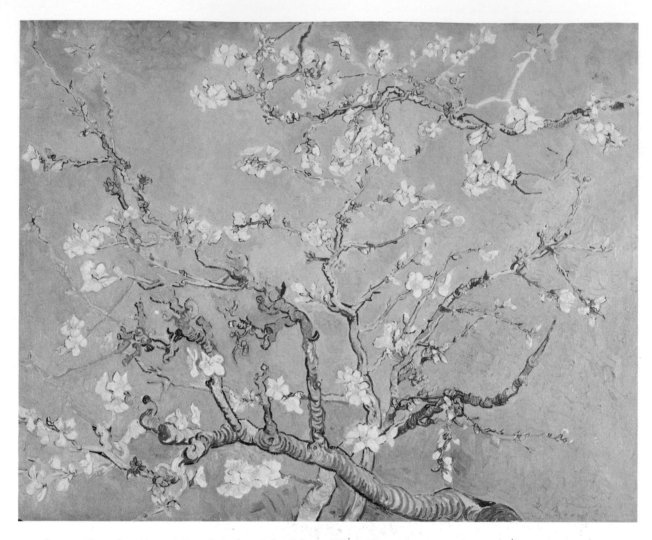

VAN GOGH: *Flowering Almond Tree Branches,* Saint-Rémy, Feb. 1890. Painted for Theo's infant son just before the artist's last attack at Saint-Rémy. Rijksmuseum Vincent van Gogh, Amsterdam

submerged himself in the exciting life of the city; it had been early spring when he first came to Arles and threw himself into his work; it had been spring when he left the hospital before coming to Saint-Rémy; and it had been spring just before his latest attack started. Work had been progressing well. His last canvas had been one of flowering branches of an almond tree against a blue sky, a canvas destined for his infant namesake. "It was possibly," he wrote to Theo, "what I have done with greatest patience and care, painted with calm and growing sureness."[90] And then his illness had cut short his work. Spring was practically gone now and the painter was unhappy to have missed it. The early southern summer was approaching; his eagerness for work was possibly increased by the knowledge that soon he would be gone. He sent Theo a substantial request for colors to be ordered from *père* Tanguy and others. Roses and irises were in bud; soon they would be in full bloom.

In May he was permitted to work again in the asylum's garden. "As soon as I went out in the park a little," he told his brother, "I recovered all my lucidity for work. I have more ideas in my head than I could ever carry out, but without being dazzled by them. The brush strokes come mechanically. I take this as a sign for daring to hope that in the North I shall get my equilibrium back, once I am delivered from this entourage and from circumstances which I don't understand or even care to understand.... The surroundings here begin to weigh on me more than I can say; well, I've been patient for more than a year, now I need air, for I feel crushed by boredom and sorrow." [96]

Theo agreed to Vincent's departure. He had met Dr. Gachet in the meantime and now wrote to him concerning Vincent: "You gave me hope that in your care he may possibly regain his normal condition. He is very well for the moment and writes me very reasonable letters. He ardently wishes to come to Paris for a few days and then to go and work in the

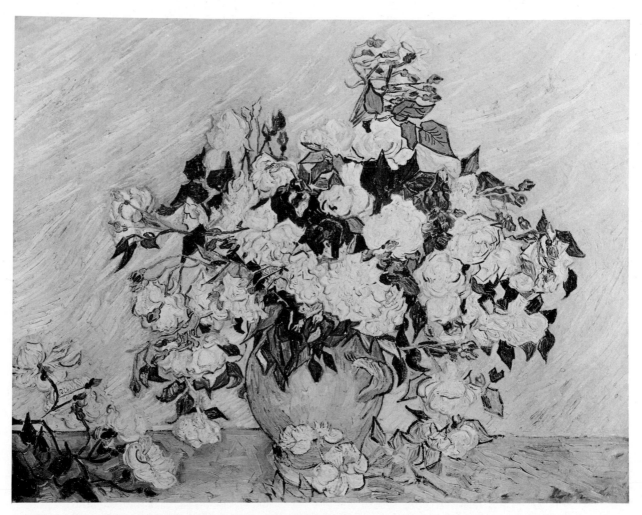

VAN GOGH: *Roses*, May 1890. 28¾ x 36". Collection The Honorable and Mrs. W. Averell Harriman, New York

country, though [he is] willing, should you feel that he would be better off in the care of an institution, to return to Saint-Rémy or to go to some other place. . . . Would it be wise to have him accompanied by somebody during the trip? He himself strenuously objects to being accompanied and begs me to let him travel alone. I should very much like to have your opinion on this."[97]

For Vincent's benefit, Theo traced a portrait of the physician: "He looks like a man who understands things well. Physically he resembles you somewhat. When you arrive here we shall go to see him; he holds consultations in Paris several times a week. When I told him how your attacks come about, he said he did not think this had anything to do with madness and that if your illness was what he thought it to be, he was convinced that he could cure you; but first he had to see you and to talk with you, so as to be able to decide with more certainty. He is a man who can be helpful to us once you get here."[93]

Letters went back and forth between Paris and Saint-Rémy on how Vincent was to make the journey. Replying to his brother's apprehensive letters, the painter pointed out that heavy attacks like the one he had suffered recently were always followed by three to four months of calm and that there was no danger of any recurrence in the near future. "I have done no harm to anybody; is it right to have me accompanied like a dangerous beast? Thanks, I protest. If a seizure occurs, in all the railroad stations people know what to do and I shall submit to them."[98] Vincent would consent only to be accompanied to nearby Tarascon, where he would board the train to Paris, alone. So as not to upset him, Theo gave in, although he shuddered at the idea of what really might happen should Vincent actually get sick and fall into the hands of strangers. It was agreed that from Tarascon Vincent would wire him to announce the time of his arrival.

And now he was about to prepare his trunk. But meanwhile the paints had arrived and the roses and irises were blooming. Vincent, who had not done any still lifes in Saint-Rémy, could not resist the temptation. "At present the amelioration continues," he wrote in May. "That horrible attack has disappeared like a storm and I work with calm and steady ardor to do a few last things here. I am working on a canvas of roses against a light green background and on two canvases of large bouquets of purple irises, one of them against a pink background, in which the effect is harmonious and soft through the combination of greens, roses and violets. The other purple bouquet (going all the way to carmine and pure Prussian blue) is quite the opposite. Standing out against a brilliant lemon yellow background, with other yellow tones in the vase and the base on which it stands, it is an effect of terribly disparate complementaries which enhance each other by their opposition. . . . The day of my departure depends on when I shall have packed my trunk and when I shall have finished my canvases. On these last I am working with such high spirits that to do my luggage seems more difficult than to do pictures. In any case it won't be long. I am very happy that this [departure] has not been delayed, for that is always unfortunate once one has made a decision."[99]

Theo had sent the money for the fare. He had signed the papers for his brother's release and Dr. Peyron had given his consent. But two days before leaving Vincent still reported: "I have just finished yet another canvas of pink roses in a green vase against a yellow-green background."[100] Was it the approach of his departure that inspired him? Was it the hope of being cured in the North? Was it the anticipation of seeing Theo again, his wife and baby? Was it the joy of relief after his recent troubles? The fact is that these last paintings of flowers are among the happiest van Gogh ever painted. Their colors are subtle even where

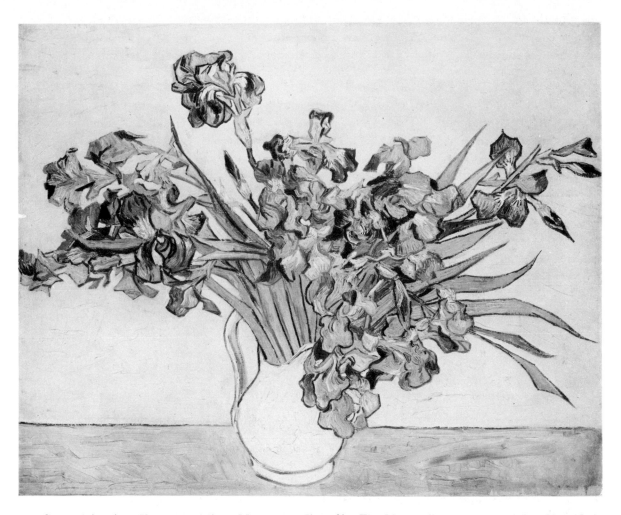

VAN GOGH: *Irises in a Vase,* Saint-Rémy, May 1890 28⅞ x 36¾″. The Metropolitan Museum of Art, New York (Gift of Mrs. David M. Levy, 1958)

they are contrasting, their execution is swift, flowing, without hesitancy and torment, their arrangements are masterly. There is nothing tortured or wild about them, nothing that reveals the urgency of creation so often apparent in his landscapes. They seem relaxed and full of joy, soft and yet of tremendous power, these large bunches of roses and irises monumentally set against uniform backgrounds, from which their blossoms, their leaves, their stems detach themselves in harmonious and graceful arabesques. Only a few months before Vincent had told his sister Wil that he felt like "asking to be pardoned for the fact that my paintings are almost like a cry of anguish."[101] But all anguish has disappeared from these radiant still lifes; if they are symbols of gratitude, as van Gogh liked to say, they are also hymns to the ever renewed splendors of nature.

These were the last paintings Vincent did in Saint-Rémy. On May 14 he went to ship his trunk to Paris. On this errand he saw the countryside again, fresh after a rain and with blooms everywhere. How many things he could still have painted! But now it was too late. "In my work," he wrote to Theo, "I feel greater assurance than when I left [Paris] and it would be ungrateful of me to speak ill of the *midi*. I must admit that it is with great sadness that I am leaving." [99]

On May 16, 1890, Vincent van Gogh left the asylum of Saint-Rémy, almost a year to the day after he had entered it. In the register of the voluntarily interned, Dr. Peyron noted the date of departure accompanied by the following remarks: "The patient, though calm most of the time, has had several attacks during his stay in the establishment which lasted from two weeks to one month. During these attacks the patient was subjected to frightful terrors and tried several times to poison himself, either by swallowing the paints which he used for his work or by drinking kerosene which he managed to steal from the attendant while the latter refilled his lamps. His last fit broke out after a trip which he undertook to Arles, and lasted about two months. Between his attacks the patient was perfectly quiet and devoted himself with ardor to his painting. Today he is asking for his release to live in the North of France, hoping that its climate will be favorable." [102]

In the column for special observations Dr. Peyron put but one word: *Cured*.

NOTES

1 V. van Gogh to his brother, [Arles, Jan. 17, 1889]; Verzamelde Brieven, vol. III, no. 571, pp. 373–75.

2 V. van Gogh to his brother, [Arles, Jan. 23, 1889]; *ibid.*, no. 573, p. 380.

3 V. van Gogh to his brother, [Arles, Jan. 28, 1889]; *ibid.*, no. 574, p. 384.

4 V. van Gogh to his brother, [Arles, Jan. 19, 1889]; *ibid.*, no. 572, p. 378.

5 V. van Gogh to his brother, [Arles, Feb. 1889]; *ibid.*, no. 577, pp. 388–89.

6 V. van Gogh to his brother, [Saint-Rémy], May 25, [1889]; *ibid.*, no. 592, p. 422. See also A. Tellegen: Vincent and Gauguin, *Museumjournaal*, no. 1–2, 1966, p. 51, on Vincent's *Sunflowers* exchange with Gauguin.

7 See V. van Gogh's letter to his brother, [Arles, Feb. 3, 1889]; *ibid.*, no. 576, pp. 387–88.

8 For the petition and the police commissioner's investigation and report, see M. E. Tralbaut: L'Heure de vérité, *Van Goghiana X*, Antwerp, 1975, pp. 10 and 13–15.

9 V. van Gogh to his brother, [Saint-Rémy, Sept. 10, 1889]; Verzamelde Brieven, vol. III, no. 605, p. 456.

10 Pastor Salles to Theo van Gogh, [Arles, March 18, 1889]; see Verzamelde Brieven, vol. I, Introduction, pp. XLIII to XLIV.

11 V. van Gogh to his brother, [Arles, March 24, 1889]; Verzamelde Brieven, vol. III, no. 581, p. 396.

12 Signac to Coquiot; see G. Coquiot: Vincent van Gogh, Paris, 1924, p. 194.

13 Signac to Theo van Gogh, [Arles, end of March 1889]; Verzamelde Brieven, vol. III, no. 581a, p. 397.

14 See V. van Gogh's letter to his sister Wil, [Saint-Rémy, Oct. 1889]; Verzamelde Brieven, vol. IV, no. W15, pp. 174–75.

15 V. van Gogh to his sister Wil, [Arles, April 30, 1889]; *ibid.*, no. W 11, pp. 166–67.

16 Pastor Salles to Theo van Gogh, [Arles, April 19, 1889]; Verzamelde Brieven, vol. I, Introduction, p. XLIV.

17 V. van Gogh to his brother, [Arles, April 21, 1889]; Verzamelde Brieven, vol. III, no. 585, pp. 405–07.

18 Theo van Gogh to his wife, [Paris, April 1889]; Verzamelde Brieven, vol. I, Introduction, pp. XLIV–XLV.

19 V. van Gogh to his brother, [Arles, April 29, 1889]; Verzamelde Brieven, vol. III, no. 587, p. 409.

20 V. van Gogh to his sister-in-law, Johanna van Gogh-Bonger, [Saint-Rémy, May 9, 1889]; *ibid.*, no. 591, p. 420.

21 Theo van Gogh to his brother, [Paris, April–May 1889]; Verzamelde Brieven, vol. IV, no. T 7, p. 264.

22 V. van Gogh to his brother, [Arles, April 30, 1889]; Verzamelde Brieven, vol. III, no. 588, p. 411.

23 V. van Gogh to his brother, [Arles, end of April 1889]; *ibid.*, no. 586, p. 408.

24 Theo van Gogh to Dr. Peyron, Paris, 8, cité Pigalle, April 24, 1889; unpublished document, courtesy the Superior of Saint-Paul du Mausolée, Saint-Rémy de Provence. The price for a first class patient was 200 francs a month, for a second class 150, for a third class 100 francs. Theo van Gogh's request that his brother be given "a half liter of wine with his meals" was not granted at first.

25 Pastor Salles to Theo van Gogh, [Arles, May 9, 1889]; Verzamelde Brieven, vol. I, Introduction, p. XLV.

26 Information courtesy the late Dr. E. Leroy, Saint-Paul du Mausolée, Saint-Rémy de Provence.

27 Observations of Dr. Peyron, [Saint-Rémy, May 9, 1889]; see V. Doiteau and E. Leroy: La Folie de van Gogh, Paris, 1928, p. 55.

28 On Vincent van Gogh's illness see the various medical publications listed in the Bibliography (the latest studies appeared in *Van Goghiana V*, Antwerp, 1968).

29 See Doiteau and Leroy, *op. cit.*, pp. 125 and 128.

30 V. van Gogh to his brother, [Saint-Rémy, Sept. 10, 1889]; Verzamelde Brieven, vol. III, no. 605, p. 459.

31 V. van Gogh to his brother and his sister-in-law, [Saint-Rémy, May 9, 1889]; *ibid.*, no. 591, pp. 420–21.

32 V. van Gogh to his brother, [Saint-Rémy, May 25, 1889]; *ibid.*, no. 592, pp. 422–25. (The sequence of certain paragraphs has been altered in this quotation.)

33 See V. van Gogh's letter to his brother, [Saint-Rémy, Sept. 10, 1889]; *ibid.*, no. 605, pp. 459–60.

34 V. van Gogh to his brother, [Saint-Rémy, June 9, 1889]; *ibid.*, no. 594, p. 430.

35 V. van Gogh to his brother, [Saint-Rémy, June 19, 1889]; *ibid.*, no. 595, p. 433.

36 V. van Gogh to his sister Wil, [Saint-Rémy, beginning of July 1889]; Verzamelde Brieven, vol. IV, no. W 13, p. 169.

37 See V. van Gogh's letter to his brother, [Saint-Rémy, June 25, 1889]; Verzamelde Brieven, vol. III, no. 596, p. 433.

38 V. van Gogh to his brother, [Saint-Rémy, June 25, 1889]; *ibid.*, no. 596, p. 434.

39 V. van Gogh to his brother, [Saint-Rémy, June 19, 1889]; *ibid.*, no. 595, p. 432.

40 Theo van Gogh to his brother, [Paris], June 16, 1889; Verzamelde Brieven, vol. IV, no. T 10, p. 267.

41 Theo van Gogh to his brother, [Paris], July 16, 1889; *ibid.*, no. T 12, p. 270. The "night effect" mentioned elsewhere in this letter refers to the painting reproduced p. 219.

42 Towards the end of August 1889 Dr. Peyron reported from Saint-Rémy to Theo van Gogh: "... He has recovered his lucidity and has started to work again as he did before. His thoughts of suicide have disappeared; nothing remains but painful dreams which begin to disappear and whose intensity is decreasing." Verzamelde Brieven, vol. III, no. 602a, p. 447.

43 V. van Gogh to his sister Wil, [Saint-Rémy, end of Sept.–beginning of Oct. 1889]; Verzamelde Brieven, vol. IV, no. W 14, p. 173.

44 V. van Gogh to his brother, [Saint-Rémy, Sept. 10, 1889]; Verzamelde Brieven, vol. III, no. 605, p. 455.

45 V. van Gogh to his brother, [Saint-Rémy, Aug. 1889]; *ibid.*, no. 601, p. 443.

46 Théo van Rysselberghe to O. Maus, [Paris, fall-winter 1887]; see M.-O. Maus: Trente années de lutte pour l'art, Brussels, 1926, pp. 64–65.

47 Cézanne to O. Maus, [Paris, Nov. 27, 1889]; *ibid.*, p. 99, and Cézanne Letters, London, 1941, pp. 189–90.

48 V. van Gogh to O. Maus, [Saint-Rémy, Nov. 20, 1889]; see M.-O. Maus, *op. cit.*, p. 100. (Not included in Verzamelde Brieven.) Of these six paintings (1) or (2) may be the one reproduced on p. 205, (3) is reproduced on p. 309, and (6) is reproduced on p. 229.

49 According to the Superior, Sister Epiphane, the nuns, though they did not like his paintings, pitied van Gogh for his misfortunes and found him polite, submissive, gentle, and well mannered. (Information courtesy the late Dr. E. Leroy, Saint-Paul du Mausolée, Saint-Rémy de Provence.)

50 See J. de Beucken: Un Portrait de Vincent van Gogh, Paris, 1953, p. 177; for further recollections of the guard Poulet see *ibid.*, pp. 195–97. Once when Poulet was taking the painter out to work in the environs of the asylum, and was descending the steps, van Gogh suddenly kicked him violently from behind. The guard immediately halted and took Vincent back to his cell. The next day van Gogh apologized to Poulet, saying that he had a vague recollection of having offended him (as he had done after throwing a glass of absinthe at Gauguin) and explaining that he had thought the guard to be a member of the secret police. Among the patients of the asylum then was a former law student who continually complained about being followed by the secret police. (Information courtesy the late Dr. E. Leroy, Saint-Paul du Mausolée, Saint-Rémy de Provence, to whom the incident was told by the guard. The version given by J. de Beucken, *op. cit.*, pp. 195–96 is altogether incorrect.)

51 On Nov. 14, 1889, Theo van Gogh wrote to Camille Pissarro: "I thank you very much for being so kind as to take the trouble to find out if there is some pension in which my brother would be comfortable; Mme Pissarro is most gracious to look into the matter also. It seems to me that if he could stay at Auvers close to that doctor you mentioned, that would be an excellent thing. According to the letters I receive from him and from his physician, it appears that he has been absolutely quiet these last weeks." (Unpublished document, courtesy the late Rodo Pissarro, Paris.) On Dr. Gachet, see chapter VIII.

52 V. van Gogh to his brother, [Saint-Rémy, middle of Sept. 1889]; Verzamelde Brieven, vol. III, no. 607, p. 464.

53 Theo van Gogh to his brother, [Paris, Oct. 22, 1889]; Verzamelde Brieven, vol. IV, no. T 19, p. 277.

54 V. van Gogh to his brother, [Saint-Rémy, Oct.–Nov. 1889]; Verzamelde Brieven, vol. III, no. 613, pp. 473–74.

55 Camille Pissarro to his son, [May 16, 1887]; see Camille Pissarro: Letters to his Son Lucien, New York, 1943, pp. 110–11.

56 V. van Gogh to his brother, [Saint-Rémy, Sept. 1889]; Verzamelde Brieven, vol. III, no. 607, pp. 462, 463. On van Gogh's copies see F. Novotny: Die Bilder van Goghs nach fremden Vorbildern *in* Festschrift Kurt Badt zum siebzigsten Geburtstage, Berlin, 1961.

57 According to an interview with B. Stokvis: Vincent van Gogh in Arles, *Kunst und Künstler*, Sept. 1929, Dr. Rey said that the painting was done in Arles and was offered by Vincent to the physician, then to M. Huard, administrator of the hospital and of the local museum, and finally to the secretary of the hospital, but nobody accepted it.

58 Van Gogh actually had painted his first *Arlésienne* after Gauguin's drawing during March or April 1889 in Arles (de La Faille no. 713, F. 542) before presumably returning the drawing to Gauguin. The later versions, executed in Saint-Rémy, were done after this initial copy rather than after the drawing.

59 V. van Gogh to Gauguin, [Auvers, June 1890]; Verzamelde Brieven, vol. III, no. 643, p. 528. (Unfinished draft, see chapter VIII, note 16.)

60 V. van Gogh to his brother, [Saint-Rémy, Jan. 1890]; *ibid.*, no. 622, p. 489.

61 V. van Gogh to his brother, [Saint-Rémy, Nov. 1889]; *ibid.*, no. 615, pp. 478–79.

62 V. van Gogh to Bernard, [Saint-Rémy, first half of Oct. 1889]; Verzamelde Brieven, vol. IV, no. B 20, pp. 231–33.

63 V. van Gogh to Bernard, [Saint-Rémy, beginning of Dec. 1889]; *ibid.*, no. B 21, pp. 233–36.

64 V. van Gogh to his mother, [Saint-Rémy, end of Dec. 1889];

Verzamelde Brieven, vol. III, no. 619, p. 485.

65 V. van Gogh to his brother, [Saint-Rémy, Nov.–Dec. 1889]; *ibid.*, no. 617, p. 481.

66 V. van Gogh to his brother, [Saint-Rémy, Jan. 1890]; *ibid.*, no. 623, p. 492.

67 Gauguin to Schuffenecker, [Le Pouldu, Jan. 1890]; see Paul Gauguin: Lettres à sa femme et à ses amis, Paris, 1949 (2nd edition), appendix, pp. 322–23.

68 Gauguin to V. van Gogh, [Le Pouldu, beginning of Feb. 1890]; unpublished document, courtesy Ir. V. W. van Gogh, Laren.

69 Aurier to his mother, [Paris, Nov. 29, 1888]; unpublished document, courtesy Mme Mahé-Williame, Aix-en-Provence.

70 See Bernard's letter to Aurier, p. 245.

71 Bernard to Aurier, [Paris, 1889]; unpublished document, courtesy M. Jacques Williame, Châteauroux. Aurier did not publish Bernard's article, sections of which are quoted in chapter I, pp. 56 and 64, note 65.

72 See chapter III, note 33.

73 Bernard to Aurier, [Paris, Jan. 1, 1889]; for other sections of this letter see note 70.

74 This passage of Aurier's article is based on the letter V. van Gogh and Gauguin had written from Arles to Bernard (quoted pp. 221–22, notes 14 and 15) and which the latter had given to Aurier.

75 A. Aurier: Les Isolés, Vincent van Gogh, *Mercure de France*, Jan. 1890; reprinted in Aurier: Oeuvres posthumes, Paris, 1893, and in: Van Gogh raconté par lui-même et par ses amis, vol. II, Geneva, 1947, pp. 59–70.

76 V. van Gogh to his mother, [Saint-Rémy, Feb. 15, 1890]; Verzamelde Brieven, vol. III, no. 627, pp. 502–03.

77 V. van Gogh to his sister Wil, [Saint-Rémy, middle of Feb. 1890]; Verzamelde Brieven, vol. IV, no. W 20, p. 180.

78 V. van Gogh to Aurier, [Saint-Rémy, Feb. 12, 1890]; Verzamelde Brieven, vol. III, no. 626a, pp. 500–01.

79 V. van Gogh to his brother, [Saint-Rémy, Feb. 12, 1890]; *ibid.*, no. 626, p. 498.

80 Rémy de Gourmont, May 1, 1893, Introduction to Aurier: Oeuvres posthumes, Paris, 1893.

81 Whereas the *Revue Indépendante* ceased to appear a short while later, the *Mercure de France* carried on for over seventy years.

82 A. H.: Les XX, *La Wallonie*, 1890, p, 133.

83 S. P. [Paul Signac]: Catalogue de l'exposition des XX, *Art et Critique*, Feb. 1, 1890.

84 See Theo van Gogh's letter to his brother, Paris, Jan. 22, 1890; Verzamelde Brieven, vol. IV, no. T 25, p. 284.

85 See M.-O. Maus, *op. cit.*, p. 100.

86 See O. Maus quoted by M. Joyant: Henri de Toulouse-Lautrec, Paris; also G. Mack: Toulouse-Lautrec, New York, 1938, p. 319.

87 O. Maus to Theo van Gogh; see Theo van Gogh's letter to his brother, [Paris, March 9, 1890]; Verzamelde Brieven, vol. IV, no. T 29, p. 287.

88 V. van Gogh to his mother, [Saint-Rémy, end of April 1890]; Verzamelde Brieven, vol. III, no. 629a, p. 506.

89 According to a supposition of P. Marois: Le Secret de van Gogh, Paris, 1957, pp. 172–73, this excursion confirmed the painter's fear that he was impotent.

90 V. van Gogh to his brother, [Saint-Rémy, middle of April 1890]; Verzamelde Brieven, vol. III, no. 628, p. 504.

91 V. van Gogh to his brother, [Saint-Rémy, April 29, 1890]; *ibid.*, no. 629, p. 505.

92 Theo van Gogh to his brother, [Paris, March 19, 1890]; Verzamelde Brieven, vol. IV, no. T 29, pp. 286–87.

93 Theo van Gogh to his brother, Paris, March 29, 1890; *ibid.*, no. T 31, p. 288.

94 See Theo van Gogh's letter to his brother, Paris, April 23, 1890; *ibid.*, no. T 32, p. 289.

95 Gauguin to V. van Gogh, [Paris, April 1890]; unpublished document, courtesy Ir. V. W. van Gogh, Laren.

96 V. van Gogh to his brother, [Saint-Rémy, May 1890]; Verzamelde Brieven, vol. III, no. 630 and 631, pp. 508–09.

97 Theo van Gogh to Dr. Gachet [spring 1890]; see P. Gachet: Deux amis des impressionnistes—Le Dr. Gachet et Murer, Paris, 1956, pp. 106–07.

98 V. van Gogh to his brother, [Saint-Rémy, May 1890]; *ibid.*, no. 631, p. 509.

99 V. van Gogh to his brother, [Saint-Rémy, May 1890]; *ibid.*, no. 633, pp. 512–13.

100 V. van Gogh to his brother, [Saint-Rémy, May 14, 1890]; *ibid.*, no. 634, p. 513.

101 V. van Gogh to his sister Wil, [Saint-Rémy, middle of Feb. 1890]; Verzamelde Brieven, vol. IV, no. W 20, p. 181.

102 See Doiteau and Leroy, *op. cit.*, facsimile of the page from the asylum register, reproduced opposite p. 85.

VIII 1890-1891 VAN GOGH'S SUICIDE AT AUVERS THE DEATH OF SEURAT

Vincent van Gogh arrived in Paris on the morning of Saturday, May 17, 1890. He had chosen this day so that his brother might have a Sunday to spend with him. Theo, after a sleepless night of anxiety caused by the fact that Vincent had insisted on traveling alone, went to meet him at the station and then took him to his new apartment in the Cité Pigalle in Montmartre. There for the first time Vincent saw his infant nephew and met his sister-in-law. Theo's wife later said that she had expected to see a sick man and was surprised to discover that the painter was "strong, with broad shoulders, a healthy color, a gay expression; his entire appearance indicated firm decision.... Apparently there had been once more one of those sudden and strange changes in his condition. 'He is absolutely well, he looks much stronger than Theo,' was my first thought."[1]

During the three days the painter spent at his brother's, the asylum was not once mentioned. Vincent was in a happy mood and got up early the first day to contemplate his pictures, of which he had never before seen so many together. Theo's apartment was filled with them; they were hanging on all available walls and many more, without stretchers, were piled up under various pieces of furniture. These were now spread out on the floor to afford a better examination.

Vincent van Gogh immediately felt a great liking for Theo's wife and was happy to see them so well adjusted to each other. Theo's brother-in-law, his old friend Andries Bonger, came to see him and soon there were a number of other visitors. There can be little doubt that *père* Tanguy showed up, probably also Lautrec, as well as Camille Pissarro with his son Lucien (Pissarro had invited Theo and his little family to spend Whitsuntide in his house at Eragny). Apparently Vincent also saw Guillaumin and Gausson, with both of whom he discussed an exchange of paintings. But he did not meet Dr. Gachet, whose Paris consultations took place on Fridays and who usually spent weekends with his children at Auvers. It is surprising that he did not see Bernard either, although the latter was then living at Vanves on the outskirts of Paris. It seems that Vincent had not even informed Bernard of his coming, which would indicate that he did not care to see him again. It may be that Bernard had reacted somewhat impulsively to van Gogh's letter reproaching him for his religious mysticism and that his reply had dampened Vincent's comradely feelings. Bernard was then going through a period of acute religious fervor and Vincent could not have been very anxious to engage in discussions on this subject with him.

Gauguin had returned to Brittany after admiring van Gogh's paintings at the Independents, but Theo unquestionably told his brother about Gauguin's plans: an inventor who had exhibited at the Paris World's Fair of 1889 had pledged a certain amount to enable Gauguin to return to the tropics. Theo was rather skeptical about the project since the inventor had not yet been paid for his patent, but Gauguin was ready to leave as soon as the sale should be concluded. "Then I shall go to Madagascar," he had informed Theo, "buy a small mud hut there and enlarge it myself, industrious sculptor that I am. I shall live like a barbarian peasant. Without worries about money, I shall be able to work there at my art as I have not yet ever been able to do. For 5,000 francs I shall deliver [to the inventor] thirty-eight canvases of which fourteen are with you and will have to be sent to him when the time comes, as well as five ceramic pots. That sum is very small but, after all, I hope that during my absence you'll do all you can to sell other works of mine.... I expect to send you from Madagascar beautiful new things, done with very great care, as there I shall have models free of charge every day. I shall not produce many pictures, but what I do will be closely knit, complete."[2]

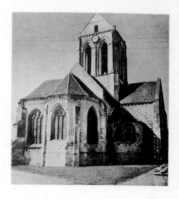

Photograph of the church of Auvers-sur-Oise

Thus happily dreaming of the future, Gauguin continued a rather drab existence at Le Pouldu, but Theo must have told Vincent how glad he was that Gauguin had left Paris again. "His stay at Schuffenecker's does him no good; he does practically no work there whereas Brittany inspires him."[3]

In spite of his great desire to see Gauguin's recent paintings, Vincent did not find time to go to Theo's gallery in order to study them there. He no doubt planned to do so whenever he came back to Paris for a few days from Auvers. But he did visit the Salon — since this could not be postponed — and greatly admired a large composition by Puvis de Chavannes (which had also impressed Gauguin). About this composition he wrote to his sister Wil: "After looking at it for a long while, one feels as if one were witnessing a total but well-intentioned rebirth of all the things in which one would have believed, which one would have desired: a strange and happy meeting of very remote antiquity with crude modernism."[4] Vincent probably also went to an exhibition of Japanese art at the Ecole des Beaux-Arts, but he abandoned his project of painting a view of a bookshop in Paris, lighted by gas, with multicolored books displayed in the window.

Four days in Paris were all van Gogh could stand. After his long isolation in Saint-Rémy, those crowded days seemed particularly long to him and he sometimes felt quite dizzy. The agitation of the city, the animated exchange of ideas with his visitors, the emotional strain of being with Theo again, the number of friends who dropped in — all this, as he had foreseen, became too much for him. On Wednesday, May 21, he was glad to leave for Auvers. He took along a letter of recommendation from Theo to Dr. Gachet: "You'll see that at present he [Vincent] is quite well. You would greatly oblige me if you would kindly look after him...."[5]

Auvers-sur-Oise had not changed very much since Pissarro, Cézanne, and Guillaumin had painted there in the early 'seventies, after the Franco-Prussian war. It was still little more than a village with thatched cottages on unpaved country lanes, though here and there appeared a few graceless, modern villas. Stretched out along a road that follows the course of the quiet Oise, it lies between the banks of the river, hidden by trees, and a gentle slope, from the top of which the view embraces on one side the lovely Oise valley and on the other an immense plain with fields of wheat. Gachet's house, a three-story structure, is situated on one of the most elevated spots, almost squeezed against the hill

Opposite: VAN GOGH: *The Church of Auvers,* June 1890. 37 x 29⅛". Formerly collection Dr. Gachet. Musée du Louvre, Paris

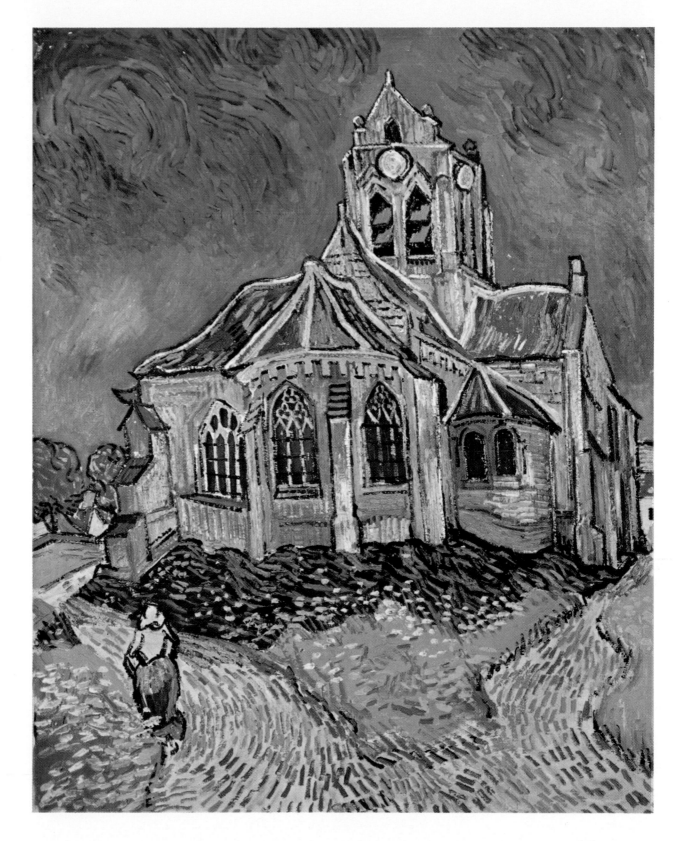

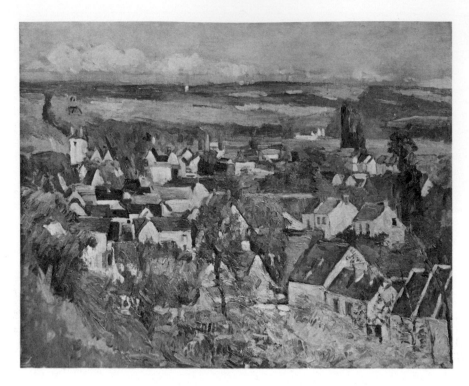

that rises immediately behind it. With the exception of the old church it dominates Auvers.

Vincent's first impression of Auvers was not as overwhelming as had been that of Arles, but then he probably did not expect as much either. "Auvers is quite beautiful," he wrote to Theo the very day of his arrival, "many thatched roofs, among others, something that is becoming rather scarce.... It is of a grave beauty, the real countryside, characteristic and picturesque."[6] Dr. Gachet took the painter to an inn where he would have to pay six francs a day, which seemed too much for him. Instead he chose to stay at Ravoux's, opposite the plain little town hall of Auvers, where he found a room and board for only three and a half francs a day. He felt certain that he would be able to produce enough in Auvers to pay his expenses.

On the subject of Dr. Gachet Vincent had this to say: "He made on me the impression of being rather eccentric, but his experience as a doctor no doubt keeps him balanced by counteracting the nervous disorder from which he certainly seems to be suffering at least as seriously as I am.... His own house is full of very, very black old stuff, with the exception of impressionist paintings."[6] Among these paintings Vincent particularly admired a snow scene by Pissarro and two flower still lifes by Cézanne, as well as a view of Auvers by the latter, which confirmed him in his desire to set to work in the village. To sum up, Vincent assured Theo: "The impression he has made on me is not unfavorable.... I do believe that we shall remain friends and that I shall do his portrait."[6]

Dr. Gachet was then in his early sixties, a fascinating and eccentric person indeed. A rabid republican (the third French Republic was not yet twenty years old), Darwinist, free-thinker, and socialist, he had been connected with the world of letters and arts since

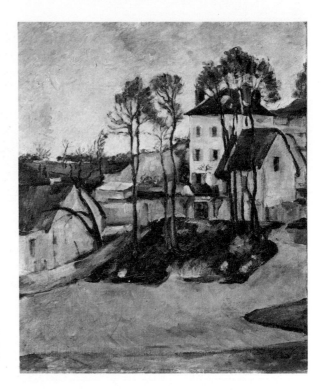

CÉZANNE: *The House of Dr. Gachet at Auvers,*
1873. 22 x 18⅛″. Formerly collection Dr. Gachet.
Collection Rudolf Staechelin, deposited with the
Kunstmuseum, Basel

his youth. He had known Courbet and Champfleury as well as Victor Hugo, had been a
friend of the etchers Bresdin and Meryon (whom he knew both before the latter's illness
and during his last years in an insane asylum), and had frequented the various cafés in
Paris where Manet and his friends used to gather. In their midst he liked to expound on
his favorite subjects: homoeopathy, cremation, free love, and many other matters which
represented advanced thinking (not to mention phrenology, physiognomy, chiromancy,
graphology, and especially anthropology). His friends did not mind these revolutionary
ideas though many resented his mania for proselytizing. Thus Gachet was bent on enlisting
all his acquaintances in a Society for Mutual Autopsy. He worked hard to obtain Renoir's
adherence, explaining to him the vital interest which the examination of the heart and
brain of a painter presented to anthropology. In order to convince the painter he quoted
the curious results yielded by a study of Gambetta's brain, but Renoir was too much in
love with life to care about the disposal of his corpse, flattering though the comparison
with Gambetta might have been.

The doctor was also convinced that science gave him infallible power to predict the
circumstances of everyone's death and made generous use of this gift of prophecy. Fortunately his predictions seldom materialized. A friend of Renoir's, who had been condemned by the physician to die at the age of twenty-five of a horrible bone disease affecting
his face, peacefully reached the age of over ninety. Gachet himself was not to be as lucky, in
spite of the fact that, while not yet fifty, he had contemplated writing a book on "The Art
of Living a Hundred Years."

Gachet's house was filled with paintings by his many impressionist friends (there

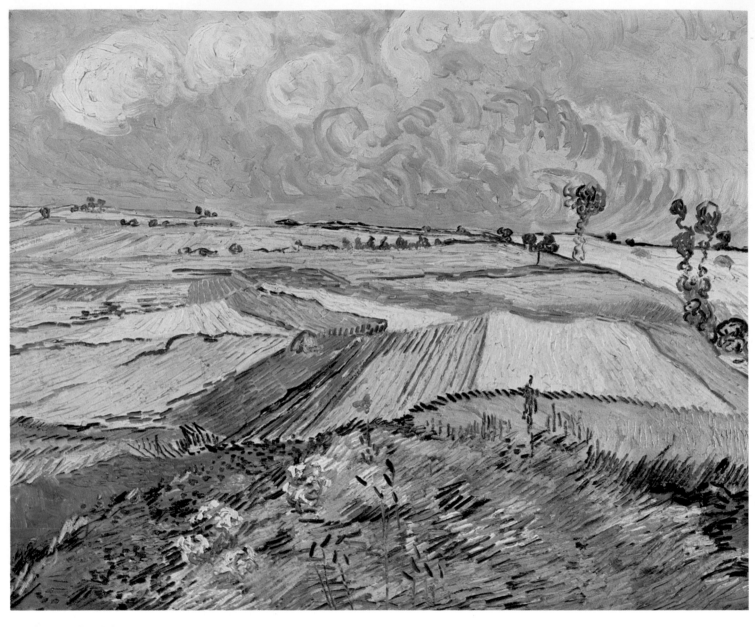

VAN GOGH: *The Plain of Auvers,* July 1890. 28¾ x 36″. Museum of Art, Carnegie Institute, Pittsburgh (Gift of Sarah Mellon Scaife Family)

were others in his Paris apartment and office) which he either bought or obtained in exchange for medical consultations; Renoir, for instance, had presented him with the portrait of a ravishing young model whom Gachet had treated during the final stages of tuberculosis. There was also a heterogeneous assemblage of what Vincent called "very black old stuff," besides an amazing multitude of animals: a dozen cats, several dogs, chickens, rabbits, ducks, pigeons, a peacock, a tortoise, and an old goat which used to startle visitors and neighbors.

"I feel," Vincent soon reported to Theo, "that in his house I shall be able to do not too bad a painting every time I go there and that he will continue to invite me to dinner every Sunday or Monday. But until now, pleasant as it has been to work there, it has been quite an ordeal to dine and lunch with him, for this excellent man makes great efforts to prepare meals of four or five courses, which is abominable for him as well as for me." And he added: "His house . . . is filled, filled, like that of an antique dealer, with things that are not always interesting. But in all that there is something good in so far as there are always useful things to arrange flowers in or to compose still lifes [Cézanne had done precisely that while working at Gachet's]."[7] Vincent also told his brother that he particularly liked a *Nude Woman on a Bed* by Guillaumin in the doctor's house. This painting was hanging there unframed and van Gogh chided his new friend for not presenting properly so fine a work of art. Gachet thereupon promised to order a frame but apparently was in no particular haste to do so.

In and around Auvers everybody knew Gachet. Of medium height, he dressed in a blue alpaca redingote or overcoat during the summer, and a white cap with a leather visor. In the winter he sported a fur cap and a fur collar, while at home he invariably wore a dark red robe. His long face was remarkable for its large forehead, blue eyes, aquiline nose, narrow mouth, and protruding chin, but above all for its abundant reddish hair.

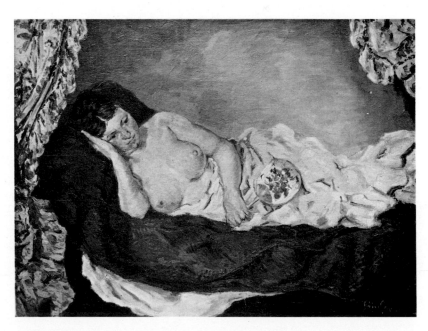

GUILLAUMIN: *Nude Woman on a Bed,* c. 1874 (?). 19¼ x 25⅝". Musée du Louvre, Paris (Gift of Paul Gachet)

There were rumors that he dyed his hair, for it always remained the same flamboyant color. One of the doctor's friends never called him anything but "Dr. Saffron."[8]

While Gachet did not practice in Auvers, he occasionally took care of friends—he had looked after Daumier during his last years in nearby Valmondois—or of poor villagers. Strangely enough, the subject of his thesis had been "Etude sur la Mélancholie" and it had been presented to the medical faculty of the Montpellier University. In Montpellier, Gachet had known Alfred Bruyas, a friend of Courbet's and a neighbor of Bazille's, whose collection Vincent had admired during his short visit there with Gauguin. A long talk about Bruyas and his paintings and the fact that Gachet shared van Gogh's admiration for Monticelli and Millet seem to have helped to break the ice between the painter and the physician.

It is not surprising that the strange personality of Dr. Gachet made such a strong impression on Vincent and immediately inspired him with the desire to paint Gachet's portrait. In the beginning the two men seem to have watched each other with mixed feelings of curiosity and benevolence, but this soon gave place to mutual understanding. Vincent detected a certain sadness and resignation in Gachet and these qualities attracted him, who had always preferred melancholy natures to self-confident and uninhibited ones. After Gachet had come to see the few paintings van Gogh had brought along, and had liked them, after they had talked at length about art and finally after the physician had unreservedly discussed Vincent's condition, the basis for a friendship was established.

The painter appeared very calm and showed no signs of his affliction. He explained his case succinctly to Dr. Gachet, who comforted him, urged him to work quietly, without haste and without thinking too much of his illness. The physician did not prescribe any medication but advised the artist to eat more regularly, preferably simple food.[9]

"He seems to me to be very reasonable," Vincent wrote to Theo after the first few days in Auvers, "but he is just as much discouraged with his profession of country doctor as I am with my painting. Whereupon I told him that I would be only too happy to exchange professions with him. Well, I believe we'll end by being good friends. By the way, he told me that if my melancholia, or whatever else it is, became too strong for me to endure, he could do something to lessen its intensity, and that I should not hesitate to be absolutely frank with him. Of course, the moment when I shall need him may very well come, although until now everything is all right. And my condition may even improve; I still believe that it was an illness of the South which I caught and that my return here will suffice to cure all that."[10]

In a letter to his mother, written a few days later, Vincent summed up the happenings of the last weeks: "To find myself among painters again, to throw myself once more into the battles and discussions, and above all to work in this small closed world of artists — all these distractions have been salutary in the sense that the symptoms of my illness, which are to some extent the thermometer of my condition, have completely disappeared these last days." But he added cautiously: "It is true that I have been warned that I cannot altogether trust this."[11]

There was still only one way in which Vincent could alleviate his illness, and that was by work. He found himself in a splendid mood to tackle the new pictorial problems that confronted him at Auvers. "I notice already," he wrote shortly after his arrival, "that it did me good to go south in order to see the North better. Things turned out as I expected: I perceive purples better where they are. Auvers is certainly very beautiful."[12] Yet he was not attracted by color alone but also planned to do a great many drawings.

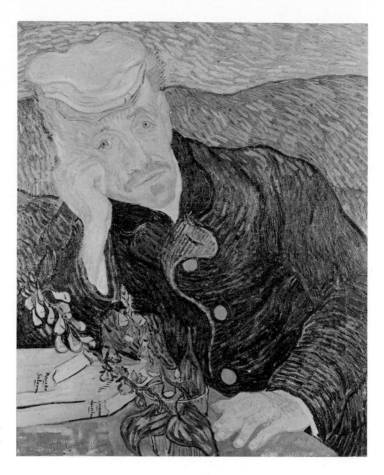

van Gogh: *Portrait of Dr. Paul Gachet* (first version), Auvers, June 1890. 26¼ x 22½″. S. Kramarsky Trust Fund, New York

Going to bed early, Vincent used to rise at five in the morning, enjoying the "calm *à la* Puvis de Chavannes" of the countryside. The first painting he did at Auvers was a landscape of old thatched cottages beyond fields of wheat and sweet peas with the hill in the background. It was soon followed by a view of the church, done in strong blues, and by studies of blossoming pink and white chestnut trees whose heavy splendor somehow compensated for the flowering almond and peach trees he had been unable to paint at Saint-Rémy. He was happy to discover that "I feel myself much more sure of my brushes than before I went to Arles."[7]

Vincent did not long delay his project of painting Dr. Gachet's portrait, especially as he hoped to find through him other willing—and possibly even paying—models. Two weeks after his first meeting with the physician, van Gogh reported to his brother: "I am working on his portrait, his head with a white cap—very blond hair, very bright; his hands also light in color, with a blue coat and a cobalt blue background. He is leaning against a red table on which there are a yellow book and a foxglove with purple blossoms.... M. Gachet is absolutely *crazy* about this portrait and wants me to do another for him, if I can, exactly like it, which I myself would also like to do."[7] Indeed, Vincent very soon painted a second version of this likeness.

In a long letter to his sister Wil, van Gogh again described this portrait of the doctor. "We became fast friends almost immediately and I shall spend one or two days every week in his house, painting in his garden, of which I have already done two studies.... I also have a larger picture of the village church, in which the building appears violet against a sky of flat deep blue, pure cobalt; the stained glass windows are like spots of ultramarine, the roof is violet and in parts orange. In the foreground a bit of blossoming greenery and rose-colored sand in the sunlight. It is almost the same as the studies I did at Nuenen [in Holland] of the old tower and the cemetery, except that now the color is probably more expressive, more sumptuous. But during my last days at Saint-Rémy I also worked like a demon, especially on bunches of flowers: roses and purple irises. For Theo's and Jo's baby I brought back a fairly large painting—which they hung above the piano—of white almond blossoms, large branches against a sky-blue background; they also have in their apartment a new portrait of an Arlésienne. My friend Dr. Gachet is decidedly enthusiastic about this last portrait of an Arlésienne (I also did a version for myself), as well as about a self-portrait, and this gives me pleasure for he will encourage me to do portraits and will, I hope, find some interesting models for me. What excites me the most in my profession, much, much more than anything else, is portraiture, modern portraiture. I endeavor to do this through color and am certainly not the only one to search in this direction. You see, I *should like*—though I am far from saying that I can do it, but at least I try—I *should like* to paint portraits which a hundred years from now will seem to the people of those days like apparitions. Thus I do not attempt to achieve this through photographic resemblance, but through our impassioned aspects, using our science and our modern taste for color as a means of expression and of exaltation of character."[4]

There can be little doubt that Vincent felt that he had come close to this aim in his portrait of Gachet, closer possibly than in any other of his likenesses, and the doctor apparently shared this conviction. Art now became a strong link between the two men and van Gogh had the unusual pleasure of painting for someone who really appreciated his work. Until then most of his portraits had been of more or less primitive though well-meaning sitters, such as the postman Roulin and his family, *père* Tanguy, Mme Ginoux, the Zouave Milliet, and the guard at Saint-Rémy, most of whom—with the exception of Tanguy—cared little for his paintings, much as they liked Vincent himself; even Dr. Rey in Arles showed no appreciation of the likeness van Gogh did of him. But now he had found at last, after his long isolation, a man who spoke his own language. Unquestionably the painter was also attracted by the resignation and indulgence which characterized Gachet's opinions on matters of art, an attitude much less antagonistic than the peremptoriness of Gauguin or the soul-searching philosophizing of Bernard.

It is not known whether van Gogh met other models through Gachet, but the physician's nineteen-year-old daughter posed for him at the piano (page 375).[13] Besides he painted likenesses of a young peasant girl, of some children, and of the daughter of the innkeepers with whom he was staying. If Dr. Gachet does not seem to have been too successful in persuading his acquaintances to commission portraits from van Gogh, he tried to be encouraging in many other ways. On several occasions Vincent went to fetch the doctor in order to show him some of his canvases. Gachet's son, who frequently accompanied his father, particularly remembered a visit after several of the paintings van Gogh had left in the South finally arrived in Auvers. Indeed, the physician saw the painter two to three times every week, kept in touch with Theo, generously expressed his admiration for some

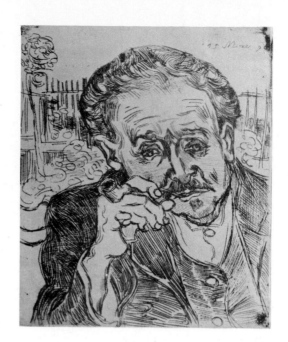

van Gogh: *Portrait of Dr. Paul Gachet,* Auvers, May 1890. Etching, 7⅛ x 5¾″. Collection Mr. and Mrs. George Greenspan, New York

of Vincent's pictures, and even asked him to copy one of these for him. He also urged his new friend to try his hand at etching.

For many years Dr. Gachet had had a passion for the graphic arts. He had done a number of etchings—among them copies after Daumier and Millet—and had eventually installed a press in his house where he could pull his own proofs. Any artist who visited him at Auvers had been invited to avail himself of this facility. Every one of the few etchings Cézanne did had been executed in Gachet's house, and Pissarro as well as Guillaumin had etched many plates, pulled many prints there.[14] Van Gogh showed himself greatly attracted by the new medium and on one of his first visits to the physician drew on copper and etched a portrait of the doctor. This was to remain the only etching he ever made, though he immediately planned to do a series of etchings—which Gachet promised to print for him—after some of his paintings of the South. He even contemplated doing some etchings in collaboration with Gauguin.

Towards the middle of June Vincent received a letter from Gauguin at Le Pouldu that made him particularly happy because he was very anxious to know how his friend liked his *Arlésienne,* painted at Saint-Rémy after Gauguin's drawing (page 328). "I have seen the canvas of Mme Ginoux [*l'Arlésienne*]," Gauguin said; "very beautiful and very strange. I like it better than my drawing. In spite of your condition you have never worked with such a degree of *equilibrium* while preserving the initial impression and the inner warmth which are indispensable for a work of art, especially at a time like ours when art is becoming something based on cold calculations established in advance." (Was this a gibe at Seurat?) And Gauguin went on to write at great length about his own new project:

"Do you remember our conversations in Arles on the subject of founding a studio of the tropics? I am about to carry this out if I can raise the small amount necessary to establish such a studio. In that case I shall go to Madagascar where the natives are gentle and live

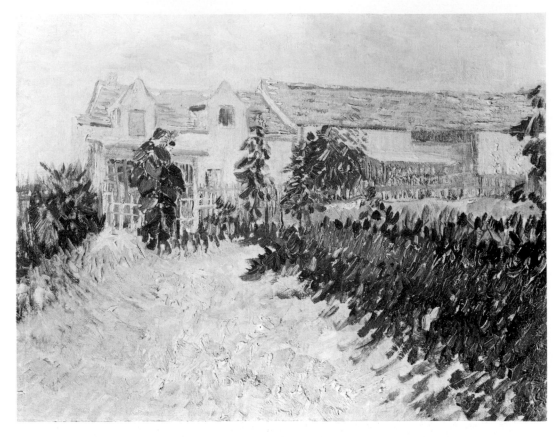

VAN GOGH: *House with Sunflowers,* June 1890. 12¼ x 16⅛″. Private collection

without money from the products of the soil. From various quarters I have obtained **very** *precise* information on this. Out of a small hut built of mud and wood I shall, with my two hands, create a comfortable house; I shall myself plant all that is needed for food, shall have chickens, cows, etc. ... and in a very short time my material existence will be assured. Those who may later wish to come there will find all that is required for working at very low cost. The studio of the tropics may possibly breed the Saint John the Baptist of the art of the future, invigorated there by a more natural, more primitive, and above all less degenerate life.''[15]

"Since my return [to the North],'' van Gogh wrote in his reply to Gauguin, "I have thought of you every day.... It gives me tremendous pleasure to have you say that you like the portrait of the *Arlésienne,* which is strictly based on your drawing.... For my part the price for painting it was another month of illness [in Saint-Rémy], but at least I know that this is a canvas that will be understood by you, by me and a very few others as we want it to be understood. Here my friend Dr. Gachet, after two or three hesitations, has now completely accepted it and has said: 'How difficult it is to be simple.'

"... I have now done a portrait of Dr. Gachet with the sad expression of our time. Perhaps it is something like what you said of your *Christ in the Garden of Olives,* not destined to be understood...." Vincent also spoke of the studies of wheat he planned to paint in Auvers and wound up by saying: "It is very likely that—if you allow me—I shall come to rejoin you for a month, to paint one or two seascapes, but above all to see you again and to meet de Haan. Then we can endeavor to create something deliberate and serious such as we probably should have done if we had been able to continue to work down there."[16] And van Gogh added a print of his portrait of Gachet to his letter.

Gauguin's reply seems somewhat less cordial than his previous letter; it was, as always, rather guarded on the subject of van Gogh's coming to Brittany: "Upon my return from a short trip [to Pont-Aven] I found your letter as well as the proof of your etching.... Your letter does not say much—whether you have seen my studies in Paris at Goupil's and what you think of them; whether my projected trip to Madagascar seems unreasonable to you. I am dreaming of it every day to the extent where I hardly do any work at present, wishing to rest a little, to gather new strength for down there. And you, you are insatiable. I see that you haven't wasted your time at Auvers. Yet it is good every now and then to give the mind and the body some rest.

"Your idea of coming to Le Pouldu in Brittany seems excellent to me if it could be carried out, for we are, de Haan and I, in a very small place far from the city, without other means of communication than a hired carriage. And for a sick person who sometimes needs a doctor that is dangerous. ... Moreover, if I manage to go through with my project

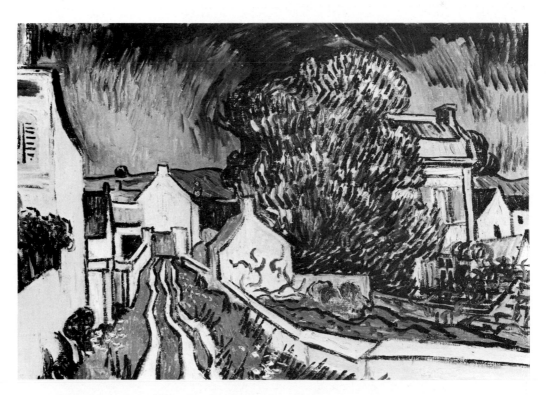

VAN GOGH: *The House of Pierre Pilon*, Auvers, May–June 1890. 19¼ x 27½". Collection Stavros S. Niarchos, Athens

to leave for Madagascar, I shall not be here at the beginning of September, nor will de Haan who is returning to Holland. This, in all frankness, is the situation, and yet God knows with what pleasure I should have liked my friend Vincent to be with us.

"I do not know Dr. Gachet, but I have heard old Pissarro talk about him many times. It must be very pleasant for you to be with somebody who understands your work, your ideas. Alas, I myself feel condemned to be less and less understood and have to be prepared to go through life *alone*, to drag out an existence without family, like an outcast. Thus solitude in the forest seems to me in the future to be a new paradise, almost a dream. The savage will return to savagery."[17]

It is not known whether Vincent now abandoned his idea of going to Brittany for a few weeks; in his letters at least he did not mention this trip any more. Instead he was tempted by Gauguin's newest plan, though he had little confidence in his friend's schemes. "Of course," he confided to Theo, "I don't think it will be possible to carry out this Madagascar project; I should prefer to have him go to Tonkin. Yet should he leave for Madagascar, I might quite possibly follow him there, for one should go there two or three together. But we are not at that point yet."[18]

Indeed Madagascar was far away while the countryside around him at Auvers literally seemed to beg van Gogh to explore its simple beauty. The low cottages, the shady river,

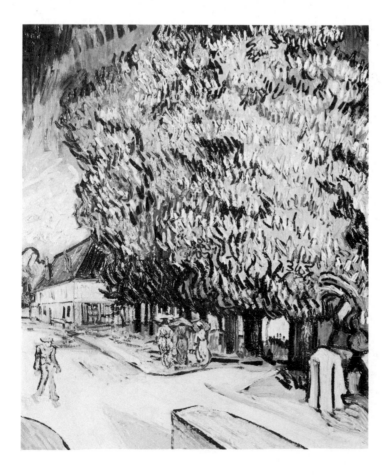

VAN GOGH: *Flowering Chestnut Trees at Auvers,* May 1890. 27½ x 23". Private collection, South America

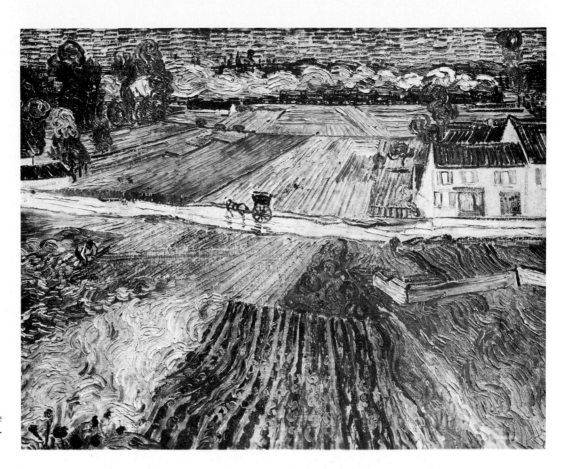

VAN GOGH: *Auvers Landscape,* June 1890. 28⅜ x 35½". Pushkin State Museum of Fine Arts, Moscow

the well-trodden steps linking streets on different levels, the massive church, the chestnut trees, the fields of wheat, the acres of potatoes and peas, the white road cutting through the patchwork of tilled, verdant soil, the field flowers, Dr. Gachet's garden and that of a large farmhouse which had belonged to Daubigny, all these provided innumerable subjects.

Invited by Dr. Gachet, Theo, his wife, and their baby had spent the Sunday of June 8 at Auvers, taking long walks with Vincent, who was in a joyous and relaxed mood. The painter was happy now to be so close to those he loved. Theo not only promised to return but actually told him that some of their friends, such as Gausson and Aurier, also contemplated visiting him at Auvers. (Theo had apparently struck up a fast friendship with Aurier who, in his series on "Les Isolés," had followed up his initial article on Vincent by studies of Pissarro and Raffaëlli, both of whom had been given one-man shows in Theo's gallery.) Theo may even have informed his brother of a projected visit to Pissarro, to whom he subsequently wrote: "As I have to go to see Monet [at Giverny] with M. Valadon [co-owner of the Goupil Galleries] on the 14th of July, I should like to invite myself with my brother-in-law [Andries Bonger] and perhaps with my brother Vincent to come and spend that day with you. We will sleep anywhere, don't bother about it."[19] But while Theo did visit Monet, he apparently did not drop in on Pissarro at Eragny, and in any event his brother did not go along on this little trip.

During Theo's early June visit to Auvers the two brothers also discussed the possibility of renting a small house in Auvers where Vincent would live either alone or with some other artist, and van Gogh had written to his friends the Ginoux family in Arles, requesting that his furniture be shipped to him. In his letter to them Vincent proudly announced: "I feel completely calm and in normal condition. The doctor here says that I should throw myself fully into my work and in this way find distraction. . . . Besides it is a fact that since I gave up drinking I do better work than before and that much at least is gained."[20] Vincent had now fully recovered his composure and even began to speak anew of one of his favorite projects, that of organizing an exhibition of his paintings in a Parisian café, either by himself or with others.[21]

Towards the end of June Theo went through some trying days; his child fell seriously ill, his wife was exhausted after many sleepless nights, he was quarreling with his superiors who showed no confidence whatever in his artistic judgment, and he began to foresee the possibility of having to live on a drastically reduced budget. Theo tried valiantly not to alarm his brother: "Don't worry about me or about us, old fellow. I want you to know that what gives me the greatest pleasure is when you are well and when you devote yourself to your work, which is admirable. You already have too much fire, and we must be in good shape to fight for a long time yet, for we shall have to battle all our lives, rather than eat the oats of charity which are doled out to old horses in good stables."[22]

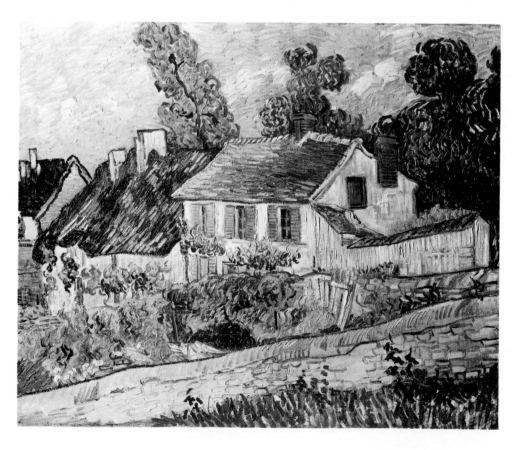

van Gogh: *Houses at Auvers,* June 1890. 24 x 30¾". Toledo Museum of Art, Toledo, Ohio (Gift of Edward Drummond Libby, 1935)

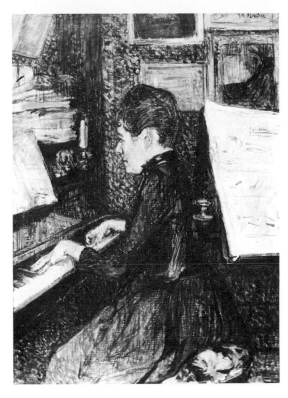 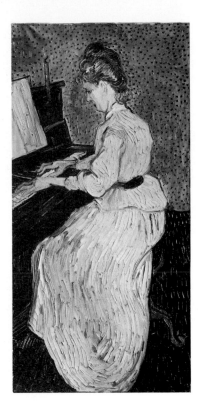

RIGHT: TOULOUSE-LAUTREC: *Woman at the Piano* (Mlle Dihau), d. 1890. Oil on cardboard, 26¾ x 19⅛". Exhibited with the Independents in March 1890. Musée Toulouse-Lautrec, Albi

Far right: VAN GOGH: *Mlle Gachet at the Piano*, Auvers, June 1890. 40⅛ x 19¾". Formerly collection Dr. Gachet. Kunstmuseum, Basel

As Theo could not come to Auvers, Vincent went for a short visit to Paris early in July. He found his brother tired and worn out. Together they explored the advisability of Theo's leaving Goupil's and opening a gallery of his own, a project that had become even more hazardous now that Theo had to support not only Vincent but also a wife and child. Vincent and Theo also discussed the desirability of Theo's taking a larger apartment because the painter was dissatisfied with the room in which his canvases were stored and shown. This time their reunion was overshadowed by grave problems, by an atmosphere of worry and strain.

As before, there was a stream of visitors for Vincent. Aurier came to meet the artist for the first time and to study his pictures in his company. Van Gogh apparently also paid a visit to Aurier, for the latter's friend Julien Leclercq later wrote: "It was at Aurier's that I saw Vincent for a moment.... I remember him as a short, blond man, nervous, with vivid eyes, a broad forehead, who seemed to feel chilly and who made me think vaguely of a Spinoza hiding a violent activity of thought behind timid manners."[23]

Vincent also went to see Gauguin's recent work. Lautrec came to lunch and did his best to cheer up his friends; he then took van Gogh to his studio to see the *Woman at the Piano* (Mlle Dihau) which Theo had admired at the Independents. Vincent must have been struck by the similarity of the composition to that of his own painting, *Mlle Gachet at the Piano*. He found Lautrec's painting "very astonishing; I saw it with emotion."[24] Guillaumin also intended to call on van Gogh, but Vincent began to feel exhausted and suddenly left for Auvers without waiting for his visit.

Theo's worries left their mark on his brother. "It is not a trifle," Vincent wrote after his return to Auvers, "when all of us feel our daily bread in danger; it is not a trifle when for other reasons also we feel that our existence is fragile. Back here, I too have felt very sad and have continued to feel the weight of the storm which threatens you. What can be done? You see, usually I try to be fairly cheerful, but my life also is menaced at its very root, my steps are unsteady too. I feared—not so much, but a little just the same—that I was an encumbrance to you, living at your expense...."[24] Fortunately an affectionate letter from Theo's wife reassured Vincent on this point, yet the germ of growing anxiety had been planted. In his last letter before going to Paris, after learning of his nephew's illness, Vincent had even mentioned in passing that his seizures might recur. After his return he reported that he had "gone back to work although the brushes almost fell from my hands."[24]

Theo tried to allay Vincent's fears: "Really, the danger is not as grave as you thought. If only all of us remain in good health which will allow us to undertake what, in our minds, may become necessary, little by little, then all will go well. Certainly there are disappointments, but we are no longer beginners and we are like the carters who, by all the efforts of their horses, have *almost* reached the top of a hill, turn back again and then, through a renewed effort, often reach the top."[25]

But Vincent was too upset to be easily cheered, although he professed to be less disturbed than during his visit to Paris. He was deeply concerned about the baby's health; he also began to worry about his monthly remittances from Theo. He was again irritable and had a violent argument with Dr. Gachet when he discovered that the greatly admired *Nude* by Guillaumin was still not properly framed.[26] Out of a clear sky he informed his brother: "I believe that we can *in no way* count on Dr. Gachet. First of all he is sicker than I am, it seems to me, or let's say just as sick; that's it. And when one blind man leads another blind man, won't both of them fall into the ditch? I don't know what to say. My last attack, which was terrible, was unquestionably brought about to a great extent by the influence of the other patients; well, the prison crushed me and old man Peyron paid not the slightest attention to it, leaving me to vegetate with the desperately afflicted."[27]

Now it was Theo's turn to worry about his brother. Did he really mean that Dr. Gachet's company might do more harm than good, did he really want to imply that the physician's eccentricity might have a corrupting influence? Theo had taken his wife and baby to Holland but had returned to Paris for a few more days. Now he wrote to his wife concerning Vincent: "If only he does not become melancholy, if only no new seizure is in the offing— everything seemed to be going so well."[28] And a few days later he reported: "I had a letter from Vincent which I again found completely incomprehensible. When will a happier time dawn for him too!—and yet he is full of goodness through and through."[29]

Meanwhile Vincent's work went on at its exhausting pace. He painted almost one canvas a day, sometimes two, occasionally working on several simultaneously. Since his dimly lit room[30]—above the Café Ravoux—was much too small to store this avalanche of freshly painted and still wet canvases, he left these, according to the Dutch painter Anton Hirschig who was also staying at Ravoux's, "helter-skelter in the dirtiest little corner one can imagine, a sort of hovel where goats were usually kept. It was dark there, the walls were of brick without any plaster, with straw hanging from them.... And every day he brought new ones in; they were strewn on the floor and hanging on the walls. Nobody ever looked at them."[31]

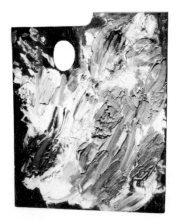

Palette van Gogh used at Auvers. Musée du Louvre, Paris

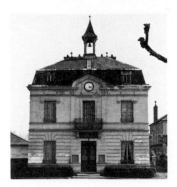

Photograph of the town hall of Auvers

Right: VAN GOGH: *The Town Hall of Auvers on Bastille Day*, July 1890. 28⅜ × 36⅝″. Presented by the artist to M. Ravoux. Private collection, England

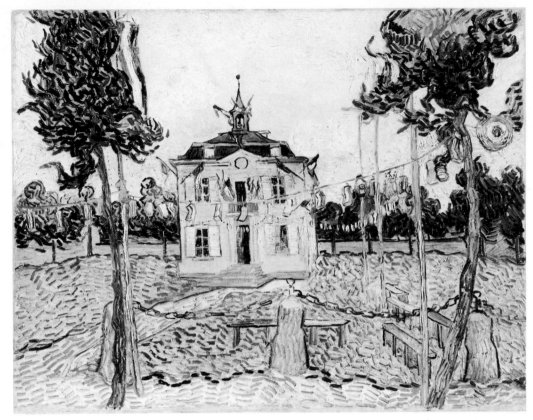

If loneliness oppressed him, van Gogh did little to relieve it. Although there were a number of painters in Auvers, among them "next door a whole family of Americans who paint day in and day out," as well as several Dutchmen, he made no attempt to associate with them. Some may have been frightened by him, for his compatriot and neighbor Hirschig later remembered "his wild eyes with a crazed expression into which I did not dare to look."[31] Thus he continued to work by himself, even more isolated now that Gachet's visits and invitations apparently had come to an end.

"I am totally absorbed," Vincent wrote to his mother in the second half of July, "by that immense plain covered with fields of wheat which extends beyond the hillside; it is wide as the sea, of a subtle yellow, a subtle tender green, with the subtle violet of a plowed and weeded patch and with neatly delineated green spots of potato fields in bloom. All this under a sky of delicate colors, blue and white and pink and purple. For the time being I am calm, almost too calm, thus in the proper state of mind to paint all that."[32]

Vincent also painted the garden of Daubigny's house with the church in the background, a subject that had interested him ever since he had arrived in Auvers. And on Bastille Day he painted the simple, gaily decorated town hall just across the road from his inn; he gave this canvas to the innkeeper M. Ravoux. But that calm, that too great calm of which he spoke, was it not the calm before the storm? Five months had elapsed since his last attack in Saint-Rémy, a longer period of grace than he was used to. Yet would it last still longer?

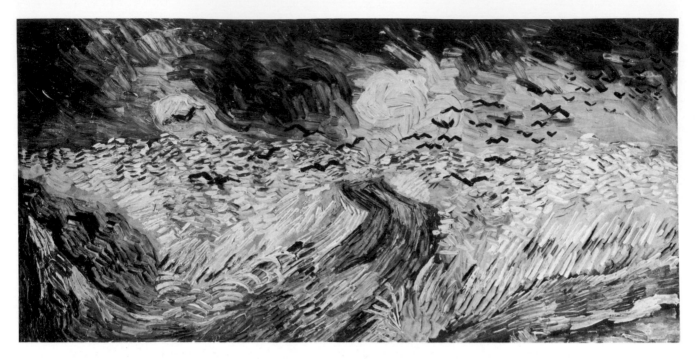

van Gogh: *Crows over the Wheat Fields,* Auvers, July 1890. 19⅞ x 39½″. Rijksmuseum Vincent van Gogh, Amsterdam

Auvers had stimulated him and the change of atmosphere had done him a world of good. He had put those five months to excellent use. But if he began to feel a rising excitement, if he had a premonition of a new seizure, then he also had to concede at last that his illness was *not* merely an ailment of the South, as he had hoped for so long; then he would have to admit that his seizures would follow him wherever he went, that he could not escape them. And once he realized this, could he evade the dreadful thought that eventually his attacks might succeed each other at an accelerated pace, with ever shorter spells of normality between them? At the end of such a series of attacks there loomed the frightening prospect of one final and uninterrupted nightmare of insanity.

Assailed by such apprehensions, how long could Vincent remain in a frame of mind conducive to work? His falling-out with Dr. Gachet must have deeply troubled him. Had he been wrong once more in his evaluation of those around him? Was he always going to be deceived by those he trusted? Now he would be all alone again in these new surroundings, just at the time when he sought at long last to re-establish himself in his own abode, his furniture being already on its way from Arles.

Theo's burden began to weigh ever more heavily on Vincent's shoulders. He had lost faith even in that community of artists for which he had worked, of which he had dreamt for years, at the very moment when Theo considered leaving Boussod & Valadon (Goupil) and becoming the salesman of the new school. But his thoughts on this subject were rather confused: "Hasn't the moment already passed a little for making [the painters] understand the usefulness of unification? And if such an alliance could be formed, wouldn't it founder if the rest should founder? Then you will say perhaps that some dealers might

378

unite for [the support of] the impressionists, but that would only be a temporary arrangement. It seems to me that personal initiative remains futile and, once the experiment has failed, would one try it again?"[33]

In one of his recent canvases of the yellow fields on that large plain above Auvers he had painted "immense expanses of wheat beneath troubled skies and I have not hesitated to express sadness, extreme solitude."[24] Sadness and solitude once more held van Gogh in their all too familiar grip.

On Sunday, July 27, Vincent sat down to write to his brother: "I should have liked to write to you about a good many things, but I feel the futility of doing so.... Since everything is well with you [at home], which is the main thing, why should I insist on things of lesser importance? *It will probably be a long time before we have a chance to talk about business matters with quiet minds....* And really, we can only speak through our paintings. Yet, my dear brother, there is one thing that I have always told you and which I am repeating once more with all the seriousness of my mental efforts, assiduously concentrated, to do as well as I can—I say again that I shall always consider you as something more than an ordinary dealer in Corots, that through me you have your share in the actual production of certain canvases which retain their calmness even in disaster. For we have reached that point and that is above all the most important thing that I have to tell you in a moment of relative crisis, a moment when things are extremely tense between dealers in pictures by dead artists and by living ones. Well, in my own work I am risking my life and half of my reason has been lost in it—good—but you are not a dealer in people, as far as I know, and you can take sides, I believe, really acting with humanity."[34]

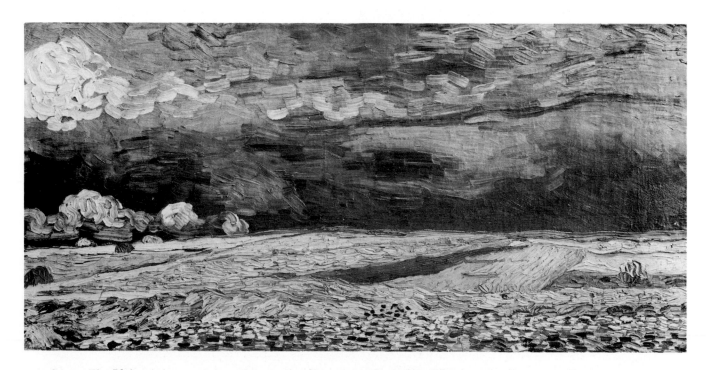

VAN GOGH: *The Plain of Auvers under a Stormy Sky,* July 1890. 19⅝ x 39⅜". Rijksmuseum Vincent van Gogh, Amsterdam

Vincent did not finish this letter. Dusk was approaching; he went out into the fields, taking a revolver along. Nobody knows where he got the revolver, but he may have borrowed it from some peasant on the pretext of shooting crows.[35] Instead he shot himself, but the bullet entered his body below the heart. He fell to the ground, yet was able to get up and start walking back to the inn. Three times on the way he fell. He had buttoned his coat so as to hide his blood-soaked shirt and went up to his small room without speaking to anybody. When he did not come down to dinner, M. Ravoux, the innkeeper, went to call for him. He found van Gogh in bed, his face turned to the wall. As Ravoux insisted that he should get up, Vincent suddenly turned around, showed his bloody chest and said: "I tried to kill myself but I missed...."[36]

Ravoux called the local physician but van Gogh asked for Dr. Gachet, who was hastily summoned and soon arrived, accompanied by his young son. Vincent immediately told Gachet that he had attempted to commit suicide while completely lucid.[37] By the light of a candle Gachet examined his wound. Extraction of the bullet seemed impossible; since there were no signs of imminent danger and since Vincent did not seem to suffer any pain, he merely dressed the wound and decided to wait. Vincent was perfectly calm and requested his pipe, which the doctor filled and lit for him. Gachet asked for Theo's home address so as to inform him of what had happened, but Vincent would not give it to him. Gachet thereupon left his seventeen-year-old son behind as a guard. During the entire night the painter was calm; he did not sleep, smoking his pipe without uttering a word.[38]

Dr. Gachet scribbled a note to Theo which he had delivered to him through Hirschig on Monday morning: "I am extremely sorry to have to trouble you. Yet I think it is my duty to write to you immediately. I was called at nine o'clock tonight, Sunday, on behalf of your brother, who wanted to see me urgently. He has wounded himself.... Not having your address, which he has refused to give me, this letter will reach you at the Goupil gallery."[39]

When the local gendarmes came to question van Gogh about what had happened, the painter replied calmly that this did not concern anybody but himself and that he felt free to do what he had done. Beyond this he would not say anything.[40]

As soon as Theo received Dr. Gachet's message he hastened to Auvers. "Missed again!" were among the first words with which Vincent greeted his brother when he entered the somber, hot room; and as Theo sobbed he told him: "Do not cry, I did it for the good of everybody." The two brothers spent the whole day together, talking most of the time.[31] But Theo found a moment to inform his wife of what had occurred, of how he had received the alarming news: "I left everything and rushed out but found him in comparatively better condition than I had expected. I should prefer not to relate details which are only too sad, yet you must know, darling, that his life may possibly be in danger.... He seems to be glad that I came and we are together almost all the time.... Poor fellow, fate has not given him much and he has no illusions left. Things are sometimes too hard, he feels so alone.... He inquired most urgently about you and the boy and said that he had not expected that life would bring him so many sorrows. If only we could give him a little courage to live! Don't be too worried; once before things looked desperate for him and yet his strong nature eventually cheated the doctors...."[41]

But this time Vincent was determined not to recover. When Theo told him that they would try to save him, he replied that Gachet's care was useless: "The sadness will last forever." Shortly afterwards he had a spell of suffocation and the next minute closed his

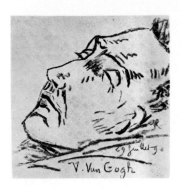

DR. GACHET: *Vincent van Gogh on His Deathbed,* Auvers, d. July· 29, 1890. Pencil, 9½ x 8⅞". Musée du Louvre, Paris

eyes. He became very quiet and did not regain consciousness.[42] At one o'clock in the morning of Tuesday, July 29, Vincent van Gogh expired in his brother's arms. He was in his thirty-eighth year. "Among his last words," wrote the heartbroken Theo to his wife, "were 'I wish I could go home now.' And thus it happened; in a few moments all was over and he found the peace he had been unable to find on earth."[43]

The funeral presented unexpected complications. The Catholic priest of Auvers refused the hearse because the painter was a suicide. The progressive municipality of a neighboring village thereupon lent its hearse and Vincent was buried on July 30 in the small cemetery of Auvers, on top of the hill, behind the church, surrounded by fields of wheat on that enormous plain which he had painted so often.

A few days later Emile Bernard wrote to Aurier: "Your absence from Paris must have kept you from learning the terrible news which I can, however, no longer withhold from you. Our dear friend Vincent died four days ago. I think you will have already guessed that he killed himself. On Sunday afternoon he went into the fields near Auvers, placed his easel against a haystack and then behind the chateau shot himself with a revolver.... Wednesday, July 30, I arrived at Auvers about 10 o'clock. Theodore van Gogh, his brother, was there with Dr. Gachet; so was Tanguy. Charles Laval accompanied me. The coffin was already closed. I came too late to see him again, who had left me three years ago[44] so full of hopes of every kind.... On the walls of the room where his body lay all his last canvases were nailed, forming something like a halo around him and rendering— through the brilliance or genius which shone from them—his death even more deplorable for us artists [Bernard himself had apparently helped Theo hang the paintings]. On the coffin a simple white drapery and masses of flowers, sunflowers which he loved so much, dahlias, and yellow blossoms everywhere. That was his favorite color if you remember, symbol of that light of which he dreamt in hearts as well as in paintings. Near him also his easel, his folding stool, and his brushes were assembled on the floor in front of the coffin.

"Many people arrived, mostly artists among whom I recognized Lucien Pissarro.... There were also people from the neighborhood who had known him a little, had seen him once or twice and who loved him, for he was so good and so human.... At three o'clock the body was removed; his friends carried it to the hearse. Some of the people present wept. Theodore van Gogh who adored his brother, who had always sustained him in his struggle for art and independence, did not stop sobbing pitifully.... Outside the sun was frightfully hot. We climbed the hill of Auvers talking of him, of the bold forward thrust he has given to art, of the great projects that always preoccupied him, of the good he has done to each of us. We arrived at the cemetery, a small new graveyard dotted with fresh tombstones. It is on a height overlooking the fields ready for reaping, under a wide blue sky which he might have loved still—maybe. And then he was lowered into the grave. He would not have cried at that moment.... The day was much too much to his liking to prevent us from thinking that he could still have lived happily....

"Dr. Gachet tried to say a few words to epitomize Vincent's life, but he too wept so much that he could only stammer a very confused farewell. He vividly recalled Vincent's efforts, indicated their sublime goal and spoke of the immense affection he himself had for him though he had known him for only a short time. 'He was,' said Gachet, 'an honest man and a great artist; he had only two aims: humanity and art. It was the art that he sought for above everything which will insure his survival....'

"And then we went back. Theodore van Gogh was completely broken by his grief...."[45]

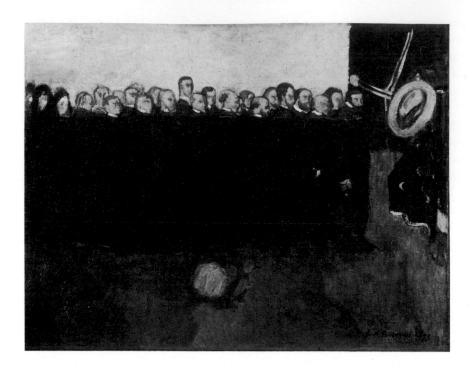

BERNARD: *The Funeral of Vincent van Gogh*
(painted from memory), d. 1893. 29½ x 36″.
Collection M.-A. Bernard-Fort, Paris

From Brittany Gauguin dispatched a short note to Theo in which de Haan joined (Gauguin's handwriting was less vigorous, more nervous than usual): "We have just learned the sad news which deeply distresses us. In these circumstances I don't want to send you phrases of condolence.—You know that to me he was a sincere friend, and that he was an *artist*, a rare thing in our times. You will continue to see him in his works.— As Vincent so often said: 'Stone will perish, but the word remains.' As for me, I shall see him with my eyes and my heart in his paintings."[46] To Schuffenecker Gauguin wrote at the same time: "I have received news of Vincent's death; it is a blessing for him, considering how much he suffered. But for his brother it is different and we owed a great deal to Vincent's influence."[47] (Gauguin obviously meant the influence Vincent exerted on Theo in favor of his painter friends). And a little later Gauguin wrote to the same: "Let us examine the situation coolly; we may be able to derive some advantage, if we are clever, from the van Gogh disaster."[48]

For several weeks Theo was too prostrated even to acknowledge the letters he received, but as soon as he was able to overcome the first shock, he had but one preoccupation: to perpetuate the work and the memory of his brother, a task that seemed almost too big for him. On account of his strained relations with Boussod & Valadon, he apparently discarded the possibility of organizing an exhibition in his own gallery, especially as he was determined not to do anything that might resemble *réclame*. Towards the end of August Theo wrote to Aurier:

"Allow me to thank you sincerely for the beautiful letter you sent me after the death of my dear brother. You were the first to appreciate him, not only for his more or less great talent for painting pictures, but you have also understood his works and have seen in them exactly the man he was. Several writers have expressed the desire to write something about him, but I have asked them to wait because I wanted to give you the chance to be the first to speak and, if you wish, to write a biography for which I could furnish you all the material, which is altogether authentic as I have had a very steady correspondence with him since 1873 and have numerous other interesting documents. I am busy preparing an exhibition which I should like to hold at the gallery of Durand-Ruel. The latter has not yet made up his mind, but I have not given up hope of obtaining his gallery. There I should like to make a catalogue with a short biography and, if you agree, we could study together the question of whether a large volume with illustrations and reproductions of certain letters should not be published." [49]

Aurier, who was absent from Paris, immediately wrote to Bernard: "You are too well aware of my admiration and my love for van Gogh's work for it to be necessary for me to tell you with what eagerness I accept this difficult but exalted task." [50] Yet Aurier apparently could not undertake this work right away, for his first novel was then about to appear. Meanwhile Theo went ahead with his plans for a show. In the middle of September he informed Dr. Gachet (who also vaguely planned to write a book on Vincent):

"As to the exhibition, I have seen Durand-Ruel, the father, who came to my apartment and found the drawings and several paintings very interesting, as he put it. But when I spoke of an exhibition, he said that the public always held him responsible whenever some people guffawed; he therefore put off his decision until he had seen the canvases [stored] at Tanguy's. He promised to call for me the following week, but he has not come back. Later I saw the son, who told me he did not think his father was undecided and that he would find it possible to provide a gallery for this purpose during the winter.... Which seems preferable to you: an exhibition at Durand-Ruel's or—if it can be obtained—a special room at the Pavillon de la Ville de Paris during the exhibition of the Independents? Signac proposed this idea and said it might not be impossible to obtain this since it is almost certain that the same thing will be done for Dubois-Pillet [who had died on August 18, 1890]." [51]

On September 18, having finally received a reply from Durand-Ruel, Theo wrote to Emile Bernard: "You may perhaps think me presumptuous to come like this to ask for your help, but this concerns myself only very little—and Vincent very much. You know that while he was still alive we had decided to move, chiefly in order to be able to show more of his paintings. We have just moved now, but the number of his canvases is staggering. I can't cope with them in assembling a group which would give an idea of his work. When I saw at Auvers how clever you were in arranging such a group, I already had the idea of asking for your help in organizing an exhibition when the time should come to hold one. Durand-Ruel having definitely refused, I can, for the time being, hang only as many as I am able to place in my home, so as to show them to anybody who manifests a desire to know his work. In short, would you be willing to help me cope with this task? But you know that unfortunately I have almost no time during the week and you have none on Sundays. As you admire Vincent's paintings, I don't have to tell you that if you will kindly accept them there are several for you in case you are willing to assist me in doing justice to Vincent's work. Next week my time is taken by a foreigner to whom I must try to sell some awful pictures. But how would Saturday be? Thus—once we have agreed on a plan—I could continue with the hanging on Sunday.... If you accept, we should have to begin in the morning, about nine for instance. Then I could go to the gallery once in the morning and once in the afternoon.... All my hope is in you." [52]

As Aurier had done, Bernard accepted this task. At the same time Theo also was in touch with Octave Maus for a memorial show of Vincent's paintings and drawings at the 1891 exhibition of the XX. In the weeks to come Theo van Gogh was thus torn between the care which Vincent's legacy demanded and the things he had to handle in his gallery. The more he lived with his brother's work, the more he realized the responsibilities which destiny so brutally had thrust upon him, and the more he came to loathe his professional dealings at Goupil's. He now led practically three separate lives: one as an employee, one as husband and father, and one of constant communion with the dead brother.

Often Theo's sorrow may have been mixed with bitter reproach: had he been right to disregard the doctor's advice by letting Vincent travel alone to Paris? Had he been right to allow Vincent to live by himself in Auvers with only distant supervision by Dr. Gachet? Had he done all that should have been done for Vincent's care? In spite of all his devotion to his brother, could he possibly have failed him? These questions forever unanswered must have burdened Theo's sensitive mind already so deeply disturbed by the many months of Vincent's sickness and yet so ill-prepared for the final tragedy. Whether a fateful heredity suddenly caught up with Theo too (a younger sister of the two brothers was to spend the greater part of her life in an institution), or whether his illness had no physical connection with Vincent's, the fact is that in October 1890 Theo van Gogh lost his mind. He had, according to Pissarro, "a violent quarrel with his employers on the subject of a painting by Decamp. Subsequently, in a moment of exasperation, he resigned from the gallery and all of a sudden went mad."[53]

On October 10, Andries Bonger summed up the situation when he wrote to Dr. Gachet: "Since yesterday, my brother-in-law van Gogh [has been] in such a state of overexcitement that we are seriously worried. If it were at all possible, we would be most grateful for you to come and see him tomorrow, while making it appear that you are paying him an impromptu visit. Everything irritates and exasperates him. His overexcitement is caused by a difference with his employers, as a result of which he wants to establish himself on his own, and this without the slightest delay. He is haunted by the memory of his brother to such a degree that he resents all those who do not espouse his views. My sister is exhausted and doesn't know what to do."[54] If Dr. Gachet did go to see Theo, he could not have done much either.

Theo's first impulses were to do precisely the things he, and especially Vincent, had always wanted to do. He sent a telegram to Gauguin: "Departure to tropics assured, money follows—Theo, Director,"[55] which created, of course, great excitement in Brittany until Gauguin, waiting in vain for the funds, convinced himself that something was wrong (he even thought of a hoax). Theo's next project was to rent the hall of Le Tambourin and to found an association of painters such as Vincent had dreamed of. But soon he became violent, apparently attacked his wife and child, and had to be taken to a clinic. As soon as he could travel, his wife took him to Holland.

Lucien Pissarro now informed his British fiancée: "You probably remember the young man who showed us some pictures at the Maison Goupil at the time of your journey to Paris. This poor man has just gone mad. It is all very sad for his family and for all the impressionist painters, for he was more than a dealer to them. Nobody took more to heart their affairs, and at this moment there is not in Paris a man able to replace him."[56]

Signac, as a newly elected member of the XX, immediately offered Maus his help for the retrospective of Vincent's works. "There are at Tanguy's nearly one hundred canvases by the poor fellow, almost all very beautiful. If his brother can't attend to this, it will be easy to make a choice for Brussels."[57]

True to his promise, Emile Bernard, together with Aurier, continued to look for a place where he could organize an exhibition of Vincent's pictures. He seems to have succeeded in a fashion, since on December 28 Johan de Meester, who had known the brothers in 1886 in Paris, sent the following report to a Dutch newspaper: "On this cold and short Christmas Day ... some Dutchmen were gathered in the tiny and sad rooms of a temporarily unoccupied apartment in Montmartre, there to admire some one hundred paintings. Their enthusiasm was tempered by sorrow: the artistic treasures assembled in this chilly and unfriendly place were the legacy of an artist who had disappeared too soon; his younger brother, very ill in turn as a result of this death, had to be taken to his homeland, leaving to the care of others—very devoted care, it is true—these relics that were so dear to him."[58]

But even this modest "exhibition" was violently opposed by Gauguin, who asked de Haan in Paris to intercede with Bernard and, in January 1891, wrote him directly: "What blundering! You know how I love Vincent's art. But in view of the stupidity of the public, this is not the time to remind people of van Gogh and his madness at the very moment when his brother, too, is in the same situation. Many people say that our painting is madness. This [exhibition] will do us harm without doing any good to Vincent. Well, do as you please, but it is *idiotic*."[59]

Theo died in Holland on January 25, 1891, less than six months after his brother; he was thirty-three years old. During his last weeks he was apparently in a complete state of apathy. His doctor tried in vain to arouse his interest by reading him an article about Vincent published in the *Handelsblad*.[58] Only Vincent's name aroused his attention. On his case sheet in the column "Cause of Illness" are the words: "Chronic illness, overstrain, and sorrow; he had a life full of emotional stress."[60] Aurier inserted a short notice in the *Mercure de France*: "We have just been informed of the death of Theo van Gogh, the kind and intelligent expert who did so much to bring to the public's attention the works of the most audacious among the independent artists of today."[61]

Theo's death seems to have affected Gauguin somewhat more than Vincent's. "If you had known [Theo] van Gogh," he later wrote to his wife, "you would have seen an earnest man devoted to the good cause. Had he not died like his brother, I should now be out of trouble."[62] And to a friend he subsequently complained: "When [Theo] van Gogh of Goupil's went mad, I was lost.... Van Gogh alone knew how to sell pictures and build up a clientele; today nobody knows how to appeal to collectors."[63]

After Theo's death his widow immediately pledged her support to Bernard as well as to Octave Maus, and no doubt also to Signac. She was ready to carry on the task that her husband had been unable to achieve. Bernard actually suggested to her that in view of the exhibition he was trying to organize, it might be better if she did not authorize the memorial show prepared by the Independents. But this she refused to do, apparently feeling that a bird in the hand was worth two in the bush. Indeed, it was not until the next year, 1892, that Bernard succeeded in finding a small gallery where he showed a group of sixteen paintings by van Gogh.

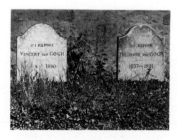

Tombstones of Vincent and Theo van Gogh at Auvers

Meanwhile Signac borrowed several canvases from Tanguy for the retrospective of the XX in February and for that of the Independents, which opened on March 20, 1891. Aurier who, besides the *Cypresses* which Vincent had painted for him, owned various pictures by van Gogh (mainly of the early Dutch period, which he had either bought from

Theo or received as presents), promptly informed his sister: "If you want to buy a painting, I know a superb bargain, a *Bouquet of Flowers* by Vincent van Gogh, which is stranded at a bric-à-brac dealer's. It can be had for some fifteen francs [a dollar was then about five francs], but it is necessary to hurry, for the van Gogh exhibition will open in about three weeks and might give the dealer an idea of the true value of the canvas."[64] Aurier's sister bought the painting, but Aurier was too optimistic in thinking that the show would drastically increase van Gogh's prices.

Whereas the retrospective of Dubois-Pillet, one of the founders of the Independents, who had died at Le Puy where he was stationed with his regiment of the National Guard, comprised sixty-four canvases, van Gogh's retrospective was much more modest: ten paintings altogether. Yet it was his show that provided the high point of the 1891 Salon des Indépendants. In March, Octave Mirbeau, always violent, outspoken, and ready to antagonize, always willing to support a forgotten or lost cause, published an article on the painter whom he had not known but whom his friends Monet and Rodin must have taught him to admire (and whose *Irises* and *Portrait of Tanguy* he was soon to purchase):

"At the exhibition of the Independents, among some happy experiments and, above all, among many banalities and even more frauds, sparkle the canvases by the greatly lamented van Gogh. In front of them, before the black veil of mourning that surrounds them and singles them out for the crowd of indifferent visitors, one is overcome by great sadness to think that this magnificently gifted painter, this instinctive, supersensitive, visionary artist is no longer among us. The loss is cruel and much more painful and irreparable for art than that of Meissonier [who had just died at the age of seventy-five], although the people were not invited to a pompous funeral, and although poor Vincent van Gogh, with whom a beautiful flame of genius had died, went to his death as obscure, as unknown as he had lived, obscure and unknown, in this world of injustice.

"And he should not be judged by the few paintings now on exhibition... though these seem greatly superior in intensity of vision, in richness of expression, in vigor of style, to all those surrounding them. Of course, I am not unaware of the search for light by Georges Seurat, whose seascapes with their exquisite and profound luminosity I like very much. I find a lively charm in the stupendous atmosphere, the feminine grace, the bright elegance of van Rysselberghe. I am attracted by Maurice Denis' small compositions, so suave in tone, bathed in such tender mysticism. I recognize in the limited realism of Armand Guillaumin, devoid of ideas but well-executed, as the saying goes, honest and robust qualities of craftmanship. And, in spite of the blacks which unduly smudge his figures, Toulouse-Lautrec shows a real power, clever and tragic, in the study of physiognomies and the understanding of character. The prints by Lucien Pissarro have verve, sobriety, and distinction. Even Anquetin, in the midst of his flagrant reminiscences, academic conventions, botched oddities, caricatured uglinesses, sometimes offers us a pleasant glimpse of light... and masterly harmonies of gray.... But none of these genuine artists—with whom one should not confound M. Signac, whose loud, dry, pretentious nothingness is irritating—captivates me as much as Vincent van Gogh. Here I feel that I am in the presence of somebody who is higher, more masterly, who disturbs me, who moves me and who leaves a profound impression."[65]

Although Mirbeau dismissed somewhat lightly the works of most of the other exhibitors, the fact remains that the Société des Indépendants was slowly gaining in importance. During the first years of its existence, Seurat and his friends had been hopelessly out-

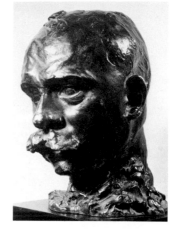

RODIN: *Portrait of Octave Mirbeau,* c. 1889. 12⅝" high. Galerie Saint-Etienne, New York

numbered by manufacturers of pitiful daubs. There had been bitter struggles between the neo-impressionists and the others. As recently as 1888—the year when van Gogh had first shown with the Independents—Signac had reported to van Rysselberghe: "Next Wednesday full reunion of the Independents; the members of the hanging committee will be named. We expect to exert some electoral pressure so as to obtain a [neo] impressionist majority. It is impossible to foresee the decisions of the hanging committee; Seurat, [Lucien] Pissarro and I are members. We shall do our best to defend our friends' interests, which are our own.... You may be sure that we shall bellow mightily... to battle against the stupid members of the committee, mad, mad, gaga, gaga."[66]

The hanging committee was still a vital issue since it afforded the only opportunity to group properly the works of those who had a real contribution to make, setting them apart from the rest. Little by little the yearly shows began to attract new talents among the younger generation. After van Gogh in 1888, Lautrec had joined in 1889 and the Belgians van Rysselberghe, Finch, and Dario de Regoyos had started to exhibit in 1890. On March 20 of that year the opening of the Independents was attended by the French President, Sadi Carnot, to whom a number of artists were introduced. Among these were Seurat and Signac, who put themselves at his disposal to explain the procedures of the "new school." But it is unlikely that he paid much attention to their involved theories (as to their political views, little did he know that they were in sympathy with the anarchist to whose bullets he was to succumb a few years hence).

In 1891 there was again a group of newcomers, and it looked as if the Independents would finally become a major factor in the Paris art season. Even Cézanne considered in 1891 showing with the Independents but eventually decided against it. Among the new adherents of 1891 were Bonnard, Denis, Vallotton, Emile Bernard, and Gauguin's acquaintance, the Dane Willumsen; Dr. Gachet also exhibited. But Seurat's friends and followers still composed by far the most numerous single group, whose works, hung together, gained considerably in impact. In 1891 this group included Angrand, Cross, the late Dubois-Pillet, Finch, Gausson, Lemmen, Luce, Petitjean, Lucien Pissarro, van Rysselberghe, Seurat, and Signac. At the same time several defections began to occur in the camp of the neo-impressionists. Whereas numerically still dominant, their little company, after the many recruits of the first years, began to show a decline at the very moment when the Société des Indépendants itself registered important gains. (Altogether 1,250 works were exhibited at the Salon des Indépendants in 1891.)

Continuous internal squabbles and rivalries had finally prompted Seurat to assert his leadership by publishing in the summer of 1890 a summary of his theories (see p. 128). At the same time he continued to keep a sharp lookout for the slightest misinterpretation of facts that might deprive him of his role as a pioneer. When, during that same summer, Fénéon—who certainly could not be suspected of unfriendliness—published an article on Signac in which Seurat detected some minor errors, he immediately wrote: "I protest and establish the dates within a margin of two weeks." He also insisted, speaking of the decisive years about 1886: "You will have to admit... that while I was unknown I none the less existed, I and my vision which you have just so superbly described...."[67]

Feeling either continually crushed by Seurat's superiority and his insistence upon it, or else being dissatisfied with his theories, several of his associates now began to abandon his group. Seurat may actually have welcomed some of these defections, which were greatly deplored by Signac. Camille Pissarro had begun a slow retreat, endeavoring to find a technique that would satisfy him better than the uncompromising dot. His son had left for London where he intended to settle, and Lucien's friend Hayet, after some hesitation, had handed his resignation to Signac:

"When I found myself won over by and drawn into the [neo] impressionist movement, I believed I had found there a group of intelligent people who assisted each other in their researches without other ambition than that of pure art. And in this I have believed for five years. But then, one day, successive clashes occurred and made me wonder. Suddenly the past came back to me, and the group which I had taken for a band of seekers, I now saw divided into two camps, some truly searching, the others merely discussing and disputing, sowing dissension (perhaps not intentionally) and having only one goal: to surpass the rest. . . . And the realization of these facts made me lose all confidence. As I cannot live in uncertainty and as I do not wish to suffer eternal torments, I have decided to isolate myself. . . ."[68]

In Belgium, Henry van de Velde was deeply disillusioned. He was disturbed by Seurat's "distrustfulness and meanness"; eventually he even came to doubt the rightness of his views. "I thought he was a greater master of the science of color," he later wrote. "His gropings, his struggles with that science, the confusion of his explanations of his 'so-called' theory threw me off. . . . Those who criticized the *Grande Jatte* for its lack of luminosity were right, as those who noticed the weak interplay of 'complementaries' saw clearly." Although van de Velde maintained his admiration for Signac who "reached the goal at which all of us aimed, we pupils of Seurat and converts to the division of color and optical mixture: luminosity," he himself decided to give up painting altogether.[69] In 1890 he had exhibited for the first and last time with the Independents. Like Hayet, van de Velde was no longer to be counted on, while Luce, never strictly a follower of Seurat, also slowly detached himself from the group.

But the most serious indictment of divisionism finally came from its first and most enthusiastic adherent, Camille Pissarro. About 1890, having vainly tried to soften the rigidity of the divisionist technique, Pissarro decided that he had been misled in following his young friends, and abandoned their theories. To him a method was valid not because its logic could be proven, but only as long as it allowed him to obtain results which satisfied his critical eye. When his works no longer met with his approbation, no scientific data could persuade him to follow a system that seemed to hamper rather than to further his artistic expression. Once he had arrived at this conviction, he articulately explained it to his friends and there must have been many sessions in which the "for" and "against" of divisionism were discussed as heatedly as in the early days. But Pissarro was firm. Eventually he explained to van de Velde:

"I believe it is my duty to write you frankly and tell you how I [now] regard the experiment I made with systematic divisionism by following our friend Seurat. Having tried this theory for four years and having then abandoned it, not without painful and obstinate efforts to regain what I had lost and not to lose what I had learned, I can no longer consider myself one of the neo-impressionists who abandon movement and life for a diametrically opposed esthetic which, perhaps, is the right thing for the man who has the temperament for it, but which is not for me, anxious as I am to avoid all narrow and so-called scientific theories. Having found after many attempts (I speak for myself) that it was impossible to be true to my sensations and consequently to render life and movement, impossible to be faithful to the effects, so random and so admirable, of nature, impossible to give an

Right: VALLOTTON: *The Waltz*, d. 1893. 24 x 19¾". Present whereabouts unknown

Far right: VUILLARD: *The Artist's Mother*, c. 1891. 8½ x 6½". Collection Mrs. William Goetz, Los Angeles

Below left: DENIS: *Annunciation*, d. 1891. 10⅝ x 16⅛". Rijksmuseum Kröller-Müller, Otterlo

Below right: TOOROP: *The Print Lover* (looking at a lithograph by Lautrec), c. 1891 (?). 25⅝ x 29⅞". Rijksmuseum Kröller-Müller, Otterlo

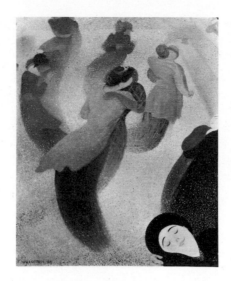

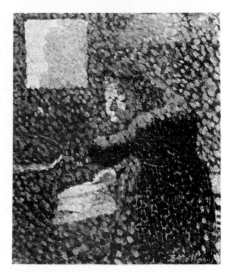

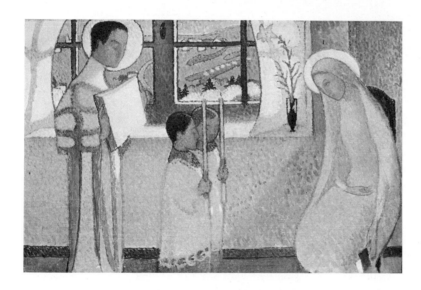

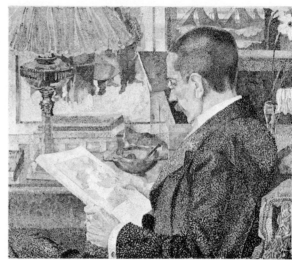

individual character to my drawing, I had to give up. And none too soon! Fortunately it appears that I was not made for this art which gives me the impression of the monotony of death!"[70]

As if to make up for these defections, some of the younger men around Gauguin's "pupil" Sérusier, such as Denis, Vallotton, and Vuillard, began to experiment with the pointillist technique. But they did so chiefly to obtain certain effects of texture—as van Gogh had done—without applying divisionism in all its rigor. Their attempts, therefore, were short-lived and without great importance for their own evolution. The ephemeral appearance of such "experimentalists" who never really joined Seurat's circle could in no way offset the defections of Pissarro, Hayet, and van de Velde, nor the death of Dubois-Pillet.

389

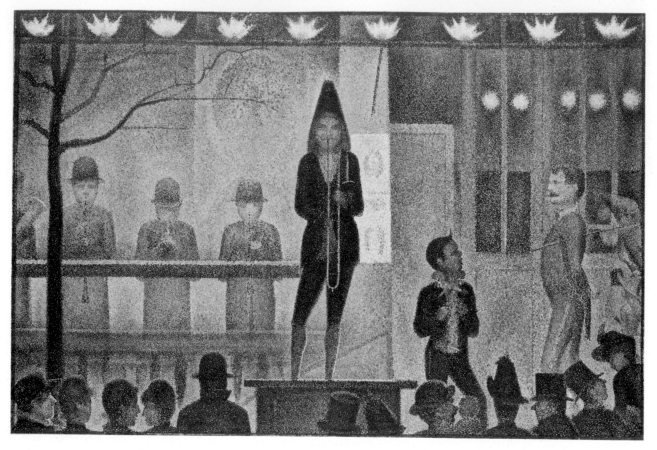

Thus matters stood in 1891 while Seurat continued his work unperturbed. During the years which had followed the completion of his *Grande Jatte,* Seurat, with the assistance of Henry's discoveries, had not only perfected his methods, he had also systematically tackled every one of the problems of painting. Only still lifes are lacking in his work, and even these can be found in sections of his large canvases. Having studied in *La Grande Jatte* the movements of people outdoors and reproduced in numerous landscapes nature in repose, Seurat had painted in turn immobile figures outdoors under artificial lighting (*La Parade,* 1887–88), immobile nudes in the studio (*Les Poseuses,* 1887–88, page 97), a portrait (*Young Woman Powdering Herself,* 1889–90, page 395), finally, moving figures indoors under artificial light (*Le Chahut,* 1889–90, page 349), and his most recent composition, *Le Cirque,* 1890–91, page 393). The figures in his paintings are dominated by monotony or by joy—there is no sadness in his pictures—and are, of course, governed by strict rules, being controlled by that play of lines and colors whose laws Seurat had studied. In these canvases Seurat had, without yielding in any way to the literary or the picturesque, rehabilitated the "subject," which had been relinquished by the impressionists.

Although Seurat was mainly concerned with integrating complicated linear schemes into his compositions, based for instance on the golden section, he maintained that he could paint only what he saw before his eyes[71] and declared that the drawing was the fundamental element in painting (this had been Ingres' dogma) and that harmony of color should flow from harmony of line. In a conversation with Gustave Kahn he once defined painting as "the art of hollowing a surface," but van de Velde was to retort that "the opposite would be just as admissible: 'the art of creating reliefs on a surface.'"[69] Yet even van de Velde later admitted that, as chief of a school, Seurat had inaugurated "a new era of painting, that of *return to style.* Destiny had decided it that way. It had made him discover a technique, that of pigment, which *inevitably* had to lead to stylization."[69]

Signac meanwhile continued to be preoccupied mostly with questions of technique and of color, his more robust temper and his fiercer character keeping him away from Henry's mathematical equations, in spite of the fact that he had occasionally collaborated with the scientist. While Seurat placed an ever stronger accent on the significance of linear directions, Signac was more concerned with colors than with Henry's theories. In an article published in 1891, Fénéon stated that in subordinating his compositions to a dominant direction, Signac did so intuitively rather than according to principles. "He has not been subjugated by those gracious mathematics; he knows that a work of art is indivisible. Besides, Henry has never claimed to furnish artists with a means to create systematically (or even to analyze) beauty, which is a rather complex thing. He has said: 'Every direction is symbolic' and this simple idea has been fecund if it has destroyed Signac's faith in hazard and fortified him in a lucid empiricism on the threshold of consciousness."[72] In reply to this article Signac had written to Fénéon: "Don't worry too much about the criticism of our Henry; he cares very little about the play of complementaries which he considers barbarous."[73]

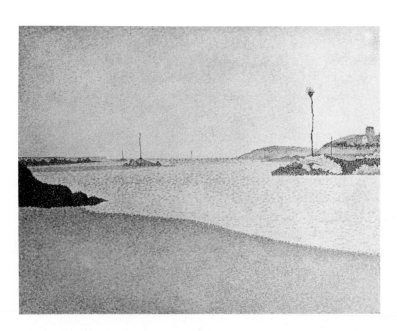

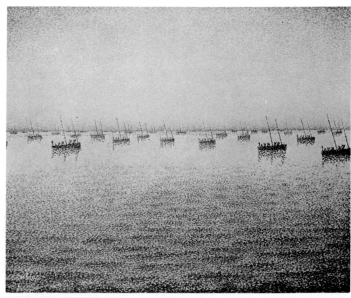

Signac: *Coast at Saint-Briac,* d. 1890. 25⅝ x 31⅞". Exhibited with the Independents in 1891. Private collection, New York

Signac: *Fishing Boats at Sunset,* d. 1891. 24¾ x 31". Collection Mr. and Mrs. John Hay Whitney, New York

Less inclined to search for "style" than Seurat, Signac progressed towards a more decorative art, stressing contrasts and technique. "We must avoid dryness," he was to write to van Rysselberghe, "slowness of execution, thinness—we must restore to the brush stroke all it can produce of luminosity and purity and yet find the means to make it inconspicuous, to harmonize it smoothly with its neighbor. Cross strives for this and so do you. We shall find the answer. The proof that we are not in a blind alley but on a sumptuous avenue, wide and airy, is that every year we modify ourselves while progressing towards harmony and light!"[74]

Signac seems to have been more deeply affected by Pissarro's withdrawal than Seurat was, but then Signac had maintained a much closer relationship with the older master than his friend. "I can still clearly recall," Signac later told Pissarro, "your enthusiasm for this technique and your expressions of satisfaction with my works. Can a thing one has liked so well suddenly appear so odious? . . . Though I am convinced that we are on the right track, I am even more certain that we have not yet reached the goal and still have a long way to go. That is all the more reason not to be discouraged; on the contrary, it is necessary to persevere and work hard."[75]

It was this conviction, this constant desire to improve, combined with a belligerent spirit, which assigned to Signac the active leadership of Seurat's circle. And conscious of his responsibilities, he was ready each year to devote all his energy to the organization of the Salon des Indépendants. In 1891 it was he who assembled the loans for Dubois-Pillet's retrospective and apparently it was Signac also who arranged the much smaller memorial exhibition of Vincent van Gogh. In spite of his efforts, most of the neo-impressionists sent less than the maximum quota of ten works, with the exception of Luce and Gausson. Anquetin, Dr. Gachet, and Gaullaumin each showed ten works, Toulouse-Lautrec nine, and the *douanier* Rousseau the same number. The various painters in the orbit of Gauguin—who himself still refused to join the Independents—were strongly represented: Denis, Vallotton, and Willumsen with ten works apiece; Maufra with nine Brittany landscapes, mostly from Pont-Aven; Bonnard also with nine works; and Bernard with six (he thus at last did participate in an exhibition where Seurat and Signac showed). Signac himself had nine paintings in the show, his *Portrait of Fénéon* (page 105) and the rest views of the Seine at Herblay and of the Atlantic coast; Seurat only five: four seascapes of Gravelines and his *Cirque* which, though not quite finished, seemed to the artist sufficiently advanced to be exhibited (a radical departure from his habits, explained possibly by the fact that the linear composition was completed and the general color scheme established).

The hanging committee, under the vice-presidency of Cross, was composed of Luce, Seurat, Signac, and Lautrec, among others. The opening was announced for the 20th of March. Early in March the committee members began their work: examination of the arrivals, grouping according to affinities, supervision of the hanging. Seurat, with Signac, spent every day in the large building which the city of Paris put at the disposal of the Independents. It was there that Seurat found himself with Angrand in the last hall, mainly devoted to the neo-impressionists, when Puvis de Chavannes entered and began to examine some drawings by Denis. "He will notice," Seurat told his friend, "the mistake I made in the horse," but Puvis passed without even stopping in front of his *Cirque*, which cruelly disappointed Seurat.[76]

A few days later Seurat went to bed with a sore throat. The year before an epidemic of influenza had struck down hundreds of victims in Paris, and again there were cases of

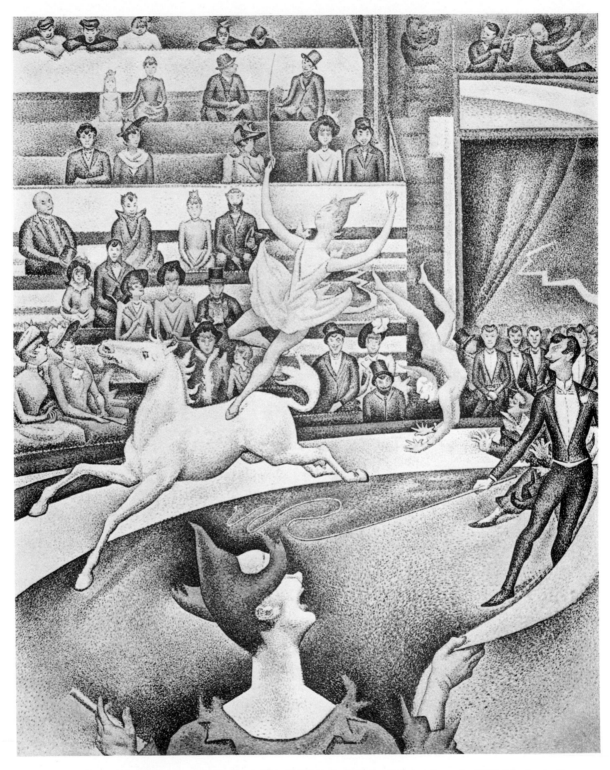

SEURAT: *Le Cirque* (unfinished), 1890–91. 73 x 59⅛". Exhibited with the Independents in 1891. Musée du Louvre, Paris (Gift of John Quinn)

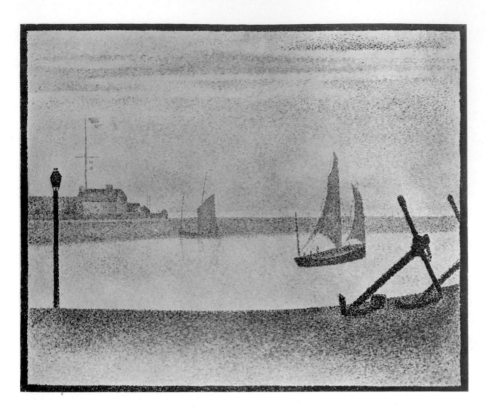

SEURAT: *The Channel at Gravelines, Evening,* 1890. 25¾ x 32¼". The Museum of Modern Art, New York (Gift of William A. M. Burden, the Donor and His Wife Retaining Life Interest)

diphtheritic influenza. Suddenly Seurat took a turn for the worse. On March 30 Signac announced to van Rysselberghe: "Awful news: our poor Seurat died yesterday morning after two days of illness. An infectious angina they say. He leaves a poor woman and—what we did not know—a beautiful baby, thirteen months old, whom he had acknowledged. The unfortunate woman is pregnant again . . . . I am too sad to write at greater length."[77] Two days later another letter informed van Rysselberghe: "Isn't it abominable, this death! I believe that I shall never get over it . . . . It seems that there was an effusion [of blood] in the brain.[78]—In a word, our poor friend killed himself by overwork. . . . He was buried yesterday. . . . Never have I seen anything as sad as this funeral. Everybody was crushed. The family organized a superb—too superb—service for him. . . . Please excuse the incoherence of this letter. I am out of my mind."[79]

It was not long before Seurat's child also succumbed; the burial took place on April 15. Although some of his most intimate friends, such as Signac and Angrand, had known about Seurat's common-law wife, Madeleine Knobloch, whom he had depicted in 1889–90 in his *Young Woman Powdering Herself,* the painter had been so secretive about his private life, even they did not know he was a father. The child that Madeleine Knobloch was expecting at Seurat's death was never born. Later that same year she suffered another loss and Signac wrote to Luce: "Did you know that the mother of that poor Knobloch girl drowned herself? She wrote me: 'Mamma drowned herself; her body was recovered at Argenteuil.—I just went to identify her at the Morgue.' . . . Poor people!"[80]

Seurat's parents, who were comparatively well off, immediately acknowledged Madeleine

394

Knobloch as their son's wife. Having decided against an auction sale of the estate, they allotted half of the painter's work to his widow. As Seurat had sold only a few pictures during his lifetime (and had given away a few others, as well as a number of drawings), practically his entire output of about ten years—the span of his artistic career—was still accumulated in his studio. (He had obtained 400 francs for his landscapes and 60 francs for his drawings; the price for his *Poseuses* had been calculated by Seurat on the basis of one year's work at seven francs a day, that is about 2,500 francs, though he was willing to accept less. Vincent van Gogh had estimated the *Poseuses* and *La Grande Jatte* at 5,000 francs each. Six years after Seurat's death a dealer asked 800 francs for the *Poseuses*, and in 1900 his family sold *La Grande Jatte* for 800, the *Cirque* for 500 and drawings for 10 francs.)

By common consent, Signac, Luce, and Fénéon—assisted by Seurat's brother—were appointed to classify his works and proceed with the division. They carefully catalogued and numbered all of Seurat's canvases, small wooden panels, and innumerable drawings,

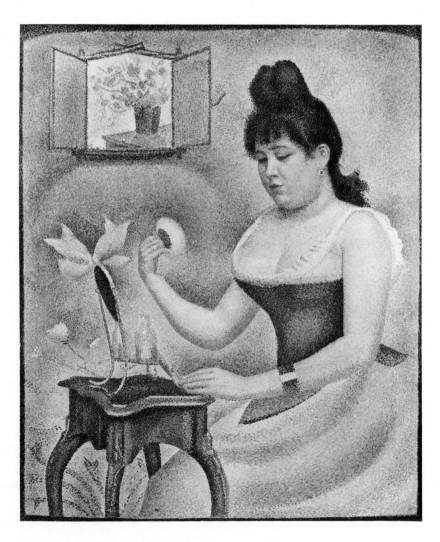

SEURAT: *Woman Powdering Herself* (Madeleine Knobloch), 1889–90. 37½ x 31¼". Courtauld Institute Galleries, London

authenticating each on the reverse and putting their own initials on the back for future identification. "I have been asked," Luce wrote to Brussels a few weeks after the artist's death, "provided the family maintains its intentions, to put aside either a panel or a drawing for each of Seurat's friends."[81] And Signac who, completely exhausted, had left Paris, reassured van Rysselberghe: "You can accept without hesitation these souvenirs of our poor friend. The family is very anxious that some of the 300 panels shall be distributed among his comrades."[82]

Since Seurat had made many friends in Belgium through his association with the XX, fourteen drawings and five panels, destined for van Rysselberghe, van de Velde, Finch, Dario de Regoyos, Mlle Boch (who had bought van Gogh's *Red Vineyard*), Verhaeren, Lemmen, Maus, Mme Gustave Kahn, and others, were taken to Brussels by Madeleine Knobloch, who planned to establish herself there as a *modiste*. But no sooner had she arrived in Brussels than she tried to convince Gustave Kahn and his wife, as well as the painter Lemmen, that she was a victim of Seurat's entourage. Thus she was able to obtain money from Kahn, to whom she said that the painter's friends were conniving to "despoil" her of his works; she accused Signac of having but one desire, that of "burying his rival Seurat," and Luce of having "finished" Seurat's *Cirque*. Deceived by her intrigues, the Kahns did not help the situation when they showed her a letter from Fénéon in which he—justifiably—expressed misgivings at seeing half of Seurat's works in the hands of Madeleine Knobloch. After her return to Paris, she continued to blurt out similar, offensive rumors which particularly aroused Signac's indignation. Eventually Theo van Rysselberghe's tactfulness put an end to the whole sad situation.[83] The Kahns admitted their transgression but "withdrew" their friendship from Madeleine Knobloch; Lemmen sent a letter of excuses to Signac. "All is finished," the latter wrote towards the end of June to van Rysselberghe, "and I hope that this gang will make up for the harm they did. The one who is most to be pitied in spite of all her irresponsibility, however great, is that poor scatterbrain, Seurat's widow who, with her idle talk and lies, like those of a crazy concierge, has now turned everybody against her."[84]

Immediately after Seurat's death, Gustave Kahn obtained from Madeleine Knobloch a great number of press clippings, concerned mostly with Seurat's various exhibitions, for a book he planned to write. He intended to ask for the collaboration of all of the painter's friends for this volume. But after what had happened, he was requested to return these documents to van Rysselberghe, who eventually restored them to Seurat's mother.

Seurat's death went practically unnoticed in the press. Only several months later did his friend Jules Christophe publish an article, lamenting: "A sudden and stupid illness carried him off in a few hours when he was in the midst of his triumph! I curse Providence and death!"[85] Verhaeren and Kahn also wrote about the painter, but the strangest obituary was composed by Fénéon: "On March 29 died, at thirty-one years of age, Seurat, who exhibited at the Salon in 1883; with the Group of Independent Artists in 1884; with the Society of Independent Artists in 1884–85, 1886, 1887, 1888, 1889, 1890, and 1891; with the Impressionists, in the rue Laffitte, in 1886; in New York in 1885–1886; at Nantes in 1886; with the XX in Brussels in 1887, 1889, and 1891; with 'Black and White,' Amsterdam, in 1888. The catalogue of his works comprises about 170 panels cigar-box size, 420 drawings, 6 sketchbooks and some 60 canvases among which are five of large dimensions (*La Baignade, A Sunday at La Grande Jatte, Poseuses, Chahut, Cirque*) and, probably, numerous masterpieces."[86]

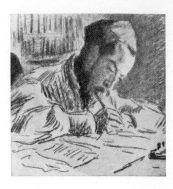

LUCE: *Portrait of Gustave Kahn,* c. 1890. Lithograph

Teodor de Wyzewa, who did not like Seurat's innovations and had already said so plainly in 1886, now wrote a somewhat mellow article, without however relinquishing his opinions: "I have several times had occasion to spend a few hours in the company of this gentle and pensive young man who had established in advance, for the next thirty years, the program of his work and who has now departed, leaving behind hardly more than the first sketches of the important accomplishment of which he dreamed. Tall, with his long beard and his naïve eyes, he gave me the impression of one of those Italian masters of the Renaissance, who were, like him, strong and yet disdainful of their power, pursuing their ideal with assured strides. And on the first evening I met him I discovered that his soul was a soul of yesteryear. The secular disillusionment which renders the task of today's artists so difficult never had any hold over him. He believed in the power of theories, in the absolute value of methods, in the continuance of revolutions. And I was overjoyed to discover in a corner of Montmartre such an admirable specimen of a race that I had thought extinct, of the race of painter-theorists, uniting practice to ideas and unconscious fantasy to reasoned effort. Yes, I sensed very clearly in Seurat a kinsman of Leonardo, of Dürer, of Poussin. I never tired of hearing him explain the details of his researches, the order in which he intended to pursue them, the number of years he planned to devote to them. Nor did he tire of revealing them to me.

"Let me add that his researches concerned the same matters that had occupied the masters of the past, the most worthy matters, to my mind, to preoccupy an artist... Georges Seurat had found solutions which he considered satisfactory. These solutions, I must admit, did not satisfy me as much as did the problems themselves which he had tackled. I could not believe that the method of pointillism, even though it might conform better to the scientific hypotheses about color, was superior to any other for the translation of color in painting, nor could I admit that it was sufficient to draw rising lines to suggest gay emotions, or that coloring a frame produced the effect of completing the harmony of a picture and of isolating it from its surroundings. But I was willing to give Seurat credit for more decisive solutions to come...."[87]

True to his conviction that the conquest of technical difficulties is not in itself an esthetic achievement, Wyzewa continued: "Experiments and rough drafts are all that remain of Seurat. His compositions of figures, *La Grande Jatte, La Parade, Les Poseuses, Le Cirque*, are obviously provisional attempts, first essays to apply step by step methods that are still vague. One always finds in them side by side superb details revealing the artist, strange details which indicate the searcher, and also details in which the neglect of this or that element is all too visible because it has been sacrificed to more singular elements. No doubt, for instance, that in due time Seurat would have managed to remove from his figures that rigid and congealed appearance which often prevents us from appreciating the authoritative purity of his draftsmanship. As to the small landscapes he has left... several are charming, lighter, more subtle than all the landscapes of today; but this daintiness and this lightness, and the delicate melancholy which accompanies them, are, I believe, due much more to the soul of Seurat than to his methods and his theories. There is, however, one field in which it seems to me that Seurat has brought to the fore all the qualities of his genius: I have seen drawings by him, marvelously artistic, sober, luminous, alive, the most expressive drawings I know of....

"Of Seurat's innovations not much remains... thus it is possible that the name of Seurat, without ever having been well known, will some day be forgotten. Death has perfidiously

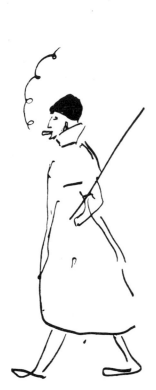

VAN RYSSELBERGHE: *Self-Portrait*, 1887. Pen and ink

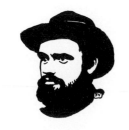

VALLOTTON: *Portrait of Maximilien Luce*. Pen and ink

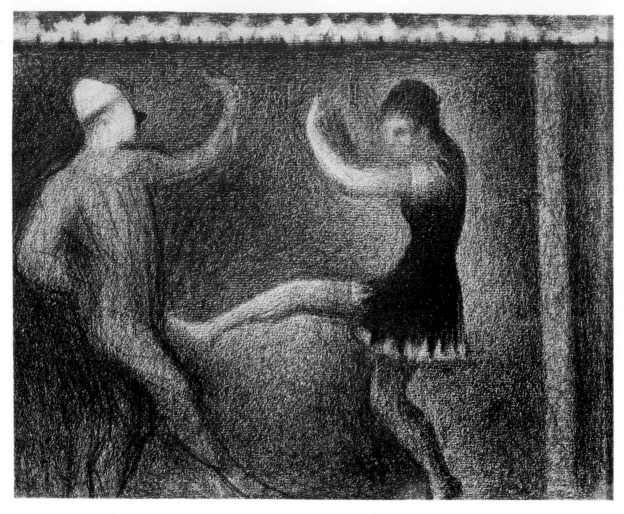

SEURAT: *Saltimbanques—Couple Dancing*, c. 1886. Conté crayon, 9½ x 12¼″. Formerly collection Paul Signac. Collection Mr. and Mrs. Leigh B. Block, Chicago

surprised him. But at least I shall be permitted to declare that he was one of the forces of the art of our time, that he was worth more than all others of his age, with a loftier curiosity and a nobler mind, and that with him vanishes one more of our hopes to see emerge a new art in the midst of the anarchy, the ignorance, and the coarseness of the contemporary artistic movement."[87]

While Pissarro, too, now expressed reservations concerning Seurat's work, he nevertheless sincerely mourned his young friend. "You can conceive," he wrote to his son Lucien in London, "the grief of all those who followed him or were interested in his artistic researches. It is a great loss for art."[88]—"Isn't it dreadful!" Lucien replied, "so young and so full of promise, having already achieved something great for so young a man, [to die] at the moment when he was probably going to enter the path of further improvements?—Pointillism has died with him!"[89] Answered his father: "I believe you are right, pointillism is finished,

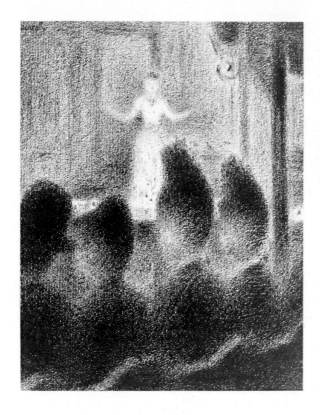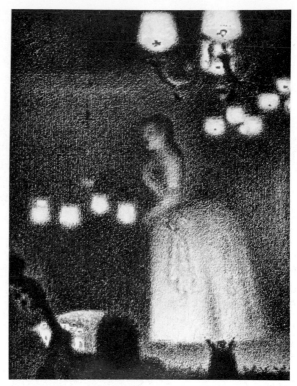

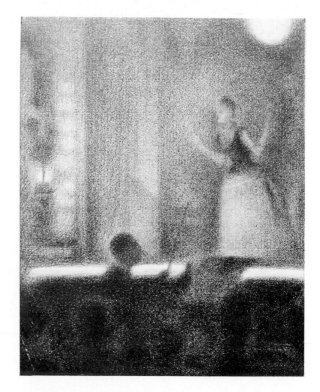

Above: Seurat: *At the "Concert Européen,"* c. 1887.
Conté crayon, 12¼ x 9⅜". The Museum of Modern
Art, New York (Lillie P. Bliss Collection)

Above right: Seurat: *Singer at the Café-Concert,* c.
1887. Conté crayon and gouache, 11⅞ x 9". Formerly
collection Theo van Gogh. Rijksmuseum Vincent van
Gogh, Amsterdam

Right: Seurat: *The Café-Concert,* c. 1887. Conté
crayon and gouache, 11½ x 8¾". Museum of Art,
Rhode Island School of Design, Providence

but I think it will have consequences which later on will be of the utmost importance to art. Seurat really added something."[90]

Under no circumstances could Signac subscribe to the view that Seurat's death spelled the end of the neo-impressionist movement. But he did realize, of course, that the leadership had now fallen upon him and that a threefold task lay ahead of him: to defend Seurat's memory, a mission in which Fénéon was to assist him with energy and subtlety; to continue the efforts which would maintain the domination of the Society of the Independents (suddenly menaced by an attempt by Anquetin to found a rival society);[91] above all, to carry on Seurat's artistic endeavors. This was an undertaking full of responsibilities, an inescapable duty which he had to shoulder because evasion of it would have amounted to an admission that he had been merely Seurat's shadow, which certainly was not the case. Signac had many of the qualities required for his new role, yet there were moments when he felt lonely and tired, conscious of the fact that the task ahead might prove to be an ungrateful one (Kahn's and Lemmen's attitude particularly had impressed this upon him).

After Seurat's death Signac went through a period of prostration. He left for Brittany, anxious to isolate himself and to plunge into work; yet in June he was back in Paris for an operation on a cyst. He was so disheartened and disgusted by what had happened in

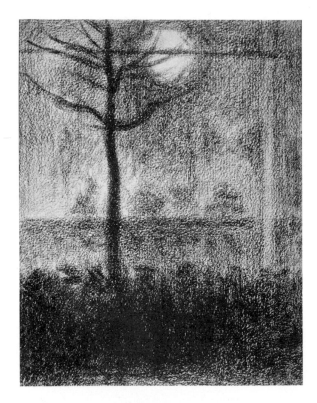

SEURAT: *Tree at Night,* study for *La Parade,* c. 1886. Conté crayon. Private collection, Paris

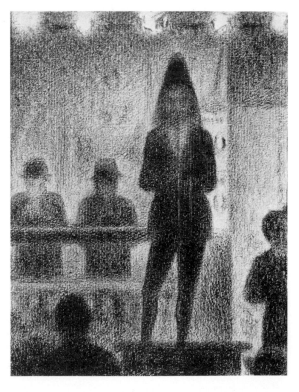

SEURAT: *Trombone Player,* study for *La Parade,* 1887. Conté crayon, 12½ x 9½". Collection Henry P. McIlhenny, Philadelphia

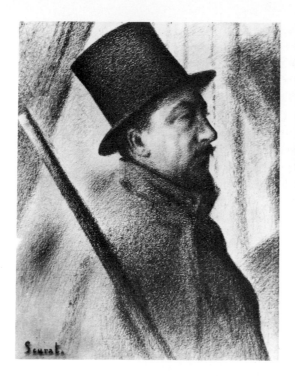

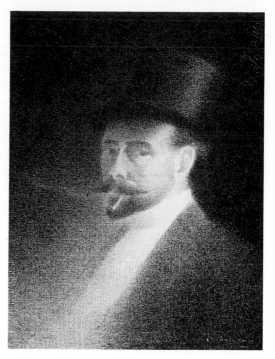

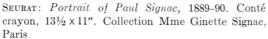

SEURAT: *Portrait of Paul Signac,* 1889–90. Conté crayon, 13½ x 11″. Collection Mme Ginette Signac, Paris

ANGRAND: *Self-Portrait,* d. 1893. Conté crayon, 24 x 17½″. The Metropolitan Museum of Art, New York (Robert Lehman Collection, 1975)

Brussels that he even considered resigning from the XX. Later on, during that same summer, he wrote a deeply discouraged letter to Camille Pissarro, in which he referred to the time when "holding each other by the hand, presenting new works and new ideas, I thought we all would courageously enter the battle together. Being the most belligerent of the group, I sacrificed myself to the interests of all. And I think that I have not been useless and that if our ideas have gained ground, I am not alien to this development. If it had to be done over again, I should do it once more and I am convinced that you would not blame me for this. If now I have quieted down somewhat, it is because at present the soil has been sown, our ideas have been diffused, our manifesto [probably an allusion to the publication of Seurat's theories] has been proclaimed.... All that remains is to work and let things run."[92]

Signac was too much of a man of action to really "quiet down" for long. Soon his optimism, his love of controversy, his intensity, his joy in crushing imbecility wherever he found it, his pride in upholding his beliefs like a provocative banner, again won the upper hand. Though he had actually no choice but to carry on where Seurat had left off, instead of doing so with resignation, he was ready to lead the fight with his old vigor and enthusiasm. By his premature death Seurat had become something like a martyr of divisionism; his actions, his theories, his works assumed the aspect of a holy legacy, inalterably established for posterity, while life brought new demands, new problems, new exigencies; and Signac was there to fulfill his destiny, even at the risk of doing so alone. But he could not help musing about the strange decisions of fate. Less than four years after Seurat's death he sadly compared van Gogh's rising fame to the oblivion that seemed to have descended upon his best friend. Dipping his pen into his prejudices against the former and his by now almost blind veneration for the latter, he confided to his diary:

"How unjust people are towards Seurat. To think that they refuse to recognize in him one of the geniuses of the century! The young people are full of admiration for [the poet] Laforgue and for van Gogh—these also dead (otherwise, would they be so admired?). And for Seurat: oblivion, silence. Yet he is a greater painter than van Gogh, who is interesting merely as an insane phenomenon ... and whose only interesting paintings are those done during his illness, at Arles. At the time of Seurat's death, the critics did justice to his talent but found that he did not leave a complete work! It seems to me, on the contrary, that he gave everything he could give, and admirably. He would certainly still have produced and progressed greatly, but his task was accomplished with finality: the black and white [drawings], the harmonies of line, composition, the contrast and harmony of colors... and even the frames. What more can one ask of a painter?"[93]

NOTES

1 See Johanna van Gogh-Bonger: Introduction to Verzamelde Brieven van Vincent van Gogh, Amsterdam, 1952–1954, vol. I, pp. XLVI–XLVII.

2 Gauguin to Theo van Gogh, [Paris, April 1890]; unpublished document, courtesy the late Albert S. Henraux; now Archives Nationales, Paris (bequest of Henraux).

3 Theo van Gogh to his brother, Paris, June 15, 1890; Verzamelde Brieven, vol. IV, no. T 37, p. 293. (This letter does not mention Gauguin by name but the reference is unquestionably to him.)

4 V. van Gogh to his sister Wil, [Auvers, first half of June 1890]; ibid., no. W 22, pp. 182–84.

5 Theo van Gogh to Dr. Gachet, Paris, May 1890; see P. Gachet: Deux amis des impressionnistes—Le Dr. Gachet et Murer, Paris, 1956, p. 110.

6 V. van Gogh to his brother, [Auvers, May 21, 1890]; Verzamelde Brieven, vol. III, no. 635, p. 516.

7 V. van Gogh to his brother, [Auvers, June 4, 1890]; ibid., no. 638, pp. 519–20.

8 On Dr. Gachet see V. Doiteau: La Curieuse Figure du Dr. Gachet, Aesculape, Aug.–Sept. 1923, as well as Tabarant's review of this article, Bulletin de la Vie Artistique, Sept. 15, 1923; also: Van Gogh et les peintres d'Auvers chez le Docteur Gachet, special issue of L'Amour de l'Art, 1952; J. Rewald: Gachet's Unknown Gems Emerge, Art News, March 1952 — The History of Impressionism, 4th ed., New York, 1973, pp. 296–301; Paul Gachet: Cézanne à Auvers, Paris, 1952 — Souvenirs de Cézanne et de van Gogh, Paris, 1953 — Vincent van Gogh aux "Indépendants," Paris, 1953 — Paul van Ryssel, Le Docteur Gachet graveur, Paris, 1954 — Deux amis des impressionnistes — Le Dr. Gachet et Murer, Paris, 1956 — Lettres impressionnistes au Dr. Gachet et à Murer, Paris, 1957; and P. Valery-Radot: Une Figure originale de médecin-artiste, La Presse Médicale, Sept. 6, 1952.

9 See P. Gachet: Deux amis des impressionnistes, p. 111.

10 V. van Gogh to his brother and sister-in-law, [Auvers, end of May 1890]; Verzamelde Brieven, vol. III, no. 637, p. 518.

11 V. van Gogh to his mother, [Auvers, beginning of June 1890]; ibid., no. 639, p. 521.

12 V. van Gogh to his brother, [Auvers, end of May 1890]; ibid., no. 636, p. 517.

13 See Paul Gachet: Van Gogh à Auvers, Histoire d'un tableau, Paris, 1953.

14 See Paul Gachet: Paul van Ryssel, op. cit.

15 Gauguin to V. van Gogh, [Le Pouldu, beginning of June 1890]; letter sent to Theo who mailed it to Vincent June 15. Unpublished document, courtesy Ir. V. W. van Gogh, Laren.

16 V. van Gogh to Gauguin, [Auvers, about June 20, 1890]. The original of this letter seems lost; it is quoted here after an unfinished draft found among van Gogh's papers, see Verzamelde Brieven, vol. III, no. 643, pp. 527–29. Gauguin's reply (see note 17), which answers various points raised in van Gogh's draft, shows that van Gogh must have sent Gauguin a letter closely resembling this draft.

17 Gauguin to V. van Gogh, [Le Pouldu, end of June 1890]; unpublished document, courtesy Ir. V. W. van Gogh, Laren.

18 V. van Gogh to his brother, [Auvers, June 17, 1890]; Verzamelde Brieven, vol. III, no. 642, p. 526.

19 Theo van Gogh to Camille Pissarro, [Paris], July 5, 1890; unpublished document, courtesy the late Rodo Pissarro, Paris.

20 V. van Gogh to the Ginoux family, [Auvers, June 1890]; Verzamelde Brieven, vol. III, no. 640a, p. 524.

21 See V. van Gogh's letter to his brother, [Auvers, June 10, 1890]; ibid., no. 640, p. 523.

22 Theo van Gogh to his brother, Paris, June 30, 1890; Verzamelde Brieven, vol. IV, no. T 39, p. 295.

23 J. Leclercq: Introduction to catalogue of "Exposition Vincent van Gogh," Bernheim-Jeune Galleries, Paris, March 15–31, 1901; courtesy the late Henry Pearlman, New York.

24 V. van Gogh to his brother, [Auvers, middle of July 1890]; Verzamelde Brieven, vol. III, no. 649, pp. 535–36.

25 Theo van Gogh to his brother, [Paris], July 14, 1890; Verzamelde Brieven, vol. IV, no. T 41, p. 296.

26 It is said that during this scene van Gogh excitedly walked up and down while clasping an object in his right coat pocket, an object which might have been the revolver with which he later killed himself (see G. Bazin, Introduction to the catalogue of the exhibition "Van Gogh et les peintres d'Auvers-sur-Oise," Orangerie, Paris, 1954, p. XXXIV). Yet it seems utterly inconceivable that Dr. Gachet would not have tried to disarm the painter and should have left a pistol in his friend's possession. See also P. Gachet, Deux amis des impressionnistes, p. 114.

27 V. van Gogh to his brother, [Auvers, middle of July 1890]; Verzamelde Brieven, vol. III, no. 648, p. 535.

28 Theo van Gogh to his wife, Paris, July 20, 1890; Introduction to Verzamelde Brieven, vol. I, p. XLVIII.

29 Theo van Gogh to his wife, Paris, July 25, 1890; ibid., p. XLVIII.

30 To show how difficult it is sometimes to ascertain even minor facts, it may be mentioned that the two surviving witnesses disagree as to the room in which van Gogh died at the Ravoux inn. According to Dr. Gachet's son he occupied a room on the second floor, whereas Ravoux's daughter maintains that it was a garret on the third floor.

31 See Hirschig's recollections in A. Bredius: Herinneringen aan Vincent van Gogh, Oud-Holland, vol. 51, no. 1, 1934, p. 44.

32 V. van Gogh to his mother, [Auvers, second half of July 1890]; Verzamelde Brieven, vol. III, no. 650, p. 537.

33 V. van Gogh to his brother, [Auvers, July 23, 1890]; ibid., no. 651, p. 537.

34 V. van Gogh to his brother, [Auvers, July 27, 1890]; ibid., no. 652, pp. 541–42. Van Gogh's last and unfinished letter, found on the painter after his death.

35 Another possibility has been suggested by Dr. Doiteau in Aesculape, March 1957.

36 Hirschig has given a somewhat different account of events. According to him they had waited for van Gogh at Ravoux's at dinnertime on that fateful Sunday, when the painter entered, "his hand pressed against his stomach. 'But Monsieur Vincent, where do you come from, what is the matter with you?'—'I was too fed up and so I killed myself'—I see him in his narrow bed in the little garret, tortured by the most terrible pain. 'But isn't there anybody to open my belly?' There was a suffocating heat under the roof. When he was dead he was terrible to behold, even more terrible than while he was alive. From his casket, which was badly constructed, ran a stinking liquid; everything was terrible about this man. I believe he suffered greatly in this world. I never saw him smile." See Herinneringen aan Vincent van Gogh, Oud-Holland, op. cit.

37 C. Mauron: Notes sur la structure de l'inconscient chez Vincent van Gogh, Psyché, Jan., Feb., March–April 1953, has pointed out that van Gogh's suicide was not committed during an attack of insanity since it was followed by a period of complete lucidity instead of the customary torpor.

38 See V. Doiteau and E. Leroy: La Folie de van Gogh, Paris, 1928, pp. 91–94.

39 Dr. Gachet to Theo van Gogh, [Auvers, July 27, 1890]; Introduction to Verzamelde Brieven, vol. I, p. XLIX.

40 See M. Gauthier: La Femme en bleu nous parle de l'homme à l'oreille coupée, Nouvelles Littéraires, April 16, 1953.

41 Theo van Gogh to his wife, Auvers, July 28, 1890; Introduction to Verzamelde Brieven, vol. I, p. XLIX.

42 See Theo van Gogh's letter to his sister Elisabeth in E. du Quesne-van Gogh: Persönliche Erinnerungen an Vincent van Gogh, Munich, 1911, pp. 75–76.

43 Theo van Gogh to his wife, [Auvers, July 29, 1890]; Introduction to Verzamelde Brieven, vol. I. p. XLIX.

44 This statement confirms the fact that Bernard did not see Vincent again after his departure for Arles, although he later pretended having painted with van Gogh on the Island of La Grande Jatte during the latter's short visit in Paris in July 1890.

45 Bernard to Aurier [Paris, Aug. 1, 1890]; see: L'Enterrement de Vincent van Gogh, Documents, February 1953. It was at the funeral that Bernard for the first time met Theo's brother-in-law, Andries Bonger.

46 Gauguin to Theo van Gogh, [Le Pouldu, beginning of Aug. 1890]; unpublished document, courtesy Ir.V.W. van Gogh, Laren.

47 Gauguin to Schuffenecker, [Moëlan, Aug. 1890]; see C. Roger-Marx: Lettres inédites de Vincent van Gogh et de Paul Gauguin, Europe, no. 194, Feb. 15, 1939.

48 Gauguin to Schuffenecker, [Moëlan, Aug.–Sept. 1890 (?)]; ibid. It is not impossible that this letter was written in 1891 and actually refers to the death of Theo van Gogh rather than to that of the painter.

49 Theo van Gogh to Aurier, Paris, Aug. 27, 1890; unpublished document, courtesy M. Jacques Williame, Châteauroux.

50 Aurier to Bernard, Châteauroux, Aug. 29, 1890; see Documents, op. cit.

51 Theo van Gogh to Dr. Gachet, [Paris, middle of Sept. 1890]; see P. Gachet, op. cit., pp. 124–25.

52 Theo van Gogh to Bernard, Paris, Sept. 18, 1890; see Bernard's introduction to: Lettres de Vincent van Gogh à Emile Bernard, Paris, 1911, pp. 2–3.

53 Camille Pissarro to his son Lucien, Paris, Oct. 18, 1890; Pissarro further reports: "It seems that Theo van Gogh was ill before his madness; he had a retention of urine. ...." See Camille Pissarro: Lettres à son fils Lucien, Paris, 1950, pp. 188–89. (This letter is not included in the American edition.) According to Dr. J.L. Foy, Theo had been afflicted with chronic nephritis.

54 A. Bonger to Dr. Gachet, Paris, Oct. 10, 1890; see P. Gachet: op. cit., pp. 125–26.

55 Theo van Gogh to Gauguin, [Paris, Oct. 1890]; see A. Alexandre: Paul Gauguin, sa vie et le sens de son œuvre, Paris, 1930, p. 108.

56 Lucien Pissarro to his fiancée, Oct. 1890; see W.S. Meadmore: Lucien Pissarro, London, 1962, p. 51.

57 Signac to Maus, Paris, Oct. 23, 1890; see M.-O. Maus: Trente années de lutte pour l'art, Brussels, 1926, pp.119–20, note.

58 Article by J. de Meester in Algemeen Handelsblad, Dec. 31, 1890; on this subject see M. E. Tralbaut in Van Goghiana I, Antwerp, 1963, pp. 23–25.

59 Gauguin to Bernard, [Le Pouldu, Jan. 1891]; see Lettres de Gauguin à sa femme et à ses amis, Paris, 1946, no. CXIII (there dated Oct. 1890), p. 204.

60 See G. Kraus: The Relationship between Theo and Vincent van Gogh, Amsterdam, 1954.

61 *Mercure de France*, March 1891.

62 Gauguin to his wife, [Tahiti, Nov. 5, 1892]; Lettres de Gauguin, *op. cit.*, p. 235, no. CXXXIII.

63 Gauguin to Daniel de Monfried, Tahiti, June 1892 and Feb. 14, 1897; see Lettres de Gauguin à Daniel de Monfreid, Paris, 1950 (second edition), pp. 58 and 99.

64 Aurier to his sister, Paris, [beginning of March 1891]; unpublished document, courtesy M. Jacques Williame, Châteauroux.

65 O. Mirbeau: Vincent van Gogh, *Echo de Paris*, March 31, 1891; reprinted in Mirbeau: Des artistes, vol. I, Paris, 1922, and in: Van Gogh raconté par lui-même et ses amis, Geneva, 1947.

66 Signac to T. van Rysselberghe, [Paris, Feb.–March 1888]; unpublished document, courtesy the late Mme van Rysselberghe, Paris.

67 Seurat to Fénéon, [Paris, June 20, 1890]; unpublished document, courtesy the late César M. de Hauke, Paris. This letter was written in connection with Fénéon's article on Signac published in *Hommes d'Aujourd'hui*, June 1890, quoted in Dorra-Rewald: Seurat, Paris, 1960, pp. XXV–XXVIII.

68 Hayet to Signac, Feb. 10, 1890; see Rewald: Seurat (French edition), Paris, 1948, p. 116.

69 Henry van de Velde, letter to the author, [Oberaegeri], Jan. 17, 1950. Van de Velde subsequently became an architect and gained fame as leader of the Art Nouveau movement.

70 Camille Pissarro to H. van de Velde, quoted from the original draft found among Pissarro's papers. The letter actually sent to van de Velde on March 27, 1896, was somewhat shorter; it was a protest against the inclusion of Pissarro's name in a list of neo-impressionists. See Rewald: Seurat, New York, 1943, 1946.

71 See G. Kahn: Introduction to Les Dessins de Georges Seurat, Paris, 1926.

72 Fénéon: Signac, reprinted in Fénéon: Oeuvres, Paris, 1948. This article was not published in *Hommes d'Aujourd'hui*, as stated in Oeuvres, but appeared in *La Plume*, Sept. 1, 1891.

73 Signac to Fénéon, April 29, 1890; unpublished document, courtesy Mme Ginette Signac, Paris.

74 Signac to T. van Rysselberghe, [Saint-Tropez, spring 1902]; unpublished document, courtesy the late Mme van Rysselberghe, Paris.

75 Signac to Camille Pissarro, Jan. 25, [1894]; see Camille Pissarro: Letters to his Son Lucien, New York, 1943, pp. 230–31 (incompletely translated).

76 See Angrand's recollections in Coquiot: Seurat, Paris, 1924, pp. 166–67.

77 Signac to T. van Rysselberghe, [Paris, March 30, 1891]; unpublished document, courtesy the late Mme van Rysselberghe, Paris.

78 It is impossible to make an exact diagnosis of the cause of Seurat's death on the basis of the few known facts: that he suffered from "infectious angina," that he died after two days, that he had an "effusion" in the brain (and that his baby died from the same disease a short while later). Under these circumstances it is unlikely that his was an ordinary angina, which could kill, but it would take longer. Nor is it likely to have been influenza, although there was an epidemic at the time. Another possible cause is diphtheria (the expression "diphtheritic influenza" is no longer used in medical language today), but two things militate against diphtheria: it could have been diagnosed even by a very mediocre practitioner at that time, and a brain hemorrhage is not at all typical of the disease. The data suggest a fulminant meningitis or encephalitis. (Epidemic encephalitis became known to the medical profession only in 1917, but it is now generally assumed that it accompanied the influenza epidemic of 1890.) Fulminant meningitis would best accord with the facts: initial angina, quick spread of the disease and rapid demise, as well as the pathological finding at death: effusion (or cerebral hemorrhage). The death of the infant also supports this assumption. Information courtesy Professor E. Ackerknecht, University of Zurich.

79 Signac to T. van Rysselberghe, [Paris, April 1, 1891]; unpublished document, courtesy the late Mme van Rysselberghe, Paris.

80 Signac to Luce, [autumn 1891]; unpublished document, courtesy Mme Ginette Signac, Paris.

81 Luce to T. van Rysselberghe, [Paris, April–May 1891]; unpublished document, courtesy the late Mme van Rysselberghe, Paris. On the inventory of Seurat's studio see also R. Rey: La Renaissance du sentiment classique, Paris, 1931, p. 144; Dorra-Rewald, *op. cit.*; and C.M. de Hauke: Seurat et son oeuvre, Paris, 1961, pp. XXVII–XXX.

82 Signac to T. van Rysselberghe, [Brittany, April–May 1891]; unpublished document, courtesy the late Mme van Rysselberghe, Paris.

83 The foregoing account is based on a series of unpublished letters exchanged by Signac and T. van Rysselberghe in 1891, courtesy the late Mme van Rysselberghe, Paris; see also Pissarro's letters of July 17 and 21, 1891, in Camille Pissarro, *op. cit.*, pp. 181–82.

84 Signac to T. van Rysselberghe, [Concarneau, June 28, 1891]; unpublished document, courtesy the late Mme van Rysselberghe, Paris.

85 J. Christophe: Georges Seurat, *La Plume*, Sept. 1, 1891.

86 Anonymous [Fénéon]: Seurat, *Entretiens Politiques et Littéraires*, vol. II, no. 13, 1891.

87 T. de Wyzewa: Georges Seurat, *L'Art dans les Deux Mondes*, April 18, 1891.

88 Camille Pissarro to his son Lucien, Paris, March 30, 1891; *op. cit.*, p. 156.

89 Lucien Pissarro to his father, [London, March 31, 1891]; Camille Pissarro: Lettres à son fils Lucien (French edition), Paris, 1950, p. 224.

90 Camille Pissarro to his son Lucien, Paris, April 1, 1891; *op. cit.* (American edition), p. 158.

91 See Camille Pissarro's letters to his son, Paris, May 9 and 13, 1891; *ibid.*, pp. 169 and 171.

92 Signac to Camille Pissarro, [Concarneau, July–Aug. 1891]; unpublished document, courtesy the late Rodo Pissarro, Paris.

93 Signac, diary, Sept. 15, 1894; see Extraits du journal inédit de Paul Signac, 1894–1895, *Gazette des Beaux-Arts*, July–Sept. 1949.

IX 1890-1891 GAUGUIN AND THE SYMBOLISTS
BREAK WITH BERNARD
GAUGUIN'S AUCTION AND HIS DEPARTURE

During the winter of 1889–90, which he had spent in Brittany, Gauguin had gone through one of the most depressing periods of his life. The "disaster" of the Volpini exhibition had deeply discouraged him, the more so as he had pinned quite unreasonable hopes on a success which he had thought certain. Theo van Gogh had been unable to be of great assistance (a fact which Gauguin ascribed in part to his recent marriage). His plans to leave for Tonkin made no progress. France had seized Indo-China less than ten years before and Gauguin had asked to be sent there as an administrator, at the expense of the government. Yet he soon realized that this request would probably be turned down. "The people who are sent to the colonies," he acidly complained, "are usually those who misbehave, rob the till, etc.... But to send me, an impressionist painter, in other words an insurgent, that's impossible!"[1] He continued nevertheless to dream of solitude under a tropical sun while at the same time his relative solitude in Brittany began to become unbearable, although he was surrounded there by the devoted de Haan, by de Chamaillard, Moret, and several others, as well as by a Countess de Nimal, whose admiration greatly flattered him.

"All that bile, that bitterness," he wrote to Bernard, "which I am accumulating under the blows of an ill fate that persecutes me, make me sick, and at the present moment I have hardly the strength, the will to work. Yet it used to be that work helped me to forget. In the end this isolation, this concentration upon myself, while all the principal joys of life are missing and all inner satisfaction is lacking, this cry of hunger, as one might call it, like an empty stomach, in the end this isolation is a lure with its promise of happiness, unless one is made of ice and absolutely insensitive. In spite of all my efforts to become so, I am not built that way, my original nature always reappears."[1]

Bernard, who was in Saint-Briac, his father having formally forbidden him to join Gauguin at Le Pouldu, likewise went through a profound depression during which he often felt doubtful about himself. At least Gauguin was generally spared such agony, for though he sometimes anxiously questioned the validity of his work, he very seldom had any doubts about his calling. In a long letter Bernard poured out all his problems to Gauguin:

"Concerning painting I am agitated and worried to the utmost degree. I do not know what fears of total impotence grip me at every moment because of the ineptitude of my productions. What I am doing appears to me, to tell you the truth, like the beginnings of rough drafts.... I have a sort of vague idea that painting is more than the product of synthesized sensations, that it is also an art intimately connected with technical processes, such as pigment, solidity, fluidity, the special quality of each thing, in a word that it is painting only as far as pigment and transcription, as far as the sensations are concerned. Besides, I have a terrible fear of losing myself in the most complete absolutism, for the more I desire to achieve something carried through and well worked out, the more I get involved, the more I approach the non-affirmative, emptiness, hollowness, to such an extent that whenever I do something that seems more or less acceptable to me, something well grasped, I do not dare touch it any more for fear of spoiling it. In a word, I no longer know at all where I am. Everywhere I see snare after snare for my poor mind. With that a great awkwardness of my hand and a total upheaval of techniques push me towards absurdity.

"Your desire for the unknown is certainly very different from my desire for completeness, since I know you to be all sensation and I see that your search tends towards simplicity whereas mine is possibly directed towards the complicated. Not for a single instant do I doubt that you will obtain good results in following that path, which always seemed to me the best and even the only possible one, yet it is rather by *perversity* than by conviction that I myself deviate from this path." Bernard went on to speak of all the paintings he had seen recently—some of them at the Paris World's Fair—works by Corot, Delacroix, Daumier, Manet, Puvis de Chavannes, Redon, Cézanne, the French primitives, etc., and confessed that he had been overwhelmed by all these impressions:

"If only this would satisfy me! But no, I should like to see more and more of those beautiful things while deluding myself with the pleasant idea of the uselessness of work on this earth, since admiration of what has been already accomplished should be enough for the man who is incapable of creating beauty but who loves it just the same. Thus stupid ideas and the difficulties which I see appear step by step on that road where we alone with our blood fertilize the barrenness of the brambles, in the words of I don't know which poetic friend; all this oppresses and kills me. I have developed an extreme anxiety, not concerning my life but concerning my possible talent, the existence of which the present situation seems more likely to make me doubt definitely than to reassure me on this subject. All the artists, except you, have rejected me; some through malice, others perhaps through logic, and I suffer greatly from this—not because I feel the need for admiration, but because if those in whom I recognize talent turn me down, then I must conclude that I have none. In short, some awkward attempts may have been the explanation for your confidence in me and all this has no doubt by now disappeared.... I thank you for all the friendship you have always shown me, it is perhaps the last stage of my hope."[2]

In an equally long reply Gauguin told his young friend: "I can see, in reading your letter, that we are all more or less in the same spot. Moments of doubt, results that are always scantier than we expect, and the slight encouragement we receive from others, all this contributes to our being flayed by thorns. Well, what can we do after that except fly into a rage, struggle with all these difficulties and, even when knocked down, say: 'still more.' Always and always. In the end painting is like man, mortal but constantly living in conflict with matter. If I were thinking of the absolute, I should stop making any effort even to live. Let us be satisfied, such as we are, with matter and completeness as far as they go. Whether I lack the patience, whether I don't feel strong enough, or whether my nature pushes me towards short cuts, hoping for completeness at the end of my career, the fact remains that I paint and live in hope.

"I do not like very much to give advice (it's so delicate) and yet I think you would do well for some time to make studies according to your inclination, well worked-out studies, since at the present moment you believe that art is absolutely connected with technical

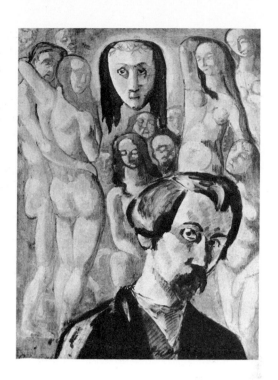

BERNARD: *Self-Portrait—Vision,* 1891. Present whereabouts unknown

processes such as pigment, fluidity, etc.... If later on you should, like me, become skeptical about this, you will do other things.... Corot, Giotto, attract me by something well beyond the solid qualities of their painting. You know how much I respect what Degas does, and yet I sometimes feel that he lacks something that is higher, a heart that beats. The tears of a child are also something, though they are not erudite. Indeed, I admire many masterpieces of all kinds, those based on sensation and those based on science; that is why something should be done in both directions.

"It is obvious that you are very gifted and even that you know a great deal. What does the opinion of imbeciles and jealous people matter to you? I can't believe that this should worry you for any length of time. What about myself? I have not been pampered very much by others, and yet I expect to become more and more incomprehensible. It doesn't matter to me! You are young and I believe that you are lacking something, but this void will soon be filled through age. It is already something to know yourself. In the midst of all that you have seen, felt, suffered, you are lost. But all this will quiet down.... You have seen too much in too short a time. Rest from seeing (for a long while)."[3]

If Emile Bernard, whom Vincent van Gogh a few weeks later warned against a revival of medieval mysticism, had only followed this advice! Yet he continued to study the masters of the past even more intently and thoroughly imbued himself with their achievements. At the same time he went through a period of deep religious gropings. "I implore God," he soon wrote to Schuffenecker, "to allow me to be what He made me or what it seems to me He wanted to make me.... These crises are followed by satanic crises of worry and impiety. It is then that I demand all kinds of pleasures which are capable of reinvigorating this nobody that I am."[4] Later on Bernard remembered that during those days "I intoxicated myself with incense, organ music, prayers, old stained glass windows, hieratic tapestries; I went back several centuries... little by little I became a man of the Middle Ages."[5] In this process Bernard strengthened his ties with the Catholic church. He also began strenuously to proselytize, trying, for instance, "to bring back to God" that old revolutionary and atheist *père* Tanguy, who obviously resisted, but at least, as Bernard subsequently said, "bore no grudge against me, knowing well that I did this only out of profound friendship and conviction."[6]

Bernard's increasing mysticism was accompanied by a slow slackening of his original boldness and incisiveness. His premature versatility gradually led to his undoing. In his religious paintings distorted forms show a growing affectation which is essentially artificial.[7] This led him farther and farther from the observation of nature, for which he substituted a conscious endeavor to draw close to the great Venetian masters. Soon he was also to abandon the use of bright colors in favor of muted harmonies, thus depriving himself of the forcefulness and originality which had attracted van Gogh to his early works.

Gauguin meanwhile strove to be somewhat more productive and not to let himself be carried away by melancholy moods. About the turn of the year both de Haan and Gauguin painted the same farmyard scene at Le Pouldu. While de Haan's canvas is dated 1889 the one by Gauguin bears the date 1890. But the similarity of the two pictures is such that the painters must have stood side by side while they worked on them. Whereas de Haan's landscape is a little clumsy and dull in color and execution, Gauguin achieved a great deli-

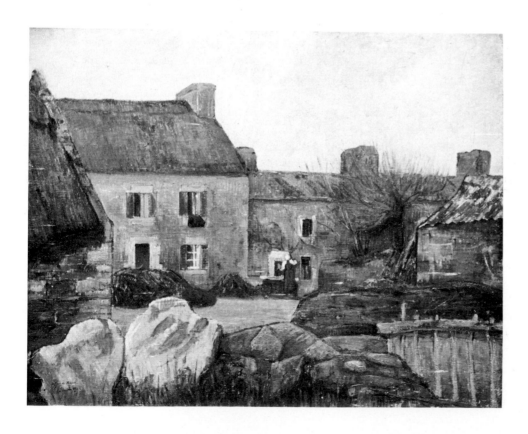

MEYER DE HAAN: *Farmyard at Le Pouldu,* d. 1889. 29 x 36⅝". Rijksmuseum Kröller-Müller, Otterlo

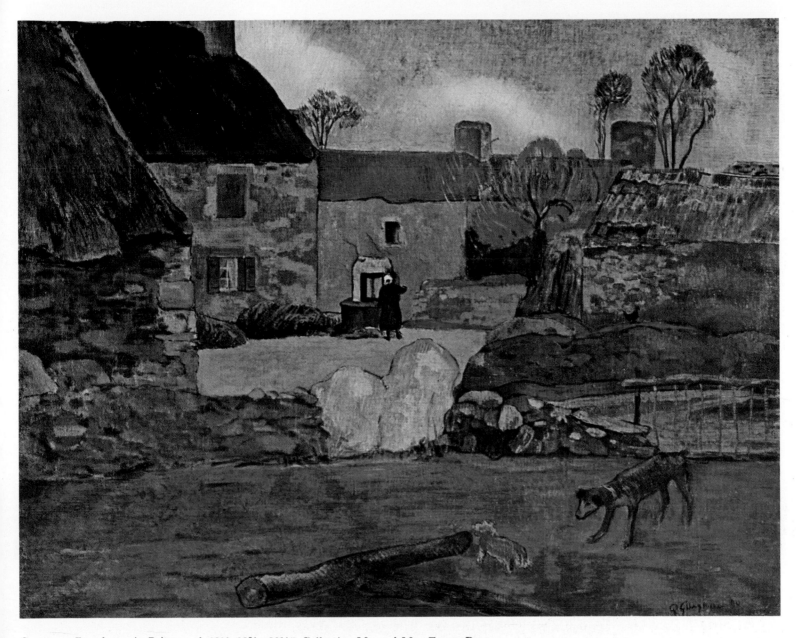

Gauguin: *Farmhouse in Brittany*, d. 1890. 28¾ x 36¼". Collection Mr. and Mrs. Emery Reves

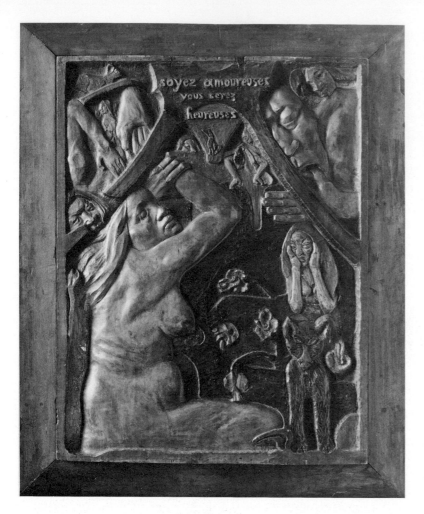

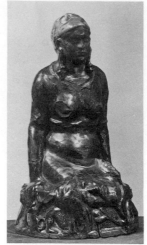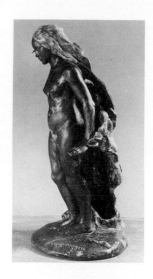

Above left: GAUGUIN: *The Black Virgin,* 1889. Glazed stoneware, 19¾″ high. Collection Harry Guggenheim, New York

Above right: GAUGUIN: *Eve,* 1888–89. Ceramic, 23⅝″ high. National Gallery of Art, Washington, D.C. (Ailsa Mellon Bruce Fund)

GAUGUIN: *Be in Love and You'll Be Happy,* Fall 1889. Painted wood relief, 37½ × 28⅝″. Exhibited with the XX in 1891. Formerly collection Emile Schuffenecker. Museum of Fine Arts, Boston (Arthur Tracy Cabot Fund)

cacy of tonalities and brushwork. His approach in this canvas was much more naturalistic than in most of his more stylized paintings of the period.

Although Gauguin was once more absolutely without money, he was soon able to work in a large attic transformed into a studio, which de Haan had rented in an isolated villa not far from Marie Henry's inn. Commanding a view of the sea, this studio, which Laval, Chamaillard, and Moret shared with their friends, was decorated with lithographs by Gauguin and Bernard, as well as with Japanese prints. There Gauguin fashioned a bas-relief in wood which Countess de Nimal—a friend of Rouvier, minister of Fine Arts—promised to have purchased by the French government, one of the many illusions to which Gauguin was always ready to succumb, only to grow more angry and bitter after their collapse. "It is the best and strangest thing I have ever done in sculpture," the artist informed Bernard, explaining the subject: "Gauguin (like a monster) taking the hand of a woman who resists, and telling her: '*Be in love and you'll be happy.*' A fox represents the Indian symbol of perversity, and in the interstices [there are] some small figures. The wood will be colored."[3]

In this spacious studio Gauguin apparently also painted a large and florid still life that in no way betrayed his worries. On the contrary, it seemed actually inspired by his dreams of the tropics, for it was dominated by a soft pink which subsequently became a favorite color on his exotic palette. Against a completely flat background are set two vases of flowers; one of these is an earthen pot in the form of a head, not unlike pre-Incan ceramics. It is one of the potteries made by Gauguin himself, probably the very one which he later offered to Emile Bernard's sister, explaining: "It represents vaguely the head of Gauguin the savage."[8] On the wall appears a Japanese print. This is one of the few instances in which Gauguin integrated such a print into a composition in the way van Gogh had frequently done. The whole canvas, colorful and subtle, seems to strike a novel note in Gauguin's work, one that can be called an anticipation of his style of the South Seas.

In other works of the period, too, this prospect began to make itself felt. On one of the wooden panels at the inn he painted a *Caribbean Woman* in a summary style and decorative pattern for which he apparently used for the first time stylistic elements derived from the sculpture of the ancient East, in this instance the fragment of a frieze that had fallen from a building of the Javanese village at the 1889 World's Fair. In his enthusiasm for the primitive and the exotic, Gauguin had picked this fragment up and taken it back to Le Pouldu.[9] He also did a sculpture of the same subject in a similar attitude.

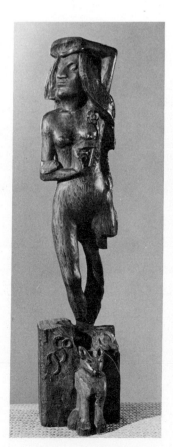

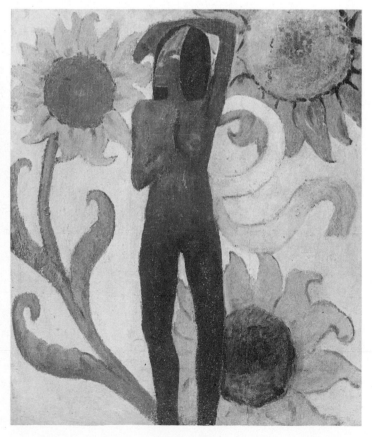

Right: GAUGUIN: *Lewdness—Caribbean Woman,* 1890–91. Painted wood, 27½" high. J. F. Willumsen Museum, Copenhagen.

Far right: GAUGUIN: *Caribbean Woman with Sunflowers,* Le Pouldu, 1889–90. Oil on wood, 26 x 21½". Collection Mrs. Harry Bakwin, New York

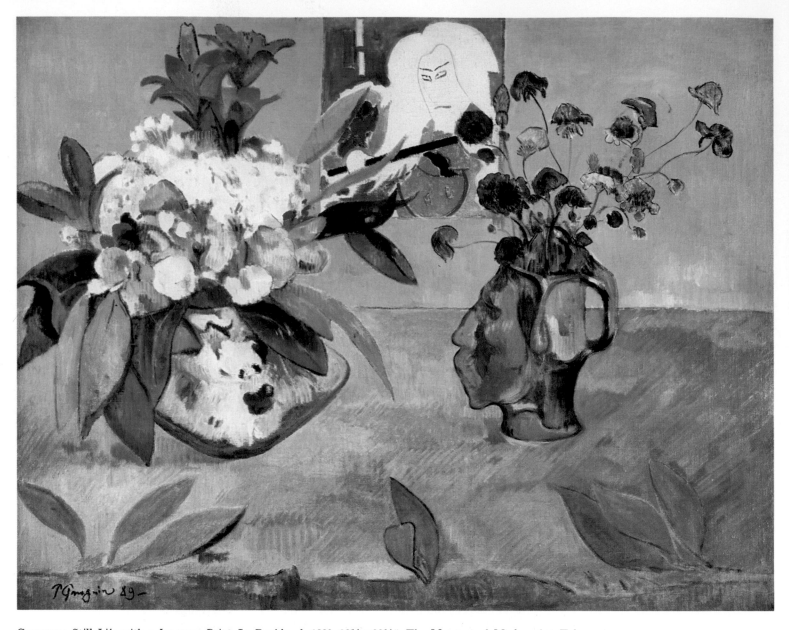

GAUGUIN: *Still Life with a Japanese Print,* Le Pouldu, d. 1889. 28½ x 36½″. The Museum of Modern Art, Tehran

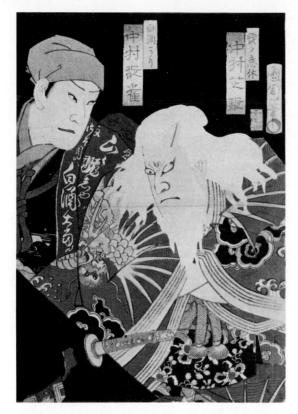

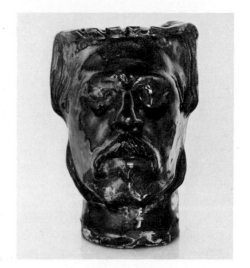

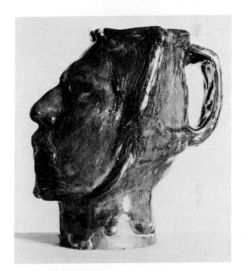

Above: KUNICHIKA: *Portrait of the Japanese Actor Hige no I kyu,* c. 1880. Color woodcut, 14 × 9⅝". Museum of Fine Arts, Boston

Right: GAUGUIN: *Self-Portrait,* 1889. Stoneware vase, 7⅝" high. Formerly collection Madeleine Bernard (?). Kunstindustrimuseet, Copenhagen. Front and side views

But occasional work and constant expectation were not enough to dispel Gauguin's depression. In moments of doubt and discouragement he confided in Bernard just as Bernard confided in him, asking his young friend to give his "opinion to guide me somewhat in the midst of my trouble."[10] Their exchange of letters during the winter of 1889–90, which they were prevented from spending together, contains an unbroken succession of complaints, generously sprinkled with expressions of compassion for each other's plight and even more generously seasoned with self-pity.

"Let them look carefully at my recent pictures," Gauguin exclaimed, "if they have any heart at all to feel with, and they will see how much resigned suffering is in them. Isn't it anything, a human cry? Well, it had to be expected. And it seems that I was meant for this, not to have any heart, to be mean, quarrelsome. I won't say any more. But you, why do you too have to suffer? You are young and you start early to carry your cross. Don't be resentful, for some day you will be happy at the thought of having resisted the temptation to hate; in the kindness of one who has suffered there is an intoxicating poetry."[10]

Eventually Gauguin managed to tear himself away from these introspective musings and vague generalities, although his financial situation was such that in January 1890 he considered giving up painting and trying to earn a livelihood otherwise, should his request to be sent to Tonkin be turned down.[11] But with the help of Schuffenecker, who early in February provided him with the fare to Paris and with a roof there, he was able to plunge once again into the more stimulating Parisian atmosphere. It was in Paris that he met a Dr. Charlopin, inventor, who promised him to buy a group of paintings—at a reduced rate—for a total of 5,000 francs, which would enable the painter to leave at last, not for Tonkin but for Madagascar. Thus he would no longer have to depend on the government for his departure, nor did he have to wait for the problematic sale of his bas-relief (which never materialized).

Gauguin got in touch with Redon, whose wife came from the French island of La Réunion in the Indian Ocean, not far from Madagascar, which she knew well. On this occasion he seems to have exchanged one of his ceramics for a work by Redon. Mme Redon told him that for 5,000 francs he could live in Madagascar for thirty years. This information was more than enough to rekindle Gauguin's hopes, infuse new strength into him, spur his imagination, stimulate his self-confidence, unleash his dreams. The "studio of the tropics" could now be created.

As Bernard was particularly downcast while at Lille, devoting three months to industrial designs in the hope of earning some money, Gauguin now told him of his plans and stretched out a helping hand: "I do not want to give you any *advice*, but with all my heart I address myself to the man who suffers, to the artist who cannot work at his art here in Europe.—If after all your efforts you do not find any satisfaction... come and join me. *Without money* you will find a secure existence in a better world. I believe that if you pull a few strings you may even obtain a free trip.... Half of my coat; that's still the best way to be a Christian."[12]

Bernard was overwhelmed by the offer. "Your letter enchants me, dazzles me, brings me back to life! To leave, to escape, far, far, all the way down there, wherever it is, as long as it is the unknown! But two questions worry me. The first is money, the second the facilities for work down there.... Oh! to leave without worrying about anything, very far, very far. To abandon this abominable European life, these pigheads, these dunces, these satiated jesters, this pestilential brood.... Ah! my beloved one (yes, I am in love, so what!) will come to join me; she can very well do that if she is really so smitten with love, and then, how wonderful it will be to get drunk with liberty to the bursting point, be able to look at the sea, be intoxicated with emptiness.... Thanks for having so well consoled me, thanks, I am filled with hope."[13]

Bernard's chaste love affair somewhat complicated things, and at the end of May 1890 he confided to Schuffenecker: "I don't know how all this will work out. On top of everything I shall have to marry a young girl who is capable of killing herself or of dying from grief if I don't do it. I myself adore her and can't live without her. So my life is ruined, lost. The bourgeois have destroyed me and yet I am still too bourgeois myself, that's why I have been so weak."[4] In a letter to Gauguin Bernard told him that his heart was torn by monsters, his love, his duty to stay in France, his desire to leave. But he was determined to

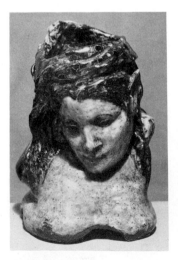

GAUGUIN: *Head of a Woman* (Mme Schuffenecker), 1888–89. Ceramic vase. Collection Mr. and Mrs. Emery Reves

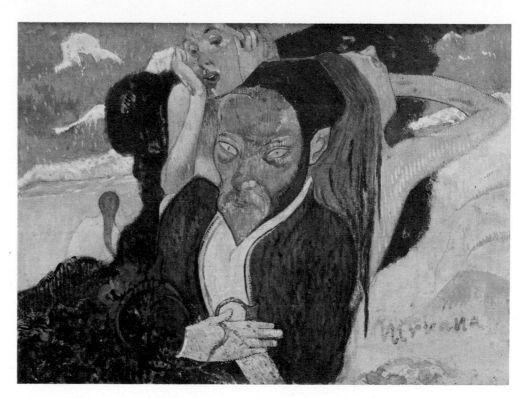

GAUGUIN: *Nirvana—Portrait of Jacob Meyer de Haan,* c. 1890. Gouache, 8 x 11⅛″ Wadsworth Atheneum, Hartford, Conn. (The Ella Gallup Sumner and Mary Catlin Sumner Collection)

raise all the money he could and to go to Marseilles once the departure was absolutely certain. Gauguin replied by stating that if he himself were a bachelor he would certainly remain one. "A [native] woman down there is a necessity, so to speak, and that will provide me with a model every day. But I can promise you that the Malagasy woman has just as much of a heart as a Frenchwoman and is much less calculating."[14]

Gauguin did his best to calm Bernard's excitement. "Be hopeful instead of going to pieces and everything will be well. In your misfortune you are still quite lucky to have found support such as mine, something that I have not found at my age. What I am doing here [by inviting you to come with me] is something I never intended to do again, having once tried the experiment with Laval [in Martinique].... If you examine the situation, you are going to begin a new life which is full of possibilities of beauty and wholesomeness, at the age of twenty-two, whereas I shall begin it at forty-two with little time ahead of me to forget the past."[15]

Having spent several months in Paris, Gauguin returned to Brittany in May or June. The date of departure for the tropics was set for the middle of August; Gauguin had hoped to be able to pay a short visit to his wife and children in Copenhagen before he left, but had to give up this project. It had now been decided to take along de Haan, who was to go first to his native Holland, undoubtedly to secure from his family the necessary funds. Meanwhile Bernard, having read Pierre Loti, suggested that Tahiti might be a better place than Madagascar. But Gauguin did not trust Loti too much, although he replied: "I admit that Tahiti is certainly delightful and that one could indeed live there (almost without money) just as we dream."[16] A little later he discussed the question again: "It is true that Tahiti is a paradise for Europeans. But the trip is much more expensive because it is in the South Seas. Besides, Madagascar offers many more possibilities as far as types, religion, mysticism, symbolism go. There you have Indians from Calcutta, black tribes, Arabs, and Hovas who are Polynesians. Just the same, get some information about the voyage via Panama [to Tahiti], etc...."[17]

But the discussions with Charlopin made no progress whatsoever and Gauguin became impatient. It was time to look for support elsewhere. Such support might possibly come from Aurier and so Bernard now undertook to appeal to him. "I am writing you," he said, "to tell you of some new developments for which your help will be of great assistance to us. Gauguin and I wish to leave for Madagascar and to do so we need money. I cannot hope for any, being too young and still too undeveloped to sell my paintings, but Gauguin who intends to take care of me and who has a better chance [of selling], having already produced the introduction to future accomplishments, has written to me to remind you of your project of an article about him; he has done so not because he wants to beat the drum or gain petty glory, but because of the importance this may have, as far as the public is concerned, for our life together. For you this would be only a small matter: to expedite (since Gauguin's talent has already convinced you), to expedite a little what you have the intention of writing. I shall provide you with all possible notes, letters, etc. Besides you know where you can see his paintings and you know his ideas through his articles in *Le Moderniste*. If you could publish this in the next *Mercure [de France]*, it would be just right, or better still in the *Revue Indépendante*, which is better known in the art world. You have written about Vincent, Pissarro, Raffaëlli. I don't know whether those (the last two) belong to the group of "Les Isolés," but Gauguin, the most isolated of them all, deserved, it seems to me, to be placed before Raffaëlli."[18]

Apparently Aurier promised to write the desired article, though he could not do it as soon as his friends hoped. Gauguin waited and did little work, except an occasional sculpture, wishing to gather strength for the long voyage. He asked Bernard to importune Charlopin, but with little result. In Le Pouldu, de Haan and Filiger were his only companions. "I am walking around like a savage, with long hair, and I do nothing; I haven't even taken my colors and palette along. I have made some darts and on the beach I practice throwing them like Buffalo Bill."[19]

The month of August came and went without any definite commitment from Charlopin and consequently without the projected departure. Gauguin now began to realize that nothing at all might come of Charlopin's promises, yet his determination to leave Europe had become so fixed that he could not abandon hope; in fact his whole existence was based on his prospective life in the tropics. Should Charlopin default, he would go to Paris and try to find someone else to finance his trip. Meanwhile he was carving a sequel to his symbolic wood relief, this one entitled *Be Mysterious*, and debated with de Haan the possibility of the latter's establishing in the tropics a trade in fine pearls as correspondent of some Dutch merchants. After abandoning his initial project of going to Tonkin, he was now about to give up Madagascar in turn and finally to decide upon Tahiti as their destination. All these were French protectorates or colonies—as was Martinique—for which the government was then making a great propaganda effort in an endeavor to develop its overseas possessions. (Tahiti, a protectorate since 1843, had become a colony in 1880; Tonkin became a protectorate in 1884 and Madagascar in 1885.) It apparently never

416

occurred to Gauguin to go to any English or Dutch colony, and when Degas subsequently recommended that he consider New Orleans—where he himself had been in 1872—Gauguin ignored this suggestion, doubtless feeling that Louisiana was not exotic enough.

When Bernard sent him the requested information on the Polynesian islands, Tahiti fired Gauguin's imagination anew. "I have a booklet published by the Colonial Department," he wrote to Schuffenecker, "which gives a great deal of information about life in Tahiti. Marvelous country where I should like to finish my life *with all my children.* I shall see later about having them follow me. There is in Paris a Society for Colonization which provides free passages.... I only live in the hope of this promised land; de Haan, Bernard, and I, and possibly later my family. With work and will power we can form there a hale and happy little circle, for you know that Tahiti is the healthiest country that exists.... The future of our children is pretty black—even with some money—in this rotten and mean Europe.... But the Tahitians, happy inhabitants of the unexplored paradises of Oceania, know only the sweet aspects of life. For them to live is to sing and to love. Here is food for thought for Europeans who complain about their existence."[20]

To Redon, who advised him earnestly against leaving and who dwelt on the future of his

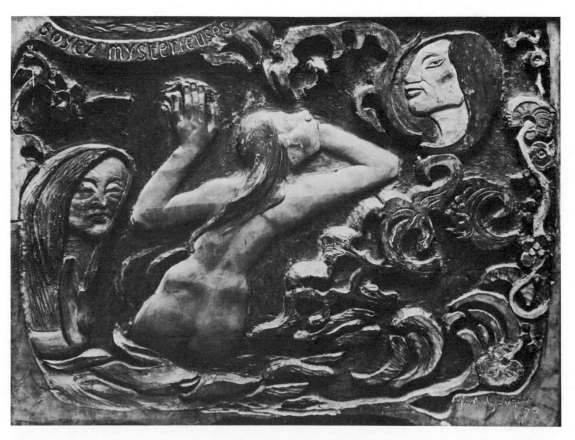

GAUGUIN: *Be Mysterious,* d. 1890. Painted wood relief, 28¾ x 37½". Exhibited with the XX in 1891. Formerly collection Emile Schuffenecker. Collection Mme d'Andoque, Béziers

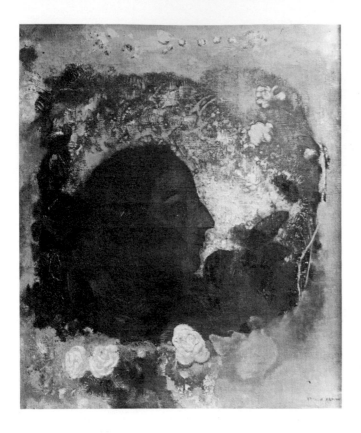

REDON: *Imaginary Portrait of Paul Gauguin,* 1900–05. Pastel, 21¼ x 23½″. Musée du Louvre, Paris

art and the position he would ultimately achieve, Gauguin now replied: "... The reasons you give me for remaining in Europe are flattering rather than made to convince me. My decision is taken, and since I am back in Brittany I have modified it. Madagascar is still too close to the civilized world. I shall go to Tahiti and I hope to end my life there. I believe that my art, which you like, is only in an embryonic stage and hope that down there I shall cultivate it for myself alone in its primitive and savage condition. For that I need calm; what do I care for fame or for the others! Gauguin will be finished here; they won't see anything by him anymore. You see how egotistic I am. In photographs and drawings I shall take along a small world of comrades who will speak to me every day. Of you I have in my head the recollection of almost everything you have created, and *a star* [possibly a reference to the work Redon had exchanged with him]; while looking at it in my hut in Tahiti, I promise you that I shall not think of death [allusion to one of Redon's lithographs published in 1888] but quite the contrary of eternal life."[21] And to the Danish painter Willumsen Gauguin explained that in Tahiti, "I want to forget all the evils of the past and to die down there unknown by those here, free to paint without any glory at all for the others.... A terrible ordeal is in store in Europe for the coming generation: the kingdom of gold. Everything is rotten, men as well as the arts."[22]

Whereas previously Gauguin had spoken only of going away for a few years, he now proclaimed that he was forever abandoning Europe to its fate. Gauguin's dreams were suddenly stimulated by the arrival in October of Theo van Gogh's telegram, in which the latter, having lost his reason, promised the money for the trip. But after a few days of excitement, Gauguin realized that something was wrong and that his situation was still as hopeless as before; it actually became even worse since de Haan's family cut off his allowance and the Dutchman had to leave for Paris for a showdown with his relatives. Unable to stand his drab and listless life in Brittany any longer, Gauguin now resolved to go to Paris himself and to try with or without Charlopin—to try at any cost—to raise the money he needed for his departure.

Gauguin apparently arrived in Paris in November 1890; he stayed again at Schuffenecker's. Among the first acquaintances he saw were Albert Aurier, for whose article he was still waiting, as well as Sérusier and Maurice Denis. The two young painters had not been idle since they had become associated with the new movement created at Pont-Aven. They had gathered a small group of friends, among them Bonnard, Vuillard, Roussel, and Vallotton, all of whom had abandoned the Académie Julian in 1890. They now called themselves the *Nabis* and were to a lesser or greater extent influenced by Gauguin's symbolist-synthesist work. Their group also included Lugné-Poë, a schoolmate of Denis' who envisioned a career in the theater and who valiantly assisted the painters through articles and attempts to sell their canvases to his colleagues of the stage. Their combined efforts had kept the issue of the new painting alive while Gauguin was in Brittany and they had established connections with the symbolist poets whose gatherings they attended and in whose discussions they took part.

"Gauguin is in Paris and bustles about a great deal," Denis in November informed Lugné-Poë, who was then doing his military service (until the end of February 1891). "There may be a serious effort attempted by him."[23] And a little later he wrote: "I have heard from Sérusier that Gauguin counts on an exhibition of his works soon to be organized, being assured of some buyers (several Jews and [Roger] Marx, Clemenceau, Antonin Proust). Let's wait and see."[24]

Meanwhile Gauguin assisted Denis with notes for an important article in which Denis, the spokesman of his youthful group, was to elaborate on his theories partly derived from Gauguin and Sérusier. "Gauguin was taken by Aurier to the Café François-Premier," Denis shortly reported to Lugné-Poë. "There Aurier presented the painter to the admiration of Stuart Merrill and a multitude of other young men. Great agitation around Gauguin.—'But we know Denis and Sérusier. Are you Gauguin, the originator of this... the originator of that...?'—He, very much surprised that in his absence we had gained for him so many and such lively sympathies. All is well."[25]

Through Aurier, Gauguin also met the latter's friends, Julien Leclercq and Jean Dolent, both of whom had collaborated with Aurier on *La Pléiade* and *Le Moderniste* before taking an active part in the founding of the *Mercure de France*. Very soon Gauguin found himself absorbed into the group of symbolist writers gathered around the editors of the *Mercure de France*; he assiduously attended their gatherings in various favorite cafés or restaurants. It was in one of these, La Côte d'Or, near the Odéon, that the poet Charles Morice, considered one of the best among the symbolists, saw the painter for the first time:

"A broad face, massive and bony, a narrow forehead, a nose neither curved nor arched, but as if broken, a thin-lipped mouth without any inflection, heavy eyelids lifting sluggishly over somewhat protuberant eyeballs whose bluish pupils rotated in their orbits to glance to left or right while his head and bust made almost no effort to turn. There was little charm about this stranger; yet he attracted one by his very personal expression, a mixture of haughty nobility, obviously innate, and of a simplicity that bordered on triviality. It was not long before one realized that this mixture was a sign of strength: aristocracy permeated by the proletariat. And if he lacked grace, his smile, though it did not suit very well his too thin, too straight lips—relaxing, they seemed to regret and to deny any admission of gaiety as if it were a weakness—Gauguin's smile had yet a strangely naïve gentleness. Above all, this head took on a real beauty in its gravity when it became illuminated and, in the heat of argument, intensely blue rays flashed suddenly from his eyes. When I perceived Gauguin for the first time on that evening, he was experiencing one of these moments. Although there were other strangers in the group which centered around him, I saw only him and, approaching, I remained standing for a long time close to the table where a dozen poets and artists were listening to him.... In a deep and slightly hoarse voice he said:

"'Primitive art proceeds from the mind and uses nature. So-called refined art proceeds from sensuality and serves nature. Nature is the servant of the former and the mistress of the latter. But the servant cannot forget her origin and degrades the artist by allowing him to adore her. This is how we have fallen into the abominable error of naturalism which began with the Greeks of Pericles. Since then the more or less great artists have been only those who in one way or another reacted against this error. But their reactions have been only awakenings of memory, gleams of common sense in a movement of decadence which, at bottom, has lasted without interruption for centuries. Truth is to be found in a purely cerebral art, in a primitive art—the most erudite of all—in Egypt. There lies the principle. In our present plight the only possible salvation lies in a reasoned and frank return to principle. And this return is the necessary action to be accomplished by symbolism in poetry and in art....'"[26]

Moréas, who was present, according to Morice "realized how right and fecund Gauguin's theories were. Without subscribing completely to them for his part, he spoke of them with respect.... With very few exceptions the poets always showed a spontaneous and profound deference to Gauguin, to the man as well as to his work, a deference logically explained by the preponderance which the artist accorded in his work to poetic thinking, or we may call it literary thinking.... At that first meeting however... there were not exactly collisions but, on the contrary, what is worse, some slight gestures of recoil, noisy objections as well as silences. The attitude of this painter who had come to lecture us on art in general and even on poetry, on its laws and its duties, offended some of us. And the very trenchant personality of the man, the broadness of his theories and of his shoulders, the incisive intuition of his gaze, the tangy carelessness of his speech in which sailors' slang and studio slang strangely clothed ideas of an absolute purity and nobility, everything in him seemed strange.... Without wanting to, Gauguin forced the others into a kind of effacement, pushed them into the background. They in turn, no doubt involuntarily, sought to regain the upper hand by taking advantage of their knowledge which was greater and more precise, at least in literature, than his. The result was a general uneasiness which he was the first to feel. He abandoned the controversial subject, asked Moréas to recite some verses and, while he listened, I could study his now motionless features. Yes, power was certainly the principal characteristic expressed by his entire being, a noble force which justified a visible claim to be a tyrant. Nevertheless, the short chin, the nose with its very fine nostrils that constantly quivered, the bitter expression of the mouth revealed, I told myself, the possibility of sudden relaxations of will power, moments of weakness or of despair,

420

carefully hidden—and these features somewhat contradicted the general impression which was of tranquil and conscious energy.... Never again, after that, in our reunions of artists and poets did he start a discussion in the doctrinaire, pedantic tone of the first day. He had understood."[26]

Gauguin soon succeeded in winning many new friends among the poets. Charles Morice, who had studied him so intently on their first meeting, was shortly to become a great admirer of his. Indeed, the painter became so quickly part of the entire group that by the end of December he found himself involved as second in one of those inevitable duels through which the various writers straightened out their differences of opinion. This one concerned Aurier's friend Leclercq and Rodolphe Darzens, both of whom used to write for the same symbolist periodicals. Jules Renard, another second, confided to his diary: "Without bragging, it would have been a pleasure for me to line up in turn.—'But we are seconds,' Paul Gauguin said to me, 'Why don't we fight too?'"[27]

Gauguin was doubtless happy to immerse himself in this milieu of writers and poets with their endless discussions of esthetic problems, since this was a radical change after the long months he had spent in practical isolation in Brittany. He needed this stimulus to clarify his own ideas, to sharpen them in contact with highly articulate intelligences, just as he had once before benefited from Bernard's philosophical monologues. It is possible that Gauguin did not always take too seriously the various theories advanced by his new friends,[28] but he certainly enjoyed being proclaimed by Morice the "chief of symbolist painting." While the poets were delighted to find in him an ally who opened new avenues

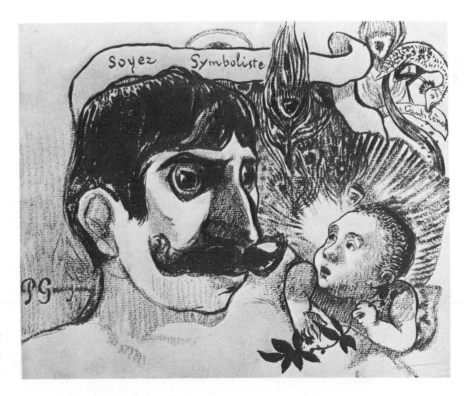

GAUGUIN: *Be a Symbolist—Portrait of Jean Moréas,* Paris, 1891. Brush and ink, 13¾ x 16½". Formerly collection Georges Renan, Paris

to their movement, they were not unaware of his pride and arrogance, so powerfully expressed in his startling features; but those were qualities of which many of them, too, could boast—and not the least Moréas. When Schuffenecker reproached his friend for the "harm he was doing himself with his haughty character," Gauguin professed to be surprised, and explained: "The people who can be of use to me are not very numerous; I know them and I don't believe that I have treated them badly. As to those who can injure me, Pissarro and company, it is more on account of my talent that they scold than on account of my character. Whatever I do, my head is always there to make them believe in my disdain; I can't do anything about it. Besides, confound it, one never gets anywhere by courting imbeciles. And I am strong enough to despise a great part of the world."[29] Having thus divided his entourage into "useful" people and the others, Gauguin began to meditate on how he could take full advantage of his new symbolist acquaintances.

Every Monday about nine o'clock in the evening the symbolists and their friends gathered at the Café Voltaire, place de l'Odéon. There Gauguin met Verlaine, sickly, walking with difficulty, Jean Moréas, Charles Morice, Albert Aurier, Jean Dolent, Julien Leclercq, Alfred Vallette, editor of the *Mercure de France*, and his beautiful wife Mme Rachilde, Henri de Régnier, Viélé-Griffin, Edouard Dujardin, Laurent Tailhade, Maurice Barrès, Brouillon (who under the name of Jean de Rotonchamp later wrote a book about Gauguin), and many others, such as Fénéon, no doubt one of the few refusing to be impressed by the painter. Indeed, Fénéon saw in him a "prey of the literati," who had succeeded in convincing the artist that he was "invested with a mission." With his biting irony, Fénéon was soon to state that—thanks to Bernard's influence—Gauguin had arrived from Brittany "full of pseudo-literary fervor, he who had until then, with the most paradoxical obstinacy, shunned bookshops as well as ideas in general."[30]

It was at a meeting at the Café Voltaire that, a short time before Gauguin's arrival, Vallette had proclaimed one evening that the symbolist movement still lacked one thing, a theater. This challenge had been taken up immediately by a young man, future poet and future brother-in-law of Emile Bernard, Paul Fort, who was then seventeen years old. Shortly afterwards Fort was to found, almost singlehanded and without any means, though he enjoyed the support of all the symbolist poets, his Théâtre d'Art, destined to rival the Théâtre Libre of André Antoine, devoted to the naturalist school. Among the painters whom Fort enlisted to do stage designs or programs for him were Emile Bernard, Sérusier, Vuillard, Bonnard, and—according to his memoirs—also Gauguin, whom Fort must have met at the Café Voltaire.[31]

Possibly inspired by his exchange of ideas with the various symbolists, Gauguin jotted down a few notes suggested by Huysmans' art studies which had appeared in 1889 under the title *Certains*. Gauguin expressed satisfaction with Huysmans' change of attitude since his naturalist days (although the *naturalist* Huysmans, in 1881, had been the first to praise the *impressionist* Gauguin), but at the same time took issue with his opinions on art. Huysmans had written about Redon in a chapter called "Le Monstre," and Gauguin objected to this with words that may have been suggested by Redon himself. "I do not see how Odilon Redon makes monsters," Gauguin wrote. "Those are imaginary beings. He is a dreamer, a visionary.... Nature has mysterious infinities, a power of imagination; it manifests these by always varying its products. The artist himself is one of nature's means and, to me, Redon is one of those chosen for the continuance of its creations. His dreams become reality through the probability he gives them [Redon himself used very similar

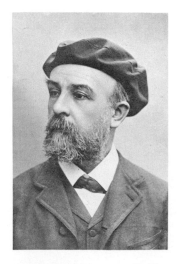

Photograph of Odilon Redon, 1890

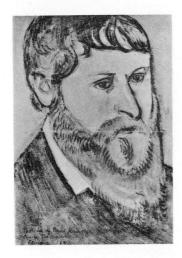
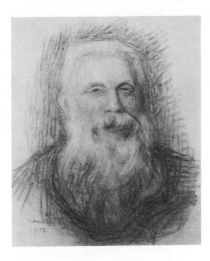
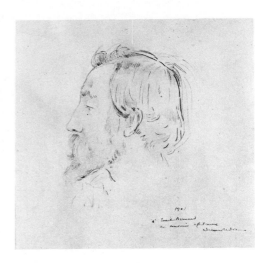

Left: BERNARD: *Portrait of Paul Sérusier,* Florence, d. 1893. 28⅜ x 22″. Collection Mlle H. Boutaric, Paris. Center: RENOIR: *Portrait of Auguste Rodin,* d. 1914. Red and white chalk. Present whereabouts unknown. Right: REDON: *Portrait of Emile Bernard,* d. 1901. Sanguine. Collection Clément Altarriba, Paris

words]. All his plants, his embryonic beings are essentially human, have lived with us; they certainly have their share of suffering.... Redon speaks with his crayon; is it matter that he is after with that inner eye? In all his work I see only the language of the heart, very human and not at all monstrous. What does the means of expression matter! Impulsive movement of the heart."

Having thus replied to Huysmans' literary and excessive tendency to see in Redon's work an accumulation of fabulous but unhealthy horrors, Gauguin went on: "Huysmans writes of Gustave Moreau with very great esteem. Well, we also have esteem for him—but to what degree? Here is a mind which is essentially not literary yet which desires to be so. Thus Moreau only speaks a language which has already been used by men of letters; it is in a certain way the illustration of ancient tales. His impulsive movement is very far from the heart and he loves the richness of material wealth. He puts it everywhere. Of every human being he makes a piece of jewelry covered with jewelry.... In fact Moreau is an excellent chaser. On the other hand Puvis de Chavannes does not attract [Huysmans]; his impulsive movements do not attract. Simplicity, nobility are out of favor. What do you want; those people will one day be very much in favor. If it isn't on our planet, it will be in another one, more favorable to beautiful things...."[32]

There can be no doubt that in his debates with the symbolists Gauguin expressed similar views. If he did not induce their admiration for Redon and Chavannes—whom they already appreciated—at least he may have helped them to better understand their aims and may have contributed to their replacing a purely literary approach by one more conscious of artistic and plastic qualities. In this way Gauguin possibly played a valuable role in the art appreciation of the symbolists.

There had been many changes in the field of the little symbolist periodicals. *La Vogue* had finally disappeared in 1889 and that same year the symbolists had abandoned the anarchist *Cravache*; by 1890 the *Revue Indépendante* had become an organ for the restoration

423

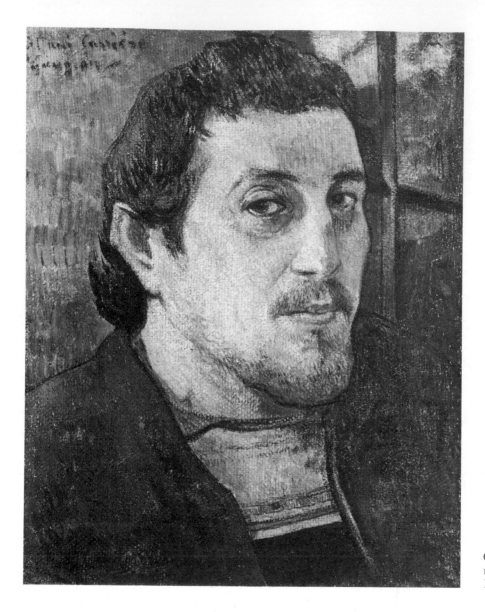

of the Orléans dynasty and for General Boulanger, who was soon to commit suicide in his Belgian exile. Instead the writers and poets had grouped themselves around some new publications: *Art et Critique* and *Entretiens Politiques et Littéraires,* both founded in 1890; at the same time the three Natanson brothers—intimate friends of the Nabis and of Lautrec—were preparing the first issue of their *Revue Blanche* which would appear later in 1891. Meanwhile the symbolists had taken over *Les Hommes d'Aujourd'hui,* a series of little four-page sheets published once a week, each issue featuring a "profile" of a single personality whose portrait appeared on the cover. Verlaine had written a great many of these articles devoted to, among others, Rimbaud, René Ghil, and Anatole France; Fénéon had written on Gustave Kahn and Signac; Lecomte on Pissarro; Jules Christophe on Seurat,

Dubois-Pillet, and Luce; Charles Morice on Redon; Emile Bernard on Cézanne and van Gogh; Wyzewa on Dujardin. Other issues concerned Henri de Régnier, Aristide Bruant, Verhaeren, Maeterlinck, and Toulouse-Lautrec. Charles Morice now prepared a number on Gauguin. But the most important new periodical was the *Mercure de France*, which had first appeared in January 1890 and in which Aurier's long-promised article on Gauguin was shortly to be published; he finished the manuscript on February 9, 1891.

Among the artists who joined the gathering at the Café Voltaire, stronghold of the *Mercure de France*, were occasionally the Nabis, sometimes Rodin, and more frequently Carrière, who had just painted a portrait of Verlaine. Gauguin became particularly friendly with Carrière, who spontaneously offered to do his portrait, although he found that Gauguin's mouth was not too kind.[33] Gauguin sat about three times, attired in a colorful embroidered shirt such as the Breton peasants wear on Sunday and which he sported in Paris; he was surprised to discover that in Carrière's likeness of him he resembled Delacroix. In exchange he presented Carrière with a portrait of himself, painted in Brittany, with strong emphasis on his powerful, massively hewn features, although it was rather subtly and delicately executed.[34] Strangely enough, Gauguin even submitted for a very short while to Carrière's

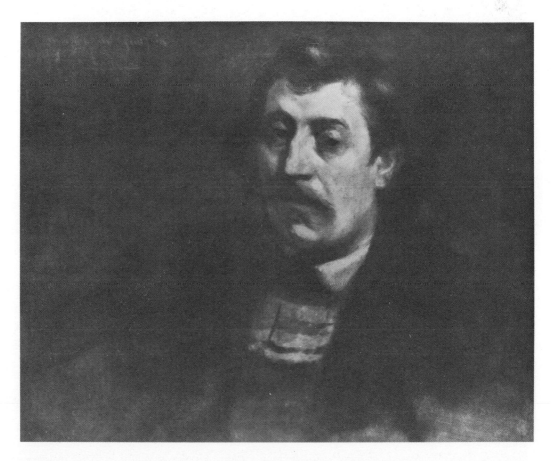

CARRIÈRE: *Portrait of Paul Gauguin,* Paris, 1891. 30 x 26″. Yale University Art Gallery, New Haven, Conn.

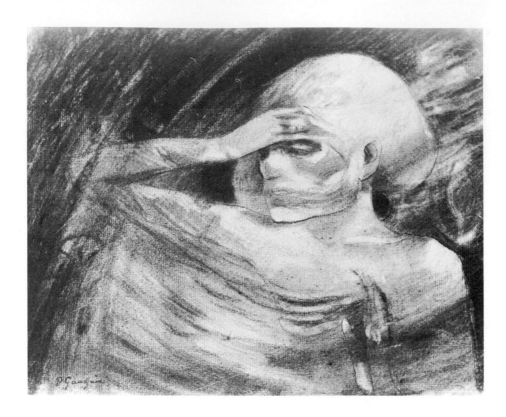

GAUGUIN: *Madame la Mort,* illustration for a play by Mme Rachilde, 1891. Charcoal and wash drawing, 9⅛ x 11½". Musée du Louvre, Paris

influence when he drew, upon Jean Dolent's recommendation, some illustrations for the publication, in book form, of a drama by Mme Rachilde. It is true that Dolent was a fanatical admirer of Carrière and that Gauguin may have wished to please his two new friends, the poet and the painter. On the whole, however, his relations with Carrière were intellectual rather than artistic, although Carrière subsequently expressed in fairly guarded words his admiration for Gauguin.[35] In any event there is no trace of Carrière's influence in the elaborate portrait of Moréas (page 421) or the incisive likeness of Mallarmé (page 451) which Gauguin was shortly to draw. He also made a sketch after one of Puvis de Chavannes' paintings which was later to appear accompanied by some of Charles Morice's verses. Gauguin subsequently etched his portrait of Mallarmé. This etching was done in the studio of Léon Fauché, one of the minor participants in the Volpini show; it was Carrière who gave Gauguin the necessary technical advice.

The portraits of Moréas and Mallarmé are among the few tangible souvenirs of those winter months of 1890–91 during which Gauguin rubbed elbows with the symbolists. After all he was only mildly interested in erudite discussions; he had come to Paris to further his own projects, and there were still more important things to do. Moreover, there was little time to be lost as he was penniless and as Schuffenecker's hospitality and patience showed signs of being exhausted. Gauguin thus began to look for a gallery where he could hold his planned exhibition. While he had been away, significant changes had occurred in the Parisian art world and Gauguin must have studied them with an eye for anything that might prove helpful to his own endeavors.

At Goupil's (the Boussod & Valadon Gallery) Theo van Gogh's position had been hastily offered to a young man, Maurice Joyant, a school friend of Lautrec's, to whom M. Boussod had said: "Our former manager, a madman of sorts, like his brother the painter... has accumulated appalling things by modern painters which have brought the firm to discredit.... You will also find a certain number of pictures by a landscape painter, Claude Monet, who is beginning to sell a little in America.... All the rest are horrors; try to manage and don't ask us for anything, otherwise the shop will be closed."[36]

Upon taking stock, Joyant was pleased to discover among the "horrors" assembled by Theo van Gogh not only numerous paintings by Monet but also several scenes of dancers by Degas, a great many landscapes by Pissarro, about a dozen canvases by Guillaumin, others by Daumier, Jongkind, Redon, Toulouse-Lautrec, sculptures by Barye, and some twenty paintings, as well as several sculptures, by Gauguin. As the majority of these had been left on consignment, the painter now retrieved most of them, among others his *Yellow Christ* and *La Belle Angèle*, which Theo van Gogh had liked so much. In view of the hostile attitude of the owners, Joyant apparently did not dare to organize an exhibition of works by Gauguin, who now began to think of holding an auction sale of a group of his pictures so as to raise the money for his trip. But at the same time he established friendly relations with Joyant, as he intended to send him his paintings from Tahiti.

Gauguin also went to see *père* Tanguy in the hope that the old man might be able to sell some paintings for him while he was away; he subsequently left at least one canvas in

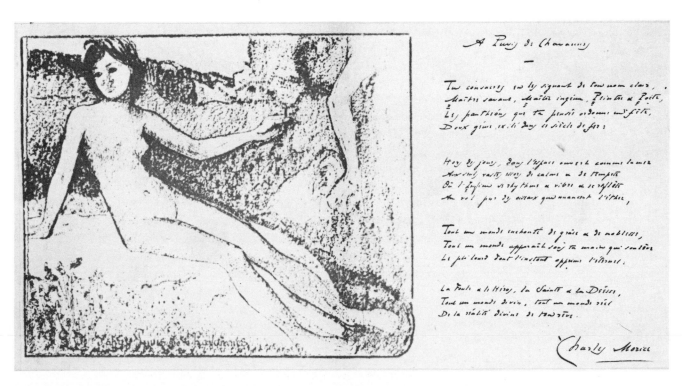

GAUGUIN: *Drawing after Puvis de Chavannes' "Hope,"* accompanied by a poem by Charles Morice, 1894. Published in the *Mercure de France,* February 1895. Present whereabouts unknown

storage at Tanguy's, with orders not to sell it. Tanguy, who was soon to move into a somewhat larger place on the same street (from no. 14, rue Clauzel, to no. 9), now had fairly numerous visitors since avant-garde artists and writers came more and more often to see the works of van Gogh, many of which Theo's widow had left with him until she could have them shipped to Holland. A German painter living in Paris in 1891 later recalled how one day, on a walk down the hill from Montmartre, he stopped, intrigued, in front of the shop-window of the color-grinder:

"In the middle lay a few tubes of colors and several brushes, symbols of his profession, but on three sides hung wild pictures of a strength and intensity of color such as we had never seen before in painting. Southern landscapes under a burning sun and still lifes of great pictorial taste, partly very much simplified and stylized and with the represented objects surrounded by heavy blue outlines, a new and daring fashion to heighten the decorative quality of the picture. A small card announced: 'Large Collection Inside.' We entered. The little narrow shop, extending to an inner court from which it received light through a large window, was stacked with piles of unframed paintings. A tiny woman who resembled an old peasant woman from Normandy, led us through and talked incessantly: 'Don't you agree, Messieurs, a good painter, a great artist. The poor fellow, to end so sadly. I always told my husband that we shall be paid some day, that he will eventually be recognized.'"[37] She asked 100 francs each for the paintings.

Gauguin, in whom his new friend Jean Dolent admired "the legitimate ferocity of a productive egotism,"[38] and who had already opposed Bernard's project for a van Gogh retrospective exhibition, may well have felt that it was a little too late now to sell Vincent's work and that the Tanguys would do better to push the production of the living.

If Tanguy had no room for a show of Gauguin's work, Durand-Ruel doubtless had no inclination to hold one. Paul Durand-Ruel, whose serious rival Theo van Gogh had threatened to become, had once more assumed practically sole command over the impressionists, although Georges Petit tried to break his monopoly (and eventually persuaded Sisley to switch to his gallery). After his short-lived contract with Theo van Gogh, Monet had refused to give any dealer the exclusive rights to his work, but it was with Durand-Ruel that he dealt most frequently. Pissarro, who had hoped to find new outlets through Theo van Gogh and thus be in a better position to ameliorate the conditions offered him by Durand-Ruel, now had once more to accept whatever prices the latter would pay him, as nobody else seemed to care for his pictures. In 1890 Durand-Ruel had even attempted to organize a new group exhibition of the impressionists, who had not shown together since 1886, but this project had to be abandoned because of Monet's refusal to participate in it. In March 1891 Durand-Ruel, increasingly and justifiably hopeful of finding a new market in America, did organize an exhibition of paintings by Monet, Sisley, and Pissarro in New York. For May 1891 he prepared in Paris a show of Monet's *Haystacks*, the artist's first attempt to retain in a series of fifteen paintings the subtle differences of light—from dawn to dusk—observed on the same object.

Since his works began to sell, Monet had been able to purchase the house in which he lived at Giverny and continued to raise his prices slowly but regularly. His recent affluence permitted him to embark in 1889–90 upon a generous project dear to his heart: the organization of a subscription among Manet's admirers for the purpose of acquiring from the artist's widow the painting *L'Olympia* and offering it to the nation. The total amount raised was 19,415 francs. The subscribers included Durand-Ruel, Fantin-Latour, Degas,

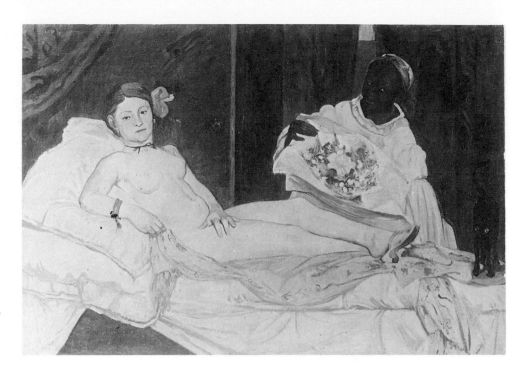

GAUGUIN: *Copy after Manet's "Olympia,"* Paris, 1891. 35 × 51⅛″. Formerly collection Edgar Degas. Collection Mrs. Annie Bergh, Oslo

Roger Marx, Puvis de Chavannes, G. de Bellio, Pissarro, Raffaëlli, Rodin, Renoir, Monet himself, Mirbeau, Mallarmé, Huysmans, Georges Petit, Geffroy, Antoine de La Rochefoucauld, Carrière, Lautrec, Caillebotte, Duret, Sargent, and many others. Only Zola refused to contribute, explaining that the work of Manet, whose earliest champion he had been, should be admitted to the Louvre in its own right and not in the form of a gift by a coterie of friends who might be suspected of trying to increase the painter's prices. Actually the administration raised unforeseen difficulties, hiding behind rules which prohibited the acceptance by the Louvre of a work by any artist who had been dead for only six years; but it promised that *L'Olympia* would enter the Louvre ten years after Manet's death, and meanwhile hung it in the Luxembourg Museum.[39] It was there that Gauguin subsequently went to paint a copy of it.

These events had once more focused the limelight on the impressionists. The increased activities of Durand-Ruel had also led to his foundation of a periodical, *L'Art dans les Deux Mondes*, which he published from November 1890 to July 1891 and which featured reproductions of works by *his* artists, together with articles on Monet and Pissarro by Mirbeau; on Renoir, Boudin, and Seurat by Wyzewa; on Sisley by Lecomte; on Degas (who disapproved of this venture), Monet, and Whistler by Geffroy, etc. The review published ample notes on art events in America as well as short paragraphs on the auction sale which Gauguin planned to organize and at which Durand-Ruel agreed to officiate as expert.

Having refused to exhibit the works of Vincent van Gogh—a decision which may possibly have been prompted by his inimical feelings for the painter's brother—Durand-Ruel was ready, on the other hand, to patronize a rather bizarre personage who called himself the "Sâr" Mérodack Joséphin Péladan and who had founded an artistic, mystic, religious, idealistic, and spiritualistic order of the Catholic Rosicrucians, largely financed by the painter Count Antoine de La Rochefoucauld. Péladan sometimes appeared at the gatherings at the Café Voltaire and had concocted a symbolism of his own, posing as the Heaven-sent defender of obsolete esthetic ideas, partly borrowed from Dante and Leonardo, and designed to renovate art through mysticism. His motto was a quotation from Pascal: "How vain is painting which tries to make us admire the representation of things which we would disdain in reality!" Among the adherents to Péladan's order was soon to be Emile Bernard.

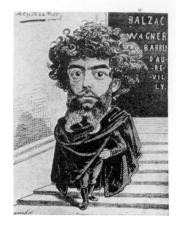

Péladan's loudly heralded emergence as an active force in the art world—he had been a novelist and Salon reviewer for many years—was yet another symptom of a growing mysticism that found increasing favor with the public at large, appearing as it did at the tail end of the symbolist movement and vulgarizing the esoteric aspirations of the poets. This mysticism was accompanied by a revival of occultism, by a general preoccupation with the forbidden, the miraculous, the terrifying, a strange whirl of spiritualistic activities. Old anarchist that he was, Pissarro was particularly worried by these trends. "Those who follow the new tendency," he wrote to his son, "are influenced by bourgeois reaction.... The purpose behind all this, my dear boy, is to check the movement [of social unrest] which is beginning to increase; we must therefore be suspicious of those who under the pretext of socialism, idealistic art, pure art, etc., etc., indeed follow a movement, but a false movement, a thousand times false, even though, perhaps, it answers the need of certain types of people, but not ours—we have to form a totally different ideal!"[40]

LE PETIT: Caricature of Sâr Péladan, 1892

The new Salon founded by Péladan for the exhibition of Rosicrucian works actually added a fourth Salon to the Parisian scene, for the official Salon had been split recently into two rival societies and there was also the Salon des Indépendants. The year 1890 had seen a revolt within the directing committee of the Société des Artistes Français, organizer of the yearly Salon, over a question of rewards (abolished once and for all by the Independents). Whereas the old society, headed by Bouguereau—hence Cézanne's expression "le Salon de Bouguereau"—clung to its prerogatives, its opponents, under the leadership of Meissonier who was shortly to die, formed the Société Nationale des Beaux-Arts with slightly more liberal rules. While the students of the Académie Julian as well as Cormon's "gang" remained with the old group, the new one counted in its ranks Puvis de Chavannes, Carolus-Duran, Stevens, Sargent, Boldini, Carrière, and Rodin. Both Sisley and Anquetin decided to show with the new society, but Renoir, who had exhibited with the old one in 1890, now resolved to abstain from both.

In March 1891 Gauguin wrote from Paris to his wife: "Meissonier's group will open this year a section of sculptural art. I received yesterday a delegate from these gentlemen, the son of [Ernest] Renan, who had been commissioned to invite me especially to exhibit my ceramics and my wood sculptures. As I am almost the only one who does work of this type, or in any event the strongest and the one most noticed, I have the possibility of obtaining a certain success...."[41]

Gauguin always combined great hopes of success with any new exhibition of his works. Having received an invitation for the 1891 show of the XX (and having asked Octave Maus to include his friend Filiger as an independent artist of talent), Gauguin had sent to Brussels two large vases, a statuette in "grès émaillé" and his two bas-reliefs in polychromed wood: *Be in Love* and *Be Mysterious*. (Finch also exhibited some faïences and two plates painted according to Charles Henry's theories on harmony, rhythm, and measure.) Among the other guests of the XX were Angrand, Chéret, Filiger, Guillaumin, Pissarro, Seurat —who died a few weeks later—and Sisley; the exhibition also included a small van Gogh retrospective. The show was immediately attacked by de Groux, the former member of the group who had been dismissed because of his opposition to van Gogh and who now singled out Gauguin for his vicious recriminations. If Gauguin received any press clippings concerning the show, he must soon have realized that his expectations had once again been cruelly disappointed.

The reactionary Belgian critics had a wonderful time at the exhibition of the XX. It was almost as if the clock had been turned back some thirty years and as if they tried to outdo their French colleagues in their earlier gibes at the impressionists. Or was it simply that Brussels was behind Paris and only now caught on to the "menace" of modern art, in spite of the fact that the XX had already waged such a courageous battle for many years? Gauguin and Seurat were most unmercifully derided, but Pissarro and van Gogh also received their share of insults.

One critic called Gauguin a "manufacturer of pornographic images whose sublime ignorance has never been surpassed by the sculptors of the Black Forest." A second wrote of the invited artists: ". . . Pissarro, Seurat, whose *Chahut*, souvenir of [the Moulin Rouge dancer] Grille d'Egout, is as good as his *Grande Jatte*, the late Vincent van Gogh who, from afar, must be enjoying a good laugh when he sees all the fools ask themselves what he means by his stupefying canvases . . ., all this is highly farcical and a kind of joke which no longer amuses. Gauguin, who invented Gauguinism, asserts with incontestable authority the most stupidly insufficient things that can be invented in order to stun a public idiotic enough to be taken in." Another qualified Gauguin as "the erotico-macabre temperament of a genius of lewdness, a dilettante of infamy who is haunted by vice," and characterized his wood relief as "the deformed sculpture of a sadistic faun, whose kisses are slobbery and disgusting, whose forked tongue sensuously licks a beard impregnated with slime." The same author was equally devastating on the subject of Seurat's *Chahut*: "This work is nothing but a frantic spasm of a panting dwarf and a rutting ghoul! Supreme hymn to palpitating flesh, though flatulent and spotted with green like the mucus of a disgorged snail, his dancers have the moldy dead color of a festering sore. Yet it is spicy in spite of everything, for it leaves me breathless, and I am sure that it causes more than one person to stick out his tongue and wring his empty hands, hypnotized by the hectic transports of a monstrous and degrading immodesty."[42]

In a similar vein another reporter wrote: "This year, as in the preceding exhibitions, it is the invited artists who succeed in attracting the greatest amount of interest. It seems right to place Seurat in the first rank, one of the mad masters who has exerted the strongest influence on the tendencies of the XX. *Le Chahut* even better than the *Grande Jatte*, so hilariously remembered, will give you an exact idea of the degree of aberration which can be reached in the practice of this doctrine of abracadabra which consists in denying everything that exists and in creating a new formula just the same. Seurat, this pontiff of the art of painting with blobs of sealing wax, this rediscoverer marked with the stamp of genius, draws and daubs with the supreme ignorance of an inmate of an insane asylum.

"The impressionists of the XX group . . . have invited to their pointillist saturnalia an incapable fellow who is worthy of them: M. Gauguin. This buffoon—I can't imagine that he takes himself seriously—carves bas-reliefs in polychromed wood which remind one,

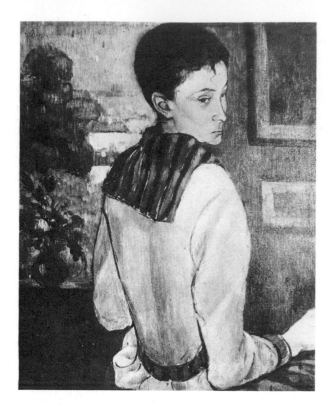

except for the subject, of course, of old Flemish shop signs. M. Gauguin has undertaken to carve, *à la* Seurat, erotico-enigmatic scenes!! These bas-reliefs: *Be in love and you will be happy* and *Be mysterious* [pages 410 and 417] go beyond all limits of insanity."[43]

As an epilogue there was a last article which repeated many threadbare jokes: "The city has ordered that the exhibition of the XX be closed; three visitors have succumbed to smallpox which they caught in front of a painting done in dots, others are stricken. A young lady in society lost her mind. Finally it is said—though this has not been confirmed—that the wife of a mayor from the provinces, who had committed the imprudence of visiting the exhibition while in an interesting condition, has been delivered of a tattooed child."[42]

If the news from Brussels was discouraging, things did not go too well in Paris either. In January 1891 Schuffenecker finally grew tired of the guest who seemed to reign over his household as if it were his own, used his studio with little consideration, and received visitors without introducing them to his host, closing the door upon the latter. Apparently Gauguin had not been satisfied to share Schuffenecker's roof, he also had tried—perhaps successfully—to share his host's attractive wife. Gauguin now had to look for new lodgings, which he found in a modest hotel in the rue Delambre, whence he subsequently moved to 10, rue de la Grande Chaumière. But even in his anger Schuffenecker could not bring himself to send his indiscreet friend to the devil; he remained civil and even agreed to keep his works in his house, as Gauguin had no place to store or show them.

"My dear Gauguin," Schuffenecker wrote on February 7, "my wife tells me that you intend to come tomorrow. As I have to go out, I am writing you so as to spare you a useless errand in case the purpose of your visit is to talk things over with me." Here Schuffenecker added: "You are made for domination whereas I am made for indifference," but he scratched this out and went on: "Neither as men nor as artists are we made to live side by side. I have known this for a long time and what has just happened proves it. I have resolved to isolate myself; everything prompts me to do so, my tastes and my interests. And this on my part without any spirit of hatred or of war, simple incompatibilty of temperament which does not prevent us from shaking hands with mutual esteem. Now, my dear Gauguin, I repeat the last paragraph of my preceding letter, concerning your canvases, potteries, and other objects which are in my house. I do not wish under any circumstances that this should cause you trouble or annoyance, as you have, I believe, plenty of worries at this moment in connection with your auction and your projects for departure. I therefore shake your hand cordially and remain your devoted friend—E. Schuffenecker." He had written at first "very cordially" and "very devotedly," but these two adverbs he scratched out.[44]

When, shortly after Gauguin had left Schuffenecker's home, Willumsen visited him at one of his several temporary abodes, he found Gauguin not far from the Café Voltaire. "He was then living in a studio at the very top of a house near the Odéon. The studio was completely empty, except for an iron bed which stood in the middle of the room and on which Gauguin was playing a guitar while at the same time a woman was sitting on his lap. The only object I saw there was a small sculpture on the mantelpiece. It was done in wood and Gauguin had just finished it. It represented a woman in an exotic style; possibly it was a dream of Tahiti by which Gauguin was then haunted. He had left the legs unfinished. Gauguin called it *Lewdness*, maybe because the woman was inhaling the perfume of a flower [page 411]. He gave it to me in exchange for one of my Brittany paintings."[45]

Fortunately Gauguin had met at Schuffenecker's one of the latter's friends, Georges-Daniel de Monfreid, a painter who had modestly participated in the Volpini show and who now offered him the use of his own studio, situated—like Schuffenecker's pavilion—in the Plaisance quarter. Thus, while living in a dreary little hotel room, Gauguin could at least continue to work, although he did not accomplish much during his agitated stay in Paris. But, inspired by all the discussions about symbolism, he did paint a large canvas in which he attempted to embody the essence of these debates.

The symbolism of this work was comparatively uncomplicated: an austere Breton landscape with a reclining nude girl holding a flower in her hand. A fox, symbol of perversity, lying near her shoulder, places one paw on her breast. In the distance, sketchily brushed in, a Breton wedding procession advances in single file along a narrow path. The title: *The Loss of Virginity* (page 434).[46] This composition was not the result of a visual experience; it was a purely intellectual product for which the artist, once he had settled upon his project, sought out an appropriate and not too pretty model.[47] Her name was Juliette Huet; she was then scarcely twenty years old and a milliner. It was Daniel de Monfreid who introduced her to the painter whose mistress she became.[48]

The Loss of Virginity, with its succession of horizontal planes, with the strong contrast of the pale nude against dark leaves, with its saturated colors, with some of its forms surrounded by heavy contours, with its flat surfaces of sea and rocks opposed to more subtly treated hills or dunes, above all with its more or less hidden meaning, combined many of the features that had already made their appearance in Gauguin's Brittany canvases. It almost seems as if he wished to sum up all his stylistic and color innovations in this ultimate translation of a vision. Less intricate than his by now much talked about *Jacob*

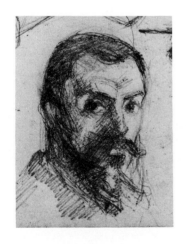

D. DE MONFREID: *Self-Portrait,* c. 1889. Formerly collection Mme Agnès Huc de Monfreid

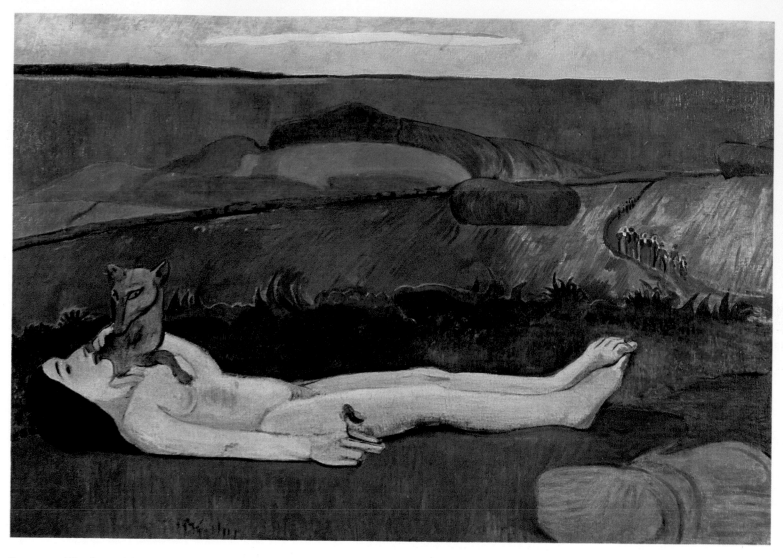

GAUGUIN: *The Loss of Virginity,* Paris, 1890–91. 35 x 52". Collection Walter P. Chrysler, Jr., New York

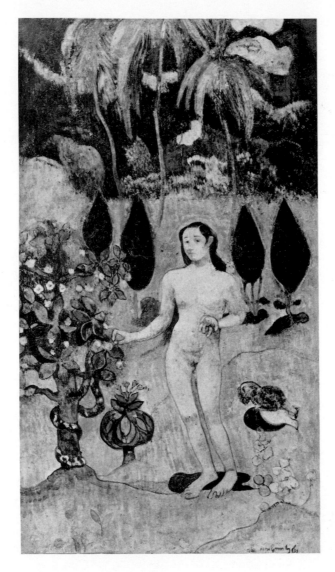

GAUGUIN: *Eve,* d. 1890. Cardboard, 17 x 9⅞". Collection M. Seydoux, Paris

Wrestling with the Angel, less subtle than his *Still Life with Two Vases,* it demonstrates more brutally and more startlingly the results Gauguin could achieve with his synthesist-symbolist vocabulary. In its colors it also suggests, like some of his previous paintings from Brittany, the palette he subsequently adopted in Tahiti.

Gauguin's preoccupation with Tahiti appears even more strongly in another work executed a little earlier—it is dated 1890—which represents an altogether exotic subject: a naked Eve in a tropical landscape. Here the artist combined recollections of Martinique (in the palm trees of the background) with elements of his new style: areas of uniform color bounded by rigid outlines. His brush strokes also vary between delicate hatchings of his impressionist phase and the entirely different application used for the flat areas. Both of these techniques were to reappear in Gauguin's first works done in Tahiti.[9]

His mind thus constantly set on the future, Gauguin was impatiently biding his time in Paris. It was all very well to be acclaimed as a master by his new friends, but this led nowhere. When de Haan, in February 1891, enthusiastically took a newly arrived compatriot, the painter Verkade, to the small restaurant in the rue de la Grande Chaumière, opposite the atelier Colarossi (where Gauguin is said to have given some painting lessons), Gauguin merely looked up from his soup "with a glance that seemed to say: 'What imbecile is de Haan bringing along now?'" According to Verkade's recollections, Gauguin, "although he was younger, gave the impression of being a man of fifty who had known difficult times but who had always withstood the blows of fate. He had long black hair which grew very low on his forehead and he wore a scanty short beard that left uncovered his mouth with its sensuous but firm lips, as well as the greater part of his yellowish cheeks. His most striking features were the heavy eyelids which gave his face a tired expression. But a prominent aquiline nose somewhat lessened this impression and revealed energy as well as perspicacity. I was introduced to the master and the other habitués—mostly foreign painters—and began to eat my soup. Gauguin was very silent, soon rose and left. After he had gone de Haan continued to talk for a long time about Gauguin's art."[49]

Although he had actually had little contact with Gauguin, Verkade left the restaurant of Mme Charlotte full of enthusiasm and thereafter returned every evening. (The owner's

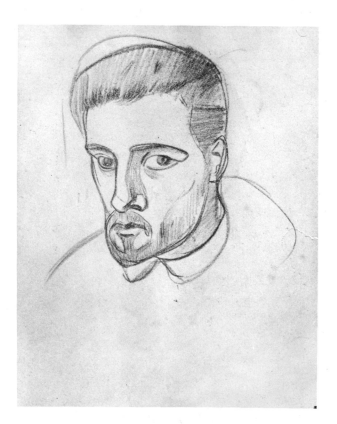

VERKADE: *Portrait of Paul Gauguin*, Paris, 1891. Drawing. Collection Dominique Denis, Saint-Germain-en-Laye

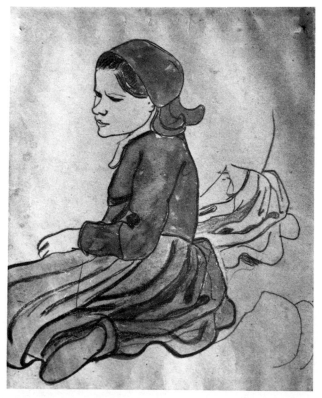

VERKADE: *Seated Breton Girl*, c. 1891. Watercolor. Collection Dominique Denis, Saint-Germain-en-Laye

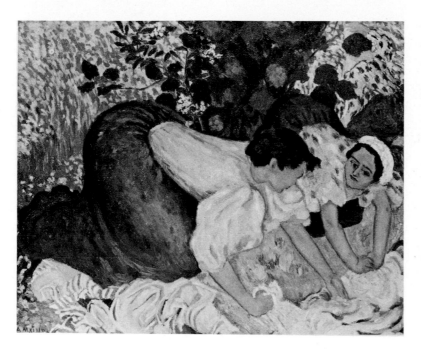

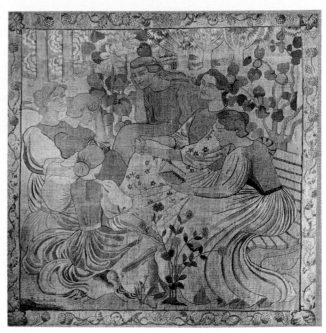

MAILLOL: *Washerwomen*, 1893. 6⁹⁄₁₆ x 8⅛". Private collection, France

MAILLOL: *Young Women in a Park*, c. 1893. Tapestry, 71 x 71". Collection Philippe Gangnat, Paris

name was Charlotte Caron; she gave Gauguin generous credit and also accepted from him and other artists paintings in payment for meals.) Through de Haan, Verkade soon met Sérusier, who introduced him to Gauguin's theories as well as to the other Nabis, into whose circle he was admitted. At about the same time the Nabis were also joined by the Danish painter Mogens Ballin—who had received introductions to Gauguin and to Pissarro from Gauguin's wife—and by Daniel de Monfreid's friend Aristide Maillol, who was then still painting and weaving tapestries, in both of which media Gauguin's influence became visible ever since Maillol had experienced a kind of revelation at the Volpini exhibition. Among the Nabis, Denis became Maillol's particular friend.

Gauguin, no doubt happy to find a few fervent admirers and followers not only among poets and writers but also among painters, maintained cordial relations with this little group. Sérusier even called him the "Dean of the Nabis." After his return from the army, Lugné-Poë shared with Bonnard a tiny studio in the rue Pigalle, where Denis and Vuillard also often came to work while Lugné-Poë was reciting his roles or giving lessons. According to his memoirs, Gauguin was among those who visited there, as well as Sérusier and the dealer Le Barc de Boutteville, who was soon to take an active interest in the young painters (and in whose small gallery Bernard was eventually to organize his van Gogh exhibition).

Among the other artists with whom Gauguin maintained contact while in Paris was Redon, whose admiration for Edgar Allan Poe he shared. While he had already told Redon that he planned to carry with him to the tropics a recollection of everything Redon had created, Gauguin certainly now immersed himself further in the older man's works. The memory of them never quite left him, for although no direct influence of Redon's art is noticeable in Gauguin's subsequent work, there sometimes appears a vague suggestion of Redon's flowers and fantasies, as if some of Gauguin's own visions had passed through the filter of Redon's mystic imagination. Gauguin himself later spoke admiringly of Redon when he called him "this extraordinary artist whom people obstinately refuse to understand. Will they ever do him justice? Yes, when all his imitators have been placed on pedestals."[50] Actually Redon had scarcely any imitators, though his admirers among the young generation, and particularly among the Nabis, began to pierce at last the isolation in which he lived and worked.

Gauguin does not seem to have seen much of Bernard and there is no record of the latter having been associated with the group that gathered at the Café Voltaire. Nor was he particularly friendly with the Nabis, although among these Denis was, like Bernard, an admirer of Cézanne and Redon, and a devout Catholic. (Denis was at least partly responsible for the fact that the Dutch Protestant Verkade and the Danish Jew Ballin soon became converted to Catholicism.) It may be that various complications in addition to his sentimental entanglement—Bernard of course never married his sweetheart—prompted the young man to renounce the trip. On the other hand Bernard was certainly not too happy to witness the acclaim received by Gauguin in literary circles while his own efforts remained completely ignored. As de Haan apparently also had given up his project of going to Tahiti, possibly because his family had denied him the necessary funds, Gauguin now began to speak openly of his intention of leaving *alone*.

Indeed, Gauguin had not come to Paris to theorize with the symbolists, to work in a borrowed studio, to establish friendly relations with fellow artists; he had come to achieve his goal of finding the means to leave Europe. As his projected organization of an exhibition had failed, he concentrated on an auction as the only means of obtaining at one stroke an adequate sum of money. In order to eliminate all possibility of a fiasco, he now set out deliberately to take advantage of the good will of all those, wherever they might be, who could be helpful to his enterprise. He knew that scruples would lead him nowhere, that only by ruthless, clever, relentless effort could he achieve his end. There was no length to which he would not go, no door on which he would not knock to assure himself the support he needed for the exploitation of that current of sympathy he had felt among the young poets and their associates.

"We are fighting against terribly ambitious 'men of genius' who are trying to crush everyone who stands in their way," Camille Pissarro told his son. "It is sickening. If you knew how shamelessly Gauguin behaved in order to get himself elected (that is the word) a man of genius, and how skillfully he went about it! One couldn't do anything but help him to climb. Anyone else would have been ashamed! Knowing that he was in such difficulties, I myself could not refuse to write to Mirbeau in his favor. He was in such despair."[51]

"I have asked our friend Monet for your address," Pissarro wrote to Mirbeau, "to inquire whether you know Gauguin's potteries, so strange, of an exotic, barbaric, savage taste and so full of style. If you have never seen them, you who appreciate all works of art, even unusual ones, you should take a look at them.... A great many of these potteries are in the custody of his friend Schuffenecker... and you will also see his paintings there."[52]

At the same time Charles Morice, who had introduced Gauguin to Mallarmé, went to see the poet to enlist his help. The latter also thought that Mirbeau's support would be most effective and wrote to him on Gauguin's behalf: "One of my young colleagues, a man of great talent and heart, a friend of the painter, sculptor, and potter Gauguin—you

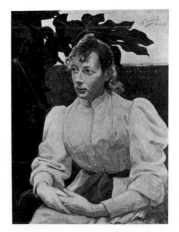

DE MONFREID: *Portrait of a Young Woman*, d. 1891. 28¾ x 21¼". Musée Toulouse-Lautrec, Albi

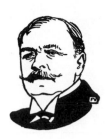

know who he is—has begged me to appeal to you as the only person who can do something. This rare artist who, I believe, has been spared few afflictions in Paris, feels the need to withdraw into isolation and almost into savagery.... What he needs, however, is an article...."[53]

Under this double-barreled assault Mirbeau gracefully yielded. "Certainly, I shall do it, and with all my heart," he replied. "I do not know Gauguin himself, but I know some of his work which interests me tremendously.... I shall be very happy to see Gauguin and Morice and if they could spend a day with me at Les Damps [Mirbeau's place in the country], it would give me great pleasure."[54] A short time later, having received the visit of the two friends, Mirbeau informed Monet:

"I have had a letter from Mallarmé, desolate about that poor Gauguin. He is completely destitute. He would like to escape from Paris and go to Tahiti... and start to work there from scratch. To help him with his projects I have been asked to write an article in *Le Figaro* in conjunction with an auction of thirty of his canvases. It has not been easy but finally Magnard has agreed to publish it. Tomorrow I am going to Paris to see some [of his] recent paintings and some potteries. Gauguin came to see me. He has an attractive character, truly tortured by suffering for art. And he has an admirable head. I liked him very much. In this nature, rather rough externally, it is not difficult to detect a very interesting intellectual side. He was greatly tormented by the desire to know what you think of his evolution towards the complication of the idea through the simplification of form. I told him that you had liked his *Jacob Wrestling with the Angel* and his potteries very much. I did well, for he was pleased."[55]

Gauguin, pinning great hopes on Mirbeau's article, now wrote to his wife: "At this moment I am gambling heavily against the future and I didn't want to reply to your letter without having some certainty of a happy outcome. The article for *Le Figaro* met with great opposition from the director, who didn't want it. At last it is promised for Tuesday; others will follow in *Le Gaulois, La Justice, Le Voltaire, Le Rappel,* and possibly in *Les Débats.* As soon as they appear I shall send you the whole batch. If you could translate the one from *Le Figaro* for a [Danish] newspaper, you would be helpful; it might have a certain influence on the Danish movement."[56] Several days later he wrote again: "I am hastily scribbling these few lines, for I am very nervous. The day of my sale is approaching: next Monday. Everything is well prepared and I am waiting to gather all the articles together before sending them to you. They have, by the way, created quite a stir in Paris and there exists in the art world a great excitement, and even in England where a newspaper mentions the sale as an event."[57]

Mirbeau's article, in which he abandoned the naturalistic views with which he had once attacked Redon, finally appeared in the *Echo de Paris* on February 16, one week before the date set for the auction. Maurice Denis called the article "the event of our week," but Gauguin's wife told her husband that she thought it "ridiculously exaggerated."

"I have just learned," Mirbeau wrote, "that M. Paul Gauguin is going to leave for Tahiti. It is his intention to live there, alone, for several years, to build his hut, to begin all over again the things that haunt him. The case of a man who flees from civilization, voluntarily seeking oblivion and silence in order to become more aware of himself, to listen better to the inner voices strangled by the noise of our passions and disputes, appears to me curious and touching. M. Paul Gauguin is a very exceptional artist, very disturbing, who has hardly shown himself to the public and of whom the public therefore knows little.

Several times I have wanted to write about him... but perhaps I hesitated because of the difficulty of such an undertaking and the fear that I might express myself poorly concerning a man for whom I have a high and very particular regard. To record in a few short and rapid notes the significance of an art as complicated and as primitive, as clear and as obscure, as barbaric and as refined as M. Gauguin's, isn't that an impossible task?..."

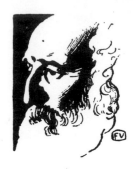

VALLOTTON: *Portrait of Camille Pissarro*. Pen and ink

Mirbeau then referred to Gauguin's Peruvian ancestors, his career as sailor and bank agent, the awakening of his interest in art, his passion for Puvis de Chavannes, Degas, Manet, Monet, Cézanne, the Japanese, but did not mention Pissarro. Nor did he mention him in connection with Gauguin's early phase as a painter, a phase during which Pissarro had exerted a vital influence on his pupil. But then—since his divisionist "aberration"—Pissarro had lost much of his value as a reference; moreover it is likely that Gauguin did not care to be reminded of his earlier non-synthesist work.

"In spite of his apparent intellectual robustness," Mirbeau went on, "M. Gauguin is essentially a restless mind, tormented by the infinite. Never satisfied with what he has accomplished, he goes on always searching for the beyond. He feels that he has not yet given of himself what he is able to give. Confused things stir within his soul; vague and powerful aspirations guide his mind towards a more abstract course, towards more esoteric forms of expression. And his thoughts go back to the countries of light and mystery which he has visited in the past. It seems to him that there he will find, still dormant, inviolate, the elements of a new art conforming to his dream. Also, there is the solitude which he needs so much.... He goes to Martinique.... He brings back a series of splendid and severe canvases in which he has conquered at last his full personality and which show enormous progress, a rapid step towards the hoped-for art.... In the majesty of contours, the dream leads him to spiritual synthesis, to eloquent and profound expression. From now on M. Gauguin is master of himself. His hand has become a slave, the obedient and loyal instrument of his brain. He will be able to achieve the works for which he has sought so long."

By insisting on the fact that a spiritual synthesis had already been achieved in Gauguin's paintings from Martinique, Mirbeau followed with docility what the painter himself had undoubtedly told him and thus, with a few words, brushed aside those prolific and ebullient months in Brittany during which Gauguin had groped for a new style in close collaboration with Emile Bernard. Bernard's share in their discoveries and clarifying discussions was not mentioned any more than was Pissarro's earlier guidance. Speaking of Gauguin's recent work, Mirbeau continued in his flowery and repetitious style — less obscure but not less wordy than that of the symbolists — to extol the artist's achievements:

"A strangely cerebral and moving work, still uneven, but poignant and superb even in its irregularities. A sad work, for in order to understand it, to feel the impact of it, one must have suffered sorrow and the irony of sorrow, which is the threshold to mystery. Sometimes it rises to the height of a mystical act of faith; sometimes it shrinks and grimaces in the frightening gloom of doubt. And always it emits the bitter and violent aroma of the poisons of the flesh. There is in his work a disquieting and savory mixture of barbaric splendor, of Catholic liturgy, of Hindu reverie, of Gothic imagery, of obscure and subtle symbolism; there are harsh realities and frantic flights into poetry, through which M. Gauguin creates an absolutely personal and altogether new art — the art of a painter and a poet, of an apostle and a demon, an art which inspires anguish.... It would seem that once M. Gauguin had reached this elevation of thought, this breadth of style, he would have achieved serenity, peace of mind, rest. But no. The dream never keeps quiet in his ardent brain; it grows and soars as it continues to acquire form. And thus the nostalgia has returned for those countries where his first dreams burst into flower. He would like to live there again, alone, for a few years.... Here he has been spared few afflictions, and great sorrows have overwhelmed him. He has lost a friend whom he loved tenderly, admired tenderly, poor Vincent van Gogh, one of the most magnificent artistic temperaments, one of the most beautiful artistic souls, on whom our hopes rested. And life has its merciless demands. The same need for silence, for meditation, for absolute solitude, which had driven him to Martinique now drives him even further, to Tahiti, where nature is better adapted to his dreams, where he hopes that the Pacific Ocean will bestow on him even more tender caresses, an old and dependable love of a rediscovered ancestor. Wherever he goes, M. Paul Gauguin can rest assured that our good wishes will accompany him."[58]

Pissarro, though at least partly responsible for his friend's intervention, now told his son: "Mirbeau, at the request of the symbolists, has written an article in which he has gone too far, as I see it, and it has caused a great sensation. I learned from Zandomeneghi that Gauguin, not daring to go to see Degas, wrote to him to ask for his support. Degas, who after all is very good and sympathetic to people who are in trouble, placed himself at Gauguin's service.... De Bellio, who had been cold to Gauguin, confessed to me that he had changed his opinion of Gauguin's work, that he considered him to have great talent, although not in sculpture. Why...? It is a sign of the times, my dear boy. The frightened bourgeoisie, astonished by the immense clamor of the disinherited masses, by the insistent demands of the people, feels it necessary to lead the people back to superstitious beliefs. Hence the bustling of religious symbolists, religious socialists, idealist art, occultism, Buddhism, etc., etc. That fellow Gauguin has sensed this tendency."[51]

Despite Pissarro's objections, Mirbeau did still better when he finally managed to get a second and shorter article accepted by the more widely read *Figaro*, where it appeared on February 18, two days after the one in the *Echo de Paris*. He now announced that the Government had taken the necessary steps to obtain, before the public sale, "a particularly delightful picture, one of the master's landscapes representing an aspect of the beautiful valley at Pont-Aven." Mirbeau congratulated the representative of the State for this decision, which he considered remarkable because Gauguin was "a very exceptional painter, one of the most interesting artists of today, one of those rare men in whom many set great and solid hopes for the future. I believe that they are right."[59]

Less florid than Mirbeau's comments, but no less full of admiration were those of Roger Marx, which appeared on February 20 in *Le Voltaire*: "Examining his work now without prejudice, while taking into consideration his individual ideal and the mode of interpretation which logically derives from it, Gauguin offers—with his supreme power of vision and expression—an example of rare decorative faculties at the service of a radiant intelligence. He appears also as an ethnologist superbly able to decipher the enigma of faces and attitudes, to extract the grave beauty of naïve images, to retain the natural gestures of rural and simple people, gestures full of rhythm and hieratic dignity."[60]

Two days later, on the eve of the sale, Gustave Geffroy also published an announcement that the French government had purchased one of Gauguin's paintings, though according to him it was a canvas from Martinique.[61] As a matter of fact, the story was a pure invention, destined to stimulate interest, and Gauguin's friends obviously had not bothered to coordinate their little lies.

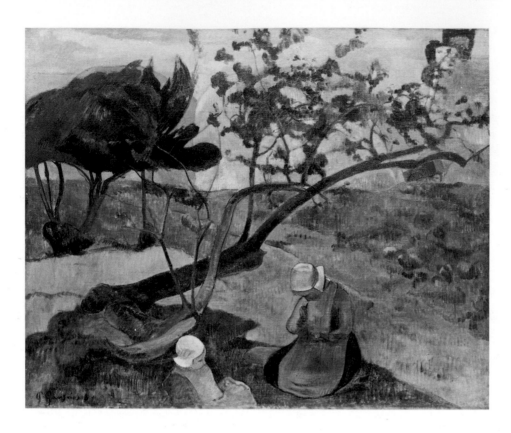

GAUGUIN: *Little Girls,* Brittany, d. 1889. 28½ x 36". Bought by Roussel at Gauguin's auction. Museum of Fine Arts, Boston (Gift of Harry Remis)

Gauguin would undoubtedly have liked to see Aurier's article also appear in time to attract more attention to his sale, but although Aurier had finished it by February 9, a week before Mirbeau's piece appeared, it could not be published until the March issue of the *Mercure de France.* Meanwhile Gauguin had Mirbeau's first article reprinted as the introduction to the catalogue of the sale.

The auction took place on February 23, 1891. Among the thirty paintings presented were works from Martinique, Arles, and Brittany. (The *Yellow Christ* was not included, having already found a purchaser in Emile Schuffenecker.) Only two canvases brought less than 250 francs each, and as this was apparently the lowest limit Gauguin had set, he himself bought back one of these. The average price obtained was 321 francs,[62] which does not compare too unfavorably with the prices at which the painter had listed in 1890 a series of pictures left with Theo van Gogh, for which he had asked an average of 380 francs. Some of the canvases priced for Theo van Gogh at 300 francs, for instance, brought 260 at the sale, and the painting of *Jacob Wrestling with the Angel,* for which Gauguin had given Goupil's a price of 600 francs, now brought 900. This was actually the highest bid obtained at the sale, the second highest, of 505 francs, being made by the dealer Manzi, a friend of Degas, whereas Degas himself (who had recently begun to collect paintings) made the third highest bid of 450 francs for *La Belle Angèle.* Among the buyers were, besides Degas and Manzi, Pissarro's patron G. de Bellio, who bought two paintings; Mallarmé's friend Méry Laurent, who purchased one; Gauguin's new acquaintance Daniel de Monfreid, who

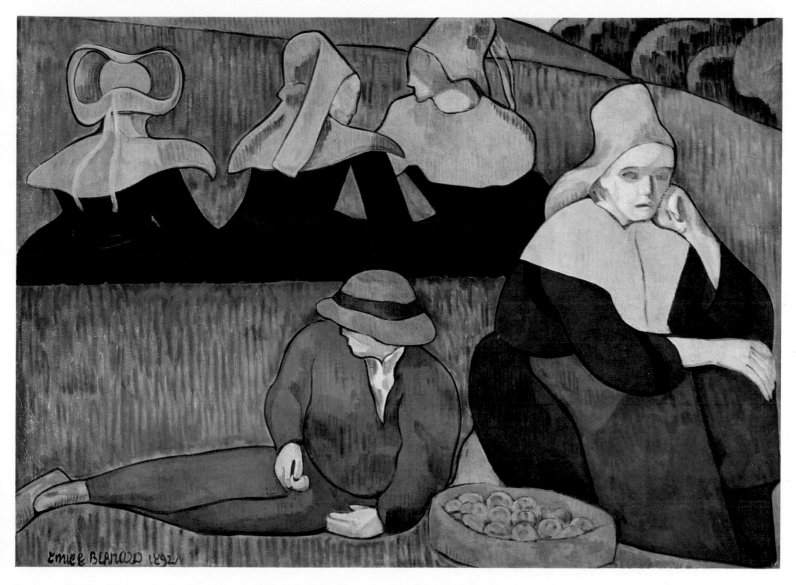

Bernard: *Breton Women in the Meadow*, d. 1892. 33 x 45⅝″. Present whereabouts unknown

acquired two; and the three Natanson brothers, founders of the *Revue Blanche*, who together successfully bid on five. The critic Roger Marx bought one painting; so did the dealer *père* Thomas, who invested 260 francs in Gauguin after never having dared to do the same for Vincent van Gogh. The painter K. X. Roussel spent 280 francs for a painting which he purchased together with the other Nabis and which each of them was to take home in rotation (page 442). As for the Count Antoine de La Rochefoucauld, he also acquired one painting (and subsequently bought another, *The Loss of Virginity*).

Mallarmé, unable to attend, sent a short note of excuse: "My dear Gauguin, an attack of grippe, without serious consequences I hope, deprives me of the pleasure of shaking your hand and also of seeing again—with a farewell in my glance—all the beautiful things I love. Have you been somewhat satisfied? I haven't seen anybody. At least have you derived from the sale a hope of departure? During this winter I have often thought of the wisdom of your resolution. Your hand! All this not for you to reply but to let you know that from near or far I am yours."[63]

Altogether the sale brought Gauguin about 9,350 francs—much more than the amount he had hoped to obtain from Charlopin—less certain expenses, such as probably the printing of the catalogue. Although Gauguin seemed to have every reason to be satisfied, he wrote the next day to his wife, whom he intended to visit shortly in Copenhagen, so as to see her and their children before his departure: "The sale took place yesterday and was successful. It wasn't overpowering in comparison with the success of the exhibition held the day before. But the moral success is tremendous and I believe that it will shortly bear fruit."[64] Gauguin's wife, who was supporting their five children by giving French lessons and doing translations—and selling occasionally some of her husband's works or paintings from his collection—promptly asked for some money but apparently received none. Instead Gauguin lent 500 francs to Charles Morice and gave instructions that his friend was to act as custodian of all additional proceeds from sales transacted during his absence.

The excitement stirred up by Gauguin's publicity campaign had aroused Bernard's ire, presumably because his own name was never mentioned. Though he himself had been anxious to have Gauguin raise the money for their trip, he now resented all the spotlights being focused exclusively on his friend. As he later said: "Many things had attached me to Gauguin: first the lack of appreciation of his talent; then his understanding of my own ideas; finally the destitution in which he found himself. I can say that I have done for him everything I could, encouraging his art, introducing him to my friends, praising him everywhere, trying to sell his paintings when I had an opportunity. I even neglected my own interests in order to serve his among writers and other people able to help him. I do not regret anything that I have done...."[65]

But now that Gauguin had succeeded to a certain extent and was neither unappreciated nor destitute, Bernard no longer felt the same towards his companion. He subsequently explained this change of attitude by the fact that Gauguin had exhibited *alone* although he had promised not to do so. Yet Gauguin could not possibly have included Bernard's works in the sale at a time when his young friend himself admitted to Aurier that his paintings did not as yet have any commercial value.[66] After all, they had exhibited together at Volpini's less than two years before, but Bernard apparently feared that whenever he subsequently showed his own recent canvases, he might be accused of having been influenced by Gauguin because of the similarity of their work. In any event, it was Gauguin's exhibition prior to his sale which brought about an open conflict between the two artists.

According to Bernard's recollections, set down almost half a century later: "My sister, witness of everything that had happened, became indignant and said to Gauguin, right in the auction room where he was trying to raise the money for his departure for Tahiti: 'Monsieur Gauguin, you are a traitor; you have violated your pledge and are doing the greatest harm to my brother, who has been the true initiator of the art which you now claim for yourself.' I then saw a strange thing," Bernard reported: "Gauguin did not answer and withdrew. Since then I have never seen him again."[65] Subsequently Bernard gave still another version of their quarrel, acknowledging however that it had been started by him and his sister, angry as they both were to see Gauguin "proclaim himself the chief of the symbolist school in painting," and adding a rather sordid touch to his memoirs when he wrote that Gauguin replied rudely to Madeleine Bernard "in a drunken outburst, for he had absorbed a great deal of absinthe that day, as his breath clearly indicated. The result was the break...."[67]

Thenceforth both Bernard and Gauguin seized every possible occasion to treat each other with the greatest contempt. Bernard insisted that he alone had been responsible for the new ideas and tendencies that were developed in 1888 in what became later known as the School of Pont-Aven: "I was the only one who established them on novel and logical foundations and it was always I who showed myself to be the most audacious and the greatest innovator, as my extreme youth (I was twenty years old), bred on independence, liberty and a passionate will, always pushed me farther ahead."[68]

Gauguin, on the other hand, in some notes which he probably intended to publish but which never appeared, took the opposite view, denying all originality to Bernard, thus being hardly any more fair-minded than Bernard himself. "Indeed," Gauguin wrote in 1895, "Bernard came to Pont-Aven in 1886 after having minutely inspected the last exhibition of the impressionists in the rue Laffitte. He then abandoned his attempts to imitate everybody—Pissarro, Manet, and Gauguin—in order to adopt the newest thing that had appeared: the little dot. That year he left behind at Gloanec's in Pont-Aven a panel exactly resembling a Seurat. At that very moment Gauguin was fighting with all his might against all these complications, although he had not yet reached the simplicity he has now attained. The following year, while Gauguin continued at Martinique along his own unchanging path, Bernard did a little bit of everything (after all, it suited his age: eighteen years); he painted holy scenes after ancient images or after old tapestries. In between he also painted still lifes in a quite different style, like Cézanne, but not signed (we do not dare believe that this was done intentionally in order to sell them as Cézannes).[69] In 1888, profiting by Gauguin's advice, he also attempted with Gauguin's chisels to do some sculptures in wood; later on his Brittany women became practically identical with Gauguin's Brittany women in wood."[70] It is remarkable, however, that in writing this acid statement, Gauguin avoided speaking of the *paintings* he and Bernard had executed side by side in 1888.

Strangely enough, Félix Fénéon, who had no particular sympathy for either Gauguin or Bernard (he abhorred *all* painters of religious subjects), in turn accused Gauguin of having borrowed left and right. Obviously aware of Gauguin's antagonistic attitude towards neo-impressionism, he now had his own moment of revenge when he wrote that among Gauguin's works at the auction, "one could recognize here some Japanese nudes, there fields by Monet, elsewhere trees by Cézanne, and his canvases from Arles looked like van Gogh's."[30] Though Fénéon considered Bernard as the innovator, he failed to mention him among Gauguin's sources.

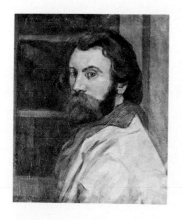

BERNARD: *Self-Portrait*, 1892. 20⅞ x 17¾". Private collection, Switzerland

What neither Gauguin nor Bernard cared to admit in the heat of resentments and recriminations was that the style they had created in Pont-Aven had been born of their close collaboration. Their friendship had been based on a continual give and take in which each tried out his new ideas on the other, in which they stimulated, criticized, and complimented each other, in which each had become more conscious of himself through comparison with the other. Advice had been liberally given and received. Their relationship had afforded to each an opportunity to escape the agonizing solitude in which one has to ask and answer questions by oneself. That some ideas originated with Bernard there can be little doubt, but the art of painting is not based solely on ideas. What counted now that their new formula had been solidly established was not so much the past but the present and the future. This present saw Bernard entangled in a vague mysticism and in the rediscovery of the principles of old masters, whereas Gauguin resolutely pursued the road on which they had started together. As to the future, it was to reveal Gauguin constantly searching for new and ever more powerful means of expression, while Bernard increasingly abandoned the promising conquests of his youth. Under these circumstances it is not surprising that outsiders showed a growing inclination to credit the stronger and more persistently revolutionary of the two with innovations that had been only partly his own (and this, of course, tremendously aggravated Bernard, who was to outlive Gauguin by almost forty years without achieving any prominence).

As if van Gogh's exhortations had borne fruit, Bernard seems to have given up, during the years 1892–93, the religious subjects to which his friend had so violently objected. Instead he concentrated on his "synthesist" endeavors in a series of works—mostly Breton scenes—which were strong in color, boldly patterned, and rhythmic in design (page 443). Interweaving flat surfaces and gracious arabesques, he appeared to sum up during those

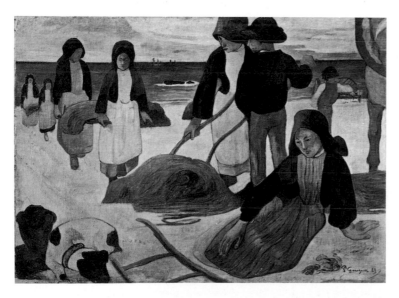

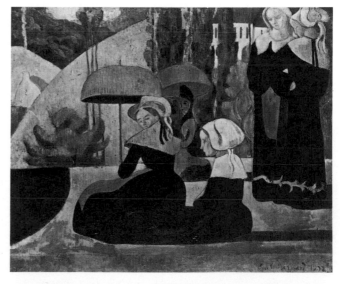

GAUGUIN: *Breton Peasants Gathering Seaweed,* d. 1889. 34½ x 48½".
Folkwang Museum, Essen

BERNARD: *Breton Women under Umbrellas,* d. 1892. 31⅞ x 39½".
Formerly collection Count A. de La Rochefoucauld. Musées Nationaux, Paris

years, while Gauguin was far away, all the new features for which they had striven together. Yet this was to be his swan song as an innovator. Leaving for Italy in 1893, he there devoted himself to a systematic study of the Renaissance masters which was to lead him steadily downward on the path of imitation and academic tradition. However, in 1891 he was still pledged to the tenets of Pont-Aven and his anger at Gauguin arose not so much from stylistic reasons as from his "betrayed" feeling.

If the split between Gauguin and Bernard really resulted from Gauguin's exhibition and sale, it was certainly irremediably widened by Aurier's article, which appeared finally about one week after the auction. This was the very article which Bernard had urged Aurier to write and for which he had promised all necessary information. In his long and elaborate piece, "Symbolisme en Peinture: Paul Gauguin," Aurier consecrated Gauguin chief of symbolist art without even once mentioning Bernard. It seems quite possible that Bernard's quarrel with Gauguin actually dates from the publication of this article rather than from Gauguin's sale. But if this is the case, Bernard obviously did not care to disclose the true source of his acrimony and thus established his more "detached" version according to which the altercation of the two former friends was brought about by a "disinterested bystander," Bernard's sister. Be this as it may, Bernard broke not only with Gauguin but now also severed relations with Aurier because of his somewhat understandable indignation over Aurier's silence concerning his own by no means negligible contribution to the creation of a symbolist-synthesist style. Actually Julien Leclercq later explained Aurier's omission by stating that the critic had decided to wait until Bernard had revealed his personality in more original works.[71] Yet Bernard himself was undoubtedly convinced that he had been ignored at Gauguin's special request, as part of what Pissarro had called his campaign "to get himself elected a man of genius," and it is quite conceivable that this was indeed the case.

Aurier's article on Gauguin was certainly the most important piece of art criticism he had written since the publication of his study on van Gogh, almost exactly a year before. It started quite dramatically with a long and poetic description of Gauguin's painting *Jacob Wrestling with the Angel* and then went on to define impressionism as an outgrowth of Courbet's naturalism, a "faithful translation of an *exclusively sensory impression without going any further.*" Parallel to the extinction of literary naturalism, hastened by a revival of idealism and even mysticism, a similar process was taking place in the fields of the visual arts, and Aurier stated the need for a different designation for the newcomers "at whose head Gauguin is marching: synthesists, ideologists, symbolists, as you please. . . .

"Paul Gauguin seems to me to be the initiator of a new art, not in the course of history, but at least in our time. . . . The normal and final goal of painting, as of all arts, cannot be the direct presentation of objects. Its ultimate goal is to express Ideas by translating them into a special language. To the eyes of the artist, that is to the eyes of him who should be the one *who expresses absolute beings* . . . objects are valueless merely as objects. They can only appear to him as *signs*. They are the letters of an immense alphabet which only the man of genius can combine into words. To write down his thought, his poem, with these signs while remembering that the sign, indispensable as it may be, is nothing in itself and that the Idea alone is everything, that is the task of the artist whose eye has been able to discern the hypostases of tangible objects. The first consequence of this principle is . . . a necessary *simplification of the writing of the sign.* . . . But if it is true that the only real beings in the world can be nothing but Ideas, if it is true that objects are but the revealing appearances of these Ideas and thus are important only as signs of Ideas... it is not less true that to our myopic eyes objects most frequently appear only as objects and nothing else, independent of their symbolic significance—to the point where, despite our sincere efforts, we can sometimes not imagine them as signs.

"The work of art, even to the eyes of a bovine populace, should never lend itself to such an ambiguity.... Consequently certain appropriate laws should prevail over pictorial imitation. The artist thus has above all the duty to avoid carefully that antinomy of all art: concrete truth, illusionism, *trompe-l'oeil*, so as not to give by his picture that fallacious impression of nature which would act on the spectator just as would nature itself.... It is logical to imagine him evading the analysis of the object in order to escape the perils of concrete truth. Indeed, every detail is actually but a partial symbol which is most frequently unnecessary to the total significance of the object. The strict duty of the ideological painter is therefore to make a rational selection among the multiple elements combined in objectivity, to utilize in his work only the general and distinctive lines, forms, colors which serve to put down clearly the ideological significance of the object, in addition to some partial symbols which corroborate the general symbol. The artist will also always have the right—an obvious deduction—to exaggerate, to attenuate, to deform these directly significant characters (forms, lines, colors, etc.) not only according to his individual vision, not only according to the form of his personal subjectivity (such as happens even with realistic art), but also to exaggerate, attenuate, and deform them according to the needs of the Idea to be expressed.

"Thus, to sum up and conclude, the work of art as I have chosen to evoke it logically will be:

1) *Ideological*, because its sole ideal is the expression of the Idea;

2) *Symbolistic*, because it expresses this Idea through forms;

3) *Synthetic*, because it presents these forms, these signs, in such a way that they can be generally understood;

4) *Subjective*, because the object is considered not merely as an object, but as the sign of an idea perceived by the subject;

5) (And therefore) *decorative*, since truly decorative painting as conceived by the Egyptians, and probably by the Greeks and the primitives, is nothing but a manifestation of art which is at the same time subjective, synthetic, symbolistic, and ideological."

But Aurier hastened to add that the artist who could read the abstract significance of every object and knew how to use these objects as a noble alphabet to express the Ideas revealed to him, would still need something else, a "psychic gift," in order to be a complete artist. "He would have to... add to this power of comprehension a still more sublime gift... the gift of *emotiveness*... this transcendental emotiveness, so great and precious, which makes the soul tremble before the undulating drama of abstractions. Oh! how rare are those whose bodies and hearts are moved by the sublime spectacle of pure Being and pure Ideas! But that is the gift *sine qua non*, that is the spark that Pygmalion sought for his Galatea, that is the illumination, the golden key, the Muse.... Thanks to this gift the symbols, that is, the Ideas, emerge from the gloom, become animated, begin to live a life which is no longer our provisional and relative life, but a splendid life which is the essential one, the life of Art.... Thanks to this gift, complete art, perfect, absolute, exists at last.

"... Thus is also the art, I believe, unless I have wrongly interpreted the meaning of his work, which that great artist of genius with the soul of a primitive and also, somewhat,

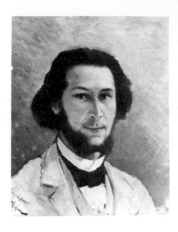

Vogler: *Portrait of G.-Albert Aurier*, d. 1891. Collection Mme Mahé-Williame, Aix-en-Provence

of a savage, Paul Gauguin, has tried to re-establish in our lamentable and putrefied country. ... Yet disturbing, authoritative and marvelous as this work may be, it is insignificant compared to what Gauguin could have produced, had he been placed in another civilization. It must be repeated that Gauguin, like all ideological painters, is above all a decorator. His compositions are confined within the restricted area of his canvases. Sometimes one is tempted to consider them as fragments of immense frescoes and almost always they seem ready to burst the frames which too closely surround them!... What, in our dying century we have only one great decorator, possibly two if we count Puvis de Chavannes, and our imbecile society of bankers and polytechnicians refuses to give to this rare artist the smallest palace, the tiniest national hovel in which to hang the sumptuous garments of his dreams! ... A little common sense, please! You have among you a decorator of genius: walls! walls! give him walls!"[72]

This article, flattering though it was for the painter, was above all a manifesto of symbolist art, just as Seurat's statement, published the preceding year, had been a manifesto of divisionism. Since he had written, in a much more poetic vein, his article on Vincent van Gogh, Aurier had progressed to the point where he now became the "official" theorist of the new movement and conferred philosophical patents of nobility upon the efforts that had germinated at Pont-Aven. It goes without saying that his provocative article aroused not only much attention but also many heated controversies.

"I am sending you," wrote Pissarro to his son, "a periodical which contains an article on Gauguin by Aurier. You will observe how this *littérateur* balances his arguments on the point of a needle. According to him, it is not strictly necessary to draw or paint in order to produce a work of art. Only ideas are required, and these can be indicated by a few signs.—Now I will grant that art is as he says, except that 'the few signs' have to be drawn more or less, after all. And it is also necessary to express one's ideas in terms of harmony—hence you have to have sensations in order to have ideas.... This gentleman seems to think we are imbeciles! The Japanese practiced this art, also the Chinese, and their signs are wonderfully natural, but then they were not Catholics, and Gauguin is a Catholic. —I do not criticize Gauguin for having painted a vermilion background, nor do I object to the two struggling warriors and the Breton peasant women in the foreground [of his *Jacob Wrestling with the Angel*], what I do mind is that he swiped these elements from the Japanese, the Byzantine painters and others. I criticize him for not applying his synthesis to our modern philosophy which is absolutely social, anti-authoritarian, and anti-mystical. —That is where the problem becomes serious. This is a step backwards. Gauguin is not a seer, he is a clever man who has sensed that the bourgeoisie are moving backwards, recoiling from the great ideas of solidarity which are sprouting among the people—an instinctive idea, but fecund, the only legitimate idea!—The symbolists belong in the same category! They must be fought like the plague!"[73]

Of course, not everybody shared Pissarro's aggressive views on the general tendencies of that *fin de siècle*. In a widely read series of interviews concerning the evolution of French literature—that is the antagonism between rising symbolism and declining naturalism— Charles Henry expressed a quite different opinion: "I do not believe in the future... of naturalism, or in general of any realistic school. On the contrary, I believe in the more or less imminent advent of a very idealistic and even mystic art, based on new techniques. And I believe this because we are witnessing a greater and greater development and diffusion of scientific methods and industrial efforts; the economic future of all nations

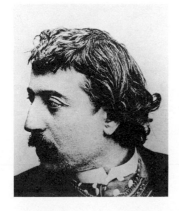

Photograph of Paul Gauguin, 1891.

is involved in it and social questions force us to follow this lead, for, after all, the problem of the progressive life of all peoples can be summed up thus: *produce much, cheaply, and in a very short time.* Europe is obliged not to let itself be annihilated or even outrun by America, which has for a long time combined its national education and its entire organization for the purpose of reaching this goal. I believe in the future of an art which would be the reverse of any ordinary logical or historical method, precisely because our intellects, exhausted by purely rational efforts, will feel the need to refresh themselves with entirely opposite states of mind. You only have to look at the singular vogue of occult, spiritualist and other doctrines, which are false because they can satisfy neither reason nor imagination."[74]

Mallarmé, in a similar interview, expressed similar views: "... In a society without stability, without unity, no stable or definitive art can be created. This unfinished social organization, which explains at the same time the restlessness of all minds, gives birth to the unexplained need for individuality of which the present literary manifestations are a direct reflection." And Mallarmé went on to define the aim of the symbolist poets in words that Aurier might have used in his article on Gauguin: "To *name* an object is to suppress three-fourths of the enjoyment of the poem which consists of the pleasure of comprehending little by little; to *suggest* it, that is the dream. It is the perfect utilization of this mystery that constitutes symbolism: to evoke an object bit by bit in order to show a mood or, conversely, to choose an object and to extract a mood from it by a series of decipherings."[75]

But Octave Mirbeau, though he respected the symbolists and freely praised Mallarmé, Verlaine, Charles Morice, and Aurier, did not subscribe to their ideas and rather shared Pissarro's opinions when he predicted that the novel of the future would be "socialistic, evidently socialistic; the evolution of ideas demands it, it is inevitable. The spirit of revolt is making progress and I am surprised that the downtrodden do not shoot millionaires more frequently when they meet them.... Yes, everything will change at the same time, literature, art, education, everything, after the general upheaval which I expect this year, next year, or in five years, but which will come, I am convinced of it!"[76]

In leaving Europe behind him, Gauguin would escape the social unrest predicted by Mirbeau, the materialistic "kingdom of gold" of which he himself had spoken, but he would take with him to a primitive island of the South Seas a mind thoroughly steeped in all the refinements of a highly articulate civilization. He, the "savage" who longed to return to savagery, would do so after having absorbed all the theories of a movement—called decadent by some—which, through its spokesmen Mallarmé and Moréas, extolled the greatest subtleties of an esoteric individualism.

While art circles buzzed with rumors concerning his flight from civilization to the primitive life, Jules Renard wrote in his diary several weeks after Gauguin's auction: "Daudet, in high spirits, told us about the 'departures' of Gauguin who wants to go to Tahiti, hoping to find nobody there, but who never leaves. So that his best friends end up by saying to him: 'You'll have to go, old man, you'll have to go.'"[77]

Early in March, Gauguin paid a short farewell visit to his wife and children in Denmark. Meanwhile Ernest Renan's son, himself an artist, who had already invited Gauguin to exhibit with the new Salon, suggested that Gauguin might obtain an "official mission," such as had been granted another painter for a trip to Indo-China (a painter whom van Gogh had met at Auvers). On March 15 Gauguin therefore wrote the following letter:

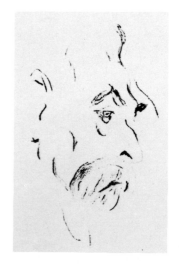

VUILLARD: *Profile of Stéphane Mallarmé,* c. 1896. Pencil. Private collection, Paris

450

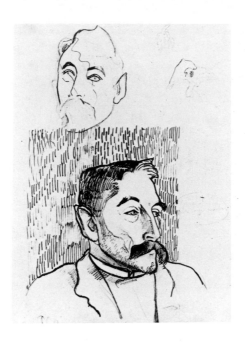

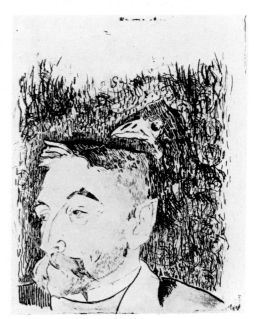

Right: GAUGUIN: *Portrait of Stéphane Mallarmé*, Paris, 1891. Pen and pencil, 10 × 7¼″. Formerly collection A. Vollard

Far right: GAUGUIN: *Portrait of Stéphane Mallarmé,* Paris, 1891. Etching, 7⅛ × 5⅝″. Collection H. M. Petiet, Paris

"Monsieur le Ministre,

"I desire to go to Tahiti in order to paint there a series of pictures representing the country whose character and light I have the ambition to explore. I have the honor to ask you to be gracious enough to entrust me with a mission, as was done for M. Dumoulin, which, though *without a salary*, would nevertheless, through the advantages pertaining to it, facilitate my studies and my transportation." [78]

This request was followed three days later by a letter signed by Georges Clemenceau, who was then editor of *La Justice* and whose intervention had been obtained by Mirbeau. On March 26 the Minister of Fine Arts, Rouvier (a friend of Countess de Nimal), not only entrusted Gauguin with an unsalaried mission but also authorized him to benefit from a 30 per cent reduction in the price of a second-class ticket from Marseilles to Nouméa. This "mission" entailed a vague promise of the purchase of a painting after Gauguin's return. But according to Charles Morice, who accompanied Gauguin to the Ministry where these privileges were granted, the artist, having at last succeeded in all his enterprises, being at last assured of imminent departure, suddenly became sad and burst into tears. The thought of the family he had abandoned and which he might never see again now gripped his heart as he was about to leave the Old World. [79]

Of course there was no longer any question of Bernard's accompanying Gauguin. The painter was perfectly ready to face the future alone and there is no trace of his having tried—now that his departure was near—to find any new companions for his venture. Gauguin, having modified his determination to leave Europe forever, now spoke of an absence of three years.

Gauguin's literary friends now decided to give a banquet in his honor, one of several at which Gauguin was present and where the various symbolist poets toasted each other. On February 2 there had been a banquet for Jean Moréas, presided over by Mallarmé, which had ended in bitter altercations. Among the invited were Henri de Régnier, Maurice Barrès, Charles Morice, Octave Mirbeau, Jules Renard, André Fontainas (with whom Gauguin subsequently corresponded), André Gide, Georges Lecomte, Anatole France, Félix Fénéon, and, representing the painters, not only Gauguin but also Redon as well as Signac and Seurat (who died the following month).[80] A few days later Gauguin joined Jean Dolent, Eugène Carrière, and Charles Morice at the dinner of Les Têtes de Bois (the Wooden Heads). But Gauguin's own banquet, though less quarrelsome than Moréas', was of course for him the most important event.

It took place on Monday, March 23, at the Café Voltaire. There were forty guests over whom Mallarmé again presided; they included Odilon Redon, Jean Moréas, Charles Morice, Jean Dolent, Alfred Valette and his wife Mme Rachilde, Roger Marx, Albert Aurier, Julien Leclercq, Eugène Carrière, Ary Renan, J. F. Willumsen, Léon Fauché, Daniel de Monfreid, Paul Sérusier, Mogens Ballin, the architect Trachsel (considered the only symbolist of his profession), and several others, among whom probably were Maurice Denis, Paul Fort, Brouillon-Rotonchamp, Verkade, de Haan, and Saint-Pol Roux. Apparently neither Schuffenecker nor Emile Bernard attended; Pissarro had not been invited either. The *Mercure de France*, in its May issue, published a partial list of guests as well as the texts of the various toasts.

Mallarmé was the first to rise and say a few words: "Gentlemen, let's do first things first; let's drink to the return of Paul Gauguin, but not without admiring his superb conscience which drives him into exile, at the peak of his talent, to seek new strength in a far country and in his own nature."

Morice recited some verses he had written for Gauguin, and Leclercq made another speech: "My dear Gauguin, when one knows you one cannot admire the great artist in you without deeply loving the man you are; and it is a real joy to be able to admire those whom one loves. During the three years of your absence, your friends will often miss the friend who has gone away; during those three years many things will happen. Those among us who are still very young—and I am one of them—you will find grown at your return; our elders will then be fully rewarded for their accomplishments. And as by then the day which is already beginning to dawn will be near, all of us will be able to proclaim your beautiful works with more authoritative voices."

There were other toasts, to those who had written about Gauguin, to Mirbeau, Dolent, Marx, Aurier, to the painters who appreciated him and to those who considered him their master. There was a recitation of Mallarmé's admirable translation of Poe's *Raven*, and then Gauguin rose to speak briefly:

"I love all of you and I am very deeply touched. I can therefore neither say much nor say it well. Some of you have created great works which everybody knows. I drink to these works, as I also drink to the works of the future."[81]

At this banquet it was decided that the next production of Paul Fort's new Théâtre d'Art would be given on May 27 for the benefit of Gauguin and Verlaine. It was to be composed of a one-act play by Verlaine and another by Maeterlinck, the Belgian poet recently "discovered" by Mirbeau; of a play in three acts by Morice; and of another recitation of *The Raven* by the young actress Marguerite Moreno, as well as of two other numbers. Paintings by Gauguin were to be on display in the foyer of the theater.

Le Figaro, which had refused to publish Mirbeau's first long article on Gauguin, announced this performance in a paragraph in which the author apparently quoted the

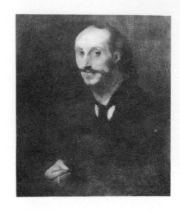

CARRIÈRE: *Portrait of Charles Morice*, 1892–93. 28¾ x 23⅝". Present whereabouts unknown

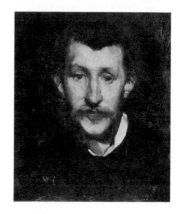

CARRIÈRE: *Portrait of Roger Marx*, 1886. Present whereabouts unknown

press release: "... My surprise increased when I read this: 'Paul Gauguin, the name—for us who dream of an idealistic renovation in literature—not only represents a painter of exceptional talent, the creator of marvelous canvases that are well known, it represents above all hatred of platitudes, return to the original symbolism of the plastic arts, a renaissance of great ideological paintings as it was conceived by Fra Angelico, Mantegna, Leonardo....'" And the writer added: "I saw at the designated spot a yellow sea, rudely drawn purple oxen, pink trees, blue rocks.... What could nature teach those people of genius who reconstruct her but don't observe her?"[82]

The performance met with little success, and neither Verlaine nor Gauguin derived any financial benefit from it (the painter had counted on some 1,500 francs as his share). By that time, however, Gauguin had already left Paris and was approaching his destination. Nor was he in Paris when the Salon of the new Société Nationale opened on May 15. This Salon included a section of "Objets d'Art" in which Gauguin was represented by three ceramics (two of them lent by Schuffenecker) and his bas-relief *Be in love....* His address in the catalogue was listed care of Boussod & Valadon, 19, boulevard Montmartre.[83]

But Gauguin must have seen the Salon des Indépendants, which opened on March 20, with its retrospectives of van Gogh and Dubois-Pillet, its large contingents of works by Anquetin, Bernard, Bonnard, de Monfreid, Denis, Lautrec, Gausson, Guillaumin, Luce, Maufra, the *douanier* Rousseau (Gauguin was one of the few not to laugh at him), Seurat, Signac, Vallotton, van Rysselberghe, and Willumsen. In his review of the exhibition, Julien Leclercq severely criticized the neo-impressionists, applauded Lautrec, though he did not consider his style "very personal," encouraged Denis, and stated that Bernard was "a very young artist of great talent who should not be judged by the canvases he shows.... One does not exhibit the product of incomplete researches." Of Daniel de Monfreid, Leclercq said: "He admires Gauguin and it shows"; of Willumsen he wrote: "Among those whom

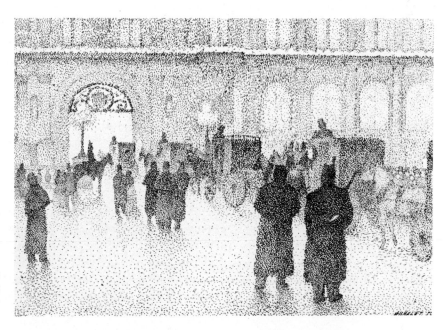

DUBOIS-PILLET: *Arrivals for a Ball at the Paris Hôtel de Ville,* 1887. Pen and ink. Drawing published in *La Vie Moderne.* Present whereabouts unknown

453

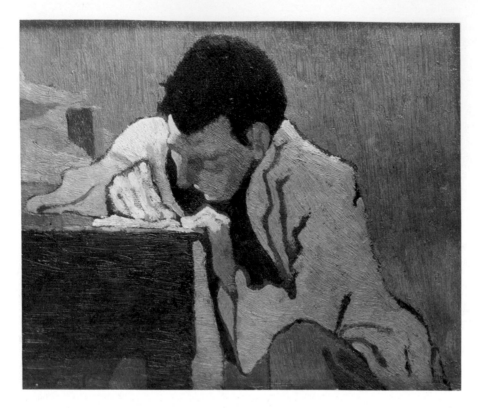

VUILLARD: *Portrait of Lugné-Poë*, 1891.
8½ x 10". Memorial Art Gallery of the
University of Rochester, Rochester,
New York

Paul Gauguin has influenced, he is one of the few whose personality clearly appears."[84] Thus
at the very moment when Gauguin prepared to leave, his ascendance over the artists of the
new generation began to be publicly acknowledged.

Gauguin's departure for Marseilles whence he was to embark took place on the evening
of April 4, 1891 (a few days after Seurat's burial). A few friends escorted him to the Gare de
Lyon; among them Sérusier, Morice, and another writer (probably Aurier), Verkade and his
friend Ballin. Apparently Gauguin's mistress, Juliette Huet, who was pregnant, discreetly
refrained from accompanying the father of her unborn child.

"The farewell was brief and emotional," Verkade later wrote. "After having embraced
us, Gauguin disappeared into the train. He was visibly moved. Once the train had left
the station, we silently went on our way; then Charles Morice suddenly broke out into
loud self-reproach, exclaiming: 'Gauguin is right! What is to become of us! But we are
wasting our time here, in this hideous Paris. Oh! If only I too could leave!'"[85]

But there were few who shared Morice's feelings. On the top of Montmartre where he
lived modestly near the newly erected basilica of Sacré-Coeur, Renoir, who patiently
awaited "his hour" that had not yet come, who still sold his paintings for a few hundred
francs and kept away from all the hubbub and the coteries of Paris, simply shook his head
upon learning of Gauguin's departure. "One can paint so well at Batignolles," he said.[86]

As for Cézanne, working in even greater isolation in his native Aix-en-Provence, he is
supposed to have accused Gauguin of "having stolen my *petite sensation* in order to roam
with it through the South Seas."[87]

NOTES

1 Gauguin to Bernard, [Le Pouldu, Nov. 1899]; see Lettres de Gauguin à sa femme et à ses amis, Paris, 1946, no. XCI, pp. 171–72. Unless otherwise indicated, all references are to this publication, on which see also p. 215, note 1.

2 Bernard to Gauguin, [Saint-Briac, autumn 1889]; unpublished document (collection Pola Gauguin), courtesy Henri Dorra, Santa Barbara, Calif.

3 Gauguin to Bernard, [Pont-Aven, beginning of Sept. 1889]; op. cit., no. LXXXVII, pp. 166–67.

4 Bernard to Schuffenecker, [Lille, May 31, 1890]; unpublished document, courtesy Mme Jeanne Schuffenecker, Paris.

5 See Bernard: L'Aventure de ma vie, in Lettres de Paul Gauguin à Emile Bernard, 1888–1891, Geneva, 1954, p. 38.

6 Bernard to Bonger, Feb. 1894; see M.E. Tralbaut: André Bonger, l'ami des frères van Gogh, Van Goghiana I, Antwerp, Jan. 1963, p. 37.

7 See H. Dorra: Emile Bernard and Paul Gauguin, Gazette des Beaux-Arts, April 1955.

8 Gauguin to Madeleine Bernard, [Le Pouldu, end of Nov. 1889]; op. cit., no. XCVI, p. 180. According to M. Bodelsen: Willumsen, Copenhagen, 1957, p. 80, note 72, the pottery presented to Madeleine Bernard was the one which appears in Gauguin's Self-Portrait, reproduced p. 284.

9 See H. Dorra: The First Eves in Gauguin's Eden, Gazette des Beaux-Arts, March 1953.

10 Gauguin to Bernard, [Le Pouldu, Nov. 1889]; op. cit., no. XCII, pp. 174–75.

11 See Gauguin's letter to Schuffenecker, [Pont-Aven, Jan. 1890]; ibid., no. XCVIII, p. 181.

12 Gauguin to Bernard, [Paris, April] 1890; ibid., no. CII, p. 187.

13 Bernard to Gauguin, [Lille, April–May 1890]; unpublished document (collection Pola Gauguin), courtesy Henri Dorra, Santa Barbara, Calif.

14 Gauguin to Bernard, [Paris, April–May 1890]; op. cit., no. CV (not June 1890), p. 192.

15 Gauguin to Bernard, [June 1890]; ibid., no. CIII (not April 1890), p. 189.

16 Gauguin to Bernard, [Le Pouldu, June 1890]; ibid., no. CVII, p. 196.

17 Gauguin to Bernard, [Le Pouldu, end of July 1890]; ibid., no. CIX, p. 198.

18 Bernard to Aurier, [July 1890]; ibid., 2nd edition, Paris, 1949, pp. 322–23.

19 Gauguin to Bernard, [Le Pouldu, August 1890]; op. cit., no. CX, pp. 199–200.

20 Gauguin to Schuffenecker, Le Pouldu, [Sept. 1890]; see A. Alexandre: Paul Gauguin, sa vie et le sens de son oeuvre, Paris, 1930, pp. 110–11.

21 Gauguin to Redon, [Sept. 1890]; Lettres à Odilon Redon, Paris, 1960, p. 193.

22 Gauguin to J.F. Willumsen, [Brittany, fall 1890]; see Les Marges, March 15, 1918.

23 Denis to Lugné-Poë, [Saint-Germain, Nov. 1890]; see Lugné-Poë: La Parade, I, Le Sot du tremplin, Paris, 1930, p. 254.

24 Denis to Lugné-Poë, [Saint-Germain, Nov.–Dec. 1890]; ibid., p. 245.

25 Denis to Lugné-Poë, [Saint-Germain, Nov.–Dec. 1890]; ibid., p. 261.

26 C. Morice: Paul Gauguin, Paris, 1920, pp. 25–29. (Morice places these recollections in 1889 but the events related by him obviously took place in 1890.)

27 J. Renard: Journal (1 vol), Paris, 1935, entry of Dec. 31, 1890, p. 56.

28 See G.-D. de Monfreid quoted by C. Chassé: Le Mouvement symboliste dans l'art du XIXe siècle, Paris 1947, p. 69.

29 Gauguin to Schuffenecker, [Brittany, 1890]; see Alexandre, op. cit., p. 154.

30 F. Fénéon: Paul Gauguin, Le Chat Noir, May 23, 1891; reprinted in F. Cachin: Fénéon, Paris, 1966, pp. 112–13. (Fénéon does not say "pseudo-literary" but uses the untranslatable word littératurière.)

31 See P. Fort: Mes Mémoires, Paris, 1944, pp. 11–12.

32 Gauguin: Huysmans et Redon; see J. Loize: Un Inédit de Gauguin, Nouvelles Littéraires, May 7, 1953.

33 See C. Morice, op. cit., p. 43.

34 The date for this Self-Portrait is somewhat in doubt; it may have been painted in 1893 after Gauguin's return from Tahiti, although it seems more likely that he would have given it to Carrière in 1891, when the latter did Gauguin's portrait (p. 425).

35 See Carrière on Gauguin in Mercure de France, Nov. 1903, reprinted in Carrière: Ecrits et lettres choisies, Paris, 1907, pp. 43–44.

36 M. Joyant: Henri de Toulouse-Lautrec, Paris, 1926, vol. I, p. 118; see also J. Rewald: Theo van Gogh, Goupil, and the Impressionists, Gazette des Beaux-Arts, Jan.–Feb. 1973.

37 H. Schlittgen: Erinnerungen, Munich, 1926, pp. 250–51.

38 J. Dolent quoted by Morice, op. cit., p. 13.

39 See G. Geffroy: Claude Monet, sa vie, son œuvre, Paris, 1924, chapter XXXIII.

40 Camille Pissarro to his son, [Eragny, July 8, 1891]; see Camille Pissarro: Letters to his Son Lucien, New York, 1943, pp. 179–80.

41 Gauguin to his wife, [Paris, March 1891]; op. cit., no. XCIX, pp. 181–82 (not Jan. 1890 as indicated).

42 Excerpts from the Belgian press quoted in L'Art Moderne, March 29, 1891.

43 Champal: Le Carnaval d'un ci-devant, reprinted in L'Art Moderne, Feb. 15, 1891.

44 Schuffenecker to Gauguin, Paris, Feb. 7, 1891; original draft, unpublished document, courtesy Mme J. Schuffenecker, Paris.

45 Information courtesy the late J.F. Willumsen.

46 See D. Sutton: La Perte du Pucelage by Paul Gauguin, Burlington Magazine, April 1949.

47 See J. de Rotonchamp: Paul Gauguin, Paris, 1925, pp. 81–82. (This usually very reliable author errs in stating that Gauguin's painting had disappeared; it is true, however, that the canvas remained hidden for over fifty years in the collection of Count Antoine de La Rochefoucauld.)

48 See C. Chassé: Gauguin et son temps, Paris, 1955, p. 88. According to Chassé she died around 1935, having long before burned all the objects and letters she had received from Gauguin.

49 W. Verkade: Le Tourment de Dieu, Paris, 1926, pp. 68–69.

50 Gauguin in Essais d'Art Libre, Feb.–April 1894.

51 Camille Pissarro to his son Lucien, [Paris, May 13, 1891]; op. cit., pp. 170–71 (here newly translated).

52 Camille Pissarro to Mirbeau, Jan. 12, 1891; see Camille Pissarro: Lettres à son fils Lucien (French edition), Paris, 1950, p. 247, note 1.

53 Mallarmé to Mirbeau, Jan. 15, 1891; see H. Mondor: Vie de Mallarmé, Paris, 1941, pp. 589–90.

54 Mirbeau to Mallarmé, [Les Damps, Jan. 1891]; ibid., p. 590.

55 Mirbeau to Monet, [Les Damps, Jan. 1891]; see Lettres à Claude Monet, Cahiers d'Aujourd'hui, no. 9, 1922.

56 Gauguin to his wife, [Paris, first half of Feb. 1891]; op. cit., no. CXIX, pp. 209–10. I have been unable to find any articles in Le Journal des Débats, and in Le Rappel. Le Gaulois published a short notice on the sale on Feb. 22, 1891, by G. Geffroy, which followed an article by Morice of Feb. 13, on "Le Symbolisme," where Gauguin was mentioned together with Puvis de Chavannes, Degas, Redon, Monet, and Carrière, among the masters of the movement. In La Justice of Feb. 22, 1891, Geffroy also wrote briefly on Gauguin, referring to Mirbeau's important article as having appeared both in L'Echo de Paris and Le Figaro.

57 Gauguin to his wife, [Paris, Feb. 19, 1891]; ibid., no. CXX, p. 211.

58 O. Mirbeau: Paul Gauguin, Echo de Paris, Feb. 16, 1891; reprinted in Mirbeau: Des Artistes, vol. I, Paris, 1922, pp. 119–29.

59 O. Mirbeau: Paul Gauguin, Le Figaro, Feb. 18, 1891 (not reprinted in Des artistes, op. cit.). This article was brought to my attention by Mr. Bengt Danielsson, Tahiti.

60 R. Marx in Le Voltaire, Feb. 20, 1891.

61 See G. Geffroy in La Justice, Feb. 22, 1891.

62 For a list of the paintings sold—though not all of them are identified—with prices and names of buyers, see the catalogue of the Gauguin exhibition, Orangerie des Tuileries, Paris, summer 1949, pp. 95–96.

63 Mallarmé to Gauguin, [Paris, Feb. 24–25, 1891]; see J. de Rotonchamp, op. cit., p. 91.

64 Gauguin to his wife, [Paris, Feb. 24, 1891]; op. cit., no. CXXI, pp. 211–12.

65 Bernard: Souvenirs inédits sur l'artiste peintre Paul Gauguin et ses compagnons lors de leur séjour à Pont-Aven et au Pouldu, Lorient, n.d. [1939], p. 12.

66 See Bernard's letter to Aurier, quoted p. 416, note 18.

67 Bernard: L'Aventure de ma vie, op. cit., pp. 45–46.

68 Ibid., p. 30.

69 This was a very unkind and mean remark, as Cézanne's works were still practically unsalable in the late '80s; moreover, Gauguin himself had been just as "guilty" of closely following Cézanne. Gauguin's statement that Bernard had painted holy images and copied old tapestries in 1887 is also not quite fair, since these works of Bernard were mostly done a little later, during his mystic-Catholic phase, after he had met Gauguin.

70 Gauguin: Notes sur Bernard [1895]; see Dorra: Emile Bernard and Paul Gauguin, op. cit.

71 See J. Leclercq's reply to E. Bernard, Mercure de France, July 1895.

72 Aurier: Symbolisme en peinture: Paul Gauguin, Mercure de France, March 1891 (article dated Feb. 9, 1891); reprinted in Aurier: Oeuvres posthumes, Paris, 1893.

73 Camille Pissarro to his son Lucien, Paris, April 20, 1891; op. cit., pp. 163–64 (here newly translated).

74 C. Henry, answer to: Enquête de Jules Huret, Echo de Paris, June 1891; reprinted in L'Art Moderne, Oct. 25, 1891.

75 Mallarmé, answer to: Enquête de Jules Huret, Echo de Paris; reprinted in L'Art Moderne, Aug. 9, 1891.

76 Mirbeau, answer to: Enquête de Jules Huret, Echo de Paris; reprinted in L'Art Moderne, Sept. 13, 1891.

77 J. Renard, diary entry of April 15, 1891 (by this time Gauguin had already left France); see Renard: Journal, op. cit., p. 66.

78 On this whole question see R. Rey's introduction to: Onze menus de Gauguin, Geneva, 1950, pp. 45–51.

79 See Morice, op. cit., pp. 29–30.

80 For Gauguin's recollections of this banquet see Gauguin: Avant et Après, Paris, 1923, pp. 27–28.

81 See Mercure de France, May 1891, pp. 318–20.

82 H. Fouquier: L'Avenir symboliste, à propos de la représentation au profit de Gauguin et Verlaine, Le Figaro, May 24, 1891.

83 Soyez amoureuses had already been shown at Boussod & Valadon's in Dec. 1890. Among the other exhibitors at this Salon were Anquetin, J.-E. Blanche, Boudin, Carolus-Duran, Carrière, H.-E. Cross, Desboutin, Hodler, Lebourg, Lépine, Liebermann, Maufra, Puvis de Chavannes, Raffaëlli, Sargent, Sisley, Stevens, Thaulow (Gauguin's brother-in-law), Whistler, and Zorn.

84 J. Leclercq: Aux Indépendants, Mercure de France, May 1891.

85 Verkade, op. cit., p. 92.

86 See A. André: Renoir, Paris, 1923, 1928, p. 49.

87 See Cézanne quoted by Mirbeau in Mirbeau, Duret, Werth, Jourdain: Cézanne, Paris, 1914, p. 9.

X   1891-1893   GAUGUIN IN TAHITI

On June 8, 1891, after sixty-three days, Gauguin at last perceived the lights of the island of Tahiti. The ship had stopped at various Australian ports and he had had to wait for almost three weeks at Nouméa before a man-of-war took him to Tahiti. He regretted having taken a second-class ticket—in spite of the reduction granted by the French government—for he might have saved five hundred francs and traveled almost as comfortably had he gone third class. But now Papeete was in sight and a new life would begin for him, although his first impression, as he saw the shore rise from the sea, was not too overwhelming.

Exactly three years before, in June 1888, Robert Louis Stevenson had for the first time sighted the Polynesian islands where he hoped to find a cure for his ailments. Before him, Melville had jumped his whaling ship in the Marquesas in 1843 and Pierre Loti had lived there in 1872 the romance he later wrote in *Rarahu*. Still others, like the American Charles Warren Stoddard, had put on paper their impressions of these fabulous isles. However, no painter had yet gone there in search of new inspiration.

When Stevenson caught his first glimpse of the Marquesas (for which Gauguin many years later was to leave Tahiti) he was moved to write: "The land heaved up in peaks and rising vales; it fell in cliffs and buttresses; its colour ran through fifty modulations in a scale of pearl and rose and olive; and it was crowned above by opalescent clouds. The suffusion of vague hues deceived the eye; the shadows of clouds were confounded with the articulations of the mountain; and the isle and its unsubstantial canopy rose and shimmered before us like a single mass.... Somewhere, in that pale phantasmagoria of cliff and cloud, our haven lay concealed."[1]

But Gauguin lost little time in contemplation. He was eager for action. The very day he set foot in Papeete he presented himself to the governor who received him cordially, thanks to the "artistic mission" with which the painter had been entrusted by the French minister of Fine Arts. Yet he was unable to dispel the governor's impression that this mission was synonymous with spying. Gauguin was quickly disgusted with the life of Papeete, which still reminded him of Europe, but was fascinated by the natives who began to arrive there for the funeral of King Pomaré, who had died three days before Gauguin's arrival. The passing of the last native ruler did not really change the situation, since the French colonial officials had already gained a firm hold over the affairs of the island. Yet Gauguin considered the death of the monarch a personal catastrophe, having apparently expected much from his protection.

Soon Gauguin was captivated by the peculiar atmosphere of Tahiti, by the deep silence of its nights, by the indolence of the natives. Towards the end of July he wrote to his wife: "It seems to me that all the hubbub of life in Europe no longer exists and that tomorrow, always, it'll be the same thing and will remain so until the end. Don't think on account of this that I am egotistical and that I am abandoning you. But let me live some time like this. Those who reproach me do not know all there is in the nature of an artist. Why do they want to impose on us duties like their own? We do not impose ours upon them."[2]

With his usual flair and ready self-deception Gauguin immediately detected prospects for profitable portrait commissions in Papeete, yet it did not take him long to decide to leave the port city and to look for a place in the still unspoiled country. One fine morning, he borrowed a horse and carriage and, accompanied by Titi, a Tahitian half-caste women whom he had met shortly after his arrival, drove along the East coast. In the district of Mataïea, some thirty miles from Papeete, he found what he was looking for: a bamboo hut, on one side the ocean, on the other a mountain hidden by a group of enormous mangrove trees. Gauguin decided to dismiss Titi but soon felt so lonely in his new residence that he called her back. After a few weeks, however, he resolved to send her away and eventually replace her by a simple native girl, less corrupted by civilization and too many lovers.

His neighbors proved to be friendly and helpful. After a little while he managed to speak a few words of their language and thus felt less isolated. Soon Gauguin began to work. As he himself later wrote, he started with notes and sketches of all kinds, "but the landscape, with its bright, burning colors dazzled and blinded me.... And yet it was so simple to paint things as I saw them, to put on my canvas a red and a blue without any of the calculations [of former times].... Why did I hesitate to let all that gold and all the joy of the sun flow directly onto my canvas?—Old routines of Europe, timidity of expression of degenerate races!"[3]

He decorated his hut with reproductions of paintings by Manet, Puvis de Chavannes, Degas, Rembrandt, Raphael, Michelangelo, and Holbein, as well as with photographs of his children and no doubt also the work presented by Redon. When a neighbor's wife admired Manet's *Olympia* and asked him whether that was his wife, it amused him to reply in the affirmative. Subsequently she agreed to pose for him. He was fascinated by the kindness, the carefree attitude, the childlike purity, the trustfulness strangely mixed with easy fright of

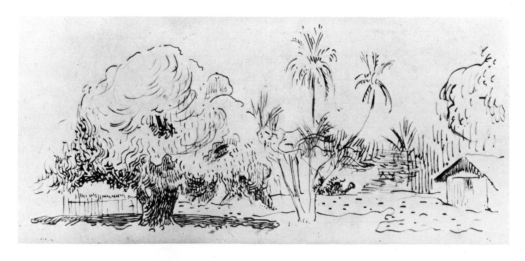

GAUGUIN: *Tahitian Landscape,* 1891–93. Pen and blue ink. Formerly collection Ambroise Vollard

458

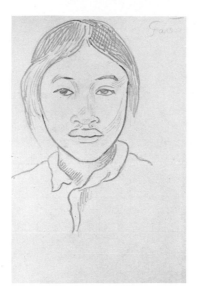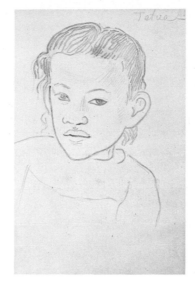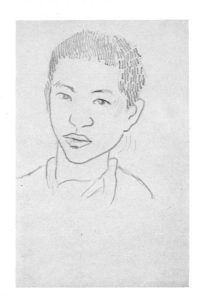

GAUGUIN: Three drawings of Tahitian children, 1891–93. Pencil and ink, 6½ x 4¼″ each. Possibly studies for the painting reproduced on page 468. Collection Mr. and Mrs. Alex M. Lewyt, New York

these guileless people who seemed ready to adopt him because he—unlike other Europeans—completely shared their way of life, subsisting on fish, roots, and fruit, drinking only water. "The majority of Polynesians," Stevenson had discovered, "are easy folk to get in touch with, frank, fond of notice, greedy of the least affection, like amiable, fawning dogs. . . . The eyes of all Polynesians are large, luminous, and melting; they are like the eyes of animals and some Italians."[4] Gauguin was deeply impressed by their beauty (although he conceded that Europeans might consider them ugly), by the natural elegance and dignity of their movements. He marveled at the almost masculine strength of the women, the rather effeminate grace of the men. They in turn took a liking to him. In the evenings they gathered beneath tufted pandanus trees over which towered lofty palms; the natives sang their strange, plaintive songs abruptly terminating in a single barbaric cry. Sometimes Gauguin played the mandolin which Filiger had helped him to master at Pont-Aven.

Later Gauguin wrote of those early weeks in Mataïea: "Every day becomes better for me; I begin to understand the language fairly well. My neighbors. . . consider me one of themselves. By continual contact with the pebbles my feet have hardened, have become used to the ground, and my body, almost constantly bare, no longer suffers from the sun. Little by little civilization is leaving me. I begin to think simply and feel hardly any hatred for my fellow men—better yet, I begin to love them. I have all the pleasures of a free life, both animal and human. I am escaping the artificial, I am penetrating nature. With the certitude of a morrow similar to the present day, just as free, just as beautiful, peace descends upon me; I am developing normally and no longer have any needless worries."[5] He felt that he was becoming a "savage" like those around him.

His neighbors came to see him work: make sketches, do some sculpture, or paint. One of the first canvases he did represents a scene he watched one day from his hut and later described: "It is morning. On the sea, by the shore, I see a pirogue and in the pirogue a woman. On the shore a man almost naked; next to him a sick coconut tree appears like a tremendous parrot whose golden tail is hanging down and who holds in its claws a big cluster of coconuts.

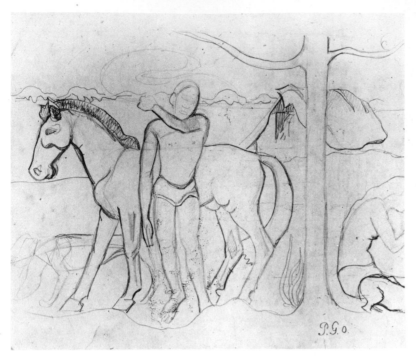

GAUGUIN: *Man and Horse in a Landscape*, Tahiti, 1891–93. Pencil, 8½ x 10⅝″. Collection M. Français, Paris

With an harmonious and subtle gesture the man raises with his two hands a heavy axe which leaves a blue mark against the silvery sky and—below—its incision on the dead tree.... On the purple soil, long serpentine leaves of a metallic yellow seemed to me like the written characters of a faraway oriental language.... In the pirogue the woman was arranging some nets. The blue line of sea was frequently broken by the green crests of the rolling surf crashing against coral reefs."[6]

With the exception of the parrot-like coconut tree all the features mentioned in Gauguin's notes appear in his painting. The glowing tropical colors are emphasized but they are of a nature quite different from those he had recently used in France. While they are strong and powerful throughout, he has avoided the sharp clashes which he had favored in some of his earlier synthesist works. His reds and blues, his purples and yellows exist side by side without feuding; in spite of their forcefulness the general aspect of this painting is less one of contrast than of harmony. Nobody before him had ever painted with such pungent colors, not even van Gogh, who had striven to accentuate complementaries; whereas here, without any emphasis on particular color oppositions, the whole canvas was pervaded by a strength of coloration that could not be surpassed. The fiery aspects of nature around him, bathed by a blazing sun, thus at last permitted Gauguin to attain a height of color which was no longer a result of his imagination but found ample nourishment in actual observation. And yet, in one of his very first letters to Daniel de Monfreid he reported: "I limit myself to delving into my innermost being rather than into nature, to learn a little how to draw—only the drawing exists!"[7] Nevertheless there can be little doubt that his South Sea paradise gave Gauguin the longed-for opportunity to become the colorist he was born to be.

He was now so deeply immersed in his creative urge, spurred by the overpowering richness

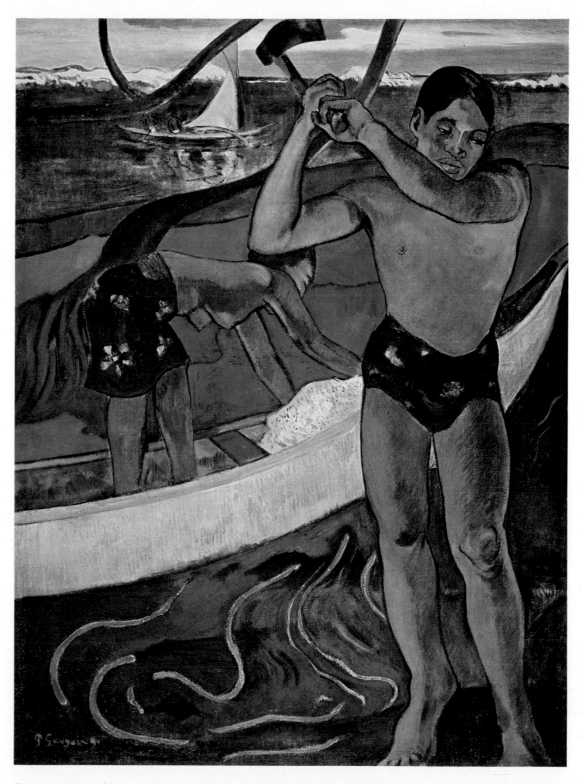

GAUGUIN: *Man with an Axe,* Tahiti, 1891. 36¼ x 27¼″. Collection Mr. and Mrs. Alex M. Lewyt, New York

of new impressions, that he felt unable to appraise his own work. When, at long last, in November, he received his first letter from France, written by Sérusier, he replied: "I have put myself to work with determination. I can't say whether it's worth anything, for it is a good deal and it is nothing. Not yet a painting but a host of researches which may prove fruitful; a great many documents which will serve me for a long time, I hope; for example in France. As a result of simplification I cannot judge the result now. It seems to me that it is disgusting. After my return, with the canvases well-dried, framed, etc. . . . I shall judge. I am quite alone in the countryside, some thirty miles from the city, with nobody to talk with about art or even in French, and I am not yet very fluent in the native language, despite all my efforts."[8]

As Sérusier apparently had written how much he owed to Gauguin, the painter modestly replied: "You are very kind to attribute your intellectual progress to me. Maybe I have a small part in it but, you see, I am convinced that artists achieve only what is already in them. The grain only grows in a fertile soil. If you make progress it is because you are meant to."[8]

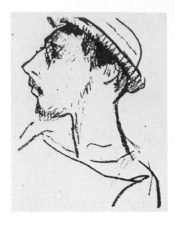

GAUGUIN: *Portrait of Pierre Bonnard*, c. 1891. Drawing. Present whereabouts unknown

Sérusier seems to have been almost the only one of his young friends and "pupils" who remembered Gauguin in his distant exile. In December 1891, at about the time when Gauguin's reply reached Sérusier, some of the Nabis and their comrades organized a small show at Le Barc de Boutteville's, in the rue Le Peletier, under the title *Impressionnistes et Symbolistes*, a name almost identical to the one Gauguin once had selected for the Volpini exhibition. Le Barc de Boutteville had just decided, according to a notice published by Aurier, to "offer a permanent shelter to the young artists, the innovators, who are still opposed by the critics, disdained by the customers, and generally scoffed at by the dealers and the juries."[9] Among the painters whom the gallery planned to represent were Anquetin, Bernard, Lautrec, Sérusier, Denis, Renoir, Signac, Bonnard, Roussel, Willumsen, Luce, Petitjean, Gausson, and several others to whom it was planned to add Filiger, Pissarro, Redon, van Gogh, and Gauguin. The first show comprised works by Anquetin, Lautrec, Bernard, Denis, and Bonnard. When a journalist went to interview these painters—interviews had become the fashion ever since Jules Huret had published in the *Echo de Paris* his interviews with Henry, Mallarmé, Mirbeau, and many others—the name of Gauguin was hardly mentioned. Among the questions the journalist asked them were: "How do you define the artistic tendencies of the young school of painting and under which labels do you group them? Who is the master whom you admire most?"

Anquetin's reply was rather evasive: ". . . Until now, unfortunately, I have submitted to various influences; but all my efforts tend to free myself from them. Symbolism, impressionism are only jokes. I care for no theories, no schools. Only temperament counts." And he added that the contemporary artists he most admired were "Cézanne and also Renoir. There are two pure geniuses to whom justice should be rendered."

Lautrec was met by the interviewer at the exhibition itself: "Very short, dark, with a full beard, spectacles on his nose. We talk. Punctuating his words with sardonic laughter, M. de Toulouse-Lautrec tells us: 'I don't belong to any school. I work in my corner. I admire Degas and Forain. . . .' And M. de Toulouse-Lautrec gives a little chuckle. He is very much the man of his paintings which, indeed, exhale a pointed irony. Do not his women, dreaming in a melancholy mood on the sofas of 'public convents,' betray qualities of a truly cruel observation?"

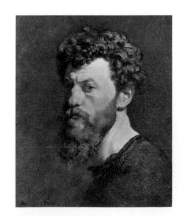

ANQUETIN: *Self-Portrait*, d. 1894. 23⅝ × 19¼". Formerly collection Mme C. du Ferron-Anquetin, Paris

The interview with Emile Bernard was much more extended, without any doubt because he was so much more voluble: "He is a searcher, a fanatic, a fellow who would rather die of inanition than make the least concession in anything concerning his art. He is also an ardent and practicing Catholic, which explains the mysticism of his paintings. At Asnières, in a small studio built of boards, and in the house where M. Bernard lives with his parents, we were able to see masses of curious sketches, very original canvases, stained glass windows of a surprising artistic beauty, panels carved with infinite care, tapestries of an extreme originality.... The impression we carried away from this visit to his studio was that M. Bernard— who has been accused of imitating Paul Gauguin—does not resemble him in the least, oh, not in the least! M. Emile Bernard is merely a hieratic and nothing else. His paintings translate only religious feelings. As to his techniques, they are very simple: few colors and exclusive use of dull, tarnished tones. M. Bernard is twenty-four years old. Tall, slender, with long hair, a pointed blond beard, blue eyes and a very gentle glance, he resembles a figure by Velásquez. His conversation is interesting, very erudite and very clear.—'I am a Christian,' he tells us, 'and I try to render the feelings which I carry in me. I dream of creating a hieratic style which would rise above modernity, above actuality. For techniques and for inspiration we should go back to the primitives: be very concise as far as technique is concerned, use line only to determine form, and color only to determine conditions. One should, in a word, create a style that would be the one of our time.'" Questioned about his admirations, Bernard replied: "Among our contemporaries I admire only Cézanne and Odilon Redon."[10]

Maurice Denis, a devout Catholic like Bernard, refused altogether to name his favorite masters. About his interview with him the reporter wrote: "It seems that at present M. Denis is engaged in researches from which he expects a satisfactory result. Although he is only twenty-one years old, he spoke to us with the moderation of an old man: 'We are not pretentious people, living with the conviction that we have discovered the *definitive Art*. We are seekers as humble as possible.... I think that above everything else a painting should be an ornament. The choice of subjects or scenes means nothing. It is through its colored surface, through the value of tones, through the harmony of lines that I attempt to reach the mind, arouse the emotion.'"

Like his friend Denis, Bonnard did not name any masters he admired, although—again like Denis—he had made a profitable study of Gauguin's work ever since he first saw it assembled at the Volpini exhibition in 1889. "M. Pierre Bonnard," the journalist reported, "is also very young. His comrades consider him an admirably gifted decorator and illustrator.... 'Painting should be mainly decorative,' M. Bonnard tells us. 'The talent will reveal itself by the way in which the lines are arranged. I do not belong to any school. I only try to do something that is personal, and I am trying, at this moment, to unlearn what I worked so hard to learn during four years at the Ecole des Beaux-Arts.'"[11]

While these painters seemed to have forgotten what they owed to Gauguin (with the exception of Lautrec and possibly Anquetin all had benefited from his liberating influence), Aurier at least proposed to do justice to his absent friend. He was then preparing an important article in which he planned to discuss the new movement and Gauguin's preponderant share in it. As Gauguin's friend Charles Morice was to proclaim a few years later: "At the present time Puvis de Chavannes, Carrière, Renoir, Redon, Degas, Gustave Moreau, and Gauguin are, in painting, directing the young artists."[12] But whether or not these young colleagues acknowledged his leading role was not then Gauguin's main concern. He seemed less troubled by the danger of being ignored by his artistic brethren than he was by the fact that those who were supposed to look after his interests also appeared to have forgotten him. Communications with France being painfully slow, he had to wait weeks from one mail to the next and he always waited in vain for promised remittances. Soon he began to complain bitterly about the negligence of his friends. Not a word from Morice who owed him 500 francs, not a word from Dolent who was supposed to pay 300 for a painting left with Tanguy, not a word from the Goupil Galleries, from Portier, etc. De Haan did not answer his letters; Bernard seemed to be intriguing against him. When Daniel de Monfreid wrote, it was to say that Juliette had given birth to the child Gauguin had not wanted, a girl who was sickly, and that she needed help. Yet Gauguin saw his funds dwindle and desperately counted on the money from Paris to arrive before his reserves were exhausted.

There was a strange contrast between the anxiety with which Gauguin continually looked forward to the next mail and the idyllic life he led. When his solitude became unbearable to the point where he felt listless, he decided to tour the island and, incidentally, look for a new companion. He followed the road along the shore to the isthmus of Taravoa, where he borrowed a horse from a gendarme and covered a few more miles. In one of the villages he was invited to a meal and introduced to a young girl who shyly expressed her readiness to become his *vahine*. She was about thirteen years old (which corresponds to the physical maturity of eighteen to twenty years in a European woman), and she soon started on the way home with him, silent, serene, beautiful. Only a somewhat mocking fold of her sensuous mouth warned Gauguin that in this bizarre adventure she might be the stronger and more inscrutable one after all.

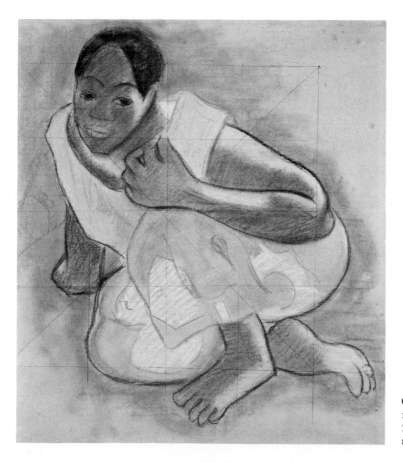

GAUGUIN: *Tahitian Woman*, c. 1892. Study for the painting reproduced on page 485. Pencil, charcoal, and pastel. 21¾ x 18¾″. The Art Institute of Chicago (Gift of Tiffany and Margaret Blake)

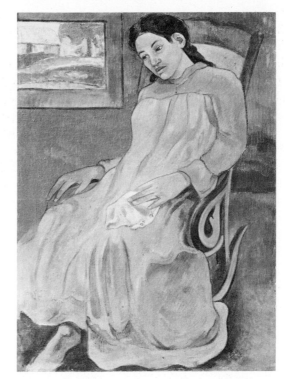

GAUGUIN: *Reverie,* Tahiti, 1891. 37 x 26¾". William Rockhill Nelson Gallery and Atkins Museum of Fine Arts, Kansas City, Mo.

Below: GAUGUIN: *Two Tahitian Women on the Beach,* d. 1891. 27⅝ x 36¼". Musée du Louvre, Paris

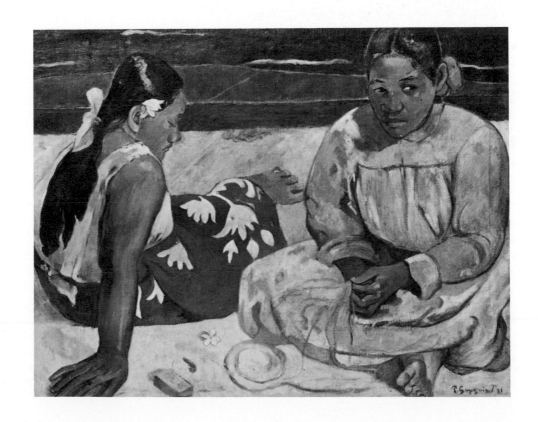

In moving and poetic words Gauguin later told[13] of his wonderful and ecstatic life with Tehura, calm, melancholy, and mocking; how he tried to penetrate her mysterious and primitive soul; how she observed him quietly without betraying her thoughts; how he began to love her; how she left him after a week to visit her family, as had been agreed, and how he feared he had lost her; how she returned after a few days, as promised, of her own free will, thus showing that she was happy with him; how after this test they entered into a truly felicitous life together, based on mutual confidence; how he took up his work again, infused with new strength; how Tehura's presence filled his hut with radiant joy; how through her he felt closer to the impermeable mind of the natives; how he soon almost shared her primitive superstitions; how submissive she was and how tender, innocent and yet knowing, independent and yet docile, sagacious but also frivolous, mature and at the same time childish, naïve and curious, loving and carefree; how he grew younger in her company and left civilization further and further behind; how he lost any notion of good and evil, for all was well that was beautiful. And Tehura was beautiful.

He painted her often, sometimes clothed, mostly in the nude. The young woman with the regular features and the straight black hair, with the slim body, the small breasts and the long powerful legs, who appears in almost all of his Tahitian pictures undoubtedly is Tehura. He painted her dreaming in a rocking chair, her slender form hidden beneath a flowing pink dress (page 465); he painted her on the beach, her golden limbs caressed by the sun, or squatting under a tree, bathing in a brook, carrying fruits; and eventually he painted her almost triumphantly as a deity of her tribe, as the *Queen of the Areois* (page 477), enthroned spendidly nude in a tropical landscape, the vivid colors of a decorative drapery setting off the glowing tone of her bronze skin.

One of the most important paintings done (like the *Man with an Axe*) in 1891, before he met Tehura, is a singular composition inspired by a religious theme similar to the subjects he had occasionally treated in Brittany. Whereas he subsequently set out to grasp the character of the native beliefs—and particularly the superstitions which Tehura imparted to him—in *Ia Orana Maria* he used a tropical setting for a Biblical scene, just as he had chosen a Breton setting for *Jacob Wrestling with the Angel*. *Ia Orana Maria* is a strange attempt to combine the luxuriance of a South Sea background with the mysticism of the faith in which Gauguin himself had been reared. In a letter to de Monfreid he explained the subject of the canvas: "An angel with yellow wings who points out to two Tahitian women the figures of Mary and Jesus, also Tahitians. Nudes dressed in pareus, a kind of flowered cotton which is wrapped as one likes around the waist. In the background somber mountains and blooming trees. A dark purple road and an emerald green foreground. To the left some bananas. I am rather pleased with it."[14]

Oddly enough, in this—one of his first major works done in Tahiti—Gauguin not only maintained a spiritual link with his religious paintings of Pont-Aven, he also drew inspiration from a photograph representing bas-relief friezes from a Javanese temple of Barabudur, a photograph which he had probably obtained at the Paris World's Fair of 1889.[15] Thus the deep impression which the arts of Asia had made upon him two years before now found its echo in the two figures of Tahitian women whose pose is copied almost literally from the Javanese frieze. Yet this unusual mixture of Catholicism, Polynesian figures, and Javanese Buddhist postures is pulled together by a masterly composition, by brilliant colors and subtle brushwork which shows clever variations of flat, uniformly and vividly colored surfaces on the one hand and softly modeled, delicately tinted details on the other.

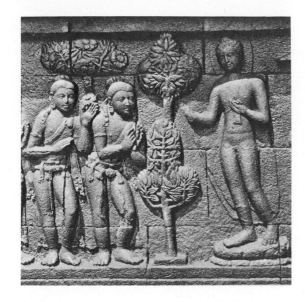

Javanese Temple of Barabudur, detail from a bas-relief frieze. The figure at the right was also the inspiration for Gauguin's drawing and watercolor, page **476**

Right: GAUGUIN: *Ia Orana Maria—Ave Maria,* Tahiti, d. 1891. 44¾ × 34½″. The Metropolitan Museum of Art, New York (Bequest of Sam A. Lewisohn)

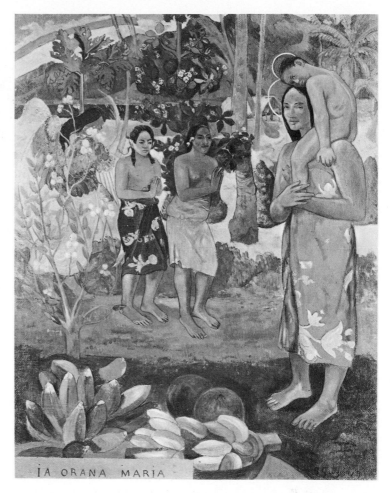

IA ORANA MARIA

During the same period, Gauguin painted a few landscapes of an almost impressionist flavor, save for their tropical harmonies. No longer bound by the rigorous requirements of his synthesist program, Gauguin's style, in these landscapes, has somewhat mellowed: lines and curves have become more gracious, the flat planes have acquired softness through slight variations of tones, and the coloration itself has lost its strong accents. But his composition nevertheless draws on the same elements: simplified forms and large expanses of uniform areas, tied together by rhythmic design (page 471).

The different approaches, the different techniques and color schemes that can be observed in Gauguin's first canvases painted in Tahiti amply explain themselves by the fact that he had not arrived there with a ready-made concept of what he planned to do. On the contrary, he almost voluptuously abandoned himself to the charm of his surroundings which he observed and absorbed. In every new work he undertook he was intent on finding an appropriate expression for the calm and luxuriance that had lured him to the South Seas, of finding plastic equivalents for the incredible beauty of landscape and human beings which all but oppressively held him spellbound.

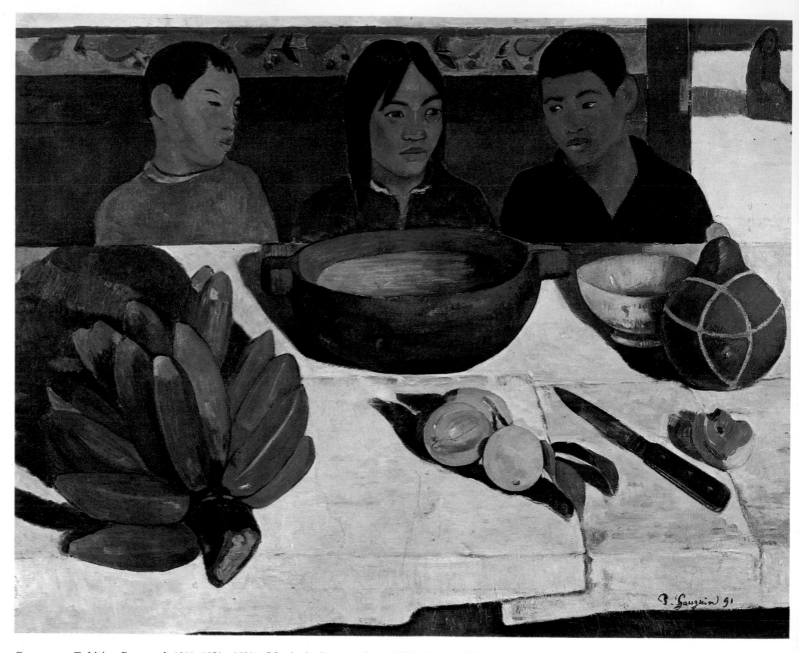

GAUGUIN: *Tahitian Repast,* d. 1891. 28¾ x 36¼". Musée du Louvre, Paris (Gift of André Meyer)

Yet the happiness of those early months away from Papeete and close to Tehura did not last long. In March 1892 the painter informed de Monfreid: "I have been rather seriously ill. Imagine, I spat blood, a quarter of a liter each day. Impossible to stop it; mustard plasters on the legs, cupping glasses on the chest—nothing helped. The doctor at the hospital was quite worried and thought I was done for. The chest was sound and even fairly strong, he said; it was the heart that played those tricks on me. That heart has suffered so many shocks that this is not surprising. Since the vomiting of blood has stopped I have been taking a digitalis treatment and now I am on my feet again without having yet had any relapses. Just the same, I shall have to be careful."[14]

Two weeks later Gauguin wrote to Sérusier: "Your letter finds me in one of those terrible moments of our existence where a man has to make a decision, knowing well that on one side or the other there are blows waiting for him. In a word, thanks to the villainy of Morice I am at the end of my rope and I shall have to go back. But how, *without money*? On the other hand I want to stay; I have not yet finished my work, I have hardly even started it, and I feel that I am beginning to do good things.... If I had another 500 francs (the 500 francs Morice owes me), I could hold out. I have been promised for May the commission of a portrait of a woman— 2,500 francs—but it is only a promise and I don't know what to think of it. From now till May I shall do everything possible and impossible to wait. If the portrait is commissioned —I have to make a portrait that pleases, in the style of [the official painter] Bonnat—and if it is paid for, then I believe I shall have one or two others to do and I shall have regained my independence.... I do not dare speak of what I am painting here, to such an extent do my canvases appall me. Never will the public accept them. They are ugly from all points of view and I shall only know what they really are once I am in Paris and you have all seen them.... What a religion, this old Oceanic religion! What a marvel! My brain is bursting with it and all the things it suggests to me will frighten everybody. So if people are afraid of my former works in a drawing room, what will they say of my new ones!"[16]

Gauguin's excitement over the Oceanic religion was caused not so much by what Tehura told him, as he later implied (Polynesian women are *not* initiated into the secrets of the ancestral beliefs of their tribes), as by a book a French colonial had lent him in Papeete, prob- ably during his sojourn at the hospital. This publication in two volumes by Moerenhout was written in 1835 and related his trips to the islands of the Pacific.[17] Consul of the United States and later also of France, Moerenhout had spent many years in Tahiti, befriending the natives and sometimes even defending them against the crude zeal of Protestant and Catholic mis- sionaries. Thus he had obtained the confidence of several Tahitian chieftains and priests and had faithfully transcribed the legends transmitted by immemorial generations soon to fade under the onslaught of Christianity. In a notebook, on the cover of which he wrote *Ancien Culte Maorie*, Gauguin copied many of these legends (some in French as well as in the native language) and adorned the manuscript with numerous drawings and watercolors.[18] Whether he already planned to use these transcriptions later for a book on his sojourn in the South Seas or whether he merely wished to acquaint himself more thoroughly with the histori- cal and mystical background against which to set off the daily life of the Polynesians as he observed it, is hard to say, but the fact remains that by copying Moerenhout's text Gauguin also envisioned subjects that he might paint, now that he had studied the nature of the superstitions and beliefs that had once governed the life of the Tahitians and that still had not died out completely.

No wonder that Gauguin felt more and more deeply attached to his surroundings and that

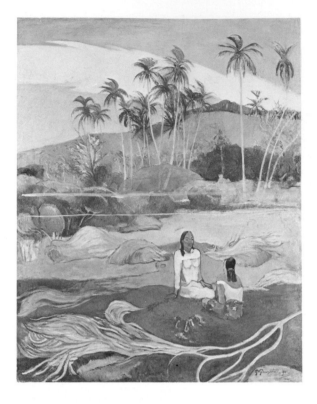

GAUGUIN: *Under the Palm Trees*, Tahiti, d. 1891. 37 x 29½". Private collection, Boston

Below: GAUGUIN: *Te ra'au rahi—The Big Tree*, Tahiti, d. 1891. 28¼ x 36". Collection Mr. and Mrs. Frank Griesinger, Cleveland

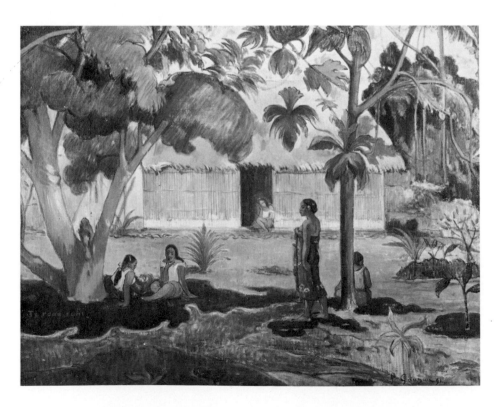

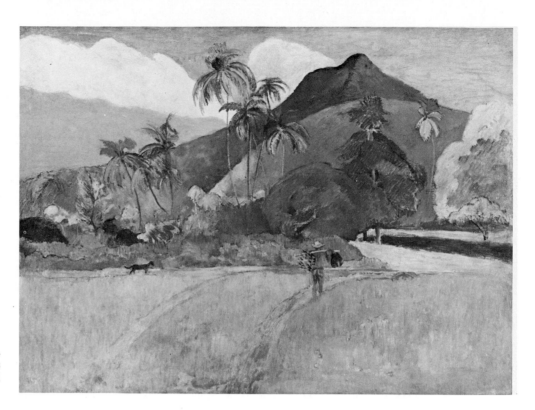

GAUGUIN: *Tahitian Landscape, c.* 1891. 26¾ x 36⅜″. The Minneapolis Institute of Arts (Julius C. Ellel Memorial Fund)

his brain was "bursting" with new projects while he feared at the same time that he might be forced to leave. The portrait commission apparently did not materialize, which can hardly have surprised the painter. Had he not exclaimed in a letter to Sérusier: "Oh, if I could only still whip up a *trompe l'oeil* picture, like the Americans, I might be able to sell a few canvases at a good price. Yet I am only, and can paint only, what I know!"[8]

But in June, when he was almost down to his last franc[19] and prepared to request from the governor his repatriation as an indigent colonist, he met a French captain who gave him 400 francs as down payment on another portrait commission, which did not come through either. This money enabled him to subsist for a few more months. Meanwhile his wife had been in Paris and gathered up some of his paintings, which she tried to sell in Denmark, even planning to organize an exhibition in Copenhagen. When she did find a few buyers, Gauguin proudly pointed out to her that his work was worth something, after all, but also requested that she send him a share of the proceeds. He carried on an active correspondence with his wife, telling her how he longed for his family but explaining at the same time that his artistic career demanded a prolonged stay in the tropics. The only others who seem to have written to him faithfully were Daniel de Monfreid, who untiringly attended to all of Gauguin's errands and interests in Paris, and Paul Sérusier.

When Mette Gauguin reproached her husband for absenting himself from Paris, he explained: "You say that I am wrong to stay away from the artistic center. No, I am right. For a long time I have known what I am doing and why I am doing it. My artistic center is in my head and nowhere else. I am strong because I am never led astray by others and because

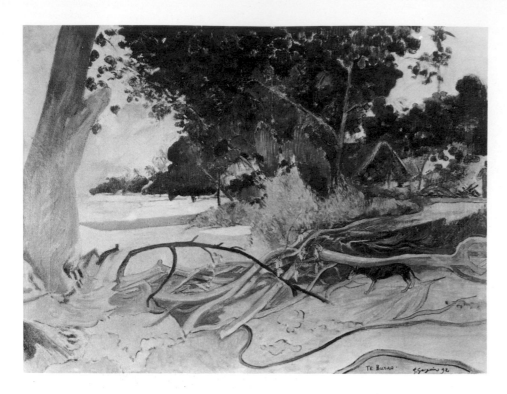

GAUGUIN: *Te Burao—The Hibiscus Tree,* d. 1892. 35½ x 26¼". The Art Institute of Chicago (Mahala Ann Winterbotham Memorial)

I do what is in me."[20] And later he told her with undisguised gratification: "I have eleven months of regular work behind me and I have done forty-four fairly important paintings." But he could not help flying immediately off into speculation by adding: "This means a year of 15,000 francs at least, supposing that the clients buy."[21]

Feeling that after one year he now really had penetrated his new surroundings, Gauguin at last admitted satisfaction with his work: "I am quite pleased with my last paintings and I feel that I am beginning to assimilate the Oceanic character. I can assure you that what I am doing here has never been done by anybody and that it is unheard of in France. I hope that this novelty will incline people in my favor.... Three months ago I sent to Paris a sample of my work which I thought well of. We shall see what Paris is going to say about it."[22]

In July he again wrote to his wife, explaining that he hoped to be able to remain in the tropics for another year while fearing that he might have to leave sooner for lack of funds. "I am hard at work, now that I know the soil and its aroma. The Tahitians whom I paint in a very enigmatic fashion are nevertheless real Polynesians and not Orientals from the Batignolles [the Paris market for professional models]. It took me almost a year to get to understand them, and now that I have reached this point and my work is well under way I may have to leave. It's infuriating."[23]

Only in September 1892 did Gauguin's first Tahitian painting appear at the Goupil Galleries (Boussod & Valadon), but there is no evidence that it caused any particular stir or even attracted much attention. Daniel de Monfreid thought highly of it, yet Schuffenecker—much to Gauguin's amusement—professed to be disconcerted and exclaimed: "But this is not Symbolism!"[24] Just as Bernard had insisted in his interview that he owed nothing to Gau-

472

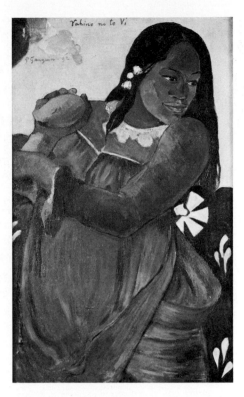

GAUGUIN: *Vahine no te Vi—Tahitian Woman with Mango,* d. 1892. 27¼ x 17½". Formerly collection Edgar Degas. Baltimore Museum of Art (Cone Collection)

Below: GAUGUIN: *I raro te oviri—Under the Pandanus Palms,* Tahiti, d. 1891. 28¾ x 36". The Minneapolis Institute of Arts

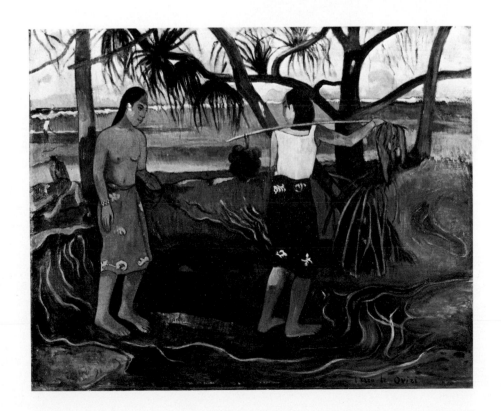

guin, the latter now stated twice in the same letter to de Monfreid that this canvas had "nothing to do with Bernard."[25] Actually this picture, painted in 1891, was not nearly as striking as Gauguin's subsequent Tahitian works; it did not yet have the specific flavor or peculiar style which he was soon to achieve in the *Man with an Axe* and *Ia Orana Maria*. It was a portrait of a native woman, obviously older than Tehura, attired in a colorful dress and holding a flower in her hand. Like so many of the artist's Tahitian paintings, it bore an inscription in the native tongue: *Vahine no te Tiare*, which Gauguin himself translated as: *Woman with a Flower* (opposite). It was possibly one of the "quieter" canvases through which Gauguin had hoped to obtain portrait commissions. Were it not for the Polynesian features of the model and the more vivid coloration, this likeness might conceivably have been done in France before Gauguin's departure. It is not surprising, therefore, that it went practically unnoticed, although it might have been accorded a more favorable reception had not the Paris art season been particularly rich in significant events.

It is not known whether Gauguin's few correspondents kept him apprised of all that was going on in Paris; his long replies to their letters speak only of his own problems and scarcely hint at any occurrences on the artistic scene. Yet exhibitions and other manifestations succeeded each other at an accelerated pace during the year of 1892.

In January Durand-Ruel had opened a complete retrospective of Pissarro's work, assembling seventy-two paintings and gouaches done between 1870 and 1892. The introduction to the catalogue was written by Georges Lecomte; an enthusiastic article by Octave Mirbeau increased the attendance. This exhibition initiated Pissarro's "comeback" after the disfavor into which he had fallen during his divisionist phase. At the close of the show Durand-Ruel himself bought all the unsold paintings.

The following month Monet exhibited in the same gallery his recent series of *Poplar Trees*, which proved once more Monet's growing popularity ("Monet now earns about 100,000 francs a year," Gauguin told his wife). Monet's exhibition was followed in May by a large Renoir retrospective—like Pissarro's, the first of its kind—for which Durand-Ruel had gathered no fewer than one hundred and ten paintings executed over the last twenty years. The success was enormous and now Renoir too was at last hailed as a great painter. The government for the first time purchased one of his canvases and his future patron Gangnat made his initial purchases.

Between the Monet and the Renoir exhibitions Durand-Ruel had opened his galleries in March to the widely heralded Salon of the Rosicrucians. Count Antoine de La Rochefoucauld, financial backer of this venture, later gleefully remembered that the preview was a "real triumph; several ambassadors—among them His Excellency the Ambassador of the United States—honored the opening of our exhibition with their presence.... The crowds were so dense in the rue Le Peletier that the public omnibuses had to be detoured."[26]

In accordance with his strange program the self-styled Sâr Péladan, "Grand Master of the Order," had banned from his show not only all historical, military, and patriotic subjects— "even if well painted"—all humorous, oriental, and illustrative works, but also "all representations of contemporary life, either private or public; portraits unless the sitters are in the costumes of an earlier age and thus achieve style; all rustic scenes, all landscapes except those executed in the manner of Poussin; seascapes and sailors; domestic animals and those used in sports; flowers, fruits, etc." Instead he had pronounced himself in favor of "the Catholic dogma and Italian subjects from Margharitone to Andrea Sacchi; the interpretation of oriental theologies with the exception of those of the yellow races; expressive or decorative

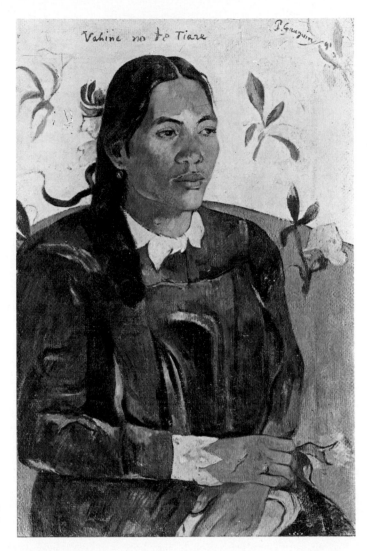

GAUGUIN: *Vahine no te Tiare—Woman with a Flower,* Tahiti, d. 1891. 27¾ x 18¼". Ny Carlsberg Glyptotek, Copenhagen

allegories; the nude exalted in the style of Primaticcio, of Correggio, or expressive heads like those by Leonardo and Michelangelo."[27]

Among the somewhat heterogeneous artists whom the Sâr had assembled were many whose connection with the new mystico-Catholic movement were rather loose and who had rallied mainly because they did not want to miss a well-advertised occasion to present themselves. Indeed, as some observers pointed out, piety not being synonymous with faith, there was a too obvious amount of the former and much less of the latter to be observed among Péladan's followers. On the other hand some of the truly devout Catholics, such as Puvis de Chavannes and Maurice Denis, as well as such real mystics as Redon and Moreau, had preferred not to join the Sâr's eager but somewhat uninspired crowd. The Pont-Aven group was represented by Filiger and Bernard, in both of whom Count de La Rochefoucauld had taken a lively interest and whom he was soon to support.

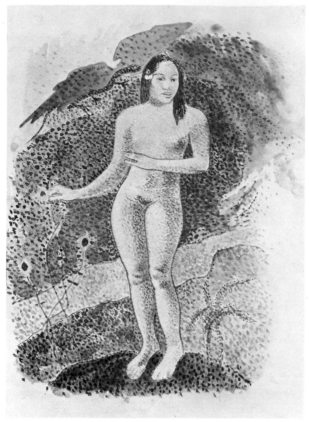

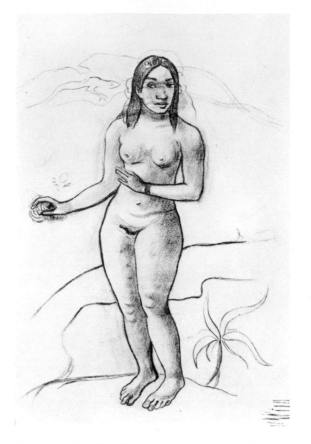

GAUGUIN: *Standing Nude,* Tahiti, 1891–93. Watercolor. Present whereabouts unknown

GAUGUIN: *Standing Nude,* Tahiti, 1891–93. Charcoal, 17½ x 11¼". Present whereabouts unknown

The general aspect of the show was one of insipidity and pallor with strong academic-religious overtones. Although he had been vastly amused by the Sâr's pompous pronouncements, Vallotton thought the exhibition much better and more dignified than he had expected and even said so in an extensive article.[28] But he was almost the only one to support this venture. Félix Fénéon was among the critics who most forcefully castigated the fallacy of the Rosicrucian tendencies: "One will never make the exhibitors understand that a painting must first of all attract through its rhythms, that a painter shows too much humility in choosing a subject which is already rich in literary significance, that three pears on a cloth by Paul Cézanne are moving and sometimes mystical whereas the entire Wagnerian Valhalla, when painted by them, is as uninteresting as the Chamber of Deputies."[29]

In spite of the great noise made about the Rosicrucian show, it was but a minor symptom of the general revival of religious interest, which also manifested itself in the fact that J.-K. Huysmans, author of *A Rebours,* which had heralded the decadent-symbolist movement, retired to a Trappist monastery and there reconverted himself to Catholicism.

Before the Rosicrucians closed their Salon, the Independents opened theirs, which featured an extensive Seurat retrospective. Altogether twenty-seven paintings, nine small wooden

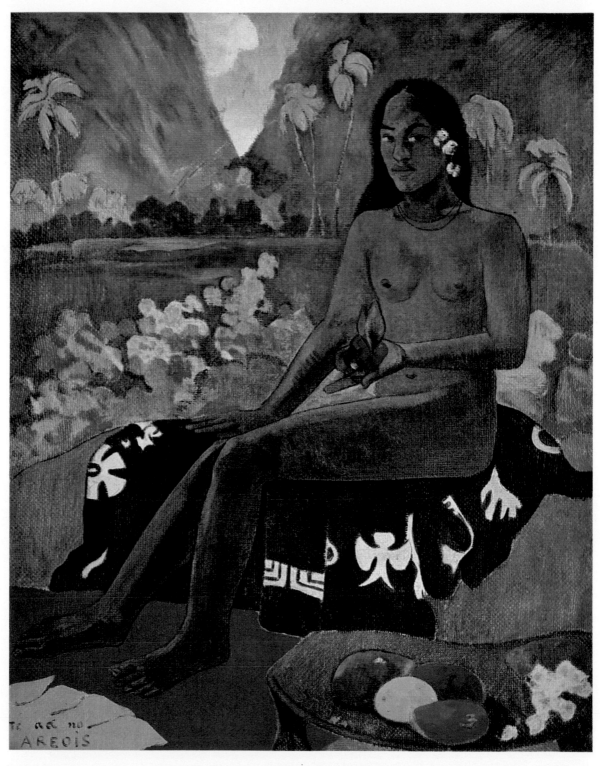

GAUGUIN: *Te aa no Areois—Queen of the Areois,* Tahiti, 1892. 36 x 28½″. Collection Mr. and Mrs. William S. Paley, Manhasset, N.Y.

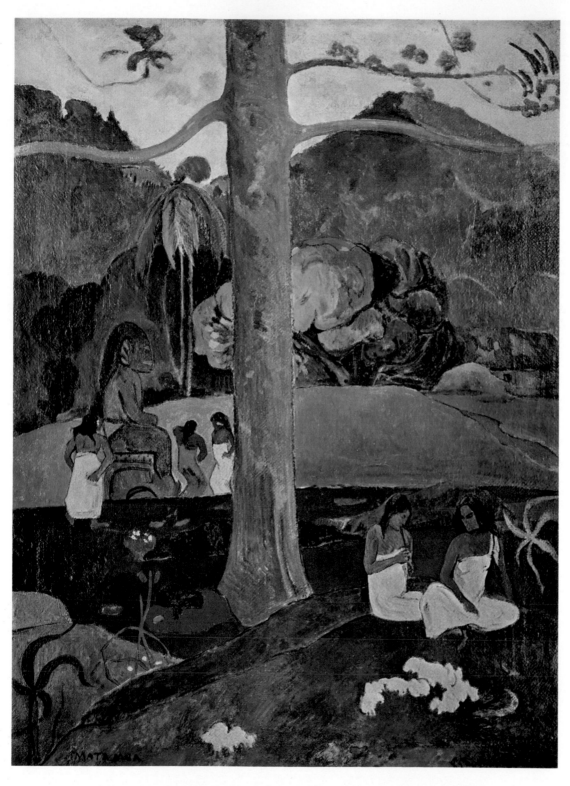

GAUGUIN: *Matamua—In Olden Times,* Tahiti, d. 1892. 36 x 27". Private collection, New York

panels, and ten drawings were shown, most of them lent by the artist's mother. Among the other exhibitors—there were 1,232 entries—were Bernard (with nine works), Bonnard, Cross, Daniel de Monfreid, Denis, Dr. Gachet, Gausson, Lemmen, Luce, Petitjean, Lucien Pissarro, the *douanier* Rousseau (with six canvases), Signac, Lautrec (with seven works, including one poster and several paintings of La Goulue), van Rysselberghe, Verkade, and Willumsen. Denis published in the *Revue Blanche* an article on the Salon des Indépendants, in the course of which he spoke of the artists who "proceed from the theories of M. Emile Bernard which were popularized by the rare talent of M. Gauguin." He particularly termed Anquetin a "victim of M. Emile Bernard, the intolerant intellectual."[30] (On the occasion of his participation in the Rosicrucian exhibition, the critic Roger Marx had already called Bernard "the founder of the so-called Symbolist school," specifying that he was "even before Gauguin, the initiator of that esthetic style which has since been described as symbolist."[31])

In April Bernard finally managed to organize at Le Barc de Boutteville's a small van Gogh

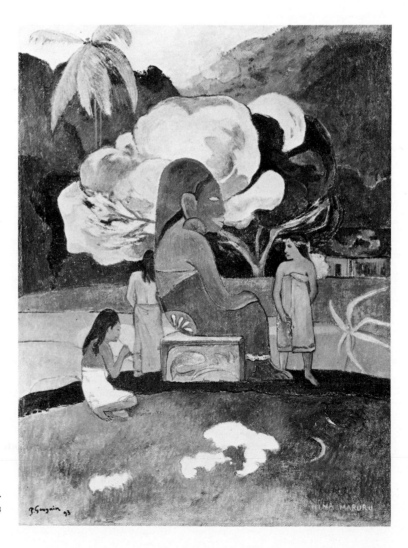

GAUGUIN: *Hina maruru—Thanks to Hina* (the Moon Goddess), Tahiti, d. 1893. 36¾ x 27¼". Present whereabouts unknown

exhibition, comprising sixteen canvases, which apparently attracted little attention. He was upset not to be supported in the press by Mirbeau, Aurier, and others on whose help he had counted.[32] (In February Verkade and Sérusier had visited Theo van Gogh's widow in Bussum, Holland, where Vincent's paintings had greatly excited them; the next year Mme Theo van Gogh-Bonger organized a van Gogh exhibition at the Panorama in Amsterdam.)

Meanwhile in Brussels the XX held another Seurat retrospective composed of seventeen paintings (*Les Poseuses*, owned by Gustave Kahn, *La Parade*, *Le Cirque*, *Woman Powdering Herself*, and a series of landscapes), a dozen small panels, and nine drawings.[33] Among those invited to their 1892 show were Mary Cassatt (color etchings), Maurice Denis, Léo Gausson, Maximilien Luce, Lucien Pissarro (woodcuts), and Toulouse-Lautrec. Signac participated in the exhibition, no longer as a guest but as a member of the group; he showed his *Portrait of Félix Fénéon* (page 105) and a series of seascapes titled *Adagio, Larghetto, Scherzo*, etc. To their tenth exhibition in 1893 the XX again invited Toulouse-Lautrec, together with Emile Bernard, Henri-Edmond Cross, and Hippolyte Petitjean. This was their last show, for Octave Maus, believing that a span of ten years was long enough for an avant-garde effort, invited the members to vote for the dissolution of the group. A majority voted as he desired, feeling that it was better to disband and leave behind the memory of a valiant venture than to see the movement created by them outlive itself. Maus subsequently founded a new organization on an entirely different basis, La Libre Esthétique.[34]

Among the other artistic events of the year 1892 were a Berthe Morisot exhibition at Goupil's and the nomination of Gustave Moreau as professor at the Ecole des Beaux-Arts, a circumstance which was to end his isolation and bring him in contact with the new generation in whose formation he thenceforth took an active part. Renoir spent the summer in Brittany, chiefly at Pont-Aven. In the fall Degas exhibited at Durand-Ruel's a series of landscape pastels; this was to be his last one-man show as he never again consented to put any collection of his works before the public. During November Le Barc de Boutteville assembled another of his group shows of young painters, hanging side by side canvases of several neo-impressionists, paintings by Lautrec, and works by such Nabis as Bonnard, Vuillard, and Denis. He also included a picture by Gauguin, whereas Bernard did not participate in the exhibition.

While the new generation now began to show up more frequently at Le Barc de Boutteville's, it did not abandon *père* Tanguy, who was of course unable to hold exhibitions on his small premises. Since the death of van Gogh and the departure of Gauguin, it appears that the neo-impressionists went there in ever greater numbers and even succeeded in rallying the old man to their cause. A young Danish painter, visiting Paris in 1892, noted in his diary: "The wretched shop of *père* Tanguy seems to be one of the most important places for synthesist and impressionist colors. It is filled with piles of canvases (of which some are without any value), doubtless left in payment for supplies. After having debated for a while with his Xantippe and having tamed her through the purchase of colors which *père* Tanguy grinds in his kitchen, one obtains permission to browse through the stacks of paintings, among which one can discover some excellent things at very modest prices.

"Van Gogh seems to have been an intimate of the house; one can see there several of his canvases, superb Provençal landscapes, a still life of fruit in beautiful colors, and a portrait of old *père* Tanguy, coarsely painted but of remarkable character. There is also a Gauguin portrait against a landscape background which appears to me of little interest. One further finds there fine paintings by Pissarro, Guillaumin, Cézanne, and Sisley who—like Anquetin

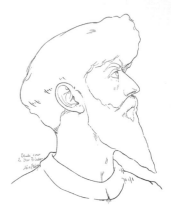

Séon: Study for a *Portrait of Sâr Mérodack Joséphin Péladan*, 1891. Exhibited at the Rosicrucian Salon

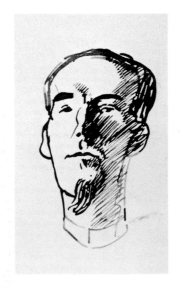

Vallotton: *Portrait of Félix Fénéon*. Pen and ink. Present whereabouts unknown

—seems on the verge of being considered an artist 'arrivé'; in any case, works by these two are now shown at the Champ-de-Mars Salon.

"Also to be seen are several paintings by a very young man who, I believe, will soon be recognized because he shows, in addition to evident talent, pleasant tendencies or, rather, because he avoids the "repulsive" aspect so frequent with the others. His name is Denis.... Among the other young painters one finds Daniel [de Monfreid] with landscapes of fine color, less strong than those of most of the others.... Léo Gausson whose colors are terrible... ; Signac with his unbearable pointillist technique, etc.

"The greater part of Tanguy's stock makes one's hair stand on end. What strikes most, however, is not any lack of talent but rather the conscious and deliberate pursuit of ugliness in the combination of colors as well as in execution. These young people are strangely doctrinaire in their multiple pseudo-scientific theories about art. They quote Chevreul and innumerable chemists or opticians, and are full of pity for those who do not understand spectral analysis.

"It is an amusing experience to buy pigments from Tanguy. When I picked one of my favorite colors—one of those that is not on the chromo-luminarist menu—he jumped as though stung by a scorpion and, in a fatherly way, advised me to give it up, not because it was less good then the others but because to use it was against the catechism."[35]

In December the neo-impressionists organized a show of their own in which practically all the members of the movement participated. That same month an artistic "scandal" shook Berlin and was reported in the *Mercure de France*: the exhibition of a young Norwegian "impressionist," Edvard Munch (who actually owed a great deal to Gauguin), so exasperated the public that his paintings had to be removed after a few days.

The political scene, meanwhile, was not less animated. The anarchists increased their activity. Bomb explosions succeeded each other. One of the leaders, Ravachol, was finally arrested, confessed his misdeeds and was executed, while anarchist outrages continued.[36] The terror was so great that, according to a chronicler, for several weeks Paris presented "the aspect of a besieged city: the streets are deserted, shops closed, omnibuses without passengers, museums and theaters barricaded; the police are invisible though present everywhere, troops in the suburbs are ready to march at the first signal. The families of rich foreigners leave, the hotels are empty, receipts of the stores dwindle...."[37] Things were not helped by the threat of a cholera epidemic in July and by the revelation of grave irregularities in the administration of the Panama Company in which many leading political figures were implicated and which caused the government to resign.

Of course all this had little bearing on Gauguin's life in Tahiti, though his own constant difficulties might have been lessened had the general situation not been so troubled. There was one event, however, which directly concerned him, although he learned about it with some delay since Morice neglected to keep him informed, as promised. In April 1892 appeared Aurier's long article, "Les Symbolistes," accompanied by numerous illustrations of works by Redon, Bonnard, Bernard, Gauguin, Sérusier, Denis, Vuillard, Anquetin, etc. It was apparently Gauguin's wife who first mentioned the publication to him, and he immediately replied: "I know Aurier and I imagine that he gives me a little share in his article. It was I who created this movement in painting and many young people are benefiting from it; they are not *without talent* but just the same it was I who formed them. Nothing of what they do derives from them; it comes from me."[21]

While Aurier did not go quite so far in his writing, he did insist on Gauguin's leadership.

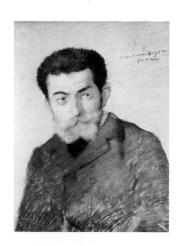

FORAIN: *Portrait of Joris-Karl Huysmans*. Pastel, 21¾ x 17½". Musée de Versailles

His article started out with a theoretical essay on art in general and symbolism in particular, covering much the same ground already covered in his study on Gauguin. He now came forth with a definition of a work of art as "a translation into a special and natural language of an intellectual idea of variable value which, in its slightest form, is a fragment of the artist's intellect and in its highest achievement represents the entire intellect of the artist in addition to the essential spirit of various objects. A complete work of art is thus *a new creation*, which one could call absolutely *alive*, since it has a soul that animates it, which is actually the synthesis of two souls: the soul of the artist and the soul of nature."[38] This was an elaborate extension of Zola's famous definition, inspired by the works of Courbet and the early endeavors of the impressionists: "A work of art is a bit of Nature seen through the eyes of a temperament." Aurier did not take into account the concept formulated by Maurice Denis in an article published in 1890: "It must be remembered that any painting—before being a war horse, a nude woman, or some anecdote—is essentially a flat surface covered with colors arranged in a certain order."[39]

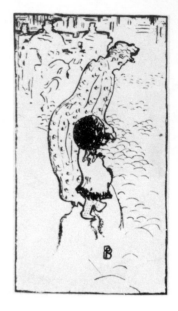

BONNARD: *In the Street.* Drawing. Reproduced in Aurier's article, 1892.

Having established the premises of his concepts, Aurier went on to discuss the works and stature of the various adherents to symbolism. "The uncontested initiator of this artistic movement—perhaps some day one may call it a renaissance—was Paul Gauguin. At the same time painter, sculptor in wood, ornamentalist, potter, he has been one of the first to affirm explicitly the need for a simplification of modes of expression, the legitimacy of a search for effects other than the servile imitation indulged in by the materialists, the right of the artist to concern himself with the spiritual and the intangible. His well-known pictorial output is already considerable. It is stamped with a profound and highly idealistic philosophy expressed through elementary means which have particularly perturbed the public and the critics. One might almost say that his work is the equivalent of Plato plastically interpreted by a savage of genius. Indeed, there are in Gauguin elements of the savage, the primitive, the Indian who, by sheer instinct, carves in ebony strange and marvelous dreams, much more disturbing than the banal reveries of the licensed masters of our academies! . . . And no doubt it was because he was vaguely conscious of this that he decided to leave our ugly civilization far behind, exiling himself to those distant and bewitching islands which have not yet been polluted by European factories, this virgin nature of barbaric and splendid Tahiti whence he will bring back, we can safely predict, new, superb, and singular works such as the anemic and senile brain of a contemporary Aryan can no longer conceive.

"Next to Gauguin one should immediately name his friend and, if not his pupil, at least his fervent admirer: Vincent van Gogh, that extreme and sublimely unbalanced artist who, alas, died too young to have left the work promised us by his genius, his powerful originality, his mad passion to create, his feverish researches, his high-minded and multiple preoccupations, but who, just the same, lived long enough to bequeath to the museum of our admirations a thousand canvases of a blinding intensity, of an unforgettable strangeness, flashing symbols of the most tormented soul that ever was.

"One should mention here also, among the bearers of the glad tidings which the young like to invoke, still another artist just as original, as profoundly idealistic, but even stranger and more terrifying, who, through his haughty disdain for materialistic imitation, through his love of dreams and of the spiritual, has acted—if not as immediately as the foregoing, at least indirectly—upon the orientation of the new artistic souls of today: Odilon Redon, whose lithographs are nightmares. His work is terrible and vertiginous, the work of a poet and a philosopher. . . . The finger of this artist seems to tear apart the veil of all the mysteries around us... and his mouth seems to cry that the result of all human science, of all thought is a shudder of fear in the infinity of the night.

"Maybe it is necessary also, in order to be complete and just, to mention the impressionists and neo-impressionists whose preoccupation with an individualistic style—subjective, instantaneous, based on sensations—and whose technical researches were certainly not without influence upon the artistic evolution we are studying here; maybe one should speak here of Degas, of Cézanne, of Monet, of Sisley, of Pissarro, of Renoir and of their efforts to achieve an expressive synthesis; of the unfortunate Seurat and his science—so sterile in itself—of decomposing light and of establishing linear rhythms; of Anquetin and his experiments in Japanese style, in *cloisonnisme*, in simplification of color and design. ...

"Let it suffice to mention, after the great names already quoted, those of some young people who, though they have not yet emerged from the period of gropings and trials, though they have not yet produced complete and definitive works, are nevertheless highly interesting for the zeal, enthusiasm and intelligence with which they prepare the hoped-for restoration of spirituality in art.

"First there is Paul Sérusier. Restricted for a time to an almost slavish imitation of Gauguin, he did not wait long to free his own personality; and his recent canvases of a poetic symbolism, of a beautiful and masterly synthesis of lines and colors indicate an artist of the first rank.

"Then there is Emile Bernard. [This was the first time that Albert Aurier, at long last, mentioned his former friend; and what he had to say about him was not likely to satisfy the latter completely.] He was, in spite of his extreme youth, one of the first to react with Gauguin against the complicated technique of the impressionists [meaning probably *neo-impressionists*]. His seems to be a very curious and artistic mind, very alert and too versatile, lacking reflection, perseverance, and direction in his researches. Once he finds his definite course, once he realizes that beauty of form is not a negligible element in art, once he gives up the too adroit clumsiness, the artful naïveté which enchant him, he will paint truly magnificent canvases, for his soul is that of a poet and his fingers are those of a real painter."[38]

Aurier then went on to discuss the "mystico-Catholic" artists of the new generation, such as Filiger and Denis; he spoke of Roussel, still under the influence of Puvis de Chavannes, of Ranson and of Bonnard, "a delightful ornamentalist, as skillful and resourceful as a Japanese and capable of embellishing all the ugly things of our life with the ingenious and iridescent flowerings of his imagination." Nor did Aurier forget Vuillard, "a rare colorist full of charm and improvisation, a poet able to communicate—not without some irony—the mellow emotions of life, the tenderness of intimate interiors."[38]

But in spite of Aurier's endeavor to extol Gauguin's genius, the painter's affairs in Paris went from bad to worse. In December 1892 the dealer Portier returned to Daniel de Monfreid his entire "stock" of Gauguin's works. "The paintings by Gauguin which I am sending back to you have been seen again and again, ever since I received them, at my place, by all my clients. It is thus quite useless for me to keep them any longer. When I return [from two or three months' absence], if you have other things of Gauguin's, I shall see whether there are any that might be more salable than those I am now returning.... I had ten paintings by Gauguin, of which I have already given back three that Mme Gauguin took to Copenhagen."[40] And in March of the following year Maurice Joyant of the Goupil Galleries, with whom de Monfreid had deposited ten paintings and five ceramics by Gauguin in January 1892, wrote a similar letter to de Monfreid: "As had been agreed, I am sending you all the canvases and

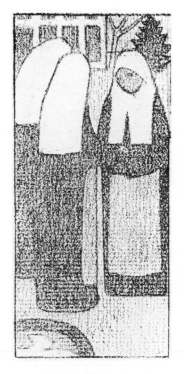

DENIS: Illustration for "Sagesse" by Verlaine, 1891. Lithograph. Reproduced in Aurier's article, 1892

ceramics by Gauguin that I have, consigned either by you or by Gauguin himself, which have not been shipped to Mme Gauguin in Copenhagen." (There follows a list of eleven paintings, six gouaches, one pastel, two wood sculptures—one of these the bas-relief *Be in Love*, reproduced page 410—nine potteries and one faïence sculpture.)[41]

But Gauguin had not waited for these new reverses. Things were already so grim during the summer of 1892, with no money arriving from France—not even a letter from Morice—that he had decided to apply for repatriation, for which he could ask only after a sojourn of more than one year abroad. Thus on June 12, 1892, Gauguin wrote to the Director of Fine Arts in Paris: "At my request you were kind enough to entrust me with a mission in Tahiti, to study the customs and scenery of the island. I hope that upon my return you will judge my works favorably. But no matter how economical one is, life in Tahiti is very expensive and the voyage very costly. I therefore have the honor to request that I be repatriated, and rely on your benevolence to make my return to France possible."[42]

It took the government a very long time to act upon Gauguin's application; meanwhile he was left once more to his own devices. While every month he hoped to hear from the governor that he could leave, and while he thus lived in continual suspense, always ready to pack his few belongings and to embark for France, he nevertheless continued to work. Besides, what else could he do? In July, however, his stock of canvas gave out and he had to stop painting. He then occupied himself with sculpture and in August was lucky enough to sell two of his

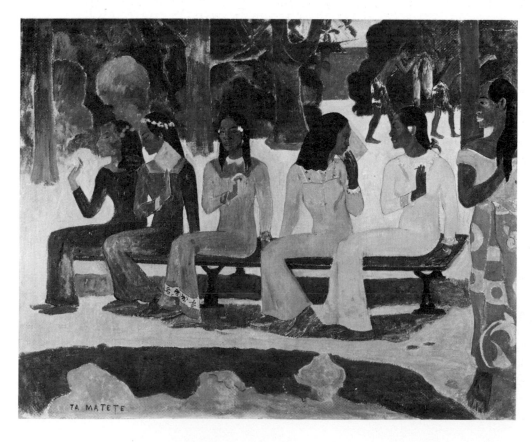

GAUGUIN: *Ta Matete—The Market*, Tahiti, d. 1892. 28¾ x 36¼". Kunstmuseum, Basel (Gift of Dr. Robert von Hirsch)

484

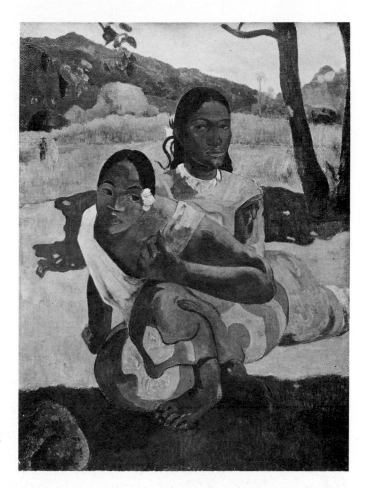

GAUGUIN: *Nafea Faaipoipo—When Will You Marry?*
Tahiti, d. 1892. 40 x 30½". Collection Rudolf Staechelin, deposited with the Kunstmuseum, Basel

wood statuettes (or bas-reliefs) for 300 francs in Papeete. This unexpected transaction was the more surprising as Gauguin was by no means well liked by the French settlers, some of whom had grown extremely wealthy by trading with the natives cheap European products for pearls and other valuables. In their eyes the painter was an intruder who preferred to live with the Tahitians rather than lead the more conventional existence of the colonists. They were never to forget what a "coarse, boastful, surly" fellow he was, how "disagreeable and how crazy, how indecently he treated all of us old residents who tried to befriend him."[43] Indeed, Gauguin did not hesitate to express his contempt for his countrymen in Papeete, but that did not mean that he was not trying to sell them some of his works.

In the fall, while he was still waiting for remittances from France or for a decision from the governor, Gauguin informed de Monfreid: "Soon I shall be a father again, in Oceania. Good Heavens! I can't help sowing my seed everywhere. It is true that this is no inconvenience here where children are well received and claimed in advance by all relatives. Everybody wants to be foster father or foster mother. For you know that in Tahiti the best present one can make is a child. Thus I don't have to worry about the fate of this one."[44]

If Gauguin did not have to worry about his new offspring, he had enough worries about himself. In November he wrote his wife: "I am growing old, and rapidly at that [he was in his forty-fifth year]. As a result of being deprived of nourishment, my stomach is in a terrible condition and I am losing weight every day. Yet I must continue the struggle, always and always. And the fault lies with society. You have no confidence in the future, but I have *because I want to.* Otherwise I would have knocked my brains out long ago. To hope almost means to live. And I must live so as to do my duty until the very end, which I can do only by straining illusions, by creating expectations in my daydreams. While every day here I eat *my piece of dry bread* with a glass of water, I manage through sheer will to believe that it is a beefsteak."[45]

It was apparently with the same bitter determination that Gauguin carried on his work, that he "did his duty" as he said. Inspired possibly by Moerenhout's writings he painted several landscape scenes with native figures gathered around a huge and clumsy idol, Hina the Moon Goddess. One he called *Matamua—In Olden Times* (page 478). It exhales a strong exotic flavor and combines in its idyllic setting a distant kinship with Puvis de Chavannes'

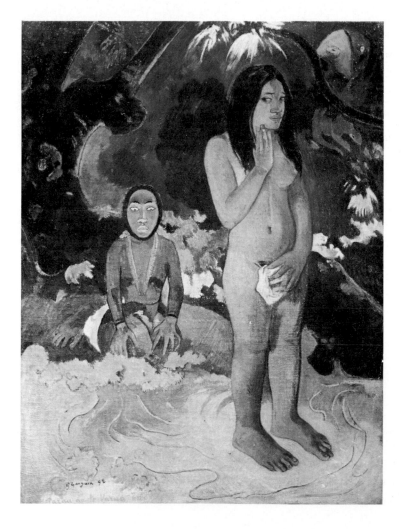

GAUGUIN: *Parau na te Varua ino—Talk about the Evil Spirit,* Tahiti, d. 1892. 37 x 27½". National Gallery of Art, Washington, D.C. (Gift of W. Averell Harriman Foundation in memory of Marie N. Harriman)

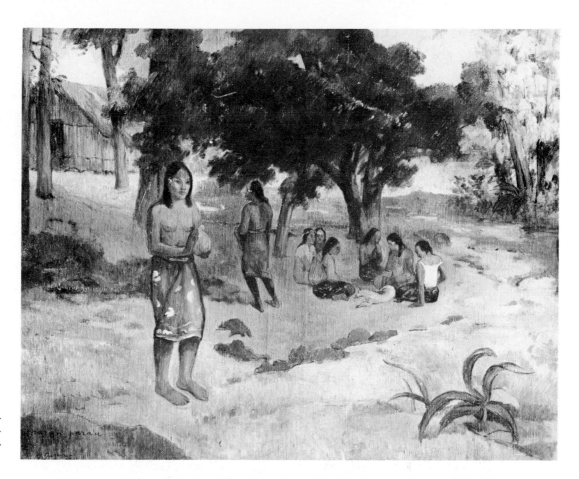

GAUGUIN: *Parau parau—Conversation*, Tahiti, d. 1892. 30 x 38″. Collection Mr. and Mrs. John Hay Whitney, New York

Elysian scenes and Redon's colorful dreams. In no way does it betray its author's anxieties and worries as it unfolds a vision of a tropical paradise. "In order to explain my Tahitian art," Gauguin later wrote, "since it is held to be incomprehensible: as I want to suggest an exuberant and wild nature and a tropical sun which sets on fire everything around it, I have to give my figures an appropriate frame. It really is open-air life, although intimate; in the thickets and the shaded brooks, those whispering women in an immense palace decorated by nature itself with all the riches Tahiti holds. Hence these fabulous colors and this fiery yet softened and silent air.

"But all this does not exist!

"Yes, it exists as the equivalent of the grandeur and profundity of this mystery of Tahiti, when it must be expressed on a canvas one meter square."[46]

On some occasions Gauguin's endeavor to find plastic equivalents for the mysteries of Tahiti inspired him to elaborate compositions in which each detail had a precise though not always obvious significance. One night upon his late return from Papeete he found Tehura waiting for him on their bed, stretched out on her stomach, her eyes widened by the fear of darkness. He discovered in this scene a subject for one of his most important paintings done in Tahiti, a painting whose symbolic character he described repeatedly and at great length:

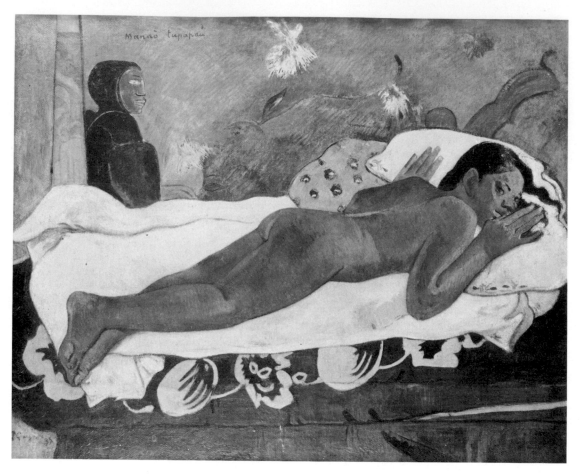

GAUGUIN: *Manao Tupapau—The Spirit of the Dead Watches,* Tahiti, d. 1892. 28⅝ x 36⅜". Albright-Knox Art Gallery, Buffalo (A. Conger Goodyear Collection)

"I painted a nude of a young girl," he wrote to his wife. "In that position, a trifle can make it indecent. And yet I wanted her that way, the lines and the action interested me. A European girl would be embarrassed to be found in that position; the women here not at all. I gave her face a somewhat frightened expression. This fright must be pretended, if not explained, and this in the character of the person—a Tahitian. These people by tradition are very much afraid of the spirits of the dead. I had to explain her fears with a minimum of literary means, unlike the way it was done in the past. To achieve this, the general harmony is somber, sad, frightening, sounding to the eye like a death knell: violet, dark blue, and orange-yellow. I made the linen greenish yellow, first because the linen of these savages is different from ours (it is made of beaten bark); secondly because it produces and suggests artificial light (the Tahitian women never go to bed in the dark), and yet I did not want any effect of lamplight (it's common); third because the yellow which connects the orange-yellow and the blue completes the musical harmony. There are some flowers in the background but, being imagined, they must not be real; I made them resemble sparks. The Polynesians believe that the phosphorescences of the night are the spirits of the dead. They believe in them and dread them. Finally, I made the ghost very simply like a small, harmless woman, because the girl can only see the spirit of the dead linked with the dead person, that is, a human being like herself."[47]

On the upper left side of the canvas Gauguin, as usual, inscribed the Tahitian title: *Manao Tupapau*. These words, according to his notes, have two meanings; either "She thinks of the spirit of the dead," or "The spirit of the dead remembers her." And he thus summed up what he had attempted to achieve in this composition: "The musical part: undulating horizontal lines, harmonies of orange and blue brought together by yellows and purples, their derivatives, which are lighted by greenish sparks. The literary part: the spirit of a living soul united with the spirit of the dead. Day and Night."[48]

As the symbolist poets had striven to clothe their ideas in a sensitive form, as they had searched for an archetypal and complex style, for mysterious ellipses and a personal vocabulary, as they had proclaimed their intention to place the development of the symbol in outright dreams, so Gauguin now endeavored to compose a personal vocabulary of colors and lines, a complex style which, coupled with a predilection for dreams, permitted him to attain a pictorial symbolism of a new kind. Based on elements derived from the island lore, haunted by things observed but reaching far beyond them, combined with the suggestive power and meaning of lines and colors, guided by the desire to simplify while never pushing abstractions beyond the recognizable, this symbolism was much more profound, more truly mystic than that of his more obvious religious compositions done in Brittany. It was thus in contact with the South Seas, with an entirely new and mysterious world untouched by European preoccupations, that Gauguin not only returned to savagery, as he called it, but also achieved a style for which the groundwork had been laid in the highly sophisticated circle of his literary friends in Paris.

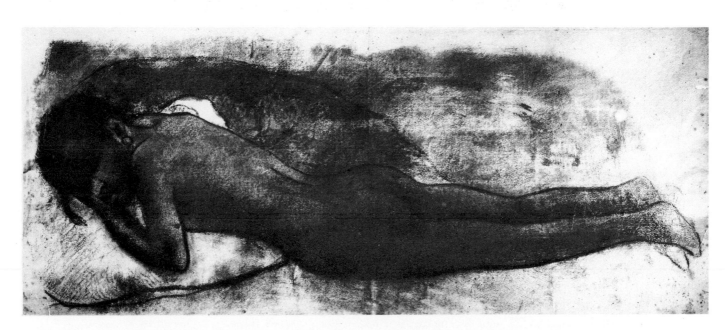

GAUGUIN: *Reclining Nude,* study for *The Spirit of the Dead Watches,* Tahiti, 1892. Charcoal. Present whereabouts unknown

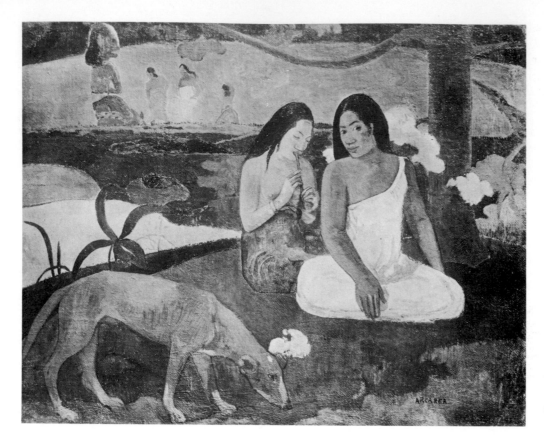

GAUGUIN: *Arearea—Joyousness,* Tahiti, 1892. 29½ × 37″. Musée du Louvre, Paris

If Gauguin may have thought of Mallarmé and his followers when he explained his picture of *Manao Tupapau*, he may likewise have remembered Redon while he painted it. Indeed, the enigmatic profile of the spirit of the dead and the sparkling flowers of the background are elements which have a certain resemblance to the apparitions of Redon's imaginary universe. Gauguin did think of Mallarmé, for he sent him a wood sculpture, a profile of a Tahitian,[49] and he also sent a drawing to Mirbeau, considering it advisable to maintain his connections with such a useful man. On the other hand Gauguin apparently neglected to send Aurier any souvenir from his exile, possibly because he felt certain of his continued and devoted support.

Among the other works which Gauguin executed before the end of the year were two compositions of a predominantly decorative character with Polynesian women and dogs beneath an ornamental tree. Here some of the flat patterns and sinuous forms appear like a continuation of the search for stylization that had manifested itself in the *Loss of Virginity*. The first of these two canvases he called *Arearea* (Joyousness), the second has—exceptionally— a French title, because he could find no Polynesian expression for its subject: *Pastorales Tahitiennes*. This last painting, with which he was particularly pleased, was completed late in December and he decided to celebrate the event by postdating it 1893.

The last weeks of 1892 were once more filled with expectations as Gauguin hoped to be able to leave in January. Through a naval officer he sent Daniel de Monfreid eight important

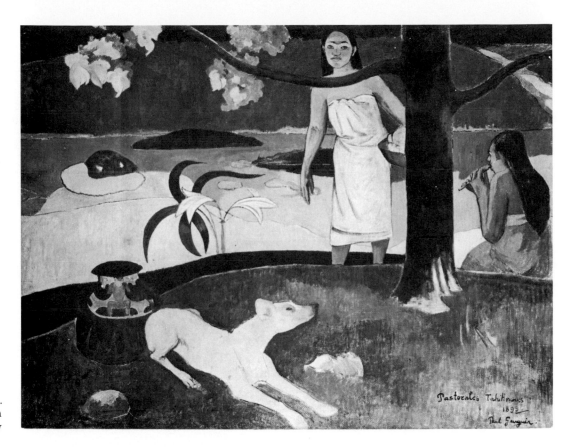

GAUGUIN: *Pastorales Tahitiennes*, Dec. 1892, d. 1893. 33⅞ x 40½". Pushkin State Museum of Fine Arts, Moscow

canvases[50] and advised his wife that she could choose some of these, insisting that she put the proceeds aside for his imminent return to France. He fixed the prices at from 600 to 800 francs, with the exception of *Manao Tupapau*, which he did not care to sell at all, at least not for under 1,500–2,000 francs. Altogether the shipment represented about 6,000 francs while by the end of December Gauguin's cash reserve was down to 50 francs, and there was no relief in sight. He was profoundly discouraged and wrote de Monfreid that he again felt his health declining and considered giving up painting altogether after his return to France. Meanwhile Sérusier made every effort in Paris to hasten Gauguin's departure. But it became clear that he could not count on leaving in January and he now began to think of April as the most likely date.

In January Gauguin's wife sent him 100 francs (she had sold 850 francs' worth of his paintings but needed the money herself). In February the painter wrote to Copenhagen that his eyesight was failing and that, during the last two months, he had not been able to spend any money on food and had subsisted on breadfruit and water. He thought of de Haan whose company he would now have appreciated; he even thought of Schuffenecker who, he felt, would have done well to send him the fare. What filled him with boiling anger was that he learned from Daniel de Monfreid that almost two years before, in May 1891, shortly after his departure from Paris, Joyant had turned over to Charles Morice the balance of Gauguin's account at Goupil's, 850 francs, the painter's share of sales totaling 1,100 francs. Gauguin was truly incensed and helplessly railed at Morice, who thus owed him altogether 1,350 francs, an amount which, he said, would have saved his life. "God, how enraged I am!" he exclaimed. "And it is even my fury that sustains me."[51] He would know how to deal with Morice upon his return!

It was in February 1893 that Gauguin received the bad news of Aurier's death. During his vacations in the South of France, in the course of which he had met Signac in Marseilles (whither he had sailed on his boat from Brittany), Aurier had been stricken with typhoid fever but had refused to see a doctor, being cared for instead by some medical students among his friends. In October 1892 he succumbed, at the age of twenty-seven. His death was a severe blow to Gauguin, coming as it did less than two years after the death of Theo van Gogh, of whom the painter thought frequently in Tahiti as the only man who might have really defended his interests during his absence. "We certainly have bad luck," he wrote to de Monfreid; "[Theo] van Gogh, then Aurier, the only critic who understood us well and who would some day have been very useful to us."[51] This seems to be an understatement, as Aurier, in fact, had already been the author of the first comprehensive article on Gauguin and had seized every opportunity to speak of his admiration for his friend. Among the small collection which Aurier left to his family were a group of important paintings by van Gogh, mostly gifts but possibly also purchases, and but one early canvas by Gauguin, dating from 1885.[52]

Shortly before his death Aurier had returned to Theo van Gogh's widow, at her request, the letters of Vincent van Gogh which he had obtained from the painter's brother. Theo's widow had begun to classify the letters herself with a view to their publication. Meanwhile Emile Bernard, who in 1893 went to Italy, thanks to subsidies from Count Antoine de La Rochefoucauld, prepared for the *Mercure de France* the publication of the letters he himself had received from Vincent van Gogh, followed by a choice of letters to Theo obviously communicated by Mme Theo van Gogh-Bonger.[53] Thus, in spite of Aurier's death, van Gogh's fascinating and beautiful letters slowly began to be made public and immediately aroused interest.

At the *Mercure de France* Aurier was succeeded by Camille Mauclair, another young hopeful from Mallarmé's entourage, who soon used his art column to exercise his youthful arrogance at the expense of Gauguin, Lautrec, Pissarro, Cézanne, etc. His vicious attacks against all new tendencies were hardly redeemed by his adulation for Monet and his enthusiasm for such minor men as Carrière, de Groux, or Hodler. His uncomprehending and indeed hostile position made all the more regrettable the untimely death of Aurier, under whom the *Mercure de France* had promised to become the leading organ of the artistic avant-garde.

To compensate for the blow Gauguin received through Aurier's death, the only encouraging news of those months was contained in a letter from Joyant: "You can't imagine how the attitude of people has changed and how all your group has come to the fore."[54] But this was meager consolation to a man who, thousands of miles from Paris, was desperately struggling for his life and work.

It seems a miracle that Gauguin, under these circumstances, was able to carry on with his painting. Nevertheless he did, and among his canvases of Tahiti are several important ones bearing the date of 1893 (though it is conceivable that some of these may have been done or at least finished in France). After *Pastorales Tahitiennes*, painted at the close of 1892, Gauguin did a modified version of *Matamua*, called *Hina Maruru* (The Feast of Hina, the Moon Goddess, page 479), and an enigmatic composition, *Hina Tefatou* (The Moon Goddess Hina and the Earth Genie Fatu), somber in color with strong accents of red (page 495).

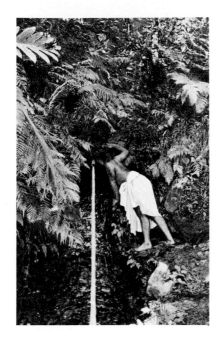

Above: Photograph of Tahitian drinking from a waterfall

Right: GAUGUIN: *Tahitian Drinking from a Waterfall*, c. 1893. Watercolor, 12½ x 8½". The Art Institute of Chicago (Gift of Mrs. Emily Crane Chadbourne). Study for the painting *Pape moe—Mysterious Water*, inspired by photograph

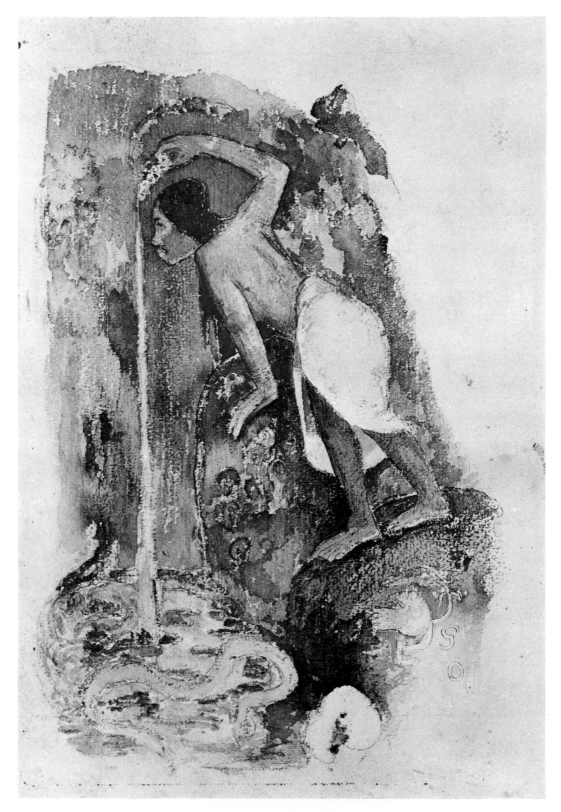

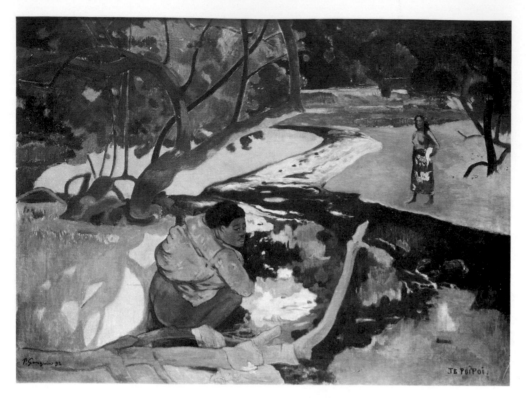

GAUGUIN: *Te Poipoi—Early Morning,*
Tahiti, d. 1892. 27 x 36¼". Collection Mr.
and Mrs. Henry B. Middleton, Amado,
Arizona

In other paintings, such as *Siesta*, Gauguin seems to depict the life of the natives with a snapshotlike directness and a flair for natural poses as if he had surprised his models unobserved. Yet the power of his colors, the contrast between intense and uniform areas and delicately brushed sections (such as the landscape background) achieve not only an extraordinary impression of heat and rest, they also confer upon his composition a static and forceful quality that transcends the instant observed. As in his more abstract canvases of studied attitudes and carefully balanced elements, Gauguin recorded the life around him with an eye for the permanent and the significant even when he was not concerned with features of symbolic meaning. Sometimes he actually used photographs for inspiration.

But in April Gauguin wrote wearily to de Monfreid: "For two months I haven't done any actual work; I am satisfied with observing, thinking, and taking notes. During a sojourn of two years, of which several months were lost, I shall have produced sixty-six more or less good paintings and several extremely savage sculptures. That's enough for one man."[55]

In March Gauguin had received 300 francs from the faithful de Monfreid. By now he was determined to leave on May 1, no matter what happened, and had found somebody in Papeete willing to lend him money, for which Gauguin agreed to pay interest and to leave a certain number of paintings as security. A few weeks later he received from Mette Gauguin 700 francs which, had they reached him sooner, he wrote, would have enabled him to go to the Marquesas where he had hoped to find an even more primitive life. But at least he was now in a position to pay his debts and his fare. He finally sailed on June 14 via Sidney for Marseilles, leaving Tehura behind.

494

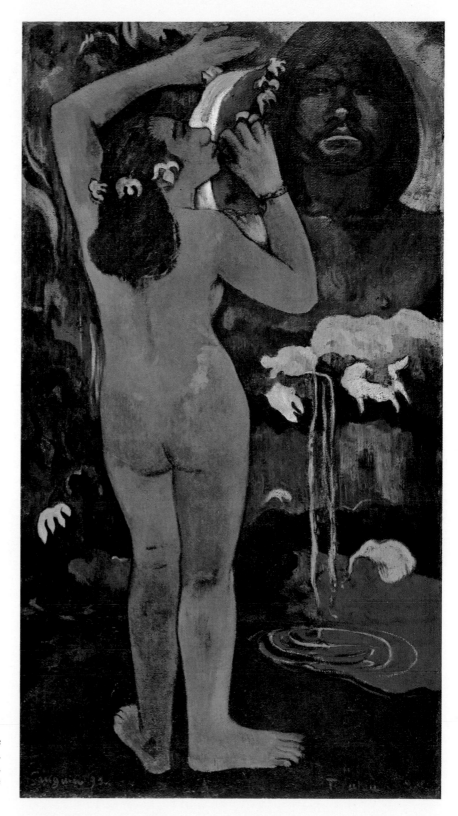

GAUGUIN: *Hina Tefatou—The Moon Goddess
Hina and the Earth Genie Fatu,* Tahiti, d. 1893.
45 x 24½″. Formerly collection Edgar Degas.
The Museum of Modern Art, New York (Lillie
P. Bliss Collection)

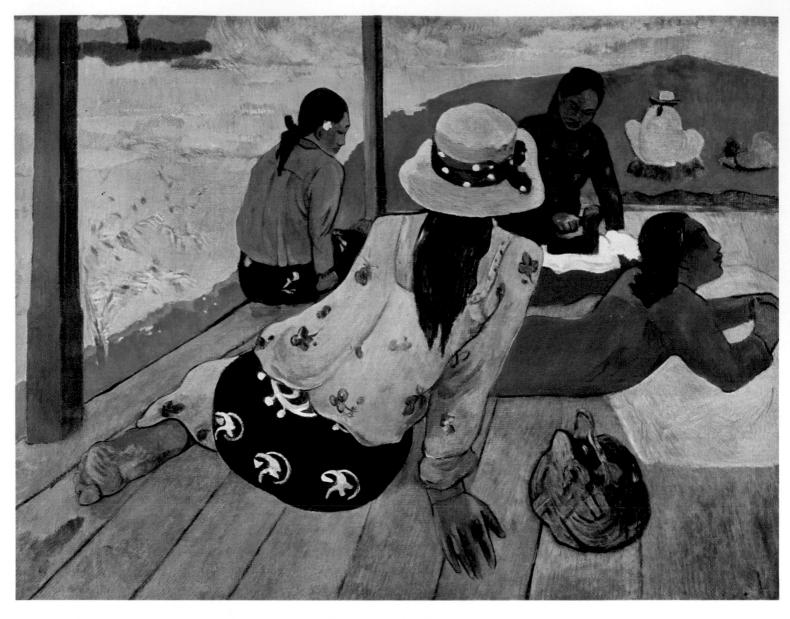

GAUGUIN: *Siesta, Tahiti,* c. 1893. 35 x 45¾". Collection Mrs. Enid A. Haupt, New York

Exactly two years after Gauguin had landed in Papeete with visions of conquest and happiness he thus departed, vanquished and penniless, his sole "booty" a series of more or less unsalable paintings and sculptures. He had left Paris in 1891 after what he himself liked to call a minor triumph: a press campaign in his favor, a successful auction, a banquet in his honor by his admiring friends. He had undertaken to circle half the globe in quest of the promised land, the Tahitian paradise whose happy inhabitants, as he had put it, "know only the sweet aspects of life," an enchanted place where one could live "almost without money." He had hoped to leave corrupt Europe far behind, to escape the "kingdom of gold," but he had discovered only too soon that even under a tropical sun, in a hut beneath palm trees, worries about money would not release him from their merciless grip. If he had found happiness in Tahiti, he had also known there the bitter feeling of being abandoned, far from the sources of his meager income, depending on the good will of friends who had a vexatious tendency to forget him. He had been sick and lonely, powerless to break a chain of mischance that persisted in following him around the earth. While he was not broken yet and still continued to hope for better days, he had to admit to himself and even to others that his trip to the South Seas had ended in failure.

But his stature as an artist had grown tremendously. At least in this respect his flight from civilization had reaped results perhaps more far-reaching than he realized. He had found himself in the tropics, had ended a long period of gestation and groping, had established the basis for a new, powerful, and original style that was to set him apart among all the painters of his time. Yet as he prepared to leave Tahiti, burdened with the weight of canvases and sculptures that he had produced in spite of all his misfortunes, he was doubtful even regarding his works. "Today," he wrote to Daniel de Monfreid, "a young group *that follows me* is active and successful, they say. As these people are much younger, disposed of more trump cards and of more cleverness, I may be crushed on the way. To save myself I count on this new phase of Tahiti; it will create a diversion from my studies of Brittany and thus it will yet take the others some time to follow me in this direction."[54]

It was with these somewhat gloomy thoughts that Gauguin drew near to France. After a difficult voyage during which several passengers died of heat in the Red Sea, he arrived in Marseilles on August 30, 1893, with exactly four francs in his pocket, just enough to wire de Monfreid and ask for help. But the latter, absent from Paris, had already approached Sérusier who had managed to raise 250 francs and deposited them in Gauguin's name in a Marseilles bank. Thus the painter was able to go to Paris where he stayed in de Monfreid's studio.

An agitated and strange span of Gauguin's life had come to an end; a new one, not less eventful, lay before him. This would bring him again in contact with the Nabis whom he persisted in calling his "followers" but who meanwhile had come into their own. It harbored new disappointments but also new successes, new accomplishments and new setbacks, new adventures and more sufferings. He was to make new acquaintances in Paris and eventually to meet a young art dealer, Ambroise Vollard, whose emergence coincided with Tanguy's death. In 1895 Vollard succeeded in tearing Cézanne away from his stubborn isolation and thus practically inaugurated a new era in the history of modern art. Indeed, Gauguin returned to Paris at a time when it was no less teeming with new events and tendencies than it had been eight years before, when Vincent van Gogh had arrived there to find his way. Paris had lost none of its vitality, its attraction, its contradiction; it was still the place where all the great battles of art were fought. Gauguin plunged once more into the exciting atmosphere of Paris and steeled himself for the endless struggle ahead.

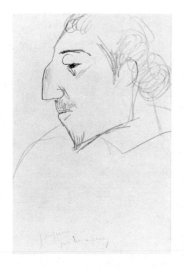

GAUGUIN: *Self-Portrait*, Tahiti, 1891–93. Pencil, 6½ x 4¼". Collection Walter P. Chrysler, Jr., New York

1 R. L. Stevenson: In the South Seas (1888–89), New York 1905, pp. 5–6.

2 Gauguin to his wife, [Tahiti, end of July 1891]; see Lettres de Gauguin à sa femme et à ses amis, Paris, 1946, no. CXXVI, pp. 218–19.

3 P. Gauguin: Noa-Noa, édition définitive, Paris, 1929, p. 46.

4 Stevenson, op. cit., pp. 11 and 10.

5 Gauguin, Noa-Noa, op. cit., p. 62.

6 Ibid., pp. 41–42.

7 Gauguin to D. de Monfreid, [Tahiti], Nov. 7, 1891; see Lettres de Gauguin à Daniel de Monfreid, Paris, 1950, no. II, p. 52.

8 Gauguin to P. Sérusier, [Tahiti], Nov. 1891; see P. Sérusier: ABC de la peinture—Correspondance, Paris, 1950, pp. 53–54.

9 G. A. A. [Aurier]: Choses d'art, Mercure de France, Feb. 1892.

10 Redon was so touched at having been mentioned by Bernard that he immediately wrote to thank him. As for Bernard's sister, who was then twenty-one years old and as mystically inclined and exalted as her brother, she wrote him at length to calm his apparently still burning resentment against Gauguin: "Why all this rage against those who offend your integrity and your personal ideas? Remain in possession of yourself while repressing these revolts which have their source in your passions although they seem well founded; work in quiet, lead a pure life free from those preoccupations with others which only result in anger, contempt or hate. We should only concern ourselves with our brethren in order to help them towards the good; we should excuse their faults and neither judge nor condemn them. I have an unshaken conviction which is that, despite everything, your artistic merit will make its way, that it will be recognized and appreciated by the seekers of beauty and the admirers of a pure ideal, expressed with faith and beauty. Leave behind those who are avid for propaganda and popularity; they have nothing to call their own; they seek the ever changing public as a prop but will eventually and forcibly be left behind, alone with their ideas. If they have none, it will be impossible for them to maintain themselves in life where they advance vacillatingly with the indecision of those who are not inwardly sustained by the principle of an Idea, an Idea they have imitated but not conceived. I have read in L'Echo de Paris the article on the young painters, and in the part which concerned you I was happy to read this: 'The impression we carried away from this visit to his studio was that M. Bernard—who has been accused of imitating Paul Gauguin—does not resemble him in the least, oh, not in the least!' You see that time, as it passes, brings about the discovery of the truth. Why then fear the perseverance of errors? Nothing lasts but truth alone. It is of you that the article speaks at the greatest length and in the most interesting manner. Do not think that your ideal is always being opposed without ever being understood; but you must speak and speak wisely. And your works will be there to sustain what you say. I am very happy to see that you are preparing an exhibition [Bernard's participation in the Rosicrucian Salon of March 1892]. Apostle of the good and of beauty, make public your doctrines and the admiration will increase. "Have your notes on art been published? If so, send them to me, I shall be happy to share the initiation which you offer to the public, which should not be treated with contempt but which one should rather try to lead towards beauty. You have the faith, you are advancing on the road of Christ, you have that glorious goal: the possession of Truth, of Light. Your soul has understood that, in following the road of the Man-God, it can by degrees reach perfection, but for this it takes patience, constant effort. It is not all of a sudden that we can manage to hold God. We are so far from Him that even in heaven, where the soul is at last freed from the bonds and passions which caused our weakness on earth, even in heaven which is the possession of God, the possession of the Infinite Good, there is still need for extension before we can hold Him completely. And it is that eternal extension towards the possession of Infinity which constitutes the blessing of Heaven...." Unpublished document, courtesy M.-A. Bernard-Fort, Paris.

11 J. Daurelle: Chez les jeunes peintres, L'Echo de Paris, Dec. 28, 1891.

12 C. Morice: Gauguin, Les Hommes d'Aujourd'hui, no. 440, 1896.

13 See Gauguin, Noa-Noa, op. cit., pp. 81–96, 107–18, 146–52.

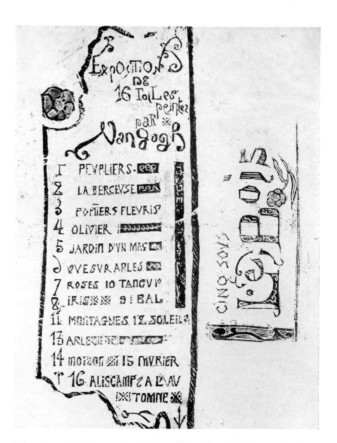

BERNARD: Catalogue for the van Gogh exhibition at Le Barc de Boutteville's, April 1892. Woodcut, 18¼ x 14⅝". Collection Fru Lone Teist-Rohde, Copenhagen

14 Gauguin to de Monfreid, [Tahiti], March 11, 1892; *op. cit.*, no. III, p. 54.

15 See B. Dorival: Sources of the Art of Gauguin from Java, Egypt and Ancient Greece, *Burlington Magazine*, Apr. 1951.

16 Gauguin to Sérusier, Papeete, March 25, 1892; *op. cit.*, pp. 58–59.

17 J.A. Moerenhout: Voyages aux îles du Grand Océan, contenant des documents nouveaux sur la géographie physique et politique, la langue, la littérature, la religion, les moeurs, les usages et les coutumes de leurs habitants, etc., Paris, 1837, 2 vol.

18 For a facsimile edition see Gauguin: Ancien culte Mahorie, Paris, 1951, with pertinent comments by R. Huyghe: Présentation de l'Ancien culte Mahorie—La clef de Noa-Noa.

19 In May 1892 Gauguin earned 36.75 francs for guarding during eleven days the furniture and objects of a man in bankruptcy. See his receipt for this amount in R. Hamon: Gauguin, le solitaire du Pacifique, Paris, 1939, p. 26.

20 Gauguin to his wife, Tahiti, [March] 1892; *op. cit.*, no. CXXVII, p. 220.

21 Gauguin to his wife, [Tahiti, Sept. (?) 1892]; *ibid.*, no. CXXVIII, pp. 225–26.

22 Gauguin to his wife, [Tahiti, June 1892]; *ibid.*, no. CXXIX, p. 227.

23 Gauguin to his wife, [Tahiti, July 1892]; *ibid.*, no. CXXX, pp. 229–30.

24 See Gauguin's letter to de Monfreid, [Tahiti], Nov. 5, 1892; *op. cit.*, no. VII, p. 60.

25 Gauguin to de Monfreid, [Tahiti, Sept. 1892, *not* March 31, 1893]; *ibid.*, no. XII, p. 67.

26 A. de La Rochefoucauld: Quelques notes sur le Salon de la Rose + Croix, sent to the author in Oct. 1948.

27 See: Salon de la Rose + Croix, Règle et Monitoire, Paris, 1891, and Catalogue du Salon de la Rose + Croix, Paris, 1892 (ill.).

28 See H. Hahnloser-Bühler: Félix Vallotton et ses amis, Paris, 1936, pp. 175–80.

29 F. Fénéon: Rose + Croix, *Le Chat Noir*, March 19, 1892 (not included in Fénéon: Oeuvres, Paris, 1948); quoted by de Larmandie: L'Entr'acte idéal—Histoire de la Rose + Croix, Paris, 1903. On this subject see also: J. Lethève: Les Salons de la Rose-Croix, *Gazette des Beaux-Arts*, Dec. 1960.

30 Pierre Louis [short-lived pseudonym of Maurice Denis]: Notes sur l'exposition des Indépendants, *Revue Blanche*, vol. II, 1892, p. 232. It may well be that this statement by Denis was responsible for the breach between him and Bernard, which originated before 1893 and lasted for some twenty years.

31 Quoted in an unsigned preface [by Emile Bernard] for: Emile Bernard, Paris, 1933, pp. 10–11.

32 On this exhibition see Bernard's introduction to Lettres de Vincent van Gogh à Emile Bernard, Paris, 1911, pp. 5–6. Bernard fails to indicate the date on which the exhibition was held, implying that it took place in 1891 prior to the retrospective assembled by Signac for the Independents in March–April 1891. But since Bernard's van Gogh show at Le Barc de Boutteville's actually took place in April 1892, his claim that he was the *first* to organize a van Gogh exhibition after Vincent's death is not substantiated by facts. However, Signac's retrospective comprised only ten paintings compared to sixteen in Bernard's exhibition.

These sixteen, according to the catalogue engraved on wood by Bernard (reproduced opposite page), were: 1. *Peupliers*; 2. *La Berceuse* [possibly the painting reproduced p. 292]; 3. *Pommiers fleuris*; 4. *Olivier*; 5. *Jardin d'un mas*; 6. *Vue sur Arles* [probably the painting corresponding to the drawing reproduced p. 202]; 7. *Roses* [possibly the painting reproduced p. 351]; 8. *Iris* [probably the painting reproduced p. 311]; 9. *Bal* [probably the painting reproduced p. 223]; 10. *Tanguy* [possibly the painting reproduced p. 45]; 11. *Montagnes* [possibly the painting reproduced either p. 322 or p. 334]; 12. *Soleils* [possibly the painting reproduced p. 205]; 13. *Arlésienne* [possibly the painting reproduced p. 239]; 14. *Moisson* [possibly the painting reproduced p. 32]; 15. *Murier*; 16. *Alyscamps à l'automne* [possibly one of the two paintings reproduced pp. 225 or 232].

33 The painter Anna Boch, a member of the XX, who had bought van Gogh's *Red Vineyard* (p. 229) in 1890, now purchased Seurat's *Seine at Courbevoie* (reproduced p. 114), exhibited in Brussels under the title *Printemps à la Grande Jatte*.

34 On La Libre Esthétique see M.-O. Maus: Trente années de lutte pour l'art, 1884–1914, Brussels, 1926.

35 J. Rohde: Journal fra en Rejse i 1892, Copenhagen, 1955, pp. 88–92.

36 Among those who contributed to a fund for the destitute children of imprisoned anarchists were Sérusier, Camille and Lucien Pissarro, Petitjean, Mirbeau, Christophe, Fénéon, de Régnier, Saint-Pol Roux.

37 See C. Simond: Paris de 1800 à 1900, vol. III, 1870–1900, Paris, 1901, p. 434.

38 Aurier: Les Symbolistes, *Revue Encyclopédique*, April 1, 1892 (with 14 illustrations); reprinted in Aurier: Oeuvres posthumes, Paris, 1893, pp. 293–309 (without illustrations).

39 Denis: article in *Art et Critique*, Aug. 23, 1890; reprinted in Denis: Théories, 1890–1910, Paris, 1912, p. 1.

40 Portier to de Monfreid, [Paris], Dec. 13, 1892; see J. Loize: Les Amitiés du peintre G.-D. de Monfreid et ses reliques de Gauguin, Paris, 1951, pp. 94–95.

41 M. Joyant to de Monfreid, [Paris], March 24, 1893; *ibid.*, p. 94.

42 Gauguin to the Director of Fine Arts, Tahiti, June 12, 1892; see R. Rey: Onze menus de Gauguin, Geneva, 1950, pp. 52–55.

43 See W. Menard: Gauguin's Tahiti Son, *Saturday Review of Literature*, Oct. 30, 1954.

44 Gauguin to de Monfreid, [Tahiti, Sept. 1892, *not* March 31, 1893]; *op. cit.*, no. XII, p. 68. Apparently no child was born; Bengt Danielsson was unable to unearth any birth record in Tahiti, nor does the local tradition mention that Tehura had any offspring by Gauguin.

45 Gauguin to his wife, [Tahiti, Nov. 5, 1892]; *op. cit.*, no. CXXXII, p. 234.

46 Gauguin: Notes à la suite de Noa-Noa; quoted in Rewald: Gauguin, Paris–New York, 1938, p. 23.

47 Gauguin to his wife, Tahiti, Dec. 8, 1892; *op. cit.*, no. CXXXIV, pp. 237–38.

48 Gauguin: Notes éparses, quoted by J. de Rotonchamp: Paul Gauguin, Paris, 1925, p. 253.

49 See C. Mauclair: Servitude et grandeur littéraires, Paris, 1922, p. 29.

50 See Gauguin's letter to de Monfreid, [Tahiti], Dec. 8, 1892;

op.cit., no. VIII, p. 62. These eight paintings were: *Parau Parau—Conversation* (reproduced p. 487); *Eaha oe féii—What, you are jealous?*; *Manao Tupapau* (reproduced p. 488); *Rarahi te maraè—There resides the Maraè*; *Woman wearing a shirt—Te Faaturuma*; *Landscape with Big Tree—Te ra'au rahi* (reproduced p. 470); *House and Horse—Te fare Maori*; *Two Women with a Dog—I raro te oviri* (reproduced p. 473). In a letter written at the same time to his wife (*op. cit.*, no. CXXXIV, p. 235), Gauguin lists the same paintings and, in addition, *Vahine no te tiare—Woman with a flower* (reproduced p. 475), which he had already shipped to Paris. He there translates *Te Faaturuma* as "Silence," *Te ra'au rahi* as "The Big Tree," *Te fare Maori* as "Tahitian House," and *I raro te oviri* as "Under the Pandanus."

51 Gauguin to de Monfreid, [Tahiti], Feb. 11, 1893; *op. cit.*, no. X, pp. 65–66.

52 The paintings by van Gogh which belonged to Aurier are listed in J.-B. de La Faille: Vincent van Gogh, Paris, Hyperion, 1939, as nos. 100 (reproduced p. 33 right), 167, 328 (probably the painting Aurier had purchased for his sister), 493 (reproduced p. 242), 584, and 695 (reproduced p. 345), all of which are now in the Rijksmuseum Kröller-Müller, Otterlo, as well as the painting reproduced p. 33 left, which is not listed in the 1939 edition of de La Faille.
The painting by Gauguin was *Conversation*, probably shown in the last impressionist group exhibition of 1886; see G. Wildenstein: Gauguin, Paris, no. 144.

53 Van Gogh's letters to Bernard appeared in the *Mercure de France* of April, May, June, and July 1893; selections from his letters to his brother were published in the Aug., Sept., Oct., Nov. 1893, Jan., March, July, Sept. 1894, and Feb. 1895 issues. See also Vallette's letters to A. Bonger in *Van Goghiana I*, Antwerp, Jan. 1963, pp. 49, 53.

54 Joyant quoted by Gauguin in a letter to de Monfreid, [Tahiti], Feb. 11, 1893; *op. cit.*, no. X, p. 65.

55 Gauguin to de Monfreid, [Tahiti, April 1893]; *ibid.*, no. XIII, p. 70.

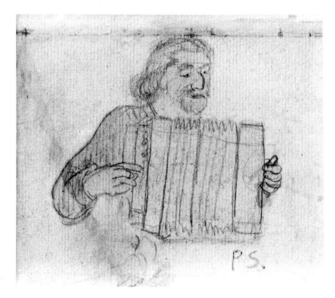

SÉRUSIER: *Gauguin Playing the Accordion,* 1889. Pencil, 4¾ x 5⅝". Collection Mlle H. Boutaric, Paris

SOURCES OF ILLUSTRATIONS

Photographs of the works of art reproduced in this volume have been provided in many cases by the owners or custodians of the works, indicated in the captions. The following list, keyed to page numbers, applies to photographs for which a separate acknowledgment is due:

Aix-en-Provence, France, Henry Ely: 448.

Albi, France, Musée Toulouse-Lautrec: 21.

Amsterdam, Gemeente Musea: 15, 25 right, 28 right, 34, 36 left and right, 54 top, 55, 56, 62 right, 66 right, 69, 70, 103 top, 175, 186, 187, 191, 194, 195, 210 left, 211, 244, 309, 324, 325 all, 327 top right, 328 bottom left, 352, 378, 379, 399 top right.

Baltimore Museum of Art: 17.

Basel, Öffentliche Kunstsammlung: 263, 265, 363, 446 left, 485. Dietrich Widmer: 29 bottom.

Beaumont-sur-Oise, France, Latarse: 445.

Brussels, Archives Centrales Iconographiques: 91, 100 top right, 110 bottom, 111 top, 247, 283 bottom right. Galerie Georges Giroux: 112 bottom.

Buenos Aires, Grete Stern for owner: 51 right.

Chicago Art Institute: 13.

Cleveland Museum of Art: 470 bottom.

Copenhagen, Ole Woldbye: 413 top and bottom right. Royal Museum of Fine Arts: 498.

Geneva, Editions Albert Skira: 157.

Helsinki, C. Grunberg: 113 bottom.

London, Grove & Sons: 75 top center, 127 center. Lefevre Gallery: 281 right. Marlborough Fine Art: 123 bottom, 377 right. Sotheby's: 114 bottom, 272 right.

Lyon, J. Camponogara: 29 top.

Minneapolis, Eric Sutherland: 323 left.

New York, Acquavella Galleries: 370. *Art News:* 208 (color). Brenwasser: 197 bottom, 328 bottom right. Geoffrey Clements: 486. Fine Arts Associates: 122 bottom. Gregoire Galleries, Inc.: 118 right. Arthur Jaffé: 355. Peter A. Juley & Son: 274, 454. Georges Keller: 264. Kate Keller: 170, 296, 495. M. Knoedler & Co.: 38 top, 49, 202 top, 235, 305 right, 311, 322, 355 right, 494. The Metropolitan Museum of Art: 317. The Museum of Modern Art: 155 bottom left, 160 (color plate from *Odilon Redon, Gustave Moreau, Rodolphe Bresdin,* © 1961, p. 75), 394, 399 top left. Otto E. Nelson: 206 right. Paul N. Perrot: 220. Eric Pollitzer: 158. J. Rewald: 88, 197 top and bottom left, 210 right, 224 right, 299 left, 304 right, 306 right, 335 left, 339 left, 376, 377 left, 385. Walter Rosenblum: 161 right. Paul Rosenberg & Co.: 62 left, 204 top, 294, 333 bottom. John D. Schiff: 89, 122

top, 386, 391 right, 459 left, center, and right. E. & A. Silberman Galleries: 276 right, 434. Star Press: 63 bottom. The Solomon R. Guggenheim Museum: 113 top, 238. Adolph Studly: 223. Soichi Sunami: 33 right, 41, 143 left, 153 left and right, 155 bottom right, 181, 227 bottom, 232, 233, 239, 272 left, 304 left, 327 bottom left, 328 top and bottom left, 400 right. Taylor & Dull, Inc.: 106, 179 bottom, 263 bottom right. *Time Magazine:* 361. Wildenstein & Co.: 24 left, 25 left, 45, 74, 81 bottom, 84, 100 bottom left and right, 101 bottom, 109, 110 top, 117 bottom left, 137, 169, 197 top, 198, 202 bottom, 207, 219, 222, 225, 283 top right, 333 top, 351, 367, 369, 391 left, 398, 401 right, 410 center and right, 412, 424, 460, 461, 465 top, 470 top, 479, 487, 496. Malcolm Varon: 19, 105, 108, 313.

Northampton, Mass., H. Edelstein: 81 top right.

Palm Beach, Fla., Lee Brian: 285.

Paris, Albin Michel: 81 top left. Alinari: 145. Arte Graphique de la Cité: 171 left, 393. Bernès-Marouteau & Cie: 32 right. Bignou Galerie: 37, 53. Braun & Cie.: 43, 75 top right, 129 left. J. E. Bulloz: 51 left, 139 left, 371. Cauvin: 58 bottom, 130, 150 bottom, 176, 184, 262 left, 286, 446 right. A. Daber: 437 right. Durand-Ruel et Fils, Editeurs: 284, 362, 423 center, 429. M. Guiet: 458. Yves Hervochon: 85. Photo Industrielle et Documentaire: 127 left. J. Rodrigues-Henriques: 92, 117 bottom right, 119, 253. Robert Schmit: 435. Service de Documentation Photographique de la Réunion des Musées Nationaux: 118 left, 150 top, 155 top, 196 left, 203 top, 224 left, 250, 282, 302, 418, 426, 465 bottom, 468, 481. Mme G. Signac: 76. Y. Vaule: 254, 255, 268 left. B. & G. Verte: 183 left. H. Roger Viollet: 493 left. Vizzavona: 27 right, 52, 57, 58 top, 68, 101 right, 121, 173 left and right, 183 center, 201 top and bottom, 234, 245, 271 right, 292, 306 left, 320, 323 right, 326, 329, 348, 373, 375 left, 400 left, 401 left, 417, 489, 490, 491. Jean Willemin: 107, 164 bottom.

Philadelphia Museum of Art: 12, 240.

Pont-Aven, France, Photo Gravier: 283 top and bottom left.

Saint-Germain-en-Laye, France, Hurault: 436 left and right.

Santa Barbara, Calif., H. Dorra: 64, 65.

Stuttgart, Stuttgarter Kunstkabinett: 269 right.

Venice, Fototeca Biennale: 117 top.

Winterthur, Switzerland, H. Wullschleger: 236 right.

The following illustrations were made after reproductions in books, periodicals, or catalogues: 24 right, 27 left, 87, 90, 100 top left, 112 top, 116, 125 top, 129 right, 133, 134, 135, 136 top and bottom, 139 right, 140, 141 top and bottom, 142, 143 right, 163, 177 right, 226 top, 252, 253 left, 259, 260 top and bottom, 261, 266, 267, 270 left, 275 right, 276 center, 337, 346 bottom, 360, 381, 396, 397 top and bottom, 407, 423 left, 427, 439, 449, 450, 451 left and right, 452 top and bottom, 453, 463 top, 480 top and bottom, 482, 483.

	CONTEMPORARY EVENTS	THE IMPRESSIONISTS	CEZANNE Born 1839	GAUGUIN Born 1848	BERNARD Born 1868
1884	economic crisis in France; unemployment Fabian Society of moderate socialists founded in England; joined by G. B. Shaw Huysmans publishes *Against the Grain* Rodin commissioned to do *Burghers of Calais* monument founding of Independents in Paris and the XX in Brussels Fénéon co-founder of *Revue Indépendante* Mallarmé professor at Lycée Janson; 1885 transferred to Collège Rolin death of Bastien-Lepage, Makart, Marie Baschkirzew Modigliani born	Manet memorial exhibition at Ecole des Beaux-Arts; sale of his estate Pissarro settles at Eragny Monet works at Bordighera, Menton, later Etretat, Giverny; participates in Petit's 3rd "Exposition Internationale" Renoir in Paris and La Rochelle; expresses dislike for impressionism Sisley works in and around Moret; lives in Les Sablons Morisot spends summer in Bougival Degas does sculpture at Mesnil-Hubert; short stay at Dieppe	works mostly in and around his native Aix; is rejected by Salon jury despite intervention of his friend Guillemet the new generation of painters greatly admires his work at Tanguy's but Cézanne seems to have been little aware of this	gives up bank job; lives in Rouen; later moves with family to Copenhagen, where he tries unsuccessfully to represent commercial firms Copenhagen exhibit of his works is closed by order of Danish Academy	shows early gifts, encouraged by his grandmother, a laundress at Lille; father insists on commercial career until a friend of the family admires the son's sketches and introduces him to Cormon father relents, lets son enter Cormon's studio, where he spends 2 years, meets Anquetin and Lautrec; they become his friends
1885	Karl Marx: *Das Kapital*, vol. II published posthumously Laforgue and Régnier publish first volumes of verse Dujardin founds *Revue Wagnérienne* *douanier* Rousseau retires from Paris customs service (about 1885) to devote himself to painting Strindberg in Paris; admires Puvis de Chavannes Rouault apprenticed to stained-glass maker Munch, first short visit to Paris death of Victor Hugo, Ulysses Grant Delaunay and La Fresnaye born	Pissarro meets Signac and Seurat; influenced by their theories Monet works at Giverny and Etretat; participates in Petit's 4th "Exposition Internationale" Renoir at Wargemont, La Roche-Guyon (with Cézanne), later Essoyes; overcomes doubts, satisfied with new work Sisley in financial difficulties Morisot works in Holland Degas makes short trip to Le Havre, Mont Saint-Michel, Dieppe where he meets Gauguin Durand-Ruel organizes exhibitions in London, Boston, Rotterdam, Berlin with little success	probably again rejected by Salon jury works in L'Estaque and Aix until May has mysterious love affair in June–July visits Renoir at La Roche-Guyon with Hortense Fiquet and their son; visits Zola at Médan where he is writing *L'Oeuvre*; in Aug. returns to Aix; works in Aix and Gardanne during rest of the year on Pissarro's advice Signac buys a landscape by Cézanne at Tanguy's	in June returns from Denmark to Paris; leaves family in Copenhagen ill in Paris; hospitalized mysterious sojourn in Brittany; meets Degas there and quarrels with him	an older pupil at Cormon's takes him to the Louvre and to Durand-Ruel's; his admiration of old and modern masterpieces helps him resist Cormon's academic influence admires Cézanne's works at *père* Tanguy's
1886	Moréas publishes Symbolist Manifesto; Fénéon publishes *Les Impressionnistes en 1886*; Zola publishes *L'Oeuvre* Mallarmé meets Monet and Renoir through Morisot; Morice, Fontainas, de Régnier, Dujardin, Whistler, etc. attend his Tuesday gatherings Durand-Ruel obtains first success in America unveiling of Statue of Liberty Bern copyright convention Clemenceau, Liszt, Dujardin, Wyzewa, etc. attend Wagner festival at Bayreuth death of Monticelli, Liszt Kandinsky (born 1866) studies law and economics in Moscow Kokoschka born Chevreul celebrates his hundredth birthday Anquetin exhibits *cloisonniste* works	May–June, eighth and last impressionist exhibition; Pissarro insists that Seurat and Signac show with group; Monet, Renoir, Sisley refuse to join; Degas and Morisot take active part in preparation of show Monet and Renoir participate in Petit's 5th "Exposition Internationale" and show with XX in Brussels; Monet visits Mirbeau, meets Geffroy Pissarro, Monet, Renoir, Sisley, Morisot, Degas, etc. shown by Durand-Ruel in New York Monet, trip to Holland; Renoir in La Roche-Guyon; Sisley in Moret; Morisot on Isle of Jersey beginning of monthly impressionist dinners at Café Riche (Monet, Renoir, Pissarro, Duret, Mallarmé, Huysmans) beginning of Renoir's friendship with T. de Wyzewa	probably again rejected by Salon jury in Paris during Feb. in March Zola publishes *L'Oeuvre*; Cézanne, deeply hurt, breaks with him on April 28 marries Hortense Fiquet in Aix in the presence of his parents his father dies Oct. 23, aged eighty-eight, leaving him a considerable fortune spends most of the year at Gardanne with his wife and son	job as bill poster quarrels with Seurat over use of Signac's studio participates with 19 paintings in impressionist show June–Nov., at Pont-Aven, Pension Gloanec; meets Laval and Emile Bernard, whom he does not receive too well in fall meets van Gogh in Paris; does ceramics with Chaplet dreams of trip to the tropics	Cormon dismisses him for insubordination; his father burns his brushes, forbids him to paint; deep crisis of discouragement; writes macabre poetry Lautrec paints his portrait with Anquetin experiments with pointillist execution notices van Gogh on farewell visit to Cormon's travels on foot through Normandy and Brittany in Concarneau meets Schuffenecker who recommends him to Gauguin; Gauguin's reception at Pont-Aven is guarded though Bernard appreciates his work

VAN GOGH Born 1853	SEURAT Born 1859	SIGNAC Born 1863	REDON Born 1840	LAUTREC Born 1864	BONNARD Born 1867
works at Nuenen, Holland, in his parents' home correspondence with van Rappard and his brother Theo paints with dark colors; his subjects mostly peasants and weavers	Feb.–March, shows *Study for Baignade* at Martinet's "Cercle des Arts Libéraux" *Baignade* rejected by Salon jury co-founder of Independents, where he meets Signac takes studio 128 bis, boulevard de Clichy on Ascension Day begins work on *Grande Jatte* spends summer in Paris shows *Baignade* with Independents in May–June; in Dec. exhibits *Landscape of Grande Jatte*, admired by R. Marx	still under influence of Monet and Guillaumin; calls on Monet co-founder of Independents; friendship with Seurat works in Paris, Asnières, Montmartre; summer in Port-en-Bessin buys painting by Cézanne at Tanguy's	co-founder of Independents; accepts vice-presidency Huysmans, writing about Redon in *Against the Grain*, for first time attracts some attention to the artist's work between 1883 and 1885 spends each year three months in Morgat, Crozon, Douarnenez (Finistère)	paints parody of Puvis de Chavannes' *Sacred Wood* occupies studio 7, rue de Tourlaque, Montmartre, for next 13 years; Suzanne Valadon at one time his neighbor	
at Nuenen with parents; paints mainly still lifes, landscapes, peasants conflict with van Rappard over *Potato Eaters*, painted in May, his most important work of this period death of his father in Nov. goes to Antwerp, studies at the Academy; starves to buy paints; near collapse	works on his *Grande Jatte* (ready in March) summer in Grandcamp (five paintings and series of small panels) after return takes up *Grande Jatte* again, introducing optical mixture in fall meets Pissarro through Guillaumin at Durand-Ruel's	meets Pissarro through Guillaumin summer in Saint-Briac, Brittany at about this time begins to gather his friends every Monday at his boulevard de Clichy studio close to Seurat's on Pissarro's advice buys a landscape by Cézanne at Tanguy's	publishes series of lithographs: *Hommage à Goya* critics and writers such as Geffroy, Morice, Caze, Huysmans praise his work invited to show with XX in Brussels death of his former master, Rodolphe Bresdin	Bruant opens cabaret, Le Mirliton, in Montmartre where Lautrec goes frequently; friendship with Bruant between 1885 and 1889 spends many evenings at the Elysée-Montmartre where he makes numerous sketches	after baccalaureat studies law at insistence of his father
in Feb. arrives in Paris; works at Cormon's meets Lautrec and Anquetin, later Bernard through Theo meets Pissarro, Degas, Guillaumin, *père* Tanguy lives with Theo, rue Laval; in June they move to 54, rue Lepic in fall meets Gauguin influenced by the impressionists, Monticelli, Japanese prints, neo-impressionism paints mostly still lifes of flowers, Montmartre landscapes, portraits does not show with Independents	shows *Grande Jatte*, 4 landscapes, 1 small panel and 3 drawings at impressionist exhibition (invited by Camille Pissarro); at Independents shows *Grande Jatte* with works from Grandcamp and Honfleur; Mirbeau, Hennequin, de Wyzewa hostile; Fénéon, Maus, Verhaeren, Henry, Kahn, de Régnier, Ajalbert, and Adam impressed, also Anquetin, Bernard, Schuffenecker, Angrand, Cross, Dubois-Pillet, Hayet, and van Gogh attends gatherings at Café de la Nouvelle Athènes *Baignade* shown by Durand-Ruel in New York	small divisionist canvas by Pissarro prompts him in March–April to paint 2 pointillist landscapes near Clichy participates in impressionist show (invited by Camille Pissarro) some of his works shown by Durand-Ruel in New York; exhibits with Pissarro and Seurat in Nantes summer with Lucien Pissarro at Petit Andely, later Fécamp friendship with Fénéon, Henry, Alexis, de Régnier, Verhaeren shows with Independents (member of hanging committee) notices pointillist paintings by Bernard who re-	invited by Guillaumin to participate in impressionist show exhibits with the XX in Brussels where his work is violently attacked by critics shows with the Independents in Paris admired by Hennequin, P. Adam, Mallarmé, but attacked by Mirbeau; contributes lithograph to *Revue Wagnérienne* birth of his first son who dies after a few months; this tragedy deeply affects the artist contact with the circle of literary symbolists becomes closer	works at Cormon's, meets van Gogh friendship with Anquetin paints portrait of Bernard starts exhibiting at Bruant's Mirliton; does illustrations for Bruant's songs Cabaret des Assassins, later called Lapin Agile (Montmartre), founded	studies law in Paris

	CONTEMPORARY EVENTS	THE IMPRESSIONISTS	CEZANNE	GAUGUIN	BERNARD
1886 cont'd					
1887	Antoine founds Théâtre Libre G. Kahn publishes *Palais Nomades* (free verse) French President J. Grévy resigns over Wilson scandal; Sadi Carnot elected Wagner's *Lohengrin* given for first time in Paris première of Verdi's *Otello* in Milan Puvis de Chavannes shows at Durand-Ruel's; commissioned to do Sorbonne murals large Millet exhibition in Paris E. Muybridge publishes portfolio of photographs, *Animal Locomotion* death of Laforgue at 27 and of A. Krupp, founder of industrial dynasty Juan Gris, Chagall, Le Corbusier born B. Berenson's first trip to Europe	Pissarro exhibits pointillist works with the XX in Brussels; his son Lucien forced to earn his living with chromo-lithography Monet visits Whistler for 2 weeks in London; at Whistler's invitation shows 4 paintings with Royal Society of British Artists Renoir exhibits *Grandes Baigneuses* at Petit's 6th "Exposition Internationale" where Pissarro, Monet, Sisley, Morisot also show Renoir paints portrait of B. Morisot's daughter Morisot pays short visit to Mallarmé at Valvins Theo van Gogh organizes small Pissarro, Gauguin, and Guillaumin exhibition at Boussod & Valadon's	probably in Aix most of the year apparently again rejected by Salon jury	does ceramics with Chaplet apparently teaches at Académie Vitti in Paris in April his wife visits him in Paris April 10 goes to Panama where he works as digger on canal, later goes with Laval to Martinique where both become ill; returns to Paris in Nov. stays with Schuffenecker, 19, rue Boulard; sees Vincent van Gogh again who admires his paintings from Martinique	about 1886–87 exhibits pointillist paintings at Asnières where Signac notices them; refuses to join Seurat's group meets van Gogh at Tanguy's, is grateful for compliments he pays him; exchanges paintings with van Gogh van Gogh works with him at Asnières and even at his father's house until the latter forbids him to return about this time evolves *cloisonniste* style together with Anquetin wanders again through Brittany
1888	Wilhelm II ascends to German throne height of nationalist Boulangist movement in France "Société des Droits de l'Homme" founded in France Institut Pasteur founded in Paris *Revue Wagnérienne* ceases to appear; Wyzewa breaks with Dujardin Ensor paints *Entry of Christ into Brussels* Castagnary, as Director of Fine Arts, buys Sisley landscape for the State Whistler has one-man show at Durand-Ruel's; Mallarmé translates Whistler's *Ten O'Clock* death of C. Cros, inventor and poet T. S. Eliot born S. Bing begins publishing *Japon Artistique* (until 1891)	Monet leaves Durand-Ruel, signs contract with Theo van Gogh (Boussod & Valadon); Jan.–April in Antibes; Mallarmé admires his paintings done there when exhibited at Theo van Gogh's; in July again visits London Renoir visits Cézanne in Aix; later in Martigues; in Dec. begins to suffer from neuralgia Sisley works in and around Moret, also at Les Sablons; considers becoming French citizen; Degas in Aug.–Sept. at Cauterets; begins to write some poetry; shows at New English Art Club Morisot works at Cimiez near Nice Pissarro exhibits at Durand-Ruel's, May–June Durand-Ruel organizes important Renoir, Pissarro, Sisley exhibition, without Monet; organizes Degas show in Paris	apparently again rejected by Salon jury beginning of year with Renoir in L'Estaque; cares for him during illness in Paris, 15, quai d'Anjou (neighbor of his friend Guillaumin) works in Chantilly and in the outskirts of Paris Huysmans publishes short article on Cézanne in *La Cravache*; from this time on Cézanne's name appears now and then in various symbolist periodicals; Aurier and Fénéon mention him occasionally	Feb.–Oct. at Pont-Aven with Bernard, Laval, de Haan; attracted by Bernard's sister paints *Jacob Wrestling with the Angel* which is refused by village priest; gives advice to Sérusier makes contract with Theo van Gogh; one-man show at his gallery early in November; Degas likes his work; Theo van Gogh sells several paintings and ceramics Oct. 23, joins Vincent van Gogh in Arles; in Dec. spends a day with him in Montpellier Dec. 23, conflict with Vincent, returns to Paris, stays with Schuffenecker	sees van Gogh off to Arles in Paris until end of April, then works again in Brittany at Saint-Briac the young critic Aurier notices his work and becomes friendly with him Aug., arrives at Pont-Aven with mother and sister, recommended to Gauguin by van Gogh; great friendship with Gauguin, continuous exchange of ideas, feverish activity, correspondence with van Gogh back in Paris, in Dec. visits Gauguin after the latter's return from Arles; deeply distressed about news of van Gogh's madness (letter to Aurier)

VAN GOGH	SEURAT	SIGNAC	REDON	LAUTREC	BONNARD
	friendship with Fénéon, Henry summer in Honfleur exhibits in Nantes; invited to show with XX in Brussels	fuses to join the neo-impressionists trip to Antwerp with Alexis and their wives(?)			
works frequently in Asnières with either Bernard or Signac organizes or participates in several small exhibitions, at *Revue Indépendante* and notably at Le Tambourin and at another restaurant on the avenue de Clichy, where he meets Seurat supposedly has love affair with La Segatori begins to drink; Paris climate and excitement affect his health does not always get along well with his brother	winter 1886–87 takes up drawing again (music halls, circus, etc.) in Feb., with Signac attends opening of XX show in Brussels where he shows *La Grande Jatte*; sells 2 paintings exhibits 8 paintings plus drawings at Independents upon its return from New York retouches *Baignade* works on *Poseuses* (1887–88); remains in Paris throughout summer; in fall begins work on *Parade* (1887–88); first experiments with colored frames attends Laforgue funeral exhibits in lobby of Théâtre Libre with Signac, van Gogh, etc. attacked by Huysmans, praised by Alexis, Kahn, and Christophe second visit from Verhaeren Luce and Gausson join his group	attends opening of the XX exhibition in Brussels with Seurat works in Comblat-le-Chateau (Auvergne) "discovers" Collioure; first contact with Southern France and Mediterranean friendship with Cross, Luce, Vincent d'Indy does etchings and lithographs exhibits at Independents where he thenceforth shows each year Nov., with Seurat, Lucien Pissarro, Dr. Gachet, Alexis, etc., assists at dinners of Independents with Seurat, van Gogh, participates in show in lobby of Théâtre Libre 1887–88, with Seurat, Dubois-Pillet, Luce, Lucien Pissarro, van Rysselberghe, Cross, and Hayet, contributes drawings to *La Vie Moderne*	shows with Independents for the last time; admired by G. Kahn illustrates works by Verhaeren and Picard whom he met through the XX	draws pastel portrait of van Gogh from 1887 to 1891 shares apartment with Dr. Bourges, 19, rue Fontaine, across the street from Degas regularly gathers his friends in his studio where van Gogh sometimes silently joins them	studies law in Paris
in Feb. leaves for Arles after visit to Seurat; intoxicated by southern color and sunlight; works in frenzy, lives in complete isolation; poor nourishment wishes to organize artists' colony in South; correspondence with Theo, Gauguin, Bernard Sept., moves into Yellow House; joined by Gauguin in Oct.; period of great activity and heated discussions; in Dec. visits Montpellier with Gauguin first mental seizure Dec. 23; cuts off his ear; taken to hospital; unconscious for 3 days; Gauguin summons Theo, leaves; Dec. 24, Theo becomes affianced to Johanna Bonger	Feb. van Gogh visits his studio spring: works with Angrand on island of Grande Jatte has argument with Signac: complains of being imitated by too many followers summer in Port-en-Bessin shows *Poseuses* and *Parade* with Independents in March–May; Fénéon criticizes colored frames 1887–88 contributes drawings to *La Vie Moderne*, together with Signac, Lucien Pissarro, Dubois-Pillet, van Rysselberghe, Cross, Luce, Hayet Belgian painters van Rysselberghe, Finch, Anna Boch, van de Velde, Lemmen, and de Regoyos adhere to divisionism	exhibits with the XX in Brussels friendship with Théo van Rysselberghe, J. Ajalbert, Mallarmé, Henry van de Velde works on the banks of the Seine, at Portrieux and at Antwerp designs program for Théâtre Libre shows with Independents considers Seurat's *Poseuses* too "divisionist"	between 1888 and 1892 spends several summers in Samois near Valvins where he sees Mallarmé almost daily writes diary: *A soi-même* Hennequin, the first and best critic of his work, drowns accidentally while visiting Redon publishes series of lithographs: *Tentation de St. Antoine* and begins work on next series inspired by and dedicated to Flaubert	exhibits 11 paintings and one drawing with the XX in Brussels renews friendship with M. Joyant with whom he had attended in 1872 the Lycée Fontanes around this time hangs group of his paintings on permanent exhibit in Bruant's Mirliton first circus painting: *Au Cirque Fernando*	fails in oral law examinations; works in Government office at the Ecole des Beaux-Arts; competes unsuccessfully for Prix de Rome studies at Académie Julian, Faubourg St. Denis, where he meets Denis, Vuillard, Ranson, Sérusier; in Oct. Sérusier returns from Brittany and reveals Gauguin's art to his friends; the Nabis begin to gather regularly interested in Japanese prints

505

	CONTEMPORARY EVENTS	THE IMPRESSIONISTS	CEZANNE	GAUGUIN	BERNARD
1889	Paris World's Fair; construction of Eiffel tower Workers' congress in Paris declares May 1 workers' holiday Huysmans publishes *Certains*, praises Puvis de Chavannes, Moreau, Degas, Cézanne, Whistler, Redon, Raffaëlli, Forain, etc. Moreau elected to the Institut de France Verlaine publishes *Parallèlement*; Bergson publishes *Données immédiates de la conscience*; B. von Sutter publishes pacifist novel *Die Waffen nieder* which impresses Alfred Nobel Moulin Rouge opens in Montmartre Kandinsky's first visit to Paris death of Chevreul, Villiers de l'Isle-Adam, Champfleury Hitler born in Austria Dec. 1889–May 1890 first sojourn of Edvard Munch in Paris last major Barbizon exhibition in New York Roger Marx named Inspector General of French Museums madness of Nietzsche	Monet organizes subscription to offer Manet's *Olympia* to the Louvre; 2 paintings by Manet bequeathed to the Metropolitan Museum, New York Monet exhibits with Rodin at Petit's (145 works), also at Theo van Gogh's in Paris, Goupil's in London, and with XX in Brussels; sojourn at Fresselines with M. Rollinat and Geffroy; works in La Creuse Renoir with Cézanne in Aix; tells Roger Marx he considers his work bad Pissarro begins to suffer from chronic eye infection; builds studio in Eragny; Durand-Ruel buys important group of his works Sisley moves to Moret; Durand-Ruel organizes first Sisley one-man show in New York (128 paintings); still in financial difficulties Degas refuses special display at World's Fair; with Boldini in Spain, also in Morocco Goupil's in London shows, "London Impressionists" (Sickert, Steer)	in Paris on quai d'Anjou with Roger Marx's help Chocquet maneuvers to have Cézanne's *Maison du pendu* shown at the World's Fair Huysmans, in *Certains*, is first to speak of Cézanne whom he calls "too long forgotten" and considers a leader of impressionism more important than Manet, though he also speaks of Cézanne's "sick retina" and "exasperated vision" in June pays short visit to Chocquet at Hattenville (Normandy) spends latter part of the year in Aix where Renoir comes to work is invited to exhibit with the XX in Brussels; declines at first but later accepts	Jan.–March, Paris, 25, avenue Montsouris returns to Pont-Aven with Laval, Sérusier; later in Le Pouldu at Marie Henry's inn with de Haan (Oct. 1889–Nov. 1890) exhibits with the XX in Brussels; the public laughs at his works during World's Fair organizes group show with Schuffenecker at Café Volpini, including works by Daniel de Monfreid, Bernard, Anquetin, Laval, Fauché, Roy; Guillaumin refuses participation, Theo van Gogh declines in his brother's name through Bernard meets Aurier; writes articles for Aurier's *Moderniste*	participates in Volpini exhibition, has largest group of works his father having forbidden him to join Gauguin, spends summer at Saint-Briac, later at Pont-Aven while Gauguin and his friends work at nearby Le Pouldu paints religious compositions for which van Gogh chides him at about this time meets Redon through Schuffenecker writes article for Aurier's *Moderniste*
1890	exhibition of Japanese Art at Ecole des Beaux-Arts Nelly Bly tours world in 72 days, 6 hours, 12 minutes and 14 seconds Puvis de Chavannes, Meissonier, Rodin, Carrière found Société Nationale des Beaux-Arts for slightly more liberal Salon Chauchard buys Millet's *Angélus* for 750,000 francs from American owner Vallette founds *Mercure de France*; Paul Fort founds Théâtre d'Art; Lugné-Poë his assistant Durand-Ruel publishes *L'Art dans les Deux Mondes* (1890 to '91) to arouse interest in the impressionists *La Plume* founded Valéry, Pierre Louys, Debussy in contact with Mallarmé	Pissarro abandons Seurat's divisionism; exhibits with XX in Brussels and in Theo van Gogh's gallery Lucien Pissarro settles in London where he devotes himself to woodcuts and typography; corresponds steadily with his father, who visits him during the summer Monet breaks with Boussod & Valadon; begins to paint series: *Fields of Poppies* (1890), *Poplars* (1890–91), *Haystacks* (1890–93); buys house at Giverny, soon begins work on water garden Renoir exhibits for last time at the Salon; on April 14, marries Aline Charigot, mother of his son Pierre (born 1885), and moves to Montmartre Morisot spends summer at Mézy where Renoir visits her Degas begins to collect art	in Jan. shows 3 canvases with the XX; is mentioned by Signac in review of exhibition in Paris, quai d'Anjou; later avenue d'Orléans spends 5 summer months with his wife and son in Switzerland (Neufchatel, Bern, Freiburg, Vevey, Lausanne, Geneva) during the fall in Aix, works at the Jas de Bouffan, probably at his *Card Players* series Bernard publishes pamphlet on Cézanne in *Les Hommes d'Aujourd'hui*	in Le Pouldu with de Haan; Jan.–June in Paris counts on subsidy from Dr. Charlopin for departure to Martinique, then Tonkin, later Madagascar, eventually Tahiti; invites Bernard and de Haan to accompany him; fails to obtain promised subsidy returns to Brittany; Nov., Eugène Boch brings together 5 friends who each buy a painting by Gauguin to help him leave Brittany Nov., Paris, stays with Schuffenecker, 12, rue Durand-Clay; friendship with de Monfreid during winter months attends symbolist gath-	makes industrial designs at Lille in vain effort to earn money religious crisis, doubts his calling April, Gauguin invites him to accompany de Haan and himself to the tropics; is overwhelmed by this offer but hesitates to leave on account of chaste love affair; eventually accepts does not see van Gogh during the latter's 2 short visits to Paris; rushes to Auvers for van Gogh's burial, helps Theo display Vincent's works is approached by Theo to help organize van Gogh memorial show publishes articles on Cé-

506

VAN GOGH	SEURAT	SIGNAC	REDON	LAUTREC	BONNARD
Jan. 7, leaves hospital but returns daily for dressing of wound beginning of Feb. taken back to hospital, suffering from persecution mania; released after about 10 days, goes back to work Feb. 28, taken anew to hospital, result of petition to Arles mayor, signed by 30 citizens; at hospital has new seizure of short duration end of March is visited by Signac has to give up yellow house; sublets two rooms from Dr. Rey; works again April 17, marriage of Theo considers enlisting in Foreign Legion, declines to go to Paris or Pont-Aven; decides to ask for voluntary internment in nearby Saint-Rémy asylum; May 8, arrival at Saint-Rémy; works in asylum garden, soon is permitted to work outside of institution July 5, learns Theo's wife is pregnant July 8, short visit to Arles; shortly afterwards has new seizure while painting in fields; for 6 weeks does not leave his room receives better food, regains will power, works with renewed energy receives invitation to show with XX wants to return to the North (Pissarro and Theo approach Dr. Gachet at Auvers) fall: begins copying reproductions, etc. chides Bernard about his mystic-religious tendencies in Nov. spends two days at Arles Dec. 22, is informed that confinement of Theo's wife approaches around Christmas has new though very short seizure considers joining Gauguin at Pont-Aven	shows *Poseuses* with the XX in Brussels summer at LeCrotoy; paints only 2 landscapes there; begins to simplify frames, instead starts painting borders directly on edges of canvas in fall, member of hanging committee of Independents; shows Le Crotoy and Port-en-Bessin landscapes with Independents begins work on *Woman Powdering Herself* (portrait of his mistress Madeleine Knobloch) and *Le Chahut* (1889–90) Fénéon criticizes the too visible linear structure of his recent works Madeleine Knobloch is pregnant moves to 39, passage de l'Elysée des Beaux-Arts near place Pigalle his friend Laurent obtains Rome prize	end of March visits van Gogh at Arles works at Cassis, Herblay, collaborates with Charles Henry on charts for latter's publications member of hanging committee of Independents	birth of his second son, Ari; thanks to doting care the child lives at about this time meets his young admirer Emile Bernard through Schuffenecker shows with Society of Painter-Engravers at Durand-Ruel's meets Mellerio, his biographer to be, who introduces him to Maurice Denis does frontispieces for books by Belgian authors Picard, Gilkin, Destrée publishes series of lithographs: *A Gustave Flaubert* Huysmans praises his lithographs in his book *Certains*	shows at Cercle Volney in Paris begins exhibiting annually with the Independents between 1889 and 1891 works frequently in the garden of M. Forest on Montmartre. opening of the Moulin Rouge where he meets Jane Avril debut of Yvette Guilbert at L'Eldorado bullfight arena opens in Paris paints *Au bal du Moulin de la Galette*	sells poster design (which Lautrec admires), decides to become an artist military service at Bourgoin
Jan., Aurier's article on van Gogh appears in first issue of *Mercure de France* Jan. 18, opening of XX show at Brussels after incident de Groux-Lautrec over van Gogh's paintings; sells his first painting there end of Jan., another short seizure after day spent at Arles Jan. 31, birth of his nephew and namesake end of Feb., new and severe seizure after 2 days spent at Arles; works during illness, tries to poison himself; unable to write until middle of April March 19, opening of Independents where he is represented by 10 paintings highly praised by Gauguin and many others decides to leave Saint-Rémy in May, works with renewed ardor, does series of flower still lifes May 16, leaves Saint-Rémy; after 3 days in Paris proceeds to Auvers-sur-Oise friendship with Dr. Gachet; paints	on Feb. 16, his child born, recognized by him member of hanging committee of Independents with whom he exhibits *Woman Powdering Herself* and *Chahut*; 6 landscapes, 2 drawings; Kahn buys *Chahut* on March 20, is presented, with Signac, to French President Sadi Carnot when he visits Independents exhibition summer at Gravelines (4 paintings, many drawings) J. Christophe publishes study on Seurat who later defines his theories in a let-	short trip to Genoa, Florence, Naples works at Saint-Briac, Herblay paints portrait of Fénéon exhibits with XX in Brussels; attends opening with Lautrec whose side he takes in incident with de Groux over van Gogh writes article on exhibition for *Art et Critique*, speaking mostly of neo-impressionists and devoting little space to van Gogh, Lautrec, etc. elected member of the XX (first non-Belgian so honored) member of hanging	exhibits with the XX in Brussels; in Feb. travels with Mallarmé to Brussels Charles Morice publishes study on Redon with portrait by Schuffenecker in *Les Hommes d'Aujourd'hui* Destrée prepares catalogue of Redon's lithographs to appear in 1891 sees Gauguin frequently, exchanges works with him; through Gauguin apparently meets Sérusier at about this time begins his friendship with the Nabis death of his friend, the botanist Clavaud	sketches at Moulin Rouge where Yvette Guilbert sings exhibits 5 paintings with the XX; attends opening of show in Brussels with Signac; provokes de Groux to duel over issue of van Gogh's work compliments Bonnard for poster shows 2 paintings with Independents his friend Maurice Joyant in Oct. succeeds Theo van Gogh at Boussod & Valadon (Goupil); from then until his death sees Joyant almost daily	military service at Bourgoin shares studio rue Pigalle with Vuillard, Lugné-Poë; Denis, Sérusier come there frequently, Gauguin sometimes his sister marries composer Charles Terrasse

CONTEMPORARY EVENTS	THE IMPRESSIONISTS	CEZANNE	GAUGUIN	BERNARD
1890 cont'd Bismarck is dismissed by the Kaiser Hamsun publishes *Hunger*; Wilde publishes *Picture of Dorian Grey* Mirbeau "discovers" Maeterlinck *Mercure de France* founded Denis publishes important definition of art Vollard arrives in France from his native island of La Réunion to study law in Paris death of Dubois-Pillet	Mary Cassatt buys Château de Beaufresnes, her permanent summer home, 27 miles from Paris; visits Japanese exhibition with Degas Sisley invited to show with XX in Brussels, but G.Petit refuses to send requested pictures there; becomes associate member of new Société Nationale des Beaux-Arts where he shows 6 paintings and obtains success; thenceforth participates in all yearly Salons, except in 1896 and 1897 Manet's *Olympia* enters the Musée du Luxembourg		erings at Café Voltaire; is acclaimed "chief" of the symbolist painters; friendship with Aurier, Morice, Redon, Mallarmé, Carrière, the Nabis; Carrière paints his portrait works on *Loss of Virginity*, for which his mistress Juliette Huet poses decides to leave without subsidy prepares auction sale	zanne and van Gogh in *Les Hommes d'Aujourd'hui* series asks Aurier to write article on Gauguin to advertise latter's auction sale
1891 suicide of General Boulanger in Brussels Antoine presents first Ibsen play in Paris; Zola, sponsor Natanson brothers found *Revue Blanche* first publication by G. B. Shaw, *The Quintessence of Ibsenism* Carrière exhibition at Boussod & Valadon's (Goupil) Puvis de Chavannes commissioned to do murals for Boston Library Hodler exhibits *Night* in Paris Whistler's *Mother* bought by French government banquet in honor of Moréas who shortly afterwards breaks with symbolism, founds "l'Ecole Romane" Le Barc de Boutteville organizes first group show of young painters, Nabis, neo-impressionists, etc. Roujon named Director of Fine Arts (hostile to all modern movements) Wilde, Maeterlinck, Verhaeren, Claudel, Redon, Vuillard, etc., attend Mallarmé's Tuesday gatherings death of Seurat, Rimbaud, Jongkind, Meissonier	Monet works during winter on the ice of the Seine, paints *Poplar* series, exhibits *Haystack* series at Durand-Ruel's; great success; in Dec. goes to London; New English Art Club shows works by Monet and Degas (also in 1892 and 1893); Durand-Ruel shows Monet, Pissarro, and Sisley in Boston Feb.–March, Renoir travels to Tamaris with Wyzewa; April at Le Lavandou, then Nîmes; short stay at Mézy with Berthe Morisot; trip to Spain Sisley works at Veneux-Nadon; his financial situation improves Degas buys painting by Gauguin at latter's auction Pissarro begins to devote more time to etchings and lithographs; has printing press set up in his new studio; makes drawings to be cut in wood by his son Lucien Mary Cassatt has first one-woman show at Durand-Ruel's 1891–92, Mrs. Potter Palmer, Chicago, begins to collect impressionist paintings	at the beginning of the year in Aix, where he sees Alexis frequently considers exhibiting with the Independents but changes his mind requests his wife and son to settle in Aix; subsequently leaves for Paris at about this time becomes a devout Catholic his paintings at Tanguy's are mentioned in *Mercure de France* (June) Bernard and Anquetin proclaim their admiration for Cézanne in interviews published in *Echo de Paris* (Dec. 28) death of Cézanne's friend, the collector Victor Chocquet prompted by Bernard, the painter Eugène Boch buys Cézanne painting from Tanguy, who is hard up	in Feb., quarrels with Schuffenecker, moves to hotel, rue Delambre, later 10, rue de la Grande Chaumière spends miserable winter; works in Monfreid's studio, does sculpture meets Verkade exhibits with the Salon du Champ de Mars; shows wood reliefs with the XX, is violently attacked by Belgian critics great activity to advertise sale; articles by Mirbeau and Aurier Feb. 23, auction with adequate results break with Bernard early in March short visit with family in Copenhagen March 23, banquet in his honor presided over by Mallarmé leaves Paris April 4 Joyant (Goupil) in May gives Morice 850 francs for Gauguin, which he fails to forward; Morice devotes an issue of *Les Hommes d'Aujourd'hui* to Paul Gauguin arrives in Tahiti June 8, three days after King Pomaré dies settles with Titi in Mataïea, far from Papeete; later sends her away his mistress Juliette in Paris gives birth to a girl	abandons plan to go with Gauguin to the tropics; is shocked by Gauguin's endeavors to have himself acclaimed as "leader of symbolist art movement" breaks with Gauguin at latter's auction; deeply hurt when Aurier neglects to mention him in eulogy of Gauguin in summer, returns to Brittany in Dec., shows with the Nabis at Le Barc de Boutteville's; in interview proclaims his admiration for Cézanne, Redon begins evolution towards more traditional art shows for first time with Independents 1891–92, contributes drawings to *La Vie Moderne*, for which all the symbolists write during the same period

VAN GOGH	SEURAT	SIGNAC	REDON	LAUTREC	BONNARD
portrait of physician greatly absorbed by his work plans month's visit with Gauguin in Brittany; early June, Theo and family spend Sunday at Auvers; end of June Theo worried by health of child and prospects of future early July, short visit in Paris, overshadowed by Theo's worries depressed after return; quarrels with Dr. Gachet July 27, shoots himself at moment when Theo plans to leave for vacation in Holland; Dr. Gachet summons Theo July 29, death July 30, burial at Auvers Theo begins to plan exhibition, also publication of Vincent's letters Oct., Theo loses his mind; is taken to Holland	ter to M. Beaubourg (Aug. 28) begins work on *Cirque* (1890–91)	committee of the Independents on March 20, is presented, with Seurat, to French President Sadi Carnot when he visits Independents exhibition Camille Pissarro, Hayet, van de Velde abandon the group Fénéon devotes an issue of *Les Hommes d'Aujourd'hui* to Signac (illustrated with his portrait by Seurat)			
Jan., Gauguin opposes Bernard's plan of organizing a van Gogh exhibition Jan. 25, death of Theo van Gogh in Holland (later buried beside his brother at Auvers cemetery) Feb., van Gogh retrospective organized by the XX in Brussels March, van Gogh retrospective organized by Signac at Independents in Paris; Octave Mirbeau writes vibrant article in memory of van Gogh	shows *Le Chahut* and 6 landscapes with the XX in Brussels in Feb. attends banquet for Moréas member of hanging committee of Independents; shows *Cirque* (unfinished) and 4 paintings from Gravelines with Independents—opening March 20 March 29, death of Seurat after 2 days of illness burial March 30 2 weeks later death of Seurat's illegitimate child in April, Signac, Luce, Fénéon appointed by Seurat family to assist the artist's brother in classifying contents of his studio (inventory dated May 5); half of estate given by parents to Madeleine Knobloch G. Kahn and Lemmen in Brussels intriguing against Signac, Luce, Fénéon; later apologize to them Wyzewa writes important article on Seurat	shows with the XX in Brussels; helps Maus in organizing van Gogh memorial exhibition member of hanging committee of Independents; helps organize large Dubois-Pillet and small van Gogh retrospectives resists Anquetin's attempt to split Société des Indépendants deeply affected by Seurat's death; participates in classification of Seurat's works works at Mont Saint-Michel, Concarneau; spends one day at Pont-Aven June, operation on a cyst attacked in article by Mirbeau	Destrée's catalogue of Redon's lithographs appears participates in "Exposition générale de la lithographie" at Ecole des Beaux-Arts gradually abandons graphic media, does pastels instead and eventually oil paintings after not having used color for several years Bernard, in interview, proclaims Redon and Cézanne as his most admired masters publishes album of lithographs, *Songes* Mirbeau apologizes to Redon for his attack of 1886 and expresses deep admiration Bernard introduces him to Theo van Gogh's brother-in-law Andries Bonger, who becomes an avid collector of Redon's works and a personal friend of the artist	exhibits at Cercle Volney in Paris member of hanging committee of Independents shows paintings in foyer of Moulin Rouge (mentioned in *Mercure de France*) does first poster for Moulin Rouge which meets with great success Lautrec's cousin, Tapié de Céleyran, arrives in Paris, works as intern in hospital; Lautrec watches and paints operations at hospital admires Yvette Guilbert at Divan Japonais issue of *Les Hommes d' Aujourd'hui* is devoted to Lautrec Dec., participates with Anquetin, Denis, Bonnard, and Bernard in group show at Le Barc de Boutteville's in interview expresses his admiration for Degas and Forain 1891–93 lives 21, rue Fontaine	exhibits 9 paintings with Independents; participates in Saint-Germain group show of Nabis one of his drawings is reproduced in *La Vie Moderne*; drawings by Gauguin, Sérusier, Filiger, Bernard, Denis, Ranson, Vuillard, Roussel, Redon, and van Gogh also appear there Dec., participates with Lautrec, Anquetin, Denis, and Bernard in first group show of young painters at Le Barc de Boutteville's; all participants are interviewed on this occasion but Bonnard avoids naming contemporary artists he admires most

	CONTEMPORARY EVENTS	THE IMPRESSIONISTS	CEZANNE	GAUGUIN	BERNARD
1892	Panama Canal scandal rocks France first show of Rosicrucians at Durand-Ruel's attracts tremendous attention Burne-Jones exhibition in Paris Huysmans becomes devout Catholic Moreau named teacher at Ecole des Beaux-Arts Debussy: *L'Après-midi d'un faune* Ravachol arrested and executed; series of anarchist bomb explosions (1892–94) Munch sends 55 paintings to Berlin art association; withdrawn after one week Aurier publishes important article on symbolist painters Mauclair succeeds Aurier as art critic for the *Mercure de France* Munich Secession founded death of Aurier (at 27), Tennyson, Ernest Renan, Guys	Pissarro has large retrospective at Durand-Ruel's; first real success; spends summer with son and Luce in London, where his son Lucien marries; buys his house at Eragny with loan from Monet Monet exhibits series of *Poplar Trees*; obtains high prices; begins *Rouen Cathedral* series; has show at St. Botolph Club, Boston Morisot exhibits at Boussod & Valadon's; death of her husband Renoir has large showing at Durand-Ruel's; great success; State buys *Jeunes filles au piano*; Gangnat begins to buy his work; second trip to Spain (with Gallimard); Aug.–Sept. in Brittany: Pornic, Pont-Aven (stays at Pension Gloanec) Oct., Degas shows series of landscape monotypes at Durand-Ruel's (his last exhibition), also with New English Art Club Sisley attacked in article by Mirbeau	in Aix and Paris, 2 rue des Lions-Saint-Paul works in Fontainebleau forest Aurier mentions him in important article among the forerunners of the new symbolist art Georges Lecomte gives lecture on Cézanne for the XX in Brussels, which is reprinted in *L'Art Moderne* (Feb. 21)	correspondence with his wife, Monfreid, Sérusier lives with Tehura Feb.–March, seriously ill, vomits blood; in Papeete hospital reads and copies Moerenhout's book on Polynesian lore Aurier's article on symbolist art appears in April thinks of leaving though wishes to stay; June 12, applies for repatriation in July, stock of canvas gives out his wife gathers pictures in Paris for sale and show in Copenhagen Sept., first Tahitian painting shown at Goupil's Tehura pregnant Nov., one of his paintings included (without his knowledge) in Le Barc de Boutteville group show sends 8 important canvases to Monfreid plans to leave Tahiti in Jan. 1893 Dec., Portier returns Gauguin's unsalable works to Monfreid	returns to Brittany, paints powerfully synthesized compositions there; expresses dislike for Pont-Aven organizes van Gogh memorial show at Le Barc de Boutteville's participates in Rosicrucian Salon; a review by M. Denis, though not unfavorable, apparently causes break that was to last 20 years shows with the Independents greatly affected by serious illness of *père* Tanguy, requests help from A. Bonger (who, in 1892, leaves Paris for his native Holland)
1893	Vaillant throws bomb in Chamber of Deputies Lugné-Poë founds Théâtre de L'Oeuvre XX dissolved; Maus founds "Libre Esthétique" Gide publishes *Voyage d'Urien* illustrated by Denis Bing organizes Utamaro-Hiroshige exhibition invention of Diesel motor Munch and Strindberg in Berlin; exhibition of Munch's "rejected" paintings there excerpts from van Gogh's letters begin to appear in *Mercure de France* Moreau's pupil Rouault fails to win coveted Prix de Rome Chicago World's Fair features Foreign Masters owned in U.S. (18 works by Degas, Manet, Monet, Pissarro, Renoir, Sisley) Mallarmé retires as teacher death of Maupassant, Gounod, Tschaikowsky, *père* Tanguy (in Feb.) at about this time Vollard opens small gallery, rue Laffitte, Paris	Monet continues *Rouen Cathedral* series though temporarily discouraged Pissarro paints Paris rue Saint-Lazare series Durand-Ruel holds Pissarro, Renoir shows of recent works Renoir spends winter at Beaulieu, summer again at Pont-Aven, where he hires Gabrielle as nurse; she soon becomes his favorite model; visits Gallimard at Benerville Berthe Morisot visits Mallarmé at Valvins, goes with him to see Sisley at Moret Mary Cassatt has second one-women show at Durand-Ruel's; Sisley has difficulties with Durand-Ruel, shows for first time at Boussod & Valadon's Toulouse-Lautrec's friend Maurice Joyant succeeds Theo at Boussod & Valadon's	in Aix and in Paris, rue des Lions Saint-Paul; works in Fontainebleau forest his self-portrait included in Le Barc de Boutteville's exhibition of "Portraits of the Next Century" (also paintings by Gauguin and van Gogh)	Jan., receives 100 francs from his wife Feb., his eyesight fails; can't work (until April); subsists on breadfruit and water; receives news of Aurier's death March, Joyant (Goupil) returns unsold paintings, ceramics, etc., to Daniel de Monfreid receives 300 francs from Monfreid and 700 from his wife; pays his debts June, sails for France; arrives Marseilles Aug. 30 with 4 francs; receives money from Sérusier in Paris stays in Monfreid's studio inherits money from an uncle in Orléans; takes studio rue Vercingétorix; meets Anna *la Javanaise*, gives weekly receptions Nov., one-man show at Durand-Ruel's (no sales); catalogue foreword by Morice with whom he plans to publish *Noa Noa* exerts influence on the Nabis	in April begins to publish in *Mercure de France* the letters received from van Gogh, followed by excerpts from Vincent's letters to Theo (until Feb. 1895) shows again and for last time (until 1902) with Independents publishes article on Redon in *Le Coeur* contributes to periodical *Le Livre d'Art*, founded by his future brother-in-law, Paul Fort helped by La Rochefoucauld, leaves for Italy, then for Constantinople, Samoa and eventually Egypt, where he remains for 10 years his sister and her fiancé, Laval, follow him; Laval dies there in 1894 of tuberculosis and Madeleine the following year

VAN GOGH	SEURAT	SIGNAC	REDON	LAUTREC	BONNARD
April, van Gogh exhibition organized by Emile Bernard at Le Barc de Boutteville's in following year, 1893, Meier-Graefe buys painting by van Gogh	large Seurat retrospective held at the Independents	member of hanging committee of Independents; helps organize large Seurat memorial show sails from Brittany through Canal du Midi to Marseilles where he meets Aurier first visit to Saint-Tropez (which he "discovers") friendship with Count Kessler Nov., marries Berthe Roblès, distant relative of Pissarro Dec., participates in Paris group show of neo-impressionists	Albert Aurier, in an important illustrated article, speaks at length about Redon as one of the leaders of symbolist painting a young Danish artist, Johan Rohde, visits him, is surprised to discover that Redon has begun to use color; he also notices the artist's modest lodgings (Redon worked in a small room of his apartment, never owned a large studio)	exhibits 9 works with the XX in Brussels, also shows at Cercle Volney; member of hanging committee of Independents; does first color lithographs, posters debut of Loie Fuller at Folies Bergère paints about a dozen scenes at the Moulin Rouge between 1892 and 1894 paints numerous brothel scenes between 1892 and 1896 constant patron of various Parisian Café-Concerts and other night spots	exhibits with Independents; participates in second Saint-Germain group show of Nabis; shows in Nov. at Le Barc de Boutteville's with Vuillard and Denis (one painting by Gauguin also included in exhibition) his work is noticed by Roger Marx and A. Aurier who reproduces 2 of his drawings in his article on symbolist art designs sets for Paul Fort's Théâtre d'Art
MATISSE Born 1869	PICASSO Born 1881	member of hanging committee of Independents attacked by Mauclair in *Mercure de France* in Oct. buys house in Saint-Tropez, then a small and unknown fishing village on Mediterranean with beautiful, protected harbor; successively invites all his friends to come there like Collioure, which he also "discovered," Saint-Tropez eventually becomes a favorite place with modern painters at about this time begins to keep a diary	Emile Bernard publishes article on Redon in *Le Coeur*, periodical founded and edited by Count Antoine de La Rochefoucauld	Jan., exhibits about 30 works together with his friend Maurin at Boussod & Valadon's (Goupil) which Joyant, successor of Theo van Gogh, was soon to leave also shows with the Society of French Painter-Engravers and with the XX in Brussels, as well as with Independents (member of hanging committee) does program illustrations for Théâtre Libre, later also for other theaters the Elysée Montmartre closes, unable to withstand competition from Moulin Rouge	exhibits with the Independents (member of hanging committee) and at Le Barc de Boutteville's does illustrations for *L'Escarmouche* and *Revue Blanche* (founded by Natanson brothers in 1891)
studies law in Paris from 1887–89; spends much time at the Louvre 1889, takes position as clerk in law office at Saint-Quentin; draws from plaster casts at local art school in summer of 1890 begins to paint returns to Paris in winter 1891–92 to study painting under Bouguereau and Gabriel Ferrier at the Académie Julian but is soon disgusted with their teaching 1892, becomes pupil of G. Moreau at Ecole des Beaux-Arts; in his studio meets fellow students Rouault and (later) Marquet, Manguin	son of a painter, lives with parents in Corunna whence family moved in 1891				

PARTICIPANTS IN THE EXHIBITIONS OF THE INDEPENDENTS — 1884–1893

	1884	1886	1887	1888	1889	1890	1891	1892	1893
Angrand	■	■	■	■	■	■	■	■	■
Anquetin				■	■	■	■	■	■
Bernard							■	■	
Bonnard							■	■	■
Cross	■	■	■	■	■	■	■	■	■
Denis							■	■	■
Dubois-Pillet	■	■	■	■	■	■	▪▪▪		
Filiger					■	■			
Finch						■	■		
(Dr.) Gachet							■	■	
Gausson			■	■	■	■	■	■	■
van Gogh				■	■	■	▪▪▪		
Guillaumin	■					■	■		
Hayet					■				
Lemmen					■	■	■	■	
Luce			■	■	■	■	■	■	■
Maufra							■	■	■
Petitjean							■	■	■
L. Pissarro		■	■	■	■	■	■	■	■
Redon	■	■	■						
de Regoyos						■		■	■
douanier Rousseau		■	■	■	■	■	■	■	■
van Rysselberghe						■	■	■	■
Schuffenecker	■								
Seurat	■	■	■	■	■	■	■	▪▪▪	
Signac	■	■	■	■	■	■	■	■	■
Toulouse-Lautrec					■	■	■	■	■
Vallotton							■		
van de Velde						■			
Verkade								■	
Willumsen							■	■	■

▪▪▪ *retrospective exhibition*

BIBLIOGRAPHY

This bibliography is meant as a *guide*. While most scholarly and more or less complete bibliographies devote equal space to the important and the trivial, the good and the bad, an attempt has been made here to limit the list to the principal publications—while including many early articles which often escape researchers—and at the same time to indicate to the reader what to expect from them.

I. The section on general literature is comparatively long. Although there are scarcely any books devoted specifically to the period studied in the present volume, there are numerous historical surveys that contain either chapters on post-impressionism or on the specific art movements and painters here considered. This general section includes many publications of personal recollections and other material which, though sometimes only indirectly connected with the present book, provide valuable background information on the years 1886–1893. Except for a few instances where books in this first section contain important chapters or new documents on individual artists, they are not listed again in section II.

II. The sections devoted to individual artists: Bernard, Gauguin, van Gogh, Redon, Seurat, and Signac, are, for greater convenience, generally subdivided as follows: *Oeuvre Catalogues; The Artist's Own Writings; Witness Accounts; Biographies; Studies of Style; Reproductions;* with a special chapter on the Pont-Aven group under the heading of Gauguin and a chapter on Medical and Psychiatric Studies under the heading of van Gogh, as well as another on Forgeries. This section also features bibliographies of the two leading critics of the period: Aurier and

Fénéon. Since some publications must be listed under more than one heading, all items are numbered and the numbers repeated wherever called for.

III–IV. The two final sections are devoted to neo-impressionism and to literary symbolism in general. The former is followed by short bibliographies devoted to the individual members of Seurat's group, the latter by short lists concerning various painters more or less closely connected with the symbolist movement.

Each section or subdivision is arranged chronologically.

The comments deal mostly with the reliability of the various publications, special emphasis being put on first-hand material. They also mention bibliographies, indexes, choice of illustrations, as well as offer an appreciation of the quality of reproductions.

Of articles published in periodicals, it has already been said that special stress is laid on those which appeared during the period studied here. Others are mentioned which contain important contributions or new documents. Among books, however, even those which may seem comparatively unimportant are listed if they have reached a large public or enjoy an undeserved reputation.

Further publications of and on the period, concerning for instance such artists as Maurice Denis and Paul Sérusier, will be dealt with in the bibliography of the planned volume on *Post-Impressionism—From Gauguin to Matisse*.

Since no attempt at completeness has been made, not all the publications consulted by the author are listed here. The reader will find references to further publications in the notes following each chapter.

I GENERAL

1 T. DE WYZEWA: Peinture Wagnérienne—Le Salon de 1885, *Revue Wagnérienne,* June 8, 1885.

2 E. DUJARDIN: Aux XX et aux Indépendants—Le cloisonnisme, *Revue Indépendante,* May 19, 1888.

3 J. DESCLOZEAUX: Les Artistes Indépendants, *La Cravache,* June 9, 1888.

4 O. MAUS: Le Salon des XX à Bruxelles, *La Cravache,* Feb. 16 and March 2, 1889.

5 P. ADAM: L'Art symboliste, *La Cravache,* March 23, 1889.

6 G. KAHN: L'Art français à l'Exposition, *La Vogue,* Aug. 1889. On Puvis de Chavannes, Moreau, Pissarro, Degas, Gauguin, etc.

7 G. LECOMTE: L'Art symboliste, *La Cravache,* May 3, 1889.

8 J. ANTOINE: Impressionnistes et Synthétistes, *Art et Critique,* Nov. 9, 1889. Review of the Volpini show.

9 J.-K. HUYSMANS: Certains, Paris, 1889. Collection of articles, notably on Puvis de Chavannes, Moreau, Degas, Cézanne, and Le Monstre [O. Redon].

10 A. H. [A. HENROTAY]: Les XX, *La Wallonie,* no. 5, 1890. Against van Gogh and Renoir, for Redon and Lautrec.

11 G. LECOMTE: Le Salon des Indépendants, *L'Art dans les Deux Mondes,* March 28, 1891.

12 E. VERHAEREN: Le Salon des Indépendants, *La Nation,* reprinted in *L'Art Moderne,* April 5, 1891.

13 J. LECLERCQ: Aux Indépendants, *Mercure de France,* May 1891.

14 T. DE WYZEWA: Le Nouveau Salon du Champ-de-Mars, *L'Art dans les Deux Mondes,* June 13, 1891. Accuses Gauguin—already on his way to Tahiti—of being influenced by Anquetin.

15 T. DE WYZEWA and X. PERREAU: Les Grands Peintres de la France (période contemporaine), Paris, 1891. With 135 engravings after works by Puvis de Chavannes,

Moreau, Manet, and also such academic artists as Cabanel, Bouguereau, and Meissonier.

16 W. G. C. BYVANCK: Un Hollandais à Paris en 1891, Paris, 1892. Chapters on Carrière, Rodin, Bruant, Moréas, Verlaine, Mallarmé, Monet, etc., most of whom the author met in Paris.

17 J. CHRISTOPHE: Le Salon de la Rose + Croix, L'Endehors, March 20, 1892.

18 R. MARX: L'Art décoratif et les "Symbolistes," Le Voltaire, Aug. 23, 1892.

19 G. GEFFROY: La Vie artistique, vols. I–VIII, Paris, 1892 to 1903. These volumes, published almost yearly, assemble most of Geffroy's newspaper articles on art until 1902. They constitute an important record of the artistic events of those years. Although their publication begins only at the time at which the present study ends, Geffroy's writings touch on many subjects related to this book. All volumes are indexed.

vol. I. 1892. Articles on Monet, Carrière, Pissarro, Japanese art, the Salons of 1890 and 1891, the Independents, etc.

vol. II. 1893. Articles on Rodin, Moreau, the Salons of 1892, the Independents, the Rosicrucians, an exhibition at Le Barc de Boutteville's, etc.

vol. III. 1894. Devoted to a "History of Impressionism" and reviews of the 1893 Salons.

vol. IV. 1895. The Salons of 1894 and 1895.

vol. V. 1897. Articles on Carrière and Cézanne, the Salons of 1896 and 1897.

vol. VI. 1900. Articles on Moreau, Gauguin, Puvis de Chavannes, Luce and Signac, Lautrec, Vuillard, Bonnard, Anquetin, Le Barc de Boutteville, etc., also the Salons of 1898 and 1899.

vol. VII. 1901. Devoted to the Paris World's Fair of 1900.

vol. VIII. 1903. Articles on Moreau, the Salons of 1900 and 1901.

20 R. MARX: Les Indépendants, Le Voltaire, March 28, 1893.

21 F. DUBOIS: Le Péril anarchiste, Paris, 1894. With numerous ill., among them drawings by Luce and C. Pissarro's sons (see p. 166, note 22).

22 A. JARRY: Minutes d'art—6e exposition chez Le Barc de Boutteville, Essais d'Art Libre, Feb.–April 1894. On Bonnard, Gauguin, Denis, Filiger, Séguin, Vuillard, Sérusier, etc.

23 C. MAUCLAIR: Lettre sur la peinture, Mercure de France, July 1894. Attack on impressionism and particularly on C. Pissarro.

24 J. LECLERCQ: La Lutte pour les peintres, Mercure de France, Nov. 1894. Reply to Mauclair with long passage on Gauguin.

25 T. NATANSON: Expositions, Revue Blanche, 1894, vol. 6, pp. 470–73.

26 Portraits du prochain siècle—poètes et prosateurs. Introduction by P. N. Roinard, Paris, 1894. Published by the review Essais d'Art Libre, this volume contains "profiles" of Mallarmé by Morice, Huysmans by R. Marx, Laforgue by Fénéon, Kahn by G. Randon, Dujardin by J. Thorel, Gide by Mauclair, Sâr Péladan by R. Nyst, Mirbeau by H. Leyret, V. Barrucand by Fénéon [not included in his Oeuvres], Willy by Fénéon, Dolent by Morice, Morice by Dolent, P. Fort by P. A. Hirsch, Aurier by J. Leclercq.

A second volume was planned, which was to include some studies of painters, but this apparently never appeared, although its contents were announced; among these figured: Fénéon by C. Saunier, Filiger by J. Bois, Anquetin by Roinard, Bernard by Ch. H. Hirsch, Gauguin by Dolent, Gausson by Frantz Jourdain, Hayet by P. Fort, Luce by Francis Jourdain, Puvis de Chavannes by Morice, van Gogh by Gauguin, Whistler and Manet by Mallarmé, Séguin, Vuillard, and Willumsen by L. P. Fargue.

27 FRANTZ JOURDAIN: Les Décorés—ceux qui ne le sont pas, Paris, 1895. Portrait sketches of a series of personalities who, the author felt, should receive the Legion of Honor. Among them are Degas, Mallarmé, Verlaine, Huysmans, Monet, Renoir, Pissarro, Maeterlinck, Lautrec, Antoine, Redon, but not Cézanne.

28 A. MELLERIO: Le Mouvement idéaliste en peinture, Paris, 1896. Mentions Puvis de Chavannes, Moreau, Redon, Gauguin, Cézanne, van Gogh, Schuffenecker, Lautrec, Anquetin, Sérusier, Vuillard, Bonnard, Ranson, Denis, Bernard, etc.

29 R. DE GOURMONT: Le 2e livre des masques, Paris, 1898. A series of "profiles" including P. Fort, Fénéon, Dujardin, Mauclair, Valette, Claudel, Fontaines, and Aurier.

30 H. VAN DE VELDE: Synthese der Kunst, Pan, no. IV, 1899.

31 A. FONTAINAS: L'Art moderne, Mercure de France, May 1900. On Seurat, on Denis-Bonnard and their group, on Gauguin-Bernard and their group, etc.

32 C. SIMOND: Paris de 1800 à 1900—La Vie parisienne au XIXe siècle, vol. III, 1870–1900, Paris, 1901. A useful, profusely illustrated guide which traces year by year all "headline" events (political, criminal, literary, artistic—the official Salons—sports, etc.) and offers month by month listings of significant occurrences.

33 J. MEIER-GRAEFE: Der moderne Impressionismus, Berlin, n.d. [1903–04]. Devoted to Lautrec, Gauguin, Japanese prints, and neo-impressionism.

34 J. MEIER-GRAEFE: Entwicklungsgeschichte der modernen Kunst, 3 vol., Stuttgart, 1904. Second enlarged ed., Munich, 1927. English translation: The Development of Modern Art, Being a Contribution to a New System of Aesthetics, 2 vol., New York, 1908. While this important publication now seems out of date—partly because the author did not have at his disposal the wealth of information we now possess—it nevertheless constitutes the first broadly conceived general history of modern art, assigning dominant places to van Gogh, Cézanne, Vuillard, Bonnard, Lautrec, Seurat, Signac, neo-impressionism in general, Rodin, Puvis de Chavannes, Monticelli, Carrière, Redon, Denis, Gauguin, the group at Pont-Aven, etc. Richly ill., index.

35 FRANTZ JOURDAIN: Propos d'un isolé en faveur de son temps, Paris, 1904. Intelligent comments on artistic innovators, particularly the impressionists and symbolists.

36 A. GERMAIN: Le Sentiment de l'art et sa formation par l'étude des oeuvres, Paris, 1904. Speaks of Seurat, Puvis de Chavannes, etc., but without offering anything new.

37 J. PÉLADAN: Les Idées et les formes—Introduction à l'esthétique, Paris, 1907. Formulation of the author's Rosicrucian principles.

38 V. PICA: Gli impressionisti francesi, Bergamo, 1908. An illustrated chapter on: Cézanne, I Divisionisti, I Sintetisti.

39 J.-C. HOLL: Après l'impressionnisme, Paris, 1910. Despite the title, this pamphlet studies the impressionists and not their successors.

39a F. RUTTER: Revolution in Art—An Introduction to the Study of Cézanne, Gauguin, van Gogh and Other Modern Painters. London, 1910. See also 19.

40 C. L. HIND: The Post-Impressionists, London, 1911. A journalistic and chatty defense of post-impressionism inspired by two exhibitions held at the Grafton Gallery in London in 1910–11. Ill., index, no bibl. On these exhibitions see also 41–43.

41 W. SICKERT: Post-Impressionists, *The Fortnightly Review,* Jan. 1911.

42 R. FRY: Post-Impressionism, *The Fortnightly Review,* May 1911.

43 D. S. MacCALL: A Year of Post-Impressionism, *The Nineteenth Century and After,* Feb. 1912.

44 L. COELLEN: Die neue Malerei, Munich, 1912. Chapters on van Gogh and Cézanne, Hodler, Gauguin, etc. No ill.

45 M. DENIS: Théories, 1890–1910, Du Symbolisme et de Gauguin vers un nouvel ordre classique, Paris, 1912. This collection of Denis' important articles contains his famous "Définition du néo-traditionnisme," as well as studies on Redon, Sérusier, Cross, Gauguin, van Gogh, Carrière, Cézanne, etc. Significant writings on the years after 1890 and on the Nabis. Reprint: Paris, 1964.

46 J.-C. HOLL: La Jeune Peinture contemporaine, Paris, 1912. Chapters on Denis, Luce, Signac, etc. No ill., no index.

47 H. R. POORE: The New Tendency in Art—Post-Impressionism, Cubism, Futurism, New York, 1913.

48 C. L. BORGMEYER: The Master Impressionists, Chicago, 1913. This book is outdated. The numerous illustrations, arranged without system, comprise not only impressionist works, but also a number of paintings by van Gogh, Gauguin, Cézanne, and Lautrec, who are discussed in the text, whereas Seurat and neo-impressionism are only mentioned in passing.

49 M. RAPHAEL: Von Monet zu Picasso—Grundzüge einer Aesthetik und Entwicklung der modernen Malerei, Munich–Leipzig, 1913. Perceptive chapters on van Gogh, neo-impressionism, Cézanne, Gauguin, etc.; few ill.

50 W. HAUSENSTEIN: Die bildende Kunst der Gegenwart—Malerei, Plastik, Zeichnung, Stuttgart–Berlin, 1914. Chapters on neo-impressionism, van Gogh and Gauguin, and on the influence of modern French art on various German movements. Few ill., index.

51 A. J. EDDY: Cubists and Post-Impressionists, Chicago, 1914; 2nd rev. ed. 1919. The introductory chapters on post-impressionism are out of date; the accent is on cubism. Black-and-white and color illustrations arranged without system. Bibl., index.

52 W. H. WRIGHT: Modern Painting, Its Tendency and Meaning, New York, London, 1915. Numerous misconceptions. The chapter on neo-impressionism includes van Gogh "who did little more than use a borrowed and inharmonious palette to express ideas wholly outside the realm of art." The chapter on the Pont-Aven School, whose activity is erroneously dated 1893, pretends that "little or nothing of lasting merit came out of this group." No bibl., few ill., index.

53 F. BURGER: Einführung in die moderne Kunst—die Kunst des 19. und 20. Jahrhunderts, Berlin, 1917. A general survey from David to German expressionism and Italian futurism, including references to, and some color plates of, works by Cézanne, Hodler, Seurat, Gauguin, van Gogh, Redon, etc. The same author also wrote: Cézanne und Hodler, Munich, 1920.

54 F. FÉNÉON [editor]: L'Art moderne et quelques aspects de l'art d'autrefois, Paris, 1919, 2 vol. 173 good black-and-white plates after works in the private collection of J. and G. Bernheim-Jeune, with poems by H. de Régnier and interesting excerpts from various writings. Includes paintings by Carrière, Cézanne, Gauguin, van Gogh, Redon, Renoir, Seurat, Cross, Signac, Lautrec, sculptures by Rodin, etc.

55 C. MAUCLAIR: L'Art indépendant français sous la troisième République, Paris, 1919. Studies on painting, literature, and music between 1890 and the first World War.

56 M. DERI: Die Malerei im XIX. Jahrhundert—Entwicklungsgeschichtliche Darstellung auf psychologischer Grundlage, 2 vol. (text and ill.), Berlin, 1919; second ed. 1923. A chapter on "Die Übergänge vom subjektiven Naturalismus in den Expressionismus" is concerned with Cézanne, Gauguin, and van Gogh. Short chapter on neo-impressionism. The text is largely composed of analytical comments on the numerous illustrations. See also 62.

57 J. DE LA ENCINA: Los Maestros del arte moderne—de Ingres a Toulouse-Lautrec, Madrid, 1920. Chapters on Puvis de Chavannes, Redon, Gauguin, van Gogh, etc. Some ill.

58 G. COQUIOT: Les Indépendants (1884–1920), Paris, n.d. [1920]. A history of the Société des Artistes Indépendants and its exhibitions, with notices on the major artists affiliated with the association. An important appendix contains an alphabetical list of artists with the years in which they exhibited; it gives the dates and places of all Salons for the period covered and reproduces the statutes of the society. Few ill., index.

59 M. PICARD: Das Ende des Impressionismus, Zurich, 1920–21.

60 C. MAUCLAIR: Les Etats de la peinture française de 1850 à 1920, Paris, 1921.

61 E. FAURE: Histoire de l'art—L'Art moderne, Paris, 1921. Excellent English translation by W. Pach, New York, 1924. The final chapters discuss briefly the position and works of Redon, Gauguin, Cézanne, Seurat, etc. Few ill., index.

62 M. DERI: Die neue Malerei, Leipzig, 1921. See also 56.

63 O. GRAUTOFF: Die neue Kunst, Berlin, 1921. More concerned with 20th-century than with 19th-century art. No ill., no index.

64 M. OSBORN: Geschichte der Kunst, Berlin, 1921.

65 O. MIRBEAU: Des artistes, 2 vol., Paris, 1922 and 1924. A collection of Mirbeau's frequently impassioned and often brilliant articles. Vol. I, Gauguin, van Gogh [the articles published in 1891], Rodin, Pissarro, père Tanguy, etc. Vol. II, Rodin, van Gogh [published in 1901], art nouveau, etc.

66 A. SALMON: Propos d'atelier, Paris, 1922. Chapters on Seurat, Degas, Redon, Renoir, Cézanne, etc.

67 FONTAINAS, VAUXCELLES, and GEORGE: Histoire générale de l'art français de la révolution à nos jours, Paris, 1922. Vol. I, La Peinture. Chapters on: van Gogh, Lautrec, Gauguin, the Pont-Aven group, Redon, Cézanne, Divisionism [Seurat, Signac, Cross, Luce], "la peinture monumentale" [Moreau, Puvis de Chavannes], etc. Ill., no bibl., no index.

68 J. GORDON: Modern French Painters, London, New York, 1923. Outdated text. Chapters on: Impressionism and Neo-Impressionism, Cézanne, van Gogh, Gauguin, etc. Ill.

69 L. WERTH: Quelques peintres, Paris, 1923. Studies on Cézanne, Renoir, van Gogh, Gauguin, Signac, Bonnard, Vuillard, etc.

70 J. W. BEATTY: The Modern Art Movement, Pittsburgh, 1924. Reprinted from The North American Review; short pamphlet mainly concerned with Cézanne, van Gogh, and Gauguin.

71 H. HILDEBRANDT: Die Kunst des 19. und 20. Jahrhunderts, Potsdam, 1924. This book, dealing on an equal basis with the best and the worst, briefly treats, among others, Puvis de Chavannes, Lautrec, neo-impressionism, Signac-Seurat, Gauguin, Carrière, Cézanne, etc. Ill., index, no bibl.

72 W. PACH: The Masters of Modern Art, New York, 1924. Chapters on: The Poles of the Modern Movement [Cézanne and Redon], and After Impressionism [Gauguin, van Gogh, Seurat]. Short bibl., ill. with notes.

73 G. COQUIOT: Des gloires déboulonnées, Paris, n.d. Studies on Carrière, Moreau, and other painters whose vogue was then waning, but among whom the author also includes Degas.

74 G. COQUIOT: Des peintres maudits, Paris, n.d. [1924]. Studies on Cézanne, Gauguin, Lautrec, Seurat, van Gogh, etc.

75 F. W. RUCKSTULL: Great Works of Art and What Makes Them Great, New York, 1925. A rambling homily (542 pages) on the virtues of academic art by an American sculptor whose first statue won an honorable mention at the Paris Salon of 1888, and who successfully avoided any contamination by modern ideas. Seurat and Lautrec are not even mentioned, whereas Rodin, Cézanne, van Gogh, and Gauguin are variously characterized as sadists, masochists, immoral, insane, etc.

76 H. KRÖLLER-MÜLLER: Die Entwicklung der modernen Malerei, Leipzig, n.d. [1925]. Ill.

77 The John Quinn Collection of Paintings, Water Colors, Drawings & Sculpture, Huntington, N.Y., 1926. An impressive catalogue of an important collection, rich in works by Cézanne, Gauguin, Puvis de Chavannes, Redon, the douanier Rousseau, Seurat, and others. Numerous illustrations.

78 M.-O. MAUS: Trente années de lutte pour l'art, 1884–1914, Brussels, 1926. A detailed and rambling history of the XX and "La Libre Esthétique" which, unfortunately, does not include itemized catalogues of the important shows organized by the XX between 1884 and 1893, but which presents a great wealth of documents, letters, recollections, sketches, etc. Index, some ill. For the archives of the XX see also Bulletin des Musées Royaux de Belgique, 1966, nos. 1–2. See also 199.

79 F. RUTTER: Evolution in Modern Art, London, 1926. Chapters on: The Legacy of Impressionism, and on The Pillars of Post-Impressionism: Cézanne, van Gogh, Gauguin, and Matisse. Few ill., short bibl., index.

80 F. RUTTER: Modern Masterpieces—An Outline of Modern Art, London, n.d. Chapters on Neo-Impressionism [Seurat, van Gogh], Reaction from Realism [Puvis de Chavannes, Redon, Gauguin], and on Cézanne. Text contains nothing new. 142 ill.

81 H. SCHLITTGEN: Erinnerungen, Munich, 1926. A little-known though very readable book of recollections on, among others, the Académie Julian, père Tanguy, and Theo van Gogh.

82 A. ZÉVAÈS: Histoire de la troisième République, 1870 à 1925, Paris, 1926. A detailed political history quoting many little known documents.

83 F. J. MATHER, JR.: Modern Painting, New York, 1927. Chapters on: Mural Painting [Puvis de Chavannes], Reaction against Impressionism [Seurat, van Gogh, Gauguin, Cézanne], and Official Art in the Nineteenth Century. Mediocre ill., index, no bibl.

84 C. BELL: Landmarks in Nineteenth Century Painting, New York, 1927. Chapters on: Seurat and Divisionism, The End of Impressionism [van Gogh, Gauguin, Denis]. Few ill., no bibl., no index.

85 K. SCHEFFLER: Die Europäische Kunst im Neunzehnten Jahrhundert, 2 vol., Berlin, 1927. Vol. II features: Geschichte der europäischen Malerei vom Impressionismus bis zur Gegenwart. Short section on neo-impressionism in the chapter: Der dekorative Impressionismus. Van Gogh, Gauguin, Munch are studied under: Der spekulative Impressionismus. Few but good ill., index, no bibl.

86 J.-E. BLANCHE: Propos de peintre, 3rd vol.: De Gauguin à la revue nègre, Paris, 1928. Studies on Gauguin, van Gogh, Monet, etc. No ill.

87 A. MICHEL: Sur la peinture française au XIXe siècle, Paris, 1928. Interesting chapter on Puvis de Chavannes, also Carrière, etc.

88 H. FOCILLON: La Peinture aux XIXe et XXe siècles, du Réalisme à nos jours, Paris, 1928. Short section on neo-impressionism included in chapter on impressionism; the academic "moderns" [Bastien-Lepage, Besnard, Henri Martin] are studied in a special chapter. Chapter: Le Nouvel Humanisme, devoted to Puvis de Chavannes. Other chapters on Cézanne, van Gogh, Gauguin, the

symbolists, etc. Profusely ill., chronological chart, index.

89 S. Bourgeois: The Adolph Lewisohn Collection of Modern French Paintings and Sculptures, New York, 1928. Handsome catalogue of an important private collection rich in works by Cézanne, Gauguin, van Gogh, Monticelli, Redon, the *douanier* Rousseau, Seurat, Lautrec, etc., all of which are reproduced and many of which are now in American museums.

90 Catalogue: First Loan Exhibition, Museum of Modern Art—Cézanne, Gauguin, Seurat, van Gogh, New York, Nov. 1929. Important foreword by A. H. Barr, Jr., 101 paintings and drawings, almost all reproduced.

91 P. Colin: La Peinture belge depuis 1830, Brussels, 1930.

92 J. Grave: Le Mouvement libertaire sous la 3e République, Paris, 1930. Recollections of the anarchist movement in France.

93 C. Mauclair: Un Siècle de peinture française, 1820–1920, Paris, 1930.

94 J.-E. Blanche: Les Arts plastiques—la troisième République, 1870 à nos jours, Paris, 1931. An intelligent and articulate observer, though mediocre painter, Blanche gives here a very complete account. Chapters on the exhibitions at the Petit Galleries, Le Barc de Boutteville's, etc., on Moreau, Redon, Lautrec, the two official Salons, the Independents, Cézanne, Gauguin, etc.; neo-impressionism, however, receives inadequate treatment. Index, no ill.

95 R. Rey: La Renaissance du sentiment classique dans la peinture française à la fin du XIXe siècle—Degas, Renoir, Gauguin, Cézanne, Seurat, Paris, 1931. A valuable study of the stylistic evolution of these five painters; the chapter on Seurat is particularly rich in new material. Extensive bibl., good ill.

96 A. Basler and C. Kunstler: The Post-Impressionists—From Monet to Bonnard, New York, 1931. A cursory treatment of Redon, Lautrec, van Gogh, Gauguin, the neo-impressionists, etc. Plates, index.

97 G. Eglington: Reaching for Art, Boston, 1931.

98 R. H. Wilenski: French Painting, Boston, 1931. A general history from the 14th to the 20th century. Chapters on: post-impressionism [Gauguin, van Gogh], on Lautrec, Cézanne, the *douanier* Rousseau; generally divided into sections on their lives and on their art, with lists of characteristic pictures. Poor ill., index, no bibl.

99 M. Denis: L'Epoque du Symbolisme, *Gazette des Beaux-Arts*, March 1934.

100 R. Cogniat: Le Salon entre 1880 et 1900. Catalogue of an exhibition at the Wildenstein Galleries, Paris, April–May 1934, containing biographical notes and reproductions of works by the most prominent official painters of the period.

101 E. F. Rothschild: The Meaning of Unintelligibility in Modern Art, Chicago, 1934.

102 T. Craven: Modern Art—The Men, the Movements, the Meaning. New York, 1934. Chapters on van Gogh, Gauguin which contain nothing new. Few ill., index.

103 T. W. Earp: The Modern Movement in Painting, special issue of the *Studio,* London, spring 1935. Short chapter on post-impressionists, some mediocre color plates.

104 J. Renard: Journal, Paris, 1935.

105 L. Katz: Understanding Modern Art, [Chicago], 1936, (3 vol.). Vol. II, chapters on van Gogh, Gauguin as well as Cézanne and Seurat. Biographical text containing nothing new. Ill., index.

106 A. Vollard: Recollections of a Picture Dealer, Boston, 1936. Slightly expanded French edition: Souvenirs d'un marchand de tableaux, Paris, 1937. Informal reminiscences of such men as Gauguin, Redon, Signac, and Sâr Péladan, whom the author had personally known. Disappointing; lacks pertinent facts. Ill., index.

107 J. W. Lane: Masters in Modern Art, Boston, 1936. Chapters on Cézanne, van Gogh, and Gauguin.

108 J. Laver: French Painting and the Nineteenth Century, London, 1937. Chapter on: The Triumph of Sciences; notes on Redon, van Gogh, Gauguin, Seurat, etc., by M. Sevier. (The book also contains the catalogue of an exhibition of French 19th-century painting, New Burlington Galleries, London, Oct. 1936.) Excellent choice of illustrations in black and white and color.

109 Les Maîtres de l'art indépendant, 1895–1937. Catalogue of an exhibition at the Petit Palais, Paris, June–Oct. 1937. Including groups of works by the *douanier* Rousseau, Suzanne Valadon, Signac, Luce, Maillol, Vallotton, Sérusier, Denis, Bernard, Bonnard, Vuillard, Rodin, and others.

110 J. Klein: Modern Masters, New York, 1938. Short, popular presentation of modern art from Manet to Gauguin with adequate black-and-white but poor color plates.

111 C. Marriott: A Key to Modern Painting, London, 1938. Dated text with chapters on Cézanne, Gauguin, and van Gogh; also, post-impressionism in England. Ill. with comments, index, no bibl.

112 W. Pach: Queer Thing, Painting—Forty Years in the World of Art, New York–London, 1938. Short chapter on Redon, as well as on the Armory Show, where, thanks to Pach, Redon was well represented. Few ill., index.

113 T. R. Bowie: Relationship between French Literature and Painting in the XIXth Century. Catalogue of an exhibition, Columbus Gallery of Fine Arts, April–May 1938.

114 La Peinture française du XIXe siècle en Suisse. Catalogue of an exhibition at the Wildenstein Galleries, Paris, 1938. Impressive catalogue of an important exhibition featuring major works by Cézanne, Gauguin, van Gogh, Redon, Lautrec, etc., from Swiss private collections. Ill.

115 C. Zervos: Histoire de l'art contemporain, Paris, 1938. Large volume, profusely illustrated in black and white, beginning with a section on Cézanne, Renoir, Gauguin, Lautrec, Seurat, van Gogh, the *douanier* Rousseau, though mainly devoted to their successors.

116 A. S. Hartrick: A Painter's Pilgrimage through Fifty Years, Cambridge, 1939. The author worked at the Académie Julian, knew van Gogh and Gauguin. Some ill.

117 J. S. Plaut: Introduction to the catalogue of the exhi-

bition: Sources of Modern Painting, Wildenstein Galleries, New York, April–May 1939. Ill.

118 E. P. RICHARDSON: The Way of Western Art, 1776–1914, Cambridge, 1939. Chapter on post-impressionism [Puvis de Chavannes, van Gogh, Gauguin, Cézanne, Seurat].

119 G. SLOCOMB: Rebels of Art—Manet to Matisse, New York, 1939. Text, more biographical than critical, relies sometimes too heavily on anecdotes dear to Vollard and others. Ill., index, no bibl.

120 C. ROGER-MARX: La Gravure originale en France de Manet à nos jours, Paris, 1939. Ill. (Hyperion).

121 H. MADSEN: Från Symbolism till Surrealism, Stockholm, 1939.

122 R. H. WILENSKI: Modern French Painters, London–New York, 1940; 2nd ed. 1945. Chapters on Seurat, Gauguin, Lautrec, etc., on the Independents, and on the years 1884–86, 1887–88, 1889, 1890–91, 1892–93, etc. An interesting but unfortunately unreliable book. Summary bibl., excellent and well chosen ill., exhaustive index. (Some of the shortcomings of the book have been pointed out by J. Rewald in the *Burlington Magazine,* Jan. 1948, pp. 27–28, with a reply by Wilenski.)

123 U. NEBBIA: La pittura del novecento, Milan, 1941.

124 L. VENTURI: Art Criticism Now, Baltimore, 1941. Chapter on: The Problem of Impressionism and Post-Impressionism.

125 S. CHENEY: The Story of Modern Art, New York, 1941. A popular book repeating popular errors, confounding impressionist and neo-impressionist doctrines. Long chapters on Gauguin, van Gogh, Seurat, Lautrec, Degas, etc. Numerous, poor ill., uncritical bibl., index.

126 K. SCHEFFLER: Die großen französischen Maler des 19. Jahrhunderts, Munich, 1942. Section on impressionists includes short studies of Cézanne and Lautrec; section on post-impressionists is limited to van Gogh and Gauguin. 110 good plates in black and white, 11 in color.

127 D. M. ROBB and J. GARRISON: Art in the Western World, New York, 1942.

128 B. DORIVAL: Les Etapes de la peinture française contemporaine, 3 vol., Paris, 1943, 44, 46. Vol. I—De l'impressionnisme au fauvisme, 1883–1905, contains chapters: La Peinture et le mouvement des idées en France vers 1889; Les Précurseurs de la peinture nouvelle [Puvis de Chavannes, Redon, Cézanne]; Gauguin et le groupe de Pont-Aven; Le Néo-impressionnisme, etc. This highly intelligent and provocative text contains many debatable assertions and analyses that in no way detract from its value as a brilliant survey of the period. Bibl. and general index in vol. III, no ill.

129 C. PISSARRO: Letters to His Son Lucien, New York–London, 1943. Edited by J. Rewald with the assistance of Lucien Pissarro. Important documents on the period in general, particularly the neo-impressionist movement. Ill., index. Third revised and enlarged edition: Mamaroneck, N.Y., 1972. French edition: Camille Pissarro—Lettres à son fils Lucien, Paris, 1950; also contains letters by Lucien to his father, amplified footnotes, and other new matter.

130 U. E. JOHNSON: Ambroise Vollard, Editeur—An Appreciation and Catalogue, New York, 1944. Although Vollard appeared on the art scene only at the time at which the present volume ends, this book is important for its lists of Vollard's publications, among them volumes illustrated by Bernard and Denis, as well as portfolios of individual prints by Bonnard, Cézanne, Cross, Lucien Pissarro, Redon, van Rysselberghe, Signac, Vallotton, Vuillard, etc. Appendices with a chronology, selected bibl. New, more complete edition: New York, 1977.

131 E. A. JEWELL: French Impressionists and Their Contemporaries, Represented in American Collections, New York, 1944. A Hyperion picture book assembled without any plan or order. Poor color plates, among them works by Carrière, Cézanne, Gauguin, van Gogh, Redon, Seurat, Signac, Lautrec, etc. The short biographical notes and bibl. by Aimée Crane are often inaccurate.

132 H. CAIRNS and J. WALKER [editors]: Masterpieces of Painting from the National Gallery of Art, Washington, New York, 1944. Some good color plates with interesting comments. The companion volume by the same editors: Great Paintings from the National Gallery of Art, Washington, 1952, contains a few more post-impressionist paintings.

133 M. GEORGES-MICHEL: Les Grandes Époques de la peinture "moderne"—De Delacroix à nos jours, New York–Paris, 1945. Text without interest, 125 ill., index.

134 J. FERNANDEZ: Prometeo—Ensayo sobre Pintura Contemporáneo, Mexico, 1945. Short chapter on Gauguin, the *douanier* Rousseau, Cézanne, of no particular interest. Ill., no bibl., no index.

135 L. VENTURI: Painting and Painters: How to Look at a Picture, from Giotto to Chagall, New York, 1945. Short considerations of Lautrec, van Gogh, Cézanne. Few ill., index, no bibl.

136 D. COOPER: George Moore and Modern Art, *Horizon,* Feb. 1945.

137 R. GOLDWATER and M. TREVES [editors]: Artists on Art, from the XIVth to the XXth Century, New York, 1945. Contains a section: Post-Impressionism and Symbolism, with excerpts from writings and utterances by Redon, Cézanne, Gauguin, Seurat, Signac, Denis, van Gogh, etc. Some ill., bibl., index.

138 A. LHOTE: Ecrits sur la peinture, Paris–Brussels, 1946. Collection of articles, among them several studies on Cézanne, Seurat, van Gogh. Few ill., no index.

139 J. REWALD: The History of Impressionism, New York, 1946. Retraces the beginnings of Gauguin as a painter and gives a detailed account of the last impressionist exhibition of 1886, in which Seurat and Signac participated. Ill., bibl., index. Fourth edition: New York, 1973.

140 P. FRANCASTEL: Nouveau Dessin—Nouvelle Peinture, Paris, 1946. Chapter on: Imitation or expression. Short bibl., few ill., no index.

141 J. E. S. JEANÈS: D'après nature—souvenirs et portraits, Geneva–Besançon, 1946. Recollections and anecdotes of Renoir, Rodin, Moréas, etc., with glances at Seurat, Signac, Lautrec, Anquetin, Degas, and others. No ill.

142 G. Bazin: L'Epoque impressionniste, Paris, 1947. Short, condensed chapters on the Independents and neo-impressionists, on symbolist painters, on *cloisonnisme*, etc. Numerous well-selected plates in black and white and color, generally of well-known works. Extensive biographical notes with selected bibl. on individual painters and on the various artistic movements.

143 C. Chassé: Le Mouvement symboliste dans l'art du XIXe siècle, Paris, 1947. Chapters on Moreau, Puvis de Chavannes, Redon, Carrière, Gauguin, Cézanne, the Pont-Aven group, etc., with many interesting quotations. Well selected ill., no bibl., index.

144 T. Natanson: Peints à leur tour, Paris, 1948. Charming portrait studies of Renoir, Monet, Degas, Redon, Pissarro, Carrière, Puvis de Chavannes, Gauguin, Seurat's friends—particularly Signac—Lautrec, Anquetin, etc., all of whom the author, an editor of the *Revue Blanche,* knew more or less well. Some ill., no index.

145 R. Pallucchini: Gli Impressionisti alla XXIV Biennale di Venezia, Venice, 1948. Introduction by L. Venturi. Elaborate catalogue of an exhibition including works by Gauguin, van Gogh, Seurat, and Lautrec. All reproduced.

146 A. M. Frankfurter: Introduction to the catalogue of an exhibition: Six Masters of Post-Impressionism: Cézanne, Gauguin, Lautrec, Rousseau, van Gogh, Seurat. Wildenstein Galleries, New York, April–May 1948. Ill.

147 J.-E. Blanche: La Pêche aux souvenirs, Paris, 1949.

148 H. Cahill: Forty Years After, *Magazine of Art,* May 1949.

149 Francis Jourdain: L'Art officiel de Jules Grévy à Albert Lebrun, special issue, *Le Point,* Paris, 1949. Interesting ill.

150 M. Raynal: History of Modern Painting, from Baudelaire to Bonnard—The Birth of a New Vision, Geneva, 1949. Introduction by H. Read; historical and biographical notes by J. Leymarie. Large volume with numerous, well-selected color plates, historical charts, bibl., etc. Sections devoted to Cézanne, Seurat, Signac, Cross, Pissarro, van Gogh, Gauguin, Redon, Ensor, Lautrec, the Nabis, etc. (Skira).

151 C. E. Gauss: The Aesthetic Theories of French Artists, 1855 to the Present, Baltimore, 1949. Chapters: From Realism to Neo-Impressionism; Symbolism and Fauvism—Gauguin, Denis, Matisse. No ill., index, extensive bibl.

152 G. di San Lazzaro: Painting in France, 1895–1949, London–New York, 1949. Ill.

153 M. Florisoone: Introduction to the catalogue of an exhibition: Eugène Carrière et le Symbolisme, Orangerie, Paris, Dec. 1949–Jan. 1950. With notes by J. Leymarie. Chronological table of symbolism, list of exhibitions, general bibl., notes with individual bibl. on Carrière, Puvis de Chavannes, Redon, Rodin, Gauguin, Moreau, Schuffenecker, van Gogh, Anquetin, Laval, Meyer de Haan, Bernard, Séguin, de Chamaillard, Sérusier, Denis, and others. A very well conceived and useful catalogue, although Carrière is given somewhat more importance than he deserves. Ill.

154 D. Sutton: The Symbolist Exhibition in Paris, *Maandblad voor Beeldende Kunsten,* July 1950.

155 K. Clark: Landscape Painting, New York, 1950. General historical survey with short but pertinent considerations of Cézanne, Seurat, van Gogh, and Gauguin as landscape painters. Few but good ill., index.

156 Liste des principales oeuvres françaises du Musée d'Art Moderne Occidental à Moscou, *Cahiers d'Art,* no. II, 1950. Contains a list with dimensions of the amazing group of 14 paintings by Bonnard, 26 by Cézanne, 29 by Gauguin, 53 by Matisse, 19 by Monet, 51 by Picasso, 10 by Redon, 13 by Renoir, 7 by the *douanier* Rousseau, 4 by Lautrec, 10 by van Gogh, 5 by Vuillard, etc., formerly in the collections of Morosov, Tchukine, and others. See also 190 and 211.

157 L. Venturi: Impressionists and Symbolists, New York, 1950. Chapters on Manet, Degas, Monet, Pissarro, Sisley, Renoir, Cézanne, Seurat, Gauguin, van Gogh, Lautrec. The text knits together well-known biographical facts and insignificant details. Some highly fortunate formulations, 217 fair ill., bibl., index.

158 E. H. Gombrich: The Story of Art, London–New York, 1950. An excellent general history with chapters on: In Search of New Standards—The Late XIXth Century [Cézanne, van Gogh, Gauguin]; Lautrec and Seurat are briefly mentioned in final chapter: Experimental Art—The XXth Century. Ill., condensed bibl., index.

159 G. Marchiori: Pittura Moderna in Europa (da Manet a Pignon), Venice, 1950. Short chapters on van Gogh, Gauguin, Seurat, Cézanne, Ensor, Lautrec, the *douanier* Rousseau. Few ill., inadequate bibl.

160 D. Wild: Moderne Malerei—Ihre Entwicklung seit dem Impressionismus, 1880–1950, Zurich (Büchergilde), 1950. Short sections on Cézanne, Gauguin, van Gogh, Seurat, the *douanier* Rousseau, Redon, Lautrec, etc., which discuss mostly the well-selected and excellently reproduced works and give summarized biographies. Bibliographical references in footnotes. 96 good plates in black and white, 8 in color. Index.

161 B. Nicolson: Post-Impressionism and Roger Fry, *Burlington Magazine,* Jan. 1951. Excellent article.

162 P. Francastel: Peinture et Société—Naissance et destruction d'un espace plastique—de la Renaissance au Cubisme, Lyons, 1951. The illustrations are accompanied by analytical comments.

163 D. M. Robb: The Harper History of Painting—The Occidental Tradition, New York, 1951. Chapters on: Landscape and Impressionism [from Constable and Corot to Seurat] and on Post-Impressionism, chiefly concerned with Seurat, Cézanne, van Gogh, Gauguin, Puvis de Chavannes, Redon, Lautrec, and the *douanier* Rousseau. Some ill., selected bibl., index.

164 G. A. Flanagan: How to Understand Modern Art, New York–London, 1951. Chapters on Cézanne, van Gogh, Gauguin, Seurat, etc. Some ill., bibl., index.

165 B. Myers: Development of Modern Art—Symbolism, *American Artist,* Nov. 1951.

166 Francis Jourdain: Né en 76, Paris, 1951. Recollections.

167 M. Raynal: The Nineteenth Century—New Sources of Emotion from Goya to Gauguin, Geneva–Paris–New York, 1951. In spite of the title, Gauguin and the other painters of "The Dawn of the XXth Century" are given a very cursory treatment and few ill. Short biographical notes with condensed bibl.; summary general bibl., index (Skira).

168 F. Novotny: Die großen französischen Impressionisten —Ihre Vorläufer und ihre Nachfolge, Vienna, 1952. Large, fair color plates including works by Lautrec, van Gogh, Gauguin, Seurat, Signac, etc., with notes on the artists and a penetrating introduction.

169 P. F. Schmidt: Geschichte der modernen Malerei—Impressionismus, Expressionismus, Kubismus, Stuttgart, 1952. Short sections devoted to Cézanne, Gauguin, Redon, Seurat, van Gogh, etc. Few but good illustrations in black and white and color. Short bibl., index. The accent of this book is on the 20th century.

170 C. Roger-Marx: Le Paysage français—De Corot à nos jours, Paris, 1952. Chapter: La Leçon de Cézanne, Gauguin, van Gogh et Seurat. Ill., index.

171 B. Taylor: The Impressionists and Their World, London, n.d. [1953]. Short introduction, 96 fair-to-poor plates in color and black and white, including works by Gauguin, van Gogh, Lautrec, Seurat, Redon, and the *douanier* Rousseau, with short biographical charts and bibl.

172 R. Benet: Simbolismo, Barcelona, 1953. Chapters on Gauguin, on neo-impressionism [Entre la geometria y el lirismo], van Gogh, Redon [Esotéricos], Lautrec, etc. 370 ill. in black and white and 28 in color. No bibl., no index.

173 M. Raynal: Modern Painting, Geneva, 1953. Material selected from previous Skira publications with short studies of Seurat, van Gogh, Ensor, Gauguin, Redon, etc.; ill. with familiar color plates (Skira).

174 V. Volavka: French Paintings and Engravings of the XIXth Century in Czechoslovakia, Prague, 1953 [in English]. Trivial notes. Fair color plates and good illustrations in black and white, including details from works by Seurat, Gauguin, and van Gogh.

175 Catalogue of the exhibition: Van Gogh's grote tijdgenoten, Stedelijk Museum, Amsterdam, and Rijksmuseum Kröller-Müller, Otterlo, summer 1953. 65 works by Cézanne, Gauguin, Lautrec, Manet, Monet, Pissarro, Renoir, and Seurat, among them many little-known ones. Profusely ill.

176 D. Cooper: The Courtauld Collection of Paintings, Drawings, Engravings and Sculpture, London, 1954. The extensive introduction devotes a chapter to: The Post-Impressionist Phase. Excellent catalogue raisonné of this important collection which comprises, among others, famous works by Cézanne, Gauguin, Seurat, van Gogh, Lautrec, the *douanier* Rousseau. 116 good ill. in black and white, detailed index.

177 A. H. Barr, Jr.: Masters of Modern Art, New York, 1954. While primarily devoted to 20th-century art, this book contains illuminating pages on Cézanne, Seurat, van Gogh, Gauguin, Redon, Ensor, etc., with illustrations in black and white and color after works owned by The Museum of Modern Art, New York.

178 W. Haftmann: Malerei im 20. Jahrhundert, Munich, 1954. The opening chapters contain short considerations on post-impressionism, neo-impressionism, van Gogh, Gauguin and the School of Pont-Aven, Cézanne, symbolism, etc. Few ill., biographical notes with summary, bibl., index. Vol. II, same title, Munich, 1955, mostly devoted to excellent ill.

179 R. Gaffé: Introduction à la peinture française—De Manet à Picasso, Paris, 1954. Contains nothing new. Ill.

180 C. Roger-Marx: Maîtres du XIXe siècle et du XXe, Geneva, 1954. Collection of the author's articles, forewords, etc., containing short chapters on Gauguin, Redon, van Gogh, Seurat, Signac, etc. Index, ill.

181 Catalogue of the exhibition: The Two Sides of the Medal—French Painting from Gérôme to Gauguin. The Detroit Institute of Arts, 1954. Interesting material, ill.

182 Dictionnaire de la peinture moderne, Paris, 1954; New York, 1955. Well-conceived reference book, profusely ill.

183 R. Cogniat: Histoire de la peinture, vol. II, Paris, 1955. From the beginning of the 19th century to today, with commentaries and notes by G. Arout. Most of the plates have previously appeared in other publications.

184 J. Rohde: Journal fra en Rejse i 1892, Copenhagen, 1955. Edited by H. P. Rohde with a preface by N. G. Sandblad, this diary of a Danish painter, kept during a sojourn in Paris in 1892, is extremely interesting because of entries concerning Tanguy, Redon, the Nabis, neo-impressionism, etc.; some ill., index.

185 G. Schmidt: Kleine Geschichte der modernen Malerei, von Daumier bis Chagall, Basel, 1955. Analyses of works by van Gogh, Gauguin, and Cézanne; ill.

186 J. Rewald: Post-Impressionism—From van Gogh to Gauguin, New York, 1956. First edition of the present book.

187 S. Hunter: Modern French Painting—Fifty Artists from Manet to Picasso, New York, 1956. Short general history with comments on the works reproduced; mediocre ill.

188 P. Francastel: Lumière et couleur après l'impressionnisme, *in* Scritti di Storia dell'Arte in onore di Lionello Venturi, Rome, 1956, v. II.

189 M. Denis: Journal, v. I, 1884–1904, and v. II, 1905–1920, Paris, 1957; v. III, 1921–1943, Paris, 1959.

190 C. Sterling: Great French Painting in the Hermitage, New York, 1958. Excellent, large volume, richly and splendidly illustrated. Post-impressionism is represented by the Tchukine and Morosov collections, now divided between the Hermitage in Leningrad and the Pushkin Museum in Moscow. Despite the title, the book covers both museums. See also 156 and 211.

191 The Niarchos Collection, catalogue of an exhibition held in 1958 in New York, Ottawa, and Boston (also in London). This collection, constituted to a great extent by the former Edward G. Robinson collection, contains important post-impressionist works; ill.

192 The Albert D. Lasker Collection—Renoir to Matisse, New York, n.d. Preface by A. Frankfurter, commentaries by W. Brockway; 60 color plates.

193 H. R. ROOKMAAKER: Synthetist Art Theories—Genesis and Nature of the Ideas on Art of Gauguin and His Circle, Amsterdam, 1959. Important publication (in English).

194 M. SERULLAZ: Les Peintres impressionnistes, Paris, 1959. Chapters on "La Réaction contre l'impressionnisme" (Cézanne, Seurat, and Signac), "Autour de l'impressionnisme" (van Gogh), "Le Symbolisme ou la rupture" (the Pont-Aven group, Gauguin, Redon). Numerous color plates, brief biographies, index.

195 S. LOVGREN: The Genesis of Modernism—Seurat, Gauguin, van Gogh and French Symbolism in the 1880's, Stockholm, 1959. Important publication (in English), ill., bibl. with indication of some little known Scandinavian studies. Second revised edition: Bloomington, Ind., 1971.

196 Les Sources du XXe siècle—Les arts en Europe de 1884 à 1914, catalogue of an important exhibition at the Musée National d'Art Moderne, Paris, 1960–61. Rich source of information with texts and excellent notices by J. Cassou and others; ill.

197 The John Hay Whitney Collection, Tate Gallery, London, 1960–61. Catalogue by J. Rewald. Collection of important impressionist and post-impressionist works; ill.

198 E. W. HERBERT: The Artist and Social Reform: France and Belgium, 1865–1898, New Haven, Conn., 1961. A scholarly record of political allegiances rather than a work of art history, with only one chapter devoted to the visual arts.

199 Catalogue of the exhibition: Le Groupe des XX et son temps, Musées Royaux des Beaux-Arts de Belgique, Brussels, and Rijksmuseum Kröller-Müller, Otterlo, Feb.–May 1962. Prefaces by Ph. Roberts-Jones, A. M. Hammacher, and F.-C. Legrand; extensive notes on the members of the group and their guests, numerous good ill. An essential publication and important supplement to 78.

200 M. MEISS [editor]: Problems of the 19th and 20th Centuries—Studies in Western Art. Acts of the 20th International Congress of the History of Art, vol. 4, Princeton, N.J., 1963. Section on: The Reaction against Impressionism in the 1880's; Its Nature and Causes. Important contributions by P. Francastel, R. Goldwater, A. M. Hammacher, and F. Novotny.

201 Catalogue of the exhibition: Cézanne-Gauguin-van Gogh-Seurat, Wegbereiter der modernen Malerei, Kunstverein, Hamburg, 1963. Text by H. Platte, numerous ill.

201a P. ANGRAND: Naissance des Artistes Indépendants, 1884, Paris, 1965.

201b H. H. Hofstätter: Symbolismus und die Kunst der Jahrhundertwende, Cologne, 1965. Important study.

202 L. NOCHLIN: Impressionism and Post-Impressionism, 1874–1904: Sources and Documents in the History of Art, Englewood Cliffs, N.J., 1966.

203 J. SANDBERG: The Discovery of Japanese Prints in the Nineteenth Century before 1867, Gazette des Beaux-Arts, May–June 1968. With additional bibliographical references.

204 P. JULLIAN: Esthètes et magiciens, Paris, 1969; English edition: Dreamers of Decadence—Symbolist Painters of the 1890s, New York, Washington, London, 1971. See also the same author's: Les Symbolistes, Neuchâtel-Paris, 1973; English edition: London, 1973. Two richly illustrated books that are entertaining but superficial; many snap judgments but few scholarly references or discussions.

204a Catalogue of the exhibition: Il sacro e il profano nell' arte dei Simbolisti, Galleria d'Arte Moderna, Turin, 1969. Prepared by L. Carluccio. 371 ill.

204b G. H. HAMILTON: Nineteenth and Twentieth Century Art, New York, 1970. Short chapter on post-impressionism and symbolism.

205 M. ROSKILL: Van Gogh, Gauguin and the Impressionist Circle, London–New York, 1970. An important publication with stylistic studies concerning, in addition, Seurat and symbolism; ill.

205a Catalogue of the exhibition: Symbolists, Spencer A. Samuels, New York, 1970. Richly ill., with extensive comments. Symbolism treated as an international phenomenon, with works by Rosicrucians and other little-known artists.

206 A. BROOKNER: The Genius of the Future: Studies in French Art Criticism. London–New York, 1971.

207 H. H. HOFSTÄTTER: Idealismus und Symbolismus, Vienna, 1972.

208 E. LUCIE-SMITH: Symbolist Art, London, 1972. Chapters on: Symbolic Art; Romanticism and Symbolism; Symbolist Currents in England; The Symbolist Movement in France; Gustave Moreau; Redon and Bresdin; Puvis de Chavannes and Carrière; Gauguin, Pont-Aven, and the Nabis; The Rose + Croix, etc.

209 C. VAN RAPPARD-ROON: Japonism: The First Years, 1856–1876, in Liber Amicorum Karel G. Boon, Amsterdam, 1974.

210 R. HUYGHE: La Relève du réel: Impressionisme, Symbolisme, Paris, 1974. Ill.

211 A. BARSKAYA: French Painting, Second Half of the 19th and Early 20th Century—The Hermitage Museum, Leningrad, Leningrad (in English), 1975. A complete catalogue with 358 fine color plates, including 44 details; biographical notes and provenance.

212 Catalogue of the exhibition: Le Symbolisme en Europe, Museum Boymans-van Beuningen, Rotterdam; also in Brussels, Baden-Baden, and Paris; 1975–76. Essays by H. H. Hofstätter, F. Russoli, G. Lacambre. Artists from Austria, Belgium, Czechoslovakia, Denmark, England, Finland, France, Germany, Holland, Italy, Norway, Poland, Russia, Spain, and Switzerland represented. Extensive catalogue notes by various authors; all works ill.; exhibitions list; bibl. A model of its kind.

213 Catalogue of the exhibition: Vom Licht zur Farbe, Nachimpressionistische Malerei zwischen 1886 und 1912, Städtische Kunsthalle, Düsseldorf, 1977. Numerous, interesting ill.

II INDIVIDUAL ARTISTS AND CRITICS

AURIER, G.-Albert (1865–1892)

Founder, editor and/or contributor: *La Pléiade, Le Moderniste, Le Décadent, Essais d'Art Libre, Le Mercure de France, La Plume.*

Writings by Aurier

1 G.-A. AURIER: Oeuvres posthumes, Paris, 1893. Introduction by R. de Gourmont. This volume contains in Section I the novel: Ailleurs; Section II: Les Psychiques, Les Intermédiaires, Les Cosmogoniques, Les Ironiques [poems]; Section III: Essai sur une nouvelle méthode de critique; Le Symbolisme en peinture—Paul Gauguin; L'Impressionnisme (a) Claude Monet, (b) Renoir; Le Néo-impressionnisme—Camille Pissarro; Le Caractérisme—Raffaëlli; Les Isolés (a) Vincent van Gogh, (b) Henry de Groux, (c) Eugène Carrière, (d) J.-F. Henner; Les Peintres symbolistes [without ill.]; Simples chroniques [on Monticelli, Gauguin, the Salons of 1891, etc.]; Section IV: Mélanges [plays and other writings]. Some ill. after drawings by van Gogh, Sérusier, Bernard, Aurier himself, etc. Not included in this volume are:

2 G.-A. AURIER: Salon review, *Le Décadent*, 1888 [cannot be located].

3 LUC DE FLANEUR [pseud. for AURIER?]: En quête de choses d'art, *Le Moderniste*, April 13 and May 11, 1889. Reports on paintings to be seen at Theo van Gogh's and at Tanguy's.

4 G.-A. AURIER: Concurrence, *Le Moderniste*, June 27, 1887.

5 G.-A. A. [AURIER]: Choses d'art, a column appearing in *Mercure de France*, 1890–92.

6 G.-A. AURIER: Introduction to the catalogue of the 2nd exhibition of "Symbolistes et Impressionnistes," at Le Barc de Boutteville's, 1892; reprinted in *Mercure de France*, July 1892.

7 G.-A. AURIER: Les Symbolistes, *Revue Encyclopédique*, April 1892. Text included in Oeuvres posthumes, but without the important ill.

See also 13 and 14.

Writings on Aurier

8 V. VAN GOGH: Letter to Aurier, [Saint-Rémy, Feb. 12, 1890]; Verzamelde Brieven van Vincent van Gogh, vol. III, Amsterdam, 1953, no. 626a, pp. 500–01.

9 *Mercure de France,* special memorial issue devoted to Aurier, Dec. 1892.

10 J. LECLERCQ: Albert Aurier in: Portraits du prochain siècle, Paris, 1894. (See General Bibl. 26.)

11 E. BERNARD: Lettre ouverte à M. Camille Mauclair, *Mercure de France,* June 1895. Bernard tells here how he met Aurier. For Leclercq's reply see Bernard 12.

12 R. DE GOURMONT: Le 2e Livre des masques, Paris, 1898. Chapter on Aurier. See also 1.

13 M. COULON: Une Minute de l'heure symboliste—Albert Aurier, *Mercure de France,* 1921. Contains some unpublished notes by Aurier.

14 E. BERNARD: L'Enterrement de Vincent van Gogh, *Arts-Documents,* no. 29, Feb. 1953. Bernard's letter to Aurier on van Gogh's funeral as well as a letter by Aurier to Bernard.

15 H. R. ROOKMAAKER: Synthetist Art Theories, Amsterdam, 1959. Chapter on Aurier.

16 G.-Albert Aurier, Special issue of *Cahiers du Collège de Pataphysique,* dossier 15, 15 Gidouille, LXXXVIII [summer 1961].

BERNARD, Emile (1868–1941)

Writings by Bernard

1 E. BERNARD: Au Palais des Beaux-Arts, Notes sur la peinture, *Le Moderniste,* July 27, 1889.

2 E. BERNARD: Paul Cézanne, *Les Hommes d'Aujourd'hui,* vol. 8, no. 387, 1890.

3 E. BERNARD: Vincent van Gogh, *Les Hommes d'Aujourd' hui,* vol. 8, no. 390, 1890; reprinted in 24.

4 From 1890 to 1895 Bernard contributed to the programs of Le Théâtre d'Art and to *Le Livre d'Art,* edited by his future brother-in-law, Paul Fort.

5 E. BERNARD: Vincent van Gogh, *La Plume,* Sept. 1, 1891.

6 E. BERNARD: Vincent van Gogh, Extraits de lettres à Emile Bernard, *Mercure de France,* April 1893; reprinted in 24. Also *ibid.,* Aug. 1893: Letters to Theo van Gogh.

7 E. BERNARD: Odilon Redon, *Le Coeur,* Sept.–Oct. 1893. See also 53.

8 E. BERNARD: Les Primitifs et la Renaissance, *Mercure de France,* Nov. 1894.

9 E. BERNARD: Ce qui fait que l'art mystique . . . , *Mercure de France,* Jan. 1895.

10 E. BERNARD: Les Ateliers, *Mercure de France,* Feb. 1895 (some recollections of Cormon's studio).

11 E. BERNARD: Art naïf et art savant, *Mercure de France,* April 1895.

12 E. BERNARD: Lettre ouverte à M. Camille Mauclair, *Mercure de France,* June 1895 (Bernard attacks Gauguin, speaks of his own role as initiator of Aurier). J. Leclercq replied in *Mercure de France,* July 1895.

13 BERNARD: Passion de l'art, *Mercure de France,* Sept. 1895.

14 E. BERNARD: Réflexions d'un témoin sur la décadance du beau, Cairo, 1902. Collection of articles first published in *Mercure de France.*

15 E. BERNARD: Article on Symbolisme, *L'Occident,* 1902.

16 E. BERNARD: Notes sur l'école dite de "Pont-Aven," *Mercure de France,* Dec. 1903. M. Denis replied in: Lettre, *Mercure de France,* Jan. 1904 (pp. 286–87), and C. Morice in: Les Gauguin du Petit Palais et de la rue

Laffitte, *Mercure de France,* Feb. 1904 (pp. 393–95).

17 E. Bernard: Odilon Redon, *L'Occident,* May 1904. On this article and Redon's reaction to it see J. Rewald: Quelques notes et documents sur Odilon Redon, *Gazette des Beaux-Arts,* Nov. 1956.

18 E. Bernard: Paul Cézanne, *L'Occident,* July 1904.

19 From May 1905 to June 1910 Bernard was editor of *La Rénovation Esthétique,* which he had founded to defend his credo: "I believe in God, in Titian and in Raphael." He wrote numerous articles not only under his own name but also under the pseudonyms Jean Dorsal, Francis Lepeseur, F. L., H. Lebreton, etc. This periodical followed an extremely reactionary line in art as well as in politics (polemics against Zola, who had died in 1903), with a slightly antisemitic bias. Among the articles by Bernard which appeared there were: Paul Gauguin et Vincent van Gogh, documents, May–Oct. 1905; L'Anarchie artistique—les Indépendants, June 1905; Louis Anquetin, Sept. 1905; Documents pour l'histoire du symbolisme pictural en France, Oct.–Dec. 1906; Souvenirs, Nov. 1907 and April 1909.

20 Jean Dorsal [pseud.]: Les Cendres de gloire, poems, Paris, 1906.

21 E. Bernard: Souvenirs sur Paul Cézanne et lettres inédites, *Mercure de France,* Oct. 1 and 15, 1905; republished in book form, Paris, 1912 and 1921. See also 31 and 33.

22 E. Bernard: Julien Tanguy, *Mercure de France,* Dec. 16, 1908.

23 E. Bernard: L'Esthétique fondamentale et traditionnelle d'après les maîtres de tous les temps, Paris, 1910.

24 Lettres de Vincent van Gogh à Emile Bernard, Paris, 1911. Published by Vollard, this volume contains "Recueil des publications sur Vincent van Gogh faites depuis son décès par Emile Bernard" preceded by a new and lengthy introduction. The reprints include Bernard's introductions to the first publications of van Gogh's letters in the *Mercure de France,* April and Aug. 1893 (6); an unpublished introduction to a general publication of van Gogh's letters to his brother, planned by the *Mercure de France* in 1895; and Bernard's short study (3). The letters themselves are incorrectly dated. Numerous ill.

For an English translation see: Vincent van Gogh, Letters to Emile Bernard, edited, translated and with a foreword by D. Lord [Cooper], London, New York, 1937. This volume does not contain Bernard's writings; the letters are competently annotated and correctly dated, but the translation is not always felicitous. Numerous good ill.

Van Gogh's letters to Bernard have since been included in the general edition of van Gogh's correspondence.

25 E. Bernard: Odilon Redon, *La Vie,* Aug. 1916.

26 E. Bernard: La Méthode de Paul Cézanne, *L'Amour de l'Art,* Dec. 1920.

27 E. Bernard: La Technique de Paul Cézanne, *L'Amour de l'Art,* Dec. 1920.

28 E. Bernard: Une Conversation avec Cézanne, *Mercure de France,* June 1, 1921. In this conversation, tran-

scribed from memory, Bernard expounds his own ideas on art. See also 31.

29 E. Bernard: Sur l'art et sur les maîtres, Paris, 1922.

30 E. Bernard: Souvenirs sur van Gogh, *L'Amour de l'Art,* Dec. 1924.

31 E. Bernard: Sur Paul Cézanne, Paris, 1925. Bernard's recollections of Cézanne, including 28.

32 E. Bernard: L'erreur de Cézanne, *Mercure de France,* May 1, 1926.

33 Lettres de Vincent van Gogh, Paul Gauguin, Paul Cézanne, J.-K. Huysmans, Léon Bloy, Elémir Bourges, Milos Marten, Odilon Redon, Maurice Barrès à Emile Bernard, Tonnerre, 1926. Planned as the first volume of a series, this book contains letters to Bernard by van Gogh, Gauguin, Redon, Cézanne, Bourges, Bloy, Marten, and Apollinaire (but not Huysmans and Barrès), with short notes by Bernard on how he met his various correspondents. In appendix: Note relative au symbolisme pictural de 1888–1890, with excerpts from writings by R. Marx, Mirbeau, C. Anet, A. de La Rochefoucauld, etc., tending to prove that Bernard was the true "father of pictorial symbolism." New edition: Lettres à Emile Bernard, with same appendix, Brussels, 1942.

34 E. Bernard: Le Juif errant—poème en vingt chants, Tonnerre, 1927.

35 Anonymous [E. Bernard]: Emile Bernard, Paris, 1933. Short unsigned introduction to a volume of 51 plates, all but six of which represent Bernard's academic style.

36 E. Bernard: Louis Anquetin, *Gazette des Beaux-Arts,* Feb. 1934.

37 E. Bernard: La Connaissance de l'art, Paris, 1935. Exhortation for a return to classicism.

38 E. Bernard: Le Symbolisme pictural, 1886–1936, *Mercure de France,* June 15, 1936; reprinted in 44.

39 E. Bernard: Gauguin et Emile Bernard, *Le Point,* Oct. 1937.

40 E. Bernard: Les Modernes—Comédie en trois actes. Introduction by A. Vollard. Paris, 1938.

41 E. Bernard: Souvenirs inédits sur l'artiste peintre Paul Gauguin et ses compagnons lors de leur séjour à Pont-Aven et au Pouldu, Lorient, n.d. [1939].

42 Lettres de Gauguin, Gide, Huysmans, Jammes, Mallarmé, Verhaeren . . . à Odilon Redon, Paris, 1960. Contains Bernard's letters to Redon.

Posthumous Publications

Mostly edited by the artist's son Michel-Ange Bernard Fort.

43 E. Bernard: La Connaissance de l'art, *Nouvelle Revue Belgique,* Sept. 30, 1942.

44 E. Bernard: Charles Baudelaire, critique d'art, Brussels, n.d. [1943]. Includes 38.

45 E. Bernard: Mémoire sur le symbolisme pictural de 1890—Gauguin et l'art nègre—Une définition du symbolisme, *Maintenant,* no. 2, April 1946.

46 E. Bernard: Deux lettres sur Courbet, *Maintenant,* no. 7, 1947.

47 E. Bernard: Affaire Vincent, *Arts-Documents,* no. 16,

Jan. 1952. On the 1892 exhibition organized by Bernard at Le Barc de Boutteville's.

48 Des relations d'Emile Bernard avec Toulouse-Lautrec, *Arts-Documents,* no. 18, March 1952. Text by E. Bernard.

49 Les Archives Emile Bernard: Mémoire pour l'histoire du symbolisme en 1890, *Arts-Documents,* nos. 26–28 and 33, Nov. 1952–Jan. 1953, June 1953.

50 E. BERNARD: L'Enterrement de Vincent van Gogh, *Arts-Documents,* no. 29, Feb. 1953. Bernard's long letter to Aurier and a letter from Aurier to Bernard.

51 E. BERNARD: Pensées, and: Petites pierres sur le chemin de ma vie, *Quo Vadis,* April–June 1953. Notes by Auriant.

52 E. BERNARD: L'Aventure de ma vie (excerpts from: Récit d'un passager voyageant à bord de la vie) published as introduction to: Lettres de Paul Gauguin à Emile Bernard, 1888–1891, Geneva, 1954. Ill.

53 Emile Bernard révèle Odilon Redon, *Arts-Documents,* Aug.–Sept. 1954. See also **7.**

54 Une lettre inédite du peintre Emile Bernard à sa mère à propos de sa première visite à Paul Cézanne, *Arts-Documents,* no. 50, Nov. 1954.

Unpublished Lectures and Writings by Bernard

55 Mes voyages et mon évolution artistique; lecture given at the Hôtel de Sens, Paris, 1913.

56 Les assises de l'art; lecture given at the Hôtel de Sens, Paris, 1913.

57 De l'impressionnisme et du symbolisme à l'art classique; lecture given at the Hôtel Jean Charpentier, Paris, Jan. 4, 1920.

58 Victor Hugo et ses dessins; lecture given at the Musée Victor Hugo, Paris, May 1934.

59 Vers-proses. Voyages—1893–94–95, avec des critiques d'art sur Redon, Cézanne, etc. Suite—1895–1897 (Voyages du Caire). Manuscript.

60 Lettres à ma famille, 1893 etc. . . . Excerpts from letters recounting Bernard's life from 1893 to 1901 [Italy, Constantinople, Jerusalem, Alexandria, Cairo, Málaga, Seville, Venice], with list of his most important paintings and frescoes done in the Orient. Manuscript.

61 La vie de Madeleine Bernard, followed by her correspondence with her brother, her father, and her mother. Manuscript.

62 Du Caire à Grenade. Diary of a trip, July–Aug. 1896. Manuscript.

63 Sur l'art de notre temps et des autres. Manuscript.

64 Sur le coloris, 1918. Manuscript.

65 Traité des harmonies des couleurs à l'usage du peintre, 1930. Manuscript.

See also **116** and **117.**

Writings on Bernard

66 J. DAURELLE: Chez les jeunes peintres, *Echo de Paris,* Dec. 28, 1891. Includes an interview with Bernard.

67 A. AURIER: Les Symbolistes, *Revue Encyclopédique,* April 1892; reprinted in Oeuvres posthumes, Paris, 1893.

68 FRANCIS JOURDAIN: Notes sur le peintre Emile Bernard, *La Plume,* 1893, pp. 392–96.

69 FRANCIS JOURDAIN: Les Peintres novateurs: Emile Bernard, *La Plume,* 1894.

70 A. MELLERIO: Le Mouvement idéaliste en peinture, Paris, 1896.

71 R. MARX: Introduction to the catalogue of Emile Bernard exhibition (Paris, Brittany, Egypt), Galerie Vollard, Paris, June 1901.

72 C. ANET: Notice on Bernard's exhibition at Vollard's, *Revue Blanche,* July 1901.

73 J. MEIER-GRAEFE: Entwicklungsgeschichte der modernen Kunst, Stuttgart, 1904. Section on Bernard in the chapter: Die Schule von Pont-Aven.

74 P. CÉZANNE, letters to his son concerning Bernard, written in 1906; see: Paul Cézanne, Letters, London, 1941.

75 L. DE MONGUERRE: Les Artistes rénovateurs, M. Emile Bernard, *La Rénovation Esthétique,* March 1906.

76 L. LORMEL: L'Individualisme et l'école traditionaliste, *La Rénovation Esthétique,* Aug. 1907.

77 M. MARTEN: Sur l'oeuvre d'Emile Bernard, *Vers et Prose,* vol. 18, 1909.

78 M. MARTEN: Introduction to the catalogue of Bernard exhibition, Musée Beaudoin, Paris, Feb. 1910; published in supplement of *La Rénovation Esthétique.*

79 P. JAMOT: Emile Bernard, *Gazette des Beaux-Arts,* 1912.

80 P. JAMOT: Introduction to the catalogue of Bernard exhibition, Galerie R. Levesque, Paris, Dec. 1912.

81 V. PICA: Attraverso gli albi e le cartelle, vol. IV, Bergamo, n.d. Chapter on Bernard as illustrator, ill.

82 P. JAMOT: Emile Bernard illustrateur, *Gazette des Beaux-Arts,* 1917.

83 C. CHASSÉ: Gauguin et le groupe de Pont-Aven, Paris, 1921.

84 L. GENTINA: Emile Bernard e il cielo umano, Venice, 1925.

85 CIOLKOWSKI: Emile Bernard, *L'Art et les Artistes,* May 1926.

86 AURIANT: Emile Bernard illustrateur, *L'Amour de l'Art,* 1928.

87 H. FOCILLON: La Peinture, XIXe et XXe siècles, Paris, 1928, pp. 290–91.

88 P. MORNAND: Emile Bernard, peintre et poète de l'amour mystique et charnel, *Courrier Graphique,* June 1939. On Bernard's work as book illustrator. Ill.

89 M. DENIS: Hommage à Emile Bernard; unpublished text of a lecture given in Bernard's studio, 15 quai de Bourbon, Paris, on July 4, 1943.

90 B. DORIVAL: Les Etapes de la peinture française contemporaine, vol. I, Paris, 1943. Chapter on Gauguin and Pont-Aven group with lengthy passage on Bernard, pp. 99–102.

91 P. JAMOT: Introduction to Bernard exhibition, Galerie Charpentier, Paris, 1943.

92 Catalogue of the exhibition: Oeuvres de Pont-Aven (1888–1893 et 1940–1941) du peintre Emile Bernard, Galerie d'Art Méda, Toulouse, Dec. 1944. No illustrations or list of paintings shown; excerpts from various writings

by A. Alexandre, P. Jamot, G. Apollinaire, etc.

93 C. MAUCLAIR: unpublished introduction to a Bernard retrospective planned in Paris in 1944.

94 U. E. JOHNSON: Ambroise Vollard, Editeur, New York, 1944. Contains list of Bernard's prints and illustrated books published by Vollard. Revised edition: New York, 1977.

95 M. MALINGUE: Emile Bernard, cet initiateur, *Les Arts et les Lettres,* July 12, 1946.

96 A. MEYERSON: Van Gogh and the School of Pont-Aven, *Konsthistorisk Tidskrift,* Dec. 1946.

97 C. CHASSÉ: Le Mouvement symboliste dans l'art du XIXe siècle, Paris, 1947.

98 AURIANT: Souvenirs sur Emile Bernard, *Maintenant,* no. 7, 1947. Fascinating and extremely important article; the most complete biographical study of Bernard.

99 F. DE LA FLICKE: Emile Bernard, *Horizon,* Revue des lettres, Nantes, 1948.

100 Catalogue of the exhibition: Carrière et le Symbolisme, Orangerie, Paris, Dec. 1949–Jan. 1950. Section on Bernard.

101 Emile Bernard et Vincent van Gogh, *Arts-Documents,* no. 17, Feb. 1952. Theo van Gogh's letter to Bernard (published also in 24), as well as letters to Bernard by Theo's widow.

102 Les Archives Emile Bernard, *Arts-Documents,* no. 21, June 1952. Reproduces a portrait by Bernard supposedly of Theo van Gogh.

103 H.-H. HOFSTÄTTER: Die Entstehung des neuen Stils in der französischen Malerei um 1890. Ph.D. thesis, Freiburg-im-Breisgau, Nov. 1954. An extensive study which analyzes individually most of Bernard's paintings and sketches of the period and their relation to Gauguin's evolution. The first comprehensive approach to the problem. Bibl., no ill.

104 J. REWALD: Emile Bernard, *in* Dictionnaire de la peinture moderne, Paris, 1954, New York, 1955.

105 H. DORRA: Emile Bernard and Paul Gauguin, *Gazette des Beaux-Arts,* April 1955 (published Dec. 1955). Interesting study with new documents and numerous illustrations.

106 J. REWALD: Quelques notes et documents sur Odilon Redon. Article chiefly concerned with Bernard's study of Redon (see 17) and the latter's reaction to it. *Gazette des Beaux-Arts,* Nov. 1956.

107 H. PERRUCHOT: Emile Bernard et Cézanne, *Le Jardin des Arts,* Jan. 1, 1957.

108 Catalogue of the exhibition: E. Bernard & Pont-Aven (1883–1896), Hirschl & Adler Galleries, New York, Feb.–March 1957. Ill.

109 P. MORNAND: Emile Bernard et ses amis [van Gogh, Gauguin, Lautrec, Cézanne, Redon], Geneva, 1957. Unimportant; the role of Bernard is exaggerated; ill.

110 FRANCIS JOURDAIN: Emile Bernard, le bon génie de Gauguin, *Connaissance des Arts,* Aug. 1958.

111 Catalogue of the exhibition: Emile Bernard, époque de Pont-Aven (1883–1893), Galerie Durand-Ruel, Paris, April–May 1959; preface by H. Perruchot, ill.

112 Emile Bernard (1868–1941), *Documents,* no. 100, 1959. Preface by H. Perruchot, study by M. Chesneau, documentation by P. Cailler. Biography, ill., bibl. copied from the present book.

113 H. R. ROOKMAAKER: Synthetist Art Theories, Amsterdam, 1959.

114 Hommage de la ville de Pont-Aven à Emile Bernard, Pont-Aven, June–Aug. 1960. Catalogue of an exhibition with texts by M. Chesneau and J. Cheyron, no ill.

115 Catalogue of the exhibition: Emile Bernard—Pont-Aven, Valley House Gallery, Dallas, Texas, March–April 1962. 26 little known works, all ill.

116 Catalogue of the exhibition: Emile Bernard, Kunsthalle, Bremen, Feb.–April 1967. Biographical outline, unpublished notes on symbolism by the artist, texts by G. Busch and H. Boek. Bibl., ill. See also 117.

117 Catalogue of the exhibition: Emile Bernard, Palais des Beaux-Arts, Lille, April–June 1967. French version of Bremen catalogue cited above, including the essay by Bernard.

118 Catalogue of the exhibition: Hommage de la Bourgogne à Emile Bernard, Musées d'Auxerre, July–Sept. 1968.

119 Catalogue of the exhibition: Emile Bernard, Göteborg, Lyngby, and Stockholm, 1969.

120 J.-J. LUTHI: Emile Bernard—L'Initiateur, Paris, 1974. Deplorable color plates. Extensive list of Bernard's writings. Bibl., list of exhibitions.

121 J.-J. LUTHI: Emile Bernard—Chef de l'Ecole de Pont-Aven, Paris, [1976]. Pamphlet.

FENEON, Félix (1861–1944)

Founder, editor, and/or contributor: *Revue Indépendante, Vogue, Décadent, Symboliste, L'Art Moderne, Revue Exotique, Cravache, Hommes d'Aujourd'hui, Art et Critique, Entretiens Politiques et Littéraires, L'Endehors* [column: "Hourras, tollés et rires maigres"], *Essais d'Art Libre, Chat Noir, Revue Blanche, Bulletin de la Vie Artistique;* translator of Poe letters and of Jane Austen's "Catherine Morland," editor of Laforgue's last poems and papers; *see also* General Bibl. 54.

Writings by Fénéon

1 F. FÉNÉON: Oeuvres, Paris, 1948. Introduction by J. Paulhan, reprinted from 38. Posthumous collection of Fénéon's writings, including his famous pamphlet: "Les Impressionnistes en 1886." Unfortunately the section of art studies is not arranged chronologically and thus distorts the evolution of Fénéon's appreciation. It includes an article on "De la représentation de la nature" which is actually by Dujardin, and omits some of Fénéon's most important articles on the neo-impressionists, as well as other writings such as:

2 F. FÉNÉON: L'Impressionnisme aux Tuileries, *L'Art Moderne,* Sept. 19, 1886.

3 F. FÉNÉON: Le Musée du Luxembourg, *Le Symboliste,* Oct. 15–22, 1886.

4 F. FÉNÉON: L'Impressionnisme, *Emancipation sociale,*

Narbonne, April 3 and 16, 1887.

5 F. FÉNÉON: Le Néo-impressionnisme, *L'Art Moderne,* May 1, 1887.

6 F. FÉNÉON: Le Néo-impressionnisme, *Le Revue Exotique,* May 4, 1887.

7 F. FÉNÉON: Le Néo-impressionnisme à la IVe exposition des Artistes Indépendants, *L'Art Moderne,* April 15, 1888.

8 F. F. [FÉNÉON]: various notes on G. Kahn, Laforgue, le Théâtre Libre, etc., in *L'Art Moderne.*

9 THÉRÈSE [FÉNÉON]: Une Affiche, *La Cravache,* Sept. 15, 1888.

10 F. FÉNÉON: 5e exposition des Artistes Indépendants, *La Vogue,* 1889, reprinted in *L'Arte Moderne,* Oct. 27, 1889.

11 F. FÉNÉON: Paul Signac, *Les Hommes d'Aujourd'hui,* vol. 8, no. 373, 1890. (Not included in 1; the study on Signac reprinted there as having appeared in *Les Hommes d'Aujourd'hui* was published in *La Plume,* Sept. 1, 1891.)

12 F. FÉNÉON: Notice on the death of Albert Dubois-Pillet, *L'Art Moderne,* Aug. 21, 1890.

13 ANONYMOUS [F. FÉNÉON]: Note on the death of Seurat, *Entretiens Politiques et Littéraires,* 1891, vol. 2, no. 13.

14 F. FÉNÉON: Au Pavillon de la ville de Paris, Société des Artistes Indépendants, *Chat Noir,* April 2, 1892.

15 F. FÉNÉON: Au Pavillon de la ville de Paris, Société des Artistes Indépendants, *L'Endehors,* April 12, 1892.

16 F. [FÉNÉON]: Léo Gausson, *Revue Blanche,* vol. 10, 1896, p. 336.

17 F. [FÉNÉON]: L'Exposition Camille Pissarro, *Revue Blanche,* vol. 10, 1896, p. 480.

18 F. FÉNÉON: Introduction to catalogue of Paul Signac exhibition, Galerie Druet, Paris, Dec. 1904.

19 F. FÉNÉON and R. DELANGE: Dialogue sur l'eau, *Cahiers d'Aujourd'hui,* Sept. 1921.

20 The Art Criticism of Félix Fénéon, Selections translated by F. Kloeppel, *Arts,* Jan. 1957.

21 F. FÉNÉON: Ecrits sur Georges Seurat, assembled as an introduction to the catalogue of Seurat's paintings by H. Dorra and J. Rewald, Paris, 1959 (see under SEURAT). Excerpts from 2, 5, 10, 11, 13, and 14, among others.

22 J. UNGERSMA: La Critique d'art au *père Peinard, Nouvelle Revue Française,* May 1, 1966. Not wholly convincing attribution to Fénéon of a text written in *argot* which appears to be too vulgar and unoriginal to be by this author.

23 F. FÉNÉON: Oeuvres plus que complètes, Paris–Geneva, 1970. 2 vol., texts assembled and annotated by Joan [Ungersma] Halperin (see also 22). Although not everything in these volumes may be by Fénéon, it is certainly good to have his various writings easily accessible and in chronological order.

See also **49.**

Writings on Fénéon

24 ANONYMOUS: Médaillon: Elie-Félix Fénéon, *Le Décadent,* Sept. 25, 1886.

25 J. MORÉAS: Peintures, *Le Symboliste,* Oct. 22–29, 1886.

Favorable review of Fénéon's: Les Impressionnistes en 1886.

26 B. DE MONCONYS [P. ADAM]: Les Personnalités symbolistes, *La Vie Moderne,* Dec. 4, 1886.

27 T. DE WYZEWA: Les Livres, *La Revue Indépendante,* Feb. 1887. Review of Fénéon: Les Impressionnistes en 1886.

28 TRUBLOT [P. ALEXIS]: Visite à la Revue Indépendante, *Le Cri du Peuple,* April 14, 1888.

29 G. VANOR: L'Art symboliste, introduction by P. Adam, Paris, 1889; pp. 32–33.

30 ANONYMOUS (WILLY [H. GAUTIER-VILLARD] and A. ERNST): Lettres de l'ouvreuse. Paris, 1890.

31 J. DE MITTY: article in *La Presse,* March 25, 1895.

32 R. DE GOURMONT: Le 2e Livre des masques, Paris, 1898; chapter on Fénéon.

33 F. DE MIOMANDRE: Vingt ans après, *Bulletin de la Vie Artistique,* Feb. 15, 1926.

34 E. DEVERIN: Fénéon l'énigmatique, *Mercure de France,* Nov. 15, 1934.

35 T. NATANSON: Ceux de la Revue Blanche: Félix Fénéon; unpublished broadcast, Radio Paris, Nov. 25, 1938.

36 E. SCHNEIDER: Félix Fénéon, *Le Courrier,* Geneva, Dec. 19, 1943.

37 J. REWALD: Georges Seurat, New York, 1943. Chapter on Fénéon.

38 J. PAULHAN: F. F. ou le critique, Paris, 1945. A clever and paradoxical essay which reveals more about the author's brilliant mind than about that of his subject. Excellent ill. Reprinted as introduction to 1.

39 M. SAINT-CLAIR [MARIA VAN RYSSELBERGHE]: Galerie privée, Paris, 1947. Excellent portrait-study of Fénéon.

40 J. REWALD: Félix Fénéon, *Gazette des Beaux-Arts,* July–Aug. 1947, Feb. 1948. Many documents, profusely ill.

41 J. ARLIN: Félix Fénéon, *Arts,* March 12, 1948, and reply by S. Kapferer: Le Vrai Fénéon, *Arts,* April 2, 1948.

42 J. TEXCIER: Félix Fénéon, curieux homme, *Le Populaire,* Jan. 9, 1949.

43 R. LONGHI: Proposte per una critica d'arte, *Paragone,* Jan. 1950. Review of 1.

44 J. REWALD: Félix Fénéon, critique d'art, *Maandblad voor beeldende Kunsten,* March 1950. Review of 1.

45 ANONYMOUS [D. COOPER]: Le Roi Fénéon, *The Times Literary Supplement,* London, April 28, 1950.

46 O. REUTERSWÄRD: Impressionisterna inför public och Kritik, Stockholm, 1952.

47 E. MILLARD [pseudonym]: Le commerce de la peinture, *Les Lettres Nouvelles,* May 1953.

48 M. RAYNAL: article on Fénéon in: Dictionnaire de la peinture moderne, Paris, 1954, New York, 1955.

49 F. CACHIN: Félix Fénéon—Au-delà de l'impressionnisme, Paris, 1966. Excellent small book with an introduction and excerpts from many writings which were previously difficult to locate.

Fénéon Collection

50 Catalogue of Collection Félix Fénéon, Sale, Paris, Dec. 4,

1941. Numerous works by Cross, Luce, Seurat, Signac, etc. Ill.

51 Catalogue of Collection Félix Fénéon, First and Second Sales, Paris, April 30 and May 30, 1947. Numerous paintings, drawings, etc., by Angrand, Cross, Luce, Seurat, Signac, and others. (Followed by a third sale of Fénéon's collection of African sculpture.)

GAUGUIN, Paul (1848–1903)

Oeuvre Catalogues

1 G. WILDENSTEIN: Gauguin—Catalogue I, Paris, 1964. A posthumously published catalogue raisonné of paintings (to be followed by a volume of drawings and documents). This book does not solve all the problems presented by Gauguin's vast production but it constitutes a good working tool until the publication of a completely revised edition, which has been announced. For an excellent review see: M. Bodelsen, *Burlington Magazine,* Jan. 1966 (235); see also 238.

2 M. GUÉRIN: L'Oeuvre gravé de Gauguin, Paris, 1927. 2 vols. Lithographs, woodcuts, and etchings, all reproduced, sometimes in various states and with preparatory drawings. 96 ill., mostly full page. A new revised edition, originally begun by C. O. Schniewind and completed by E. Mongan, is in preparation. See also 167.

3 CH. GRAY: Sculpture and Ceramics of Paul Gauguin, Baltimore, 1963. A conscientious and well-presented—though not always satisfactory—endeavor to assemble the artist's three-dimensional works and to trace the sources of his inspiration. Profusely ill. For a review see: W. V. Andersen, *Art Bulletin,* Dec. 1964.

4 M. BODELSEN: Gauguin's Ceramics, London, 1964. While more restricted in scope than 3, this study provides infinitely more information on the previously insufficiently explored subject of the artist's ceramic works. Exhaustive text, good ill. in color and black and white.

Following are some important exhibition catalogues:

5 Exposition d'oeuvres récentes de Paul Gauguin, Paris, Galeries Durand-Ruel, Nov. 1893. Introduction by C. Morice. Small catalogue of great historical importance, listing Gauguin's most representative works of his first trip to Tahiti; no ill.

6 Catalogue of the Gauguin Sale, Paris, Hôtel Drouot, Feb. 18, 1895. With a long letter by Strindberg to Gauguin and the latter's reply [the two documents are reproduced in 95, pp. 148–53]. For a list with buyers and prices see 24.

7 Gauguin retrospective, Salon d'Automne, Paris, 1906; introduction by C. Morice. 277 items.

8 Gauguin, exposition rétrospective, Paris, Dec. 1926. Introduction by C. del Pomar and G. D. de Monfreid.

9 Sculptures de Gauguin, Musée du Luxembourg, Paris, 1927. Catalogue by C. Masson and R. Rey.

10 Gauguin, sculpteur et graveur, Musée du Luxembourg, Paris, Jan.–Feb. 1928. Catalogue by C. Masson and M. Guérin; ill.

11 Gauguin Ausstellung, Kunsthalle, Basel, July–Aug. 1928.

Introduction by W. Barth; bibl., ill.

12 Gauguin Ausstellung, Galerien Thannhauser, Berlin, Oct. 1928. Introduction by W. Barth; ill.

13 The Durrio Collection of Works by Gauguin, Leicester Gallery, London, May–June 1931; no ill.

14 Gauguin, ses amis, l'école de Pont-Aven et l'académie Julian, Paris, Galerie Beaux-Arts, Feb.–March 1934. Introduction by M. Denis, catalogue by R. Cogniat.

15 R. COGNIAT: La Vie ardente de Paul Gauguin, Paris, n.d. [1936]. Biographical text with catalogue of an exhibition, Galerie Wildenstein-Gazette des Beaux-Arts. Introduction by H. Focillon. Interesting new formula for a catalogue; ill.

16 Gauguin exhibition, Wildenstein Galleries, New York, March–April 1936. Introduction by R. Cogniat.

17 Gauguin exhibition, Baltimore Museum of Art, May–June 1936. Introduction by H. Focillon.

18 Paul Gauguin, Exhibition of Paintings and Prints, San Francisco Museum of Art, Sept.–Oct. 1936. Introduction by G. L. McCann Morley; chronology, selected bibl., ill.

19 Georges Daniel de Monfreid et son ami Paul Gauguin, Paris, Galerie Charpentier, Oct. 1938. Introduction by M. Denis.

20 Gauguin—Aquarelles, Monotypes, Dessins—Tahiti, 1891–93. Galerie Marcel Guiot, Paris, May–June 1942. Introduction by M. Guérin. Works assembled by Gauguin in a portfolio under the title: "Documents, Tahiti." Good cat., ill.

21 Gauguin, Wildenstein Galleries, New York, April–May 1946. Introduction by R. Cogniat; abundantly ill.

22 Paul Gauguin, Ny Carlsberg Glyptotek, Copenhagen, May–June 1948. Excellent catalogue by H. Rostrup, listing many little-known works in Danish collections (the majority of which were originally sold by the artist's wife); no ill.

23 Gauguin et ses amis, Galerie Kléber, Paris, Feb. 1949. Introduction and catalogue by M. Malingue.

24 Gauguin, Exposition du Centenaire, Orangerie des Tuileries, Paris, summer 1949. Introduction by R. Huyghe; catalogue by J. Leymarie. Excellent catalogue (116 items) with unpublished documents, bibliography, list of Gauguin exhibitions, ill., etc.

25 Gauguin, Kunstmuseum, Basel, Nov. 1949–Jan. 1950. 153 works, among them some little-known ones. Excellent catalogue with short bibliography listing many books on Tahiti in general, good ill.

26 Eugène Carrière et le Symbolisme, Orangerie des Tuileries, Paris, Dec. 1949–Jan. 1950. See General Bibl. 153.

27 Gauguin et le Groupe de Pont-Aven, Musée des Beaux-Arts, Quimper, July–Sept. 1950. Introduction by R. Huyghe: catalogue by G. Martin-Méry. Good catalogue, documents, few ill.

28 Commémoration du cinquantenaire de la mort de Paul Gauguin—Exposition d'oeuvres de Paul Gauguin et du Groupe de Pont-Aven, Pont-Aven, Aug.–Sept. 1953. Introduction by T. Briant, no ill.

29 Paul Gauguin, His Place in the Meeting of East and West, Museum of Fine Arts, Houston, March–April 1954. Introduction by H. Dorra. Interesting material, fine

catalogue, excellent ill.

30 Paul Gauguin—Paintings, Sculpture and Engravings, Edinburgh Festival, 1955. Introduction and excellent notes by D. Cooper; chronology, brief bibl., few ill.

31 Gauguin, Wildenstein Galleries, New York, April–May 1956. Forewords by R. Goldwater and C. O. Schniewind. Profusely ill.

32 Gauguin og hans Venner, Winkel & Magnussen, Copenhagen, June–July 1956. A group of little known works by Gauguin and his friends: Ballin, Bernard, Denis, Filiger, Laval, Monfreid, O'Connor, Schuffenecker, Séguin, Sérusier, Verkade, Willumsen, etc. Preface by H. Rostrup; extremely interesting ill.

33 Paul Gauguin, G.-D. de Monfreid et leurs amis, Perpignan, 1958. Typed catalogue, listing works by Gauguin, Monfreid, Maillol, Terrus, etc. Bibl. 317 appeared simultaneously.

34 Gauguin—Paintings, Drawings, Prints, Sculpture, Art Institute of Chicago and Metropolitan Museum of Art, New York, Feb.–May 1959. Preface by T. Rousseau, chronology, condensed bibl., detailed notes on the works exhibited. Excellent catalogue, numerous ill.

35 Cent oeuvres de Gauguin, Galerie Charpentier, Paris, 1960 (two editions). Prefaces by R. Nacenta and J. Leymarie, chronology by M. Malingue. Summary list of the works shown, ill. Unfortunately this exhibition included a number of works of doubtful authenticity, some of which are reproduced in the catalogue; they are also illustrated in a special issue of *Art et Style:* Gauguin, with preface by R. Nacenta, published simultaneously.

36 Paul Gauguin, Haus der Kunst, Munich, April–May 1960. Preface by H. Joachim, chronology by M. Malingue, condensed bibl. Summary list of 200 works shown, numerous good ill.

37 Paul Gauguin, Belvedere, Vienna, June–July 1960. Texts by G. Bazin and H. Joachim; chron., bibl., ill.

38 Paul Gauguin, Tokyo, Kyoto, Fukuoka, 1969. Richly illustrated catalogue with French captions and introductions.

39 Gauguin i Söderhavet, Ethnographic Museum, Stockholm, 1970. An important exhibition on the exotic sources of Gauguin's work, assembled by B. Danielsson with texts (in Swedish) by him and R. S. Field, excerpts from the artist's letters, and ill.

See also A. Joly-Segalen: Catalogue of exhibition: Victor Segalen—Poète de l'Asie, Galerie-Librairie Palmès, Paris, Oct.–Nov. 1950. Introduction by R. Cogniat. Items 62–92 relate to Gauguin (letters, documents, sketches, etc.), ill.

Writings by Gauguin—Texts

40 P. GAUGUIN: Notes synthétiques (c. 1886); published by H. Mahaut in *Vers et Prose,* July–Sept. 1910; reprinted in 252; reissued in a facsimile edition of the entire sketchbook in which they were jotted down, with prefaces by R. Cogniat and J. Rewald, Paris–New York, 1962.

41 P. GAUGUIN: Notes sur l'art à l'Exposition Universelle,

Le Moderniste, June 4 and 13, 1889.

42 P. GAUGUIN: Qui trompe-t-on ici? *Le Moderniste,* Sept. 21, 1889.

43 P. GAUGUIN: Huysmans et Redon, [c. 1889–91]; see J. Loize: Un inédit de Gauguin, *Nouvelles Littéraires,* May 7, 1953.

44 P. GAUGUIN: Ancien Culte Mahorie [Tahiti, 1892–93]. Excellent facsimile edition of Gauguin's illustrated manuscript: Paris, 1951. With an illuminating commentary by R. Huyghe, providing "la clef de Noa-Noa."

45 P. GAUGUIN: Cahier pour Aline [Tahiti, 1893]. Excellent facsimile edition with comments by S. Damiron, Paris, 1963.

46 P. GAUGUIN: Noa-Noa, [Paris, c. 1893–94].

P. GAUGUIN and C. MORICE: Noa-Noa. First published in *La Revue Blanche,* beginning Oct. 15, 1897.

P. GAUGUIN and C. MORICE: Noa-Noa, Paris, Editions La Plume, n.d. [1900]; 2nd ed. 1908; Editions Crès, Paris, 1924.

P. GAUGUIN: Noa-Noa, Voyage de Tahiti. Superb facsimile edition of Gauguin's illustrated manuscript (presented to the Louvre by Daniel de Monfreid in 1925), Berlin, n.d. [1926]. Reprint: Stockholm, 1947 (facsimile).

P. GAUGUIN: Noa-Noa (édition définitive), Paris, 1929; with two chapters and poems by C. Morice. Inadequate English translation by O. F. Theis, New York, n.d.

P. GAUGUIN: Noa-Noa, Paris, 1954. Facsimile edition of Gauguin's first draft [Paris, c. 1893–94], originally given to Morice; no ill., no comments.

P. GAUGUIN: Noa Noa—Voyage to Tahiti, Oxford, n.d. [1962]. Translated by J. Griffin, with an important Postscript by J. Loize, with numerous illustrations from the 1926 German edition.

P. GAUGUIN: Noa Noa, Paris, 1966. Edited by J. Loize with more extended comments than in the Oxford edition.

See also J. LOIZE: Gauguin écrivain, ou les sept visages de "Noa-Noa," Paris, 1949 (this text does not take into account Gauguin's original draft, published for the first time in 1954).

47 P. GAUGUIN: Natures mortes, *Essais d'Art Libre,* Jan. 1894.

48 P. GAUGUIN: Sous deux latitudes, *Essais d'Art Libre,* Feb.–April 1894.

49 P. GAUGUIN: Préface à l'exposition d'oeuvres nouvelles d'Armand Séguin, Galerie Le Barc de Boutteville, Paris, Feb.–March 1895; reprinted in *Mercure de France,* Feb. 1895.

50 P. GAUGUIN: Diverses choses, 1896–97. Manuscript.

51 P. GAUGUIN: L'Esprit moderne et le catholicisme, d. 1897–98. Unpublished manuscript, illustrated with monotypes and woodcuts, The St. Louis Art Museum. For excerpts and illustrations see H. S. Leonard: An Unpublished Manuscript by Paul Gauguin, *Bulletin of the City Art Museum of St. Louis,* summer 1949. *See also* Cat. No. 1, N. A. Kovach, Los Angeles, 1933 (item no. 120).

52 P. Gauguin: *Les Guêpes,* periodical published in Papeete 1898–1902 (articles by Gauguin appeared in 1899 and 1901). On this subject see B. Danielsson and P. O'Reilly: Gauguin journaliste à Tahiti et ses articles des "Guêpes," Musée de l'Homme, Paris, 1966.

53 P. Gauguin: *Le Sourire* [Papeete, 1899–1900]. Excellent facsimile edition: Le Sourire de Paul Gauguin, Paris, 1952. Includes the 9 issues and 3 supplements of the periodical published by Gauguin at Papeete in those years; introduction and notes by L.-J. Bouge; bibl.

See also Gauguin: Le Sourire—Journal sérieux; excerpts in French with English translation by K. Botsford, *Poetry New York,* no. 3, 1950.

54 P. Gauguin: Racontars de Rapin, [Marquesas Islands, Atuana, Sept. 1902]. Text published in full by A. Joly-Segalen, Paris, 1951. Extensively though not always correctly quoted in 95.

55 P. Gauguin: Avant et Après, [Marquesas Islands, Atuana, 1903]. Superb facsimile edition of Gauguin's most important manuscript: Leipzig (Kurt Wolff), 1918. With reminiscences (on van Gogh, among others), considerations on art, some ill. Reprinted: Copenhagen, n.d. [1951]. Regular edition: Paris, 1923. Condensed English translation by Van Wyck Brooks: The Intimate Journals of Paul Gauguin, New York, 1921, and subsequent editions: London, 1930. See also 58.

56 P. Gauguin: Reflections sur l'art et la nature de l'homme. Manuscript. Excerpts in Catalogue no. 324, Librairie Auguste Blaizot, Paris, n.d. [1966], nos. 1013–1014.

Writings by Gauguin—Letters

57 Lettres de Gauguin à Daniel de Monfreid, Paris, 1919. Introduction by V. Segalen. All names of contemporaries unfavorably referred to by Gauguin have been disguised by false initials. New edition: established by A. Joly-Segalen, Paris, 1950. All names are given in full, some deleted passages restored, extensive notes and new documents in appendix, notably letters by D. de Monfreid and C. Morice to Gauguin, by Sérusier and Mette Gauguin to D. de Monfreid, etc. Ill. Condensed and inadequate English translation: New York, 1922.

58 Lettres de Gauguin à André Fontainas, Paris, 1921. Introduction by A. Fontainas relates how Gauguin entered into correspondence with him and tells the story of the manuscript of Avant et Après (55), which Gauguin had sent him from Atuana shortly before his death. For an English translation see 60. Fontainas' letter to Gauguin, Paris, Dec. 19, 1902, is reproduced in 95, pp. 212–13. Letters incorporated in 61.

59 Lettres de van Gogh, Gauguin, Redon, Cézanne, Bloy, Bourges, etc. à Emile Bernard, Tonnerre, 1926. With short explanatory notes by Bernard; dates not always correct. New edition: Lettres de Paul Gauguin à Emile Bernard, 1888–91, Geneva, 1954. With a long unpublished text by Bernard: L'Aventure de ma vie. Dates not always correct; ill. Letters incorporated in 61. For an additional letter to Bernard see: Vincent van Gogh—

Letters to Emile Bernard, London–New York, 1938, no. XXIII, pp. 106–07.

60 P. Gauguin: Letters to Ambroise Vollard and André Fontainas, San Francisco, 1943. Edited by J. Rewald [translated by G. Mack]. See also Rewald: Gauguin and Vollard, *Art News,* May 1959, with an additional letter to Vollard.

61 Lettres de Gauguin à sa femme et à ses amis, Paris, 1946. Edited by M. Malingue. 2nd, augmented edition, Paris, 1949. 182 letters to the artist's wife, Schuffenecker, Bernard, Aurier, Mallarmé, Strindberg, Alexandre, Denis, Morice, Fontainas, etc.; also letters by Mette Gauguin to Schuffenecker. Unfortunately these letters are rather carelessly transcribed and not always correctly dated. Chronology, some illustrations. Very inaccurate English translation: Gauguin—Letters to his Wife and Friends, London, 1949. Not included, beside the letters to Vollard, are the following:

62 C. Roger-Marx: Lettres inédites de Vincent van Gogh et de Paul Gauguin, *Europe,* Feb. 15, 1939. (Letters to Schuffenecker; see also 133).

63 J. Ribault-Menetière: Lettres inédites de Gauguin, *Arts,* Jan. 11 and Sept. 27, 1946, March 28, 1947.

64 R. Rey: Introduction to: Onze Menus de Paul Gauguin, Geneva, 1950. Contains letters to Rouvier, Minister of Fine Arts, written in Paris, March 15, 1891, and in Tahiti, June 12, 1892.

65 P. Gauguin: Letter to the Danish painter Willumsen [written at Pont-Aven, autumn 1890], *Les Marges,* March 15, 1918.

66 P. Gauguin: Letter to O. Maus [autumn–winter 1890–91]; see M.-O. Maus: Trente années de lutte pour l'art, Brussels, 1926, p. 119.

67 P. Gauguin: Two letters to P. Sérusier [Tahiti, Nov. 1891 and March 25, 1892]; see P. Sérusier: ABC de la Peinture—Correspondance, Paris, 1950, pp. 52–55 and 58–60.

68 P. Gauguin: Letter to the editor of *Le Journal des Artistes,* [Paris, Nov. 14, 1894], in reply to: Enquête sur l'évolution des industries d'art, *Journal des Artistes,* Nov. 18, 1894. See also *Prisme des Arts,* no. 1, March 15, 1956.

69 P. Gauguin: Two letters to the editor of the newspaper *Le Soir,* Brussels; *Le Soir,* April 23 and May 1, 1895.

70 Interview of Gauguin by E. Tardieu, *Echo de Paris,* May 13, 1895.

71 P. Gauguin: Letters to a journalist, to Dr. M. Marx, and to M. Maufra [1894–96], reproduced in appendix of 24.

72 P. Gauguin: Letter to G. Fayet [Atuana, March 1902], *Arts Décoratifs,* Nov. 1925, p. 64; reprinted with Fayet's letter to Gauguin in 57, 2nd ed., pp. 201–03.

73 P. Gauguin: Letters to C. Siger and to E. Petit, Governor of Tahiti [Ivava, Nov. 1902]; *Mercure de France,* Aug. 1904.

74 P. Gauguin: Letter to a Judge in Papeete [Atuana, Jan. 1903]; recopied by Gauguin in Avant et Après (ed. Paris, 1923, pp. 141–45).

75 P. Gauguin: Letter to M. Porlier, capitaine au cabotage [Atuana, April 5, 1903]; see P. Borel: Les derniers jours et la mort mystérieuse de Gauguin, *Pro Arte et Libris*

(Geneva), Sept. 1942.

76 H. Rostrup: Gauguin et le Danemark (see 118) ; a letter to Mette Gauguin of Aug. 15, 1886, pp. 73–74.

77 Lettres de Gauguin, Gide, Huysmans, Jammes, Mallarmé, Verhaeren . . . to Odilon Redon, Paris, 1960. Six letters written 1889–94.

    B. Danielsson is preparing a book containing excerpts from unpublished letters to Gauguin's lawyer in Papeete (1902–03).

78 P. Gauguin: Oviri—Ecrits d'un sauvage, edited by D. Guérin, Paris, 1974. Excerpts from Gauguin's writings and letters.

    An edition of Gauguin's letters to Theo and Vincent van Gogh is being prepared by Ir. Dr. V. W. van Gogh.

    For a letter by Theo van Gogh to Gauguin see M. Bodelsen: An Unpublished Letter by Theo van Gogh, *Burlington Magazine,* June 1957.

    For van Gogh's letters to Gauguin see: V. van Gogh: Verzamelde Brieven, vol. III and IV, Amsterdam, 1953, 1954.

    See also Oeuvres écrites de Gauguin et Van Gogh, catalogue of an éxhibition, Institut Néerlandais, Paris, 1975. Introduction by Ir. V. W. van Gogh.

    A complete edition of Gauguin's correspondence, with numerous new documents, is being prepared by J. Rewald in collaboration with M. Bodelsen and B. Danielsson.

Witness Accounts

79 J. Huret: Paul Gauguin devant ses tableaux, *Echo de Paris,* Feb. 23, 1891.

80 C. Morice: Paul Gauguin, *Le Soir,* Paris, Nov. 23, 1894.

81 C. Morice: L'Atelier de Paul Gauguin, *Le Soir,* Dec. 4, 1894.

82 C. Morice: Le Départ de Paul Gauguin, *Le Soir,* June 28, 1895.

83 V. Segalen: Gauguin dans son dernier décor, *Mercure de France,* June 1904. See also the same author's introduction to 57.

84 O. Mirbeau: Lettres à Claude Monet, *Les Cahiers d'Aujourd'hui,* no. 9, 1922.

85 A. Gide: Si le grain ne meurt, Paris, 1924. (Encounter with Gauguin in Le Pouldu, completely quoted in the present vol.)

86 W. Verkade: Le Tourment de Dieu—Etapes d'un moine peintre, Paris, 1926.

87 A. Vollard: Recollections of a Picture Dealer, Boston, 1936. See General Bibl. 106; on Vollard's dealings with Gauguin see 60.

88 C. Pissarro: Letters to His Son Lucien, New York–London, 1943.

89 Auriant: XII lettres inédites de Charles Filiger, *Maintenant,* no. 6, July 1947. (Letters to J. Bois, relating an incident in Brittany, 1894.)

90 J. Loize: Les Amitiés du peintre Georges-Daniel de Monfreid et ses reliques de Gauguin, Paris, 1951. Rich documentation though full of trivia.

91 G. Kjellberg: Hänt och sant [Events and Truths], Stockholm, 1951. Chapters 4–6 deal with the author's life with the Molard family, who were Gauguin's neighbors in Paris after his return from Tahiti in 1893. Included also are recollections by Judith Gérard, Mme Molard's daughter. On this subject see also an article by Judith Gérard's son, G. Gérard-Arlberg: 6, rue Vercingétorix, *Utlandsvenskarna* [Swedes Abroad], no. 9, 1961.

92 Jénot: Le Premier Séjour de Gauguin à Tahiti (1891–93) ; see 118.

93 G. Le Bronnec: Les Dernières Années, reprinted in 118 from an article published originally in *La Revue de la Société des Etudes Océaniennes,* Papeete, 1954, with information collected in Atuana in 1910.

See also 95, 97, 98, 107, 129, 132, 138, 185, and 198.

Biographies

94 C. Morice: Paul Gauguin, *Les Hommes d'Aujourd'hui,* no. 440, vol. 9, 1896.

95 J. de Rotonchamp [pseud. for Brouillon]: Paul Gauguin, Weimar, 1906; Paris, 1925. The most important biography of Gauguin, written by a man who knew him but who based his account to a large extent on the documentation assembled by their mutual friend D. de Monfreid. Numerous quotations from letters, manuscripts; lists of paintings, auction catalogues, etc. Ill.

96 B. Lázár: Gauguin, Paris, 1908. Text of a lecture given in Budapest on the occasion of a Gauguin exhibition in May 1907.

97 C. Morice: Paul Gauguin, Paris, 1920. With Rotonchamp's book (95), the major biography written by a friend of the artist; Morice actually knew Gauguin much better than Rotonchamp, though his book is less methodical. Abundantly ill., no bibl., no index.

98 A. Alexandre: Paul Gauguin, sa vie et le sens de son oeuvre, Paris, 1920. Based to a great extent on Schuffenecker's recollections and on Gauguin's letters to Schuffenecker, many of which are quoted here for the first time (and some of which are not included in 61 and 62). Profusely ill.

99 J. G. Fletcher: Paul Gauguin, His Life and Work, New York, 1921.

100 K. Zelenina: Paul Gauguin, Moscow, 1926.

101 J. Dorsenne: La Vie sentimentale de Paul Gauguin, Paris, 1927. Based on Gauguin's letters to his wife, of which excerpts appeared here for the first time. Dated since the publication of 61.

102 W. Barth: Paul Gauguin—Das Leben, der Mensch und der Künstler, Basel, 1929. Biography combined with analyses of paintings; 50 good ill.

103 F. C. del Pomar: Arte y Vida de Pablo Gauguin, Madrid, 1930. Short bibl., ill., no index.

104 B. Ternovitz: Paul Gauguin, Moscow, 1934.

105 P. Vasseur: Paul Gauguin à Copenhague, *Revue de l'Art,* March 1935, pp. 117–26.

106 R. Burnett: The Life of Paul Gauguin, London, 1936. A very conscientious and readable biography; ill., index, no bibl.

107 Pola Gauguin: My Father Paul Gauguin, New York,

1937. This competent biography contains few personal recollections as the author hardly knew his father. Ill., index, no bibl.

108 C. KUNSTLER: Gauguin, Paris, 1937. Ill.

109 H. GRABER: Paul Gauguin—Der Künstler erzählt sein Leben, Basel, 1938. By the same author: Paul Gauguin—nach eigenen und fremden Zeugnissen, Basel, 1946. More or less clumsy translations of material first published elsewhere, without any indication of sources or even acknowledgment of the fact that the documents were not actually gathered by the author. R. Goldwater, in a review (*Art Bulletin,* June 1945) has justly censured Graber's "methods" as *piracy.* 60 good ill., no bibl., no index.

110 R. HAMON: Gauguin, le solitaire du Pacifique, Paris, 1939. A journalistic report on the places where Gauguin lived in Tahiti and the Marquesas Islands, on his descendants there, etc. Some documents, numerous photographs. By the same author: Sur les traces de Gauguin en Océanie, *L'Amour de l'Art,* July 1936.

111 H. PERRUCHOT: Gauguin, sa vie ardente et misérable, Paris, 1948. Largely based on Gauguin's writings, this is a competent book though presented with a slight tendency toward "fictionalizing"; no new material. Few ill., bibl., no index.

New ed., Paris, 1961. A more thorough study with particular attention to numerous details. Unfortunately the author neglects to provide sources for specific information. Few ill., extensive bibl., chron., no index.

112 L. VAN DOVSKI: Paul Gauguin—Das abenteuerliche Leben des großen Malers, Bern, 1948.

113 C. CHASSÉ: Les Démêlés de Gauguin avec les gendarmes et l'Evêque des Iles Marquises, *Mercure de France,* Nov. 15, 1948. See also 116.

114 B. VILLARET: Les Dernières Années de Gauguin, *Revue de Paris,* Feb. 1953.

115 L. and E. HANSON: Noble Savage—The Life of Paul Gauguin, London–New York, 1954–55. Though based on extensive research, this book reveals that the authors have a regrettable penchant for fiction and are insufficiently acquainted with questions of art.

116 C. CHASSÉ: Gauguin et son temps, Paris, 1955. Excellent analysis of the anarchist attitude of the symbolists; chapters on Gauguin's grandmother, on Gauguin at Pont-Aven (better organized than the same author's 132), on Gauguin in Tahiti (see also 113), his literary friends, etc. 21 ill.

117 C. CHASSÉ: Du Nouveau sur Gauguin, *Prisme des Arts,* Dec. 1956; on a thesis by Mme Vandenbroucke (see 118).

118 Gauguin, sa vie, son oeuvre, collection of texts, studies, and documents, edited by G. Wildenstein, Paris, 1958 (published also as a special issue of the *Gazette des Beaux-Arts,* Jan.–April 1958). This essential volume contains a genealogy of the Gauguin family; U. F. MARKS-VANDENBROUCKE: Gauguin, ses origines et sa formation artistique; H. ROSTRUP: Gauguin et le Danemark; G. WILDENSTEIN: Gauguin en Bretagne; Y. THIRION: L'Influence de l'estampe japonaise dans l'oeuvre de Gauguin; JÉNOT: Le Premier Séjour de Gauguin à Tahiti (1891–93) [see 92]; G. WILDENSTEIN: L'Idéologie et l'esthétique dans deux tableaux-clés de Gauguin; L.-J. BOUGE: Traduction et interprétation des titres en langue tahitienne inscrits sur les oeuvres océaniennes de Paul Gauguin [the translations are not always reliable]; J. LOIZE: Gauguin sauvé du feu; G. LE BRONNEC: Les Dernières Années [see 93]; documents (Gauguin's account books; the inventory of his belongings, May 27, 1903; the sale of works of art, books, and objects having belonged to Gauguin, Sept. 2, 1903); and numerous highly interesting ill., including photographs of his Breton landscape subjects.

119 J. REWALD: Gauguin and Vollard, *Art News,* May 1959; see also 60.

120 L. VAN DOVSKI: Gauguin—The Truth, London–Geneva, 1961. The title is too ambitious. This book summarizes most known facts, adds nothing new, and neglects many of the recent findings, thus repeating a number of errors; poor ill. First published in Germany in 1959. New German edition: Darmstadt, 1973; revised "catalogue."

121 P. BOMPARD: Ma Mission Paul Gauguin aux Marquesas Paris, 1962. Not very interesting.

122 G. BOUDAILLE: Gauguin, Paris, 1963. Among the numerous illustrations are several of doubtful authenticity.

123 B. DANIELSSON: Gauguins Söderhavsar, Stockholm, 1964. English edition: Gauguin in the South Seas, London, 1965, New York, 1966. An important book in which the author combines perfect knowledge of the South Sea islands where Gauguin lived with the fruit of patient and meticulous research. Ill.

124 C. CHASSÉ: Gauguin sans légendes, Paris, 1965. Ill.

125 P. O'REILLY: La Mort de Gauguin et la presse française, n.d. [1903], *Le Vieux Papier,* fasc. 212, April 1965.

126 F. CACHIN: Gauguin, Paris, 1968. A competent biography; ill.

127 W. ANDERSEN: Gauguin's Paradise Lost, New York, 1971. For a review see the *Times Literary Supplement,* May 25, 1973; mentioned in the *Chronique des Arts,* Oct. 1973, p. 32.

See also 15, 75, 252, 255, 259, and 324.

Gauguin and the Group at Pont-Aven

128 ANONYMOUS: Gauguin et l'école de Pont-Aven, by "un de ses admirateurs de l'école de Pont-Aven," *Essais d'Art Libre,* Nov. 1893.

129 A. SÉGUIN: Paul Gauguin, *L'Occident,* Jan.–June 1903.

130 M. FACY: Gauguin, *Brittia,* May 1914.

131 CAREIL: article on Gauguin in Brittany, *Le Fureteur Breton,* Nov.–Dec. 1919.

132 C. CHASSÉ: Gauguin et le groupe de Pont-Aven, Paris, 1921. Based on extensive research done in Brittany and on information provided by those who knew Gauguin there; long quotation from a report by Mothéré, husband of Marie Henry. But this important material is poorly organized (essential parts of it are much better presented in 116). Abundantly illustrated, yet unfor-

tunately the reproductions are not dated. Neither bibl. nor index.

133 A. SALMON: Chamaillard et le groupe de Pont-Aven, *L'Art Vivant,* July 1, 1925.

134 R. REY: A propos des peintures murales exécutées par Gauguin au Pouldu, *Bulletin de la Société de l'Histoire de l'Art Français,* 1926. See also the same author's: "La Belle Angèle" de Paul Gauguin, *Beaux-Arts,* April 1, 1927.

135 L. TUAL: Mademoiselle Julia de Pont-Aven, Concarneau, 1928.

136 R. J. GOLDWATER: Primitivism in Modern Painting, New York–London, 1938. Chapter on: Gauguin and the School of Pont-Aven.

137 C. CHASSÉ: De quand date le synthétisme de Gauguin? *L'Amour de l'Art,* April 1938.

138 A. S. HARTRICK: A Painter's Pilgrimage through Fifty Years, Cambridge, 1939. Recollections.

139 A. ARMSTRONG WALLIS: The Symbolist Painters of 1890, *Marsyas,* vol. I, 1941. Important article, ill.

140 B. DORIVAL: Les Etapes de la peinture française contemporaine, vol. I, Paris, 1943. Chapter on Gauguin and the Pont-Aven group.

141 C. CHASSÉ: Importance pour la Bretagne de l'école de Pont-Aven, *Nouvelle Revue de Bretagne,* no. 2, March–April 1946.

142 C. CHASSÉ: Gauguin et ses amis en Bretagne, *Paris, Les Lettres et les Arts,* April 26, 1946.

143 A. MEYERSON: Van Gogh and the School of Pont-Aven, *Konsthistorisk Tidskrift,* Dec. 1946.

144 R. MAURICE: Reflets du mouvement symboliste sur l'art en Bretagne, *Nouvelle Revue de Bretagne,* Nov.–Dec. 1947.

145 ANONYMOUS: Unknown Gauguin—Painted in a French Inn, It Turns Up in New York, *Life,* May 1, 1950.

146 W. JAWORSKA: Gauguin-Slewinski-Makowski, *Sztukai Krytka* [Art and Criticism], Warsaw, nos. 3–4, 1957 (in Polish).

147 Catalogue of the exhibition: Hommage à Sérusier et aux peintres du groupe de Pont-Aven, Musée des Beaux-Arts de Quimper, July–Sept. 1958.

148 Catalogue of the exhibition: Gauguin et ses amis, Hôtel de Ville, Pont-Aven, Aug.–Sept. 1961. Preface by M. Malingue, no ill.

149 Catalogue of the exhibition: Gauguin and the Pont-Aven Group, Tate Gallery, London, 1966. Introduction by D. Sutton; ill.

150 Catalogue of the exhibition: Pont-Aven—Gauguin und sein Kreis in der Bretagne, Kunsthaus, Zurich, 1966. Introduction by D. Sutton. This is a different publication from 149, with different ill.

151 Catalogue of the exhibition: Pont-Aven und Nabis, Galleria del Levante, Munich, 1966. Text by M. Malingue; ill.

152 W. JAWORSKA: W Kregu Gauguina malarze szkoly Pont-Aven, Warsaw, 1969. Ill. English edition: Gauguin and the Pont-Aven School, Boston, 1972. An important book, richly ill., with many reproductions of little-known works by Gauguin's followers.

153 W. ANDERSEN: Gauguin's Motifs from Le Pouldu—Preliminary Report, *Burlington Magazine,* Sept. 1970.

154 M. GUICHETEAU (with the collaboration of P. H. BOUTARIC): Paul Sérusier, Paris, 1976. Long text; detailed biographical table; ill. catalogue of 419 paintings, drawings, and watercolors (mixed together); list of exhibitions; selected bibl. Good ill., in black and white and color. Documentation was assembled by Boutaric but published without her knowledge.

See also the catalogues of the sales, Paris, Hôtel Drouot, Feb. 6 and 7, 1956 (O'Connor estate); March 16 and June 24, 1959 (Coll. Marie Henri).

See also Bernard Bibl. for various writings and exhibitions.

See also 14, 26, 27, 28, 32, 85, 86, 89, 187, 189, 205, 208, 211, 217, 218, 219, 264, and 288.

On Gauguin's Ceramics, Sculptures, and Woodcuts

155 R. MARX: A propos des oeuvres céramiques de Paul Gauguin, *Revue Encyclopédique,* Sept. 15, 1891.

156 L. VAUXCELLES: A propos des bois sculptés de Paul Gauguin, *L'Art Décoratif,* Jan. 1911.

157 G. VARENNE: Les Bois gravés et sculptés de Paul Gauguin, *La Renaissance,* Dec. 1927.

158 R. REY: Les Bois sculptés de Paul Gauguin, *Art et Décoration,* Feb. 1928.

159 W. BARTH: Eine unbekannte Plastik von Gauguin, *Das Kunstblatt,* June 1929.

160 L. VAUXCELLES: La sculpture de Paul Gauguin, *Art Décoratif,* 1935.

161 DARAGNÈS: Les bois gravés de Paul Gauguin, *Arts Graphiques,* no. 49, 1935, pp. 35–42.

162 C. O. SCHNIEWIND: Two Woodcuts by Paul Gauguin, *Bulletin of the Art Institute of Chicago,* Dec. 1940.

163 A. M. BERRYER: A propos d'un vase de Chaplet décoré par Gauguin, avec une liste de ses céramiques, *Bulletin des Musées Royaux d'Art et d'Histoire,* Brussels, Jan. 1944, pp. 13–27.

164 J. RIBAULT-MENETIÈRE: "Que sommes-nous?"—Un panneau sculpté par Gauguin, *Arts,* Sept. 12, 1947.

165 M. BODELSEN: The Missing Link in Gauguin's Cloisonnism, *Gazette des Beaux-Arts,* May–June 1959. Important article.

166 M. BODELSEN: Gauguin Ceramics in Danish Collections, Copenhagen, 1960. Important study (in English) with a detailed catalogue of 11 potteries, ill. See also 4.

167 L. SYKOROVA: Les Gravures sur bois de Paul Gauguin, Prague, 1963. With reproductions of a few works not listed in 2.

168 T. GOTTHEIMER: Some Unknown Blocks for Woodcuts by Gauguin, *Burlington Magazine,* April 1967.

169 B. LANDY: The Meaning of Gauguin's 'Oviri' Ceramic, *Burlington Magazine,* April 1967.

See also 2, 3, 4, 9, 10, 233, 239, and 261.

Studies of Style

170 J.-K. HUYSMANS: L'Art moderne, Paris, 1883.

171 P. Adam: A propos de la 8e exposition [of the Impressionists], *Revue Contemporaine,* 1886.

172 J. Antoine: Impressionnistes et Synthétistes, *Art et Critique,* Nov. 9, 1889 (review of the Volpini show).

173 O. Maus: Le Salon des XX à Bruxelles, *La Cravache,* Feb. 16, 1889.

174 O. Mirbeau: Chronique—Paul Gauguin, *Echo de Paris,* Feb. 16, 1891; reprinted in Mirbeau: Des artistes, vol. I, Paris, 1922.

175 G.-A. Aurier: Le Symbolisme en peinture—Paul Gauguin, *Mercure de France,* March 1891; reprinted in Aurier: Oeuvres posthumes, Paris, 1893.

176 G.-A. Aurier: Les Symbolistes, *Revue Encyclopédique* April 1, 1892; reprinted in Aurier: Oeuvres posthumes, Paris, 1893.

177 C. Merki: Apologie pour la peinture, *Mercure de France,* June 1893 (attacks on Gauguin, van Gogh, and Signac).

178 C. Morice: Paul Gauguin, *Mercure de France,* Dec. 1893.

179 T. Natanson: Oeuvres récentes de Paul Gauguin, *Revue Blanche,* Dec. 1893.

180 R. Marx: Paul Gauguin, 1894; reprinted in Marx: Maîtres d'hier et d'aujourd'hui, Paris, 1914.

181 C. Mauclair: Choses d'art, *Mercure de France,* June 1895; article against Gauguin.

182 C. Mauclair: Choses d'art, *Mercure de France,* May 1896. Says of Gauguin's Tahitian paintings: "This is Papuan art, revolting in its coarseness and its screaming violence. . . ."

183 A. Fontainas: article on Gauguin, *Mercure de France,* Jan. 1899; English translation in 60. This article prompted Gauguin to write to Fontainas and is responsible for their ensuing correspondence; see 58 and 60.

184 C. Morice: Paul Gauguin, *Mercure de France,* Oct. 1903.

185 C. Morice: Quelques opinions sur Paul Gauguin, *Mercure de France,* Nov. 1903. Includes short statements on Gauguin by Carrière, Dolent, Durrio, Geffroy, A. de La Rochefoucauld, Luce, R. Marx, Redon, H. de Régnier, L. Roy, A. Séguin, Signac, etc.

186 O. Mirbeau: article on Gauguin in *Revue Universelle,* Oct. 15, 1903.

187 M. Denis: L'Influence de Paul Gauguin, *L'Occident,* Oct. 1903; reprinted in Denis: Théories, 1890–1910, Paris, 1912.

188 J. Meier-Graefe: Der moderne Impressionismus, Berlin, n.d. [1903–04]. Chapter on Gauguin.

189 M. Denis: Letter to the Editor, *Mercure de France,* Jan. 1904. Reply to an article by E. Bernard.

190 C. Morice: Les Gauguin du Petit Palais et de la rue Laffitte, *Mercure de France,* Feb. 1904.

191 J. Meier-Graefe: Entwicklungsgeschichte der modernen Kunst, Stuttgart, 1904. Chapter on Gauguin.

192 M. Denis: De Gauguin, de Whistler et de l'excès des théories, *L'Ermitage,* Nov. 15, 1905; reprinted in Denis: Théories, 1890–1910, Paris, 1912.

193 P. Jamot: Le Salon d'Automne de 1906, *Gazette des Beaux-Arts,* 1906, pp. 466–71.

194 C. Morice: article on Gauguin in *Art Moderne,* no. 80, 1909.

195 M. Denis: De Gauguin et de van Gogh au classicisme, *L'Occident,* May 1909; reprinted in Denis: Théories, 1890–1910, Paris, 1912.

196 J.-E. Blanche: Gauguin, *Revue de Paris,* May 1920; reprinted in Blanche: De Gauguin à la revue nègre, Paris, 1928.

197 C. Chassé: Gauguin et Mallarmé, *L'Amour de l'Art,* Aug. 1922.

198 G. Kahn: Paul Gauguin, *L'Art et les Artistes,* Nov. 1925 (special issue devoted to Gauguin).

199 H. Hertz: Paul Gauguin, *Art in America,* April 1927.

200 G. Tschann: Paul Gauguin et l'exotisme, *L'Amour de l'Art,* Dec. 1928.

201 R. Rey: La Renaissance du sentiment classique, Paris, 1931. Very important chapter on Gauguin.

202 L. Venturi: Gauguin, *L'Arte,* March 1934, pp. 136–65.

203 D. C. Rich: Gauguin in Arles, *Bulletin of the Art Institute of Chicago,* March 1935.

204 J. Rewald: Camille Pissarro, His Work and Influence, *Burlington Magazine,* June 1938; on Pissarro's influence on Gauguin and Gauguin's early impressionist work see also Rewald: The History of Impressionism, New York, 1946.

205 K. van Hook: A Self-Portrait by Paul Gauguin from the Chester Dale Collection, *Gazette des Beaux-Arts,* Dec. 1942.

206 A. Merlin: Gauguin e l'exotismo *Emporium,* Nov. 1943.

207 R. Goldwater: The Genesis of a Picture: Theme and Form in Modern Painting, *Critique,* Oct. 1946. Analysis of Gauguin's "Whence Do We Come? What Are We? Where Are We Going?"

208 R. Goldwater: Gauguin's "Yellow Christ," *Gallery Notes,* Albright Art Gallery, Buffalo, no. XI, 3, 1946, pp. 3–13.

209 C. Maltese: Gauguin e la pittura giapponese, *Emporium,* Jan. 1947, pp. 2–10.

210 P. Marois: Des goûts et des couleurs, Paris, 1947. Chapter on: Gauguin ou l'Eve des derniers temps.

211 D. Sutton: "La Perte du Pucelage" by Gauguin, *Burlington Magazine,* April 1949.

212 D. Sutton: Paul Gauguin, *Maandblad voor Beeldende Kunsten,* April–May 1949, pp. 106–10 (in English).

213 D. Sutton: article on Paris Gauguin Exhibition, *Burlington Magazine,* Oct. 1949.

214 B. Dorival: Sources of the Art of Gauguin from Java, Egypt and Ancient Greece, *Burlington Magazine,* April 1951. Extremely important article with new documents, ill.

215 G. R. [G. Rosenthal]: Gauguin's "Woman with Mango," *News,* The Baltimore Museum of Art, March–April 1952.

216 H. Dorra: The First Eves in Gauguin's Eden, *Gazette des Beaux-Arts,* March 1953. Important article.

217 F. Dauchot: Le "Christ Jaune" de Gauguin, *Gazette des Beaux-Arts,* July–Aug. 1954.

218 H. H. Hofstätter: Die Entstehung des "Neuen Stils"

in der französischen Malerei um 1890; mimeographed thesis, Freiburg im Breisgau, Nov. 1954. Important and detailed analysis of Gauguin's and Bernard's artistic evolution before and during their collaboration at Pont-Aven.

219 H. DORRA: Emile Bernard and Paul Gauguin, *Gazette des Beaux-Arts,* April 1955 [published Dec. 1955]. Important article.

220 H. READ: Gauguin—Return to Symbolism, *Art News Annual,* 1956. Important text, profusely illustrated in black and white and color.

221 D. SUTTON: Notes on Paul Gauguin apropos a Recent Exhibition, *Burlington Magazine,* March and Aug. 1956.

222 H. ROSTRUP: Nye Oplysninger om Gauguin of Hans Forhold Til Danmark (1883–1893), *Meddelelser fra Ny Carlsberg Glyptotek,* 1956 (see also 118).

223 Y. THIRION: L'Influence de l'estampe japonaise dans l'oeuvre de Gauguin (see 118).

224 G. WILDENSTEIN: L'Idéologie et l'esthétique dans deux tableaux-clés de Gauguin (see 118).

225 F. DAULTE: L'Art de "transposer" le sujet chez Gauguin, *Connaissance des Arts,* Feb. 1959.

226 H. R. ROOKMAAKER: Synthetist Art Theories—Genesis and Nature of the Ideas on Art of Gauguin and His Circle, Amsterdam, 1959. Important book with bibl., numerous notes, index, no ill.

227 J. RICHARDSON: Gauguin at Chicago and New York, *Burlington Magazine,* May 1959.

228 H. ROSTRUP: Eventails et pastels de Gauguin, *Gazette des Beaux-Arts,* Sept. 1960.

229 M. BODELSEN: Gauguin and the Marquesan God, *Gazette des Beaux-Arts,* March 1961. Important article.

230 A. CHASTEL: Seurat et Gauguin, *Art de France,* no. 2, 1962.

231 M. BODELSEN: Gauguin's Cézannes, *Burlington Magazine,* May 1962. Important article. See also 242 and 243.

232 M. ROSKILL: An Unexpected Gauguin Discovery, *Bulletin, Boston Museum of Fine Arts,* Nov. 1964.

233 M. BODELSEN: Paul Gauguin som Kunsthändvaeker—to Arbejder i Norsk Privateje, *Konst og Kultur* (Oslo), 1964. Gauguin as craftsman, with summary in English.

234 M. BODELSEN: The Dating of Gauguin's Early Paintings, *Burlington Magazine,* June 1965.

235 M. BODELSEN: The Wildenstein-Cogniat Gauguin Catalogue, *Burlington Magazine,* Jan. 1966.

236 W. M. KANE: Gauguin's "Le Cheval Blanc"—Sources and Syncretic Meanings, *Burlington Magazine,* July 1966. Important article.

237 H. DORRA: More on Gauguin's "Eves," *Gazette des Beaux-Arts,* Feb. 1967.

238 B. DANIELSSON: Gauguin's Tahitian Titles, *Burlington Magazine,* April 1967. Correction of many erroneous translations in 1.

239 M. BODELSEN: Gauguin Studies, *Burlington Magazine,* April 1967.

240 W. A. ANDERSEN: Gauguin and a Peruvian Mummy, *Burlington Magazine,* April 1967.

241 K. MITTELSTAEDT: Paul Gauguin—Self-Portraits, Oxford, 1968. Ill.

242 M. BODELSEN: Gauguin og Impressionisterne, Copenhagen, 1968. A detailed study of Gauguin's collection; ill. See also 231 and a condensed English version, 243.

243 M. BODELSEN: Gauguin, the Collector, *Burlington Magazine,* Sept. 1970. Important article with extensive list of all impressionist works owned by Gauguin that could be identified; ill. See also 231 and 242.

244 M. ROSKILL: Van Gogh, Gauguin and the Impressionist Circle, London, New York, 1970. Important chapters on Impressionism, Japanese prints, Seurat and his theory, but especially on Van Gogh, Gauguin and Bernard, Van Gogh and Gauguin at Arles, Symbolistic Art, etc. Numerous ill., extensive notes, appendices, bibliography, and index.

245 Z. AMISHAI-MAISELS: A Gauguin Sketchbook: Arles and Brittany [Album Huyghe], *The Israel Museum News,* April 1975. Ill. See also 264.

246 H. DORRA: Munch, Gauguin, and Norwegian Painters in Paris, *Gazette des Beaux-Arts,* Nov. 1976.

247 G. SVENAEUS: Gauguin and van Gogh, *Bulletin of the Rijksmuseum Vincent van Gogh* (Amsterdam), vol. 4, no. 4, 1976.

248 E. PEARSON: Three Paintings by Gauguin: Evidence in a Letter from Daniel de Monfreid, *Burlington Magazine,* Nov. 1977.

See also 102, 127, 132, 136, 137, 139, 140, 153, 251, 266, 270, 271, 272, and 324.

Reproductions

249 E. WIESE: Paul Gauguin, Leipzig, 1923. Short text, 32 poor black-and-white plates (small), among which are many little-known works, notably from Russian museums.

250 P. GIRIEUD: Paul Gauguin, Paris, 1928 (Album d'Art Druet).

251 R. REY: Gauguin, Paris, 1928. Interesting text, 40 fair ill. (small), bibl.

252 J. REWALD: Gauguin, Paris, London, New York, 1938. Short biographical text, bibliography, numerous fair plates in black and white and color, unfortunately arranged by subjects rather than chronologically (Hyperion).

253 R. COGNIAT: Gauguin, Paris, 1938. 60 small but good black-and-white plates (Collection des Maîtres).

254 L. HAUTECOEUR: Gauguin, Paris, 1938; Geneva, 1942. Large color plates (Skira).

255 M. MALINGUE: Gauguin, Monaco, 1943. Large volume, profusely illustrated with good black-and-white but poor color plates, chronologically arranged. The introduction contains some new documents; excerpts from contemporary articles, bibl. The plates include many little-known works but also one canvas (p. 57) actually painted by C. Camoin. See also 259.

256 A. DE WITT: Paul Gauguin, Milan, 1945. Short text, biographical notes, extremely extensive bibliography (by G. Scheiwiller); 35 very poor black-and-white plates (small).

257 R. COGNIAT: Gauguin, Paris, 1947. Numerous good

but small black-and-white plates (Tisné).

258 J. E. Payro: Paul Gauguin, Buenos Aires, 1947.

259 M. Malingue: Gauguin, Paris, 1948. Large volume, with introduction, bibliography, and numerous, often mediocre plates in black and white and color (among which are many little-known works), chronologically arranged. The attributions of some of the works reproduced seem questionable.

260 René-Jean: Gauguin, Paris, 1948. Small color plates (Braun).

261 Paul Gauguin: Dreizehn Holztafeldrucke von Paul Gauguin, Basel, 1948. 13 good reproductions of woodcuts.

262 F. Elgar: Gauguin, Paris, 1949. Introduction and 20 mediocre color plates not chronologically arranged.

263 R. Rey: Onze Menus de Paul Gauguin, Geneva, 1950. Superb facsimile reproductions of 11 rather whimsical menus done in watercolors in Tahiti. The introduction contains some new documents.

264 R. Huyghe: Le Carnet de Paul Gauguin, Paris, 1952. Excellent facsimile edition of a sketchbook from Brittany and Arles (c. 1888–90). Huyghe's comments and notes are almost more interesting than the somewhat minor sketches. See also 245.

265 J. Taralon: Gauguin, Paris, 1953. Short introduction accompanied by 65 small black-and-white illustrations and 16 large color plates. Biographical appendix with photos (Chêne).

266 C. Estienne: Gauguin, Geneva, 1953. Highly readable text, biographical chart, bibliography, list of exhibitions, index, numerous well selected plates, all in color. (Skira Collection "The Taste of our Time").

267 J. Rewald: Gauguin, New York, 1954. Portfolio with 16 good color plates with comments (Abrams).

268 J. Rewald: Paul Gauguin, New York, 1954. Some black-and-white and 20 mostly poor color plates (small) with comments (Abrams—Pocket Library of Great Art).

269 B. Dorival: P. Gauguin—Carnet de Tahiti, Paris, 1954. Excellent facsimile edition of an interesting sketchbook from Gauguin's first trip to Tahiti (1891–93) with pertinent comments.

270 R. Goldwater: Gauguin, New York, 1957. Introduction and commentaries for 50 color plates. Important book (Abrams).

271 J. Rewald: Gauguin Drawings, New York–London, 1958. 126 good illustrations—among which there are unfortunately several of doubtful authenticity—with commentaries.

272 R. Huyghe: Gauguin, Paris, 1959. Numerous plates in black and white and color, condensed bibl.

273 J. Leymarie: Paul Gauguin—Aquarelles, pastels et dessins en couleurs, Basel, 1960. 31 mediocre color plates with commentaries, provenance, preface, and bibl.

274 P.-F. Schneeberger: Gauguin—Tahiti, Lausanne, 1961. 28 small and mediocre color plates.

275 M. Gauthier: Gauguin, Paris, 1961.

276 R. Cogniat: Gauguin, New York, 1963.

277 A. Langer: Gauguin, Leipzig, 1965.

278 D. Vallier: Gauguin, Bergamo, 1965.

279 G. Legrand: Gauguin, Paris, 1966. Particularly atrocious color plates assembled without any order.

279a R. Pickvance: Gauguin Drawings, London, 1970. Numerous color plates of only fair quality and mostly of works reproduced in 271 and 273.

See also 1, 2, 3, 4, 20, 21, 31, 34, 38, 39, 40, 46, 55, 60, 95, 97, 98, 102, 107, 108, 109, 118, 122, 123, 132, 149, 150, 152, 167, 198, 214, 231, 242, 243, 244, and 324.

Miscellaneous Writings on Gauguin

280 A. Chainaye: Le Carnaval d'un ci devant; reprint of an attack on Gauguin on the occasion of his showing with the XX in Brussels, L'Art Moderne, Feb. 15, 1891.

281 Documents à conserver—A propos des XX; reprint of unfavorable reviews, L'Art Moderne, March 29, 1891.

282 Article on Gauguin in Art et Critique, 1891 (cannot be located).

283 J. Leclercq: Exposition Paul Gauguin, Mercure de France, Nov. 1894.

284 T. Natanson: M. Paul Gauguin, Revue Blanche, Dec. 1, 1898.

285 L. Hevesi: Paul Gauguin, March 21, 1907 (review of an exhibition at the Galerie Miethke, Vienna); also by the same author: Noa-Noa, March 3, 1907. Reprinted in Hevesi: Altkunst-Neukunst, Wien 1894–1908, Vienna, 1909 (pp. 514–18 and 519–25).

286 L. Lormel: Gauguin, Revue Illustrée, 1907.

287 B. Zuckerkandl: Zeitkunst, Wien, 1901–1907, Vienna–Leipzig, 1908. Chapter on Gauguin.

288 D. de Monfreid: Gauguin, L'Ermitage, Dec. 1908. (See also the same author's article in La Dépêche de Toulouse, Oct. 10, 1903.)

289 M. Puy: Paul Gauguin, L'Art Décoratif, 1911, pp. 177–88.

290 J. Rivière: Etudes, Paris, 1911. Chapter on Gauguin.

291 W. Hausenstein: Van Gogh and Gauguin, Stuttgart–Berlin, 1914.

292 A. Salmon: Gauguin, L'Europe Nouvelle, Oct. 18, 1919.

293 G. de Chirico: Gauguin, Convegno (Milan), March 1920.

294 M. Puy: Gauguin, Les Marges, July 1920.

295 J. G. Goulinat: Les Collections Gustave Fayet, L'Amour de l'Art, 1925, pp. 131–42.

296 Anonymous: Autour de Gauguin, Bulletin de la Vie Artistique, Oct. 1, 1925 and Nov. 1, 1926.

297 R. Rey: Gauguin, L'Art Vivant, March 1927.

298 R. Rey: Paul Gauguin, L'Amour de l'Art, May 1928.

299 Anonymous: Gauguin fut-il assassiné?, Beaux-Arts, Aug. 12, 1934.

300 E. Campagnac: Paul Gauguin et Emile Schuffenecker, Le Matin, Paris, Feb. 10, 1935.

301 K. Miterwa: Gauguin i van Gogh w Arles, Glos Plastikow, Dec. 1935 (in Polish).

302 C. Chabot: Paul Gauguin, Art et Vie, 1935, pp. 209–15.

303 M. Boudot-Lamotte: Le Peintre et collectionneur Claude-Emile Schuffenecker, L'Amour de l'Art, 1935.

304 A. M. Frankfurter: Gauguin, *Art News,* March 1936.

305 W. Gaunt: Paul Gauguin, *London Studio,* Nov. 1938.

306 M. Florisoone: Gauguin et Victor Segalen, *L'Amour de l'Art,* Dec. 1938.

307 G. Visenti: La moglie di Gauguin, Florence, 1942.

308 R. Brest: Gauguin, *Ver y Estimar* (Buenos Aires), special issue, Oct.–Nov. 1948.

309 J. Leymarie: L'Exposition Gauguin, *Bulletin des Musées de France,* June 1949.

310 A. Joly-Segalen: Paul Gauguin and Victor Segalen, *Magazine of Art,* Dec. 1952.

311 W. Menard: Gauguin's Tahiti Son, *Saturday Review,* Oct. 30, 1954.

312 E. Göpel: Paul Gauguin, Munich, 1954.

313 A. Leclerc: Gauguin, Wiesbaden, n.d.

314 W. K. Zinsser: Footnote to Gauguin's Art, *New York Herald Tribune,* Nov. 23, 1956.

315 H. Nevermann: Polynesien und Paul Gauguin, *Baessler Archiv,* Neue Folge, v. IV [1956]. Gauguin's work examined from a purely ethnological viewpoint. The author quotes numerous books on Tahiti, among which: H. Melville: Typee, New York, 1845; F. O'Brien: White Shadows in the South Seas, New York, 1920; A. K. Nielsen: Aloha, Berlin, 1944; K. von den Steinen: Die Marquesaner und ihre Kunst, Berlin, 1923, 1928; O. Bunzenzahl: Tahiti und Europa, Leipzig, 1935; H. Tischner: Kunst der Südsee, Hamburg, 1954. A. Breton: L'Art magique, Paris, 1957. Chapter on: Deux grandes synthèses—Gustave Moreau et Paul Gauguin.

316 B. Danielsson: Forgotten Islands of the South Seas, London, 1957.

317 R. Puig: Paul Gauguin, G.-D. de Monfreid et leurs amis, Perpignan, 1958.

318 G. Reyer: Paul Gauguin, *Match,* Sept. 20, 1958. Interesting documents, though the photograph of a painter in Papeete does *not* represent Gauguin.

319 C. Chassé: Le Sort de Gauguin est lié au Krach de 1882, *Connaissance des Arts,* Feb. 1959.

320 M. Malingue: Du nouveau sur Gauguin, *L'Oeil,* July–Aug. 1959. Interesting article with reproductions of unknown works from a photographic album which once belonged to Marie Henry.

321 M. Malingue: Encore du nouveau sur Gauguin, *L'Oeil,* Oct. 1959. Interview of Pola Gauguin, illustrated mostly with portrait photographs.

322 M. de Sablonière: Paul Gauguin, Amsterdam, 1960.

323 V. W. van Gogh: Enkele notities over Gauguin op Martinique—1887, *Museumjournaal,* July 1960; ill.

324 Gauguin, Paris, 1960. A collection of Gauguin studies by: H. Perruchot: La Vie; G. d'Angelis: L'Homme; B. Dorival: Le Milieu; F. Nourissier: Sa Place dans la mêlée symboliste; M. Malingue: L'Homme qui a réinventé la peinture; R. Field: Plagiaire ou Créateur? [very interesting study]; C. Roger-Marx: Ce que lui doit la peinture contemporaine; M. Rheims: La Cote des Gauguin; R. Huyghe: Initiateur des temps nouveaux. Chronology, index, numerous ill. in black and white and color.

325 P. O'Reilly: "Les Amours d'un vieux peintre aux Marquises" ou Paul Gauguin héros d'une comédie en vers écrite de son vivant, *Journal de la Société des Océanistes,* Dec. 1962.

326 B. Danielsson: När Gauguin censurerades i Stockholm (When Gauguin was censored in Stockholm—1897–98), *Svenska Dagbladet,* Nov. 11, 1964.

327 M. Tavernier and P. O'Reilly: L'Écriture de Gauguin—Etude graphologique, Musée de l'Homme, Paris, 1968.

328 D. Desanti: Flora Tristan—La Femme révoltée, Paris, 1972. A fascinating biography of Gauguin's maternal grandmother.

Fiction

329 C. Sternheim: Gauguin und van Gogh, Berlin, 1924.

330 S. W. Maugham: The Moon and Sixpence, London, 1929. The story of the painter Karl Strickland derives many details from Gauguin's life, but also differs from it too frequently and too intentionally to be considered merely a fictionalized biography of Gauguin.

331 B. Becker: Paul Gauguin—The Calm Madman, New York, 1931. The bibliography lists many publications on Tahiti in general.

332 C. Gorham: The Gold of Their Bodies, New York, 1955.

333 C. Francolin: La Vie passionnée de Paul Gauguin, Paris, 1958.

GOGH, Vincent van (1853–1890)

Bibliography

1 C. M. Brooks, Jr.: Vincent van Gogh—A Bibliography, New York, 1942. An extremely useful and methodical book. Unfortunately it does not separate the trivial publications—and there are many—from the essential ones (the short excerpts given often quote unimportant or insignificant passages). Numerous misprints.

Only a selection of the publications listed by Brooks is given in the present bibliography, augmented by some which escaped his vigilance, and by those which appeared after 1942.

Oeuvre Catalogues

2 J. B. de la Faille: L'Oeuvre de Vincent van Gogh, catalogue raisonné, Paris–Brussels, 1928, 4 vols. (I, text, paintings; II, illustrations, paintings; III, text, drawings; IV, illustrations, drawings.) The works are not arranged in strict chronological order. This publication is a monument of patient work, but it is, unfortunately, marred by the inclusion of a number of paintings, for the most part from the Wacker Galerie, Berlin, which the famous trial involving that gallery established as forgeries. See also this bibliography under "Studies on Forgeries."

In a subsequent volume:

3 J. B. de la Faille: Les Faux van Gogh, Paris–Brussels,

1930. The author collects and reproduces a total of 134 van Gogh forgeries, 33 of which he himself had catalogued as genuine in his 1928 volumes (2). Some of the other 80 paintings included in this catalogue of forgeries had been authenticated by E. Bernard. The volume also contains 21 spurious drawings and watercolors, indicating how extensively the work of van Gogh was being copied and forged within a few decades after his death. In a second edition of his catalogue raisonné, however, comprising only paintings:

4 J. B. DE LA FAILLE: Vincent van Gogh, Paris, London, New York, 1030 (Hyperion), the author failed to clarify in this second edition of the 1928 catalogue raisonne (2) some of the thorny problems of authenticity. He included six of the Wacker paintings which appeared there but which were declared to be spurious in his 1930 volume on forgeries (3); his occasional explanations for accepting these paintings once more as genuine works of van Gogh are not persuasive. Furthermore, this 1939 edition contains one painting (Forgery no. 141, Hyperion no. 395) which the author states he had on three previous occasions branded as spurious; no reasons for his altered judgment are set forth. At the same time it lists as a forgery a painting which had originally been published as genuine (F 761) and which de la Faille has since redeclared authentic when confronted with proof that it was sold by Theo van Gogh's widow in 1908 to German dealer Paul Cassirer. This second edition omits 35 paintings included in the 1928 catalogue raisonné. In all, there are 42 works about which the author revised his judgment during a period of eleven years. The frankness with which such revisions are acknowledged is admirable. Nonetheless, the scholar and the connoisseur could wish, in consulting this second edition of the catalogue raisonné, that the author had chosen to justify, or at any rate explain, his altered judgments by specific analytical pronouncements and stylistic discussions. For example, in the case of the two versions of the *Jardin de Daubigny* (Hyperion nos. 758 and 765), which have been the subject of extended controversies (see under "Forgeries": 262–66), de la Faille contents himself with the declaration: ". . . I have not come to a decision. I do not believe No. 758 to be a fake, but to doubt the authenticity of No. 765 seems to me worse than a crime, it is a blunder." Again, the author pronounces genuine the questioned *Self-Portrait* (Hyperion no. 508) and dismisses in one sentence the weighty arguments advanced against its authenticity (see under "Forgeries": 260). Such pronouncements *ex cathedra* are of scant assistance to the student in this difficult field. At the time of his death in 1959, de la Faille was preparing a new, revised edition of his oeuvre catalogue.

5 J. B. DE LA FAILLE: The Works of Vincent van Gogh— His Paintings and Drawings, New York, 1970. This much needed and admirably presented volume was published after de la Faille's death by a committee of Dutch editors headed by A. M. Hammacher. While it endeavors to solve many of the vexing van Gogh problems, it still leaves much to be desired.

Represented are four major categories:

A. Paintings and drawings considered genuine by both de la Faille and the editors; these form the bulk of this publication.

B. Paintings and drawings considered forgeries by both de la Faille and the editors but previously accepted by the former; these include 43 oils and 6 drawings, reproduced separately on pp. 588–97 under the heading "Rejected Works." (Among these are the Wacker paintings, some of which de la Faille had accepted in 1928, branded as fakes in 1930, readmitted in 1939 [see 2, 3, 4], and subsequently eliminated once more.) In addition, there are forgeries from other sources, such as the *Self-Portrait* (Hyperion no. 508), the authenticity of which de la Faille had still defended in 1939.

C. Works rejected by de la Faille but accepted by the editors (among them one painting from Wacker which seems, indeed, to be genuine). There are 6 works (plus 1) in this category, and they are reproduced, with one exception, at their chronological place within the catalogue.

D. Works accepted by de la Faille but rejected—and rightly so—by the editors. Seventeen of these have been allowed to remain in the catalogue, where they are reproduced next to unquestionably genuine works. Only by reading the accompanying notes or by checking with lists hidden on p. 597, and *not* mentioned in the table of contents, can the reader locate them. Thus no. 185a is duly catalogued, though with question marks as to date and place, but with no other reservations stated either in the note that accompanies the reproduction or in the back pages to which additional data on exhibitions and provenances are relegated; however, on p. 597, no. 185a is listed as *rejected* by the editors. (It is true that a more explicit statement appears on the very last page, 703, among the "Errata and Addenda.") Stranger still is the case of no. 203a, listed on p. 105 with the note that it has been removed from the Nuenen period and shifted to Antwerp; on p. 108 it is reproduced among works "redated to Antwerp" with the editors' comment: "The attribution seems doubtful." But on p. 597 the painting is no longer considered "doubtful" since it is unequivocally listed among the works *rejected* by the editors. It is difficult to understand why the reader of this reference book should be involved in the "redating" of a picture in the authenticity of which the editors do not believe. If it was not painted by van Gogh, it cannot be assigned to either his Nuenen or his Antwerp period!

In addition to these four categories there are still others. One consists of forgeries about which nobody— not even de la Faille—entertained any doubts; many of these were published by him in his volume on fakes (see 3). But there are also works that have come to light since the death of de la Faille, some authenticated by Tralbaut (see 119), which have simply been left out here, the implication being that the editors do not believe them to be genuine. This should have been clearly stated, the more so as they do accept and publish other recent discoveries, mostly in a section of "Supplementary Paintings," pp. 570–73, which includes an oil rejected by de la Faille (no. SP 1672a), though with good reason judged authentic by the editors, who neglected, however, to indicate this on their list on p. 597. There is also an important section of "Supplementary Drawings," pp. 574–86, many of which became known in de la Faille's lifetime. Why these were not included at their respective places in the catalogue is hard to understand. As for the special section of juvenile drawings, it does not precede the general section of drawings, where it obviously belongs, but instead follows it.

For some disputed pictures, such as the two versions of the *Jardin de Daubigny*, the editors provide extensive notes that go far beyond de la Faille's often inept statements and document their views as clearly as can be done in the available space. But there are still other paintings which remain doubtful, such as nos. 221 and SP 1670; obviously, there will always be differences of opinion. More serious are many inconsistencies and lapses of scholarship. Thus M. Florisoone established in an article in 1953 that the Zouave *bugler* and the Zouave *officer* Milliet were two different persons (see 351); yet here there is a specific reference on p. 197, no. 423, to the fact that the name of the bugler was Milliet, while the officer's likeness is catalogued later on, under no. 473, as *Portrait of Milliet*.

Another example of carelessness concerns no. 803, for which the editors' comment reads: "J. Rewald . . . identifies subject as the chapel of Saint Paul's Hospital at Saint-Rémy. P. Leprohon . . . : the picture represents the church of Labbeville, a village in the neighborhood of Auvers." This is simply not true. Leprohon has made no positive identification but has stated guardedly: "In spite of some recent restorations, it seems to us that we can recognize here the old church of Labbeville. . . ." Since van Gogh is not known to have ever worked at Labbeville and since the church of the asylum in Saint-Rémy still stands and can be identified without too much trouble, the editors had the *duty* to make their own verification. [The painting and a photograph of the church, though *not* taken from the spot where Vincent painted it, are reproduced on p. 339 of the present volume.] While this may appear to be a minor matter, it does have a direct bearing on the dating of the work. De la Faille, having previously assigned the picture to the Auvers period, had accepted the Saint-Rémy identification and had dated the picture Oct.–Nov. 1889. But the editors, preferring the Labbeville "attribution," list it under Auvers as of the end of June 1890. Not one word is said about the colors, which tie in much more readily with Vincent's paintings of the South than with those of his last weeks in Auvers.

But the most maddening aspect of this monumental publication is the fact that the editors have chosen to reinstate the numbering of de la Faille's first catalogue of 1928 (2), with numerous a's, b's, and c's for additional works. At the same time, they have tried to establish a sorely needed and stricter chronology, especially for the Paris period, from which hardly any letters exist to provide precise dates of execution. De la Faille originally had lumped everything together under "Epoque de Paris" without even attempting any differentiations, and the editors are to be praised for their attempt to be more specific. However, by maintaining the numerical order of the 1928 publication, they fail to offer a "visual chronology" of the evolution of van Gogh. For example, on pp. 136–39, concerning the Paris period, the bewildered reader finds the following sequence of reproductions and notes:

No. 269 verso—summer 1887; no. 270—early 1887; no. 270a—May 1887; no. 271—early winter 1886; no. 272—winter 1886; no. 273—summer 1886; no. 274—summer 1886; no. 275—May 1887; no. 276—May 1887; no. 277—summer 1887; no. 278—autumn 1886.

To give precedence to the numbering of a woefully inadequate publication of more than forty years ago over a chronology that at last brings some order into the production of van Gogh cannot be called anything but exasperating.

Yet this is not all. The many works redated by the editors have been assembled as a group at the end of each period. As a result, the reproductions (which are excellent) and corresponding catalogue entries do *not* really follow the numerical order of the 1928 catalogue. Indeed, with works shifted to other periods or left out because they are spurious, the actual succession of entries on pp. 176–80 (for the Paris period) presents itself as follows:

No. 382; no. 383; no. 384 (Arles period, see after no. 607); no. 385 (see Rejected Works); no. 386 (Arles period, see after no. 607); no. 387 (see Rejected Works); no. 388 recto (Nuenen period, see after no. 203a); no. 388 verso.

Here now follows a group of works "Redated to Paris" in this order:

No. 28; no. 61 verso; no. 77 verso; no. 109 verso; no. 177a; no. 178 verso; no. 179 verso; no. 180; no. 181; no. 197; no. 201; no. 203; no. 207a; and no. 208.

If there exists a more confusing way to present a catalogue, the editors apparently could not find it.

6 J. B. DE LA FAILLE: L'Epoque française de van Gogh, Paris, 1927. 45 ill.

7 W. SCHERJON: Catalogue des tableaux par Vincent van Gogh décrits dans ses lettres—périodes Saint-Rémy et Auvers-sur-Oise, Utrecht, 1932. This catalogue endeavors to separate the spurious from the authentic paintings by accompanying the illustrations with excerpts from the artist's letters. As such it limits itself to those works which van Gogh discussed in his correspondence. This correspondence was not completely known to the author since new and important letters, notably those to the artist's sister Wil, have since come to light. See 53.

8 W. SCHERJON and J. DE GRUYTER: Vincent van Gogh's Great Period—Arles, Saint-Rémy and Auvers-sur-Oise (complete catalogue), Amsterdam, 1937. Augments 7. Separates van Gogh's paintings into those mentioned in his letters and those not mentioned, and also—unlike 7—

includes unmentioned paintings the authors consider genuine.

9 W. VAN BESELAERE: De Hollandsche Periode (1880–1885) in het werk van Vincent van Gogh, Amsterdam, 1938. French edition: Catalogue de la période hollandaise [de Vincent van Gogh], Antwerp, [1938].

For catalogues of various exhibitions see:

10 Van Gogh exhibition at the Panorama in Amsterdam, 1892–93, organized by Johanna van Gogh-Bonger. Introduction by R. N. Roland-Holst. The exhibition comprised 104 paintings and drawings; the catalogue contains some illustrations and excerpts from van Gogh's letters. On this exhibition see H. V. [H. VAN DE VELDE?]: L'Exposition van Gogh à Amsterdam, L'Art Moderne, Jan. 8, 1893.

11 Exposition Vincent van Gogh, Galerie Bernheim-Jeune, Paris, March 15–31, 1901. Introduction by J. Leclercq. 65 paintings (some lent by Vollard, A. de La Rochefoucauld, E. Schuffenecker, Mirbeau, Rodin, C. Pissarro, T. Duret, J. Leclercq) and 6 drawings; no ill. On this exhibition see 201; this show gave impetus to the "fauve" movement.

12 Vincent van Gogh exhibition, Amsterdam, Stedelijk Museum, 1905. Introduction by J. Cohen-Gosschalk (second husband of Johanna van Gogh-Bonger). 474 items. For reviews of this exhibition see Brooks nos. 384, 754, and 755.

13 100 Teekeningen van Vincent van Gogh uit de Verzameling Hidde Nijland in het Museum de Dordrecht, Amsterdam, 1905. 100 plates of early drawings.

14 Van Gogh exhibition, Galerie Bernheim-Jeune, Paris, Jan. 1908. 100 paintings.

15 Van Gogh exhibition, Galerie Druet, Paris, Jan. 1908. 35 paintings.

16 Van Gogh exhibition, Leicester Galleries, London, Dec. 1923. Introduction by Sir M. Sadler. Second van Gogh exhibition at the same galleries, Nov.–Dec. 1926.

17 Vincent van Gogh, Gemälde, Paul Cassirer Galerie, Berlin, Jan. 1928. Introduction by J. B. de la Faille. 92 paintings, many reproduced. This show brought about the discovery of the Wacker forgeries when W. Feilchenfeldt of the Cassirer Gallery compared paintings purchased from Wacker with genuine pictures loaned to the exhibition. See under "Forgeries."

18 Vincent van Gogh en zijn Tijdgenoten, Stedelijk Museum, Amsterdam, Sept.–Nov. 1930. Illustrated catalogue.

19 Vincent van Gogh, Museum of Modern Art, New York, 1935. Profusely illustrated catalogue edited by Alfred H. Barr, Jr., with excerpts from the artist's letters grouped by subject, a chronology, a list of books van Gogh read as mentioned in his letters (see also 227 and 228), extensive notes on the works exhibited (with quotations from van Gogh's letters), selected bibl. First important show in the United States.

20 Van Gogh, sa vie, son oeuvre, catalogue of an exhibition at the Paris World's Fair, 1937. Special issue of L'Amour de l'Art, edited by R. Huyghe, M. Florisoone, and J. Rewald. Profusely ill., numerous documents.

21 The Art and Life of Vincent van Gogh, Wildenstein Galleries, New York, Oct.–Nov. 1943. Introductions by A. M. Frankfurter and G. de Batz. 68 paintings and 12 drawings and watercolors, mostly from American collections, all reproduced.

22 Vincent van Gogh, Museums voor Schoone Kunsten, Luik, Bergen; Paleis voor Schoone Kunsten, Brussels, Oct. 1946–Jan. 1947. Introduction by E. Langui. 171 works with notes, almost all reproduced; poor ill. in black and white and color.

23 Catalogus Vincent van Gogh, Stedelijk Museum, Amsterdam, n.d. Edited by W. Steenhoff. Works by van Gogh and his contemporaries, mostly from the collection of Ir. V. W. van Gogh. Ill.

24 Vincent van Gogh, Musée de l'Orangerie, Paris, Jan.–March 1947. Introduction by R. Huyghe. 172 paintings and drawings, mostly from the collection of Ir. V. W. van Gogh and the Rijksmuseum Kröller-Müller, Otterlo. Ill.

25 Catalogue of the van Gogh exhibition, Kunsthalle, Basel, Oct.–Nov. 1947.

26 Work by Vincent van Gogh, Cleveland Museum of Art, Nov.–Dec. 1948. Introduction by H. S. Francis. 38 paintings and 12 drawings and watercolors from American collections, all reproduced.

27 Catalogus van 264 Werken van Vincent van Gogh, Rijksmuseum Kröller-Müller, Otterlo, 1949. Notes on many works, good illustrations in black and white and color. See also 30.

28 Van Gogh, Paintings and Drawings, Metropolitan Museum of Art, New York, and Art Institute, Chicago, 1949–1950. Introduction by D. C. Rich, catalogue and notes by T. Rousseau, Jr. Numerous illustrations in black and white, 4 good color plates.

29 Vincent van Gogh, Contemporary Arts Association, Houston, Texas, Feb.–March 1951. Introduction by T. Rousseau, Jr. Ill.

30 Catalogue of 270 Paintings and Drawings of Vincent van Gogh belonging to the collection of the State Museum Kröller-Müller, Otterlo, 1952. In English; ill. New ed.: 1959; detailed catalogue with full documentation for 272 works and an essay on van Gogh's childhood drawings by J. G. van Gelder; small ill.

31 Vincent van Gogh, Rijksmuseum Kröller-Müller, Otterlo, and Stedelijk Museum, Amsterdam, summer 1953. Mostly works from the Köller-Müller and Ir. V. W. van Gogh collections; some private loans. Good illustrations in black and white and color.

32 Vincent van Gogh, City Art Museum, Saint Louis; Philadelphia Museum of Art; Toledo Museum of Art, Oct. 1953–April 1954. Introduction by Ir. V. W. van Gogh. 181 works from the Kröller-Müller and Ir. V. W. van Gogh collections. Illustrations in black and white, 12 inadequate color plates.

33 Van Gogh et les peintres d'Auvers-sur-Oise, Orangerie des Tuileries, Paris, Nov. 1954–Feb. 1955. Introductions by P. Gachet and G. Bazin; very complete notes on every work included by A. Chatelet. Some ill.

34 Van Gogh, Wildenstein Galleries, New York, March–April 1955. Introduction by J. Rewald. Numerous illus-

trations in black and white, 3 mediocre color plates.

35 Vincent van Gogh en zijn Hollandse Tijdgenoten, Antwerp, Zaal C. A. W., May–June 1955. Introduction by M. E. Tralbaut. 84 works; 25 black-and-white ill. and 13 color plates.

36 Vincent van Gogh, Stedelijk Museum, Amsterdam, summer 1955. Introduction by V. W. van Gogh (almost all the 243 paintings and drawings are from his collection). Numerous ill. in black and white, 12 not always adequate color plates.

37 Vincent van Gogh—Quelques oeuvres de l'époque 1881–1886 provenant de collections particulières néerlandaises, Gallery van Wisselingh, Amsterdam, Feb.–March 1956. 34 works, some ill.

38 Vincent van Gogh, Musée Cantini, Marseilles, March–April 1957, with a text by C. Mauron on "Vincent et Monticelli" and a study by J. Latour. 88 works from the van Gogh Foundation.

39 Vincent van Gogh, Municipal Art Gallery, Los Angeles, July–Aug. 1957. Preface by J. Rewald. 39 works from American collections; ill.

40 Vincent van Gogh—Leben und Schaffen, Dokumentation, Gemälde, Zeichnungen, Villa Hügel, Essen, Oct.–Dec. 1957. Important exhibition organized by M. E. Tralbaut with extensive photographic documentation assembled by him. Preface by Tralbaut, detailed chronology, genealogy, geographic charts, numerous good ill. The show combined original works with photographs of the subjects; the catalogue notices are accompanied by detailed comments. Excellent publication. See also 41, 43, and 119.

41 Vincent van Gogh—Leven en Scheppen in Beeld, Stedelijk Musuem, Amsterdam, May–June 1958. Exhibition of the documents assembled by Tralbaut, similar to 40, but with different originals and different ill.

42 Van Gogh en Provence, Pavillon Vendôme, Aix-en-Provence, Oct.–Nov. 1959. 62 works from the coll. of V. W. van Gogh and the Rijksmuseum Kröller-Müller; ill.

43 Vincent van Gogh, Musée Jacquemart-André, Paris, Feb.–May 1960. Exhibition similar to 40 and 41, with documentation by Tralbaut but with different paintings and different ill. Preface by L. Hautecoeur.

44 Van Gogh Self Portraits, Marlborough Galleries, London, Oct. 1960. Prefaces by A. M. Hammacher (see also 242) and by O. Kokoschka; ill.

45 Van Gogh—Aquarelles et dessins de l'époque 1881–85 provenant de collections particulières néerlandaises, van Wisselingh & Co., Amsterdam, April–May 1961. 40 works, ill.

46 Vincent van Gogh dessinateur, Institut Néerlandais, Paris, Jan.–March 1966; ill.

47 Vincent van Gogh—Drawings, Watercolors, Dallas Museum of Fine Arts, Philadelphia Museum of Art, The Toledo Museum of Art, National Gallery of Canada, Ottawa, Oct. 1967–April 1968; ill.

48 Vincent van Gogh—Paintings and Drawings: A Choice from the Collection of the Vincent van Gogh Foundation, Amsterdam, 1968; ill.

49 Paintings and Drawings from the Collection of the Vincent van Gogh Foundation, Amsterdam, Hayward Gallery, London, Oct. 1968–Jan. 1969.

50 Vincent van Gogh—Paintings and Drawings, Baltimore Museum of Art, M. H. de Young Museum, San Francisco, Brooklyn Museum, Oct. 1970–April 1971. (This is the last itinerant exhibition of the collection of the artist's nephew before its permanent installation in the new museum of the Vincent van Gogh Foundation in Amsterdam.)

See also:

51 Van Gogh's grote Tijdgenoten, Stedelijk Museum, Amsterdam, and Rijksmuseum Kröller-Müller, Otterlo, summer 1953. 65 works by Cézanne, Gauguin, Lautrec, Manet, Monet, Pissarro, Renoir, and Seurat, among them many little-known ones. Profusely ill.

52 Collectie Theo van Gogh, Stedelijk Museum, Amsterdam, 1953. This catalogue, which does not contain any of Vincent van Gogh's works, lists 104 works, some of which are reproduced, among them paintings and drawings by Bernard, Bock, Corot, Daubigny, Daumier, Forain, Gauguin, Gausson, Guillaumin, Koning, Manet, Mauve, Millet, Monticelli, C. and L. Pissarro, Raffaëlli, Lautrec, Vignon, etc., but does not comprise the complete collection of Theo van Gogh. See also 348.

Writings by van Gogh

53 A complete collection of Vincent van Gogh's letters in 4 vol. was published in Holland: Verzamelde Brieven van Vincent van Gogh, Amsterdam, 1952–1954. Vol. I, introduction by J. van Gogh-Bonger, letters to his brother from 1872 to 1882; vol. II, letters to his brother from 1882 to 1885; vol. III, letters to his brother from 1885 to 1890, also letters to the artist's mother, to Gauguin, Signac, Russell, Aurier, etc.; vol. IV, letters to van Rappard, to the artist's sister Wil (here published for the first time), to Emile Bernard, as well as Theo van Gogh's letters to Vincent, and various documents assembled by Ir. V. W. van Gogh. The letters are published in their original version, that is, in Dutch, French, and occasionally in English; some of the documents quoted are in German. Profusely illustrated with sketches from the letters and documents; index in vol. IV; the footnotes might have been more explicit.

A new edition with two additional letters, assembled in two volumes, appeared in Amsterdam in 1955.

English translation: The Complete Letters of Vincent van Gogh, 3 vol., Greenwich, Conn., n.d. [1958]. Contains some additional letters but not the documents in vol. IV of the Dutch edition.

Some errors in the chronology of the letters from the Hague and from Nuenen have been pointed out by J. Hulsker (articles in *Maatstaf,* Sept. 1958, Aug.–Sept. 1960, and Jan. 1961) and reported by M. de Sablonière: Encore une fois Vincent van Gogh, *Museumjournaal,* Aug.–Sept. 1959, pp. 59–60; see also M. de Sablonière: De Volgorde van den Brieven van Vincent van Gogh aan zijn Broer Theo, *Museumjournaal,* Nov.–Dec. 1960.

The complete edition of his letters renders obsolete all previous publications of the artist's correspondence, listed by Brooks under nos. 1–54. However, for convenience, some earlier publications of letters are given below:

54 Lettres de Vincent van Gogh à Emile Bernard, Paris, 1911. English edition: Vincent van Gogh—Letters to Emile Bernard, edited, translated, and with a foreword by D. Lord [pseud. for D. Cooper], London–New York, 1938. The letters are here for the first time grouped in chronological sequence; ill. Translation not always accurate.

55 VINCENT VAN GOGH: Brieven aan zijn Broeder, Amsterdam, 1914. First complete edition in 3 vol., with introduction and notes by Johanna van Gogh-Bonger. English edition (partly translated by Johanna van Gogh-Bonger, who died before the completion of the work): The Letters of Vincent van Gogh to his Brother, 1872–1886, London–Boston, 1927, and Further Letters of Vincent van Gogh to His Brother, 1886–1890, London–Boston, 1929.

56 E. V. LUCAS: A Wanderer's Notebook—Van Gogh Again, Sunday Times, London, Feb. 17, 1929. Letter to H. M. Livens.

57 Letters to an Artist—from Vincent van Gogh to Anton Ridder van Rappard, 1881–1885, London, 1936. 58 letters translated from the Dutch by R. van Messel and published here for the first time. Index, ill.

58 Dear Theo—The Autobiography of Vincent van Gogh, edited by I. Stone, Boston, 1937. Stone's aim was to "edit the 1670 pages of material down to a swiftly flowing, continuous, normal-sized book." He has achieved this by "editing" the artist's letters beyond recognition, with more concern for a "swiftly flowing" prose than for van Gogh's personality, thought, and very individual style. For H. Read's highly critical review of this book see Brooks no. 599.

59 H. THANNHAUSER: Van Gogh and John Russell, Some Unknown Letters and Drawings, Burlington Magazine, Sept. 1938; also L'Amour de l'Art, Sept. 1938.

60 C. ROGER-MARX: Lettres inédites de Vincent van Gogh et de Paul Gauguin, Europe, Feb. 15, 1939. An important and long letter to Gauguin.

61 VINCENT VAN GOGH: Lettres à sa mère, Paris, 1952. Small volume with letters translated from the Dutch by L. Roelandt; also contains letters to Gauguin and to van Gogh's friends, the Ginoux family in Arles (the latter were first published in 94).

62 J. B. DE LA FAILLE: Een onbekende Brief van Vincent [illustrated letter to the Belgian painter Eugène Guillaume Boch], Kroniek van Kunst en Kultuur, March 1954. This letter was included in the two-volume edition of Verzamelde Brieven, 1955 (see under 53).

63 The Letters of Vincent van Gogh, edited and introduced by M. Roskill, London, 1963. A selection.

64 Vincent van Gogh on England, compiled from his letters by his nephew, Amsterdam, 1968; ill. This is the first of several planned publications in which excerpts from the artist's letters will be assembled by subject. Accompanied by reproductions of period woodcuts from the artist's extensive collection.

65 Letters of Vincent van Gogh, 1886–1890, a facsimile edition. Introd. by V. W. van Gogh; chronology by J. Hulsker. In preparation, London–Amsterdam.

Witness Accounts

66 B. v. H. [Boele van Hensbroek]: Les van Gogh, De Nederlandsche Spectator, Aug. 26, 1893. (Reprinted in 87.)

67 E. H. DU QUESNE–VAN GOGH: Persoonlijke Herinneringen aan Vincent van Gogh, Baarn, 1910. English edition: Personal Recollections of Vincent van Gogh, translated by K. S. Dreier, London, 1913. Written by one of the artist's sisters, this book is rewarding only for van Gogh's early years; the chapters on the painter's French period are very unreliable. Ill.

68 N. B. MENDES DA COSTA: Persoonlijke Herinneringen aan Vincent van Gogh, Algemeene Handelsblad (Amsterdam), Dec. 2, 1910. German translation: Die persönlichen Erinnerungen N. B. Mendes da Costas an seinen Lateinschüler Vincent van Gogh, Kunst und Künstler, Nov. 1911.

69 E. BERNARD: Introductions to: Lettres de Vincent van Gogh à Emile Bernard, Paris, 1911. These comprise earlier writings by Bernard which had appeared in Les Hommes d'Aujourd'hui in 1890 and in Mercure de France in 1893 (see Bernard Bibliography). These texts are not included in the English translation, 54.

70 JOHANNA VAN GOGH–BONGER: Introduction to Vincent van Gogh—Brieven aan zijn Broeder, Amsterdam, 1914 (see 55). Her writing about the brother-in-law whom she knew only briefly but about whom she had learned much through her husband is one of the most restrained, most beautiful, and most moving texts on van Gogh.

71 M. BRUSSE: Vincent van Gogh als Buchhandlungsgehilfe, Kunst und Künstler, Aug. 1914.

72 P. GAUGUIN: Avant et Après [written in Atuana, Marquesas Islands, 1903], Leipzig, 1918; Paris, 1923. Gauguin's version of his stay with van Gogh at Arles.

73 E. BERNARD: Souvenirs de van Gogh, L'Amour de l'Art, Dec. 1924.

74 H. SCHLITTGEN: Erinnerungen, Munich, 1926. Some recollections of Theo van Gogh and père Tanguy, whom the author met in Paris between 1888 and 1891.

75 M. BRAUMANN: Bei Freunden van Goghs in Arles, Kunst und Künstler, 1928.

76 B. STOKVIS: Vincent van Gogh in Arles, Kunst und Künstler, Sept. 1929 (interview with Dr. Rey).

77 THEO VAN GOGH: Lettres à son frère Vincent, Amsterdam, 1932. With a biography of Theo van Gogh by his widow. Contains only 41 letters (of the several hundreds which Theo must have written and which the painter apparently lost); of these, 35 are from Theo to Vincent (in French) and 5 from Johanna van Gogh-Bonger to Vincent (in Dutch, with French translations). This material has since been included in 53.

For some letters by Theo van Gogh to Dr. Gachet see P. Gachet: Deux amis des impressionnistes—Le Docteur Gachet et Murer, Paris, 1956, pp. 106–10.

For a letter to Gauguin see M. Bodelsen: An Unpublished Letter by Theo van Gogh, *Burlington Magazine,* June 1957.

78 A. BREDIUS: Herinneringen aan Vincent van Gogh, *Oud Holland,* no. 1, 1934. Short article with recollections of Anton Hirschig, who knew van Gogh at Auvers.

79 A. S. HARTRICK: A Painter's Pilgrimage through Fifty Years, Cambridge, 1939. The author knew both van Gogh and Gauguin in Paris, 1886–88; some of the material was first published in 1916 (see Brooks no. 337).

80 T. J. HONEYMAN: Van Gogh—A Link with Glasgow, *The Scottish Art Review,* vol. II, no. 2, 1948. Recollections of the art dealer Alexander Reid, who knew van Gogh in Paris.

81 E. BERNARD: L'Enterrement de Vincent van Gogh, *Arts-Documents,* Feb. 1953. Bernard's letter to Aurier on the funeral.

82 M. GAUTHIER: La Femme en Bleu nous parle de l'Homme à l'oreille coupée, *Nouvelles Littéraires,* April 16, 1953. Interview of Mme Guilloux, daughter of the innkeeper Ravoux at Auvers, of whom van Gogh had painted three portraits as a young girl in blue. See also A. CARRIÉ: La Femme en Bleu revient à Auvers, *Nouvelles Littéraires,* Aug. 12, 1954.

83 P. GACHET: Souvenirs de Cézanne et de van Gogh—Auvers, 1873–1890, Paris, 1953. Recollections of the son of Dr. Gachet. Ill.

84 P. WEILLER: Nous avons retrouvé le Zouave de van Gogh, *Lettres Françaises,* March 24–31, 1955. Article on the Zouave Milliet with his recollections of van Gogh, written after Milliet's death. See also 351.

85 J.-N. PRIOU: Van Gogh et la famille Roulin, *Revue des PTT de France,* May–June 1955. Article on the Roulin family based on interviews of Roulin's daughter, who was still an infant when van Gogh painted her in her mother's arms.

86 V. DOITEAU: Deux "copains" de van Gogh inconnus, les frères Gaston et René Secrétan—Vincent tel qu'ils l'ont vu, *Aesculape,* March 1957.

87 M. E. TRALBAUT: *Van Goghiana I,* privately printed for P. Peré, Antwerp, Jan. 1963. Important article (in French) on: André Bonger, l'ami des frères van Gogh, with a text by Bonger's widow, interesting letters from Tanguy's widow, etc. According to Theo's son, however, the author exaggerates the role of his uncle, A. Bonger (who was more interested in Redon than in Vincent).

88 H. BONGER: Un Amstellodamois à Paris—Extraits des lettres écrites à Paris entre 1880 et 1890 par Andries Bonger à ses parents à Amsterdam, in Liber Amicorum Karel G. Boon, Amsterdam, 1974.

See also 94, 97, 103, and 145.

Biographies

89 J. MEIER-GRAEFE: Impressionisten, Munich, 1907. Chapters on Guys, Manet, van Gogh, Pissarro, Cézanne. The author subsequently published the long, illustrated chapter on van Gogh separately as:

90 J. MEIER-GRAEFE: Vincent van Gogh, Munich, 1910, 1912, 1918, 1922. With 50 mediocre ill.

91 J. HAVELAAR: Vincent van Gogh, Holland, 1915; Zurich, 1920; Amsterdam 1929, 1943.

92 T. DURET: Van Gogh—Vincent, Paris, 1916; second "définitif" edition, 1919. This by now completely obsolete biography has the sad distinction of being the first publication to feature among its illustrations several spurious drawings and paintings, some of them incredibly poor. The scourge of forgeries had thus begun within twenty-five years after the artist's death. In justice to the forgers it must be added that their products have since been considerably improved.

93 J. MEIER-GRAEFE: Vincent, 2 vol., Munich, 1921, 1925. A biography treated more like a novel. English editions: London, 1922, with 102 good plates; New York, 1933, with 61 poor ill.

94 G. COQUIOT: Vincent van Gogh, Paris, 1923. This rambling biography would be completely obsolete if it did not contain some recollections of van Gogh, such as Signac's, and various unpublished letters, since included in 53.

95 F. FELS: Vincent van Gogh, Paris, 1928.

96 K. PFISTER: Vincent van Gogh—Sein Werk, Potsdam, [1922], 1929. With 6 color plates and 62 black-and-white ill.

97 L. PIÉRARD: La Vie tragique de Vincent van Gogh, Paris, 1924, 1939. English edition: Boston–New York, 1925. Almost completely devoted to the early periods of van Gogh's life with emphasis on his stay in the Borinage, of which the author was socialist deputy and where he has gathered important material. See also the same author's: Van Gogh au pays noir, *Mercure de France,* 1913, and: Van Gogh à Auvers, *Les Marges,* Jan. 1914.

98 C. TERRASSE: Van Gogh—Peintre, Paris, 1935. Profusely ill. See also the same author's introduction to 4.

99 J. REWALD: Vincent van Gogh, Supplement to *La Renaissance,* July 1937.

100 J. DE BEUCKEN: Un Portrait de Vincent van Gogh Liège, 1938; Brussels, n.d.; Paris, 1953. Biography written in a journalistic style with a slight tendency toward fictionalizing; contains nothing new.

101 T. W. EARP: Van Gogh, London–Edinburgh, n.d. [1934]. With 6 mediocre color plates.

102 C. NORDENFALK: Vincent van Gogh, Stockholm, 1943; Copenhagen, 1946, Holland and Norway, 1947. English edition: The Life and Work of van Gogh, New York, 1953. A good biography which, though it does not contain any new material, presents the known facts in a clear and logical fashion. Selected bibl., 68 ill., 4 mediocre color plates, no index.

103 Van Gogh raconté par lui-même et par ses amis, vol. II, Geneva, 1947. Excerpts from writings about van Gogh which have all previously appeared elsewhere. Short bibl., ill. Vol. I was never issued.

104 F. ELGAR: Van Gogh—Peintures, Paris, 1947.

105 F. HOLMER: van Gogh, Stockholm, 1947.

106 A. PARRONCHI: van Gogh, Florence, 1947.

107 G. SCHMIDT: Vincent van Gogh—Leben und Werk, Bern, 1947. With good though small ill. (Scherz Bücher).

108 W. WEISBACH: Vincent van Gogh—Kunst und Schicksal. Vol. I, Die Frühzeit (50 ill.), Basel, 1949; vol. II, Künstlerischer Aufstieg und Ende (83 ill.), Basel, 1951. An extremely thorough and extensive biography based on the artist's writings and on his work. Well-selected and good ill., index.

109 A. M. HAMMACHER: Vincent van Gogh, Amsterdam, n.d. Competent text with 62 good ill., among them some documents and details of paintings, 2 color plates. Short bibl.

110 J. LEYMARIE: Van Gogh, Paris–New York, 1951. A very thorough text, accompanied by well-selected documentary illustrations and followed by a few of van Gogh's letters. 160 good and well-chosen plates in black and white and color; ample appendix with excerpts from writings by Aurier, Mirbeau, Bernard, and van Gogh; detailed chronological chart with references to paintings reproduced in the volume (but which does not list the various exhibitions of the Independents and of the XX); analytical notes on the works reproduced; extensive bibl., list of exhibitions, index. A valuable book (Tisné).

111 P. GACHET: Vincent van Gogh aux "Indépendants," Paris, 1953. With catalogues of van Gogh's works shown at the Independents in 1888, 1889, and 1890, as well as of his retrospectives of 1891, 1905, and 1926. Ill.

112 M. E. TRALBAUT: Vincent, Theo, Johanna [van Gogh], a lecture published by the Stedelijk Museum, Amsterdam, 1953.

113 M. DE SABLONIÈRE: Vincent van Gogh, Amsterdam-Antwerp, n.d. [1954?]. In Dutch.

114 H. PERRUCHOT: La Vie de van Gogh, Paris, 1955. Conscientious biography based mainly on van Gogh's letters, with a good chronological chart, selected bibl. No index, no ill.

115 L. and E. HANSON: Passionate Pilgrim—The Life of Vincent van Gogh, New York, 1955. Written with a regrettable penchant for fictionalizing and an insufficient acquaintance with matters of art. Short bibl., index, 22 ill.

116 P. MAROIS: Le Secret de van Gogh, Paris, 1957. Conscientious and readable text, although containing nothing new. No ill., no bibl., no index.

117 J. HULSKER: Who Was Vincent van Gogh?, The Hague, 1958. Small vol. for the general public, with text in Dutch, English, French, and German; ill.

118 F. ELGAR: Van Gogh, Paris and New York, 1958. Good text, richly illustrated in black and white and color; bibl., index.

119 M. E. TRALBAUT: Van Gogh (le peintre par l'image), Paris, 1960. Along with works of van Gogh, this book contains numerous photographs of his subjects, of documents, and of his various friends. This picture-biography is based on the documentation presented by its author in the exhibitions organized by him (see 40, 41, and 43). See also 123.

120 P. LEPROHON: Tel fut Van Gogh, Paris, 1964. A detailed biography liberally sprinkled with anecdotes but containing very few new elements; ill.

121 J. LEYMARIE: Qui était Van Gogh, Geneva, 1968. Biography and fine study of van Gogh's artistic evolution; numerous excellent ill. in black and white and color.

122 C. BOURNIQUEL, P. CABANNE, G. CHARENSOL, R. COGNIAT, F. DURET-ROBERT, J. PARIS, M. ROBERT, Y. TAILLANDIER: Van Gogh, Paris, 1968. A series of essays, mostly popularizations; ill.

123 M. E. TRALBAUT: Vincent van Gogh, New York, 1969. A large and handsome volume by a man who has toiled for years under a kind of "spell" cast on him by van Gogh. This is truly a labor of love, though at moments it may appear to be an almost blind love. Indeed, nothing that concerns the painter, down to the last bit of trivia, ever escapes Tralbaut; but his devotion to his subject is so touching, his eagerness so tremendous, his patience so amazing that one cannot help but admire this single-minded pursuit of his obsession. This massive book contains many previously unknown details and documents, also numerous excellent reproductions in black and white and color.

124 Vincent: Bulletin of the Rijksmuseum Vincent van Gogh, Amsterdam, 4 vols., 1970–76. Illustrated periodical that appeared two to four times a year and carried many interesting and well-documented studies on the artist (in English). Suspended publication after vol. 4, no. 4, 1976.

125 B. WELSH-OVCHAROV: Vincent van Gogh—His Paris Period, 1886–1888, Utrecht–The Hague, 1976. A very useful study on a frequently neglected phase of Vincent's evolution, with new documents, a list of rejected works, as well as a chronological list of his works done in Paris. Unfortunately, the text is written in a rather clumsy vernacular. For a review, see B. PETRIE, *Burlington Magazine*, Nov. 1977.

See also 70, 288, and 315.

Medical and Psychiatric Studies

126 DE MEESTER: Over kunstenaar-zijn en Vincent van Gogh, *De Gids*, 1911.

127 K. JASPERS: Strindberg und van Gogh, Arbeiten zur angewandten Psychiatrie, Berlin, 1922. French edition: Strindberg et van Gogh—Hölderlin et Swedenborg, Paris, 1953.

128 A. J. WESTERMANN-HOLSTIJN: Die psychologische Entwicklung van Gogh, *Imago*, vol. X, no. 4, 1924. See also 163 and 177.

129 GRUNDY: The Childishness of van Gogh, *The Connoisseur*, vol. 68, 1924.

130 W. RIESE: Über den Stilwandel bei Vincent van Gogh, *Zentralblatt für die gesamte Neurologie und Psychiatrie*, May 2, 1925.

131 V. DOITEAU: La Folie de Vincent van Gogh, *Progrès Médical*, nos. 1 and 3, 1926.

132 H. EVENSEN: Die Geisteskrankheit Vincent van Goghs, *Allgemeine Zeitschrift für Psychiatrie und psychischgerichtliche Medizin*, Berlin–Leipzig, vol. 84, Feb. 15, 1926 (pp. 133–54).

133 E. LEROY: Le Séjour de Vincent van Gogh à l'Asyle de

Saint-Rémy-de-Provence, *Aesculape,* May, June, July 1926.

134 W. Riese: Vincent van Gogh in der Krankheit—Ein Beitrag zum Problem der Beziehung zwischen Kunstwerk und Krankheit, *Grundlagen des Nerven- und Seelenlebens,* Munich, Fasc. 125, 1926.

135 J. Thurler: A propos de Vincent van Gogh. Doctoral thesis presented at the medical faculty of the University of Geneva, 1927.

136 G. Duthuit: Le Drame des Alyscamps, *L'Amour de l'Art,* 1927.

137 V. Doiteau and E. Leroy: La Folie de van Gogh, Paris, 1928. Based on the records of the Saint-Rémy asylum (of which Dr. Leroy was medical chief), as well as on van Gogh's letters and other related material. Numerous ill., short bibl. See also 131, 133, and 145.

138 H. Prinzhorn: Genius and Madness, *Parnassus,* Jan. 1930.

139 Bataille: La Mutilation sacrificielle et l'oreille coupée de Vincent van Gogh, *Documents,* no. 8, 1930.

140 Hutter: De vijf diagnoses van de ziekte van Vincent van Gogh, *Nederlandsch Tijdschrift voor Geneeskunde,* 1931.

141 J. A. M. Meerloo: De diagnostische strijd over Vincent van Gogh, *Psychiatrische en Neurologische Bladen,* 1931.

142 A. Bader: Künstlertragik—Karl Stauffer und Vincent van Gogh, Basel, 1932.

143 F. Minkowska: Van Gogh—Les Relations entre sa vie, sa maladie et son oeuvre, *L'Evolution Psychiatrique,* vol. III, 1932. See also 188.

144 Rijnsaburo Shikiba: Vincent van Gogh—His Life and Psychosis, Tokyo, 1932. In Japanese.

145 V. Doiteau and E. Leroy: Vincent van Gogh et le drame de l'oreille coupée, *Aesculape,* July 1932. Quotes the recollections of the policeman to whom van Gogh's ear was given at the bordello in Arles.

146 E. Schindeler: Van Gogh's "Insanity," *Museum of Modern Art Bulletin,* Dec. 1935.

147 J. Beer: Essai sur les rapports de l'art et de la maladie de Vincent van Gogh. Doctoral thesis, Strasbourg, 1936. See also 160.

148 J. Beer: La Maladie de Van Gogh, *Beaux-Arts,* Jan. 10 and 17, 1936.

149 Cochrane: Van Gogh's Madness, *Art Digest,* April 15, 1936.

150 S. Hedenberg: Van Gogh, om hans sjukdom och konst, *Svenska Läkartidningen,* vol. XXXV, 1938.

151 M. Rose and M. J. Mannheim: Vincent van Gogh im Spiegel seiner Handschrift, Basel–Leipzig, 1938. With numerous facsimile reproductions of van Gogh's letters.

152 G. Kraus: Vincent van Gogh en de Psychiatrie, *Psychiatrische en Neurologische Bladen,* Sept.–Oct. 1941. Extensive discussion (in Dutch) of the various theories concerning van Gogh's illness, followed by an exhaustive bibliography on which the present section draws heavily. (This bibliography also includes a number of general books on psychiatry and on the relationship between genius and madness which are not listed here.)

153 A. J. Kaes: Een vergelijkend onderzoek naar de beeldende kunst van gezonden en geesteszieken, Arnhem, 1942.

154 W. Nigg: Religiöse Denker—Kierkegaard, Dostojewski, Nietzsche, van Gogh, Bern–Leipzig, 1942.

155 W. Born: The Art of the Insane, *Ciba Symposia,* Jan. 1946.

156 I. H. Perry: Vincent van Gogh's Illness, *Bulletin of the History of Medicine* (Johns Hopkins), 21, 1947.

157 J. Beer: Notes sur la maladie de Van Gogh, *Psyché,* Mar. 1947.

158 D. E. Schneider: The Psychoanalyst and the Artist *in* Three Modern Painters, New York, 1949.

159 D. E. Schneider: Psychic Victory of Talent—A Psychoanalytic Evaluation of van Gogh, *College Art Journal,* 1950, no. 9. (With a reply by Buckman, *ibid.,* no. 10.)

160 J. Beer: Diagnosis of the Tragedy, *Art News Annual,* 1950. See also 147.

161 J. Schnier: The Blazing Sun: A Psychoanalytic Approach to Van Gogh, *American Imago,* 7, 1950.

162 F. Minkowska: Notes sur Van Gogh, *Revue Esthétique,* 1951.

163 A. J. Westermann-Holstijn: The Psychological Development of Vincent van Gogh, *American Imago,* 8, 1951. Translation of the German original (128). See also 177.

164 C. Mauron: Notes sur la structure de l'inconscient chez Vincent van Gogh, *Psyché,* nos. 75–78, Jan.–April 1953. Very important study. See also 196.

165 C. Mauron: Vincent et Théo van Gogh—Une symbiose; lecture published by the *Instituut voor moderne Kunst,* Amsterdam, no. 1, 1953. See also 196.

166 G. Kraus: The Relationship between Theo and Vincent van Gogh; lecture given at and published by the Rijksmuseum Kröller-Müller, Otterlo, 1953.

167 L. Roelandt: Les Maladies de Van Gogh, *Aesculape,* 34, 1953; 35, 1954.

168 J. A. M. Meerloo: Three Artists, An Essay on Creative Urge and Artistic Perturbation, *American Imago,* 10, 1953.

169 W. R. Bett: Vincent van Gogh (1853–90) Artist and Addict, *British Journal of Addiction,* 1–2, 1954.

170 G. Aigrisse: L'Evolution du symbole chez Van Gogh, *Psyché* (France), no. 91, 1954.

171 G. Aigrisse: La Ronde des Prisonniers, *De Tafel Ronde,* special van Gogh issue, May–June 1955. Excerpts from a thesis at the Institut International de Psychologie, Geneva. (On this subject see G. Bazin: Van Gogh s'est suicidé pour ne pas tuer Théo, *Arts,* May 1–7, 1957.) The author sees in van Gogh's copy after Doré (see ill. p. 326) a significant example of his desire to return to his mother's womb as well as to escape from it by trying to identify himself with the sun, symbol of the Ideal father. This psychoanalytical study leads one to question whether the author is sufficiently conversant with van Gogh's artistic problems. See also 172 and 173.

172 G. Aigrisse: Psychoanalyse de Vincent van Gogh; short

article in *Het cahier—de nevelvlek,* Antwerp, special van Gogh issue, May–June 1955. See 171.

173 G. AIGRISSE: Une interprétation jungienne de van Gogh, C. G. Jung (Festschrift), Brussels, 1955. See 171.

174 J. J. GILLON: Le Symbole sexuel chez Van Gogh, *Concours Medical,* 1955.

175 H. GASTAUX: La Maladie de Vincent van Gogh envisagée à la lumière des conceptions nouvelles sur l'épilepsie psychomotrice, *Annales médico-psychiatriques,* 2, 1956, 196.

176 H. P. BLUM: Van Gogh's Chairs, *American Imago,* 13, 1956.

177 A. J. WESTERMANN-HOLSTIJN: The Psychological Development of Vincent van Gogh, *Journal of Mental Science,* Jan. 1957. Revised version; differs from 128 and 163.

178 L. ROELANDT: Vincent van Gogh et son frère Théo, Paris, 1957. This is an extremely biased study which tries to prove that the relationship of the two brothers was poisoned by misunderstandings and disagreements, and that Theo's widow edited Vincent's letters in such a way as to put her husband in a favorable light. Although certain problems are ably discussed and the numerous quotes well selected, the author's prejudices harm the credible aspects of his thesis. The book examines in great detail the relationship of the two brothers before the painter's arrival in Paris but is much less convincing concerning the later and more decisive years during which the brothers were much closer to each other. No ill., no bibl., no index. See also 352.

179 A. KUHN-FOELIX: Vincent van Gogh—Eine Psychographie, Bergen II, Obb. (Germany), 1958.

180 F. WÜRTENBERGER: Vom milieubedingten zum existentialistischen Künstlertum, *Studium General,* Jahrg. 11. Heft 2, 1958. Chapter on van Gogh.

181 C. MAURON: Van Gogh au seuil de la Provence, Marseilles, 1959. Pamphlet.

182 A. J. LUBIN: Vincent van Gogh's Ear, *Psychoanalytical Quarterly,* 30, 1961.

183 R. E. HEMPILL: The Illness of Vincent van Gogh, *Proceedings of The Royal Society of Medicine,* London, Dec. 1961.

184 E. VAN ZIEGLER: Vincent van Gogh und seine Ärzte, *Schweizerische Medizinische Wochenschrift,* 32, 1961.

185 J. L. FOY: Vincent van Gogh—The Crisis in Identity, *in* Proceeding of the Third World Congress of Psychiatry, University of Toronto Press, 1963.

186 J. A. M. MEERLOO: Vincent van Gogh's Quest for Identity, *Nederlands Kunsthistorisch Jaarboek,* 14, 1963.

187 H. R. GRAETZ: The Symbolic Language of Vincent van Gogh, London, 1963. The author is so wrapped up in Freudian theories and so unfamiliar with the problems of creative production that he completely overlooks one basic fact, namely, that a painting or drawing contains not only more or less unconscious elements, but also obeys artistic and compositional necessities. Thus, a repetition which he considers "important as a symbol of frustration" (p. 27) is probably merely a device to fill an empty space. And it seems equally far-fetched to stress the fact that the woman in the *Potato Eaters* "looks down while pouring coffee into the cups" (p. 34). Could she possibly do otherwise while filling four cups? For reviews see: *Times Literary Supplement,* July 16, Nov. 19, and especially Dec. 10, 1964 (letter from M. Roskill).

188 F. MINKOWSKA: Van Gogh, sa vie, sa maladie et son oeuvre, Paris, 1963. Three articles, republished posthumously. See also 143.

189 P. W. MILLER: Provenience of the Death Symbolism in Van Gogh's Cornscapes, *Psychoanalytical Review,* 54, 1965.

190 R. H. FAIRBAIRN: Vincent van Gogh—His Psychopathology as Reflected in His Oil Paintings, *Canadian Psychiatric Association Journal* (Ottawa), 11, Oct. 1966.

191 H. NAGERA: Vincent van Gogh—A Psychological Study, London, 1967.

192 R. W. PICKFORD: Studies in Psychiatric Art; Its Psychodynamics, Therapeutic Value, and Relationship to Modern Art, Springfield, Ill, 1967.

193 M. ROBERT: Le Génie et son double, *Preuves,* 204, 1968; also *in* Van Gogh, Collection Génies et Réalités, Paris, 1968.

194 A. J. LUBIN: The Second Vincent van Gogh, *Stanford Today,* summer 1969.

195 J. B. TRAINER: Resemblance of Sex to Epilepsy—Medical Aspects of Human Sexuality, 1970.

196 C. MAURON: Van Gogh—Etudes psychocritiques, Paris, 1976. A posthumously assembled collection of the author's writings on van Gogh.

See also the declaration of H. Gaustaut *in* Kommentaar bij het van Gogh-Symposium, *Van Goghiana V,* Antwerp, 1968, p. 40.

Studies of Style

197 G.-A. AURIER: Les Isolés—Vincent van Gogh, *Mercure de France,* Jan. 1890; reprinted in Oeuvres posthumes, Paris, 1893.

198 E. BERNARD: Vincent van Gogh, *Les Hommes d'Aujourd'hui,* vol. 8, no. 390, 1890.

199 O. MIRBEAU: Vincent van Gogh, *Echo de Paris,* March 31, 1891; reprinted in: Des artistes, vol. I, Paris, 1922, and in 103.

200 C. SAUNIER: Vincent van Gogh, *L'Endehors,* April 24, 1892.

201 H. VON HOFMANNSTHAL: Die Farben (Aus den Briefen eines Zurückgekehrten, [Paris], May 26, 1901); Gesammelte Werke, vol. II, Berlin, 1924, pp. 210–14. French translation in 103, pp. 142–48.

202 J. MEIER-GRAEFE: Entwicklungsgeschichte der modernen Kunst, Stuttgart, 1904. Chapter on van Gogh.

203 J. COHEN-GOSSCHALK: Vincent van Gogh, *Zeitschrift für bildende Kunst,* 1908.

204 M. DENIS: De Gauguin et de van Gogh au classicisme, *L'Occident,* May 1909; reprinted in Théories, Paris, 1912, pp. 154–70.

205 R. Meyer-Riefstahl: Vincent van Gogh, *Burlington Magazine,* Nov. and Dec. 1910.

206 P. Godet: Vincent van Gogh, *L'Art Décoratif,* Sept. 1911.

207 L. Coellen: Die neue Malerei, Munich, 1912. Chapter on van Gogh and Cézanne.

208 W. Hausenstein: Van Gogh und Gauguin, Stuttgart–Berlin, 1914.

209 H. Hertz: Van Gogh, *Art in America,* Aug. 1923.

210 R. Fry: Transformations—Critical and Speculative Essays on Art, London, 1926. Chapter on van Gogh. New edition: New York, 1956.

211 W. F. Douwes: Vincent van Gogh, Amsterdam, n.d. [1930]. 62 ill.

212 K. Scheffler: Van Gogh als Grenzstein, *Kunst und Künstler,* April 1932.

213 W. Pach: Vincent van Gogh—A Study of the Artist and His Work in Relation to His Times, New York, 1936.

214 C. Cunningham: Roulin the Postman by van Gogh, *Bulletin of the Museum of Fine Arts,* Boston, Feb. 1936.

215 J. Rewald: Van Gogh en Provence, *L'Amour de l'Art,* Oct. 1936. Juxtaposition of photographs and motifs. See also 219 and 226.

216 F. Novotny: Van Gogh's Teekeningen van het "Straatje te Saintes-Maries," *Maandblad voor Beeldende Kunsten,* Dec. 1936. Important article. See also 232 and 252.

217 M. Florisoone: Van Gogh, Paris, 1937. A philosophical approach to van Gogh's personal tragedy and art. Profusely ill. with good reproductions. Selected bibl.

218 W. Gaunt: Vincent, an Appreciation of van Gogh, *London Studio,* Dec. 1938.

219 J. Rewald: Van Gogh versus Nature, *Art News,* April 1–14, 1942; see also 215 and 226.

220 M. Schapiro: On a Painting of van Gogh, *View,* fall 1946; reprinted in *Perspectives U.S.A.,* vol. I, no. 1, 1952, pp. 141–53.

221 C. Nordenfalk: Van Gogh and Sweden; C. Derkert: Theory and Practice in van Gogh's Dutch Painting; C. Derkert, H. Eklund, and O. Reutersvärd: Van Gogh's "Landscape with Corn Shocks"; C. Nordenfalk and A. Meyerson: The Date of the Stockholm "Landscape with Corn Shocks"; A. Meyerson: Van Gogh and the School of Pont-Aven, *Konsthistorisk Tidskrift,* Dec. 1946, special issue: Swedish van Gogh Studies (in English). Series of interesting articles, profusely ill.

222 J. G. van Gelder: Vincent van Gogh—The Potato Eaters, London, n.d. [1947?]. With 18 illustrations of drawings and studies for, and details of, van Gogh's most important early work. See also 248.

223 M. E. Tralbaut: Vincent van Gogh in zijn Antwerpsche Periode, Amsterdam, 1948. With 57 illustrations after documents and works by the artist, among them many unpublished sketches. Extensive synopsis of van Gogh's letters from Antwerp. Four mediocre color plates, index.

224 M. Buchmann: Die Farbe bei Vincent van Gogh, Zurich, 1948. Color in van Gogh's work studied on the basis of individual paintings and quotations from his letters. Excellent analysis. Section on van Gogh's historical position. Bibl.

225 C. Nordenfalk: Van Gogh and Literature, *Journal of the Warburg and Courtauld Institute,* London, 1948.

225a W. Hausenstein and G. Jedlicka: Vincent van Gogh—"Sommerabend bei Arles," *in* Hauptwerke des Kunstmuseums Winterthur, 1949.

226 W. Gaunt: The Man and His Time; J. Rewald: The Artist and the Land; S. Spender: The Painter and the Poet; J. Beer: Diagnosis of the Tragedy; M. Pease: The Hand and the Brush; *Art News Annual,* special van Gogh issue, 1950. Profusely ill. Reprinted as album with 19 color plates: Van Gogh, New York, 1953.

227 F. Bonger–van der Borch van Verwolde: Vincent van Gogh als Lezer, *Maandblad voor Beeldende Kunsten,* March 1950.

228 J. Seznec: Literary inspiration in van Gogh, *Magazine of Art,* Dec. 1950.

229 M. Serullaz: Van Gogh et Millet, *Etudes d'Art,* Musée d'Algers, V, 1950.

230 P. Guastalla: Essai sur van Gogh, Paris, 1952. No ill.

231 F. Novotny: Die Popularität van Goghs, *Alte und Neue Kunst,* no. 2, 1953. See also 252.

232 F. Novotny: Reflections on a Drawing by van Gogh, *The Art Bulletin,* March 1953. See also 216 and 252.

233 P. Gachet: Van Gogh à Auvers—Histoire d'un tableau, Paris, 1953. On van Gogh's "Mlle Gachet at the Piano" representing the author's sister; ill.

234 G. Mazzariol: Proposte per uno studio su Van Gogh, *Atti del seminario di Storia dell' Arte,* Pisa-Viareggio, July 1–15, 1953.

235 W. J. de Gruyter: Theo and Vincent van Gogh (in English); M. E. Tralbaut: Van Gogh's Japanisme (in Dutch with very interesting ill.); J. Leymarie: Symbole et réalité chez van Gogh. Van Gogh Symposium issue of *Mededelingen* (The Hague), nos. 1–2, 1954. See also 350.

236 M. E. Tralbaut: Vincent van Gogh in het Caf' conc' of het raakpunt met Raffaëlli, Stedelijk Museum, Amsterdam, 1955. With 24 illustrations among which are 9 unknown sketches of the Paris period.

237 V. W. van Gogh: Madame Roulin—La Berceuse—door Vincent van Gogh en Paul Gauguin, *Museumjournaal,* Oct. 1955.

238 D. Cooper: Two Japanese Prints from Vincent van Gogh's Collection, *Burlington Magazine,* June 1957.

239 M. de Sablonière: Inleiding tot de Kunst van van Gogh, Amsterdam, 1958.

240 L. Gans: Vincent van Gogh en de Schilders van de "Petit Boulevard," *Museumjournaal,* IV, Dec. 1958.

241 J. Stellingwerff: Werkelijkheid en Grondmotief bij Vincent Willem van Gogh, Amsterdam, 1959 (Doctoral thesis with 21 ill., index).

242 A. M. Hammacher: Van Gogh Selbstbildnisse, Stuttgart, 1960. Booklet with 16 ill. See also 44.

243 F. Novotny: Die Bilder van Goghs nach fremden Vorbildern, *in* Festschrift Kurt Badt, Berlin, 1961. See also 252 and 256.

244 K. Badt: Die Farbenlehre van Goghs, Cologne, 1961. An important book; 32 ill. in black and white and color.

245 F. Novotny: Zu einem unbekannten Selbstbildnis von Van Gogh, *Alte und Moderne Kunst,* Sept.–Oct. 1962.

246 F. Novotny: Die Zeichnungen van Goghs in der Albertina, *Albertina Studien,* Heft 1, 1963.

247 F. Erpel: Van Gogh—Selfportraits, Oxford, 1964 (original German edition: Berlin, 1963). A rather uncritical approach since three of the paintings are considered spurious. On the subject of self-portraits, see also K. Bromig-Kolleritz von Novisancz: Die Selbstbildnisse Vincent van Goghs—Versuch einer kunsthistorischen Erfassung der Darstellungen, Munich, 1955.

248 A. Boime: A Source for Van Gogh's "Potato-Eaters," *Gazette des Beaux-Arts,* April 1966.

249 A. Tellegen: Vincent and Gauguin; Vincent and de Chamaillard, *Museumjournaal,* 1–2, 1966.

250 M. Roskill: Van Gogh's "Blue Cart" and His Creative Process, *Oud Holland,* 81, 1966.

251 A. Szymanska: Unbekannte Jugendzeichnungen Vincent van Goghs und das Schaffen des Künstlers in den Jahren 1870–1880, Berlin, 1968. Ill. Some of these drawings, though far from all, have been included among the "Juvenilia" of 5. The reproductions here are better and are accompanied by an extensive study.

252 F. Novotny: Über das "Elementare" in der Kunstgeschichte und andere Aufsätze, Vienna, 1968. Contains reprints (in German) of 216, 231, 232, and 243.

253 M. Roskill: Van Gogh, Gauguin and the Impressionist Circle, London–New York, 1970. Important chapters on van Gogh, Gauguin, and Bernard, also on van Gogh and Gauguin at Arles, followed by "Coda—The Personal Relationship between van Gogh and Gauguin."

254 R. Pickvance: English Influences on Vincent van Gogh, University Art Gallery, Nottingham, 1974. Profusely illustrated, excellent text exploring an uncharted field in an exemplary manner, including, among others, reference to Goupil's in London. On other art dealers, Pickvance refers to: B. Gould: Two van Gogh Contacts: E. J. Van Wisselingh, Art Dealer; Daniel Cottier, Glass Painter and Decorator, London, 1969.

255 De Verzameling Engelse prenten van Vincent van Gogh, Rijksmuseum Vincent van Gogh, Amsterdam, 1975. Exhibition catalogue containing detailed chronology of the years 1853–1876, with quotes from the artist's letters and ill.

256 C. Cheltham: The Role of Vincent van Gogh's Copies in the Development of His Art, New York–London, 1976. An extremely thorough and well-documented investigation. Ill. See also 370.

See also 90, 96, 107, 108, 109, 125, 313, 317, and 356.

Studies on Forgeries

See especially 3.

257 P. Fierens: Les Faux van Gogh, *Journal des Débats,* April 25, 1930.

258 E. Faure: A propos des faux van Gogh, *L'Art Vivant,* April 1930.

259 J. B. de la Faille: Réponse à l'article de M. Elie Faure, *L'Art Vivant,* 1930.

260 G. Poulain: Dans le maquis des faux, *Comoedia,* Dec. 10, 1931. Interview with the painter Judith Gérard, stepdaughter of Gauguin's friend Molard, who declares that she copied van Gogh's "Self-Portrait" (Hyperion 508) from the painting (Hyperion 505) which Gauguin had left with her parents.

261 C. Veth: Schoon schip—expertise naar echtheid en onechtheid inzake Vincent van Gogh, Amsterdam, 1932. German translation: Falsche Expertisen? Falsche Experten? Berlin, n.d. [1932?]. On the Wacker pictures.

262 A. Pfannstiel and M. J. Schretlen: Van Gogh's "Jardin de Daubigny," *Maandblad voor Beeldende Kunsten,* May 1935.

263 A. Hentzen: Der Garten Daubignys von Vincent van Gogh, *Zeitschrift für Kunstgeschichte,* vol. IV, 1935.

264 W. Überwasser: Le jardin de Daubigny, das letzte Hauptwerk van Goghs, Basel, 1936. A detailed discussion of the authenticity of the two versions, concluding against the version F 776 [Hyperion no. 758] (see also 3). Profusely ill. [Brooks's contention in 1 (no. 728, p. 56) that Überwasser may be a pen-name for R. Staechelin, owner of the other version which is here declared solely authentic, is wholly unfounded.] This study brought about further controversies.

265 A. Hentzen: Nochmals "der Garten Daubignys" von Vincent van Gogh, *Zeitschrift für Kunstgeschichte,* vol. V, 1936.

266 M. de Sablonière: Over echte en valse van Goghs, *Vrij Niederlande,* Dec. 23, 1950. See also the same author's two small publications: Een "echte" van Gogh? Leiden, 1948, and: Over u een Studie bij Kaarslicht, Leiden, 1954.

267 M. M. van Dantzig: Vincent?—A New Method of Identifying the Artist and His Work and of Unmasking the Forger and His Products, Amsterdam, n.d. [1953?] (in English). The author has established a list of 93 "characteristic features" of van Gogh's paintings, to which are added 82 others, subdivided by subjects and three great periods of his work. By examining individual paintings in the light of these and establishing numerically their "positive" and "negative" features on a percentage basis, he purports to be able to distinguish authentic from forged works. It is to be questioned whether this purely mechanical test is an adequate substitute for visual experience and the insight which can only be gained by patient study of the painter's works. 36 small ill. See also 275.

268 L. Anfray: Plus de 500 tableaux de Vincent van Gogh ont échoué à la brocante, *Arts-Documents,* Feb. 1953. The author of this article was a retired French naval officer who interested himself in the work of van Gogh after having discovered in the Paris flea market a painting which he and J. B. de la Faille attributed to van Gogh. (It was subsequently rejected—and rightly so—by the editors of 5.) The author approached his subject from a strictly logical point of view, with little analysis based upon artistic insight. As a result, his

publications (269–73, 276, 346, 347, 349) are more confusing than illuminating. See 274. Together with de la Faille this author issued in 1957 *Les Cahiers de van Gogh* (two numbers appeared), brimming with polemics.

269 L. ANFRAY: "Les Mangeurs de Pommes de Terre" dans l'oeuvre de Vincent van Gogh, *Arts-Documents,* April 1953.

270 L. ANFRAY: Van Gogh—Catalographie de son oeuvre, *Arts-Documents,* Dec. 1953.

271 L. ANFRAY: Méthode d'examen d'un tableau, *Arts-Documents,* Dec. 1953, Jan. 1954.

272 L. ANFRAY: Une énigme van Gogh, *Arts-Documents,* Dec. 1953, March 1954, June 1954.

273 L. ANFRAY: La Vérité torturée, *Arts-Documents,* April and May 1954.

274 L. GANS: Een vermeende versie van "de Aardappeleters"—onjuiste interpretatie van van Gogh's brieven, *Museumjournaal,* Dec. 1955. Excellent refutation of Anfray's theories.

275 Expertise et Contre-Expertise d'un van Gogh par M. VAN DANTZIG, H. L. C. JAFFÉ et A. M. HAMMACHER, *Connaissance des-Arts,* Oct. 1957. In this particular case the method of van Dantzig (see 267) turns out to be just as subjective as the "unscientific" method which it was supposed to replace.

276 L. ANFRAY: Guerre froide autour d'un portrait de van Gogh—"Etude à la bougie," *Les Cahiers de van Gogh,* no. 2, n.d. [1957]. See also 266.

See also 92, 221, and 299.

On forgeries *see also:* Brooks (1), nos. 57, 135, 170, 236, 300, 301, 322, 354, 421, 427, 428, 429, 430, 434, 435, 518, 637, 640, 641, 642, 647, 648, 650, 651, 673, 695, and 704.

Reproductions

277 H. P. BREMMER: Vincent van Gogh—Vier-en-twintig teekeningen mit zijn Hollandsche periode, Amsterdam, 1907. The earliest portfolio devoted to the artist, containing 24 poor plates after drawings of his Dutch period.

278 H. P. BREMMER: Vincent van Gogh, introduction to a portfolio of poor reproductions, Amsterdam, 1911.

279 H. P. BREMMER: Vincent van Gogh—Reproducties naar zijn werken in de verzameling van Mevrouw H. Kröller-Müller, privately printed in the Hague, 1919. First publication on the Kröller-Müller collection, in the assembling of which Bremmer had a leading part, and which has since grown into the Rijksmuseum Kröller-Müller, Otterlo (see also 27 and 30). Numerous ill.

280 Vincent van Gogh, 16 facsimiles after drawings and watercolors published by the Marées-Gesellschaft, Munich, 1919. Introduction by O. Hagen. Superlative reproductions.

281 C. GLASER: Vincent van Gogh, Leipzig, 1921 (Seemann).

282 G. F. HARTLAUB: Vincent van Gogh, Berlin, 1922, 1930. 49 small, fair ill., not chronologically arranged.

283 R. GREY: Van Gogh, Rome (in English) and Paris, 1924. Small plates.

284 F. FELS: Vincent van Gogh, Paris, 1924. 20 very poor and small plates.

285 Vincent van Gogh, Seemanns Künstlermappe No. 66, Leipzig, [1924]. Eight color plates with introduction by A. Seemann.

286 J. H. NIJLAND: Portfolio of 24 reproductions after drawings of van Gogh's Dutch period, Amsterdam, 1924. See also 13.

287 W. GEORGE: Van Gogh, Paris, n.d. Short introduction with 24 mediocre plates (Album d'art Druet).

288 R. COLIN: Van Gogh, Paris, 1925: English edition, London–New York, 1926. 40 small and mediocre plates, bibl.

289 Vincent van Gogh—facsimile reproductions after watercolors and drawings published by the Marées-Gesellschaft, Munich, 1926. Superlative reproductions.

290 J. MEIER-GRAEFE: Vincent van Gogh der Zeichner, Berlin, 1928. Long introduction, 52 good plates chronologically arranged.

291 A. BERTRAM: Vincent van Gogh, London–New York, 1929. 24 small plates.

292 F. KNAPP: Vincent van Gogh, Leipzig, 1930. 28 black-and-white and 16 color plates (Velhagen & Klasing Künstler Monographien).

293 C. TERRASSE: Introduction to van Gogh portfolio, Paris–Leipzig, 1931. 8 color plates.

294 KARDAS: Van Gogh à Arles, *L'Art Vivant,* Sept. 1933. See also by the same photographer: Subjects of van Gogh as They Appear Today, *London Studio,* Aug. 1934.

295 L. PIÉRARD: Vincent van Gogh, Paris, 1936. Small but good plates, not chronologically arranged (Collection des Maîtres).

296 G. BENSON: Introduction to Vincent van Gogh portfolio of 12 color plates published by the New York Graphic Society, New York, 1936.

297 W. UHDE: Vincent van Gogh, Vienna, 1936. Large volume of excellent black-and-white but poor color plates of paintings, drawings, and watercolors, not chronologically arranged (Phaidon).

298 L. VITALI: Vincent van Gogh, Milan, 1936. Small plates with an extremely extensive though not always reliable bibl. by G. Scheiwiller (see also 305 and 306).

299 INOSOUKE HAZAMA (comments by): Recueil important des oeuvres de Vincent van Gogh, Tokyo [1936], in French and Japanese. 3 vol. of poor color plates. Vol. I, Paysage; vol. II, Portraits et nus (20 plates including some of van Gogh's copies but no nudes); vol. III, Nature morte (20 plates including some of spurious paintings).

300 J. KLEIN: Vincent van Gogh, New York, [1937]. Portfolio of reproductions with foreword.

301 A. DORNER: Vincent van Gogh—Blumen und Landschaften, Berlin, [1937]. 10 color plates.

302 R. HUYGHE: Van Gogh, Paris, n.d. [1937]. Portfolio of 30 excellent black-and-white reproductions after drawings and watercolors, with short introduction.

303 R. HUYGHE: Vincent van Gogh, *L'Illustration,* Dec. 1937. Numerous color plates.

304 A. M. ROSSET: Van Gogh, Amsterdam–Antwerp–Paris, 1941.

305 M. VALSECCHI: Vincent van Gogh, Milan, 1944. Small and rather poor plates after drawings and watercolors; bibl. by G. Scheiwiller (see also 298 and 306).

306 R. FRANCHI: Vincent van Gogh, Milan, 1944. 33 small and poor plates, genealogy and chronology; bibl. by G. Scheiwiller (see also 298 and 305).

307 L. HAUTECOEUR: Van Gogh, Monaco–Geneva, 1946. 100 fair to poor black-and-white and color plates, more or less chronologically arranged (many captions inaccurate); bibl.

308 E. BRINER: Vincent van Gogh, Zurich, 1947. Two portfolios with short text and comments and 6 good color plates each.

309 A. RÜDLINGER: Vincent van Gogh, Bern, 1947. 24 drawings and lithographs with excerpts from van Gogh's letters.

310 P. FIERENS: Van Gogh, Paris–New York, 1947. Short introduction with 32 fair to poor color plates.

311 W. MUENSTERBERGER: Vincent van Gogh—Drawings, Pastels, Studies, Bussum–New York, 1947. 106 plates of good black-and-white reproductions, a few mediocre color plates.

312 P. JAMES: Van Gogh, London, 1948. Introduction and notes, 11 fair color plates (Faber Gallery).

313 M. SCHAPIRO: Vincent van Gogh, New York, 1950. 50 large, good color plates, chronologically arranged, with penetrating comments and an introduction, illustrated with excellent black-and-white reproductions of drawings and watercolors (Abrams).

314 M. SCHAPIRO: Vincent van Gogh, New York, n.d. Portfolio with 10 color plates previously published in 313 (Abrams).

315 F. S. WIGHT: Van Gogh, New York, n.d. Biographical text with 34 good black-and-white reproductions and 12 mediocre color plates. Selected bibl.

316 Van Gogh et les peintres d'Auvers chez le docteur Gachet, special issue of L'Amour de l'Art, Paris, 1952. Excellent reproductions in black-and-white and color, enlarged details of paintings, photographs, documents.

317 C. ESTIENNE: Van Gogh, Geneva, 1953. Study of van Gogh's style with biographical text by C. H. Sibert. Numerous small color plates. Selected bibl., list of exhibitions, index.

318 A. ANDRIESSE: The World of Van Gogh, The Hague, 1953. Introduction by W. J. de Gruyter. Volume of beautiful photographs, mostly of Provence and Auvers, depicting the artist's world without attempting to reproduce his motifs.

319 A. M. HAMMACHER: Van Gogh, Milan, 1953. 34 excellent plates of well-selected drawings, chronologically arranged.

320 A. M. HAMMACHER: Van Gogh—The Land Where He was Born and Raised, The Hague, 1953. Small volume of documentary photographs.

321 D. COOPER: Drawings and Watercolours by Vincent Van Gogh, Basel–New York, 1955. Fair color plates with comments.

322 R. COGNIAT: Van Gogh, New York, 1959. Small biography with 36 color plates.

323 H. W. GROHN: Vincent van Gogh, Leipzig, 1959 (2nd ed.). Long study with numerous plates in black and white and color.

324 P. HUISMAN: Van Gogh—Portraits, Lausanne, 1960. 28 color plates.

See also 2, 4, and 5.

Miscellaneous Writings on Van Gogh

325 A. H.: Les XX, La Wallonie, 1890, p. 133.

326 FRANCIS: Exposition van Gogh chez Le Barc de Boutteville, La Vie Moderne, April 24, 1892.

327 C. MERKI: Apologie pour la peinture, Mercure de France, June 1893. Attacks on van Gogh, Gauguin, Signac.

328 T. NATANSON: Exposition van Gogh, Revue Blanche, 1895, vol. 8, p. 572. Exhibition organized by Vollard.

329 J. MEIER-GRAEFE: article on van Gogh in Die Insel, May 1900.

330 L. HEVESI: Vincent van Gogh, article published Jan. 17, 1906, on an exhibition at the Galerie Miethke, Vienna, reprinted in L. Hevesi: Altkunst–Neukunst—Wien 1894–1908, Vienna, 1909, pp. 526–29.

331 A. SHERVASCHIDZE: Van Gogh, Apollon, Sept. 1913 (in Russian).

332 H. F. E. VISSER: De Literatur over Vincent van Gogh, De Beweging, Amsterdam, May–June 1917.

333 W. PACH: Vincent van Gogh, International Studio, Nov. 1920.

334 S. STREICHER: Vincent van Gogh, Zurich–Leipzig, [1928].

335 E. LEROY: La Provence et van Gogh, Revue des Pays d'oc, June 1932.

336 K. MITERWA: Gauguin i van Gogh w Arles, Glos Plastykow, Dec. 1935 (in Polish).

337 J. REWALD: Les Amitiés de Vincent van Gogh et ses lettres à van Rappard, Le Point, Nov. 1937.

338 E. BLOMBERG: Den barocke van Gogh, Konstrewy, vol. XX, No. 3, 1944.

339 R. JOSEPHSON: Vincent van Gogh, naturalisten, Stockholm, 1944.

340 BRIELLE, FIERENS, and DORIVAL: articles on van Gogh in Les Beaux-Arts (Brussels), no. 348, 1946.

341 FRANCIS JOURDAIN: A propos de Vincent van Gogh, Arts de France, No. 11–12, n.d. Some recollections of père Tanguy.

342 A. ARTAUD: Van Gogh, le suicidé de la société, Paris, 1947.

343 M. ARLAND: Chronique de la peinture contemporaine, Paris, 1949. Short chapter on van Gogh.

344 J. REWALD: Gachet's Unknown Gems Emerge, Art News, March 1952. On Gachet and his collection, ill.

345 P. COURTHION: Van Gogh écrivain, Arts-Documents, March 1953.

346 L. ANFRAY: L'Evolution picturale de van Gogh, Arts-Documents, March, Aug.–Sept., and Oct. 1953. On Anfray see 268.

347 L. Anfray: Hommage à Vincent van Gogh, *Arts-Documents,* June 1953.

348 V. W. van Gogh: Theo van Gogh without Vincent, *Art News,* Oct. 1953. See also 52.

349 L. Anfray: Vincent van Gogh devant ses contemporains et devant la postérité, *Arts-Documents,* Nov. 1953.

350 M. E. Tralbaut: Vincent van Gogh, privately printed for P. Peré, Antwerp, 1953. Collection of various studies on van Gogh, notably on his "japonaiseries" (in Dutch and French). See also 87, 123, 223, 235, 236, 354, 356, 358, 361, 365, 369, and statement at the end of this section.

351 M. Florisoone: Vincent van Gogh, peintre de Zouaves, *Revue Internationale d'Histoire Militaire,* no. 13, 1953.

352 L. Roelandt: Le Légende des frères van Gogh, *Arts-Documents,* March 1954. An attempt to minimize the importance of Theo van Gogh's role in his brother's life. The author announces a book on this subject; see 178.

353 M. Guerrisi: L'Errore di Cézanne, Pisa, 1954. Chapters on Cézanne, van Gogh, Gauguin, Matisse, Picasso.

354 M. E. Tralbaut: In van Gogh's voetspoor te Nuenen en omgeving, *De Toerist,* Antwerp, April 16, May 1 and June 1, 1955.

355 11 × Vincent van Gogh, *De Tafel Ronde,* special van Gogh issue, Antwerp, no. 8–9, May–June 1955. Articles by V. W. van Gogh, G. Aigrisse (see 171), M. Florisoone, J. G. van Gelder [on van Gogh's early drawings], H. Jaffé, M. de Sablonière [important article on Sien], H. Sandberg, M. E. Tralbaut, and others. Some new documents and ill.

356 *Het cahier—de nevelvlek,* special van Gogh issue, Antwerp, May–June 1955. Contributions by V. W. van Gogh, M. E. Tralbaut, J. Vandiest, C. Mauron, M. de Sablonière, R. Magritte, G. Aigrisse (see 172), E. Buckman, etc. Among the ill. some unpublished sketches by van Gogh.

357 H. Perruchot: La Fin énigmatique de van Gogh, *L'Oeil,* Oct. 1955.

358 M. E. Tralbaut: Van Gogh & Gauguin, privately printed for P. Peré, Antwerp, 1956. Reprints of a few articles in Dutch and French with a list of the author's writings on van Gogh. (The title is misleading; the book does not treat the relationship between the two painters.) See also 350.

359 P. Gachet: Deux amis des impressionnistes, le Docteur Gachet et Murer, Paris, 1956.

360 H. L. C. Jaffé: L'Apport de van Gogh à la critique d'art, *in* Scritti di Storia dell'Arte in onore di Lionello Venturi, Rome, 1956, v. II.

361 M. E. Tralbaut: Van Gogh, début et évolution (in French); van Gogh & Rembrandt (in Dutch), privately printed for P. Peré, Antwerp, Jan. 1957.

362 *Les Cahiers de van Gogh,* Geneva, n.d. [1957], nos. 1 and 2 have appeared; see 268.

363 F. Würtenberger: Vom milieubedingten zum existentialistischen Künstlertum, *Studium General,* Jahrg. 11. Heft 2, 1958.

364 J. Hulsker: Van Gogh's dramatische Jaren in den Haag, *Maatstaf,* Sept. 1958.

365 M. E. Tralbaut: Richard Wagner in het vizier von vier grote schilders—Fantin-Latour, Redon, Renoir, van Gogh, privately printed for P. Peré, Antwerp, Jan. 1959.

366 P. Gachet: A propos de quelques erreurs sur Vincent van Gogh, *Revue des Arts—Musées de France,* 1959, no. 2.

367 J. Hulsker: Van Gogh's opstandige Jaren in Nuenen, *Maatstaf,* May 1959.

368 F. de Hérain: Peintres et sculpteurs écrivains d'art—De Léonard à van Gogh, Paris, 1960.

369 M. E. Tralbaut: Un Document inédit sur van Gogh, *Connaissance des Arts,* Aug. 1960.

370 J. G. van Gelder: Een amerikaans proefschrift over Vincent van Gogh, *Museumjournaal,* Feb. 1961. On a thesis by C. S. Cheltham: "The Role of Vincent van Gogh's Copies in the Development of His Art." See also 256.

371 E. Plüss: Ungemalte Bilder von Vincent van Gogh, *in* Festschrift Kurt Badt, Berlin, 1961.

372 P. Ripert: Van Gogh et Monticelli, *Marseille,* Revue Municipale, no. 45, July–Sept. 1961.

373 M. Robin: Van Gogh, ou la remontée vers la lumière, Paris, 1964.

374 A. Sheon: Monticelli and van Gogh, *Apollo,* June 1967.

375 J. Rewald: Vincent van Gogh, 1890–1970, *Museumjournaal,* Sept. 1970. The posthumous fate of van Gogh (in English).

376 Van Gogh's Sources of Inspiration, Brooklyn Museum, Feb.–April 1971. Introduction by J. Miller; ill.

Museumjournaal, published jointly by the Dutch museums of Eindhoven, Kröller-Müller, and Stedelijk in Amsterdam, frequently contained small articles on van Gogh or reports and condensations of studies which have appeared elsewhere.

From 1953 to the beginning of 1975, M. E. Tralbaut published nearly every year a small booklet of collected essays (articles, lectures) concerned almost exclusively with van Gogh and privately printed for P. Peré in Antwerp. The texts are in French or Dutch; see 87, 350, 358, 361, and 365. From Jan. 1963 to Jan. 1975, these booklets formed a series called *Van Goghiana,* of which ten issues appeared. Many of the author's findings have been incorporated in 123.
See also 124.

Fiction

377 M. Irwin: How Many Miles to Babylon? London, 1913. Semibiographical novel.

378 M. Elder: La Vie apostolique de Vincent Vingeame, Paris, 1917. Novel.

379 H. Kasack: Vincent—Schauspiel in 5 Akten, Potsdam, 1924. Play.

380 C. Sternheim: Gauguin und van Gogh, Berlin, 1924.

381 W. Sauer: Van Gogh—Drama eines Menschen in 5

Aufzügen, Munich, n.d. Play.

382 M. GEISSLER: Die Fahrt zur Unsterblichkeit, Leipzig, [1929]. Novel.

383 L. DE LAFORGUE: Hölle im Hirn—Der Roman des dämonischen und genialen Malers Vincent van Gogh, Berlin, 1931. Novel.

384 I. STONE: Lust for Life, New York–Toronto, 1934, 1936 (ill. edition), 1939, etc.; London, 1935; Copenhagen, 1935; Berlin, 1936; Baarn [Holland], 1936; Oslo, 1936; Palestine, 1936; Paris, [1938]; Riga, 1938; Helsinki, 1939. This best-selling novel did much to popularize van Gogh in the United States, yet readers will get a better picture of the man from his letters (see 53, 54, 55, and 57) and of his life from such reliable biographies as 70, 97, 102, 108, 110, and 123. The book is of scant value to scholars. A motion picture was made (1956) based on this novel.

385 V. DRNAK: Hlavou proti zdi, Prague, 1935. Novel.

386 S. POLLATSCHEK: Flammen und Farben—Das Leben des Malers van Gogh, Vienna, 1937. Novel.

387 D. BURKE: Van Gogh—A Play in Six Scenes, London, 1938.

388 M. JENISON: True Believer, *Harper's Monthly Magazine,* Aug. 1938. Semi-fictional short story.

389 N. STÉPHANE: Le Pauvre Vincent, Paris, 1954. Novel.

390 J. POLDERMANS: Vincent, New York, 1962.

391 N. EMILE-LAURENT: Vincent van Gogh—en religion: Saint Vincent de la Folie de la Croix, typed in 100 copies, Fécamp, 1962.

REDON, Odilon (1840–1916)

Oeuvre Catalogues

1 J. DESTRÉE: L'Oeuvre lithographique d'Odilon Redon, Brussels, 1891. Ill. Limited to 75 copies.

2 A. MELLERIO: L'Oeuvre graphique complet d'Odilon Redon, Paris, 1913. More complete than 1; extensive text, catalogue of 205 etchings and lithographs with small illustrations: bibl. includes many newspaper articles from which important excerpts are quoted; list of exhibitions. Excellently reprinted in New York, 1968.

3 K. BERGER: Odilon Redon—Fantasy and Colour, New York, London, n.d. [1965]; first published in Germany, 1964. This weighty study of Redon's life and work is accompanied by excerpts from the artist's writings, a chronology, a list of exhibitions, a selected bibliography, and diagrams of the shapes of vases used by the artist in his work (many of these vases still exist and could have been photographed but are of no great interest since they offer scant clues for a chronology). There are numerous good black-and-white illustrations, as well as many often slightly garish color plates. All dimensions have been left in centimeters.

But the essential feature is an oeuvre catalogue that is possibly the most frustrating one ever conceived. It consists of a list of 785 paintings, pastels, watercolors, and drawings (obviously quite incomplete for the last two categories) *without a single reproduction.* Since the thematic range of Redon's work is rather limited, consisting mainly of numerous flower still lifes and mythological or fantastic scenes, it is practically impossible to locate any given work. Moreover, the author has divided the oeuvre into various groups with such vague headings as: "Intimate Nature Studies, 1870–95," "Visions and Allegories I, Fantasy, 1860–1900," "Visions and Allegories II, Colour, 1901–14," "Religious Mood, 1895–1905 (1910)," "Myth: Orpheus, Angelica, Phaeton, 1905–10," "Bodies, Faces, Profiles, (1882) 1900–12," "Poetry of the Sea, 1900–13," "Still Lifes, 1900–15," "Flower Pieces I, Early Works, before 1900," "Flower Pieces II, Objective Portrayal of Space, 1900–04/05," "Flower Pieces III, Decorative Phase, 1905–09/12," and "Flower Pieces and Butterflies IV, Crystalline Synthesis, 1909–15."

Unless the user knows beforehand in which section a specific work is listed, he will find it extremely difficult to locate, for instance, a *Bunch of Flowers* ("objective," "decorative," or "crystalline"?), especially since there is *no list of owners.* Worse still is the fact that the author does not stick to his own classifications: one *Perseus and Andromeda* (no. 131), dated circa 1908, is catalogued under "Myth: Orpheus, Angelica, Phaeton, 1905–10," but another work of the *same title* and with the *same date* (no. 170) is to be found under "Bodies, Faces, Profiles, (1882) 1900–12." Even if the reader is familiar with the date assigned to a work in previous publications, this will be of little help in locating it. Indeed, the author has chosen to indicate divergent dates in brackets, without explanations, and—above all—to ignore the artist's own notes relating to matters such as sales and titles, which Redon's son generously made available to scholars and which are essential for any chronology. (All dates for bibl. 24 were established with the cooperation of the artist's son.) Berger has been satisfied with a general statement on p. 181, invoking "stylistic analysis" and Redon's "philosophical outlook," which certainly offer less precision than the master's private notes.

All this makes the catalogue highly impractical; what renders it even less useful as a working tool is the fact that not even the reproductions in his own volume were cross-referenced by the author. Looking for a specific picture of *Apollo's Sun Chariot with Four Horses,* the reader will discover no fewer than twelve versions of this subject, nos. 153–164; should he fancy that the one he wants also shows a dragon and is owned by Alexander M. Bing of New York, he will find that it is illustrated under no. 16 in the catalogue of a Redon exhibition held at the Paul Rosenberg Gallery in New York in 1959. He will therefore start to hunt for this not always easily accessible publication. There is *no indication anywhere* in the catalogue notice that a color plate of this very painting is to be found on p. 95 of Berger's own book!

Next to the monstrous lack of method and organization, the fact that there is an oil listed as a drawing (fig. 10), that there are drawings reproduced but not featured in the catalogue (fig. 5 and pl. 51), and that the reproductions follow neither a chronological order nor the sequence of the catalogue are very minor flaws.

For a review of this book, see R. Pickvance, *Burlington Magazine,* Sept. 1969.

See also Odilon Redon—Oeuvre graphique complet, 2 vols., The Hague, n.d. [1913]. No text, 192 good, large plates of lithographs only.

See also 49.

Catalogues of various exhibitions follow:

4 Exposition Odilon Redon—Dessins, Portraits et Lithographies. Introduction by A. Mellerio. Galeries Durand-Ruel, Paris, March–April 1894.

5 Odilon Redon Ausstellung, Galerie Paul Cassirer, Berlin, Feb. 1914. Introduction by J. Elias.

6 Exhibition of Etchings and Lithographs by Odilon Redon. Introduction by W. Pach. R. R. Donnelly & Sons, Co., Chicago, 1919.

7 Odilon Redon, Musée des Arts Décoratifs, Paris, March 1926. Introduction by J. Morland. For review, see 179.

8 Paintings, Pastels and Drawings by Odilon Redon, Art Institute of Chicago, Dec. 1928—Jan. 1929.

9 Odilon Redon, Galerie Dru, Paris, May–June 1929. Introduction by C. Roger-Marx.

10 Lautrec-Redon, Museum of Modern Art, New York, Feb.–March 1931. For review, see 184.

11 Eugène Carrière et le Symbolisme, Orangerie des Tuileries, Paris, Dec. 1949–Jan. 1950. Introduction by M. Florisoone, notes by J. Leymarie. Important section devoted to Redon. Contains extensive bibl.

12 Odilon Redon—Pastels and Drawings, Cleveland Museum of Art; Walker Art Center, Minneapolis; Jacques Seligmann & Co., New York, 1951–52. Introductions by G. Seligmann, H. S. Francis, and A. Leblond. List of exhibitions, ill.

13 Redon, Drawings and Lithographs—Picasso, His Graphic Art, Museum of Modern Art, New York, winter 1952. Text by W. S. Lieberman. Ill.

14 Odilon Redon, Society of the Four Arts, Palm Beach, Fla., March–April 1955. Ill.

15 Visionaries and Dreamers. An exhibition illustrating the influence of the French symbolist artists on succeeding generations. Corcoran Gallery of Art, Washington, D.C., April–May 1955. Interesting catalogue; text by Henri Dorra. Ill., short bibl.

16 Odilon Redon, Orangerie des Tuileries, Paris, Oct. 1956–Jan. 1957. Forewords by J. Bouchot-Saupique and C. Roger-Marx; excellent catalogue by R. Bacou with biography, list of exhibitions, bibl., documents, and 64 ill. See also 91.

17 Odilon Redon, Municipal Museum, The Hague, May–June 1957. Forewords by V. Bloch and F. W. M. Bonger-van der Borch van Verwolde (in French and Dutch), biographical chart, ill.

18 Odilon Redon, magicien du noir et blanc, Galerie S. Higgins, Paris, June–Sept. 1958. Foreword by C. Roger-Marx, ill.

19 Odilon Redon, Kunsthalle Bern, Aug.–Oct. 1958. Paintings, pastels, drawings, watercolors, lithographs, etc.; some ill.

20 Odilon Redon, New Gallery, New York, Nov. 1958; some ill.

21 Odilon Redon, Paintings and Pastels, Paul Rosenberg Gallery, New York, Feb.–March 1959. All works included are reproduced.

22 Odilon Redon, Matthiesen Gallery, London, May–June 1959. Excellent catalogue of an important exhibition (paintings, drawings, pastels); all 85 works shown are reproduced; good ill.

23 O. Redon, Gradska Galerija Suvremene Umjetnosti, Zagreb, Feb. 1961.

24 Redon—Moreau—Bresdin, Museum of Modern Art, New York, and Art Institute of Chicago, Dec. 1961–April 1962. Text on Redon by J. Rewald; on his prints by H. Joachim. Numerous ill. in black and white and in color; condensed bibl. English translations of Redon's writings on Bresdin.

25 L'Oeuvre gravé de Odilon Redon, Maison Pulliérane, Lausanne, Sept. 1966. Preface by H. R. Hahnloser.

26 Odilon Redon, Galerie Krugier, Geneva, Feb. 1967 (also New York), with texts by C. Roger-Marx and H. R. Hahnloser (see 25); ill.

27 Odilon Redon—Rare Graphics and Drawings, University of Pennsylvania, Philadelphia, April 1967.

28 Fine Lithography by Odilon Redon, Sotheby, London. Catalogue of a special sale, March 26, 1968; fully illustrated.

29 Odilon Redon (Drawings, Etchings, Lithographs), Galerie Le Bateau Lavoir, Paris, 1969, with excerpts from critical writings on the artist and little-known drawings among the illustrations.

30 Odilon Redon, Acquavella Art Galleries, New York, Oct.–Nov. 1970. Text by K. Berger, 50 plates, many in color.

Writings by Redon

31 O. REDON: Salon de 1868, *La Gironde,* May 19, June 9, July 1, 1868. Salon review with appreciations of works by Courbet, Manet, Pissarro, Jongkind, and Monet, but no mention of those by Degas, Renoir, Sisley, Morisot, and Bazille. Excerpts quoted in 24, 83 and in J. Rewald: History of Impressionism, New York, 1973 (4th ed.), p. 188.

32 O. REDON: Confidences d'artiste [Letter to E. Picard, June 15, 1894], *L'Art Moderne,* Aug. 25, 1894. Excerpts quoted in 2.

33 O. REDON: Sur Paul Gauguin, *Mercure de France,* Nov. 1903; see Gauguin Bibl. 185.

34 O. REDON: Rodolphe Bresdin, introduction to the catalogue of a retrospective exhibition, Salon d'Automne, Paris, 1908. English translation in 24.

35 O. REDON: Confidences d'artiste, 1909, reprinted in 36.

36 O. REDON: A soi-même—Journal (1867–1915)—Notes sur la vie, l'art et les artistes, Paris, 1922. Introduction by J. Morland. Important text, exquisitely written, which offers an intimate self-portrait of the artist rather than a picture of his time. Significant reflections on Moreau, Millet, Ingres, Puvis de Chavannes, Courbet, Bresdin, the impressionists, Delacroix, etc. (Unfortunately does not reprint 31.) For inadequately translated excerpts,

see *Tricolor,* Feb. 1945, pp. 68–87. New ed.: Paris, 1961.

37 Lettres d'Odilon Redon, 1878–1916, published by his family, Paris–Brussels, 1923. Introduction by M.-A. Leblond. 105 beautiful letters, written notably to Theo van Gogh's brother-in-law, Andries Bonger (one of the artist's first admirers), to Mellerio, the artist's son, and others. Sketches in the text, no index. (Unfortunately this collection is far from complete; it does not include letters to Hennequin, Bernard, Maus, Picard, Faure, the American painter W. Pach, and the artist's brother, Ernest Redon; see also 38, 39, 47, and 84.)

38 Lettres de Vincent van Gogh, Gauguin, Cézanne, Huysmans, Bloy, Bourges, Marten, Redon, Barrès à Emile Bernard, Tonnerre, 1926. Contains 13 letters to Bernard with a short introduction to the latter.

39 Auriant: Des lettres inédites d'Odilon Redon [with quotations from Hennequin's article on Redon of March 4, 1882], *Beaux-Arts,* June 7, 1935; Redon et E. Hennequin, Lettres inédites (suite), *Beaux-Arts,* June 14, 1935. For further letters to Hennequin see 84.

For a letter to Emile Bernard's father and another to Elie Faure, as well as Redon's comments on 66, see 195.

For letters to Ernest Redon see 84.

Some unpublished letters to Andries Bonger are at the Prentenkabinett, Rijksmuseum, Amsterdam; several are quoted in 51.

40 Lettres de Gauguin, Gide, Huysmans, Jammes, Mallarmé, Verhaeren . . . à Odilon Redon, Paris, 1960. Foreword by Arï Redon, with texts and detailed notes by R. Bacou. Contains quotations from various unpublished letters by Redon. Some ill., no index.

Witness Accounts

41 A. MELLERIO: Les Artistes à l'atelier—Odilon Redon, *L'Art dans les Deux Mondes,* July 4, 1891.

42 Hommage à Odilon Redon, *La Vie,* Nov. 30 and Dec. 7, 1912. With important testimonials by Bonnard, Denis, Fontainas, H. de Groux, G. Kahn, P. Laprade, Mellerio, de Monfried, Sérusier, L. Valtat, etc.

43 J. DOIN: Odilon Redon, *Mercure de France,* July 1, 1914. One of the best studies of the artist, based on numerous consultations with him.

44 C. OULMONT: Souvenirs sur Odilon Redon, *Le Gaulois* (Supplément du dimanche), May 22, 1920.

45 T. NATANSON: Peints à leur tour, Paris, 1948. Chapter on Redon.

46 A. REDON: Odilon Redon dans l'intimité, *La Revue des Arts,* Oct. 1956.

47 A. LEBLOND: J'ai vu Odilon Redon face à face avec Rembrandt, *Arts,* Oct. 24–30, 1956; Mon ami Mallarmé par Odilon Redon, *Arts,* Oct. 31–Nov. 6, 1956; Huysmans, mon grand frère, par Odilon Redon, *Arts,* Nov. 7–13, 1956; Odilon Redon et Francis Jammes (with some unpublished letters by Redon to Jammes) (see also 149). The conversations with Redon, as reported here, were recreated with more or less fidelity.

48 A. LEBLOND: Redon et l'impressionnisme, *Le Peintre,* Oct. 1, 1957. The articles by A. Leblond (47, 48) were to be part of a volume of souvenirs on which the author was working at the time of his death.

See also Bernard's text in 38, the introduction of Arï Redon to 40, as well as 2, 49, 53, 149.

Biographies

49 A. MELLERIO: Odilon Redon—Peintre, dessinateur et graveur, Paris, 1923. Extremely well-documented book by a lifelong friend and admirer of the artist, who himself provided his biographer with a great deal of material and information. In appendix, a catalogue of Redon's etchings and lithographs (more complete than 1 and 2 but without ill.), bibl., list of exhibitions, and list of works in museums and collections, index. Profusely ill.

50 C. FEGDAL: Odilon Redon, Paris, 1929. Excellent text, 60 good plates, bibl.

51 R. BACOU: Odilon Redon, Geneva, 1956, 2 vols. I is devoted to the life and work of Redon (with numerous new documents) and to a study of his style; II features a list of unpublished documents, a list of exhibitions, a detailed bibl., and 107 ill. in black and white and in color, chronologically arranged, with notes on the works reproduced. An essential book. See also 40.

See also 24.

Studies of Style

52 TRIOLET [pseud. for E. HENNEQUIN]: Le Rêve, *Le Gaulois,* March 2, 1882.

53 E. HENNEQUIN: Odilon Redon, *La Revue Littéraire et Artistique,* March 4, 1882. Extensively quoted in 39.

54 E. HENNEQUIN: "Les Origines" par Odilon Redon, *Revue Libérale,* April 1884.

55 E. HENNEQUIN: Notes d'art, *La Vie Moderne,* Feb. 27, 1886.

56 ANONYMOUS [O. MAUS?]: Odilon Redon, *L'Art Moderne,* March 21, 1886.

57 O. MIRBEAU: L'Art et la nature, *Le Gaulois,* April 26, 1886; reprinted in *Beaux-Arts,* April 2, 1935.

58 P. GAUGUIN: Huysmans et Redon [written c. 1889–91]; see J. Loize: Un Inédit de Gauguin, *Nouvelles Littéraires,* May 7, 1953.

59 H. VAN DE VELDE: Notes d'art, *La Wallonie,* no. 5, 1890.

60 A. SYMONS: A French Blake, *The Art Review* (London), July 1890. See also the same author's: Color Studies in Paris, New York, n.d.; chapter on Redon.

61 C. MORICE: Odilon Redon, *Les Hommes d'Aujourd'hui,* vol. 8, no. 386, 1890.

62 G.-A. AURIER: Les Symbolistes. *Revue Encyclopédique,* April 1892; reprinted in Oeuvres posthumes, Paris, 1893.

63 A. MELLERIO: Le Mouvement idéaliste en peinture, Paris, 1896.

64 M. DENIS: Exposition Odilon Redon, *L'Occident,* April 1903; reprinted in Denis: Théories, 1890–1910, Paris, 1912.

65 J. VETH: Odilon Redons lithographische Serien, *Kunst und Künstler,* Dec. 1903.

66 E. BERNARD: Odilon Redon, *L'Occident,* May 1904. For

Redon's comments on this article, see 195.

67 J. Meier-Graefe: Entwicklungsgeschichte der modernen Kunst, Stuttgart, 1904. Short chapter on Redon.

68 W. Pach: Odilon Redon, New York, 1913.

69 G. Janneau: Au chevet de l'art moderne, Paris, 1913. Chapter on the last romanticist: Odilon Redon.

70 W. Pach: The Masters of Modern Art, New York, 1924. Chapter on: The Poles of the Modern Movement [Cézanne and Redon].

71 H. Hertz: Odilon Redon, *Art in America,* Oct. 1924.

72 C. Roger-Marx: Odilon Redon, *Burlington Magazine,* June 1926.

73 R. Miedema: Odilon Redon en Albrecht Dürer, Amsterdam, 1928.

74 W. Born: Der Traum in der Graphik des Odilon Redon, *Graphische Kunst,* 1929.

75 J. Morland: Odilon Redon et le Symbolisme, *Mercure de France,* 1936, tome 269, pp. 143–62.

76 S. Barazetti: Odilon Redon et la logique de ses formes imaginaires, *Beaux-Arts,* May 15, 1940.

77 M.-A. Leblond: Les Fusains d'Odilon Redon, Paris, 1941.

78 H. Edwards: Redon, Flaubert, Vollard—Drawings for "The Temptation of Saint Anthony," *Art Institute of Chicago Bulletin,* Jan. 1942.

79 B. Dorival: Les Etapes de la peinture française contemporaine, vol. I, Paris, 1943. Chapter on: Les précurseurs de la peinture nouvelle [Redon].

80 J. Seznec: The Temptation of Saint Anthony in Art, *Magazine of Art,* March 1947.

81 L. Krestovsky: La Laideur dans l'art à travers les âges, Paris, 1947. Chapter on Redon.

82 J. B. Oosting: Odilon Redon, *Maandblad voor beeldende Kunsten,* July 1949. On Redon's works in the collection of Mevrouw Bonger.

83 A. Chastel: L'Episode "symboliste" et ses vestiges: Redon, Carrière et Rodin, *Cahier du Sud,* no. 298, 1949. On the exhibition 11.

84 S. Sandström: Le Monde imaginaire d'Odilon Redon, Lund, 1955. The first extensive investigation of the iconology of Redon's work. While this book is rather unimaginative, it is an extremely valuable addition to the small group of scholarly publications on the artist. Profusely illustrated; appendix with unpublished letters (see 39); thorough bibl., index.

85 C. Roger-Marx: Odilon Redon, peintre et mystique, *L'Oeil,* May 1956.

86 K. Berger: The Pastels of Odilon Redon, *College Art Journal,* fall 1956.

87 A. Masson: Redon: Mystique with a Method, *Art News,* Jan. 1957. Important article.

88 B. Montifroy: Odilon Redon, les étapes d'un peintre vers la lumière, *Triades,* no. 2, summer 1957, v. V.

89 J. Jacquinot: Huysmans et Odilon Redon, *Bulletin de la Société J.-K. Huysmans,* no. 33, 1957.

90 J.-E. Bersier: Odilon Redon et nous, *Etudes d'Art* (Algiers), no. 13, 1957–58.

91 K. Berger: The Reconversion of Odilon Redon—Reflections on an Exhibition, *Art Quarterly,* summer 1958.

On the exhibition at the Orangerie, Paris (16).

92 T. Reff: Redon's "Le Silence"—An Iconographic Interpretation, *Gazette des Beaux-Arts,* Dec. 1967. Important article.

Reproductions

93 V. Pica: Attraverso gli Albi e le Cartelle—Sensazioni d'arte; vol. I, Artisti macabri, Bergamo, 1896.

94 C. Roger-Marx: Odilon Redon, Paris, 1925. Short text, numerous small and mediocre ill.

95 C. Roger Marx: Redon-Fusains, Paris, 1950. Short introduction with 16 excellent plates of well-selected charcoal drawings.

See also 1, 2, 3, 12, 13, 16, 21, 22, 24, 49, 50, 51, 65, 67, 77, 78, 82, 84, and 195.

Miscellaneous Writings on Redon

96 A. Pigeon: Odilon Redon, *Le Courrier Républicain,* May 15, 1881.

97 J-K. Huysmans: Notice on Redon, *Le Gaulois,* March 2, 1882.

98 J.-K. Huysmans: A. Rebours, Paris, 1883.

99 J.-K. Huysmans: L'Art moderne, Paris, 1883.

100 J.-K. Huysmans: Le Nouvel Album d'Odilon Redon, *Revue Indépendante,* Feb. 1885.

101 G. Geffroy: Odilon Redon, *La Justice,* March 6, 1885.

102 C. Morice: "L'Hommage à Goya" par Odilon Redon, *Petite Tribune Républicaine,* April 2, 1885.

103 J. Destrée: Odilon Redon, *La Jeune Belgique,* Feb. 1, 1886.

104 G. Geffroy: "La Nuit" par Odilon Redon, *La Justice,* March 15, 1886.

105 L. Rouanet: Les Artistes nouveaux—Odilon Redon, *Le Petit Toulousain,* April 17, 1886.

106 R. Darzens: Exposition des Impressionnistes, *La Pléiade,* May 1886.

107 Azelbert: Odilon Redon, *La Revue Moderne* (Bordeaux), June 20, 1886.

108 J.-K. Huysmans: Croquis parisiens, Paris, 1886. Mentions Redon, p. 147 and following.

109 J. Moréas: Redon (poem) in: Petit Bottin des Lettres et des Arts, Paris, 1886.

110 G. Kahn: Chronique de la littérature et de l'art, *Revue Indépendante,* Jan. 1888.

111 J. Staphorst: Impressies, *De Nieuwe Gids,* April 1888.

112 Anonymous: La "Tentation de Saint-Antoine" par Odilon Redon, *L'Art Moderne,* Oct. 21, 1888.

113 J.-K. Huysmans: Certains, Paris, 1889. G. Coquiot in Le vrai J.-K. Huysmans, Paris, 1912, p. 78, quotes Huysmans as expressing himself rather unfavorably on Redon and on what he had written about him in Certains and elsewhere.

114 G. Mourey: Trois Dessins d'Odilon Redon, *Feuille Libre,* April 24, 1890.

115 Anonymous: Yeux clos, *L'Art Moderne,* Dec. 28, 1890.

116 Anonymous: article against Redon, quoted in *L'Art Moderne,* Oct. 25, 1891.

117 Paulet: Exposition des Peintres-Graveurs, *Le Jour,* April 17, 1892.

118 E. Bernard: Odilon Redon, *Le Coeur,* Sept.–Oct. 1893. A dithyrambic article. On this article see: Emile Bernard révèle Odilon Redon, *Arts-Documents,* Aug.–Sept. 1954. See also 179.

119 J.-E. Schmitt: Exposition Odilon Redon, *Le Siècle,* March 31, 1894.

120 G. de Beaurégard: Exposition de M. Odilon Redon, *La Patrie,* April 2, 1894.

121 H. M.: Odilon Redon, *La Paix,* April 4, 1894.

122 A. Barbey: Odilon Redon, *Mémorial Artistique,* April 7, 1894.

123 R. Robbe: Le Tourment de l'inconnu, *Famille-Revue,* April 8, 1894.

124 J. Lorrain: Un Etrange Jongleur, *Echo de Paris,* April 10, 1894.

125 C. Morice: Odilon Redon, *Le Soir,* April 10, 1894.

126 G. Soulier: Odilon Redon, *L'Art et la Vie,* April 15, 1894.

127 A. Paulet: L'Exposition Odilon Redon, *La Famille,* April 15, 1894.

128 Thiébault-Sisson: Odilon Redon, *Le Temps,* April 17, 1894.

129 P. Forthuny: Odilon Redon, *L'Oeuvre d'Art,* April 25, 1894.

130 C. R.: Exposition Odilon Redon, *La Paix Sociale,* April 28, 1894.

131 C. Mauclair: Exposition Odilon Redon, *Mercure de France,* May 1, 1894.

132 Notice on the banquet in honor of Redon, organized by "Les Têtes de Bois" on April 7, 1894, *Mercure de France,* May 1, 1894.

133 E. Leclerc: Les Lithographies d'Odilon Redon, *Revue des Arts Graphiques,* May 1, 1894.

134 E. Pilon: Oeuvres d'Odilon Redon, *La Plume,* May 1, 1894.

135 T. Natanson: Exposition Odilon Redon, *Revue Blanche,* May 1894.

136 Anonymous: Odilon Redon, *Nieuwe Rotterdamsche Courant,* July 4, 1894.

137 C. Mauclair: Choses d'art, *Mercure de France,* Oct. 1894.

138 A. Mellerio: "La Tentation de Saint-Antoine" par Odilon Redon, *L'Avenir Artistique et Littéraire,* Aug. 1, 1896.

139 M. Denis: Odilon Redon, *L'Art et la Vie,* Oct. 1896.

140 E. Pilon: Redon, *Revue Blanche,* 1896, vol. 11, pp. 135–37.

141 A. Mellerio: La Femme et l'enfant dans l'oeuvre d'Odilon Redon, *L'Estampe et l'Affiche,* Feb. 15, 1898.

142 G. Babin: Le Salon d'Automne, *Echo de Paris,* Oct. 14, 1904.

143 E. Cordonnier: Le Salon d'Automne, *La Grande Revue,* Nov. 15, 1904.

144 Anonymous: Odilon Redon Exhibition, *New York Herald,* March 1, 1906.

145 L. Vauxcelles: Exposition Odilon Redon, *Gil Blas,* March 6, 1906.

146 H. Eon: Odilon Redon, *Le Siècle,* March 13, 1906.

147 E. Charles: Odilon Redon, *La Liberté,* March 14, 1906.

148 Y. Rambosson: La Peinture et la sculpture au Salon d'Automne, *L'Art Décoratif,* VIII, 1906.

149 F. Jammes: Odilon Redon—Botaniste, *Vers et Prose,* tome VII, 1907.

150 P. Forthuny: Odilon Redon, *Le Matin,* Nov. 16, 1908.

151 H. Eon: Odilon Redon, *Le Siècle,* Nov. 20, 1908.

152 A. Plasschaert: Over Odilon Redon en over en soort van konstenaars, *De Amsterdamer,* Sept. 10, 1911.

153 J. Cohen-Gosschalk: Odilon Redon, *Zeitschrift für bildende Kunst,* Dec. 1910.

154 A. Salmon: Odilon Redon, *L'Art Décoratif,* Jan. 1913.

155 F.-J. Gregg: The International Exhibition of Modern Art, *Buffalo Academy Notes,* April 1913.

156 A. Alexandre: La Semaine artistique—Floralies, *Comoedia,* Nov. 1, 1913.

157 H. P. Bremmer: Odilon Redon, *Beeldende Kunst,* 1913–1914.

158 A. Mellerio: Odilon Redon, son oeuvre gravée et lithographiée, *La Nouvelle Revue,* Feb. 14, 1914.

159 J. Doin: Odilon Redon, *Mercure de France,* July 1, 1914.

160 M. Leblond: Odilon Redon, *L'Oeuvre,* July 7, 1916.

161 L. Vauxcelles: Odilon Redon, *L'Evénement,* July 8, 1916.

162 E. Bernard: Odilon Redon, *La Vie,* Aug. 1916.

163 J. Sacs: L'obra de Odilon Redon, *Revista Nova* (Barcelona), July 31, 1916.

164 Anonymous: Odilon Redon, [London] *Daily Mail,* Aug. 15, 1916.

165 A. Fontainas: Odilon Redon, *Mercure de France,* Aug. 16, 1916.

166 Thiébault-Sisson: La Vie artistique—un isolé, Odilon Redon, *Feuilleton du Temps,* Nov. 12, 1916.

167 T. Leclère: Odilon Redon, *Larousse Mensuel Illustré,* Oct. 19, 1917.

168 F. Jammes: Odilon Redon, der Mensch, and K. Pieper: Odilon Redon, die Kunst, *Das Kunstblatt,* vol. I, 1917.

169 R. Rey: Odilon Redon, *Art et Décoration,* Aug. 1919.

170 C. Roger-Marx: Odilon Redon ou les droits de l'imagination, *Feuillets d'Art,* April 25, 1920.

171 P. Sérusier: Les Arts et les lettres—Odilon Redon, *La Vie,* May 15, 1920.

172 C. Roger-Marx: Odilon Redon, *L'Amour de l'Art,* June 1920.

173 G.-Jean Aubry: La Renommé d'Odilon Redon, *La Renaissance de l'Art Français,* Aug. 1920.

174 R. Rey: Odilon Redon, *Art et Décoration,* Aug. 1920.

175 A. Mellerio: Odilon Redon, 1840–1916, *Gazette des Beaux-Arts,* Aug.–Sept. 1920.

176 W. Pach: The Etchings and Lithographs of Odilon Redon, *The Print Connoisseur,* Oct. 1920.

177 A. Mellerio: Trois peintres-écrivains—Delacroix, Fromentin, Redon, *La Nouvelle Revue,* April 15, 1923.

178 G. Biermann: Odilon Redon, *Der Cicerone,* April 1924.

179 L. Benoist: Exposition Odilon Redon et Fayet—Musée des Arts Décoratifs, *Beaux-Arts,* March 15, 1926.

180 H. P. Bremmer: Odilon Redon, *Beeldende Kunst,* 1927.

181 M. D. Henkel: Die Sammlung A. Bonger in Amsterdam, *Der Cicerone,* 1930.

182 K. G. Sterne: Odilon Redon Viewed Again, *Parnassus,* March 1931.

183 Anonymous: List of important Redons in the U.S., *Parnassus,* April 1931.

184 G. Pène du Bois: Lautrec-Redon Exhibition—Museum of Modern Art, *Arts,* March 1931.

185 R. Flint: Gauguin, Cézanne and Redon shown at Durand-Ruel's, *Art News,* March 1932.

186 C. Roger-Marx: Les Tentations de Saint-Antoine, *La Renaissance,* March 1936.

187 E. Schaub-Koch: Odilon Redon, peintre de la vie intérieure, *La Revue Bleue,* 1936.

188 A. Sterner: Odilon Redon, *Prints,* Dec. 1937.

189 M. Gauthier: L'Art français du XIXe siècle dans les collections russes, *Beaux-Arts,* no. 285, 1938.

190 P. Girou: Des decorations oubliées de Redon à Fontfroide, *Beaux-Arts,* no. 308, 1938.

191 R. Mesuret: La Maison natale d'Odilon Redon, *La Renaissance,* March 1939.

192 P. du Colombier: Odilon Redon, *Beaux-Arts,* May 10, 1942.

193 U. E. Johnson: Ambroise Vollard, Editeur, New York, 1944. Revised edition: New York, 1977. On Vollard's 1938 publication of *La Tentation de Saint-Antoine.*

194 G. Bazin: Ephémérides impressionnistes, *L'Amour de l'Art,* 1947.

195 J. Rewald: Quelques notes et documents sur Odilon Redon, *Gazette des Beaux-Arts,* Nov. 1956. This article contains some new documents, among them Redon's comments on Bernard's article (see 66).

196 P. Roumequère: Le Mystère Odilon Redon, *La Vie Médicale—Art et Psychopathologie,* Dec. 1956.

197 T. Mullaly: Odilon Redon and the Symbolists, *Apollo,* Dec. 1957.

198 T. W. Strieter: Odilon Redon and Charles Baudelaire —Some Parallels, *Art Journal,* Fall 1975.

SEURAT, Georges (1859–1891)

Oeuvre Catalogues

1 H. Dorra and J. Rewald: Seurat—L'Oeuvre peint, biographie et catalogue critique, Paris, 1959 [issued in 1960]. Contains: F. Fénéon: Ecrits sur Georges Seurat (many of which were not included *in* Fénéon: Oeuvres (see Fénéon Bibl. 1); Rewald: La Vie et l'oeuvre de Georges Seurat; Dorra: The Evolution of Seurat's Style; a catalogue raisonné of 211 paintings with preparatory drawings, accompanied by numerous excerpts from writings on Seurat from 1884 to the date of publication (in English and/or French); a list of exhibitions; detailed bibl.; indexes of works and of owners; photographs of details and of "motifs"; documents, diagrams, a genealogy, etc., 322 ill.

2 C. M. de Hauke: Seurat et son oeuvre, 2 vols., Paris, 1961. This superbly presented publication devotes one volume to paintings and another to drawings (not recorded in 1 unless related to oils). Though there is hardly any text, there are some facsimiles of the artist's rare letters, as well as important documents on the posthumous inventory of Seurat's studio, in which Fénéon took part. As a matter of fact, Fénéon assisted the author in preparing this catalogue. His notes and recollections were invaluable for the early provenance of many works, which he often knew from their inception, bought from the heirs or sold for them, exhibited, and followed from owner to owner. His provenances therefore are generally more precise and detailed than those of 1, the existence of which de Hauke simply chose to ignore (there are *no* cross-references or mentions of this "rival" publication). That de Hauke was thoroughly familiar with it and even used it for more recent changes of ownership (Fénéon's notes were completed in 1939–40, fully twenty years before these volumes went to print) can be proven since an admittedly "planted" false provenance in 1 was copied by de Hauke and even embellished so as to hide its origin.

Just the same, these volumes are absolutely indispensable for the study of Seurat. The quality of the reproductions (especially of the drawings) and the wealth of other material, such as facsimiles of frequently hard-to-locate catalogues, installation photographs of some recent exhibitions, and a small section of forgeries under the heading "Pilori," amply make up for the author's lack of generosity.

Following are some catalogues of important exhibitions:

3 Exposition Georges Seurat, Galerie Bernheim-Jeune, Paris, Dec. 1908–Jan. 1909. Important exhibition, organized by F. Fénéon; no ill. in the catalogue.

4 Georges Seurat, Galerie Bernheim-Jeune, Paris, Jan. 1920. Short introduction by Signac. Exhibition organized by F. Fénéon; 35 paintings and 27 drawings, of which only 4 are reproduced in the catalogue.

5 Paintings and Drawings by Georges Seurat, Brummer Gallery, New York, Dec. 1924. 20 paintings and 11 drawings.

6 Exhibition of Pictures and Drawings by Georges Seurat, Lefevre Galleries, London, April–May 1926. Ill.

7 Dessins de Georges Seurat, Galerie Bernheim-Jeune, Paris, Nov.–Dec. 1926. Short introduction by L. Cousturier. Exhibition organized by F. Fénéon; 140 drawings, none reproduced.

8 24 Paintings and Drawings by Georges-Pierre Seurat, Renaissance Society, University of Chicago, Feb. 1935.

9 Seurat, Galerie Paul Rosenberg, Paris, Feb. 1936. 51 paintings and 78 drawings; only 4 reproduced.

10 Seurat—Paintings and Drawings, Knoedler Galleries, New York, April–May 1949. 24 paintings and 61 drawings, most of which are reproduced and accompanied by detailed notes. Unfortunately the authenticity of a few works included seems doubtful.

11 Seurat—Paintings and Drawings, Art Institute of Chicago and Museum of Modern Art, New York, Jan.–May

1958. Important exhibition, 152 works. Catalogue with chronology; a study on Seurat's paintings by D. C. Rich and on his drawings by R. L. Herbert; numerous ill. See also 89, 90, 91, and 93.

See also under Neo-Impressionism some catalogues of exhibitions devoted to "Seurat and his friends."

Writings by Seurat

12 F. FÉNÉON: Notes inédites de Seurat sur Delacroix, *Bulletin de la Vie Artistique,* April 1, 1922; reprinted in 123.

13 G. CACHIN-SIGNAC: Autour de la correspondance de Signac, *Arts,* Sept. 7, 1951. Letters by Seurat and Pissarro to Signac.

14 R. L. HERBERT: Seurat and Emile Verhaeren—Unpublished Letters, *Gazette des Beaux-Arts,* Dec. 1959.

For Seurat's important letter to Beaubourg (quoted p. 128), see 1, 23, 27 (where it was quoted for the first time), and 57.

For Seurat's letter to O. Maus, see M.-O. MAUS: Trente années de lutte pour l'art, Brussels, 1926.

For Seurat's letters to Fénéon, see 3.

For some of Seurat's letters to Signac, see J. REWALD: Georges Seurat, Paris, 1948 (the chapter with these documents does not appear in the American edition), and 1.

For a letter to T. van Rysselberghe, see 158.

Witness Accounts

15 A. ALEXANDRE, G. KAHN, *et al.:* Georges Seurat (1859–1891), [Brussels, 1895]. According to R. L. Herbert (Bibl. 101, p. 166, note 1), this is the first book on the artist, "unnoticed by previous scholars. It was apparently produced by his friends in 1895 in Brussels, though it bears no date or imprint. It is a gathering of short articles, most of which had appeared in newspapers and reviews, plus letters of thanks to Mme Seurat from the recipients of Seurat's drawings and paintings, . . . and the funeral oration of E. Valton who was president of the *Société des Artistes Indépendants* at the time of Seurat's death." I have not been able to see a copy of this volume.

16 G. KAHN: Seurat, *L'Art Moderne,* April 5, 1891; see also 114.

17 T. DE WYZEWA: Georges Seurat, *L'Art dans les Deux Mondes,* April 18, 1891.

18 E. VERHAEREN: Sensations, Paris, 1927. (First published in 1891.)

19 H. DE RÉGNIER: Vestigia Flammae, Paris, 1929. Poems, among them one on Seurat, quoted in 23, French edition, p. 154.

20 C. PISSARRO: Letters to his Son Lucien, New York–London, 1943. Ed. by Rewald. Rev. ed.: New York, 1972.

21 F. AMAN-JEAN: L'Enfant oublié, Paris, 1963. Recollections of the son of Seurat's friend; first chapter: L'Ile de la Grande Jatte.

See also 22 and 23, which quote various witness accounts, and 1, 37, and 57.

Biographies

22 G. COQUIOT: Georges Seurat, Paris, 1924. The text includes recollections of Seurat by his friends, commentaries on his work, his followers, etc. Insufficient list of his works. Ill., no index, no bibl.

23 J. REWALD: Georges Seurat, New York, 1943, 1946. First complete biography with numerous new documents, profusely illustrated, extensive bibliography, index. French edition: Paris, 1948; contains an additional chapter with hitherto unpublished documents, more complete bibl. See review by: W. I. HOMER: *The Art Bulletin,* Sept. 1960.

24 DR. J. SUTTER: Recherches sur la vie de Georges Seurat, Paris, 1964. Published in 80 typewritten copies. Minute accumulation of dates and facts concerning Seurat's ancestors, his parents, their children and descendants. Many hitherto unknown biographical details, though mostly of a minor nature.

25 H. PERRUCHOT: La Vie de Seurat, Paris, 1966. Despite his tendency to write in a somewhat "lively" and "colorful" vernacular, the author has provided a sober and very conscientious biography, even adding a few unknown though not very important facts. This is a most extensive and detailed account of the painter's life, with a number of generally documentary ill., a bibl., but no index.

See also 1 and 122.

Studies of Style

26 F. FÉNÉON: Les Impressionnistes en 1886, Paris, 1886. Reprinted in Fénéon: Oeuvres, Paris, 1948.

27 J. CHRISTOPHE: Seurat, *Les Hommes d'Aujord'hui,* vol. 8, no. 368, 1890.

28 H. VAN DE VELDE: Notes sur l'art: Chahut, *La Wallonie,* no. 5, 1890.

29 H. VAN DE VELDE: Georges Seurat, *La Wallonie,* April 1891.

30 J. CHRISTOPHE: Chromo-Luminaristes—G. Seurat, *La Plume,* Sept. 1, 1891. (Special issue: Peintres Novateurs.)

31 ANONYMOUS: Ouverture du Salon des XX—L'Instaurateur du néo-impressionnisme—Georges Pierre Seurat, *L'Art Moderne,* Feb. 1892.

32 P. SIGNAC: D'Eugène Delacroix au Néo-Impressionnisme, Paris, 1899. A basic book.

33 J. LECLERCQ: Exposition Georges Seurat, *Chronique des Arts,* March 31, 1900.

34 E. VERHAEREN: Georges Seurat, *L'Art Moderne,* April 1, 1900.

35 J. MEIER-GRAEFE: Entwicklungsgeschichte der modernen Kunst, Stuttgart, 1904. Chapter on Seurat.

36 A. CHERVACHIDZE: Georges Seurat, *Apollon* [Moscow], July 1911.

37 L. COUSTURIER: Georges Seurat, *L'Art Décoratif,* June 20, 1912, and Les Dessins de Seurat, *L'Art Décoratif,* March 1914. Excellent articles with a good description of Seurat (based on Signac's recollections); reprinted together in one volume: see 111.

38 A. Salmon: Georges Seurat, *Burlington Magazine,* Sept. 1920.

39 Bissière: Notes sur l'art de Seurat, *Esprit Nouveau,* Oct. 15, 1920.

40 J. M. Langaard: Georges Seurat, *Kunst og Kultur* [Norway], 1921.

41 A. Salmon: La Révélation de Seurat, Brussels, 1921.

42 W. Pach: Georges Seurat, *The Arts,* March 1923.

43 G. Eglington: The Theory of Seurat, *International Studio,* 1925; reprinted in: Reaching for Art, Boston, 1931.

44 J. B. Manson: La Baignade, *Apollo,* 1925.

45 A. Ozenfant: Seurat, *Cahiers d'Art,* Sept. 1926.

46 A. Salmon: Seurat, *L'Art Vivant,* 1926.

47 R. Rey: A propos du "Cirque" de Seurat, *Beaux-Arts,* 1926.

48 O. Sitwell: Les Poseuses, *Apollo,* 1926.

49 R. Fry: Transformations—Critical and Speculative Essays on Art, London, 1926. Chapter on Seurat.

50 C. Zervos: Idéalisme et naturalisme dans la peinture moderne, *Cahiers d'Art,* 1927.

51 C. Roger-Marx: Georges Seurat, *Gazette des Beaux-Arts,* 1927.

52 F. Fels: Les Dessins de Seurat, *L'Amour de l'Art,* 1927.

53 R. A. Parker: The Drawings of Georges Seurat, *International Studio,* Sept. 1928.

54 C. Zervos: "Un Dimanche à la Grande Jatte" et la technique de Seurat, *Cahiers d'Art,* no. 9, 1928. This important and profusely illustrated article constitutes the first attempt to study Seurat's technique on the basis of his preparatory works for a large composition. On the same subject, see also 60.

55 C. Roger-Marx: Les Dessins de Seurat, *L'Europe Nouvelle,* Jan. 12, 1929.

56 R. Fry: Seurat's "La Parade," *Burlington Magazine,* 1929.

57 R. Rey: La Renaissance du sentiment classique dans la peinture française à la fin du XIXe siècle—Degas, Renoir, Gauguin, Cézanne, Seurat, Paris, 1931. The important chapter on Seurat presents the first extensive study of his style; appendix with valuable notes, bibl., ill. F. Fénéon assisted the author with information.

58 J. F. van Deene: Georges Seurat, *Maandblad voor Beeldende Kunst,* no. VIII, 1931.

59 B. E. Werner: Georges Seurat, *Die Kunst,* Feb. 1932.

60 D. C. Rich: Seurat and the Evolution of "La Grande Jatte," Chicago, 1935. A pictorial analysis of Seurat's most important work, accompanied by diagrams, lists of preliminary and associated works, a selected bibliography, and 60 illustrations of drawings, small panels, details of the large painting, etc. Since the publication of this important work, a few more preliminary studies have reappeared. See also 54.

61 M. Schapiro: Seurat and "La Grande Jatte," *Columbia Review,* XVII, 1935.

62 J. Helion: Seurat as a Predecessor, *Burlington Magazine,* 1936. See also the same author's: Poussin, Seurat and Double Rhythm in M. Evans: The Painter's Object, London, 1937.

63 M. Schapiro: Nature of Abstract Art, *Marxist Quarterly,* New York, Jan.–March 1937.

64 G. Jedlicka: Die Zeichnungen Seurats, *Galerie und Sammler* (Zurich), Oct.–Nov. 1937.

65 J. A. [J. Abbot]: Two Drawings by Seurat, *Smith College Museum of Art Bulletin,* June 1939.

66 R. Goldwater: Some Aspects of the Development of Seurat's Style, *The Art Bulletin,* June 1941. Important article, ill.

67 H. Hope: Letter to the Editor, *The Art Bulletin,* June 1941. Concerning 66.

68 B. Nicholson: Seurat's "La Baignade," *Burlington Magazine,* Nov. 1941.

69 G. Paulsson: Konstverkets byggnad, Stockholm, 1942.

70 A. C. R. [A. C. Ritchie]: An Important Seurat, *Gallery Notes,* Albright Art Gallery, Buffalo, May 1943.

71 B. Dorival: Les Etapes de la peinture française contemporaine, vol. I, Paris, 1943. Lengthy discussion of Seurat.

72 B. Stillson: Port of Gravelines (Petit Fort Philippe) by Georges Seurat, *The Bulletin of the Art Association of Indianapolis,* Oct. 1945.

73 G. Seligmann: The Drawings of Georges Seurat, New York, 1945. Analysis of Seurat's method of drawing, with some diagrams of drawings which themselves are not reproduced. The author distinguishes between "independent" drawings and those related to paintings, but unfortunately confines himself to drawings located in the United States. Numerous other drawings owned in this country have escaped his attention; others have since come here. Extensive notes on 59 drawings, bibl., 46 good plates.

74 G. Duthuit: Georges Seurat, voyant et physicien, *Labyrinthe,* Dec. 1946.

75 D. Cooper: Georges Seurat—"Une Baignade, Asnières." London, n.d. [1946]. Analysis of Seurat's first large composition, accompanied by 23 illustrations of preparatory studies and details of the painting. Not all preliminary studies have been included.

76 J. M.: Seurat—Master Draftsman, *Bulletin of the California Palace of the Legion of Honor,* July 1947.

77 R. Huyghe: Trois Poseuses de Seurat; J. Bouchot-Saupique: Trois dessins de Seurat, *Bulletin des Musées de France,* Aug. 12, 1947.

78 L. Venturi: The Art of Seurat, *Gazette des Beaux-Arts,* July–Dec. 1944 (published Sept. 1947).

79 H. Naef: Zur zeichnerischen Kunst von Seurat, *Du,* 1948.

80 A. Chastel: Le Mutisme de Seurat et la psychologie de l'art, *Cahiers du Sud,* III, 1948.

81 J. Rewald: Seurat—The Meaning of the Dots, *Art News,* April 1949.

82 F. Minkowska: De van Gogh et de Seurat aux dessins d'enfants, *Revue de l'Esthétique,* April–June 1949.

83 F. Schmidt: Georges Seurat, *Die Kunst,* July 1949.

84 R. Longhi: Un Disegno per la "Grande-Jatte" e la cultura formale di Seurat, *Paragone,* Jan. 1950.

85 M. Berthe: Les Dessins de Georges Seurat, *Arts Plastiques,* July–Aug. 1950.

86 F. Roh: Das Geheimnis der Stille—Seurat als Zeichner, *Das Kunstwerk,* 1956–57, 1–2.

87 W. I. Homer: Seurat's Port-en-Bessin, *Minneapolis Institute of Arts Bulletin,* summer 1957. Important article. See also the same author's: Further Remarks on Seurat's Port-en-Bessin, *Minneapolis Institute of Arts Bulletin,* Oct.–Dec. 1959.

88 H. Dorra: Re-naming a Seascape by Seurat, *Gazette des Beaux-Arts,* Jan. 1958.

89 D. C. Rich: The Place of Seurat, *Art Institute of Chicago Quarterly,* Feb. 1, 1958.

90 M. Schapiro: New Light on Seurat, *Art News,* April 1958. Important article.

91 R. L. Herbert: Seurat in Chicago and New York, *Burlington Magazine,* May 1958. Important article.

92 R. L. Herbert: Seurat and Chéret, *Art Bulletin,* June 1958. Important article.

93 W. I. Homer: Seurat's Formative Period—1880–84, *Connoisseur,* Aug. 1958. Important article.

94 A. Chastel: Une Source oubliée de Seurat, *Etudes et Documents sur l'Art Français,* t. XXII (1950–57) [issued in 1959]. Important article.

95 R. L. Herbert: Seurat and Puvis de Chavannes, *Yale University Art Gallery Bulletin,* Oct. 1959.

96 H. R. Rookmaaker: Synthetist Art Theories, Amsterdam, 1959. Short chapter on Seurat.

97 S. Lovgren: The Genesis of Modernism—Seurat, Gauguin, van Gogh and French Symbolism in the 1880's, Stockholm, 1959. Important chapter on "L'Ile des Iridées." Second edition: Bloomington, Ind., 1971.

98 A. Chastel: Seurat et Gauguin, *Art de France,* no. 2, Paris, 1962.

99 B. Nicolson: Reflections on Seurat, *Burlington Magazine,* May 1962.

100 A. Scharf: Painting, Photography, and the Image of Movement. *Burlington Magazine,* May 1962. See reply by W. I. Homer: Concerning Muybridge, Marey, and Seurat, *Burlington Magazine,* Sept. 1962.

101 R. L. Herbert: Seurat's Drawings, New York, 1962. Excellent text, the first comprehensive study of Seurat's evolution as a draftsman. Among the 173 ill. are many not previously published; some color plates. Extensive notes, bibl., annotated list of ill., and index. See review by H. Dorra: *The Art Bulletin,* June 1971.

102 W. I. Homer: Seurat and the Science of Painting, Cambridge, Mass., 1964. The author has set out to explore and explain the basis of Seurat's theories of color and expression in nineteenth-century science. A valuable contribution with extensive notes, a selected bibl. with special emphasis on scientific literature, and an index. See review by H. Dorra: *Burlington Magazine,* April 1966.

103 M. Schapiro: Seurat—Seurat Reflections, *Art News Annual* 29, 1964.

104 A. Boime: Seurat and Piero della Francesca, *The Art Bulletin,* June 1965. New information.

105 J. Russell: Seurat, London, New York, 1965. A perceptive study that puts Seurat in excellent perspective; well written. With 225 ill. but poor color plates. See

review by H. Dorra: *Burlington Magazine,* April 1966.

106 H. Dorra and S. C. Askin: Seurat's Japonisme, *Gazette des Beaux-Arts,* Feb. 1969. Ill. Important article.

107 H. Dorra: Charles Henry's "Scientific" Aesthetic, *Gazette des Beaux-Arts,* Dec. 1969.

108 H. Dorra: Seurat's Dot and the Japanese Stippling Technique, *The Art Quarterly,* vol. 33, no. 2, 1970.

109 M. Roskill: Van Gogh, Gauguin and the Impressionist Circle, London–New York, 1970. Contains chapter on: The Importance of Seurat and His Theory.

110 J. H. Rubin: Seurat and Theory—The Near-Identical Drawings of the Café-Concert, *Gazette des Beaux-Arts,* Oct. 1970.

See also Dorra's study in 1, as well as 113, 123, 127, 146, 150, and 153.

Reproductions

111 L. Cousturier: Georges Seurat, Paris, 1921; second edition with more illustrations: Paris, 1926. See also 37.

112 A. Lhote: Georges Seurat, Rome, 1922.

113 W. Pach: Georges Seurat, New York, 1923. Lengthy introduction, 14 plates not chronologically arranged.

114 G. Kahn: Les Dessins de Seurat, 2 vol., Paris, 1926. 128 superb plates assembled by F. Fénéon, with a short introduction by Kahn. Major publication on the subject.

115 W. George: Seurat, Paris, 1928. Short introduction with 24 fair plates (Album d'Art Druet).

116 C. Roger-Marx: Seurat, Paris, 1931. Short introduction and 32 small but good ill., short bibl., and list of exhibitions.

117 J. de Laprade: Georges Seurat, Monaco, 1945. Short introduction, 91 fair black-and-white and 10 color plates, chronologically arranged. Short bibl. All oils are listed as "on canvas," even those executed on wooden panels.

118 H. Bertram: Seurat—Tegninger, Copenhagen, 1946.

119 A. Lhote: Seurat, Paris, 1948. Short introduction with 16 excellent and well-selected plates of drawings (Braun).

120 U. Apollonio: Disegni di Seurat, Venice, 1947. 17 plates.

121 J. Rewald: Seurat, Paris, 1949. Short text, small but good plates (Collection des Maîtres).

122 R. H. Wilenski: Seurat, London, 1949 (Faber Gallery).

123 J. de Laprade: Seurat, Paris, 1951. Biographical and analytical text with numerous poor ill. in black and white and good color plates. Unfortunately these comprise several works of highly doubtful authenticity. Appendix with Seurat's "Notes on Delacroix" (see 12), list of exhibitions, and short bibl.

124 R. Cogniat: Seurat, Paris, n.d. [1951?]. Small ill. (Hyperion).

125 J. E. Muller: Seurat, Paris, 1960. 20 small color plates (Hazan).

126 J. E. Muller: Seurat—Dessins, Paris, 1960. 36 good though small ill. (Hazan).

127 P. Courthion: Seurat, New York, n.d. [1968]. 48 fair color plates, a certain number after small panels not

previously reproduced in color, accompanied by mostly short comments; also good reproductions (Abrams) of drawings and a few documents. The selected bibl., inexplicably, does not list 25.

See also 1, 2, 11, 23, 54, 57, 60, 66, 73, 75, 78, 81, 101, and 105.

Miscellaneous Writings on Seurat

128 R. MARX: Le Salon, *Le Progrès Artistique,* June 15, 1883.

129 Notice in *The Bat* (London), May 25, 1886.

130 A. J. WAUTERS: Aux XX, Seurat, La Grande Jatte, *La Gazette* (Brussels), Feb. 28, 1887.

131 J.-K. HUYSMANS: Chronique d'art, *Revue Indépendante,* April 1887.

132 A. ALEXANDRE: Le Mouvement artistique, *Paris,* Aug. 13, 1888.

133 E. PICARD: La Peinture, *L'Art Moderne,* 1891, pp. 3–4.

134 ANONYMOUS [F. FÉNÉON]: Seurat (obituary), *Entretiens Politiques et Littéraires,* vol. 2, no. 13, 1891.

135 J. ANTOINE: Georges Seurat, *Revue Indépendante,* 1891, pp. 357–58.

136 E. VERHAEREN: Chronique artistique—Les XX, *La Société Nouvelle,* 1891, pp. 248–54.

137 T. NATANSON: Un Primitif d'aujourd'hui—Georges Seurat, *Revue Blanche,* April 15, 1900.

138 E. VERHAEREN: Notes—Georges Seurat, *Nouvelle Revue Française,* Feb. 1, 1909.

139 F. DE MIOMANDRE: article in *L'Art et les Artistes,* Feb. 1909.

140 J. CARRÉ: Le Grand Art—Georges Seurat, *La Vie,* Sept. 1, 1922.

141 ANONYMOUS [F. FÉNÉON]: Précisions sur Seurat, *Bulletin de la Vie Artistique,* Aug. 15, 1924.

142 ANONYMOUS [F. FÉNÉON]: Le "Cirque" de Seurat, *Bulletin de la Vie Artistique,* March 15, 1926.

143 F. FÉNÉON: Georges Seurat und die öffentliche Meinung, *Der Quersechnitt,* Oct. 1926.

144 F. FELS: Seurat, *ABC Magazine,* Nov. 1927.

145 ANONYMOUS: Quelques esquisses et dessins de Georges Seurat, *Documents,* no. 4, Sept. 1929.

146 P. JAMOT: Une Etude pour le "Dimanche à la Grande Jatte" de Seurat, *Bulletin des Musées de France,* Paris, 1930.

147 K. NIEHAUS: Georges Seurat, *Elsevier's Geilustred Maandschrift,* Amsterdam, 1930.

148 F. WALTER: Du paysage classique au sur-réalisme, Seurat, *Revue de l'Art,* 1933.

149 A. WATT: The Art of Georges Seurat, *Apollo,* March 1936.

150 G. DUTHUIT: Seurat's System, *The Listener,* Feb. 3, 1937.

151 P. MABILLE: Dessins inédits de Seurat, *Minotaure,* 1938.

152 A. NEWMARCH: Seurat, *Apollo,* July 1940.

153 H. KAHNWEILER: La Place de Georges Seurat, *Critique,* nos. 8–9, Jan.–Feb. 1947.

154 J. REWALD: From Ingres to Seurat, Introduction, catalogue of an exhibition of drawings, California Palace of the Legion of Honor, San Francisco, March 1947.

155 H. HILDEBRANDT: Seurat, *Aussaat,* nos. 3–4, Aug.–Oct. 1947.

156 U. APOLLONIO: Disegni di Georges Seurat, Introduction to the catalogue of an exhibition of Seurat drawings, Catalogue of the XXVth Biennale of Venice, 1950, pp. 175–79.

157 L. VENTURI: Piero della Francesca—Seurat—Gris, *Diogenes,* Spring 1953, pp 19–23.

158 G. POGU: Théo van Rysselberghe, sa vie, n.d. [Paris, 1963?]. Small pamphlet with a not very important letter from Seurat to T. van. Rysselberghe and various documents concerning the intrigues centering on Seurat's estate.

159 J. F. REVEL: Charles Henry et la science des arts, *L'Oeil,* Nov. 1964.

See also Fénéon, Signac, and Neo-Impressionism Bibls.

SIGNAC, Paul (1863–1935)

Oeuvre Catalogues

A catalogue raisonné of Signac's paintings is presently being prepared by the artist's daughter and granddaughter. See also 10.

Following are some exhibition catalogues:

1 Paul Signac, Galerie Druet, Paris, Dec. 1904. Foreword by Fénéon (see also 6).

2 Signac, Galerie Bernheim-Jeune, Paris, May 1930. 56 ill. arranged in chronological order; no text.

3 Signac, Peintures-Aquarelles, Musée de Mulhouse, Jan.–Feb. 1950. Foreword by F. Jourdain.

4 Signac, Musée National d'Art Moderne, Paris, Oct.–Dec. 1951. Foreword by J. Cassou; biographical notes: 37 paintings and numerous drawings, watercolors, lithographs (not individually listed); some ill.

5 Signac, Fine Arts Associates, New York, Nov. 1951. Excerpts from the artist's diary (see 17), reproductions of some little known works.

6 Signac, Marlborough Gallery, London, March–April 1954. Forewords by G. Besson, P. Gay, and F. Fénéon (see 1); 65 paintings, watercolors, drawings, lithographs, etc. Important catalogue, good ill., short bibl.

7 P. A. WICK: Paul Signac Exhibition, *Bulletin of the Museum of Fine Arts,* Boston, Oct. 1954. Study of Signac's graphic art, followed by a catalogue of watercolors, drawings, and prints shown at the Boston Museum.

8 La Création de l'oeuvre chez Paul Signac, Marlborough Gallery, London, April–May 1958. Foreword by P. Gay, excerpts from the artist's diary (see 17), chronology, numerous ill., some in color.

9 Signac, Musée du Louvre, Paris, Dec. 1963–Feb. 1964. Excellent catalogue by M.-T. Lemoyne de Forges with length notes on every painting shown and even on some of the drawings and watercolors. Extensive bibl., much more complete than the present one; it is indeed so detailed and long that it could not be incorporated here. Publications are listed in chronological order and divided, as here, in various categories. See also 57.

10 E. W. KORNFELD and P. A. WICK: Catalogue raisonné de l'oeuvre gravé et lithographie de Paul Signac, Bern, 1974. 27 prints.

10a Paul Signac et ses amis à Saint Tropez, 1892–1914. Musée de l'Annonciade, Saint-Tropez, 1975.

Writings by Signac

11 P. SIGNAC: Letter to Trublot [P. Alexis] protesting his being under suspicion as a Prussian spy while painting in the Cantal Department, *Le Cri du Peuple,* June 23, 1887.

12 NÉO [pseud. for P. SIGNAC]: Les XX—Lettre à Trublot [P. Alexis], *Le Cri du Peuple,* Feb. 9, 1888.

13 NÉO [pseud. for P. SIGNAC]: IVe exposition des Artistes Indépendants—Lettre à Trublot [P. Alexis], *Le Cri du Peuple,* March 24, 1888.

14 P. SIGNAC: Letter [to Jules Christophe], Sept. 19, 1888, *L'Art Moderne,* 1888, p. 326; first published in *La Cravache.*

15 S. P. [P. SIGNAC]: Catalogue de l'exposition des XX, Bruxelles, *Art et Critique,* Feb. 1, 1890.

16 ANONYMOUS [P. SIGNAC?]: Impressionnistes et révolutionnaires, *La Révolte,* June 13–19, 1891.

17 Extraits du journal inédit de Paul Signac—I, 1894–1895; II, 1897–1898; III, 1898–1899. Introduction and notes by J. Rewald, *Gazette des Beaux-Arts,* July–Sept. 1949, April 1952, July–Aug. 1953. Profusely ill. See also P. Signac: Fragments de journal, *Arts de France,* no. 11–12, 1947, and no. 17–18 [n.d.].

18 P. SIGNAC: D'Eugène Delacroix au Néo-Impressionnisme, Paris, Editions de la Revue Blanche, 1899; new edition: Paris, 1911. First published as a series of articles in *La Revue Blanche,* beginning May 1898. New edition: Paris, 1964, edited by F. Cachin, the artist's granddaughter, with a useful introduction and excellent footnotes. Basic text. See Neo-impressionism Bibl. 59.

19 P. SIGNAC: Jongkind, Paris, 1927. Short chapters on Jongkind's vision, his drawings, etchings, and watercolors (of which 129 are reproduced, among them many belonging to Signac); no paintings.

20 P. SIGNAC: Fondation de le Société des Artistes Indépendants, *Partisans,* Jan. 1927.

21 P. SIGNAC: Charles Henry, *Cahiers de l'Etoile,* Jan.–Feb. 1930 [special issue devoted to Henry].

22 P. SIGNAC: Short introduction to the catalogue of an exhibition of 23 Soviet artists, Galerie Billiet, Paris, April–May 1933.

23 P. SIGNAC: Le Néo-Impressionnisme—Documents. Introduction to the catalogue of an exhibition "Seurat et ses amis" (see Neo-impressionism Bibl. 73, 77); reprinted in *Gazette des Beaux-Arts,* Jan. 1934.

24 P. SIGNAC: Les Besoins individuels et la peinture, *Encyclopédie Française,* vol. XVI, Paris, 1935; chapter II. Important text.

25 P. SIGNAC: Letter to Edouard Fer, written c. 1918, quoted *in* E. Fer: Solfège de la couleur, Paris, 1954.

For Signac's letters to O. Maus, see M.-O. Maus: Trente années de lutte pour l'art, 1884–1914, Brussels, 1926.

For his letters to C. and L. Pissarro, see Camille Pissarro: Letters to His Son Lucien, New York–London, 1943; also J. Rewald: Georges Seurat, Paris, 1948.

For his letters to T. and V. van Gogh, see Vincent van Gogh: Verzamelde Brieven, vol. III, Amsterdam, 1953.

For his recollections of V. van Gogh, see G. COQUIOT: Vincent van Gogh, Paris, 1924, p. 194 (letter to Coquiot).

For his letters to Lucie Cousturier, see 38.

26 G. CACHIN-SIGNAC: Autour de la correspondance de Signac, *Arts,* Sept. 7, 1951.

27 Notes on Stendhal, unpublished manuscript.

Writings on Signac

28 F. FÉNÉON: Paul Signac, *Les Hommes d'Aujourd'hui,* vol. 8, no. 373, 1890 [see p. 132, note 81]. See also various texts by Fénéon in Oeuvres, Paris, 1948.

29 F. FÉNÉON: Paul Signac, *La Plume,* Sept. 1, 1891. Included in Oeuvres.

30 A. DE LA ROCHEFOUCAULD: Paul Signac, *Le Coeur,* May 1893.

31 C. MERKI: Apologie pour la peinture, *Mercure de France,* June 1893 (attacks on Signac, van Gogh, Gauguin).

32 C. MAUCLAIR: Choses d'art, *Mercure de France,* March 1894 (diatribe against Signac and the opening of a special gallery devoted to neo-impressionism).

33 C. MAUCLAIR: Choses d'art, *Mercure de France,* April 1895 (against Signac, Pissarro, Lautrec, etc.).

34 H. VAN DE VELDE: Les Expositions d'art—à Bruxelles, *Revue Blanche,* vol. 10, 1896, pp. 284–87.

35 J. MEIER-GRAEFE: Entwicklungsgeschichte der modernen Kunst, Stuttgart, 1904. Chapter on Signac.

36 A. ALEXANDRE: Paul Signac, Président des Indépendants, *Comoedia,* March 26, 1910. Long though not very interesting article.

37 H. GUILBEAUX: Paul Signac et les Indépendants, *Les Hommes du Jour,* April 22, 1911.

38 L. COUSTURIER: Paul Signac, *La Vie,* March 23, 1912 (with some letters).

39 J.-C. HOLL: La Jeune Peinture contemporaine, Paris, 1912. Chapter on Signac.

40 L. COUSTURIER: Paul Signac, Paris, 1922. Written by his friend and pupil, this book, the first important one on the artist, offers a lively account of the man, his conversation, his studio, etc. 20 reproductions of paintings, 24 of watercolors and drawings, some photographs; numerous ill. of pen drawings in the text.

41 J. GUENNE: Entretien avec Paul Signac, *L'Art Vivant,* March 20, 1925.

42 G. BESSON: Paul Signac, Paris, 1935. Short text, 32 ill., chronologically arranged.

43 B. DORIVAL: Les Etapes de la peinture française contemporaine, vol. I, Paris, 1943. Chapter on neo-impressionism with long, and generally unfavorable, section devoted to Signac.

44 G. BESSON: Paul Signac, *Arts de France,* no. 2 [n.d.].

45 H. HILDEBRANDT: Neo-impressionisten—Paul Signac, *Aussaat,* May–July 1947.

46 T. NATANSON: Peints à leur tour, Paris 1948. Chapter on

"L'École de Seurat" concerns itself with Signac.

47 G. Besson: Paul Signac, Paris–London–New York, n.d. [1948?]. Short text, 60 excellent though small ill., chronologically arranged (Collection des Maîtres).

48 G. Besson: Paul Signac—Dessin, Paris, 1950. Superb and well-selected plates.

49 Francis Jourdain: Paul Signac, Art-Documents, no. 13, Oct. 1951.

50 M. Breuning: Signac's Science, Art Digest, Nov. 15, 1951.

51 H. E. Bates: French Painters—Signac and Cross, Apollo, May 1952, ill.

52 C. Roger-Marx: Maîtres du XIXe siècle et du XXe, Geneva, 1954. Short chapter on Signac.

53 J. Rewald: Paul Signac, in Dictionnaire de la peinture moderne, Paris, 1954. New York, 1955.

54 M. Sandoz: L'Oeuvre de Paul Signac à La Rochelle, Croix-de-Vie, Les Sables d'Olonne, de 1911 à 1930, Bulletin de la Société de l'Histoire de l'Art Français, Année 1955, Paris, 1956.

55 M. Sandoz: Signac et Marquet, Dibutade IV, 1957. Ill.

56 E. C. Flamant: Signac, ses amis, ses tableaux, ses yachts, Connaissance des Arts, Nov. 1963.

57 M.-T. de Forges: L'Exposition Paul Signac au Musée du Louvre, Revue du Louvre, no. 6, 1963.

58 J. Arguëlles: Paul Signac's "Against the Enamel of a Background Rhythmic with Beats and Angles, Tones and Colors, Portrait of M. Félix Fénéon in 1890, Opus 217," Journal of Aesthetics and Art Criticism, Fall 1969. Important article.

59 F. Cachin: Le Portrait de Fénéon par Signac—Une Source inédite, Revue de l'Art, no. 6, 1969. Important article.

60 F. Cachin: Paul Signac, Paris, 1971. Richly documented biography with numerous good ill., extensive bibl.; the author is the artist's granddaughter.

III   NEO-IMPRESSIONISM

1 F. Fénéon: Les Impressionnistes en 1886, Paris, 1886; reprinted in 84.

2 R. Darzens: Exposition des Impressionnistes, La Pléiade, May 1886.

3 P. Adam: Peintres Impressionnistes, Revue Contemporaine, May 1886.

4 Anonymous: L'Exposition des Impressionnistes, Revue de Demain, May–June 1886. Review of the last impressionist show with interesting comments on Seurat, Pissarro, and Signac; unfavorable ones on Gauguin.

5 J. Le Fustec: Exposition des Artistes Indépendants, Journal des Artistes, Aug. 22, 1886.

6 P. Adam: Les Artistes Indépendants, La Vogue, Sept. 6–13, 1886.

7 E. Hennequin: L'Exposition des Artistes Indépendants, La Vie Moderne, Sept. 11, 1886.

8 L.-P. de Brinn'Gaubast: Les Indépendants, Le Décadent, Sept. 18, 1886.

9 F. Fénéon: L'Impressionnisme aux Tuileries, L'Art Moderne, Sept. 19, 1886.

10 J.-K. Huysmans: Chronique d'art, Revue Indépendante, Nov.–Dec. 1886.

11 T. de Wyzewa: L'Art contemporain, Revue Indépendante, Nov.–Dec. 1886.

12 A. Alexandre: Critique décadente, L'Evénement, Dec. 10, 1886.

13 E. Verhaeren: Le Salon des XX à Bruxelles, La Vie Moderne, Feb. 26, 1887.

14 Trublot [P. Alexis]: L'Exposition des Artistes Indépendants, Le Cri du Peuple, March 26, 1887.

15 M. Fouquier: L'Exposition des Artistes Indépendants, XIXe Siècle, March 28, 1887.

16 G. Kahn: La Vie artistique, La Vie Moderne, April 9, 1887.

17 J. Le Fustec: Exposition des Artistes Indépendants, Journal des Artistes, April 10, 1887.

18 J. Christophe: Les Evolutionnistes du Pavillon de la Ville de Paris, Journal des Artistes, April 24, 1887.

19 F. Fénéon: Le Néo-impressionnisme, L'Art Moderne, May 1, 1887.

20 Anonymous: De l'emploi des couleurs pour la peinture et la décoration, L'Art Moderne, 1887, pp. 253–54, 292–93, 301–03, 326–27.

21 A. Michel: Le Néo-impressionnisme, La Flandre Libérale, Feb.–Mar. 1888; reprinted in L'Arte Moderne, Mar. 10, 1888.

22 E. Verhaeren: Chronique bruxelloise—L'Exposition des XX à Bruxelles, Revue Indépendante, March 1888.

23 Anonymous: Le Salon des XX—L'ancien et le nouvel impressionnisme, L'Art Moderne, 1888, pp. 41–42.

24 F. de Faramond: article on the exhibition of the Indépendents, La Vie Franco-Russe, March 24, 1888 [cannot be located].

25 A. Alexandre: La Semaine artistique, Paris, March 26, 1888.

26 G. Kahn: Exposition des Indépendants, Revue Indépendante, April 1888.

27 G. Geffroy: Pointillé-Cloisonnisme, La Justice, April 11, 1888.

28 F. Fénéon: Le Néo-impressionnisme à la IVe exposition des Artistes Indépendants, L'Art Moderne, April 15, 1888.

29 P. Adam: Les Impressionnistes à l'exposition des Indépendants, La Vie Moderne, April 15, 1888.

30 J. Christophe: Le Néo-impressionnisme au Pavillon de

la Ville de Paris, *Journal des Artistes,* May 6, 1888.

31 ANONYMOUS: Néo-impressionnisme, *L'Art Moderne,* Nov. 11, 1888.

32 ANONYMOUS: Aux XX, *L'Art Moderne,* Feb. 3, 1889.

33 ANONYMOUS: L'Art japonais et le néo-impressionnisme, *L'Art Moderne,* 1889, pp. 50–52.

34 O. MAUS: Le Salon des XX à Bruxelles, *La Cravache,* Feb. 16, 1889.

35 P. M. O. [P. M. OLIN]: Chronique de l'art—Peinture, les XX, *La Wallonie,* no. 2, 1889.

36 A. GERMAIN: L'Exposition des Indépendants, *Art et Critique,* Sept. 15, 1889.

37 F. FÉNÉON: 5e Exposition de la Société des Artistes Indépendants, *La Vogue,* Sept. 1889; reprinted in *L'Art Moderne,* Oct. 27, 1889.

38 G. LECOMTE: L'Exposition des Néo-Impressionnistes—Pavillon de la Ville de Paris, *Art et Critique,* March 29, 1890.

39 G. LECOMTE: Société des Artistes Indépendants, *L'Art Moderne,* March 30, 1890.

40 ANONYMOUS: L'Exposition des XX, *L'Art Moderne,* 1890, pp. 25–27.

41 J. L. [J. LECLERCQ]: Aux Indépendants, *Mercure de France,* May 1890.

42 G. LECOMTE: Le Salon des Indépendants, *L'Art dans les Deux Mondes,* March 28, 1891.

43 E. VERHAEREN: Le Salon des Indépendants, *La Nation;* reprinted in *L'Art Moderne,* April 5, 1891.

44 A. GERMAIN: Théorie des Néo-Luminaristes, *Moniteur des Arts;* reprinted in *L'Art Moderne,* July 12 and 16, 1891.

45 A. GERMAIN: Théorie Chromo-Luminariste, *La Plume,* Sept. 1, 1891.

46 J. ANTOINE: Critique d'art—Exposition des Artistes Indépendants, *La Plume,* III, 1891, pp. 156–57.

47 E. VERHAEREN: Exposition des XX, *Art et Critique,* Feb. 13, 1892.

48 E. COUSTURIER: Société des Artistes Indépendants, *L'Endehors,* March 27, 1892.

49 P. M. OLIN: Les XX, *Mercure de France,* April 1892.

50 F. FÉNÉON: Au Pavillon de la Ville de Paris—Société des Artistes Indépendants, *Le Chat Noir,* April 2, 1892.

51 G. LECOMTE: L'Art contemporain, *La Revue Indépendante,* 1892, pp. 1–29.

52 C. SAUNIER: L'Art nouveau, *La Revue Indépendante,* 1892, pp. 30–48.

53 Y. RAMBOSSON: Exposition des peintres néo-impressionnistes, *Mercure de France,* Jan. 1893.

54 A. GERMAIN: Pour le beau, *Essais d'Art Libre,* special issue, Feb.–March 1893; chapt. III: Le Chromo-Luminarisme.

55 O. MIRBEAU: Néo-impressionnistes, *Echo de Paris,* Jan. 23, 1894.

56 G. G. [G. GEFFROY]: L'Art d'aujourd'hui—Néo-impressionnistes, *Le Journal,* Jan. 28, 1894.

57 TIPHERETH [pseud.?]: Néo-impressionnistes, *Le Coeur,* July 1894.

58 *Pan,* first issue, 1898. Excerpts from Signac's book (see 59 below) with original lithographs by Signac, Petitjean,
Luce, van Rysselberghe, Cross, and reproductions after 2 drawings by Seurat.

59 P. SIGNAC: D'Eugène Delacroix au Néo-Impressionnisme, Paris, 1899. The first important book on the subject, giving the historical background for the neo-impressionist theories as well as these theories themselves and their practical application. A basic book by the most articulate member of the movement.

60 A. FONTAINAS: Art moderne, *Mercure de France,* May 1900.

61 J. MEIER-GRAEFE: Der moderne Impressionismus, Berlin, n.d. (1903–04). Chapter on neo-impressionism.

62 H. KESSLER: Ueber den Kunstwert des Neo-Impressionismus—Eine Erwiderung, Berlin, 1903. Short pamphlet.

63 C. MAUCLAIR: L'Impressionnisme—son histoire—son esthétique—ses maîtres, Paris, 1904. Contains a confused and ill-informed chapter on: Le Néo-impressionnisme et la théorie du pointillisme—Seurat, Signac, Denis, van Rysselberghe, Bonnard, Vuillard, Gauguin, Anquetin, etc.

64 J. MEIER-GRAEFE: Entwicklungsgeschichte der modernen Kunst, Stuttgart, 1904. Contains 2 chapters on neo-impressionism.

65 C. MORICE: Le XXIe Salon des Indépendants, *Mercure de France,* April 15, 1905.

66 C. HERRMANN: Der Kampf um den Stil, Berlin, 1911. Written by a painter who became a divisionist around 1904, this book examines the artistic situation at the turn of the century and hails neo-impressionism as the style of the future. (The author's wife translated Signac's book, see 59, into German.)

67 M. RAPHAEL: Von Monet zu Picasso, Leipzig, 1913. Chapter on neo-impressionism.

68 H. KELLER and J. MACLEOD: The Application of the Physiology of Color Vision in Modern Art, *Annual Report, Smithsonian Institution,* 1917, pp. 723–39: originally published in *Popular Science Monthly,* Nov. 1913.

69 E. FER: Les Principes scientifiques du néo-impressionnisme, *Pages d'Art,* Dec. 1917 and May 1918. See also the same author's: Solfège de la couleur, Paris, 1954.

70 G. COQUIOT: Les Indépendants, Paris, n.d. [1920]. Chapter on neo-impressionism.

71 G. MARZYNSKI: Die Methode des Expressionismus—Studien zu seiner Psychologie, Leipzig, 1920. The chapter on the method of impressionism is devoted mainly to neo-impressionism.

72 G. KAHN: Au temps du pointillisme, *Mercure de France,* April 1924.

73 Seurat et ses amis—La Suite de l'impressionnisme, catalogue of an exhibition, Galerie Wildenstein, Paris, Dec. 1933–Jan. 1934. Introduction by P. Signac. Excellent catalogue with notes on the various painters, ill. Signac's text also appeared separately: Le Néo-impressionnisme—Documents, *Gazette des Beaux-Arts,* 1934, ill. See also 77.

74 R. ESCHOLIER: Seurat et ses amis, *Le Journal,* Dec. 20, 1933.

75 A. LÉVY-GUTMANN: Seurat et ses amis, *Art et Décoration,* 1934.

76 Schilderyen uit de Divisionistische School van Georges

Seurat tot Jan Toorop, catalogue of an exhibition, Boymans Museum, Rotterdam, Dec. 1936–Jan. 1937. Introduction by D. Hannema. In addition to works by Angrand, Cross, van Gogh, Lemmen, Luce, van Rysselberghe, Seurat, Signac, Lautrec, and van de Velde, this exhibition also included paintings by such Dutch followers as J. J. Aarts, H. P. Bremmer, Gestel, F. Hart Nibbrig, Thorn Prikker, and J. Toorop. Altogether 71 paintings and drawings, of which 31 are reproduced. See also 93 and 97.

77 Seurat and his Contemporaries, catalogue of an exhibition, Wildenstein Galleries, London, Jan.–Feb. 1937. Introduction by Signac (same as 73). Works by Angrand, Cousturier, Cross, Delavallée, Dubois-Pillet, Gausson, Hayet, Luce, C. Pissarro, van Rysselberghe, Seurat, Signac (and L. Pissarro in supplement). Notes on each painter, chronological table, good ill.

78 R. Escholier: La Peinture française—XXe siècle, Paris, 1937. Chapter on neo-impressionism.

79 Les Néo-Impressionnistes, catalogue of an exhibition, Galerie de France, Paris, Dec. 1942–Jan. 1943.

80 B. Dorival: Les Etapes de la peinture française contemporaine, vol. I, Paris, 1943. Chapter on neo-impressionism.

81 F. Maret: Les Peintres luministes—L'Art en Belgique, Brussels, 1944. On Belgian impressionism and divisionism (here called "luminisme"). Among the neo-impressionists, only van Rysselberghe receives full consideration, whereas Finch, Lemmen, and van de Velde are merely mentioned. Short bibl., 32 good ill., among which are 11 plates devoted to van Rysselberghe. A comprehensive study of Seurat's followers among the XX still remains to be written. See also 91 and 97.

82 H. Rostrup: Pointillisme, *Meddelelser fra Ny Carlsberg Glyptotek,* Copenhagen, 1947. Ill.

83 M. Saint-Clair [Mme Maria van Rysselberghe]: Galerie privée, Paris, 1947. Excellent portrait studies of Verhaeren, Cross, Fénéon, Théo van Rysselberghe, Gide, etc., whom the author knew intimately.

84 F. Fénéon: Oeuvres, Paris, 1948. Reprints of some, though far from all, of Fénéon's basic writings on neo-impressionism. For a more complete and better organized edition, see F. Fénéon: Oeuvres plus que complètes, J. U. Halperin, ed., 2 vols. Paris–Geneva, 1970.

85 C. E. Gauss: The Aesthetic Theories of French Artists— 1855 to the Present, Baltimore, 1949. Chapter on: From Realism to Neo-impressionism.

86 Pointillists and Their Period, catalogue of an exhibition, Redfern Gallery, London, Nov.–Dec. 1950. Introduction by H. E. Bates. Includes more works by their contemporaries than by neo-impressionists. Ill.

87 Seurat and His Friends, catalogue of an exhibition, Wildenstein Galleries, New York, Nov.–Dec. 1953. Introduction by J. Rewald. Paintings and drawings by nearly all the members of the movement, with short notes on them. Profusely ill.

88 F. Marti Ibañez: An Experiment in Correlation: The Psychological Impact of Atomic Science on Modern Art, *Arts and Architecture,* Jan., Feb., and March 1953.

89 G. Cachin-Signac: Un poète turc a-t-il inspire les néo-impressionnistes? *Lettres Françaises,* Jan. 7, 1954.

90 G. Pogu: Sommaire de technologie divisionniste, *in* catalogue of H. Petitjean exhibition, Paris, Galerie de l'Institut, April 1955.

91 L'Impressionnisme en Belgique avant 1914, catalogue of an exhibition, Casino Communal, Knokke-le-Zoute, Albert Plage, July–Aug. 1955. Introduction by P. Fierens. Includes works by Anna Boch, Ensor, Evenepoel, G. Lemmen, van Rysselberghe, and van de Velde. Bibl., ill.

92 G. Habasque: Le Contraste simultané des couleurs et son emploi en peinture depuis un siècle, *in* I. Meyerson: Problèmes de la couleur, Paris, 1957.

93 A. B. Loosjes-Terpstra: Moderne Kunst in Nederland 1900–1914, Utrecht, 1958; revised: 1959. Information on the Dutch neo-impressionists.

94 Les Néo-impressionnistes, catalogue of an exhibition, Galerie J.-C. & J. Bellier, Paris, June–July 1961. Ill.

95 G. Pogu: Néo-impressionnistes étrangers et influences néo-impressionnistes, Paris, 1963. Inept.

96 Neo-Impressionists and Nabis in the Collection of Arthur G. Altschul, catalogue of an exhibition, Yale University Art Gallery. New Haven, Conn., 1965. Catalogue edited by R. L. Herbert.

97 Neo-Impressionism, catalogue of an exhibition, The Solomon R. Guggenheim Museum, New York, 1968. Exhibition assembled and texts written by R. L. Herbert. Unquestionably this was the most important and thorough exhibition on this subject, with notes on every painter, as well as most of the works shown; all are reproduced, some in poor color plates. One may wonder why Laugé, Le Sidaner, and Selmersheim-Desgrange were included in the section on "Neo-Impressionists" rather than among their "Contemporaries"; on the other hand, the sections on the Belgian and Dutch neo-impressionists are fine additions to the scant literature on these artists. With the inclusion of fauve and cubist works, however, it becomes clear that the subject of this fascinating show was not so much neo-impressionism as *pointillism,* since Herbert had patiently assembled a wide range of paintings executed in dots—or merely featuring dots (Gris, Klee, Mondrian, Severini, and even one Marevna Vorobieff). The hanging of the exhibition was somewhat deceptive, since it attempted a chronological presentation; thus, major canvases by Seurat or Signac were almost obscured by surrounding works of their epigones. This kind of historical survey looks better in a book than on museum walls. But this catalogue is very well conceived; there is a list of exhibitions and a chronology, as well as a condensed bibl.

98 Homage to Seurat—Paintings, Watercolors, and Drawings by the Followers of Seurat, Collected by Mr. and Mrs. W. J. Holliday, Tucson, Ariz., 1968. Very few of the works are by true followers of Seurat; most are by artists who do not have any historical, artistic, or stylistic connection with him, not to mention those who do not even apply a pointillist technique (some of those who do would have been disowned by Seurat). It is ironic that the lone panel by Seurat himself looks suspiciously like

the one published by C. de Hauke in his "pilori" (see Seurat Bibl. 2, vol. 1, p. 298). The catalogue notes are almost unreadable.

99 L'Aube du XXe siècle—Néo-impressionnistes et autour du néo-impressionnisme, Petit Palais, Geneva, n.d. Works from the O. Ghez collection, of which the most important ones were included in 97.

100 J. SUTTER, ed.: Les Néo-Impressionnistes, Neuchâtel, Paris, 1970. A handsome, richly ill. volume with black-and-white and color reproductions as well as portraits and documents, divided into chapters by various contributors: Seurat, by Sutter; Les Théories de Seurat et le néo-impressionnisme, by R. L. Herbert; Signac, by Sutter; Cross, by I. Compin; Angrand, by P. Angrand; Dubois-Pillet, by L. Bazalgette; Lucien Pissarro, by A. Fern; Hayet, by Sutter; Petitjean, by Bazalgette and Sutter; Cavallo-Peduzzi, by P. Eberhart; Luce, by Sutter; Gausson, by Sutter and Eberhart; Delavallée, by Sutter; texts on the members of Les XX are quoted from 91 and 95; two chapters on the Indépendants; condensed bibl.

VARIOUS NEO-IMPRESSIONISTS

Angrand, Charles (1854–1926)

1 F. Fénéon: Catalogue des trente-trois, *La Cravache,* Jan. 19, 1889; reprinted in Fénéon: Oeuvres, Paris, 1948.

2 C. ANGRAND: Henri-Edmond Cross, *Les Tempes Nouveaux,* July 23, 1910.

3 Article on Angrand in *Par Chez Nous* (revue normande), Feb.–March 1921.

4 ANONYMOUS [F. FÉNÉON?]: Charles Angrand, *Bulletin de la Vie Artistique,* April 15, 1926.

5 Inédit de Charles Angrand, *La Vie,* Oct. 1, 1936.

6 ANONYMOUS: Foreword to the catalogue of a Charles Angrand exhibition, Galerie André Maurice, Paris, Dec. 1960–Jan. 1961.

See also G. COQUIOT: Seurat, Paris, 1924, for Angrand's recollections of Seurat.

See also Signac's Diary, *Gazette des Beaux-Arts,* July–Sept. 1949, April 1952, July–Aug. 1953.

Cross, Henri-Edmond (1856–1910)
[real name: Delacroix]

1 COMPIN: H.-E. Cross, Paris, 1964. A biographical and critical study, based on many unpublished letters, presents the first systematic study of this too frequently neglected artist. It is followed by what the author calls "Premier essai de catalogue de l'oeuvre peint." Though not complete, this catalogue offers a great deal of information and reproduces most of the works—at least all major ones—as well as a few drawings and watercolors. There is an extensive list of exhibitions and a chronologically presented bibl., much more complete than the present one.
Some of the more important publications are:

2 F. FÉNÉON: Article on H.-E. Cross, *Le Chat Noir,* March–April 1892.

3 E. VERHAEREN: Introduction (in form of a letter to the artist), catalogue of the exhibition, H.-E. Cross, Galerie Druet, Paris, March 21–April 8, [1905].

4 M. DENIS: Introduction, catalogue of an exhibition, H.-E. Cross, Galerie Bernheim-Jeune, Paris, April–May 1907; reprinted in Denis: Théories, Paris, 1912, pp. 152–55.

5 C. ANGRAND: Henri-Edmond Cross, *Les Temps Nouveaux,* July 23, 1910.

6 M. DENIS: Introduction, catalogue of a posthumous exhibition, H.-E. Cross, Galerie Bernheim-Jeune, Paris, Oct.–Nov. 1910; reprinted in Denis: Théories, Paris, 1912, pp. 156–60.

7 [F. FÉNÉON]: Les Carnets d'Henri-Edmond Cross, I–VII, *Bulletin de la Vie Artistique,* May 15, June 1, July 1, Sept. 1 and 15, Oct. 1 and 15, 1922.

8 L. COUSTURIER: H.-E. Cross, Paris, 1932. Valuable introduction and 32 ill.

9 M. SAINT-CLAIR [MME MARIA VAN RYSSELBERGHE]: Galerie privée, Paris, 1947. Exquisite portrait study of the artist.

10 J. REWALD: Introduction, catalogue of an exhibition, H.-E. Cross, Fine Arts Associates, New York, April–May 1951. Ill.

11 H.-E. CROSS: Carnet de dessins, 2 vols., Paris, 1959. Foreword by J. Rewald. Facsimile of a sketchbook.

Dubois-Pillet, Albert (1846–1890)

1 J. CHRISTOPHE: Albert Dubois-Pillet, *La Cravache,* Sept. 15, 1888.

2 J. CHRISTOPHE: Dubois-Pillet, *Les Hommes d'Aujourd'hui,* vol. 8, no. 370, 1890.

3 F. F. [F. FÉNÉON]: Notice on the death of A. Dubois-Pillet, *L'Art Moderne,* Aug. 21, 1890.

4 J. CHRISTOPHE: Le Commandant Dubois, *Art et Critique,* Aug. 30, 1890.

5 J. ANTOINE: Dubois-Pillet, *La Plume,* III, 1891, p. 299.

6 L. BAZALGETTE: Albert Dubois-Pillet, sa vie et son oeuvre (1846–1890), Paris, 1976. Richly documented and illustrated, with lists of exhibitions and other important information, this book suffers somewhat from what must be called "too vivid" writing.

Finch, A. William (1854–1930)

R. SIHTOLA: A. W. Finch—maalari, graafikko, keraamikko, in: L. Wennervirta and Y. A. Jäntti: Suomen Taiteen Vuosikirja 1945, Helsinki, 1945. Finnish text, ill.

Gausson, Léo (1860–1944)

1 F. [F. FÉNÉON]: Léo Gausson, *Revue Blanche,* vol. 10, 1896, p. 336.

2 C. MAUCLAIR: Choses d'art, *Mercure de France,* May 1896. Attack on Gausson and Gauguin.

Lemmen, Georges (1865–1916)

M. Nyns: Georges Lemmen, Antwerp, 1955.

Luce, Maximilien (1858–1941)

1 J. Christophe: Maximilien Luce, *La Cravache*, July 28, 1888.
2 G. Kahn: Chronique de la littérature et de l'art, *Revue Indépendante,* Oct. 1888.
3 J. Christophe: Maximilien Luce, *Les Hommes d'Aujourd'hui,* 1890.
4 Anonymous: Maximilien Luce, *Les Hommes du Jour,* no. 60, March 13, 1909.
5 J.-C. Holl: La Jeune Peinture contemporaine, Paris, 1912. Chapter on Luce.
6 A. Tabarant: Maximilien Luce, Paris, 1928. Biographical and analytical text by a friend of the artist; 50 good ill.
7 G. Turpin: Dix-huit peintres indépendants, Paris, 1931. Chapter on Luce.
8 J. Texcier: Les Peintres et la vie—Maximilien Luce, *Le Populaire,* April 10, 1949.
9 J. Sutter *et al.:* Maximilien Luce, Lausanne, 1971. Many ill.

Petitjean, Hippolyte (1854–1929)

1 Souvenirs du peintre Jules Joëts recueillis par M.-A. Bernard, *Art-Documents,* no. 50, Nov. 1954. Letters by Camille and Lucien Pissarro to Petitjean.
2 Hippolyte Petitjean, catalogue of an exhibition, Galerie de l'Institut, Paris, April 1955, with a "Sommaire de technologie divisionniste" by G. Pogu.

Pissarro, Lucien (1863–1944)

1 G. Lecomte: En Angleterre—Lucien Pissarro et ses amis, *Art et Critique,* March 12, 1892.
2 Anonymous: Note on Lucien Pissarro, *L'Art Moderne,* Aug. 6, 1893.
3 L. P. [Lucien Pissarro]: Letter to the editors, *Les Temps Nouveaux,* Dec. 7–13, 1895.
4 C. Ricketts and L. Pissarro: De la typographie et de l'harmonie de la page imprimée—William Morris et son influence sur les arts et métiers, London, 1898.
5 Article on the "Eragny Press," *Books and Bookplates,* vol. IV, no. 1, 1903.
6 E. Willrich: Lucien Pissarro als Buchkünstler, *Zeitschrift für bildende Kunst,* Nov. 1906. Ill.
7 J. B. Manson: Lucien Pissarro's Wood-Engravings, *Imprint,* April 1913.
8 J. B. Manson: Lucien Pissarro as Painter, *The Studio,* Nov. 15, 1916.
9 Clément-Janin: Peintres-Graveurs contemporains—Lucien Pissarro, *Gazette des Beaux-Arts,* Nov.-Dec. 1919, pp. 337–51, ill.
10 C. Marriott: Modern Movements in Painting, London, 1920.
11 F. Rutter: Some Contemporary Artists, London, 1922.
12 Camille Pissarro: Letters to His Son Lucien, New York—London, 1943. Edited by J. Rewald with the assistance of Lucien Pissarro. Essential documents on the divisionist phase of father and son, and on the period in general; richly ill., index. Rev. ed.: Mamaroneck, N.Y., 1972. French edition: Paris, 1950, also contains many letters from Lucien Pissarro to his father. See also 16.
13 Catalogues of the Memorial Exhibitions of Lucien Pissarro, Leicester Galleries, London. Part I, Jan. 1946: paintings and watercolors, with an appreciation by R. Mortimer. Part II, Dec. 1947: wood-engravings, drawings, and books, preface by P. James.
14 W. R. Sickert: A Free House, edited by O. Sitwell, London, 1947.
15 B. Robb: The Wood-Engravings of Lucien Pissarro, *Signature,* no. 6, 1948.
16 J. Rewald: Lucien Pissarro—Letters from London, 1883–1891, *Burlington Magazine,* July 1949. See also 12.
17 Designs and Engravings for the Eragny Press, catalogue of an exhibition: Arts Council of Great Britain, 1950. Introduction by P. James.
18 F. L. Gwynn: Sturge Moore and the Life of Art, London, 1952.
19 J. Rothenstein: Modern English Painters—Sickert to Smith, London, 1952.
20 Catalogue of Retrospective of the Works of Lucien Pissarro, Ohana Gallery, London, Nov. 1954. Introduction by V. Abul-Huda.
21 Lucien Pissarro: Notes on the Eragny Press, and a Letter to J. B. Manson, presented by A. Fern with a study on the artist and his work, Cambridge, 1957. A charming little book, ill.
22 W. S. Meadmore: Lucien Pissarro—Un Coeur simple, London, 1962. Detailed biography, based on the artist's correspondence, the recollections of his daughter, his friends, etc. Ill., index. Short preface by J. Rewald.
23 Catalogue of the centenary exhibition of paintings, watercolors, drawings, and graphic work: Lucien Pissarro, 1863–1944, Arts Council of Great Britain, London and other cities, 1963. Introduction by R. Pickvance; chronology; a few ill. Bibl. taken from the present book.
24 Lucien Pissarro, catalogue of an exhibition, Findlay Galleries, New York, April–May 1966. Introduction by R. Pickvance (reprinted from 23).

Rysselberghe, Théo van (1862–1926)

1 E. Verhaeren: Théo van Rysselberghe, *L'Art Moderne,* 1898.
2 E. Verhaeren: Théo van Rysselberghe, *Ver Sacrum,* Zeitschrift der Vereinigung bildender Künstler Österreichs, Leipzig, no. 11, 1899.
3 J. Meier-Graefe: Entwicklungsgeschichte der modernen Kunst, Stuttgart, 1904. Section on van Rysselberghe.
4 L. Hevesi: Acht Jahre Secession, Vienna, 1906. Chapter on van Rysselberghe.
5 M. Denis: Introduction to the catalogue of an exhibition, Théo van Rysselberghe, Galerie Giroux, Brussels, Nov.-Dec. 1927; reprinted in 7.

6 G. VAN ZYPE: Notice on Théo van Rysselberghe with chronological list, in *L'Annuaire de l'Académie*, Brussels, 1932.

7 P. FIERENS: Théo van Rysselberghe, Brussels, 1937. Excellent study with reprint of M. Denis' foreword (5), bibl., and 49 good plates.

8 M. SAINT-CLAIR [MARIA VAN RYSSELBERGHE]: Galerie privée, Paris, 1947. Excellent chapter on van Rysselberghe by the artist's widow.

9 F. MARET: Théo van Rysselberghe, Antwerp, 1948. Short biography with bibl. and 26 good ill. See also the same author's: Les Peintres luministes—L'Art en Belgique, Brussels, 1944.

10 Théo van Rysselberghe, catalogue of an exhibition, Musée des Beaux-Arts, Ghent, July–Sept. 1962. Extensive notes on some paintings and introduction by P. Eeckhout; study of the artist by G. Chabot; useful short biographical notes on some of the painter's friends; good ill.; bibl. (more complete than the present one).

11 G. POGU: Théo van Rysselberghe, sa vie, [Paris, 1963]. Small pamphlet.

12 M.-J. CHARTRAIN-HEBBELINCK and P. MERTENS, eds.: Van Rysselberghe's Letters to O. Maus, *Bulletin des Musées Royaux de Belgique,* no. 1–2, 1966.

See also M.-O. MAUS: Trente années de lutte pour l'art, Brussels, 1926, on van Rysselberghe and the XX.

See also Signac's diary, *Gazette des Beaux-Arts,* July–Sept. 1949, April 1952, July–Aug. 1953. See Signac Bibl. 17.

IV LITERARY SYMBOLISM

1 E. HENNEQUIN: J.-K. Huysmans, *La Revue Indépendante,* July 1884.

2 T. DE WYZEWA: La Littérature Wagnérienne, *Revue Wagnérienne,* June 1886.

3 L. D'ORFER: article on Symbolism, *Le Scapin,* Sept. 1, 1886.

4 J. MORÉAS: Le Symbolisme, *Figaro Littéraire,* Sept. 18, 1886. The famous "Symbolist Manifesto."

5 G. KAHN: Réponse des Symbolistes, *L'Evénement,* Sept. 28, 1886.

6 P. ADAM: Le Symbolisme, *La Vogue,* Oct. 4–11, 1886.

7 P. ADAM: La Presse et le symbolisme, *Le Symboliste,* Oct. 7, 1886.

8 R. GHIL: Notre école, *La Décadence,* Oct. 15, 1886. See also 33.

9 A. VALLETTE: Les Symbolistes, *Le Scapin,* Oct. 16, 1886.

10 B. DE MONCONYS [P. ADAM]: Les Personnalités symbolistes, *La Vie Moderne,* Dec. 4, 1886.

11 ANONYMOUS [P. ADAM, J. MORÉAS, O. MÉTÉNIER, F. FÉNÉON]: Petit Bottin des lettres et des arts, Paris, 1886.

12 JACK PLOWERT [pseud. for P. ADAM]: Petit Glossaire pour servir à l'intelligence des auteurs décadents et symbolistes, Paris, 1888.

13 J. CHRISTOPHE: Symbolisme, *La Cravache,* June 16, 1888.

14 T. DE WYZEWA: Les Origines de la littérature décadente, *L'Art Moderne,* April 14, 1889.

15 A. GERMAIN: Du Symbolisme, *Art et Critique,* Oct. 5, 1889.

16 G. VANOR: L'Art symboliste, Paris, 1889; preface by P. Adam.

17 J. MORÉAS: Les Premières Armes du Symbolisme, Paris, 1889.

18 T. DE WYZEWA: Edouard Dujardin, *Les Hommes d'Aujourd'hui,* vol. 8, no. 388, 1890.

19 E. HENNEQUIN: Quelques écrivains français, Paris, 1890. Among others, an important essay on Huysmans' A Rebours.

20 J. HURET: Enquête sur l'évolution littéraire, *Le Figaro,* March–July, 1891; partly reprinted in *L'Art Moderne* (Brussels). Replies by Mallarmé, Mirbeau, and Henry are quoted in chapter IX.

21 ANONYMOUS: Les Préludes, *La Vie Moderne,* June 14 and 21, 1891. History of the symbolist periodicals.

22 G. KAHN: Les Origines du symbolisme, *Revue Blanche,* Nov. 1, 1901.

23 G. KAHN: Symbolistes et Décadents, Paris, 1902. Also 52.

24 C. MENDÈS: Le Mouvement poétique français de 1867 à 1900, Paris, 1903. Important volume with extensive bibliographical and critical dictionary.

25 A. RETTÉ: Le Symbolisme, Paris, 1903.

26 J.-K. HUYSMANS: A Rebours (originally published in 1884), Paris, 1903. This reprint features an important introduction written 20 years later.

27 G. COQUIOT: Le Vrai J.-K. Huysmans, Paris, 1912. Chapter on Huysmans as art critic.

28 A. BARRE: Le Symbolisme—Essai historique sur le mouvement poétique en France de 1885 à 1900, Paris, 1912.

29 E. RAYNAUD: La Mêlée symboliste, 3 vols., Paris, 1918–1922. See also the same author's: En marge de la mêlée symboliste, Paris, 1938.

30 A. ANTOINE: Mes souvenirs sur le Théâtre Libre, Paris, 1921. Vol. II, Mes souvenirs sur le Théâtre Antoine et sur l'Odéon, Paris, 1933. See also 70.

31 C. MAUCLAIR: Servitude et grandeur littéraires, Paris, 1922. A highly articulate account of the author's "souvenirs d'arts et de lettres de 1890 à 1900," about the

symbolists and their periodicals, the avant-garde theaters, some artists, dealers, musicians, etc.

32 G. Michaud: Message poétique du Symbolisme, 3 vols., Paris, 1922.

33 R. Ghil: Les Dates et les oeuvres—Symbolisme et poésie scientifique, Paris, 1923. See also the same author's: Choix de poèmes, Paris, 1928, with a summary exposé of his theories.

34 E. Dujardin: La Revue Wagnérienne, *La Revue Musicale,* Oct. 1923.

35 G. Kahn: Silhouettes littéraires, Paris, 1925. Chapters on Mallarmé, Huysmans, Verlaine, Rodin, etc.

36 Willy [pseud. for H. Gautier-Villard]: Souvenirs littéraires . . . et autres, Paris, 1925.

37 M. L. Henry: Stuart Merrill, la contribution d'un américain au symbolisme français, Paris, 1927.

38 E. Verhaeren: Impressions—De Baudelaire à Mallarmé—Parnassiens et Symbolistes, Paris, 1928. Studies on symbolism, Moréas, de Régnier, Huysmans, etc.

39 A. Fontainas: Mes Souvenirs du symbolisme, Paris, 1928. One of the best books on the subject, it strikes a balance between the author's perceptive views and his personal recollections. Chapters on symbolist reviews, Huysmans, Moréas, Kahn, Verlaine, le Théâtre d'Art, Verhaeren, Mallarmé, etc. A chapter on painters and sculptors speaks briefly of Moreau, Redon, Puvis de Chavannes, Aurier, Bernard, Monet, Rodin, Sérusier, the Nabis.

40 Rachilde [Mme A. Vallette]: Portraits d'hommes, Paris, 1930. Portraits of the "équipe" of the *Mercure de France* (A. Vallette, Verlaine, Tailhade, Moréas, de Gourmont, etc.), founded and edited by the author's husband.

41 P. Martino: Parnasse et Symbolisme, Paris, 1930.

42 Lugné-Poë: La Parade, vol. I, Le Sot du tremplin—Souvenirs et impressions de théâtre, Paris, 1930. Very rewarding recollections, particularly concerning the Nabis, the author's personal friends; with many documents and letters. See also 74.

43 H. de Régnier: Mallarmé et les peintres, *L'Art Vivant,* April 1, 1930. See also 64.

44 H. de Régnier: Nos rencontres, Paris, 1931.

45 E. Dujardin: Le Monologue intérieur, Paris, 1931.

46 H. de Régnier: De mon temps . . ., Paris, 1933. Recollections, among others, of Mirbeau, de Wyzewa, Verhaeren, de Gourmont.

47 I. de Wyzewa: La Revue Wagnérienne—Essai sur l'interprétation esthétique de Wagner en France, Paris, 1934. History of this important periodical, with a list of articles published in it. Extensive bibl. on Wyzewa; see also 75.

48 H. Trudgian: L'Esthétique de J.-K. Huysmans, Paris, 1934.

49 V. Stock: Memorandum d'un éditeur, Paris, 1935. Introduction by J. Ajalbert. Recollections and documents.

50 A. Jaulme and H. Moncel: Le Mouvement symboliste—Etudes bibliographique et iconographique, catalogue of an exhibition, Bibliothèque Nationale, Paris, 1936. Intro. by E. Jaloux. A model of its kind, this catalogue presents a detailed chronology from 1876 to 1900, as well as sections on: the forerunners and the masters of symbolism, the "Decadents," the symbolist periodicals, foreign influences, Wagner and Wagnerism, the first-generation symbolists (Laforgue, Kahn, Verhaeren, Moréas, Merrill, Morice, de Régnier, Viélé-Griffin, Fénéon, Dujardin, Ajalbert, Maeterlinck, and others, with excellent short biographies), "free verse," peripheral figures (Tailhade, Barrès, Adam, Aurier, and others), the second-generation symbolists (de Gourmont, Paul Fort, Gide, Valéry, Mauclair, Leclercq, and others), symbolism and the theater (Vuillard, Lautrec, Denis, Bonnard, Munch, H. de Groux, Anquetin, van Rysselberghe, and others), symbolism and music (Debussy), symbolism and painting (Puvis de Chavannes, Moreau, Gauguin, van Gogh, Ary Renan, Redon, A. Point, Anquetin, Bernard, Filiger, Laval, A. Séon, H. de Groux, Ensor, Denis, Sérusier, and others), the Rosicrucian movement, and so on. An indispensable and well-organized source of information about the intellectual currents of the time. Ill.

51 E. Jaloux, Saint-Pol-Roux, H. Charpentier, Auriant, A. Mockel, H. Strentz: Cinquantenaire du symbolisme, special issue of *Visages du Monde,* April 15, 1936. Ill.

52 G. Kahn: Les Origines du symbolisme, Paris, 1936. Reprint of introduction to 23.

53 P. Valéry: Existence du symbolisme, Maestricht, 1938.

54 J. Ajalbert: Mémoires en vrac—Au temps du symbolisme—1880–1890, Paris, 1938. Ill.

55 H. Mondor: Vie de Mallarmé, Paris, 1941. The most complete and most authoritative biography of the poet.

56 L. Hautecoeur: Littérature et peinture en France du XVIIe au XXe siècle, Paris, 1942.

57 H. Mazel: Aux beaux temps du symbolisme, 1890–1895, Paris–Brussels, 1943. Recollections.

58 A. Dinar: La Croisade symboliste, Paris, 1943.

59 Special issue of *Le Point,* Feb.–April 1944, devoted to Mallarmé. Contains a chronological chart: Mallarmé et la peinture de son temps. Profusely ill.

60 R. de Casteras: Avant le Chat Noir—Les Hydropathes, Paris, 1945.

61 L. Hourticq: L'Art et la littérature, Paris, 1946. Chapter on symbolism.

62 G. Michaud: La Doctrine symboliste, Paris, 1947.

63 H. Clouard: Histoire de la littérature française du symbolisme à nos jours, de 1885–1914, Paris, 1947.

64 T. Natanson: Près de Mallarmé—Le Paysage de Valvins et les peintres, *Maandblad voor Beeldende Kunsten,* Oct. 1948. Ill. See also 43.

65 C. F. Ramuz: Les Grands Moments du XIXe siècle français, Lausanne, 1948. Series of lectures on French literature with occasional sidelights on painting.

66 M. Raymond: From Baudelaire to Surrealism, New York, 1950. Survey of the evolution of French literature with a chapter on symbolism.

67 A. G. Lehmann: The Symbolist Aesthetic in France (1885–1895), London, 1950.

68 K. Cornell: The Symbolist Movement, New Haven, 1951.

69 M.-J. DURRY: Jules Laforgue, Paris, 1952.

70 M. ROUSSOU: André Antoine, Paris, 1954. See also 30.

71 A.-M. SCHMIDT: La Littérature symboliste, Paris, 1955.

72 R. BALDICK: Life of J.-K. Huysmans, Oxford, 1955.

73 H. AMER: Huysmans et la peinture, *La Tour Saint-Jacques,* May–June 1957. Special Huysmans issue.

74 J. ROBICHEZ: Le Symbolisme au théâtre—Lugné-Poë et les débuts de "L'Oeuvre," Paris, 1957. See also 42.

75 E. LIVERMAN DUVAL: Téodor de Wyzewa—Critic without a Country, Geneva–Paris, 1961. A biography with excerpts from Wyzewa's diary (in French) and an extended bibl., both of Wyzewa's writings and publications concerning him. See also 47.

76 Les Mardis—Stéphane Mallarmé and the Artists of His Circle, catalogue of an exhibition, University of Kansas Museum of Art, Lawrence, Kans., n.d. [1968]. Excellent catalogue with several essays.

77 M. COLLIE: Jules Laforgue, London, 1977. On the poet's life and work: an attempt at a precise chronology of the latter and some views on him. Selected bibl., index.

VARIOUS SYMBOLIST PAINTERS

Carrière, Eugène (1849–1906)

1. G.-A. AURIER: Eugène Carrière, *Mercure de France,* May 11, 1891; reprinted in Oeuvres posthumes, Paris, 1893.

2 A. REMACLE: Eugène Carrière, *La Plume,* 1891, pp. 89–94.

3 E. BRICON: Psychologie d'art—Les maîtres de la fin du XIXe siècle, Paris, 1900. Chapter on Besnard and Carrière.

4 G. SÉAILLES: Eugène Carrière, l'homme et l'artiste, Paris, 1901.

5 G. GEFFROY: L'Oeuvre d'Eugène Carrière, Paris, 1902. See also General Bibl. 19.

6 C. MAUCLAIR: Eugène Carrière, *L'Art Décoratif,* May 1902.

7 C. MAUCLAIR: Eugène Carrière, *Art et Décoration,* Feb. 1906.

8 G. GEFFROY: Souvenirs d'Eugène Carrière, *Les Arts,* April 1906.

9 G. GEFFROY: Eugène Carrière, peintre de portraits, *L'Art et les Artistes,* May 1906.

10 P. JAMOT: Eugène Carrière, *Gazette des Beaux-Arts,* May 1906.

11 C. MORICE: Eugène Carrière, l'homme et sa pensée, l'artiste et son oeuvre, Paris, 1906.

12 M. DENIS: Le Renoncement de Carrière—La Superstition du talent, *L'Ermitage,* June 15, 1906; reprinted in DENIS: Théories, Paris, 1912.

13 E. CARRIÈRE: Ecrits et lettres choisies, Paris, 1907.

14 E. FAURE: Eugène Carrière, peintre et lithographe, Paris, 1908.

15 Collection Jean Dolent, sales catalogue, Hôtel Drouot, Paris, Feb. 24 and 25, 1910. (Dolent was one of the artist's closest friends.)

16 G. SÉAILLES: Eugène Carrière, essai de biographie psychologique, Paris, 1911; new edition: Paris, 1922.

17 L. DELTEIL: Eugène Carrière, Lithographies—Le peintre-graveur illustré, vol. VIII, Paris, 1913.

18 FRANTZ JOURDAIN: Au pays du souvenir, Paris, 1922. Chapter on Carrière and the Salon d'Automne.

19 JAN-TOPASS: Eugène Carrière, *Art in America,* 1928, pp. 254–59.

20 A. MICHEL: Sur la peinture française au XIXe siècle, Paris, 1928. Chapter on Carrière.

21 H. PIERQUIN: Eugène Carrière—La Sensibilité et l'expression de son art, *L'Art et les Artistes,* Nov. 1930.

22 J.-P. DUBRAY: Eugène Carrière, essai critique, Paris, 1931.

23 T. NATANSON: Peints à leur tour, Paris, 1948. Chapter on Carrière.

24 Eugène Carrière et le Symbolisme, catalogue of an exhibition, Orangerie des Tuileries, Paris, Dec. 1949–Jan. 1950. Introduction by M. Florisoone, notes by J. Leymarie. Contains extensive bibl.

25 Musée National du Louvre—Peintures, Ecole française, XIXe siècle, Paris, 1958, vol. 1: A.–C. 61 paintings by Carrière catalogued and reproduced.

26 J. R. CARRIÈRE: De la vie d'Eugène Carrière—Souvenirs, lettres, pensées, documents, Toulouse, 1966. Ill., no index.

27 Eugène Carrière—Seer of the Real, catalogue of an exhibition, Allentown Art Museum, Allentown, Pa., 1968–69. Introduction by R. T. Hirsch, who is preparing a book on Carrière.

Ensor, James (1860–1949)

1 L. TANNENBAUM: James Ensor, New York, 1951. Published by the Museum of Modern Art with catalogue of an extensive retrospective; numerous ill. in black and white and color. Selected bibl. (compiled by H. B. Muller) listing Ensor's major writings and illustrations, catalogues of his prints, books and articles on him, as well as catalogues of and comments on important exhibitions. Other important publications are:

2 G. COQUIOT: La Vie artistique, *La Vogue,* Feb. 1899.

3 V. DENIS: James Ensor, *Ulisse,* July 1950; special issue devoted to the XXV Biennale di Venezia.

4 F. ARCANGELI: Ensor, pittore perplesso, *Paragone,* Sept. 1950.

5 F. S. WIGHT: Masks and Symbols in Ensor, *Magazine of Art,* Nov. 1951.

6 Ensor, catalogue of an exhibition, 10 paintings. Feigl Gallery, New York, Feb. 1953.

7 P. HAESAERTS: James Ensor, London, 1957.

8 James Ensor, catalogue of an exhibition, Marlborough Galleries, London, April–May 1960. Numerous ill.

9 James Ensor—The Early Work, catalogue of an exhibition, Allan Frumkin Gallery, New York and Chicago, n.d.

10 Ensor, catalogue of an exhibition, World House Galleries, New York, Sept.–Oct. 1960; foreword by A. Werner; some ill.

11 Ensor, catalogue of an exhibition, Art Institute of Chicago and Solomon R. Guggenheim Museum, New York, 1976–77. Introduction by J. D. Farmer.

Hodler, Ferdinand (1853–1918)

1 F. BURGER: Cézanne und Hodler, Munich, 1917. Study of style; ill.
2 Catalogue of Hodler exhibition, Kunstmuseum, Bern, Aug.–Oct. 1921. Bibl. and ill.
3 Catalogue of Hodler exhibition, Kunstmuseum, Bern, May–June, 1938. Ill., no bibl.
4 E. BENDER and W. Y. MÜLLER: Die Kunst Ferdinand Hodlers, Zurich, 1941; 2 vol.: I—Das Frühwerk bis 1895, by Bender; II—Reife und Spätwerk, by Müller. Basic publication with hundreds of fine ill., extensive bibl., index.
5 W. HUGELSHOFER: Ferdinand Hodler, Zurich, 1953. Biography with 168 excellent black-and-white and 18 color plates; no bibl., no index.

Moreau, Gustave (1826–1898)

1 P. LEPRIEUR: Gustave Moreau et son oeuvre, Paris, 1889.
2 J.-K. HUYSMANS: Certains, Paris, 1889.
3 R. MARX: Moreau, *Pan,* no. 1, 1897.
4 L. THÉVENIN: L'Esthétique de Gustave Moreau, Paris, 1897.
5 A. RENAN: Gustave Moreau, *Gazette des Beaux-Arts,* Jan., March, April, July, Nov., and Dec. 1899; profusely ill.
6 P. FLAT: Le Musée Gustave Moreau; l'artiste, son oeuvre, son influence, Paris, 1899.
7 G. GEFFROY: L'Oeuvre de Gustave Moreau, Paris, 1900.
8 E. SCHURÉ: L'Oeuvre de Gustave Moreau, *Revue de Paris,* Dec. 1901. See also the same author's: Précurseurs et révoltés, Paris, 1904.
9 L. DIMIER: L'inspiration de Gustave Moreau, *Minerva,* Nov. 15, 1902.
10 P. FLAT: Le Musée Gustave Moreau, Paris, 1904. Catalogue with a great deal of information. New edition: Paris, 1926.
11 E. DE MONTESQUIEU: Foreword to the catalogue of a Moreau exhibition, Galeries Georges Petit, Paris, 1906.
12 M. VAUCAIRE: Salomé à travers l'art et la littérature, *Nouvelle Revue,* 1907.
13 CATTEAU: L'Esthétique de Gustave Moreau et son fatalisme, Paris, 1907.
14 ABBÉ LOISEL: L'Inspiration chrétienne du peintre Gustave Moreau, Paris, 1912.
15 J. LARAN: Gustave Moreau, Paris, n.d. [1913]. Numerous ill.; chronologically arranged, short bibl.
16 G. DESVALLIÈRES: L'Oeuvre de Gustave Moreau, Paris, 1913.
17 R. MUTHER: Aufsätze über bildende Kunst, Berlin, 1914.
18 L. BENEDITE: Notre art—Nos maîtres: Puvis de Chavannes, Gustave Moreau et Burne-Jones, Paris, 1922.
19 H. EVENEPOEL: Gustave Moreau et ses élèves. Lettres d'Evenepoel à son père, Paris, 1923.
20 G. CHARENSOL: Gustave Moreau, *L'Art Vivant,* 1926, pp. 252–54.
21 G. ROUAULT: Gustave Moreau—A propos de son centenaire, *Le Correspondant,* April 10, 1926.

22 G. ROUAULT and A. SUARÈS: Gustave Moreau, special issue of *L'Art et les Artistes,* April 1926. Ill.
23 G. ROUAULT: Souvenirs intimes, Paris, 1927.
24 M. PETITBON: Gustave Moreau—Originalité de sa pensée et de son oeuvre, *Bulletin des Musées de France,* 1931.
25 IRONSIDE: Gustave Moreau, *Horizon,* no. 1, 1940.
26 J. LEJAUX: L'Oeuvre de Gustave Moreau, *Le Dessin,* no. 1, 1947.
27 C. CHASSÉ: Le Mouvement symboliste dans l'art du XIXe siècle, Paris, 1947. Chapter on Moreau.
28 Eugène Carrière et le Symbolisme, catalogue of an exhibition, Orangerie des Tuileries, Paris, Dec. 1949–Jan. 1950. Introduction by M. Florisoone, notes by J. Leymarie. Section on Moreau and his studio, with bibl.
29 M. PROUST: Contre Sainte-Beuve, suivi de Nouveaux Mélanges, Paris, 1954. Chapter on Gustave Moreau.
30 C. BEURDELEY: Gustave Moreau, *Connaissance des Arts,* Nov. 15, 1955.
31 I. CREMONA: Moreau sconosciuto, *Circolare Sinistra,* 4–5, 1955.
32 Visionaries and Dreamers, catalogue of an exhibition, Corcoran Gallery of Art, Washington, D.C., April–May 1956. Text by H. Dorra.
33 A. BRETON: L'Art magique, Paris, 1957.
34 R. von HOLTEN: Oedipe et le Sphinx—Gustave Moreaus genombrottsverk, Special issue: "Symbolister," *Tidskrift for Konstvetensk,* XXXII, 1957.
35 R. von HOLTEN: Gustave Moreau sculpteur, *Revue des Arts,* nos. 4–5, 1959.
36 G. ROUAULT et A. SUARÈS: Correspondance, Paris, 1960.
37 R. von HOLTEN: L'Art fantastique de Gustave Moreau, Paris, 1960. First modern and well-documented study on the artist. Numerous good ill. in black and white and in color; chronology, extensive bibl. Short, separate, foreword by A. Breton. Essential monograph. See also 48.
38 Gustave Moreau, catalogue of an exhibition, Musée du Louvre, Paris, June 1961. Forewords by J. Cassou and J. Paladilhe; detailed notes by R. von Holten; biography, short bibl., ill.
39 ANONYMOUS: The Splendrous Art of Gustave Moreau, *Life,* July 21, 1961; color reproductions.
40 R. von HOLTEN: Le Développement du personnage de Salomé à travers les dessins de Gustave Moreau, *L'Oeil,* July–Aug. 1961.
41 Redon—Moreau—Bresdin, catalogue of an exhibition, The Museum of Modern Art, New York, and The Art Institute Chicago, Dec. 1961–April 1962. Text on Moreau by D. Ashton; numerous ill. in black and white and color; short bibl.
42 R. von HOLTEN: Gustave Moreau, Illustrateur de La Fontaine, *L'Oeil,* July–Aug. 1964.
43 J. KAPLAN: Gustave Moreau's "Jupiter and Semele," *The Art Quarterly,* Winter 1970, pp. 393–414.
44 P.-L. MATHIEU: Documents inédits sur la jeunesse de Gustave Moreau (1826–1857), *Bulletin de la Société de l'Histoire de l'Art Français, année 1971,* Paris, 1972, pp. 259–79.
45 L. FRONGIA: I miti classici nelle opere della maturità di Gustave Moreau, *Storia dell'Arte,* no. 13, 1972.

46 J. Kaplan: Gustave Moreau, catalogue of an exhibition, Los Angeles County Museum of Art, July 23–Sept. 1, 1974. Richly ill., well-documented catalogue, with chronology.

47 S. Alexandrian: L'Univers de Gustave Moreau, Paris, 1975. 37 color plates.

48 P.-L. Mathieu: Gustave Moreau—Sa vie, son oeuvre, catalogue raisonné de l'oeuvre achevé, Paris, 1976. The best, most indispensable book on the artist, with excellent plates in black and white and color.

49 H. H. Hofstätter: Gustave Moreau (in preparation), Cologne. Numerous ill. chronology, list of exhibitions, bibl., index. Announced for 1978.

See also General Bibl. 19.

Puvis de Chavannes, Pierre (1824–1898)

1 E. Aynard: Les Peintures décoratives de Puvis de Chavannes au Palais des Arts de Lyon, Lyon, 1884.

2 R. Caze: La Foire aux peintures, *Lutèce,* nos. 172–75, 1885. Salon review.

3 G. Kahn: Chronique—Exposition Puvis de Chavannes, *Revue Indépendante,* Jan. 1888.

4 Aman-Jean: Puvis de Chavannes, *L'Art dans les Deux Mondes,* Nov. 29, 1890.

5 C. Florisoone: Puvis de Chavannes, Amiens, 1893.

6 M. Vachon: Puvis de Chavannes, Paris, 1895; new edition: 1900.

7 Puvis de Chavannes, special issue of *La Plume,* Nov. 15, 1895.

8 K. Cox: Puvis de Chavannes, *The Century Magazine,* Feb. 1896.

9 Puvis de Chavannes, special issue of *La Revue Populaire des Beaux-Arts,* no. 17, 1898.

10 Puvis de Chavannes, special issue of *Le Figaro Illustré,* Feb. 1899.

11 C. Mauclair: Puvis de Chavannes, *Nouvelle Revue,* June 15, 1899.

12 J. Buisson: Pierre Puvis de Chavannes—Souvenirs intimes, *Gazette des Beaux-Arts,* July and Sept. 1899. Ill.

13 G. Mourey: Some Sketches by Puvis de Chavannes, *International Studio,* Nov. 1899.

14 L. L. Road: P. Puvis de Chavannes, Boston, 1899.

15 J. La Farge: Puvis de Chavannes, *Scribner's Magazine,* no. XXVII, 1900, pp. 672–84.

16 M. Goldberg: Puvis de Chavannes, Paris, 1901.

17 T. de Wyzewa: Peintres de jadis et d'aujourd'hui, Paris, 1903. Chapter on Puvis de Chavannes.

18 M. Adam: Les Caricatures de Puvis de Chavannes, Paris, 1906.

19 G. Scheid: L'Oeuvre de Puvis de Chavannes à Amiens, 1907.

20 C. Ricketts: Modern Painters, *Burlington Magazine,* April 1908. Section on Puvis de Chavannes.

21 L. Thévenin: Puvis de Chavannes, 1909.

22 C. de Mandach and L. Wehrle: Lettres de Puvis de Chavannes, *Revue de Paris,* Dec. 15, 1910, Feb. 1, 1911.

23 T. Tugendhold: Puvis de Chavannes, Saint-Petersburg, n.d. (in Russian).

24 A. Michel and J. Laran: Puvis de Chavannes, Paris, n.d. [1911].

25 L. Riotor: Puvis de Chavannes, Paris, 1914.

26 A. Segard: Fresques inédites de Puvis de Chavannes, *Les Arts,* March 1914.

27 R. Jean: Puvis de Chavannes, Paris, 1914; new edition: 1933.

28 L. Benedite: Notre art—Nos maîtres—Puvis de Chavannes, Gustave Moreau et Burne-Jones, Paris, 1922.

29 H. Galtier: Puvis de Chavannes, Paris, 1924.

30 L. Werth: Puvis de Chavannes, Paris, 1926. Profusely ill.

31 C. Mauclair: Puvis de Chavannes, Paris, 1928. Extensive biography, 33 plates, bibl., index.

32 A. Declairieux: Puvis de Chavannes et ses oeuvres, Lyon, 1928.

33 A. Michel: Sur la peinture française au XIXe siècle, Paris, 1928. Chapter on Puvis de Chavannes.

34 M. Lagaisse: Puvis de Chavannes et la peinture lyonnaise du XIXe siècle, Lyon, 1937; catalogue of an exhibition with extensive bibl.

35 R. Goldwater: Puvis de Chavannes—Some Reasons for a Reputation, *Art Bulletin,* March 1946.

36 C. Chassé: Le Mouvement symboliste dans l'art du XIXe siècle, Paris, 1947. Chapter on Puvis de Chavannes.

37 T. Natanson: Peints à leur tour, Paris, 1948. Chapter on Puvis de Chavannes.

38 Eugène Carrière et le Symbolisme, catalogue of an exhibition, Orangerie des Tuileries, Paris, Dec. 1949–Jan. 1950. Introduction by M. Florisoone, notes by J. Leymaric. Section on Puvis de Chavannes, with bibl.

39 Visionaries and Dreamers, catalogue of an exhibition, Corcoran Gallery of Art, Washington, D.C., April–May 1956. Text by H. Dorra.

40 Puvis de Chavannes and the Modern Tradition, catalogue of an exhibition, Art Gallery of Ontario, Toronto, 1975. Prepared by R. J. Wattenmaker. Richly ill.

41 Puvis de Chavannes, catalogue of an exhibition, Grand Palais, Paris, 1976, and National Gallery of Canada, Ottawa, 1977. Catalogue published in French and English editions. Texts by J. Foucart and A. Brown Price. Extensive catalogue notes by various authors; all 228 works (paintings, watercolors, and drawings) fully documented and ill.; also numerous reproductions of important works, such as murals, not included in the exhibition. Chronology, bibl., list of exhibitions. A most valuable source of information, based on recent scholarship.

Willumsen, Jens Ferdinand (1863–1958)

1 N. V. Dorph: Moderne Kunst in Dänemark, *Pan,* no. 2, 1898.

2 J. Rohde: J. F. Willumsen, *Kunst und Künstler,* July 1906.

3 H. Öhman: J. F. Willumsen, 1921 (with the artist's own comments on his works).

4 J. F. Willumsen—Pictures, Sculptures, Ceramics, 1929. 68 ill. with a biographical preface by V. Jastrau.

5 J. F. Willumsen—Peintures, Nice, 1932. 23 ill. but no text.

6 S. Schultz: J. F. Willumsen, Copenhagen, 1948. Danish text, bibl., 70 plates (several with comments by the artist).

7 S. Schultz: J. F. Willumsen *in* Weilbachs Kunstnerleksikon, Copenhagen, 1952, vol. 3. Detailed biography with extensive bibl.

8 J. F. Willumsen: Mine Erindringer fortalt til E. Mentze (recollections as told to E. Mentze), Copenhagen, 1953.

9 M. Bodelsen: Willumsen i halvfemsernes Paris, Copenhagen, 1957. Danish text with English summary. Important study of Willumsen's relationship with Gauguin and Redon, among others, correcting information provided by the artist himself. Excellent ill., several in color, short bibl.

10 M. Bodelsen: Willumsen i 90'ernes Paris *in* Festskrift for Professor Ragnar Josephson, Stockholm, 1957.

11 Anonymous: J. F. Willumsen—Litografier og Raderinger, Copenhagen, 1960. Ill.

INDEX

photograph, *ill.* 213

mentioned 11, 15, 16, 17, 20, 22, 23, 24, 25, 34, 35, 39, 40, 41, 42, 43, 60, 66, 67, 68, 69, 70, 103, 168, 176, 178, 181, 182, 183, 186, 192, 194, 196, 199, 209, 211, 212, 213, 214, 215 (note 42), 217, 218, 219, 221, 222, 223, 224, 228, 233, 236, 241, 243, 245, 246, 250, 256, 257, 258, 259, 261, 264, 281, 284, 285, 291, 292, 295, 297, 298, 299, 300, 301, 302, 307, 308, 309, 310, 311, 312, 315, 317, 318, 320, 321, 322, 323, 324, 326, 329, 330, 335, 336, 338, 339, 340, 343, 344, 345, 346, 347, 348, 349, 350, 352, 353, 354, 356, 359, 360, 362, 365, 366, 367, 368, 372, 373, 374, 375, 376, 378, 379, 380, 381, 382, 383, 384, 385, 418, 427, 428, 429, 442, 480, 492

Gogh, Vincent van

early years as an artist, 19–20

arrival in Paris, 11

and impressionism, 16, 17, 18

at Cormon's, 20, 22, 27, 71 (note 20)

offers to marry Theo's mistress, 23

rooms with Alexander Reid, 24–25

paints flower still lifes, 25–26, 65

friendship with Toulouse-Lautrec, 28–29

friendship with Anquetin, 29–30

artistic evolution in Paris, 33–35

friendship with Camille Pissarro, 34–35, 56, 71 (note 40)

friendship with Guillaumin, 35

friendship with Hartrick, 35–36

meets Gauguin in Paris, 39

distressed by petty squabbles among Paris painters, 39–40, 60

difficulties with his brother, 40

his personality, 40–43

meets *père* Tanguy, 43–46

meets Cézanne at Tanguy's [?], 46

meets Angrand, 46

friendship with Signac, 51, 52–53

on pointillism, 55, 72 (note 62)

friendship with Bernard, 56, 57, 60

on Barbizon painters, 60

organizes exhibition at Le Tambourin, 61–64

organizes exhibition at another restaurant (43, avenue de Clichy), 62–63

relationship with La Segatori, 61–62, 66

relationship with Seurat, 64, 65, 70, 72 (note 62), 73, 99, 177

exhibits at Théâtre Libre, 64

exhibits at *Revue Indépendante* [?], 65

and Japanese prints, 65–66, 72 (note 76)

admires Gauguin's Martinique paintings, 68, 171

depressed by Paris, 69

decides to go south, 69–70

leaves for Arles, 70

trip to Arles, 192

impressions of Provence, 192

first work at Arles, 192–99

on working from imagination, 198

his technique at Arles, 199, 206

drawings at Arles (reed pen), 199–205, 216 (note 55)

meets Belgians Boch and McKnight in Arles, 196

friendship with Milliet, 206–09

on portraiture, 209

considers his work "ugly," 209

symbolism of colors, 185, 210–11, 218

correspondence with Gauguin, 185

considers going to Pont-Aven, 185

invites friends to join him in Arles, 185

invites Gauguin to Arles, 222–23

dreams of studio of the South, 185

suggests exchange of paintings to Gauguin, Bernard, 185–86, 191–92

correspondence with his brother, 211–12

on his brother's "share" in his work, 212–13

receives financial help from Theo, 212, 216 (note 65)

sees through Gauguin's attitude towards Theo, 214

prepares himself for Gauguin's arrival at Arles, 217–18

pace of work, 217

paints *The Rhône River at Night*, 218; *ill.* 219

fears becoming sick, 218, 219

speaks of madness, 218–19

first days with Gauguin, 221

on Gauguin (letter to Bernard), 221

critical of Gauguin's budget, 222–23

work with Gauguin at Alyscamps, 224, 228

copies Brittany painting by Bernard, 228

paints *Red Vineyard*, 228

Gauguin's influence, 231–36

paints "abstractions," 232

discussions and disagreements with Gauguin, 235

his portrait painted by Gauguin, 238, 240, 247 (note 36); *ill. in color* 244

incident at café, 240–41

Gauguin decides to leave, 241

visit to Montpellier, 241

Gauguin reconsiders leaving, 241

distrusts Gauguin's decision to stay, 241

learns of Theo's engagement, 241

"attacks" Gauguin, 243, 246

cuts off ear, 243, 245, 246, 248 (note 45)

brings ear to brothel, 243, 245, 248 (note 45)

hospitalized, 245, 246

visited by Theo, 246

writes to Gauguin, 246

released from hospital, 291

bitter about Gauguin, 291

on his condition, 291, 292, 297, 299–300

return to hospital because of persecution mania, 292

paints again (Mme Roulin), 293

thirty Arles citizens request his confinement in an asylum, 293–95

drinking, 298, 299, 300, 374

visited by Signac, 298

permitted to leave hospital grounds, work again, 298

speaks of suicide, 299, 301

considers confinement in Saint-Rémy asylum, 299–300, 301

declines to go to Pont-Aven or Paris, 300, 301, 321

considers enlisting in Foreign Legion, 301

arrival at Saint-Rémy, 303

description of asylum, 303–04

Dr. Peyron's diagnosis, 305

character of van Gogh's illness, 305–07

"treatment" at Saint-Rémy, 307

describes his quarters and life at Saint-Rémy, 308

works in garden, 310, 311

thinks of Gauguin and Bernard, 310, 312, 322, 323, 330

intrigued by cypresses, 311–12, 344

first excursion to Arles, 316

receives news of Johanna van Gogh's pregnancy, 316, 318

Women Picking Green Sprouts in the Snow, 347; *ill.* 348
Yellow Corn—Cypresses at Saint-Rémy, ill. 303
Yellow House (the artist's house at Arles), 210; *ill.* 210
Zinnias, ill. 25
Gogh, Vincent W. van (son of Theo van Gogh), 343, 346, 352, 354, 368, 373, 374, 375, 376, 380, 384
Gogh, Wilhelmina van (sister of Theo and Vincent van Gogh), 40, 41, 65, 67, 193, 298, 310, 316, 343, 348, 355, 360, 368
Goncourt, Edmond and Jules de, 64–65, 73, 135, 336
Goulue, La, 14, 27, 143, 479
Goupil Galleries (Boussod & Valadon), 11, 12, 13, 16, 24, 43, 67, 68, 71 (note 9), 213, 236, 339, 341, 350, 371, 373, 375, 378, 380, 382, 384, 385, 427, 442, 453, 464, 472, 480, 483, 491
Gourmont, Rémy de, 139, 141, 346
portrait by Vallotton, *ill.* 141
Goya, 161, 162
Grand Café des Beaux-Arts, *see* Volpini
Grandcamp, 83, 84, 92, 94, 98
Gravelines, 392, 394
Greenaway, Kate, 86
Grévy, Jules, 30
Grille d'Egout, 14, 431
Groupe Impressionniste et Synthétiste (exhibition), 259–61; catalogue of exhibition, 289 (note 14)
Groux, Henri de, 346, 347, 431, 492
Guillaumin, Armand, 12, 16, 17, 18, 35, 39, 45, 51, 64, 65, 66, 67, 68, 76, 152, 199, 212, 213, 237, 249, 256, 257, 265, 321, 340, 349, 350, 359, 360, 365, 369, 375, 376, 386, 392, 427, 431, 453
Nude Woman on a Bed, 365, 376; *ill.* 365
Quai de la Rapée, Paris, *ill.* 52
Self-Portrait, ill. 36

Haan, Meyer de, *see* Meyer de Haan
Hague, The, 20, 326
Hamsun, Knut, *Hunger*, 212
Hartrick, A. S., 35, 36
Hayet, Louis, 102, 116, 138, 318, 374, 388, 389
Place de la Concorde, Paris, ill. 109
Helmholtz, Hermann von, 79, 137
Hennequin, Emile, 161–62, 163
Henry, Charles, 13, 89, 90, 91, 125, 126,

127, 128, 130, 131 (note 38), 133, 135, 137, 138, 139, 140, 390, 391, 431, 449, 462
his research, 89–90, 165 (note 3)
his publications, 90, 125, 132 (notes 83 and 85)
his theories, 99, 126
his influence, 134–35, 166 (note 30)
Henry, Marie (Le Pouldu), 267, 270, 271, 272, 275, 290 (note 61), 410
photograph of Marie Henry's inn, *ill.* 272
Herblay, 392
Hiroshige, *Ohashi Bridge in Rain, ill.* 66
Hirschig, Anton, 376, 377, 380, 403 (note 36)
Hobbema, 192
Hoschedé, Ernest, 62
Hodler, Ferdinand, 151, 152, 456 (note 83), 492
Night, 151; *ill.* 151
Hokusai, 66
Holbein, Hans, 11, 458
Holland, 192, 213, 214, 220, 222, 233, 298, 302, 305, 346, 368, 372, 376, 384, 385, 415, 428, 480
Hommes d'Aujourd'hui, Les (periodical), 424
Honfleur, 92, 93, 94
Huet, Juliette, 433, 454, 455 (note 48), 464
Hugo, Victor, 13, 133, 363
Les Misérables, 195
Huysmans, Joris-Karl
secedes from Zola's group, 135, 156
"discovers" Moreau and Redon, 135, 144
on Moreau, 144, 146
on Cézanne, 163
portrait by Forain, *ill.* 418
mentioned, 137, 138, 148, 161, 162, 163, 165, 336, 422, 423, 429, 476
A Rebours (Against the Grain), 135, 162, 476 [des Esseintes, 135, 146]
Certains, 163, 422

Ibsen, Henrik, 13
impressionism, impressionists, 12, 17, 21, 29, 30, 35, 39, 62, 64, 65, 68, 80, 83, 87, 88, 89, 90, 91, 92, 93, 120, 129, 134, 137, 142, 143, 144, 148, 151, 152, 156, 163, 167, 168, 172, 185, 191, 192, 199, 212, 213, 257, 259, 260, 261, 264, 288, 291, 298, 319, 339, 340, 341, 344,

363, 379, 405, 422, 428, 429, 431, 445, 447
Independents, Society of and Salon, 30, 32, 33, 51, 61, 62, 71 (note 37), 75, 76, 84, 85, 86, 87, 91, 92, 102, 103, 109, 129, 152, 176, 288, 318, 319, 323, 345, 346, 348, 349, 375, 383, 385, 386, 387, 391, 392, 393, 396, 400, 430, 453, 479
India, 265
Indo-China, 238, 405, 450
Ingres, Jean-Dominique, 73, 70, 235, 251, 391
Isaäcson, 318, 340, 343
Italy, 447, 492

Japan; Japanese art, artists, prints, 30, 45, 51, 65, 66, 72 (note 76), 143, 168, 173, 176, 177, 180, 181, 185, 192, 193, 194, 200, 205, 211, 213, 220, 230, 275, 282, 321, 335, 360, 410, 411, 440, 449, 483
Java, 265, 411, 466
Joan of Arc, 183
Jongkind, Johann, 427
Joyant, Maurice, 427, 483, 491, 492
Julian, Académie, *see* Académie Julian
Julian, Rodolphe, 250–51, 254; *ill.* 252
Justice, La (newspaper), 439, 451, 456 (note 56)

Kahn, Gustave, 13, 89, 90, 127, 130, 134, 136, 137, 138, 139, 141, 144, 146, 148, 163, 166 (note 13), 168, 171, 213, 260, 289 (note 18), 391, 396, 400, 424, 480
Palais Nomades, 137
Knobloch, Madeleine, 394, 395, 396
portrait by Seurat, *ill.* 395
Koning, A. H., 64
Kropotkin, Prince, 14, 141
Kunichika, *Portrait of the Japanese Actor Hige no I kyu, ill.* 413

Laforgue, Jules, 89, 90, 130, 134, 135, 136, 137, 139, 143, 402
Lagadu, Marie, 286
portraits, *ill.* 269, 287
Lapin Agile, Le, 14
La Rochefoucauld, Antoine de, 429, 430, 444, 455 (note 47), 474, 475, 492
Laurent, Ernest-Joseph, 118
Laurent, Méry, 442
Laval, Charles, 39, 62, 67, 167, 168, 173, 180, 182, 185, 195, 214, 215 (notes 9

and 24), 217, 257, 258, 259, 260, 261, 272, 289 (note 14), 381, 410, 415
portrait by Gauguin, *ill.* 169
Bathers, ill. 179
Martinique, ill. 171
Self-Portrait, dedicated to Vincent van Gogh, 191–92; *ill.* 191
Le Barc de Boutteville (Paris art dealer), 437, 462, 479, 480
Leclercq, Julien, 261, 375, 419, 421, 422, 447, 452, 453
Lecomte, Georges, 90, 137, 141, 424, 429, 452, 474
Lefebvre, Jules, 253, 254
Lehmann, Henri, 73
Lemmen, Georges, 102, 119, 387, 396, 400, 479
Thames Scene, The Elevator, ill. 112
Lenbach, Franz von, 11
Leonardo da Vinci, 11, 397, 430, 453, 475
Le Petit, Caricature of Sâr Péladan, *ill.* 430
Le Pouldu, 228, 254, 267, 268, 270, 272, 273, 274, 276, 280, 281, 283, 286, 287, 288, 315, 339, 350, 360, 369, 371, 405, 408, 411, 416
Le Puy, 386
Le Sidaner, H.-E.-A., 118
Lhermitte, Léon, 16
Libre Esthétique, La (Brussels), 480
Lille, 414
Liszt, Franz, 14
Loti, Pierre, 233, 293, 415, 457
Louvre Museum, Paris, 11, 23, 60, 73, 264, 344, 429
Luce, Maximilien, 81, 102, 119, 120, 130, 136, 137, 138, 139, 141, 142, 213, 249, 350, 387, 388, 394, 395, 396, 453, 462, 479
portrait by Signac, *ill.* 127
portrait by Vallotton, *ill.* 397
Portrait of Camille Pissarro, ill. 88
Portrait of Gustave Kahn, ill. 397
Portrait of Paul Signac, ill. 127
portraits of Seurat, *ill.* 129
View of Montmartre, ill. 103
Lugné-Poë, 419, 437
portrait by Vuillard, *ill.* 454
Lutèce (periodical), 135
Luxembourg Museum, Paris, 60, 429

McKnight, Dodge, 196
Madagascar, 265, 360, 369, 372, 414, 415, 416, 418

Maeterlinck, Maurice, 137, 139, 425, 452
Maillol, Aristide, 151, 262, 264, 437
Washerwomen, ill. 437
Young Women in a Park (tapestry). *ill.* 437
Mallarmé, Stéphane
and impressionists, 142–43
and Redon, 143
and Gauguin, 438–39, 444–45, 452
portrait by Renoir, *ill.* 142
portrait by Vallotton, *ill.* 135
portrait by Vuillard, *ill.* 450
portraits by Gauguin, *ill.* 451
mentioned, 13, 14, 67, 133, 135, 136, 137, 138, 139, 141, 142, 143, 144, 152, 162, 163, 164, 165, 426, 429, 438, 439, 442, 444, 450, 451, 452, 462, 490, 492
Manet, Edouard, 13, 16, 21, 30, 39, 51, 62, 83, 88, 136, 142, 143, 163, 186, 256, 288, 363, 406, 428, 429, 440, 445, 458
Olympia, 172, 428, 429, 458 (copy by Gauguin, *ill.* 429)
Mantegna, 453
Manzi (Paris art dealer), 442
Marquesas Islands, 457, 494
Marseilles, 70, 293, 304, 415, 451, 454, 492, 494, 497
Martin, Henri, 118
Martin, *père* (Paris art dealer), 17
Martinique, 62, 67, 68, 69, 168, 171, 172, 214 (notes 4 and 9), 220, 223, 238, 256, 258, 274, 415, 416, 435, 440, 441, 445
Marx, Karl, 141
Marx, Roger, 257, 419, 429, 441, 444, 452, 479
portrait by Carrière, *ill.* 453
Massenet, Jules, 270
Mataïea District, Tahiti, 458, 459
Mauclair, Camille, 141, 492
Maufra, Maxime, 272, 392, 453, 456 (note 83)
Maupassant, Guy de, 13, 336
Maurer, Alfred, 252
Maus, Octave, 91, 137, 319, 346, 347, 384, 385, 396, 430, 480
portrait by van Rysselberghe, *ill.* 91
Maxwell, James, 79
Meissonier, Ernest, 16, 343, 344, 386, 430
Mercure de France, Le (periodical), 142, 342, 343, 346, 385, 416, 419, 422, 425, 442, 452, 481, 500 (note 53)
Merrill, Stuart, 136, 137, 139, 141, 419

Meryon, Charles, 363
Meyer de Haan, Jacob, 183, 249, 257, 267, 270, 271, 272, 273, 274, 275, 282, 290 (note 61), 316, 318, 321, 339, 350, 371, 382, 385, 405, 408, 408, 410, 415, 416, 417, 419, 436, 437, 438, 452, 464, 491
bust by Gauguin, 271; *ill.* 271
portraits by Gauguin, *ill.* 271, 415
Breton Women Stretching Hemp, 272; *ill.* 273
Farmyard at Le Pouldu, ill. 408
Portrait of Marie Henry, 270
Self-Portrait, ill. 270
Michelangelo, 30, 458, 475
Millet, Jean-François, 16, 17, 18, 60, 61, 65, 192, 323, 324, 327, 337, 369; *ill.* 324, 327, 331
Milliet, Zouave, 206, 207, 210, 238, 368
portrait by van Gogh, *ill.* 214
Minerve, La (periodical), 136
Mirbeau, Octave
attacks Redon, 156–61
article on Gauguin, 439–41, 456 (note 56)
mentioned, 18, 44, 141, 156, 260, 311, 386, 429, 438, 439, 440, 441, 442, 450, 451, 452, 456 (notes 52–56, 58, 59, 76, 87), 462, 474, 490, 499 (note 36)
bust by Rodin, *ill.* 386
portrait by Vallotton, *ill.* 439
Mirliton, Le, 15
Moderniste, Le (periodical), 260, 261, 265, 290 (note 30), 340, 341, 342, 416, 419
Moerenhout, J. A., 469, 486, 499 (note 17)
Monaco, 92
Monet, Claude, 12, 13, 16, 17, 18, 30, 46, 51, 60, 62, 65, 67, 73, 76, 83, 84, 87, 91, 136, 143, 199, 213, 249, 252, 256, 272, 310, 318, 373, 386, 427, 428, 429, 438, 439, 440, 456 (note 56), 474, 483, 492
Haystacks, 428
Poplar Trees, 474
Poplars at Giverny, Sunrise, ill. in color, 19
Monfreid, Georges-Daniel de, 257, 258, 259, 289 (note 14), 433, 437, 442, 452, 453, 460, 464, 466, 469, 471, 472, 479, 481, 483, 485, 490, 491, 492, 494, 497
Portrait of a Young Woman, ill. 438
Self-Portrait, ill. 433

Proust, Antonin, 419
Provence, 69, 220, 222, 318, 330, 335, 480
Puvis de Chavannes, Pierre
  admired by symbolist writers, 148
  his art, 148
  Wyzewa on, 148–49
  admired by younger painters, 151
  bust by Rodin, *ill.* 12
  mentioned, 11, 12, 16, 27, 60, 67, 135, 136, 143, 147, 148–51, 152, 154, 162, 163, 172, 192, 230, 252, 262, 285, 330, 360, 367, 392, 406, 423, 426, 429, 430, 440, 449, 456 (notes 56, 83), 458, 463, 475, 483, 486
  Poor Fisherman, ill. 150; copy by Seurat, *ill.* 150
  Sacred Wood Dear to the Arts and the Muses, 28, 151, *ill.* 29; parody by Toulouse-Lautrec, 28, 151, *ill.* 29
  Vision of Antiquity—Symbol of Form, ill. 149

Quimper (river), 267

Rachilde, Mme (wife of Alfred Vallette), 422, 426, 452
Raffaëlli, Jean-Francois, 12, 16, 87, 136, 138, 163, 373, 416, 429, 456 (note 83)
Rameau, Jean-Philippe, 90
Ranson, Paul, 253, 483
  sketch by Sérusier, *ill.* 255
Raphael, 11, 235, 458
Rappel, Le (newspaper), 439, 456 (note 56)
Ravachol, 141, 481
Ravoux, 362, 376, 377, 380, 403 (note 30)
Reclus, Elysée, 141
Redon, Odilon
  Salon review (1868), 153
  first exhibitions, 161
  praised by Hennequin, 161–62
  cofounder of Independents, 32, 152
  discontinues participation, 92
  and Mallarmé, 143, 165
  and symbolist writers, 152, 156, 162–63
  on impressionism, 152
  on imagination, 153–54
  his art, 153–54, 163
  attacked by Mirbeau, 156–61
  praised by Huysmans, 162, 163
  admired by Bernard, 61, 165
  reappraised by Mirbeau, 165

exchanges works with Gauguin, 414, 459
  letter from Gauguin, 417–18
  Gauguin's notes on Redon, 422–23
  Aurier on Redon, 482–83
  photograph, *ill.* 422
  mentioned, 12, 61, 91, 92, 135, 136, 143, 144, 152–65, 318, 346, 406, 414, 417, 437–38, 439, 452, 456 (note 56), 458, 462, 463, 475, 481, 487, 490, 498 (note 10)
  Apparition, ill. 153
  Armor, ill. 154
  Child and Aurora Borealis, ill. 164
  Cyclops, ill. in color 157
  Flowers in a Vase, ill. in color 158
  Green Death, ill in color 160
  Imaginary Portrait of Paul Gauguin, ill. 418
  Incense Burner, ill. 156
  Marsh Flower (charcoal), *ill.* 156
  Marsh Flower (lithograph), *ill.* 161
  Mysterious Head, ill. 155
  Owl, ill. 153
  Phantom, ill. 161
  Portrait of Emile Bernard, ill. 423
  Portrait of Mlle Violette H., ill. 164
  Profile, ill. 154
  Reverie, ill. 155
  Skeleton, ill. 161
  Spider, ill. 155
  Vase with Anemones, ill. in color 159
Régnier, Henri de, 129, 135, 137, 139, 141, 146, 422, 425, 452, 499 (note 36)
Regoyos, Dario de, 102, 387, 396
  Fishermen at San Sebastian, ill. 112
Reid, Alexander, 24, 25
  portrait by van Gogh, *ill.* 24
Rembrandt, 11, 237, 323, 344, 458
Renan, Ary, 430, 450, 452
Renan, Ernest, 336, 430, 450
Renard, Jules, 421, 450, 452
Renoir, Pierre-Auguste, 12, 13, 16, 18, 27, 46, 60, 62, 67, 84, 87, 91, 136, 143, 147, 152, 212, 256, 318, 346, 363, 365, 429, 454, 462, 463, 474, 480, 483
  Bathers, 60; *ill.* 63
  Portrait of Auguste Rodin, ill. 455
  Portrait of Stéphane Mallarmé, ill. 142
  Seated Bather, 60; *ill in color* 50
  The Tresses (Suzanne Valadon), *ill.* 27
Réunion, La, Island of, 414
Revue Blanche, La (periodical), 142,

424, 444, 479
Revue Contemporaine, La (periodical), 136
Revue Exotique, La (periodical), 137
Revue Indépendante, La (periodical), 65, 87, 125, 129, 130, 135, 136, 138, 176, 177, 416, 423
Revue Moderne, La (periodical), 137
Revue Wagnérienne, La (periodical), 14, 130, 136
Rey, Dr., 248 (note 45), 291, 292, 298, 300, 316, 320, 368
  photograph, *ill.* 293
  portrait by Vincent van Gogh, *ill.* 292
Rhône (river), 198, 218
Rimbaud, Arthur, 13, 137, 165 (note 3), 424
  Illuminations, 13
"Ripipoint," 274, 290 (note 42), *ill.* 274
Robert (Arles policeman), 243, 248 (note 45)
Robert-Fleury, Joseph, 252
Robinson, Theodore, 87
Rodin, Auguste, 32, 60, 67, 91, 136, 310, 386, 425, 429, 430
  portrait by Renoir, *ill.* 423
  Bust of Puvis de Chavannes, ill. 12
  Portrait of Octave Mirbeau (bronze), *ill.* 386
Rood, O. N., 73, 76, 79, 82, 88, 109
Rosicrucians, Order of, 430, 474, 475, 476
Rothenstein, William, 252
  Caricature of M. Julian, ill. 252
Rotonchamp, J. de, *see* Brouillon
Roulin, Joseph (Arles postman), 206, 216 (note 57), 237, 240, 246, 248 (note 47), 291, 293, 301, 368
  portrait by van Gogh, *ill.* 206
Roulin, Mme, 237, 293
  La Berceuse—Mme Roulin, by van Gogh, *ill.* 292
  portraits by van Gogh and Gauguin, *ill.* 236
Rousseau, Henri, *le douanier,* 12, 179, 256, 350, 392, 453, 479
Rousseau, Théodore, 235
Roussel, Ker-Xavier, 419, 442, 444, 462, 483
Rouvier (Minister of Fine Arts), 410, 451
Roy, Louis, 256, 257, 258, 260, 272, 289 (note 14)
Rubens, Peter Paul, 11, 33

poster, *ill.* 259

Voltaire, Le (newspaper), 439, 441

Voltaire, 336

Vuillard, Edouard, 253, 279, 389, 419, 422, 437, 481, 483
The Artist's Mother, ill. 389
Portrait of Lugné-Poë, ill. 455
Profile of Stéphane Mallarmé, ill. 450

Wagner, Richard, 14, 51, 69, 130, 133, 134, 136, 193, 255, 271, 276
Lohengrin, 14
Tannhäuser, 14

Wallonie, La (periodical), 136, 346

Watteau, Jean-Antoine, 90

Wauters, Emile, 218, 219; *ill.* 247

Weber, Karl-Maria von, 140

West Indies, 192

Whistler, James McNeill, 13, 91, 132 (note 68), 136, 143, 163, 429, 456 (note 83)

Whitman, Walt, 137

Wilde, Oscar, 13

Willumsen, Jens Ferdinand, 280, 387, 392, 418, 433, 452, 453–54, 462, 479
Men Working in a Quarry, ill. 280
Two Breton Women Parting after a Chat, ill. 280

World's Fair, *see* Paris World's Fair

Wyzewa, Teodor de, 13, 14, 131, 136, 137, 138, 139, 140, 142, 143, 146, 147, 148, 152, 162, 163, 341, 397, 425, 429
caricature by Anquetin, *ill.* 139
photograph, *ill.* 138

Young, Thomas, 109

Zandomeneghi, Federico, 441

Ziem, Félix, 235

Zola, Emile, 13, 23, 32, 51, 64, 88, 118, 133, 135, 156, 192, 336, 429, 482
portrait by Vallotton, *ill.* 134
L'Oeuvre, 13, 32

Zuloaga, Ignacio, 252